The North Carolina Continentals

*This volume is sponsored
by the North Carolina Society
of the Cincinnati
as evidence of its purpose
to illuminate our country's path today
with a knowledge and understanding
of those who pledged their lives
to bring it into being.*

The North Carolina Continentals

by Hugh F. Rankin

The University of North Carolina Press
Chapel Hill

For Hugh and Ida Lefler

Preface

Perhaps the most surprising revelation about the North Carolina Continental Line is that it was able to survive the American Revolution, especially after 1780. Among other disabilities, the state was poor, while its population was more divided in loyalties than is generally realized. There was also the lack of strong executive leadership, a characteristic sorely needed in periods of great stress. This is not intended to damn the wartime governors of North Carolina, but to admit that they were handicapped by constitutional and legislative restrictions. And the legislature did not always seem so cooperative as it might have been in the war effort, for too often it appeared more interested in present and future political considerations than in more pressing military matters. Such considerations were not wrong, but only poorly timed.

Throughout this study of the North Carolina Continentals there will be evident inconsistencies. For example, for the sake of continuity, I have followed the progress of the state's Continentals in the Northern Department until they were ordered south in late 1779 to aid in the defense of Charleston. As a result, in Chapter 9 I have had to swing back to the state to pick up those events that had occurred in the absence of these regulars. Not only does this maintain the train of events in the Northern Department, but allows a continuing narrative for the southern campaign. There are some events that by contrast appear thin, but this has been by neither intent nor judgment;

it was dictated by a paucity of sources. In the latter stages of the war, soldiers were neither so enthusiastic nor so diligent in reporting their experiences in the field as they had been in the earlier stages of the conflict.

The designations "regiment" and "battalion" were used interchangeably by the North Carolina Continentals. Inasmuch as they customarily fancied the use of "regiment" I have used that designation throughout.

Many people were more than helpful in furthering my efforts. Staff members in the search rooms at the Library of Congress, the National Archives, the New York Public Library, the New-York Historical Society, the Public Record Office, and the British Museum were most kind in bringing forth the necessary manuscripts and books.

At the William L. Clements Library of the University of Michigan I am much in debt to Howard Peckham and William Ewing. At the Southern Historical Collection of the University of North Carolina at Chapel Hill, Dr. J. Isaac Copeland and Dr. Carolyn Wallace made my visits to that collection most rewarding, as did Mr. William Powell, curator of the North Carolina Collection of that same institution. At the North Carolina Department of Archives and History at Raleigh Dr. H. G. Jones, Mr. Fred Coker, and those tireless and wonderful people in the search room did everything in their power to make my task easier. Dr. Curtis Carrol Davis of Baltimore was most generous in lending both printed and manuscript items from his personal collection.

I am particularly grateful to Mrs. Elizabeth H. Drew of New York City, who, while working with me on another project, turned up a number of items that proved valuable to this study. Mr. Jerry Cashion of the University of North Carolina at Chapel Hill utilized his extensive knowledge of North Carolina in reading parts of the manuscript and making several valuable suggestions. Dr. John Sellers of the Library of Congress was kind enough to call my attention to a number of items that he discovered while working on his own study of the Virginia Continentals. As always, I must pay tribute to my wife, whose keen editorial eye was instrumental in curbing an unruly penchant for grandiloquent prose. And last, but by no means least, I have found it a delightful experience to work with the Publications Committee of the North Carolina Society of the Cincinnati, who placed no restrictions upon me and offered only their constant encouragement and aid.

Tulane University
New Orleans, Louisiana

Hugh F. Rankin

Contents

The North Carolina Continentals

Chapter 1
War Comes to North Carolina

". . . teizing and fretting the people here. . . ."

In the years just before the outbreak of the rebellion in the American colonies, violence and civil strife were peculiar characteristics of a bitter political struggle. In North Carolina this struggle was particularly venomous for, it has been said, the colony contained a greater number of loyalists in proportion to its population than any other. Some Carolinians seemed to take the actions of Great Britain as a personal affront, and in 1774 Samuel Johnston had written from Edenton, "The Ministry from the time of passing the Declaratory Act, on the repeal of the Stamp Act, seemed to have used every opportunity of teizing and fretting the people here as if on purpose to draw them into Rebellion or some Violent opposition to Government. . . ."[1]

1. Samuel Johnston to Alexander Elmsley, 23 September 1774, Samuel Johnston Papers, North Carolina Department of Archives and History, Raleigh, N.C.; Robert O. DeMond, *The Loyalists in North Carolina during the Revolution* (Durham, N.C., 1940), p. vii. Both of the Carolinas had heavy concentrations of loyalists. In fact, one might disagree with DeMond's conclusion and claim that South Carolina had a greater number of Tories in proportion to her white population. Yet it should be remembered that the South Carolina loyalists were most active and came out in greater numbers when that state was occupied by British troops.

The Whigs, as the most rebellious element termed themselves, early began to take the initiative, so much so that Janet Schaw, a loyalist visitor was led to record a doleful lament in her journal: "Oh Britannia, what are you doing, while your true obedient sons are thus insulted by their unlawful brethren; are they also forgot by their natural parents?" But these "true obedient sons" grew weary of passively turning the other cheek and they too began to organize into a party of the opposition.[2]

The logical leader for these adherents to the Crown was the royal governor, Josiah Martin. The governor was a young man of thirty-six years, energetic and attractive, but possessed of a penchant for overenthusiasm, while his approach to political problems was seldom tactful or cautious. He seemed always to be chasing a will-o'-the-wisp, with the grass always greener in other pastures. Life, he seemed to feel, had been particularly unkind to him in distributing material wealth to less deserving individuals. Born in Antigua in 1737, he had entered the local militia at the age of seventeen and three years later had purchased a commission in the Fourth Foot Regiment of the regular army. By 1764 he had been able, through the assistance of his family, to purchase a lieutenant colonel's commission in the Twenty-Second Regiment, but in 1764 he was transferred to the Sixty-Eighth, stationed in Antigua, at which place he had been appointed a member of the governor's council. In 1761 he had visited the mainland where his uncle Josiah, for whom he was named, was living on Long Island in New York. There he met his cousin Elizabeth, and although she was five years older, he married her in that same year. The couple were to have eight children.[3]

Although Martin pleaded ill health as the reason for selling his army commission in 1769, a more likely explanation is that he was experiencing financial difficulties. Through the influence of his brother Henry, Josiah was appointed royal governor of North Carolina on December 14, 1770. It was not an appointment that would make a man wealthy, but Martin had his eye on a position that would, an additional job as agent for Lord Granville's grant, comprising roughly about one-half of North Carolina.[4]

In general, North Carolinians seemed pleased with the appoint-

2. Janet Schaw, *Journal of a Lady of Quality; Being the Narrative of a Journal from Scotland to the West Indies, North Carolina and Portugal, in the Years 1774 to 1776*, ed. Evangeline Walker Andrews and Charles McLean Andrews (New Haven, Conn., 1932), p. 192.

3. *Ibid.*, pp. 264–66; Blackwell P. Robinson, *The Five Royal Governors of North Carolina, 1729–1775* (Raleigh, N.C., 1963), p. 63.

4. Josiah Martin's letters to his brother Samuel in London are filled with

ment; Samuel Johnston wrote before Martin's arrival, "As we hear a very amiable Character of him [we] are not uneasy of the approaching Change." The new governor, complaining of his health, did not arrive in the colony until July 11, 1771. On August 12, he met his council for the first time and took the oath of office in the magnificent new governor's residence in New Bern, constructed by his predecessor, William Tryon. Before his departure to assume his new appointment as governor of New York, Tryon talked with Martin, and it was he who probably suggested to Martin that he make a tour of the back country, the scene of the recent Regulator uprising. In the summer of 1772, in company with his family, the new governor toured the Regulator country, but in the light of later events, this trip was not as successful as he at first imagined.[5]

Martin's gubernatorial difficulties began in his first assembly. When the legislature repealed a tax law of 1748, the governor vetoed the repeal on the grounds that the statute should be retained. In retaliation, Richard Caswell, Speaker of the House of Commons, advised the sheriffs not to collect the taxes; they obeyed the Speaker despite the governor's proclamation demanding that the levies be collected. Martin refused to call another assembly until January, 1773, when the legislature, in a routine renewal of a court statute, attached a rider to the bill allowing the assembly to attach or confiscate the North Carolina property of nonresidents. When Martin refused to agree to the bill, the high courts of the colony did not sit, leaving the governor to struggle along with the emergency courts that he created under the royal prerogative. In March one visitor was led to comment: "The present state of North Carolina is really curious—there are but five provincial laws in force through the colony, and no courts at all in being. No one can recover a debt, except before a single magistrate, where the sums are within his jurisdiction, and offenders escape with impunity. The people are in great consternation about the matter; what will be consequence is problematical."[6]

Faced with the prospect of a legislature that might become increasingly stubborn, Martin sought a more congenial climate. When he heard that the governor's places in South Carolina and Virginia

---

pleadings for the position as Granville's land agent. Martin Papers, British Museum, London, Additional Manuscripts 41361.

5. Samuel Johnston to Thomas Barker, 10 June 1771, Samuel Johnston Papers.

6. Robinson, *Five Royal Governors of North Carolina*, pp. 65–66; Josiah Quincy, *Memoir of the Life of Josiah Quincy Jun. of Massachusetts* (Boston, 1825), p. 123.

were possible vacancies, Martin dismissed both possibilities with the observation that the people of South Carolina were "vain, luxurious, & pompous, to the highest degree. They are not less ostentatious in Virginia, so that in either place I should be exposed to expence. . . ." His most promising rumor was that Tryon was not only ill, but was "weary of the toils of government," and was entertaining thoughts of relinquishing the governor's chair in New York. Martin wanted the position, explaining that "the Climate of that Province is genial to my constitution & its vast emoluments would soon improve my future to the height of my wishes."[7]

There was another rebuff for the governor when the assembly met in December, 1773; that body refused to sanction an appropriation to meet the obligations of Martin's emergency courts. The governor complained to his brother that "the late Session of the General Assembly, abortive of every thing but ill humour & reproach of Government, hath left me to bewail, the wretched state to which its rank & unpolitical Councils have reduced this Country." Seemingly, he was now convinced that the "Patriots," as he now termed the recalcitrants, would so inflame the people that rebellion was inevitable. He solicited his brother's aid in seeking permission from Lord Barrington, secretary at war, to allow Martin to raise a battalion of Highlanders in the state, and to restore his old commission in the army "for which I feel an inclination."[8]

At the same time that the December assembly was sitting, local events in Massachusetts were to affect not only that province, but all of the remaining colonies. A mob, masquerading under crude disguise as "Mohawks," boarded British tea ships and threw some 342 chests of East India Company tea into Boston harbor. Parliament's original Tea Act had not seemed to have had strong repercussions in North Carolina, but when subsequent coercive measures were passed to punish the Bostonians for their effrontery, the Carolinians began to argue that if such acts were allowed to stand, similar statutes might be applied to other colonies. And there were some who could see no end to the dispute between England and her colonies. Samuel Johnston wrote with sarcastic pen of a *"Mr* Pettigrew, who comes over for a Commission from the Bishop to prepare the Americans for death, and a World where they will no longer be liable to be taxed by a British Parliament. . . ."[9]

7. Josiah Martin to Samuel Martin, 27 January 1774, Martin Papers.
8. *Ibid.*
9. William L. Saunders (ed.), *The Colonial Records of North Carolina* (Raleigh, N.C., Goldsboro, N.C., etc., 1886–98), X, viii–ix, hereafter cited as *Colonial*

There was an effective organization to maintain a measure of unity among the defiant North Carolinians. The December assembly, following the lead of Virginia, had selected a Committee of Correspondence composed of John Harvey, John Ashe, Cornelius Harnett, Robert Howe, Edward Vail, William Hooper, Samuel Johnston, and Joseph Hewes, possibly the most influential political leaders in the colony. As its mission, the committee was charged "to obtain early information of any acts of the British government in regard to the colonies, and to correspond with committees of other colonies as to their plans of resistance." One of their first public statements was to declare that the cause of Boston was the cause of all, pledging their cooperation with the other colonies and asserting that "a Continental Congress was an absolute necessity." Josiah Quincy, Boston patriot traveling for his health, passed through North Carolina in March and April, 1773. His observations on the North Carolina leaders with whom he dined on March 30, 1773, are worthy of notice: "Dined with about twenty at Mr. William Hooper's—find him apparently in the Whig interest,—has taken their side in the House—is caressed by the whigs, and is now passing his election through the influence of that party. Spent the night at Mr. Harnett's, the Samuel Adams of North Carolina (except in point of fortune). Robert Howe, Esq., Harnett, and myself made the social triumvirate of the evening. The plan of continental correspondence highly relished, much wished for, and resolved upon, as proper to be pursued."[10]

From the Boston Committee of Correspondence came the declaration that their city was "suffering in the common cause." The Wilmington area sprang into action, and within a short time "a considerable sum was subscribed. . . ." Parker Quince of Brunswick offered his *Penelope*, and a Captain Budd and his crew agreed to sail a cargo of provisions to Boston without pay. A committee composed of James Moore, George Hooper, Robert Howe, Archibald Maclaine, William Hooper, John Ancrum, Robert Hogg, and Francis Clayton supervised the collection of 2,096 bushels of corn, 22 barrels of flour, and 17 barrels of pork, which, although originally consigned to Salem, was eventually unloaded at Marblehead, Massachusetts.[11]

The business was not without its humorous byplay. When the

Records; Samuel Johnston to Alexander Elmsley, 23 September 1774, Samuel Johnston Papers.

10. Quincy, *Memoir of the Life of Josiah Quincy Jun.*, p. 120.

11. *Boston Gazette*, 22 August 1774, 5 September 1774; *Collections of the Massachusetts Historical Society*, 4th Series (Boston, 1858), IV, 22–26, 22n–25n, 45, 86–88; William Hooper to James Iredell, 5 August 1774, Iredell Papers, Duke University, Durham, N.C.

ladies of Edenton swore off tea and those of Wilmington burned theirs "in solemn procession," Arthur Iredell commented in a letter from England:

> Is there a Female Congress in Edenton too? I hope not, for we English-men are afraid of the Male Congress, but if the Ladies, who have ever, since the Amasoien ara, been esteemed the most formidable Enemies, if they, I say, should attack us, the most fatal consequences is to be dreaded. So dex-trous in the handling of a Dart, each wound they give is Mortal; whilst we are so unhappily form'd, by Nature, the more we strive to conquer them, the more the Conquest! The Edenton Ladies conscious of this Superiority on their side, by former Experience are willing, I imagine to crush into Atoms, by their Omnipotency, the only Security on our Side, to prevent the impend-ing Ruin, that I can perceive is, the probability that there is that but few of the places in America who possess so much female Artillery, as Edenton.[12]

By June, things had worsened to such a point that Martin was little more than a figurehead on the North Carolina political scene. Some, such as William Hooper, were in virtual rebellion against the "mistaken policy" of England. Hooper declared, "The only appology I can find for them [the English ministry] is to charge the depravity of their hearts upon the weakness of their heads—Infatuated people!" When Massachusetts and Virginia issued calls for a continental con-gress to meet in Philadelphia during September, the North Carolina Committee of Correspondence urged all southern colonies to follow the lead of Virginia and, if the governors refused to summon the as-semblies, to form associations. Martin, knowing full well that the North Carolina Assembly would defy his instructions and elect dele-gates to a continental congress, refused to call the assembly into ses-sion. Colonel John Harvey, Speaker of the House, announced that if the governor persisted in his refusal to summon the legislature, a con-vention would be called. In July, a mass meeting in Wilmington, led by Cornelius Harnett, William Hooper, and Edward Buncombe, called for a provincial congress to meet in New Bern on August 23, 1774. The three-day session of North Carolina's first Provincial Congress was presided over by John Harvey, who was named modera-tor. After resolutions critical of British policy (although including protestations of loyalty to the Crown), and of sympathy for the suf-fering inhabitants of Boston, the idea of a continental congress was proposed and endorsed. William Hooper, Richard Caswell, and Joseph Hewes were elected as delegates to the Continental Congress and "invested with such powers as may make any Acts done by them

12. Schaw, *Journal of a Lady of Quality*, p. 155; Arthur Iredell to James Ire-dell, 31 January 1775, Charles E. Johnston Collection, North Carolina Department of Archives and History, Raleigh, N.C.

or any of them or consent given in behalf of this Province, Obligatory in honor upon every Inhabitant thereof." Before adjourning, the delegates to the Provincial Congress gave Harvey the authority to call another meeting of the body when he deemed necessary.[13]

Royal government crumbled, weakened by the erosion of turbulent passions. As early as March, 1775, Martin heard of troop embodiments in New Hanover and Brunswick counties. In April his council deserted him. Yet he was optimistic because of the loyalist sentiment evident in the colony, although he was forced to admit that "the movement of this part of the Continent, will be governed by the impulses of the people of New England. . . ." On the other hand, Archibald Neilson and others who deplored the idea of the Carolinians taking their cues from "the violence to the Northward,— the illiberal wild impolitic and profane violence, transacted there, can not be for Sacred Liberty— which Induces only what is wise and Virtuous.—Now it is Folly, all madness and wickedness. . . . I am more and more convinced that there are many vile men in popular Consideration to the Northward; Hypocrites and traitors to the cause they ostensibly defend. . . ."[14]

Overestimating his powers of persuasion, Martin issued a call for the assembly to meet in New Bern on April 4. Once again John Harvey frustrated the governor by issuing a call for a provincial congress to meet in the same place on the day before the assembly was to gather, its declared purpose "to act in union with our neighboring colonies," and to elect new delegates to the second Continental Congress. Only one of the assembly's fifty-seven delegates was not listed among the sixty-seven members of the Provincial Congress. John Harvey, Speaker of the House, served in a similar capacity as moderator for the Congress. In their meeting Governor Martin was denounced; the right to petition the Crown for a redress of grievances was asserted; and Hooper, Hewes, and Caswell were re-elected as delegates to the Continental Congress. A Committee of Safety was created not only for each town and county, but for the colony as a whole. Harvey was authorized to call another provincial congress unless his

---

13. W. P. Palmer *et al.* (eds.), *Calendar of Virginia State Papers and Other Manuscripts* (Richmond, Va., 1875–93), VIII, 58–59, 64–65; William Hooper to James Iredell, 21 June 1774, Iredell Papers; Resolution of North Carolina Provincial Congress, 5 April 1775, Miscellaneous Papers, Papers of the Continental Congress, National Archives, Washington, D.C.

14. Josiah Martin to Thomas Gage, 16 March 1775, Thomas Gage Papers, William L. Clements Library, University of Michigan, Ann Arbor, Mich.; Archibald Neilson to ———, 25 January 1775, Miscellaneous Papers, 1697–1912, North Carolina Department of Archives and History, Raleigh, N.C.

present illness proved fatal. Under such a circumstance, Harvey's authority was to pass to Samuel Johnston.[15]

For all of his faults, Josiah Martin was a courageous man. In his address to the assembly on Tuesday, April 4, he urged its members to resist "the monster, sedition," who "dared raise his impious head in America." So passionate were his words that one newspaper termed his address "a high-flying, abusive, anti-American speech, in which he spoke hard things of all the colonies, congresses, committees, and people on the continent, except those of his own stamp, and begged of his assembly not to approve of sending delegates to the Congress in May." The governor's words might as well never have been spoken, for the members of the assembly continued to discuss those matters with which they had occupied themselves the day before in the Provincial Congress, and voted a formal resolution voicing approval of the Continental Congress. Within four days an angry governor had dissolved the legislature, shortly after he had written Lord Dartmouth, secretary of state for the colonies, that "government here is as absolutely prostrate as impotent, and nothing but the shadow of it is left." He concluded his dispatch with the prophetic warning that "unless effectual measures such as British Spirit may dictate are speedily taken, there will not long remain a trace of Britain'[s] dominion over the colonies."[16]

Even before the meeting of the assembly, efforts had been made by the rebels to secure the powder supply within the colony. Militia units had been alerted to raise money for the purchase of powder and lead "that they may be provided against the Incursions on the frontier which seems probable." The situation was only intensified when the news of the battles of Lexington and Concord reached New Bern on May 6. After this Samuel Johnston noted that "Tom Polk is raising a very pretty spirit in the back country. . . ." The rumor that the governor was planning to muster Negroes and Indians to his defense added fuel to the flames. Although Martin denied any such intentions, a number of Negroes were accused and punished, and armed bands of runaways were discovered hiding in the swamps and forests along the coast. In Chatham County "a deep Laid Horrid Tragick Plan, Laid for distroying the Inhabitants of this Province without respect of persons, Age or Sex" was put down by hastily raised light horse

15. Hugh T. Lefler and Albert R. Newsome, *North Carolina: The History of a Southern State* (Chapel Hill, N.C., 1954), pp. 189–90; Martin to Gage, 16 March 1775, Thomas Gage Papers.

16. *Colonial Records*, IX, 1194, 1214–15; Frank Moore (ed.), *Diary of the American Revolution from Newspapers and Original Documents* (New York, 1863), I, 63.

troops recruited from the militia. Such accusations led Martin to complain that he was "not supported by a single man, an helpless and disagreeable situation that almost breaks my heart." Robert Howe seems to have assumed the direction of the militia. The entire colony took on a martial air as groups drilled to the unlikely rhythm of the thump of the drum and the scrape of the fiddle. Ridiculous as one such "review" appeared to Janet Schaw, she appended an ominous warning in her journal: "But the worst figure there can shoot from behind a bush and kill even a General Wolfe."[17]

Yet despite these martial and even belligerent rumblings in the province, the North Carolina delegates to the Continental Congress felt that the colony had not shown the zeal or exertion displayed by other colonies who had "taken an honourable share in the line of Defence armed and equipped to avert the Calamity, dreading a civil War as the most awful scourge of Heaven. . . ." And, added Hooper, Caswell, and Hewes, "North Carolina alone remains an inactive Spectator of the general Armament. Supine and careless, she seems to forget even the Duty she owes to her own local Circumstances and Situations."[18]

Governor Martin remained under the constant surveillance of the New Bern Committee of Safety. Not only the town's militia company, but those of the surrounding country were embodied. On May 23, the local committee called on the governor. Abner Nash, according to Martin, their "Oracle" and "a principal promoter of sedition here," came forward to request that the cannon usually before the governor's palace and recently dismounted by Martin be returned to their original positions. Martin was furious, convinced that Nash used this demand as "a mere pretext for insulting me." Yet he held his tongue. Apparently the governor's explanation that new gun carriages sturdy enough to stand the salutes of the upcoming celebration of the king's birthday were under construction satisfied the committee, for Nash led them away.[19]

17. *Colonial Records*, X, 9–11, 94–95, 118; Schaw, *Journal of a Lady of Quality*, pp. 189–90, 199; Martin to Gage, 26 May 1775, Thomas Gage Papers; John Drayton, *Memoirs of the American Revolution, From Its Commencement to the Year 1776, Inclusive: as Relating to the State of South-Carolina and Occasionally Referring to the States of North-Carolina and Georgia* (Charleston, 1812), I, 277-82; Samuel Johnston to Joseph Hewes, 27 June 1775, Samuel Johnston Papers; John Simpson to Richard Cogdill, 15 July 1775, Richard Cogdill Papers, North Carolina Department of Archives and History, Raleigh, N.C.

18. *Colonial Records*, X, 21; Joseph Hewes to Samuel Johnston, 11 May 1775, Samuel Johnston Papers.

19. Martin to Dartmouth, 30 June 1775, British Headquarters Papers, Colonial Williamsburg, Inc., Williamsburg, Va.

This display of open resistance to matters even of a minor nature led Martin to conclude that he could no longer maintain the fiction of effective government in New Bern. Mrs. Martin, who expected a child soon, and the other children were placed aboard a small vessel and taken to the comparative safety of her father's house on Long Island. Shortly afterwards "a certain old soldier" in Carolina on business reported to the governor that a sloop with a cargo of arms was on its way to Martin. Because, or so the governor reported, these arms would probably never reach him if unloaded in conventional ports, he decided to station himself in Fort Johnston near the mouth of the Cape Fear. With the aid of a few faithful servants he spiked the cannon and buried all ammunition and military accouterments beneath the cabbage bed in the palace garden. Then, with the announced intention of paying a visit to Chief Justice Hand, he fled to Fort Johnston, arriving at that post on June 2.[20]

Fort Johnston offered little more protection than the governor's palace; Janet Schaw declared that she could "take this fort with a regim't of blackguard Edinburgh boys without any artillery, but their own pop-guns." But there was the added protection of the *Cruizer,* an eight-gun sloop of the Royal Navy anchored in the Cape Fear off the post. Under normal conditions the fort was garrisoned by a housekeeping complement of twenty-five men, but desertions had reduced that number to less than half. The fort had been low on powder for some time, and Captain John Collet, the commanding officer, had been desperately attempting to supplement his supply from the *Cruizer* since early May. But Francis Parry, commander of the sloop, refused to part with more than two and one-half barrels because of the threats of the Carolinians that they would send a fleet of armed vessels down upon him.

Despite this depressing prospect, Martin decided upon an aggressive course of action. The majority of his council now ignored him, and only five attended his meeting within the walls of Fort Johnston on June 25. Although Captain Collet swore that his powder supply would not allow him to defend even his own artillery, the council went along with the governor's optimism, authorizing him to issue militia commissions, recruit replacements for the garrison, and petition General Thomas Gage for funds with which to repair the fort.

20. Martin to Dartmouth, 30 June 1775, British Headquarters Papers; J. Almon, *The Remembrancer: or Impartial Repository of Public Events for the Year 1776* (London, 1776), Part I, p. 114; *Virginia Gazette* (Williamsburg), 21 October 1775; Walter Clark (ed.), *The State Records of North Carolina* (Goldsboro, N.C., Winston, N.C., etc., 1895–1914), XI, 368, hereafter cited as *State Records.*

But in general, thought Martin, the council were "afraid to take a becoming part, I firmly believe from apprehensions of personal insult. . . . As for himself, "The situation in which I find myself at present is indeed most despicable and mortifying to any man of greater feelings than a Stoic. . . ." And now, since the people of Mecklenburg had taken such a strong stand against royal government in their resolves of May 31, 1775, Martin felt that things were coming to a head and that the resolves "surpass all the horrible and treasonable publications that the inflamatory spirits of this Continent have yet produced. . . ."[21]

Martin was so isolated that he did not receive formal notification of the battles of Lexington and Concord until two months after the events, and by that time "first impressions [had] taken deep root in the minds of the vulgar here. . . ." To Lord Dartmouth he reiterated his conviction that he could raise a battalion of Highlanders within the colony and once again he requested the restoration of his commission. His enthusiasm seems to have been generated after Allan McDonald, a person of influence among his countrymen and husband of the famous Flora, had journeyed down to Fort Johnston with the proposal that a battalion of "good and faithful Highlanders" be raised among the recent arrivals of the McDonald and McLeod clans. The rising spirit of opposition seemed to stamp a note of finality upon any hope of negotiations. Now there were reports that armed bands were forcing people to sign the Association, and recruiting parties from South Carolina were enlisting men in North Carolina. Those who were suspected of contacting Martin had been branded as "false and seditious" incendiaries.[22]

John Harvey had died in May, but Samuel Johnston seemed reluctant to exercise the authority that had passed onto him. Perhaps the explanation lies in a later letter of Joseph Hewes, who asked that he postpone the meeting until a complete journal of the proceedings of the Continental Congress could be laid before the North Carolina Provincial Congress. Then too, said Hewes, "It will never do to harrass our people by calling them too often to meet in Conven-

21. *Colonial Records*, X, 38–40; Capt. Collet to Capt. Parry, 20 May 1775, PRO Ad. 1/485; Admiral Samuel Graves to Charles Stephens, 16 July 1775, Frances Parry to Admiral Graves, 26 July 1775, British Museum, London, Additional Manuscripts 14039; Martin to Dartmouth, 30 June 1775, British Headquarters Papers; Samuel Graves, Conduct of Vice Adml Graves, Brit. Mus. Add. MSS 14038; Schaw, *Journal of a Lady of Quality*, p. 142.

22. Martin to Dartmouth, 30 June 1775, British Headquarters Papers; *Colonial Records*, X, 73; J. P. Maclean, *An Historical Account of the Settlement of Scotch Highlanders in America Prior to the Peace of 1783 together with Notices of Highland Regiments and Biographical Sketches* (Cleveland, Ohio, 1900), p. 115.

tion. . . ." In July, the Committee of Safety demanded that Harvey call an early congress, arguing that every passing day allowed the governor additional time in which to spirit up the back country or perhaps even the slaves, while at the same time he could be strengthening the walls of Fort Johnston. The reports of a slave insurrection only increased the fears of Martin's influence.[23]

These supposed activities of the governor posed a problem for the Wilmington Committee of Safety, especially since Fort Johnston constituted a bridgehead from which protection could be afforded for the disembarkation of troops sent from General Thomas Gage's force in Boston. It was evident from intercepted letters that Martin was striving mightily to raise a force of sufficient strength to regain the province for his royal master. To prevent Martin from using available manpower and also to strengthen themselves, a number of seamen aboard the merchant vessels in the river who were familiar with the operation of artillery were "seduced" by the Carolinians through a five-pound bounty. Captain John Collet, who had succeeded Robert Howe as commander of Fort Johnston in 1773, was used as a justification for an attack upon the fort. The Wilmington Committee of Safety declared that he was readying the fort to receive expected reinforcements, that he was wantonly detaining merchant vessels when they applied for bills of health, he had constantly defied local magistrates, and he had embezzled government property. When the sheriff had served proper writs upon him for debt, Collet had replied "with the shameful contempt of wiping his b--k s-de with them." And Martin later was to admit that most of these charges were substantially accurate. An attack on the fort was planned. Summons were sent out to all militia and independent companies to turn out to dislodge "that notorious freebooter."[24]

Robert Howe's command of nearly five hundred militia and minutemen marched out of Brunswick on July 15. There was no attempt at secrecy. A letter signed by "The People" informed the governor that since it had been learned that Captain Collet intended to dismantle the post, they had come to take the cannon from its walls. There was little chance that the garrison could put up a respectable

23. *Colonial Records*, X, 91–92, 94–95; *State Records*, XI, 255; Hewes to Johnston, n.d., North Carolina Letters from the Emmet Collection, New York Public Library (transcripts), North Carolina Department of Archives and History, Raleigh, N.C., hereafter cited as Emmet Collection; Cornelius Harnett to the New Bern Committee of Safety, 13 June 1775, Samuel Johnston Papers.

24. *Colonial Records*, IX, 798–99, X, 93, 113–14, 234–35; Collet to Parry, 20 May 1775, PRO Ad. 1/485; Parry to Admiral Graves, 26 July 1775; Brit. Mus. Add. MSS 14039.

defense. Nearly the entire garrison had deserted, and Collet cried that he could not be expected to hold the fort with the three or four men that he could depend upon. Back in March Martin had informed Gage that the fort in its present state was indefensible against a force of any size and now declared it to be "a most contemptible thing, fit neither for a place of Arms, or an Asylum for the friends of Government." The artillery was dismantled and placed on the beach under the protection of the guns of the sloop. All provisions were removed aboard a transport, while Martin remained aboard the *Cruizer,* "my best asylum in the present time of Confusion in this Country." Between two and four o'clock on the morning of July 19, Howe began the destruction of the fort by firing the home of Captain Collet within the walls. After sunrise Martin looked on as a "savage and audacious mob" under the leadership of Howe, John Ashe, and Cornelius Harnett burned the fort and the surrounding buildings. On the following day, the Americans, parading under three British colors, put the torch to the remaining fortifications "with a degree of wanton malice."[25]

On August 8, Governor Martin, almost a prisoner aboard the *Cruizer* and "reduced to the deplorable state of being a tame Spectator of Rebellion spreading over this Country," resorted to his pen and issued a lengthy document. In this "Fiery" proclamation he blamed the Committees of Safety, especially that of Wilmington, for leading the people of the colony onto the path of rebellion through "the basest and most scandalous Sedition and inflamatory falsehoods. . . ." Not only did he flay the Provincial Congress, but likewise the "resolves of a set of people stiling themselves a Committee for the County of Mecklenburgh most traitorously declaring the entire dissolution of the Laws, Government, and Constitution of this country and setting up a system of rule and regulation repugnant to the Laws and subversive of His Majesty's Government. . . ." Even Martin must have realized that he was but whistling into the teeth of a whirlwind.[26]

Samuel Johnston finally called for a provincial congress. It assembled at Hillsborough on Monday, August 21, 1775. Joining the delegates were Joseph Hewes, William Hooper, and Richard Caswell, who traveled from Philadelphia to lay before the North Carolinians the various resolves of the Continental Congress. Although there was a pressing need for action, Samuel Johnston sarcastically commented

25. *Colonial Records,* IX, 1167, X, 96–97, 105, 108–9; Martin to Admiral Graves, 8 July 1775, PRO Ad. 1/485.
26. *Colonial Records,* X, 141–51, 232.

that "We have more orators than men of business among us, which occasions great delays." This observation was proved when it was decided that the first order of business should be an answer to Governor Martin's proclamation. Their resolution declared "that the said Paper is a false, Scandalous, Scurrilous, malicious, and seditious Libel, tending to disunite the good people of this province, and to stir up Tumults and Insurrections, dangerous to His Majesty's Government, and the safety of the Inhabitants. . . ." The governor's proclamation was ordered burned by the public hangman. Once Martin had been disposed of, a provisional government was established with a Council of Safety and a congress, with additional committees of safety in each military district, county, and town. On August 23, Maurice Moore, William Hooper, Robert Howe, Richard Caswell, and Joseph Hewes were named a committee to prepare an address to the people, "stating the present Controversy in an easy familiar stile and manner obvious to the very meanest Capacity, calling upon them to unite in defense of American liberty. . . ." There was need for such a statement, for the time had come to consider the problems of raising an army. It was not an unexpected development. Earlier Samuel Johnston had suggested that the principal concern of the congress should be the raising of troops.[27]

In early June, in response to a petition from the Massachusetts Congress, the Continental Congress in Philadelphia had taken over the armed mob then besieging the British army in Boston. This move had been followed by the selection of the tall delegate from Virginia, George Washington, as "General and Commander-in-Chief of the Army of the united Colonies" and the resolve to raise a continental army of fifteen thousand men. On August 24 the North Carolina Congress had discussed, then pledged payment of its quota of the funds required for such a military force. Not until the last day of August did a formal resolution pass the body that one thousand troops should be embodied as state troops, with the expectation that eventually they would be absorbed into the Continental Line as stated in a June 6, 1775, resolution of the Continental Congress. On the following day, September 1, details were worked out so that the thousand men were to be divided into two regiments of five hundred men each, with the men stationed in the military districts of Wilmington, Salis-

27. *Ibid.*, pp. 88, 164–80; Lefler and Newsome, *North Carolina*, p. 196; Adelaide L. Fries (ed.), *Records of the Moravians in North Carolina* (Raleigh, N.C., 1922–47), II, 861, hereafter cited as *Moravian Records*; Almon, *Remembrancer . . . for . . . 1776*, Part I, pp. 110–11; Johnston to Iredell, 5 September 1775, in Griffith J. McRee, *The Life and Correspondence of James Iredell* (New York, 1857–58), I, 262.

bury, New Bern, and Edenton. Field officers for the First Regiment were to be Colonel James Moore, Lieutenant Colonel Francis Nash, and Major Thomas Clark. Robert Howe was to command the Second Regiment, with Alexander Martin as Lieutenant Colonel and John Patten as Major.[28]

Provisions were made for local minutemen and militia, with one battalion of ten companies of fifty men each to be raised in each of the six military districts of Edenton, Salisbury, Halifax, Hillsborough, Wilmington, and New Bern. These men were to be uniformed in hunting shirts, leggings, or splatterdashes with black gaiters and were to be enlisted for six months. When called into service, they were to be subject to the same rules and regulations as the Continental forces. Edward Vail, Nicholas Long, Thomas Wade, James Thackston, Richard Caswell, and Alexander Lillington were appointed commanders of the various districts with the rank of colonel. Commanding officers, who were to rank below the comparable rank of minutemen, were also appointed for each county.[29]

The colonel of the First North Carolina Regiment, thirty-eight-year-old James Moore, had long been prominent in the affairs of the lower Cape Fear. There is some evidence to suggest that he had served in the French and Indian War and that by the time he was twenty-eight he had been appointed a colonel in the local militia. In Tryon's expedition against the Regulators he had served as colonel of "all the artillery and artillery company of volunteers." He appears to have been a quiet sort of man, but when he did speak, he spoke with that authority that demanded attention. The perceptive but loyalist Janet Schaw noted that Robert Howe seemed to be intriguing for command of all North Carolina troops and, although he was a man to be feared, she went on to observe:

I wish he may get the command with all my heart, for he does not appear to me half so dangerous as another candidate, a Coll. Moor, whom I am compelled at once to dread and esteem. He is a man of free property and a most unblemished character, has amiable manners, and a virtuous life has gained him the love of everybody, and his popularity is such that I am assured he will have more followers than any other man in the province. He acts from a steady tho' mistaken principle, and I am certain has no view or design, but what he thinks right and for the good of the country. He urges not a war of

28. *Colonial Records*, X, 174, 186–87; Worthington C. Ford *et al.* (eds.), *Journals of the Continental Congress, 1774–1789* (Washington, 1904–34), II, 87, 100, 107.

29. *Colonial Records*, X, 196–200, 204–5; Louis van Loan Naisawald, "The Military Career of Robert Howe" (M.A. thesis, University of North Carolina, 1948), p. 3.

words, and when my brother told him he would not join him, for he did not approve the cause, "Then do not," said he, "let every man be directed by his own ideas of right or wrong." If this man commands, be assured, he will find his enemies work. His name is James Moor: should you ever here him mentioned, think of the character I gave him.[30]

Moore's kinsman, Robert Howe, was seven years older, a fine-living, proud man with a keen mind and a devilish sense of humor. As in Moore's case, there is the possibility that he too served briefly in the French and Indian War. Twice he had served as commandant of Fort Johnston, 1765–67 and 1769–73, and he had been a member of the assembly since 1760. His name, according to Governor Martin, had originally been Howes, but now "commonly called Howe, he having impudently assumed that name for some years past in affectation of the noble family that bears it, whose least lenient virtues have been ever far beyond his imitation." Janet Schaw thought him a flirt and something of a devil with the women. A man of many facets was this Robert Howe,

or as he is called here Bob Howe. This Gentleman has the worst character you ever heard thro' the whole province. He is however very like a Gentleman, much so indeed than anything I have seen in the Country. He is deemed a horrid animal, a sort of woman-eater that devours everything that comes in his way, and that no woman can withstand him. . . . I do assure you they overrate his merits and as I am certain it would be in the power of mortal woman to withstand him, so I am convinced he is not so voracious as he is represented. But he has that general polite gallantry, which every man of good breeding ought to have. . . .

Yet from the masculine viewpoint, the New Englander, Josiah Quincy, was fascinated by this "most happy compound of the man of sense, the sword, the senate, and the buck. A truly surprising character. . . . He was formed by nature and his education to shine in the senate and the field—in the company of the philosopher and the libertine—a favorite of the man of sense and the female world. he has faults and vice—but alas who is without them."[31]

While Moore and Howe were readying their commands for possible military action, others busied themselves with potential political enemies. The loyalists, or Tories as they were derisively termed by the Whigs, were pressured to switch their allegiance, sometimes with tar and feathers as the primary instrument of persuasion. Yet, it should be noted that in the early days of the rebellion such persecu-

30. Schaw, *Journal of a Lady of Quality*, pp. 166–67; James Sprunt, *Chronicles of the Cape Fear River* (Raleigh, N.C., 1914), pp. 50, 119.
31. *Colonial Records*, VII, 436, X, 98; Schaw, *Journal of a Lady of Quality*, p. 167; Sprunt, *Chronicles of the Cape Fear River*, pp. 50, 119.

tion was usually reserved for the poorer sort, while those of gentility sought to protect themselves through argument. A number of loyalists fled to the protection of the *Cruizer,* there to be sustained by Captain Parry until they were able to gain passage on some departing vessel. The Regulators, supposedly of loyalist inclinations, and whose aid Governor Martin hoped to enlist against the rebels, were visited by agents of the Continental Congress, some of whom carried accounts of the battle of Bunker Hill as an illustration of the vulnerability of British regulars. Although some of these back-country men expressed apprehension in denying the oath of allegiance administered them by Governor Tryon, enough of them signed the test oath required by the rebels so that "we apprehend no danger from them."[32]

Recruiting officers fanned out through the colony. Moore sent Alexander Martin into Guilford Country and by October 4 the first company marched through the Moravian settlements on its way for training in the bivouac at Salisbury. Those who owned no arms were furnished with weapons purchased, by receipt, from the people of the neighborhood. Some recruiting officers were not above practicing a bit of chicanery in their recruiting activities in that they purposely neglected informing prospects that they were liable for service in colonies other than North Carolina. They were uniformed in hunting shirts and moccasins, some of which were acquired from the Moravians, who showed some reluctance in accepting the paper money issued by the Continental Congress, "but dared not refuse, as that would have led to oppression and resentment." Moore was able to acquire some lead and gunpowder from the supply controlled by the Wilmington Committee of Safety.[33]

In the meantime, the Continental Congress, acting on a report of a committee that had visited the army near Boston, reorganized the Continental army. There were some who feared the step. Samuel Ward of Rhode Island thought that the new alterations would be disgusting both to officers and men. To his brother he grumbled that "under the idea of the new modelling, I was afraid that we should destroy our army. Southern gentlemen wish to remove that attachment, which the officers and men have to their respective colonies, and make them look up to the continent at large for their support or promotion." Under this new arrangement it was hoped that twenty thousand men could be maintained in the lines around Boston, while

32. Peter Force (comp.), *American Archives,* 4th Series (Washington, 1837–46), III, 679; Parry to Admiral Graves, 26 July 1775; Brit. Mus. Add. MSS 14039.
33. *Moravian Records,* II, 850, 885, 941–42; *Colonial Records,* X, 263–64, 286, 292.

an additional five thousand could be dispatched upon an expedition into Canada. Four new regiments were to be raised for the defense of South Carolina and Georgia, while New Jersey was to raise two and Pennsylvania one.[34]

The committee that had visited the Continental army had not been impressed by the caliber of the officers of that force, at least Thomas Lynch of South Carolina had not been. He held little respect for those "Pittyfull wretches," and he suggested to Washington that he not suffer his new officers "to sweep the Parade with the skirts of their Coats or bottoms of their Trowsers, to cheat or mess with their Men, to skulk in battle or sneak in Quarters." Perhaps it was because of the reported poor quality of the officers that, to attract better men, the pay of the lower three grades was increased; captains to twenty-six and two-thirds dollars, lieutenants to eighteen dollars, and ensigns to thirteen dollars per month. Henceforth each Continental regiment was to consist of 728 men, including officers, and was to be divided into eight companies. The complement of each company was to be a captain, two lieutenants, one ensign, four sergeants, four corporals, two drummers or fifers, and seventy-six privates.

Ration issues as established by Congress for men of the ranks were: one pound of beef, three quarters of a pound of pork or one pound of salt fish per day; one pound of bread or flour per day; three pints of peas or beans a week, or other vegetables in proportion (peas and beans cost six shillings per bushel); one pint of milk per day; one-half pint of rice, or one pint of Indian meal per week; and one quart of spruce beer per man, or nine gallons of molasses for each company of one hundred men per week. Each company was to receive three pounds of candles and twenty-four pounds of soft soap or eight pounds of hard soap per week.[35]

From Philadelphia, Joseph Hewes urged that the North Carolina regiments be raised and uniformed as quickly as possible for he felt that the troops would shortly be taken into the Continental Line. He suggested that North Carolina follow the procedures that had seemed to work well for the troops at Boston—that the colony purchase cloth and have it made into uniforms, deducting ten shillings a month from each man's pay.[36]

34. Edmund C. Burnett, *The Continental Congress* (New York, 1941), pp. 104–8.

35. *Colonial Records*, X, 314–15; Burnett, *Continental Congress*, pp. 104–8.

36. *Colonial Records*, X, 314–15; Ford, *Journals of the Continental Congress*, III, 322.

There was a little popgun war going on down on the Cape Fear. The *Cruizer* was sending shot crashing toward the shore in retaliation for the rifle balls that the Americans sent winging through her rigging. On November 11 another sloop, the *Scorpion*, arrived to relieve the *Cruizer*. Governor Martin, however, refused to allow the *Cruizer* to leave, declaring that she was not seaworthy enough to make the voyage to Boston. It seems more likely that he was attempting to assemble all of the armaments possible, no matter what the ship's condition. In fact, he had been begging Admiral Samuel Graves in Boston to send additional naval vessels to the Cape Fear to prevent smuggling of military stores into the colony, despite his conviction "that the time for restoring Lawfull Gevernment [*sic*] in this Province, by its own internal strength, is past and gone."[37]

Shortly after the arrival of the *Scorpion* several field guns were sent down from Wilmington for James Moore to erect a battery at Brunswick. Still there was the lingering apprehension that this would not be enough. So strong was the fear that Martin's two sloops would sail upriver to bombard and fire Brunswick that the Wilmington Committee of Safety sent a group into that town to place values on those buildings likely to be burned by enemy action.[38]

Perhaps it was a growing concern about developments in North Carolina that led the Continental Congress to take action relative to the North Carolina troops. On November 28, 1775, after the usual debates, a resolution was passed: "Resolved that the two Battalions which Congress directed to be raised in the Province of North Carolina be increased to the Continental Establishment, and kept in pay at the expense of the United Colonies for one year from this time, or until the further order of Congress, as well as for the purpose of defending the good people of that Colony against the attacks of Ministerial oppression, as assisting the adjacent Colonies."

In like manner, it was recommended that Pennsylvania and South Carolina send all the gunpowder they could spare to North Carolina, while the colony's delegates in Congress were directed to purchase drums, fifes, and colors, and that all the gunsmiths and blacksmiths in North Carolina be immediately employed in the making of muskets and bayonets. Once the news arrived that their troops were on the Continental establishment, the Provincial Council decided that the Carolina soldiers should be dressed in something better than hunting shirts and splatterdashes. Cloth was ordered to be

37. *Colonial Records*, X, 236, 321–27; Martin to Graves, 8 July 1775, PRO Ad. 1/485.
38. *Colonial Records*, X, 335–36, 337.

purchased and made into coats, waistcoats, and breeches, which, along with the haversacks and cartouches furnished the troops, were to be paid for by a monthly deduction of ten shillings from each man's pay. This was but optimistic projection, for there were not even enough arms or sufficient ammunition to put the troops into the field.[39]

Tension lengthened with the stirrings of the Tories in back-country South Carolina and when Virginia's royal governor, Lord Dunmore, initiated military action to regain his lost authority. Emotions grounded in political passions are not easily curbed, and in North Carolina the Whigs began to act in a more belligerent fashion toward the loyalists. Some fled to Virginia and the protection offered by Lord Dunmore. Samuel Johnston, despite his own political leanings, was shocked at one instance of mob action. After a certain Abraham Pollock had been brought before the Wilmington Committee of Safety and had answered their questions to their satisfaction, some of the officers who had arrested him heard "that he had spoke disrespectfully of them. . . ." With a party of soldiers and "such Scoundrels as they could prevail with to join, "they broke into Pollock's home, confiscated his liquor, and forced money from him when Pollock's whiskey proved too little to slake their thirst. A short time later, at the courthouse, Pollock underwent a coating of tar and feathers while his wife, standing by, "half naked . . . rent the Air with the most affecting Shrieks and Cries imaginable, at last quite exhausted she fainted and was carried home more dead than alive." Such incidents took the revolution away from political oratory into unpleasant domestic aspects, and it became evident that tar and feathers were no longer reserved for the poorer sort.[40]

In the South Carolina backcountry, the loyalists, or "Scovelites" as they were called (after their leader) had arisen, attacked, and besieged the fort at Ninety-Six, but more important, they had also seized the powder stored in that post. The South Carolina Provincial Con-

39. Force, *American Archives*, 4, III, 1925; *Colonial Records*, X, 360–61, 338–39; *State Records*, XV, 685; R. W. Gibbes (ed.), *Documentary History of the American Revolution* (New York, 1853–57) I, 240, 247; Edmund C. Burnett (ed.), *Letters of Members of the Continental Congress* (Washington, 1921–36), I, 251; Ford *Journals of the Continental Congress*, II, 307–8; Samuel Johnston to Joseph Hewes and others, 10 march 1776, Hayes Collection (transcripts), North Carolina Department of Archives and History, Raleigh, N.C.; Thomas McKnight to Rev. Dr. McKnight, 26 December 1775, Miscellaneous Papers, William L. Clements Library, University of Michigan, Ann Arbor, Mich.

40. Samuel Johnston to Joseph Hewes, 10 March 1776, American Loyalist Claims, 1775–1789 (transcripts), North Carolina Department of Archives and History, Raleigh, N.C.

gress dispatched a punitive expedition under the command of Colonel William Richardson. In response to that colony's plea for aid, North Carolina sent a detachment of between 160 and 200 Continentals: one company of the First Regiment under Captain George Davidson and a company of the Second Regiment under John Armstrong, the whole under the command of Alexander Martin. The North Carolina Continentals in this group had volunteered for service in this campaign. In addition there were 900 Rowan and Mecklenburg County militia under Colonels Thomas Polk, Griffith Rutherford, and Richard Caswell. And it should be mentioned that the Third South Carolina State Regiment (not yet on the Continental establishment) was composed of as many North Carolina recruits as those from South Carolina. A junction was made with Richardson's force as they passed the Saluda River. Abandoning Ninety-Six, the loyalists under Joseph Robinson and Patrick Robinson fled into the Cherokee country where they, along with other loyalist groups, were captured. Actually the North Carolina troops were engaged in little more than rounding up scattered Tories although William, the son of Thomas Polk and considered "a fine youth," was wounded in one of the few skirmishes. But at this time young Polk was an officer of a South Carolina regiment. On Christmas day, 1775, the North Carolinians were dismissed to return to their homes. This expedition, in reality, was little more than an exercise in marching, and is sometimes referred to as the "snow campaign," because of an uncommon two-foot snow that fell during one thirty-hour period and remained on the ground for eight days.[41]

More alarming to North Carolinians was the situation in Virginia. Forced to flee the governor's palace in Williamsburg, Governor Dunmore had taken refuge aboard the *Fowey*, a man-of-war in the York River. Gathering a following, he had led them on a series of raids and plundering expeditions. Even more disturbing was the report that Dunmore not only planned to arm the Indians but had issued a proclamation of freedom to those rebel-owned Negroes who

41. *Colonial Records*, X, xi, 340–41; *State Records*, XI, 264–65; David Duncan Wallace, *South Carolina: A Short History* (Chapel Hill, N.C., 1951), p. 269; Chalmers G. Davidson, *Piedmont Partisan: The Life and Times of Brigadier-General William Lee Davidson* (Davidson, N.C., 1951), p. 35; David Ramsay, *The History of the Revolution in South Carolina* (Trenton, N.J., 1785), pp. 70, 76; Gibbes, *Documentary History of the American Revolution*, I, 246–48; "Autobiography of William Polk," in W. H. Hoyt (ed.), *The Papers of Archibald D. Murphey* (Raleigh, N.C., 1914), I, 210, II, 401n, hereafter cited as Hoyt, *Murphey Papers;* Drayton, *Memoirs of the American Revolution*, II, 66–67, 116–32. William A. Graham, *General Joseph Graham and His Papers on North Carolina Revolutionary History* (Raleigh, N.C., 1904), p. 198.

came in and joined his force. One Philadelphian, quoted in a London newspaper, cried out that "Hell itself could not have vomited anything more black than this design of emancipating our slaves." This sentiment was echoed in North Carolina, especially since an intercepted letter of Governor Martin's had pointed out that since the Negroes in Maryland and Virginia outnumbered the whites, their employment in a military way would hasten the reduction of the southern colonies. And the *Maryland Gazette* noted that by the first of November Dunmore had enlisted some three hundred Negroes under Major Thomas Boyd. Termed the "Royal Regiment of Ethiopians," they were uniformed in military garb with "Liberty to Slaves" emblazoned across their chests. Then there were reports that Dunmore had sent agents into the Albermarle region of North Carolina to incite the slaves to insurrection. After one traveler who had stopped overnight in Dunmore's camp stated that the Virginia governor planned to march into North Carolina, Howe's Continentals and the Edenton Minute Men were ordered to march into Pasquotank and Currituck. There they were to station themselves along the Virginia border, not only to oppose such a move by Dunmore, but to prevent the Negroes in the area from running away to join him. It was also suggested that they awe the inhabitants of the area, reported to be the most disaffected in the province.[42]

Howe, although there is no evidence suggesting that he had been given proper authorization, wrote to Colonel William Woodford of Virginia offering the assistance of troops under his command. Although Woodford at first declined the offer, feeling that his own command could take care of the situation, the Virginia Convention countermanded his refusal to accept the aid of North Carolina. Only the 150 volunteer militia men from the Halifax District under Nicholas Long arrived in time to participate in the battle of Great Bridge, December 9, 1775, when Woodford's Virginia Continentals and volunteers crushed a detachment of Dunmore's army as they rushed across the narrow causeway crossing a swamp. The North Carolinians, it was said, "who . . . were in the action . . . did honour to their country."[43]

42. *Morning Chronicle and London Advertiser*, 20 January 1777; Martin to Dartmouth, 30 June 1775, Sir Henry Clinton Papers, William L. Clements Library, University of Michigan, Ann Arbor, Mich.; *Maryland Gazette* (Annapolis), 14 December 1775; Samuel Johnston to Joseph Hewes, 14 November 1775, PRO Ad. 1/485; *The Lee Papers* in *Collections of the New York Historical Society for the Year 1871 . . . 1872 . . . 1873 . . . 1874* (New York, 1872–75), I, 384–86; R. D. W. Connor, *History of North Carolina* (New York, 1919), I, 383.
43. Force, *American Archives*, 4, IV, 76, 224, 538; Almon, *Remembrancer* . . .

Five days later, when Woodford marched into Norfolk, he was joined by Howe and the 428 officers and men of the Second North Carolina regiment, along with several field pieces. By this time the North Carolina volunteers and militia men had been discharged and allowed to return to their homes. The intricacies of command seem to have imposed themselves with Howe's arrival, for although he was not a Virginian, Howe, rather than Woodford, assumed the command of the the combined forces. Howe, said Woodford, "mentioned to me in a very genteel manner his appointment by the Congress, & his Right of precedence by that appointment." Woodford assented to this arrangement, but continued as commander of the Virginia troops. Among the prisoners captured at Great Bridge were a number of British regulars who had been sent to gratify Dunmore's "Request as a Guard to his Person only." In the negotiations for a prisoner exchange, Howe demonstrated that he was no military novice and held his own with Dunmore as the flurry of notes passed back and forth.[44]

Anchored offshore was the insolent little fleet under Dunmore's command, the frigate *Eilbeck,* the *Liverpool* with twenty-eight guns, the *Otter* with sixteen, along with an eight-gun sloop and a number of small tenders. Howe refused to allow provisions to go out to the enemy vessels, some of which were crowded with loyalist refugees. All foraging parties attempting to come ashore were driven back by a heavy fire. Dunmore had frequently threatened to burn Norfolk, and now he announced that on January 1, 1776, he would begin a bombardment with that in mind. Howe requested more time to allow the evacuation of women and children. Dunmore refused, and Howe prepared to resist any attempt to carry the town, convinced "that Virginia and North Carolina must stand or fall together, and then if they fall Norfolk will be the cause."[45]

On New Year's day, between three and four o'clock in the afternoon four British ships carrying over sixty guns moved in within range and began a seven-hour bombardment of the town. The North Carolina and Virginia Continentals were stationed along the shore.

for . . . *1776*, Part I, p. 355; *State Records*, XI, 353; *Virginia Gazette*, 16 December 1775; Samuel Johnston to _____, 21 December 1775, Samuel Johnston Papers.

44. *Colonial Records*, X, 365–69; *State Records*, XI, 353; J. D. to Earl of Dumfries, 14 June 1776, PRO CO5/40/122; Samuel Johnston to _____, 21 December 1775, Samuel Johnston Papers; Morning Return of the Forces Now Under the Command of Col. Robert Howe at Norfolk, 29 December 1779, Military Collection, North Carolina Department of Archives and History, Raleigh, N.C.; *Virginia Gazette*, 16 December 1775; *Richmond College Historical Papers*, I (June, 1915), 127.

45. *Colonial Records*, X, 372, 381–82; Force, *American Archives*, 4, IV, 452, 474, 538–39; *State Records*, XI, 262–63, 353.

It was rough duty, some men having to stand duty for a forty-eight hour stretch. Even then there was a carefree air about the business. Some of Howe's North Carolina sentinels, or so it was charged, deliberately drew the fire of the enemy as they stood on the wharves making lewd and obscene gestures in the direction of the British vessels. Late in the afternoon, British landing parties came ashore and fired the parts of the city that had escaped the bombardment. When the flames were at their height Dunmore, expecting that the fire would throw the American troops into confusion and panic, sent parties in toward the shore. One group managed to drag a field piece into the middle of town, but were driven back to their boats before they could gain a foothold. For raw troops, fighting in the midst of a holocaust of smoke and flame, the Americans did well.[46]

The British kept up sporadic artillery fire until 2:00 A.M. on January 2, 1776. The fire burned for two days and it was said that four-fifths of the houses in the town were reduced to ashes. Shortly afterwards the Whigs, feeling that Norfolk was but little more than a "nest of Tories," put the torch to all but twelve of the remaining buildings. Howe split his forces, stationing detachments at such strategic points as Kemp's landing, Great Bridge, and Suffolk. Dunmore left the Chesapeake in February and it was later claimed that he sold a number of his Negro troops into slavery in the West Indies. He himself was to join the British force in New York. After the departure of Dunmore, and at the request of the other field officers, Howe went up to Williamsburg to advise the Virginia government concerning defensive operations.[47]

The appreciation of the Virginia Convention sitting at Williamsburg had been expressed earlier in a resolution of December 22, 1775: "Resolved unanimously, That the thanks of this convention are justly due to the brave officers, gentlemen volunteers and soldiers of North Carolina, as well as the brethren of that province in general, for their prompt and generous aid in defence of our common rights against the enemies of America and of the British Constitution, and that the president be desired to transmit a copy of this resolution to Colonel Howe."[48]

And from Philadelphia came a glowing letter from John Penn: "I have the pleasure to assure you that our Province stands high in

46. *Colonial Records*, X, 381–82; *State Records*, XI, 353; Samuel Inglis to Robert Morris, 6 January 1776, in Stanley V. Henkels, *Confidential Correspondence of Robert Morris* (Philadelphia, 1917), p. 191.

47. Force, *American Archives*, 4, IV, 53, 293, 946; Council of Officers, 9 January 1776, Emmet Collection.

48. *Colonial Records*, X, 364.

the opinion of Congress. The readiness with which you marched into Virginia and South Carolina hath done you great credit."[49]

The North Carolina Council of Safety seemingly felt that the events in Virginia held the key to the future for, despite the critical situation in their own colony, they addressed a letter to the Virginia Convention offering to allow Howe to remain in Virginia as long as needed, or until such time as North Carolina felt that she needed her troops for her own defense. In reply, the Virginians promised to release the North Carolina troops as quickly as possible, and at the same time praised Howe as "a brave, prudent & spirited Commander." But North Carolina was to feel the need for troops much earlier than it had originally seemed to expect, and by February 18, 1776, the Virginia Committee had relieved Howe's troops to return to their homes.[50]

49. *Ibid.*, p. 455.
50. *State Records*, XI, 270, 274–75.

Chapter 2
The Moore's Creek Bridge Campaign

"King George and Broad Swords!"

That most frustrated of all men, Josiah Martin, although held "in an inglorious captivity" aboard the *Cruizer*, still laid schemes and dreamed grand dreams of conquest. Shortly after his arrival at Fort Johnston, he had instructed a business acquaintance to send him a royal standard, bed and bedding fit for the field, and a tent, "of the size of the Colonel's tent in the army."[1]

With an imagination that knew no limits, Martin forwarded to Lord Dartmouth a lofty design for the subjugation of North Carolina, requesting that it be submitted to the consideration of the Crown. His strategy was not limited to one colony but encompassed details for a restoration of all the southern colonies to royal jurisdiction. The first and basic phase involved arms and ammunition, supposedly to be acquired from General Thomas Gage in Boston. With an adequate supply of weapons, he claimed that at least three thousand of the settlers from the Scottish Highlands could be embodied. With this small army offering protection, Martin estimated that nearly twenty thousand of North Carolina's fighting men would

1. *Colonial Records*, X, 16; Martin to Samuel Martin, 15 November 1775, Martin Papers.

repair to the king's standard. Then, he felt, with such a sizable force on her borders, Virginia would stand "in awe" and would send no reinforcements to the Carolinas and the latter could be overrun with a minimum of effort. In addition to ten thousand stand of arms, six brass six-pounders, and all other supplies necessary to sustain an army in the field, the governor once again requested the restoration of his commission.[2]

As additional insurance for the adoption of his plan, Martin persuaded Alexander Schaw to travel to London and lay before Lord Dartmouth his extensive knowledge of the country. Schaw, a customs officer on the island of St. Christopher and brother of Janet Schaw, was at the time on leave attending the business affairs of his Carolina plantation, "Schawfields."[3]

Dispatches from other southern governors seemed to substantiate Martin's claims. One writer who had traveled through the South in 1773, pictured a region that could be conquered with but little effort:

The Southern Provinces may be entirely thrown out of the Question, not only as being thinly peopled & enervated, But from the great Majority of Negroes intermixed, which exposes them to immediate ruin whenever we detach a small Corps to support an Insurrection. There are besides a Body of hardy Men in their back frontiers whom at present they can scarce keep under, & who bid fair in a few years to dispute the possession of the Country . . . the rest are a mixture of people of different Religions, principles of government, neither United in Interest nor Affection, composed of Breeding people incumber'd with large familys of Children, in so much that there is not half the proportion of effective men to the number of people in British America that there are in the other parts of the World. And even few of these to be spared from providing Sustenance for their familys—the Americans, from the Cheapness of provisions & facility of procuring Land, marrys soon, begetts Children & establishes himself, & is besides too much at his ease to stand the hardships of War.[4]

In England it was generally felt that, with the exception of Georgia, North Carolina was the weakest colony in America. According to some loyalist accounts, the primary opposition in North Carolina would be encountered in the coastal plain. The settlers from the Highlands of Scotland would of a certainty take up arms for the gov-

---

2. *Colonial Records*, X, 45–47; Martin to Samuel Martin, 9 September 1775, Martin Papers.

3. Martin to Dartmouth, 6 July 1775, British Headquarters Papers; Schaw to Dartmouth, 31 October 1775, Dartmouth Manuscripts (transcripts), North Carolina Department of Archives and History, Raleigh, N.C.; Declaration of the Account of Josiah Martin, Esqr., Audit Office Records (transcripts), North Carolina Department of Archives and History, Raleigh, N.C.

4. Reflections on the Means Necessary to Reduce the Americans, March, 1775, Liverpool Papers, British Museum Additional Manuscripts 38374.

ernment, and the Regulators, or "back-Settlers," would at least remain neutral if they did not join the forces of the king. This in itself was reassuring to London, for it was the general impression there that the people of eastern North Carolina "stood in perpetual awe of the Regulators." John Stuart, royal superintendent of Indian Affairs in the Southern Department, reported that the greater number of the frontiersmen were loyalist in sentiment and, given a choice, would support the Crown. He also suggested Indian uprisings in conjunction with possible military action in the low country. As an indication of the low esteem other colonies held of the resistance capabilities of the North Carolinians, one Pennsylvania loyalist wrote: "North Carolina is in general the poorest country on the Continent, Nova Scotia excepted, and one of the Floridas. With a few very honourable exceptions, much of the same character must be given of the people. The bulk of them are renegades from other Colonies."[5]

The sum of these reports concerning the general weakness of North Carolina and Martin's estimates of the number of loyalists generated enthusiasm among certain of the officials in Whitehall. There was some pressure on the ministry to order immediately a battalion of regulars from Boston to support Governor Martin in his bid to reclaim the province. The government, however, refused to act hastily, for the dispatches of other southern governors were equally as optimistic and the conclusion was that any of the southern colonies would act quickly to avail themselves of any military aid.[6]

A southern campaign, with troops from England acting in harmony with a detachment from Gage's army in Boston, was discussed in Privy Council. A proposal was put forth that the first attempt should be against Charleston. The loss of this port, the most important in the South, would not only block importation of rebel supplies, but would also provide an excellent base of operations in any future campaign in the South. It was then that Martin's emissary, Alexander Schaw, proved his worth, ably arguing the cause of a first strike against North Carolina. He suggested that if the province was first returned to royal control, the reduction of Charleston would prove

5. *Annual Register for the Year 1776* (London, 1776), XIX, 156; Lord Townshend to Dartmouth, 21 July 1775, Dartmouth Manuscripts; John Andrews, *History of the War with America, France, Spain and Holland; Commencing in 1775 and Ending in 1783* (London, 1785), II, 171; Force, *American Archives*, 4, IV, 317; Historical Manuscripts Commission, *Report on the Manuscripts of Mrs. Stopford-Sackville of Drayton House, Northamptonshire* (London, 1904), II, 18, hereafter cited as *Report on the Manuscripts of Mrs. Stopford-Sackville.*

6. Sir John Fortescue (ed), *The Correspondence of King George the Third from 1760 to December 1783* (New York, 1928), III, 266–67, 360; *Report on the Manuscripts of Mrs. Stopford-Sackville*, II, 10–11.

much easier, since a route to the "well-affected people" in the back settlements would be opened, thereby affording a source of provisions and possible recruits from among the loyalists. The campaign in North Carolina, he argued, would delay the expedition for only a short while, and once the colony was overrun and under control of the numerous loyalists, it would remain true to the Crown, which "I wish one could be sure of . . . in South Carolina."[7]

Apparently Schaw's polemics were convincing, for a strike at North Carolina was included in the basic plan of operations. Troops from the Irish station under the command of Lord Cornwallis were to be convoyed by a fleet under Sir Peter Parker. The draft of this plan was communicated to General William Howe, Gage's successor as commanding general of British troops in America, and a duplicate was sent to Governor Martin. Howe was instructed to dispatch a detachment from Boston to the Cape Fear, there to make a junction with the seven regiments under Cornwallis, the combined force to act under the direction of a general officer selected by Howe. Dartmouth, just before he was replaced as secretary for the American Department by Lord George Germain, expressed apprehension concerning the success of the Cape Fear operations, especially since later information had implied that the larger vessels of the fleet would be unable to cross the bar at the mouth of the river, thereby losing the support of the guns of the fleet in any amphibious operation. Should such an operation appear feasible, however, an agreed number of troops were to be put ashore in North Carolina with the remainder to continue toward the primary objective—the reduction of Charleston. In a letter dated December 22, 1775, Germain reported that the troops from Ireland were ready for embarkation and were to be convoyed by nine warships of the Royal Navy.[8]

Dartmouth's dispatches outlining the proposed expedition reached Martin on January 3, 1776, and the governor immediately began to implement the local phases of the strategy. On January 10 he issued a proclamation declaring the royal standard to be raised in North Carolina and calling upon all loyal subjects to unite in suppressing the rebellion. On the same day loyalist leaders in the counties of Anson, Cumberland, Chatham, Guilford, Mecklenburg, Rowan, Surry, and Bute were issued the necessary authorization to recruit a

7. Schaw to Dartmouth, 8 November 1775, Dartmouth Manuscripts.

8. Dartmouth to William Howe, 22 October 1775, Germain Papers, William L. Clements Library, University of Michigan, Ann Arbor, Mich.; Germain to William Howe, 8 November 1775, Dartmouth to Martin, 7 November 1775, British Headquarters Papers; *Colonial Records*, X, 364.

militia, commission officers, seize rebel arms and ammunition, and impress all necessary provisions and transportation resources. Once this was accomplished, they were to march from a to-be-announced rendezvous to Brunswick, so timing their arrival that they would be at that town no later than February 15, at which time the fleet should have appeared.[9]

The key to Martin's plan of mobilization was the embodiment of the Highlanders in Cumberland County. As late as November, 1775, a ship of Scottish immigrants had arrived in the Cape Fear, with the wily Martin granting them lands only after they had renewed their oaths of allegiance to the Crown and sworn to "their readiness to lay down their lives in the defence of his Majesty's Government." The Highlanders had long been known for their fighting abilities; the British termed them "naturally warlike" and the Continental Congress had early attempted to enlist their support. In November, 1775, the Congress had directed two Presbyterian ministers to go among these people to explain the nature of the dispute with Great Britain, in an effort to counteract the royalist preachings of one John McLeod, the Presbyterian minister with the Highlanders in North Carolina. This well-intentioned scheme met with meager success because of the inability of these pious envoys to speak Gaelic.[10]

Although Martin had boasted of the fidelity of the Highlanders, he still entertained some doubts, especially concerning those who had been longest in the colony. In 1766 they had demonstrated rebellious tendencies in a public protest against the Stamp Act which they had printed in the *North Carolina Gazette*. In October, 1775, he had felt some alarm when they had declared themselves neutral as a result of the activity of a committee of the Provincial Congress, a committee that had included one of their number, Farquard Campbell. Martin had relied upon Campbell for support and at these first rumors of his defection had angrily condemned him as "an ignorant man." But less than a month later the governor was once again declaring that the Highlanders were almost "without exception staunch to government." This temporary attachment to neutrality by the Highlanders may well have been a result of increasing commercial restrictions imposed by the Committee of Safety. One such order specified that no salt was to be sold at the "landing places" unless the purchaser

9. *Colonial Records*, X, 364, 397, 406, 441–42.
10. *Ibid.*, pp. 327, 577; Anon., *Impartial History of the War in America between Great Britain and Her Colonies, from Its Commencement to the End of the Year 1779* (London, 1780), p. 307; Ford, *Journals of the Continental Congress*, III, 388; Burnett, *Letters of Members of the Continental Congress*, I, 296; MacLean, *Scotch Highlanders in America*, p. 116.

could produce a certificate from the committee identifying him as a good "Liberty Man." This prohibition seems to have been temporary insofar as the Cross Creek merchants were concerned, for they were soon advertising salt again without discrimination to all those who could afford their inflated prices.[11]

Martin had described the loyalists and the military inclinations of the Highlanders in such glowing terms that North Carolina had come to be considered a prime potential pool of recruits for the British army. Agents of General Gage had attempted to enlist some eight hundred men from among the Highlanders and had actually signed up that many from among the more recent arrivals, but the counterefforts of the Whigs frustrated any actual mobilization of those who had signed. Disregarding this reversal, Gage had, in July, 1775, ordered two Scottish-born officers to North Carolina to enlist recruits for a battalion of the Royal Highland Emigrant Regiment, carrying letters from Dartmouth soliciting Martin's aid. Each of the officers, Lieutenant Colonel Donald MacDonald and Captain Donald McLeod, had participated in the battle of Bunker Hill where Mac-Donald, a veteran of the battle of Culloden, had been wounded.[12]

When MacDonald and McLeod had landed at New Bern the Committee of Safety there was immediately warned, "There is reason to suspect their errand of a base nature." In the ensuing investigation, however, the two strangers convinced the committee that they were officers so severely wounded at Bunker Hill that they could no longer serve in the military and had come to North Carolina to seek out friends and possibly settle among them. They were allowed to go their way with a warning and caution against the activities of the loyalists.[13]

Meanwhile Governor Martin saw his dreams of martial glory punctured when Lord Dartmouth refused to restore his commission. The refusal had been based on the opinion of Attorney General Alexander Wedderburn that colonial governors should have no authority over any troops other than the provincial militia, with Dartmouth adding that Martin's power as governor was sufficient to exe-

11. MacLean, *Scotch Highlanders in America*, p. 110; *Colonial Records*, X, 266; *Moravian Records*, II, 861.

12. *Collections of the New-York Historical Society for the Year 1882* (New York, 1893), p. 356; Certificate of Colonel MacDonald, English Records Transcripts, Foreign Office, 1783–1794, North Carolina Department of Archives and History, Raleigh, N.C.; Martin to Alexander McLeod, 4 July 1775, British Headquarters Papers.

13. *Colonial Records*, X, 117, 325; *Gentleman's Magazine*, XLVI (June 1776), 281–82; Almon, *Remembrancer . . . for . . . 1776*, Part II, p. 74.

cute all measures expected of him. Many loyalists of Brunswick County were now coming out to the *Cruizer*, complaining bitterly of harsh treatment received from their former friends and neighbors. Repeatedly they assured the governor that at the proper time they could embody between two and three thousand troops in the area. There were reports, they declared, that the rebels were low in ammunition and arms, which, in turn, suggested that the time for action was near. Martin was determined to draw upon the vast manpower pool he felt existed in the interior of the province—the Highlanders and the Regulators—planning to unite them with the coastal loyalists and hold off the rebels until the arrival of the fleet. To inform the loyalist chieftains of the interior of these developments, he selected one of the Brunswick citizens as a messenger, but this supposed loyalist promptly handed over his information to the Whigs.[14]

Martin then sent Alexander McLean to contact local Tory leaders to determine the number of men each could bring into the royal standard and to emphasize that they were to have their recruits on the coast no later than February 15. At Cross Creek, McLean was assured that no less than three thousand men could be embodied, but there were no more than one thousand stand of arms. Nevertheless, McLean's dispatch to Martin reporting the Highlanders in "high spirits and very fast collecting," and it was his personal estimate that an army of six thousand men, well equipped with horses and wagons, could be raised. It had been decided, however, that the entire force should not march, but that at least a thousand men were to be left in Cross Creek to protect the families and property of those who had marched for the coast. The main body of loyalist troops expected to be in possession of Wilmington as early as February 20, and certainly no later than February 25.[15]

It had been McLean's enthusiasm that had led Martin to issue his proclamation on January 10. McLean dispatched a circular letter calling upon all loyalist leaders to meet in Cross Creek on February 5. It was a stormy gathering. All the Highland chieftains were present, but only four loyalists came from other sections of the colony. Their

14. *Colonial Records*, X, 248, 486–90; Alexander Wedderburn to Dartmouth, n.d., Thomas Gage Papers.
15. *Colonial Records*, X, 487; Alexander McLean, A Narrative of the Proceedings of a Body of Loyalists in North Carolina, in Genl. Howe's Letter of the 25th April 1776, English Records, Colonial Office, 1776 (transcripts), North Carolina Department of Archives and History, Raleigh, N.C., hereafter cited as McLean, Loyalist Narrative. Alexander McLean was but one of the authors of this narrative, apparently written shortly after the battle of Moore's Creek Bridge. The shortage of firearms among the Highlanders possibly may be traced to British orders disarming the Scots after the battle of Culloden in 1746.

earlier enthusiasm somewhat cooled, the Scots were now of the opinion that they should wait at least until March 1 before assembling the troops—unless the British fleet arrived before that date. Other leaders, including those from the Regulator country, were almost abusive in their refusals to consider delay. Since the latter supposedly controlled the greater number of men, the Highlanders conceded to their demands, but now declared that in this circumstance they could be held responsible for raising only seven hundred men. The back-country men shrugged this aside with the boast that rather than the three thousand they had previously promised, they would now bring five thousand men into the field. Why, even now, they bragged, they had collected five hundred men who were ready to march at a moment's notice. Calling their bluff, the council decided that Captain Donald McLeod, as a regular officer of the British Army, should return with these loyalist leaders and conduct their recruits to Cross Creek.[16]

Governor Martin had appointed Donald MacDonald brigadier general of militia "for the time being," and given him command of the loyalist forces. Donald McLeod was made second in command with the militia rank of lieutenant colonel, while the selection of other officers in Martin's forces was to be left to the council of Tory leaders at Cross Creek. The three hundred recruits that MacDonald had already enlisted for the Royal Emigrant Regiment were to be included in the march to the coast. As commanding general, Mac-Donald issued a manifesto calling upon all loyal subjects to repair to the royal standard, and at the same time assuring them no harm would come to their women, children, or property. All provisions taken by the king's troops were to be paid for, while fearful retaliation was promised for any who harmed the families of the men who joined the loyalist force.[17]

In the back country, despite the promises and optimism of the local leaders, the loyalists were finding it difficult to organize. In the Yadkin valley, many of those who were so bold as to voice an affection for George III were forced to flee their homes and hide in the forests, thus gaining for themselves the sobriquet of "Outlyers." Only with the news that the loyalists were rallying at Cross Creek did they creep out of hiding and, in small groups, cautiously make their way

16. McLean, Loyalist Narrative; *Colonial Records*, X, 441–42.

17. *Colonial Records*, X, 443; Charles Stedman, *The History of the Origin, Progress, and Termination of the American War* (London, 1794), I, 179; Certificate of Colonel MacDonald, English Records Transcripts, Foreign Office, 1783–1794.

to Cross Creek. The Tories of Surry County were speedily dispersed by the Whig faction, while the Guilford contingent had been opposed by a hastily organized company under Captain William Dent. In the ensuing skirmish Dent was killed, thereby becoming the first battle casualty of the campaign. Although this Tory company resolutely pushed on toward Cross Creek, others in the Regulator country concealed their political views, with their leaders complaining that there was a scarcity of arms among them, since the Regulators had been forced to surrender their arms to Governor William Tryon after their unsuccessful uprising in the spring of 1771. They did promise, however, that they would rise when the Highlanders returned from the coast and could offer them protection. These people also suffered from a lack of leadership; there was not a man of property or political leadership among them to whom they could look for direction.[18]

The five hundred men that Donald McLeod had been sent to escort to Cross Creek were a churlish and raucous lot. The young officer was not impressed by their appearance, while the rough and tumble backwoodsmen disliked the idea of a spit-and-polish officer in command. To counter their resentment, a hogshead of rum was brought out, "which most of them visited industriously." When a rumor spread through the celebrants that a large body of Whigs was marching against them, the five hundred Tories disappeared even more rapidly than had the hogshead of rum. McLeod, suddenly alone in a strange country, was unable to persuade anyone to guide him to Cross Creek. An embarrassing situation was avoided when he was joined by four Highland officers. Urgent messages were dispatched to the cocksure back-country men who had sat in the council at Cross Creek. They were not to be found. The messenger was informed by their neighbors that "they were Sculking & hiding themselves through Swamps & such concealed places." The unhappy McLeod returned to Cross Hill, the place now designated as the loyalist rendezvous.[19]

Cross Hill was alive with activity. The British had offered a number of enlistment benefits, and the thrifty Scots were taking full advantage of their opportunities. There was a standing offer of two hundred acres of land to all Highlanders in America who would offer their services to the Crown. In addition, Lord Dartmouth had authorized Martin to promise that they would be issued arms, receive

18. *Moravian Records*, III, 1026; *Colonial Records*, X, 599; Andrews, *History of the War with America, France, Spain and Holland*, II, 171; Samuel Johnston to Joseph Hewes, 10 March 1776, Hayes Collection.

19. *Moravian Records*, III, 1026; McLean, Loyalist Narrative. Cross Hill is present-day Carthage, N.C.

the same pay as regular troops, be liberally compensated for any personal equipment including horses and wagons furnished, and not be required to fight beyond the boundaries of North Carolina. As a bonus, all arrears in quitrents were to be forgiven, with a twenty-year future quitrent exemption to be granted. Many Scots enlisted because they had only recently been forced to renew their oaths of allegiance to the king, and they had not been in the country long enough to have gained any attachment to the rebel cause. Most of the older settlers among the Highlanders refused to commit themselves. On the whole, the Tory army was made up of newcomers and the poor. With the exception of the leaders, there was not a man among them who owned property worth as much as £100. Perhaps the most outstanding of the local group was Thomas Rutherford, formerly a member of the Provincial Congress but now termed a "poor Creature" by his former associates. Other loyalist leaders of prominence were Samuel Williams, James Colson, and Dr. John Pyle.[20]

There were about five hundred Highlanders gathered at Cross Hill, and Rutherford had assured MacDonald that he would join him at Cross Creek with an additional five hundred recruits. After deciding to unite these two units as quickly as possible, MacDonald arrived at Cross Creek on February 12 but found no sign of either Regulators or other back-country loyalists. The Guilford County unit, reputed to be one of the strongest expected at the rendezvous, had met with adversity. Seven of their leaders had been arrested and clapped into the jail at Halifax, whereupon their followers turned back and marched homeward. Small groups of the Regulator and other back-country loyalists drifted into Cross Creek, expecting to find Governor Martin and at least one thousand British regulars as had been promised by their fast-talking leaders. Angered at this duplicity, they also turned on their heels and left for their homes. A council of officers resolved to send Donald McLeod and Alexander McLean into the Regulator country in an effort to revive the earlier enthusiasm of these people. About thirty-five miles out of Cross Creek the two officers met Dr. John Pyle and near forty men on their way to the rendezvous. After escorting these newcomers back to camp, and listening to their report of conditions in the west, it was decided that McLeod and McLean should remain with the army, for the situation

20. *Collections of the New-York Historical Society for the Year 1882*, p. 222; *Colonial Records*, X, 308; Johnston to Hewes, 10 March 1776, Hayes Collection. This was the same Dr. John Pyle who was later involved in the so-called "Pyle's Massacre," February 23, 1781, when his group of loyalists were annihilated by Henry Lee's Legion and Andrew Picken's militia about three miles southwest of Graham in Alamance County.

had now grown tense and throughout the province emotions were on the verge of combustion. Yet despite the obvious disaffection shown by many of the back-country men, the gathering at Cross Creek was still referred to by many as "the Regulators."[21]

The activity in the Highland settlements and the bands of armed men marching toward Cross Creek had not gone unnoticed and had alarmed the Whigs of North Carolina. The governor's ambitions for the restoration of the colony to royal control were well known, as were some of his plans for doing it. As early as July, 1775, there had been the idea that "he intends kindling the flames of a Civil War," and county committees of safety had been cautioned to keep a "strict look out" for signs of increasing activity among the Tories. A desperate plea was sent to neighboring governments for aid in relieving the dire shortage of arms and ammunition in North Carolina. The Provincial Council of Virginia lent five hundred pounds of gunpowder and one hundred pounds of lead, while South Carolina responded with an offer of one thousand pounds of gunpowder. Yet firearms were so scarce that the Wilmington Committee of Safety borrowed fifty muskets from the townspeople to arm some of the troops of James Moore's First Regiment.[22]

The western part of the colony, far removed from the scene of action, was a hotbed of rumors. In early December, 1775, a report had been circulated through the area that William Tryon had landed on the coast with a detachment of seven hundred men and had made a junction with Governor Martin, who led an additional seven hundred Scots from the Cape Fear region. Even now, or so ran the rumor, this force was marching on Rowan and Mecklenburg Counties. No sooner had this gossip been disproved than a story, based on more or less reliable information, was circulated that Captain William Fields of Guilford County had received orders from the east directing him to hold his loyalist militia in readiness for immediate action. The people of the upper Yadkin, supposedly neutral, had been angered by reports that the Cross Creek merchants refused to purchase surplus produce, or sell iron, sugar, and salt unless the vendor or purchaser agreed to take an oath of allegiance to George III.[23]

21. McLean, Loyalist Narrative; Johnston to Hewes, 10 March 1776, Hayes Collection; Force, *American Archives*, 4, IV, 1488; *State Records*, XI, 282–83; *Colonial Records*, X, 491–92; J. Blair to Nelly Blair, 21 February 1776, Iredell Papers.

22. *Colonial Records*, X, 118, 124; *State Records*, XI, 271, 272, 273.

23. *Moravian Records*, II, 891, 892; Lyman C. Draper, *King's Mountain and Its Heroes: History of the Battle of King's Mountain October 7th, 1780, and the Events Which Led to It* (Cincinnati, Ohio, 1881), p. 432.

These whisperings led to a semimobilization of the militia and minutemen, and when word did come of the embodiment of the loyalists, many Whig units were ready to march with a minimum of preparation. Although orders required each unit to bring six week's provisions with them, many detachments chose to march unencumbered. Several of these companies on their way to the rendezvous at Hillsborough, marching through the Moravian towns, seized all available lead and commandeered other provisions from the stores. They promised payment at a later date, but the gentle Moravians were of the opinion that they would never receive compensation.[24]

It was the same in the coastal region, although the proceedings were more orderly. On February 10, the lower Cape Fear was alerted to the danger then being fomented at Cross Creek, and when word was received that Captain Fields and his western Tories were on the move toward Cross Creek, mobilization orders were issued to local militia commanders. Colonel Alexander Lillington, militia commander of the Wilmington area, was ordered to alert his command. The New Bern Committee of Safety ordered out the district's militia and minutemen under Colonel Richard Caswell. This unit was equipped with artillery, and Caswell was empowered to purchase necessary wagons and provisions along his line of march. The military units of Dobbs, Johnston, Pitt, and Craven Counties were instructed to join Caswell.[25]

The town of Wilmington suddenly retired behind hastily thrown-up earthworks. Defensive preparations had been initiated upon receipt of information that the *Cruizer* was on its way upriver to attack the town. Martial law was declared, and all those who refused to submit to an oath to support the Whig cause were forced to work on the fortifications. Twenty known Tories were taken into custody. Artillery was mounted on the parapets; fire rafts were prepared, and the women and children were sent to safety outside the town.[26]

These frantic preparations proved worthwhile. When the *Cruizer* approached the town, the sloop was frightened away by the formidable appearance of the works, for its primary mission was not to bombard Wilmington, but to aid the loyalists upstream. An attempt was made to bypass Wilmington by sailing through the channel on

24. Thomas Polk to Ely Kershaw, 23 February 1776, Miscellaneous Papers, 1697–1912; *Moravian Records*, IV, 1877; Bromfield Ridley to John Williams, 14 February 1776, John Williams Papers, Duke University, Durham, N.C.

25. Force, *American Archives*, 4, IV, 1129; *Colonial Records*, X, 444–45.

26. *Colonial Records*, X, 465–67.

the west side of Grand Island, which lay opposite the town. Shallow water forced back the vessel. After a slight skirmish during which a landing party was driven back to the sloop, the *Cruizer* dropped downstream to Brunswick, harrassed by rifle fire from each side of the river[27]

At Cross Creek, MacDonald was industriously applying his talents to the organization of his loyalist army. On February 15 a return of his troops revealed that of approximately 1,400 men present, only 520 possessed firearms. A hastily organized light cavalry detachment sent raiding through the countryside brought in 130 stand of arms confiscated from local Whigs. Powder that had been stored with the Cumberland County Committee of Safety was seized and supplemented through purchases from local merchants. Provisions were also purchased, but such rare items as British colors were made from "camp equipage" by the more talented members of the army.[28]

Time was fast running out for MacDonald and his loyalists. Not only was the estimated time of arrival of the British fleet near, but the Whigs were gradually drawing in a tight circle of men around Cross Creek. Colonel James Moore and a reported 2,000 men were within seven miles of the town and had fortified the bridge across Rockfish Creek, blocking the most direct route to the sea. Moore, with a much smaller force than that reported to MacDonald, had arrived at Rockfish Creek on February 15. With his five fieldpieces giving him a decided advantage in firepower, he decided to assume the defensive at the bridge, giving him time to allow reinforcements to come up. Intelligence of MacDonald's movements was gained from the nearly sixty residents of the vicinity of Cross Creek who made their way into Moore's camp. By February his force numbered approximately 1,100, including a number of small militia and minuteman units who had drifted in. The loyalist strength was estimated at about 1,500. Outnumbered, Moore's best chance of victory lay in defensive operations.[29]

On February 18, MacDonald made his move. He hoped to bluff his way through the blockade at the bridge, and that night the loyalists lay within four miles of Moore's position. The following day he

27. *Ibid.*, pp. 467–68.
28. McLean, Loyalist Narrative; Declaration of the Account of Josiah Martin, Esq., Audit Office Records; Memorial of Donald McDougall, American Loyalist Claims, 1775–1789.
29. *State Records*, XI, 283, 628.

paraded his troops, inspected their gear, and made preparations for battle.[30]

Despite this martial display, MacDonald was in no mood to do battle. As an officer in the British army, his primary responsibility was to deliver the recruits of the Royal Emigrant Regiment to the coast, thence to be transported to the main army by sea; his command of the loyalist militia was of but secondary importance. To avoid combat, a messenger under a flag of truce was sent into Moore's camp, bearing a letter containing a copy of Martin's proclamation and MacDonald's manifesto. In his covering letter the Tory general pointed out to Moore that he apparently was not familiar with these documents or he would have enlisted in the service of the king. He warned that unless the Whigs had not come over to the royal standard by noon of the following day, it would be necessary to consider them as enemies and "the necessary steps for the support of royal authority" would be undertaken.[31]

Moore still played for time. His reply was couched in evasive language with no suggestion concerning his future course of action. He assured the Tory commander that, insofar as he was concerned, neither his duty nor his inclinations would permit him to accept any terms offered by MacDonald. He went on to say that before any definite reply could be composed, the other officers in the vicinity must be consulted. A final decision was promised by noon of the following day.[32]

It was obvious to MacDonald that Moore was procrastinating, for his reply had implied a rejection of any terms. Any determination for immediate action was forestalled as both commanders had designated noon of the following day as the hour of decision. When MacDonald's council of officers announced the possibility of a battle on the next day, two companies of Colonel James Cotton's Anson County loyalist regiment, lead by Captain Samuel Snead, picked up their arms and returned home. This sudden reduction not only decreased manpower, but armaments, with the latter shortage the more alarming.[33]

Farquard Campbell, on parole from the Whigs, came into MacDonald's camp with the word that Richard Caswell and a force of six hundred men was on the march to join Moore. This, in the face

30. McLean, Loyalist Narrative.
31. *State Records*, XI, 276–77.
32. *Ibid.*, p. 277.
33. McLean, Loyalist Narrative.

of the recent defection among his own troops, dictated a change in strategy. The younger officers insisted upon immediate action, but cooler heads prevailed, and a motion for evasive movement was adopted. Campbell offered a suggestion. He proposed that the loyalist army fall back on Cross Creek, cross the Cape Fear at Campbell Town, then strike east for Negro Head Point on the coast before the Whigs could reorganize their forces to block their progress. He promised that he would report Moore's movements. MacDonald recognized the expediency of Campbell's advice and placed his command under marching orders for the following day.[34]

Promptly at noon on February 20, Moore's reply was delivered to MacDonald. He reported that his officers were unanimous in agreeing with his sentiments in their great cause, "the defense of the liberties of mankind." He enclosed for MacDonald a copy of the test oath advocated by the Continental Congress. In conclusion, MacDonald was chided for his perjury when appearing before the New Bern Committee of Safety when he first entered North Carolina.[35]

With military protocol and niceties behind him, the Tory general made preparations for his march. Drawing up his troops in formation, he addressed them in stirring tones, terming them the instrument through which the country was to be restored to their king, which in itself would be a method of ridiculing "those base rascals" who had deserted the night before. In concluding he seemed to be carried away by his own verbiage. In dramatic overtones he called upon all those so fainthearted as not to want to conquer or die to make their decision now. Offered this alternative of glory or death, twenty men stepped from the ranks of Colonel Cotton's regiment and, declaring that "their Courage was not Warproof," laid their arms upon the ground and quietly disappeared into the forest. But among the remainder of his command, MacDonald had so fanned the flames of patriotism that a general "huzza" rang across the field as they moved out.[36]

On the other side of Rockfish, Moore's intelligence failed. Expecting an attack and drawn up behind his earthworks, he did not learn of MacDonald's departure until the following day. Anticipating their objective, he dispatched messengers to all commanders in the field, shifting their troops to block all roads to the sea. An express

34. *Ibid., North Carolina University Magazine,* VII (November, 1857), 139; *Colonial Records,* X, 595.
35. *State Records,* XI, 277–78; *New England Chronicle* (Boston), 25 April 1776.
36. McLean, Loyalist Narrative.

to Colonel Caswell directed that militia officer to take a post at Corbett's Ferry on Black River. Colonels James Martin and James Thackston were ordered to occupy Cross Creek, thus eliminating the last refuge for the Tories. Colonels Alexander Lillington and James Ashe were sent from Moore's command as reinforcements to Caswell, and if a junction could not be made, they were to secure the crossing at Moore's Creek Bridge. Moore marched his own Continentals and militia to Elizabeth Town with an expectation of intercepting the loyalists on the march for Corbett's Ferry. If MacDonald crossed the Black River before his arrival, Moore planned to fall in behind the enemy, harassing the troops until they could be brought to battle, then close in on their rear in an enveloping action. By these skillfully executed maneuvers, James Moore slammed the gateways to the sea in MacDonald's face.[37]

Upon the reception of Moore's orders, Caswell moved in on Corbett's Ferry and deployed his troops. "Old Mother Covington and her daughter," as the two light-artillery pieces were affectionately termed, were so positioned as to cover the approaches to the river crossing. Riders were sent through the countryside, instructing the inhabitants to destroy all bridges in the path of the enemy. To prevent the use of the river for either transportation or succor for the Tories, narrow points along the Cape Fear were secured. Colonel William Purviance, commanding the defenses of Wilmington, threw a heavy boom across the river above that port.[38]

The loyalists, unaware of these efforts to check their progress, crossed the Cape Fear at Campbell Town. To discourage pursuit, they destroyed their boats, but at the same time they created a gap in their own route of escape. As the troops were formed on the northern bank of the stream, Donald McLeod was ordered to mount one hundred Highlanders with a mission to scout and secure bridges in advance of the main body.[39]

MacDonald's army moved eastward at a sluggish pace. Inasmuch as bridges were a luxury in eighteenth-century North Carolina, the country people had not completely destroyed them upon the approach of the Tories. Nevertheless, a number of the bridges required strengthening before the wagons could cross safely. Information that Caswell had changed his line of march was obtained through

37. *State Records*, XI, 284.

38. *Colonial Records*, X, 467–68; E. W. Carruthers, *Interesting Revolutionary Incidents: And Sketches of Characters, Chiefly in the "Old North State,"* (Philadelphia, 1854), p. 92.

39. McLean, Loyalist Narrative.

the capture of one of the riders who had been sent out to alert the countryside. This "Spy," as he was termed by the loyalists, apparently refused to reveal Caswell's ultimate destination, but the knowledge that the Whigs might be marching toward him led MacDonald, fearing ambush, to move with extreme caution.[40]

As the Tories neared the Black River on February 23, word was sent back from the vanguard that Caswell was encamped at Corbett's Ferry, only four miles ahead. A halt was called and the troops were drawn up in battle formation. All broadswords, or claymores, the traditional hand weapon of the Scots, were collected and reissued to a company of volunteers under Captain John Campbell. Intended to act as shock troops, this special unit was to be stationed in the center of the battle formations. With this reorganization, MacDonald marched forward, half expecting that the time for battle had come. A five-man enemy scouting party was captured; interrogation of the prisoners revealed that Caswell had entrenched himself on the far side of the river. The army went into camp while measures to counteract this new development were considered.[41]

McLeod's mounted troops scouted upstream. Four miles above the ferry they met a Negro who told them that he knew of a "flat" sunk on the far side of the river that could be raised with little trouble. This man was employed to raise the boat as a message was dispatched to MacDonald informing him of the find. McLeod remained to guard his find and initiate the construction of a bridge.[42]

Before marching to this site, MacDonald detached a small group "to amuse Caswell" and cover his own movements. This unit stationed itself across the river from Caswell's entrenchments, moving noisily through the trees, playing bagpipes, beating drums, and punctuating this bedlam with an occasional rifle shot to keep Whig heads down.[43]

As the main army came up to take over construction of the bridge, McLeod and his horsemen crossed to the far shore and resumed their scouting operations. Three miles beyond the river a supply train of twenty-one bullocks and two wagons loaded with flour destined for Caswell was captured. Twenty men and two officers were taken prisoner. From them it was learned that Caswell was expecting reinforcements.[44]

Construction of the bridge was completed, and by eight o'clock

40. *Ibid.*
41. *Ibid.*
42. *Ibid.*; *State Records*, XI, 284.
43. McLean, Loyalist Narrative.
44. *Ibid.*

on Monday, February 26, the passage of the river had been achieved. Detachments were called in and the march to the sea was resumed. The unopposed river crossing had so inflated the spirits of the loyalist troops that the general feeling was that Caswell should be attacked at the first opportunity, "the Army being in Motion for that Purpose."[45]

Caswell, in the meantime, discovered that he had been duped by a few rifles, drums, and bagpipes and that the loyalists had successfully negotiated a passage of the river. Colonel Moore was still at Elizabeth Town, awaiting supplies for Caswell's troops, when a message arrived from Caswell with the information that the Tories had outmaneuvered him. Moore moved fast. Caswell was ordered to march at once for Moore's Creek Bridge, and if this did not prove expedient, he was to close in on the rear of MacDonald's army in a harassing action. Moore loaded his troops aboard boats and floated downriver some sixty miles to Dollison's Landing, from where he planned to move overland to Moore's Creek. He arrived at Dollison's late in the afternoon of February 26 and camped for the night, awaiting daylight to collect the horses needed to draw his artillery. Late that night dispatch riders brought the news that Caswell had made a junction with Lillington at Moore's Creek and had entrenched after destroying a portion of the bridge.[46]

Moore's Creek Bridge provided a perfect defensive situation, a narrow bridge in an area that was more swamp than dry land. The creek itself flows into the Black River about ten miles above that tributary's confluence with the Cape Fear. At the bridge site the stream is about fifty feet wide with a depth of five feet and a tidal variation of three feet. Here the creek crawls through the marsh in a series of twisting loops. Beneath the dank waters lay a bottom miry with the accumulation of years of swamp wastes. The bridge itself was located on a sand bar, the highest point in the area.

Colonel Alexander Lillington had been the first to occupy the position and had fortified a slightly elevated knoll on the east bank of the creek. Caswell, arriving on the scene with eight hundred men, assumed the command since Lillington's force was made up only of the Wilmington battalion of minutemen. Some time after his arrival Caswell had the men cross the bridge and throw up new entrenchments on the west bank.[47]

45. *Ibid.*
46. *State Records*, XI, 284.
47. *Colonial Records*, X, 482; Force, *American Archives*, 4, V, 62–63.

The Tories had examined Caswell's camp site at Corbett's Ferry after his departure, which had been executed in such haste that several footsore horses and some provisions had been left behind. Mac-Donald increased his rate of march, but when his troops were within six miles of Moore's Creek, his scouts reported that Caswell had won the race.[48]

Donald MacDonald was an old man; one contemporary claimed he was "near seventy years of age." He had long been active in the service of his king, but the forced marches and constant tensions of the campaign had so exhausted him that he fell ill.[49]

To secure information of Caswell's position, James Hepburn, MacDonald's secretary and a former member of the Provincial Congress, was sent as a messenger under a flag of truce into the Whig camp. In his message to Caswell, MacDonald urged him to submit, have his men lay down their arms, take the oath of allegiance, and accept the pardon of the Crown. He strengthened his offer with the threat that unless the rebels complied with his terms he would be forced to "take the necessary steps to Conquer and Subdue you." The usual copy of Martin's proclamation and MacDonald's manifesto accompanied the ultimatum.[50]

Caswell flatly refused to consider the contents of the message, but Hepburn's primary mission was accomplished. The Tory messenger had used his eyes while in the camp of the enemy, yet not well enough. When he returned he reported that Caswell was encamped on the near side of the creek and, with this barrier at his rear, it was practicable to attack his position.[51]

MacDonald, following the accepted military procedure of the day, called a council of his officers. Sentiment was divided as to the practicability of attacking the entrenched rebels. MacDonald, according to his later statements, was not in favor of closing with Caswell, for not only did he feel that he was outnumbered, but half of his men were without firearms. But so persuasively did the younger and more aggressive faction argue that it was eventually unanimously agreed to take the offensive the following morning. MacDonald, tired

48. McLean, Loyalist Narrative.

49. J. F. D. Smyth, *A Tour of the United States of America* (London, 1784), I, 232. MacDonald's age varies in all accounts, with some giving it as low as fifty, others as high as eighty.

50. MacDonald to Caswell, 26 February 1776, Donald MacDonald Papers, North Carolina Department of Archives and History, Raleigh, N.C.

51. McLean, Loyalist Narrative.

and sick, was in no condition to stand the rigors of combat, and Donald McLeod was appointed to lead the assault.[52]

The hour for attack was set for daybreak. This called for an immediate implementation since the loyalists were still six miles from the battleground. The severe shortage of firearms became even more evident since only 500 men of approximately 1,600 were found to be properly equipped for combat. The approach march began at one o'clock in the morning. The loyalists, unfamiliar with the terrain, were soon lost and floundering in the mire. This so delayed them that it was only an hour before dawn when the dying flames of Caswell's campfires were sighted through the trees. To take full advantage of the element of surprise, McLeod divided his troops into three columns. They entered the enemy's camp in silence, only to discover that Caswell had decamped during the night, leaving his fires burning to cover his movement.[53]

It was still dark and difficult to determine the exact location of the bridge. McLeod ordered his troops back into the cover of the trees while the three columns were reformed into a battle line. A rallying cry, so dear to the hearts of Highland warriors, "King George and Broad Swords!" was passed along the line. The signal for the attack was to be three cheers. As the line was being formed, rifle shots rang out near the spot where the bridge was thought to be. The impetuous McLeod could wait no longer. As the three cheers rang out, the drums began to roll and the shrill squeal of bagpipes bit through the cool morning air. The line, with Campbell's broadswordsmen in the center, moved forward.[54]

Alexander McLean, leading a patrol, had come upon the bridge quite unexpectedly. A challenge from Caswell's sentries floated across the stream. McLean answered that he was a friend. "A friend to whom?" was the answering challenge. With McLean's reply, "to the king," the dim shapes on the far shore fell to the ground. McLean, still believing them to be his own men who had somehow managed to cross the bridge, issued a challenge in Gaelic. When there was no answer, he ordered his men to take cover and open fire on the opposite bank of the stream.[55]

McLeod, followed by Campbell's broadswordsmen, hurried for-

52. Certificate of Colonel MacDonald, English Records Transcripts, Foreign Office, 1783–1794; McLean, Loyalist Narrative.

53. McLean, Loyalist Narrative; *State Records*, XI, 368.

54. *State Records*, XI, 368; Carruthers, *Interesting Revolutionary Incidents*, p. 190.

55. McLean, Loyalist Narrative.

ward to determine the cause for this sudden outburst of firing. Examining the bridge, they discovered that approximately half the planking had been removed. To make the crossing even more difficult, Caswell had ordered the two bare log stringers to be greased with soft soap and tallow.[56]

McLeod, on one of the slippery logs, Campbell on the other, led the Highlanders on a foolhardy charge across the bridge. The broadswordsmen maintained their footing by thrusting the points of their weapons into the sleepers. As the leaders reached the far shore, "Old Mother Covington and her daughter" boomed their disapproval, echoed by the sharp crackle of musket fire. With this "very proper reception," both McLeod and Campbell fell, mortally wounded. McLeod, a brave soldier who "would have done honor to a good cause," tried to struggle to his feet, shouting encouragement to his men and waving his sword forward in the direction of the enemy until a sudden volley snuffed out his life. The first blast of lead swept the bridge clean. Many Highlanders, wounded, toppled into the creek and drowned. Others, thrown from the bridge by the shock of the sudden volley, were pulled beneath the dark waters by the weight of their heavy clothing. All of those who managed to cross the bridge were shot down, with McLeod's body within a few paces of Caswell's earthworks.[57]

On the opposite shore some Highlanders took cover and returned the fire of the Whigs. Many of the Regulators and other loyalists fled the field; rallying efforts by their officers were feeble. Colonel Cotton fled at the first fire, while Thomas Rutherford "ran like a lusty fellow." In the grey light of the misty dawn, the fire of the Highlanders was hasty and wild, the majority of their shots singing high above the heads of Caswell's men. Their aim was not improved by the precipitate flight of their officers and comrades, and they soon joined in the rout. There was a general rush for the spot where the wagons had been left. But wagons are not fit vehicles for headlong flight; horses were cut loose from their harness and, with as many as three men mounted on one animal, ridden away in the direction of the camp of the night before.[58]

56. Smyth, *Tour of the United States of America*, I, 231; Stedman, *History of the . . . American War*, I, 181; Carruthers, *Interesting Revolutionary Incidents*, pp. 184–85.

57. *North Carolina University Magazine*, VII (November, 1857), 139; *State Records*, XI, 285, XV, 784–85.

58. *Pennsylvania Evening Post*, 23 March 1776; Force, *American Archives*, 4, V, 170; McLean, Loyalist Narrative; Stedman, *History of the . . . American War*, I, 181; Moore, *Diary of the American Revolution*, I, 209–10.

The Whigs, with a shout of triumph, leaped over the parapets in pursuit. A few loyalists, not so fleet of foot as their companions, were captured. The victors, however, did not immediately follow up their advantage but halted to pillage Tory baggage and collect the wounded. Only two of their number were wounded and only one, John Grady of Anson County, seriously so—he was to die of his wounds four days after the battle. It was impossible to determine loyalist losses. There were at least thirty, but a number had disappeared beneath the murky waters of the creek, while others were presumed to have died of their wounds in the swamp. Caswell's first estimate was later revised upward to seventy by Moore. An examination of McLeod's body revealed that he had been riddled by nine musket balls and twenty-four swan shot.[59]

Moore and his army arrived in Caswell's camp several hours after the battle. He immediately organized a pursuit. Patrols were dispatched to determine the escape route of the enemy, with orders to collect all articles of value thrown away by the enemy. Detachments of troops were deployed to strategic locations to discourage further loyalist attempts to reach the coast. Other parties were ordered out with instructions to take into custody all suspicious persons and to disarm all Highlanders and Regulators, no matter what their political affiliations. The troops of the Wilmington garrison were ordered out for the chase. With reports that the enemy was fleeing toward Cross Creek, Moore dispatched a rider to Colonel James Martin, commanding the occupation troops in that place, with orders to close in on the Tories.[60]

The defeated loyalists had crashed wildly through the swamps to their camps of the night before, there to discover General MacDonald sleeping peaceably in his tent, unaware of the disaster that had overtaken his army. The remaining officers were immediately summoned into council while a survey was being taken of the supplies still on hand. Only two barrels of flour remained to feed the survivors. A proposal was advanced that the army return to Cross Creek, fortify the town, and hold out until further instructions were received from Governor Martin. This suggestion was discarded when it was learned that James Martin had occupied the town. The final decision was to divide the remaining ammunition among the sur-

59. S. A. Ashe, *History of North Carolina* (Greensboro, N.C., 1908–25), I, 504; *Colonial Records*, X, 482; Force, *American Archives*, 4, V, 63; *State Records*, XI, 285; Moore, *Diary of the American Revolution*, I, 209; *Virginia Gazette*, 22 March 1776; *The North Carolina Historical Review*, XXX (January 1953), 50–55.

60. *North Carolina University Magazine*, VII (November, 1857), 140; *Virginia Gazette*, 22 March 1776; *State Records*, XI, 285.

vivors and then disband. For protection, it was felt best for the men to march in a body to Smith's Ferry, some twenty-five miles above Cross Creek, and from there make their way home as best they could.[61]

MacDonald, too weak to travel, remained in his tent and was soon captured. Taken to Moore's camp, he still retained enough military dignity to insist upon a formal surrender. He tendered his sword to Colonel Moore, who, following the usual military practice of the day, returned it to him, assuring his prisoner that he would be well treated. After his baggage had been searched for papers, the Tory general was conducted to Halifax by way of New Bern.[62]

The loyalist army soon suffered the same fate as its general. The survivors had marched only a few miles to Black Mingo Creek when they suddenly found themselves surrounded by a small group of mounted Whig militia demanding their surrender. To resist would have been futile—the Tories laid down their arms. They were marched to Smith's Ferry by their captors, who were joined there by 500 men under Colonel Nicholas Long. The prisoners were searched, their arms, ammunition, and wagons seized. Nearly 850 of the rank and file were paroled and allowed to return to their homes on their oaths not to take up arms against the patriot cause in the future. The officers, however, were incarcerated in the tiny jail at Halifax, which was soon bulging with loyalist prisoners of war. In addition to Donald MacDonald, there were at least thirty other officers confined, among them Allan MacDonald, Flora's husband.[63]

In addition to prisoners, much of material worth had been taken. Listed among the booty seized from the loyalists (including noncombatants) were 350 gun and shot bags; nearly 150 dirks and swords; 1,500 stand of firearms; and two medicine chests that had just arrived from England, one of which was valued at £300. Thirteen wagons, complete with teams, were taken. In Cross Creek a Negro revealed the hiding place of a chest, buried beneath the floor of a stable, containing £15,000 sterling in gold coins.[64]

This was the official list of goods seized by the province, but the Highlanders and other loyalists suffered additional indignities as a

61. Carruthers, *Interesting Revolutionary Incidents*, p. 91; McLean, Loyalist Narrative.

62. Force, *American Archives*, 4, VI, 613–14.

63. *Colonial Records*, X, 486; Carruthers, *Interesting Revolutionary Incidents*, pp. 108–9; *State Records*, XI, 503; McRee, *Life and Correspondence of James Iredell*, I, 273.

64. *Virginia Gazette*, 23 March 1776; *Colonial Records*, X, 485–86. The 1,500 stand of arms must have included those gathered from Tories and other suspected persons after the battle, for the greatest number of firearms listed in MacDonald's force at any one time was 650.

result of the deluge of troops that had descended upon the Cape Fear region. The large stocks of merchandise in the shops of the Scottish merchants were sources of great temptation for the poorer sort of the back-country settlements. The militia detachments occupying Cross Creek called a conference of their officers wherein it was resolved that each member of the militia would be entitled to one bushel of Tory salt if he would assume the responsibility of transporting it to his home. The merchants of the community were also taken to Halifax and held for a short time, but were soon released on bond and allowed to resume their business activities. Other inhabitants suffered in various ways; when the Surry County militia passed through the Moravian towns on their way home it was noticed that many were wearing "Scottish clothes."[65]

Plundering, however is never a prerogative limited to the victors. Those sullen Regulators who had stormed out of Cross Creek during the mobilization of the loyalists had organized themselves into bands, some totaling as many as 180 men, and had bettered their economic status by raiding the farms of those professed Whigs who were so unfortunate as to lie on their homeward route. In retaliation, as the militia of the upper Yadkin valley returned from the campaign, they "scoured" the forests of Wake County, flushing out a number of Tories, one of whom they peremptorily hanged.[66]

Josiah Martin, the person indirectly responsible for these outbursts of turbulent passions, was still aboard the *Cruizer* and still writing lengthy dispatches to England. He shrugged off the Moore's Creek Bridge affair as only a "little check the loyalists here have received," meanwhile stubbornly insisting that the prospects of returning North Carolina to royal authority were as promising as ever. He did feel, however, that any future expedition should be planned with an expectation of making a junction with the loyalists in the interior rather than on the coast. To intimidate the local inhabitants, and possibly in imitation of the British coastal raids the British navy had been carrying out in New England, Martin used the threat of the *Cruizer*'s guns in requisitioning supplies from the citizens of Wilmington. The townspeople called his bluff, refused his demands, and quietly strengthened their fortifications. As an added precaution, Colonel

65. John Graham, Diary, William A. Graham Papers, North Carolina Department of Archives and History, Raleigh, N.C.; *Moravian Records*, III, 1029, 1058. In July, 1776, two hundred bushels of salt were requisitioned from the merchants of Cross Creek to be distributed among the veterans of the Moore's Creek campaign who lived in Wake and Granville counties. (*Colonial Records*, X, 690.)

66. McRee, *Life and Correspondence of James Iredell*, I, 273; Draper, *King's Mountain and Its Heroes*, p. 432.

Moore moved his First Regiment of Continentals into the port town, but the militia and minutemen were ordered home, as were the irregulars stationed at Cross Creek under Colonel Martin.[67]

As these groups returned to their homes and the hysteria of the moment subsided, rebellion once again became an emotional rather than a martial experience. Violence once again became a community affair. Despite their paroles, many loyalists were not allowed to return to their homes by their former neighbors. Many hid in the forests, some not daring to come out until the British invasion of North Carolina in 1781. Others, although they returned to their homes, would scurry to the protection of the nearest swamp or thicket at the report of Whig militia in the neighborhood. And the Provincial Congress, enmeshed in the passions of a civil war, refused to concern themselves with either the families of these men, or the dependents of those Tory officers who were sent as prisoners to Philadelphia. These people, often living among vindictive neighbors, were in constant terror. Pillaging Whigs declared open season upon them, and no less often were they the victims of marauders masquerading as loyalists.[68]

In some instances, the excuse of loyalist control was employed as an instrument to seize political power. William Rand, appointed to inventory Tory property at Cross Creek, set himself up as a local dictator, seizing power through the appointment of local justices. So harsh were his measures that from Whig and Tory alike rose the cry, "We have not the Shadow of liberty among us!"[69]

The legislature also sought its share of the spoils. By November, 1776, an act confiscating loyalist property was passed, and the following April a similar statute ordered the death penalty for certain crimes committed against the state in the name of loyalism. Many loyalists, especially those who had held office under the Crown, sailed for the British strongholds of New York and Nova Scotia on the first ships on which they could book passage.[70]

The victory at Moore's Creek Bridge and the decline of British authority in North Carolina had a salutary effect on what had promised to be a major problem—the fear of a British-inspired slave insurrection. Shortly after the battle one planter wrote, "The Negroes at Cape Fear were never known to behave so well as they have lately."[71]

---

67. *Colonial Records*, X, 492–93; *State Records*, XI, 279–81, 285.
68. Memorial of James Green, American Loyalist Claims, 1775–1789; *State Records*, XI, 829.
69. *State Records*, XI, 627–30.
70. *Ibid.*, pp. 756–66, XXIII, 985–86, XXIV, 9–12. Later laws confiscating loyalist property were passed in 1778, 1779, 1781, 1782, 1784, and 1787.
71. Force, *American Archives*, 4, V, 170.

Yet the defeat of the loyalists excited little interest in England, perhaps an indication of the growing low esteem in which the ministry held the loyalists as a potential military force, certainly not a force that could act independently of the regular army. In London, the battle was generally disregarded or brushed aside without comment. The official news organ of the government, the *London Gazette*, completely ignored the affair, while the *Gentleman's Magazine* dismissed it with the observation that the business was of no importance, as the Americans "only reduced a body of their own people, supported by no one company of regular troops." Only the *Annual Register*, of the leading periodicals, saw the danger the rebel victory foretold, and warned that the loyalists could not be expected to rise so readily another time. The attention of its readers was directed to the rapid manner in which the colony had raised approximately ten thousand men, and to the fact that "they [the Whigs] had encountered Europeans [the Highlanders] (who were supposed to hold them in the most sovereign contempt, both as men and soldiers) and had defeated them with an inferior force."[72]

In the northern colonies, this victory was exaggerated to an importance out of all perspective. This was one of the first absolute decisions won by force of American arms, and the abilities of the North Carolina colonels, even those who had played but minor roles, were inflated beyond recognition. Ezra Stiles reflected the general jubilation of New England in his diary: "The Colonels *Moore, Martin, Caswell, Polk, Thackston, Lillington & Long*, have great Merit; any one of these Gent. in this Country would be an over match for a *Howe, Burgoyne*, or a *Clinton*. Their knowledge of the Country and necessary Modes of Attack would frustrate any Attempt fallen upon by the Characters last mentioned. The Whole Province in general consider Regulars in the Woods an easy Conquest."[73]

As in so many battles, this victory was to eventually end in controversy, albeit of a local nature. The point of argument was, Who had been in command at Moore's Creek Bridge, Lillington or Caswell? This controversy, long to be argued in eastern North Carolina, even saw the Lillington adherents setting their protest to doggerel:

Moore's Creek field, the bloody story,
Where Lillington fought for Caswell's glory.

From the available evidence there seems but little doubt that Cas-

72. Almon, *Remembrancer . . . for . . . 1776*, Part II, p. 155; *Gentleman's Magazine*, XLVI (June, 1776), 281; *Annual Register for 1776*, pp. 157–58.

73. Franklin Bowditch Dexter (ed.), *The Literary Diary of Ezra Stiles, D.D., LL.D., President of Yale College* (New York, 1901), II, 6–7.

well was the commander in the field, but the argument fails when the consequences are fully weighed.[74]

The real hero of the campaign was James Moore, although he was not a participant in the ultimate battle. It was Moore who, with all the finesse of a master chess player, maneuvered his troops in such a fashion as to effectively seal off the loyalists from their objective and force them to do battle on ground of his own choosing.

The Moore's Creek Bridge campaign, viewed from a perspective of nearly two hundred years, assumes greater importance than in 1776. Had the loyalists reached the sea, it is not unreasonable to suppose that their ranks would have been swelled considerably by the Tories of the coastal areas. If a junction had been made with Governor Martin, and arms in sufficient number acquired, large numbers of loyalists and Regulators would have flocked in to the royal standard. But time, terrain, the sea, Richard Caswell, and James Moore all cooperated to frustrate Tory hopes.

One of the intangibles fell on the negative side. The success of the militia in this engagement so raised appreciation of the occasional soldier that North Carolina consistently fell short of her quota of troops for the Continental Line throughout the remaining years of the American Revolution.

Perhaps the most positive result of the victory was that it possibly played a significant role in North Carolina's decision, on April 12, 1776, to instruct her delegates in the Continental Congress "to concur with the delegates of the other colonies in declaring Independency. . . ." As early as April 5, Samuel Johnston had suggested this when he wrote from Halifax that "all our people here are up for Independence."[75]

74. McRee, *Life and Correspondence of James Iredell*, I, 272.
75. *Colonial Records*, X, xviii; McRee, *Life and Correspondence of James Iredell*, I, 275.

Chapter 3
The British in North Carolina

"Nothing is left but to fight it out...."

In the flush of enthusiasm following the victory at Moore's Creek Bridge, North Carolinians evaluated only the immediate results and seemingly gave little consideration to the future. The initial jubilance of the people soon waned into complacency. By the middle of April the militia had been disbanded and allowed to return home, while the Provincial Congress had fulfilled its public obligations by formally extending the thanks of that body to Caswell and his men.[1]

For some reason, North Carolina did not seem to take the threat of a British invasion seriously, despite the warning by the Continental Congress on January 1, 1776, that the British ministry was apparently planning an attack upon the Carolinas and Virginia. It had been suggested that the Committees of Safety of the three provinces meet together to consider joint action in the event of such an invasion. These committees ignored the proposal. Perhaps the apathy of the colony was partially the result of impressions gained from the October 26, 1775, speech by George III in which that monarch had implied that he wished no more than to have the colonies returned to the same status within the empire that they had occupied in 1763.

1. *Colonial Records*, X, 513, 515.

This had given rise to the speculation that there was some conciliatory move in the offing.[2]

Yet warnings continued to come from Philadelphia. Even before Moore's Creek Bridge Joseph Hewes had noted that "all accounts from England seem to agree that we shall have a dreadful storm bursting on our heads thro' all America in the Spring." As for the rumors of possible peace negotiations, Hewes warned that the British "are to treat under the influence of a mighty Fleet & Army, [and] what are we to expect from the mouth of a Cannon or the point of a Bayonet?" And he was to add later, "nothing is left but to fight it out, and for this we are not well provided, having but little ammunition, no Arms, no money, nor are we unanimous in our Councils, we do not treat each other with that decency and respect that was observed heretofore, Jealousies, ill natured observations and recriminations take the place of reason and Argument, our Tempers are soared. . . ." John Penn reported that he had seen an Irish newspaper that had contained a story to the effect that seven regiments were being dispatched to Governor Martin and added, "I hope we to the Southward shall act like men determined to be free." His letter ended with the plea, "For God's sake, my Good sir, encourage our People, animate them to dare even to die for their country."[3]

The British expedition to the southern colonies had met with many delays, brought about by bureaucratic fumblings and foul weather. Some eight months after the approval of the plan, seven regiments finally sailed from Cork, under the command of General Charles Cornwallis and convoyed by the fleet of Admiral Sir Peter Parker. In Boston, General William Howe selected General Henry Clinton to command the operations after the junction with Cornwallis's troops in the Cape Fear. Charleston was the primary objective, for, as Lord George Germain had noted, that port was "the Seat of Commerce in all that part of America, and consequently the place where the most essential Interest of the Planters are concentrated, the restoration of legal Government there, must & will, have very important consequences." If an attack upon Charleston did not prove feasible, Clinton was to operate in any of the southern colonies where an opportunity presented itself, perhaps even cooperate with Governor Dunmore in the Chesapeake. But in no instance was Clinton to haz-

2. Force, *American Archives*, 4, IV, 1627; *Colonial Records*, X, 395–96.
3. *Colonial Records*, X, 446–47, 449, 455–56; Burnett, *Letters of Members of the Continental Congress*, I, 349; Ford, *Journals of the Continental Congress*, IV, 222n; William Hooper to Samuel Johnston, 6 February 1776, Emmet Collection.

ard his troops, and if matters took a critical turn, he was immediately to rejoin Howe in the northern colonies.[4]

On January 20, 1776, Clinton sailed aboard the frigate *Mercury*, accompanied by the armed sloop *Scorpion* and three transports. Aboard were two companies of light infantry along with some Scottish Highlanders. The latter, it was hoped, would be useful in recruiting loyal Scots in North Carolina. By February 4, Clinton's little flotilla dropped anchor in New York harbor. By coincidence, Major General Charles Lee, his skinny frame wracked with gout, arrived in the city about the same time with seven hundred American troops. Expecting an attack upon the city, he sent for an additional regiment. Clinton, however, pledged his word that his troops had not come to attack the city, and stated that his only purpose in coming in was to visit his old friend, Governor William Tryon. This Lee felt to be "the most whimsical piece of civility I ever heard of." In fact, Clinton was audacious enough to state that his true destination was North Carolina where he was to be joined by troops from overseas, an announcement that Lee termed "certainly a droll way of proceeding; to communicate his full plan to the enemy is too novel to be credited." Yet Clinton sailed within the week, leaving matters even more confusing than when he arrived.[5]

Lee had been preparing to assume the command of an expedition to Canada, and was unhappy when those plans were changed. Now he was to assume the command of the newly created Southern Department, comprising the provinces of Virginia, North Carolina, South Carolina, and Georgia. At the same time that Lee's orders were changed, the Continental Congress created six new brigadier generals: Lord Stirling (William Alexander), William Thompson, John Armstrong, Andrew Lewis, James Moore, and Robert Howe, the last four of whom were destined to serve under Lee in the Southern Department. Lewis and Howe were directed to assume the command of the Continental troops in Virginia, Armstrong to command in South Carolina, while Moore was to be the commanding general of North Carolina. Under the practice of the day, in actual rank they were listed in the order, Armstrong, Thompson, Lewis, Moore, Stirling,

4. Germain to Major General Clinton or the Officer appointed to command an expedition to the Southern Colonies, 6 December 1776, PRO CO5/243/97; Precis of the Expedition to the Southern Colonies, Germain Papers; *English Historical Review*, LXVI (October, 1951), 54.

5. Force, *American Archives*, 4, X, 412–13, 420–21; *Colonial Records*, X, 428–29; *Lee Papers*, I, 271–72.

and Howe. Lee, after visits to Philadelphia and Baltimore, arrived at Williamsburg in Virginia on March 26, 1776.[6]

Clinton's fleet arrived off the Cape Fear on March 12, to discover not only that the loyalists had met with disaster at Moore's Creek Bridge but that the troops from Ireland under Lord Cornwallis had not yet arrived. Clinton was not unexpected. For the past week rumors had suggested his destination, and a British packet captured in the Chesapeake had carried a letter stating that North Carolina was his immediate objective. His fleet appeared larger than it actually was; ten or twelve sail of the estimated twenty had been taken as prizes on the voyage southward. It was guessed that the British troops aboard the transports numbered between four hundred and seven hundred men. Every day Clinton exercised his men, landing them upon little Battery Island, near enough to the men-of-war to be protected by their guns, and distant enough from the shore to escape harassing fire by the Americans. Knowing that his men might be called upon to take Charleston, Clinton drilled them in street fighting.[7]

Captain John Collet, former commander of Fort Johnston, had returned aboard the armed vessel, *General Gage*. This "pert audacious little scoundrel" seems to have returned to North Carolina for just one reason—revenge for his humiliation when the rebels burned the fort. After the citizens of Brunswick fled, Collet burned Bellfont, the elegant home of William Dry, formerly a member of Martin's council and collector of the customs for the Port of Brunswick, "for no other crime than being a friend to his country." The new home of William Hooper some three miles below Wilmington and not yet complete was also put to the torch, with Hooper commenting, "That hopeful youth made a Bonfire of a country house of mine. . . . I suffered little more than the mortification of having given Martin an opportunity to triumph at my expense." Hooper barely escaped kidnapping when a boat from the *Cruizer* came within a hundred yards of his seashore home before it was detected.[8]

6. *Lee Papers*, I, 342–43, 343–44; Ford, *Journals of the Continental Congress*, IV, 174, 180–81; *Colonial Records*, X, 482–83; John Hancock to Lee, 1 March 1776, Papers of the Continental Congress.

7. *State Records*, XI, 281–82; *Virginia Gazette*, 29 March 1776, 5 April 1776; *Lee Papers*, I, 398–400; Force, *American Archives*, 4, V, 733, 928, 1517.

8. *Virginia Gazette*, 5 April 1776; Anderson Galleries, *The Library of Dr. Geo: C. F. Williams* (New York, 1934), p. 166; Alfred M. Waddell, *A History of New Hanover County* (Wilmington, N.C., 1909), I, 179; Benson J. Lossing, *The Pictorial Field Book of the Revolution; or, Illustrations by Pen and Pencil, of the History, Biography, Scenery, Relics, and Traditions of the War for Independence* (New York, 1851), II, 383.

At the request of the Wilmington Committee of Safety, James Moore, now wearing the pink ribbon of a brigadier general, marched his troops to the Cape Fear, including 120 men of Howe's Second Regiment in addition to 449 of his own First Regiment. A number of militia and minutemen swelled the total to 1,847. Caswell was on the march with an additional 600 minutemen of Craven County. Moore estimated British strength at "no less than 7,000 men," and he was certain that Clinton would drive inland. He also expressed the fear that the militia would not turn out in any appreciable number, "being at this season engaged in the farming business." Lacking the artillery to make a move in strength against Clinton, Moore confined his operations to harassing actions and to keeping the enemy under close observation. The channel below Wilmington was blocked by sinking hulks in the river. The fortifications of the city were strengthened. Two newly erected batteries were armed with a few six- and nine-pounders, which were felt adequate to drive off any shallow draft vessel that might attempt to negotiate the river. Detachments were kept out along the river banks, keeping an eye out for British landing parties. In one "brush" with a redcoat unit, one officer and five men were taken prisoner. One enemy landing party with a design to "disturnish" Kendall, the home of Robert Howe, took away valuables worth at least £1,500, but was driven away before it could fire the house. But Moore was limited to defensive operations, for his position would allow him to do little other than brace the coast for a possible invasion when Clinton's reinforcements arrived from Ireland.[9]

The expedition was far off schedule. Not until February 13, 1776, did Sir Peter Parker's fleet convoying Cornwallis's troops sail from the Irish port of Cork. Five days out it ran into weather so foul that several vessels were forced back into port. After battling high winds and heavy seas for more than two months, the first arrivals limped into the Cape Fear anchorage on April 18. Not until May 3 was the entire fleet reassembled. As soon as the major portion of his troops arrived Clinton issued a proclamation urging the citizens of the Carolinas to return to their duty as loyal subjects of George III, denouncing the rebellion, and promising a pardon to all those who

9. *State Records*, XI, xi; *Lee Papers*, I, 449, 450, 398–400, 401–2; Force, *American Archives*, 4, V, 62, VI, 404, 405; Nicholas Long to Jethro Sumner and Philemon Hawkins, Jr., April 1776, Emmet Collection; John Armstrong to _____, 23 April 1776, Historical Society of Pennsylvania Collection (photostats), North Carolina Department of Archives and History, Raleigh, N.C.; Return of the Regular Troops, Minute Men, Militia, Volunteers & Independents at Wilmington, 29 March 1776, Troop Returns, Military Collection.

would come in and reaffirm their allegiance—except Cornelius Harnett and Robert Howe.[10]

As the number of masts grew in the lower Cape Fear anchorage, the Provincial Congress expedited measures for filling the new regiments created for Moore's command. Even the newest recruits were hastened forward as fast as they could be enlisted. Additional militia units were ordered out. Wilmington was evacuated of all noncombatants. It was estimated that Moore would soon have at least five hundred men under his command, but for the present there was little that could be done other than harassing outposts and patrols. The British began to disembark on both sides of the river, the greater number encamped near the ruins of Fort Johnston, with young Lord Rawdon complaining bitterly of the forest of "miserable thin-topped pine, which springs from white sand."[11]

The long confinement aboard ship had created a restlessness and the troops were "as keen for action as ever men were." Clinton himself led them on one night raid. It was a rather large detachment of four battalions of foot and two companies of light infantry. Their objective was the post guarding the bridge at Orton Mill. With muffled oars they rowed upstream for about fifteen miles, pulling into shore at Kendall, Robert Howe's plantation, between two and three o'clock on Sunday morning, May 11. The soldiers, however, made so much noise that they were discovered by sentries, who shot down one British soldier after they had given the alarm. Clinton halted, ordering his men to fix bayonets as the surrounding darkness was shattered by drums beating to arms. The post of ninety men of the First North Carolina Regiment was commanded by Major William Davis, who used Clinton's brief delay to good advantage, retiring with most of his baggage and two small swivel guns. The British did not attempt a pursuit, but did burn Orton Mill before returning to their boats, plundering those unfortunates whose homes lay along their way.[12]

Clinton's foray held no real significance; it was little more than a military exercise to relieve boredom. The general had already de-

10. Charles Ross (ed.), *Correspondence of Charles, First Marquis Cornwallis* (London, 1859), I, 21; Stedman, *History of the . . . American War*, I, 183; Henry B. Dawson, *Battles of the United States by Sea and Land* (New York, 1858), I, 135; *Colonial Records*, X, 591–92; Clinton Proclamation, 5 May 1776, Miscellaneous Papers, William L. Clements Library.

11. Force, *American Archives*, 4, IV, 432; *Report on the Manuscripts of Mrs. Stopford-Sackville*, II, 177–78; *State Records*, XI, 296–97, 555.

12. *Virginia Gazette*, 31 May 1776; Almon, *Remembrancer . . . for . . . 1776*, Part II, p. 189; _____ to Richard Cogdill, n.d. [1776], Richard Cogdill Papers.

cided that the British could do little good in North Carolina, especially after the disaster at Moore's Creek Bridge. With the colony under the political control of the rebels, there was no chance of enlisting loyalists, nor was there an opportunity of obtaining enough horses to draw his artillery. One regiment, the Forty-Sixth, was almost prostrate because of illness. Because of the lateness of the season and the British aversion to military operations in southern regions during the warm months, Clinton seemed inclined to bend his attention toward the Chesapeake. Sir Peter Parker, however, was a single-minded person. His original objective had been Charleston and he appeared determined that an attack should be carried forward against that post. Governor William Campbell, royal governor of South Carolina, supported him in his arguments. A sloop, sent on a scouting mission to Charleston, returned with the information that the fort the rebels were constructing on Sullivan's Island in Charleston harbor was only partially completed and the ships of the fleet would have little difficulty in sailing past the works to attack the town. Josiah Martin bore some of the responsibility for the fortifications in Charleston, for he had sailed there in early December and had persuaded Captain Tallemache of the sloop-of-war *Scorpion* to bring his vessel to the Cape Fear. Once the ship had left the harbor the South Carolinians had started construction of a redoubt on Sullivan's Island. With Clinton persuaded that Charleston could be an easy conquest, the British fleet put to sea and sailed southward on May 30, 1776.[13]

The British semi-invasion of North Carolina had not been without its salutary effects. The Provincial Congress had been spurred to greater efforts and had accelerated its normally leisurely pace of legislation. There was need for action. The Continental regiments, because of the original short-term enlistments, were dwindling. Some of the enlistments of the regiments had been on the verge of expiration when the North Carolina troops had been inducted into the Continental Line. In some instances the captains of privateers sought their crews among the line regiments, for the men welcomed a chance to share in the prize money divided aboard such pseudo-warships. In Robert Howe's Second Regiment, some 250 of the 350 men stationed at Edenton, whose original enlistments had been for only six months, were persuaded to re-enlist only after they had been promised immediate ten- to twelve-day furloughs. The situation became

13. Precis of the Expedition to the Southern Colonies, Germain Papers; Stedman, *History of the . . . American War*, I, 184; *State Records*, XI, 265–67; Almon, *Remembrancer . . . for . . . 1776*, Part II, p. 189.

more critical since the response of the militia in the back country had been disappointing and reports ran that some "obstinately refuses to march & Says they will die before they will go."[14]

The Provincial Congress had assembled in Halifax on April 4, 1776. There was an almost rampant spirit of independence underlying the surface emotions of the delegates. Not only did they instruct their representatives in the Continental Congress to concur in independence should it be proposed, but many, almost before the messenger bearing their resolves had clattered off to Philadelphia, were thinking seriously of drawing up a document under which they could erect an independent government. As early as April 20, Samuel Johnston had written James Iredell that "we have not yet been able to agree on a Constitution. We have a meeting on it every evening, but can conclude nothing." And, he said, "The great difficulty in our way is how to establish a Check on the representation of the people to prevent them assuming more power than would be consistent with the Liberties of the people," although Johnston felt this to be a "strange piece of patch work." This spirit of urgency carried over into military matters. On Tuesday, April 9, the Congress resolved itself into a Committee of the Whole for a consideration of "the expediency of employing a military force for its defence against foreign invaders." The members of the committee were so enthusiastic in their planning that they seemed to "have lost all idea of expense, in the zeal of preparing for defence." The Continental Congress had already resolved, almost unanimously, that North Carolina could raise two additional Continental regiments "if they think necessary," and had followed this by elevating Moore and Howe to the rank of brigadier generals. But so ardent was the North Carolina Congress that it resolved to raise four battalions, or regiments, or two more than the Continental Congress had suggested. The additional regiments were authorized when it was agreed that the militia could not be relied upon to act as a regular army, nor could it be expected to remain in the field for any length of time without veering to the edge of mutiny. There was also the proposal, possibly by some of the more romantic members, that three companies of light horse be raised, though there were no provisions for such troops on the Continental establishment. Although Abner Nash had sought the command of the First or Second Regiments, his supporters were unable to gain him the post. To replace Moore and Howe, Francis Nash and Alexander Martin were promoted to colonels, while Majors Thomas Clark and

14. *Lee Papers*, I, 399–400; *Colonial Records*, X, 511–12, 579; William Bryan to John Ashe, 12 June 1776, Miscellaneous Papers, 1697–1912.

John Patten were elevated to lieutenant colonels, with William Davis and John White as majors of the First and Second Regiments.[15]

For the Third North Carolina Regiment, Jethro Sumner, prosperous tavern-keeper of Warren County, was appointed colonel, with William Alston as lieutenant colonel and Samuel Lockhart as major. For the Fourth, there were Thomas Polk, James Thackston, and William Davidson; the Fifth, Edward Buncombe, Henry Irwin, and Levi Dawson; and the Sixth, Alexander Lillington, William Taylor, and Gideon Lamb. The captains for the three light-horse companies were John Dickerson, Martin Pfifer, and James Jones. The privates of the Continental regiments were to be enlisted for two years, six months. Inasmuch as the captains of the line companies could take rank only when their companies reached full complement, there was a suggestion that the quality of the rank and file would not be of the best. The rules and regulations drawn up as guidelines for recruiting officers are worthy of notice:

1. They are to inlist none but able-bodied men, fit for service, capable of marching well, and such whose attachment to American liberties they have no cause to suspect; young, hearty, robust men, whose birth, family connections, and property bind them to the interests of their country, and well practiced in the use of fire arms, are much to be preferred.

2. They are as much as possible to have regard to moral character, particularly sobriety.

3. They are not to inlist any imported servant, nor, without the leave of his master, any apprentice.

4. They are to be careful in inlisting such men for Serjeants and Corporals, whose ability and diligence make them fit for that appointment; they are also to appoint a Fifer and Drummer.

5. They are to exert themselves to complete their companies, and punctually to report to their Colonels.

6. That the soldiers be allowed 1 s[hilling] per day for their subsistence.

7. They are to take notice that the Colonels of their battalion, or some field officer appointed by him, are to inspect their men, and to reject such as are not fit for service.

8. They are to furnish the subaltern officers of their companies with a copy of their instructions.

9. They are to inlist their men according to the following form, viz:

10. "I have this day voluntarily inlisted myself as a soldier in the American Continental Army, and do bind myself to conform in all instances to

15. *Colonial Records*, X, 498, 506, 507–9; *Lee Papers*, I, 397, 400; Burnett, *Letters of Members of the Continental Congress*, I, 409; Samuel Johnston to James Iredell, 20 April, Charles E. Johnston Collection; Samuel Johnston to _____, 3 March 1776, Samuel Johnston Papers; John Hancock to James Moore, 1 March 1776, Resolution of the North Carolina Congress, 13 April 1776, Papers of the Continental Congress.

such rules and regulations as are or shall be established for the government of the said army; as witness my hand," etc.

11. That they inlist no soldier under 5 feet 4 inches high, able bodied men, healthy, strong made, and well limbed, not deaf, or subject to fits, or ulcers on their legs, or ruptures.

12. That they pay to each soldier they shall inlist 40s. bounty, and £3 advance; and that every recruit take the following oath:

"I _____, do swear, that I will be faithfull and true to the United Colonies; that I will serve the same, to the utmost of my power, in defence of the just rights of America, against all enemies whatsoever; that I will to the utmost of my abilities, obey the lawful commands of my superior officers, agreeable to the Ordinances of Congress, and the Articles of War to which I have subscribed and lay down my arms peacebly, when required so to do by the Continental Congress. So help me God."[16]

At the insistence of General Moore, the Provincial Congress provided for five independent companies, and allowed them the same pay and rations as line troops. Because of the possibility that the Continental troops might be ordered out of North Carolina, these independent companies of eighty-three officers and men were to be stationed at strategic points along the coast. The North Carolina Congress also expressed the hope that not only the two additional regiments but that the independent companies would be placed on the Continental establishment by the Continental Congress. In like manner, an artillery company of fifty rank and file, under the command of Captain John Vance, was to be raised immediately and rushed to the support of General Moore. To arm these new troops, all arms confiscated from the Tories, as well as those that could be purchased, including those forcibly bought from the pacifist Quakers, Moravians, and Dunkards, were to be brought forward immediately. Armorers were engaged to repair broken weapons and to hammer out bayonets. Manufactories were established for the making of muskets and bayonets to the following specifications: "Each firelock to be made of 3/4 bore, and of a good substance at the breach, the barrel to be 3 feet 8 inches in length, a good lock, the bayonet to be 18 inches in the blade, with a steel ramrod, the upper end of the upper loop to be trumpet mouthed." The iron works on Deep River and in Guilford County were to be employed "for casting pieces of ordnance, shot, and other warlike implements." Because of the urgency of the moment, all re-enlistment furloughs granted to Howe's Second Regiment were cancelled. New troops, as fast as they could be enlisted,

16. *Colonial Records*, X, 508, 516, 519, 520, 528–29, 545; Recruiting Instructions, Military Collection; Miscellaneous Papers, 1697–1912; Ford, *Journals of the Continental Congress*, IV, 332–33.

were rushed to Moore on the Cape Fear. To supply these men, Nathaniel Rochester was appointed deputy commissary general.[17]

The acquisition of uniforms of similar design and colors posed a problem for troops raised on such short notice. Rochester was ordered to issue the osnaburgs, Dutch stripes, romals, and check cloth that had been purchased by North Carolina for the use of her Continentals; the same materials were issued to the crews manning the armed vessels of the colony. Coarse linens were to be purchased for making shirts and undergarments. Despite the ambitious program outlined by the Provincial Congress, money was so scarce that the legislature authorized Alexander Martin to borrow £2,000 to make a partial payment on the wages owed the men of his Second Regiment, to be secured by a draught on the Continental Congress.[18]

Despite the first flush of enthusiasm for independence, the Provincial Congress assumed an air of hesitancy in taking definitive action. Perhaps many of its members felt it proper that Congress make the first move, or perhaps it was the presence of the British fleet in the Cape Fear that discouraged any idea of an immediate and permanent constitution. On May 2 it was proposed that a Council of State and county councils be established, the former to sit permanently and the latter to meet at periodic intervals. But nothing was done and apparently the general feeling was that it was best to await the outcome of current events.[19]

The Continental Congress was quick to place the newly raised North Carolina troops on the regular establishment. So placed also were the three independent companies, although they were destined to become lost in the haze of inactivity through most of the remaining years of the war. Nicholas Long was made deputy quartermaster general with the rank of colonel. Twelve fieldpieces were ordered sent to the North Carolina troops along with three tons of powder, three medicine chests, and one hundred pounds of Peruvian, or Jesuit's, bark with which to treat malaria. There was one disappointment in that the Congress refused to take the colony's mounted troops into the Continental service, "being found by experience to be too expensive." Similar troops in South Carolina had already been converted into foot regiments. Joseph Hewes, however, reported from Philadelphia that he had been unable to purchase muskets for the North Carolina troops at any price. Other agents, traveling through the back country

17. *Colonial Records*, X, 494–95, 524, 539, 540, 546, 555, 572, 575.
18. *Ibid.*, pp. 576, 578–79, 629; Thomas Burke to Charles Lee, 6 May 1776, Papers of the Continental Congress.
19. *Colonial Records*, X, 591.

of the province, found it equally difficult to purchase firearms from the inhabitants, who refused to disarm themselves, fearing Indian attacks.[20]

Robert Howe, returning from Virginia where he had been on personal business, stopped at Halifax at the request of the Provincial Congress, who referred all military matters to him for advice. He also reported regularly to General Lee, who had stationed himself at Williamsburg, fortifying that place and Yorktown lest Governor Dunmore strike at those towns from his position on Gwynne's Island. Lee also harbored the suspicion that Clinton would sail from the Cape Fear to the Chesapeake to make a junction with the expatriate Virginia governor. Lee's agile mind explored every possible move by the British. There were so many contingencies that he complained to Washington, "I am like a dog in a dancing school—I know not where to turn myself, where to fix myself." Still, just as soon as defensive operations were complete in Virginia he planned to go to North Carolina "which we have reason to think will be the first scene of their diabolical operations." Brigadier general John Armstrong was sent with his Virginia troops to the southward with the injunction, "Charleston must be defended with the utmost obstinacy."[21]

Although the Continental Congress did not approve of North Carolina's forming light-horse troops, Lee did, for "it is a species of troops without which an army is a defective and lame machine." He argued that they added to the mobility of any body of troops with their quick strikes, especially when it was realized that each dragoon could carry a foot soldier behind him on his horse. With respect to the critical shortage of muskets, Lee suggested that all hunting rifles be collected to arm the men and that spears be issued to ease the shortage of bayonets.[22]

Frantic letters from North Carolina pleaded with Lee to hasten to the colony or send additional protection. From Robert Howe came the rumor, gained from British deserters, that the enemy was only awaiting a shipment of bombs before bombarding and setting fire to

20. Joseph Hewes to Samuel Johnston, 16 May 1776, Samuel Johnston Papers; *Colonial Records*, X, 604–5; Burnett, *Letters of Members of the Continental Congress*, I, 448; Ford, *Journals of the Continental Congress*, IV, 332–33, V, 624; William Bryan to John Ashe, 12 June 1776, Miscellaneous Papers, 1697–1912.

21. *Lee Papers*, I, 376–78, 383–84, 398–400, 409–10; Drayton, *Memoirs of the American Revolution*, II, 279; Thomas Jones to James Iredell, 28 April 1776, Charles E. Johnston Collection; McRee, *Life and Correspondence of James Iredell*, I, 277; Lee to Hancock, 19 April 1776, Papers of the Continental Congress.

22. *Lee Papers*, I, 417–18.

Wilmington. From Halifax there were Thomas Burke's denounce-
ments of the "Intestine Enemy in our bosom" who was daily gaining
strength. He also reported the latest hearsay that the British planned
to land troops at Little River, thirty miles south of Cape Fear, and
penetrate the province by way of Lake Wiggaman [Waccamaw] to
make a junction with the Highlanders and Regulators, who were by
no means dejected by their defeat at Moore's Creek Bridge. Yet, Burke
went on to say, despite the critical shortage of artillery, "every thing
may be expected from our people which a generous warmth and active
enterprising disposition and an invincible love of liberty can impel
men to perform." In the face of all these alarums and requests, Lee
still procrastinated, claiming "important busyness" held him in Virginia. Just as soon as these affairs were cleared he promised that he
would set out for North Carolina, "both for the public service, and my
own gratification in making the acquaintance of Mr. Howe."[20]

South Carolina also clamored for the guiding hand of Lee, whose
presence, it felt, "was equal to a reenforcement of 1000 men. . . ."
And that colony needed a firm hand in control. When General John
Armstrong reached Charleston he did not find a single soldier of that
colony on the Continental establishment. Among other things, the
government of South Carolina objected to the Continental regulations for disciplining the troops as "too mild for the perverse Soldiery
of this Meridian, to whom 39 lashes wou'd prove but a light breakfast." It also took exception to the time of enlistment, while the prospect of an officer being drummed out of the army after conviction by
a court martial was an unhappy thought for many of the more aristo-
cratic element from which the officer corps would be drawn. Yet the
colony had about two thousand men under arms, but on the provincial rather than the Continental establishment.[24]

Reports such as these contained in letters from Armstrong and
the growing number of enemy vessels dropping anchor in the Cape
Fear finally prompted Lee to action. He persuaded the Virginia Assembly to send aid to North Carolina; he had previously dispatched
a battalion of riflemen toward Halifax, their rifles slung over their
shoulders, and each carrying a thirteen-foot spear. By May 19, there
were a reported sixty or seventy British ships in the Cape Fear, and

23. *Ibid.*, pp. 420, 438–40, 446, 448.

24. *Ibid.*, II, 10–11; William Moultrie, *Memoirs of the American Revolution,
So Far as It Related to the States of North and South Carolina, and Georgia* (New
York, 1802), I, 141; John Armstrong to John Hancock, 7 May 1776, Papers of the
Continental Congress.

the following day Lee was in Halifax. His arrival changed the pattern of conversation in town. The usual small talk about fine horses was channeled into prattle centered around Lee and his dogs:

... among others, the general will not suffer Spado [his dog] to eat bacon for breakfast (a practice very general both with ladies and gentlemen in this part of the country) lest it make him stupid—this piece of satire, however, has not prejudiced him in their good opinion: he is considered as a very polite, well-bred, and sensible gentleman by every one I have ever heard speak of him, making allowances for a few oddities, which all great men are indulged in, and which were not so many as they had reason, from report, to expect.[25]

Lee planned to march for the coast just as soon as the Virginia riflemen rendezvoused at Halifax. Yet the general could see no real objective for the British in North Carolina unless it was "rage and revenge (which at present alone seems to actuate the King and his accursed instruments)" which may inspire them before their departure with the lust of destroying Wilmington." But Lee was troubled by the "disorderly, mutinous, and dangerous disposition of the 8th Regt" of Virginia, who seemed such strangers to discipline. And the North Carolina troops also were a cause for apprehension, possibly because their officers had recruited such large numbers of the Scotch-Irish in the back country who seemed to possess a penchant for desertion once they had collected the enlistment bonus. There was also friction between the Continentals and the militia. The militiamen were unhappy because they felt they were doing all of the dirty work and because there was discrimination in the distribution of provisions and supplies. The spirit of unrest among the regular soldiers stationed at Wilmington became so acute that it finally flamed forth in what was termed an "unhappy Mutiny," and it required the militia force of Brigadier John Ashe before it was put down. This unrest among Moore's troops, according to the Council of State, was only because of "an Anxious desire" to carry the war to the enemy, and "not from any dislike or Aversion to the Services of their Country." The news of this uprising among the North Carolina Continentals, however, was suppressed, so much so that there are but guarded references to it in most of the records.[26]

From Halifax, where he had impressed Samuel Johnston as "that

25. *Lee Papers*, II, 18–19, 22–23, 28, 30–31; McRee, *Life and Correspondence of James Iredell*, I, 297–98.

26. *Lee Papers*, II, 34–35; *Colonial Records*, X, 684; William Purviance to Provincial Council, 29 February 1776, Council of Safety to John Ashe, 25 July 1776, Papers in the Office of the Secretary of State, North Carolina Department of Archives and History, Raleigh, N.C.

Original," Lee traveled to Wilmington by way of Tarboro and New Bern. By June 1 he had arrived in Wilmington, just missing an opportunity to observe the enemy, who had weighed anchor and stood out to sea only the day before. Many local authorities felt that the enemy was bound for Charleston, and although Lee was still unconvinced he dispatched Colonel Peter Muhlenberg's Eighth Virginia Regiment along with detachments from the First, Second, Third, and Fourth North Carolina regiments, around seven hundred men, marching for Charleston. Arms were so scarce that before the North Carolina units began their march, muskets were taken from the militia so that the regulars would have some semblance of a military appearance. The shortage of arms, however, could not be attributed to the North Carolina Congress, who had become "involved in an immense Load of Debt by its Spirited exertion in the Common Cause." In reality there was an acute shortage of all manner of weapons. Lee stripped North Carolina of 1,600 pounds of gunpowder. Still he could not bring himself to believe that the enemy was heading for Charleston and, to protect the Chesapeake area, dispatched a messenger to turn back the Virginia militia who had been marching for Wilmington.[27]

By June 4, while Lee and his retinue were still on their southward journey, an estimated fifty-one British sail were rocking at anchor on the far side of the bar that blocked the entrance to Charleston harbor. Lee, finally convinced of the British interest in Charleston, immediately dispatched a request to the Continental Congress for regiments from Pennsylvania and Maryland.[28]

So it was that the North Carolina Continentals, raised in haste to repulse a possible invasion, were sent to defend a colony of which it had been said, "From time immemorial South Carolina has manifested a singular jealousy of North Carolina, affecting a contempt whose frequent expression affords a most practical denial of its reality."[29]

27. *Lee Papers*, II, 50–51; *State Records*, XI, 300–301; *Colonial Records*, X, 1038–39; Samuel Johnston to James Iredell, 20 April 1776, Charles E. Johnston Collection; Cornelius Harnett to John Hancock, 24 June 1776, Papers of the Continental Congress.

28. *Lee Papers*, II, 53–54; Ford, *Journals of the Continental Congress*, V, 485; Lee to Brig. Genl. Lewis, 6 June 1776, Papers of the Continental Congress.

29. McRee, *Life and Correspondence of James Iredell*, I, 407.

Chapter 4
Siege of Charleston, 1776

"It was brave to the last degree."

The Charlestonians had been busy, but not busy enough. In early November, 1775, the Continental Congress had resolved that Charleston should be fortified "immediately." Yet the work had gone along slowly, perhaps because that same resolution had stated that "the expence [is] to be paid by the said Colony." They had demonstrated some imagination, if no great industry, in adapting their fortifications to their peculiar geography. The city lay on the arrowhead peninsula formed by the confluence of the Ashley and Cooper rivers, so that there was only one direction to approach by land. Bordering the mainland were low sandy islands, overgrown with palmettoes, myrtle thickets, and scrub oak. Most were separated from the mainland by meandering streams, turgid inlets, and grassy marshes. Some six miles out was the entrance to the harbor, protected by its massive sand bar, which effectively blocked the passage of heavily loaded ships of deep draught. On the south shore of the harbor lay James Island, on which stood Fort Johnson, heavily armed and protected by an additional battery, in all a total of forty-three guns.[1]

Nearer the town and on the north side of the harbor was Sulli-

1. Ford, *Journals of the Continental Congress*, III, 326.

van's Island, a strip of sand some four miles long and only about a mile wide at high tide. To the north of Sullivan's Island, separated by a narrow inlet termed the "Breach" lay unfortified Long Island. A small battery had been erected on Haddrel's Point to the rear of Sullivan's Island, while other batteries and strong points had been thrown up around the town. The fortifications that were to prove most important in the struggle for Charleston were on the southern end of Sullivan's Island. Construction on Fort Sullivan had been initiated in January, but in early June it was no more than half complete. The walls were two parallel rows of palmetto logs sixteen feet apart, the interval between filled with sand. This redoubt and supporting batteries contained thirty-four pieces of artillery. The Second South Carolina Regiment of 413 men and the 22 men of the Fourth Artillery Company manned the guns and parapets. Colonel William Moultrie was in command [2]

The South Carolinians welcomed Lee, whose presence "excited the public ardour." Some were irritated by the general's eccentricities, perhaps best expressed in the observations of C. C. Pinckney: "General Lee appears very clever, but is a strange animal; however . . . we must put up with ten thousand oddities in him on account of his abilities and his attachments to the rights of humanity." Many of the local military disagreed with him concerning the enemy's designs, while others grumbled when Lee criticized Fort Sullivan, which he termed a "slaughter pen," and the local soldiery, who refused to work on the earthworks until forced. The general made the citizens demolish the houses on the wharves and replace them with earthworks and other "military mince-pies." Although the South Carolina troops were not on the Continental establishment, John Rutledge, president of the South Carolina Provincial Congress, delegated the proper command function, especially after it was learned, on June 8, that Clinton and Cornwallis were landing troops on Long Island, thereby constituting a threat to the unfinished fort on Sullivan's Island.[3]

There were now about 750 North Carolina Continentals of the First Regiment under Lieutenant Colonel Thomas Clark in Charleston. It has also been claimed that the South Carolina company commanded by Captain C. C. Pinckney was composed largely of men

2. Gibbes, *Documentary History of the American Revolution*, II, 5; *Lee Papers*, II, 66.
3. Gibbes, *Documentary History of the American Revolution*, II, 8; *Lee Papers*, II, 56, 57; Force, *American Archives*, 4, IV, 1188; Drayton, *Memoirs of the American Revolution*, II, 280; Moultrie, *Memoirs of the American Revolution*, I, 14; Richard Hutson to Isaac Hayne, 24 June 1776, Richard Hutson Papers, Duke University, Durham, N.C.

recruited in North Carolina. The Second Regiment under Lieutenant Colonel John Patten had begun its march for South Carolina, but had halted south of Wilmington to await Lee's further orders. It had been discovered that the British fleet off Charleston was being supplied by foraging parties operating from small vessels that worked their way into the smaller streams along the North Carolina coast. Already some forty head of cattle had been taken in the vicinity of Lockwood's Folly, and there was the possibility that additional enemy sloops might slip in over the bar at Little River or Shallotte Inlet to gather water and provisions. Patten camped at Little Creek, sending out detachments to observe and guard critical points. Lee was a bit miffed that Moore had allowed Patten to halt and sent a dispatch urging the resumption of his march as quickly as possible.[4]

In Charleston, the North Carolinians were stationed on the left flank in an old field known as Lynch's pasture adjacent to Haddrel's Point and behind the inlet separating the mainland from Sullivan's Island. For the present they acted in reserve for the South Carolina rural militia some two hundred yards in front of them. Although this militia group was placed under the command of Robert Howe, the North Carolinians constituted a special reserve acting directly under the orders of Lee. Actually Howe seems to have acted as something of a super-adjutant for Lee throughout the Charleston operations. Lee had little confidence in his troops, "the officers being all boys, and the men raw recruits." Despite white British sails in plain view, the American troops did not appear to take them too seriously, working leisurely on the entrenchments ordered by the general. Perhaps their lethargy may be attributed to the lack of funds, for the North Carolina troops had set up a "clamore for their pay." But by June 19 it had become obvious to even the lowliest of militiamen that an attack was in the offing and they all applied the pick and the shovel more industriously. On that day, Lee's general orders sounded a note of pleading:

the continental troops, provincials, and the militia, are, therefore, most earnestly conjured to work with no less alacrity, than fight with courage. Courage alone will not suffice in war: true soldiers and magnanimous citizens must brandish the pick-axe and spade, as well as the sword, in defence of their country; one or two days labour at this critical juncture, may not only save many worthy families from ruin, but many worthy individuals from loss of limbs and life.[5]

4. *Lee Papers*, II, 72–73; *State Records*, XI, 307; McRee, *Life and Correspondence of James Iredell*, I, 325.
5. *Lee Papers*, II, 65, 73–74, 100–101; *State Records*, XI, 298; Robert Howe

Lee's greatest concern was for the fort on Sullivan's Island. Isolated from the mainland and not easily reinforced, the post, with its incomplete defenses in the rear, invited encirclement. Then too, there was no proper route of retreat, and Lee's proposal of a crude pontoon bridge of barrels and planks proved impracticable and unstable after Thomas Clark, leading 200 of his North Carolinians across the bobbing structure, sank so low in the water that they were obliged to return. When Clinton first landed troops on Long Island, Lee rushed forward Lieutenant Colonel William Thompson's Third Regiment of South Carolina Rangers with orders to attack and drive off the invaders. This order was quickly rescinded when the enemy began to land additional men. Thompson was reinforced with 200 men of Clark's First Regiment along with 200 South Carolina militia under Daniel Horry. The Raccoon Company of 50 riflemen brought Thompson's command to 750 troops to oppose any British attempt to cross the Breach. There were two pieces of artillery, an eigtheen-pounder and a brass six-pounder.[6]

The troops were skittish, taking pot shots at targets on the far side of the Breach. After a time this desultory firing exploded into a long-range "sham battle." The British had long held an almost unnatural fear of the American riflemen, and Lee feared that this apprehension would fade into contempt if these supposed experts took too many wild shots. On June 21, his orders to Thompson commanded "that not a man under your Command is to fire at a greater distance than an hundred and fifty yards at the utmost—in short that they never fire without almost a moral certainty of hitting their object—distant firing has a double bad effect, it encourages the Enemy, and adds to the pernicious perswasion of the American soldiers—vizt *that they are no match for their antagonists at close fighting*—to speak plainly, it is almost a sure way of making 'em Cowards."[7]

Sir Peter Parker was having trouble getting his heavy men-of-war across the bar at the entrance of the harbor. Two weeks had passed before the guns on the two largest warships were removed and they

---

Orderly Book, William L. Clements Library, University of Michigan, Ann Arbor, Mich.; Drayton, *Memoirs of the American Revolution*, II, 294–95.

6. Edward McCrady, *The History of South Carolina in the Revolution, 1775–1780* (New York, 1901), p. 140; Dawson, *Battles of the United States*, I, 140; Moultrie, *Memoirs of the American Revolution*, I, 142; Archibald Maclaine Howe, "Memoir of Genl. Howe," Robert Howe Papers, Southern Historical Collection, The University of North Carolina at Chapel Hill, Chapel Hill, N.C.; John Armstrong to John Hancock, 12 August 1776, Papers of the Continental Congress.

7. *Lee Papers*, II, 76; Richard Hutson to Isaac Hayne, 24 June 1776, Richard Hutson Papers.

rode high enough in the water to negotiate the barrier. On the morning of June 28, in a movement almost majestic in execution the British fleet moved in. The ships, with springs on their cables, dropped anchor some four hundred yards from Moultrie's fort on Sullivan's Island. All that hot, sultry day the guns of the fleet and the artillery within the fort exchanged broadsides. Parker's men shuddered as the balls from Moultrie's guns plowed into their ships, while their own shot buried themselves into the sand and spongy palmetto logs of the fort. The fire, with the exception of an hour's lull when Moultrie ran low on powder, continued until half past nine in the evening. By eleven, Parker's ships had slipped their cables and pulled back to their previous anchorage in Five Fathom Hole. They left the frigate *Actaeon* behind, badly damaged and wedged so tightly on a sand bar that her crew was forced to abandon her after setting her afire.[8]

Thompson's command across from Long Island had been reinforced during the battle with Muhlenberg's Eighth Virginia Regiment. Originally British strategy had been for Clinton's troops to ford the Breach and hit the unfinished fort on Sullivan's Island from the rear. Intelligence had assured them that the Breach was shallow and even the locals felt that the inlet "at low water, is fordable." But sands have a habit of shifting, and the Breach not only proved too deep for fording, but adverse winds had piled the water in the gut even deeper. Clinton had far too few boats to attempt to ferry his troops across the channel and could aid the cause little more than by presenting a threat by lobbing over a few shells from his field pieces. He positioned an armed sloop and an armed schooner, the *Lady William,* as if to provide fire cover for a crossing, and twice he made diversionary moves to suggest that his troops were coming across. Both times the small detachments were driven back onto Long Island by the concentrated musketry and artillery fire from Thompson's command, which "spread Havoc, Devastation and Death, and always made them retire faster than they advanced."[9]

8. Dawson, *Battles of the United States*, I, 136–38; Christopher Ward, *The War of the Revolution*, ed. John R. Alden (New York, 1952), II, 675–76; Precis of the Expedition to the Southern Colonies, Germain Papers; *South Carolina and American General Gazette* (Charleston), 2 August 1776; Drayton, *Memoirs of the American Revolution*, II, 296, 299; Moultrie, *Memoirs of the American Revolution*, I, 174–80.

9. *Lee Papers*, II, 91–92; John Richard Alden, *General Charles Lee: Traitor or Patriot?* (Baton Rouge, La., 1951), pp. 126–27; Gibbes, *Documentary History of the American Revolution*, II, 9; *South Carolina and American General Gazette*, 2 August 1776; Richard Hutson to Isaac Hayne, 24 June 1776, Richard Hutson to Thomas Hutson, 30 June 1776, Richard Hutson Papers; Robert Howe to _____, 29 June 1776, Robert Howe Papers, Southern Historical Collection.

British casualties were heavy. Moultrie's losses numbered only ten killed and twenty-two wounded; Thompson reported no casualties although there was one man wounded among the Americans at the Breach. Lee fairly strutted in his dispatches. Praise was lavished on Moultrie's defense, although the general was forced to confess it "astonished me; it was brave to the last degree." He did not mention, as it was later claimed, that he had sent Francis Nash, on the morning of the battle, with orders to relieve Moultrie, but the British fleet had opened fire before Nash could reach Sullivan's Island. Lee was proud of the work of Thompson's detachment. Not only did he praise Muhlenberg's Virginians, but he included the North Carolina troops as "equally alert, zealous and spirited." To Washington he reported that the North Carolina Line was made up of "admirable soldiers," while his dispatch to the Continental Congress gave the North Carolinians and the South Carolina Rangers all the credit for repulsing Clinton's diversionary attempts.[10]

The British men of war "sheared off next morning like earless dogs," and dropped down to their previous anchorage. There they lay for over three weeks. The redcoated soldiers were shifted from one island to another. Deserters constantly crept into the American lines, complaining of the sickness and lack of provisions among the king's soldiers. From them it was learned "that the consequences of the action have been more decisive than we then thought." Nevertheless, Lee kept his troops constantly at work on the fortifications. He entertained a notion of making a strike at Clinton's force, and made plans to that end until it became obvious that the redcoats were preparing to embark again and Lee was unable to collect enough boats for any amphibious operation. His total strength had begun to decline in "that the Virginians and North Carolina Troops are falling down in sickness." Lee attributed their illnesses to bad drinking water, constant exposure to the broiling sun during the day and sleeping on the damp ground at night. Some men were so near naked that they became badly sunburned, and as the temperature soared, the general suggested that they "march gently." The North Carolinians were ordered out of the old field in which they had been stationed to a bivouac in the shade of nearby trees. The water situation was partially alleviated by an increased issuance of rum.[11]

10. Charles Lee to Edmund Randolph, 14 July 1776, Papers of the Continental Congress; *Lee Papers*, II, 92–94, 101–3, 107–9; Robert Howe Orderly Book; Robert Howe to _____, 29 June 1776, Robert Howe Papers, Southern Historical Collection; Drayton, *Memoirs of the American Revolution*, II, 315; Richard Hutson to Thomas Hutson, 30 June 1776, Richard Hutson Papers.

11. *Lee Papers*, II, 139–40, 148–49; *Colonial Records*, X, 659–60; Robert

There were some who disagreed with Lee that the next British objective would be the Chesapeake, arguing that the British fleet was so battered that it could offer little support to the troops. They opposed Lee's suggestion that he take his southern army to Virginia, arguing that there were still problems requiring immediate attention for the American troops in the area. There was the matter of the current expedition against the Cherokees, already termd "most Tyrannical and bloody," but this was mostly carried on by Griffith Rutherford and his "Chosen Rifle-men." The Georgia frontier was being harassed through raids from St. Augustine and Pensacola. Florida Tories crossed the border to carry off cattle, seizing Negroes and murdering those so bold as to offer even token resistance. Some insisted that this could all be stopped by an expedition against St. Augustine, as that enemy post was but lightly garrisoned. The Georgians cried for aid, but the South Carolinians offered little more than sympathetic cluckings. Knowing that the North Carolina and Virginia Continentals might be ordered northward at any moment, they wished to keep their own troops at home. On the other hand, neither the North Carolinians nor the Virginians were eager to go on a southern expedition, arguing that the South Carolinians should be willing to go to the aid of Georgia, just as the troops from the northward had come to her assistance. It was finally agreed that Muhlenberg's Virginians, supported by some South Carolina troops and Colonel Jethro Sumner's Third North Carolina Regiment would begin a march for Savannah. Yet this was delayed until a court of inquiry had settled a dispute over rank between Muhlenberg and Sumner. Because Sumner refused to appear before such a court and the records were sparse, Muhlenberg was given temporary rank over the North Carolinian.[12]

Just as soon as it became evident that the British were going to leave Charleston without further hostile actions, Lee made his own preparations to march. He wasn't sure that the North Carolina Continentals would be able to march because of their "wretched condition . . . for want of cloaths." Thomas Polk's Fourth North Carolina

---

Howe Orderly Book; Robert Howe to _____, 29 June 1776, Robert Howe Papers, Southern Historical Collection; Drayton, *Memoirs of the American Revolution*, II, 315; John Armstrong to John Hancock, 12 May 1776, Papers of the Continental Congress.

12. Alden, *General Charles Lee*, pp. 131–32; *Lee Papers*, II, 114–17, 125, 129, 153, 157–60; Robert Howe Orderly Book; Moultrie, *Memoirs of the American Revolution*, I, 184; Thomas Jones to James Iredell, 23 July 1776, Charles E. Johnston Collection; copy of Cornelius Harnett Letter, 16 July 1776, Miscellaneous Papers, 1697–1912.

Regiment was so ragged that it was excluded from the southern expedition, but instead was ordered to station itself just beyond the southern boundary of North Carolina in such a manner as to prevent the enemy from making predatory raids into the inlets of the area between Little River and Fort Johnston. But even its march was held up by a court of inquiry that cleared Captain William T. Coles of the regiment of charges termed only as "extraordinary."[13]

By late July there were frantic reports of British men-of-war off Savannah. The North Carolinians under the over-all command of Robert Howe, and the South Carolinians under Isaac Huger, were ordered to make preparations for an immediate march to Purysburg. To quiet the "Clamours of the Troops," the North Carolina Council of Safety was obliged to dispatch a paymaster posthaste to Charleston. The troops were so destitute of personal covering that Lee begged two hundred pairs of "negroe shoes" from Colonel Moultrie, while a dispatch to Colonel Moore urged that haversacks be forwarded immediately to the North Carolina soldiers.[14]

Robert Howe was not overly enthusiastic about the prospect of an expedition to the southward. The objectives, he felt, "can not be very important." General John Armstrong, ill from the excessive heat, and also considered for the command, was equally sour on the project and to withdraw his own name from consideration praised Howe as "a genius amongst our American best." Yet he could not forbear a facetious footnote extolling Howe's social graces: "Howe has a thousand qualifications for this meridian & not a foible known to me that will preponderate the opposite scale, and he is able to wash off all the dryness incidental as it was, with half a dozen of Madeira, or a single dance with the ladies will shake it off as we do the dust from our feet."[15]

On August 12, in the midst of these preparations, there was the electrifying news that the Continental Congress had declared the colonies independent. Although the celebration in Charleston assumed an air of solemnity as the chief officials and high military officers paraded slowly through the streets, it was "amidst loud acclamations of thousands who always huzza when a proclamation is read." Perhaps it was during the excitement of the moment that Lee began planning a great move that many of the officers closest to him were

13. *Lee Papers*, II, 164, 165; Robert Howe Orderly Book.
14. *Lee Papers*, II, 168–69; *State Records*, XI, 307–8; Moultrie, *Memoirs of the American Revolution*, I, 173.
15. *Lee Papers*, II, 184–88; Robert Howe Orderly Book; Armstrong to Hancock, 12 August 1776, Papers of the Continental Congress.

not aware of, an expedition to East Florida. This, he felt, would take some of the pressure off the Georgia frontier. By August 3, Lee was urging Jethro Sumner to cross the Ashley River; such a move, he felt, would make it more difficult for the North Carolinians to desert when he revealed the true objective of the expedition. Although Congress had taken the South Carolina regiments into the Continental establishment on June 18, President Rutledge of South Carolina seemed reluctant to allow his provincial troops to assume Continental status under Lee. The general was quick to answer that if North Carolina had hoarded her troops in South Carolina's hour of need, Charleston would now be in enemy hands. He and Howe made a hurried inspection trip to Port Royal where several British transports laden with sick redcoats had put in to allow the men to recuperate on shore. Ever the showman, Lee paraded the North Carolina and Virginia Continentals before he marched. He began his address to them by commending them for their past services. Then, "He told them he had planned a secret expedition as a means of rewarding them—that the service was such as they had been used to; being without danger—and secure of success: and, that a very large booty, of which he would resign his share to them, attended their steps. That he did this, as a favour to the troops; but did not mean to force any of them to acquire booty; for volunteers only were to undertake that expedition." Soon after Lee marched with 1,500 men, but without a single artillery piece or even a medicine chest, to join the large body of militia stationed in the vicinity of Port Royal. When the British sailed away, Howe was left in the area to straighten the "Damnable Hobble" of the "Hotch Potch Camp" of the troops stationed there. Lee himself started out for Savannah, leaving the grubbier details of the march to Howe, who followed on August 8 with the regulars. By August 18 they had arrived at that Georgia port, with a number of smaller detachments of North Carolina troops stationed at small Georgia communities along the way.[16]

In Savannah and other Georgia towns, the situation grew worse than it had been in Charleston. Of the troops stationed at Sunbury, for instance, fourteen or fifteen men died each day as a result of disease. Howe came to regard the business as "a fatiguing, pointless expedition." The troops groused continually as the supplies dwindled.

---

16. *Lee Papers*, II, 186–87, 198, 201, 204, 207–8, 222; Robert Howe Orderly Book; *State Records*, XI, 344–45; Ford, *Journals of the Continental Congress*, V, 461–62; Drayton, *Memoirs of the American Revolution*, II, 334–36; Charles Lee to Jethro Sumner, 3 August 1776, Jethro Sumner Papers, North Carolina Department of Archives and History, Raleigh, N.C.

Too often rations amounted to no more than rice or "Journey-cake." Entire houses were sometimes pulled down by the soldiers for use as fire wood. As the discontent grew, rather desperate measures were undertaken to preserve discipline. Recalcitrants were sentenced for a specified number of days in "the Black Hole" on a diet of "Rice and Water." The South Carolinians, many of whom had grown wealthy supplying the army, now took advantage of the situation and charged exorbitant prices for necessities. The resentment against that province was such that Lee predicted that if the British once again attacked Charleston there would be "a dangerous repugnance" among the Virginia and North Carolina troops to march once again to their aid. A number of deerskins were eventually collected and doled out to the ragged soldiers so that they might fashion their own moccasins and leggings. The "harum skarum" Georgians were not much more helpful. Because the royal governor, James Wright, had remained so long in their province they had made few preparations for their defense and now were so anxious and apprehensive, said Lee, that they would agree to anything, even to "mounting a body of mermaids on Alligators."[17]

Lee's southern career was nearing its end. The Continental Congress had grown alarmed with the growing strength of the British army in New York. Inasmuch as Lee's star was in the ascendancy as a result of the astounding repulse of the British at Charleston, he was desired not only as a subordinate to Washington but also as a general who could assume the command of the army should anything happen to the commander in chief. James Moore was to assume the command of the Southern Department.[18]

Lee left Savannah in early September, leaving Howe in command of the troops in Georgia. The Virginia and North Carolina troops were ordered to follow Lee, but at Charleston Rutledge persuaded the general to leave the North Carolina Line in South Carolina, especially since that province's troops had been left in Georgia. Lee did take seventy men from both the First and Second Regiments whose enlistments were about to expire to act as something of an

17. *Lee Papers*, II, 246, 254; Drayton, *Memoirs of the American Revolution*, II, 336; Robert Howe Orderly Book; Howe to Caswell, 10 April 1777, Caswell Letterbook, North Carolina Department of Archives and History, Raleigh, N.C.

18. Alden, *General Charles Lee*, p. 137; Burnett, *Letters of Members of the Continental Congress*, II, 56–57; Ford, *Journals of the Continental Congress*, V, 638; Moultrie, *Memoirs of the American Revolution*, I, 186, II, 336–37; Lee to Harnett, 16 August 1776 (copy), Miscellaneous Papers, 1697–1912; Howe to Rutledge, 20 September 1776, George Washington Papers, Library of Congress, Washington, D.C.; Hancock to Lee, 8 August 1776, Papers of the Continental Congress.

honor guard for him through North Carolina. A number of those troops left in Charleston were kept busy working on the fortifications. In Georgia, Howe made a feeble attempt to carry through Lee's expedition toward St. Augustine. The effort ended in dismal failure as British reinforcements, transportation breakdowns, an outbreak of malaria, and a lack of cooperation by Governor Houstoun of Georgia frustrated all designs.[19]

Lee, however, did North Carolina irreparable harm before his departure. Because of the shortage of men in the ranks of the South Carolina and Georgia Continental regiments, and the seeming inability of their officers to attract additional recruits, Lee's orders on September 8, 1776, allowed some men of the North Carolina regiments to be "translated" into the lines of those two states. A number of the men took advantage of this irregularity to gain an additional enlistment bounty, enough so that Edward Rutledge of South Carolina was to later state, "We raised our complement of men in the neighboring colonies." Captain Cosmo Medici of the North Carolina mounted troops also allowed a number of his command to be taken into the cavalry of other states, thereby inviting a court of inquiry for himself. When, in late October, the North Carolina Council of Safety became aware of this transaction, it immediately dispatched orders to Howe to "reclaim" these men and also to return all North Carolina troops stationed to the southward to home soil. When Howe attempted to follow through he met with a rather bluff rebuttal from the Council of South Carolina, who demanded a return of the six pounds, five shillings paid each man as an enlistment bounty. Howe finally advised the members of the North Carolina Council to resign themselves to their loss, for if the men in question were discharged from the South Carolina Line they would be technically free of military obligations and there was no assurance they would re-enlist in the the North Carolina regiments. Yet Howe did not bother to explain why he had consented to Lee's action in the first place, and in November was urging that South Carolina be allowed to recruit in the state. The North Carolina protest seems to have been a result of a feeling of being put upon more than anything else, for within a month after the council protest, the Provincial Congress of North Carolina, because of North Carolina's greater white population, was allowing South Carolina recruiting officers to attempt to fill their line regiments with men from North Carolina.[20]

19. Howe to Rutledge, 20 September 1776, Howe to Rutledge, ? September 1776, Lincoln to Washington, January 28–29, 1780, George Washington Papers; Hancock to Lee, 8 August 1776, Papers of the Continental Congress.

20. Extract from Council Minutes, 25 October 1776, Jethro Sumner Papers,

The recall of Lee from the South did not set at ease the fears of the Continental Congress. On September 3, 1776, it resolved that two North Carolina regiments should be sent, if expedient, to bolster Washington's army near New York. Two weeks later this resolution was altered to allow the North Carolina Council of State to decide when the state's troops were ready for combat, "according as they shall think it most conducive to public service, and the safety of their particular state." The council, after examining the returns of General James Moore, agreed that the units were not only far from complete in numbers, but were too "sickly and ill provided with Cloathing and by no means prepared to march to a Northern Climate." Then too it was feared that the removal of the troops would render the state defenseless in the event of another invasion by the enemy. And there was some reason for alarm. From the delegates in the Continental Congress had come the warning, "The Southern Colonies are a tempting morsel to them & they have not forgot their disgraceful expedition at Charleston and no doubt will strain every nerve to retrieve their Honour." All line troops within the borders of the state were ordered to the vicinity of Wilmington and New Bern to recruit both their health and their numbers. In an effort to protect the men from the rigors of the approaching winter months Nathaniel Rochester, commissary of stores, was ordered to have tents made and to busy his tailors in making woolen short coats and breeches.[21]

In the meantime, each breeze seemed to carry a new cluster of rumors. To the northward, deserters who came into Washington's camp swore that General William Howe was planning another expedition to Charleston. Such stories were repeated too often to be taken lightly. And when a large fleet was sighted off the Jersey coast

Southern Historical Collection, The University of North Carolina at Chapel Hill, Chapel Hill, N.C.; *State Records*, XI, 356–57, 361–62, XV, 683; *Colonial Records*, X, 928–29; Ford, *Journals of the Continental Congress*, III, 489; Howe to Caswell, 15 January 1776, Caswell Letterbook and Governors' Papers, North Carolina Department of Archives and History, Raleigh, N.C.; Caswell to Howe, 7 March 1777, Governors' Papers; Robert Howe Orderly Book; Howe to President of Council, 6 November 1776, Robert Howe Papers, Southern Historical Collection.

21. Each battalion, or regiment, was to be provided with tents in the following fashion: thirty yards were designated as sufficient to sew a tent to shelter eight men, twenty yards for a tent to protect arms, thirty-five yards for a tent for the noncommissioned officers in each company, and one hundred yards of canvas to be used in sewing together a hospital tent. *State Records*, XI, 353; *Colonial Records*, X, 878–79; John C. Fitzpatrick (ed.), *The Writings of George Washington* (Washington, 1931–1944), IV, 24; Burnett, *Letters of Members of the Continental Congress*, II, 95–96; Ford, *Journals of the Continental Congress*, V, 733–34, 762; North Carolina Delegates in Congress to Council of Safety, 26 September 1776, Continental Congress Delegates' Papers, North Carolina Department of Archives and History, Raleigh, N.C.; Hancock to James Moore, 3 September 1776, Papers of the Continental Congress.

sailing southward, even more credence was given the rumors. No one seemed to feel that the enemy had any real designs upon North Carolina; most people seemed to agree with Samuel Johnston that North Carolina "is found too inconsiderable to attract the attention of the British Ministry at a time when they had so many others of so [much] greater importance to attend to, and I am not without hopes that we shall soon return to our former obscurity which I once thought our best Security. . . ." The Continental Congress, on November 16, 1776, hastily resolved that General Moore station his troops in such a situation as to render aid quickly if the enemy fleet bore down once again upon Charleston. In addition, two battalions of volunteers were to join Moore's command in South Carolina, but it was specifically stated that they were not to be enlisted in the South Carolina Line.[22]

The South Carolina delegation in the Continental Congress clamored for aid. "Stating the weakness of that Colony and its incompetency to its own defence, if attacked by a formidable force of the Enemy, its reliance upon North Carolina for that succour which it had little reason to expect from any other source," it persuaded the Continental Congress to call for the embodiment of five thousand militia and to have Moore concentrate on the defense of South Carolina. On November 29, 1776, the formal resolve sending Moore's command into South Carolina was passed by the North Carolina Assembly. It was also decreed that soldiers in the line whose enlistments were near expiration could re-enlist for an extra three months or the duration of the war. Even when it was discovered that the rumors had been started by "a set of water Gruel Sons of B———s," and that the fleet of transports sailing from New York were returning empty to England, there was still an element of doubt and the Continental Congress recommended that North Carolina construct fortifications and obstructions to protect the entrance to the Cape Fear.[23]

The troops of James Moore had missed the earlier action at Charleston. During that period they had been held in the vicinity of Wilmington because the *Falcon, Scorpion,* and *Cruizer,* along with fifteen other British ships, lay in the Cape Fear, posing a constant threat to that area. There had also been the need to protect the newly constructed and vital salt works from British shore parties. In Wilmington, the Continentals had been allowed to use the militia bar-

22. *Colonial Records,* X, 871, 899, 903–5, 908, 928–29; *State Records,* XI, 357; Burnett, *Letters of Members of the Continental Congress,* II, 153–54; Samuel Johnston to _____, 17 August 1776, Samuel Johnston Papers.

23. *Colonial Records,* X, 947; Burnett, *Letters of Members of the Continental Congress,* I, 155–56, 154; Ford, *Journals of the Continental Congress,* VI, 657, 908, 952.

racks for fear that "much of the Lumber will be stole." This led to antagonism between the regulars and the militia, with each group spying on the other to determine if they received more than their share of rations and supplies.[24]

Not until early October had the British weighed anchor, after burning three vessels no longer fit for service. Since early fall the regiment had been sickly. Between sixty and seventy men were constantly in the hospital and an even larger number were ill but ambulatory. Because of the prevalence of disease among the troops a large number were moved some eight miles out from Wilmington to an isolated location called the "Jumping Gulley." Those who were not down with fevers were drilled twice a day. There was always the fear of another uprising among the Tories. Perhaps to alleviate the boredom, Moore marched out three hundred men against the loyalists, promising "you shall have fighting for your money if the enemy can be brought to any kind of action." It amounted to little more than a stroll around the countryside. When the Provincial Congress assembled at Halifax, the Regiment of Colonel Francis Nash was marched to that town to protect it from the enemies of the state. After three days encampment in one of Nicholas Long's old fields along the banks of the Roanoke the troops were returned to Wilmington. This had been the nearest thing to action Moore's troops had seen.[25]

Moore's command looked stronger on paper than it was. The total number in the returns was 2,035, but of this number 81 men of the First Regiment, 75 of the Second and all but 37 of the Third Regiment were "On Command" in Georgia under Robert Howe. Even the 37 of the Third Regiment were not under the direct command of Moore, but were at Salisbury under Colonel Alexander Martin, guarding the stores gathered at that spot. Despite their role as the elite of the North Carolina troops, most of these Continentals not only lacked most of the martial graces but many military necessities. They were ill-trained, ill-fed, ill-housed, ill clothed, without sufficient arms, ammunition, blankets, and tents. And while the Provincial Congress so dawdled over pressing matters that Samuel Johnston complained, "God knows when there will be an end of the trifling here," Moore was forced to borrow $6,250 (South Carolina currency) from Thomas Polk to feed his troops. Despite the daily hardships, there

24. *Colonial Records*, X, 564, 743, 744; Harnett to Council of Safety, 30 August 1776, Papers in Office of Secretary of State.
25. *State Records*, XI, 340, 341, 833, XXII, 749–50, 751; Armstrong to Hancock, 7 October 1776, Papers of the Continental Congress; Samuel Ashe to Council of Safety, 13 August 1776, Papers in Office of Secretary of State.

seemed an undercurrent of enthusiasm among the North Carolina regulars that allowed them to feel that they were the equals of Europe's best.[26]

In January, 1777, Moore's brigade marched southward in two columns. One group, under Colonel Francis Nash, traveled by way of Lockwood's Folly to Beaufort and thrived in the excellent bivouac discovered in the latter place. In addition to their daily drills, the troops cleared one hundred acres of land for the owner of the tract. Moore's troops were not so fortunate. Arriving in Charleston in early January, they encamped on sandy Haddrell's Point five miles from town. There a steady diet of fresh pork and rice and the lack of clothing, blankets, and suitable shelter took their toll. A large number of those who contracted colds developed pneumonia because of constant exposure. Moore discovered that there were a large number of blankets within the city, but the Charleston merchants refused to part with them until they held cash in hand. To compound the misery, there were no funds with which to pay the troops. As a result, despite the warnings issued by their officers, and because of the high enlistment bounty offered by South Carolina recruiting officers, many of the North Carolina Line slipped away to join the South Carolinians. Moore returned to North Carolina on January 8 and, inasmuch as Robert Howe was in command of the troops within the city and at Fort Johnson, the North Carolinians were placed under Colonel Francis Nash, under the over-all command of Brigadier General Moultrie of South Carolina.[27]

At this time things were not going well with the main army in the North. Despite Washington's success at Trenton, the general's total situation had grown more critical. The short-term enlistments of many of the men of the army had expired the first of January and not only had there been few re-enlistments, it was unlikely there would be many in the near future. One reason, or so it was felt by Thomas Burke, was that the New England states were "very languid: the troops do not at all come forward." Since the situation bordered on the critical, the Continental Congress attempted to put more men

26. *Colonial Records*, X, 858–59; Ford, *Journals of the Continental Congress*, IX, 992–93; Samuel Johnston to James Iredell, 4 December 1776, Charles E. Johnston Collection.

27. James Moore to Caswell, 22 January 1777, William Lord to Caswell, 28 February 1777, Caswell Letterbook; *State Records*, XI, 367, 399, 707–9, 834; Moultrie, *Memoirs of the American Revolution*, I, 188–89; Robert Howe Orderly Book; North Carolina Orderly Book, 1777, Historical Society of Pennsylvania Collection; Howe to Hancock, 26 February 1777, Papers of the Continental Congress.

into the field through an extensive recruiting campaign, offering a rather generous bounty of twenty dollars and a hundred acres of land to every soldier who signed up for the duration of the war. Francis Nash was elevated to the rank of brigadier general and Congress urged that he be sent into the western portions of North Carolina to "use his personal influence" in recruiting the small farmers of that area. These men were to act as partial replacements for the Continental regiments in North and South Carolina which, on February 15, were ordered to march for the Northern Department as near March 15 as possible. Several of the older units were still incomplete and Moore was ordered to fill them from the new units as quickly as possible. In the future, units as small as companies were to be rushed forward as quickly as they could be readied. Yet so many officers used recruiting as an excuse for staying at home that the assembly ordered all those without specific recruiting commissions to join Washington's main army without delay.[28]

And in Congress there was a growing spirit of sectionalism and distrust that was to be reflected in the Continental army. The southern members of that body had begun to express "some apprehensions of combinations in the Eastern States to derive to themselves every possible advantage from the present war, at the expense of the rest." William Hooper had expressed this fear when he wrote, "If I am a Slave let me have one rather than 60,000 Masters." Perhaps it was these misgivings that caused the southern delegates to lead the floor fight to have a regular system established for the selection of general officers. North Carolina, Virginia, and Maryland argued that the states were entitled to such officers in proportion to the men they furnished the regular army—a brigadier general for every three regiments or battalions, a major general for every nine such units. When this proposal was defeated in favor of a promotion policy based on "quota, and . . . merit," the North Carolina delegates refused to vote on those names placed before the Congress for promotion to major general. They also joined with New Jersey, Pennsylvania, and South Carolina in expunging from the journals a "pompous paragraph" censuring General Washington, a resolution that had been supported by the New England states, Georgia, and Virginia. In like manner, the North Carolinians were beginning to fear domination by the Virginia delegates

28. Burke to Caswell, 5 February 1776, Caswell to James Moore, 6 February 1777, Moore to Caswell, 7 March 1777, Caswell Letterbook; *State Records*, XI, 383, 461; Moultrie, *Memoirs of the American Revolution*, I, 189; Ford, *Journals of the Continental Congress*, II, 32, VI, 104, VII, 90–91; Burnett, *Letters of Members of the Continental Congress*, I, 235–36, 256; Resolution of North Carolina Congress, 1 May 1777, Emmet Collection.

in the Congress and felt that they were "best calculated to check the ambitions of Virginia."[29]

The march northward was hampered not only by the lack of money to pay the troops, but by the constantly changing directives from the Continental Congress. Further delays were experienced when Howe, contrary to the orders of Moore, refused to allow the North Carolina line regiments to leave South Carolina. The continuing raids upon the Georgia frontier by the Indians and Tories from East Florida posed a constant threat and there were the persistent rumors of another descent upon the South Carolina coast by the enemy. Washington had also suggested the possibility of a strike against St. Augustine. And Georgia, notwithstanding Howe's urging the "absolute necessity of immediately proceeding to place your Country (already too long neglected) in a proper State of defence," seemed unable to bring order out of the confusion existing in that state.[30]

Other problems included such matters as an adequate supply of provisions along the route of march and muskets for those soldiers who were still unarmed. The only immediate source of firearms was the purchase of the cargoes of two prizes that had been brought into New Bern by privateers. Blankets were so scarce that it was suggested that the people weave them in their homes for distribution to the soldiery. Prices had so risen that those who had contracted to supply the troops resigned rather than suffer bankruptcy. Financial affairs had reached such a critical state that Governor Richard Caswell urged the state treasurer, John Ashe, "For God's sake, give every assistance in your power to facilitate the marching of the Troops." This desperate situation, plus dissatisfaction with the method of selecting officers adopted by the Continental Congress, led many officers to resign, including Colonel Alexander Lillington of the Sixth Regiment, who pleaded his advanced age, and who apparently felt that his future lay in political rather than military pursuits.[31]

29. Burke to Caswell, 10 February 1777, Caswell Letterbook; *State Records*, XI, 380–81, 384, 420; Burnett, *Letters of Members of the Continental Congress*, II, 40–41, 146–47; Ford, *Journals of the Continental Congress*, VII, 132, 149–50, 150n.
30. Fitzpatrick, *Writings of Washington*, VII, 297–98; James Moore to Caswell, 1 April 1777, Preston Davie Collection, Southern Historical Collection, The University of North Carolina at Chapel Hill, Chapel Hill, N.C.; Moultrie, *Memoirs of the American Revolution*, I, 188–89; James Searle Letter, November 1776, Miscellaneous Papers, 1697–1912; Robert Howe to Caswell, 13 February 1777, Governors' Papers (Caswell); Howe to _____, 11 December 1776, George Washington Papers; Howe to Hancock, 26 February 1777, Papers of the Continental Congress.
31. James Moore to Caswell, 8 February 1777, Caswell to Moore, 8 March 1777, Burke to Caswell, 11 March 1777, Caswell to Moore, 13 March 1777, Cas-

Yet despite the obvious shortcomings and understrength of the regiments in the field, the state legislature in late November, 1776, had created three new regiments to be placed on the Continental establishment. James Hogun was to command the Seventh Regiment, with Lott Brewster, Robert Mebane, and Shelby Harney as majors; James Armstrong of the Eighth and John Williams of the Ninth were not immediately given subordinate officers above the rank of captain until they had enlisted a sufficient number of men.

In addition to these difficulties, there was the threat of an uprising along the frontier by the Cherokees and the Creeks, which necessitated dispatching troops to those areas to quell any sudden uprisings by the savages. Governor Patrick Henry offered the aid of Virginia, yet felt it best to postpone all operations "till corn is planted." Commissioners had been appointed to treat with the Indians, but the proceedings had been so bumbled that there seemed little prospect of success.[32]

Through it all, the state government appeared unconcerned about military matters perhaps because of the new and inexperienced legislators whom Samuel Johnston termed "fools and knaves who by their low Arts have worked themselves into the good graces of the populace." In this time that bordered on the critical, the General Assembly during the first two weeks it sat in the spring of 1777 accomplished "little more than settle the decorum to be observed between each House, and the method of doing business." When the need for cutting red tape was so desperate, the new government was so cautious and fearful of establishing precedents that it neglected immediate concerns. There was a flurry of wild rumors. Some said, even in the Continental Congress, that Washington had as many men as he could possibly use and that there was no need of reinforcements from the South. And despite the need to fill the ranks of those regiments already established, the General Assembly created a new Continental regiment, the Tenth, to be recruited by Colonel Abraham Sheppard. At this time Sheppard was in command of a "volunteer" militia regiment in South Carolina and pleading to be rescued from "the most miserable part of God's creation, both men and lands." There is the suggestion, however, that this was a proposal by Caswell to reward Sheppard for past favors, and the governor went so far

well to John Ashe, 13 March 1777, Peter and Daniel Mallet to Caswell, 1 April 1777, Caswell Letterbook; *State Records*, XI, 376, 411, 412–13, 416, 424–26, 427, 439, 443–45, 706–7, 707–9, 709–10, 713–14.

32. Henry to Caswell, 18 March 1777, Henry to Caswell, 1 April 1777, Howe to Caswell, 10 April 1777, John Page to Caswell, 17 April 1777, Caswell to Henry, 11 April 1777, Caswell Letterbook; *State Records*, XI, 438–39, 446, 447–48, 451.

as to write the Continental Congress on the colonel's behalf. Sheppard had served as a lieutenant colonel at the battle of Alamance in 1771, and once again had been with the governor at Moore's Creek Bridge in command of the Dobbs County militia. He had raised a battalion to go to the assistance of South Carolina during the "Snow Campaign," where "he behaved well." When Sheppard first proposed that he be allowed to raise a regiment, he had indicated that the men were practically enlisted and formed once the word was given. He had assured the governor that his regiment would be ready to march by July 1, and had agreed that the privates would draw no pay until three hundred had been enlisted. He was given the privilege of selecting his own officers. Caswell appeared to think that he would soon have an elite corps. Nevertheless certain restrictions were placed upon Sheppard by the General Assembly and were incorporated into the resolve of the Continental Congress that gave him the command.[33]

Confusion was compounded when North Carolina lost the one military figure who might have acted as a catalyst and pulled the many strings together. On April 15, 1777, General James Moore, a great spirit in a frail body, died of what was diagnosed as "a fit of Gout in his Stomach." His death robbed North Carolina of probably its greatest military mind. Certainly he had been the balance wheel between the new military and civil organizations and had managed to mold a reasonable facsimile of an army, though there were those who deplored his lack of discipline and that he had allowed himself "to be guided by the silliest fellows in the world." Although Moore had not been personally engaged in a single military action, his astute direction of troops had been largely responsible for the eventual victory at Moore's Creek Bridge. His actions had held the promise of greatness.[34]

At the time of Moore's death, Howe had finally released the North Carolina Continentals stationed in Charleston upon his return from "a fatiguing, fruitless, expedition to Georgia." He released

33. Samuel Johnston to Thomas Burke, 19 April 1777, Johnston to Burke, 26 June 1777, Thomas Burke Papers, Southern Historical Collection, The University of North Carolina at Chapel Hill, Chapel Hill, N.C.; Caswell to Burke, 20 April 1777, Sheppard to Caswell, 16 March 1777, Caswell Letterbook; *State Records*, XI, 453–55, 456–57; Ford, *Journals of the Continental Congress*, VIII, 450, 475; _____ to Burke, [1777], Thomas Burke Papers, North Carolina Department of Archives and History, Raleigh, N.C.; Caswell to _____, 8 March 1777, Recruiting Instructions issued to Colonel Abraham Sheppard, 9 May 1777, Governors' Papers.

34. Samuel Johnston to Burke, 19 April 1777, Thomas Burke Papers, Southern Historical Collection; *State Records*, XI, 453–54; _____ to _____, n.d. [1777], Thomas Burke Papers, North Carolina Department of Archives and History.

them, however, with reluctance, arguing that the regiments of South Carolina were filling so slowly that "the Troops of North Carolina were in case of Exigence the only Reliance it had. . . ." They had arrived in Wilmington in early April. Despite the poor physical condition of the Carolina Line, Moore had planned to march them northward as quickly as possible. After Moore's death, and because Howe could not leave his position in South Carolina and Georgia, Francis Nash abandoned his recruiting mission in the western part of the state, hurrying down to Wilmington to assume command of the troops. A rendezvous was established at Halifax and the march to join Washington was to begin just as soon as all units were assembled. The situation now held an atmosphere of urgency. Intelligence suggested that the British would make an assault upon Annapolis or Baltimore. Troops were needed desperately, for the New England states had turned "very languid" in their attitude toward the war, although there was some justification for their not sending troops since their own shores were being threatened with British coastal raids. There was also the possibility that the North Carolina troops might be better supplied with Washington's army than in their own state, for supplies from France had begun to arrive in northern ports.[35]

Jethro Sumner's Third Regiment was the first unit to arrive at Halifax. The Third was far from full strength, considerably weakened by those men who had enlisted in the South Carolina and Georgia Lines. Even now Georgia recruiting officers were trying to persuade North Carolina mounted troops to enlist in their own units. Things had become so desperate in that state that it had been proposed that the Georgia Line be filled with deserters from the British army. Numbers in the North Carolina Line were further depleted by those who were "now every night running off." In fact, the situation grew so desperate that Governor Caswell offered to pardon all deserters who rejoined their units. And among other things, there were disputes over rank, with one argument being settled by recognizing Jacob Turner as first captain of the regiment.

Abraham Sheppard was also experiencing difficulty in recruiting his regiment, despite an enlistment bounty of thirty dollars, a suit

35. Caswell to Burke, 20 April 1777, Caswell to _____, 20 April 1777, Richard Caswell Papers, Southern Historical Collection, The University of North Carolina at Chapel Hill, Chapel Hill, N.C.; *State Records*, XI, xiii, 456–57, 460–62, 436–37; North Carolina Orderly Book, Historical Society of Pennsylvania Collection; Howe to Caswell, 10 April 1777, Governors' Papers; Howe to Washington, 14 May 1777, George Washington Papers; Howe to Hancock, 8 May 1777, Papers of the Continental Congress.

of clothes, and 100 acres of land for those who enlisted for three years, or 250 acres for those who agreed to remain in service until the end of the war. Sheppard, however, was hampered somewhat by the restrictions laid upon him by the General Assembly, who had enjoined him to recruit only "young, hearty, robust men, whose birth, family connections, and property, bind them to the interest of their country. . . ." In short, the assembly was instructing the colonel to enlist only the cream of the younger generation as privates, a group that normally would have sought an officer's commission rather than serve in the ranks.[36]

Nash's soldiers slowly gathered at Halifax, subsisting in part on fish seined from the Roanoke River. Then, because of the prevalence of smallpox in the vicinity of the camp, they marched in early May. Colonel John Williams was left in command of the Halifax camp to organize and send forward recruits as fast as they came in. Three officers from each of the nine regiments were left to continue recruiting efforts in the state. Nash remained behind long enough to establish recruiting procedures, with about 1,500 men sent forward under Alexander Martin. Cosmo Medici's mounted troops were detailed to escort prisoners taken at Moore's Creek Bridge to Philadelphia.[37]

The North Carolina Continentals marched through Virginia by way of Petersburg to Williamsburg, where they rested for two days before continuing to Richmond. At Richmond they met with the only resistance they encountered during the march. As they trooped through the town a doughty little shoemaker stood in the doorway of his shop shouting, "Hurrah for King George!" At first, the soldiers ignored him as a harmless nuisance and paid little attention even that night when he invaded their camp outside of town, sauntering through their ranks and still shouting lustily for his sovereign. When, however, he began to follow Nash and his aides around with his continual hurrahing for his king, tolerance turned to irritation. With

36. *State Records*, XI, 465–66, 467, 716–17, XV, 699–700; Sumner to Caswell, 27 April 1777, Settlement of Officers, 18 April 1777, Sheppard to Caswell, 7 May 1777, Instructions for Col. Abraham Sheppard, Caswell Letterbook; North Carolina Orderly Book, Historical Society of Pennsylvania Collection; Howe to Caswell, 10 April 1777, Governors' Papers; George Walton to Washington, 28 August 1777, George Washington Papers; Caswell to Burke, Papers of the Continental Congress; Recommendation of Third Regiment, 14 April 1777, Revolutionary Papers, Southern Historical Collection, The University of North Carolina at Chapel Hill, Chapel Hill, N.C.

37. John Williams to Caswell, 3 June 1777, Cosmo Medici to Caswell, 31 May 1777, Caswell Letterbook; Alexander Martin to Hancock, 10 May 1777, Papers of the Continental Congress.

a rope tied around his middle the stubborn little Tory was sawed back and forth across the river until he was almost drowned. Yet every time he managed to get his head above water, he would sputter forth another "Hurrah for King George!" In exasperation, Nash finally had him dipped headfirst in a barrel of tar and then sprinkled liberally with feathers taken from the shoemaker's own mattress. Still he hurrahed and kept doing so until the general had him drummed out of camp with the threat that he would be shot if he returned. There were no further demonstrations from the people, who stood on either side of the road as the long line of soldiers shuffled past toward Fredericksburg.[38]

At Alexandria, according to a recent resolve of the Continental Congress, a station for inoculation for smallpox had been established for the Continental troops. After the arrival of the vanguard of the North Carolina troops under Alexander Martin, it was discovered that some two hundred had had the dread disease and were thereby immune. They were sent on to the main army under the commands of Colonels Sumner and Lytle. General Nash had himself inoculated before any of his men were subjected to the scratch on the arm and the pus from the pustules of a smallpox victim rubbed into the little opening in the skin. The operation began around eight o'clock on the morning of May 21 and continued until after two in the afternoon. After the men had undergone a mild case of the disease, they crossed the Potomac some eight miles above Georgetown and continued their journey. It was claimed that only one man was lost as a result of the inoculation, a private named Griffin, who died after a swim in the Potomac following his supposed recovery from his illness. Yet there were enough complaints from both the North Carolina and Virginia regiments that had undergone inoculation at Alexandria that Dr. William Rickham was suspended from duty because of his neglect of officers and men.[39]

The effects of the smallpox inoculation immobilized the troops from three to four weeks. After the men had fully recovered their strength they were marched to Philadelphia to await further orders.

38. *State Records*, XI, xiii–xv, 486, 834–36.

39. *Ibid.*, pp. 479, 836, XV, 702; Alexander Martin to Washington, 16 May 1777, George Washington Papers; John Bush Orderly Book, Southern Historical Collection, The University of North Carolina at Chapel Hill, Chapel Hill, N.C.; Henry B. Livingston to Lt. Col. Ramsey, 7 May 1777, Revolutionary Papers, Southern Historical Collection; Morning Report, Col. Sumner's Detachment, 11 June 1777, Jethro Sumner Papers, Southern Historical Collection; Ford, *Journals of the Continental Congress*, VII, 110, 292, 317, IX, 1038; David Mason to Washington, George Washington Papers.

They camped within a mile of the city, in fact close enough so that Nash was lodged in the house of Thomas Burke, one of North Carolina's delegates to the Continental Congress.

On July 8, the Continental Congress ordered them to Billingsport, where they were to join the militia of New Jersey and Pennsylvania in completing the fortifications for the defenses of the Delaware River, The Virginia Continental troops in the neighborhood were temporarily placed under Nash's command. Soon after they were directed by Washington to join his army, but the general soon countermanded these orders. Nash's troops were now to remain at Trenton until the next move of General Sir William Howe could be ascertained. If Howe did make an attempt on Philadelphia, the North Carolinians, aided by local militia, were to fight a holding action until Washington could come up in the enemy's rear. Nash's brigade had been so reinforced by local troops and an artillery company that the troops under his command now numbered nearly two thousand.[40]

In the meantime, the two hundred who had marched forward from Alexandria under Sumner and Lytle had joined Washington's army, then in camp at Morristown, New Jersey. There they sat while the commander in chief attempted to determine the next move of the British general. The North Carolinians, as were all troops in camp, were drilled and whipped into some semblance of a military force. Arms were inspected and repaired, although some of those belonging to the North Carolina troops were in such bad condition that they were found to be beyond repair and were discarded. Although soldiers were prohibited from bathing during the heat of the day, and then were not to stay in the water very long for fear of falling ill, other steps were taken to promote "Decency & Clendlyness" among the men. To instill better discipline, officers were ordered to exercise their commands in person on the parade ground rather than leaving routine drills to the sergeants as in the past. There were still desertions. Dennis O'Bryan, a private of Sumner's Third Regiment, was convicted of desertion by a court martial, but as he was considered "a stupid Foolish Person," and not worthy of harsh punishment, he was dismissed from the service and drummed out of camp.[41]

By June 30, 1777, the British had evacuated all their posts in

40. Ford, *Journals of the Continental Congress*, VIII, 538, 608; Fitzpatrick, *Writings of Washington*, VIII, 415; *State Records*, XI, 510–11, 733, 739; Francis Nash to Sally Nash, 25 July 1777, Francis Nash Papers, Southern Historical Collection, The University of North Carolina at Chapel Hill, Chapel Hill, N.C.

41. Jacob Turner Orderly Book, North Carolina Department of Archives and History, Raleigh, N.C.; Fitzpatrick, *Writings of Washington*, VIII, 362; Alexander Martin to Hancock, 10 May 1777, Papers of the Continental Congress.

New Jersey, and by July 8 had begun to embark an estimated 18,000 troops aboard the great fleet of over 260 vessels that had been assembling in New York harbor for the past two months. Inasmuch as General John Burgoyne had arrived in Canada in May, Washington was "almost certain" that this armada would transport the British army up the Hudson to make a junction with Burgoyne, driving southward from Canada. Still there was enough doubt in the general's mind to admit that his situation was "truly delicate and perplexing." Other possible enemy objectives were felt to be Philadelphia, the Chesapeake, or even a second attack upon Charleston.[42]

When Howe first began his embarkation of troops, Washington felt that he should move to a point on the Hudson to prevent a junction with Burgoyne. On July 10, the baggage wagons were sent forward and the army was ordered to march early the following morning. The North Carolina troops, in the division commanded by Major General Nathanael Greene, camped that night with the rest of the army at Pompton Plains, eighteen miles out. For two days they lay there, soaked by the "foul weather," but by July 14 they were in bivouac at Smith's Clove in the New York highlands, not too far from West Point. Once the tents were pitched, the rank and file were set to work putting their arms in condition because their officers had allowed them to neglect their weapons. Wagons were repaired so that there would be no delay should there be sudden orders to march. The Carolina Line was not so troubled with desertions as other units, but when Levi Springer of the Fourth North Carolina enlisted in the Tenth Virginia to claim the bounty offered by the recruiting officers of that state, he was sentenced to receive fifty lashes "on his bare back."[43]

Washington still worried himself concerning Howe's next move. On July 9 he learned, to his "Chagrine and Suprise," that the fort at Ticonderoga had fallen to Burgoyne with a minimum of resistance. Howe's conduct, he felt, was "puzzling and embarrassing beyond measure," as was "the information I get." By July 21 it was apparent that Howe would soon sail and Washington ordered his force to be ready to march at a moment's notice. Howe finally sailed July 23, 1777. The following day Washington received the information that

42. Leonard Lundin, *Cockpit of the Revolution* (Princeton, N.J., 1940), pp. 312–21; Fitzpatrick, *Writings of Washington*, VIII, 355; Ambrose Serle, *The American Journal of Ambrose Serle, Secretary to Lord Howe, 1776–1778*, ed. Edward H. Tatum, Jr. (San Marino, Calif., 1940), p. 241; John Penn to Caswell, 25 June 1777, Caswell Letterbook.

43. Jacob Turner Orderly Book; Fitzpatrick, *Writings of Washington*, VIII, 424–25.

the enemy fleet had gone down the river and had passed Sandy Hook. Heavy American detachments were sent to Philadelphia, followed by the main body at a more leisurely pace. But because of the depredations on previous marches, orders were issued against "destroying fences and seizing horses" along the way. Too many people had turned their faces from the cause of liberty with their "distress from the Plundering and wanton destruction of their Property." Brief halts were made at Trenton and Morristown until July 31 when intelligence was received that the enemy fleet had been sighted off the Delaware Capes. Sumner's men were now in Muhlenberg's brigade in Greene's division and were encamped near Chester, Pennsylvania. Nash's brigade was still in the vicinity of Trenton.[44]

Despite the obvious, Washington still seemed to feel that things were falling into place too easily and could not bring himself to believe that Philadelphia was the true British objective. His doubt was expressed to General Horatio Gates: "Gen'l Howe's in a manner abandoning Genl. Burgoyne is so unaccountable a matter, that till I am fully assured it is so, I cannot help casting my Eyes continually behind me." And so the army sat and waited, although no furloughs were granted and the troops were ordered to hold themselves in readiness to march "soon and sudden." All women camp followers, "especially those who are Pregnant or have Children," were to leave the army, except those whose presence was felt absolutely necessary to do laundry and other housekeeping chores around camp.[45]

As late as August 21, Washington was still convinced that Howe's puzzling maneuvers amounted to little more than a skillful feint to draw his attention away from Burgoyne's movement down the Hudson. After a council of general officers convinced themselves that the real British objective was Charleston, Washington once again marched northward to secure a position from which he could block Burgoyne's thrust down the Hudson. He had made camp in the meadows bordering the Neshaminy River some twenty miles north of Philadelphia when he received word that the British fleet was standing in to Chesapeake Bay; the next day the information was that they were well inside the Capes. It was now obvious that Howe, rather than attempting the defenses of the Delaware River, planned to disembark at the head of Chesapeake Bay and march the fifty-five

44. Fitzpatrick, *Writings of Washington*, VIII, 386, 414, 454, 460–68, 496, 497, 499; Serle, *American Journal of Ambrose Serle*, p. 241; *Pennsylvania Archives*, 3rd Series, V (1894), 415; Jacob Turner Orderly Book; Cornelius Harnett to Caswell, 11 August 1777, Caswell Letterbook; *State Records*, XI, 569–70; North Carolina Orderly Book, Historical Society of Pennsylvania Collection.

45. Fitzpatrick, *Writings of Washington*, IX, 17; Jacob Turner Orderly Book.

miles overland to Philadelphia. It was something of a relief for the American general, for with the plan of the enemy now obvious, no longer would he be "compeld to wander about the country like the Arabs in search of corn." At four o'clock on the morning of August 23 Washington once again moved toward Philadelphia and that night lay in camp near Germantown.[46]

In early August the brigade of Francis Nash had been stationed at Chester, but on August 6 the men and wagons had been sent by boat up to Trenton. His force was not so large as it had been, although it numbered nearly two thousand. While marching through Philadelphia eighty mounted troops and their officers (enough men and officers for three troops of thirty men each) had been dropped, their horses so poor and unfit for service that they were sold. The Continental Board of War refused to purchase new mounts because the men had enlisted for only twelve to eighteen months and had refused to enlist for the duration of the war. There was the suggestion that they be taken into Colonel George Baylor's Third Continental Dragoons or be transferred to the infantry. Some, such as Silas Dollahide of Clark's First Regiment, were detached to help man Continental naval vessels on the Delaware. But no sooner did Washington near Philadelphia than Jethro Sumner requested that his North Carolina troops be allowed to rejoin Nash.[47]

While the Commander in Chief was maneuvering the main army, Nash lay encamped in an orchard near Trenton. Although ordered to hold himself ready for immediate action, Nash was to remain where he was while "the Enemy's real intentions still remain ambigious and uncertain." It was reported that the North Carolina troops were "in high spirits." Nash spent much of the time drilling his brigade as a unit and many off-duty hours in policing the camp site. In general, the average soldier of the American revolutionary army was a rather dirty animal and those of the North Carolina Brigade were no different from the Continentals of other states. In Nash's command the artillery company was the worst offender, "throwing Bones, and Scraps of Meat and other things about their Tents." Respiratory diseases incapacitated many, and the men were cautioned against bathing too frequently. During the continuing rains, extra whiskey rations were

46. Fitzpatrick, *Writings of Washington*, VIII, 1–5; IX, 107, 113, 114, 110n, 155–56, 119; Hancock to Caswell, 22 August 1777, Papers of the Continental Congress.

47. Richard Peters to Washington, 19 August 1777, Muster Roll of the Frigate Washington's Crew, 26 October 1777, George Washington Papers; Commissions Grants, 25 August 1777, Revolutionary War Rolls, Adjutant General's Office, National Archives, Washington, D.C.

issued in an attempt to keep down illness. Frequent courts-martial tried soldiers charged with deserting, stealing, sleeping on duty, insulting officers, and disobeying orders. Two received the death penalty for desertion, and even after mercy was recommended, Washington decreed that they not be given their reprieves until "after carrying them thro' all the forms of an execution." In general, the usual punishment for the enlisted men was fifty lashes at the cart's tail, while convicted officers were either reprimanded or cashiered from the service.[48]

The officers, especially those of field grade, voiced their discontent with the promotion policy as practiced by the North Carolina Brigade. This dissatisfaction arose when James Ingram of the Eighth Regiment resigned as lieutenant colonel of that regiment and Samuel Lockhart of the Third was elevated to that rank. A dangerous discontent had been simmering since Gideon Lamb and Archibald Lytle of the Sixth Regiment had been promoted to colonel and lieutenant colonel as vacancies had occurred. Other lieutenant colonels in other regiments argued that they should have received the promotions by reason of their seniority. On June 13, a board of general officers of the Continental army had decided that all promotions up to major should be made from within the regiment, but higher ranks should be made from the state line as a whole, and the malcontents used this as a basis for their argument. When the dispute was submitted to General Washington, he ruled that the decision of the board was the proper promotions policy of the Continental army but that the promotions of Lamb and Lytle should be allowed to stand. This seemed to placate the complainers for the time being since less grumbling was heard in the camp of the North Carolina brigade.[49]

More alarming was the rumor that the Continental Congress had appointed Dr. Edward Hand of Pennsylvania as a brigadier general of North Carolina troops to replace James Moore. Even worse, Thomas Burke, North Carolina delegate, had actively cam-

48. Francis Nash to Sally Nash, 25 July 1777, Francis Nash Papers, Southern Historical Collection; John Bush Orderly Book, Southern Historical Collection; Jacob Turner Orderly Book; Harnett to Caswell, 11 August 1777, Caswell Letterbook; State Records, XI, 745, 751–53; G. W. Greene, Life of Nathanael Greene (New York, 1867–71), I, 438–39; Washington to Nash, 3 August 1777, Washington to Alexander Martin, 17 August 1777, Washington to Nash, 5 August 1777, George Washington Papers; North Carolina Orderly Book, Historical Society of Pennsylvania Collection.

49. John Bush Orderly Book, Southern Historical Collection; Jacob Turner Orderly Book; Fitzpatrick, Writings of Washington, IX, 80–81; Burnett, Letters of Members of the Continental Congress, III, 497n; State Records, XI, 562–63.

paigned for Hand's appointment. Professing no ill will against Hand, sixteen field officers of the North Carolina regiments dispatched a bitter remonstrance to the Congress, declaring the action to be "a reflection on that State, which appointed us, and a stab to Military honour throughout the Continent in general." Burke ignored a request for a report by the officers for his part in urging the promotion of Hand, and in a letter to Nash he raged, "Their Behavior in this Instance has determined me to forego all particular attention to them. I hope they will so distinguish themselves that their Merit alone will be sufficient for their Promotion, without standing in need of any assistance which I could give."[50]

As Washington approached Philadelphia, he was persuaded to parade his army in a display of force calculated not only to awe the large loyalist element in the city, but to raise the spirits of those who supported the rebellion. Every soldier, to offset his shabby appearance, was ordered to wear in his hat a "green sprig, emblem of hope." General orders demanded that all "carry their arms well" and cautioned that anyone who dared break ranks would be punished with thirty-nine lashes, well laid on his bare back. There was almost a pathetic admonition to the drummers and fifers to play a quick step, "but with such moderation that the men may step to it with ease and without *dancing* along, or totally disregarding the music." The long columns began their march around three o'clock in the morning of Sunday, August 24, and by seven were entering the environs of the city. The rain that had threatened to damp the proceedings stopped just as the march began to wind down Front Street and up Chestnut. For two hours they trudged by. General Washington, with the young Lafayette by his side, rode at the head of the nearly 16,000 men marching twelve abreast. The very mass of them concealed many defects. The spectacle made John Adams "feel secure," but in a letter to his wife he reported military imperfections that disturbed his politician's eye: "Our soldiers have not yet quite the air of soliders. They don't hold up their heads quite erect, nor turn out their toes exactly as they ought. They don't all of them cock their hats; and such as do, don't all wear them the same way."[51]

---

50. Remonstrance of N.C. Field Officers, 14 August 1777, Jethro Sumner Papers, Southern Historical Collection; Alexander Martin to Washington, 17 August 1777, George Washington Papers; Burke to Nash, 16 August 1777, Thomas Burke Papers, N.C. Dept. Arch. & Hist.

51. Fitzpatrick, *Writings of Washington*, IX, 125–27; Charles Francis Adams (ed.), *Familiar Letters of John Adams and His Wife Abigail Adams* (New York, 1876), p. 298; *Pennsylvania Magazine of History and Biography*, XVI (1892), 147; *Pennsylvania Journal* (Philadelphia), 25 August 1777.

Nash, who had been ordered to bypass Philadelphia on a previous move down to Chester, was now ordered to join the main army. Perhaps to make the army appear larger than it was, Nash's brigade and Colonel Thomas Procter's regiment of artillery were to march through the city on Monday, passing along the same streets as had the main army the day before. Thomas Burke joined other members of the Continental Congress along the route of march and reported the North Carolina brigade "appeared very well." So impressed had he been that his hopes were "now very high that a capital blow will be given the enemy in every quarter." Alexander Graydon was equally optimistic and felt the soldiers appeared as though "they might have faced an equal number with a reasonable prospect of success."[52]

Within two days the army lay encamped at Wilmington, Delaware, checking weapons and drawing additional ammunition. One hundred of the best rank and file were selected for inclusion in the elite Corps of Light Infantry then forming. Colonel Alexander Martin was detached to command them. By now word had come that Howe's army was landing at Head of Elk, Maryland, and would soon be on its march toward Philadelphia. Washington, accompanied by Greene and Lafayette, his aides, and two troops of light horse, rode forth to personally reconnoiter the enemy. From the top of a hill within two miles of the British camp he attempted to estimate their numbers by counting their tents.[53]

Washington, well aware of the morale factor involved should Philadelphia fall, refused to give up the city without a fight. He was ready, as Alexander Graydon noted, "to scuffle for liberty." On September 7 the army moved up near the little village of Newport, less than ten miles from where Howe lay encamped at Iron Hill. At three in the morning of the eighth the alarm guns were fired, the tents struck, and the troops paraded. And then, as so often happens in military organizations, the men stood around and awaited orders until nine o'clock. At last they were marched out and stationed in a

52. John Bush Orderly Book, Southern Historical Collection; Jacob Turner Orderly Book; *State Records*, XI, 593; Alexander Graydon, *Memoirs of His Own Times with Reminiscences of the Men and Events of the Revolution*, ed. John Stockton Littell (Philadelphia, 1846), p. 291; Fitzpatrick, *Writings of Washington*, IX, 116; *North Carolina Gazette*, 19 September 1777.

53. John Bush Orderly Book, Southern Historical Collection; Jacob Turner Orderly Book; Fitzpatrick, *Writings of Washington*, IX, 128, 147, 451–52; Greene, *Life of Nathanael Greene*, I, 444; *State Records*, XIII, 263; Washington to Nash, 25 August 1777, George Washington Papers.

battle line along Red Clay Creek, anxiously awaiting the onset of the battle the general was so sure was in the offing. Nothing happened.

That night the enemy camped within two miles of the American position. During the night intelligence reported that Howe had ordered his troops to divest themselves of their heavy baggage and tents, a move that suggested a flanking operation with a token force left behind to amuse Washington. The general thereupon ordered his own men to discard their packs and place them in the baggage wagons, retaining only their blankets and great coats—if they had them. At two o'clock in the morning of September 9, he put his troops in motion and put Brandywine Creek between his army and that of Howe. He took a position on the high ground behind one of the likelier stream crossings, Chad's Ford. Each night a hundred North Carolinians joined with other detachments in acting as pickets. Washington could do no more than await his opponent's next move in this game of military chess.[54]

The men of the North Carolina Line, on the eve of battle, were no different from other soldiers. Some were nervous, some were scared, while others moved about in that daze that so often overcomes soldiers when combat is near. And all they could do was wait.

54. Fitzpatrick, *Writings of Washington*, IX, 140, 179, 197; Graydon, *Memoirs of His Own Times*, pp. 282–83; *State Records*, XIII, 757–58.

Chapter 5
Brandywine and Germantown

"Trophies lay at our feet. . . ."

Brandywine Creek seemed a logical place to make a stand. If the British Army could not be stopped here, it seemed inevitable that Philadelphia would fall to the enemy. The Brandywine was not a particularly formidable obstacle when considered in the light of military geography. The position's primary advantage lay in the stream's depth, a factor that would force a marching army to use a ford to make a crossing. Unfortunately, there were a number of such crossings on the Brandywine that could be selected by Sir William Howe. But at Chad's Ford the terrain on either side of the stream favored a defensive operation. The Brandywine proper begins with the confluence of two streams known as the East and West branches some six miles upstream from Chad's Ford. The stream wanders through a valley of varying widths, sometimes very narrow between rather steep hills, sometimes widening into spacious meadows on either bank. But everywhere the shore rises upward from the creek, at times rising in a gentle slope to a height of almost two hundred feet, at others almost leaping upwards.[1]

Washington had chosen to position the center of his defense

1. Douglas Southall Freeman, *George Washington*, (New York, 1948–57), IV,

on the high ground above Chad's Ford. Here the Brandywine was about 150 feet wide. It was a good defensive site, for not only did it provide a good base from which the other fords could be covered, but there was a good route for withdrawal. The center was under the command of Major General Nathanael Greene, the division in which Nash's brigade had been assigned. Anthony Wayne's Pennsylvania Continentals were posted near the brow of the hill behind the slight earthworks that had been thrown up near Chad's house. The division commanded by Major General John Sullivan held down the right wing, some two miles upstream in wooded hilly terrain. To the left, where there were no good roads to invite a sudden retreat, were stationed the Pennsylvania militia under John Armstrong. Brigadier General William Maxwell with his eight hundred light infantry, including a number of Continentals detached from the North Carolina Brigade, were thrown across to the southern, or far side of the stream. Nash's brigade was held in reserve behind the center of Greene's division. Thomas Burke, who had ridden out from Philadelphia reported the North Carolina Continentals to be "in high spirits." Burke was so carried away with the excitement of the moment that he was led to boast, "Our army is supposed superior, and the enemy is very shy."[2]

Washington used every crumb of psychology at his command to inspirit his troops, even suggesting that the Almighty was indeed their shepherd. Among other things there was a sermon preached to the men by the Reverend Joab Trout, who took as his text, "All they that take the sword shall perish with the sword." In eloquent bombast he thundered that "the doom of the British is near! Think me not vain when I tell you that beyond the cloud that now enshrouds us, I see gathering thick and fast the darker form and blacker storm of Divine indignation." And the need for aid, both physical and supernatural, was becoming critical. That night Howe's army lay at Kennett Square, just six miles away. When scouting parties reported that Washington had concentrated his strength in the vicinity of Chad's Ford, a surprise was planned for the American general.[3]

As dawn broke on the morning of September 11, 1777, fog clung to the ground. But before eight the mist had burned away and alread the sun was beginning to bear down with an intensity that

471; Christopher L. Ward, *The Delaware Continentals, 1776–1783* (Wilmington, Del., 1941), p. 195; Ward, *War of the Revolution*, I, 341.

2. Ward, *War of the Revolution*, I, 342; Willard M. Wallace, *Appeal to Arms* (New York, 1951), pp. 122–23; *State Records*, XI, 613, 621.

3. *Magazine of American History*, XIII (1885), 281.

promised a hot and sultry day. Alarm guns were fired. Those on the heights above the ford could make out the green coats of the loyalist rangers and the riflemen of Patrick Ferguson in the vanguard of the British force driving down to the ford. Maxwell's light infantry engaged them briskly, inflicting severe casualties until nearly ten o'clock when the sheer force of numbers sent them splashing back across the ford. Among the Americans were the North Carolinians who had been detached to that elite corps and were serving therein under the command of Colonel Alexander Martin. Captain Jacob Turner of the Third Regiment particularly distinguished himself by his gallantry in this early stage of the battle.[4]

Maxwell reformed on the north bank with detachments occasionally slipping back across the stream to harass the enemy advance. An artillery duel began to develop as the British brought up their field guns. Upon several occasions the fire of the Americans forced the British to pull back from the far shore. But between ten-thirty and eleven the enemy had pushed forward under the cover of their artillery and had formed a line of battle along the banks of the Brandywine. Then a strange silence fell over the battlefield. Only the desultory popping of musketry and an occasional boom of a cannon kept up the suggestion of a battle in progress.[5]

By this time Washington should have guessed Howe's strategy. He should have anticipated the enemy movement, so similar to that of the year before on Long Island that one is led to suspect that the American general underestimated the intelligence of his opponent. By eleven o'clock it should have been clear that the enemy was making no real effort to force a crossing and was only amusing Washington, while the major force was detached on a flanking move. And this was Howe's plan. The Hessian general, von Knyphausen, had been sent down to engage Washington's attention at Chad's Ford while another division under Cornwallis, and accompanied by Howe, was marching upstream. The plan was for Cornwallis's command to cross the streams above the fork, turn the American flank and then fall upon the rear of the defenders at Chad's Ford.[6]

---

4. Burke to Caswell, 17 September 1777, Caswell Letterbook; James T. Talman (ed.), *Loyalist Narratives from Upper Canada* (Toronto, 1946), p. 162; *State Records*, XIII, 262; Martin to Caswell, 4 November 1777, Governors' Papers.

5. Fitzpatrick, *Writings of Washington*, VIII, 206; Ward, *War of the Revolution*, I, 342–43; Freeman, *George Washington*, IV, 473–74; *State Records*, XIII, 620–21; *Historical Magazine*, XI (1867), 181.

6. Ward, *War of the Revolution*, I, 344–45; George F. Scheer and Hugh F. Rankin, *Rebels and Redcoats* (Cleveland, Ohio, 1957), p. 267; Dawson, *Battles of the United States*, I, 275.

Sometime after eleven o'clock reports began to come in that a large body of British troops was marching upstream on the far side of the Brandywine. Washington immediately started two divisions moving toward Birmingham Meeting House, three and one-half miles from Chad's Ford. That area commanded the most likely route to Philadelphia. Washington could not bring himself to believe that Howe would commit so great a blunder as to split his forces, but he could not afford to take the chance that Howe had not divided his command. His troops were already on the march when a note arrived from General John Sullivan on the right wing. Sullivan reported that he had just talked with a militia major who had spent the greater part of the morning on the far side of the Brandywine and had neither seen nor heard of any large troop movement on the north bank. Therefore, concluded Sullivan, the previous intelligence was false. Washington immediately recalled his troops and once again settled back to await the frontal attack across Chad's Ford that he felt certain would soon be coming.[7]

Then, in the midst of semicomplacency, the world seemed to explode! A hatless, coatless, barelegged farmer burst into camp on a heaving, sweating horse, demanding to see the general. After identifying himself as Squire Thomas Cheney and a good patriot, he declared that he had heard the firing that morning and had gone out to look around. From the top of the hill at Birmingham Meeting House he had spotted the British marching up the far side of the Brandywine. Despite Cheney's howls of outraged dignity, Washington could not believe the story. He was almost ready to ride out on a personal reconnaissance when a rider brought in another message from Sullivan. Colonel Theodorick Bland, wrote Sullivan, while scouting with his troop of light horse had sighted the enemy not too far from Birmingham Meeting House. Three divisions were sent marching for the meeting house, but Washington decided to remain with Greene for he still believed that the primary attack would be directed at Chad's Ford.[8]

It was around four-thirty in the afternoon when the ominous growl of artillery, interspersed with the sharp crackle of musketry, finally convinced Washington that he had been outflanked. Sullivan, who had moved his command upstream toward the meeting house, was hit by Cornwallis before all the American troops could be brought

7. Burke to Caswell, 17 September 1777, Caswell Letterbook; Freeman, *George Washington*, IV, 475–76; Ward, *War of the Revolution*, I, 345–46.
8. Freeman, *George Washington*, IV, 477–79; Ward, *War of the Revolution*, I, 346–47; Scheer and Rankin, *Rebels and Redcoats*, pp. 236–37.

up in battle formation. On the far side of the Brandywine Knyphausen heard the distant firing and his own cannon began to bark as he stepped up the attack on the ford. After ordering Greene, with Nash's brigade in support, to march to the aid of Sullivan, Washington rode rapidly across country to personally direct the operations at the meeting house. Wayne's Pennsylvania Continentals were left to hold the ford.[9]

The British had advanced against Sullivan at Birmingham Meeting House with their music playing the "Grenadier's March," but once contact was made the fighting was fierce. Out-numbered by more than two to one, the Americans fought well. Cornwallis constantly kept them off balance by gradually working his troops to the right toward Dilworth and the road to Philadelphia. Five times his men drove the Americans back and five times they rallied and came surging forward. One British officer described the fighting in graphic terms: "There was a most infernal fire of cannon and musquetry. Most incessant shouting, 'Incline to the right! Incline to the left! Halt! Charge! etc.' The balls plowing up the ground. The trees crackling over one's head. The branches riven by the artillery. The leaves falling as in autumn by the grapeshot."[10]

The constant pressure finally forced the Americans backward after an hour and a half of angry fighting. The order to retreat was issued. As Sullivan's men fell back on Greene's division, what had been an orderly retreat became a rout. Thomas Burke, who was on the field but who had no military authority, rode forward and attempted to stem the tide of fleeing men. Greene's men refused to panic, but opened their ranks and allowed the fugitives to pour through before closing in to present a wall of resistance to the pursuing British. Possibly the greatest casualties of the afternoon occurred when, in the heavy pall of smoke that hung over the ground, George Weedon's Third Virginia Regiment was fired on by another American unit who mistook it for the enemy. Yet the retreat continued in an orderly fashion as first one platoon and then another would break off and cover the others as they fell back.[11]

9. Freeman, *George Washington*, IV, 480–84; Ward, *War of the Revolution*, I, 350–51.

10. Freeman, *George Washington*, IV, 481–83; Ward, *War of the Revolution*, I, 352; Dawson, *Battles of the United States*, I, 275–76; *Pennsylvania Magazine of History and Biography*, XVI (1892), 149–50, XXIX (1905), 368, XXV, (1911), 104–5; *Magazine of American History*, III (1879), 568; *Historical Magazine*, XI (1867), 81.

11. Burke to Caswell, 17 September 1777, Caswell Letterbook; *State Records*, XI, 620–22; George Weedon to John Page, 11 September 1777, George Weedon

Nash's North Carolina Brigade did not get into action that hot, dusty afternoon. It had been held in reserve, but had been near enough to the action to see the haze of battle and be stung by the pungent odor of burnt powder. Upon one occasion the men were within fifty yards of the enemy and were prepared to meet them with the bayonet when the British were driven back. That night they fell back to Chester, the designated rendezvous, where they added to the mounting confusion when the army was gradually reassembled as the troops straggled in.[12]

Back at Chad's Ford, Anthony Wayne and his Pennsylvanians had waged a valiant resistance, even after the enemy began "cutting them up in grand style." Time and time again the British attacked, accompanied by "an incessant clap of thunder." Still the Americans held on until near sunset when Knyphausen finally was able to muster a sustained drive and force Wayne's men from their positions. Several artillery pieces were lost as Wayne fell back on the main army at Chester.[13]

Although the army at Chester was defeated, it was not discouraged. The men knew that except for the mistakes by the generals, their side had acted in a most "agreeable" manner. Captain Enoch Anderson of the Delaware Continentals remembered that night as one in which he saw "not a despairing look nor . . . a despairing word." Timothy Pickering found "the troops in good spirits." Brigadier George Weedon whose brigade had borne the brunt of covering the retreat, found time to muse that "such another victory would establish the rights of America, and I wish them the honor of the field again tomorrow on the same terms." Even the Continental Congress, that body of would-be generals who fought every battle so well in their debates, could not bring itself to heap its usual criticism on the commander in chief. They voted thirty hogsheads of rum for the army "in compliment . . . for their gallant behaviour," with each soldier to receive "one gill per day, while it lasts." The North Caro-

---

Papers, Chicago Historical Society, Chicago, Ill.; Burnett, *Letters of Members of the Continental Congress,* II, 519–20.

12. Ward, *War of the Revolution,* I, 352–53; Dawson, *Battles of the United States,* I, 280–82; *Pennsylvania Magazine of History and Biography,* XVI (1892), 150, XX (1896), 421, XXXV (1911), 104–5; *Trumbull Papers: Collections of the Massachusetts Historical Society,* 7th Series (Boston, 1902), II, 142–43; Noah Brooks, *Henry Knox, a Soldier of the Revolution* (New York, 1900), pp. 268–69.

13. Burke to Caswell, 17 September 1777, Caswell Letterbook; *State Records,* XI, 622–23; Ward, *War of the Revolution,* I, 352–53; *Journal of American History,* I (1901), 449.

lina delegates in Congress were quick to predict that "General Howe is making his last effort, if he meets with a defeat he is undone, as he is a considerable distance from his fleet, his situation is truly critical." Even the usually critical Thomas Burke could find nothing disparaging to report about the behavior of the troops. Actually Burke was too busy trying to have John Sullivan removed from his command. Burke placed all the blame for the failure at Brandywine on Sullivan, who, he said, had "ever been the Marplot of our Army, and his miscarriages . . . owing to a total want of Military Genius."[14]

Washington found little time to compliment himself on the fine showing made by his army. On the morning following the battle of Brandywine he marched his army out of Chester, crossed the Schuylkill, and encamped on the edge of Germantown facing the enemy. When he realized that he might be forced into a pocket between the Schuylkill and Delaware rivers, he recrossed the Schuylkill and on September 15 lay in the woods near Warren's and White Horse taverns on the Lancaster road. Now he was between the British Army and Swede's Ford on the Schuylkill, the road he expected Howe would take to Philadelphia.[15]

Since that sultry day on the Brandywine the weather had turned. On September 13 the breeze had shifted to a stiff northwest wind as temperatures dropped sharply. On the fifteenth the wind velocity rose as a gale began blowing out of the northeast, and the skies grew darker and black, angry clouds scudded from one horizon to the other. Nevertheless when Washington learned on the following day that Howe was near Goshen Meeting House and advancing toward him he went out to meet the enemy despite the weather.[16]

Howe had selected a prime position on high ground near the White Horse Tavern. Washington first formed his troops in the valley below on ground so spongy that his artillery could not be brought up. His officers persuaded him to pull back to the high ground across the valley from Howe. By this time the initial skirmishes were underway, or were supposed to be. Count Casimir Pulaski, the redoubtable Polish ally for the Americans, had been sent out with three hundred

14. *Historical Society of Delaware Papers*, XVI (1896), 29; Greene, *Life of Nathanael Greene*, I, 156; Fitzpatrick, *Writings of Washington*, IX, 207–8; George Weedon to John Page, 11 September 1777, George Weedon Papers; Ford, *Journals of the Continental Congress*, VIII, 738; *State Records*, XI, 625–26; Burnett, *Letters of Members of the Continental Congress*, II, 496–97.

15. Ward, *Delaware Continentals*, pp. 213–14; Scheer and Rankin, *Rebels and Redcoats*, p. 238; *Historical Society of Delaware Papers*, LVI (1910), 173–74.

16. Greene, *Life of Nathanael Greene*, I, 462; Ward, *Delaware Continentals*, p. 214.

cavalry and infantry to slow up any advance the enemy might attempt. At the first British volley the foot soldiers "fled shamefully" and harassed the enemy not at all.[17]

The first real encounter between the two forces came about as the commands of Wayne and Maxwell were scouting along the Dilworth-Chester road. Near Boot Tavern they fell in with the vanguard of a column commanded by Knyphausen, the jaegers and grenadiers under Colonel von Donop. Wayne and Maxwell immediately formed on high ground covered with corn fields and orchards. The Hessians wheeled into their battle line and rushed forward, "ducking behind fences around the fields and woods," firing as they ran. The Americans retired into the fields behind them. And then the rains came.[18]

By this time the two main armies had formed and were almost ready to begin what might have become the battle of Goshen. As the troops began their initial maneuvers the deluge came. "It came down so hard," said one Hessian major, "that in a few moments we were drenched and sank in mud up to our calves." Ammunition was rendered useless as the downpour soaked cartouche boxes. Four hundred thousand American cartridges were ruined—"a most terrible stroke to us," reported Henry Knox. The howling wind drove the rain directly into the faces of the British, prohibiting the use of the bayonet. The valley between the armies became a quagmire as Washington filed off. Through the remainder of the day and a good part of the night the shivering men, nearly a thousand of whom were without shoes, slogged through the cold rain. They were to march only eleven miles to Yellow Springs, where they camped on the brow of a hill—without tents. The rain continued for thirty straight hours. Much of that period was spent by Washington's army in crawling through the mud. After the troops had been suppled with fresh cartridges at Warwick, and it appeared as though Howe was attempting to envelop both American flanks, Washington, on September 19, recrossed the Schuylkill.[19]

17. Greene, *Life of Nathanael Greene*, I, 462–63; Ward, *Delaware Continentals*, pp. 214–16.

18. Bernhard A. Uhlendorf (Trans. and ed.), *Revolution in America: Baurmeister Journals—Confidential Letters and Journals 1776–1784 of Adjutant General Major Baurmeister of the Hessian Forces* (New Brunswick, N.J., 1957), p. 18; G. D. Scull (ed.), *The Montresor Journals: Collections of the New-York Historical Society for 1881* (New York, 1882), p. 453.

19. Uhlendorf, *Baurmeister Journals*, pp. 18–19; Scull, *Montresor Journals*, pp. 451–53; Greene, *Life of Nathanael Greene*, I, 462; Fitzpatrick, *Writings of Washington*, IX, 229, 231, 238–39; *Historical Society of Delaware Papers*, LVI (1896), 175; John Penn to Caswell, 5 October 1777, Governors' Papers; *State Rec-*

Anthony Wayne's division of 1,500 men was left behind with instructions to harass the enemy's rear. During the night of September 20, a British detachment led by Major General Sir Charles Grey fell upon Wayne's men and massacred a number of them before they were able to make their escape. Then Howe, by making a quick feint toward the rebel supply depot at Reading Furnace forced Washington to march northward to protect it. The British general quickly reversed his line of march, slipped down the river under the cover of night, crossed the Schuylkill, and on September 26 sauntered into Philadelphia without opposition. The Continental Congress had already "decampted with the utmost precipitation. . . ." Leaving three thousand of his finer troops, the Grenadiers, in Philadelphia, Howe stationed his main force at Germantown, some five miles northwest of Philadelphia. He refused to allow his troops to fortify their positions lest the move be interpreted as a sign of weakness.[20]

Strangely enough, the loss of Philadelphia did not bring down any great censure upon Washington. The city was no longer considered a supply center since the stores had been removed. There were still the forts protecting the Delaware and preventing British supply ships and transports from reaching the city. Reinforcements were on the way to bolster Washington's army. With a strong force astride the highways and with the water approaches controlled by the Americans, it was quite possible that Howe would evacuate Philadelphia of his own volition. As Cornelius Harnett observed from the temporary seat of Congress at Lancaster, Pennsylvania, "should he [Howe] meet with a severe check now, his situation will be rendered uneasy to him, if he is not entirely ruined." Many would have agreed with Ben Franklin, who observed that "Philadelphia has captured Howe."[21]

In the past Washington had often been censured for his lack of decision, even by his greatest disciple, Nathanael Greene. And the French volunteer, de Kalb, had noted that although the general was one of the most amiable and kindest of men, "as a General he is too

ords, XI, 641–42; *Pennsylvania Magazine of History and Biography*, XXXIV (1910), 229–30.

20. Scull, *Montresor Journals*, pp. 356, 455; Fitzpatrick, *Writings of Washington*, IX, 248–49, 259, 262, 270–75; Ford, *Journals of the Continental Congress*, VIII, 752; Burke to Caswell, 20 September 1777, Caswell Letterbook; *State Records*, XI, 631–32; *Proceedings of the American Antiquarian Society*, New Series, XL (1930), 87; *Pennsylvania Magazine of History and Biography*, XXXIV (1911), 231–32; Burnett, *Letters of Members of the Continental Congress*, II, 494n, 498–99, 502.

21. Harnett to Caswell, 27 September 1777, Caswell Letterbook; *State Records*, XI, 636–37; Scheer and Rankin, *Rebels and Redcoats*, p. 239; *Pennsylvania Magazine of History and Biography*, I (1877), 3–4.

slow, too indolent and far too weak; besides he has a tinge of vanity in his composition, and overestimates himself. In my opinion, whatever success he may have will be owing to good luck and the blunders of his adversaries, rather than his abilities. I may even say that he does not know how to improve upon the grossest blunders of the enemy." But this was a new Washington who, although he realized his troops were badly in need of rest, appeared anxious to renew the attack. He had even wanted to throw his army at Howe before the British could enter Philadelphia.[22]

On September 23, a council of general officers urged caution and refused to sanction any move it considered reckless until reinforcements came in. Still, Washington gradually moved his army nearer the enemy. He had moved down the Skippack Road to the spot where the highway crossed Skippack Creek, within sixteen miles of Germantown, when the time to strike seemed near. Through two intercepted letters he learned that a substantial number of Howe's troops had been detached to strengthen the attack upon the Delaware forts, while others had been sent off to escort supplies moving into the city by land. This time the council of general officers agreed that an attack should be launched against Germantown if all conditions were favorable. In preparation, each man was furnished rations for two days and issued forty rounds of ammunition. There was also a general issue of new clothing in which all nine of the North Carolina regiments shared.[23]

The houses of Germantown, each neatly enclosed by its own rail fence, stretched out for two miles along the Skippack Road. They ranged from the humble but neat homes of the poorer sort to the massive stone mansions of the wealthy, well-built homes that could be utilized as fortresses if necessary. There were few crossroads as such but there were several intersecting lanes, each bordered with fences that could shelter a force large enough to check an army moving down the big road.[24]

Washington's plan of attack reflected a reading of classical liter-

22. Greene, *Life of Nathanael Greene*, I, 468; Friedrich Kapp, *Life of John Kalb* (New York, 1884), p. 127; *State Records*, XI, 636–37; Scheer and Rankin, *Rebels and Redcoats*, p. 277.

23. Harnett to Caswell, 27 September 1777, Penn to Caswell, 5 October 1777, Caswell Letterbook; Ward, *Delaware Continentals*, p. 222; Fitzpatrick, *Writings of Washington*, IX, 278–79; *Historical Society of Delaware Papers*, LVI (1896), 188; *Pennsylvania Magazine of History and Biography*, XVI (1892), 152, XVIII (1894), 340–42; Return of Clothing Issued . . . 23rd Septr. 1777, George Washington Papers.

24. Freeman, *George Washington*, IV, 502–3; Ward, *Delaware Continentals*, pp. 222–23.

ature, for basically it was the same strategy used by both Hannibal at
Cannae and Scipio Africanus at Ilipa. It was, in essence, a giant pin-
cer movement, with two divisions driving in to crush the center while
two wings closed in on the flanks. Although John Sullivan was under
heavy criticism from Congress for his behavior at Brandywine, Washington chose him to make the frontal attack along the Skippack, or
Chestnut Hill, road. Sullivan's command was to be made up of his
own and Wayne's divisions, with the brigade of Brigadier General
Thomas Conway in the van. Greene, with his own division and that
of Adam Stephen, with Alexander McDougall's brigade out in front,
was to march by the Lime Kiln Road and hit the enemy's right wing.
This route along the Lime Kiln Road was roughly four miles longer
than the march to be made by Sullivan. It paralleled the Skippack
Road, gradually curving inward toward it to intersect it between the
main part of the village and the British encampment. Inasmuch as the
force opposed to Greene's was considered to be the best of the enemy,
Greene's command was composed of nearly two-thirds of the American army. Still another mile to the northeast beyond Greene the Maryland militia under William Smallwood and the New Jersey militia
under Daniel Forman were to march by the Old York Road to slip in
behind the British. John Armstrong, with almost a thousand Pennsylvania militiamen, was to march by the Manatawny Road across the
Wissahiccan Creek and turn the left flank of the enemy. The light
horse was supposed to coordinate movements between the marching
columns. The reserve under Lord Stirling was to consist of the light
infantry brigade of William Maxwell and Nash's North Carolinians.[25]

The troops were to begin their march by 7:00 P.M. on the evening of October 3, 1777. At 2:00 the following morning they were to
halt within two miles of the enemy pickets, and by 4:00 the final dispositions for the attack were to have been made. At 5:00 they were to
launch the attack against the picket posts with "charged bayonets
without firing." In the grim, gray dusk of the early morning it would
be difficult to distinguish friend from foe, and the men were instructed
to wear white pieces of paper in their caps for identification. All in
all, it was a grand scheme, conceived in grand design, but was completely unworkable except for the most disciplined of troops. Too
much attention had been given to the over-all action and too little
thought paid to details; for instance, when the troops charged the

25. Fitzpatrick, *Writings of Washington*, IX, 307–8; Ward, *Delaware Continentals*, p. 224; Otis G. Hammond (ed.), *Letters and Papers of Major-General
John Sullivan, Continental Army* (Concord, N.H., 1930–31, 1939), I, 544; *Pennsylvania Magazine of History and Biography*, I (1877), 399–400.

picket posts, no allowances had been made for the fences that lay between them and their objective. The success of the entire movement rested upon precision and almost split-second timing between four marching columns over a space of seven miles. With the best trained troops of the day it would have been a most intricate operation, and Washington had inexperienced officers in his command, most of whom had learned their soldiering from fighting Indians or from one of the popular military manuals of the day. Although the rank and file had proved they could stand and fight, they had also demonstrated that they were such complete strangers to discipline that the entire maneuver, on paper, would seem to have been doomed before it ever began. This was, perhaps, Washington's most desperate gamble of the entire war.[26]

The reports that came to the Continental Congress stated that Washington had, on the afternoon of the third, harangued his troops and promised that if they defeated Howe he would allow them unrestricted plundering of the Tories of Philadelphia. The soldiers, it was said, were "in high spirits." The army began to move out at seven on the evening of October 3, 1777, although Sullivan's division, with the shortest distance to travel, did not move out of its encampment on Methuchen Hill until nine o'clock. Nash's brigade, in reserve, moved out even later. Many of the men had little sleep the night before and were near exhaustion; their weariness could impair their effectiveness in battle. The roads were rough and many of the poorly shod men limped along in pain. They had to be rested often. The schedule was lost. To complicate matters even more, the early morning mist thickened into fog, obliterating and distorting landmarks.[27]

On October 3, the British could scarce believe those intelligence reports that suggested Washington planned to force another action in the immediate future. Nevertheless, pickets were strengthened and orders stressed the need for extreme vigilance. Around 3:00 A.M. patrols had learned that the Americans were on the march. Although all regiments had been ordered under arms, most of the officers felt there was no real need for alarm and shrugged off those on the road as little more than a "flying party." And as the fog rolled in the gen-

26. Fitzpatrick, *Writings of Washington*, IX, 307–8; Sir John Fortescue, *A History of the British Army* (New York, 1899–1900, London, 1902), III, 221.

27. Fitzpatrick, *Writings of Washington*, IX, 307; *North American Review*, XXIII (October, 1826), 425; Hammond, *Letters and Papers of Major-General John Sullivan*, I, 544; *New Jersey Historical Society Proceedings, 1922–1923* (Newark, N.J., 1924), pp. 34–35; Walter Stewart to Joseph Reed, 12 October 1777, Joseph Reed Papers, New-York Historical Society, New York, N. Y.

eral conviction was that the Americans would not attack in such foul weather.[28]

Many of the British had relaxed when Sullivan began his attack at almost six o'clock. Because of the many delays, the assault was an hour late and the sun was just beginning to penetrate the fog. At Mount Airy, the picket post a mile from Germantown was overrun, but not before its defenders had fired two fieldpieces to give the alarm. The Second Light Infantry rushed forward to the support of the post, as did Lieutenant Colonel Thomas Musgrave and his Fortieth Regiment. Sullivan was forced to wheel his column into a line of battle. Wayne's division, still smarting under the memory of the Paoli Massacre, drove in with the bayonet, shouting "Have at the Bloodhounds! Revenge Wayne's affair!" The British mustered several countercharges, but each time were forced back. Following each charge, Wayne's men, despite the cries of their officers, took no prisoners, using the bayonet to finish off all those who were wounded or attempted to surrender. The raucous strains of a British bugle cut through the haze, sounding the retreat.[29]

Sullivan drove the enemy before him. His men, performing with unusual discipline, advanced at a dog trot, tearing down rail fences as they advanced in order to maintain their line. For a mile they drove Musgrave's men, who resisted at every step. Howe came up angrily shouting, "For shame, Light Infantry. I never saw you retreat before. Form! Form! It's only a scouting party." But the rattle of grapeshot through the branches of the chestnut tree above him convinced him that it was more than a minor operation and Howe rode off to direct the forming of supporting units in the rear. There was no breeze; the powder smoke mixing with the fog held close to the ground, cutting visibility to about thirty yards.[30]

28. *Pennsylvania Magazine of History and Biography*, XXII (1898), 484; Howe to Clinton, Sir Henry Clinton Papers; Henry Belcher, *The First American Civil War* (London, 1911), II, 274.

29. George Weedon to John Page, 4 October 1777, George Weedon Papers; *Historical Magazine*, IV (November, 1860), 341–42; Hammond, *Letters and Papers of Major-General John Sullivan*, 544–46; Wayne to Mrs. Wayne, 6 October 1777, Wayne to Polly Wayne, 6 October 1777, Anthony Wayne Papers, Pennsylvania Historical Society, Philadelphia, Pa.; Walter Stewart to Joseph Reed, 12 October 1777, Joseph Reed Papers.

30. Weedon to Page, 4 October 1777, George Weedon Papers; *Historical Magazine*, IV (November, 1860), 347; Hammond, *Letters and Papers of Major-General John Sullivan*, I, 545; Oswald Tilghman, *Memoir of Lieut. Col. Tench Tilghman, Secretary and Aid to Washington, Together with an Appendix, Containing Revolutionary Journals and Letters, Hereto Unpublished* (Albany, N. Y., 1876), 160–61; Isaac Q. Leake, *Memoir of the Life and Times of General John Lamb* (Albany, N.Y., 1857), p. 183; John Penn and Cornelius Harnett to Caswell, 20 October 1777, Emmet Collection.

With visibility shortened by the haze, Musgrave was able to pull out nearly 120 men to barricade themselves in Cliveden, the massive stone house of Pennsylvania Chief Justice Benjamin Chew and known locally as the Chew House. Sullivan's men drove the other redcoats before them through the town into their camp without noticing Musgrave's actions. When the reserve came up, muskets blazed from the windows of the Chew House. Nash's brigade had previously been ordered out to the flank and had pushed forward. Back at the Chew House, Washington held a conference with his staff. Some maintained that a regiment should be detached to amuse Musgrave while the remaining troops pushed on ahead. Henry Knox argued from the lessons of history, declaring that in any penetration of the enemy's lines a general "must not leave an occupied castle in your rear." A young lieutenant colonel sent forward under a white flag to demand Musgrave's surrender was fatally wounded. Artillery was brought forward, but the heavy balls rebounded from the thick walls and proved as useless as the musketry of Maxwell's men.[31]

By the time the futility of pounding the walls became evident, half an hour had been lost. Maxwell's men were ordered to disregard the Chew House and to keep out of range. The advance of Sullivan's men was further obscured as the enemy fired the hay and stubble in the fields as they retreated. Yet they pushed on forward through the blinding, choking cloud, across fields, across fences, into the outposts of the British camp, "which fell into our hands as recompence for our valour & courage." Before them the enemy "ran lustily." To keep the pressure on, Nash's brigade had been ordered up. Wayne's men continued to take their revenge for Paoli with the bayonet. Washington pushed forward with the men, exposing himself so recklessly that Sullivan was finally forced to ask him to retire. Although each man had been given the usual battle issue of forty rounds of ammunition, they had fired so often that they were running out of cartridges. Still they fought on.[32]

As mistakes began to multiply in this "most horrid fog," confusion was compounded. Greene had arrived on the enemy's right half

31. *North American Review*, XXIII (May, 1837), 427–28; Hammond, *Letters and Papers of Major-General John Sullivan*, I, 544–45; Hugh Hastings, *Public Papers of George Clinton, First Governor of New York, 1777–1795—1801–1804* (Albany, N. Y., 1904), II, 369; Ward, *Delaware Continentals*, pp. 226–27.

32. Hammond, *Letters and Papers of Major-General John Sullivan*, I, 547–48; Wayne to Polly Wayne, Anthony Wayne Papers; Walter Stewart to Joseph Reed, 12 October 1777, Joseph Reed Papers; Hastings, *Public Papers of George Clinton*, II, 368; *Newport* [Rhode Island] *Gazette*, 6 November 1777; Ephraim Kirby to Abraham Kirby, 12 November 1777, Ephraim Kirby Papers, Duke University, Durham, N. C.

an hour late, but his march had been longer and his guide had lost his way. He had to drive his men to make it as early as he had. Contacting the enemy at Luken's Mill he fought his way almost to the center of the British line. McDougall never did get into position, thereby exposing the flanks. Adam Stephen, who went into the battle drunk, heard the artillery fire and musketry at the Chew House and, acting without orders, swung his division to the right and marched for the scene, thereby weakening the basic battle plan. In a like manner, Anthony Wayne, hearing these sounds of battle in the rear and supposing that Sullivan had run into trouble, turned back to help him. His division ran into that of Stephen's and that group, but faintly viewing Wayne's men through the dense fog and mistaking them for the enemy, formed into battle line and delivered a volley. Wayne's men returned a smart fire. Then both units broke and ran. Some said that Stephen had given the order to retreat, although he later maintained that he had attempted to halt the rush by shouting that they were running from victory. The seeds of panic had been planted.[33]

It was almost at this moment, feeling that victory was within his grasp, that Washington was about to give the order for a general advance toward Philadelphia. Then suddenly, from out of the fog, came fleeing, hysterical men all about him. Sullivan's division had become terror-stricken when an unidentified light horseman appeared among them shouting that they were surrounded. Not even the prospect of booty within the British camp could lessen the bite of fear. Back they came, running toward the rear. Officers rode among them, swinging their swords, alternately cursing and pleading in an effort to stem the great wave of fugitives who jammed the roads and spilled over into the fields. By ten o'clock it was all over. There was little that the general could do other than attempt to bring some order out of the rout. And the retreat continued until the army reached Pennypacker's Mill, some twenty miles from the field of battle.[34]

The North Carolina Line did not flee with the rest, although panic may well have set in when Francis Nash was wounded. Although it has often been stated that the North Carolinians were not

33. Weedon to John Page, 8 October 1777, George Weedon Papers; Ephraim Kirby to Abraham Kirby, 12 November 1777, Ephraim Kirby Papers; Walter Stewart to Reed, 12 October 1777, Joseph Reed Papers.

34. *Pennsylvania Magazine of History and Biography,* II (1878), 288–89; Weedon to Page, 12 October 1777, George Weedon Papers; Greene, *Life of Nathanael Greene,* I, 478–79; Fitzpatrick, *Writings of Washington,* IX, 310; Wayne to Washington, 4 October 1777, Wayne Papers; John Armstrong to Thomas Wharton, 8 October 1777, Joseph Reed Papers.

actually engaged with the enemy that October day, they did their share "and some pushed bayonets." During the battle they were nearly all engaged in combat and according to reports, "behaved well," and "with great resolution." It has been claimed that Nash's men were in actual possession of sixteen pieces of enemy artillery when, after the clash in the fog and the beginning of the retreat, a volley from the left raked his line. Anthony Wayne had formed a rear guard to protect the withdrawal, and after the flight of the Pennsylvania militia exposed the American right flank, Nash moved his North Carolina brigade into place and began a stubborn resistance as he slowly fell back. He was forced to abandon the captured cannon and increase the rate of his withdrawal to prevent the encirclement and isolation of his brigade. He was sitting astride his horse directing his men when a cannon ball smashed into his left thigh, mangling his body in horrible fashion and killing his mount. A musket ball grazed his head, blinding him. Although Nash was not instantly killed, it was almost immediately evident that his days were numbered. His men hurriedly made a litter of brush and poles and tenderly carried him from the field. Thomas Polk, who was himself wounded shortly afterwards, said that as Nash was carried from the field he reached out his right hand and whispered "Farewell." When Thomas Paine saw him some distance from the field, he said he was unable to recognize General Nash.[35]

No one seemed able to determine just why Washington's strategy, impossible though it seemed, had broken down so completely when victory seemed so near. There were claims that the enemy lost four men to every American who fell, and during the battle young Ephraim Kirby "rode through the field over the dead bodies where they lay as thick as the stones in a stony plowfield, shocking to behold!" One observer noted that "the Enemy were astonished at our retreat as they looked upon every thing as lost with them. . . ." Nathanael Greene maintained that the Americans "fled from Victory." Thomas Burke railed that "it appears our miscarriage sprung from the usual source—want of abilities in our superior officers and want of order

35. *Pennsylvania Magazine of History and Biography*, II (1878), 288–89; Cosmo Medici to Caswell, 21 October 1777, Harnett to Caswell, 10 October 1777, Penn to Caswell, 16 October 1777, Penn and Harnett to Caswell, 20 October 1777, Caswell Letterbook; *North Carolina Gazette*, 31 October 1777; *State Records*, XI, 647–50, 654, 659, 661, XIII, 262; Brooks, *Henry Knox*, pp. 110–11; Hammond, *Letters and Papers of Major-General John Sullivan*, I, 546–47; Alfred Hoyt Bill, *Valley Forge: The Making of an Army* (New York, 1952), p. 72; Hoyt, *Murphey Papers*, II, 207; Penn and Harnett to Caswell, 20 October 1777, Emmet Collection; Penn to Caswell, 20 October 1777, Caswell Papers; Alexander Martin to Caswell, 4 November 1777, Governors' Papers.

and discipline in our army." No one could quite place the blame, although Adam Stephen was to be court-martialed for his behavior that day. Some, like Lieutenant James McMichael of the Pennsylvanians, felt that Stephen's Virginians were responsible for the breakdown in battlefield discipline. McMichael, who had an almost compulsive penchant for recording his adventures in doggerel, noted in his journal:

> But to my grief tho' I fought sore, yet we had to retreat
> Because the cowardice of those on our left was great.[36]

Some complained of the fog, others of Greene's late arrival, while still others, including Washington, felt that the delay at the Chew House had been responsible for the defeat. In retrospect, it would seem that the breakdown in communications played a most important role, although no one at the time seemed to consider it significant. It was, perhaps, as George Weedon observed: "Trophies lay at our feet, but so certain were we of making a general defeat of it that we pass them by in pursuit and by that means lost the chief part of them again, for when the unlucky idea struck our men to fall back, the utmost exertions to rally them again was in vain. . . ."[37]

Yet there was none of that gloom so characteristic of defeat and, in general, there was an air of cheerfulness in the army. Alexander Martin's report to Caswell bragged that "though we retreated from them at Chad's Ford and at Germantown Yet they have nothing to boast of but their keeping the field." In York, Pennsylvania, members of the Continental Congress heard that "the British officers have long faces," and that Howe refused to allow anyone on the field of battle lest the extent of his casualties become known. Congressmen cheered what they considered the worst drubbing the British had received since Bunker Hill. When it was reported that Washington once again had his army on the move, one Germantown diarist noted, "British seem afraid." The American troops were "in high spirits," and, according to Thomas Paine, seemed "to be sensible of a disappointment, not a defeat." And George Weedon probably spoke for the

---

36. Wayne to Polly Wayne, Anthony Wayne Papers; Hammond, *Letters and Papers of Major-General John Sullivan,* I, 545–46; [John Miller] Journal, Joseph Reed Papers; *State Records,* XI, 649; *Pennsylvania Magazine of History and Biography,* XVI (1892), 153; Burnett, *Letters of Members of the Continental Congress,* II, 542; Ephraim Kirby to Abraham Kirby, 12 November 1777, Ephraim Kirby Papers.

37. Weedon to Page, 12 October 1777, George Weedon Papers; Walter Stewart to Reed, 12 October 1777, Joseph Reed Papers; Adam Stephen to Washington, 7 October 1777, George Washington Papers; Fitzpatrick, *Writings of Washington,* IX, 310, 436–39; *Pennsylvania Magazine of History and Biography,* XXVI (1902), 104–7, XXXV (1911), 66.

majority of the officers when he wrote, "Though the enterprise miscarried, it was worth the undertaking." Washington felt that "the day was rather unfortunate than injurious" and came out of the engagement with considerably more pride in his army than he had formerly demonstrated. He was confident that fortune would smile upon it and his men would "merit by more substantial services the further applause of the country." And he himself, through his own behavior on the battlefield, had gained stature in the eyes of those who served under him.[38]

The night after the battle, after collecting his men, Washington had camped at Pennypacker's Mill. General Nash was carried on one of the hospital wagons. For three days he stubbornly fought death, although it was apparent to everyone that it was but a question of time before his broken body would find the solace of death. On October 7, 1777, Francis Nash died. On October 9, at ten o'clock in the morning, the North Carolina brigadier was buried at the crossroads near Washington's headquarters at Toemensing. In the general orders for the day the commander in chief urged all officers who possibly could to "attend and pay their respect to a brave man who died in defense of his country." Shortly afterwards the Continental Congress was to vote $500 for a monument to perpetuate the memory of Francis Nash. Thomas Clark, no mean poet in the classical tradition, penned a heroic verse to this "Genius of Freedom":

> ... with the fatal wound,
> Tho' tortur'd, weltering, on the hostile ground,
> "Fight on my troops," with smiling ardor said,
> " 'Tis but the fate of war, be not dismay'd."[39]

As after every battle, there was a counting of heads. Colonel Edward Buncombe and Lieutenant Colonel Henry Irwin of the North Carolina Line had been reported as prisoners of the enemy. At the time it was felt that they were unhurt and had only been captured because they were lame and could not keep up with the retreat. Later it was discovered that Irwin had been killed during the battle,

---

38. Penn to Caswell, 10 October 1777, Caswell Letterbook; *State Records*, XI, 649–50; [John Miller] Journal, Joseph Reed Papers; Paine to Franklin, 26 May 1778, *Pennsylvania Magazine of History and Biography*, II (1878), 289; Fitzpatrick, *Writings of Washington*, IX, 310–11, 351–52, X, 28; R. B. Douglas (trans. and ed.), *Charles Albert, Comte de More, Chevalier de Pontgibaud, a French Volunteer in the War of Independence* (New York, 1898), p. 42; Alexander Martin to Caswell, Governors' Papers.

39. *State Records*, XI, 651, 669–70; Ford, *Journals of the Continental Congress*, II, 312; Fitzpatrick, *Writings of Washington*, IX, 342; *The North Carolina University Magazine*, I (April 1844), 79.

while Buncombe of the Fifth Regiment had been wounded and had fallen into the hands of the enemy and had been carried a prisoner to Philadelphia and paroled. In May, 1778, while walking in his sleep, he fell down a flight of stairs, resulting in an opening of his old wounds, which led to his death. Captain Jacob Turner and Lieutenant John McCann had been felled by musket fire, while Major Thomas Polk had been shot through both jaws. Other wounded officers included Captain John Armstrong, Lieutenant Joshua Hadley, and Ensign John Daves. There was no accurate count taken at the time of the men lost in battle. Colonel Henry Irwin, Captain Jacob Turner, and Adjutant David Lucas were buried in a common grave along with six North Carolina privates.[40]

Alexander Martin, who as oldest colonel was in command of the brigade, nevertheless was charged with cowardice by "some officers of the 4th Battalion." And, on November 6, 1777, a court of enquiry headed by James Armstrong investigated the conduct of Gideon Lamb, who had been charged with abandoning his troops leaving the field during the battle of Brandywine. He was acquitted "with honor." Conversely, Captain Edward Vail of the Second Regiment was to be tried for cowardice and convicted. His behavior was to be published in the newspapers with the comment "and that it should be deemed scandalous for any officer to associate with him." Other irregularities were discovered. Captain Thomas Granbury of the Third Regiment was cashiered from the service, not only for demanding kickbacks from the enlistment bounties of new recruits, but also for forging and selling discharges. Captain Daniel Jones of the Third Regiment was found guilty of disobedience of orders and absenting himself without leave. This rash of charges against officers may well have been the result of the "censorious spirit" that seemed to prevail in the army. Generals Sullivan, Stephen, Wayne, and Maxwell all were forced to face charges levied by subordinate officers. Most of the charges were found to be false but some were justified. Many of the field officers of the North Carolina regiments were discontented, and were particularly anxious to have one of their number elevated to the rank of brigadier general in place of Nash or James Moore. Jethro Sumner and Thomas Clark appeared to be favorites to receive the promotions, but even then it was rumored that if they did receive the

40. Penn and Harnett to Caswell, 20 October 1777, Caswell Letterbook; *State Records,* XV, 859–60, 677, 761–62; *North Carolina Gazette,* 20 February 1778; Hoyt, *Murphey Papers,* II, 404; John C. Daves (ed.), *Minutes of the North Carolina Society of the Cincinnati* (n.p., n.d.), II, 227.

elevation in rank, a number of the other colonels would resign their commissions in protest.[41]

The men of the North Carolina Brigade were pathetic in their nakedness. On October 13 a survey was made to determine clothing shortages. The North Carolina Line was found to be in desperate need of 415 coats, 461 waistcoats, 752 pairs of breeches, 779 pairs of stockings, 456 pairs of shoes, 521 shirts, 78 hunting shirts, 62 overalls, 381 hats, and 618 blankets. For a brief change, there was sufficient food, since some 283 fat cattle had been driven into camp and slaughtered. Critical shortages were found among the North Carolina mounted troops. The men of these detachments had been forced to fight on foot during the last two battles because of the lack of mounts. They had arrived in the northern theater on horses so unfit for combat that they were ordered sold. There had been about eighty men and enough officers for three troops. Some of the officers and men had been transferred to Colonel George Baylor's Third Continental Dragoons. In early August a resolve of the Continental Congress had stated that if the men of the troops of Captains Martin Pfifer, Cosmo Medici, and Samuel Ashe would re-enlist for the duration of the war they would be equipped with good horses and proper accouterments. A year later Cornelius Harnett was to charge that the North Carolina Light Horse had been "shamefully neglected" with regard to equipment, while newer-formed units of other states were quickly equipped by the Continental Congress.[42]

There were still, however, internal troubles within the regiments. A sizable number of men attempted to gain their discharges, claiming that their times had expired. Apparently this misunderstanding was the result of the recruiting practices of Captain Griffith McRee, who, in order, to enlist his quota of men, had promised prospects shorter terms of service than authorized. Then there was a question of promotion of the officers. Colonel Alexander Martin, commanding the North Carolina Brigade since the death of Nash, called together a board of officers to recommend promotions. To replace the late

41. James Armstrong to Sumner, n.d., Jethro Sumner Papers, Southern Historical Collection; *State Records*, XI, 790–94, XV, 709; Harnett to Burke, 19 November 1777, Thomas Burke Papers, Southern Historical Collection; Hastings, *Public Papers of George Clinton*, II, 372–73; *North Carolina Gazette*, 8 November 1777; Alexander Martin to Caswell, 4 November 1777, Governors' Papers; Fitzpatrick, *Writings of Washington*, X, 191.

42. *State Records*, XI, 784, 799–800, 807–8, 811, XII, 64; Mary Elinor Lazenby, *Catawba Frontier, 1775–1781* (Washington, 1950), p. 17; Fitzpatrick, *Writings of Washington*, IX, 118; Burnett, *Letters of Members of the Continental Congress*, III, 383; Ford, *Journals of the Continental Congress*, VIII, 627, 696.

Henry Irwin, Major William Lee Davidson of the Fourth Regiment, as the eldest major, was promoted to lieutenant colonel of the Fifth. Major Levi Dawson of the Fifth was elevated to a similar rank in the Eighth Regiment in place of Samuel Lockhart, who had resigned two weeks after Germantown. Captains Henry Dixon, John Armstrong, and Thomas Hogg were promoted to majors to replace Lockhart, Davidson, and Dawson. It was Lockhart's departure, plus a rash of resignations by officers of lower rank, that brought a vote of censure by the North Carolina Assembly upon those who "should quit their posts and resign the several offices to which they had been appointed." Every officer who resigned in the future was to be prohibited from holding either military or civil office in North Carolina.[43]

While the British battered and finally reduced the American forts guarding the Delaware, Washington marched his army in restless maneuvers and, at times, in an almost aimless fashion. One bright spot was the news of the surrender of Burgoyne to Horatio Gates at Saratoga. In celebration, on October 15 Washington drew up his troops in parade formation. After the chaplains had delivered what the general was pleased to term "short discourses," thirteen artillery pieces burst forth in thunderous salute. Then, just before sunset, with the army drawn up in two lines, and using blank cartridges, there was the firing of a rolling *"feu-de-joy,"* followed by three loud huzzas. Then the troops were disbanded.[44]

During the night of October 18/19, Sir William Howe evacuated Germantown, pulling all of his troops back into Philadelphia where they were set to work strengthening the fortifications around the city. During this period reinforcements, some from posts on the Hudson River, came into the American camp, and once again Washington felt strong enough to test the enemy. Because the time of the Massachusetts troops would expire by the end of November, Washington called a council of general officers to consider an attack upon Philadelphia. The officers answered "in the Negative unanimously," bearing out the observation of Cornelius Harnett that "we suffer ourselves to be Attacked instead of Attacking."[45]

43. Proceedings of a Court of Enquiry, 22 November 1777, Jethro Sumner Papers, N.C. Dept. Arch. & Hist.; Commissions Granted 8th Carolina Regt., 27 November 1777, Proceedings of a Board of Officers, 9 November 1777, Revolutionary War Rolls, Adjutant General's Office; *North Carolina Gazette,* 20 February 1778; *State Records,* XV, 708–9.

44. Fitzpatrick, *Writings of Washington,* IX, 390–91; *Pennsylvania Magazine of History and Biography,* XVI (1892), 154; Burnett, *Letters of Members of the Continental Congress,* II, 526n.

45. *Pennsylvania Magazine of History and Biography,* XIX (1895), 75; Har-

The American general then moved over to White Marsh with the intention of hovering near Philadelphia and awaiting an opportunity to strike. His presence disturbed Howe. British efforts on the night of December 4 to make a surprise attack were discovered and Howe was forced to take post on Chestnut Hill. For awhile it was almost certain there would be another battle. Howe went so far as to attempt his favorite maneuver, a flanking movement, but was forced to abandon his plans when his circling troops were discovered. Upon several occasions skirmishes and small fire fights threatened to evolve into a full scale battle, but Howe pulled back into the city on December 7, 1777.[46]

Four days later Washington was almost caught in an embarrassing position. On December 11, for no apparent reason he broke camp at White Marsh and began to cross the Schuylkill at Matson's Ford over a bridge of thirty-six wagons connected by rails. Suddenly there were redcoats on the hill on the far side of the river, a force of 3,500 on a foraging expedition under the command of Lord Cornwallis. After a few minutes of awkward staring, Washington recalled his troops, broke his bridge, and fell back to White Marsh.[47]

It was growing cold. The pleasant hues of autumn had given way to stark, bare trees. White patches of snow spotted the ground after the increasingly frequent flurries. Washington knew, and it should have been apparent to everyone else, that his half-naked, half-starved army was in no condition to fight in heavy weather, and he refused to listen to a committee from Congress who urged a "Winter's Campaign with vigor and success." He finally selected a place called Valley Forge for his winter encampment. On the surface, the site held few advantages. It had been an American supply depot, but on September 20 the British had encamped there and had either destroyed or carried off all supplies. Foraging by both armies had swept away all the livestock in Chester County. Washington had traded much for a position near the enemy and its only advantage was a location where he would be able "to cover this Country against the

nett to Burke, 8 December 1777, Thomas Burke Papers, Southern Historical Collection.

46. *Historical Society of Delaware Papers,* LVI (1910), 265; William B. Reed, *Life and Correspondence of Joseph Reed* (Philadelphia, 1847), I, 351n; Fitzpatrick, *Writings of Washington,* X, 156; *State Records,* XI, 693.

47. *Historical Society of Delaware Papers,* LVI (1910), 265; *Pennsylvania Magazine of History and Biography,* XXI (1897), 305; Reed, *Life and Correspondence of Joseph Reed,* I, 354; Fitzpatrick, *Writings of Washington,* X, 156; Harnett to William Williamson, 8 December 1777, Cornelius Harnett Papers, Southern Historical Collection, The University of North Carolina at Chapel Hill, Chapel Hill, N.C.

Horrid rapine and Devastation of a wanton Enemy." But not even the general could forecast the months of frigid purgatory that lay before him and his soldiers.[48]

During all of this maneuvering in weather that grew increasingly colder, the North Carolina troops were not well. On November 10 there had been 227 of the rank and file ill, and on December 3 there were 258 unfit for duty of a total of 1,033 enlisted men. The selection of a general to succeed Nash remained a perplexing question. Although Alexander Martin was the choice of many politicians, it was feared that his elevation in rank would set off widespread resignations among other field officers of the brigade. But once he had been cleared of the charges against him, Martin settled that question by resigning on November 22, 1777. He pleaded exhaustion as a result of his arduous duty with the light infantry. Lieutenant Colonel John Patten was elevated to the rank of colonel and given the command of Martin's Second Regiment, with Selby Harney as second-in-command. Jethro Sumner seemed to be the choice of many of the field officers for North Carolina's brigadier, but there was still the chance that Edward Hand might be appointed to command them. For awhile the North Carolina Brigade was under the command of Alexander McDougall of New York. Although the officers did not question the qualities of his leadership, they did question whether it would not appear "contemptible in the eyes of the Army, not having one General Officer from our State." And according to their quota of men to be furnished by the state, they felt that North Carolina was entitled to one major general and two brigadiers.[49]

By the time the army reached Valley Forge, there was still no brigadier for the North Carolina Brigade, and on December 20 it was placed under the command of Brigadier General Lachlan McIntosh of Georgia. It was not a command to be envied. In numbers, the brigade now totaled 1,384, and of the 1,051 on duty at Valley Forge on December 20, 1777, some 353 were sick and another 164 were declared "unfit for want of cloaths." But all of the ambulatory sick joined the

48. Charles J. Stillé, *Major-General Anthony Wayne and the Pennsylvania Line in the Continental Army* (Philadelphia, 1893), p. 137; Scull, *Montresor Journals*, pp. 455–56; Harnett to William Williamson, 28 December 1777, Cornelius Harnett Papers, Southern Historical Collection.

49. *State Records*, XI, 676, 690, XIII, 263–64; Harnett to Burke, 8 December 1777, Thomas Burke Papers, Southern Historical Collection; Alexander Martin to Caswell, 4 November 1778 [1777], Caswell Letterbook; Fitzpatrick, *Writings of Washington*, X, 94–95; Proceedings of a Board of Officers, 23 November 1777, Revolutionary War Rolls, Adjutant General's Office.

healthy in constructing huts to protect them against the chill of winter.[50]

And so it was that the year 1777 ended on "a very gloomy aspect," for an army that was in need of "breeches, shoes, stockings, blankets and . . . in want [of] flour." Still, it was not a beaten army. It was an army whose general, even in an interval of distress and despair, spent Christmas day preparing "Orders For a Move That was Intended Against Philadelphia by Way of Surprise."[51]

50. Fitzpatrick, *Writings of Washington*, X, 180; *State Records*, XI, 700, 824; Harnett to William Williamson, 28 December 1777, Cornelius Harnett Papers, Southern Historical Collection.

51. William Duane (ed.), *Extracts from the Diary of Christopher Marshall, Kept in Philadelphia and Lancaster, during the American Revolution, 1774–1781* (Albany, 1877), p. 172; Fitzpatrick, *Writings of Washington*, X, 202.

Chapter 6
Valley Forge, 1777-1778

"A train of evils might be enumerated. . . ."

Back in North Carolina the recruiting business had not gone
well. Too many hands were reaching for the available men. South
Carolina was having difficulty in filling her regiments; the state was
too wedded to a plantation economy, and a large number of slaves
and far too few small farmers could not provide the numbers necessary. Many South Carolinians who had exhibited enthusiastic support for the war effort considered themselves prime officer material
and were not interested in joining the ranks. And then too, South
Carolina, in proportion to her population, probably had a greater
political division among her white residents than any other state,
and Tories did not take kindly to enlistment in the Continental Line.
Georgia, a mere lass among colonies when the Revolution began, was
not only sparsely settled, but her borders were constantly harassed by
raids from East Florida. Because of the large numbers of small farmers in the western part of the state, North Carolina had become the
primary recruiting ground in the lower South. Recruiting officers
from South Carolina and Georgia, along with some from Virginia,
probed the back country, holding out enticing recruiting bounties
for all those who would enlist in their state lines.[1]

1. Robert Howe to the North Carolina Council of Safety, 6 November 1776,
Robert Howe Papers, Southern Historical Collection.

124

Despite the plaintive cry from the Congress, "For God's sake fill up your Batalions, lay Taxes, put a stop to the sordid & avaritious Spirit which has infected all ranks & Conditions of Men," the North Carolina Assembly that met in the spring of 1777 had done little of military importance. Too much time had been spent in "trifling matters." Too often, pressing matters, including those involving the enlistment of state troops, were ignored while time was consumed in specious debate. Wordings of resolutions relative to the Continental Line were argued at great length, but there was little attempt to find a solution to immediate problems. Conversely, there were also sweeping resolves directing commanders in the field on such matters as marching their troops, and demanding so many detailed reports that officers would have little time with their men if they followed them to the letter. Too often, immediate matters were shifted to a committee for further study.[2]

When Francis Nash had marched northward with his troops, Colonel John Williams of the Ninth Regiment had been left at Halifax in command of the camp on Quankey Creek. As quickly as recruits for the older regiments were brought in, they were sent on, in small groups, to join their units. Not only recruits but invalids and deserters were brought into Halifax, the deserters brought before a court of enquiry to determine if they were entitled to the discharges that so many of them claimed. If it was proved that they had indeed deserted, they were sent forward to join Washington's army, although many took the first opportunity to slip away again. Governor Caswell promised a pardon to all deserters who rejoined their units, but few accepted this clemency. A number of the new recruits walked off because there was no money to pay the promised enlistment bounties. The most successful effort was in the artillery company where some forty or fifty men had been persuaded to enlist for three years or the duration of the war.[3]

Alexander Martin had earlier discovered "that it is vain to attempt inlisting Volunteers in any part of the State when the Militia have gained such a preference to the regular Service." In fact, the only solution he could suggest was for the General Assembly to draft vagrants and persons of little property into the Continental services. One exception was one Arthur Boyes, who appeared happy to enlist to escape his debts and the daily struggle to survive. A married man,

2. Caswell to Burke, 13 May 1777, Caswell Letterbook; *State Records*, XI, 470, XII, 8, 9, 12–13, 22, 33, 93; Harnett to Burke, 16 December 1777, Cornelius Harnett Papers, Southern Historical Collection.

3. *State Records*, XI, 467–77, 500–501, XII, 14–15, 80–81, XXII, 912; Simon Alderson to Caswell, 8 June 1777, Caswell Letterbook; Burke to Caswell, 23 May 1777, Caswell to Burke, 17 June 1777, Governors' Papers.

he seemed fond of his wife, "But what is worst of all, her fathers character is so bad I wou'd rather quit her altogether than she shou'd stay 12 months near him, my own folly brought my distress upon me and death alone frees me."[4]

In addition, the Seventh, Eighth, and Ninth Regiments were being organized at Halifax. Colonel James Hogun of the Seventh was having his troubles with the officers of his regiment. Many officers felt they needed to remain at home to look after personal affairs until Hogun assumed a firm attitude and "they were told to proceed immediately or lay down their command. . . ." At least seven officers of the Eighth Regiment refused to serve when pressured to come into the field. Recruiting officers from the regiments that had already marched were also scouring the state for recruits. Loyalists attempted to hinder enlistments through a whispering campaign, declaring Washington's army was being decimated and that "a very fatal infectious disease prevails in our army." In like manner, prisoners taken during the Moore's Creek campaign and on parole in Halifax had been able to persuade some of the recruits of the Ninth Regiment to desert. To remove this evil, the General Assembly declared that henceforth these prisoners were properly the charges of the Continental Congress and sent them, under guard, to Philadelphia. This action was possibly hastened by the disclosure of a plot to assassinate "all the leading men" of North Carolina. And above all, the lag in recruiting was a result of the abiding and ridiculous faith in the ability of the militia, a faith often expensive and often betrayed by ignorance and incompetence, perhaps because so many members of the assembly were, or had been in the past, militia officers.[5]

By the middle of July John Williams had collected some 300 recruits for all nine regiments, including 130 for his own Ninth Regiment, although at least 50 were without arms. But the men refused to march until they had been given their back pay. Some 14 of the new men had deserted and others were showing obvious signs of discontent. In fact, when Williams decided to move out of town across the river to a better camp site, the troops threatened mutiny and refused to move until they had been paid, and Williams was forced to countermand his orders. Lieutenant Colonel Henry Irwin arose from his

4. Alexander Martin to Caswell, 20 April 1777, Arthur Boyes to Caswell, 19 August, 1777, Governors' Papers.

5. *State Records*, XI, 510–11, 573, 517–18, 518–19, 561–62; *North Carolina Gazette*, 24 July 1777; J. G. Blount to Caswell, 5 July 1777, Caswell to Davidson, 10 July 1777, Caswell Letterbook; Davidson to Caswell, 2 July 1777, Caswell to _____, 17 June 1777, Governors' Papers.

sick bed when about thirty malcontents "made an attempt" on Tarborough. Leading twenty-five Continentals, Irwin disarmed them and made them take the oath of allegiance to the United States. Forty men stationed at Wilmington veered to the periphery of mutiny because they had been unpaid, but they were quieted before they resorted to violence. Some officers became disgusted and tried to resign. At least three captains and three subalterns flatly refused to heed orders to come in and rejoin their units. There was a continuing struggle for men with the recruiting officers of Abraham Sheppard's Tenth Regiment, who, to fill their own quotas, made promises that all those who enlisted in their regiment would not be required to leave the state. Then there were the militia officers in the back country who hampered recruiting among militia privates lest their own commands be depleted.[6]

It was almost impossible to recruit men in such areas as Guilford County. There were reports that a rather large group was planning to march on Cross Creek to loot the salt stores there. And, or so the reports ran, these fellows drank the king's health and damned all those who did not hold with their views. There was also the persistent rumor that the leading patriot leaders in each county were to be killed and all those who refused to swear allegiance to the king would be slaughtered.[7]

Although few of his men had arms, John Williams exercised his Ninth Regiment by marching them toward Cross Creek to protect the salt from the thousand men now reported marching in that direction. And because of this threatened insurrection among the Tories, powder destined for the magazines at Salisbury and Washington County was held at Halifax. The militia was called out to cooperate with Williams and to guard critical supply points. And when it was learned that Howe's army had sailed from New York, many supposed that this was a move to cooperate with the loyalists in another attempt upon the North Carolina coast. Others felt that any uprising over salt would be brought about by the greed of "the cursed Scottish race," who controlled so much of the civilian salt supply at Cross Creek.

6. John Carter to Caswell, 5 July 1777, Williams to Caswell, 15 July 1777, Robert Mebane to Caswell, 17 July 1777, Governors' Papers; *State Records*, XI, 520–21, 557, XXII, 759–60; Davidson to Caswell, 4 August 1777, Historical Society of Pennsylvania Collection; Caswell to Sheppard, 16 June 1777, Selby Harney to Caswell, 17 July 1777, Governors' Papers; Williams to Caswell, 15 July 1777, Caswell Papers, Duke University, Durham, N.C.

7. Allen Jones to Burke, 6 August 1777, Thomas Burke Papers, N.C. Dept. Arch. & Hist.; *State Records*, XI, 526–27, 530, 533–34, 535–36, 538, 539.

Still others feared a gradual infiltration, by twos and threes, into critical areas by those "damn rascals, the Torys."[8]

By July 29, 1777, there were indications that the alarm had been little more than a tempest in a teapot. Further investigations suggested little likelihood of an uprising among the Tories, although it was reported from Cross Creek "that upwards of two thirds of this County intend leaving the State and are already become Insolent and it is apprehended will be troublesome." There had been a meeting on July 21 as reported, but it had been in Chatham rather than Guilford County, and had been a level-headed discussion that resulted in the decision to send a delegation to Cross Creek to negotiate with the Scot merchants there. The Cross Creek merchants, perhaps intimidated by the rumors, forestalled possible violence by selling their salt at reasonable prices. And when one unruly group of nearly 140 men who had caught the plundering fever refused to listen to reason and marched from Duplin and Johnston Counties, threatening to take the salt by force, they were dispersed by a company of volunteers under Robert Rowan.[9]

By now, John Williams had enlisted a total of 399 effectives and was eager to march northward. Although the danger of a loyalist uprising was now past, the men refused to move until they had been paid. It was not until early August, 1777, that the state received $300,000 in Continental currency and ordered the men paid by August 20. Yet when this news reached Williams' camp on Quankey Creek, a number of officers tendered their resignations rather than leave the state. Colonel Williams refused to accept the resignations. By the first of September the men had been paid and began their march toward Pennsylvania and the Grand Army. Behind they left Lieutenant Colonel John Luttrell to supervise recruiting activities within the state.[10]

8. J. Bradley to Caswell, 7 June 1777, Williams to Caswell, 23 July 1777, Thomas Craike to Caswell, 23 July 1777, John Simpson to Caswell, 26 July 1777, Caswell to John Ashe, 26 July 1777, Wiliam Bryan to Caswell, 27 July 1777, William Kenan to Caswell, 28 July 1777, Ashe to Caswell, 28 July 1777, John Vance to Caswell, 28 July 1777, Caswell Letterbook; *State Records*, XI, 541–43, 544–45, 546, 547–48; Return of the 9th Bn., 18 July 1777, Troop Returns, Military Collection; John Williams to Caswell, 3 June 1777, Williams to Caswell, 23 July 1777, Caswell Papers, Duke University.

9. David Smith to Caswell, 29 July 1777, Frederick Harget to Caswell, 2 August 1777, John Ashe to Caswell, 4 August 1777, Robert Rowan to Ashe, 30 July 1777, Caswell to Ashe, 6 August 1777, Caswell Letterbook; Irwin to Caswell, 16 July 1777, Irwin to Caswell, 15 August 1777, Governors' Papers; *State Records*, XI, xv, 548–49, 554.

10. Williams to Caswell, 16 August 1777, Caswell to Penn, 2 September 1777, John Luttrell to Caswell, 2 September 1777, Caswell Letterbook; *State Records*,

By early August, Abraham Sheppard's Tenth Regiment was being assembled and organized at Kinston (then Kingston); 328 men had been enlisted, but they were, in general, the sickly offscourings of the back country. They had been ordered north in September, but this was no more than an optimistic whistling for effect, for even to the unpracticed eye it was obvious that the condition of the men was such that to march them off to war would be sentencing them to death without benefit of trial. Sheppard had been allowed, through a special resolve of the assembly, to appoint his own officers, and to speed recruiting efforts a bonus of twenty shillings was allowed every officer for every private he enlisted. This was a far greater incentive than had been allowed the previous nine regiments. So eager was the General Assembly to get men into the field that Captain Cosmo Medici's company of light horse was sent forward in small groups as soon as they could be mounted. All in all, the actions of the legislature were haphazard; the legislature concerned itself too often with petty civil affairs and cast but occasional side glances at more immediate military matters. As Francis Nash noted, "Our Assembly . . . I believe has done nothing." And Samuel Johnston complained that the new government he had helped to create had fallen into the hands of "tools and knaves" of "narrow and contracted principles supported by the most contemptible abilities."[11]

Money was scarce, despite the assembly's claim that adequate sums had been appropriated. Sheppard's officers, first using their personal funds, and then borrowing more, had been unable to recruit the required three hundred men by the July 1, 1777, deadline. During their recruiting campaign a number of deserters had been rounded up and forced to rejoin their old regiments, but most of this group deserted once again when they found an opportunity. There were some doubts that another regiment should be raised in North Carolina until the ranks of the older units had been filled, but on June 12, 1777, the Tenth Regiment had been placed on the Continental establishment. Sheppard was ordered to march forward to join Washington as soon as he had enlisted three hundred men. Captain John Vance's artillery company was placed in Continental service at the

XI, 557–58, 560, 564–65, 565–66, 579–80, 602, 605–6; David Smith to Caswell, 26 July 1777, Caswell to Robert Smith, 27 July 1777, Governors' Papers.

11. *State Records*, XI, 479, XII, 19, 67; Caswell to Burke, 15 July 1777, Richard Caswell Papers, Southern Historical Collection; Johnston to Burke, 26 June 1777, Thomas Burke Papers, Southern Historical Collection; Roster, Colonel Sheppard's Bn., 19th April until 1st July 1777, Troop Returns, Military Collection.

same time, although it was specified that it was not to be attached to any particular regiment.[12]

By late August Governor Caswell was beginning to demonstrate his displeasure with Sheppard's seeming procrastination and "endeavoured to excite Colonel Sheppard and his officers to a discharge of their duty by urging them on every principle of honor, love of liberty and of their country. . . ." Only three companies had appeared at the rendezvous at Kinston and they were troops from the immediate area. Recruiting officers who had been sent out into the country apparently had done little. Caswell not only reminded Sheppard that he was under orders to march northward, and had been since June, but suggested that the true needs of the regiment could not be determined until it was assembled. Sheppard's record-keeping was so sloppy that it was not only difficult to determine just how many men had been enlisted but equally hard to ascertain the actual number in camp with him. The governor complained of the lethargy of the officers of the Tenth, saying, "For God's sake, and your Country's sake, for your own honor and that of your Regiment, let me entreat you, nay order and command, immediately to order your officers to repair to Head Quarters at Kingston. . . ." Yet when Caswell wrote to members of the Continental Congress two weeks later, he boasted that the regiment was being recruited with the "utmost expedition," that the artillery company had been ordered north, and that he expected them to march within "a few days."[13]

On September 15, Caswell, his patience exhausted, ordered Sheppard to march northward no later than Thursday, September 25, with Vance's artillery company to be attached to the Tenth Regiment until it joined the main army. Although Sheppard was supposed to march directly to Richmond to await further orders from Caswell, by October 6, he had moved no farther than the Roanoke River, two miles from Halifax. Sheppard, for some unexplained reason, left his troops encamped on the banks of the river and returned to his home in Dobbs County. Ordered back to his regiment by the governor, he returned in a few days with a memorial from his officers, complaining of their treatment. Bread was scarce, and the men of the Tenth

12. *State Records*, XI, 479, XII, 19, 67; Caswell to Burke, 15 June 1777, Richard Caswell Papers, Southern Historical Collection; Johnston to Burke, 26 June 1777, Thomas Burke Papers, Southern Historical Collection; Roster, Colonel Sheppard's Bn., 19th April until 1st July 1777, Troop Returns, Military Collection.

13. Caswell to Sheppard, 22 August 1777, Caswell Letterbook; *State Records*, XI, 587, 602–3, XXII, 781; Fitzpatrick, *Writings of Washington*, VIII, 242; Caswell to Penn, 2 September 1777, Governors' Papers.

were near naked; Sheppard's command had received only 111 pairs of breeches, not a single pair of stockings, no hats, and less than half of their assigned supply of tents, blankets, and shoes. Yet they had received more than similar units. Already the men were grumbling and accusing the officers of "breach of promise." When Sheppard finally began his march he was forced to leave forty-seven behind who were too ill to take the rigors of a long march.[14]

The departure of the Continental troops from North Carolina did not mean an end of recruiting activities within the state. Major General Robert Howe was still attempting to gain permission for South Carolina and Georgia recruiting officers to carry out their operations within North Carolina and had gone so far as to suggest that they exert pressure upon the state. All North Carolina regiments still had recruiting officers roaming the state. The Sixth Regiment had experienced so many desertions from fear of an Indian uprising in the west that an officer had been left behind just to round them up. Recruiting officers still had to contend with some militia officers who, fearful they might lose their commissions if their commands were depleted, were paying bonuses out of their own pockets to those who refused to enlist in the Continental regiments. And to add to the confusion, the colonel of the Fourth Georgia Continentals, marching his command through North Carolina, posed a subtle threat to authority by warning Caswell that unless the state granted him a loan to feed his men, he would turn them loose on the land. Although the state was desperate for supplies of all kinds, James Mease, clothier general of the Continental army, sent almost arrogant demands that all military materiel in the state be sent immediately to the main army.[15]

Those troops already in the field with the main army were unhappy; their letters overflowed with bitterness. They were "uneasy," or so they said, because there was no general officer from their own

14. Caswell to Sheppard, 15 September 1777, Caswell to Vance, 15 September 1777, Sheppard to Caswell, 22 October 1777, Caswell Letterbook; Sheppard to Caswell, 15 October 1777, Governors' Papers; *State Records*, XI, 614–15, 616, 651–52, 672, 680–81, XXII, 781–82; Caswell to the General Assembly, 29 November 1777, Caswell Papers, North Carolina Department of Archives and History, Raleigh, N.C.; A List of Men Left Behind belonging to the 10th Regt. Commanded by Col. Abraham Sheppard, Troop Returns, Military Collection.

15. Benjamin Stedman to Caswell, 8 October 1777, Governors' Papers; Nicholas Edmunds to Caswell, 3 December 1777, James Mease to Caswell, 3 December 1777, James Mease to Caswell, 3 December 1777, Caswell Letterbook; *State Records*, XI, 619, 679, 685–87, 688–89; Robert Howe to Washington, 3 November 1777, George Washington Papers; Howe to Hancock, 3 November 1777, Papers of the Continental Congress.

state to command them. They argued that North Carolina was entitled to at least two brigadier generals, and since the death of Francis Nash there had been no general officer with them. In response to urgent letters from Jethro Sumner, Cornelius Harnett suggested that the General Assembly immediately recommend one or more of the North Carolina colonels for promotion. Alexander Martin had been first in line for promotion, but he had complicated matters by his resignation. Jethro Sumner and Thomas Clark were next in line, although it was understood that if either of the two were elevated to general rank, other officers would be so irritated that a number would immediately resign. This internal friction, coupled with Thomas Burke's seeming antipathy toward the North Carolina colonels, was possibly the reason that promotions in the line were delayed as long as they were.[16]

Some felt that solutions to military problems would come out of the General Assembly that was to meet in New Bern in November, 1777. The members of the legislature were late in arriving, but the entire town went wild on the night of November 7 with the arrival of the news of Burgoyne's surrender to Horatio Gates at Saratoga. While the rest of the town buzzed with excitement, the members of the council and those legislators in town went to the governor's palace to join Caswell in "many Patriotic toasts." The three cannons before the mansion boomed out salutes, while many windows in the town were illuminated with flickering candles. It was a striking display, and perhaps engendered a spirit of optimism that overshadowed possible legislation designed to benefit the North Carolina Continentals.[17]

On Saturday, November 15, 1777, after the arrival of a quorum, the assembly sat for its first session. The situation at the time would suggest that one of the first items on the agenda would be the introduction of bills designed to correct some of the evils existing in the military. But after appointing a committee to look into the conduct of the officers of the Tenth Regiment, the assembly turned its attention to a consideration of the land policy of the state.[18]

And when military concerns finally were considered, too often personalities or private interests were involved. One dispute involved Caswell and the assembly over the status of Captain John Vance of the artillery company. For "misbehaviour in office," Vance had "been broke and declared unworthy of the command of the said company by

16. *State Records*, XI, 681–83, 639–95.
17. *North Carolina Gazette* (Supplement), 8 November 1777.
18. *North Carolina Gazette*, 21 November 1777; *State Records*, XII, 114–15.

the General Assembly. . . ." Caswell had reinstated the officer; the legislature demanded his reasons for acting contrary to its wishes. Caswell admitted knowing that the young officer had been broken, but denied having any knowledge that Vance had been declared unfit for command. When the position had fallen vacant and there had been no other candidates for the position, Vance had presented a petition, signed by all but two members of the artillery company, requesting that he be reinstated. With the advice of his council Caswell had reappointed Vance. The senate, still convinced that Vance was unworthy of the post, was not satisfied by the governor's explanations and demanded the young officer's removal, sending in its own recommendations for filling the vacancy. Caswell complied with its wishes but facetiously suggested that in the future the senate appoint all officers and he would issue the commissions, pointing out that had it taken the trouble to recommend a successor when it declared Vance ineligible there would have been no trouble. Yet Vance was not relieved of his commission; the field officers of the North Carolina Brigade presented a memorial and remonstrance to Washington. Inasmuch as Vance's commission was a Continental rather than a state rank, the general forwarded the petition to the Continental Congress.[19]

The conduct of Abraham Sheppard and the officers of the Tenth Regiment also fell under the scrutiny of Archibald MacLaine's senate committee and a similar group in the House headed by Willie Jones. In general, the committee reports charged Sheppard and his officers with procrastination, and there was the suggestion that they had been more than reluctant to march northward to join the Grand Army. And the assembly seemed to be quite willing to accept the word of Thomas Craike, commissary of stores, that the critical supply situation within the Tenth Regiment had been more the fault of Sheppard than of any state agency. There had been two rather shocking revelations. Benjamin Sheppard, paymaster of the Tenth, and Alexander Outlaw, the quartermaster, were declared unworthy of holding office when they were suspected of counterfeiting. Outlaw's name was fitting in that he had "long labored under a bad character" and had forfeited bail for failing to appear at the last court of oyer and terminer at Wilmington. There had also been irregularities in the recruiting business, with testimony from one witness declaring that he had purchased from one of the officers of the regiment a certificate ex-

19. *State Records*, XII, 114, 117, 123–24, 136, 140–41, 271, 281–82, 290–91, 299, 307; Fitzpatrick, *Writings of Washington*, XI, 444; Caswell to the General Assembly, 19 November 1777, Emmet Collection.

empting him from all military duty. The conclusion of the committee was that "Colonel Sheppard and the officers under his command have disobeyed orders on frivolous and insufficient reasons; that their conduct casts a shade, not only on themselves, but in some measure draws a reflection on this State; and that, to do away with this, the only proper way is to behave like soldiers for the future." Caswell, acting in response to a resolution of the assembly, ordered Sheppard to begin his march immediately. Money was hurriedly appropriated for pay and supplies to eliminate further cause of complaint.[20]

In addition, the assembly concerned itself with a resolution of the Continental Congress having to do with a monument to Francis Nash, who had given his life as "an offering to purchase freedom and independence for his posterity." Then there was an inquiry into the state of Continental stores within the state; a pension for John Singletary, who had lost an arm by accident while in service; rewards for the apprehension of deserters; and an angry resolution that officers who henceforth resigned their commissions would be incapable of holding either military or civil office in the state of North Carolina.[21]

The absence of a brigadier general to command the North Carolina troops hung like a backdrop to other military affairs. The delegates in the Continental Congress, even after the resignation of Alexander Martin, seemed to feel that there was still a movement afoot to promote him to general rank. They warned that such would not be prudent since his name would not receive a satisfactory vote in Congress, his "having been charged with want of courage soon after the Battle on the Brandywine." John Penn, who seemed more interested than the other delegates in the Congress, appeared to favor the promotion of Thomas Clark. Finally, on December 15, 1777, the General Assembly got around to a resolution instructing its representatives in the Continental Congress to press for the election of Thomas Clark and Jethro Sumner. But the North Carolina General Assembly that met in November, 1777, was not a body that did a great deal to promote the actual war effort. In terms of bulk of matters considered, it would seem that the body had devoted much attention to military problems, but upon a closer examination, the greater questions were either ignored or bypassed with little more than a figura-

20. *State Records*, XII, 131–35, 156–57, 268, 270, 293–97, 318, 326, XXII, 782, 783.
21. *State Records*, XII, 123, 135, 148, 203, 278–79.

tive shrug. One is tempted to term them, as did Joseph Hewes, an assembly of "wise acres."[22]

There was a different spirit among the members of the assembly when they reconvened at New Bern on April 14, 1778. Perhaps the re-election of Richard Caswell had something to do with it, or perhaps the accounts of the sufferings of Washington's army at Valley Forge had twinged a conscience here and there. For the first time there was a concentrated effort to fill the nine regiments already active in the field. Despite the difficulty in recruiting Continentals, the assembly did offer to send 5,000 militia to Washington's Grand Army. The Continental Congress offered a solution in the resolve that militia, who were to be termed "drafts," be drafted to serve nine months in Continental battalions. The North Carolina Assembly followed this with an act that 2,648 militia be drafted "as expeditiously as possible," for a period of nine months. And to lessen the hardship, it was decreed that after serving this time, these drafts were to be exempted from all military service for three years. Each county was allotted a quota in proportion to the number of militia enrolled. After the captains and field officers of each county determined the number to be drafted, the militia was to vote on those to be drafted, casting its ballot for those who could be best spared from the life of the community. Each private so selected was to receive a bonus of fifty dollars, while those who voluntarily offered their services were to have one hundred dollars. An additional three dollars was allowed each soldier who provided his own musket. In addition, the county was to provide each draftee a pair of shoes and stockings, two shirts, a hunting shirt, a waistcoat, a pair of breeches along with a pair of trousers, a hat, and a blanket.[23]

And now no one objected, as in the past, when the state's supply of powder was sent to Washington's army. Because of the obvious discontent and the resignations of so many officers, the law censuring and declaring unfit for future military and political office all those who quit the service was repealed. The governor was authorized to appoint agents to purchase supplies and clothing throughout the

22. *State Records*, XII, 284–85, 298, 300, 350, 367, 379, 386, 436, XIII, 61–62; Burnett, *Letters of Members of the Continental Congress*, III, 10, 65–66; Ford, *Journals of the Continental Congress*, IX, 861; Resolution of the House of Commons, 20 November 1777, George Washington Papers.

23. *State Records*, XII, viii, 574–77, 661–63; *North Carolina Gazette*, 8 May 1777; Ford, *Journals of the Continental Congress*, X, 200, 202; An Act for raising Men, to complete the Continental Battalions belonging to this State, Papers of the Continental Congress.

state. If those possessing material needed for the troops refused to sell at the prevailing price, these agents were empowered to seize the goods, giving certificates that could be redeemed at the next session of the General Assembly. A quota for clothing was given each county, and it was directed that such pacifist religious sects as Quakers, Mennonites, Dunkards, and Moravians furnish more than other people in return for their exemption from the draft. In like manner, officers in the field were to be allowed to purchase clothing at one-third the customary price. The governor was authorized to draw additional funds without recourse to the legislature, and was given greater freedom in the procurement of supplies. Although the assembly continued to focus its attention upon matters more civil than military, it now seemed to take the war more seriously and appeared more resigned to its responsibility for supplying the troops in the field.[24]

The North Carolina troops with Washington's army needed all the help anyone could give them. They had suffered, as did the entire army, all during that desperate winter at Valley Forge. Perhaps American soldiers have suffered more in other wars, but it seems unlikely that soldiers have ever felt so abandoned by the very people they were supposed to be fighting for. On December 17, 1777, before they reached the bivouac, Washington's general orders had explained his reasons for moving into such a desolate spot:

> ... the General ardently wishes it were now in his power to conduct the troops into the best winter quarters. But where are these to be found? Should we retire to the interior parts of the State, we should find them crowded with virtuous citizens, who sacrificing their all have left Philadelphia and fled thither for protection. To their distresses humanity forbids us to add. That is not all; we should leave a vast extent of fertile country to be despoiled and ravaged by the enemy from which they draw vast supplies and where many of our firm friends woud be exposed to all the miseries of the most insulting and wanton depredations. A train of evils might be enumerated, but these will suffice.[25]

The place called Valley Forge was bleak and desolate. Trees, with their vegetation stripped by the cold hand of winter, held up their branches toward the gray skies as if pleading for a new garb of green. The few houses near the junction of Valley Creek and the Schuylkill could hardly be termed a village. Once there had been a forge, but it had been destroyed and all supplies and provisions had been taken up by the British army when it swept through the area

24. *State Records*, XII, 556, 558–60, 574–77, 580–81, 605, 615, 639–41, 644–45, 653, 661–64, 680, 713, 720, 744, 747–51, 752.
25. Fitzpatrick, *Writings of Washington*, X, 167–68.

in September. As a site for a winter encampment, Vallely Forge could offer little other than timber for huts and a strong defensive position that could not be easily overrun. Johann de Kalb, accustomed to European practices, declared that such a position could only have been selected by a land speculator, a traitor or a council of idiots. The camp was pitched on a thickly wooded slope some two miles long, rising from the river to a long ridge that terminated in an eminence called Mount Joy. Here, on a windy, gray December 18, 1777, George Washington's army had pitched their tents.[26]

Huts were built, but the army shivered and huddled together in their ragged tents while the construction was brought forward. Because of the scarcity of draught animals, many men yoked themselves to the wagons and in this fashion were able to haul timber onto the ground. Soldiers were divided into parties of twelve, each group to build its own hut, fourteen by sixteen feet, six and one-half feet high. As an incentive, Washington offered a prize of twelve dollars to the group in each regiment who produced the best hut in the shortest period of time. Tom Paine was reminded of beavers as he observed that "everyone was busy; some carrying logs, others mud, and the rest fastening them together." The soldiers of the Continental army lived more like animals in crude burrows rather than troops in barracks. Comfort became little more than a memory of the past and a hope for the future.[27]

There were some in Congress who complained to Washington that he should have maintained an active army in the field, constantly harassing and attempting to destroy the enemy. They seemed to disregard the fact that full bellies and bodily comfort are as necessary to keep an army in the field as arms and ammunition. Just before the army had reached Valley Forge, a thanksgiving proclaimed by Congress for Gates's victory at Saratoga had been celebrated by a ration issue to each man of "half a gill of rice and a tablespoonful of vinegar." And on December 23, 1777, an angry Washington reported to Congress that not only were many soldiers confined to the hospital for want of shoes but blankets were so scarce that large numbers of men were forced to sit up by the fires all night to keep from freezing to death. In sarcastic refrain the general noted that "it is a much easier and less disturbing thing to draw remonstrances in a comfort-

26. Bill, *Valley Forge*, pp. 95–96; Kapp, *Life of John Kalb*, p. 137; Scheer and Rankin, *Rebels and Redcoats*, pp. 333–34.

27. William S. Stryker, *The Battle of Monmouth* (Princeton, 1927), pp. 3–4; Bill, *Valley Forge*, p. 96; Moncure Daniel Conway, (ed.), *The Writings of Thomas Paine* (New York, 1894–96), I, 392.

able room by a good fireside than to occupy a cold bleak hillside and sleep under frost and snow without clothes or blankets. However, although they seem to have little feeling for the naked and distressed soldiers, I feel superabundantly for them and, from my soul, I pity those miseries, which is neither in my power to relieve or prevent."[28]

There was an inconsistency in the attitude of the state of North Carolina. Although those troops already on the Continental establishment were freezing and starving, the General Assembly was even now offering to raise additional troops, while Robert Howe, shortly after his elevation to major general, was still urging that South Carolina and Georgia be allowed to recruit within the state. Of the 1,051 North Carolina Continentals stationed at Valley Forge near the end of December, 327 were on the sick rolls, while an additional 164 were listed as "Unfit for Duty for want of Cloathing." Under such circumstances the Continental Congress was reluctant to recruit additional North Carolina soldiers as further drains on the supplies still on hand.[29]

And for all of the sound and fury leveled at Abraham Sheppard's Tenth Regiment, by mid-February it was no farther north than Tottopomey Creek in Hanover County, Virginia. By this time, it was little more than a skeleton unit; in addition to the 47 left behind at the beginning of the march, 118 men had deserted along the route, an average of almost 1 every mile. A large number had fallen ill, and 20 had died and had been buried in shallow graves along the way. The regiment had been so long in recruiting and so long on the march that it was already clamoring for replacements for worn-out clothing. It did not reach the smallpox inoculation camp at Georgetown on the Potomac until early March. Only six men died as a result of the inoculation, but a much larger number were lost as a result of the measles epidemic that swept through the camp. To many observers it was already clear that Sheppard's Tenth Regiment would be more of a hindrance than any great aid to the war effort. The unit was soon to fade into obscurity as a result of continued desertions. The pitiful few who finally reached Valley Forge were disbanded and attached to the First and Second Regiments.[30]

28. *State Records*, XIII, 361; [Joseph Plumb Martin], *A Narrative of Some of the Adventures, Dangers and Sufferings of a Revolutionary Soldier* (Hallowell, Me., 1830), p. 73; Fitzpatrick, *Writings of Washington*, X, 295–300.

29. Fitzpatrick, *Writings of Washington*, X, 300–2; Return of the N.C. Brigade Commanded by Gen. McIntosh, Dec. 20th, 1777, Revolutionary War Rolls, Adjutant General's Offices.

30. Harnett to Caswell, 10 February 1778, Sheppard to Caswell, 16 February 1778, Sheppard to Caswell, 7 April 1778, Governors' Papers; *State Records*, XI,

The days grew even colder in that slough of despondency called Valley Forge. Cornelius Harnett, warm and comfortable by his fireside in York, Pennsylvania, listened to local gossip, believed it, and reported that the "huts are very warm and comfortable" in Washington's camp. But in camp one soldier wrote that it was "colder than one can think," while Surgeon Albigence Waldo complained that the continuous "cold and smoke make us fret." Often as many as three men were forced to huddle together under one blanket to keep from freezing, while clothing was so scarce that sentinels were seen standing in their hats to keep their rag-wrapped feet out of the snow. According to Waldo, many men lived on a steady diet of "firecake and water, sir," sometimes varied by such a delicacy as "a bowl of beef soup full of dead leaves and dirt." Some of the troops were without bread or meat as long as forty-eight hours, and throughout the camp rose the plaintive cry, "No bread, no meat, no soldier!"[31]

In late December Washington had estimated that 2,898 men, or nearly one-third of his total number of troops, were useless because of the scarcity of proper clothing and blankets. Anthony Wayne guessed that nine of every ten deaths or desertions could be laid to the frugal diet and scanty clothing. Although many officers, especially those of general rank, were housed better than the rank and file, they fared little better. Clothing had been lost, stolen, or had simply worn out with no way of replacement because of the rapid depreciation of the Continental currency. Foreign officers who had crossed the Atlantic to fight with the Americans declared that no European would, or could, stay in the field under such conditions, and expressed their amazement when they saw officers mounting guard in old dressing gowns or with blankets wrapped around them.[32]

There must have been times when Lachlan McIntosh cursed the day that he had been given command of the North Carolina Brigade. None of the regiments held their full quotas of 300 privates. In fact, the total number of men in all nine regiments in camp during January and February averaged 1,035 men, and of these few were well enough equipped or healthy enough to take the field on sudden notice. About 107 of this number were constantly "On Com-

703, XIII, 37–38, 48–49, 82–83, XXII, 94; Return of the Men Absent from the 10th N.C. Bn., Commanded by Colonel Abraham Sheppard in Camp in Hanover County, Virginia, Feb. 26, 1778, Troop Returns, Military Collection.

31. *State Records*, XIII, 370–71; *Pennsylvania Magazine of History and Biography*, XXI (1897), 301–19; Stryker, *Battle of Monmouth*, pp. 2–7.

32. Kapp, *Life of John Kalb*, pp. 197–200; Fitzpatrick, *Writings of Washington*, X, 326; Bill, *Valley Forge*, pp. 99–101; Hastings, *Public Papers of George Clinton*, II, 843–44.

mand," scouting and foraging around the countryside. There were an average of 88 soldiers sick in camp, while another 219 were carried as "sick absent" in the various hospitals scattered around Pennsylvania and New Jersey. So many of the Second North Carolina were "sickly" that it was considered imperative that they be removed from the dank tents and huts. In fact, according to Washington, the North Carolina Brigade was more sickly, for want of provisions and clothing, than any other unit at Valley Forge. For the better part of this period there was an average of 199 unfit for duty because of the lack of shoes and clothing. Some of the healthier members of the brigade were detached to man the galleys that plied the upper reaches of the Delaware and Schuylkill. The North Carolina units were by this time so depleted that Washington ordered McIntosh to combine all nine regiments into the First, Second, and Third regiments, while the supernumerary officers were to return to North Carolina to recruit enough men to reactivate their units.[33]

Until late February no more than half of the North Carolina Brigade was fit for duty at any one time. By then there had been captures of several ships at sea whose cargoes of clothing had been purchased and distributed to the more destitute soldiers. Governor Caswell had been particularly active in the purchase of woolens and other cloths as well as some shoes and stockings and a quantity of tanned leather and deerskins. By the end of the month there were only thirty North Carolina soldiers listed as unfit for duty because of the lack of shoes or clothing. Some fifty men of the brigade had died of various ailments during the first two months of 1778. Some might have been saved had there had been more than one medical man in the brigade, Dr. William McClure of the Second Regiment. One Dr. Colley of the Fifth, despite the pleas of McIntosh, had insisted upon returning to North Carolina with supernumerary officers, "leaving so many of his brave Country men to perish without assistance." The absent physician, cried the infuriated McIntosh, "deserves still further marks of Resentment from his Country." Although the situation was infinitely better in the late winter, the usually optimistic Harnett had begun to fear that "our Continental Army will cut a poor figure in the Spring."[34]

The rate of desertion at Valley Forge had been extremely high,

33. *State Records*, XIII, 42, 46, 66, 67–68, 365, 366, 377, 374–75; Greene, *Life of Nathanael Greene*, I, 563; Fitzpatrick, *Writings of Washington*, X, 268–69, XI, 105, 120, 135, 169–70, XII, 43.

34. Caswell to Burke, 15 February 1778, Caswell to Clothier General, 14 March 1778, Lachlan McIntosh to Caswell, 20 March 1778, Caswell Letterbook; *North Carolina Gazette*, 30 January 1778.

for "The Love of Freedom which once animated the Breasts of those born in the Country is controuling by Hunger, the keenest of necessities." Yet the only bright spot insofar as the North Carolina Brigade was concerned was that it had fewer desertions than the line of any other state. Perhaps this can best be explained in terms of distance—the North Carolinians were farther away from home than most of the troops in the encampment at Valley Forge. Even had they been fortunate enough to steal a horse, the few horses that survived the ordeal would have been too weak to carry them very far.[35]

The only explanation for the survival of the army during the desperate months at Valley Forge is that the troops had become conditioned to adversity beyond the recognition of ordinary mortals. Much credit should be given those officers who remained with their men. At times the entire army was about to mutiny and one wonders why it did not. Perhaps the explanation lies in the simple fact that so many of the soldiers were not dressed well enough to attempt desertion, for the records suggest that many had no body clothing other than a blanket in which they wrapped themselves.[36]

The situation became even more discouraging with the knowledge that many farmers in the neighborhood had barns bulging with provisions, but preferred the hard money paid out by the British in Philadelphia to the paper currency offered by the American commissaries. Christopher Marshall, an apothecary of Philadelphia who had exiled himself to Lancaster, confided to his diary the excesses of that "monster of rapine, General Howe." The British, he noted, made "frequent excursions twenty miles together, destroying and burning what they please, pillaging, plundering men and women, stealing boys above ten years old, deflowering virgins, driving into the City for their use droves of cattle, sheep [and] hogs; poultry, meat, cider, furniture and clothing of all kinds, loaded upon our horses." Not only were there attempts to block these enemy raids, but other steps were taken to aid the American troops. Parties were sent into the countryside to thresh wheat, all wagons with horses able to pull them were in continuous use, hauling in all the provisions that could be gathered up. Meat was rare, and "though America abounds with provisions we cannot get sufficient for a few Thousand men without expending Millions in the purchase of it." Mounted troops ranged

35. James Varnum to Nathanael Greene, 12 February 1778, George Washington Papers.

36. James Thacher, *A Military Journal During the Revolutionary War* (Boston, 1827), p. 128n; Kapp, *Life of John Kalb*, pp. 142–43; Fitzpatrick, *Writings of Washington*, X, 268, 436.

as far away as Maryland, collecting cattle and driving them back to camp. There was even a plan to truck in pork from North Carolina, while local farmers were urged to establish markets within the limits of the camp. None of these schemes were very successful. Johann de Kalb, whose European sensibilities were outraged by what he saw, complained, "How sad that troops of such excellence, and so much zeal, should be so little spared and so badly led." And Nathanael Greene lifted up his prayer, "God grant we may never be brought to such a wretched condition again."[37]

The physical sufferings were topped by mental disturbances that threatened to wreck the entire army. Washington had long been a whipping boy for those politicians who fancied themselves military experts, perhaps because he had almost accomplished the impossible at Germantown and then had seen victory slip from his grasp. Of those congressmen who had endorsed him as commander in chief in 1775, only six remained in the Continental Congress. Even John Adams, who had been the first to support the nomination, feared that the masses might begin to think of the general as "a deity or savior." Others agreed with Jonathan Sargent, attorney general of Pennsylvania, who disparaged Washington's efforts with: "Two battles he has lost for us by such blunders as might have disgraced a soldier of three months standing, and yet we are so attached to the man I fear that we shall rather sink with him than throw him off our shoulders."[38]

There was, or so it seemed to many, a plot to remove Washington as commander in chief and replace him with the "Saratoga hero," Horatio Gates. This supposed conspiracy had come to light when Gates's aide, James Wilkinson, had revealed a phrase from a letter to Gates from Thomas Conway: "Heaven has been determined to save your country; or a weak General and bad Councellors would have ruined it." Conway, an Irishman who had formerly served in the French army, now held an American rank of major general and inspector general. He was greatly resented by other American generals whom he had been so foolish as to term "fools, cowards and drunkards in public company. . . ." His unbridled arrogance had won him few

---

37. Fitzpatrick, *Writings of Washington*, X, 467, 474, 491, 513, 524; Ford, *Journals of the Continental Congress*, X, 62–63; Greene, *Life of Nathanael Greene*, I, 557; Duane, *Extracts from the Diary of Christopher Marshall*, p. 153; Burnett, *Letters of Members of the Continental Congress*, III, 128; Varnum to Greene, 12 February 1778, George Washington Papers.

38. Adams, *Familiar Letters of John Adams and His Wife Abigail Adams*, p. 323; Jonathan Sergeant to James Lovell, 20 November 1777, Samuel Adams Papers, New York Public Library, New York, N.Y.

friends. An additional irritant to the officers in Washington's command was the praise heaped upon Gates for his victory over Burgoyne. Then many of the officers at Valley Forge, including Washington, felt that a "damned faction" in the Continental Congress, including many of the New England delegates, were forming a "cabal" with the design of removing Washington from command. One officer in the North Carolina Line vented his emotions in a letter to William Lee Davidson: "You are right when you think I enjoy every kind of honor, or respect shown the General. I really do, I venerate his Character, and look only to him and Heaven for salvation, men will do for him, what they will not for a Cabal that is now despised, most heartily, by all that know them, or their transactions."[39]

Before it was all over, Conway had been wounded in a duel with General John Cadwalader of the Pennsylvania militia and, thinking himself dying, had penned a most abject letter of apology to Washington. And he seemed surprised when Congress accepted his subsequent resignation. Whether there was a cabal or not is not significant, but the fact that Washington thought there was became an important factor. The general came out of the affair stronger than ever. Nathanael Greene expressed the opinion of many officers when he wrote: "The poor and shallow politicians unmasked their batteries before they were ready to attempt any execution."[40]

Physical discomforts and mental anguish were forgotten as soughing spring breezes began to melt the snow. On February 23, a fabulous character had ridden into camp. Calling himself Friedrich Wilhelm August Heinrich Ferdinand, Baron von Steuben, he claimed to have been a lieutenant general on the staff of Frederick the Great. He had never been higher in rank than captain under that great military leader, but there was just enough of the truth woven into the embroidery of his past to make his boasting seem plausible. Stout, bald, and with a large red nose dominating his round face, the baron was possessed of a disarming personality. From Paris he had brought letters from Benjamin Franklin and Silas Deane, and had been shrewd enough to write Washington, "I would rather serve under your Excellency as a volunteer than be a subject of discontent to such deserving officers as have already distinguished themselves amongst you." It was not only a refreshing sentiment but a gracious

39. Fitzpatrick, *Writings of Washington*, X, 29, 249, 264–65, 440, 508–9, 517; *State Records*, XIII, 111–12; _____ to William Lee Davidson, 18 February 1777 [1778], Miscellaneous Papers, 1697–1912.

40. *Pennsylvania Magazine of History and Biography*, XXXI (1908), 168–70; Greene to MacDougall, 5 February 1778, Alexander MacDougall Papers, New-York Historical Society, New York, N.Y.

one, especially since it came so hard on the heels of the Conway affair. So impressed was the commander in chief that he recommended to Congress that it appoint Steuben temporary inspector general, an appointment to be made permanent just as soon as Conway could be relieved.[41]

Within a short period it was reported that this ebullient imposter had "hit the taste of the officers, gives universal satisfaction, and I am assured has made an amazing improvement in discipline." Yet the baron faced a seemingly insurmountable task in readying the army to take the field against a well-trained enemy. Among other things, he discovered regiments larger than brigades, while one regiment had only thirty men and the entire strength of one company was one lonely corporal. To Steuben's horror he also discovered that there was not even a standard set of drill regulations for the Continental army. He wrote his own, a modification of the Prussian system, thereby lending all future American armies a Teutonic flavor. Among those things that he had to overcome was the English tradition that drilling troops was beneath the dignity of commissioned officers and should be left to the sergeants. Some officers had to be threatened with arrest and punishment for not attending drill. They were reminded that "nothing conduces more to the Honour of an Officer than to march well, salute with good Grace, in short to be knowing in every particular Part of his Profession. . . ." Steuben became the drillmaster to one hundred picked men. From six in the morning until six in the evening his guttural commands rebounded from the muddy parade ground at Valley Forge. At times, driven to exasperation by the ineptness of his students, he would loose a volley of oaths in French, then in German, and end by lustily swearing in both languages at the same time. And because his English was so poor he would sometimes call out to his aides, "My dear Walker and my dear Duponceau, come and swear for me in English. These fellows won't do what I bid them."[42]

Although the Americans seemed inclined to cling to the English way of doing things, Steuben wrote to a friend that he had proved that his "sauerkraut" was best for them, even though it sometimes

41. Freeman, *Washington*, IV, 616–17; John M. Palmer, *General von Steuben* (New York, 1937), pp. 114–15; Henry Laurens to Washington, 19 February 1778, Papers of the Continental Congress.

42. Burnett, *Letters of Members of the Continental Congress*, III, 153–54; Palmer, *General von Steuben*, pp. 115, 157; *Pennsylvania Magazine of History and Biography*, LXIII (1939), 219; Josiah Harmar Orderly Book, William L. Clements Library, University of Michigan, Ann Arbor, Mich.

had to be done by a flurry of hearty "God-dams." He reduced the manual of arms to ten simple commands:

1. Poise Firelock.
2. Shoulder Firelock.
3. Present Arms.
4. Fix Bayonet.
5. Unfix Bayonet.
6. Load Firelock.
7. Make Ready.
8. Present (later changed to "Take Sight").
9. Fire.
10. Order Firelock.[43]

The troops, who seemed to realize their desperate need for such training, cooperated. Within a month even the meticulous Steuben admitted that he had experienced the satisfaction "to see not only a regular step introduced into the army, but I also made maneuvers with ten or twelve battalions with as much precision as the evolution of a single company." The army had learned to march in compact columns, eliminating the hazards of loose discipline, limping stragglers, and time lost in forming for battle. Now it could deploy from a line of march into a line of battle with a minimum of time. In early May, when intelligence reported that Lafayette might be surrounded by the enemy, the entire army was under arms, formed, and ready to march within fifteen minutes after the first alarm gun sounded. Young John Laurens seemed almost eager for another brush with the enemy, for "we shall be infinitely better prepared to meet him than ever we have been."[44]

Other changes promised a better future. Thomas Mifflin, who had served as quartermaster general in a disinterested fashion, resigned his post. As an example of his poor operations, a committee from Congress had discovered badly needed supplies stored in a haphazard manner with no apparent record of them. Nathanael Greene was persuaded to accept the post although he was unhappy about it. The appointment, said Greene, "is flattering to my fortunes, but humiliating to my Military pride," and he insisted upon also retaining his command in the field. The Commissary Department,

43. Palmer, *General von Steuben*, pp. 114–15; Thomas Ewing, *George Ewing, a Gentleman, a Soldier at Valley Forge* (Yonkers, N.Y., 1928), pp. 33–35.

44. Palmer, *General von Steuben*, pp. 114–15; John Laurens, *The Army Correspondence of Colonel John Laurens in the Year 1777–8, Now First Printed from Original Letters Addressed to His Father, Henry Laurens, President of Congress, with a Memoir by William Gilmore Simms* (New York, 1867), p. 152; *State Records,* XIII, 137–38; Fitzpatrick, *Writings of Washington,* XI, 387; Jacob Turner Orderly Book.

which had gone steadily downhill since the illness of Joseph Trumbull, received new life with the appointment of Jeremiah Wadsworth as commissionary general. This change proved beneficial for the North Carolina Brigade, for within a month they were issued new blankets.[45]

On February 6, 1778, the treaty between France and the United States had been signed. Washington did not receive the news until May 1, and on May 5 the union was announced to the army. There were the usual discourses by the chaplains, the usual artillery salutes, and the inevitable *feu de joie*. The whole was conducted in a happy fashion and the firing was intermingled with frequent "huzzas" from the troops. Even Washington, it was said, lowered his usual stout reserve to join the huzzas.[46]

With the warm weather, the North Carolina Brigade cleared its backlog of military charges. Captain Daniel Jones of the Third Regiment had already been convicted of disobedience of orders and absenting himself without leave, when Colonel Thomas Clark became the president of a court-martial to hear the charges against a number of officers and men. Captain Thomas Granbury was acquitted of drawing more money and provisions than he had in his company and for giving bonuses to "imagined" recruits. Captain John Medaris of the Third was reprimanded in orders for unintentional forgery. The court ruled that Lieutenant Matthew McCalley of the Tenth be reprimanded for allowing a prisoner to escape. Private Julian Burton received fifty lashes in front of the entire brigade for stealing a pair of shoes from another soldier and giving them to his doxy. Other men of the ranks received sentences of from twenty-five to fifty lashes for such offenses as drunkenness on duty, absence without leave and for "countermanding desertion." One John O'Neal, who had developed a racket of forging and selling discharges, was sentenced to receive a total of 225 lashes, with 125 to be applied the first day and 100 additional lashes two days later before the welts had time to heal. Captain Clement Hall was brought before the court charged with illegally seizing three and one-half barrels of cider, a barrel of whiskey, and another lot of seventy-eight gallons of whiskey. It was proved in court, however, that those who charged him were themselves guilty

---

45. Greene, *Life of Nathanael Greene*, II, 42–45; Ford, *Journals of the Continental Congress*, X, 210, 293, 305, 356–57; Burnett, *Letters of Members of the Continental Congress*, III, 166, 175; Nathanael Greene to William Greene, 15 May 1778, Nathanael Greene Papers, William L. Clements Library, University of Michigan, Ann Arbor, Mich.; Fitzpatrick, *Writings of Washington*, XII, 65.

46. *Pennsylvania Packet* (Philadelphia), 12 May 1778; Jared C. Sparks (ed.), *The Writings of George Washington* (Boston, 1834–35), V, 357n.

of selling spirits to the soldiers without proper license and the conscientious captain was absolved of all blame. The court went even further, confiscating the evidence for the use of the troops.[47]

The North Carolina Brigade, although still proudly divided into nine regiments, did not contain one-half the rank and file needed to bring it up to full strength. The Sixth Regiment had been so reduced in manpower that its officers had been sent home in early February to recruit enough men to fill the ranks, although there were no funds with which to pay enlistment bounties. In April the North Carolina General Assembly had passed a bill in an attempt to bring the state units up to full strength, but the Continental Congress had, on May 29, decided upon another course of action. It had agreed that there should be a consolidation of the North Carolina regiments then in camp to best utilize the men. The captains with the longest terms of service in the regiments that were to be broken up were to be retained in the consolidated regiments and were to be allowed to select the men from their old units for their new companies.[48]

The state of North Carolina was to raise four additional regiments, or battalions, but they were to remain within the state until further orders. The remaining regiments were now to be reduced to four; the Sixth Regiment was consolidated with the First with Colonel Thomas Clark commanding; the Fourth was combined with the Second under Colonel John Patten; and the men of the Fifth were added to the Third Regiment under Colonel Jethro Sumner. Washington had finally become tired of waiting for Abraham Sheppard's Tenth Regiment and had sent an officer to hurry it on in. And once it had arrived, inasmuch as Sheppard had not filled his regiment, his men were distributed among the older regiments. Colonels Thomas Polk and James Hogun, with a large number of supernumerary officers were sent back to North Carolina to aid in recruiting and to officer the new regiments.[49]

47. *Historical Magazine*, III (1868), 244–46; Fitzpatrick, *Writings of Washington*, X, 486; *State Records*, XIII, 130–31; *North Carolina Gazette*, 6 February 1778.

48. *State Records*, XIII, 42–43, 111–12, 122–23, 151–52, 154, XV, 710–11; Davidson, *Piedmont Partisan*, p. 49; David Schenck, *North Carolina, 1780–81* (Raleigh, 1889), p. 31; Ford, *Journals of the Continental Congress*, XI, 551, XII, 1193–94; Resolution of Congress, 29 May 1778, Revolutionary Papers, Southern Historical Collection.

49. Caswell to Burke, 15 February 1778, Caswell to Henry Laurens, 2 May 1778, Caswell to Laurens, 6 May 1778, Caswell to James Hogun, 7 June 1778, Caswell Letterbook; *North Carolina Gazette*, 8 May 1778; *State Records*, XIII, 392, 426; Extracts from the Minutes of the Continental Congress, 28 May 1778, Caswell Papers, N.C. Dept. Arch. & Hist.; Fitzpatrick, *Writings of Washington*, XII, 8–9.

There was a change in the top echelon of command. On May 15, Lachlan McIntosh was assigned to the command of Fort Pitt on the frontier. Thomas Clark was given the command of the North Carolina Brigade. Samuel Ashe's First troop of North Carolina Dragoons was also sent to Fort Pitt with McIntosh. It was expected that since Ashe's men had but recently been completely equipped, they would remain in the field for an extra two months. They didn't. All but fourteen took their leave soon after their arrival at Fort Pitt. This made the Continental Congress so unhappy that it ordered the discharge of all North Carolina dragoons as of January 1, 1779.[50]

But the Americans now had a new ally, a new spirit, and an army that had been hammered into shape by a Prussian drillmaster at a place called Valley Forge. It was spring, and spring is the season when armies take the field.

50. Fitzpatrick, *Writings of Washington*, XI, 202–3, 388–89, 460–61; Extracts from the Minutes of the Continental Congress, 28 May 1778, Caswell Papers, N.C. Dept. Arch. & Hist.

Chapter 7
*M*onmouth and the New York Highlands

". . . beat out with heat and fatigue. . . ."

As spring breezes tempered the bite of winter, Washington became restless. He was eager to leave Valley Forge and take the field against the enemy. His army had swelled considerably in numbers and now totaled, including convalescents, about 11,600. By recalling outlying detachments, and including the militia expected to turn out, the general could expect well over 20,000 troops in the field, over twice the number of British soldiers in Philadelphia. Yet the enemy's plans remained unknown, and other generals did not share the commander in chief's optimism. A council of war recommended that the army remain in Valley Forge to await further developments rather than risk an offensive action. Perhaps influenced by Steuben, the council suggested that the time in camp be utilized in building up the cavalry and training and strengthening the infantry.[1]

Washington now had a new adversary whose moves could prove unpredictable. On April 23 he learned that Sir William Howe had been granted permission to return to England and had been suc-

1. Fitzpatrick, *Writings of Washington*, XI, 363–65, 385; Benjamin Franklin Stevens (ed.), *Facsimiles of Manuscripts in European Archives Relating to America, 1773–1783* (London, 1889–95), 825; Nathanael Greene to R. L. Hooper, Joseph Reed Papers.

ceeded in the command by Sir Henry Clinton. What Washington did not know was that when France entered the war the entire complexion of the war changed, and British strategy was now diverted into new channels. Of primary importance was the French naval base on the West Indian Island of St. Lucia. Clinton had been ordered to detach five thousand troops for the expedition to St. Lucia while another three thousand were ordered southward to protect Florida. Philadelphia was to be evacuated and New York was to be held, pending the outcome of peace negotiations then in progress. If it was possible for Washington to take New York, Clinton was to make Rhode Island his primary base. It was learned at Valley Forge that this news had been received with "great commotions" by the British officers, who expressed "loud dissatisfaction at the appearance of an unfavorable change of officers, & the Citizens clamoring their apprehensions of what might happen to them."[2]

By mid-May intelligence reports indicated that the British were planning to evacuate Philadelphia. Still their total operations were confusing to Washington, enough so that he was never sure of the enemy's intentions. Lafayette was sent out with his division, which included Clark's brigade, to observe enemy action. He was very nearly surrounded at Barren Hill before he was able to extricate himself when the enemy "managed very badly" and "the Marquis displayed great Generalship." Posting small detachments at strategic points, Washington decided to wait until the enemy made a definite move. It was well that he did; a sudden epidemic of minor ills temporarily weakened his force.[3]

Washington seemed impatient for action. Finally, on June 18, he learned that the last British soldiers had evacuated Philadelphia, destroying the bridges over which they marched. It was now apparent that Clinton planned to march overland to New York. His water transportation had been used to convey the troops of two Hessian regiments who, it was feared, might desert at the first opportunity, and several thousand loyalists who were fleeing the city with their possessions. The following day Benedict Arnold led American troops into the city. Washington immediately ordered six divisions under

2. *Journal of Modern History*, XIX (1947), 111–13; Hancock to Caswell, 24 April 1778, Papers of the Continental Congress.

3. General Orders, 17 June 1778, Laurens to Caswell, 26 May 1778, Papers of the Continental Congress; Fitzpatrick, *Writings of Washington*, XI, 397–98, 405, 418–19, 428, 447, 451, 484; Louis Gottschalk, *Lafayette Joins the American Army* (Chicago, 1937), pp. 186 ff., *State Records*, XIII, 130–31; Burnett, *Letters of Members of the Continental Congress*, III, 285; Adam Boyd to Caswell, 20–22 March 1778, Governors' Papers.

Charles Lee and Anthony Wayne to begin their march towards Coryell's Ferry on the Delaware. At five the next morning, June 19, 1778, three divisions under Lafayette, de Kalb, and Stirling were to follow the same route. The North Carolina Continentals, along with Charles Scott's Virginia Continentals and William Woodford's command, were brigaded under Lafayette.[4]

Washington knew that a defeat of the British army at this time, following so closely upon the defeat of Burgoyne, might well change the entire complexion of the war. But any move he made would have to be predicated on the route Clinton took to New York. So the American general marched and waited, his army hovering like a great hawk ready to pounce once the prey had committed himself. By June 23 the American army, alternately drenched by driving rain and broiled by a dull sun burning through the humid haze, had crossed the Delaware at Coryell's Ferry. On the following day it reached Hopewell, within fifteen miles of the British encampment at Allentown. By now it was obvious that Clinton would take the road to Sandy Hook, there to meet the transports that would convey him over to New York. The British general originally had planned to strike for South Amboy, but there was a persistent rumor that Horatio Gates was marching his army down from upper New York and would make a stand at the Raritan.[5]

Already the American troops in the field were harassing the British. William Maxwell with 1,300 Continentals and Philemon Dickinson with 800 New Jersey militia were hanging off the left flank of the British column. John Cadwalader with nearly 300 Continentals and a few militia were popping away at the enemy's rear. Maxwell and Dickinson performed their tasks so well, destroying bridges, felling trees across the road, and filling in wells, that the long red column managed to crawl only thirty-four miles in six days. The British right flank was exposed to attack.[6]

Washington called a council of war. Perhaps he took the total eclipse of the sun on June 24 as a good omen. Other general officers, however, seemingly chose to regard it as an evil sign, or they had fallen under the influence of Charles Lee. Lee had been captured by the enemy, but had been exchanged in May and was now strutting

4. Fitzpatrick, *Writings of Washington*, XII, 74, 107, 82–83, 85, 86–87, 90, 107; *Lee Papers*, II, 408–10; [John Miller] Diary, Joseph Reed Papers.

5. Fitzpatrick, *Writings of Washington*, XII, 110; Reed, *Life and Correspondence of Joseph Reed*, I, 368; Clinton to George Germain, 5 July 1778, Sir Henry Clinton Papers.

6. Stryker, *Battle of Monmouth*, p. 75n; John André, *Major André's Journal, 1777–1778*, ed. Henry Cabot Lodge (Boston, 1902), p. 78.

around camp with his dogs at his heels. He dominated the council of war. The British army, Lee said, was in such fine condition and so well disciplined that, if necessary, the Americans would be justified in building "a bridge of gold" to hasten the march of the enemy across New Jersey rather than attempting to fight them. A defeat, he argued, might well jeopardize the alliance with France; it was Lee's opinion that Washington should march directly for White Plains without molesting Clinton. His passionate discourse convinced the majority of the generals that it would be "criminal" to attack the British army. They would sanction no bolder action than strengthening the force on the enemy's left flank and holding the remainder of the army in readiness to take advantage of any opportunities that might develop. This decision, snorted young Alexander Hamilton, "would have done honor to the most honorable society of midwives and to them only."[7]

Some generals had second thoughts, while others wrote out statements clarifying their positions. Nathanael Greene, for example, explained, "We are now in the most awkward position in the world and have come to our grief repeatedly—marching until we get near the enemy and then our courage fails and we halt without attempting to do the enemy the least injury. . . . People expect something from us and our strength demands it. I am by no means for rash measures but we must preserve our reputations and I think we can make a very serious impression without any great risk and if it should amount to a general action I think the chance is greatly in our favor. However, I think we can make a partial attack without suffering them to bring us to a general action."[8]

Washington felt bound by the counsel of his generals and thrust aside any thoughts of a general action. Charles Scott with nearly 1,500 men was sent out to annoy the enemy's left flank and rear; included in his command was the Second North Carolina Regiment. Daniel Morgan, with his relatively small detachment of 600 men, was ordered out to vex the right flank of the enemy; several days earlier two light infantry companies from the North Carolina Brigade had been attached to Morgan's command. The British advance column was under the command of the Hessian general, Knyphausen,

7. Marquis de Lafayette, *Memoirs, Correspondence and Manuscripts of General Lafayette* (New York, 1837), I, 50–52; Fitzpatrick, *Writings of Washington*, XII, 113, 116, 140; *Pennsylvania Magazine of History and Biography*, II (1878), 140–42; Francis S. Drake, *Memorials of the Massachusetts Society of the Cincinnati* (Boston, 1873), pp. 142–43; *North Carolina Gazette*, 26 June 1778; Harnett to Sumner, 1 April 1778, Jethro Sumner Papers, Southern Historical Collection.
    8. Greene to Washington, 24 June 1778, George Washington Papers.

followed by the baggage train, said to be composed of some four hundred wagons and stretching out along the road for twelve miles. The second column was under the command of Lord Cornwallis, although Clinton rode with him. On June 25 the long red column began to crawl toward Monmouth Court House, nineteen miles away, the brassy sun sending the temperature soaring to 100 degrees. A number of the soldiers, still in heavy uniforms, fell dead of heatstroke. On the night of June 26 they bivouacked at Monmouth Court House; a heavy thunderstorm that night coupled with the sheer exhaustion of the men made it inadvisable to march farther until they were rested.[9]

Had they not been so tragic, the events occurring in the American army on June 25 might have been termed comic. Washington, leaving his heavy baggage at Hopewell, moved up to Rocky Hill and Kingston. Unhappy with the previous advice of his generals, he detached the Pennsylvania troops of Anthony Wayne and Enoch Poor's New Hampshire Brigade to join the forces of Scott, Maxwell, Morgan, and Dickinson. The senior brigadier general of the troops acting on the flanks and rear of the enemy was William Maxwell, a man whose military abilities were not admired by all. His reputation had been declining since Brandywine when "we had opportunities and anybody but an old woman would [have] availed themselves of them—He is sure to be a damned bitch of a General. . . ." This attitude, coupled with the fact that the advance force needed a unified command, led Washington to attempt to persuade Charles Lee to take over the operation. Lee, in his most pompous style, declined, reasoning that such a command was "a more proper business of a young, volunteering general, than of the second in command of the army. . . ." Washington immediately assigned the post to the Marquis de Lafayette, who was delighted. When Lee discovered that Lafayette's command was to be composed of almost half the army he changed his mind and demanded that he be given the position. It was, however, agreed that Lafayette should be allowed the honor of making the first contact.[10]

That night the army marched to Cranbury. The next day, June

9. Fitzpatrick, *Writings of Washington*, XII, 114–15, André, *Major André's Journal*, pp. 77–78; Diary of James McHenry, William L. Clements Library, University of Michigan, Ann Arbor, Mich.; Freeman, *George Washington*, V, 22n. The fact that Patten's Second North Carolina was with Scott is found in the Table of Organization in Samuel Stelle Smith's *The Battle of Monmouth* (Monmouth Beach, N.J., 1964), p. 28. Smith arrived at this conclusion by studying the testimony at Lee's court martial, for Lee kept no field returns on the day of the battle.

10. Fitzpatrick, *Writings of Washington*, XII, 110, 120, 140; *Lee Papers*, II, 417; Freeman, *George Washington*, IV, 535n.

26, was miserable; after a morning of steaming heat, the troops were subjected to "a very great gust of rain" in the afternoon. At five the following morning, Saturday, June 27, the Americans marched six miles up the road toward Englishtown and pitched camp. The soldiers busied themselves in twisting branches from trees to build "booths" to protect themselves from the blistering sun. Each man was issued forty rounds of ammunition and ordered to check his firearm.[11]

Back from the advance group came word from Lafayette that Lee was showing no inclination to attack the enemy the following day, although reconnaissance indicated that the enemy was in a vulnerable position. Washington decided that it was now or never. Lee was ordered to begin the attack the minute the enemy renewed his march, although that eccentric fellow seemed reluctant to press the British for fear they would turn and strike back.[12]

On the morning of June 28, Steuben and Colonel John Laurens reconnoitered the enemy position and discovered that the British were moving out, with the second column under Cornwallis just beginning their march. Washington dispatched orders for Lee to attack. Philemon Dickinson's militia was already skirmishing with the enemy as Lee moved up. Despite the confusing orders of Lee, something of a ragged battle line was formed with Lafayette on the right, Wayne in the center and Scott and the North Carolina regiments on the left. Scott's command aided in repulsing a charge by enemy cavalry on one of the advance units, but when units on the right started falling back and neither he nor Lafayette could get additional orders from Lee, he was forced to order his own troops to file off rather than be outflanked.[13]

Both Wayne and Scott felt that they had been in a most advantageous position and had been near "obtaining a most glorious and decisive victory." In general, there had been no concerted plan of attack and the troops scurrying aimlessly about resembled more an exercise in mass hysteria than an orderly movement of trained sol-

11. Martin, *Narrative of the Sufferings of a Revolutionary Soldier*, p. 91; *Historical Magazine*, XI (1867) 83; Friedrich Kapp, *The Life of Frederick William von Steuben, Major General in the Revolutionary War* (New York, 1859), p. 158; Fitzpatrick, *Writings of Washington*, XII, 124.

12. Diary of James McHenry; Gottschalk, *Lafayette Joins the American Army*, p. 52; Fitzpatrick, *Writings of Washington*, XII, 141–42; *Lee Papers*, III, 7.

13. Diary of James McHenry; *Pennsylvania Magazine of History and Biography*, II (1878), 140–42; Fitzpatrick, *Writings of Washington*, XII, 142; André, *Major Andre's Journal*, p. 79; *Magazine of American History*, III (1879), 355–56, 577; Josiah Quincy (ed.), *Journal of Major Samuel Shaw, First American Consul at Canton* (Boston, 1847), p. 46.

diers. Lee compounded confusion by issuing orders without informing subordinates of his intentions. Under the protection of his artillery, Clinton began to bring up his heavy columns, or so it was
reported to Lee. Some troops began to fall back, and when it appeared that undue pressure might be brought upon Scott's position
a general withdrawal was ordered. Yet when Washington's aide rode
forward to determine why Lee was not pressing the attack, the answer
was, "Tell the General I am doing well enough." Lafayette displayed
near genius in the ambuscades he planned in covering the retreat,
disputing every inch of ground with the Guards and Grenadiers,
whose several bayonet charges failed to turn the retreat into a rout.[14]

Washington, earlier that sultry Sunday morning, had pulled in
his outlying detachments and at eight had begun his march toward
Englishtown, five miles away. The dull thunder of artillery could
be heard in the distance. The men were ordered to lay aside their
knapsacks and blankets and push on. They were past Englishtown and
within two and a half miles of the courthouse when Lee's command
suddenly came pouring back upon them. There was confusion as the
two groups came together, but Washington and his officers managed
to form them into some semblance of a battle line. Coming up with
Lee, Washington demanded the reasons for the retreat. Some said that
Lee stammered a bit as he replied. "Sir, these troops are not able to
meet British Grenadiers." "Sir," cried the seething Washington, "they
are able, and by God they shall do it." Others said that when Lee
attempted to explain his actions, he was cut off with, "All this may be
very true, Sir, but you ought not to have undertaken it unless you
intended to go through with it." Lee himself admitted that Washington used "very singular expressions" upon this occasion.[15]

Lee requested, and received, permission to direct the holding
force that would give Washington time to consolidate his position.
He performed this task with skill and courage. In the center, out in
front of the main battle line, Wayne's men under Walter Stewart
along with the Third Maryland under Nathaniel Ramsey had taken
a position in an orchard beside a road that ran between two hills.
Lieutenant Colonel Jeremiah Olney came forward with his Rhode

14. Anthony Wayne to his wife, 1 July 1778, Anthony Wayne Papers; *Lee
Papers*, II, 438, III, 180–84; *Magazine of American History*, III (1879), 355–56,
577.

15. *Historical Magazine*, XI (1867), 83; *Magazine of American History*, III
(1879), 83; Thomas W. Balch (ed.), *Papers Relating Chiefly to the Maryland Line
During the Revolution* (Philadelphia, 1857), pp. 103–4; Henry J. Johnston (ed.),
Memoirs of Colonel Benjamin Tallmadge (New York, 1904), p. 40; *Lee Papers*, II,
435, III, 191–92.

Island detachment and two pieces of artillery. Together they fought off the early series of attacks by the British light horse and Grenadiers. Throughout the area, or so a British account ran, there was "scarce a bush that had not a fellow under it." To the rear, Washington, astride a new white horse, personally supervised the establishment of the principal line of resistance, constantly exhorting his men and exposing himself to the fire of the enemy. "He unfolded surprising abilities," said James McHenry, "which produced uncommon results." Steuben was invaluable in placing troops. His duties over, after supervising the holding force, Charles Lee rode off to round up the stragglers and did not return to the battle that day.[16]

Washington had formed his line behind Wayne's position on a rise on the west side of the ravine carved by a branch of Wemlock Brook. The regiments wheeled into line with a precision that reflected the months of training at Valley Forge. Washington commanded the center in person, Stirling was on the right, while Nathanael Greene was in command of the left flank. Lafayette was in charge of the reserve. In the final arrangement of the troops, Wayne remained in front of the center, his three regiments of Pennsylvania Continentals and one each from Maryland and Virginia posted in a barn and along a hedgerow that bordered the orchard. On the main line of defense a piece of open ground, protected by a morass, made it difficult for the enemy to turn the left flank, while the ravine and wood dictated any plan of attack on the right. Steuben was sent to the rear to collect the remnants of Lee's command who had fallen back along the Germantown road. Artillery stationed on each flank enfiladed British troops approaching the primary position. Wayne's troops fought fiercely, allowing Washington additional time in which to solidify his battle line.[17]

Clinton brought up his artillery and posted it on a hill across from Washington's lines. It was now eleven o'clock and the sun bore down with smoldering fury. The cannon of both armies began to bark at each other. The first major assault by the enemy was directed at

16. Alden, *General Charles Lee*, pp. 222–23; Diary of James McHenry; Wayne to his wife, 1 July 1778, Wayne Papers; *New York Gazette and Weekly Mercury*, 20 July 1778; *Pennsylvania Magazine of History and Biography*, III (1879), 355, 358; George Washington Custis, *Recollections and Private Memories of Washington* (New York, 1860), p. 220.

17. Diary of James McHenry; *Magazine of American History*, III (1879), 358–59; Kapp, *Life of Steuben*, p. 162; D. Griffith to "Hannah," 30 June 1778, Monmouth County, New Jersey, Historical Association; Laurens, *Correspondence of Colonel John Laurens*, p. 198.

Stirling's division on the right. The light infantry, the Forty-Second Foot, and the Black Watch pushed forward. As they moved through the open fields they were shelled from the left wing by Edward Carrington's First Regiment of Continental Artillery; at the time it was said to have been the "severest artillery fire ever heard in America." Washington's great white horse had died from the heat and exhaustion, and he now galloped along the lines on a chestnut mare, encouraging his men as they poured volley after volley into the advancing red line. When the First and Third New Hampshire and the First Virginia moved out through the thick woods on the left and "fell with great vigor" on the right flank of the enemy, the British fell back to regroup.[18]

The heat had drained a great deal from both sides, but the British, still dressed in heavy woolen uniforms, suffered more than the Americans. The next assault, led by Cornwallis in person, was directed at Greene's division on the right and was executed by the finest troops in the British army. Enfilading fire from the American artillery on Comb's Hill shredded their ranks. Greene's musketry blazed in a solid sheet of flame. Still the British pushed forward. Then, caught in artillery crossfire and faced with the concentrated musketry to the front, they once again retreated.[19]

At the same time that this attack was launched on Greene, the Light Infantry, Dragoons, and Grenadiers thrust at Wayne's position in front of the American lines. They came forward at a dog trot. From within the barn and from behind the hedgerow Wayne staggered them with a blast of sudden fire. They stumbled back. After reforming, they drove forward once again. Once again Wayne held his fire until they were nearly upon him and sent them reeling backwards. After the passage of an hour, the British reformed for another try, now only five hundred feet from the American forward positions. Wayne's men could hear Lieutenant Colonel Henry Monckton encouraging his men. They dashed forward. Wayne held his order to fire until the enemy was within forty yards; his volley crumpled the ranks of the charging redcoats. The gallant Monckton fell so near the hedge fence that several of the bolder of Wayne's men leaped out and dragged in his body, along with the British colors. Once again

---

18. Stryker, *Battle of Monmouth*, pp. 209–10; Diary of James McHenry; André, *Major André's Journal*, p. 80; *Magazine of American History*, III (1879), 359; *Pennsylvania Archives*, 2nd Series, X, 317–18.

19. Diary of James McHenry; *Magazine of American History*, III (1879), 359–60.

the enemy formed. But it was now obvious that enough fresh troops were being brought up for Wayne's position to be flanked on both sides. Wayne withdrew to the American main line.[20]

The battle settled into a series of probing skirmishes, with the British artillery pounding away with monotonous regularity. Clinton now realized that he could no longer force his exhausted men into the field. It was nearly five o'clock in the afternoon. Washington sensed the opportunity for the victory that had so long eluded him. Steuben was ordered to bring up fresh troops to pursue the retreating enemy. William Woodford's Virginians were to drive around the British left flank while Enoch Poor with his own regiments and the North Carolina Brigade under Thomas Clark were to bear in from the right. The North Carolina regiments had been posted behind a creek near Englishtown and did not come forward quickly, for, like the rest of the army on that hot day, they were "beat out with heat and fatigue." They had advanced out beyond the front line when darkness fell and the fire on both sides gradually died away. "We remained looking at each other," wrote John Laurens, "with the defile between us, till dark. . . ." That night Washington slept on the lines, beneath a tree in an orchard, wrapped in a cloak.[21]

The army lay on its arms that Sabbath night. Washington expected a renewal of the conflict in the morning, but around one o'clock in the morning of June 29 Clinton, taking advantage of the bright "Moon Shine," slipped away and resumed his march toward Sandy Hook. At dawn the Americans were in high spirits, but Washington decided not to pursue Clinton. It was another hot day, the roads ahead were sandy, the troops were weary, and the militiamen seemed determined to return home to cultivate their crops. Daniel Morgan, who never seemed to tire, was sent, along with the Dragoons of Stephen Moylan, to harass the flanks and rear of the British as they plodded toward the Hudson. From sunrise on deserters, especially from the Hessian regiments, flowed in a steady stream into the American lines. Estimates were that the British dead, wounded, prisoners, and deserters amounted to between 1,000 and 1,500 men. Burial de-

20. Diary of James McHenry; *Magazine of American History*, III (1879), 358–59; *Pennsylvania Archives*, 2nd Series, X, 317–18; Wayne to his wife, 1 July 1778, Wayne Papers; Stryker, *Battle of Monmouth*, pp. 215–18; Fitzpatrick, *Writings of Washington*, XII, 145.

21. *Lee Papers*, III, 96; Lloyd A. Brown and Howard Peckham (eds.), *Revolutionary War Journals of Henry Dearborn* (Chicago, 1939), p. 128; Lafayette, *Memoirs*, p. 54; Laurens, *Correspondence of Colonel John Laurens*, p. 198; *Magazine of American History*, III (1879), 359, 570; *New York Journal*, 13 July 1778; Clinton to Germain, Sir Henry Clinton Papers; Fitzpatrick, *Writings of Washington*, XII, 139–46.

tails stacked the British dead in piles on the battlefields before rolling them into the mass graves prepared for them. Lieutenant Colonel Monckton was buried with the full honors of war as befitting a brave officer. Washington lost 61 killed, 162 wounded, and 130 missing. Actual British battlefield casualties closely paralleled those of the Americans, but the enemy had lost more through heat and fatigue. The only two casualties suffered by the North Carolina Brigade were Sergeant Stephen White of the First Regiment and Private Willie Upton of the Second, both dead of fatigue.[22]

Although the jubilant Americans boasted, "Victory Declared for us, the British Courage failed and was forced to give place to American Valour," the Battle of Monmouth was more a drawn contest than a victory for either side. Victory or not, Washington had no intention of celebrating. On June 29 he marched his army back to Englishtown where James McHenry noted in his diary, "the soil very sandy—water very scarce—drink the wells dry." There the army rested for two days and, despite the water shortage, the troops were ordered "to wash themselves . . . and appear as decent as possible," for the thanksgiving celebration to the "supreme Disposer of human Events for the Victory. . . ."[23]

On June 29 there began an interesting exchange of letters between Charles Lee and George Washington. Since the battle Lee had been asserting that he deserved great praise for his masterful retrograde maneuver at Monmouth Court House. His letter, received by Washington on July 1, contained expressions of outraged dignity and confidently declared that he could justify his battlefield actions "to the Army, to the Congress, to America, and to the world in general." He boasted that the success of the day at Monmouth was owing entirely to his judicious disposition of troops. He accused the commander in chief of "cruel injustice" and suggested that he had fallen under the influence of "dirty earwigs who will forever insinuate themselves around persons of high office."[24]

That same day Anthony Wayne and Charles Scott felt called upon to write Washington, charging Lee with failure to exercise the

22. Diary of James McHenry; *Historical Magazine*, XI (1867), 83; Fitzpatrick, *Writings of Washington*, XII, 128, 144, 128–30; Quincy, *Journals of Major Samuel Shaw*, p. 48; Wayne to his wife, 1 July 1778, Wayne Papers; Johnston, *Memoirs of Colonel Benjamin Tallmadge*, p. 41; Stillé, *Anthony Wayne and the Pennsylvania Line*, pp. 153–54; *Southern Literary Messenger*, XXVIII (1859), 299; *Pennsylvania Archives*, 2nd Series, X, 317–18.

23. Wayne to his wife, 1 July 1778, Anthony Wayne Papers; Diary of James McHenry; Fitzpatrick, *Writings of Washington*, XII, 131.

24. *Lee Papers*, II, 435–70; Fitzpatrick, *Writings of Washington*, XII, 132–33.

command that could have brought victory. And when an angry Washington suggested that Lee justify his actions or be thought guilty of "making an unnecessary, disorderly and shameful retreat," Lee demanded a court-martial. Thomas Clark was one of the members of the board which sat with Lord Stirling as president. Lee was to be found guilty of misbehavior on the battlefield and for disrespect to the commander in chief. His sentence of suspension from the army for twelve months was sent to the Continental Congress for approval. Later Lee, unable to contain his paranoiac tendencies, dispatched an insulting letter to the Congress that led that body to close the issue with a resolve that there was "no further occasion for his services in the army of the United States."[25]

On June 30, the first divisions of the army began to march northward. There was no longer any intention of pursuing Clinton. By the time Washington could catch up with the British, they would be boarding the transports waiting to take them over to New York. At Sandy Hook the terrain was so flat and devoid of cover that the guns of the fleet could cover the embarkation. So Washington marched for the Hudson highlands, from where he could cover the New England states, which some felt would be the next objective of the enemy. And New York might become vulnerable should Clinton weaken the garrison to make a strike elsewhere. By July 1 the Americans had crossed the Raritan at New Brunswick. The temperature still hung in the high ranges and Washington was led to complain that the march had been "distressing"; the army had had to travel through "about twenty miles of deep sand, without a drop of water, except at South River...."[26]

At New Brunswick the troops celebrated the anniversary of the Declaration of Independence with the customary thirteen-gun salute, *feu de joie*, and cheering, a spectacle James McHenry described as "a beautiful exhibition." The North Carolina Continentals had been assigned to Steuben's division. During the early morning hours of July 5 the troops were paraded in column. When the rear of the division was ready to march a drum began to beat; when it was answered by another drum from the front of the column the army began its march. Despite such martial display, it was not an orderly movement. Some of the rank and file, and even some officers, too often slipped out from

25. *Lee Papers*, II, 435–40; Fitzpatrick, *Writings of Washington*, XII, 132–33; Ford, *Journals of the Continental Congress*, XVI, 33; *Magazine of American History*, III (1879), 360.
26. Diary of James McHenry; D. Griffith to "Hannah," 30 June 1778, Monmouth County, New Jersey, Historical Association; Fitzpatrick, *Writings of Washington*, XII, 145, 150.

the ranks to plunder houses and orchards alongside the road. By July 9 the army was passing through Newark and on July 11 had bivouacked at Paramus, a small Dutch settlement in the rugged hills north of Passaic. Then, by leisurely moves, with the army resting every third day, Washington crossed over the Hudson and made camp at White Plains. The general derived great pleasure from the fact that the two armies had returned to almost the same positions they had occupied two years earlier, for "the offending party in the beginning is now reduced to the use of the pick and spade for defence."[27]

Now the French alliance became evident for the first time, since Vice Admiral Comte d'Estaing had arrived with twelve ships of the line, four frigates, and four thousand crack French troops. The admiral lay off Sandy Hook, but no pilots could be persuaded to guide his deep-draught ships across the bar to attack the British naval vessels in the harbor in coordination with an American attack from the land side. So, sailing away to Newport, Rhode Island, d'Estaing participated in a joint attack with the Americans under Major General John Sullivan against the British garrison stationed there. It was an abortive affair, with the French behaving in such a fashion as to shake the very foundations of the alliance itself.[28]

Washington fretted in his camp at White Plains, waiting for Sir Henry Clinton's next move. There was no way for him to know that the future course of British strategy had been changed by the entrance of France into the war. Not only were there British possessions in the Caribbean to be protected, but French sugar islands to be taken. And on the continent the Southern colonies, with their subtropical products fitted much better into the scheme of British mercantilism than did the commercially minded northern areas. New York was to be held, but not at the expense of more desirable British possessions. Washington waited for Clinton to inaugurate a major operation, but had to settle for no more than a series of teasing skirmishes.[29]

The camp at White Plains became a model of routine. On July 22, 1778, the army had been rearranged into right and left wings with a second line. The North Carolina Brigade was placed in the second wing under the command of Major General Alexander McDougall. Sheer boredom made the soldiers restless, so much so that all units were assembled twice a day for roll call to prevent the men from wan-

27. Brown and Peckham, *Revolutionary War Journals of Henry Dearborn*, p. 130; Diary of James McHenry; Carlos E. Godfrey, *The Commander-in-Chief's Guard, Revolutionary War* (Washington, 1904), p. 280; Fitzpatrick, *Writings of Washington*, XII, 154, 343; Jacob Turner Orderly Book.
28. Ward, *War of the Revolution*, II, 587-93.
29. *Journal of Modern History*, XIX (1947), 111-13.

dering off. Enlistments in the North Carolina regiments began to expire and few of the men were willing to re-enlist unless it was agreed that they would be furloughed and allowed to return home during the winter months. Troops were drilled four hours a day and when on duty were required "to come off with Clean hands and faces, hair combed and powdered, and are to appear in all respects as decent and Soldier-like as circumstances will permit." Arms were checked, the camp was constantly policed. Tempers grew short and there was an increase in the number of courts-martial. Some seven privates of the First Regiment were sentenced to one hundred lashes each for plundering and one, Thomas Glover, was condemned to be hanged. Lieutenant Levi Gatlin of Patten's Second North Carolina was dismissed from the service upon his conviction for "Neglect of Duty and disobedience of orders." Enlisted men experienced the usual lashings for smiliar offenses. And Lieutenant James Verrier, adjutant of the Third Regiment, was tried for "Cruelly and unnecessarily beating the Fife Major of the same Regiment while in the execution of his duty." Verrier was found guilty of beating the man, but "not cruelly."[30]

In September, the army was once again rearranged with Putnam, Gates, Stirling, de Kalb, and McDougall each commanding a division. It was generally felt that the enemy would soon be forced to leave New York: Thomas Clark chuckled, "They are like wandering Israelites, equally cursed by their maker; this Campaign, I think, will deprive them of any foot hold in America." That part of the North Carolina Brigade then in camp was sent under de Kalb to Fredericksburg (present-day Patterson, New York) where the headquarters of the army had been located. Putnam was detached to West Point, Gates and McDougall to Danbury, Connecticut, and Stirling to a point between Fredericksburg and New York. After inoculation for smallpox at Carlisle, Pennsylvania, James Hogun arrived with his newly raised Seventh Regiment from North Carolina, made up of over five hundred nine-months men drafted from the militia. Under his command were the newly completed mounted troops of Cosmo Medici. Hogun had marched within six miles of Fredericksburg when, to his great "Mortification," he was ordered to West Point where his command was placed on work detail. He didn't like the place, describing it as "disagreeably situated" between the river and the rock-studded mountains. Hogun disliked the idea of building fortifications, he disliked the idea of living in tents through the winter months, he was unhappy because Washington had ordered him to

30. Jacob Turner Orderly Book; Fitzpatrick, *Writings of Washington*, XII, 358, 415, XIII, 137–38, 145.

the army before his men had been fully inoculated against smallpox, and he complained that the new arrangement of the army was "a little mysterious." Hogun actually had little reason to grumble, for his men were too poorly armed to be considered a combat unit; Washington had to procure four hundred muskets for them from Albany. And most of the weapons that had been brought from North Carolina were in such poor repair that they could not be used in battle.[31]

In October there was a clothing windfall when a large shipment of uniforms arrived from France. The waistcoats and breeches were all alike, and although all of the coats were faced in red, some were blue while others were brown. Inasmuch as all troops with the main army clamored for the blue coats, they were assigned to the different states by lots. On the first drawing, North Carolina, Maryland, New York, and New Jersey drew the blue. When a large number of blue coats remained after the initial issuance, a second drawing was held, whereby the Massachusetts, Virginia, and Delaware Lines were also issued the preferred color. The main army, at least until the new issue wore out, was now to present some semblance of a uniformed force.[32]

And winter was coming.

31. Elizabeth Steele to Ephraim Steele, 17 October 1778, John Steele Papers, North Carolina Department of Archives and History, Raleigh, N.C.; Fitzpatrick, *Writings of Washington*, XII, 403, 409, 422, XV, 234-35, 176, 195, 202, 210, 213, 221, 225; *State Records*, XIII, 470-71, 478, 488, XIV, 15-16; _____ to Caswell, 9 July 1778, Caswell Papers, N.C. Dept. Arch. & Hist.

32. Fitzpatrick, *Writings of Washington*, XIII, 173, 173n, 353, XIV, 184.

Chapter 8
Stony Point and the Hudson

". . . perpetual and galling fire. . . ."

Cold winds sweeping up the Hudson brought the first bite of winter. In November the American Army went into winter quarters. The troops were strategically placed, not only in areas where provisions were likely to be more plentiful but in positions where they could block possible moves by the enemy. With Washington's headquarters at Middlebrook, other posts were estabilshed at Elizabeth and Ramapo, New Jersey; West Point and Fishkill, New York; and Danbury, Connecticut. This great semicircle, drawn in a forty-mile radius around New York, not only protected the more vital areas in the highlands, but also kept open the routes of communications with New England. Mounted troops operated in the intervals, not only scouting the enemy, but foraging over a large area. Hogun's Seventh Regiment still labored on the fortifications at West Point. Until early December, 1778, Thomas Clark and his regiments had been stationed at Smith's Clove where Clark had been responsible for sending out detachments to guard the mountain passes. On December 11 they moved to Paramus, where their chief function was blocking communications between the inhabitants of that area and the British in New York. They also took in British deserters, who were beginning to come from New

York in increasing numbers. Clark attempted to hold a taut rein over his troops and went so far as to assure Washington, "I will take care that the Soldiers do not burn the fences or commit any disorderly acts." Some of the sufferings of the North Carolina troops were explained when Nathan Nuthall, quartermaster to the Third Regiment, was found guilty not only of "behaving in an infamous manner unbecoming an Officer and a Gentleman," but also for embezzling stores and "applying them to his own use."[1]

Major General Benedict Arnold, commandant at Philadelphia, requested Washington to send him a regiment or two of Continentals to guard the stores and perform the necessary garrison duties in that city. The local militia, said Arnold, complained bitterly of being turned out just to perform military routine. Possibly because Hogun's regiment was made up of short enlistment troops, Washington selected them for this duty. As he explained it, "They are a tender set of people, but illy provided with Cloathing and therefore require warm quarters." He also suggested to Hogun that he collect all convalescents with him. On December 13 Washington wrote Arnold that he was detaching the Seventh North Carolina to Philadelphia, which was "as much as I can with propriety spare." Lieutenant Colonel William Lee Davidson was ordered to leave early, marching by way of Trenton where he was to leave a captain and fifty men to guard the magazine of stores at that place.[2]

Leaving his sick behind him, Hogun withdrew from the Hudson sometime after the middle of December and arrived in Philadelphia shortly before January 19, 1779. The rough march through bitter cold was somewhat compensated for by the barracks that were available in the Pennsylvania city. The North Carolina delegates to the Continental Congress were burdened with the task of procuring warm clothing for these troops inasmuch as they were to be in Continental service for such a short period. Hogun was to be held responsible for and the state of North Carolina charged for all supplies issued from Continental stores, except those that could be spared "without detriment to the service. . . ." It was hard duty in Philadelphia. Most of the enlistments were to expire on April 20, and with one company stationed at Trenton and a daily duty roster of 82 to be drawn from only

1. Greene to Washington, 27 October 1778, Joseph Reed Papers; Fitzpatrick, *Writings of Washington,* XIII, 75–76, 82–83, 85–87, 115–16, 183, 350–52; Francis Vinton Greene, *The Revolutionary War and the Military Policy of the United States* (New York, 1911), pp. 155–56; Thomas Clark to Washington, 18 December 1778, George Washington Papers.

2. Fitzpatrick, *Writings of Washington,* XII, 371–73, 392–93, 436; Washington to Davidson, 19 December 1778, George Washington Papers.

165 rank and file, some of the men had to pull double duty. In fact, by April 23, 1779, Lieutenant Colonel Davidson was in command of a company whose entire complement was 2 lieutenants, 6 sergeants, and 26 rank and file. In like manner Cosmo Medici's company of light horse was having so much difficulty finding adequate mounts that the troop was ordered disbanded in January, 1779. After Benedict Arnold's resignation as commandant of Philadelphia in March, 1779, Hogun held that post until November 22, 1779.[3]

The winter of 1778–79 was severe, but nothing like the desperate hours spent at Valley Forge. Clark's force had been ordered to Smith's Clove to defend that pass and render aid to West Point if necessary. The primary reason for this station, however, was that the Convention troops taken at Saratoga were being marched to a camp in Virginia and Washington wanted a force between them and the British in New York. After the prisoners of war had passed, Clark was ordered to Paramus to protect American lines of communication. To the eastward, Robert Mebane was stationed with two hundred men at King's Ferry to cut enemy supply lines into New York city and stand ready to lend assistance to West Point or any other post in the highlands. Clark's command was not sufficiently strong to repel a British thrust in strength, but it was felt that he could act as a holding force until help arrived.[4]

Once again the soldiers built huts, but their pace was leisurely and their tents provided adequate protection during the early part of the winter. The weather, according to Surgeon James Thacher, was "remarkably mild and temperate," though the men did suffer from the severe storms that accompanied each cold front that pushed through. Although the soldiers were warmly clad, there was a critical shortage of shoes and blankets, and Washington feared that his army would soon be barefoot. Summer or winter, there was always an insufficiency of food. The Continental currency was so depreciated that the general was to write that "a waggon of money will scarcely purchase a waggon load of provisions." Even then, grumbled Nathanael Greene, the Congress was so parsimonious with its appropriations that the amounts were "no more equal to our wants than a sprat in a

3. *State Records*, XIV, 15–16, 290, 294; Burnett, *Letters of Members of the Continental Congress*, III, 547; Ford, *Journals of the Continental Congress*, XIII, 15, 337, XV, 355–56; Washington to Alexander MacDougall, 7 December 1778, Washington to Lafayette, 3 July 1778, George Washington Papers; Roll of Lt. Col. Davidson's Co., 23 April 1779, Revolutionary War Rolls, Adjutant-General's Office.
4. Fitzpatrick, *Writings of Washington*, XIII, 282–83, 330, 346, 362–63, 367–68, 437, 466–67, 489.

whale's belly." At Paramus, Clark's men fared better than most of the army for they were billeted in houses. A number of enlistments expired in the North Carolina Line. Clark, using his powers of persuasion and paying the usual enlistment bounty, paid out $19,840 to eighty-one men in the First Regiment and eighty-three in the Second. Each of those who re-enlisted was paid an average of $121.[5]

The Third North Carolina Regiment under Lieutenant Colonel Robert Mebane was moved down with Washington at Middlebrook. The regiment was fast disintegrating because of the expiration of enlistments. In March there had been 400 rank and file, but even then there were only 20 in camp fit for duty. Fifty-five of the total number, however, were on detached duty, while reports indicated that there were "Sick Present," 178; sick absent, 29; and recovering from inoculation, 110. By August, 1779, there were only 171 rank and file in the entire regiment. By the middle of April the Continental Board of War ordered Mebane to return the Third Regiment to North Carolina, including all those whose enlistments had some time to go, with the hope that they could be used as a nucleus in bringing the regiment up to full strength. The officers of the Third were loud in their complaints that the state of North Carolina had forgotten them, and addressed petitions to the General Assembly for relief.[6]

On January 9, 1779, North Carolina finally got the two brigadier generals for which it had been clamoring so long. Washington had also urged that the state be given at least one officer of general rank to command the North Carolina Brigade, which Thomas Clark still commanded as a colonel. Although Clark's and Sumner's names had been placed in nomination before the Continental Congress on February 10, 1778, and again on December 29, that body preferred to wait until the other states had indicated their preferences for promotions so that the business could be disposed of at one time. There seemed to be little or no objection to the forty-five-year-old Sumner, termed four years earlier a man of "violent principles" in politics, but "a person lusty, rather handsome, with an easy and genteel address." Clark was the youngest colonel in line for promotion, yet he had much going for him. Although it was generally agreed that his elevation to general's rank might bring about resignations in the line, one

5. James Thacher, *Military Journal of the American Revolution* (Hartford, Conn., 1862), Fitzpatrick, *Writings of Washington*, XIII, 376–77, 445–46; Greene to Charles Pettit, 2 January 1779, Nathanael Greene Papers; Clark to Washington, 17 March 1779, George Washington Papers.

6. *State Records*, XIV, 70, 80, 89–90, 292–93; Returns of the Third Regiment, 16 August 1779, Troop Returns, Military Collection; Order, Continental Board of War, 17 April 1779, Governors' Papers.

unidentified member of the North Carolina General Assembly countered with, "I wish to God many of them would resign, for, between
ourselves, they are a sorry set of fellows." Not only was Colonel Clark
a stern disciplinarian but "at the same time, by constant attention to
the wants of the soldiers, and a singular humanity in relieving them,
is beloved by the whole army." Seniority, it was argued, should give
way to merit.[7]

Although he had told Harnett that he would not oppose the
nomination, Thomas Burke was the greatest hurdle in Clark's path
to promotion. Burke had talked with "a gentleman, who came immediately through the camp," and from him had learned that the
recommendation of Clark for promotion to brigadier general had led
to "great uneasiness" in that it violated the principles of military
seniority, and was considered by many of the officers of the North
Carolina units "as a violence to military rank and honor, and by all
resented." As a result of this information, Burke seemed determined
to block Clark's nomination. The North Carolina delegation proceed-
ed to inform the Congress of the seniority in the North Carolina Line.
The name of James Hogun was placed in nomination, but not by the
delegates of the state—apparently Burke persuaded some other member of the Congress to do that. Honest John Penn, who seldom spoke
in Congress, argued that the Congress should follow instructions from
the General Assembly, but Burke was the better talker. Burke admitted that it had not been Clark's fault that he had been unable to distinguish himself at Germantown, being "restrained by Superior Authority." Yet Hogun did have a chance in that battle and "behaved
with distinguished intrepidity." Hogun, he noted, also had seniority
in rank. Although Burke did vote for Clark as the delegates had been
instructed, Hogun's seniority won out over Clark's popularity with
the state legislature. Perhaps Clark's chances were lessened because
his brother-in-law, William Hooper, was no longer a member of the
Congressional delegation. With each state casting one ballot for each
position, the final vote was Sumner, 13; Hogun, 9; and Clark, 4. Clark,
who had every right to expect the promotion and seemingly deserved
the rank, swallowed his pride and remained in the field.[8]

7. Burke to Caswell, 10 January 1779, Governors' Papers; Burnett, *Letters
of Members of the Continental Congress*, III, 148, IV, 20; Fitzpatrick, *Writings of
Washington*, XII, 120, 275; McRee, *Life and Correspondence of James Iredell*, I,
394n; Ford, *Journals of the Continental Congress*, X, 142; Member of General
Assembly to Burke, n.d., Thomas Burke Papers; J. F. D. Smyth, *A Tour in the
United States of America* (Dublin, 1784), pp. 70–71.

8. George W. Connor (ed.), *Autobiography of Benjamin Rush* (Princeton,
N.J., 1948), p. 153; Burnett, *Letters of Members of the Continental Congress*, IV,

Although it was guessed that Clinton would make no major move, there was fear that he would sally forth against a single encampment and crush it before help could arrive. There were a number of transports swaying at their anchors in New York harbor, suggesting that the next British move would be in some more distant field. Clinton kept the Americans along the Hudson off balance by several raids on river towns. Upon one occasion Washington came up to Paramus after the enemy had landed and set fire to a few small buildings near the river. But Clinton made no significant moves until warmer weather.[9]

Washington's greatest fear had been a strong move against West Point. Clark had been stationed in such a position that he was able to furnish support to several stations. Smaller detachments were scattered throughout the area to block communications with New York. The basic defense of the highlands had been left to Major General Alexander McDougall and five regiments in addition to the two North Carolina regiments under Clark. And it was Clark's First and Second North Carolina Regiments that received the first spring thrust by the British. On May 16, 1779, two columns of five hundred redcoats each crossed the river and attempted to close in on Clark. Clark sent a captain's command of light infantry and a few militia to hang on their flanks to "prevent pillaging." On a personal reconnaissance Clark discovered that the enemy had changed direction and was now marching for New Bridge. The militia came pouring in. That night the North Carolina Continentals and the local militia slept on their arms. From the several deserters who came in, Clark learned that his troops had been the objective of the two columns that were to converge on him at Paramus Church. One group had missed its landing place while the other had lost its way. After rounding up all the cattle and plundering several houses, the enemy fell back across the river. Clark's only casualties were three men wounded in the several skirmishes along the enemy's line of march.[10]

The first formal defenses of the Hudson River lay at the small unfinished fort on Stony Point and across the river on the east side, on

---

30–31, 34; Ford, *Journals of the Continental Congress*, XII, 1260, XIII, 46; John Penn to Jethro Sumner, 16 January 1779, Emmett Collection.

9. Greene to John Hancock, 20 December 1778, *American Historical Record*, II (1873), 513–14; Fitzpatrick, *Writings of Washington*, XIII, 370–71, XIV, 119, 168, 254n; Washington to Clark, 4 December 1778, Washington to Clark, 7 December 1778, Washington to Clark, 9 December 1778, Washington to Clark, 21 December 1778, Clark to Washington, 6 December 1778, Clark to Washington, 18 December 1778, George Washington Papers.

10. Clark to Washington, 17 May 1779, George Washington Papers; Fitzpatrick, *Writings of Washington*, XIV, 190–91, 396–97, XV, 94.

Verplanck's Point, the small detached post called Fort Lafayette. The latter was garrisoned by Captain Thomas Armstrong and seventy North Carolina Continentals, remnants of the Second and Fifth Regiments. On May 31, Clark sighted a large force of British on the river, but he could no more than observe their movements. Six thousand British troops disembarked from a fleet of 70 ships and 150 flat-bottomed boats on both sides of the river. Neither fort had much of a chance. The garrison at Stony Point fell without resistance, its forty men burning the log blockhouse and fleeing before the enemy. The North Carolinians in Fort Lafayette were more stubborn. The fort was not a particularly strong structure, but it had been palisaded and was surrounded by a double moat and an abatis. It may have been able to withstand an infantry assault, but was vulnerable to artillery bombardment. British troops kept up a steady fire on the land side, while the ships in the river lobbed shot after shot into the enclosure. After the fall of Stony Point the enemy turned its full force upon Fort Lafayette. The fort surrendered, with Clinton allowing the officers to march out wearing their side arms, an honor accorded them in admiration of their stubborn resistance.[11]

The forts had not been that important to Clinton; his primary objective had been to entice Washington out into the open and crush the American army. But when Washington refused to take the bait, Clinton strengthened the works, placed a rather heavy garrison in each and sailed back down the river. To Washington, the most vexatious thing about the loss of Stony Point, other than the blow to his pride, was that it prevented the Americans from making use of King's Ferry. The general moved his headquarters down to Smith's Clove to better study the situation. Although at first Washington felt that "an attempt to dislodge them . . . would require a greater force and apparatus than we are masters of," he soon began to feel that retaking the forts was not an impossible task.[12]

The day after Clinton sailed downriver, Washington suggested to Anthony Wayne that he get a spy into Stony Point. Allan McLane,

---

11. Stephen Kemble, *Kemble Journals, 1773–1789: Collections of the New-York Historical Society for 1883* (New York, 1884), I, 179; Fitzpatrick, *Writings of Washington*, XV, 176, 195, 202, 208, 210, 213, 221, 223, 225, 234–35; W. H. Smith (ed.), *The St. Clair Papers: The Life and Public Services of Arthur St. Clair* (Cincinnati, Ohio, 1882), I, 472; Clark to Washington, 31 May 1779, George Washington Papers; *State Records*, XIV, 158–159; C. M. Lawrence to Sumner, 29 August 1782, Jethro Sumner Papers, Southern Historical Collection.

12. Clinton to Germain, 5 July 1779, Sir Henry Clinton Papers; Fitzpatrick, *Writings of Washington*, XV, 260, 261, 280, 292, 313; Archibald Robertson, *Diaries and Sketches in America* (New York, 1930), p. 196; Kemble, *Kemble Journal*, I, 179.

of Delaware, after slipping into the fort in disguise, reported that several of the batteries were incomplete and this, together with other weak points, would allow the fort to be retaken. Washington personally reconnoitered the vicinity of Stony Point, while mounted patrols were sent on a reconnaissance to spy out the various approaches.[13]

Wayne was assigned the task of retaking the post. Recently, in late June, he had been given command of the brigade of light infantry, composed of four regiments of two battalions each, in all a force numbering about 1,350. When Wayne had been given the appointment, Daniel Morgan, who was probably fitted better for the post, resigned from the army in bitter protest. This elite corps had been drawn from the troops of every state. They were all combat veterans, twenty to thirty years old and ranging in height from five feet, five inches to five feet, nine inches tall. They had been subjected to rigorous training and were especially adept in the use of the bayonet. Included were two companies of 178 picked men from the North Carolina Continentals under the command of Major Hardy Murfree of the Second Regiment.[14]

It was not to be an easy task. For nearly half a mile along the west bank, Stony Point thrust itself up almost angrily, rising to a height of nearly 150 feet above the water that lapped three-fourths of its base. The sides toward the river presented a rugged, steep, and formidable prospect. To the west, or the shore side, the land dropped down in crazy pattern to the wide morass formed by the stream that ran from the northern to the southern base of the prominence. High tide made this swampy area a veritable lake that could be crossed only at a narrow causeway and a bridge—unless one chose to wade the treacherous marshy area.[15]

Wayne drew up his command on Sandy Beach, fifteen miles above Stony Point. It was near noon. A vain man, Wayne had insisted that his command be "well shaved and fresh powdered." The soldiers marched by a circuitous route, sometimes over rocky paths so narrow that it became necessary to walk in single file. At nearly eight-thirty that evening they halted in a defile about a mile and a half from

13. Ward, *Delaware Continentals*, pp. 295–96; Henry P. Johnston, *The Storming of Stony Point on the Hudson, Midnight, July 15, 1779; Its Importance in the Light of Unpublished Documents* (New York, 1900), pp. 62–63.

14. Wayne to Washington, 17 July 1779, George Washington Papers; Johnston, *Storming of Stony Point*, pp. 69–71; Fitzpatrick, *Writings of Washington*, XV, 283, 421; *American Historical Review*, XXXI (1926), 455; *State Records*, XIII, 487.

15. Johnston, *Storming of Stony Point*, pp. 83–84.

Stony Point. Here, for the first time, most of the men discovered what their objective was to be. As fast as the men came in they were formed into two columns. On the right were the regiments of Christian Febiger and Colonel Return Jonathan Meigs, followed by the battalion of Major William Hull. The Pennsylvanians of Colonel Richard Butler led the left column with Hardy Murfree's North Carolinians in the rear. Lieutenant Colonel François Fleury led a picked detachment of 150 men in advance of the right column; his mission was to send out small patrols to secure the sentries and tear away the abatis. Every man wore a bit of white paper in his hat identifying him as a friend. The principal reliance was to be upon the bayonet and all muskets were unloaded except in Murfree's command. In fact, if any soldier did attempt to fire his piece, Wayne's orders were that he should be put to death instantly by the nearest officer. To preserve the utmost secrecy, the inhabitants in the neighborhood were taken into custody and any dog who was so bold as to bark at the shadowy figures moving through the darkness was to be bayoneted.[16]

At eleven-thirty that evening, July 15, 1779, the columns moved out. It was high tide and the water was several feet deep as they began wading through the morass. When they reached the stream proper, the two columns diverged toward the north and south. Murfree's command peeled off and approached the fort from directly in front; once the attack began he was to deliver "a perpetual and galling fire," to mask the approach of the two primary columns. British sentries spied Wayne's men while they were still struggling through the morass. They gave the alarm and opened fire. Murfree's men pushed forward firing as they came. Musket balls and grape shot rained down upon them.[17]

Not another gun sounded, although some sources state that one soldier in the attacking columns fired his piece and was instantly run through by a nearby officer. The two assault columns rushed forward through the muck, across the solid ground to the line of abatis. Axmen swung at the fallen trees, cutting paths for those behind. As the muddy men poured through the gaps in the abatis, Murfree increased his fire. Wayne fell to the ground, his head creased by a musket ball. Ever mindful of the value of the dramatic, he cried out that his wound was fatal and begged his men to carry him within the walls of the fort to

16. Dawson, *Battles of the United States*, I, 523–24; *State Records*, XIV, 326–27; William Abbatt (ed.), *Memoirs of Major-General William Heath, by Himself* (New York, 1901), p. 193.

17. Dawson, *Battles of the United States*, I, 525; Johnston, *Storming of Stony Point*; H. B. Dawson, *The Assault on Stony Point* (Morrisiana, N.Y., 1863), pp. 47–48.

die. His troops, placing their wounded general on their shoulders, gave a mighty shout, then swept up and over the ramparts.[18]

In less than half an hour the entire fort was overrun. The two columns had driven the defenders into each other until they began to throw down their arms, huddling together as they cried for mercy. The artillery officers who accompanied Wayne rushed to the guns and turned them upon the British sloop *Vulture*, anchored offshore. The vessel slipped her cable and dropped downstream. A number of rounds were arched over toward the British in Fort Lafayette but seem to have done little harm, for the fire was not returned.[19]

British losses were heavy: 63 killed, over 70 wounded and 543 taken prisoner. The Americans lost only 15 killed and 83 wounded; among the severely wounded was Captain John Daves of the Carolinians. There was also valuable booty in the form of fifteen cannon and a cache of stores, which, added together, were appraised at a value of $180,655. This amount, on the suggestion of Wayne, was divided among the soldiers who had taken part in the affair. In his dispatches, Wayne praised Murfree for his "good conduct & intrepidity."[20]

Verplanck's Point and Fort Lafayette was the next objective. Major General Robert Howe was to be involved in this undertaking. He had been replaced as commanding general in the South by Benjamin Lincoln. It was generally supposed that he had been replaced because he had allowed the British to take Savannah, but there were more subtle reasons. The general's recall had been more political than usually suspected. As early as August 20, 1777, the South Carolina Assembly had passed a resolution questioning Howe's right to command in that state. The dispute with Christopher Gadsden continued with such acrimony that on August 30, 1778, Howe and Gadsden fought a duel, with both missing at eight paces. Joseph Hewes wrote that Howe's recall had been because of a "little ridiculous matter he has been concerned with in South Carolina, with regard to a female [which] has induced the Delegates of Georgia and South Carolina to desire his recall. Congress complied with their request, but do not intend to enter into the private amours of their Generals. I hope our friend (should the war continue) will have an opportunity of display-

18. George A. Billias (ed.), *George Washington's Generals* (New York, 1964), p. 274; Abbatt, *Memoirs of Major-General William Heath*, p. 223; Thacher, *Military Journal of the American Revolution*, p. 176.

19. Dawson, *Battles of the United States*, I, 525; Clinton to Germain, 5 October 1779, Sir Henry Clinton Papers.

20. Henry Johnson to Clinton, 24 July 1779, Clinton to Germain, 24 July 1779, Sir Henry Clinton Papers; Johnston, *Storming of Stony Point*, p. 87; *State Records*, XIV, viii, 337; Ford, *Journals of the Continental Congress*, XIV, 890.

ing his abilities (which Congress acknowledge) in the field of Mars, as well as of Venus." Howe had been with Washington's army since May 19, 1779, but had been incapacitated for over a month, suffering from injuries received in a fall.[21]

Howe was sent across the river to cooperate with Israel Putnam in the attempt to capture Verplanck's Point. The planning had been deplorable. Assuming that Howe would have sufficient artillery, Washington ordered him to concentrate heavy fire on Fort Lafayette, "beating the block House about their Ears." But, for some strange reason, few artillery pieces had been sent along; equally baffling was the absence of ammunition for those several guns that were available. There were no entrenching tools, no provisions, and no wagons to transport either had they been present. There was no question of taking the fort by storm for the engineer with the group, after an examination of the fortifications, declared such a bold venture to be "ineligible." On June 18 a small reinforcement of British soldiers were landed from the river. Shortly afterwards there was intelligence that a sizable enemy detachment was marching upriver to cut off the Americans from the land side. Howe felt that "Duty and Prudence enjoin me to avoid the Snare," and "that no time should be lost to effect a Retreat." Washington called off the siege.[22]

This meant the end for Robert Howe in future military plans. He was to hold relatively insignificant commands from this time on. Howe seemed to realize that his military career was fading fast. He wrote Washington: "Oh: My Dear General What a Soul Piercing Wound has the unexpected delay of Yesterday given to Dear Sir your very Respectful and truly affectionate. R Howe." Some cried that Robert Howe had missed a golden opportunity for glory through his procrastinations. Brigadier General William Irvine charged that Howe was "suspected by many for having a *talent* (at least on that occasion) of finding many supposed obstructions, and barely plausible pretences for his delay. . . ." Washington, however, vindicated Howe, blaming the misfortunes on several of his dispatches going astray and the lack of entrenching tools and proper artillery. And Verplanck's Point had not been that important in the general's plans. Feeling that Stony Point was not worth the force required to retain it, Washington had the cannon and supplies removed from that

21. Burnett, *Letters of Members of the Continental Congress*, III, 512; Richard Walsh (ed.), *The Writings of Christopher Gadsden, 1746–1805* (Columbia, S.C., 1966), pp. 124–25, 128, 135, 151; *State Records*, XV, 766–67.
22. Washington to Howe, 17 July 1779, Howe to Washington, 17 July 1779, Howe to Washington, 18 July 1779, George Washington Papers; Fitzpatrick, *Writings of Washington*, XV, 428, 429, 433–34; *State Records*, XIII, 304–5; Harnett to Caswell, 24 November 1779, Caswell Letterbook.

strongpoint and left it to be reoccupied by Sir Henry Clinton. He had managed to embarrass the enemy and had allowed Anthony Wayne to lay the groundwork for his own legend.[23]

Despite the glory of Stony Point and a similar exploit agains Paulus Hook by Henry Lee during the night of August 19, 1779, times were once again bad. The North Carolina troops were now stationed in the general vicinity of West Point in the division of Major General Alexander MacDougall. The majority of the men of the North Carolina Brigade were not particularly happy when they were stationed on Constitution Island near West Point. Eighty-four were once again detached to serve in the Light Infantry and once again were commanded by Hardy Murfree. Some of those who remained on the island spent their time in building and repairing fortifications, while others acted as watermen on the ferries of the neighborhood. Clothing was short and there appeared to be no relief before winter. "Many of our poor fellows," wrote General Irvine, "have been two years in service and never had a blanket to this day." Many troops were near naked. Provisions were still scarce and the bite of hunger gripped bellies more every day. A severe drought had so lowered the water level in so many mill ponds that it was difficult to get grain ground into flour. And the hard money of the British and agents for the French fleet was much preferred by the merchants and farmers to the depreciated currency of the Americans.[24]

By the middle of the summer of 1779 it had become obvious that the British were planning to make the southern states a major objective in coming campaigns. Southern legislatures began to clamor for the return of their state troops. At first the Continental Congress denied the requests on the grounds that such a move "would be attended with Consequences, fatal to their health, and such as must deprive the public of their Services everywhere, during this Campaign, if not forever." Yet when it was agreed that the southern troops would be sent home, they did not march immediately.[25]

Washington finally agreed that the North Carolina Continentals

23. Alexander MacDougall to Washington, n.d., Alexander MacDougall Papers; Reed, *Life and Correspondence of Joseph Reed*, II, 117; Howe to Washington, 18 July 1779, George Washington Papers; Fitzpatrick, *Writings of Washington*, XV, 439, 449; Howe to _____, 2 July 1779, Historical Society of Pennsylvania Collection.

24. Reed, *Life and Correspondence of Joseph Reed*, II, 128; Freeman, *George Washington*, V, 133; Clark to Washington, 12 July 1779, George Washington Papers; Fitzpatrick, *Writings of Washington*, XV, 436–37, 461–62, 502; XVI, 11, 432.

25. *State Records*, XIV, 101–2, 154, 129, 326; Caswell to Hogun, 26 May 1779, Caswell Letterbook; Ford, *Journals of the Continental Congress*, XVI, 1087–1193; *State Records*, XIV, 101–2, 154, 129, 326; Harnett to Burke, 9 October 1779, Thomas Burke Papers, Southern Historical Collection.

would perhaps be better used in the South, and although they had been ordered south on August 10, they did not begin to leave until September. The Carolina troops, perhaps because of their distance from home, seemed to be wanting for clothing more than any other state contingent. Congress decided that they should be dressed as uniformly as quickly as possible. The North Carolina, South Carolina, and Georgia Continentals were to wear blue coats, with blue button holes edged with lace or white tape. The buttons and linings of the coats were to be white. The officers of the brigade were so ragged and threadbare that the Continental Congress advanced the North Carolina Delegates $100,000 to clothe their officers.[26]

The Brigade had marched no farther than Trenton when the Continental Congress ordered them to wait there for further orders. When the situation in the South appeared to take a turn for the better, and Washington began planning a joint operation with the French, Hogun, who had assumed the command, was ordered to march his troops back to the main army. When the planned joint operations failed to materialize, the general went into winter quarters with his headquarters at Morristown. The North Carolina Continentals were first ordered to their old position at Paramus where, upon any movement by the enemy, they were to fall back to the mountain gorge near Suffern, New Jersey. Finally, on November 19, 1779, they were once again ordered south, the only reinforcements that Washington felt he could spare for Benjamin Lincoln. The brigade at this time consisted of 33 command and staff officers, 90 non-commissioned officers, and 705 rank and file. Murfree's light infantry men were returned to their regiments. Captain John Kingsbury's North Carolina Independent Artillery Company was also ordered detached from the main army and sent southward with Hogun. There was no way of knowing that these men were marching into defeat.[27]

26. Ford, *Journals of the Continental Congress*, XIV, 820, XV, 1138; Fitzpatrick, *Writings of Washington*, XIV, 469–70, XVI, 235–36, 235n, XVII, 105, 210; Washington to Laurens, 20 November 1779, Revolutionary Papers, Southern Historical Collection.

27. Fitzpatrick, *Writings of Washington*, XVI, 241, 242n, 282, 360, 363–64, 382, 383–84, 384n, 407–8, 469–70, 473, XVII, 111n, 124–25, 134–35, 150–51, 171, 174–75, 209–10; Laurens to Clark, 5 October 1779, Papers of the Continental Congress; Hogun to Sumner, 7 November 1779, Jethro Sumner Papers, Southern Historical Collection.

Chapter 9
The Carolinas, 1778-1779

*"We have always been haughtily treated
by South Carolina. . . ."*

The year 1778 had been a busy year for the little town of Halifax.
It had continued as a rendezvous for recovered deserters, new re
cruits, and Continental soldiers returning from furlough. Some had
been assigned the task of guarding the magazine at that place. Re
cruiting officers had scoured the state, but they had met with little suc
cess; there were few funds with which to pay the bounties and it be
came increasingly difficult to persuade persons to accept contracts for
clothing new enlistees. Early in February, 1778, the officers of the
Sixth Regiment had been sent home as supernumeraries with orders
to seek out new recruits to reactivate the regiments. A number be
came discouraged at the lack of money and were little inclined to take
the field again. Even such glamorous units as Cosmo Medici's and
Samuel Ashe's light horse were finding it difficult to attract recruits.
A number of officers, including Captain William Caswell of the Fifth
Regiment, spent their time rounding up deserters from the North
Carolina Brigade.[1]

1. James Richardson to Caswell, 21 January 1778, Caswell to Allen Jones, 1
February 1778, J. Luttrell to Caswell, 20 February 1778, Caswell Letterbook;

Colonel James Hogun, after his return from Valley Forge, had worked diligently in the recruiting service, although many of those who returned to the state with him lacked his enthusiasm; in fact, a number of officers seized the first opportunity to tender their resignations. Recruits, when they could be persuaded to enlist, deserted as soon as they received the bounty. One of the more ingenious was William Watson of the Fifth Regiment, who managed to desert upon five different occasions before slipping away for good. Others signed, took the bounty, but lingered near the warmth of their own firesides rather than coming in to the rendezvous. Some seemed to be hanging back because of the rumor that William Pitt, Lord Chatham, had returned to head the British ministry and soon would bring about a cessation of hostilities. There were no men to fill the four additional regiments that Congress had authorized when the North Carolina troops had been consolidated in May, 1778.[2]

Yet almost every post rider brought urgent pleas that men be forwarded to Washington's army as soon as they could be signed, even if they were not properly equipped. And they were ill-equipped, so much so that there was a story going the rounds that North Carolina did less to supply its officers and men than any other state. Washington felt that sending them on, even if not properly fitted out, would give the new recruits less time to desert. The shortages were not because of a lack of effort on the part of Governor Caswell, who was utilizing all of his powers to supply the state's Continental troops. Caswell prohibited the exportation of all meat from the state. He bought cloth wherever he could find it, whether the material was regulation or not. Even then a shortage of wagons held up the delivery of supplies to the troops.[3]

By June, 1778, and after the planting season, recruiting picked up, especially in Orange County where a large number of volunteers came forward. Perhaps this had been a result of the vague promises of recruiting officers who implied that nine months' service in the Continentals would exempt recruits from all further military duty, either regular or militia service. Some of the volunteers may have been ex-

State Records, XIII, 12, 13–14, 26, 42–43, 50; General Orders, 1 July 1778, Miscellaneous Papers, Military Collection; Cosmo Medici to Caswell, 21 March 1778, Governors' Papers; *North Carolina Gazette*, 5 December 1778.

2. Hogun to Caswell, 22 March 1778, Caswell to Hogun, 27 March 1778, Horatio Gates to Caswell, 28 March 1778, Caswell to Mathew Locke, 31 March 1778, Thomas Craike to Caswell, 11 April 1778, Caswell Letterbook; *State Records*, XIII, 69, 74, 75–76, 81–82, 84–85; *North Carolina Gazette*, 13 March 1778.

3. Fitzpatrick, *Writings of Washington*, XI, 139; Ford, *Journals of the Continental Congress*, XI, 551; Caswell to Washington, 15 February 1778, George Washington Papers; *North Carolina Gazette*, 13 February 1778.

cited by the news of the alliance with France, which had been received in North Carolina in May. In every county men were drafted to do nine months' duty with the Continentals, although there were seldom weapons with which to arm them; those muskets available "would not be such as would be received in the Continental Army." In some counties there was little need for a draft since there was a rather large number of volunteers who wished to collect the substantial bounties that were not always paid. In some instances men were chosen by the ballot of the local militia.[4]

Just as soon as a county's quota had been achieved, Hogun sent officers to march the recruits to Camp Quankey at Halifax. From there they were sent on to Peytonsburg, Virginia, where they were to be placed under the command of Lieutenant Colonel James Thackston. These men were to be marched as quickly as possible, for their nine months' service began the moment they reached camp. At Peytonsburg there were complications. The state of Virginia had agreed to provide food for the troops gathered there but had failed to furnish "one ounce of provisions." And throughout the camp there was the sound of the lash as each deserter was flogged "on his bear back," as many as ten times in a single morning. Thackston was finally forced to drop back to Dixon's Ferry on the Dan River where food was said to be more plentiful.[5]

In some instances it seemed that the militia deliberately elected those men who they were confident would be turned down once they reached the rendezvous. An inordinate number of men limped into Camp Quankey, "having sore legs and ruptures which render them incapable of duty." For example, Hardy Coker, who had been selected in Craven County, not only had only one eye but was termed "sickly" and the sole support of a "sickly wife and three small children." In Anson County, among others, the draft seems to have been seized upon as an opportunity to wreak revenge for past discomforts; among the first selected from that county were a circuit judge, a state senator, a tax collector, and a subsheriff. Others so chosen were either fugitives from justice or "idle bread eaters, answering the purposes of base Tools which are hurtful to our Country." Some were little more than "mere Boys," especially those who had volunteered. Many

4. Thomas Craike to Caswell, 2 June 1778, William Bryan to Caswell, 6 June 1778, Caswell Letterbook; *Life and Correspondence of James Iredell*, I, 39–92; Allen Jones to Caswell, 8 June 1778, Historical Society of Pennsylvania Papers.

5. *State Records*, XIII, 146–47, 148–49, 151–52, 460; *North Carolina Gazette*, 22 May 1778; General Orders, 1 July 1778, Miscellaneous Papers, Military Collection.

of these who had voluntarily enlisted refused to take a step until they had their bonus in hand.[6]

Matters were further complicated to the eastward, in the Beaufort County area, where a group of some thirty armed loyalists were persuading the draftees to desert and making public declarations that their guns would prevent them from being taken up by Continental officers. These bold fellows had "become so outrageous and daring that every person who wishes well to his country is insulted by them." Although some counties followed milita custom and elected officers, James Hogun, after he began organizing the new Seventh Regiment, established a "court of line" to recommend company grade officers for commissions to be granted by the General Assembly. Some of the older officers, disgusted with the haphazard arrangement of the line and their failure to receive promotions under the reorganization, resigned their commissions. Governor Caswell was unhappy with the rampant democracy that had caused "in many Counties a Most scandalous abuse of the powers Lodged with the People at large. . . ."[7]

The ranking officer of the North Carolina Line, Jethro Sumner, had been ill since his return from Valley Forge. His health improved, Sumner arrived at Halifax on July 6 and attempted to bring some order and organization there. Some of the older soldiers who had been in North Carolina on furlough were alerted for an immediate return to Washington's army. Colonel John Williams ranged out from the camp on Quankey Creek rounding up strays from all regiments and collecting wagons. Still so many misfits were sent into the camp from the various counties that the officers were shocked at the strange specimans of humanity who were considered fit enough to be soldiers by their fellow men.[8]

The supply situation became even more critical as an August hurricane ripped through the eastern part of the state, destroying the crops not yet harvested. The Continental Congress sent only one-fifth of the funds necessary to start the troops on their northward

6. John Bryan to William Bryan, 6 June 1778, John Crawford to Caswell, 11 June 1778, James Martin to Caswell, 11 June 1778, Thomas Bonner to Caswell, 4 July 1778, Hogun to Caswell, 9 July 1778, Caswell Letterbook; William Bryan to Caswell, 7 June 1778, Caswell to Hogun, 7 June 1778, Caswell to Hogun, 29 June 1778, Caswell to Hogun, 5 July 1778, Governors' Papers.

7. *State Records*, XIII, 148–49, 149–50, 150–51, 152, 158–59, 179–80, 187–88, 188–89, 191, 451; Caswell to Sumner, 12 July 1778, Governors' Papers.

8. Sumner to Caswell, 9 July 1778, Hogun to Caswell, 9 July 1778, Caswell to Hogun, 12 July 1778, Caswell to Sumner, 12 July 1778, Governors' Papers; *North Carolina Gazette*, 14 August 1778; Robert Raiford to Sumner, 31 August 1778, Jethro Sumner Papers, N.C. Dept. Arch. & Hist.; *State Records*, XIII, 189–90, 190–91, 192–93, 193–94.

march. There was enough to pay the bounties owed Hogun's Seventh Regiment of "nine-months" Continentals so that they might start their march in July. When North Carolina complained, the Congress replied that the funds had not yet been sent forward because of sloppy bookkeeping and that the state had not yet sent its military accounts to Philadelphia. It was also argued that North Carolina had already received more Continental funds "than any State in the Union." Cornelius Harnett, the only North Carolina delegate in attendance at Congress at the time, pointed out that the expenses of the Moore's Creek Campaign, the Snow Campaign, and the expedition against the Cherokees, plus the upkeep of ten battalions already put in the field, had impoverished an already poor state. Although he felt that North Carolina had been "wantonly sported with" by the Philadelphia assembly, he felt that additional funds would be sent if the state would only straighten out her accounts. And, Harnett added, much of the blame for the situation should fall on a "Congress [that] seems to go on in the old way, some times disputing upon trifles, and neglecting the greater matters of the Law. . . ."[9]

The recruiting situation may have been further complicated by the activities of one Monsieur Chariol de Placer, a colorful Frenchman who appears to have captured the imagination of many of the state's leaders. Monsieur Chariol, as he was generally known, was possessed of dreams of martial glory, and he persuaded the state to authorize him to raise a regiment of marines on the Continental establishment "to be composed of French Sailors or other natives of France, or the French West Indies." There is, however, the suggestion that he used subtle blackmail to gain his commission; he had been in possession of eight thousand pounds of badly needed gunpowder and the evidence implies that he engaged in "teasing" the North Carolina authorities until he received the necessary authorization to raise his regiment. Then too, it was argued that this would be something of a gesture of good will in recognition of the French alliance.[10]

In the beginning it seemed as though Chariol's regiment might be a credit to the state. He persuaded Baron de Bottecele, an officer

9. Caswell to John Penn, 13 August 1778, Harnett to Caswell, 27 August 1778, Harnett to Caswell, 15 September 1778, Caswell Letterbook; *State Records*, XIII, 207–8, 211–12, 218–19; Burnett, *Letters of Members of the Continental Congress*, III, 334, 382–84; Ford, *Journals of the Continental Congress*, X, 86, 90.

10. Caswell to Rawlins Lowndes, 6 May 1778, Petition of Monsieur Chariol, 15 April 1778, Governors' Papers; James Green, Jr., to Caswell, 7 February 1778, Caswell to Patrick Henry, 6 May 1778, Caswell Letterbook; *State Records*, XIII, 34–35, 119–20, 122.

of twenty-five years' experience, to become his lieutenant colonel, while several other persons of prominence and of French extraction accepted lesser commissions. Chariol's recruiting activities ranged as far south as Charleston and northward to southern Virginia. One company of predominantly French descendants formed in Williamsburg, Virginia, expressed a wish to join the regiment if the consent of Governor Patrick Henry could be gained. Chariol, by concentrating his activities in seaports, reported the enlistment of eleven sailors off of one French ship, and boasted that he expected to recruit at least fifty more.[11]

Chariol's high-handed methods, or so they seemed to the townspeople, set off a riot in New Bern. A young French sailor, one Julian Laborcet, was enlisted in that town. Immediately James Davis, Jr., claimed Laborcet as an indentured servant working as a seaman aboard one of his ships. Davis's father, James Davis, Sr., publisher of the *North Carolina Gazette*, immediately swore out a warrant. The French sergeant in charge of the local barracks refused to allow Davis and his son to reclaim their alleged property. The Davises immediately gathered a mob, shouting "the Liberty we have been fighting for so long was about to be taken by the damned French!" They abused Chariol and the local magistrates, with Davis crying that he would have Chariol's commission revoked and swearing that "he would have justice done, or he would the night following head a party to put every Frenchman to death in town, or drive them out of it." There might have been violence had not Abner Nash used his persuasive powers to disperse the mob.[12]

The following night, Davis, with sailors from his own and other vessels, surrounded the school house that was being used as a barracks. Forcing its way into the building, the mob gave the French recruits therein a severe beating with cudgels. The justices of the peace were so intimidated by this action that, although Davis could produce no indenture or other document to prove ownership, they ordered Laborcet to be confined in jail until the matter could be settled in court. Chariol called the Davis bluff; he remained in town and actually met with some success in his recruiting efforts. On June 10, 1778, the local court declared Laborcet a free man. As the noise died, the general conclusion was that the affair had been staged by Davis in an

11. Chariol de Placer to Caswell, 20 May 1778, Governors' Papers; *State Records*, XIII, 129–30.

12. R. Cogdell to Caswell, 29 May 1778, Cogdell to Caswell, 30 May 1778, Caswell Letterbook; *State Records*, XIII, 142–43, 144–45, 155–56, 162; Alonzo Thomas Dill, *Governor Tryon and His Palace* (Chapel Hill, N.C., 1955), pp. 190–91.

attempt to embarrass one of the justices, Dr. Alexander Gaston. Not only had Gaston been born in France, but Davis had charged that Gaston had earlier killed one of his prize bulls.[13]

Whether Davis was responsible for Chariol's losing his commission, or whether it was because it was felt that the Frenchman was enlisting men who might have joined one of the regular regiments, the General Assembly, sitting in Hillsborough in August, decided to abandon the idea of a French marine regiment in the state line. Certainly Chariol's activities were utilizing funds that might have been spent on one of the older regiments. Although the fidelity or ability of Chariol's officers were not questioned, the assembly noted that there were not enough "privates of the French Nation" within North Carolina to fill the ranks of the regiment. All of those privates already enlisted were dismissed. Chariol returned to France shortly afterwards. Although he had spent over £1,000 of his own money, it is to be suspected that his stiff formality alienated many and may well have been a factor in recalling his commission.[14]

Although Caswell had called the extra session of the legislature at Hillsborough to "consult on the weighty and arduous Affairs of the said State," the legislature, despite the worsening military situation, seemed inclined toward perfecting the independent civil government it had not yet won. It refused to heed the governor's plea for money for the line, and suggested that he apply to the Continental Congress. Little was done for the state regiments other than establishing a board to determine the officers who were to remain on duty with the state regiments. Supernumerary officers were to be relieved of duty but would be given preference when vacancies occurred. The drafting of militia having proved such an unsatisfactory stopgap, recruiting officers were directed to enlist all men in the future, if possible, either for three years of for the duration of the war. All recruits who accepted such terms were to be furloughed until March 1, 1779. All "nine-months" Continentals who were now in the field would also

13. *State Records*, XIII, 425, 429–30; Deposition of Alexander Gaston, 5 June 1778, Miscellaneous Papers, Military Collection; R. Cogdell to Caswell, 9 June 1778, Governors' Papers.

14. *State Records*, XII 811, 873, XIII, 222–23, 226–27, XXII, 762–63; Caswell to Washington, 14 September 1778, Caswell to Henry Laurens, 16 September 1778, Caswell Letterbook; Ford, *Journals of the Continental Congress*, XIII, 472–73; Caswell to Patrick Henry, 16 September 1778, Chariol to Caswell, 20 September 1778, Caswell to Washington, 22 September 1778, Governors' Papers; Caswell to Laurens, 14 September 1778, Papers of the Continental Congress. The following year the people of French extraction in South Carolina attempted to raise a regiment similar to that proposed by Chariol in North Carolina. (Ford, *Journals of the Continental Congress*, XIII, 443–44.)

be granted furloughs if they would agree to serve an additional nine months. Inasmuch as commanders in the field had been forced to borrow money in order to provide for their men, it was felt that furloughing these men with pay would be cheaper than clothing them through the winter months when there was usually little need for them in the field.[15]

From Philadelphia came warnings from Henry Laurens, president of the Continental Congress, and Cornelius Harnett that the enemy seemed intent upon evacuating New York and Rhode Island and might be sailing southward. Some feared that North Carolina was the objective, so much so that at almost every report of enemy movements many of the residents of Edenton left the town. Harnett felt that North Carolina's new levies should be recalled from their furloughs and marched to South Carolina, which he felt was the enemy's real objective. William Hooper agreed with him and felt this to be the result of the desire of "General Clinton to gratify a personal picque, to convince the world of his own prowess & to wipe away the stain which the British had suffered in a former attempt upon Charlestown. . . ." Perhaps because of a feeling of guilt on the part of South Carolina and Georgia for having insisted upon Robert Howe's recall or perhaps because of the reputation Caswell had gained at Moore's Creek Bridge, the South Carolina delegates proposed that Caswell be placed in command of all North Carolina troops in the field with the rank and pay of a major general. Yet the proposal might have been motivated mainly by flattery, for Caswell was also reminded that "in this you will no doubt consider the interest of North Carolina and the propriety of being absent from your Government." In any event he would have been outranked by Howe's replacement, Major General Benjamin Lincoln of Massachusetts.[16]

By the middle of October, 1778, the Continental Congress was demanding that the state dispatch three thousand troops to South Carolina immediately. The same directions were sent to Virginia, but the legislature at Williamsburg considered the alarm "altogether visionary," and would do no more than authorize the governor to send men to repel an invasion force. Thomas Burke may have been partially responsible for this attitude on the part of the Virginia leg-

---

15. *State Records*, XII, 795, 808, 820, 848–49, XIII, 455, 469–70; Burnett, *Letters of Members of the Continental Congress*, III, 402.

16. Penn, Harnett, and John Williams to Caswell, 29 September 1778, Harnett to Caswell, 4 October 1778, Penn to Caswell, 18 October 1778, Caswell Letterbook; Burnett, *Letters of Members of the Continental Congress*, III, 426, 430–31, 461; *State Records*, XIII, 224–26, 234–36, 237–38, 239–40, 242–44; J. Blair to James Iredell, 7 May 1778, Charles E. Johnston Collection.

islature for he was in Williamsburg at the time, declaring that Clinton would never be so foolish as to split his army. The alarm, he felt, was the result of "the credulity of some Southern Gentlemen in Congress, and from the high idea of the importance of their Country." The business, he added, would "end in mere smoke."[17]

Within the state there were some who agreed with William Hooper, who insisted that Charleston could offer little to the enemy, who could do no more than "pilfer a parcel of Jew merchants, burn their shops, and then with his army Starve upon rice gruel or perish with a putrid fever for the honor of Great Britain." He argued that South Carolina would "entrap all of our countrymen into their own regiments." Allen Jones, after declaring that "Charles Town is too trifling an acquisition for British Arms," then went on to voice his real objections to sending North Carolina troops into the neighboring state:

We have always been haughtily treated by South Carolina, till they wanted our assistance, and then we are sisters, but as soon as their term is served, all relationships ceases. So. Carolina is so well aware of our resentment that they despaired of succeeding, should they apply themselves, therefore have got Congress to make a requisition, thinking no doubt of respect to that Body, we should overlook their former treatment, In short, Sir, our State either one way or other appears to be sacrificed to So. Carolina, and that we are very little consequence in the eyes of Congress.[18]

Governor Caswell, however, acted with characteristic zeal, immediately publishing a proclamation recalling the furloughed troops and ordering the militia to be in the field by November 10, 1778. For a while it seemed that he had done the right thing, for there were reports that the British were embarking troops in preparation for sailing from New York. Yet there was no way of knowing whether they were sailing for the West Indies or the southern states. Caswell's proclamation met with an unfavorable response throughout the state. Some declared that troops could not come out on such short notice; others voiced doubt that the governor had the authority to send the militia out of the state. And Allen Jones, although he complied with the governor's directive, protested that it was an unnecessary expense and persisted in reminding Caswell that Virginia had not yet sent a man past her southern border. By now Caswell had decided not to

17. John Penn to Caswell, 22 October 1778, Caswell Letterbook; *State Records*, XIII, 244–45, 247; Ford, *Journals of the Continental Congress*, XII, 951; Henry Laurens to Caswell, 26 September 1778, Papers of the Continental Congress; Archibald Hooper to James Iredell, 17 November 1778, Iredell Papers.

18. *State Records*, XIII, 245–47; McRee, *Life and Correspondence of James Iredell*, I, 405; Archibald Hooper to Iredell, 17 December 1778, Iredell Papers.

accept the command of the North Carolina troops and attempted to have the commission given to John Ashe.[19]

With the sailing of the British fleet from New York, communications from Congress assumed a frantic note. They ordered an additional two thousand men to be raised in North Carolina and sent to the aid of South Carolina and Georgia. Caswell, as any good wartime executive must, placed his own interpretations upon state laws when they seemed to conflict with what he felt was proper. He ordered troops to rendezvous at Kinston and Elizabeth City no later than November 25 where, he promised, there would be sufficient funds to pay bounties. Once assembled, they were to push on to Charleston as quickly as possible. Various supply contractors were urged to drive in cattle and hogs and, to save time, they were not to be slaughtered but driven along with the troops as they marched southward. Although the militia had fairly well-organized commissary departments, the newly recruited Continentals were not so fortunate. No contractors could be persuaded to supply them. A plague of the Hessian fly had ravaged grain crops in the southern states so that there was very little flour for the troops, and the flour that was collected was very bad.[20]

Arms were short, and in reply to Caswell's request, Governor Rawlins Lowndes of South Carolina reported that his state was suffering a similar shortage. The North Carolina militia units, if they had surplus arms, refused to give them up; indeed, many of their number had run off and were now "hiding in the woods." Not only muskets but tents and camp kettles were in short supply. All manner of excuses came in from the militia concerning why it could not take the field. Those in the western counties proclaimed their preoccupation "in the suppression of the Savages and other inhuman hostile wretches, who have their livelihood from Carnage and Rapine." Those in the coastal counties felt it necessary to guard their homes against small enemy raiding parties.[21]

Some of Caswell's enthusiasm seemed to abate when it became

19. Gideon Lamb to Caswell, 24 October 1778, W. Skinner to Caswell, 25 October 1778, Griffith Rutherford to Caswell, 25 October 1778, Butler to Caswell, 28 October 1778, Caswell to John Ashe, 28 October 1778, Caswell Letterbook; Harnett to Caswell, 24 October 1778, Allen Jones to Caswell, 28 October 1778, Governors' Papers; *State Records*, XIII, 248, 249, 249–51, 252, 253–54, 255–56; Burnett, *Letters of Members of the Continental Congress*, III, 455.

20. Caswell to Rawlins Lowndes, 5 November 1778, Caswell to Griffith Rutherford, 7 November 1778, Caswell Letterbook; Caswell to Allen Jones, 7 November 1778, Caswell to Peter Mallet, 8 November 1778, Allen Jones to Caswell, 15–23 November 1778, Samuel Jarvis to Caswell, 16 November 1778, Governors' Papers; *State Records*, XIII, 265, 265–66, 267–69, 269–70, 271.

21. Lowndes to Caswell, 10 November 1778, Anthony Lytle to Caswell, 13 November 1778, John Butler to Caswell, 14 November 1778, Rutherford to Cas-

doubtful that the British fleet was sailing for South Carolina. Yet the Continental Congress continued to press North Carolina to send troops southward to join General Benjamin Lincoln in an expedition against East Florida. But affairs in that British stronghold were too distant to generate much interest in North Carolina, despite the promise of the Continental Congress of rather generous land grants to all those who took part in the campaign.[22]

As the discontent within the state grew, those Tories who had remained quiet now began a whispering campaign "to the disadvantage of the glorious cause of Freedom. . . ." In Johnston County there were near riots, while a number of loyalists hid out in the woods "and swears to kill any person that shall offer to enlist them." Others embodied themselves into a semimilitary organization and laid out along the Johnston-Nash County line, sweeping back and forth across the boundary on destructive raids. When some of their number were apprehended and placed in jails, mobs broke them out. So many threats were made against militia officers that they began to fear for their lives.[23]

Still Caswell was determined to send troops at least as far south as Charleston, especially after a conference with Generals Lincoln and Sumner and other state officers at Kinston on November 19, 1778. Sumner rode off in an attempt to collect additional troops. Caswell remained at Kinston, sending out a barrage of letters to anyone who might aid the war effort in any fashion. He agreed wholeheartedly with the observation of Cornelius Harnett: "I am one of those old Politicians who had much rather see my neighbour's house on fire than my own, but at the same time would lend every assistance in my power to quench the flames. St. Augustine, during the continuance of this War (from her situation) will constantly have it in her power, not only to destroy our *poor frontier State of Georgia* by land but to embarass and almost ruin the trade of the four Southern States by their Privateers."[24]

For some time Caswell entertained the notion of accepting the

well, 15 November 1778, Caswell Letterbook; *State Records*, XIII, 276, 278, 280–81, 282–83, 285–86; Henry Laurens to Lowndes, 18 December 1778, Papers of the Continental Congress.

22. Ford, *Journals of the Continental Congress*, XII, 116–18; Laurens to Caswell, 14 November 1778, Caswell Letterbook; Laurens to Caswell, 18 October 1778, Papers of the Continental Congress.

23. Caswell to Butler, 20 November 1778, Caswell to Lytle, 20 November 1778, William Bryan to Caswell, 23 November 1778, Governors' Papers; *State Records*, XIII, 20–71, 279, 292–93, 294, 295.

24. Harnett to Caswell, 10 November 1778, Hewes to Caswell, 24 November 1778, Caswell Letterbook; *State Records*, XIII, 297–98, 299, 305–6; Burnett, *Letters of Members of the Continental Congress*, III, 456–57.

commission of Major General that had been proposed by the Continental Congress and accompanying the troops to South Carolina. But after discussing the situation with General Lincoln during the three days that Lincoln spent in Kinston, an expedition to the southward lost it attractions for the governor. John Ashe was given command of the North Carolina troops in the south until Sumner was fully recovered from his illness. It wasn't much of a command. The troops, although on Continental pay for nine months, were poorly armed, if at all. Only the men from the Edenton district were fairly well equipped, by virtue of the recent arrival of a cargo of muskets, cartouche boxes, and a few blankets. Despite Caswell's efforts, in early December only two hundred nine-months Continentals and one thousand militiamen had crossed the Neuse on their march south by way of Elizabeth Town.[25]

Some of the supernumerary officers of the Continental Line were placed in command of militia units from their home counties. Despite Lowndes's protests that South Carolina had no spare muskets, Caswell learned from Lincoln that there were Continental muskets in that state that would be issued to the North Carolina troops when they arrived on the scene sometime around Christmas day. The North Carolina regiments were by no means full, "owing to individuals who have undertaken to find fault with the measures now pursuing." Remembering the last occasion when troops were sent to the assistance of South Carolina, Caswell cautioned Ashe not to allow the state's militia to be enlisted into the Continental regiments of any other state. And these men were to be discharged from service by April 10, 1779, if not earlier.[26]

By December 22, 1778, it was fairly obvious that the British were planning a campaign to retake the southern states. William Haslan, a North Carolina loyalist who had served aboard the British transport *Neptune*, gave his disposition in Savannah in early December. Georgia, he swore, was the true objective of the British fleet that had sailed from New York, and orders had been issued "to burn and destroy all who would not submit." From Henry Laurens came the plea "that

25. Hewes, Smith, and Allen to Caswell, 24 November 1778, Gideon Lamb to Caswell, 25 November 1778, Caswell to Hewes, Smith and Allen, 29 November 1778, Caswell Letterbook; Caswell to Joseph Hewes, 29 November 1778, Caswell to Lamb, 29 November 1778, Caswell to John Ashe, 5 December 1778, Governors' Papers; *State Records*, XIII, 300–301, 301–2, 307–8, 308–9, 315.

26. Lytle to Caswell, 5 December 1778, Caswell to Benjamin Lincoln, 8 December 1778, Caswell to John Ashe, 8 December 1778, Caswell Letterbook; *State Records*, XIII, 316–17, 320–21, 322–23, Caswell to Ashe, 29 December 1778, Richard Caswell Papers, Southern Historical Collection.

North Carolina will on this, as on former occasions be nobly distinguished by patriotic Exertions in the great cause of Liberty and Prosperity."[27]

By the end of 1778 only about nine hundred North Carolinians had joined Lincoln, driving their cattle and hogs before them. Bread was scarce. Despite his pleas for aid, and despite the fact that these fresh troops were without arms, Governor Lowndes stood adamant against issuing arms to the troops of another state. South Carolina had also given its executive officer more authority over its Continental troops than the general commanding the Southern Department. Robert Howe had complained that the southern army had "been in an abject dependence upon the civil authorities," an observation with which Lincoln readily agreed. No South Carolina troops could march without the governor's consent, and Lowndes also controlled the supply situation in that state, prerogatives he guarded jealously. When Lincoln requested that he arm the North Carolinians, it was reported that the governor cried that he "would be betraying a trust reposed in him to do it; — they were purchased for the defence of this State— It would never do to leave them defenceless—No· he would deliver them, should he receive an order of Congress for it." But Benjamin Lincoln was a persuasive man, and Lowndes was finally prevailed upon to pass out some seven hundred stand of arms to the North Carolina troops. The artillery situation was even more critical, for none of the six fieldpieces belonging to the Continental forces was serviceable.[28]

Around the first of the year Lincoln had started marching southward for Savannah and was within twenty-eight miles of the city when a dispatch from Robert Howe informed him that the British had routed his force and the town had fallen to the enemy on December 29, 1778. On September 25, 1778, Major General Robert Howe had been ordered to join Washington's army and turn over the southern

27. Lincoln to Caswell, 22 December 1778, Caswell Letterbook; Testimonial of William Haslan, 6 December 1778, Governors' Papers; Moultrie, *Memoirs of the American Revolution*, I, 249–51; Laurens to Caswell, 23 January 1779, Laurens to Lincoln, 23 January 1779, Papers of the Continental Congress; *State Records,* XIII, 332, 332–34.

28. Peter Mallett to Caswell, 23 December 1778, Lowndes to Caswell, 27 December 1778, Governors' Papers; Caswell to Ashe, 29 December 1778, Lincoln to Caswell, 31 December 1778, Caswell Letterbook; *State Records,* XIII, 336–37, 338, 338–42, 342; Billias, *George Washington's Generals,* p. 198; Burnett, *Letters of Members of the Continental Congress,* III, 540; Lincoln to Laurens, 19 December 1778, Papers of the Continental Congress; Lincoln to Washington, 19 December 1778, George Washington Papers; Lincoln to Houston, 25 December 1778, Benjamin Lincoln Papers, Massachusetts Historical Society, Boston, Mass.

command to Lincoln. Howe did not seem unhappy about the change for he had earlier complained "it is an embarassing Command to me, and a circumstance of anxiety & fatigue." Word of the change of command had been delayed because of the illness of the messenger, and when Howe finally received the orders, an invasion of Georgia seemed imminent. Feeling that he could not leave until Lincoln arrived, he hurried to Georgia to take command of the defenses of that state.[29]

In the meantime, on November 27, 1778, Lieutenant Colonel Archibald Campbell with 3,500 troops had sailed from Sandy Hook with a fleet of transports convoyed by Commodore Hyde Parker. General Augustine Prevost, commanding British troops in East Florida, was to march overland and make a junction with Campbell. Their combined forces, it was felt, were sufficient to take the town of Savannah. The British fleet dropped anchor off Tybee Island on December 23, awaiting the arrival of Prevost. Howe, with 700 Georgia and South Carolina Continentals and 150 militia, had taken a stand at Sunbury, thirty miles south of Savannah. Then, leaving a portion of his force at Sunbury to check Prevost, he fell back to the defense of Savannah.[30]

Howe did his best in the face of little cooperation from the Georgia authorities. There was little artillery to support those troops under his command. Governor John Houstoun of Georgia, seemingly fearful of the diminution of his own authority, not only refused to heed Howe's suggestions, but went so far as to openly condone outright disobedience by the officers of the Georgia militia. When there was a threat to Savannah and Howe attempted to repair the dilapidated defenses of the town, the governor procrastinated in furnishing entrenching tools or labor in answer to the general's request. Some Georgia troops were allowed to return to their homes despite the obvious threat to the state. Howe struggled on as best he could with what he had at hand.[31]

Learning from deserters that the force opposing him was thin in

29. *State Records*, XIII, 498; Ford, *Journals of the Continental Congress*, IX, 823, XII, 951; Howe to Caswell, 10 April 1777, Governors' Papers; Laurens to Howe, 6 October 1778, John Hancock to Howe, 27 October 1778, Howe to Hancock, 24 November 1778, Papers of the Continental Congress; Lincoln to Henry Laurens, 31 December 1778, Benjamin Lincoln Papers.

30. *Collections of the New-York Historical Society for 1879* (New York, 1880), pp. 241–42, 250–51, 265–67; Howe to Lincoln, 24 December 1778, Benjamin Lincoln Papers.

31. Dawson, *Battles of the United States*, I, 472; George White (ed.), *Historical Collections of Georgia* (New York, 1855), p. 209; *Collections of the New-York Historical Society for 1879*, p. 280; Howe to _____, 25 December 1778, Revolutionary Collection, Duke University, Durham, N.C.

numbers, and uncertain of Prevost's arrival, Campbell decided to launch an attack against the town on December 29. Savannah, which one Englishman described as appearing as though a city had been built atop the cliffs of Dover, had been fortified since the French and Indian War, but its defenses had been allowed to fall into decay. Howe's disposition of troops on the strong ground on the east side of town where his flanks were protected by marshes has been termed well chosen, but he was outnumbered four to one. His numbers were such that he would have been hard pressed to repel a frontal attack, and to properly guard against flanking actions it would have been necessary to spread his thin ranks even farther.[32]

Campbell, learning from a Negro of a path through the swamp on the American right flank, sent one group over this route while dispatching another unit to demonstrate in front of Howe. When Howe's jittery militiamen discovered Campbell's flanking force in their rear they fled willy-nilly, a number of them drowning as they attempted to make off through the marshes and across the streams. In all, more than five hundred Americans were drowned, killed, or captured. After Prevost joined Campbell, Augusta fell in early January, 1779. The significance of the fall of Savannah is perhaps best summed up in the observation of Chief Justice Anthony Stokes: "This place is the key to the southern provinces, and the Gibraltar of the Gulf passage; for to the south of this province there is not a port on the continent that will receive a sloop of war."[33]

Archibald Campbell boasted, "I may venture to say, Sir, that I have ripped one star and one stripe from the Rebel Flag of America." Indeed he had, and the British force in Georgia now stood poised like a dagger pointed toward the heart of South Carolina. Howe, already in disfavor with the Georgia and South Carolina politicians, bore the greater part of the blame. Although he was subsequently acquitted "with the Highest Honor" by a court-martial, he was, from this time on, destined to sink into military oblivion.[34]

Howe's defeat made it necessary for Caswell to increase his

32. Campbell to Germain, 16 January 1779, Germain Papers; Dawson, *Battles of the United States*, I, 479; John R. Alden, *The South in the Revolution, 1763–1789* (Baton Rouge, La., 1957), pp. 232–35; *American Historical Review*, IV (1899), 482.

33. Moore, *Diary of the American Revolution*, II, 228; David Ramsey, *The History of the American Revolution* (London, 1793), II, 130–31; Moultrie, *Memoirs of the American Revolution*, I, 252–54; Howe to Washington, 30 December 1778, George Washington Papers; Howe to Laurens, 30 December 1778; Lincoln to Laurens, 31 December 1778, Papers of the Continental Congress; General Elbert's Testimony, n.d., Robert Howe Papers, Southern Historical Collection.

34. *Collections of the New-York Historical Society for 1879*, pp. 310–11.

efforts to put troops in South Carolina, for that state had suddenly become North Carolina's first line of defense. Militia were called out and, on the advice of the Continental Congress, the furloughs of all nine-months Continentals were cancelled and they were ordered into the various rendezvous points. Some refused to heed the call, arguing that their time would be up in April. Those who assembled at Kinston were fortunate enough to be issued "good new arms," which had been sent to South Carolina by the Continental Congress but had been intercepted along the way. Money, however, was still scarce. And the general attitude throughout the state had changed. Many of those who had formerly opposed sending troops to South Carolina now reversed themselves, although the militia continued to show a reluctance to turn out. Efforts were further hampered by the steady winter rains, which swelled the streams over their banks.[35]

By the first of February, however, 438 North Carolina nine-months Continentals and a substantial number of militia had joined Lincoln at Purysburg on the South Carolina side of the Savannah River, although many were poorly armed. William Moultrie noted that "those continentals from North-Carolina, are as undisciplined troops, as any militia." Field officers commanded detachments no larger than companies. Colonel Sumner, Lieutenant Colonels Thackston and Lytle, and Majors Dixon, Armstrong, and Nelson commanded units ranging from thirty-eight to fifty-three men. John Ashe's militiamen had arrived on January 3, but they had no more than pitched camp than they began to cry that their time was up and they were going home. Others began to listen to South Carolina recruiting officers who were promising a $500 bonus to each North Carolinian who would enlist in their line for sixteen months. After the fall of Augusta the North Carolina troops were moved up to that area to prevent a river crossing in that vicinity. Yet spirits were high as a result of General William Moultrie's success in a skirmish with the enemy at Beaufort. Caswell's abiding optimism had led Lincoln to expect more troops than he received from North Carolina. Although the governor was busy with troubles in the western part of the state, Lincoln chided him: "It is truly mortifying that the enemy, with so contemptable a number compared with the force these states might bring into the field, are submitted to remain in

35. Caswell to Lincoln, 13 January 1779, Caswell to Lowndes, 13 January 1779, Caswell Letterbook; *State Records*, XIV, 4–5, 7, 13–14, 15; Ford, *Journals of the Continental Congress*, XIII, 132; Lincoln to Laurens, 19 December 1778, Papers of the Continental Congress.

quiet, and entertain an idea that they have conquered one of the thirteen United States."[36]

Moultrie's repulse of a British turning movement at Beaufort on February 3, 1779, followed by the defeat of seven hundred North Carolina loyalists under a Colonel Boyd at Kettle Creek on February 14, created some optimism in Lincoln's camp. Although the militiamen seemed to turn out with more enthusiasm, those of South Carolina were insistent that they were not to serve beyond March 1, and Lincoln complained that "they leave camp and even their posts when they please with impunity." And there was "a buzzing in the North Carolina camp," where it had been decided that the soldiers' time would expire on April 10 and the men were demanding that they be allowed to begin their homeward march no later than March 10. It was felt that their presence was needed at home to awe the Tories and interrupt British communications with the Indians in the back country. If any use was to be made of the services of these men it was obvious that some move would have to be made soon.[37]

Lincoln sent Brigadier General Andrew Williamson with 1,200 South Carolina militia to the east bank of the river opposite Augusta. Griffith Rutherford and about 800 North Carolina militia marched to take post at Black Swamp. John Ashe, with 1,200 militia and some 200 nine-month North Carolina Continentals organized into a light infantry detachment under Lieutenant Colonel Anthony Lytle, moved down to Brier Creek south of Augusta to "cover the upper part of the Country." Ashe was strengthened there by 70 Georgia Continentals and 200 militia who had been collected by Colonel Samuel Elbert before he had been driven back across the river by Campbell. Ashe did not want to take this position, for his men were exhausted by the long march from North Carolina and were ill equipped, so much so that they could do nothing to prevent the enemy's free use of the river. Well-rested and well-equipped men remained behind in the camp at Purysburg because General Lincoln interpreted South Carolina law as preventing the state's militia from being sent out of

36. Caswell to Allen Jones, 5 March 1779, Caswell Letterbook; *State Records*, XIV, 17–18, 20–22, 30–31; Moultrie, *Memoirs of the American Revolution*, I, 270, 309–10; John Ashe to Lincoln, 21 February 1779, Emmet Collection; Lincoln to Washington, 19 December 1778, George Washington Papers; A Return of the Continental Soldiers together with the New Series from Hillsborough and Salisbury Districts . . . Commanded by Colo. Jethro Sumner, Jany 29, 1779, in possession of Mr. Curtis Carroll Davis of Baltimore, Md.

37. Gibbes, *Documentary History of the American Revolution*, II; *State Records*, XIV, 33, 39–40 Lincoln to Henry Laurens, 28 January 1779, Papers of the Continental Congress.

the state without the prior approval of the legislature. Ashe also complained that his position was not easily defended.[38]

The British, receiving false information that Ashe's command numbered no less than eleven thousand men, evacuated Augusta and began the march for Savannah, burning the bridge over Brier Creek behind them. So hastily did they decamp that they left twelve freshly killed beeves on the ground. With his men on short rations, Ashe began to rebuild the bridge. His position, examined by later generations, has been considered a strong one, with one flank resting on a swamp and the Savannah River, while a deep stream protected his front. He had sufficient light horse to scout out ahead to give warning of the enemy's approach. But Ashe was inexperienced in formal military matters and he had grown careless with the retreat of the enemy.[39]

In the meantime Prevost had constructed secret fortifications in an effort to ambush Ashe on the drive toward Savannah. After waiting two days for the Americans to come up and learning of Ashe's true strength from spies, the British commander made new dispositions of his troops. Major McPherson and his First Battalion of the Seventy-First Regiment, with a Tory artillery detachment armed with two three-pound pieces called "grasshoppers," were sent to demonstrate in front of Ashe's position. Lieutenant Colonel Prevost took the Second Battalion of the Seventy-First, Sir James Baird's corps of light infantry, and three grenadier companies of the Florida Brigade and began marching in a long half-circle sweep of some fifty miles to come up behind Ashe. Detachments were sent off to harry and distract those units of Lincoln's command that might come to Ashe's assistance.[40]

Ashe's patrols had not only seen signs of the enemy but one group had actually exchanged fire with a British detachment; yet no one had sent word back to Ashe. And during the afternoon of Tuesday, March 2, 1779, when enemy groups were sighted in the neighborhood, Ashe did little in the way of defensive preparations. On the advice of

38. *State Records,* XIV, 33, 51–52; Council of War, 1 March 1779, Emmet Collection; Lincoln to John Jay, 27 January 1779, Papers of the Continental Congress.

39. *State Records,* XIV, 51–52; Stedman, *History of the . . . American War,* II, 196–99; Henry Lee, *Memoirs of the War in the Southern Department of the United States,* ed. Robert E. Lee (New York, 1870), pp. 123–24; Moultrie, *Memoirs of the American Revolution,* I, 291–95, 301, 317–19; Lincoln to Laurens, 6 February 1779, Papers of the Continental Congress.

40. Prevost to Germain, 6 March 1779, Germain Papers; Dawson, *Battles of the United States,* I, 493; "A Spy" to Lincoln, n.d., Benjamin Lincoln Papers, Southern Historical Collection, The University of North Carolina at Chapel Hill, Chapel Hill, N.C.

Brigadier General William Bryan and Colonel Elbert, he decided to march out and disperse what were believed to be no more than small parties. The drums rolled out their "beat to arms." On Wednesday, March 3, Ashe formed his command in two lines and sallied out to disperse the enemy. Some time was lost in serving out cartridges, for powder had been ruined earlier because of the absence of cartouche boxes. Even in this business of deadly seriousness, the Americans were ludicrous in appearance, "some carrying their cartridges under their arms, others in the bosoms of their shirts, and some tied up in the corners of their hunting shirts." It was felt that Lytle and his light infantry would not be needed and they were left posted at a bridge a mile and a half from camp.[41]

Mounted units on the far side of the stream gave the alarm around three o'clock in the afternoon. Fifteen minutes after Ashe received this intelligence, Prevost's column made its appearance in the rear of the Americans. The British were in three columns, six abreast; when they came within 150 yards of Ashe's troops they deployed into a line of battle. The drums rolled out the alarm as Ashe's troops hurried into a loose formation.[42]

The Georgia Continentals were the first to open fire. After delivering two or three rounds they began a short advance, but began to drift over to the left in front of the New Bern militia regiment, which, in turn, prevented that unit from firing. The Edenton regiment was forced to slide to the right, thereby leaving a gap in the line. Someone (later it was said to be William Bryan), shouted that the American flank had been turned. The men of the Halifax Regiment, in the second line, took to their heels without firing a shot. It should be noted, however, that much of the ball ammunition issued this unit was of the wrong caliber to fit the muskets used. The Wilmington regiment moved to their right to prevent being flanked and, along with the New Bern unit, delivered several volleys. By this time Lytle had come up with his light infantry and a brass field piece, just in time to see the Edenton regiment break. As the American lines disintegrated, Lytle moved off in good order, protecting the rear of the fugitives. The Georgia Continentals held fast until the situation became hopeless and Colonel Elbert surrendered. The actual battle had lasted but a little more than five minutes.[43]

41. Ashe to Caswell, 17 March 1779, Caswell Letterbook; *State Records*, XIV, 39–40; Dawson, *Battles of the United States*, I, 489–93; Moultrie, *Memoirs of the American Revolution*, I, 337.

42. *State Records*, XIV, 33, 40–43; Dawson, *Battles of the United States*, I, 490–91.

43. Lincoln to Caswell, 7 March 1779, Ashe to Caswell, 17 March 1779, Cas-

The rout was complete. Ashe and other officers rode among the fugitives, attempting to turn them. Their efforts were useless. They surged through the swamps and forests like a great tidal wave. More would have been taken prisoner had not the British halted to plunder the American encampment. Some of the Americans splashed through Brier Creek, while others attempted to swim the Savannah. Some threw together crude rafts and poled across the river. Some drowned and others died of exhaustion as they wandered through the swamps or fell into the lagoons. Ashe made it to Matthew's Bluff some four miles away where Griffith Rutherford's brigade of North Carolina militia was stationed. Gathering all available canoes, General Ashe sent the brigade back to ferry the survivors across the river.[44]

Ashe lost somewhere between 150 and 200 men killed, while 11 officers and 162 rank and file had been captured. Many of the militia continued the flight until they reached the safety of their own firesides. On the night of March 3, 1779, 106 privates were still missing and more were to disappear during the next few days. Of the 721 privates in William Bryan's militia brigade, only 242 were still ready for combat. Lytle's light infantry command of 200 nine-months Continentals remained intact. A number of the militia suddenly began to plead illness and return to their homes. Ashe, acting on the orders of Caswell and Lincoln, offered an additional bounty to those militia privates who would remain in the field until reinforcements came up; only one man agreed to stay.[45]

Some blamed the disaster on the "negligence" of Ashe, and his life was made even more miserable through the unbridled criticism of William Bryan, whom Ashe termed "a scoundrel, that has neither honor nor truth, and who was so panick-struck that he was not capable of making any observations, either on my conduct or on the action." Bryan's "unhappy temper" had previously created a breach between the two generals on the march from North Carolina, and now his carping observations on Ashe's strategy led Ashe to feel that

---

well Letterbook; *State Records*, XIV, 40–43; Dawson, *Battles of the United States*, I, 490–91; Lee, *Memoirs of the War in the Southern Department*, p. 124; Moultrie, *Memoirs of the American Revolution*, I, 323–25, 337; Prevost to Germain, 6 March 1779, Germain Papers; Lincoln to John Jay, 7 March 1779, Papers of the Continental Congress.

44. Ashe to Caswell, 17 March 1779, Caswell Letterbook; *State Records*, XIV, 41–42, 45; Ashe to Lincoln, 3 April 1779, Jethro Sumner Papers, N.C., Dept. Arch. & Hist.

45. Ashe to Caswell, 17 March 1779, Ashe to Caswell, 3 April 1779, Caswell Letterbook; *State Records*, XIV, 45, 51; Lee, *Memoirs of the War in the Southern Department*, p. 124; General Return of Bryan's Brigade of Militia after action at Bryar Creek, March 3d 1779, Troop Returns, Military Collection.

his actions would "ever render him contemptible to me." After the remnants of his command were assembled at Purysburg, a court of enquiry found Ashe guilty of "negligence," but he was acquitted of "every imputation of a want of personal courage in the affair at Bryar Creek, and think he remained in the field as long as prudence and duty required him." Ashe's greatest fault was that he had not laid out a route of withdrawal or designated a rendezvous in the event of defeat. William Bryan shortly afterwards resigned his commission as brigadier general of militia, claiming that he was too ignorant of military affairs to command a unit in the field.[46]

Prevost, by his bold action, had made the recovery of Georgia even more difficult for the Americans. Many agreed with Ashe that "things here wear a melancholy appearance." The militia had lost all enthusiasm for combat. When the terminal date of April 10 arrived, the men in Ashe's command refused to heed entreaties or promises of extra pay if they remained in the field and returned to their homes. But the North Carolinians were not alone in this, for the South Carolina militia showed a similar antipathy for martial life. In truth, the North Carolina militiamen proved to be of little use throughout the campaign, for they had spent so much time on the march to South Carolina that they had little time to learn even the basic patterns of battlefield formations and were on their march homeward after only a short time in the field. Then, too, it was spring and spring was the time for planting.[47]

46. Ashe to Caswell, 17 March 1779, Court of Enquiry to John Jay, 20 March 1779, Ashe to Lincoln, 3 April 1779, Caswell Letterbook; *State Records*, XIV, 41-42, 51-55, 74-75; Moultrie, *Memoirs of the American Revolution*, I, 323-24, 353; Ashe to Lincoln, 3 April 1779, Jethro Sumner Papers, N.C. Dept. Arch. & Hist.

47. *State Records*, XIV, 32, 51, 54, 66, 68; [Ashe] to _____ 3 April 1779, Miscellaneous Papers, 1697–1912.

Chapter 10
Stono Ferry

*"... barbarous warfare
of which the details would shock an Arab."*

Despite the burning resentment of the people of North Carolina toward the state of South Carolina, they continued to send aid to the best of their abilities and resources. So timely was this relief that Charles Pinckney had waxed rhapsodic: "They have been so willing and ready upon all occasions to afford us all the assistance in their power, that I shall ever love a North Carolinian, and join with Gen. Moultrie in confessing they have been the salvation of this country." But past efforts now had to be intensified, for intelligence indicated that the British in Georgia were expecting reinforcements from New York in the immediate future.[1]

Soon after Ashe had marched for South Carolina, Jethro Sumner had recovered his health enough to gather 759 nine-months Continentals who had been furloughed to their homes. Sumner pushed southward and in late March had arrived in General Lincoln's camp at Black Swamp. Although the men were in good health, they were badly in need of clothing. Clothier Thomas Craike had a rather sub-

1. Gibbes, *Documentary History of the American Revolution*, II, 107–8; *State Records*, XIV, 56.

stantial amount of cloth in varying patterns but Lincoln refused to allow Continental clothing to be issued to the nine-months men because of the limited time they were to remain in the field. Once in camp, these temporary Continentals were divided into two regiments which Sumner termed the Fourth and Fifth North Carolina Continentals. Some strength was added when some of the militia were persuaded to enlist as "substitutes" for a term of sixteen months. There was a shortage of officers of lower rank. Many of those who had been returned from Washington's army as supernumeraries were still in North Carolina on recruiting duty. The men were now "very naked," and appeared even more ragged when they were paraded with the well-clothed South Carolina troops. In demanding that the state send suitable clothing for its men, Lincoln pointed out that he felt that this obvious discrimination was hurting their morale—yet he refused to allow Craike to issue them Continental clothing supplies.[2]

Although several additional militia units joined Lincoln at Black Swamp, there was little chance of getting more men from North Carolina in the immediate future, for that state was now threatened. A British force had landed in Portsmouth, Virginia, and raided Suffolk. There was the rumor, and the subsequent fear, that the enemy might strike southward into North Carolina. Even "The Virginians," said Joseph Hewes, "who seem to have been in a kind of stupor, begin now to turn out." The militia from Perquimans and Tyrrell Counties began to come out with dispatch, but those of Chowan were termed "a sett of lazy Raskalls that hate to leave the fire side." But when the British fell back on Portsmouth and began to fortify that port, the militiamen were allowed to return to their homes with the promise that they would be called out again the moment the enemy threatened North Carolina again.[3]

South Carolina, now apprehensive about the setbacks in Georgia, took drastic measures, although it paid no heed to Congress's suggestion that Negro battalions (with white officers) be raised, with compensation for the owner and freedom for the black soldiers. The recently elected governor, John Rutledge, was given dictatorial powers

2. Sumner to Caswell, 28 March 1779, Lincoln to Caswell, 7 April 1779, Sumner to Caswell, 10 April 1779, Caswell Letterbook; Lincoln to Caswell, 3 April 1779, Governors' Papers; *State Records*, XIV, v, 48, 56, 61–62, 64, 310–11; Diary of John Graham, William A. Graham Papers; Return of Genl. Sumner's Brigade, 15 May 1779, Thomas Craike to Sumner, 14 June 1779, Jethro Sumner Papers, Southern Historical Collection.

3. Joseph Hewes to Caswell, 23 May 1779, Caswell Letterbook; Hewes to Caswell, 12 May 1779, Caswell Papers, N.C. Dept. Arch. & Hist.; *State Records*, XIV, 94–95; *North Carolina Historical and Genealogical Register*, II (April, 1901), 195.

and granted the privilege of "doing every thing that appeared to him and the council necessary for the public good." With the almost frantic aid of the state Legislature, Rutledge took decisive measures to strengthen South Carolina's martial posture. The South Carolina militia rushed into the field faster than ever before. In North Carolina Governor Caswell hurried down to Charlotte to speed the militia from the state's southern counties on toward Lincoln's position. From there he pressed on to New Bern where the assembly was sitting, who, he hoped, would make better arrangements for aiding the troops in the field.[4]

As reinforcements flowed into his camp, Lincoln grew ambitious, especially after intelligence indicated that the enemy did not have a large enough force to allow an expedition into South Carolina. Acting on the advice of a council of officers, Lincoln prepared to take the field in an offensive action. Leaving approximately a thousand men with General William Moultrie for the defense of Purysburg and the post at Black Swamp, Lincoln designated some four thousand troops for his own direction. Yet when the militiamen discovered that Lincoln planned to cross the river into Georgia, a "Great Mutiny" took place as they declared they could not be forced to leave South Carolina. After nightfall, around four hundred militiamen slipped away and were so cunning in their flight that none were captured. On April 23, 1779, Lincoln crossed the Savannah and marched for Augusta, his design to cut the enemy's communication with the back country, force him into a more limited area around Savannah, and protect the Georgia legislature, which had been summoned to meet in Augusta the first of May.[5]

General Prevost anxiously watched these moves by Lincoln. Although he had fewer men than Lincoln, their superior training, experience, and discipline would allow them to better than hold their own on any open battlefield against the American troops. To draw the Americans from Georgia, Prevost, at the head of 2,400 British troops and a sizable number of Indians slipped across the Savannah into South Carolina on April 29. At Purysburg, Lieutenant Colonel

4. Ramsay, *Revolution in South Carolina*, II, 18, 19; Lee, *Memoirs of the War in the Southern Department*, p. 125; Caswell to Lincoln, 5 April 1779, Caswell Papers, N.C. Dept. Arch. & Hist.; Ford, *Journals of the Continental Congress*, XIII, 387–88.

5. Dawson, *Battles of the United States*, I, 495; Lee, *Memoirs of the War in the Southern Department*, p. 125; Ford, *Journals of the Continental Congress*, XIII, 465–66; Moultrie, *Memoirs of the American Revolution*, I, 374–79; Diary of John Graham, William A. Graham Papers; Lincoln to Henry Laurens, 23 June 1779, Papers of the Continental Congress.

Alexander McIntosh with only about 220 men under his command, the Second and Fifth South Carolina Continentals, fell back upon Moultrie at Black Swamp. As Prevost swung towards Moultrie, that general retreated, destroying bridges as he marched. Riders were sent to Lincoln and to Charleston. During the night of May 7, Moultrie marched into Charleston, to be received with open arms by the terrified citizens, who had fallen into a "general confusion and alaram."[6]

Had Prevost driven straight to the gates of Charleston, the city surely would have fallen to him. But the plantation homes with their promise of booty were as effective in slowing the British advance as a strong rear-guard action. Prevost even weakened himself by detaching groups to escort flour and other loot back to Georgia. One such detachment of an officer and sixteen men were captured by the North Carolina militia. Not until May 9 did the British cross the Ashley River and march down Charleston Neck, there to be confronted with hastily thrown-up earthworks and abatis. Count Casimir Pulaski who had but recently arrived in South Carolina with his Legion of mounted troops and infantry, sallied out against the enemy dragoons in an attempt to draw them into an ambuscade. The enemy refused to take the bait; in fact, they gave the count a rather sound thrashing when some of his men broke from their concealment too soon. The only other action happened one night when a group of South Carolinians, placing some wagons in the line to be used as fortifications, were fired upon by their own people. Seven or eight were killed, including Major Benjamin Huger.[7]

Prevost's demands for the surrender of the town were countered by the amazing proposals of Governor Rutledge; the city would be turned over to the enemy if Prevost would guarantee the neutrality of the harbor and the rest of the state for the duration of the war! In rejecting the governor's proposals, Prevost declared that unconditional surrender was the only terms he could accept. Before he could muster any attempt upon the city, however, an intercepted letter revealed that Lincoln was hurriedly marching to the relief of Charles-

6. Thomas Bee to Caswell, 5 May 1779, Governors' Papers; *State Records*, XIV, 78–79; Dawson, *Battles of the United States*, I, 496–97; Lee, *Memoirs of the War in the Southern Department*, p. 125; Moultrie, *Memoirs of the American Revolution*, I, 403–13; Thomas Bee to Patrick Henry, 5 May 1779, Papers of the Continental Congress; Moultrie to Lincoln, 4 May 1779, Miscellaneous Papers, William L. Clements Library.

7. Moultrie, *Memoirs of the American Revolution*, I, 426–27; Dawson, *Battles of the United States*, I, 497–98; *State Records*, XIV, 118–20; Diary of John Graham, William A. Graham Papers.

ton. During the night of May 12 Prevost filed off to the coast and camped on John's Island to await water transportation back to Georgia. To protect his rear, earthworks were thrown up on the mainland at Stono Ferry.[8]

Lincoln arrived in the vicinity of Charleston shortly after Prevost's withdrawal. His army, including the North Carolina troops of Jethro Sumner, went into camp at Dorchester. A number of the militia light horse were sent out on patrols to intercept the large number of Negro slaves who had fled into the enemy camp in search of the freedom promised by the British. But the primary group was held back while Lincoln deliberated his next course of action. The general had been given permission to turn over the command to William Moultrie and return northward, but could not seem to be able to bring himself to leave in a time of crisis. There is also the suggestion that he felt he had to prove himself to those who had criticized him for marching into Georgia and leaving Charleston undefended.[9]

This delay allowed the enemy the time necessary to construct three solid redoubts on the mainland across from John's Island, each surrounded by a thick abatis of fallen trees. Prevost collected all the boats in the neighborhood and used them in the construction of a floating bridge across Stono Inlet to the island. By June 9 British transports, protected by men of war, dropped anchor off John's Island. They brought provisions but no reinforcements. In a dispatch from Governor Patrick Henry of Virginia there was additional bad news: the British in that state had embarked and might possibly join Prevost.[10]

On June 16, however, the outlook appeared more favorable as Prevost began to embark some of his troops aboard the transports. The great bulk of the booty and the slaves gathered on the march through South Carolina were first placed on board. To protect the embarkation, a battalion of the Seventy-First Highlanders, the weak von Trumback Hessian regiment, and Lieutenant Colonel John Hamilton's loyalist regiment made up of Tories from North and South

8. Moultrie, *Memoirs of the American Revolution*, I, 426–37; Lee, *Memoirs of the War in the Southern Department*, I, 497–98; Oliver Hart Diary (copy), Duke University, Durham, N.C.; Moultrie to Lincoln, 16 May 1779, Miscellaneous Papers, William L. Clements Library.

9. Diary of John Graham, William A. Graham Papers; Lincoln to Caswell, 6 June 1779, Governors' Papers; Laurens to Lincoln, 15 May 1779, Lincoln to Jay, 21 June 1779, Papers of the Continental Congress; *State Records*, XIV, 112–13.

10. John Rutledge to Caswell, 9 June 1779, Caswell Letterbook; Lee, *Memoirs of the War in the Southern Department*, pp. 128–29; Dawson, *Battles of the United States*, I, 499; Stedman, *History of the . . . American War*, II, 116; Moultrie, *Memoirs of the American Revolution*, I, 464–71.

Carolina were left on the mainland under the command of Lieutenant Colonel John Maitland. The boats used in the bridge had now been taken up for use in embarking the troops. Prevost made no effort to replace the bridge, since he wished to leave no easy avenue of retreat open to the men of the mainland garrison. His sick, the spare baggage, and his horses were ferried across to John's Island.[11]

Lincoln's intelligence indicated that the enemy redoubts were but poorly defended. On June 15 the general had met with his officers and Governor Rutledge and this council had decided to move against the enemy. Now that Prevost had appearently weakened the garrison at Stono Ferry, the chances for victory had improved considerably. John Butler's North Carolina militiamen, who had joined Lincoln on April 26, would be leaving for home when their time expired on July 10, while Sumner's nine-months Continentals would have to be discharged on August 10. The Virginia militia planned to march for home on July 15. Lincoln, if he was to make any use of these troops, would have to make an early move. And he would gain a distinct advantage if he could hit the British while they were engaged in embarkation.[12]

Lincoln however, was never one to make a hasty move, and it was not until June 19 that a council of officers decided that the attack should be launched the following morning. Moultrie, as Lincoln's second in command, was to lead a detachment from Charleston and move down to James's Island, adjoining John's Island, so that his forces might be seen by Prevost, who would send no aid to Maitland for fear of an attack in his rear. Boats were carried along to ferry Moultrie's men over to John's Island in cooperation with the attack on the redoubts. Moultrie did not immediately execute these orders; it has been charged that he deliberately procrastinated in order to enjoy the conviviality of a Charleston social event. By the time his command reached James's Island it had lost the tide and the current was flowing too swiftly to allow any use of small boats. Some complained that "from mismanagement, they did not reach their place of destination till the action was over."[13]

11. Stedman, *History of the . . . American War,* II, 116; Lee, *Memoirs of the War in the Southern Department,* pp. 129–30; Dawson, *Battles of the United States,* I, 499; *State Records,* XIV, 120; Butler to Caswell, 17 June 1779, Caswell Letterbook.

12. Rutledge to Caswell, 9 June 1779, Butler to Caswell, 17 June 1779, Lincoln to Caswell, 17 June 1779, Governors' Papers; *State Records,* XIV, 112–13, 119–20, 126–27; Moultrie, *Memoirs of the American Revolution,* I, 479; Lincoln to John Jay, 21 June 1779, Papers of the Continental Congress.

13. Ramsay, *Revolution in South Carolina,* II, 29; Moultrie, *Memoirs of the American Revolution,* I, 488–91; Joseph Johnson, *Traditions and Reminiscences*

American intelligence, so vague that at times it appeared almost ludicrous, suggested that the enemy was evacuating its redoubts. Lincoln, with 1,200 men, began his march shortly after midnight on the morning of June 20. After an eight-mile march, the ineptness and confusion of his guides led the general to form his battle line nearly a mile from the enemy post. Jethro Sumner commanded the right wing, made up of Butler's North Carolina militia and the nine-month Continentals with two fieldpieces. The left wing of Georgia and South Carolina Continentals with four guns was under the direction of General Isaac Huger of South Carolina. Colonel Marquis Francis de Malmedy and Lieutenant Colonel John Henderson led the light companies that protected the flanks. Pulaski's cavalry, including a detachment under Major William R. Davie, and Colonel David Mason's Virginia militia with its two artillery pieces made up the reserve.[14]

Lincoln had planned to outflank the enemy, but communications grew more capricious as the troops advanced. The right wing struggled through thickets of scrub oaks and pine saplings, while those on the left found the going much easier through an open forest of stately pines. On the right, contact was made with outlying enemy pickets about seven in the morning. They were driven in by Sumner's advance. The first real action was by John Henderson's light infantry over on the left flank. Two companies of the Seventy-First Highlanders had been posted out from the redoubts to intercept the American light infantry that of late had been conducting a series of early morning raids on the British outposts. Despite an inferiority in numbers, the well-disciplined Scots advanced to the attack with characteristic Highland daring . The American light infantry drove in with the bayonet and engaged them in hand-to-hand combat. The Highlanders "stood as obstinate as mules," until all but eleven privates had either been killed or wounded. As the survivors fell back toward the safety of their own lines the Americans pushed forward.[15]

Chiefly of the American Revolution in the South (Charleston, S.C., 1851), p. 225; Dawson, *Battles of the United States*, I, 499; Ford, *Journals of the Continental Congress*, XIV, 585–86; Ramsay, *History of the American Revolution*, II, 119.

14. Moultrie, *Memoirs of the American Revolution*, I, 491–99; Blackwell P. Robinson, *William R. Davie* (Chapel Hill, N.C., 1957), pp. 33–44.

15. Moultrie, *Memoirs of the American Revolution*, I, 491–99; Lee, *Memoirs of the War in the Southern Department*, pp. 130–31; Stedman, *History of the . . . American War*, II, 117; John Butler to Caswell, n.d., Rutledge to Caswell, n.d., Governors' Papers; *State Records*, XIV, 129–30; Timothy Pickering to Washington, 18 July 1779, George Washington Papers; John Rutledge to the South Carolina Delegates in Congress, 22 June 1779, Papers of the Continental Congress.

Maitland kept his troops within the fortifications, with the remainder of the Seventy-First Regiment on the right, the Hessians on the left, and Hamilton's loyalists in the center. Either Lincoln had not sent out proper reconnaissance, or he had paid little attention to intelligence reports. Not only were the redoubts stronger than he expected but he had overlooked, by his own admission, a deep creek running in front of the redoubt on his right which prevented the Continentals from storming the position. The defenders held their fire until the attacking force was within sixty yards of the abatis, then loosed a devastating volley.[16]

Sumner drove in and forced the von Trumbach regiment from its position. Those Hessians who fled and crowded aboard the few boats on the shore were sighted by the North Carolinians as they attempted an escape across Stono Inlet. Some were killed by musket fire while others drowned as they leaped overboard. Maitland and the Seventy-First stood firm until the majority of the Hessians could be rallied. Lincoln held back, feeling that the North Carolinians had not been "so broken to service" as to charge the enemy with the bayonet. So for the next hour there was an almost continuous fire. The American artillery was too light to make an impression upon the enemy works, yet upon several occasions American cannon fire wiped out the crews working the British guns. Lincoln's men began to run short of ammunition, even as enemy reinforcements were sighted crossing the inlet from the island. The order to retreat was carried out in an orderly fashion, the wounded and the artillery brought off under the protection of the mounted units and the Virginia militia. Maitland, with no cavalry, returned to his post after a brief pursuit. Over two hours had elapsed since the first contact had been made, although the primary battle lasted no longer than fifty-six minutes.[17]

American casualties numbered 146 killed and wounded, with 155 missing. It seems, however, that many of those among the missing simply continued their retreat until they reached the safety of their chimney corners. The loss among the nine-months North Carolina

---

16. Lee, *Memoirs of the War in the Southern Department*, pp. 131–32; Moultrie, *Memoirs of the American Revolution*, I, 500; Lincoln to Jay, 21 June 1779, Papers of the Continental Congress.

17. Stedman, *History of the . . . American War*, II, 117; John Butler to Caswell, n.d., Rutledge to Caswell, n.d., Governors' Papers; Dawson, *Battles of the United States*, I, 500–504; *State Records*, XIV, 120–21, 137–38; Prevost to Germain, 4 August 1779, Germain Papers; Moultrie, *Memoirs of the American Revolution*, I, 492–93; Lincoln to Jay, 21 June 1779, Papers of the Continental Congress; Diary of John Graham, William A. Graham Papers.

Continentals was ten killed, and five sergeants and twenty-six rank and file wounded. Andrew Jackson's older brother Hugh, a volunteer serving under Davie, died soon after the battle from excessive heat and fatigue. Colonel Armstrong, Lieutenant Colonel Lytle, Major Hal Dixon, Captains Joseph Rhodes and Davie, and Lieutenants Campbell and Charlton all suffered wounds. Only Dixon and Charlton, however, had serious wounds; the latter died soon after. The North Carolina militia suffered two rank and file killed with three officers and seventeen privates wounded. The British loss was three officers and twenty-three men killed, with ninety-three wounded and one man missing.[18]

After the battle each side attempted to harass the other through long-distance firing but inflicted little damage. There was some joy among the Americans as they witnessed two large row galleys sent out by Moultrie from James's Island capture a British schooner loaded with plundered household furniture. Three days after the battle the British moved down to Port Royal Island where Maitland was left in command of the post they established at Beaufort.[19]

There were frequent showers of rain almost every day. But even had he been so inclined Lincoln would have been able to do little in the way of offensive action. With the time of the militiamen near expiration, they stubbornly refused to engage in hazardous duty. The general spent much of his time composing dispatches to Caswell urging the governor to fill his battalions and send them on, at the same time grumbling because the Virginia Continentals were so slow in arriving. Because the enlistments of the nine-months men were running out, a number of the Continental officers were sent back to North Carolina to aid in recruiting. Lincoln could do little more than move down to Sheldon, where he could keep an eye on Maitland, although the thinness of his ranks prohibited offensive measures. Then, too, the "sultry season had set in; which, in this climate, like the frost in the North, gives repose to the soldiers. Preparations for

18. Dawson, *Battles of the United States,* I, 500; Rutledge to Caswell, n.d., Governors' Papers; *State Records,* XIV, 120–21; Prevost to Germain, 4 August 1779, Germain Papers; Robinson, *William R. Davie,* pp. 44–45; Moultrie, *Memoirs of the American Revolution,* I, 505–6, II, 3–10; Return of the Killed, Wounded and Missing in the Division of North Carolina Troops Commanded by Brig. Genl. Sumner in the Action at Stono Ferry the 20th June 1779, Troop Returns, Military Collection; A Return of the Killed, Wounded & Missing in the Action of 20 June 1779, Papers of the Continental Congress.

19. Diary of John Graham, William A. Graham Papers; Prevost to Germain, 4 August 1779, Germain Papers.

the next campaign, and the preservation of the health of the troops, now engrossed the attention of the hostile generals."[20]

Recruiting remained the greatest problem in North Carolina. The Continental Congress, in its new arrangement of the Continental Line, had established the quota for the state as six battalions or regiments. The Third, Fourth, Fifth, and Sixth Regiments were to be raised as quickly as possible and sent south to replace the nine-months Continentals then in the field. For home defense, the Congress authorized North Carolina and Virginia to raise battalions of men enlisted for only one year, to be allowed the pay and other benefits of Continental soldiers, a $200 bounty, and the promise that they would not be forced to serve north of Virginia. Enlishments lagged, perhaps because of the reluctance of many officers to engage in such mundane duty as recruiting. In eastern North Carolina the inhabitants were thrown into a panic when it was reported that the British were leaving South Carolina, possibly for North Carolina, and many along the coast began "packing up their alls expecting a visit every moment." William Hooper thought the fear of an attack on North Carolina was a bit silly. "What could the enemy get by it?" he asked, "To rob the pine trees and bear away the sandhills? . . . but I forgive you, local prejudices are unaccountably strong, and I have heard of a man in New England, who in his prayers always thanked Heaven that he lived on Cape Cod (the desert of God's deserted work)." Then the persistent rumor that the Tories were planning to rise once again killed the desire of many who might have enlisted.[21]

The Council of State took under consideration a new plan of the assembly whereby it was hoped that as many as two thousand men might be raised. For every man who could be persuaded to enlist as a Continental for eighteen months, ten militia men in his county were to be excused from military service. Such enlistees were to be termed "hired men." This plan was made even more attractive by the offer of additional enlistment bounties, but there were few takers. Almost in desperation it was decided to draft a quota of men for the militia

20. *State Records*, XIV, 126–27; Lee, *Memoirs of the War in the Southern Department*, pp. 132–33; Moultrie, *Memoirs of the American Revolution*, II, 10–11.

21. Lincoln to Caswell, 22 June 1779, Robert Mebane to Caswell, 30 June 1779, Lillington to Caswell, 5 July 1779, Caswell to Allen Jones, 7 July 1779, Caswell to Rutledge, 11 July 1779, Caswell to Rutherford, 19 July 1779, Caswell to Robert Raiford, 19 July 1779, Caswell Letterbook; Ford, *Journals of the Continental Congress*, XIII, 298, 387–88; McRee, *Life and Correspondence of James Iredell*, I, 428.

from each county who were to remain in the field for three months after they left the boundaries of the state. Despite the acute manpower shortage, no consideration was given the suggestion of Congress that Negro battalions, officered by white men, be raised in the South. And history repeated itself when Governor Caswell gave Count Pulaski permission to recruit men for his Legion from among the militiamen of the state.[22]

There was a concentrated effort to round up all deserters, whose numbers were increased by new enlistees running away. In some counties, particularly Edgecombe, Nash, Johnston, and Dobbs, there were subversive groups led by Samuel Godwin, Thomas Davis, Enoch How, and one Barswell, whose primary aim was the prevention of the militia being drafted and the releasing of those deserters who had been apprehended. There was also trouble in Burke County, where a body of bandits were operating and not only were plundering the inhabitants but were openly boasting that as soon as the harvest was gathered in they were going "to put to death the principal Friends to the Cause and March off to the Enemy. . . ." They had already participated in one jail break to release some of their friends from the Salisbury prison. Matters were further complicated by British recruiting officers prowling the area enlisting men for loyalist battalions. So desperate was the situation that the enlisting of Continental soldiers became a secondary consideration when Griffith Rutherford marched a large body of militia into the district to put down this rowdy set.[23]

Brigadier General Jethro Sumner fell into a "low state of health," and returned home to recover his strength and, as soon as he was able, to aid in recruiting and regimenting the newly enlisted Continentals. A number of other officers were also returned to aid in gathering recruits, as were a substantial group of sick and wounded from those troops already in the field. Yet on this detached duty these officers suffered even more than they would have in the field, for money had so depreciated that they found it difficult to support themselves, even after the council had granted them an extra ten dollars per diem.[24]

Despite such hardships, it was imperative that recruiting go for-

22. *State Records*, XIV, 126–27, 136, 140–41, 142–43, 151, 168–69, 171; Laurens to Caswell, 2 May 1779, Papers of the Continental Congress; Burnett, *Letters of Members of the Continental Congress*, IV, 136.

23. Caswell to Rutherford, 23 July 1779, Thomas Bonner to Caswell, 3 August 1779, Caswell Letterbook; *State Records*, XIV, 175–76, 184, 319–21.

24. Sumner to Caswell, 16 July 1779, Caswell Letterbook; *State Records*, XIV, 157–58, 322; Moultrie, *Memoirs of the American Revolution*, II, 16.

ward as expeditiously as possible. The southern army was losing men so rapidly that it was impossible for General Lincoln to engage in anything other than defensive moves; it would have been difficult to maintain any posts should the enemy attempt a move in force. By July 3 a number of the North Carolina short-term Continentals were returning home. The first to depart Lincoln's camp were the "sick and weak," who numbered 202. The remainder marched July 10, first turning in the arms that had been issued them when they came into the field. Most of the North Carolina militia had been discharged on July 2 and now the South Carolina militia clamored for release. But these men were held in camp because other militia groups refused to take the field.[25]

As a result of the action taken by the North Carolina Continental officers at West Point in the Spring of 1779 who had threatened to resign to a man unless North Carolina took some notice of their distressed situation, the General Assembly was forced into action. To slow the resignation of officers the legislature had, on May 13, 1779, passed a resolution offering officers half pay for life, the right to purchase personal supplies and one uniform a year at the same prices existing at the beginning of the war, exemption from taxation on lands granted for military service while the officers remained in the army, and a pension for the widows of those killed in action.[26]

Despite the poor state of his health, Jethro Sumner worked diligently in building up the state forces, and as soon as arms could be procured, he sent men marching for the rendezvous in the high hills of the Santee for further training. From this position they could move quickly into the low country if their services were required. By the middle of August, the "hired men" sent by the militia into the Continental service were being embodied. Governor Caswell labored to persuade men to come into the field, despite threats on his life, including that of John Barefoot who "watched several days for an opportunity to get a loaded gun and said if he could get one he would be damned to hell if he did not waylay the Road from your house to Kingston and kill you as you passed, for you passed every day that way." Caswell paid little heed to such threats. Those men recruited

25. Moultrie, *Memoirs of the American Revolution*, II, 8–9, 15–17, 20, 27; Diary of John Graham, William A. Graham Papers; Laurens to Caswell, 12 August 1779, Lincoln to Jay, 1 September 1779, Papers of the Continental Congress; *State Records*, XV, 745–46.

26. *State Records*, XIV, viii, 301–2, 335; Gideon Lamb to Caswell, 18 August 1779, Gideon Lamb Papers, North Carolina Department of Archives and History, Raleigh, N.C.

from the Edenton, New Bern, and Halifax districts were embodied at Kinston under Colonel Reading Blount where they were issued "good new arms" and marched to Camden where they were joined by the men from Wilmington. Yet despite this fairly auspicious beginning, Caswell warned that not above more than three hundred men could be raised in North Carolina, although he did promise to try to get as many as two thousand militiamen in the field. There were still a few North Carolina Continentals in South Carolina. These included nine-months men whose time would not expire until the first of December and some "old soldiers," in all amounting to about ninety men. Lincoln embodied them into companies and stationed them in Charleston.[27]

Lincoln still wanted to give up the southern command. Strange fevers and a troublesome old wound from Saratoga had so depressed him that he again requested permission to resign his southern command and return to Washington's army. Moultrie was recommended for a promotion to major general and succession to the command, a move that would not have rested well with the North Carolinians. Congress had granted Lincoln's request, but things happened too fast, and in August that body requested that he remain at his post "if the state of his health will permit, until he shall receive further direction from Congress," especially since the governor and council of South Carolina had requested that the general defer his departure.[28]

The summer drowsed away, with the days still hanging heavy with heat in September. General Lincoln had been ill much of the summer and was still convalescent when late intelligence forced him to leave his bed. All during the late spring and early summer the Continental Congress, Lincoln, and Governor Rutledge had sent appeals to the French admiral Comte d'Estaing, then operating in the West Indies, to join the southern army in a joint effort to dislodge the enemy at Savannah. Comte d'Estaing was a man of many and sudden impulses, and unexpectedly word came on September 3, 1779, that the French admiral with his fleet and four thousand soldiers was off Savannah. He was dogmatic in his insistence that he would remain

27. Stephen Cobb to Caswell, 26 July 1779, Caswell to Rutledge, 8 August 1779, Caswell Letterbook; *State Records*, XIV, 176–77, 188–89, 335, 337–38, 340–41; Lincoln to John Jay, 1 September 1779, Papers of the Continental Congress; Caswell to John Rutledge, 8 August 1779, Preston Davie Collection, Southern Historical Collection; Caswell to Sumner, 17 August 1779, Jethro Sumner Papers, Southern Historical Collection.

28. Ford, *Journals of the Continental Congress*, XIII, 149, 153, 465–66, XIV, 942; Laurens to Lincoln, 12 August 1779, Papers of the Continental Congress.

off American shores for only two weeks, for the hurricane season was at hand.[29]

Gathering every available man, including the ninety North Carolinians stationed in Charleston, Lincoln marched southward through the piney woods. On September 16 he marched into the Frenchman's camp pitched among the huge moss-hung oaks some three miles below Savannah. To Lincoln's consternation he discovered that the vain admiral had already summoned the enemy garrison to surrender to France, omitting any reference to the American forces. But in Prevost, d'Estaing met a master of procrastination, who stalled until additional troops could come in from Beaufort. Then he began to act "strong and so very saucy."[30]

Then it rained. Guns were manhandled into position through the mire and, just as soon as the weather cleared, siege lines were thrown up. On October 5 the French and American artillery began to saturate the town with artillery bombardment. Day and night they pounded the defenses with a steady fire. But the French admiral was an impatient fellow and he feared the heavy weather that might suddenly burst upon him. A cantankerous individual, he was constantly bickering with Lincoln over the most minute details and dismissing matters of some import with a wave of the hand. Even a number of the French officers began to grow unhappy with their commanding officer. "Of all the scourges of the human race," complained one, "an ambitious master of its fate is the worst." Over the angry protests of Lincoln and several of the French military men, d'Estaing insisted upon launching an all out frontal attack upon the town. There was little that Lincoln could do but acquiesce in the mad scheme.[31]

In the early morning of October 9 five columns were to advance against the town, with three to be made up of the French troops. One of the American columns was to be composed of the Second South Carolina Continentals and the Charleston militia under the

29. Ward, *War of the Revolution*, II, 688–89; Moultrie, *Memoirs of the American Revolution*, II, 33, Laurens to Lincoln, 15 May 1779, Laurens to Moultrie, 15 May 1779, Laurens to Jay, 5 September 1779, Papers of the Continental Congress.

30. Alexander A. Lawrence, *Storm Over Savannah: The Story of Count d' Estaing and the Siege of the Town in 1779* (Athens, Ga., 1951), pp. 30–59; Charles C. Jooe, Jr. (ed.), *The Siege of Savannah in 1779, as Described in Two Contemporaneous Journals of French Officers in the Fleet of Count d'Estaing* (Albany, N.Y., 1874), pp. 56–61; Lincoln to Samuel Huntington, 22 October 1779, Papers of the Continental Congress.

31. Lawrence, *Storm Over Savannah*, pp. 84–85; Lincoln to Huntington, 22 October 1779, Papers of the Continental Congress.

command of Brigadier General Isaac Huger and Colonel John Laurens; the other included the First and Fifth South Carolina Continentals with few Georgia regulars under Brigadier General Lachlan McIntosh. There is no record of the disposition of the ninety North Carolina Continentals, but it is only reasonable to suppose that they were included in one of the two South Carolina battalions.[32]

From the beginning, one error amplified the other until there seemed to be little left to expect other than a foregone conclusion of disaster. A deserter saw to it that the British were informed of the time and nature of the attack. The French were late in arriving at the point of departure, and when they did arrive d'Estaing led them to the assault without waiting for the other columns to get into position. Other mistakes and a dreadful lack of communication confused matters even further, but the South Carolinians under John Laurens flung themselves against the British parapet after the French were driven back. The French flag and the standard of the Second South Carolina Regiment were placed on the ramparts of the Spring Hill redoubt before the attackers were repulsed. The fighting was fierce, so fierce that the ditch in front of the British redoubt was filled with bodies and it was reported that "many hung dead and wounded on the abatis," while beyond "the plain was strewed with mangled bodies." The Americans were driven back. Between them, the allies had lost a total of 16 officers and 228 men killed and 63 officers and 521 wounded, almost one-fifth of the men engaged in the battle. Among the dead was the colorful Pole, Casimir Pulaski. British losses totaled 40 killed, 63 wounded, and 52 missing.[33]

Despite this setback, Lincoln wished to continue the siege, but the count had lost his taste for land warfare. His crews were ill with scurvy and his ships lay in the path of possible fall hurricanes. Lincoln's pleas fell on deaf ears and on October 18 the siege was lifted. The following day Lincoln pulled his troops back across the Savannah. The French began their retirement the next day.[34]

The defeat of the allies before Savannah held greater implications than just a battlefield disaster. Had the British been driven from

32. Ward, *War of the Revolution*, II, 692; Moultrie, *Memoirs of the American Revolution*, II, 37–40; Lincoln to Huntington, 22 October 1779, Papers of the Continental Congress.

33. Franklin B. Hough, *The Siege of Savannah, by the Combined American and French Forces, under the Command of Gen. Lincoln, and the Count d'Estaing, in the Autumn of 1779* (Albany, N.Y., 1866), pp. 160–74; Lawrence, *Storm Over Savannah*, pp. 100–123; Moultrie, *Memoirs of the American Revolution*, II, 40–41.

34. Lawrence, *Storm Over Savannah*, pp. 122–45; Lincoln to Huntington, 22 October 1779, Papers of the Continental Congress.

the town, the enemy would have been deprived of a base from which to launch a southern campaign. This is not to say that they would not have attempted such an expedition, but without Savannah the task would have been infinitely more difficult, and the departure of the French fleet left the sea lanes open. In this failure lay the genesis of a "barbarous warfare of which the details would shock an Arab."[35]

It was because of the desperate situation in the Southern Department that Washington was finally led to release the North Carolinians stationed to the northward, especially after it became apparent that no aid could be expected from d'Estaing in a joint attack upon the British forces in New York. Marching orders had been issued to Hogun and the North Carolina Continentals on November 18, but they were unable to move before November 24 because of the torrential rains. Some clothing had been issued them, but not nearly enough and that given out had been of many hues and many patterns. By December 5 they were in Philadelphia attempting to arrange water transportation to the South. Although many of the seven hundred men in the brigade lacked proper clothing, the Continental Congress ordered them to begin their march overland without waiting for ships since the latest intelligence from New York was that the enemy was embarking a considerable body of troops, presumably for an expedition to the South. The Board of War, although "extremely embarrassed" because of its inability to secure the necessary ships to transport the North Carolinians, did make arrangements to ferry them across Chesapeake Bay.[36]

With the prospect of an enemy strike against South Carolina, North Carolina became increasingly more important as a primary source of aid. Lincoln not only pleaded with Caswell to speed up recruiting activities but to also keep an eye on the back country to prevent the Tories from rising and marching to the coast to make a junction with the enemy. But the practice of employing "hired men" had exempted so many of the militia from military duty outside the state that any body of men sent to the southward would of necessity be small. The need for manpower in the southern army grew more desperate with each passing day, for on December 24 the first troop ships in New York had weighed anchor and had dropped down to Sandy Hook. Charleston, it appeared, was their objective, with intelligence stating that "their Destination is so well ascertained as to be out of Doubt. . . ." It was generally felt that the troops march-

35. William Sharpe to Caswell, 5 December 1779, Caswell Letterbook.

36. *State Records,* XIV, 230–31, 357; Ford, *Journals of the Continental Congress,* XV, 1092–93, 1138, 1256, 1362.

ing from the northward would arrive too late to be of much aid.[37]

The march of the men of the North Carolina Brigade southward from Petersburg, Virginia, was probably one of the worst experiences of their military careers. The weather turned bitter cold. In many places the snow lay drifted three feet deep with a hard frozen crust that cut through skimpy footwear like a knife. Yet to Hogun's credit, he pushed his soldiers as hard as their physical condition would permit, then demanded just a bit more. After overcoming many "obsticles," they reached Wilmington by February 19, 1780, but there was no rest for the weary North Carolinians. They learned that the British had already landed in the vicinity of Charleston. And so they pushed on to their doom.[38]

37. Lincoln to Caswell, 15 December 1779, Henry Lee to Congress, 26 December 1779, Caswell Letterbook; *State Records*, XIV, 233–34, 239–40, 351, 359; Laurens to Lincoln, 11 November 1779, Laurens to Caswell, 11 November 1779, Papers of the Continental Congress.

38. Hogun to Washington, 19 February 1779, George Washington Papers; William Sharpe to Caswell, 5 December 1779, Historical Society of Pennsylvania Collection (also in Caswell Letterbook); Laurens to Caswell, 13 July 1779, Papers of the Continental Congress; *State Records*, XIV, 798, XV, 187–88.

Chapter 11
Charleston, 1780

"...as if the stars were tumbling down."

The repulse of the allies before Savannah was significant beyond local considerations. With the sea lanes open, Sir Henry Clinton was able to proceed with his plans for returning the South to the royal fold. The time was ripe for it was felt that the loyalists, after the successful defense of Savannah, would flock to the royal standard. After Charleston had fallen, the upper South could be regained at leisure. In September, 1779, the British had evacuated Newport, Rhode Island. Then, after persuading Vice Admiral Marriot Arbuthnot that it would be foolish to seek out the French navy rather than escort the British army to the South, Clinton began to embark his troops. The rather formidable armada numbered ninety transports, escorted by five ships of the line and nine frigates, in all bearing a total of 650 guns.[1]

Just missing becoming icebound when New York harbor froze over, the massive fleet cleared Sandy Hook on December 26, 1779. The thirty-eight day voyage was a journey of terror. Just two days out a storm struck off Cape Hatteras. Many of the vessels that steered out to sea were caught in the Gulf Stream, making southward prog-

1. Uhlendorf, *Baurmeister Journals*, pp. 331–32.

ress even more difficult. One transport, the *Anna*, with two hundred Hessians aboard, was swept across the Atlantic to Europe. All but three hundred horses were lost, as were a number of artillery pieces and an inestimable amount of supplies. North Edisto inlet, just south of Charleston, had been the original destination of the British fleet but was bypassed in favor of putting into Savannah for repairs, reorganization, and time enough to allow the troops to regain their health. On January 30, 1780, sixty-one vessels dropped anchor off Tybee Island.[2]

The arrival of Clinton in the South came as no surprise to Lincoln. Some time earlier the Continental Congress had passed on that intelligence. In fact, as it turned out, the intelligence received was fairly accurate in reporting British strategy and plans for the future. The Congress had also been responsible for Washington's releasing the North Carolina Brigade for the defense of "Devoted Charles Town," although Robert Howe prophesied that "their aid is too feeble to save it, even supposing they should arrive in time, which is almost impossible they should." The sailing of the enemy fleet had forced Lincoln to abandon plans for an expedition against St. Augustine. This change in plans, however, was not too distasteful, for he had been against this move ordered by Congress, feeling it to be "fruitless." He had written a letter to the delegates of Massachusetts Bay in Congress requesting that they oppose it. Now the problem was where Lincoln should station his troops: along the overland route where he could oppose the enemy at important river crossings, or in Charleston lest the British come by water.[3]

The news that the enemy fleet had sailed, presumably for the South, discouraged new enlistments in North Carolina, and many of those who had earlier accepted enlistment bonuses now proved faint of heart and deserted. Some North Carolina officers in Charleston were sent home by Lincoln to assist General Sumner in rounding up deserters. When bonus money was exhausted, new recruits refused to march until they had received their bounty and back-ration allow-

2. Sir Henry Clinton, *The American Rebellion: Sir Henry Clinton's Narrative of His Campaigns, 1775–1782*, ed. William B. Willcox (New Haven, Conn., 1954), pp. 156–60.
3. *State Records*, XIV, 358–59, XV, 323–24; John Penn, Thomas Burke, and Allen Jones to Caswell, 21 January 1780, Lincoln to Caswell, 24 January 1780, Caswell Letterbook; Lincoln to Washington, 23 January 1780, Lincoln to Washington, 28 January 1780, George Washington Papers; Lincoln to Richard Howley, 19 February 1780, Miscellaneous Papers, William L. Clements Library; Lincoln to the Massachusetts Delegates in Congress, 9 July 1779, Preston Davie Collection, Southern Historical Collection; Intelligence, n.d., Caswell Papers, N.C. Dept. Arch. & Hist.

ances. Officers were forced to borrow money to meet personal expenses, and when they could no longer find funds they returned to their homes. Tories went on the prowl, which hampered recruiting activities.[4]

Lincoln, like most Continental generals, did not particularly want militia in his command, but in these desperate hours he grasped at every straw. He felt that calling out the militia resulted in

such a waste of time in marching to and from Camp, such sporting with the public monies by the extraordinary expence in keeping up an army in this way, such loss of husbandmen from the fields (being double their number absent from their homes to those really in arms) besides the more melancholy evils which arise from a call so frequently of different men into Camp, many of whom are lost before they become seasoned to it, and the distresses brought on the families of those who are hurried away before they have an opp'y of making the necessary provisions for their subsistence while absent, are misfortunes much to be regretted and guarded against if possible.[5]

But it proved easier to call the militia into the field than to recruit Continentals in North Carolina, even though it was difficult to persuade these men to serve beyond the boundaries of the state. Supplies and provisions for both militia and Continentals were hard to come by. It had been a hard winter, leading Thomas Hart to muse, "I wonder truly how many poor Sons of Bitches with tears in their Eyes have I seen within these Six weeks past . . . all declaring themselves broken. . . ." Although the state had promised a bounty to all those militiamen who would agree to serve outside North Carolina, those regiments that did march were frightfully thin in numbers and poorly equipped. Many were without arms, accouterments, tents, or camp kettles, but Edward Rutledge of South Carolina promised to provide them with such necessities just as soon as they reached Charleston. When it became apparent that there would be no funds to pay the promised bonuses, those militiamen who had already reached South Carolina became "very uneasy, and at sometimes were almost ready to mutiny. . . ." In some instances, better discipline resulted when supernumerary Continental officers, including Archibald Lytle, solicited and secured command of the militia units. Although Lincoln cried for reinforcements of any kind, Governor John Rutledge of South Carolina urged that a large body of militia be held in North Carolina to

---

4. Peter Mallet to Caswell, 4 January 1780, James Long to Caswell, 17 January 1780, Sumner to Caswell, 30 January 1780, Caswell Letterbook; *State Records,* XV, 314, 316–18; Lincoln to Caswell, 3 March 1780, Governors' Papers; *The Collector,* LXXV (1962), 76.

5. Lincoln to Caswell, 3 January 1780, Caswell Letterbook; *State Records,* XV, 312–13.

"hover on our Frontiers, & on the least prospect or Apprehension of an Insurrection amongst our disaffected, march in to crush it."[6]

A number of North Carolina militia units were in Charleston by early January. Lincoln's orders were confusing, and for awhile they were posted in Dorchester before they were called into Charleston on January 28. Other small units trickled in each day. Their general, Alexander Lillington, wished to establish greater discipline and pleaded that regular officers, preferably Continental field-grade officers, be assigned to his command. There was little time for training, since the North Carolina troops became something of a labor force, assigned to work on the fortifications when the planters in the vicinity refused to allow their slaves to come into town to work for fear of smallpox. Despite promises, most of the militiamen were still without tents or supplies. Technicalities complicated the supply situation. Although the North Carolina militia commissaries had collected a fair amount of provisions, they could not issue them to Lillington's men because once they passed the state boundary they fell under the jurisdiction of Thomas Rutledge, commissary general of the Southern Department. Lincoln was able to find the muskets with which to arm them. By February 10, 1780, a total of 1,248 North Carolina militiamen were under Lillington's command, encamped just beyond the city limits.[7]

Hogun's North Carolina Brigade of Continentals, accompanied by the artillery company, after overcoming "the many Obsticles that has Tended to the Impeding my March to the Southward," arrived in Wilmington in mid-February. Their stay was short, but they were supplied with sufficient quantities of rum, sugar, and coffee. Few of the officers could afford the blue and white uniforms authorized by the Continental Congress although they were issued linen to make into shirts. The troops were badly in need of uniforms, hats, and boots, and the commissaries had no money. Some of the men, their

6. Lillington to Caswell, 10 January 1780, James Long to Caswell, 17 January 1780, John Butler to Caswell, 20 January 1780, Lytle to Caswell, 28 January 1780, John Rutledge to Caswell, 31 January 1780, Caswell Letterbook; *State Records*, XV, 317, 318, 320–21, 329, 332–33; Caswell to Lincoln, 22 December 1779, Miscellaneous Papers, William L. Clements Library; Alice Barnwell Keith (ed.), *The John Gray Blount Papers*, (Raleigh, N.C., 1952), I, 9.

7. Lytle to Caswell, 28 January 1780, Lillington to Caswell, 12 February 1780, Rutherford to Caswell, 17 February 1780, Charles Jewkes to Caswell, 1 March 1780, Lincoln to Caswell, 3 March 1780, Caswell Letterbook; Return of N.C. Militia under Lillington in Camp near Ch'ston, 10 February 1780, Troop Returns, Military Collection; *State Records*, XV, 336–37, 347–48, XXII, 1022; Lincoln to Committee of Correspondence, 2 December 1779, Papers of the Continental Congress; Gibbes, *Documentary History of the American Revolution*, II, 129.

pay in arrears for the past few months, refused to march farther south "till they had justice done them." Their leader, Sergeant Samuel Glover of the Second Regiment, a veteran of Brandywine, Germantown, and Stony Point, was taken up and shot as an example to the others. They marched.

By February 19, Hogun's troops had completed their crossing of the Cape Fear at Wilmington and were on the march for Charleston. During the evening of March 3 they paraded into Charleston, an occasion that gave "great spirits to the Town and confidence to the Army." The strength of the brigade, composed of Clark's First and Patten's Second regiments, was six hundred rank and file. Each regiment needed an additional two hundred men to complete its complement. The enlistment of fifty-five men had expired during the march south while twelve privates had deserted as the brigade passed through North Carolina, a surprisingly low number in view of the time they had been away from home. Some essential personnel such as wagoners and artificers belonging to the brigade had been kept with Washington's army.[8]

The Third Regiment had arrived in Charleston no later than late December or early January, long enough for a considerable number to have deserted and returned home by January 8. Actually, the men were supposed to have arrived as early as June, when the governor's council, acting on a resolve by the Continental Congress of May 7, 1779, ordered them to join Lincoln. Sumner and other Continental officers were urged to take up the deserters and return them to the army, while Lincoln suggested to Governor Caswell that if the deserters found it impossible to live in their neighborhoods when they got home, the practice of deserting would be stopped. Two officers from the regiment were sent back home to round up those who were absent without leave.

Back in April, 1779, the enlistments of the noncommissioned officers and of the rank and file had expired. Robert Mebane, along with other officers, had been ordered back to North Carolina to rebuild the strength of the Third Regiment. Recruiting had lagged because of the illness and general unhappiness of the officers. Many of the supernumerary officers from other regiments who had been returned

8. Hogun to Washington, 19 February 1780, Lincoln to Washington, 4 March 1780, Washington Papers; Harnett to Burke, 22 February 1780, Thomas Burke Papers; Return of the N.C. Brigade of Foot Commanded by B. G. Hogun, Feby 1780, Troop Returns, Military Collection; *State Records*, XIV, 798–99, XV, 187–88, 325, 352; Hogun to Caswell, 16 July 1779, Robert Rowan to Caswell, 7 March 1780, Caswell Letterbook; Lincoln to Huntington, 4 March 1780, Papers of the Continental Congress.

to the state had given up their commissions, declaring that they had been treated in an ignominious fashion by the General Assembly. The recruiting of Continentals, mostly nine-months "hired men" from the militia, had not gone well. Such success as had been achieved in recruiting was because of the almost unrelenting efforts of Gideon Lamb. In general, these men were poorly armed, with the exception of those from the Kinston area, where a shipment of Continental arms on the way to South Carolina had been intercepted. A number of these men had been sent to Camden or the high hills of the Santee because of the food problem before they were ordered on to Charleston. Before Gideon Lamb became very active in military affairs he first had to be cleared of charges of improper conduct on the battlefield at Brandywine. On November 5, 1779, a court of enquiry held in Halifax acquitted him "with honor." The command of the Third Regiment, nevertheless, was given to Lieutenant Colonel Robert Mebane, with Lieutenant Colonel Selby Harney and Major Thomas Hogg as his chief subordinates. There were 162 men in the regiment, 130 of whom were privates.[9]

On January 23 a British cargo vessel had been "decoyed" into Charleston harbor and captured. From papers aboard that vessel it was discovered that Charleston was the primary objective of the British expedition. This was confirmed less than a week later when Commodore Whipple captured and brought in two sloops with about fifty British dragoons aboard. Intelligence reports revealed that British plans called for the subjugation of both Carolinas by May and that the attack on Charleston would employ different strategy than that used in 1776. Clinton, it was reported, "will make a Rigorous push for it, for I believe he thinks it necessary to do something to distinguish himself before he returns to England."[10]

Perhaps Lincoln should have evacuated the town at this time to save his southern army, but the Continental Congress, since 1776, had constantly recommended a strong defense of Charleston and stationed Continental vessels there. In 1779 the French engineer Lieutenant Colonel Cambray-Digny had been sent to superintend the construction of fortifications for the city. To have abandoned Charleston would have left the most important port in the southern colonies

9. Timothy Pickering to Caswell, 17 April 1779, Mebane to Caswell, 10 May 1779, Mebane to Caswell, 30 June 1779, Caswell Letterbook; State Records, XIV, 289–90, 292–93, 337–38, 351–52, 816, 817, XV, 314, 316–17, 320–21, 398, XXII, 955; Lincoln to Caswell, 8 January 1780, Governors' Papers.

10. Intelligence, n.d., Governors' Papers; Lincoln to Washington, 23–24 January 1780, Lincoln to Washington, 28–29 January 1780, Papers of the Continental Congress.

in the hands of the enemy. Not only did the port serve South Carolina, but it was the chief export area for back-country North Carolinians who used the rivers flowing in a southeasterly direction to get their goods to market. Then, too, Lincoln was expecting aid. In December a communication from Henry Laurens, president of the Continental Congress, had reported that a diversionary force was being sent against the Floridas. Although this expedition had not yet materialized, it was suggested that both Spain and France also would send "a naval Force & troops sufficient" to aid the southern army.[11]

Lincoln began to push the work on the fortifications around Charleston. Continentals stationed in outlying areas were called in. Letters pleading for speedy assistance were dispatched to Governors Caswell and Jefferson. In the event of an enemy attack, Caswell was requested to embody militia and station them along the border to prevent the Tories from rising. A letter to Comte de Grasse pleaded for aid from the French fleet under his command. A message to Brigadier General William Woodford, in command of the Virginia Continentals detached from Washington's army, urged that he abandon his baggage and wagons and hurry forward as "Your speedy arrival is most ardently wished for & it is not more so than Necessary."[12]

Once the ships of the British fleet were again seaworthy, they weighed anchor on February 10, 1780, and put out to sea. The following day, to the accompaniment of the distant booming of alarm guns in Charleston, troops were disembarked on Simmon's Island on North Edisto Inlet. By February 16 Stono Ferry had been secured by the establishment of a light-infantry post. The weather worsened; fog and an almost constant rain hampered operations. As the transports continued to come in, artillery was landed, depots were established, and small boats and seamen were pulled into shore to be use in transporting the troops across the various cuts and streams. The British general gradually worked his way onto James's Island.[13]

11. Lincoln to Caswell, 24 January 1780, Governors' Papers; *State Records,* XV, 24–25, 326; *Original Papers Relating to the Seige of Charleston, 1780* (Charleston, S.C., 1898; reprinted from the *Charleston Year Book for 1897* [Charleston, S.C., 1898]), p. 27; Laurens to Lincoln, 18 December 1779, Papers of the Continental Congress; Lincoln to Sumner, 24 June 1780, Jethro Sumner Papers, Southern Historical Collection; [Franklin Benjamin Hough], *The Siege of Charleston, By the British Fleet and Army under the Command of Admiral Arbuthnot and Sir Henry Clinton* (Albany, N.Y., 1867), p. 27.

12. Lincoln to Washington, 23–24 January 1780, Lincoln to Washington, 28–29 January 1780, Lincoln to William Woodford, 11 February 1780, George Washington Papers; Lincoln to Caswell, 24 January 1780, Lincoln to Caswell, 29 January 1780, Governors' Papers; Burnett, *Letters of Members of the Continental Congress,* V, 11.

13. *American Historical Review,* V (April, 1899), 483–89; Lincoln to Samuel

Except in naval strength, Charleston's defense system was not so formidable as it had been in 1776. Nine armed vessels, ranging in armament from sixteen to forty-four guns, under the command of Commodore Abraham Whipple, lay at anchor in the harbor. Three French frigates that had planned to winter in Charleston upped anchor and sailed just as soon as it became obvious that the British were going to attack the place. Fort Moultrie (formerly Fort Sullivan), on Sullivan's Island, and Fort Johnson, on James Island, had been allowed to fall into ruins and little had been done to repair them until attack seemed imminent. On March 6, Clinton took Fort Johnson by attacking it from the rear. This allowed the British to afford protection for their own ships once they crossed the bar, annoy American shipping, or even send an occasional nuisance shell toward the Charleston waterfront.[14]

The construction of the American fortifications was pushed forward, with one observer noting that "like mushrooms they sprang from the soil." The South Carolina legislature invested Governor Rutledge with almost dictatorial powers and he immediately impressed six hundred slaves to labor on the earthworks. A ditch, or moat, approximately a mile and a half long, was thrown across the peninsula, its flanks anchored on the Ashley and Charles rivers and with the extremities further protected by wide marshes. Behind this "broad canal" were strong breastworks and redoubts, bristling with fraise work and protected by a double abatis. Wolf traps were scattered throughout these tangled trees to discourage those inclined to creep or charge through the obstruction. Sixty-six guns and a number of mortars were mounted in the works. In the center of this protective line was a substantial "horn work," constructed of masonry and known as the "Citadel." A redoubt mounting sixteen guns was thrown up at the south end of the town, while smaller forts containing four to nine guns were thrown up at strategic points. The British almost received complete diagrams of the Charleston defenses when one Hamilton Ballard attempted to slip through the lines, but he was betrayed by his two Negro guides at the last American outpost and hanged.[15]

Huntington, 14 February 1780, Lincoln to Huntington, 22 February 1780, Papers of the Continental Congress; [Hough], Siege of Charleston, p. 30.

14. Rutledge to Caswell, 31 January 1780, Lincoln to Caswell, Caswell Letterbook; Clinton to Huntington, 29 February 1780, Papers of the Continental Congress; State Records, XV, 332-33.

15. Bernhard A. Uhlendorf (trans. and ed.), The Siege of Charleston, with an Account of the Province of South Carolina: Diaries and Letters of Hessian Officers. From the von Jungken Papers in the William L. Clements Library (Ann Arbor,

This strong fortification convinced Clinton that his six thousand men were not enough to take the town by assault. Transports were sent back to New York for reinforcements, while General James Paterson was ordered to bring up the diversionary force that had been left in Georgia. By the middle of April, Clinton was to have ten thousand troops under his command, plus the use of the five thousand sailors under Arbuthnot.[16]

Lincoln could not hope to summon additional strength, although Governor Rutledge, who in the past had appeared almost lax in his efforts, now cooperated fully. When called, the South Carolina militiamen hung back, fearing that once they were cooped up within the city smallpox would become prevalent. Others had grown faint of heart because of the magnificent stand made by the British at Savannah. Lincoln now called upon Caswell for the militia stationed on the North Carolina border, "for I am convinced on it depends the Salvation or loss of the State; and with it your State may suffer." All of these things seemed to bear out an observation made by John Mathews, South Carolina delegate to the Continental Congress. In January he had deplored the "want of vigour" in his state and had noted: "In passing through No. Carolina and Virginia, whenever I urged the necessity of their sending men to our aid, the constant reply was how can South Carolina expect we will send our men to their support, when they will do nothing for themselves. Our men go there, sacrifice their healths, their lives, and the So. Carolina Militia are snug at their own homes. It is too much for them to expect us to fight their battles for them."[17]

With the British army in the state, the Tories began to rise and harass and plunder their former tormenters, presaging the vicious civil war that was to rage in South Carolina for the next two years. Rutledge requested Caswell to send the North Carolina militia under Griffith Rutherford into the area of the "Snow Campaign" of 1775 to awe the loyalists of that neighborhood into activity. Lincoln countermanded this request, inasmuch as every possible man was needed for the defense of Charleston. Because Spain had recently entered the

---

Mich., 1938), p. 211; R. Cogdell to Caswell, 10 March 1780, Caswell Letterbook; *State Records*, XV, 42, 353–54; [Hough], *Siege of Charleston*, pp. 68–69; Ramsay, *History of the American Revolution*, II, 151–52; John Laurens to Washington, 9 April 1780, Washington Papers.

16. Clinton, *American Rebellion*, pp. 160–63.

17. Lincoln to Caswell, 14 March 1780, Governors' Papers; Rutledge to Caswell, 14 March 1780, Caswell Letterbook; Burnett, *Letters of Members of the Continental Congress*, V, 11; *State Records*, XV, 349–50; Gibbes, *Documentary History of the American Revolution*, II, 129; [Hough], *Siege of Charleston*, p. 37; Ramsay, *Revolution in South Carolina*, II, 40.

war, Congress authorized Lincoln to "correspond & concert with the Governor of the Havannah." Lincoln secretly sent an emissary, Lieutenant Colonel John Tennant, to Havana requesting Spanish aid in the form of men and ships. The request was refused.[18]

On March 20, 1780, after waiting more than a week for the high tides of the full moon, Arbuthnot began to move the vessels of his command across the bar. The little American flotilla could find no position that would effectively allow it to offset the firepower of the enemy. The ships were pulled back into the Cooper River in the channel between the town and the island called Shute's Folly. Four frigates and several merchant vessels were sunk in the mouth of the Cooper River, providing anchors for the log and chain boom blocking the entrance to the river. The remaining ships were anchored in the river behind the boom, but the guns and crews of all vessels except the twenty-gun *Ranger* and the twenty-eight gun *Queen of France* were brought ashore to strengthen American firepower. By removing his guns and heavy equipment, Arbuthnot gradually worked his heavy ships across the bar into the deep water of Five Fathom Hole. By March 25, the British vessels seemed only to be awaiting a favorable breeze to bring them opposite the town.[19]

This display of seapower and the seeming withdrawal of Commodore Whipple's ships led to an increasing uneasiness among the militia within the town, especially among the men from North Carolina. The term of service for the greater part of them expired on March 24 and they immediately left, most of them paying scant heed to Governor Rutledge's offer of a bounty of $300 and a new suit of clothes if they would remain. Others, whose discharges were due April 6, fearful lest they become trapped within the city, clamored for an immediate release. Lincoln refused to listen to their demands. Many deserted. Those militiamen who were being raised in North Carolina to replace this group were slow in coming out. Calling out the militia in North Carolina for the relief of Charleston was more of a disadvantage than an advantage, for these men constantly soaked up badly needed supplies originally destined for Hogun's Continentals. On April 7, the desperate situation looked some brighter when, "to the

18. McCrady, *History of South Carolina in the Revolution,* II, 445; Lincoln to Caswell, 3 March 1780, Rutledge to Caswell, 5 March 1780, Caswell Letterbook; *State Records,* XV, 354–55; Huntington to Lincoln, 18 December 1779, John Tennent to Lincoln, 23 March 1780, Lincoln to Huntington, 24 March 1780, Papers of the Continental Congress.

19. Lincoln to Caswell, 14 March 1780, Lincoln to Caswell, 25 March 1780, Caswell Letterbook; Clinton, *American Rebellion,* p. 162; *State Records,* XV, 355, 362–63; John Laurens to Washington, 4 April 1780, William Woodford to Washington, George Washington Papers; Lincoln to Huntington, 24 March 1780, Papers of the Continental Congress.

great joy of the Garrison," General Woodford and 750 Virginia Continentals came in, having marched 505 miles during the past thirty days. Accompanying them were 120 North Carolina militiamen under Lieutenant Colonel William Henry Harrington.[20]

Lincoln had attempted to maintain a line of communication and a withdrawal route by holding the upper fords of the Cooper River. General Isaac Huger with about 500 men had been stationed near Biggins Bridge near the forks of the Cooper, some thirty miles north of Charleston. To defend the three miles of fortifications about Charleston there were now approximately 2,650 Continentals and 2,500 militiamen. Only about one-third, chiefly militia and armed volunteers, were from South Carolina. To make matters worse, the civil authorities and merchants constantly questioned Lincoln's decisions.[21]

On March 29, 1780, Clinton crossed the Ashley River in force. Lincoln's light infantry, stationed at an advanced post along the river, slowly pulled back toward the town, skirmishing as it retreated. A detachment of the North Carolina Line, operating as light infantry under Lieutenant Colonel John Laurens, and acting as a rear guard in the withdrawal had a "brush" with the advance of the enemy on March 30. Captain Joseph Bowman of the First Regiment was killed and became the first casualty of the North Carolina Brigade, a loss that was "much lamented." On April 1, at distances ranging from 600 to 1,100 yards from the American works, Clinton broke ground, laying out saps and parallels in the classic European style of siege warfare. His men worked slowly as some American shells "disquieted them and interrupted their operations." British preparations had been thorough, so much so that massive mantelets had been constructed in New York before the expedition sailed, providing great portable shields to protect the men as they dug. Additional mantelets were constructed on the spot from the timbers of houses torn down in the neighborhood.[22]

Lincoln was not sure that Fort Moultrie, in its present state,

---

20. Lincoln to Caswell, 25 March 1780, Caswell Letterbook; *State Records,* XV, 327–68, *passim,* 800; Woodford to Washington, 9 April 1780, George Washington Papers; Lincoln to Huntington, 24 March 1780, Papers of the Continental Congress; Moultrie, *Memoirs of the American Revolution,* II, 67; [Hough], *Siege of Charleston,* p. 123.

21. Ward, *War of the Revolution,* II, 698; Lynn Montross, *Rag, Tag and Bobtail: The Story of the Continental Army, 1775–1783* (New York, 1952), p. 356.

22. Clinton, *American Rebellion,* p. 163; Uhlendorf, *Siege of Charleston,* pp. 39, 231; John Laurens to Washington, 9 April 1780, Woodford to Washington, 9 April 1780, Lincoln to Washington, 9 April 1780, George Washington Papers; Ramsay, *Revolution in South Carolina,* II, 50; Moultrie, *Memoirs of the American Revolution,* I, 65.

would be able to withstand an attack from the sea. When he questioned a council of war concerning whether Fort Moultrie should be abandoned or reinforced, a negative answer was received to each query, with all of the North Carolina officers present voting against both proposals. During the afternoon of April 8, Arbuthnot took advantage of a brisk southern breeze and led his squadron out of Five Fathom Hole for a run past Fort Moultrie. Eight warships, followed by six armed transports, sailed by Sullivan's Island, with the *Roebuck* and the *Richmond* exchanging a heavy fire with the twenty guns mounted in Fort Moultrie. Little damage was inflicted by either group. The *Richmond* was partially dismasted, while the supply ship *Aeolus* ran aground and was burned after her cargo was removed. British losses were seven killed and twenty wounded. Now Charleston was almost completely invested from both land and sea, with the only escape route across the Cooper and to Monck's Corner, still held by Isaac Huger. All that night and part of the day on April 9, a steady stream of civilians crossed the Cooper, taking their valuables and livestock with them.[23]

On April 9, the British first parallel was completed and on the following day Clinton and Arbuthnot sent in a formal demand for surrender. Lincoln declined, pointing out that he had already had sufficient time to evacuate the city and now "Duty & Inclination point to the propriety of supporting it to the last Extremity."[24]

At about ten in the morning of Thursday, April 13, the British batteries opened up with the full force of their dreadful thunder. Within an hour, two heavy fires flamed within the town and were not extinguished until late that evening. The soldiers were pulled off the parapets to fight the flames, since most of the townspeople crowded into cellars to escape the bombardment. A child, its nurse, and a sergeant and a private of Hogun's brigade was killed. Another North Carolina sergeant was killed the following day as enemy artillery fire continued to saturate the town.[25]

Governor Rutledge was persuaded to slip out of the town with

23. Journal of John Philip Hooke, William L. Clements Library, University of Michigan, Ann Arbor, Mich.; Clinton, *American Rebellion*, p. 164; *Original Papers Relating to the Siege of Charleston*, pp. 9–10; Uhlendorf, *Siege of Charleston*, p. 53; John Laurens to Washington, 9 April 1780, George Washington Papers; *State Records*, XIV, 800–801.

24. Uhlendorf, *Siege of Charleston*, p. 55; *Original Papers Relating to Siege of Charleston*, p. 38; Journal of the Siege, Lincoln to Clinton and Arbuthnot, 10 April 1780, Papers of the Continental Congress.

25. Journal of John Philip Hooke; John Lewis Gervais to Henry Laurens, 17 April 1780, George Washington Papers; Moultrie, *Memoirs of the American Revolution*, II, 70.

the hope that he could rally the militia in the back country and hurry on those troops of Griffith Rutherford's who were supposed to be on the march from North Carolina. Several of the governor's council went out with Rutledge as a method of preserving the executive authority of the state. On April 16, in the face of superior bombardment from the enemy, Lincoln called upon his general officers to advise him concerning whether or not the city should be evacuated by the troops while the escape route was still open. Lachlan McIntosh proposed that the Continentals, at least, should cross the Cooper and march along the eastern shore to safety. The other generals appeared hesitant. Lincoln made the fatal mistake of listening to the pleas of the civil authorities that a vigorous defense of the city be maintained. A day later it made no difference.[26]

At three o'clock of the morning of April 14, Lincoln's primary escape route was sealed. Banastre Tarleton's British Legion, reinforced by Major Patrick Ferguson's American Volunteers, struck at Huger's command at Monck's Corner. So sudden was the attack that all those who were not immediately struck down fled terror-stricken through the darkness. Seventeen American officers and men were killed, while both Clinton and Tarleton claimed that one hundred of Huger's men were taken prisoner, along with the capture of four hundred fine dragoon horses and fifty wagons loaded with arms, ammunition, and clothing. American reports were that only thirty saddle horses and twenty wagons with their teams were lost. The following day two British regiments moved in to occupy Huger's former bivouac. The ring around Charleston was now made fast.[27]

The artillery duel continued as British working parties dug their way forward in a slow advance, disturbed only by occasional raiding parties. "The rebels," said one Scot officer, "throw their shells better than we do, but did no harm." And as if to bear out his statement, on Tuesday, April 18, a great number of shells fell into the North Carolina camp, but only one man was killed and two wounded. Lincoln had not had the time to construct his works high enough and more and more American artillery pieces were dismounted by enemy fire. Ammunition grew short, and Lincoln's men loaded their artil-

26. John Lewis Gervais to Henry Laurens, 17 April 1780, George Washington Papers; Gibbes, *Documentary History of the American Revolution*, II, 130–31; Alden, *South in the Revolution*, p. 240; *Original Papers Relating to the Siege of Charleston*, p. 18; Journal of the Siege, Papers of the Continental Congress.

27. Banastre Tarleton, *A History of the Campaigns of 1780 and 1781, in the Southern Provinces of North America* (Dublin, 1787), pp. 15–18; Clinton, *American Rebellion*, p. 166; Uhlendorf, *Siege of Charleston*, pp. 61, 387; Gervais to Laurens, 17 April 1780, George Washington Papers.

lery pieces with broken glass and scrap iron to fire when the British working parties were within range. But still they continued to dig. And just to show the Americans the firepower that they were facing, the British artillery hefted a dead thirteen-inch mortar shell into the town. The situation seemed even more hopeless when Lincoln learned that Clinton had received a reinforcement of 2,600 men from New York.[28]

With enemy lines now within 250 yards of the defensive works, Lincoln once again called his general officers, including James Hogun, into conference. He laid the state of the garrison before them and pointed out that supplies were fast diminishing and that there was little hope of reinforcement. The generals agreed that an attempt to retreat now "would be attended with many distressing inconveniences." The civil authorities "were utterly averse to it, and intimated in Councils, if it was attempted [a withdrawal], they would counteract ye measure." Civilian advice to Lincoln was that he should make a proposal to Clinton that all resistance would cease if he would allow the American army to withdraw and also give assurances that the lives and properties of the inhabitants would be protected.[29]

Around noon on April 21, Lincoln beat a parley and sent out a young officer under a flag, with the proposal that a six-hour truce be observed while terms of capitulation were discussed. Lincoln's proposals were, to say the least, fantastic. He was quite willing to surrender Charleston, he said, as long as the citizens were protected, American naval vessels were allowed to put out to sea unmolested, and he and his army were given thirty-six hours to march away with full honors of war, carrying with them all artillery, ammunition, supplies, and wagons. At eight o'clock that evening, Lincoln received his answer. Clinton and Arbuthnot not only rejected his terms but gave him until ten o'clock to surrender unconditionally. At that hour the bombardment was resumed "more violently than ever before."[30]

It was apparent that Charleston was experiencing its last spasms of resistance. General William Moultrie noted that in the lines "fa-

28. Journal of Lieutenant John Peebles, Cunningham of Thornton Muniments, Scottish Record Office, Edinburgh, Scotland; Uhlendorf, *Siege of Charleston*, p. 63; *Original Papers Relating to the Siege of Charleston*, p. 20; Moultrie, *Memoirs of the American Revolution*, II, 72.

29. *Original Papers Relating to the Siege of Charleston*, pp. 18–20; Journal of the Siege, Minutes of Council, 20 and 21 April 1780, Papers of the Continental Congress.

30. *Original Papers Relating to the Siege of Charleston*, pp. 19–20, 43–45; Uhlendorf, *Siege of Charleston*, pp. 67, 258–59; Clinton, *American Rebellion*, p. 168; Lincoln to Clinton, 21 April 1780, Clinton to Lincoln. 21 April 1780, Papers of the Continental Congress.

tigue . . . was so great that, for want of sleep, many faces were so swelled they could scarcely see out of their eyes." By April 23, the British had advanced their third parallel to "within a stone's throw of the enemy's abatis." To disrupt their steady progress, Lincoln sent out a sortie composed of about three hundred Continentals, twenty-one of whom were from the South Carolina Line and the remainder selected from Hogun's brigade and Woodford's Virginia Continentals. Commanding was Lieutenant Colonel John Henderson of Virginia, but originally hailing from Granville County, North Carolina. The Americans went in quietly, without being discovered until the workers on the line spied their dark outlines in the darkness. The British fled, crying out, "Damn me the rebels are here!" A hot fight followed, with between fifteen and twenty British put to the bayonet and twelve of their number taken prisoner. The Americans lost Captain Thomas Moultrie of South Carolina. When the British attempted a pursuit they were driven back by the American artillery firing improvised canister shot made of "old burst shells, broken shovels, pickaxes, flatirons, pistol barrels, broken locks, etc., etc." Clinton's men inflicted the greatest loss upon themselves when they mistakenly fired upon a group retreating to the second parallel, inflicting casualties upon one officer and twenty workmen.[31]

By Wednesday, April 26, the British were beginning to move their heavy artillery into positions in the third parallel. The Frenchman, Brigadier General Louis du Portail, chief engineer of the American army, who had been ordered south by the Continental Congress, arrived from Philadelphia on April 25. After an inspection of the works he reported to Lincoln's council of war "that the works are not tenable" and suggested an evacuation of the town; in fact, it was du Portail's opinion that the British could have taken the town ten days earlier had they only put forth the effort. He wished to leave Charleston, but Lincoln refused permission on the grounds that "it would dispirit the troops." Lincoln once again posed the question to his generals whether the Continental troops should not be evacuated; they were unanimous in their opinion that evacuation was "not expedient, as being impracticable." When the townspeople heard of these latest deliberations, some of them burst into the council chamber "and declared to General Lincoln that if he attempted to withdraw the troops and leave the citizens, they would cut up his boats

31. Gibbes, *Documentary History of the American Revolution*, II, 132; Moultrie, *Memoirs of the American Revolution*, II, 78–80; Uhlendorf, *Siege of Charleston*, pp. 264–65; Journal of the Siege, Papers of the Continental Congress.

and open the gates to the enemy." There was no alternative to continued resistance.[32]

After British reinforcements arrived from New York on April 19, Clinton slowly closed his trap. A small post manned by North Carolina Continentals on Haddrell's point was overrun. Lord Cornwallis took post at Mount Pleasant, and Tarleton managed to kill or disperse the remainder of Huger's troops. Ditches were dug to drain the moat in front of the American lines. Fort Moultrie still held out and its commander, in answer to a summons to surrender, sent back the insolent reply, "Tol, lol, derol, lol, Fort Moultrie will be defended to the last Extremity." Yet on May 7, when Arbuthnot landed a force of marines and seamen from the *Richmond* on Sullivan's Island, this same commanding officer lowered his flag without resistance. A storm of the walls was the next step. As early as May 5, a number of American ladies came to Clinton "to desire I should permit them to go into town to take leave of their sons, as they knew I intended storming in a day or two."[33]

Even the most ardent advocates of continued resistance came to realize that little could be gained by holding out until the bitter end. Food was low. A search of private homes for provisions proved unsuccessful. On May 8, Clinton, in a summons, warned of the "vindictive Severity exasperated Soldiers may inflict on the unhappy People whom you devote by persevering in a fruitless Defence." Of the fifty-one officers attending Lincoln's council, only nine advised against asking for terms, and four of these were the captains of Continental vessels. All North Carolina Continental officers voted for terms. And Lieutenant Governor Christopher Gadsden and his council were now in agreement, sending Lincoln suggestions for the protection of the citizens and their property, which they wished to be included in the surrender terms.[34]

Late in the afternoon of May 9, Clinton rejected Lincoln's terms,

32. Moultrie, *Memoirs of the American Revolution,* II, 79–80; *Original Papers Relating to the Siege of Charleston,* pp. 20–21; Minutes of Council, 26 April 1780, du Portail to President of Congress, 17 May 1780, Papers of the Continental Congress; Minutes of Council, 26 April 1780, Preston Davie Collection, Southern Historical Collection.

33. Journal of John Philip Hooke; William B. Willcox, *Portrait of a General: Sir Henry Clinton in the War of Independence* (New York, 1964), p. 308; Journal of the Siege, Papers of the Continental Congress; [Hough], *Siege of Charleston,* pp. 127, 167; *State Records,* XV, 29.

34. *Original Papers Relating to the Siege of Charleston,* pp. 11–13, 46–47; Walsh, *Writings of Christopher Gadsden,* pp. 167–68; Clinton to Lincoln, 8 May 1780, Lincoln to Clinton, 8 May 1780, Minutes of Council, 8 May 1780, Papers of the Continental Congress; Gadsden to Lincoln, 5 May 1780, Preston Davie Collection, Southern Historical Collection.

calling them "Terms, you certainly have no claims to," especially referring to those clauses concerned with the protection of the militia and the civilian population. That night the bombardment was resumed. For General William Moultrie the shells made a grand yet terrible experience: "It was a glorious sight to see them like meteors crossing each other and bursting in the air; it appeared as if the stars were tumbling down. The fire was incessant almost the whole night; cannon-balls whizzing and shells hissing continually amongst us; ammunition chests and temporary magazines blowing up; great guns bursting, and wounded men groaning along our lines. It was a dreadful night! It was our last great effort, but it availed us nothing."[35]

Then, said Moultrie, "We began to cool, and we cooled gradually. . . ." No longer were the townspeople so intent on securing guarantees for the protection of their property. They had been pounded into submission. The enemy, advancing by saps, were within twenty-five yards of the walls. Petitions from a number of the militia along with two others signed by over four hundred citizens urged sending out another flag to accept whatever terms the British wished to impose. On Thursday, May 11, Lincoln received a communication from Gadsden and his council, stating that they felt that the general should no longer seek terms but should request the best possible conditions for surrender. A council of general officers suggested capitulation. On that same day Lincoln accepted the articles of surrender as prepared by Clinton and Arbuthnot on May 8, with Lieutenant Colonel John Tennant and Major John André arranging the procedures to be followed. The fall of the city, predicted Benjamin Smith, "will give a rude Shock to the Independence of America."[36]

At eleven in the morning of May 12, 1780, marching out with colors cased and their drums mournfully beating out the "Turk's March," the North Carolina Continentals participated in the greatest American surrender of the war. One Britisher's description of the surrender ran: "Lincoln limped out at the head of the most ragged rabble I ever behold." Another officer registered a somewhat different impression in his diary: "They are a ragged dirty looking set of People as usual, but more appearance of discipline than what we have

35. *Original Papers Relating to the Siege of Charleston*, pp. 46–47; Moultrie, *Memoirs of the American Revolution*, II, 96; Journal of the Siege, Clinton to Lincoln, May, 1780, Papers of the Continental Congress.

36. *Original Papers Relating to the Siege of Charleston*, pp. 50–53; Walsh, *Writings of Christopher Gadsden*, p. 169; Petitions, 10 and 11 May 1780, Minutes of Council, 11 May 1780, Papers of the Continental Congress; Clinton to Lincoln, 8 May 1780, Clinton to Arbuthnot, 12 May 1780, Preston Davie Collection, Southern Historical Collection; [Hough], *Siege of Charleston*, pp. 85, 115.

seen formerly & some of their Officers decent looking men." The militia, later in the day, straggled out and piled their arms.[37]

Over 5,466 Continental soldiers, militia, and armed citizens participated in the surrender. William Moultrie, however, complained that this figure included the "aged, the timid, the disaffected, and the infirm, many of them who had never appeared during the whole siege, which swelled the number of militia prisoners to, at least, three times the number we had on duty." Lincoln's official returns indicate that he surrendered 1,977 Continental rank and file and 246 officers, of which number at least 500 were either sick or wounded. Included were 814 Continentals from North Carolina; 64 officers and men of Captain John Kingsbury's artillery company, 287 of Clark's First Regiment, 301 of Patten's Second, and 162 of Mebane's Third. Militia prisoners from the state totalled 1,231 men. In addition, British booty included 391 artillery pieces, 5,916 muskets, fifteen regimental colors, 33,000 rounds of ammunition, 8,000 round shot and 376 barrels of flour, plus other military stores. For such a long siege, casualties were surprisingly light; the British lost 76 killed and 189 wounded, while American losses were 89 killed and 138 wounded. Of this number, Captain Bowman along with two sergeants and two privates of the North Carolina Brigade had been killed, while the officers among the wounded included Captain Joseph Montford, Lieutenant James Campen, Lieutenant Arthur Cotgrave, and Lieutenant John Hall. The latter's leg had been broken by grape shot from the British batteries. At least four privates of the brigade had been wounded. None of the men of the militia had suffered death or injury because they had been bivouaced in an area that had not been subjected to bombardment.[38]

Among the higher ranking officers of the North Carolina Line taken prisoner were Brigadier General James Hogun, Colonels Thomas Clark and John Patten, Lieutenant Colonels Robert Mebane, Archibald Lytle and Selby Harney, and Majors Thomas Hogg and John Nelson. Other prisoners of war from the unit included eleven captains, four captain lieutenants, twenty lieutenants, seven ensigns, four regimental surgeons, one brigade commissary of military stores, and one wagon master.[39]

Continental officers were permitted to return to the city, collect

37. Journal of Lieutenant John Peebles, Cunningham of Thornton Muniments, Scottish Record Office; [Hough], *Siege of Charleston*, pp. 129–30.

38. Ward, *War of the Revolution*, II, 708; Moultrie, *Memoirs of the American Revolution*, I, 65, 70, 72, 81, 82, 83, II, 109–10; *State Records*, XIV, 814–15, 816.

39. *Original Papers Relating to the Siege of Charleston*, pp. 78–87.

their baggage, and sign their paroles before being sent over to Haddrel's Point. The British idea was that they would hold these men nearby as prisoners so that a ready exchange could be effected for the officers of Burgoyne's army taken at Saratoga. Housing was a problem on Haddrel's Point and many officers were forced to build small huts to shelter themselves, clearing little plots in which they could plant vegetables to supplement their meager diet. The efforts of Chaplain Adam Boyd to secure food and clothing for the officers were in vain. He and Hardy Murfree attempted to collect indigo to be sold, but their efforts bore no fruit. Later some were allowed to go to other localities until their exchange could be arranged, with some permitted to travel to Virginia, others to Philadelphia.[40]

The British offered to parole James Hogun to some other community, but he declined, declaring that he wished to share the hardships of confinement with the men of his brigade. He feared that in his absence enemy recruiting officers would find greater success in recruiting North Carolina prisoners for service in British regiments in the West Indies. And it has been claimed that at least five hundred American prisoners did seek this way out when they were assured that they would not be forced to fight their former comrades in arms. Several accepted commissions in loyalist corps of the British army. Many of those who remained had a tendency to "behave so much amiss" that it was necessary to hold frequent courts-martial. Hogun tried to maintain a military atmosphere among the prisoners, but he was not a strong man. During the winter of 1780 his health began to fail, and on January 4, 1781, James Hogun died on Haddrel's Point.[41]

Many of the militiamen were allowed to return to their homes on parole. A substantial number, however, were kept as prisoners of war, along with the Continental rank and file. Although these men supposedly received the same treatment as the regulars, a greater proportion of them died as prisoners of war. Nearly a year later it was reported that "Militia men . . . are detained from their suffering families, & are themselves lingering in a pestilential region, friendless, decrepid & pennyless."[42]

The fall of Charleston marked a sad day for the South. Some saw in the surrender of the city the beginning of the end. Ezekiel Cornell,

40. Moultrie, *Memoirs of the American Revolution*, II, 109, 115, 116; *Original Papers Relating to the Siege of Charleston*, p. 78; *State Records*, XIV, 820, 834–35; Adam Boyd to Nash, 5 June 1780, Governors' Papers.

41. *State Records*, XIV, 854, 861.

42. Stephen Moore to Commanding Officer of the Southern Army, 5 December 1780, Historical Society of Pennsylvania Collection; Copy of Parole of John Hamilton, 19 May 1780, Miscellaneous Papers, Military Collection.

Rhode Island delegate to the Continental Congress, observed that "it is agreed on all hands the whole state of So. Carolina hath submited to the British Government as well as Georgia. And I shall not be surprised to hear N. Carolina hath followed their example."[43]

43. Burnett, *Letters of Members of the Continental Congress*, V, 226.

Chapter 12

The Brief Command of Horatio Gates

*"... it was an unseasonable hour
for gentlemen to call."*

With the fall of Charleston, North Carolina was to rely almost entirely upon the militia for protection against an almost certain invasion by the enemy. It was not a happy prospect.

Back in February, 1780, Governor Caswell had attempted to call the assembly into session, but that body had failed to find a quorum. Those who did come in returned to their homes after waiting for ten or twelve days. On April 17, after some delay, the legislature was finally convened at New Bern. Richard Caswell had served three consecutive one-year terms as governor and was no longer eligible to hold that office. Abner Nash of New Bern was elected chief executive of North Carolina. He was not to be a happy governor. His trouble began almost immediately when the assembly went beyond what Nash felt to be its constitutional powers and appointed Caswell a major general in command of the state militia, four thousand of whom were to march into South Carolina as quickly as possible. Caswell was also given the authority to appoint staff officers, again usurping what Nash felt to be a prerogative of the executive. Hoping that a Continental officer might well persuade some of the militia to en-

235

list in the regulars, Caswell prevailed upon Jethro Sumner to allow Lieutenant Colonel Henry Dixon to accept a temporary command in the militia.[1]

Despite the critical military situation in Charleston, and the opinion that "Our affairs at this time wear not the most pleasing aspect," the assembly followed its customary pattern of concerning itself more with civil affairs than the more urgent military matters. Although Charleston was already under siege, the governor was authorized to raise no more than eight thousand troops to send to the aid of South Carolina, and then only if "absolutely necessary." Even as the situation grew more acute, this number was later revised downward to four thousand, with a quota established for each county, the men to be drafted into active service for a specified term of service. A militia law was passed to tighten discipline and procedures, and the usual platitudinous efforts toward filling the Continental regiments were made. Blithely, the legislators provided for the immediate enlistment of three thousand Continentals who were to serve for three years or the duration of the war. Generous inducements were held out to prospective recruits. Each enlistee was to receive $500 in currency when signed and an equal amount at the conclusion of each year of service. Those who served out their three years, or the duration, were to receive one "prime slave" between the ages of fifteen and thirty, in addition to three hundred acres of land in the tract set aside for that purpose in the western part of the state. Those disabled in service were to receive the same bonuses, as were the heirs of those who were killed or who died while on duty. On the surface these were liberal measures but hardly adequate to take care of the situation then at hand. In a state where loyalties were divided and the populace reluctant to turn out and leave their homes unguarded, a mechanism for drafting regulars should have been established, no matter how undemocratic it might have seemed. Democracy can sometimes become a major handicap in a country torn by civil war.[2]

Notwithstanding its seemingly confident legislation, the assembly realized the futility of attempting to raise additional Continental regiments. Nash was directed to write the president of the Continental Congress requesting "further aid from the Regular Army." On the other hand, the assembly did little in response to Nash's plea that it

1. *State Records,* XIV, x, XV, 341; Harnett to Burke, 22 February 1780, Thomas Burke Papers, N.C. Dept. Arch. & Hist.; Caswell to Sumner, 8 May 1780, Caswell Papers, N.C. Dept. Arch. & Hist.; Samuel Ashe to Alexander Lillington, 29 May 1780, Lillington Papers, Southern Historical Collection, The University of North Carolina at Chapel Hill, Chapel Hill, N.C.

2. *State Records,* XXIV, 331–32, 335–37, 339–41, 826.

do something about supplying the North Carolina troops then in Charleston, although it did vote substantial supplies, almost to the point of luxury, for the militia supposed to go to the aid of South Carolina. To some, it was already obvious that no effectual aid could be sent before Charleston fell.[3]

But North Carolina was a destitute state. Not only did it have to feed its own troops in the field, but also those military units who had marched through on their way to Charleston. The marches and countermarches of the militia had stripped the land as clean as would a plague of locusts. When there were provisions to be purchased, there was no money. Nash hounded the legislature to appropriate adequate funds, but there were bureaucratic delays all along the line. Not until May 10 was even an estimate submitted concerning the supplies needed for the four thousand militiamen who were to be sent to the aid of South Carolina. Shortly afterwards the entire state fell into despair when the news arrived of the surrender of Charleston. When Lincoln had marched out of that city on May 12, North Carolina was left without a single Continental unit in the field. Only those officers who had been on leave were available, and they had only a scattering of recruits to command.[4]

Toward the end of April, 1780, former governor Richard Caswell's son, Brigadier General William Caswell, with about four hundred of a brigade of North Carolina militia, was at Lanier's Ferry on the Santee River in South Carolina where Governor John Rutledge of that state was attempting to rally his own militia. Few South Carolinians answered his call, for they were "so apprehensive of their families being killed (& their properties destroyed) by the tories & Indians, who daily threaten Hostilities while they are absent from their Districts. . . ." Caswell had been joined by Colonel Abraham Buford's 350 Virginia Continental dragoons, and a small detachment of mounted men under Colonel William Washington, all under the command of Brigadier General Isaac Huger. With the news of the fall of Charleston they began to fall back toward the north, with Caswell marching for Cross Creek and Buford striking for Hillsborough by way of Charlotte.

In the meantime Cornwallis had been sent from Charleston into the Camden area; he dispatched Banastre Tarleton and his British Legion in pursuit of Buford, paying no attention to Caswell's militia. Mounting his infantry behind the cavalry, Tarleton covered 154

---

3. Nash to the President of Congress, 24 April 1780, Papers of the Continental Congress; *State Records*, XIV, 802, 806, 811–12.

4. *State Records*, XIV, 506, 811–12.

miles in fifty-four hours, with several of his horses falling dead of exhaustion. He caught up with Buford in the area near the North Carolina border known as the Waxhaws. Buford refused Tarleton's demands to surrender. After the British horses swept across them, the Americans raised the white flag. Even as Buford's men grounded their arms, Tarleton rushed forward with bayonet and sabre. Buford and a few of his men managed to escape the ensuing slaughter, but behind they left 113 killed and over 200 wounded. From this time on, the phrase "Tarleton's Quarters" became synonymous with wanton bloodshed and cruelty.[5]

This incident did little to help matters in North Carolina. Many of those Continental officers in the state had been assigned the duty of searching out and taking up deserters and sending them back to their units—only now there were no units to send them back to. Many of these officers and those on recruiting duty had now begun to submit their resignations because of sheer "Poverty." Others returned to their homes because now it was almost certain that there would be an invasion of North Carolina by the enemy. A man by the name of Weickerman, who lived in Salisbury, was apprehended coming from the British lines. Weickerman, who had talked with Josiah Martin in Charleston, reported that the former royal governor of North Carolina had assured him that he would be in Cross Creek within a fortnight and had offered himself as leader of the loyalist militia so that he could speedily re-establish royal government. Although such a rapid movement by the enemy seemed improbable, there was little doubt that the next objective of the British was North Carolina.[6]

By the end of May it was difficult to separate rumor from fact. There was talk of a drive against Cross Creek by the Royal Highland Emigrant Regiment, who expected to be joined by the Scot settlers in that area. Enemy magazines of provisions, it was said, would be established at Brunswick and Wilmington. So alarmed was Governor Rutledge that he was urging other governors and members of the Continental Congress to detach Continental troops from other areas to the southern states, and to drive the British from South Carolina.[7]

Jethro Sumner, with some financial aid from the state government, was attempting to gather recruits so that the North Carolina Line might be reorganized. The militiamen were reluctant to come

5. *Ibid.*, pp. 821–24, 829–30, 832–33; William Caswell to Nash, 3 June 1780, Caswell Letterbook; John Rutledge to Nash, 24 May 1780, Governors' Papers.

6. *State Records*, XIV, 799, 819–20, 822, 848, 858; *The Collector*, LXXV, No. 12 (1962), 76; Rutledge to Nash, 16 May 1780, Papers of the Continental Congress.

7. *State Records*, XIV, 822–23.

out, and if they had, there would have been little in the way of weapons and supplies with which to equip them. Many sympathized with the eighteen militia volunteers and 112 draftees of Bertie County who refused to march for any rendezvous until they had received the bounty that had been promised them. Others banded together and hid out in the woods, determined to "defend themselves to the Utmost Rigger." The only hopeful signs were that segments of the Maryland Line had crossed the Roanoke River on their march to Hillsborough. Colonel Charles Armand, the Marquis de la Rouerie, with his Legion, was at Wilmington planning to join with the remnants of Pulaski's command. Colonel William Washington, who had been skirmishing with the enemy in South Carolina with the remains of Baylor's, Bland's, and Moylan's mounted troops, was also in the state attempting to reform and remount his troopers. The presence of these units led to grumblings, for their quartermasters sometimes went about with armed escorts, appropriating provisions with little regard for proper procedures.[8]

Not all news wore such an air of gloom. For some weeks Lord Cornwallis had cautioned the North Carolina loyalists to lie quiet until after the harvests were in before rising; this would allow him time to subdue South Carolina and his troops would not be forced to make an exhausting march in hot weather. But the loyalists would not wait. A large number responded to the call of Colonel John Moore, who had returned after a stay with Cornwallis in South Carolina. By June 20, there were at least 1,300 at the Tory rendezvous at Ramsour's Mill, although at least a fourth of them were unarmed. In a counteraction, 800 militiamen had responded to Griffith Rutherford's call and were assembling at Charlotte. Another 400 came in to Mountain Creek to serve under Francis Locke. In an attempt to surprise the Tories, Locke moved against them on June 19 and attacked them the following day. The loyalists were defeated, although each side lost about 150 men. Only about 300 of Moore's men were able to join Cornwallis in South Carolina. Impressive as the victory was, it had an adverse effect. The politicians were now so convinced that the militia could be used successfully against the enemy that they paid even less attention to filling the Continental regiments.[9]

Hillsborough had been designated as the general Continental rendezvous in the state. A new commanding general of the Southern

8. *Ibid.*, pp. 827, 829–32, 835–36, 837–38, 847; Arthur Brown to Nash, 9 June 1780, Thomas Benbury to Nash, 12 June 1780, Governors' Papers.

9. *State Records*, XIV, 866–67, XV, 7; DeMond, *Loyalists in North Carolina during the Revolution*, pp. 126–27.

Department was to meet the Continentals there. By a resolution in the Continental Congress on June 14, 1780, Major General Horatio Gates, the hero of Saratoga, was selected to succeed Benjamin Lincoln. Gates had not been Washington's choice; the general had favored Nathanael Greene for this command. Washington, it was said, was eager to have Greene designated as his successor should death strike him down before the end of the war. Gates, however, was a man of jovial personality and one on whom fortune seemed to smile with regularity. More important, he had powerful friends in Congress, including a number who had grown weary of Washington's command. And Greene had but recently irritated many members of the Congress by his resignation as quartermaster general, and his caustic criticisms of that body. There were some who claimed that he had given Washington unsound advice.[10]

Major General Johann de Kalb, the Bavarian giant, who had been marching south with the Maryland and Delaware Continentals, along with the Virginia artillery, became ranking general in the South after the fall of Charleston until the arrival of Gates. He was not to be envied. Crop failures had left a barren land. Provisions were so scarce that the daily ration for the men was little more than adequate for bare subsistence. The situation was not helped by the Tories in the southern part of the state who were terrorizing the area and preventing the gathering of supplies.[11]

Near the end of June provisions grew so scarce in the vicinity of Hillsborough that de Kalb decided to move down near the Peedee River in South Carolina. Reports had it that food was abundant in that country and that the site would allow a reasonable base to reorganize the army as well as a post from which the enemy could be observed. Yet de Kalb had journeyed no farther than Deep River when he was forced to bivouac at Coxe's Mill, his men placed on short bread rations until enough could be collected to resume the march.[12]

Gates first stopped at Hillsborough, where he discovered "the most unpromising Prospect my Eyes ever beheld." But his confidence

10. *State Records*, XIV, 843–44; Burnett, *Letters of Members of the Continental Congress*, V, 307, 314–16, 398; Graydon, *Memoirs of His Own Times*, pp. 103n, 299.

11. *State Records*, XIV, 381–83, 858–59, 865; John Penn to Burke, 21 June 1780, Thomas Burke Papers, N.C. Dept. Arch. & Hist.; Henry Laurens to Nash, 9 May 1780, Laurens to Lincoln, 14 May 1780, Nash to Laurens, 15 July 1780, Papers of the Continental Congress; Nash to Washington, 6 October 1780, George Washington Papers.

12. *State Records*, XIV, 503–4; de Kalb to the Board of War, 20 June 1780, George Washington Papers.

was not dimmed; on July 25 he swaggered into the camp at Coxe's Mill, the salute of eight artillery pieces burning badly needed gunpowder in a show of martial fluff. De Kalb turned over the command with no regret. He reported to Gates his plan of marching southward by way of Salisbury and Charlotte through a country where the people were Whiggish and provisions relatively plentiful. Then, perhaps, should the opportunity present itself, a strike might be launched against the British outpost at Camden.[13]

Gates dismissed de Kalb's plans as calling for too circuitous a route and planned a more direct move against Camden, fifty miles shorter, but through a sterile and infertile region of pine barrens, peopled principally by angry and hostile Tories. To the protests that this was no country through which to march an army already on a starvation diet, Gates replied smugly that "provisions, rum, salt, and every requisite will flow into camp . . . [and] with a liberal hand be distributed." And then, to the astonishment of the hungry men, the general issued orders that they hold themselves in readiness to march at a moment's notice. Ignoring the advice of his close friend, Charles Lee, who had warned, "Take care lest your Northern laurels turn to Southern willows," Gates was determined to risk the valuable little southern army in an effort to boost morale and his own dignity. Throughout the preparations the general exuded a confidence strangely out of keeping with the stark reality of the situation. Yet his spirit was so infectious that Elizabeth Steele was led to comment that "before this year be done, the brittish & Tories will be all cooped up in charlestowne."[14]

Food was collected by use of threats and even violence. Quartermasters turned horses loose in grain fields and allowed the animals to graze them clean, all "attended with much Insolence, and a conduct extremely disgusting to the people, which have produced much murmuring, indignation and complaint. . . ." Thomas Burke's plantation was violated by roving foragers, leading to a vigorous protest by that politician. Wagons and horses were impressed for the use of the army without any statement of authority. Soldiers were quartered in private homes, and some houses were taken over for use as barracks by

13. William Johnson, *Sketches of the Life and Correspondence of Nathanael Greene* (Charleston, S.C., 1822), I, 294, 486; Scheer and Rankin, *Rebels and Redcoats,* pp. 404–5; Gates to Samuel Huntington, 20 July 1780, Papers of the Continental Congress.

14. Johnson, *Sketches of Greene,* I, 486; Scheer and Rankin, *Rebels and Redcoats,* pp. 404–5; Elizabeth Steele to Ephraim Steele, 27 July 1780, John Steele Papers.

the military. Many expressed their disgust "with the haughty manners of the Commissaries, and therefore will deliver them nothing."[15]

On July 27 Gates marched off at the head of the collection of men he termed his "grand army." It was a spectacle of military ineptitude. None of his rashly promised provisions arrived. The country through which his men marched had been previously gleaned of food by the North Carolina militia under Griffith Rutherford and Richard Caswell. The Virginia militia, marching at the rear of Gates's column, intercepted and devoured the few provisions that had been sent down from the North. The troops were forced to forage in the fields and orchards and eat the green corn and green peaches that they gathered there. Molasses was used as a substitute for the daily rum ration. Officers used their hair powder to thicken soup. The effect of such a diet upon the gastronomical tract is better imagined than described. Even Gates was brought to believe that his army was now so near exhaustion and starvation that they could no longer fight effectively.[16]

Gates's intelligence was not only poor, it was misleading. Although Caswell passed on the word that his sources had stated that the British at Camden were determined to march out and fight, Gates preferred to believe the intelligence that Cornwallis had gone to Savannah and had weakened Camden by withdrawing troops from that post. The general grew impatient and wanted to get on with the business of victory. He fretted because Caswell and his militia had not joined the main force; in fact, Caswell was blamed for the wretched supply situation. Food destined for the army, Gates claimed, had all been consumed in Caswell's camp. He deplored what he charged was a tendency on the part of Caswell to add to his military reputation by attacking minor objectives. He felt that Caswell's ambitions should be checked "by a rap over the knuckles," but Gates feared that if he disciplined the militia general, the "militia would disperse, and leave this handful of brave men without even nominal assistance." And without the North Carolina militia, Gates's own ambitions could be dashed.[17]

By August 7, a junction was made with Caswell's, 2,100 North Carolina militiamen. The militia officers had come into the field in high style. Colonel Otho Williams was amazed at the baggage they had brought along: "Tables, chairs, bedsteads, benches, and many

15. *State Records*, XV, 769–76.

16. Johnson, *Sketches of Greene*, I, 487; Gates to Caswell, 4 August 1780, Caswell Papers, N.C. Dept. Arch. & Hist.; Gates to Nash, 3 August 1780, Governors' Papers.

17. Johnson, *Sketches of Greene*, I, 488–89; *State Records*, XV, 17–18; Caswell to Nash, 5 August 1780, Governors' Papers.

other articles of heavy and cumbrous household stuff, were scattered before the tent doors in great disorder." The confusion in the militia camp was partially a result of the unusual number of high-ranking officers; Caswell actually began one dispatch with, "Sir, General W———, my aid de camp." In general, militia discipline was sloppy, and one officer of the day rode all one night through their lines and encampment without once being challenged. When he went to Caswell's marquee to complain, the officer who answered him suggested that "it was an unseasonable hour for *gentlemen to call.*"[18]

Francis, Lord Rawdon, commandant of the British post at Camden, pulled in his outposts as Gates approached. This, coupled with the arrival of Brigadier General Edward Stevens with seven hundred Virginia militiamen, led Gates to feel that victory was now within his grasp. What Gates did not know was that Lord Cornwallis, now in command of the British army in the South, alarmed by the exaggerated estimates of the size of Gates's army, had hurried to Camden with reinforcements for Rawdon. After surveying the situation and "seeing little to lose by a defeat and much to gain by a victory," he resolved "to take the first good opportunity to attack the rebel army." At ten o'clock on the night of August 15, 1780, he set out to attack the American encampment at dawn.

Strangely enough, Gates chose the same time to move toward Camden, hoping to be within seven miles of that town by sunrise. Although Gates had estimated that his force numbered almost 7,000 men, actual returns showed only 3,052. Murmuring that "these are enough for our purpose," Gates issued the orders to march.

They had been marching for some four hours when they reached the open area between the two branches of Gum Swamp. Suddenly the vanguard slammed into the mounted troops leading Cornwallis's column. Both groups stumbled back to the protection of their own forces after a few minutes of stabbing pistol fire and shouts in the darkness. Gates called a council of war—at least thirteen general officers attended—and in answer to Gates's query as to their next step, the majority agreed with Edward Stevens's observation, "Is it not too late *now* to do anything but fight?"[19]

The engagement that took place the following morning in the open field between the two branches of Gum Swamp should not be dignified by the term "battle." Gates had no battle plan and seemed disposed to await events. He gave no orders. The enemy pressed forward just as soon as the battle was joined. British infantry, under

18. Johnson, *Sketches of Greene,* I, 489–91.
19. *Ibid.,* pp. 494–95.

Lieutenant Colonel James Webster, hit with such force that first the Virginia militiamen, then the North Carolina militiamen, broke and ran. In their terror they threw away equipment, ammunition, and arms, some muskets never having been fired. They ran, said one observer, "like a Torrent and bore all before them." Among the North Carolinians, only that part of the brigade under the command of Lieutenant Colonel Henry Dixon stood fast long enough to fire three rounds, and, it was said, "pushed Bayonets to the last." The flight of other units allowed the enemy to bend additional strength against them. Together with the Delaware and Maryland Continentals they fought as long as they could, "making great havoc among the Enemy," and then forced a passage through the enemy to make their escape. Gates, trying desperately to rally his army, was caught up in the stream of humanity and was carried from the field with them.[20]

Only the Delaware and Maryland Continentals continued to fight. They fell back, rallied, fell back, and rallied once again. They stood fast against a bayonet charge. Only when Cornwallis noted that there were no mounted troops to protect their flanks and threw in his dragoons did they give way. The battle was over. The British victory was complete. One interested and happy spectator of the day's proceedings was Josiah Martin, who saw the victory as the first step toward his restoration as royal governor of North Carolina.[21]

Three hundred and twenty-four of Cornwallis's men lay either dead or dying upon the field, but the battle of Camden, coming so hard upon the fall of Charleston, was for the Americans a disaster. No accurate casualty lists were ever compiled of American losses, but the British estimated that Gates lost between 800 and 900 killed and wounded and another 1,000 made prisoners, including General Griffith Rutherford of the North Carolina militia. The American army lost all of its artillery, its baggage, most of its 400 wagons, and a majority of its muskets. The gallant de Kalb was stripped of his uniform even as he lay dying upon the field. Of the known dead, 162 were Continentals, 12 were South Carolina militiamen, 3 were Virginia militiamen, and 63 were North Carolina militiamen. Most of the North Carolinians were from Dixon's command. In general, the North Carolina militiamen had simply vanished, "Most of them preferring the shortest way home, scattered through the wilderness. . . ."

20. Nash to Washington, 6 October 1780, George Washington Papers; Nash to Laurens, 23 August 1780, Gates to Huntington, 28 August 1780, Papers of the Continental Congress.

21. Johnson, *Sketches of Greene*, I, 495–97; *State Records*, XV, 49–55, 60, 269–76, 383–85; Gates to Huntington, 28 August 1780, Papers of the Continental Congress.

Ten days after the battle, 700 Continentals assembled at Hillsborough, 180 miles from Camden. Gates had covered that distance in three days. When Gates reached Salem, one of the pious Moravians noted that "General Gates breakfasted with us this morning, but seemed in haste."[22]

No one could bring himself to believe that the disaster had been so complete. Colonel John Bannister of Virginia wrote, "Gov. Nash informs me that the defeat is by no means so disastrous as was first represented; and adds that in a few days they [the militiamen] should be able to face about and confront their enemies, who have been severely handled in this action, and had not advanced from their post at Camden." Gates's dispatches to Washington reflected none of the gloom that hung over North Carolina.[23]

Troops that had been on the march to join Gates before Camden trickled into the state. They aroused little enthusiasm. Two mounted troops from Virginia preyed upon the community almost as though they had declared war on the local inhabitants. In the southern part of the state, Caswell was trying to rally the militia. There was but little response. Most of the men who were brought in had been drafted, and spent most of their time sulking and complaining. In general, those militiamen who had fled the field at Camden spread terror among their compatriots. About the only things to cheer about were the exploits of William R. Davie, who was harassing British outposts and raiding parties just across the South Carolina boundary.[24]

Governor Abner Nash was desperate. He had inherited an impossible situation and his own nervous apprehensions did little to improve the situation. The office of governor had been conceived as a weak peacetime executive, and had been allotted none of those sweeping powers so necessary to control a disorganized community in the midst of a civil war. Frustrated, sick, and with a heart saturated with a sense of failure almost at the very beginning of his term, he began to look for someone to help shoulder his burden.

The assembly met at Hillsborough in early September, 1780. The situation now demanded that it devote more attention to military

22. Johnson, *Sketches of Greene,* I, 496–98; *Magazine of American History,* V (October, 1880), 221, 278, 496; William Seymour, *A Journal of the Southern Expedition, 1780–1783* (Wilmington, Del., 1896), p. 7; Nash to Laurens, 23 August 1780, Papers of the Continental Congress; *State Records,* XV, 161–67.

23. Theodorick Bland, *The Bland Papers,* ed. Charles Campbell (Petersburg, Va., 1840–43), I, 33.

24. *State Records,* XV, 48–49, 65–66; Robinson, *William R. Davie,* pp. 67–69; Caswell to Nash, 19 August 1780, Caswell Papers, N.C. Dept. Arch. & Hist.; Nash to Washington, 6 October 1780, George Washington Papers.

demands rather than arguing political dispositions of the future. A specific provision tax was laid on the people, who were required to deliver a percentage of their produce to designated warehouses around the state. Yet the assembly did little to encourage the rebuilding of the North Carolina Continental establishment, preferring instead to rely upon militia calls or militia drafts for the next three months. On the other hand, militia calls to take the field were so frequent that only a small manpower pool from which to recruit Continentals was available. Governor Nash complained that his council would neither attend called meetings nor otherwise lend its assistance to the conduct of the war. On September 6 he reported to the legislature that "as I have only one of the Council to aid and advise me, permit me to recommend to the General Assembly the expediency of appointing a board of war in aid of the executive, and that the vacancy in the Council be filled up."[25]

The assembly took Nash at his word and created a Board of War, but went far beyond the governor's request to create an advisory body. The new agency was given powers that exceeded limitations imposed by the state constitution. Its members were given extraordinary powers in raising, organizing, and equipping the military forces of the state. They were to concert with the commanding officer in the state a plan of operations, requiring prompt troop returns and accurate records. Their authority included the right to remove or suspend all military officers of the state and appoint others in their places. The executive was required to carry through with all measures formulated by the board "as necessary and expedient for the public safety."

Five members of the board were elected by a joint ballot of both houses: Archibald MacLaine, Thomas Polk, Alexander Martin, John Penn and Oroondates Davis, the latter a lawyer and a member of the assembly from Halifax. MacLaine and Polk refused to serve. No one was appointed in their stead. And not only was Nash unhappy with the authority granted the board, but the appointment of its members was unpopular with the army. "Nothing could be more ridiculous," complained William R. Davie, "than the manner this Board was filled. Alexander the Little, being a Warrior of great fame, was placed at the head of the board—Penn who was fit only to amuse children, and O. Davis knew nothing but the game of Whist composed the rest of the Board." The assembly had indeed created a body of so much more power than that requested by the governor

25. *State Records*, XIV, 344–47, XV, 76–77; Gates to Laurens, 27 September 1780, Nash to Huntington, 8 October 1780, Papers of the Continental Congress.

that Nash cooperated with the board no more than absolutely necessary. In essence, it had but added to the general confusion already existing in North Carolina.[26]

Recovered from his chronic illness, and in view of the critical situation within the state, Jethro Sumner accepted the command of the militia of the Hillsborough District, under the over-all command of Richard Caswell. Supernumerary officers of the Fourth, Fifth, and Sixth Regiments were persuaded to assume temporary commands in the militia. Some officers among the supernumeraries and invalids refused to come back into the field to starve, or to leave their destitute families, especially since the majority of them were owed considerable sums in back pay.

Sumner marched his troops southward in early September, his mission to act as a scouting and holding force between the main body of the militia and the enemy. He was to risk no general engagement, "as another Defeat would be attended with Consequences to Fatal to mention—Skirmishing will encourage the Militia & give them Spirits." Sumner had the governor's permission to impress provisions if the people did not voluntarily furnish supplies for the army. His command was sickly, with some sixty of seventy men too ill to march. Some of those left at Chatham Court House were to die, "and them that is still alive, are almost naked." Even by militia standards, Sumner's troops promised little in the military way. Most of their arms were in ill repair, while nearly one-third were constantly employed in threshing the wheat gathered along the line of march.[27]

Serving under Sumner was William Lee Davidson. When the North Carolina Brigade had marched through North Carolina on its way to Charleston, Davidson had been granted leave to visit his family, whom he had not seen in three years. Charleston had fallen before his leave had expired. The assembly had commissioned him brigadier general of the Salisbury District in place of Griffith Rutherford who

---

26. George Doughtery to Sumner, 16 September 1780, Sumner Papers, William L. Clements Library, University of Michigan, Ann Arbor, Mich; Robinson, *William R. Davie*, pp. 82 03; Hugh T. Lefler and Paul Wager (eds.), *Orange County—1752–1952* (Chapel Hill, N.C., 1953), p. 50; *State Records*, XIV, 347–48, 355–57.

27. Sumner to Gates, n.d., Sumner to Nash, 3 September 1780, Gates to Sumner, 17 September 1780, Gideon Lamb to Sumner, 24 August 1780, Sumner Papers, William L. Clements Library; Nash to Sumner, 3 September 1780, Jethro Sumner Papers, N.C. Dept. Arch. & Hist.; Neal Scarlock to John Penn, 2 September 1780, Penn to Sumner, 21 September 1780, Board of War Papers, Military Collection; *State Records*, XV, 117–18, 118–19, 236, 369–70, 403–4, 770; Nash to Laurens, 23 August 1780, Papers of the Continental Congress; Sumner to Nash, 1 September 1780, Governors' Papers; Sumner to John Armstrong, 23 August 1780, Emmet Collection.

had been captured at Camden. Yet Davidson refused to relinquish his Continental commission and stood ready to resume his command once his regiment was reactivated.[28]

As he marched into Rowan County, Sumner found himself in a predicament that could only be described as gloomy, a plight brought about by Gates's precipitate flight to Hillsborough: "The effects of it are . . . worse than those of his defeat. It has frightened the ignorant into despair, being left without cover & support to defend themselves against the whole force of the enemy." When Davidson joined him with "His Brigade," his command consisted of no more than "upwards of 20 privates fit for duty." There was little hope of increasing the troops in the field since Tories were roaming the countryside doing "a great deal of mischief" and the militiamen hung close to their firesides to protect family and property. Loyalist harassments led militia leaders to disregard the orders of Caswell and Sumner and stray off in search of the marauders. Some hurried into the back country where the force of Patrick Ferguson posed a continuing threat. One group of Tories reported to be on their way to join the enemy were discouraged by a detachment of three hundred men sent by Sumner to block their progress.[29]

There were only fourteen North Carolina Continentals in the field, a small number of recruits and a few deserters who had been taken up and returned to active duty. All were, in general, "very naked." Those drafted militia who had been forced to do duty kept insisting that their time had expired and were so poorly equipped that they were of little use. On the other hand, many of the militiamen from Mecklenburg, just as soon as they had removed their families to places of safety, began to come into camp. But the general inconsistency of such soldiers created a fluid situation, for they were "quite inconsiderable; frightened, too, and irresolute—one day in camp, another away to save their property—so that one-half will undoubtedly vanish upon the approach of the enemy," Many of those already in the field seized the first opportunity to desert and, once beyond military jurisdiction, organized themselves into bands to plunder Whig and Tory alike. In Nash County, many of those who

28. *State Records*, XXII, 117–19; Davidson, *Piedmont Partisan*, p. 62.
29. Davidson to Sumner, 18 September 1780, Locke to Sumner, 23 September 1780, Sumner Papers, William L. Clements Library; Penn to Sumner, 21 September 1780, Board of War Papers, Military Collection; Sumner to Gates, 24 September 1780, George Washington Papers; *State Records*, XIV, 785, 786–87; Sumner to Nash, 5 September 1780, Governors' Papers; John Innes to Cornwallis, 12 September 1780, PRO 30/11/164.

were drafted only answered the call to duty after they were threatened with hanging.[30]

Although Gates was convinced that the British would not march northward in the near future, Sumner, upon receiving intelligence that the British had planned an invasion of North Carolina, marched into Charlotte at six o'clock in the morning of September 25. At this time reports were coming in that the British were only twelve miles away. Leaving Davie to cover his withdrawal, Sumner gathered those stores and provisions that he could transport and retreated toward Salisbury.[31]

Sometime earlier Cornwallis had decided to carry the war into North Carolina. The time was right, for the British general had earlier assured the North Carolina loyalists that he would come to their aid no later than September. Fourteen hundred Tories, over half of whom were from Rowan County, a community that had in the past been considered a hotbed of North Carolina Whiggery, had come into the British army. To Josiah Martin, this exodus from the state was "great proof . . . of the loyalty of North Carolinians."[32]

The British offensive was designed as a three-column thrust. Major James Craig was to be sent up the coast to take Wilmington, thereby controlling the Cape Fear River as a supply route to Cross Creek. The center column was to be the main army under Cornwallis, who planned to march for Hillsborough by way of Charlotte. The left flank, on the side of the mountains, was to be controlled by the force made up mainly of back-country Tories and commanded by Patrick Ferguson.

As the enemy approached Charlotte on September 26, Sumner and Davidson moved toward Salisbury, with the country people "flying before us in confusion." William R. Davie was ordered "to attend the enemy's motion and skirmish with their front." Davie, always the bold one, went beyond the intent of his orders and fought what almost amounted to a pitched battle with the entire British army, holding back Tarleton's vaunted British Legion. "The whole of the British

30. Sumner to John Penn, 29 September 1780, Sumner Papers, William L. Clements Library; *State Records*, XV, 118–19, 236, 369–70, XXII, 776–77; Return of the Troops commanded by General Sumner, 5 September 1780, Jethro Sumner Papers, Southern Historical Collection; Gates to Huntington, 27 September 1780, Papers of the Continental Congress.

31. *State Records*, XIV, 787–88.

32. *Report on the Manuscripts of Mrs. Stopford-Sackville*, II, 170–71, 174; Ross, *Cornwallis Correspondence*, I, 57; Gates to Huntington, 5 September 1780, Papers of the Continental Congress.

army," said Cornwallis's commissary, "was actually kept at bay, for some minutes, by a few mounted Americans, not exceeding twenty in number." Joined by reinforcements, Davie continued to harass the enemy for several hours and, it was estimated, killed twenty of the enemy and wounded even more.[33]

The British built their brush huts in a great circle around Charlotte, foraging parties sweeping the countryside in ever-widening circles to strip it of all produce. Within the town, Josiah Martin was handing out paroles and certificates of protection to the inhabitants of Mecklenburg County, signing them "Governor of North Carolina." This paroling of the local people, along with the distribution of generous quantities of liquor, convinced many that the British were attempting to subjugate the people of North Carolina in much the same fashion as they had in South Carolina.[34]

Charlotte soon proved untenable for the British. Cornwallis was constantly harassed by "Davie and other irregular troops who have committed the most shocking cruelties, and the most horrid murders on those suspected of being our friends, that I ever heard." Riflemen lay about the skirts of the village, and "nabbed them if they set out their heads," bringing on a shortage of supplies and forage in the British camp.[35]

Out of the southwest came the news that Ferguson, "his great Western Bugbear," had been killed and his command wiped out at a place called King's Mountain. Cornwallis and a number of his men fell ill. Pressure was constantly applied to the outposts until the British "situation at Charlotte hath been rendered very troublesome by the close Attention paid them by Davidson and Davie, who, with Colonel Morgan are now hanging on and greatly distress them."[36]

When Cornwallis made the decision to fall back into South Carolina to rebuild his army of invasion, there were few protests. An aide to the general was to observe that "Charlotte is an agreeable village,

33. Stedman, *History of the . . . American War*, II, 240; *State Records*, XV, 83, 89; Davidson to Gates, 26 September 1780, George Washington Papers; Sumner to Gates, 29 September 1780, Papers of the Continental Congress.

34. Sumner to Gates, 1 October 1789, Sumner Papers, William L. Clements Library; Board of War to Nash, 7 October 1780, Board of War Papers, Military Collection; *State Records*, XIV, 779, 780; Davidson to Nash, 26 September 1780, Governors' Papers.

35. Sumner to Gates, 1 October 1780, Papers of the Continental Congress; Sumner to John Penn, 1 October 1780, Preston Davie Collection, Southern Historical Collection.

36. Davidson to Sumner, 13 October 1780, Alexander Martin to North Carolina Delegates in Congress, 17 October 1780, Papers of the Continental Congress; Sumner to Gates, 10 October 1780, Sumner Papers, William L. Clements Library.

but in a d——d rebellious country." The retirement began at sunset, October 9, but their guide, William McCafferty, a Charlotte merchant, deserted them shortly after nightfall. The British, panic-stricken, wandered through the darkness and become so disorganized that they were not again united until noon of the following day. Just as soon as the news of the retreat reached the American camp, Davie and other partisans were sent out "to gall the Enemy in their Rear," and skirmished with the large detachment sent back to accommodate them. The main army, with their sick general jolting along in a baggage wagon, hurried to Winnsboro. Five miles from Charlotte the British abandoned thirty wagons, later recovered by the Americans. This retrograde movement left the North Carolinians jubilant; they along with other southerners, began to speak confidently of the early capture of the British army.[37]

In the fall of 1780, the situation was so gloomy that even a small success was construed as an omen of victory.

37. Board of War to Nash, 25 October 1780, Board of War Papers. Military Collection; Davidson to Nash, 22 October 1780, Governors' Papers; William A. Graham, *General Joseph Graham*, pp. 270–71; Moore, *Diary of the American Revolution*, II, 352; Reed, *Life and Correspondence of Joseph Reed*, II, 348; Fortescue, *A History of the British Army*, III, 330; *State Records*, XIV, 779, XV, 111; Benjamin Franklin Stevens (ed.), *Clinton-Cornwallis Controversy Growing Out of the Campaign in Virginia, 1781* (London, 1888), I, 308.

Chapter 13
A New General for the South

"This is really making bricks without straw."

The withdrawal of Cornwallis had given a false ray of hope to the people of North Carolina. Hillsborough continued to be a rendezvous for the southern army. The village was soon swarming with soldiers, many of whom openly boasted that once they took the field again they would thrash the British army. As their numbers swelled they overflowed into the surrounding countryside. There were frequent clashes between the military and civilians, especially among the militiamen, who seemed to hold little respect for civil authority. Their officers did little to develop an attitude of responsibility among their men. As in previous encampments at Hillsborough, provisions and forage were taken without regard for ownership, exposing "the Inhabitants of this Country to rapine without remedy."[1]

Now that the people had time to reflect upon Gates's behavior at Camden, they held three major grievances against him. One was his failure to provide a rendezvous for his army in the event of a defeat. Not properly securing the baggage wagons had led to irreparable losses of supplies for the southern army. And, "thirdly in quit-

1. *State Records*, XV, 779–89.

ting the field of Action some time before the Regulars gave way and riding post to Hillsbo 230 Miles in about 75 Hours, he is indeed execrated by the Officers, Unrevered by the Soldiers & Citizens have lost all confidence in the Man and wou'd esteem it a happy circumstance cou'd he be recall'd or coax'd away from the Command in the Southern Department."[2]

The supply situation blackened the picture. The Board of War authorized the issuance of certificates to the owners of grain taken for the army, but wandering bands of foragers often confiscated wheat and corn without such formalities. The courthouse had been designated as a warehouse, but there was little surplus to be stored therein; certainly it was not as full as the church that had been converted into a hospital. The men of the Maryland and Delaware lines were barefoot and "in want of every thing except arms. . . ." A number of Virginia militiamen who had fled the field at Camden returned to the army, "mortified at the reception they met with in Virginia, and so ashamed of their past conduct. . . ." But this group wore little more than their shame, for they had "no Cloathing—No Arms—& no provisions with them." Some were so poorly clad that they refused to leave their huts or tents. Those arms that were available, although belonging to the North Carolina militia, were issued to those Continental troops who had lost their weapons at Camden. The Board of War collected all available hides, placed the local tannery under state authority, and established a shoe factory under the supervision of John Taylor. Everyone capable of leather work was pressed into service making and repairing shoes. Tailors and all those women handy with a needle were put to work repairing and sewing uniforms. Letters pleading for additional supplies were dispatched to every possible source, while a desperate search for salt was initiated. There was no money; the state had more than exhausted its treasury in attempting to equip Gates's army before Camden.[3]

Gates, "sadly low dispirited," grew short tempered and, brooding about his future, "made everyone unhappy that had to Communicate with him." Yet he did not neglect his military responsibilities. The Maryland and Delaware Continentals were consolidated into one regiment under the command of Colonel Otho Williams.

2. Oroondates Davis to Willie Jones, 27 September 1780, Board of War Papers, Military Collection.

3. *State Records*, XV, 79; Gates to Henry Laurens, 27 September 1780, Papers of the Continental Congress; Board of War to Nash, 17 September 1780, Board of War Papers, Military Collection; Gibbes, *Documentary History of the American Revolution*, II, 270; Nash to Washington, 6 October 1780, George Washington Papers; Gates to Nash, 11 September 1780, Governors' Papers.

The remnants of several cavalry troops were united under Colonel William Washington. Some recruits, along with some Virginia artillery came in. Supernumerary officers were sent home to recruit.[4]

Despite many efficient operations, the Board of War went beyond the supply problem and made something of a nuisance of itself. Its three members, an ex-Continental officer, a politician, and a lawyer, prepared minute instructions for the artillery, detailing movements and operations of such military matters as how to approach the enemy, how to fight and, if necessary, how to retreat. The very fact that it was felt necessary to issue these written precepts suggests that the Board of War no longer held much confidence in Gates. To add to the confusion in Hillsborough, Governor John Rutledge of South Carolina, who had fled before the advance of the enemy, was attempting to run the affairs of his state from within such protection as was afforded by Gates's army. His influence was such that he was able to persuade the Board of War to dispatch funds (which it didn't have) for the support of the South Carolina militia although those of North Carolina were not properly provided for.[5]

There was one bright spot in a picture that otherwise appeared to grow steadily more gloomy. Colonel Daniel Morgan, who had voluntarily retired from the army in July, 1779, because of what he considered to be ill treatment by Congress and a dispute over command, returned to active duty after the Camden disaster. Gates put together a light infantry corps and placed it under Morgan's command. Shortly afterwards, the burly backswoodsman was marching his troops toward the Yadkin, where he arrived in time to aid in the harassment of the British in Charlotte. On October 13, Congress made Daniel Morgan a brigadier general.[6]

The Board of War, in essence, was now running the state. Because North Carolina was in a near state of civil war with a formidable enemy on her doorstep with an obvious intent to invade the state, military problems were of the greatest importance, and the Board of War ran the military. Martin and Davis were absent a great deal of the time attending to personal affairs at home. For some time John Penn became something of a dictator, for it was not until November and December that Martin and Davis played active roles as members of the board.[7]

4. Gibbes, *Documentary History of the American Revolution*, II, 270; Lee, *Memoirs of the War in the Southern Department*, pp. 208–9.

5. *State Records*, XV, 417.

6. *Ibid.*, p. 117.

7. *Ibid.*, XIV, 389–406.

Perhaps because of the influence of Gates, who constantly blamed his defeat at Camden on the "rascally behaviour of the militia," the assembly seemed to have lost faith in the ability of local officers. Former governor and now major general of militia Richard Caswell was removed as commanding general of the North Carolina militia, ostensibly because "he could not conveniently immediately take the field." In view of the behavior of most of Caswell's troops at Camden, this might have been expected, especially since the Continental Congress was to remove Gates from command and turn over the choice of a successor to Washington. Yet the most galling development to most North Carolina military men was that the command of the local militia was given to Brigadier General William Smallwood of the Maryland Continentals. Smallwood had done little better than Caswell at Camden, having been separated from his troops by the horde of fleeing militia, but he, along with everyone else except Gates and the militia, had received the "thanks of Congress" for his efforts in that action. The nearest thing to an explanation by the North Carolina Assembly for the selection of Smallwood was "your Character as a Soldier is highly respected, while your Behavior as a Gentleman is engaging."[8]

At New Bern an angry Caswell confronted Governor Nash. The meeting began in a cordial fashion, with Caswell waiting upon "His Excellency for any Command he might deliver him relative to his Duty as a Major General, saying he was ready to take the Field & waited his Orders only." Nash explained that the assembly, in the creation of a Board of War, had practically removed the militia from executive jurisdiction. When Caswell demanded if the governor still considered him to be a general officer, Nash replied that "he did not, that the Resolution appointing General Smallwood to the Command of the Militia of this State, a Supersedas to General Caswell's Command as Major General." Caswell, resigning in a huff, also resigned his position on the Board of Trade. Nash importuned the Board of War on Caswell's behalf, suggesting that the former governor had been treated in a rather shabby fashion. The situation created so much resentment and discussion that Alexander Martin suggested that a separate command be created for Caswell.[9]

Jethro Sumner, as a brigadier general of the North Carolina Line, must have been equally unhappy to have been superseded by

8. *Ibid.*, XIV, 401, XV, 131, 771.

9. Affidavit of John Sitzgreaves, 5 January 1781, Historical Society of Pennsylvania Collection; *State Records*, XIV, 435, XV, 131; Martin to Nash, 25 October 1780, Board of War Papers, Military Collection.

an officer from the line of another state. Equally disturbing to his pride was the information that Gates had also placed the few North Carolina Continentals in the field under Smallwood's direct command. Although keeping his irritation to himself, he must have agreed with a friend who wrote that "I must confess I was somewhat Nettled."[10]

When the British had approached Charlotte, Sumner pulled back to the Yadkin within one-half mile of Salisbury. He was ordered to maintain that position as long as possible; in fact Gates had warned that "you must be answerable if it is too soon abandoned." On the other hand, John Penn warned against any action that might lead to a general engagement "lest another defeat be more than American patriotism could stand." It is unlikely that Sumner would have been so foolish as to risk any engagement, even had he been so inclined. Atlhough some of his men seemed eager for action, two militia regiments insisted that their time was up and clamored to be allowed to return to their homes. To make matters even more difficult for the North Carolina brigadier, Gates insisted that he send dispatches every six hours if not oftener, and the Board of War also demanded regular reports of all military activities. Smallwood was delayed by illness in assuming command of the militia; actually he appeared more interested in remaining in Hillsborough to reorganize and re-equip the Maryland and Delaware Continentals than he was in taking over as commanding general of the North Carolina militia. Sumner, isolated by distance from the main army, was forced to spend much of his time in searching out provisions, for Gates had held back all supplies for his troops at Hillsborough, including those items earmarked for the militia. He received little aid from the Board of War, for when he needed positive decisions he got only evasive answers.[11]

Sumner had little inclination to begin offensive action before the arrival of Smallwood. He, along with a majority of the officers of the line serving with the militia had decided to "decline command of

10. George Doughtery to Sumner, 16 September 1780, Sumner Papers, William L. Clements Library; *State Records*, XV, 772; Gates to Smallwood, 3 October 1780, Papers of the Continental Congress.

11. Gates to Sumner, 30 September 1780, Davidson to Sumner, 1 October 1780, Sumner to Gates, 1 October 1780, Sumner to John Butler, 6 October 1780, Sumner to _____, 12 October 1780, Sumner Papers, William L. Clements Library; Gates to Sumner, 2 October 1780, Sumner Papers, N.C. Dept. Arch. & Hist.; Penn to the North Carolina Delegates in Congress, 5 October 1780, Martin to Davidson, 7 November 1780, Board of War Papers, Military Collection; Sumner to Gates, 29 September 1780, George Washington Papers; *State Records*, XV, 773, 780; Sumner to Smallwood, 15 October 1780, Papers of the Continental Congress.

the militia of this State as being treated scandalously and with great partiality." The brigadier brooded about the legislature's apparent lack of confidence in him in appointing Smallwood. Although he had agreed to serve under Caswell, a militia major general, Caswell had been a North Carolinian. Alexander Martin appealed to Sumner's patriotism, saying, "Should you leave the Service at this critical Juncture in the Face of the Enemy, the Board will sincerely regret it and wish the brave and virtuous Soldiers will dispense with immediate Inconveniences & will not for the little punctilio of Honour suffer his Country to be given into the Hands of a Merciless Enemy." But Jethro Sumner and his officers were proud men, and this was an age in which pride and honor were important to those who considered themselves gentlemen.[12]

As wounded pride undermined an already crumbling local military organization a furious Nash accused the board of attempting to usurp the prerogatives of the executive and being itself a threat to constitutional government. Had not the general situation been so critical, the feud might well have erupted into a bitter struggle. But the exigencies of the moment would not allow a complete breakdown of the machinery of state.[13]

Shortly after the British had struggled out of Charlotte the rains came in a downpour as heavy as "ever poor fellow ever lived thro'." Powder was soaked. Daniel Morgan and his light troops had managed to get across the river before the rains began, but for a week the rising Yadkin prevented any move by Sumner until October 17. Smallwood's procrastination in assuming the militia command left Sumner with no definite plan of operation and he felt it inexpedient to act on his own and commit his successor to actions he had not anticipated. Shortly after Smallwood arrived in the middle of October, Sumner submitted a brief statement to him: "I feel myself distressed to signify my declining any further Command of the Line of Militia." Then he, along with other unhappy Continental officers who had been serving with the militia, made their way home. Militia officers throughout the state, equally dissatisfied with Smallwood's appointment, began to find excuses not to serve under his command.[14]

12. Sumner to Gates, 10 October 1780, Sumner Papers, William L. Clements Library; Martin to Sumner, 13 October 1780, Martin to Nash, 25 October 1780, Board of War Papers, Military Collection; *State Records*, XIV, 785, 787–88; Penn to Sumner, 13 October 1780, Preston Davie Collection, Southern Historical Collection.

13. Davis to Nash, 15 December 1780, Martin to Nash, 21 December 1780, Board of War Papers, Military Collection.

14. Sumner to Gates, 13 October 1780, Davidson to Sumner, 13 October 1780,

Food had grown short in the vicinity of Hillsborough. The Board of War, now that winter was coming, had decided that Orange County could no longer support the army. It persuaded Gates that an adequate supply of provisions could be found farther south in the Salisbury area. Smallwood was also urging Gates to join him, arguing that their combined force could "change the prospect." Alexander Martin felt that the army should take a post nearer the British, for the "operations of the Enemy seem rather daring & wear a countenance of seriousness." And Gates had recaptured some of his former optimism. From somewhere he had gained the idea that a large French fleet would soon be off the South Carolina coast to cooperate with him. On November 2, he sent off about 1,000 men, the Maryland, Delaware, and Virginia Continentals, along with the two artillery pieces of Captain Anthony Singleton's artillery company. Several days later the general left Hillsborough with an escort of 130 Continental mounted troops. No matter how confident he appeared, Gates was in no condition to fight. At least 55 per cent of his men were sick or incapacitated with such ailments as dysentery, diarrhea, rheumatism, dropsy, ulcerated legs, or were "billious," "lame," or wounded.[15]

Gates knew full well that there were not sufficient supplies in Rowan County. Jethro Sumner had constantly complained of the lack of food and forage. Thomas Polk, Continental Commissary, had done his best, but his efforts had been so unsuccessful that "his conduct was deemed doubtful and suspicious." Polk had become so angered by such accusations that he had submitted his resignation, to become effective when he had completed those projects in which he was now engaged.[16]

Sumner to Smallwood, 15 October 1780, Davie to Sumner, 16 October 1780, John Peasley to Sumner, 16 October 1780, Davie to Sumner, 17 October 1780, Sumner to Davidson, 16 October 1780, Philip M. Taylor to Sumner, 16 October 1780, Sumner to Smallwood, 17 October 1780, Sumner to Smallwood, 20 October 1780, Sumner Papers, William L. Clements Library; Martin to Nash, 25 October 1780, Board of War Papers, Military Collection; *State Records,* XIV, 463–64, 790; Davidson, *Piedmont Partisan,* p. 92.

15. *State Records,* XIV, 405–6, XV, 160–61; Penn to Nash, 27 September 1780, Emmet Collection; Return of the General Hospital at Hillsborough, N.C., 5 November 1780, Papers of the Continental Congress; Martin to Nicholas Long, 5 November 1780, Martin to the North Carolina Delegates in Congress, 7 November 1780, Board of War Papers, Military Collection; Elizabeth Merritt (ed.), *Calendar of the General Otho Williams Papers in the Maryland Historical Society* (Baltimore, 1940), pp. 27, 30; Penn to Nash, 27 September 1780, Martin to Nash, 10 November 1780, Governors' Papers.

16. *State Records,* XV, 416; Penn to Polk, 4 October 1780, Board of War Papers, Military Collection.

Shortly after Gates marched southward another major general rode into Hillsborough, seeking the southern army. In answer to the rising waves of criticism of Gates after Camden, Congress had suggested to General Washington that he select a new commanding general for the Southern Department. Washington's choice had been Nathanael Greene of Rhode Island. The appointment was generally popular with the army, and Robert Howe had written, "Gen'l Greene will deserve success whether he obtains it or not." At this time, Greene was thirty-eight years old, somewhat corpulent, but taller than the average man and of a fair complexion. An old injury had left him with a limp. "His health," wrote Henry Lee, "was delicate, but preserved by temperance and exercise." Greene had long been a favorite of Washington's and the commanding general feared the consequences of the appointment, for "in the command he is going into he will have every disadvantage to struggle with." Washington warned Congress that unless that body gave increased support to Greene, "the history of this war is a history of false hopes."[17]

Greene had set out for the South on October 23. He stopped by Philadelphia for nine days to urge the Congress and the state of Pennsylvania to furnish him with more of the necessities of warfare. But to his supplications "poverty was urged as a plea, in bar to every application. They all promised fair, but I fear will do little: ability is wanting with some, and inclination with others." Leaving Philadelphia he stopped by both Annapolis and Richmond. In both state capitals he was promised greater aid than he knew he would receive; yet promises were something to live on until reality intervened. Nathanael Greene was an ambitious man, endowed with a strong sense of history and fearful of judgments when his contributions were evaluated in the future. He expressed his fears to Washington: "My only consolation is, that if I fail, I hope it will not be accompanied by any marks of personal disgrace. Censure and reproach ever follow the unfortunate. This I expect, if I don't succeed; . . . the ruin of my family is what hangs most heavily upon my mind. My fortune is small, and misfortune or disgrace to me must be ruin to them."[18]

17. Fitzpatrick, *Writings of Washington*, XX, 242, 244–45; *State Records*, XIV, 527, XXII, 527; Howe to Nash, 23 October 1780, Robert Howe Papers, Southern Historical Collection; Lee, *Memoirs of the War in the Southern Department*, p. 221; Burnett, *Letters of Members of the Continental Congress*, V, 411, 421, 432.
18. Jared Sparks (ed.), *Correspondence of the American Revolution: Being Letters of Eminent Men to George Washington, From the Time of His Taking Command of the Army to the End of His Presidency* (Boston, 1853), III, 137–39, 150–51; John C. Hamilton (ed.), *The Works of Alexander Hamilton* (New York, 1856), I, 204.

Baron von Steuben, who had been assigned to the Southern Department as inspector general, had ridden with Greene as far as Richmond. Because of the presence of the British in Chesapeake Bay, Greene appointed Steuben as military commander in Virginia and charged him to whip the local recruits into some semblance of a military organization. Steuben had other duties. A steady supply of flour was to be shipped regularly from the Virginia grist mills, as well as the lead from the mines of Fincastle County. Continental supplies stored in the state were to be inspected, while those materials sent down from the North were to be forwarded to Greene's army as quickly as possible. The larger number of broken arms in Virginia were to be repaired. The recruiting service in Virginia was to be overhauled and fresh troops were to be sent to Greene just as soon as they were ready for the field. In all, it was a task to try even the capabilities of the irrepressible Steuben.[19]

Greene, who had expected to find the army in Hillsborough, remained in that place but a short while. Governor Nash was not in town. With the news of the landing of British troops under General Alexander Leslie in the Chesapeake, thereby posing the threat of an invasion of North Carolina, Nash had dashed to Halifax to rouse the inhabitants of that community. Irritated, Greene wrote a short note to the Governor, suggesting that Nash could better utilize his talents and attention in preparing the state militia to meet the greater threat of an invasion from the south by Lord Cornwallis.[20]

A dispatch to Jethro Sumner enlisted his aid in the rehabilitation of the North Carolina Continental Line. All physically disabled officers were ordered retired from active duty, while all deserters and former prisoners of war who had escaped from the enemy were to be assembled as quickly as possible. Sumner was authorized to grant pardons to all deserters who rejoined the army. Hillsborough was designated as the rendezvous. In that town Greene found James Thackston, who had been assigned the task of rounding up deserters and collecting new recruits by the Board of War. At the time there were only sixteen soldiers under his command. Greene then rode out over the muddy roads to Salisbury, only to discover that Gates had marched to Charlotte.[21]

19. Kapp, *Life of Frederick William Von Steuben*, pp. 347–49.
20. James Graham, *The Life of General Daniel Morgan, of the Virginia Line of the Army of the United States, with Portions of His Correspondence Compiled from Authentic Sources* (New York, 1856), pp. 244–45; Merritt, *Calendar of the General Otho Williams Papers*, p. 27; Greene, *Life of Nathanael Greene*, III, 64–68.
21. *State Records*, XIV, 792; Thackston to Sumner, 16 November 1780, Sumner Papers, William L. Clements Library.

Arriving in Charlotte on December 2, Greene found that Gates had discovered that the Salisbury area could not furnish his troops with provisions. Despite the fact that the countryside around Charlotte had been stripped clean of provisions and forage by the British army and the Mecklenburg and Rowan militia, Gates became convinced that the place was a proper site for winter quarters. When the new general rode into the village the army was busily constructing huts gainst the chilling winds of winter.[22]

Despite the rumored ill feeling between the two men, the new commanding general was received by the old with cordiality and respect. General orders for December 3, 1780, carried the news of the change in command. Later in the day Greene reviewed the troops and paid his predecessor the compliment of confirming all of his standing orders.[23]

A tour of inspection revealed little more than added causes for discouragement. Greene's first evening in camp had ended with an all-night discussion with Colonel Thomas Polk relative to military supplies and the resources of the country. Polk was to later declare that Greene, on the following morning, better understood the situation of the country than Gates had in the entire period of his command. There was only a three-day supply of provisions on hand, and ammunition was dangerously low. The inhabitants were hiding those cattle that had escaped Cornwallis's foragers.[24]

Many factors had contributed to the desperate supply situation. The drafting of farmers to serve in the militia had "deranged the agriculture of the country." Droughts in the highlands and floods in the lowlands had ruined crops the previous year so that there was no surplus on hand. Although the crops in western North Carolina were reported to have been good this year, they did the army little good, for even had there been wagons to transport the grain there were no draught animals to pull them.[25]

Colonel Thaddeus Kosciuszko, chief engineer of the southern army, had been dispatched to survey the area around the Peedee River in South Carolina where supplies were said to be plentiful. Alexander Martin, a close friend of Smallwood's who was in Char-

---

22. Johnson, *Sketches of Greene*, I, 510.
23. John H. Wheeler, *Historical Sketches of North Carolina From 1584 to 1851* (Philadelphia, 1851), II, 263; Johnson, *Sketches of Greene*, I, 495.
24. Hamilton, *Works of Alexander Hamilton*, I, 205; Winslow C. Watson (ed.), *Men and Times of the Revolution: or, Memoirs of Elkanah Watson* (New York, 1856), p. 269; Stedman, *History of the . . . American War*, II, 216–17n.
25. Thomas Burke, William Sharpe, and Samuel Johnston to John Laurens, 16 January 1781, Revolutionary Collection.

lotte at the time, urged that Greene establish a line of posts reaching south toward the enemy. The general's laconic reply was that it would take "some time to inform himself of the Country, not choozing to be in surprizing Distance of Lord Cornwallis until he was strong enough to fight him."[26]

The southern army, on paper, had a total operative force of 2,307 men, over half of whom were militiamen. But of the total number, only about 800 were properly equipped for action. A large number had no weapons and it was discouraging to realize that there were something like 5,000 muskets in North Carolina that were "useless for want of some trifling repairs" because of the lack of gunsmiths. Greene was horrified to discover that Gates had been so lax in his administrative duties that many important army accounts had been lost or destroyed. To his frend Joseph Reed he complained that "General Gates has lost the Confidence of the Officers; and the Troops all their Discipline: and so addicted to plundering that they were a terror to the Inhabitants." There were no maps. The army with which Greene was to drive the enemy from the South was little more than a ragged undisciplined mob, using the exigencies of war as excuses for plundering. The militia, customarily employed as infantry, insisted upon coming into the field on horseback. Foraging for their mounts added to the privations of an already ravaged countryside. The situation had worsened to such an extent that when the militiamen were not looting the inhabitants they plundered each other. Officers were openly criticized for their conduct of military affairs, for "With their militia everybody is a general." In short, Greene's army was, in his opinion, "but the shadow of an army in the midst of distress."[27]

Much of Greene's time was spent in composing pleading letters to anyone who might offer aid, but the situation had grown so acute that he had to resort to every expedient. All the sheeting and osnaburg in the neighborhood was taken up and sent to the women of Salisbury to be made into overalls. Because of the shortage of funds, Greene suggested that these seamstresses be paid in salt. Despite such stopgaps, and despite the need for good mounted troops, the plight of Major Nelson's Virginia cavalry was so hopeless that the entire group was sent home, with Greene suggesting to Governor Jefferson that they should not be returned to the army until they had been properly

26. Martin to Nash, 21 December 1780, Board of War Papers, Military Collection.

27. Greene, *Life of Nathanael Greene*, III, 70; *State Records*, XIV, 768; *Portfolio*, 3rd Series (1813), I, 203–6, 290–91; Greene to Reed, 9 January 1781; Joseph Reed Papers; Nash to Washington, 2 February 1781, Papers of the Continental Congress.

equipped and clothed. Many officers felt that Jefferson was too intent in courting the popularity of the people to concentrate upon the business of winning the war.[28]

The army seemed a complete stranger to discipline; desertions were frequent and returns fluctuated widely as men came and went as they pleased without the formality of furloughs. Determined to halt the practice, Greene himself initiated the rumor that the first deserter caught would be made an example. The men still wandered off. To assert his authority, Greene speedily court-martialed and condemned to death the first deserter returned to camp. The entire army was drawn up to witness the execution. That night, to determine the reaction of the men, officers strolled among the campfires. One unidentified philosopher was heard to utter the terse observation, "It is new Lords, new laws."[29]

The army, in spite of, or perhaps because of Gates's attempts at reorganization, was in a ferment of inefficiency. The Virginia Continentals, for example, were considered "deranged" and were "destitute of Cloathing and consequently dirty and exceedingly deficient in Discipline." Orders issued under his loose command structure had been both confusing and contradictory. The decrees of Governor Nash and the Board of War, the orders issued by Gates and Smallwood were all boiling in the same cauldron with the new changes made by Greene. There was no alternative to a sweeping reorganization and the institution of new policies and precepts. To aid in administrative details, the brilliant Marylander, Otho Williams, was made adjutant general, a position that he had filled briefly under Gates. In the quartermaster department the inefficient but "very honest young man" holding the job of deputy quartermaster general was replaced by Colonel Edward Carrington of Virginia.[30]

The office of commissary general was held by Colonel Thomas Polk, who had fallen into ill favor with both Gates and Smallwood. Weary of Smallwood's accusations and Gates's censures, and the charges that he refused to supply any but Continental troops, Polk had resigned, his resignation to become effective when he delivered

28. *State Records*, XV, 181; Palmer, *Virginia State Papers*, I, 398; Merritt, *Calendar of the General Otho Williams Papers*, p. 37; *Pennsylvania Magazine of History and Biography*, XVIII (1904), 241–42.

29. William Gordon, *The History of the Rise, Progress, and Establishment of the Independence of the United States of America: Including an Account of the Late War and of the Thirteen Colonies, from Their Origin to That Period* (London, 1788), IV, 28.

30. Greene, *Life of Nathanael Greene*, III, 73–74; Davidson, *Piedmont Partisan*, p. 97; Merritt, *Calendar of the General Otho Williams Papers*, p. 31.

the supplies he was then engaged in collecting. Shortly after Greene's arrival, Polk had asked that he be relieved of duty, explaining, "I am too far advanced in years to undergo the tasks and fatigues of a Commissary-General." As a result of a resolution by the Continental Congress, one Robert Forsyth had been appointed deputy commissary general of purchases for the Southern Department, but Greene needed a capable officer with his immediate command. On the same day that he received Polk's request for relief, Greene wrote William R. Davie, offering him the post, listing Davie's special qualifications of health, education, and popularity with the inhabitants of the region. Davie, who at this time was attempting to recruit "a kind of Legion" to serve with Daniel Morgan's light corps, demurred, declaring that he knew little of keeping accounts. Greene blunted this excuse by pointing out that there was not a single dollar in the military chest, nor was there a prospect of securing any for the near future. After his acceptance, Davie's duties were not limited to the procurement of provisions. Often he was to lead foraging expeditions in person and it was the rule rather than the exception to buy from the willing and extort from the reluctant.[31]

Although the nondescript army was beginning to show some signs of rehabilitation, a new factor was beginning to creep in that threatened to shake the structure if not destroy it entirely. Dissension had appeared among the officers, with William Smallwood as the chief protagonist. Smallwood had been promoted to major general on September 15 and the elevation in rank seemed to have filled him with delusions of grandeur. Earlier there were those who had whispered that Smallwood had been the original instigator of the discrediting rumors of Gates's conduct at Camden, and Gates himself suspected that Smallwood was trying to supplant him. Greene felt that Smallwood had expected to be given command of the Southern Department and had been greatly disappointed when he had not been given consideration. Smallwood, rather than reveal the true reasons for his discontent, refused to serve so long as von Steuben outranked him in the southern army. He proposed to Greene that he petition Congress to date Smallwood's promotion to major general two years forward, which would rank him above Steuben and allow him to assume the command should anything happen to the com-

31. Gates to the North Carolina Board of War, 17 November 1780, Jethro Sumner Papers, Southern Historical Collection; Robinson, *William R. Davie*, pp. 97–100; Greene, *Life of Nathanael Greene*, III, 76–77; *State Records*, XIV, 490, 737; Victor Leroy Johnson, *The Administration of the American Commissariat During the Revolutionary War* (Philadelphia, 1941), p. 186; Oroondates Davis to Nash, 1 December 1780, Board of War Papers, Military Collection.

manding general in the Southern Department. Greene refused to even consider this proposal. He had been a witness to, and even a participant, in the so-called "Conway Cabal," and could see in Smallwood's suggestion a fuse that, if burned to the end, could throw the entire army into discord. Greene, feeling that Smallwood was basically a valuable officer, attempted to persuade him to drop his demands, but the stubborn Marylander refused to listen. Realizing the dangers inherent when a high-ranking officer spent time sulking in his tent, Greene mentioned the quarrel to Congress. On December 19, Smallwood was sent north, ostensibly to gather and forward supplies from Maryland to the southern army, but in reality to give him a base near the seat of Congress with whom he personally settled his differences. To lead the North Carolina militia Greene appointed Brigadier General William Lee Davidson, subject to the approval of the state's General Assembly.[32]

Kosciuszko returned from his scouting mission to the south to report the prospect for supplies to be good along the Peedee River and to suggest that the army could fare better in that South Carolina bivouac. Before marching orders could be issued the rains came. While waiting for the downpour to cease, Nathanael Greene made the decision that was to shape his destiny as well as the course of the war in the South: he split his army. Perhaps as a result of a suggestion by William Lee Davidson, the general ordered Daniel Morgan to the southwest to take a position near the Broad River, there to harry the enemy, collect provisions and forage, give protection to those who supported the American cause, and in general "spirit up the people."[33]

On December 20, after a steady rain for eleven days, the two armies marched off in different directions. The roads were deep in mire, and Greene's army did not complete the eighty-mile march to the camp on Hick's Creek on the Peedee until the day after Christmas. Although the prospects for provisioning the army were brighter, Greene complained that "this is no Egypt." Many of his soldiers were so naked that they were unable to perform the most menial of tasks. A large number wore only a portion of a blanket wrapped Indian-

32. *Year Book: City of Charleston, S.C., 1899* (Charleston, S.C., 1899), pp. 71–72; Burnett, *Letters of Members of the Continental Congress*, V, 361–62; Reed, *Life and Correspondence of Joseph Reed*, II, 344–46.

33. *State Records*, XIV, 759; Theoderas Baily Myers (ed.), *Cowpens Papers: Being the Correspondence of General Morgan and Prominent Actors* (Charleston, 1881), pp. 9–10; Sparks, *Correspondence of the American Revolution*, III, 189–91; Burke, Sharpe, and Johnston to _____, Greene Papers, Duke University, Durham, N.C.

fashion around the waist. The weary general and his men settled down in what he termed "a camp of repose; and no army ever wanted it more."[34]

The high esteem in which North Carolina had held the militia since the battle of Moore's Creek Bridge had been magnified by the victory at King's Mountain. Greene constantly nagged the North Carolina Board of War, demanding that they complete their Continental battalions rather than coddling the militia. The general had, in fact, turned down one "class" of North Carolina militiamen who had been called out. The Board of War in reply suggested that the militiamen be employed in partisan warfare until they could be replaced with Continental levies. This the board knew full well Greene would never do, for to turn the militiamen into the field under only their own officers would be only giving them license to plunder. The Board of War, however, did notify the general that Continental recruits were being raised, but they would not be sent immediately to Greene "lest they disturb as to provisions." Then, adding insult to injury, the Board stated that these new levies would not be ordered forward until Greene had gathered enough strength to "offend the enemy." This affection for the occasional soldier appeared to prevail in the other states that comprised the Southern Department, and if he created a force of any effectiveness Greene would be forced to discard his dream of a well-disciplined Continental command and utilize the militia. Still, he repeated his conviction that "the enemy will never relinquish their plan, nor people be firm in our favor, until they behold a better barrier on the field than a voluntary militia, who are one day, out, and the next, at home."[35]

The improvement in the supply situation lasted but a short while. The inhabitants appeared reluctant to sell to any army that could pay only with promises. To remedy the acute shortage of shoes, the Moravian Society in North Carolina was contacted and the hides of the cattle slaughtered for food were offered in exchange for footwear. To the protests of a merchant whose salt had been confiscated, Greene answered, "In such a situation remote evils must be submitted to, to prevent an immediate misfortune." Investigation revealed that many supplies destined for the southern army never reached camp. Provisions collected in the immediate neighborhood were in such

34. Myers, *Cowpens Papers*, pp. 10–11; Alexander Gregg, *History of the Old Cheraws* (New York, 1867), p. 352; Greene to Thomas Sumter, 15 January 1781, Greene Letterbook, New York Public Library, New York, N.Y.

35. Reed, *Life and Correspondence of Joseph Reed*, II, 346; *State Records*, XIV, 485; Greene to Sumter, 8 January 1781, Greene Letterbook.

danger of attack from local Tories that mounted guards had to be detached to guard the wagons. The greatest danger, however, came not from the enemy but from the American army itself. Agents at small posts along the supply lines waylaid wagons moving south and appropriated needed articles, especially if their freight contained rum. Greene issued directives prohibiting agents from stopping supply trains unless they possessed a signed order from the general. To the Commissary at Cross Creek he explained, "It is the consumption of Posts that starve the Army, and this evil must be remedied."[36]

The army was not only hungry but sick. There was the constant threat that an outbreak of smallpox would immobilize the troops. Bickerings and petty jealousies among the officers threatened the little spirit of unity that existed. Such was the organization with which Nathanael Greene was supposed to drive the enemy from the South. It seemed an insurmountable task. "This," he murmured, "is really making bricks without straw."[37]

36. Greene to the Head of the Moravian Society, 8 January 1781, Greene to Robert Gillies, 9 January 1781, Greene to Fletcher, n.d., Greene Letterbook; Johnson, *Sketches of Greene*, I, 341.
37. Myers, *Cowpens Papers*, pp. 10–11.

Chapter 14
The Race to the Dan

*". . . nakedness, the want of provisions,
poor horses, broken harness, and bad roads."*

In general, the appointment of Nathanael Greene had been welcomed in North Carolina. Both Governor Nash and the Board of War felt that a firm hand on the reins of the floundering military machine would bring some order out of a steadily increasing chaos, and Greene had built himself something of a reputation for methodical planning. They also hoped that a change in the top command would induce those Continental officers who had returned home to come back into the field and assist in an active recruiting campaign.

Yet there were few who felt that Greene would be able to work the miracle so desperately needed. For one thing, there seemed little chance that he would receive the proper state cooperation needed to supplement his own efforts. A bitter Abner Nash felt that his powers had been usurped by the creation of the Board of War and that that body had proved to be a meddlesome and inefficient organization. By the last of December the continuing antipathy between the board and the chief executive was gathering momentum.[1]

By the time the General Assembly met in Halifax in late Janu-

1. *State Records,* XIV, 481–83.

ary, Nash had grown weary of his role as chief executive. Bitterness and disappointment laced his address to the legislature. Admitting that he had felt it necessary that an organization similar to the Board of War be created, he went on to say that it had not been his intention that he be made a servant to any such body, nor had he intended that the governor be stripped of all military authority. He concluded his remarks with an ultimatum: "In short, Gentlemen, I hold at present but an empty title, neither serviceable to the people nor honorable to myself. It will therefore become an act of necessity, however disagreeable at a time like this, that I resign my office, unless you restore it to a condition as respectable as it was when you did me the honor to confer it upon me."[2]

Shortly afterwards the assembly abolished the Board of War and replaced it with the Council Extraordinary, composed of Richard Caswell, Alexander Martin, and Allen Jones, Although the legislature had gone along with Nash in his demand for doing away with the board, the governor still indicated that he had no wish to succeed himself.[3]

Soon after he reached North Carolina, Greene had urged Sumner and other Continental officers to leave off their sulking, return to active duty, and bend their efforts toward re-establishing the Continental regiments. Because so many line officers had been captured at Charleston, the reactivation of regiments posed problems. Many of those officers in captivity, because of seniority, were still entitled to ranks in the regiments although they were physically unable to serve with their units. A number of Continental officers had been allowed to return to their homes to take care of domestic affairs, while others were serving with the militia. Others had gone into retirement and had been placed on half-pay; included in this group were Colonels James Armstrong of the Fifth Regiment and Gideon Lamb of the Sixth, Lieutenant James Thackston of the Fourth and William Lee Davidson of the First, Captain Francis Child of the Third and Micajah Lewis of the Fourth. Some of those still active were now ordered to replace those Maryland officers whom Gates and Smallwood had stationed in key positions around the state.[4]

Suddenly there was a note of optimism, for there was a victory to celebrate. Brigadier General Daniel Morgan, after leaving Greene at Charlotte, had marched to the southwest toward the British outpost and loyalist stronghold at Ninety Six in South Carolina. Lord

2. *Ibid.*, XVIII, 719–20.
3. *Ibid.*, XVII, 707, 785–86.
4. *Ibid.*, XIV, 792, XV, 420–22, XVI, 610.

Cornwallis could not tolerate this threat to the loyalists, the harassment of his patrols, or a possible attack upon his flanks should he move again toward North Carolina. Banastre Tarleton, with his British Legion and a part of the Seventy-First Regiment were sent in pursuit of Morgan, with Tarleton confident of an easy victory over Morgan's little force composed of Maryland and Delaware Continentals and militia units from North Carolina, South Carolina, and Georgia.

Morgan fell back before Tarleton, moving so fast that many of his troops cursed him for acting the coward and retreating to avoid combat. It appeared that Morgan planned to cross the Broad River to take a position near Thicketty Mountain where the terrain was better suited to his style of battle. When he neared the Broad he discovered that stream to be running wide and deep, swollen almost out of its banks by recent rains. To have attempted a crossing could possibly have exposed his troops to a deadly fire should Tarleton come up on them while they were in the water. Intelligence indicated the British to be closing in fast. Morgan's reasoning in deciding not to cross the Broad was expressed in a later statement: "Had I crossed the river, one-half of the militia would immediately have abandoned me."

Near sunset on January 16 Morgan arrived at a place known locally as "Hannah's Cowpens," near the crest of a long, gently sloping ridge, covered with open woods, the underbrush cleared away by grazing cattle. To the rear, the swollen Broad discouraged retreat and Morgan's exposed flanks invited encirclement. It was a situation calculated to give victory to the side with the best cavalry, and Tarleton's British Legion was considered by many to be the best mounted unit serving with the British forces in America. On the other hand, Morgan felt that the lack of a route of withdrawal would force his men to stand and fight.

There, in an unorthodox, but a veritable little gem of a battle, fought in the early morning hours of January 17, 1781, Daniel Morgan inflicted a smashing defeat on the arrogant and impetuous Banastre Tarleton. Perhaps no other general could have done what Morgan did on that cold, gray winter morning, for he had a way with militiamen and they, in turn, considered him one of their own. For example, when the British formed and rushed forward with a typical "Huzza," Morgan, galloping among his men, shouted, "They give up the British halloo, boys, give them the Indian halloo, by God!" And his "boys" responded by giving the enemy a disastrous volley. Morgan had also known that the militiamen, whom he had placed in the front line, would become frightened and take to their heels, so he promised them that if they would give the British but two volleys they might retire from the field. They did just that.

As the militiamen fled, Tarleton's dragoons rode in among them but were thrown into disorder when charged by William Washington's cavalry, who stormed up from the rear of the American infantry where they had been held in reserve. The British infantry was now charging upon Morgan's second line where the Continentals had been posted. When the second line, not so long as that of the advancing enemy, was in danger of encirclement the flanks were ordered to fall back to meet this threat. The center, thinking an order to retreat had been issued, also began to drift to the rear, although maintaining their places. Although to all appearances a retreat, Morgan, riding among the troops shouting, "Old Morgan was never beaten," ordered them to continue moving to the rear until he gave the signal to turn and fire. The British, thinking an American rout eminent, broke formation and, shouting as they came, pressed forward. The Americans, continuing their withdrawal for about fifty yards, reached the spot designated by Morgan, suddenly faced about and at a range of about ten yards fired a volley into the faces of their astonished foes. Troops that but a moment before were an example of British discipline and bravery now found themselves becoming a frightened and milling mob. Morgan's men charged forward. The British, thrown into an "unaccountable panick," discarded their muskets and cartouche boxes as they "did the prettiest sort of running away." The battle was over.

Daniel Morgan had won an overwhelming victory over a force with which he would have been happy to fight a draw. With a motley army of between 900 and 1,000 men, over 600 of whom were militiamen, he had defeated a British force of approximately 1,000 well-trained and disciplined British soldiers. Morgan's casualties were amazingly light: 12 killed and 60 wounded. By contrast, British losses were staggering. Ten officers were among the 110 killed. Prisoners of war totaled 700, 200 of whom had been wounded, and there were 29 officers among the prisoners.

Much valuable military equipment had been captured: two small fieldpieces, eight hundred muskets, one traveling forge, thirty-five wagons, and one hundred horses, along with "all their music." All this had been taken in an engagement that had lasted less than an hour.[5]

Although he reported that he had given Tarleton "a devil of a

5. This account of the battle of Cowpens has been condensed primarily from Hugh F. Rankin, "Cowpens: Prelude to Yorktown," *North Carolina Historical Review*, XXXI (July, 1954), 336–37.

whipping," Morgan had no intention of remaining on the scene and becoming the object of Cornwallis's wrath. There was little doubt that the British general would soon be marching his entire army against Morgan to recover the prisoners and remove some of the tarnish from British glory, and Morgan decided to preserve the splendor of the day by a strategic withdrawal. After paroling the British officers and dispatching news of his victory to Greene, he marched toward the Catawba River with his prisoners before the sun had set. Colonel Andrew Pickens and the local militia were left behind to bury the dead and collect the wounded. After placing the wounded of both armies in tents with a guard under a flag of truce, Pickens dismissed the militia and hurried after Morgan.[6]

The battle of Cowpens, a small engagement when measured by the yardstick of the numbers engaged, was far-reaching in its results. For Cornwallis, it was the first link in a chain of circumstances that led to Yorktown and ultimate disaster. Critics of Banastre Tarleton have maintained that the defeat at Yorktown can be traced to the fall of the light troops at Cowpens. Indirectly, it meant an end to all efforts to bring the North Carolina Line up to strength, for the state was to suffer invasion by the enemy just as soon as Cornwallis received reinforcements.[7]

On January 23, 1781, Major Edward Giles, Morgan's aide de camp, rode into Greene's bivouac on the Peedee with the electrifying news of the victory. The whole camp went wild. Scarce gunpowder was burned in a celebration that Otho Williams described for Morgan: "We have had a *feu de joie*, drunk all your healths, swore you were the finest fellows on earth, and love you, if possible more than ever." Within twenty-four hours Major Giles was riding for Philadelphia, carrying the news to the Continental Congress. To victory-starved people along the way, Cowpens was a miracle that led to exaggerated hopes and brags: "This one Blow Secures us from the Southern quarter, and totally ruins this Campaign to the Enemy."[8]

Greene's first impulse was to lead his army into the vicinity of Ninety Six to strike a blow in the rear of the British army. But he

6. Morgan to William Snickers, 26 January 1781, Horatio Gates Papers, New-York Historical Society, New York, N.Y.; James P. Collins, *Autobiography of a Revolutionary Soldier*, ed. John M. Roberts (Clinton, La. 1859), p. 59.

7. Stedman, *History of the . . . American War*, II, 327; *Annual Register for 1781* (London, 1781), p. 86; Roderick Mackenzie, *Strictures on Lt. Col. Tarleton's History "Of The Campaigns of 1780 and 1781, in the Southern Provinces of North America"* (London, 1787), p. 89.

8. Graham, *Life of General Daniel Morgan*, p. 323; *South Carolina Historical and Genealogical Magazine*, XVIII (July, 1917), 131; Robert Smith to James Iredell, 30 January 1781, Charles E. Johnston Collection.

was forced to discard this plan when he realized that the Virginia militiamen of General Edward Stevens were preparing to leave for their homes just as soon as their time expired in the immediate future. Utilizing their services until the last, Greene ordered them forward to join Morgan and charged them with the responsibility of escorting the prisoners of Cowpens into Virginia.[9]

Cornwallis, after receiving reinforcements, fell in behind Morgan in full pursuit. Neither the army of the Peedee or Morgan's force was strong enough to face the British alone, and Greene wanted to unite the two groups at the first opportunity. To gain the necessary time to make this junction, he planned to range fairly close to the British and govern the movements of Morgan's troops by those of the enemy.[10]

The army of the Peedee was placed under the command of Brigadier General Isaac Huger of South Carolina, who had replaced Smallwood as second in command. Huger was ordered to proceed to Salisbury for a junction with Morgan's command. With the assurance that the army would march no later than January 29, Greene, with a small escort of dragoons, rode across country to join Morgan.[11]

Cornwallis was beginning to gain on Morgan, whose pace was slowed by his prisoners. Cornwallis had halted at Ramsour's Mill and burned his wagons and excess baggage to increase his mobility and rate of march. Two men were mounted on every available horse. He conducted his approach to the Catawba in a series of short marches, a maneuver designed to confuse the Americans concerning the ford he planned to use to cross the river.[12]

The news of Cornwallis's approach, added to the tales of British atrocities and plunderings in South Carolina, spread consternation throughout southern North Carolina. Many men, craving companionship in their fear, huddled together in forest hideaways. Furniture, clothing, food and all articles of value were hidden, some buried in the ground, some concealed in hollow trees. Horses and cattle were hidden in dense thickets, while some men resorted to the expedient of driving their livestock to the summits of high hills on the assumption that the British would not search for valuables in such unlikely spots. The few schools in the community were dismissed

9. Henry Lee [Jr.], *The Campaign of 1781 in the Carolinas: with Remarks Historical and Critical on Johnson's Life of Greene* (Philadelphia, 1824), pp. viii–ix.

10. *Ibid.*, p. 109.

11. Merritt, *Calendar of the General Otho Williams Papers*, p. 41.

12. *North Carolina Historical Review*, IX (July, 1932), 287–90; Edward Carrington to Steuben, Steuben Papers, New-York Historical Society, New York, N.Y.

as rumors convinced the more gullible that Tarleton was ranging the countryside, kidnapping young lads to provide the British army with drummer boys.[13]

Yet the news of the victory at Cowpens had given spirit to the North Carolina militiamen. Morgan, in their eyes, had assumed the guise of a giant-killer, but he was in no condition to direct their operations. Wracked with "Ceatick" pains and a severe case of piles, he had requested Greene to relieve him of his command. Nevertheless, once he reached the Catawba, Morgan overcame his agony and began to prepare defenses against a river crossing by Cornwallis. Obscure fords were made impassable by felled trees, and small detachments were posted nearby to frustrate British attempts to clear the passage. The principal ford of the area, Beatty's, was defended by eight hundred militiamen under William Lee Davidson. By January 30 patrols reported that the British were within a few miles of the river.[14]

It was around two-thirty in the afternoon of January 31 when Greene joined Morgan at Beatty's Ford. After a short review of the situation by Morgan, Greene and Davidson retired to a nearby log to discuss the defensive preparations. Davidson was complaining of the lack of response by the militia when a large body of British mounted troops appeared on the far side of the stream and an officer, thought to be Lord Cornwallis, surveyed the American position through a spyglass. At the conclusion of a twenty-minute discussion, Greene and Morgan rode off toward Salisbury, leaving Davidson to check a British crossing of the Catawba.[15]

Greene was not yet out of sight when Davidson went into action; one-half of his troops were dispatched to Cowan's Ford, a private crossing about four miles down the river. Davidson went with this group, leaving the detachment at Beatty's under the command of a Captain Farmer of the Orange County militia. On his march to the lower ford, Davidson was overheard to say that "though General Greene had never seen the Catawba before, he appeared to know more about it than those who were raised on it." Davidson had divided his command because of Greene's warning that Cornwallis

13. Collins, *Autobiography of a Revolutionary Soldier*, p. 65; Robert Henry, *Narrative of the Battle of Cowan's Ford* (Greensboro, N.C., 1891), p. 8.

14. Merritt, *Calendar of the General Otho Williams Papers*, pp. 37–38; Graham, *Life of General Daniel Morgan*, pp. 336–37; Graham, *General Joseph Graham*, p. 288; Greene to Campbell, 30 January 1781, Preston Davie Collection, Southern Historical Collection.

15. Graham, *General Joseph Graham*, pp. 289–90; Greene to Francis Locke, 31 January 1781, Nathanael Greene Papers, New-York Historical Society, New York, N.Y.

would probably attempt to get his cavalry across the river at some isolated crossing during the night so it could attack the defending force from the rear on the following morning. Davidson did not reach Cowan's until after sunset, the darkness preventing him from properly surveying the situation and deploying his troops so as to take best advantage of this situation.[16]

Greene had ordered Morgan to proceed as quickly as possible to Salisbury, sending all extra baggage ahead to Guilford Court House. It was now imperative that the army of the Peedee be joined with Morgan's men, for Greene was "not without hopes of ruining Ld. Cornwallis if he persists in his mad scheme of pushing through the country." A successful delaying action by the militia at the Catawba would allow the necessary time to unite his command with expected reinforcements at Salisbury. If this could be accomplished, the British could be forced to do battle at a time and place of Greene's choosing.[17]

But Cornwallis had his own plans. One detachment was ordered to Beatty's Ford to create a diversion. The main body was to cross at Cowan's, which was reported to be lightly guarded. The march began at one in the morning, and the darkness slowed progress. Cowan's was reached just before daybreak. Through the mist rising from the surface of the river, the flickering lights of campfires could be seen on the far shore, the number indicating the strength of the defenders to be greater than reported. The Catawba was still rising as a result of recent rains, but the troops were ordered into the water, with orders not to fire until they reached the other shore.[18]

Led by a Tory guide, the men of a unit of light infantry were the first to wade into the cold, muddy waters, their empty muskets with bayonets fixed, slung high over their left shoulders. Many carried long staves with which to brace themselves against the swirling current, but eventually men and officers were forced to lash themselves together to prevent their being carried downstream. Major General Alexander Leslie's horse was swept from beneath him, but the officer was saved by the quick thinking of an alert sergeant. The mount of Brigadier General Charles O'Hara lost its footing and rolled over, but "the brigadier, no doubt . . . thoroughly wet from this accident . . . received no other injury."[19]

By the time the British had reached midstream, their splashings

16. Graham, *General Joseph Graham*, pp. 290–91.
17. Greene to Huger, 30 January 1781, Greene Letterbook.
18. Ross, *Cornwallis Correspondence*, I, 503–4.
19. Graham, *General Joseph Graham*, p. 29; *United Services Journal* (1832), p. 570.

were heard by an American sentry, who promptly gave the alarm by firing his musket. The British guide fled. Awakened, Davidson's men rushed to defensive positions to pour a "steady and galling fire" towards the dark shadows in the river. The British struggled on.[20]

As they emerged from the water, the light infantry deployed into battle lines. After their guide fled, they had missed a turn in the ford and had not come ashore at the usual place. Davidson shifted his men. The light infantry loaded their muskets and fired a volley as a covering fire for those of their comrades still in the stream. As the British came forth from the river to form their lines and fire, Davidson moved his men to positions that afforded greater cover. Many frightened militiamen refused to halt and continued a rather rapid drift to the rear. General Davidson, mounting his horse to rally these recalcitrants, was shot in the heart and instantly killed. This, along with the seeming endless stream of dripping soldiers materializing out of the mist and water accentuated fear. The light infantry charged. The militia fled in wild disorder, making what one participant described as "straight shirt tails."[21]

No sooner had Cornwallis reached shore than he sent Tarleton out to prevent harassment of the military train while it was still in the water. Despite the near surprise of Davidson and his men, the crossing had been costly. Cornwallis's official report of one officer and three rank and file killed and thirty-six wounded was disputed by others. One American report claimed thirty-one of the enemy were killed, while another estimated that at least a hundred lost their lives as a large number of bodies were caught up in fish traps. For some time afterwards, it was claimed, the "river stunk with carcasses." One loss not carried in official reports was a beaver hat, found some ten miles downstream, and marked inside, "Property of Josiah Martin, Governor."[22]

Tarleton rode through a steady rain. Several wandering American militiamen were captured. From them it was learned that the militiamen of Mecklenburg and Rowan counties were expected to join the fugitives from the fords at Torrance's Tavern by two o'clock that afternoon.[23]

20. Stedman, *History of the . . . American War*, II, 327–28; Tarleton, *Campaigns of 1780 and 1781*, p. 224.

21. Graham, *General Joseph Graham*, pp. 294–95; Henry, *Narrative of the Battle of Cowan's Ford*, pp. 13–16; Stedman, *History of the . . . American War*, II, 328–29.

22. Henry, *Narrative of the Battle of Cowan's Ford*, p. 14; Graham, *General Joseph Graham*, pp. 298–99; *Annual Register for 1781*, p. 60.

23. Tarleton, *Campaigns of 1780 and 1781*, pp. 225–26.

The sounds of battle coming from the fords had set the entire country in motion, many people loading their most valued possessions in wagons and fleeing before the advance of the enemy. Many sought the protection of the militia assembling at Torrance's. The day was raw, wet, and cold, and rum was brought outside by the pailful. With the appearance of Tarleton and his mounted troops, many fled to the protection of the surrounding trees, still carrying their pails of rum. The militia made hurried preparations to fight.[24]

When Tarleton came in sight of the tavern he saw what he later claimed to be five hundred militiamen assembling. Appealing to his men to erase the shame of Cowpens, he gave the order to charge. The soldiers were met by a scattered and sporadic fire. The sight of the flashing cold steel of cavalry sabres was too much for the undisciplined militia. They fled, closely pursued by the dragoons. Tarleton's losses, he said, were seven killed and wounded, with twenty horses lost. Fifty Americans, he claimed, had been killed. The tavern, operated by the widow of a Whig casualty of the battle of Ramsour's Mill, was burned by the main British army when it marched by the following day.[25]

These skirmishes at the fords and the tavern, although small, were significant in that the people of the neighborhood did not dare rise again until the British had crossed the Yadkin, thereby depriving Greene of expected reinforcements. All enthusiasm for enlisting in the Continental Line was dampened.

The failure of the militia to hold the fords forced Greene to re-evaluate his strategy. Huger was ordered to change his line of march and make his way to Guilford Court House rather than attempting a junction at Salisbury. All public stores were ordered to Hillsborough and, if necessary, wagons were to be impressed from their owners to facilitate this task. Circular letters to militia leaders in western North Carolina urged them to call out their men to join Greene. General Greene had been at David Cain's farm, near Oliphant's Mill, which had been designated as a rendezvous should the British force a passage of the river and prevent the embodiment of the militia at Torrance's Tavern. The general waited at Cain's until past midnight, but not a man appeared. He rode on into Salisbury.[26]

24. Graham, *General Joseph Graham*, pp. 295–98.

25. Tarleton, *Campaigns of 1780 and 1781*, p. 256; Graham, *General Joseph Graham*, p. 300.

26. Greene to Huger, 1 February 1781, Greene to Colonels McDowell and Black, 1 February 1781, Greene to Thomas Sumter, 3 February 1781, Greene Let-

At Salisbury, Greene supervised the removal of military stores from that place. He was distressed to find that nearly 1700 stand of arms collected there for the use of the militia had been stored so poorly that they were nearly useless. The sight of the rusted muskets so irritated the general that he was led to exclaim, "These are the happy effects of defending the Country with Militia from which the good Lord deliver us!" Once the stores had been removed, Greene hurried to join Morgan at the Yadkin River.[27]

When Cornwallis reached Salisbury on February 3, he was informed that Morgan's troops were at the Trading Ford on the Yadkin but had not yet effected a crossing. A detachment under General Charles O'Hara sent forward to prevent Morgan from crossing was slowed by rain, darkness, and muddy roads. As they neared the stream around midnight, the British were greeted by rifle fire. They drove off the riflemen. Several defenders of the ford were captured, and from them it was learned that they were but part of a small detail left to guard the wagons of the "country people" flying before the British. Morgan's men, they reported, had already crossed the river in flat boats. These boats were now on the opposite shore, tied up under the bluff that dominated the crossing. Daybreak came and with it a view of the rising waters of the Yadkin, an occasional uprooted tree rolling along with the current and the river much too deep and dangerous to attempt a crossing. The artillery with the British column was brought up and Morgan's position on the far side of the river was subjected to a brief cannonade.[28]

With Morgan's troops safely across the Yadkin, there was little possibility that Cornwallis could block a junction with the army of the Peedee. To prevent possible heavy losses in a crossing at the Trading Ford, Cornwallis decided to push on to the shallow fords up the river, eliminating further delays. Tarleton was sent upstream to reconnoiter. At Grant's Creek he was opposed by approximately a hundred militiamen under Colonel Francis Locke, who had been engaged in destroying the bridge at that place. Tarleton was held up about three hours until the mounted troops who had been dispatched upstream circled around and hit the defenders from the rear. The militia fled, pursued by the dragoons. Despite the time consumed in this fire fight, there was only one casualty, a member

terbook; Robert Rowan to Thomas Wooten, 4 February 1781, Commissary Correspondence, Military Collection.

27. J. Hall Pleasants *et al.* (eds.), *Archives of Maryland* (Baltimore, Md., 1930), XLVII, 88.

28. Tarleton, *Campaigns of 1780 and 1781*, p. 227.

of Locke's militia who was wounded while fleeing the scene. Tarleton continued his reconnaissance but met no further resistance. Cornwallis immediately marched by way of the shallow fords and crossed over into the Moravian towns.[29]

Greene realized that a confrontation between the two forces was now inevitable, but he was determined to command an adequate force before he gave battle. He explained to Huger that "If Ld. Cornwallis knows his true interest he will pursue our army. If he can disperse that, he completes the reduction of the State, and without that, he can do nothing to effect." On February 4 he marched his army away from the Yadkin. Progress was slow, the muddy roads having been cut to pieces by the vehicles of the local inhabitants fleeing before the advance of the enemy.[30]

Nathanael Greene had long favored Guilford Court House as a rendezvous after a retreat, or as a battleground if forced to stand and fight. He had earlier gone so far as to project a chain of magazines from his camp on the Peedee to Guilford, but there had not been enough time to accomplish this. Apparently he had given the terrain a thorough inspection on his ride south.[31]

Morgan and his troops reached Guilford Court House on February 6 and camped there while awaiting further developments. The local militia were beginning to assemble and their officers were instructed to hold them in readiness until Cornwallis's next move could be determined. Greene expected that he would have to fight soon and the militiamen were instructed to bring only five days' provisions into the field with them. The possibility of reinforcements inspired optimism, but Greene was a prudent man and he refused to allow promises to overshadow his ingrained New England caution. Because of the possibility that the British might attempt an encircling movement, Huger was ordered to halt until Cornwallis showed his hand.[32]

Intelligence of February 8 revealed that Cornwallis was marching for the upper reaches of the Yadkin. Huger was ordered to resume his march, while the militia was urged to march night and day until it reached the courthouse. The hospital and all surplus stores were sent across the Dan River to prevent capture or destruction in the event of a defeat. The following day, February 9, Huger's tattered army, accompanied by Henry Lee's Legion, joined Greene. These

29. *Ibid.*, pp. 227–28; Graham, *General Joseph Graham*, pp. 307–8.
30. Greene to Huger, 5 February 1781, Greene Letterbook.
31. I. Burnett to John Gunby, 6 January 1781, Greene Letterbook.
32. Greene to Major Blair, 6 February 1781, Greene to Andrew Pickens, 6 February 1781, Greene to Huger, 7 February 1781, Greene Letterbook.

new arrivals promised little in the way of adding combat strength to the army. The march from the Peedee had been marked by adversity, brought about by "nakedness, the want of provisions, poor horses, broken harness and bad roads." Many men were without shoes and their feet, cut by the frozen ground, left bloody tracks as they limped along.[33]

Greene called his staff and unit commanders together in a council of war. The wretched condition of the army of the Peedee and the failure of the militia to turn out as anticipated dampened enthusiasm for an immediate action. Desertions daily sapped the army of its strength; one unit of 300 had dwindled to 36 within a week, and the truants had carried off their muskets, which were of Continental issue. The American army now numbered approximately 2,000 men, while the estimated strength of the British was 2,500 well-disciplined troops. Greene seemed anxious to give battle and take advantage of an enemy who had "risqued everything to subdue North Carolina." He feared a continuation of the retreat would dishearten the people of the Carolinas and Virginia. But the idea of an immediate engagement was discouraged by subordinate officers, who persuaded their general to exercise caution and continue the withdrawal to the comparative safety of the far side of the Dan River.[34]

Such a movement had its problems. Cornwallis was now less than twenty-five miles away and was as near the shallow upper crossings of the Dan as was Greene and in a position to intercept the march. Lieutenant Colonel Edward Carrington suggested the use of Boyd's and Irwin's ferries on the lower Dan. Although the waters were not fordable, these ferries were only four miles from each other, and the boats at Dix's Ferry twenty miles upstream could be floated down to facilitate the crossing. This plan won approval and a small detachment under Carrington hurried forth to assemble the boats before the arrival of the army.[35]

To cover his retreat to the river, Greene organized a light corps. The mounted troops were taken from the cavalry of the First and Second Maryland regiments and 240 dragoons of Lee's Legion, all

33. Greene to John Butler, 8 February 1781, Greene to Marberry, 8 February 1781, Greene Letterbook: *Collections of the New-York Historical Society for the Year 1875* (New York, 1875), p. 477; *South Carolina Historical and Genealogical Magazine*, XVIII (October, 1917), 133; Greene to Steuben, 8 February 1781, Nathanael Greene Papers, William L. Clements Library.

34. Greene to Steuben, 8 February 1781, Nathanael Greene Papers, William L. Clements Library.

35. Greene to Abner Nash, 9 February 1781, Greene Letterbook; Lee, *Memoirs of the War in the Southern Department*, p. 236.

under the command of Henry Lee. Colonel John Eager Howard of the Maryland Continentals led the foot soldiers, made up of 250 picked Continental infantrymen, 60 Virginia riflemen, and the infantry of Lee's Legion. As a military courtesy, the command of the light corps was offered to Daniel Morgan, although it was apparent that his physical condition would not allow him to accept. Just three days earlier, Morgan had insisted that he be relieved of active duty for, in addition to his sciatica, his piles had grown so painful that it was impossible for him to sit a horse. Despite such handicaps, Greene was reluctant to part with the services of so able a leader and attempted to persuade Morgan to remain with the army in an advisory capacity. When Morgan refused, he was relieved and allowed to return to his home in Virginia. The over-all command of the light troops was given to Colonel Otho Williams, Greene's adjutant general.[36]

On February 9 the army moved out toward Virginia. The light troops remained until the following day when Williams broke camp and moved his command into a position that would enable him to intercept the British line of march should Cornwallis pursue the main force.

From Tory informants Cornwallis learned that the lower reaches of the Dan were too deep for fording and were virtually impassable in the winter months without the use of boats. He was assured that the number of boats in the vicinity of the lower ferries was too small to ferry even a small detachment across the stream. The British general was of the opinion that it would be to his advantage to force an engagement before Greene could be reinforced from Virginia. It was his judgment that the only recourse open to Greene was to cross by the shallow upper fords. He moved his troops in a direction calculated to intercept the enemy and force him to battle.[37]

The first contact came when the British were engaged by Williams's troops. Since the British vanguard was far in advance of the regular column, it was necessary for Cornwallis to close his files before moving forward to investigate the strength of the force blocking his progress.[38]

Even as Cornwallis probed forward with patrols, Williams moved, having delayed his lordship for several hours. This maneuver

36. Graham, *Life of General Daniel Morgan*, pp. 354–55; Don Higginbotham, *Daniel Morgan: Revolutionary Rifleman* (Chapel Hill, N.C., 1961), p. 153; Proceedings of a Council of War, 9 February 1781, Papers of the Continental Congress; Lee, *Memoirs of the War in the Southern Department*, p. 237; *Archives of Maryland*, XLVII, 83.

37. Ross, *Cornwallis Correspondence*, I, 504–5.

38. *Ibid.*

forced the British general to slow his rate of march, for the threat of ambush compelled him to regulate his pace to that of his slowest unit. Williams moved obliquely to the northeast and continued his march on an immediate road between the British and American armies. This placed Cornwallis to his left rear and Greene to his right front, a position designed to allow him to intercept an enemy movement toward the American army. Williams marched fast; his men were on the move every morning by three o'clock. When his infantry slept, the mounted troops patrolled in shifts to prevent surprise.[39]

Williams's moves convinced Cornwallis that Greene's destination was Dix's Ferry. He crossed to the road leading to that ferry, actually the same road along which Williams was retreating. Early in the morning of February 13, while Williams's men were eating breakfast, a farmer rode into camp with the information that the British were only four miles to the rear. Lee was sent to investigate. His detachment made contact with the point of the enemy's vanguard. A running fight followed in which Lee claimed that his men killed eighteen and captured several of the enemy while losing only one of his own men—a young bugler.[40]

Williams decided that Greene had had ample time to cross the Dan and, with the British army hot on his heels, struck out overland for Irwin's Ferry. Lee's mounted troops, acting as a rear guard, managed to gain the protection of Williams's column with no further casualties. By this time, Cornwallis was pushing his men unmercifully, and sometimes was so near that the advance of the British column could be seen by the American rear guard.[41]

The weary Americans marched until after dusk with no rest. A feeling of dismay fell over them as the flames of many sputtering campfires could be seen through the trees. These fires could only be those of the American army and Williams feared that he led the enemy straight to Greene. Apprehensions were lessened when it was learned that although these were the remains of the fires of Greene's army, some were twenty-four hours old. Williams marched on until he was certain that the British had halted for the night. There was little time for sleep. Near midnight there were scattered attacks on the American pickets. Williams roused his sleepy men and continued his drive for the river. Around noon of the following day, February 14, a messenger arrived with the information that Greene's army was safe across the Dan. Williams pressed on for Boyd's Ferry and late

39. Lee, *Memoirs of the War in the Southern Department*, pp. 238–39.
40. *Ibid.*, pp. 239–43.
41. *Ibid.*, pp. 243–44.

that afternoon crossed the river. Between eight and nine o'clock that evening Lee's mounted troops, still acting as the rear guard, had been transported to the far shore. Lieutenant Colonel Carrington, who had been at the ferry to meet the light troops, crossed in the last boat with Lee.[42]

Shortly after Williams had completed his crossings, the British appeared on the banks of the river. Cornwallis had marched his men nearly forty miles during the past twenty-four hours. Realizing that the time in which he had to bring the Americans to action was limited, he had ordered out his troops at four o'clock that morning, leaving their packs behind with the sick and wounded.[43]

Cornwallis had lost the race to the Dan, a race that had consumed nearly a month of valuable time, and whose course was the breadth of North Carolina. Frustrated, he reviewed his position. He had allowed himself to be out-generaled and out-maneuvered in a dash that even Tarleton admitted was "judiciously designed and vigorously executed." He had extended his line of communication 150 miles from his primary base of supplies. Now he considered his army to be too ill-equipped to enter so powerful a province as Virginia. His troops were suffering from a lack of supplies and provisions. After resting them until his wagons and stragglers came up, he planned to proceed in a series of easy marches toward Hillsborough.[44]

The race to the Dan had been a dramatic affair. Greene's plans had contained that fluid quality that had allowed him to substitute one move if another did not work. Nathanael Greene was a man who thrived on adversity and appeared at his best when the future seemed darkest, although he complained bitterly upon such occasions. His superiority over Cornwallis in the first phase of the North Carolina campaign was demonstrated by one very evident fact: he had won the race to the Dan.

42. *Ibid.*, pp. 245–47.
43. Stedman, *History of the . . . American War*, II, 332; *North Carolina Historical Review*, IX (October, 1932), 367.
44. Ross, *Cornwallis Correspondence*, I, 505.

Chapter 15

The Road to Guilford

"I shall attempt to gall his rear."

Dramatic as Greene's retreat was, it had held many disadvantages. For one thing, it had kept Greene constantly on the move, thereby complicating the supply situation. His army was desperately in need of shoes, and his men still left bloody footprints as they trudged across the frozen ground.[1]

The rapidity of Cornwallis's pursuit had discouraged the recruiting of Continentals and had prevented any real embodiment of militia. Some disgusted officers charged that the people of North Carolina were more interested in saving their property through flight than in fighting for it. Many of the inhabitants in the vicinity of Guilford Court House had loaded their valuables in wagons and had sought the protection of Greene's army, thereby inhibiting the mobility of his force. The militiamen of the army, including some who held ranks as high as captain and major, frequently absented themselves without leave. By the time Greene reached the Dan, there were no more than eighty North Carolina militiamen still under his command. Thirty North Carolina Continentals were listed in the re-

1. Sparks, *Correspondence of the American Revolution*, III, 234.

284

turns, apparently under the command of James Thackston and attached to one of the other Continental regiments.[2]

When Greene crossed the Dan and moved to Halifax Court House in Virginia, he was still of the opinion that Cornwallis's primary objective was the complete destruction of the southern army. Halifax, in North Carolina, where many American supplies were stored, seemed a logical objective for the British. Greene reasoned that if the British did take that town, Cornwallis would then move on to Petersburg and make a junction with "Mr. Arnold," who was then ranging about the Virginia countryside. Greene ordered all stores removed from Halifax and Colonel Kosciuszko was ordered to fortify the town. Major General Richard Caswell, now acting as commandant of militia in eastern North Carolina, was requested to send men to aid the engineer and garrison the town once the fortifications were completed.[3]

Intelligence from the far side of the river indicated that British foraging parties were scouring the countryside, collecting enough provisions to last ten days, a suggestion that Cornwallis was planning an early move. One possibility was that he would cross the Dan and force Greene into battle. The Americans were in no condition to fight, and their general was convinced that the continued existence of his army in the field was of the utmost importance to the total war effort. If the southern army was driven from the field, hope would die in the South.[4]

But if Greene's army was to survive, it would have to be greatly strengthened. Greene had nurtured dreams of converting his command into a dashing "flying army" with a strong nucleus of Continental troops, but such romantic notions had to be discarded. Now he was forced to turn to the militia. Governor Jefferson was requested to call out the Virginia militia. To insure greater discipline and provide experienced leadership, he asked that these troops be placed under the command of supernumerary or retired Continental officers. To avoid time-consuming legislation, Jefferson was asked to bestow upon Greene extreme emergency powers that would allow the

2. Greene to Nash, 17 February 1781, Greene Letterbook; *Collections of the New-York Historical Society for 1875,* p. 481; R. W. Carruthers, *A Sketch of the Life and Character of the Rev. David Caldwell, D.D.* (Greensboro, N.C., 1829), p. 209; Gordon, *The History of the . . . Independence of the United States,* IV, 44; Merritt, *Calendar of the General Otho Williams Papers,* p. 39.

3. Greene to Steuben, 15 February 1781, Greene to Joseph Clay, 17 February 1781, Greene to Caswell, 16 February 1781, Greene Letterbook.

4. Greene to Robert Lawson, 17 February 1781, Greene to Caswell, 16 February 1781, Greene Letterbook.

general to circumvent certain legal procedures. Jethro Sumner was also urged to assign Continental officers to militia units for the time being. By the time Sumner received these dispatches, a number of the North Carolina Continental officers had already volunteered for such duty.[5]

It was only natural that a general who stressed mobility as much as Greene should place great emphasis upon well-mounted cavalry and dragoons. Although Jefferson had told him to "take Horses to mount your cavalry, and I will attempt to have it justified," he was later to lodge a bitter protest against the manner in which this authorization was carried out. Colonel William Washington was instructed to bring his unit up to strength, but was cautioned to treat the inhabitants "with tenderness" and to give receipts with true estimates of worth of the impressed animal while explaining to the owner that the taking of the animal was absolutely necessary for the war effort. The first impressments brought cries of anguish as the best horses, even prize stallions, were wrested from their owners. A mild reprimand suggested that Washington conduct this business "with great delicacy," but there was little apparent change.[6]

The Virginia militiamen were enthusiastic in their response to the request for reinforcements. Greene attempted to shame Governor Nash by boasting of Virginia's response and suggested that North Carolina would do well to emulate her sister state's example. Colonel Thomas Polk was endorsed to succeed to the militia command held by the late General Davidson, and so confident was Greene that his recommendation would be upheld by the legislature that he immediately wrote Polk and instructed him to call out five hundred riflemen to join the southern army. A dispatch to the North Carolina Assembly, however, appealed to that body to complete its Continental quota and ease their reliance upon the militia for, he said, sending large bodies of militia into the field would be but playing into the hands of the enemy.[7]

The general nevertheless knew that much of his future strength

5. Greene to Jefferson, 15 February 1781, Greene Letterbook; Sumner to _____, 21 February 1781, Sumner to Greene, 24 February 1781, Jethro Sumner Papers, Southern Historical Collection.

6. Greene to William Washington, 16 February 1781, Greene to Washington, 17 February 1781, Greene Letterbook; Johnson, *Sketches of Greene*, I, 445; Margaret Burnham MacMillan, *The War Governors in the American Revolution* (New York, 1943), p. 206.

7. Greene to Lawson, 17 February 1781, Greene to Nash, 17 February 1781, Greene to the North Carolina Legislature, 19 February 1781, Greene Letterbook; Greene to Steuben, 18 February 1781, William Preston to Greene, 18 February 1781, Nathanael Greene Papers, William L. Clements Library.

would have to come from the militia and he planned accordingly. He wanted to strike one quick blow at the British, dismiss the militia, and then execute a quick withdrawal before the enemy. In preparation for this movement, he explained to militia commanders that he wanted their men to be lightly equipped and to bring only enough provisions with them to last from six to ten days. To conserve forage, these troops, other than their officers, were to bring no horses into the field.[8]

Virginia militiamen poured into camp in ever-increasing numbers. More were reported to be on the march. To utilize their services, Greene planned an early recrossing of the Dan with "hopes of giving Ld. Cornwallis a run in turn. At any rate, I shall attempt to gall his rear."[9]

To observe and report the movements of the enemy as well as to keep the Tories subdued, Greene dispatched Lee's Legion, two companies of Maryland infantry and the South Carolina militia corps back across the river on February 18. This detachment was to be under the command of Andrew Pickens, who was already on the North Carolina side of the Dan, recruiting militia in the rear of the British forces. He had been joined by a considerable group from the Salisbury District. Moving to a site on the road between Hillsborough and the Haw River, this group pitched camp and sent out patrols and foraging parties. That night Greene, accompanied by a small guard of dragoons, joined them. After an all-night discussion and planning of operations, Greene left Pickens and Lee just before daybreak to rejoin his men at Halifax Court House.[10]

Important information was awaiting Greene when he returned to camp. On February 18 Cornwallis had left the plantation of one Hugh Dobbins, where he had been resting his men and had moved toward Hillsborough. Pickens was ordered to make a junction with the troops of Colonel John Campbell, then on the march from Virginia, and harass the enemy enough so that patrols and foraging parties would be kept close to town. This would allow enough time for those Virginia militia still on the march to join Greene's army. The hare was beginning to turn on the hound.[11]

8. Greene to Lewis Burwell, 17 February 1781, Greene Letterbook.

9. Greene to Caswell, 16 February 1781, Greene Letterbook.

10. Lee, *Memoirs of the War in the Southern Department*, p. 263; Greene to William Preston, 24 February 1781, Nathanael Greene Papers, William L. Clements Library.

11. Greene to Pickens, 19 February 1781, Greene Letterbook; William Pierce to Greene, 19 February 1781, Nathanael Greene Papers, William L. Clements Library.

One event had gone almost unnoticed. In late January the British force under Major James Craig had come up the Cape Fear and had taken Wilmington. This meant that the mouth of the river was now open for the entry of supplies for the enemy, which could be water-borne upstream as far as Cross Creek. Cornwallis reached Hillsborough on February 20. Inasmuch as the town was supposed to be the center for a heavy concentration of loyalists, Josiah Martin, still traveling with the army, attempted to re-establish something akin to royal government.[12]

Despite the claims of royalist newspapers that Tories were flocking in to the royal standard, and the proud boast that seven hundred of their number had enlisted in the British army in one day, little local strength was recruited. Many loyalists rode into Hillsborough to learn the news, inspect the king's troops, and discuss Cornwallis's latest proclamation. Few expressed a desire to enter British service. Many were bitter because little effort to assist them had been made since the beginning of the war, thereby exposing them to the persecutions of their Whig neighbors. Others expressed the view that British military forces were spread far too thin to offer more than a promise of security. And Cornwallis had miscalculated loyalist strength in the Hillsborough area. He had failed to discount those who had been lost as a result of premature uprisings or those who had grown timid and had journeyed to South Carolina to enjoy the protection of His Majesty's arms. Others had grown cautious because of the miscarriage of British plans in the past. The oppressions of the Whigs had broken the spirits of many. Many of those who had opposed the Whigs were not Tories but had been driven into opposition by the nefarious practices of Colonel William O'Neil, in charge of drafting local militia for the American forces. He had grown wealthy on bribes from those wishing to escape compulsory military service. For a payment of seventy-five pounds, or a good horse, a man whose name had been chosen could be excused and another's name drawn to replace his.[13]

And the Americans were growing bolder. British soldiers, in search of whiskey, and wandering beyond the picket lines around Hillsborough, were often shot or captured by rebels hiding in the woods just beyond the fringes of the town. A group of mounted militia under the command of Captain Joseph Graham attacked the British detachment guarding Hart's Mill, within a mile and a half of

---

12. Ashe, *History of North Carolina*, I, 91–92.

13. Tarleton, *Campaigns of 1780 and 1781*, p. 231; Mackenzie, *Strictures on Lt. Col. Tarleton's History*, p. 152; Stedman, *History of the . . . American War*, II, 332–33; Carruthers, *Life and Character of the Rev. David Caldwell*, pp. 213–16.

Hillsborough. Nine were killed and nineteen British soldiers were taken prisoner.[14]

Before the arrival of Cornwallis in Hillsborough the notorious Tory partisan, Colonel David Fanning, had received word of the approach of the British army. Exceeding his authority, Fanning immediately published an advertisement offering inducements to all those rallying to the British cause. The generous terms of this circular promised a bounty of three guineas to each recruit, assurances that he would serve only in the two Carolinas and Georgia, and a generous grant of land to be awarded by the Crown at the conclusion of the war. These promises, along with Lord Cornwallis's proclamation calling upon all those of loyalist inclinations to repair to the royal standard, resulted in the embodiment of around four hundred Tories in the area between the Haw and Deep rivers, under the leadership of a loyalist colonel, Dr. John Pyle. A request for protection was sent to Cornwallis, who notified Pyle that Tarleton would meet them near Colonel John Butler's plantation, a few miles distant from Hillsborough. The Tories made a lark of their assembly, strolling around the neighborhood in a group, bidding their friends farewell and drinking innumerable toasts to each other and their cause.[15]

Tarleton's departure from Hillsborough was reported by scouts, and at first there was speculation that Tarleton was the vanguard of a move by the entire British army. When Cornwallis showed no signs of moving, Pickens and Lee decided to attempt a surprise attack against Tarleton. As they trailed the British Legion they came upon a farmer who reported that Tarleton had made his midday stop just three miles ahead and apparently had felt so secure that he had neglected to post pickets. The pursuers quickened their pace. Near Tarleton's reported position they deployed. Their charge, punctuated with shouts, met no opposition; Tarleton had moved on. Two British staff officers, who had remained behind to settle accounts with the loyalists who had supplied them with provisions, were captured. Interrogation of the prisoners revealed that Tarleton planned to camp for the night at the plantation of Colonel William O'Neil, only six miles ahead. Pickens and Lee pushed forward.[16]

14. Graham, *General Joseph Graham*, pp. 313–18.

15. A. W. Savory (ed.), *Col. David Fanning's Narrative of His Exploits and Adventures as a Loyalist of North Carolina in the American Revolution, Supplying Important Omissions in the Copy Published in the United States* (Toronto, 1908), pp. 14–15; Ross, *Cornwallis Correspondence*, I, 505; Tarleton, *Campaigns of 1780 and 1781*, p. 232.

16. Lee, *Memoirs of the War in the Southern Department*, p. 256; Gordon, *History of the . . . Independence of the United States*, IV, 48–49.

As they hastened along the road they were suddenly halted by two armed men. Conversation revealed that they were Pyle's men who had been sent on ahead to locate Tarleton and had mistaken the green tunics of Lee's Legion for the similar dress of Tarleton's British Legion. They reported that Pyle was in the path ahead. Pickens and Lee felt Tarleton to be the more important objective and decided to pass the Tories and drive on toward the camp of the British Legion. One of the loyalists, still under the impression that he had contacted Tarleton, and accompanied by two dragoons, was returned to Pyle with the request that he give the mounted troops the right of way as the troopers were weary and wished to reach their camp before nightfall. The militia infantry were ordered to circle around the loyalists through the dense woods on either side of the road.[17]

The ruse almost succeeded. Pyle obligingly stationed his men on the side of the road. Lee, with his ever-present flair for military dramatics, carried his deception to the limit by extending his hand to the Tory leader. The sounds of battle at the end of the column discouraged further theatrics. The local mounted militia had been placed at the rear of Lee's Legion. Apparently their officers had not been informed of the scheme to bypass the Tories. A number of the men, recognizing the red strips of cloth in the hats of Pyle's men as the badge of Toryism, questioned their officers with respect to their own security. To allay their fears, Captain Joseph Eggleston, an officer of the Legion temporarily commanding militia cavalry, rode up to a member of the other group who appeared to be an officer and inquired concerning his allegiance. When the stranger replied, "To the King," Eggleston immediately drew his sabre and struck him in the head. His men, seeing their officer giving an obvious signal for the attack, rushed in.[18]

The terrified Tories, even after the attack, thought they were the victims of a horrible mistake, repeatedly crying out, "You are killing your own men!" "I am a friend to his Majesty!" and "Hurrah for King George!" The members of Lee's Legion, new to the area and unfamiliar with local distinctions between Whig and Tory, asked each man to which side he belonged before striking him down. One group of twelve or fifteen loyalists, determined to sell their lives as dearly as possible, banded together and began to fire wildly in every direction. Their shots resulted in only one casualty—a horse—as the Legion cavalry rode them down. Many of the homemade blacksmith's swords

17. Lee, *Memoirs of the War in the Southern Department*, pp. 58–59.
18. Graham, *General Joseph Graham*, pp. 58–59.

belonging to the militia were broken or bent as the men hacked away at their victims.[19]

The Tories fled. Behind they left ninety of their number dead, and most of the survivors, including Pyle, were wounded. Pyle, according to tradition, concealed himself in a small pond near the scene of the massacre until his enemies had departed. The men of Pickens and Lee escaped injury and their only loss was the one horse.[20]

Soon after the slaughter, a band of Catawba Indians, fighting on the side of the Americans under the command of a Captain Oldham, arrived on the scene. The sight of fresh spilled blood fired primitive instincts and before they could be stopped, the savages had thrust their spears into the bodies of seven or eight of the wounded loyalists.[21]

After collecting their men, Pickens and Lee decided that the noise of the encounter had alerted Tarleton and eliminated any element of surprise. The pursuit was abandoned and they returned to camp.

The sounds of the massacre had not been heard in Tarleton's camp. His first knowledge of the disaster came when several of Pyle's wounded loyalists stumbled into his camp. Still thinking that they had been attacked by the British Legion, these men complained bitterly to Tarleton of the cruelty of his dragoons. Shortly afterwards a message from Cornwallis ordered the Legion back to Hillsborough; Greene was reported to have recrossed the Dan and advanced in the general direction of the British position.[22]

Back in Virginia the situation had grown so encouraging that Greene had indeed determined to cross back into North Carolina at the earliest opportunity. Over two thousand Virginia militia had come in and more were reported to be on the march. As a diversionary move, he directed Thomas Sumter in South Carolina to upset the routine of the enemy by launching a series of attacks against the small outposts of the enemy, destroying the mills used for grinding grain for the army and disrupting recruiting activities among the loyalists.[23]

---

19. *Ibid.*, pp. 219–20; Copy of General Joseph Graham's Declaration for a Pension, Joseph Graham Papers, North Carolina Department of Archives and History, Raleigh, N.C.

20. Lee, *Memoirs of the War in the Southern Department*, p. 260; Lee to Greene, 26 February 1781, Nathanael Greene Papers, William L. Clements Library.

21. Graham, *General Joseph Graham*, p. 320.

22. Tarleton, *Campaigns of 1780 and 1781*, pp. 231–33, 251.

23. Palmer, *Virginia State Papers*, I, 520, 526, 553; Greene to Pickens, 20 February 1781, Greene to Sumter, 21 February 1781, Greene Letterbook.

Despite the fact that his army was low on ammunition, provisions, and stores of all kinds, Greene made the decision to move, especially after he heard rumors that the loyalists were streaming into Hillsborough. Notwithstanding the shortages, Greene justified his action by reasoning that "it was best to put on a good face, and make the most of appearances."[24]

The passage of the river was effected on February 23. Greene made a strong display of force in a feint toward Hillsborough. The massacre of Pyle's loyalists seemed to magnify the size of the American army in the eyes of Cornwallis's informants. It was this information that had led to the recall of Tarleton. Because of the serious supply situation, Cornwallis soon moved out of Hillsborough to a position on Alamance Creek between the Deep and Haw rivers.[25]

British mistakes and American aggressiveness combined to further alienate the loyalists from Cornwallis's army. For example, as one group of the more resolute Tories was marching into Tarleton's camp on Deep River, it was fired upon by a nervous picket. Without further investigation, the dragoons charged the huddled loyalists. Those who were not ridden down fled in terror. The error was soon realized, but the party sent out to reassure and bring in the frightened Tories met with little success. The following night a patrol of William Washington's cavalry met a group driving in beeves to the British army. Twenty-three of the herdsmen were killed. These little affairs, coupled with the slaughter of Pyle's men, lost nothing in the telling and completely subdued the spirits of the loyalists in the district. Many of those who had joined the British now slipped away to see to the defense of their homes.[26]

Meanwhile Greene's army was gradually gathering strength. He kept his command on a constant move to gain the time to allow the militia to come in. Yet the increase was not constant; every skirmish was reflected in a fluctuation in the returns. A large number of the men under his command were volunteers and were subject to few restrictions. Every wild shot fired by a timorous picket was a signal for a reduction in their numbers, going home, said Greene, "to tell the news."[27]

The response of the North Carolina militia, however, was greater

24. Reed, *Life and Correspondence of Joseph Reed,* II, 349.

25. Stedman, *History of the . . . American War,* II, 335–36; Greene to Steuben, 29 February 1781, Nathanael Greene Papers, William L. Clements Library.

26. Palmer, *Virginia State Papers,* I, 555, 563; *Collections of the New-York Historical Society for 1875,* p. 483; Greene to Steuben, 5 March 1781, Nathanael Greene Papers, William L. Clements Library.

27. Reed, *Life and Correspondence of Joseph Reed,* II, 349.

than had been anticipated. The mountain men, fighters by necessity, had formerly refused to leave their homes unprotected against the Cherokees and Chickasaws, who had taken up the hatchet as British allies. These tribes, defeated by a force led by Colonel Arthur Campbell, were now willing to discuss peace. Greene, perhaps exceeding his authority, immediately appointed Campbell a commissioner to negotiate with the Indians. This meant that a number of the men of the mountains could be released for service in the lowlands.[28]

Little aid could be expected from the eastern part of the state because the Tories had grown bolder since the occupation of Wilmington by Major Craig. Ardent Whigs remained close to their homes, refusing to "leave their Families exposed to a Set of Villians, who Dayley threatains their Destruction."[29]

There was little hope that there would be an increase among the few North Carolina Continentals under Greene's command. Cornwallis's presence in the state and the increased activities of the Tories had all but stopped recruiting efforts. Times were so uncertain that few citizens wished to commit themselves to military service for three years. And the recent mutiny of the Pennsylvania Line had so disrupted the Northern Department that little aid could be expected from that quarter.[30]

The division of his army had functioned so successfully in the latter phases of the retreat to the Dan that Greene resorted to the same stratagem to guard against surprise. Otho Williams was once again placed in command of a light force and ordered to maneuver between the British and American forces. The appearance of these troops had confused Cornwallis and had led him to detach Tarleton in an effort to discover the intentions of his adversary.[31]

British foraging parties reported American patrols in the area supposedly controlled by the British. Tarleton's entire corps was ordered into the sector. Scouts reported his progress to Henry Lee, who planned a surprise for his British counterpart. By now, Lee's Legion had been reinforced by a sizable group of local militia and some Catawba Indians. Near Clapp's Mill on Alamance Creek Lee's men were extended in formation behind a rail fence, their flanks protected by the cavalry.

28. Palmer, *Virginia State Papers*, I, 507; Greene to Campbell, 26 February 1781, Greene Letterbook.

29. M. L. Brown to Alexander Lillington, 19 February 1781, Lillington Papers, Southern Historical Collection.

30. Burnett, *Letters of Members of the Continental Congress*, V, 585.

31. Lee, *Memoirs of the War in the Southern Department*, p. 263; Ross, *Cornwallis Correspondence*, I, 506.

The unsuspecting Tarleton rode into the well-planned ambush. As soon as the confusion resulting from the first American volley was brought under control, Tarleton retired to cover and deployed his troops. They advanced on the American position. At the first British shot, the Indians melted away into the woods behind them. The British fire, as usual, was high, but by a curious twist of fate, was highly effective. The militiamen, some of whom were under fire for the first time, grew restless and uneasy. Bark and leaves, cut down by the whining lead, fell among them, accentuating their fears. After a short interval of desultory fire, they began to fall back without orders. Lee attempted to rally them, but just as soon as he calmed one group and turned to another, the first would resume its retreat. It was obvious that these men would never hold against a pressing attack, and there were rumors that the enemy was bringing up reinforcements. Lee ordered the troops to assemble in a defile to the rear. There he separated the men into small groups and returned them to camp by different routes, confusing the enemy and making an organized pursuit impossible. Casualties were surprisingly light in view of the numbers engaged. The British admitted to losses of one officer and twenty men killed and wounded. American losses were listed as eight men killed and wounded.[32]

Returning to camp, Lee sent out small units to annoy Tarleton's picket lines. A British squad sent out to disperse them was driven back into the camp and its sergeant captured. Excited British sentries fired wildly into the night. It was then that Tarleton, rushing out with a detachment to destroy his tormenters, ran into a large group of Tories marching in to meet Cornwallis. Believing them to be rebels, Tarleton cut them down.[33]

As these intermediate troops were sparring back and forth, the two main armies drew off, each awaiting the other to show his hand. In the interim, representatives of the two forces met and arranged an exchange of prisoners of war.[34]

Cornwallis knew full well that, unless forced, Greene would not fight until he had built up his strength through reinforcements. Patrols reported Greene still on the far side of the Haw, but Williams's light troops were maintaining a position between him and the

---

32. Tarleton, *Campaigns of 1780 and 1781*, pp. 234–36; Graham, *General Joseph Graham*, pp. 329–35; Sparks, *Correspondence of the American Revolution*, III, 359–60; Ross, *Cornwallis Correspondence*, I, 506.

33. Graham, *General Joseph Graham*, pp. 339–40.

34. Tarleton, *Campaigns of 1780 and 1781*, p. 237.

British army. Williams's troops were described as carelessly posted on separate plantations as an expedient adopted to simplify subsistence. The British general made up his mind to attack these units, drive them back into Greene's army, and then, if possible, invest the Americans in total combat. At five-thirty on the morning of March 6, Cornwallis began his move toward the Haw River.[35]

That same morning, Otho Williams had hoped to take advantage of an early morning fog to storm and seize the small British garrison at a mill about a mile from his camp. But intelligence revealed that Cornwallis had broken camp and was even then hastening along a road that would lead him into a position commanding the left flank of Williams's camp. At the time of this report, the British were estimated to be only two miles away. The American troops were immediately put in motion toward Wetzel's Mill on Reedy Fork Creek. Two British stragglers were brought in, who revealed that Cornwallis's destination was also Wetzel's Mill, and that he planned to travel on a parallel road leading to the ford.

Small parties were sent out to annoy the enemy. The British were not slowed. The vanguard of the pursuing troops, Lieutenant Colonel James Webster's brigade and Tarleton's cavalry, pushed hard to intercept Williams's troops before they could reach the stream crossing. So fast were their movements that the American rear guard often found itself on the flanks rather than in front of the enemy. The chase continued for about ten miles.[36]

The pursuit was so hot that the crossing at Wetzel's now appeared a dangerous maneuver. Williams formed a party to provide covering fire for those men crossing the Reedy Fork. This detail was formed of the men of Colonel James Preston and William Campbell, aided by the South Carolina and Georgia militia. Dragoons from Lee's Legion and Washington's command were posted on the flanks. They delivered a blistering fire as the British advanced. The enemy fell back in disorder.

By the time the British had reformed Williams had crossed the creek with a number of men to form on the north bank to furnish protecting fire for the crossing of the covering party. Cornwallis deployed his troops along the south bank of the Reedy Fork and a fording party was formed under the command of Colonel Webster.

35. Ross, *Cornwallis Correspondence*, I, 506; *North Carolina Historical Review*, IX (October, 1932), 382.

36. Johnson, *Sketches of Greene*, I, 463; Graham, *General Joseph Graham*, p. 342.

The British line was longer than that of the defenders and the extremities poured in a murderous enfilade fire upon the flanks of the Americans.[37]

As Colonel Webster, in the face of heavy fire, led his men into the stream, Cornwallis brought up his artillery. The creek was not wide, and Webster's men were soon able to cross and form a line on the opposite shore, although one British soldier later declared it to be "hot work." The right flank of the Americans began to fold, allowing the British to gain a hill commanding Williams's position. When Williams issued the order to retreat, a large number of his men fled pell-mell through the woods. Williams formed a few small covering parties who gave the British several checks. After a pursuit of near a mile the British turned back. Williams retreated five miles before he gave the order to halt. Major Burnett, Greene's aid, arrived with instructions for Williams to cross over to the north side of Haw River since Greene planned to remain on that side of the stream to keep his line of communication open to allow the militia to join him without fear of molestation.[38]

Both sides claimed light casualties in the skirmish at Wetzel's Mill. Tarleton declared that a hundred Americans were killed and wounded while British losses numbered no more than thirty men. On the other hand, the Americans said that their losses were light, while reporting that British deserters had informed them that enemy losses were nearly a hundred.[39]

The greatest American loss was not in killed and wounded but the sudden decrease in militia numbers. The Salisbury militiamen who had come out on horses were unhappy at being dismounted and used as infantry; a number were leaving for home. Those from the back country of South Carolina and Georgia suffered from injured pride. They claimed that they had been discriminated against and had been needlessly exposed to enemy fire in covering the crossing of the regulars at Wetzel's Mill. Their commanding officer, Andrew Pickens, came into Greene's camp to confer with Governor John Rutledge of South Carolina. When he returned to the light camp Pickens found his South Carolinians sulking and remaining only long enough to determine if he would return with them. Both Greene

37. Graham, *General Joseph Graham*, p. 346.

38. Johnson, *Sketches of Greene*, I, 463; George L. Fowler (ed.), *A Narrative of the Life and Travels of John Robert Shaw, the Well Digger, Now Resident in Lexington, Kentucky, Written by Himself* (Lexington, Ky., 1807), p. 60; Sparks, *Correspondence of the American Revolution*, III, 259–60.

39. Tarleton, *Campaigns of 1780 and 1781*, p. 238; Palmer, *Virginia State Papers*, I, 563.

and Rutledge advised him to go with his men. Pickens was assured that the American army would return to South Carolina just as soon as Greene had an opportunity "to break this fellow's [Cornwallis's] leg." Pickens was to attempt to keep his men together and throw the British in South Carolina off balance through a series of nuisance raids.[40]

The action at Wetzel's Mill had demonstrated to Greene that his army was not invulnerable to attack, and he remained constant in his determination not to fight Cornwallis until he had numerical superiority. So many militiamen came into his camp and then left that Jefferson was led to comment that "they seem only to have visited and quitted them." To gain the necessary time, Greene continued to keep his army constantly on the move, seldom spending two nights on the same camp site. The dense wilderness hampered British pursuit. Greene's movements were unhampered by surplus baggage; he had brought only a few wagons with him when he recrossed the Dan and only enough tents were carried to shelter the firearms in the event of a steady rain.[41]

As Greene moved along the north bank of the Haw, the British maintained a parallel course on the opposite shore at a distance of ten to twelve miles. On March 10 a large number of reinforcements had joined the American army at High Rock Ford on the Haw River. Among these new arrivals were two brigades of North Carolina militia under Generals John Butler and Thomas Eaton, a similar brigade from Virginia commanded by General Robert Lawson, along with four hundred new Continental troops from Maryland. Greene now commanded a force of respectable size, but the inclination of the militia to leave on short notice and without permission might well reduce his strength at any moment. The general had come to the conclusion that only an overwhelming defeat would drive Cornwallis from the South, although he held some doubts that his army was capable of administering that defeat. And if Greene suffered a defeat, it was possible that his enemy could be so weakened that he could be destroyed in any subsequent action. Then, too, a battle, even if it resulted in a draw, would arouse the spirits of the people, many of whom had begun to doubt the effectiveness of the southern army. The morale of his command was high, and the talk around the camp-

40. A. L. Pickens, *Skyagunsta, The Border Wizard Owl: Major-General Andrew Pickens (1739–1807)*, (Greenville, S.C., 1934), p. 89; Pickens to Greene, 5 March 1781, Nathanael Greene Papers, William L. Clements Library.

41. Reed, *Life and Correspondence of Joseph Reed*, II, 350; Greene to Joseph Reed, 18 March 1781, Joseph Reed Papers; Greene to Steuben, 11 March 1781, Nathanael Greene Papers, William L. Clements Library.

fires was that of the coming battle. The movements of the enemy also suggested that Cornwallis was maneuvering to gain a strategic advantage and force Greene into combat. On March 12 Greene moved away from High Rock Ford and marched in the general direction of Guilford Court House.[42]

Both sides were ready and almost eager for battle. They would not have long to wait.

42. Sparks, *Correspondence of the American Revolution*, III, 259–60, 267–68; Gordon, *History of the . . . Independence of the United States*, IV, 53; Palmer, *Virginia State Papers*, I, 570; Henry Knox to Lincoln, 3 April 1781, Miscellaneous Papers, William L. Clements Library.

Chapter 16

The Battle of Guilford Court House

"I never saw such fighting since God made me."

Charles, Lord Cornwallis, was obsessed with the idea of bringing Greene to battle and destroying him. He had allowed the American general to lead him out of an area of relative security, and he now felt that his enemy had to be eliminated if his own army was to survive. He had directed Major Craig to forward supplies by water from Wilmington to Cross Creek, but Greene had so positioned himself that by a forced march he could intercept British supplies coming up the Cape Fear. A move toward Cross Creek by the British could prove disastrous for it would leave the Americans free to launch an attack upon the British rear at a time and place of their own choosing. And Cornwallis's army was shrinking. Despite the British general's claims that he had suffered only 101 casualties on the march through North Carolina, his returns indicated the loss of 227 men in the month of February alone.[1]

When Greene moved to Speedwell Iron Works on Troublesome Creek, eighteen miles north of Guilford Court House, Cornwallis

---

1. Tarleton, *Campaigns of 1780 and 1781*, p. 270; *The London Magazine: Or, Gentleman's Monthly Intelligencer* (June, 1781), p. 300; Stevens, *Clinton-Cornwallis Controversy*, I, 376.

found himself handicapped in seizing the initiative. With the ford of the upper Dan in the rear of the Americans, there was no way to force them to stand and fight. Cornwallis's supply situation was even more critical than Greene's; a large number of his men were desperately in need of shoes. Yet he could not move too far from Greene without leaving doubts in the minds of the loyalists concerning the superiority of British arms.[2]

To offer the loyalists one final opportunity to demonstrate their allegiance, as well to gather provisions, Cornwallis marched his army to the forks of Deep River and camped near the Quaker Meeting House at that place.

On March 14 word was received that Greene had been joined by a large number of reinforcements and was expecting additional men in the near future. Some intelligence indicated that the Americans were maneuvering to attack the British army. That afternoon scouting parties notified Cornwallis that Greene had reached Guilford Court House about twelve miles distant and apparently had camped for the night. These reports were confirmed during the night. Cornwallis resolved to surprise Greene in his bivouac. Sending his baggage and wagons to Bell's Mill on Deep River, Cornwallis marched at daybreak for Guilford Court House.[3]

British movements were reported to Greene. Henry Lee's mounted troops were sent out to determine Cornwallis's intentions. Their first contact with the enemy came about four miles from New Garden Meeting House and was between Tarleton and the vanguard of Lee's Legion. Lieutenant Head, in command of the advance unit, led Tarleton into the partial ambush set up by Lee. When fired upon, Tarleton fled with his mounted troops to the protection afforded by the muskets of his Legion infantry. In expectation of preventing the junction, Lee took up the pursuit. A sharp skirmish followed. When the Americans appeared to be gaining the upper hand, Cornwallis sent forward the Twenty-Third Regiment. Lee immediately executed a rapid withdrawal to the main army, reporting that he had suffered "little injury," while the British were to admit to the loss of one captain and thirty rank and file killed or wounded in the skirmish.[4]

Feeling that he had reached the limit of his manpower expecta-

2. Palmer, *Virginia State Papers*, I, 551; Ross, *Cornwallis Correspondence*, I, 506.

3. Cornwallis to Lord George Germain, 17 March 1781, Cornwallis Papers, PRO 30/11/76; Ross, *Cornwallis Correspondence*, I, 507.

4. Lee, *Campaign of 1781*, p. 170; Tarleton, *Campaigns of 1780 and 1781*, p. 271; Lee, *Memoirs of the War in the Southern Department*, pp. 273–74; Stedman, *History of the . . . American War*, II, 337.

tions, Greene had chosen this time to provoke a fight. The short-term enlistments of many of the militiamen were soon to expire and he could anticipate but few replacements in the immediate future. His force now numbered approximately 4,400, of whom 1,490 were Continentals. British strength was near 2,200. The disadvantages of the lack of battle experience and discipline in the American forces was supposedly equalized by superior numbers.[5]

Guilford Court House was located on a hill from which the ground sloped gradually downward for a mile and a half to the west, the toe of the slope resting in a small stream. The ground was mostly covered with a fairly dense growth of trees, intermittently spotted with old fields at the lower end of the slope. Just above the creek there were several large interconnecting fields. The road from Hillsborough to Salisbury bisected the area. Near the courthouse this highway was joined by an intermediate road leading to Reedy Fork Creek. On either side of the general area there was broken terrain that could serve as anchors for the lines of battle. The position appeared ideal to offset the battlefield techniques favored by the British. Even as Greene positioned his troops, the sounds of the skirmish between Lee and Tarleton could be heard in the distance.[6]

Greene's deployment of troops for battle, though on a much larger scale, was similar to the arrangement of Morgan's troops at Cowpens. This may have resulted from Morgan's letter, written to Greene but a short time earlier, outlining such a disposition. Yet there were differences. Greene held none of his troops in reserve, and his lines were not in supporting distance of each other. But these inconsistencies, other than the lack of a reserve because of the manpower shortage, were dictated by the terrain.[7]

The American army was posted in three lines of battle. The first was composed of the North Carolina militia under Eaton and Butler. They were stationed behind a rail fence that rambled along the skirts of the woods. Directly in front of them were the open fields, offering an excellent field of fire. On the Salisbury road, which cut this line near its center, were posted two of Greene's four six-pounders under the command of Captain Anthony Singleton, so positioned as to

5. Greene, *Life of Nathanael Greene*, III, 190; Cornwallis claimed that his strength at the time of the battle was only 1,360, but this appears to be an understatement in view of the fact that on April 1, 1781, his returns listed 1,723 rank and file "present and fit for duty," while his casualties at Guilford were listed as 469 killed and wounded. This would have given him around 2,192 men under his command on March 15, excluding officers and noncommissioned officers.
6. Lee, *Memoirs of the War in the Southern Department*, p. 274n.
7. Graham, *Life of General Daniel Morgan*, p. 370.

cover all approaches to the front line. Greene considered this first line to be his weakest for it was made up of militiamen and he despised the militia. He hoped that the threat to their homes would inspire them beyond their capabilities.[8]

The second line was also made up of militia, but this was Virginia militia and considered to be stronger than the usual citizen soldiery furnished by the other states. For one thing, many of the rank and file had previously served as Continentals, and a number of supernumerary Continental officers had been placed in positions of responsibility. Many of those, after they had taken their places in the line, constructed semibarricades of "brushwood." General Edward Stevens, commanding the brigade, had been humiliated by the flight of the Virginia militiamen at Camden, and was determined to prevent a repetition of that disgrace. Twenty paces to the rear of the second line he posted forty picked riflemen with orders to shoot the first man who deserted his post. This line was placed in the woods on either side of the road, three hundred yards to the rear of the first line.[9]

In the clearing around the courthouse, four hundred yards to the rear of the Virginia militia, Greene stationed his third and final line. Here were the Continentals, the elite of his command. They were posted on rising ground overlooking a ravine. To take advantage of the contour of the hill and to command the open fields with their fire, these troops were drawn up in double-front formation. The right front was made up of the Fourth and Fifth Virginia Continental regiments of Colonel John Green and Lieutenant Colonel Samuel Hawes, both units under the command of Brigadier General Isaac Huger. The two Maryland regiments, the First and Second, under Colonel John Gunby and Lieutenant Colonel Benjamin Ford, were on the left and under the command of Otho Williams. The two remaining cannon under the immediate command of Captain Samuel Finley were located between the two fronts. The only veteran Maryland troops were Gunby's; Ford's Second Regiment had joined Greene only recently. Their strength lay in their officers, all of whom had battlefield experience. Greene held no troops in reserve, for he knew Cornwallis's strength and he realized that the British general

---

8. Greene to the President of Congress, 18 March 1781, Nathanael Greene Papers, William L. Clements Library.

9. Lee, *Campaign of 1781*, pp. 181–83; Greene to the President of Congress, 18 March 1781, Nathanael Greene Papers, William L. Clements Library; A. D. L. Cary and Stouppe McCace, *Regimental Records of the Royal Welch Fusiliers (Late the 23rd Foot)* (London, 1921), I, 180–81.

would have to commit his entire force to prevent his lines being out-flanked by those of the Americans.[10]

As security for the right flank, Lieutenant Colonel William Washington's 86 dragoons and Captain Robert Kirkwood's 110 Delaware Continentals were posted, supported by 200 Virginia riflemen under Colonel Charles Lynch. Lynch's and Kirkwood's troops were slightly to the rear of the first line. On the left there was Lee's Legion of 75 cavalry and 82 infantry. A short distance behind them were the 200 Virginia riflemen of Colonel William Campbell.[11]

Greene, after posting his troops, rode along the first line, promising the North Carolina militiamen that if they gave the enemy two good volleys they could retire from the field. He attempted to fire their spirits by reminding them that they were fighting for liberty and independence, and that they should show themselves worthy of the cause. But Greene was never noted for his ability to make inspirational speeches, and it remained for the colorful Henry Lee to cheer the uneasy militiamen, for Lee was a man who could almost literally strut on horseback. Soon after the Legion commander rejoined the army, he rode the length of the front line, exhorting the militia to stand firm and not to be afraid of the British. Why, he swore, he had already whipped them three times that morning and promised that he would do it again.[12]

Around one-thirty in the afternoon the British arrived on the field. Cornwallis surveyed the terrain and made his plans for the attack. Dense woods limited the use of mounted troops. The only unobstructed passage for his artillery to be moved forward was the road running through the middle of the field, and that was defended by Singleton's artillery and the enfilading fire of the defensive lines. The trees of the left appeared less dense and the British general decided to concentrate his attack upon that sector. As the British troops were brought up, Singleton's two six-pounders opened up on them. Corn-

10. Lee, *Memoirs of the War in the Southern Department,* 432; Greene to the President of Congress, 18 March 1781, Nathanael Greene Papers, William L. Clements Library; Henry Knox to Lincoln, 3 April 1781, Miscellaneous Papers, William L. Clements Library.

11. Greene to the President of Congress, 18 March 1781, Nathanael Greene Papers, William L. Clements Library.

12. Alexander Garden, *Anecdotes of the American Revolution, Illustrative of the Talents and Virtue of the Heroes of the Revolution, Who Acted the Most Conspicuous Parts Therein* (Brooklyn, N.Y., 1865), I, 30; Jesse Turner to David Schenck, 14 June 1893, David Schenck Papers, North Carolina Department of Archives and History, Raleigh, N.C.; Carruthers, *Interesting Revolutionary Incidents,* p. 155. Both the Turner letter and the Carruthers volume record reminiscences of survivors of the Revolution.

wallis brought up his two fieldpieces to answer them. Under their covering fire, the infantry began to form, although it was still subjected to artillery and sporadic rifle fire. Even as these men wheeled into line a young lieutenant of the Royal Artillery was killed by sniper fire. The North Carolina militia watched in awe as the well-disciplined British regulars quickstepped into position.[13]

The right front of the British line was composed of the Regiment du Bose and the Seventy-First Regiment under the command of Major General Alexander Leslie. On the left were posted the Twenty-Third and Thirty-Third regiments under the command of Lieutenant Colonel James Webster. The light infantry of the Guards and the Hessian Yagers under Brigadier General Charles O'Hara were held in the trees to the rear of Webster and to the left of the artillery in the road. The mounted troops remained on the road, just out of artillery range, and were to be used as circumstances dictated.[14]

The order to advance came. The troops slogged across a field but lately ploughed and muddy from the recent rains. Still they moved forward at a steady pace until slowed by a "most galling and destructive fire." A captain of the Seventy-First Regiment was to later declare that half his men "dropt on the spot." The British answered with an occasional volley, firing only upon command of their officers.[15]

When the Brtish reached a spot approximately forty yards from the rail fence, they could see the long line of musket muzzles, seemingly aimed in their faces. The red line wavered, paused, and appeared on the verge of breaking. Lieutenant Colonel Webster rode out in front of his troops shouting, "Come on, my brave Fuziliers!" He ordered a volley, to be followed by a charge. They fired and then rushed forward.[16]

As the British quickstepped across the field, bayonets fixed, the North Carolina militiamen stood for a moment, transfixed by the sight of cold steel. Then they broke, throwing away weapons, cartouche boxes, and everything else that threatened to impede their flight. Some said their hasty withdrawal was triggered by the miscon-

13. Cornwallis to Germain, 17 March 1781, Cornwallis Papers, PRO 30/11/76; Tarleton, *Campaigns of 1780 and 1781*, p. 273.

14. Cornwallis to Germain, 17 March 1781, Cornwallis Papers, PRO 30/11/76; Ross, *Cornwallis Correspondence*, I, 507.

15. *United Services Journal* (1832), p. 56; Carruthers, *Life and Character of the Rev. David Caldwell*, p. 237; Cary and McCace, *Regimental Records of the Royal Welch Fusiliers*, I, 180–81.

16. R[oger] Lamb, *An Original and Authentic Journal of Occurrences During the Late American War, From Its Commencement to the Year 1783* (Dublin, 1809), p. 361.

duct of a militia colonel who shouted to another officer that they were in danger of being surrounded. Eaton and Butler attempted to stem the tide, but no one listened to their shouts. Lee rode among them, crying out that if they did not halt he would charge them with his dragoons. They were wasting their breath. Singleton's two fieldpieces were hastily wheeled back to the third line and placed upon the left flank. Unfortunately for the British the flight of the militia obliqued toward the flanks, leaving the advancing troops exposed to the fire of the second line.[17]

The panic engendered by the first line was not communicated to the Virginia militia of the second line. General Stevens had warned his men that the North Carolinians would probably withdraw in some haste and had instructed his troops to open ranks and allow the fugitives to pass through if they retreated to the rear.[18]

The fire from the second line and from the flanks grew so fierce that Cornwallis was forced to bring up his reserves and change his front. The first battalion of Guards were brought up to strengthen the right wing and, accompanied by the Regiment du Bose, drove toward the flank protected by Lee's infantry and Campbell's riflemen. The Yagers and light infantry were brought up on the left to make a thrust against Washington and Lynch. Tarleton's corps was still held in reserve, with particular orders not to join the battle unless in prompt support of some unit in danger of being overrun. These mounted troops now constituted the only reserve that remained at the disposal of Lord Cornwallis.[19]

With this additional strength to protect his flanks, Webster led his troops forward at a slow trot against the Virginians. Bayonets had been fixed but they were not too effective in the thick underbrush. An orderly line of battle was difficult to maintain, and there was a tendency for the fight to break up into a series of small skirmishes. This was particularly true on the right flank where the trees were thickest.[20]

The Virginians of the second line put up a stubborn defense, holding the enemy in check with such tenacity that Tarleton was to declare that "at this period the event of the action was doubtful, and victory alternately presided over each army." Even after General Stevens received a musket ball in the thigh and was carried from the

17. Lee, *Memoirs of the War in the Southern Department*, p. 279; *United Services Journal* (1832), p. 570; Ramsay, *History of the American Revolution*, II, 242.

18. Lee, *Campaign of 1781*, pp. 182–83.

19. Cornwallis to Germain, 17 March 1781, Cornwallis Papers, PRO 30/11/76.

20. *Ibid.*

field, his men fought on. Cornwallis personually led the charge that broke the resistance of the Virginians, although the general's horse was shot from beneath him. The men of one of the Virginia regiments became panicky when there was a rumor that enemy units were maneuvering in their rear. Fearing encirclement, they fled, their energetic flight rivaling that of the North Carolina militia a short time earlier.[21]

The way now clear, the first battalion of the Guards was the first British group to break through into the unobstructed area around the courthouse. The ever-zealous Webster, without waiting for supporting troops to come up, charged the First Maryland Regiment. Gunby's men drove him back with a heavy and withering fire. Webster fell back to the shelter of a nearby ravine to await support. During the charge Webster received a musket ball through his knee, a wound that eventually was to prove fatal. As the two armies regrouped, Greene rode along the American third line, beseeching his men to stand firm and administer a killing blow to the British when they renewed the attack.[22]

General O'Hara strengthened Webster by bringing up the second battalion of Guards under Lieutenant Colonel Stuart. The two little three-pounders were brought forward to a small knoll about 250 yards from the courthouse, allowing them a field of fire upon the American position and furnishing covering fire for a second assault. Tarleton believed that Greene's failure to occupy this knoll spelled the difference between victory and defeat.[23]

Stuart led his men in a charge against the green troops of Ford's Second Maryland Regiment. As they rushed forward, bayonets gleaming in the sunlight, the raw recruits broke and ran. Singleton's two six-pounders, placed on the left flank of the Marylanders, were quickly overrun and taken.[24]

Colonel Gunby ordered a counterattack by the First Maryland. No sooner had he issued the command than his horse was killed and the colonel pinned to the ground by the body of his mount. The command of the regiment fell to Lieutenant Colonel John Eager Howard. Howard wheeled the regiment into a position that could

21. Tarleton, *Campaigns of 1780 and 1781*, p. 273; Lee, *Campaign of 1781*, p. 173n; *Magazine of American History*, VII (September, 1880), 41; St. George Tucker to Fanny Tucker, Coleman-Tucker Papers, Colonial Williamsburg, Inc., Williamsburg, Va.
22. Lee, *Memoirs of the War in the Southern Department*, p. 279.
23. Tarleton, *Campaigns of 1780 and 1781*, pp. 277–78.
24. Lee, *Campaign of 1781*, p. 175; Lee, *Memoirs of the War in the Southern Department*, p. 280.

intercept the left flank of the Guards, poured in a volley at close range, and followed it with a bayonet charge. Colonel Washington, who had been forced to fall back with the retreat of the second line, was ordered to charge with his cavalry.

The British assault disintegrated before this unexpected onslaught and the troops began to fall back to the protection offered by their artillery. Singleton's two guns were retaken by the Americans. Cornwallis, sensing a possible rout, attempted to rally his troops. Failing to halt them, he galloped over to his artillery and ordered a round of grape shot fired at Washington's dragoons. General O'Hara protested the order, pointing out that the Guards were in the line of fire. Cornwallis was adamant; the guns were fired. A number of the Guards fell, killed or wounded by their own artillery.[25]

This desperate measure arrested the charge of the Americans and allowed time for the Twenty-Third and Seventy-First regiments to come up. The appearance of these troops, plus the fire of the artillery, forced Washington and Howard to fall back to their original positions. As the British launched another drive forward against the Continentals, Singleton's guns were once again captured, as were the remaining two manned by Captain Finley's men.

The flight of the Second Maryland had so weakened the left side of the American third line that its flank was soon turned. There were reports of enemy units operating in the rear of the Virginia Continentals; other reports indicated that the right flank was on the verge of folding. These developments suggested an encirclement and possible destruction of the Continentals. The American artillery had been lost because the draught horses had been killed, and the savagery of the fighting had prevented their removal by manpower. Greene's troops had by now become so dispersed that it was impossible to concentrate enough strength in any one place to halt the British advance. Greene decided that a strategic withdrawal would be the most prudent move to save his army. He placed the Virginia Continentals under General Huger as a rear guard.[26]

The retreat was orderly and well conducted. Cornwallis ordered the Twenty-Third and Seventy-First regiments to pursue, but he was

25. Lee, *Campaign of 1781*, p. 175; Lee, *Memoirs of the War in the Southern Department*, p. 280; Ramsay, *History of the American Revolution*, II, 243; Fortescue, *History of the British Army*, III, 378; Tarleton, *Campaigns of 1780 and 1781*, p. 275; Ross, *Cornwallis Correspondence*, I, 508.

26. Greene to the President of Congress, 18 March 1781, Nathanael Greene Papers, William L. Clements Library; Merrit, *Calendar of the Otho Williams Papers*, pp. 42–43.

quick to recall them when he became aware of the extent of his casualties.[27]

The battle still raged on the fringes of what had been the right flank where Lee and Campbell were engaged by the first battalion of the Guards and the Regiment du Bose under General Leslie. The Legion infantry and Campbell's riflemen had proved difficult to dislodge and their fire had taken a heavy toll among British troops. Units had become separated and fighting had waned into a number of isolated engagements. The thick underbrush limited the use of bayonets, and the riflemen frequently concealed themselves in thickets until a British group had pushed by and then would pour in a devastating fire upon their rear.

The Americans, however, were gradually pushed back to a nearby promontory where they attempted to make a stand. The Guards scrambled up the slope. Reaching the summit, they provided covering fire for the Regiment du Bose, who drove off the Americans. As these British and Hessian troops halted, awaiting further orders, a small group of Virginia riflemen made their way into the trees at the rear of the enemy and annoyed them with long-range rifle fire. Cornwallis, at the courthouse, heard this fire and sent Tarleton's dragoons to investigate. A charge dispersed the riflemen. Campbell was later to complain that Lee's cavalry was no more than two hundred yards distant when this charge was executed but had ridden off in another direction. Lee's troops circled through the woods until they came to the Salisbury road. They followed this highway until they found the intermediate road leading to Greene's designated rendezvous at Speedwell Iron Works on Troublesome Creek.[28]

So ended the battle of Guilford Court House, an engagement that had lasted but an hour and a half, but whose results were to be felt at Yorktown.

Greene, after leaving the field of battle, retired approximately three miles until he had crossed Reedy Fork Creek. There he halted long enough to allow the stragglers to rejoin the column. Rain had begun to fall. The road was muddy and it was nearly daylight on the morning of March 16 when the army arrived at its destination at Speedwell Iron Works.[29]

Greene was physically exhausted, but he brushed fatigue aside

27. Stedman, *History of the . . . American War*, II, 341.

28. *Ibid.*, p. 342; Tarleton, *Campaigns of 1780 and 1781*, p. 276; Lee, *Campaign of 1781*, p. 194; Johnson, *Sketches of Greene*, II, 2n–3n; Draper, *King's Mountain and Its Heroes*, pp. 394–95.

29. Graham, *Life of General Daniel Morgan*, pp. 372–73.

and personally directed defensive preparations, for he expected Cornwallis to follow up his victory with an attempt to destroy the American army. Despite the continuing rain, the weary soldiers threw up earthworks on the bluffs overlooking Troublesome Creek. Morale was high and among the rank and file there was talk of a second action. Greene's orders of the day suggested such a possibility: "The General requests the officers will take every precaution to procure their Arms and Ammunition, and make every necessary precaution for another Field Day." Greene had not removed his clothing nor enjoyed the comfort of a bed for the past six weeks. On the night of March 16 he fainted; the following night he collapsed again.[30]

As he waited, Greene reviewed the condition of his army. It was almost impossible to make an accurate estimate of his losses. His casualties numbered 1,255 men, but the majority of these were listed as wounded or missing. Of this number, 576 were charged to the fleet-footed North Carolina militia, who had lost only 7 killed and 6 wounded. It was assumed that most of these men had made their way home, although the British were to later claim that every house for miles around was filled with American wounded. This claim, if true, indicates that militia losses were greater at Guilford than official records reveal. The greatest American loss, and one most damaging for future operations, was the 290 casualties among the Continentals.[31]

Greene also bemoaned the loss of his four brass six-pounders, his entire supporting artillery. Two of these fieldpieces had served alternately as trophies of war for both sides; originally they had been captured by Morgan at Saratoga, retaken from Thomas Sumter at Fishing Creek by Tarleton, recaptured at Cowpens, and now were once again in British hands. Greene had not, however, lost his sense of humor. It was reported that he sent a message to Cornwallis, under the protection of a flag, "to make him the offer of four more cannon on the same terms if he would accept them."[32]

The battle of Guilford Court House had been a vicious and bitterly contested fight in which the fortunes of war had determined

30. Palmer, *Virginia State Papers*, I, 574; *State Records*, XV, 430–31; Reed, *Life and Correspondence of Joseph Reed*, II, 350; Greene to Washington, 18 March 1781, Nathanael Greene Papers, William L. Clements Library; General Orders, 16 March 1781, Greene Papers, N.C. Dept. Arch. & Hist.; General Orders, 16 March 1781, Jethro Sumner Papers, Southern Historical Collection.

31. Greene, *Life of Nathanael Greene*, III, 205; Carruthers, *Interesting Revolutionary Incidents*, p. 151; *Annual Register for 1781*, p. 70; Fitzpatrick, *Writings of Washington*, XXI, 413.

32. Merritt, *Calendar of the Otho Williams Papers*, p. 36; Carruthers, *Life and Character of the Rev. David Caldwell*, p. 239; *Historical Magazine*, 2nd Series, VI (December, 1867), 359.

the victor, although Greene declared the outcome to be the result of superior British discipline. Both generals had displayed great personal courage and each had been in danger of capture by the enemy. Cornwallis had been slightly wounded, but would not allow his name to be included on the casualty list. Two horses had been killed beneath the British general. He is reported to have later made the statement, "I never saw such fighting since God made me. The Americans fought like demons." And Greene was convinced that he had dealt the British Army a crippling blow.[33]

For a general who had just been driven from the field, Nathanael Greene was in surprisingly good spirits. He must have agreed with his young aide, Lewis Morris, who said, "Like Peter the Great we shall profit by defeat, and in time learn to beat our Enemy—one more such action and they are ruined." Reports from the British army indicated that it had been severely hurt, and Cornwallis would be forced into a withdrawal just as soon as he could care for his wounded. But Greene's pride had been damaged and he complained that he could never gain a reputation through defeat, or while forced to operate under so many disadvantages. Yet after thinking over the events of March 15, he admitted to Steuben that "the Enemy got the ground the other Day, but we the victory. They had the splendor, we the advantage, and tho' it was not glorious for me, it is beneficial to the community."[34]

A few of the militiamen, on the march while the battle was taking place, were still straggling into camp. Two days after the battle a company of North Carolina mounted militiamen under the Frenchman, and former Continental officer, Marquis de Malmedy, rode into camp, and offered their services. Greene, knowing full well Malmedy's reputation as a troublemaker, ordered the group to maneuver in the counties south of Hillsborough to keep the Tories under control. This area was one through which Cornwallis would have to pass if he moved down to Cross Creek. Malmedy's mission was to so awe

33. Greene to the President of Congress, 18 March 1781, Nathanael Greene Papers, William L. Clements Library; Carruthers, *Interesting Revolutionary Incidents*, p. 152; Lamb, *An Original and Authentic Journal*, p. 363; Ross, *Cornwallis Correspondence*, I, 86; *Annual Register for 1781*, p. 69; Palmer, *Virginia State Papers*, I, 582; A. A. Gunby, *Colonel John Gunby of the Maryland Line* (Cincinnati, Ohio, 1902), p. 48; Nash to Washington, 19 March 1781, George Washington Papers.

34. Reed, *Life and Correspondence of Joseph Reed*, II, 350; Greene to Washington, 18 March 1781, Nathanael Greene Papers, William L. Clements Library; *Collections of the New-York Historical Society for the Year 1875*, p. 484; Greene to Steuben, 2 April 1781, Steuben Papers.

the loyalists that they would discourage any inclinations to join the British army.[35]

These sparse reinforcements were offset by the numbers of militiamen who were leaving daily "to return home to kiss their wives and sweet hearts." The Virginia militia had come into the field for a six-weeks period, and a number of these men, worried about the planting of their crops, were leaving before the expiration of their service.[36]

Nathanael Greene was an ambitious man and could not force himself to hide his disappointment about the outcome of the battle. "Here," he said, "has been the field for the exercise of genius, and an opportunity to practice all the great and little arts of war. Fortunately we have blundered through without meeting capital misfortune." Despite the observations of those such as Captain Singleton, who was nearer the front line than Greene and who had noted that "the militia, *contrary to custom*, behaved well for militia," Greene was harshly critical of the North Carolina militia. The defeat at Guilford was blamed on its swift withdrawal from the field. At least half of the men, he declared, had fled the field without firing a shot, although the day after the battle he did say that most of them had fired at least one shot. He later wrote Horatio Gates attempting to reconcile his predecessor to the defeat at Camden by drawing a parallel between the poor conduct of the militiamen at Camden and their similar behavior at Guilford. Part of the general's bitterness stemmed from "the shameful waste which Prevails among the NCarolina Militia," who had run away with the muskets and cartouche boxes issued by Greene. His criticism of the militia was so caustic and so unrestrained that his friend Joseph Reed cautioned him to temper his public expressions of contempt and not attempt to attribute all of his failures in the South to the behavior of the militia. Reed warned that an attitude of superiority by Continental officers would be resented and could alienate "the bulk of the country." He suggested that in the future Greene adopt an attitude toward the militia that one should hold toward a wife:

> Be to their faults a little blind
> And to their virtues very kind.[37]

35. *State Records*, XXII, 128–31.

36. Greene to Joseph Reed, 18 March 1781, Joseph Reed Papers; Reed, *Life and Correspondence of Joseph Reed*, II, 350; Palmer, *Virginia State Papers*, I, 582.

37. Greene to Reed, 18 March 1781, Reed to Greene, 16 June 1781, Joseph Reed Papers; Sparks, *Correspondence of the American Revolution*, III, 267–68; Reed, *Life and Correspondence of Joseph Reed*, II, 296, 350, 355; Charles Caldwell,

Three days were spent at Speedwell Iron Works, preparing for a second battle that never came. Word came that Cornwallis was retiring toward the Yadkin River. More reliable intelligence a few hours later revealed that the British were moving toward Bell's Mill. Greene issued orders to break camp.[38]

Since the end of the battle the uninjured troops of Cornwallis had been kept busy caring for the wounded of both armies. They were without tents or provisions and were near exhaustion as a result of their early morning march and the intensity of the subsequent battle. Despite their weariness, they were put to work burying the dead and caring for the wounded—the American wounded were treated with their own. Rain fell throughout the night, a night torn by the cries of the wounded and the groans of the dying. It was estimated that at least fifty men died during that night of horror. The wagons and supplies did not arrive from Bell's Mill until between three and four o'clock on the afternoon of March 16, but even then there was little food for the hungry troops. The gravity of the situation was well expressed by one British officer who noted that "here, time, place, and numbers, all unite against the British."[39]

At eight o'clock on the morning of March 17, seventeen wagons left Guilford Court House on the road to New Garden Meeting House. Each was loaded to capacity with those wounded who could not walk or ride a horse. Later in the day the women with the army were sent off along the same route.[40]

British casualties had been heavy. Ninety-three had been killed, with 413 wounded and 26 missing. There was no way that the British general could estimate the losses of his opponent. Few prisoness had been taken, for the thick woods had facilitated the escape of many. His foraging parties, however, reported that the houses in the neighborhood were crowded with American wounded. The capture of American supplies had been limited to ordnance: 4 brass sixpounders, 160 round shot, 50 case shot, and 2 ammunition wagons.

Memoirs of the Life and Campaigns of the Hon. Nathaniel Greene (Philadelphia, 1819), pp. 175–76; Graham, *Life of General Daniel Morgan*, pp. 372–73; Kapp, *Life of Steuben*, pp. 175–76; Marquis de Chastellux, *Travels in North American in the Years 1780, 1781, and 1782*, trans. George Greive (London, 1787), II, 67; Greene to Steuben, 22 March 1781, Steuben Papers; Greene to Jefferson, 16 March 1781, Nathanael Greene Papers, William L. Clements Library.

38. Graham, *Life of General Daniel Morgan*, p. 372.

39. *North Carolina Historical Review*, IX (October, 1932), 389; Stedman, *History of the ... American War*, II, 346–47; Greene to Cornwallis, 17 March 1781, Nathanael Greene Papers, William L. Clements Library.

40. *North Carolina Historical Review*, IX (October, 1932), 388–89.

The greatest prize had been the capture of 1,800 stand of small bore weapons; some were distributed to local loyalists, others destroyed on the field.[41]

British troops remained at Guilford until noon, Sunday, March 18. Despite a poor response by the loyalists, Cornwallis still maintained the pose of a conqueror. Before leaving the courthouse he issued a proclamation claiming a "compleat victory" and inviting all loyal subjects to join his victorious army. The last act of the British before leaving Guilford was to burn the house of a Mr. Campbell, a prominent Whig of the community. Shortly afterward Cornwallis moved off the field on which he had won his hollow victory.[42]

At New Garden his wagons and camp followers were waiting. Cornwallis discovered that a number of his wounded men were in no condition to travel. Seventy were left behind in the improvised hospital in the meeting house, since the British general knew that the gentle Quakers of the neighborhood would not allow them to go unattended.[43]

After their arrival at Bell's Mill on March 19 the tired British troops were allowed to rest for two days. The physical appearance of the army discouraged prospective recruits. Many of the inhabitants rode into camp, shook the hand of the British general, told him that they were happy that he had beaten Greene, and then rode home again. Cornwallis began to move toward Cross Creek in a series of easy marches, the slow pace dictated by the condition of his wounded.[44]

Greene had set out in pursuit just as soon as he received word of the British departure from Guilford. He left his wounded at the courthouse, later writing the Quakers at New Garden, reminding them that he had once been a member of their sect and soliciting their aid in comforting his wounded men.[45]

His army was in good spirits and spoiling for a fight. But he had to make contact with the enemy in the near future, for many of his

41. Ross, *Cornwallis Correspondence*, I, 509; *London Magazine* (June, 1781), p. 300; *Bulletin of the New York Public Library*, IX (November, 1905), 464.

42. Cornwallis to Germain, 17 March 1781, Cornwallis Papers, PRO 30/11/76; Stevens, *Clinton-Cornwallis Controversy*, I, 371; *Royal Gazette* (Charleston), 28 March 1781.

43. Carruthers, *Interesting Revolutionary Incidents*, p. 175; *The American Museum: Or Repository of Ancient and Modern Fugitive Pieces, &c., Prose and Poetical*, VI (September, 1789), 214; Merritt, *Calendar of the Otho Williams Papers*, p. 43; St. George Tucker to Frances Tucker, 18 March 1781, Coleman-Tucker Papers.

44. Clinton to Germain, 18 April 1781, Cornwallis Papers, PRO 30/11/76; Stevens, *Clinton-Cornwallis Controversy*, I, 396–97.

45. *American Museum*, VI (September, 1789), 213.

troops would soon be leaving because their terms of enlistments were expiring. One of these units had been a well-equipped troop of seventy-five or eighty volunteers from Halifax, mostly young gentlemen under Captain Samuel Lockhart. Included in their number was Willie Jones, a member of the Continental Congress.[46]

Greene had not yet recovered his own strength and his eyes were giving him trouble. His sources of intelligence were faulty. He assigned Lee the task of placing a spy within the enemy's camp. And to demonstrate to the people along Cornwallis's route that the American army was not beaten, Lee's Legion was sent to range off the flanks of British column. The straggling formation of the enemy aided this operation and a number of prisoners were taken during each day's march. Along the way one Solomon Slocum of the Second Maryland Regiment was court-martialed for deserting to the enemy and then returning to the American camp as a spy. Found guilty, he was hanged to a tree along the roadside so that the troops might view his body as they marched by.[47]

Lee sent back word that Cornwallis had halted at Ramsey's Mill on Deep River to comfort his wounded and procure provisions. Troops had been set to work building a bridge across the stream. They were able to work in relative peace, harassed upon only one occasion when Colonel Malmedy and "about twenty of the gang of plunderers that are attached to him" galloped in among the sentries and carried off three Hessian Yagers. Greene had halted his own march to await a supply of arms and ammunition. Lee and his Legion were ordered to cross the river ten miles above the British encampment and work their way down the opposite shore. There they were to attempt to dislodge the British bridgehead, destroy the bridge, and refuse passage of the stream to Lord Cornwallis until Greene could bring up the main force and attack the British from the rear. In some fashion Cornwallis discovered this strategy and on March 28 broke camp, crossed the stream, and marched rapidly for Cross Creek. His departure was so sudden that he left unburied several men who had but recently died of their wounds. Lee and his Legion arrived too late to prevent the destruction of the bridge by the rear guard.[48]

46. Lee, *Campaign of 1781*, appendix, ix–x; *Southern Literary Messenger*, IX (February 1845), 146–47; *Rhode Island Historical Society Publications*, XX (October, 1927), 107.

47. Lee, *Memoirs of the War in the Southern Department*, p. 287; Merritt, *Calendar of the Otho Williams Papers*, p. 43; Seymour, *A Journal of the Southern Expedition*, p. 22; Robert Kirkwood, *The Journal and Orderly Book of Captain Robert Kirkwood of the Delaware Regiment of the Continental Line*, ed. Joseph Brown Taylor (Wilmington, Del., 1910), p. 15.

48. Sparks, *Correspondence of the American Revolution*, III, 282; Abner Nash

Greene reached Ramsey's Mill the following day and decided to discontinue the pursuit. His troops were dwindling in number and there was little hope of securing reinforcements in the "vile toryish country from Hillsborough to Cape Fear." The pine barrens along Cornwallis's route promised little in the way of subsistence for two armies.[49]

Greene remained at Ramsey's Mill for several days, resting his troops and preparing detailed drafts of future operations. Then there was the tidying of loose ends that was always necessary when the army rested for a few days. A court-martial acquitted Captain William Lytle of the North Carolina Continentals, who allegedly had refused to obey Colonel John Gunby's orders when the latter officer was temporarily stationed at Hillsborough. The same court tried Private Thomas Hall of the North Carolina troops, who was charged with deserting and joining the enemy. Found guilty, Hall was sentenced to one hundred lashes on his bare back and required to make up the time he had been absent from his unit. The flogging was carried out that same afternoon. Food was scarce in this semiwilderness of pine barrens and an early move was dictated by the scarcity of provisions. A number of men collapsed each day, worn thin by malnutrition. The people of the community were of divided political opinions and engaged in a little civil war so vicious that it threatened to flame into something greater.[50]

Greene prepared a fluid master plan that allowed him the necessary latitude to cope with unforseen emergencies. His basic move was a return of the army to South Carolina. By this maneuver he hoped to be able to intercept British lines of communications between their posts outside Charleston. This, he hoped, would force Cornwallis to return to that state. The presence of the southern army would bolster the sagging morale of the people of South Carolina, who were complaining that they were being neglected. And it was hoped that a return to South Carolina would benefit the people of North Carolina. With the war drawn from its doorsteps, perhaps the state legislature would be able to complete its quota of Continental troops. If Greene

to Washington, 4 April 1781, George Washington Papers, Library of Congress; Greene to Lafayette, 29 March 1781, Nathanael Greene Papers, William L. Clements Library; Stevens, *Clinton-Cornwallis Controversy*, I, 395–99.

49. Burnett, *Letters of Members of the Continental Congress*, VI, 5; John Russell Bartlett (ed.), *Records of Rhode Island and Providence Plantations in New England* (Providence, R.I., 1864), IX, 380–81.

50. *Year Book of the City of Charleston, 1899*, pp. 85–86; Tarleton, *Campaigns*, pp. 32–41 Nathaniel Pendleton Orderly Book, Library of Congress, Washington, D.C.

remained in North Carolina, it was possible that the enemy would be able to maintain a measure of control over both states.[51]

Greene's plans included a check for the British should Cornwallis decide to march into Virginia. The Marquis de Lafayette had been sent south with his troops to join the southern army. Dispatches also carried the information that Major General Anthony Wayne had been ordered south with his Pennsylvania Line to join Greene. Greene ordered Lafayette to assume the military command in Virginia and authorized him to use the Pennsylvania Line when and if Wayne arrived. Steuben was to devote his energies to securing supplies and forwarding Continental recruits to the southward but was requested to coordinate his efforts with those of Lafayette. Should the British initiate a serious campaign in Virginia, Greene planned to place the southern army under General Huger and assume the command of the troops opposing Cornwallis.[52]

To protect his rear against a sudden strike from Craig at Wilmington, the general instructed Jethro Sumner to collect those troops he could and maintain a close watch on Cornwallis. If the enemy indicated a return to South Carolina, Sumner was to place his troops between the two armies and attempt to sustain a holding action until the main army could come up in support.[53]

The governor of North Carolina was urged to remove all military stores from near the coast to Hillsborough, a move calculated to make the coastal towns less attractive as military objectives. The more critical supplies were ordered to be moved to Charlotte where they would be more readily accessible to South Carolina.[54]

Greene's greatest problem was the lack of men. The six-weeks term of enlistment for the Virginia militia had come to an end and, with spring planting in the offing, the men refused to remain longer in the field. All the southern states seemed to have lost interest in filling their Continental quotas. The enemy garrisons in South Carolina were small enough to more nearly equal Greene's depleted force

51. Greene to Samuel Huntington, 9 June 1781, Greene Papers, Duke University; *Collection of the Rhode Island Historical Society* (Providence, 1867), VI, 382–83; Hastings, *Public Papers of George Clinton*, VI, 910; Sparks, *Correspondence of the American Revolution*, III, 278.

52. Greene to Samuel Huntingon, 9 June 1781, Greene Papers, Duke University; Greene to Sumner, 11 April 1781, Jethro Sumner Papers, Southern Historical Collection; Greene to Steuben, 2 April 1781, Steuben Papers.

53. *State Records*, XVII, 1048.

54. *Ibid.*, XV, 435–36; Joshua Potts to Philemon Hawkins, 19 April 1781, Jethro Sumner Papers, Southern Historical Collection; Greene to Washington, 29 March 1781, George Washington Papers.

and a campaign against these detached posts promised some success.[55]

The general also had his personal problems. His mobility had been limited when his favorite horse was stolen. He requested that the state of North Carolina supply him with adequate mounts.[56]

Word came that Thomas Sumter had recovered from wounds and was once again active in partisan warfare in South Carolina. The aid of Francis Marion was enlisted in stockpiling provisions against the return of the army. On Monday, April 2, 1781, Lawson's Virginia militiamen were assembled and after the resolution of the Congress praising Morgan for his victory at Cowpens was read to the troops, they were dismissed and allowed to return to their homes. The following day the army was alerted and placed under marching orders. General John Butler of the North Carolina militia was to remain at Ramsey's Mill to collect those militia who could be persuaded to come out, as well as forward to Greene all supplies that could be collected. On April 6 the return march to South Carolina began, with Greene still harboring misgivings that this withdrawal might serve to damage his military reputation.[57]

The beginnings of this march marked the end of the contest between Greene and Cornwallis. It had been a disastrous campaign for the British general. He had been outmaneuvered and outgeneraled by his American opponent and the fact that his tired troops never had an opportunity to fully recover from the effects of the campaign must be considered an important link in the chain of events that led to Yorktown.

Greene had made blunders, but his blunders had been offset by his practice of trying to anticipate eventualities. He had made a science out of retreat and, inveterate planner that he was, his designing of retrograde movements showed greater genius than some of those times when he was striving for victory on the field of battle. He be-

55. Sparks, *Correspondence of the American Revolution*, III, 279; Greene to Steuben, 2 April 1781, Steuben Papers; Abner Nash to Washington, 4 April 1781, George Washington Papers.

56. Greene to Sumner, 11 April 1781, Jethro Sumner Papers, Southern Historical Collection.

57. *Year Book: City of Charleston, 1894* (Charleston, S.C., 1894), pp. 6–7; William Dobein James, *A Sketch of the Life of Brig. Gen. Francis Marion and a History of His Brigade from Its Rise in June 1780 Until Disbanded in December 1782* (Marietta, Ga., 1948), pp. 30, 34; Greene, *Life of Nathanael Greene*, III, 217; Sparks, *Correspondence of the American Revolution*, III, 279; John Butler to Thomas Wooten, 8 April 1781, Commissary Correspondence, Military Collection; Greene to Steuben, 2 April 1781, Steuben Papers; Pendleton Orderly Book; John Butler to Sumner, 11 April 1781, Jethro Sumner Papers, Southern Historical Collection; General Orders, 1 April 1781, Robert Lawson Papers, Duke University, Durham, N.C.

came respected as a worthy foe and for his ability to strike, withdraw, and then strike again, perhaps best expressed in the observations of a British officer serving farther north: "Greene is however entitled to great praise for his wonderful exertions; the more he is beaten the farther he advances in the end. He has been indefatigable in collecting troops and leading them to be defeated."[58]

The importance of the campaign in the Carolinas lay not in its great battles but in the results of its many skirmishes and small engagements. The more observant British officers had foreseen the results of customary military practices in America, and as early as 1775 one British general had written: "our army will be destroyed by damned driblets . . . America is an ugly job . . . a damned affair indeed." And by 1781 the staid *Annual Register* noted: "Most of these actions would in other wars be considered as skirmishes of little account, and scarcely worthy of a detailed narrative. But these small actions are as capable as any of displaying military conduct. The operations of war being spread over that vast continent . . . it is by such skirmishes that the fate of America must be necessarily decided. They are therefore as important as battles in which a hundred thousand men are drawn up on each side."[59]

For Cornwallis, the campaign of 1781 in the Carolinas had been a study in frustration, with the British general desperately trying to strike the decisive blow that would destroy the southern army and Greene seeking the ever-elusive victory by which he hoped to gain a reputation and lasting military glory.

58. Frederick Mackenzie, *Diary of Frederick Mackenzie* (Cambridge, Mass., 1930), II, 673.
59. Fortescue, *History of the British Army*, III, 171; *Annual Register for 1781*, p. 83.

Chapter 17
South Carolina, 1781

"We fight, get beat, rise, and fight again."

Nathanael Greene had been able to do something of which Horatio Gates had seemingly been incapable: arouse the flagging spirits of the Continental officers of North Carolina. There are several possible explanations for this change of attitude. For one thing, Gates was noted for his great faith in and reliance upon the militia. Greene, on the other hand, despised the militia and rested all of his hopes in an army of Continentals. Then, too, Greene appeared more energetic and professional than his predecessor, and had captured the imagination of many officers who had suffered disillusionment. And the British invasion of the state had brought some into the field who otherwise might have remained at home.

Certainly Jethro Sumner appeared much happier with Greene in command of the Southern Department. In January, in response to an appeal from Greene, Sumner came out of his self-imposed exile and supervised the removal of military stores from Guilford and Caswell counties. He called together the Continental officers to discuss the reconstitution of the North Carolina Line. They suggested that if agreeable to the legislature, they raise four Continental regiments to be placed under the command of Lieutenant Colonel John B.

Ashe and Majors Murfree, Dixon, and James Armstrong. A group of these officers traveled to Halifax before the meeting of the assembly to solicit the support of early-arriving members in restructuring the state line.[1]

There were local complications, reaching back to January 27, 1781. On that day a fleet of eighteen vessels flying the British ensign had dropped anchor in the Cape Fear River off Wilmington. On board were 450 redcoats under the command of Major James Craig. Despite their bold boasts in the past, the nearly 1,000 inhabitants of the city were unprepared to defend their homes. After an unsuccessful attempt to gain favorable terms, 200 men marched out of the town to lay down their arms, after first spiking the seventeen nine- and twelve-pounders in the two batteries protecting Wilmington. Governor Rutledge of South Carolina was so disgusted that he wrote, "6 of the Town's people left it, the rest received the Enemy with 3 huzzas." Craig landed his troops "without the least opposition," and immediately set them to work throwing up fortifications around the town.

The delay in landing had allowed time for a considerable amount of military stores, arms, and ammunition to be moved up the Northeast River in small craft. To intercept them, Craig led out one detachment, while Andrew Barkley, commanding the naval vessels, dispatched a Lieutenant Winters with a galley and two gunboats up the river. All of the fleeing boats were captured except a schooner and a sloop loaded with arms and ammunition that had run aground and had been burned by their crews to prevent them falling into enemy hands.

Patrols were sent out to round up all prominent Whigs in the community. Some attempted to escape. Thomas Bloodworth, the tax collector, loaded all of his papers and records into a boat and sent it up the river. Craig's troops, after a twenty-mile ride across country, captured and burned the boat.[2]

Other patrols, mounted on the best horses of the lower Cape Fear region, and sometimes joined by Tories, rode constantly. Cornelius Harnett, who had been proscribed by Governor Josiah Martin and declared an outlaw by Sir Henry Clinton, attempted to flee with the money entrusted to him for the purchase of military supplies and clothing. After getting the money to a place of safety, Harnett fell ill

1. *State Records*, XV, 421, 426.
2. Andrew Barkley to Admiral Arbuthnot, 12 February 1781, Proposals for Capitulation, Wilmington, 27 January 1781, PRO Ad. 1/486; *State Records*, XV, 543, XVI, ix.

with the gout and accepted the hospitality of Colonel James Spicer of Onslow County, whose home was some thirty miles above Wilmington. Captured by Craig's marauders, his hands and feet trussed with rope, Harnett was carried back to town, slung across a horse like a sack of meal. He was thrown into a blockhouse that had no roof. There, exposed to the elements, the frail fifty-eight year old Harnett died on April 28, 1781.[3]

John Ashe, brigadier general of militia, suffered a similar fate. His hiding place in the swamps had been betrayed to the enemy by a servant. Attempting to escape, Ashe was wounded in the leg. In prison, while recovering from this wound, he fell victim to smallpox. Although paroled, he was so weakened by these experiences that he died soon after he reached his home at Clinton in Sampson County. Other prominent Whigs were brought into Wilmington by the Tories. Because of these incidents, the militia of eastern North Carolina had been restricted to the Wilmington area in an attempt to prevent the British from roaming too far afield.[4]

In general the townspeople did not give Craig much trouble. It was reported that Thomas Maclaine and John Huske were the only two men in all Wilmington who refused to sign a "petition to be admitted to a dependence upon Great Britain." By February 12, Andrew Barkley was able to boast that "the Inhabitants remaining in Town and in the Neighbouring parts have delivered up their Arms, and I have given them Paroles, they most ardently wish once more for the blessings of Peace and a re-union with the Mother Country." These events complicated and almost eliminated chances of recruiting Continental soldiers in southeastern North Carolina. Similarly the water route into the interior was blocked to supplies destined for the North Carolina military forces. M. L. Brown of Elizabeth Town summed up the situation: "The greatest part of the good People in this Country, is Ingaged back against the Toryes: and seems very Loth to go against the Brittish and Leave their Families Expos'd to a set of Villians; who Dayley thriettans their Destruction."[5]

3. R. D. W. Connor, *Cornelius Harnett* (Raleigh, N.C., 1909), pp. 196–98.
4. *State Records*, XVI, ix; Nash to Washington, 4 April 1781, George Washington Papers.
5. Andrew Barkley to Admiral Arbuthnot, 12 February 1781, PRO Ad. 1/486; *South Carolina Historical and Genealogical Magazine*, XVIII (July, 1917), 135; Thomas Burke, William Sharpe, and Samuel Johnston to John Laurens, 10 January 1781, Revolutionary Collection, Duke University; M. L. Brown to Alexander Lillington, 19 February 1781, Charles E. Johnston Collection. Volume XV of the *State Records* identifies the writer as Colonel Thomas Brown, but the manuscript is signed M. L. Brown, probably Morgan Brown.

Because of the unstable military situation, and the presence of both Craig and Cornwallis in the state, the recruiting of Continental soldiers throughout the remainder of the state was virtually halted. Greene requested Sumner and other Continental officers to present themselves to Major General Richard Caswell to aid in arranging and temporarily commanding those militiamen supposed to be collecting under the former governor. Sumner was willing to cooperate, but he feared the resentment of militia officers serving with Caswell, although a number of Continental officers were serving with the militia. Others had offered their services to Greene to serve in a capacity where they would be most useful. There was some feeling that the militia should be placed under Sumner's command until the Continentals could be reformed. Although such an arrangement would have pleased Sumner, he was quite willing to serve under Caswell if he was given a militia brigade to command.[6]

It was statute law and not the persuasive powers of recruiting officers that solved the manpower problem for the North Carolina Continentals. As explained to Washington by Abner Nash, "The State is now busily imployed in drafting their regulars for our four Batalions, and as the militia by a late law are subjected in case they desert their Colours in time of action, & run away, to the condition of Continental Soldiers during the war, we expect to derive some good for the Evil they did in running away from the Enemy in action of the 15th at Guilford." By the first of April those who had so hurriedly absented themselves from the field at Guilford and who could be found, were being conscripted as Continental soldiers, but their term of service was usually for twelve months rather than for the duration of the war. Their punishment actually went beyond forced military service, for these draftees were given no bounty and issued no clothing and the state was not required to furnish support for their families while they were in service.[7]

A measure originally proposed by the Board of War in early January was implemented by Nash and his Council Extraordinary and was designed to improve the supply situation. Every area of the state, except those regions gleaned by the two armies, was now required to give up one-fifth of their bacon and other salted meat for the use of the army. On the surface this expedient appeared reason-

6. *State Records*, XV, 425–26, 429–30.

7. Nash to Washington, 4 April 1781, George Washington Papers; *State Records*, XVII, 930–31; Nash to Greene, 3 April 1781, Benedict Arnold Papers, New-York Historical Society, New York, N.Y.

able, but to some one-fifth was surplus, while to others it could mean a starvation diet.[8]

Because of Greene's magnetism, some Continental officers were coming back into service with an almost religious fervor. Collection points for those persons drafted into the army were established at Edenton, Smithfield, Duplin Court House, Halifax, Hillsborough, and Salisbury, with Hillsborough designated as a general rendezvous. Sumner, for the time being, stationed himself at Hillsborough to assist in the gathering of provisions for the 2,000 or 3,000 men he expected to arrive at that place in the near future. Arms he hoped to borrow from Virginia. General John Butler, still at Ramsey's Mill, had already collected 240 of those militiamen who had fled at Guilford, and it was his intention to send them on to Hillsborough just as soon as Continental officers arrived to take charge of them. There was no time to arrange them into proper units for Greene was so impatient for reinforcements that he urged Sumner not to wait until he had sufficient men to form a regiment, but to send them on to the southern army as fast as they came in.[9]

There was still the problem of the enemy in eastern North Carolina, hampering recruiting and the rounding up of wayward militiamen in that quarter. The little civil war raging in the coastal plains had grown more intense, with the two factions "killing one another so fast that it seemed likely to Depopulate that Country." The Tories, under the protection supplied by Craig's troops, had taken a vengeful trail, plundering and forcing many of Whig inclinations to "Lay out in the woods." Some loyalists were captured and brought in as prisoners by wandering Whig parties.[10]

It was no easy task for Jethro Sumner to pull all of the loose ends together. Communications were disorganized or nonexistent. Those militiamen drafted into Continental service were sometimes brought in to rendezvous points only to discover that there were no Continental officers on hand to take command. Some officers complained that they were not informed concerning where they were to

8. William Hooper to James Iredell, 29 March 1781, Charles E. Johnston Collection; *State Records*, XV, 484–86; Nash to Greene, 3 April 1781, Benedict Arnold Papers; Nash to Washington, 4 April 1781, George Washington Papers; Burke to the President of Congress, 7 August 1781, Papers of the Continental Congress.

9. *State Records*, XV, 433–34, 435; Butler to Sumner, 11 April 1781, Jethro Sumner Papers, Southern Historical Collection; Greene to Sumner, 8 April 1781, in possession of Mr. Curtis Carroll Davis of Baltimore, Md.

10. *State Records*, XV, 437, 438; Burnett, *Letters of Members of the Continental Congress*, VI, 60–61.

meet their men, nor what they were expected to do with them once they assumed command. And as time passed it became apparent that an army of two thousand was a dream, even with "such recruits, delinquents and others liable to be taken into the Continental Army." Yet Sumner still expected to rendezvous a considerable number of men at Hillsborough by April 25, while those from the eastern and southern districts were expected to arrive no later than May 5.[11]

The produce tax had not proved productive enough to support half the troops then in the field, and this was complicated by the shortage of wagons to transport those provisions that had been collected. Available wagons, along with provisions, were dispatched to Greene's army rather than to Sumner's troops. The inadequate food supply had been created by a drought in 1779 and floods in 1780. Virginia troops, on their march to join Greene, had been provisioned by North Carolina when they passed through the state. In addition to food deficiencies, there was little money with which to pay the Continental troops. The state treasury, as usual, was empty, and Greene was obliged to offer a loan from his already thin military chest. And the recruiting was not helped by Greene's attitude toward all militiamen and especially those of the state. "North Carolina," he wrote Joseph Reed, "has got next to no regulars in the field, and few militia, and those are the worst in the world, for they have neither pride nor principle to bind them to any party, or to a discharge of their duty."[12]

Greene, in the meantime, had directed his course toward Camden in South Carolina with an idea of laying siege to the force of Lord Rawdon, the commandant at that outpost. To protect his rear, the general ordered Sumner to maneuver in North Carolina in such a manner as to keep himself between the American and British armies. But Sumner had not the strength to operate in such a fashion, for many of those Continentals in the field who should have been under

11. Sumner to _____, 18 April 1781, John Stewart to Sumner, 18 June 1781, Jethro Sumner Papers, N.C. Dept. Arch. & Hist.; Sumner to Joshua Potts, 18 April 1781, Commissary Correspondence, Military Collection; *State Records*, XV, 440–41.

12. Sumner to Greene, 20 April 1781, Jethro Sumner Papers, N.C. Dept. Arch. & Hist.; Greene to Sumner, 19 April 1781, Jethro Sumner Papers, Southern Historical Collection; *State Records*, XV, 442; Greene to Davie, 14 April 1781, Davie to Greene, 23 April 1781, William R. Davie Papers, Southern Historical Collection, The University of North Carolina at Chapel Hill, Chapel Hill, N.C.; Gordon, *History of the . . . Independence of the United States*, IV, 86–87; Thomas Burke, William Sharpe, and Samuel Johnston to John Laurens, 16 January 1781, Revolutionary Collection, Duke University.

his command appeared to be marching aimlessly from one place to another. Those who had come into Halifax had found a smallpox epidemic. Continuing on to Hillsborough they found the same disease raging there.[13]

Recruiting, or even the drafting of the militia into the Line, was not aided by the news of another defeat of Greene before Camden. After leaving Ramsey's Mill he had marched 140 miles in fourteen days and pitched camp on Hobkirk's Hill, a mile and a half from Camden. Thomas Sumter, Francis Marion, Andrew Pickens, and Henry Lee were out in the countryside acting as diversionary groups, "but their Endeavours rather seem to keep the contest alive than lay a Foundation for the Recovery of the States." With Greene were 250 North Carolina militiamen under the command of Colonel James Reed. Feeling that he was too weak to launch an attack, the general camped on the high ground awaiting reinforcements and supplies.[14]

Greene had his army pitch camp in battle lines on the slope facing Camden. Just before daybreak on April 19, provisions had arrived. The men had stacked their arms while a two-day food supply and a gill of rum were being distributed. Some were washing their clothes in a nearby creek. At about ten o'clock there was the crackle of a musket shot, then another, followed by the crash of a full volley. Drums rattled out a call to arms.

Young Lord Rawdon had arrived at the conclusion that his only hope lay in surprising Greene before reinforcements arrived. Army cooks, drummers, and convalescents were issued arms and marched out with the rank and file to meet the enemy. The surprise was complete, but Captain Robert Kirkwood and his little band of Delaware Continentals managed to delay Rawdon until Greene's men could rush to their battle positions.[15]

Greene's three six-pounders opened up with canister and grape shot as soon as the enemy came within range. When he noticed Rawdon's forces advancing on a narrow front, Greene ordered William Washington's dragoons to make a wide sweep and hit the British rear. These mounted troops poured across the flank, taking prisoners, and for a moment, held Rawdon captive. When the counterattack came, Washington's men were encumbered with so many prisoners that they

13. *State Records,* XV, 444–45, 449.

14. Greene to Sumner, 21 April 1781, Jethro Sumner Papers, Southern Historical Collection; *State Records,* XV, 444; Hastings, *Public Papers of George Clinton,* VI, 910–14.

15. Tarleton, *Campaigns of 1780 and 1781,* pp. 482–84; Ross, *Cornwallis Correspondence,* I, 97; *American Historical Record,* II (March, 1873), 105.

were obliged to fall back. Hastily paroling those officers whom he had taken, Washington sped back to the protection of his own lines.[16]

Rawdon brought up his second line to extend his front, but at the time it seemed a futile move. The Virginia and Maryland Continentals in Greene's first line pushed their way forward. Then, as so often happens in battles, an innocent order led to the collapse of the American army. The center of Colonel John Gunby's crack First Maryland Regiment, in their forward thrust, had managed to distort their line in a huge bow. Gunby's order halting the center to allow the wings to catch up, coupled with a bayonet charge by the enemy, caused the regiment to fall apart. Its panic was communicated to the Second Maryland whose commander, Lieutenant Colonel Benjamin Ford, was struck down at this moment. It was followed by the troops of Colonel Richard Campbell's First Virginia Regiment, who broke and ran. Only Lieutenant Colonel Samuel Hawes's Second Virginia stood steady and checked what might have been the beginning of a disastrous rout. It continued to stand firm until Greene, fearful of being outflanked, ordered its withdrawal.[17]

Captain John Smith with his light company of the Maryland Line were dragging off the artillery by hand when the British came up. In the fight that followed, most of Smith's command had been struck down when Washington's troopers returned from their mission behind the enemy lines. Hastily dumping his prisoners, Washington charged the British and drove them back. Hitching some of his mounts to the fieldpieces, he pulled them out of danger. Although not mentioned in Greene's dispatches, the North Carolina militiamen under Colonel Reed had been attached to Washington, and some said that they aided in holding off the enemy long enough to make possible Greene's withdrawal.

The American general managed to keep his command intact and was able to bring his men together three miles from the battle site. Rawdon was not strong enough to pursue and had halted his men on Hobkirk's Hill. That afternoon Greene fell back another three miles and made camp on Sanders Creek near the spot where Horatio Gates had met disaster nine months before.[18]

16. *American Historical Record*, II (March, 1873), 106–9; Tarleton, *Campaigns of 1780 and 1781*, pp. 483–84; Greene to Steuben, 27 April 1781, Steuben Papers.

17. Stedman, *History of the . . . American War*, II, 355–58; Greene, *Life of Nathanael Greene*, III, 239–54; Tarleton, *Campaigns of 1780 and 1781*, p. 484; Greene to Steuben, 27 April 1781, Nathanael Greene Papers, William L. Clements Library.

18. Greene to Steuben, 27 April 1781, Steuben Papers; Greene to John Butler,

American casualties were 1 officer and 18 men killed, 7 officers and 108 men wounded, while 136 were missing. British losses totalled 258 of whom 38, including 1 officer, had been killed. Thirteen officers had suffered wounds. Rawdon, although he had won the field, had been hurt enough so that he felt that he was no longer strong enough to hold Camden and shortly afterwards he abandoned the town and fell back to Charleston.[19]

Four of the prisoners taken during the battle were discovered to be deserters from Continental units who had enlisted in the British army, including one Thomas Wood of the Fifth North Carolina Regiment. A court found all five guilty and sentenced them to be hung. Greene, although not agreeing with the sentence, approved the court's action for "desertion is a Crime so dangerous to an Army that policy has directed a Mode of Correction—the Indispensable necessity of giving some serious example of the Recent Misfortune the troops have suffered by the perfidy of some of their unworthy Companions forbid the exercise of Lenity & Compel the General to admit the force of Martial Law." All five were hanged the following afternoon at four o'clock.[20]

Greene was not discouraged about the outcome of the battle of Hobkirk's Hill, nor did he blame Gunby for his "unfortunate order." In fact, the court-martial that later exonerated Gunby criticized the confusion in orders as "the only cause why we did not obtain a Complete Victory." "War is a critical business," Greene wrote Abner Nash, "and the fate of the Day after every possible precaution depends upon the most trifling incident." To Baron von Steuben he noted that "this repulse, if repulse it may be called, will make no Alteration in our general plan of Operation." And his strategy was summed up in a letter to the French minister, the Chevalier La Luzerne, "We fight, get beat, rise, and fight again."[21]

But Hobkirk's Hill was not taken so lightly by the people of North Carolina. Greene had been in two major battles since he had

n.d., Greene Papers, Library of Congress, Washington, D.C.; Nathaniel Pendleton Orderly Book.

19. Greene, *Life of Nathanael Greene*, III, 250–54; Tarleton, *Campaigns of 1780 and 1781*, pp. 484–85; *Magazine of American History*, VII (December, 1881), 431.

20. Pendleton Orderly Book; *Journal and Orderly Book of Captain Robert Kirkwood*, p. 17.

21. Greene to Nash, 2 May 1781, Greene Papers, Library of Congress; Greene, *Life of Nathanael Greene*, III, 253; Pendleton Orderly Book; Greene to Joseph Reed, 4 May 1781, Joseph Reed Papers; Stedman, *History of the . . . American War*, II, 398–99.

come south and in both instances he had been forced to yield the field, at the time an important yardstick of victory. Matters within the state were further complicated when Cornwallis, on April 19, marched out of Wilmington, his destination unannounced. Sumner was ordered to hold those men under his command in readiness; if Cornwallis went into Virginia, Sumner was to join Steuben, and if his Lordship marched south towards Camden, he was to join Greene.[22]

It had been evident for some time that Cornwallis was planning a move. A detachment sent out by him to destroy American magazines had been frustrated when arms and ammunition were removed from their path. After he marched, militia from the eastern counties had been called out, not to offer battle but to control the loyalists along the British line of march. Operating off the flanks of the marching columns, the militiamen prevented Tories from bringing in fresh beef to Cornwallis. They frequently found themselves in running fights with the loyalists, who sometimes inflicted "a pretty little Switching." In reality the militia acted more as a force escorting the British out of North Carolina than as an opposing force.[23]

There was one group of North Carolina Continentals in the field, although in many contemporary accounts and in all later studies they were identified as militiamen. In reality these men were draftees from the militia that had fled at Guilford Court House, but Greene and others had complained so bitterly of their behavior that no one in the field would dignify their presence by terming them Continentals. This little band of ragged men was to prove them wrong.

Major Pinkethan Eaton, formerly of the Third and Fifth Regiments under the old establishment, was in command. General Sumner had called Eaton back into service in late January to replace Colonel John Gunby of the Maryland Continentals at Hillsborough, who had been stationed there by Gates to gather supplies and recruits. Of late Eaton had been active in the removal of supplies from the path of the British.[24]

Eaton became commanding officer by default. He had been at Chatham Court House when 170 draftees had been brought in by

22. *State Records*, XV, 455–56; Greene to Sumner, 5 May 1781, Jethro Sumner Papers, Southern Historical Collection.
23. John Johnston to _____, 3 May 1781, Robert Smith to James Iredell, May 1781, Charles E. Johnston Collection; James Armstrong to William Caswell, 17 May 1781, Caswell Papers, N. C. Dept. Arch. & Hist.; Edward Hill to Joshua Potts, 5 June 1781, Commissary Correspondence, Military Collection; James Emmet to Greene, 28 April 1781, Miscellaneous Papers, New-York Historical Society.
24. *State Records*, XV, 422.

Colonel William Linton, who turned the men over to Eaton and left. There was no Continental officer accompanying the troops. Poor Eaton was in a quandary. Although he was directly responsible to Sumner, Greene had left specific orders that all recruits brought into Chatham Court House be marched directly to his headquarters. On April 17 Eaton, with about 180 men, marched for Greene's camp, with 41 of his men almost immediately deserting. Although Sumner ordered Major Henry Dixon to send Eaton enough Continental officers to take care of the command problem, by the middle of April there was only one such officer, Lieutenant John Campbell, with him. Shortly afterwards he was joined by Captain Robert Smith of the old Fourth Regiment.[25]

It was not a desirable command. Apparently Lieutenant Colonel Linton had used little discretion in assembling the men, arbitrarily selecting them without resorting to proper procedures or investigation. The men deserted at every opportunity, "and complain heartily of the injustice done them, having never had a Tryall as they many of them declare."[26]

Eaton was near Rugeley's Mill, within a short distance of Camden, when Captain Daniel Conyers of Greene's staff met him with orders to join Francis Marion. At this time, there were 140 ragged and hungry men under Eaton's command, mostly from the Halifax District, "that are turned into the Continental service for twelve months."[27]

Apparently these orders were later countermanded, for Eaton and his men acted briefly with Henry Lee in late April and in early May were in Greene's camp. It was then that twenty-five of his men were detached to Lee's Legion, where they were placed under the command of Lieutenant Andrew Manning, under whom they were to serve for the remainder of their terms. Eaton was still suffering from a lack of Continental officers, with only himself, Captain Smith, and Lieutenant Campbell with the troops. Shortly after Eaton joined Greene, he was detached, along with Captain Finley and a six-pounder, to join Lee and Marion in the reduction of Fort Motte, a fortified private residence located near where the Congaree and

25. *Ibid.*, pp. 438, 444, 460, XIX, 910; Eaton to Sumner, 13 April 1781, Preston Davie Collection, Southern Historical Collection; Edward Carrington to Greene, 24 April 1781, Nathanael Greene Papers, William L. Clements Library.

26. *State Records*, XV, 440–41; Eaton to Sumner, 17 April 1781, Jethro Sumner Papers, Southern Historical Collection.

27. Eaton to Greene, 17 April 1781, William Pierce to Eaton, 18 April 1781, Eaton to Greene, 29 April 1781, Nathanael Greene Papers, William L. Clements Library.

Wateree came together to form the Santee River. This mansion, belonging to Mrs. Rebecca Motte, was situated on a commanding knoll and had been strongly fortified by a stockade, moat, and abatis. Its importance lay in the fact that it was a primary depot on the British line of communications between Charleston and the posts in the interior. The fort was garrisoned by Captain John McPherson and 150 infantry. A small detachment of dragoons, carrying dispatches from Camden to Charleston, had joined McPherson upon the approach of Lee and Marion on May 8.

Regular siege procedures were initiated, much of the work on the earthworks done by slaves from neighboring plantations. On May 10 surrender summons were sent in. McPherson refused. That evening word was received that Rawdon had evacuated Camden, and beacon fires on distant hills conveyed the good news to those in Fort Motte that help was on the way. This intelligence forced the besiegers to abandon regular siege operations.

It was decided to burn the defenders out by shooting fire arrows onto the roof of the main building within the stockade. Mrs. Motte, after viewing the crude bow and arrows that had been prepared, presented Lee with a "bow and its apparatus imported from India." Another flag was sent in demanding McPherson's surrender. Once again it was refused.

Lee and Marion brought their troops forward into the lines for an assault. Flaming arrows arched their way onto the roof of the mansion. McPherson sent men to rip off the shingles. Finley's six-pounder drove them off, "and no other effort to stop the flames being practicable, McPherson hung out the white flag."

Shortly after the surrender, Greene, accompanied by a small escort, rode into camp. Marion was ordered to take Georgetown, while Lee was ordered to take Fort Granby on the Congaree. Although Henry Lee, in his *Memoirs*, did not mention Eaton and his men, Greene noted that they were "indefatigable in proceeding the siege."[28]

Greene was ready to take the field again with his army. Conditions throughout South Carolina were favorable. On May 10 Rawdon had evacuated Camden because the "whole interior country had revolted." Lee and Marion had taken Fort Watson on the Santee and had forced the surrender of Fort Motte. Marion had moved down against Georgetown and there was little doubt that that post would soon fall. Thomas Sumter, who liked to conduct a war of his own

28. Lee, *Memoirs of the War in the Southern Department*, pp. 347–48; *State Records*, XXI, 93; Greene to Samuel Huntington, 14 May 1781, Nathanael Greene Papers, William L. Clements Library.

without interference from Greene or any other commanding general, had forced the surrender of the garrison at Orangeburgh on May 11. Andrew Pickens was operating in the vicinity of Augusta. An intercepted letter revealed that Rawdon had ordered Colonel John Cruger to evacuate Ninety Six. Greene decided to force the surrender of that place to prevent Cruger's garrison from reinforcing the British in Charleston. Lee swept up the Congaree to take Fort Granby, where "His gallantry and elegant military address frightened the garrison into an immediate surrender." The hard-riding Lee's next assignment was to assist Pickens and Elijah Clarke in the reduction of Augusta before joining Greene at Ninety Six.[29]

Eaton's command was now reformed as light infantry and on May 16 was ordered to escort the artillery to Lee. Contact was made with Lee at noon on May 17, shortly after the fall of Fort Granby. Lee pushed the men hard for three days, for word had been received that the annual presents from the king to the local Indians had arrived at Fort Galpin on the north side of the Savannah River, twelve miles from Augusta. Not only would these articles be useful to the American army, but Colonel Brown, the commandant at Augusta, had detached two infantry companies to man the stockade at Fort Galpin. Mounting as many of his infantry as he could accommodate behind his dragoons, Lee pushed on to Galpin, with Eaton and the remainder of the Legion posted in such a manner as to prevent help from Augusta. Fort Galpin, sometimes referred to as Fort Dreadnought, proved to be a surprisingly easy conquest. Lee, joined by some South Carolina and Georgia militia, made a feint at the stockade. When the defenders sallied out, Captain Michael Rudolph rushed in with the Legion infantry from another direction and took possession of the post. The enemy lost only three or four men, while Lee's only casualty was one man who died "from the heat of the weather."[30]

Major Eaton made his junction with Brigadier General (of the South Carolina militia) Andrew Pickens at Cherokee Ponds, six miles from Augusta. With the fall of Fort Galpin, Lee detached Major Joseph Eggleston, with the cavalry, to join Pickens and Clarke. But Eggleston was a man whose temperament was similar to that of his commanding officer, for no sooner had he reached the outskirts of

29. *State Records*, XV, 460; Lee, *Memoirs of the War in the Southern Department*, pp. 350–52; Lee to Greene, 28 April 1781, Nathanael Greene Papers, William L. Clements Library; *Magazine of American History*, VII (December, 1881), 432; Greene to Lee, 16 May 1781, Greene Papers, Duke University.

30. Lee, *Memoirs of the War in the Southern Department*, pp. 354–55; Hugh McCall, *The History of Georgia* (Savannah, 1811–16), II, 370–71; Lee to Greene, 22 May 1781, Revolutionary Collection, Duke University.

Augusta than he sent in a flag to Colonel Thomas Brown, the commandant, informing him of the proximity of a formidable force, the investment of Ninety Six, and urging that resistance was futile and that blood not be spilled needlessly. In this move Eggleston, perhaps acting on Lee's orders, was usurping the authority of Pickens, and probably this was why Brown treated the summons with contempt. He refused to give a written answer to the demand, and told the messenger that he wished no further communications on the subject of surrender.[31]

Augusta lay on a level plain on the south side of the Savannah River, washed by the river on the east and to the west terminating in thick woods, interspersed with swamps and lazy streams. Fort Cornwallis, the town's principal defensive work, stood near the center of town. It was a well-constructed fortification that not only commanded the river but had a field of fire of eight hundred yards in every direction. On the west a deep gully ran from the river. On the west bank of this ravine, and about half a mile west of Fort Cornwallis, stood Fort Grierson, named for the Tory who commanded its garrison.[32]

On May 23, 1781, the ground was reconnoitered by the high-ranking officers and a plan of attack decided upon. The basic strategy was to dislodge Grierson and intercept his troops should they attempt to withdraw to Fort Cornwallis. Pickens and Clarke were to attack from the northwest with their South Carolina and Georgia militia, while Eaton's North Carolina Continentals, supported by some Georgia militiamen under a Major Jackson were to pass down the river and attack from the northeast. Lee, with his Legion and the artillery, took a position south of the fort to support Eaton and prevent aid from coming to Grierson as well as to block his progress should the Tory forces attempt to retreat to Fort Cornwallis.[33]

Pickens and Eaton pushed hard upon Fort Grierson. Brown, realizing Grierson was in a critical situation, sallied forth from Fort Cornwallis, with a part of the garrison and two fieldpieces. When he saw Lee's command ready to intercept him, Brown fell back into the fort, content to cannonade Lee, who returned the compliment with his six-pounder.

Grierson, realizing that resistance was futile, resolved to throw his men into Fort Cornwallis. Opening the gates, he and his men

31. Lee, *Memoirs of the War in the Southern Department*, p. 355; McCall, *History of Georgia*, II, 372–73.

32. Lee, *Memoirs of the War in the Southern Department*, p. 356; McCall, *History of Georgia*, II, 372.

33. Lee, *Memoirs of the War in the Southern Department*, p. 356; McCall, *History of Georgia*, II, 372.

rushed down the gully to the river bank from where some of his men reached the safety of Fort Cornwallis. Eaton came up with his men and, with Pickens, killed thirty of the enemy and either wounded or captured another forty-five. Two artillery pieces were taken.

Pinkethan Eaton, "who had on all occasions sought the post of danger," was the major casualty for the American forces: he "fell gallantly at the head of his battalion in the moment of victory." Lee and Pickens received intelligence that Eaton was taken prisoner after suffering a wound and was put to death with his own sword. An angry protest deploring this "impious deed" was sent in to Brown.[34]

With Eaton's death, Captain Smith assumed command of the unit under the over-all direction of Pickens. Throughout the remainder of the siege the North Carolina corps "behaved perfectly soldierlike." The primary strategy now was to take Fort Cornwallis by regular siege procedures, a policy dictated by the fact that the Americans had only one piece of artillery. The digging went slowly, and Brown showed no inclination to surrender. Lee proposed the construction of a "Maham Tower." This tower had been originally suggested by Colonel Hezikiah Maham of the South Carolina militia as a means of gaining elevation to bring fire on the defenders of a stockaded position, and had been successfully used in the reduction of Fort Watson in April.[35]

This tower was little more than a square of logs, raised to about thirty feet and built strongly enough to support a six-pounder. It was located behind an old frame house that Brown had left standing near the fort. On the night of May 28, Brown sent out detachments to force the Americans from their works. They were driven back after an obstinate fight. The following night they came out again and once again they were pushed back by a vigorous use of the bayonet. The majority of the North Carolinians missed this engagement since they were stationed near the river with the town between them and the fort. It was felt that with no experienced officer in command that they would not be too effective in positions near the enemy.

The log tower, filled with earth and stones to give it stability, was nearly thirty feet high. Two "rifle citadels" were constructed within thirty yards of the enemy's parapet. On the night of May 31, fearing that Brown would attempt to destroy the tower, Lee and Pickens strengthened their lines. Shortly before midnight the attack came.

34. Lee, *Memoirs of the War in the Southern Department*, p. 357; McCall, *History of Georgia*, II, 374; *State Records*, XV, 481; Pickens to Greene, 25 May 1781, Revolutionary Collection, Duke University; Pickens and Lee to Greene, 5 June 1781, Lloyd Smith Collection, Morristown National Historical Park, Morristown, N. J.

35. Pickens and Lee to Greene, 5 June 1781, Lloyd Smith Collection.

The fighting was fierce on the river side. The North Carolinians, fighting alongside the Legion troops of Captain Michael Rudolph gave the enemy a "warm reception" and drove them back. This move, however, proved to be but a feint, for Brown, with the elite of his garrison, drove out and hit the South Carolina militia from the rear. For awhile Pickens's men held fast, but a bayonet charge drove them out of their trenches and they fell back until Captain Handy of the Maryland Line came up with his regulars and drove the enemy into the fort.[36]

Brown brought his two heaviest artillery pieces to a platform on the bastion opposite the tower and attempted to destroy it. Lee's men worked on, and by June 1 the structure was complete. Finley's six-pounder was manhandled to the top. Under the direction of the artillery captain, the enemy's two heavy guns were dismounted and the defenders of Fort Cornwallis driven to shelter.

Brown now resorted to stratagem. He sent out a Scot sergeant, under the guise of a deserter, to burn the tower if possible. This sergeant reported to Lee and Pickens that the garrison was in good spirits and likely to hold out for some time. He went on to say, however, that he could direct the fire of the six-pounder on the tower so that a well-placed red hot shot would blow up the magazine. Lee was delighted and sent the man to the tower. Upon reflection, he recalled the man and placed him under arrest.

Lee and Pickens, for some unexplained reason, had carelessly allowed the frame house before the tower to stand. Brown had placed a substantial charge of explosives beneath the building, perhaps anticipating Pickens' plan to place riflemen in the upper story of the building to cover a final assault against the fort. During the night of June 3 Pickens examined the house to determine the number of men who could be placed in it the next day. At about three o'clock the following morning the darkness was rent by a shattering blast as Brown, assuming that troops were already in the house, set off the charge. No one was injured.

At daylight on June 4 the troops of Pickens and Lee were stationed in columns around Fort Cornwallis, preparatory to making the final attack. The defenders were given one last chance to surrender. Brown repeated his determination to defend his post "to the last extremity." For some reason, the assault was postponed for a day. At about nine o'clock on June 5 a British officer, under the protection of a flag, came out of Fort Cornwallis with a request that the terms

36. *Ibid.*

granted in a surrender be honorable as a result of Brown's "desire to lessen the distresses of war."[37]

There was some haggling, but Brown was finally persuaded to accept the terms offered by Lee and Pickens. On June 6 the men of the garrison marched out as prisoners of war. One incident marred the victory. An unidentified man rode up to the room in which Grierson was confined and, without dismounting, shot and killed the prisoner. A major in the room ran outside and was shot in the shoulder as the murderer sped away. Although a pursuit was organized the man escaped. Grierson was buried with full military honors. Some whispered that the deed had been done by a North Carolinian who was unhappy at the manner by which Eaton met his death. Yet it seems more likely that the killing was the result of Grierson's past misdeeds, for he had been one of those responsible for the hanging of twenty-nine prisoners after Elijah Clarke's unsuccessful attack on Augusta in September, 1780. Some reports suggested that the killer was Captain Samuel Alexander of the Georgia militia. Greene was to offer a reward of £100 for information leading to the capture of the murderer; no one ever claimed it.[38]

Brown was placed under a tight guard to prevent similar treatment being visited upon him by those who had suffered in the past at the hands of this "fiend of darkness." Shortly afterwards he was paroled and sent to Savannah under guard. Because of the antipathy toward the other prisoners and the fear that the officers would be set upon if they were paroled and allowed to make their way to Savannah, they were sent across the river and escorted to Charleston by way of Ninety Six. A part of the guard was made up of some of the North Carolinians under Captain Smith.[39]

Lee, in response to orders from Greene, marched immediately for Ninety Six. Just as soon as arrangements were made for the transportation of the booty taken at Augusta Pickens and the troops under his command followed.

After he had left Camden Greene had planned to place his army

37. Brown to Pickens, 31 May 1781, Lee and Pickens to Brown, 3 June 1781, Brown to Pickens and Lee, 3 June 1781, Brown to Pickens and Lee, 5 June 1781, Lloyd Smith Collection.

38. Proclamation of Major General Greene, 9 June 1781, Nathanael Greene Papers, William L. Clements Library; Lossing, *Pictorial Field Book of the Revolution*, II, 718.

39. Lee, *Memoirs of the War in the Southern Department*, pp. 363–71; McCall, *History of Georgia*, II, 375–80; Dawson, *Battles of the United States*, I, 375–79; Ward, *War of the Revolution*, II, 814–15; Gibbes, *Documentary History of the American Revolution*, III, 91–92; Pendleton Orderly Book.

between that of Lord Rawdon and the forces of Lee, Sumter, and Marion to protect them as they attacked British outposts. By May 10 he learned that Rawdon, after burning the mill, jail, a number of private houses, and all of his surplus stores, and leaving behind the sick and wounded, both British and American, had evacuated Camden. An intercepted letter to John Harris Cruger, the New York Tory who commanded the post at Ninety Six, contained orders to evacuate that force. This meant that Cruger's men could swell reinforcements for Rawdon. On May 15, after receiving intelligence of the fall of Fort Granby, Greene moved westward toward Ninety Six.[40]

Ninety Six, according to tradition, received its name because it was ninety-six miles from Fort George on the Keowee River. Around this village on a flat plain was a stockade protected by a moat and an abatis. The town jail had been fortified to protect the stream from which the town received its water and was now termed "Fort Holmes." On the bank of the stream opposite the jail were two blockhouses, each of which was surrounded by a stockade and abatis. They were connected with the town by a covered way.

The primary fortification, however, was the Star Fort, nearly two hundred feet in diameter and containing ten salients, or star points. Cruger commanded six hundred tough Tory troops, recruited primarily from New York and New Jersey. There were also a number of South Carolina loyalists under his command.

Greene had nearly twice as many troops as Cruger, but the town was too strongly fortified to be overrun by a direct assault; a siege was the only solution. After his arrival at the town during the night of May 22 Greene spent the hours before daylight in getting his troops to throw up earthworks for a three-gun battery, 130 yards from the enemy fortifications. The work was completed despite a desultory fire by the enemy. The battery opened fire on the enemy redoubt on May 24.[41]

Thaddeus Kosciuszko laid out the siege lines in the classic pattern of European warfare and the troops were set to work digging the first parallel. According to the military niceties of the day, Greene should have paid Cruger the courtesy of summoning him to surrender before launching the actual siege, but Cruger was a Tory and perhaps, in Greene's mind, was not entitled to military courtesies. Cruger was

40. *Year Book of the City of Charleston, 1895* (Charleston, S.C., 1895), pp. 99–100; Gibbes, *Documentary History of the American Revolution*, III, 69–74; Gordon, *History of the Independence of the United States*, IV, 88–89.

41. Kirkwood, *Journal and Orderly Book of Captain Robert Kirkwood*, pp. 18–19.

determined "to teach him to his cost to shew a little more respect." He brought his three three-pounders to a platform opposite the American battery and began to lob shells into the position. That night a party of thirty men put several of the working party to the bayonet, drove off the others, loaded up Negro slaves with American entrenching tools, and retired to the protection of the fort.[42]

This experience had a sobering effect upon Greene's strategy. Kosciuszko was given orders to begin a new parallel at a more respectful distance from the enemy stockade, some 1200 yards away and out of gunshot range. And from this time on, general orders contained the admonition that entrenching tools were to be carefully collected at sunset and deposited at the rear of the artillery. The digging went slowly, but on June 3 the earthworks were far enough along that Greene felt he was able to beat the chamade and send in Otho Williams with a summons for an immediate surrender of the town. Cruger's reply was that "both duty and inclination pointed to the propriety of defending it to the last extremity."[43]

Once again the men began to push their way forward by pick and shovel. An attempt was made to burn the houses within the stockade by the use of fire arrows; Cruger ordered all roofs removed from the buildings. When the trenches reached the spot where Kosciuszko had so optimistically begun digging the first parallel, a new plan was presented: dig a tunnel under the walls, so that a mine could be placed to blow an opening through which the defenders could be rushed. An almost continuous cannonade kept Cruger's men under cover.[44]

On June 8 Henry Lee arrived from Augusta. Later that same day Pickens came in with the prisoners. Perhaps to impress the enemy, Greene allowed Lee to indulge himself in a bit of arrogance that one British officer declared to be the "gratification of a little mind." The men of the Augusta garrison, preceded by fife and drum and with the British colors reversed, were marched by in full view of the defenders of Ninety Six.[45]

Lee, after surveying the situation, boldly suggested to Greene that the siege had begun on the wrong side, opposite the strongest works. Lee was then stationed on the far, or east, side and Greene

---

42. Stedman, *History of the . . . American War*, II, 408; Mackenzie, *Strictures on Lt. Col. Tarleton's History*, pp. 146–48.

43. Pendleton Orderly Book; Mackenzie, *Strictures on Lt. Col. Tarleton's History*, pp. 149–50; Lee, *Memoirs of the War in the Southern Department*, p. 372; *Year Book: City of Charleston, 1899*, p. 104.

44. Stedman, *History of the . . . American War*, II, 409–10; Pendleton Orderly Book.

45. Mackenzie, *Strictures on Lt. Col. Tarleton's History*, pp. 154–55.

ordered him to begin digging parallels and attack the water supply of the fort as quickly as possible. The North Carolina troops were brigaded with the infantry of Lee's Legion. On June 9 Cruger sent out two groups, one against each position. The mouth of the mine leading to the star fort was discovered. One of the casualties in the brief fight here was Colonel Kosciuszko, who received a painful bayonet wound while inspecting the works. On the left those sent out against Lee's position fell in with a working party, a number of whom were put to the bayonet and the officer in charge taken prisoner. So successful were these forays that from this time on Cruger sent out similar raiding parties as a means of keeping the Americans off balance.[46]

A dispatch from Thomas Sumter received on June 11 contained discouraging information. A British fleet with reinforcements had arrived at Charleston on June 3. Troops had been quickly disembarked and Rawdon was now on his march to the relief of Ninety Six. Greene increased the tempo of the siege. A sergeant, leading nine privates of the Legion infantry, slipped toward the stockade under the cover of a storm and an artillery barrage, their mission to blow a hole in the wall. Six men, including the sergeant, were shot down; the other four made it back to their own lines.[47]

For Cruger, the siege had reached a critical stage. Lee's position on the east endangered the water supply, since many of those who were sent out were shot. An attempt to dig a well inside the fort proved fruitless. Naked Negroes were sent out under the cover of darkness to bring in water for the garrison. But there was never enough to satisfy the men in the sultry June weather. A Maham tower was erected by Greene, forcing the defenders of the fort to throw up a wall of sandbags, but with loopholes to return the fire.[48]

On June 17 a countryman rode leisurely through the American camp. Thinking him to be a sightseer, no one paid much attention to him until, when at a point nearest the stockade gate, he put spurs to his horse, shouting and waving aloft a paper as he raced toward the gate. Hastily fired shots missed him as he rode into the stockade. Happy shouts and the rolling thunder of a *feu de joie* signified to

46. *Ibid.*, pp. 156–57; Pendleton Orderly Book; *Year Book: City of Charleston, 1899*, p. 109; Miecislaus Haiman, *Kosciuszko in the American Revolution* (New York, 1953), pp. 113–14.
47. Mackenzie, *Strictures on Lt. Col. Tarleton's History*, p. 158; Lee, *Memoirs of the War in the Southern Department*, pp. 373–74; Gibbes, *Documentary History of the American Revolution*, III, 89–90.
48. Stedman, *History of the . . . American War*, II, 412.

Greene that this bold messenger had brought the news of Rawdon's relief column.[49]

Greene was faced with two alternatives: to abandon the siege and march to meet Rawdon in open battle or storm the works of Ninety Six. Though inclined to the former, the knowledge that he had only half as many regulars as Rawdon led prudence to dictate to his instincts. And the time factor decreed an immediate mass assault on Ninety Six. The cavalry of William Washington and Henry Lee were ordered out to join Thomas Sumter, its mission to initiate skirmishes and hamper Rawdon's progress. Then, if Greene's attack were successful, he could turn to make a junction with Sumter and oppose Rawdon in force.[50]

Ninety Six was to be attacked in two simultaneous assaults by Lieutenant Colonel Richard Campbell with a detachment of Virginia and Maryland Continentals. On the west the attack was to be made by the Legion infantry, the North Carolinians and the Delaware Continentals.

The signal gun was fired at noon on June 18. Captain Michael Rudolph led his troops forward, crossed the moat, and after an hour of fighting forced his way into Fort Holmes, the former jail. When the enemy fled, Rudolph halted his men to await the developments arising out of Campbell's attack.[51]

Campbell ran into a stout and bloody resistance. Under the cover of fire from the artillery and from the trenches and tower he moved forward. Gaps appeared in the abatis as the axmen did their jobs among the tangle of fallen trees. Fascines were thrown into the ditch to make a bridge for the infantry. Men equipped with hooks began pulling down sandbags from the top of the parapet. The defenders could not fire down upon the attackers without exposing themselves to the riflemen on the tower.

Two parties of Oliver De Lancey's loyalist regiment slipped out of the sally port, turned in opposite directions and came in with bayonets upon the flanks of the axmen and hookmen. The fighting was bloody. When the leaders of the forlorn hope were struck down, the survivors fell back to the American lines. The battle was over.

Rawdon had swept wide on his march to Ninety Six and had avoided Sumter. Now he was too near Ninety Six for Greene to or-

49. Lee, *Memoirs of the War in the Southern Department*, p. 374; Stedman, *History of the . . . American War*, II, 413.

50. Lee, *Memoirs of the War in the Southern Department*, p. 375; *Year Book: City of Charleston, 1899*, pp. 106–7; Pendleton Orderly Book.

51. Kirkwood, *Journal and Orderly Book of Captain Robert Kirkwood*, p. 19.

ganize and execute another assault. After ordering a withdrawal of his troops because of the "Circumstances of War," Greene sent in a flag requesting a truce to bury his dead. Cruger refused. The Americans had lost 185 men killed and wounded, while British casualties numbered 85.[52]

Greene began his withdrawal on the evening of June 19 and had cleared the area by the following day. On June 21 Rawdon's relief column arrived. He pursued Greene as far as Fish Dam Ford on Broad River before turning back.[53]

The siege had proved that such operations were not listed among Greene's better military talents, nor was his army suited for such action. He would not attempt siege warfare again.

52. Lee, *Memoirs of the War in the Southern Department*, pp. 375–79; Mackenzie, *Strictures on Lt. Col. Tarleton's History*, pp. 156–60; Pendleton Orderly Book; *State Records*, XV, 497; Greene to President of Congress, 20 June 1781, Nathanael Greene Papers, William L. Clements Library.

53. Pendleton Orderly Book; John Armstrong to Sumner, n.d., Jethro Sumner Papers, Southern Historical Collection.

Chapter 18
Eutaw Springs

"... a Confidence
which does honour to young Soldiers."

As long as Cornwallis remained in North Carolina Jethro Sumner had been able to do little to recruit Continental troops. Benedict Arnold was rampaging his way through Virginia, and no one could promise that he would not turn south to make a junction with Lord Cornwallis. Sumner could do little other than wait. Greene's dispatches, on the other hand, seemed to assume that Sumner had a considerable body of North Carolina Continentals under his command.

Little support was received from the state administration. Governor Nash was attempting to bring together a legislature to supply the funds and authority to actively support both Greene and Sumner. Even after the assembly met at Wake Court House, it provided little aid, for "we have gone (as usual) the wrong track, nothing will ever set us right, we are a cowardly revengeful set of wretches too contemptible to merit a blessing or exact a damn."[1]

There had been difficulty in establishing a rendezvous for the

---

1. Abner Nash to Greene, 7 April 1781, Autographs of Americans Collection, Pierpont Morgan Library, New York, N.Y.; Robert Smith to James Iredell, 3 July 1781, Charles E. Johnston Collection.

drafted Continentals. Smallpox was still raging in Halifax and Hillsborough, making it dangerous to bring together a large concentration
of troops. There were other disadvantages: Hillsborough and its environs had been devastated by two armies, while Halifax was on the
route of the British army should Cornwallis decide to march to Virginia. Harrisburg in Granville County was designated as a collection
point for recruits. There were not enough Continental officers on active duty to aid the militia in marching in volunteers and draftees to
the central collecting stations. Some Continental officers were still
serving in the east with Alexander Lillington's militia brigade, who
had been stationed in Duplin County to observe the movements of
the enemy. Others, including Hardy Murfree, were collecting and im-
pressing supplies and provisions for Greene's army. So scattered were
the Continental officers that it became difficult to coordinate their activities. Arms were scarce. Allen Jones was sent into Virginia on a procurement mission but discovered that all spare weapons in that state
had already been sent to Greene. At this time Sumner had only
enough muskets to outfit sixty men.[2]

Once Cornwallis left Wilmington in late April, Sumner found it
difficult to carry out Greene's fluid plan to march south to join him,
or north to make a junction with Lafayette, depending upon the
route his Lordship took. At the time, Sumner did not have enough
men under his command to comply with either alternative. He was
constantly in the saddle, attempting to consolidate the draftees into a
single group. Many of those Continental officers who might have
aided in the organization had been forced to hide out when the British marched through their communities. Further complications became evident when the Tories began disrupting lines of supply and
communications.[3]

Near the end of May Greene's dispatches carried contradictory
orders. Sumner was to join Lafayette and Steuben in Virginia as early
as possible, but not until all horses were removed from the path of the
enemy. But almost immediately the general sent word for the draftees
from the Salisbury and Halifax districts to join him at once. This last
order appears to have been seized upon as an expedient to provide an

2. *State Records*, XV, 442–50, 456; Sumner to Greene, 8 April 1781, Greene
to Sumner, 11 April 1781, Benjamin Seawell to Greene, 21 April 1781, Jethro
Sumner Papers, Southern Historical Collection; Murfree to Nash, 8 June 1781,
Governors' Papers.

3. *State Records*, XV, 440–61; Greene to Sumner, 21 April 1781, Benjamin
Seawell to Sumner, 21 April 1781, Greene to Sumner, 23 May 1781, Jethro Sumner
Papers, Southern Historical Collection; Greene to Steuben, 23 May 1781, Steuben
Papers.

escort for Greene's heavy baggage and several artillery pieces that had been stored on the Catawba River and were now needed for the siege of Ninety Six.[4]

Jethro Sumner never knew the exact number of men supposed to be under his command. Frequent desertions led to fluctuating returns from the collection points. Because of the unpopularity of the draft law, local courts were reluctant to hand out severe sentences, and chose only to "chastise" guilty culprits. In some units as many as one-third of the draftees deserted. The number of desertions, it was said, was increased by the practice of Tories who volunteered for service in the Continental army and then, with the bounty money safely in their pockets, slipped away home. Many of those who remained were poor examples of military men. John Armstrong complained that he was "sorry that I ever had anything to do with such sloathful Officers and neglected soldiers; there is a number of them almost Nacked. . . . When cold weather sets in they must be discharged for no Officer would pretend to put them on duty." There were cries from the officers in the field that something be done about the high rate of desertion and demanding that "an Example of Death must be made. Genl , and that shortly of Such offenders." The situation had grown so shameful that Sumner apologized to Greene, "I assure you, Sir, that it is with great mortification to me . . . at this alarming season to make you a return of my Strength in its present Low Ebb."[5]

High Rock Ford on Haw River had been designated as a supply depot and by early June the supply situation seemed to have improved, although there were never enough wagons to bring in the provisions collected. Most of the available wagons had been placed in service hauling supplies to Greene's army. And now draftees and volunteers had begun to come into Camp Harrisburg in a steady stream. Sumner organized one regiment and expected to have another organized by the end of June when he intended to march them into Virginia, where he hoped that they could be supplied with arms. The most critical personnel shortage was still that of Continental officers, for now many were sulking "by reason of the Shamefull neglect of the State, we seem rather a burthen than a benefit to them, we are tossed to and fro like a ship in a storm."[6]

4. *State Records*, XV, 465, 468; Greene to Sumner, 23 May 1781, John Armstrong to Sumner, 26 May 1781, Jethro Sumner Papers, Southern Historical Collection.

5. *State Records*, XV, 469–70, 504–5; John Armstrong to Sumner, 1 July 1781, Jethro Sumner Papers, Southern Historical Collection; Sumner to Greene, 15 May 1781, Frederic Kirkwood Collection, Columbia University, New York, N.Y.

6. *State Records*, XV, 473, 475–76, 481, 494–96; John Armstrong to Sumner,

On June 29 an express rider rode into Sumner's camp at Harrisburg bringing dispatches from Stephen Drayton. Drayton had been sent north by Greene, not only with dispatches but with a mission of securing greater aid from the state government of North Carolina. He had stopped at Hillsborough long enough to write Sumner and send on Greene's dispatches before riding on to Wake Court House where he expected to confer with Thomas Burke, the recently elected governor of North Carolina. One dispatch, dated June 20, ordered Sumner to join Greene's southern army. The troops at Camp Harrisburg were immediately placed under marching orders. There were nearly five hundred men under Sumner's command but only about two hundred had weapons. An express to Steuben requested that three hundred muskets be delivered as quickly as possible to Guilford Court House.[7]

Because of the possibility that the British might strike into North Carolina after he had marched, Sumner took precautionary moves designed to protect the state. General John Butler was ordered to call out the militia from Orange, Granville, and Caswell counties and station them in the vicinity of Boyd's Ferry on the Dan River, while a group of Granville riflemen were posted at Kemp's Ferry on the Roanoke. These river passes were fortified with earthworks and abatis.[8]

On July 1 Sumner marched southward by way of Hillsborough and Salisbury, a large part of his command made up of "delinquents & old Continental Soldiers." Uniforms had been hastily sewn together from all of the osnaburg and other coarse cloth that could be gathered. It was a slow march. Time was needlessly spent foraging for food since the county commissioners had been negligent in collecting provisions as ordered. Desertions were so frequent that the general approved the sentences of a court-martial that condemned two deserters to death. One was shot, the other reprieved at the last moment; that evening three men deserted. The army had marched no farther than Salisbury by July 10. Four days later enough arms had been gathered for three hundred men to be outfitted with good arms and cartouche boxes, but none had bayonets.[9]

---

1 July 1781, Jethro Sumner Papers, Southern Historical Collection; Sumner to Nash, 21 June 1781, Governors' Papers.

7. *State Records*, XV, 496–97, 499–501; Sumner to Steuben, 29 June 1781, Stephen Drayton to Sumner, 29 June 1781, Jethro Sumner Papers, Southern Historical Collection; Greene to Sumner, 20 June 1781, Greene Papers, Duke University.

8. Sumner to Butler, 10 July 1781, Jethro Sumner Papers, Southern Historical Collection; Thomas Burke to Greene, 3 September 1781, Lloyd Smith Collection.

9. *State Records*, XV, 506, 528–29, 530–31.

This detachment was placed under the command of Lieutenant Colonel John Baptiste Ashe, who on July 14 was ordered to march the men to Greene's headquarters in the high hills of the Santee in South Carolina. Once with Greene, Ashe was to combine his group with the draftees from the Salisbury district who had earlier marched with John Armstrong and the remnants of Eaton's command into the First Regiment of the North Carolina Line, to be the first of the four regiments recently authorized for the state by the Continental Congress. Sumner remained at Salisbury to form incoming draftees into the Second Regiment.[10]

By July 18 Ashe had marched no farther than Charlotte and was complaining that he was "much plagued" by his troops. He was forced to remain at Charlotte for several days because of the lack of wagons and the "bad mismanagement of the Staff at this place." From Charlotte south there was little prospect of subsistence, with one recent arrival from Greene's army reporting that "when I arrived at Charlotte, I was near 40 hours without having taken bread."[11]

Within ten days Sumner was regretting that he had sent Ashe forward. Lafayette reported that Cornwallis had evacuated Williamsburg in Virginia and that the British troops were embarking at James town perhaps to sail to Charleston. Greene guessed that Tarleton would lead his Legion, along with other mounted troops of the army, through North Carolina on a dash to join the British in South Carolina. Recruits who might have been sent to the southern army were now employed in removing supplies and livestock from Tarleton's possible route. Major Thomas Hogg, a Continental officer, was sent out with militia to subdue those disaffected who showed an inclination to aid the enemy should Tarleton enter the state.[12]

Tarleton's southward march did not materialize. Sweeping through southwest Virginia on a destructive raid, he turned back to join Cornwallis on the Chesapeake. Now the general impression was that the British in Virginia would soon sail for New York. Sumner could now devote his efforts to sending aid to Greene, but there were continuing problems to complicate even the smallest task.[13]

10. *Ibid.*, pp. 533, 541; *A Sidelight on History: Being the Letters of James McHenry, aide-de-camp of the Marquis de Lafayette to Thomas Sim Lee, Governor of Maryland, Written During the Yorktown Campaign, 1781* (Southampton, N.Y., 1931), pp. 30–33; Sumner to Greene, 25 June 1781, Jethro Sumner Papers, Southern Historical Collection.

11. *State Records*, XV, 546; *South Carolina Historical and Genealogical Magazine*, XXXVIII (July, 1937), 79.

12. *State Records*, XV, 541, 545–46, 547–48, 549, 550, 551, 566, 572; Greene to Sumner, 23 July 1781, Jethro Sumner Papers, Southern Historical Collection.

13. *State Records*, XV, 589.

Those Continental officers who had come into the field were now both confused and angry. Some were unable to stand the financial sacrifices and resigned their commissions. Others who had expected to command regiments under the new establishments, had discovered only paper organizations and had gone home in bitter disappointment. Among those who found the situation confusing was Colonel Gideon Lamb, who at this time was engaged in marching draftees to collecting points. To Sumner he penned a plaintive "Pray let me know Where, Who, and What I am." Sumner sent him into the Edenton district to apprehend deserters and delinquents and forward draftees to the army. These orders he "cheerfully Obey'd, as far as in my Power," even though he was beginning to suffer from the "bilious fever" of which he was to die four months later.[14]

With Craig protecting them, Tories were now roaming as far inland as Cross Creek and were beginning to take revenge for the real or imagined wrongs they had suffered in the past. The militia, when it was called out against these marauders, was so ruthless in its own retribution that Craig was led to complain to both William Hooper and Abner Nash that the loyalists were "being put to death without trial or examination many hours and sometimes days after they were taken, by order of Militia officers commanding parties and acting under authority of your present Government."[15]

Despite this critical situation within the state and because of the positive orders of Greene, Sumner marched the Continentals under his command for South Carolina around the middle of July. He was near Hanging Rock, South Carolina, when a warning was received from Lafayette that Cornwallis now appeared as though he might turn south again and Sumner's aid was requested in slowing the British army so that Lafayette's army could hit him from the rear. Before resuming his march to join Greene Sumner pointed out that the North Carolina militia stationed at the principal fords could perform that service.[16]

It was shortly after the first of August when Sumner reached the southern army. His people were a welcome addition, although Greene seemed disappointed in the general response of the state of North Carolina. This was not entirely the fault of the state administration.

14. *Ibid.*, pp. 562–63, 571, 578, 672–73; Gideon Lamb to Sumner, 22 July 1781, Jethro Sumner Papers, Southern Historical Collection.

15. Craig to Hooper, 20 July 1781, Jethro Sumner Papers, Southern Historical Collection; Craig to Nash, 20 June 1781, Governors' Papers.

16. William Pierce to Sumner, 27 June 1781, Jethro Sumner Papers, N.C. Dept. Arch. & Hist.; *State Records*, XV, 501; Sumner to Lafayette, 27 June 1781, Jethro Sumner Papers, Southern Historical Collection.

Isaac Shelby had raised over seven hundred riflemen and was on the march for Greene's army when a dispatch arrived from Andrew Pickens. Pickens seemed to have taken it upon himself to determine the future course of action for the southern army. Pickens reported that Rawdon, after the relief of Ninety Six, had fallen back to Orangeburgh and probably would retreat all the way to Charleston, and he implied that Greene intended pursuing the British to the very gates of Charleston. Short on supplies, and with the weather too warm for an extended forced march by his men, Shelby allowed them to return to their homes until there was further word from Greene.[17]

Pickens and Thomas Sumter also had been responsible for the reduction of the North Carolina representation in still another manner. After Eaton's death these two militia leaders had recruited men under a procedure known as "Sumter's law." Because South Carolina had no regular government and no Continentals in the field, and because the militia could be called out for sixty days at a time, Sumter had proposed that "State troops" be enlisted for ten months, receiving confiscated slaves as enlistment bonuses and pay. Not only were Eaton's men recruited into these South Carolina units, but Colonel William Polk had been sent into Mecklenburg and Rowan counties to enlist men as South Carolina State troops. Complications initiated by this practice were long-lasting; suits were later brought against a number of North Carolina natives who had taken advantage of this offer. Not until 1788 did South Carolina masters cease suing for a return of their slaves, and then only after a North Carolina law made it mandatory that the judgment in such cases be for the defendant.[18]

Greene had been awaiting the arrival of reinforcements from North Carolina before moving against the enemy. Just the week before Sumner's arrival, William Pierce, Greene's aide, had written, "Mischief is a-brewing by the General, who keeps us in constant hot water, and never fails to make us fight."[19]

Sumner formed his men as a Second Regiment under John Armstrong and joined them with Ashe's command as the North Carolina brigade. Francis Malmedey (or Malmady, Malmédy), the Frenchman who held a North Carolina militia commission, came into camp with

---

17. *South Carolina Historical and Genealogical Magazine*, XVI (July, 1915), 104; *North Carolina Historical Review*, III (April, 1927), 211.

18. *South Carolina Historical and Genealogical Magazine*, XVIII (July, 1917), 142n; *The Public Acts of the General Assembly of North Carolina* (New Bern, 1804), p. 447; Gibbs, *Documentary History of the American Revolution*, III, 48.

19. *Magazine of American History*, VII (December, 1881), 436; William Pierce to St. George Tucker, 23 July 1781, Tucker-Coleman Papers; Graham, *Life of General Daniel Morgan*, pp. 395–96.

nearly four hundred militiamen. Others from North Carolina were supposed to be on the march under John Butler, but many of those who had begun the march with Butler refused to cross the boundaries of their militia districts, declaring that state law did not require them to leave their homes undefended. Greene wasted no time in preparing the new arrivals for combat. Every day, from early morning until the torrid August sun drove them from the field, the troops underwent drills and battlefield training. Fire discipline was instilled by the regular firing of blank cartridges only upon the command of the officers.[20]

Some of the North Carolina officers spent their time in sitting on an almost continuous court-martial. A number of the rank and file of the line were brought before them on various charges. One B. Holley pleaded not guilty to a charge of desertion but was sentenced to fifty lashes. Sampson Sykes was found guilty of forging Lieutenant Colonel Ashe's name to a pass and received a hundred lashes. On the other hand, John Sullivan, charged with desertion, claimed that he was an indentured servant and had been kept from the field by his master. After hearing his story the court decided that he had suffered enough at the hands of his master and allowed him to rejoin his regiment. Francis Weston had been taken prisoner at Charleston and had joined the British army to improve his lot but asked for mercy in that he had acted only as a hostler and had not carried arms. Although he was found guilty and sentenced to death, the court recommended mercy. Greene pardoned the man.[21]

Others were not so fortunate. John Rogers of the North Carolina Line was hanged with two other deserters from the Maryland Line in the late afternoon of August 10. Josias Lahier was executed for bearing arms against the United States. At the same court Josiah Saylers of the North Carolina Line was sentenced to death by hanging but several of the officers of the brigade came forward to plead his case, asserting that Saylers had returned to camp of his own accord, that he had vowed to atone for his past misconduct, and that he had three brothers who were now serving with the southern army. They begged that he be pardoned. Greene agreed with them.[22]

The greatest topic of conversation in camp, however, was the case of Colonel Isaac Hayne of South Carolina. Hayne had been cap-

---

20. Theodore Thayer, *Nathanael Greene: Strategist of the Revolution* (New York, 1960), p. 373; Pendleton Orderly Book; Francis Locke to Greene, 25 August 1781, Revolutionary Collection, Duke University; Guilford Dudley to John Butler, 5 July 1781, Miscellaneous Papers, 1697–1912.
21. Pendleton Orderly Book.
22. *Ibid.*

tured in May, 1780, when Charleston fell, and had been paroled to his plantation. When ordered to join the British army in 1781, he considered his parole invalidated and he took the field as a militia colonel. Later, when recaptured by the British, he had been brought before a court of enquiry on charges of espionage and treason and then, without further trial, was hanged in Charleston on August 4, 1781. Greene felt that something had to be done, especially after receiving a petition signed by all of the officers of his army, protesting Hayne's treatment. The mood of the army was such that the militia might well desert in body. He thereupon issued a proclamation promising retaliation upon regular British officers and not "those deluded inhabitants who have joined their Army." This move quieted somewhat the clamor for revenge and allowed the general to get on with the war.[23]

By this time, Greene had his army on the march. Lee, whom Greene sometimes referred to as his "right eye," had been scouring the countryside and sending back information since early August. On the thirteenth he suggested that the enemy, lethargic from the constant heat and humidity, was in no mood to fight. If given the opportunity, he said, many of the British soldiers would desert. He urged an attack upon Lieutenant Colonel Alexander Stewart, the successor to Lord Rawdon in command of the area. Stewart, reported Lee, had found a Negro who was willing to lead the British along a secret trail through the swamps to attack Greene's encampment in the high hills of the Santee. There were also rumors that Lord Cornwallis was returning to Charleston.[24]

Stewart had taken a position on the west side of the Congaree near the point where that stream was joined by the Wateree to form the Santee. Under his command were two thousand men, the greater part of them British regulars, supported by three artillery pieces. He had been in bivouac at Center Swamp, near the now-deserted Fort Motte, only sixteen miles from Greene's camp, but the two rivers lay between them and were now swollen into lakes by recent rains. The rivers, Stewart felt, would serve as a protection against surprise. He sent out few patrols and allowed his army to take its ease. Greene

23. Officers of the Army to Genl. Greene, 20 August 1781, British Headquarters Papers; Greene to Lafayette, 26 August 1781, Proclamation, 26 August 1781, Nathanael Greene Papers, William L. Clements Library; Moore, *Diary of the American Revolution*, II, 474–75; Lee, *Memoirs of the War in the Southern Department*, pp. 449–62.

24. Lee to Greene, 17 August 1781, Siege of Yorktown Papers, Pierpont Morgan Library, New York, N.Y.; Lee to Greene, 20 August 1781, Nathanael Greene Papers, William L. Clements Library.

seemed to feel the same way, for he received no intelligence when Stewart moved his command down to Eutaw Springs to better protect the supply trains from Charleston.[25]

Because of the drowned canebrakes on either side of the rivers, Greene was forced to take a circuitous route to make contact with Stewart. By August 22, he was ready to move, with nearly 2,200 men under his command. At five the following morning he moved out with the two regiments of Sumner's North Carolina Brigade leading the way. Part of the brigade was detached to the rear as a "Bullock Guard," whose duty it was to act as herdsmen for the beef that had been brought along on the hoof and were to be slaughtered as needed. The afternoon before he broke camp Greene had drawn up his army to practice firing blank ammunition, for one of the greatest disadvantages of commanding raw troops in the field was the indiscriminate firing before proper commands were given.[26]

Greene marched only during the cooler hours of the early morning or the late afternoon. At Camden he established a "Flying Hospital" for the men who had fallen ill along the way. Because of the desperate need for men, an officer was left behind to bring on "all the convalescents who will be able to march or who may be in a fair way of recovery." When the troops halted for any length of time they were drilled in battle techniques. On August 30, after a march of ninety miles, they reached Howell's Ferry on the Congaree. All invalids and convalescents were left here to guard the heavy baggage and tents. The soldiers were allowed to take only their camp kettles and provisions from Howell's Ferry on. The militia was issued twenty rounds of ammunition per man, the Continentals thirty. The men were confident, many agreeing with Otho Williams's comment, "If Colonel Stewart . . . thinks proper to risk an action, he will be beaten."[27]

It was at Howell's Ferry that Greene learned that Stewart had moved to Eutaw Springs. Several days were spent at Fort Motte, awaiting the arrival of Francis Marion and his troops, who had been carrying on partisan operations in the vicinity of Charleston. The men spent their time resting, repairing weapons, washing clothing, and being drilled in basic warfare. By August 15, the army was at Stouteman's plantation of Maybrick's Creek, with Greene making final preparations and practicing deployments as outlined in his battle

25. Stewart to Cornwallis, 15 August 1781, Cornwallis Papers, PRO 30/11/70.
26. Pendleton Orderly Book.
27. *Ibid*; Osmond Tiffany, *A Sketch of the Life and Services of Gen. Otho Williams* (Baltimore, 1851), p. 23; Merritt, *Calendar of the Otho Williams Papers*, pp. 48–49.

plan. On the night of September 7, after a twenty-mile march, the southern army was encamped at Burdell's plantation, seven miles from Eutaw Springs. That day Greene had been joined by 100 additional North Carolina Continentals under Major Reading Blount. Sumner, by placing some of the more experienced men among the new recruits, was able to enlarge his brigade to three regiments under Ashe, Armstrong, and Blount. Just the day before Greene had been joined by the South Carolina brigade of Francis Marion, bringing his total effective strength up to 2,300. General orders that night stated that "This Army will March at 4 oClock tomorrow Morning by the right to attack the Enemy."[28]

Stewart, feeling secure in his comfortable bivouac, allowed his intelligence to lag and had no word of Greene's approach. Eutaw Springs was a delightful spot near Nelson's Ferry, just off the road leading to Monck's Corner. It had received its name because of two springs that boiled up from an underground stream and then flowed into Eutaw Creek. The creek ran between steep banks covered with heavy thickets of blackjack oak until it emptied into the Santee near the ferry. Near the head of the creek stood a fine brick house of two stories and an attic, looking out over a cleared area of some eight acres. This clearing was bisected by the east-west river road, which, just beyond the house, forked off toward Charleston, sixty miles away. Between the house and the creek there was a palisaded garden. Little underbrush grew beneath the great oaks and cypresses in the woods surrounding the clearing. Stewart's encampment lay within the clearing. About a hundred years earlier this land had been the site of a battle between the Indians and whites, and in the field there was a mound, "said to have been erected over the bodies of the brave Indians who fell in defence of their country."[29]

On the morning of September 8 at four in the morning Greene broke camp and set his men in motion toward Eutaw Springs. They marched in four columns. Lee's Legion led the way, followed by the South Carolina state troops under Lieutenant Colonel John Henderson. The second column consisted of the North and South Carolina militia under Malmedy, Pickens, and Marion. The third was made up of the three Continental brigades, the Marylanders under Otho Williams, the Virginians under Lieutenant Colonel Richard Camp-

---

28. Pendleton Orderly Book; William Hooper to James Iredell, 1 October 1781, Iredell Papers; Seymour, *A Journal of the Southern Expedition*, pp. 30–31; Kirkwood, *Journal and Orderly Book of Captain Robert Kirkwood*, pp. 22–23; *Virginia Magazine of History and Biography*, LI (April, 1943), 147.

29. Dawson, *Battles of the United States*, I, 712; *Graham's Magazine* (December, 1847), p. 258; Tiffany, *Otho Williams*, p. 26.

bell, and the North Carolinians under Jethro Sumner. The fourth group held Washington's cavalry and Kirkwood's little band of Delaware Continentals who were to act as a reserve. This marching order allowed the troops to wheel into battle formation with the least possible confusion.[30]

After a three-mile march the columns were halted while Greene opened his rum casks to allow the men to take "a little of that liquid which is not unnecessary to exhilirate the animal spirits upon such occasions." A short time later the men were formed into their battle lines, for the general felt that he needed the "time for his raw troops to form with coolness and recollection."[31]

Once again Greene used the Cowpens pattern, with the militia in the front line acting as shock troops and the more experienced and better disciplined troops making up the second line. When formed, the units on the front line were the South Carolina militia under Marion on the right, Malmedy's two battalions of North Carolina militia in the center, and the South Carolina militia on the left, commanded by Pickens. Captain-Lieutenant William Gaines, who had just arrived the night before with dispatches from Lafayette, was in charge of the two three-pounders in the center of the first line.[32]

Sumner's North Carolina Brigade of 350 men were on the right of the second line. In the center Campbell directed the Virginia Brigade of 350 men, divided into two regiments commanded by Major Smith Snead and a Captain Edmunds. The Maryland Brigade of 250 men of the regiments of Lieutenant Colonel John Eager Howard and Major Henry Hardman under Otho Williams were posted on the left. Two six-pounders under the Marylander, Captain William Brown, were centered in this line.

Lee's Legion made up the right flank. On the opposite flank were the South Carolina State troops led by Lieutenant Colonels Wade Hampton, William Polk (of North Carolina), and Charles Middleton, the whole under the command of Lieutenant Colonel John Henderson. Washington's cavalry and Kirkwood's Delawares made up the reserve. Once formed, the soldiers moved slowly through the woods for fear of losing contact with each other.[33]

30. *Magazine of History with Notes and Queries*, Extra Number 139, XXV (1928), 73–74; Greene to Benjamin Lincoln, 11 September 1781, Nathanael Greene Papers, William L. Clements Library.

31. Tiffany, *Otho Williams*, pp. 23–24; *Graham's Magazine* (December, 1845), p. 257.

32. *Pennsylvania Magazine of History and Biography*, XXX (1906), 359–60; *Southern Literary Messenger*, XXIX (October, 1859), 291–92.

33. *Pennsylvania Magazine of History and Biography*, XXX (1906), 360–61;

There were more North Carolinians on the field that warm September day than were indicated in the returns. A large part, even a majority, it is sometimes said, of the commands of Polk, Hampton, and Middleton had been enlisted in North Carolina and had joined to take advantage of "Sumter's law" to gain a slave. They had been recruited in the area between the Catawba and Yadkin rivers, in Mecklenburg and Rowan counties.[34]

Strangely enough, Stewart was not yet aware of the approach of Greene. Because of the shortage of bread, the British commander had been sending out foraging parties each morning to dig sweet potatoes. At five o'clock on the morning of September 8 he had sent out about 100 men on such a mission. Two hours after they had left, two deserters from Greene's command, who had left the American camp the night before, came in with the information that Greene was marching to the attack. Stewart thought them to be spies and ordered them confined. Nevertheless, to settle all doubts, he sent out loyalist Major John Coffin with 140 infantry and fifty cavalry to reconnoiter and to recall the "rooting party."[35]

Around eight o'clock, and within less than four miles of the British camp, Coffin's cavalry were sighted by the North Carolina mounted troops under Major John Armstrong who were scouting out before the main body. Coffin rushed forward; Armstrong fell back, drawing the Tory on toward the American army. Word was sent back to Lee, who hastily contrived an ambush with his infantry stretched across the road and his cavalry in the trees on either side of the road. Coffin, an impetuous fellow, charged. He was met by a shower of lead. The Legion's mounted troops under Major Joseph Eggleston swung around to the rear of Coffin. In the short fight that followed, Coffin managed to escape, but at least forty of his men were killed or taken prisoner. Some accounts say that the rooting party came out of the woods when the skirmish began, and that at least sixty of their number were killed, wounded or taken prisoner. In his first report to Lord Cornwallis, Stewart stated that they had been captured, but ten days later in a "private" letter to the general he said that they had joined him after the battle and he seems to have felt they would have been of

---

Gibbes, *Documentary History of the American Revolution,* III, 141–42, 144; *Magazine of History with Notes and Queries,* Extra Number 139, XXXV (1928), 74–75; *State Records,* XXII, 153.

34. Hoyt, *Murphey Papers,* II, 296.

35. Stewart to Cornwallis, 9 September 1781, Cornwallis Papers, PRO 30/11/70; Lee, *Memoirs of the War in the Southern Department,* p. 604; Stedman, *History of the ... American War,* II, 420; Gibbes, *Documentary History of the American Revolution,* III, 144.

help during the battle. On the other hand, Otho Williams said that they were taken. The truth seems to be that a sizable number of the foragers were taken, but those who escaped made it back to the British camp after the battle of Eutaw Springs.[36]

Stewart could only stand and fight. Coffin reported a large party of cavalry with the enemy, and to have withdrawn would have furnished an opportunity to the American mounted troops to inflict considerable damage on his own column. He formed his troops, almost equal in numbers to Greene's army, with one flank near the creek, the other "in the air," but supported by Coffin's infantry and cavalry. Major John Majoribanks with the Guards and Grenadiers were stationed some distance from the British right flank in a thicket of blackjack oak near the creek, the thick underbrush discouraging harassment by enemy cavalry. Stewart's artillery, two six-pounders and a four-pounder, were placed in the road, flanked on either side by Cruger's loyalist veterans from Ninety Six.[37]

Small infantry detachments were sent out as skirmishers, with Stewart hoping they would be able to slow the American advance long enough for him to post his own troops. To aid Lee, who was out in front of Greene's army, the general sent forth skirmishers of his own. Also sent forward was Captain William Gaines with his two three-pounders, his guns protected by a guard of a lieutenant and twenty-two infantry detached from Sumner's brigade. Gaines and his escort pushed forward for nearly a mile until they overtook Lee, who advised Gaines that the enemy were rapidly advancing. Even as Lee spoke, the enemy appeared, Gaines unlimbered and pointed his grasshoppers. Holding his fire until the advancing enemy was within between twenty-five and fifty yards, Gaines staggered the enemy with a round of canister shot. By the time the British had reformed, Greene's first line had come up. The little fieldpieces continued a heavy fire until they were disabled when the straps holding the trunions broke under the strain.[38]

The militiamen of the first line, firing as they advanced, fought well. Never in the South had these occasional soldiers stood up so well

---

36. Lee, *Memoirs of the War in the Southern Department*, p. 466; Kirkwood, *Journal and Orderly Book of Captain Robert Kirkwood*, p. 22; *Magazine of History with Notes and Queries*, Extra Number 139, XXXV (1928), 79; Stewart to Cornwallis, 9 September 1781, Stewart to Cornwallis, 19 September 1781, Cornwallis Papers, PRO 30/11/73; Gibbes, *Documentary History of the American Revolution*, III, 144.

37. Lee, *Memoirs of the War in the Southern Department*, pp. 467–68.

38. *Southern Literary Messenger*, XXIX (October, 1839), 291–92; Gibbes, *Documentary History of the American Revolution*, III, 148–49; *State Records*, XXI, 96.

before British regulars. It was said that they delivered seventeen rounds before the pressure grew too great. Francis Marion, commanding the South Carolina militia to the right of Malmedy's North Carolina militia in the center, later declared that the latter began to fall back after delivering only three rounds. In North Carolina the word at a later date was that "but for the shameful conduct of Col. Farmer (Ruthy's husband) who headed them damped their spirits & lessened the execution which might have otherwise been expected of them." Still, Greene was pleased with their behavior and in official dispatches praised them, saying, "General Marion, Colonel Malmady, and General Pickens conducted the troops with great gallantry, and good conduct, and the Militia fought with a degree of Spirit and firmness that reflects the highest honor upon this class of soldiers." And to Steuben he commented that "such conduct would have graced the soldiers of the great King of Prussia."[39]

On the right, Marion's command, made up of South Carolina militia and deserters from the British army, were subjected to a withering fire. They behaved well, and when they did break, they quickly reformed and drove forward again. Enemy fire began to widen the gaps in their line and the troops began to drift back before the enemy's advance. It was then that Sumner was ordered forward. To counteract these fresh troops, Stewart brought up the infantry of his reserve on the left. Greene must have held some reservations about ordering the North Carolinians into action, especially those raw troops who had just arrived the day before with Reading Blount. The General was pleasantly surprised when "they fought with a degree of obstinacy that would do honor to the best veterans and I can hardly tell which to admire most, the gallantry of the Officers or the bravery of the Troops. They kept up a heavy and well directed fire, and the Enemy returned it with equal Spirit, for they really fought with a degree of courage worthy of a better cause, and great execution was done on both sides."[40]

The situation on the left had become critical. The flank of the South Carolina militia under Pickens and protected by Henderson's

39. Gibbes, *Documentary History of the American Revolution*, III, 148, 160–61; *South Carolina Historical and Genealogical Magazine*, XVIII (July, 1917), 139–40; William Hooper to James Iredell, 1 October 1781, Iredell Papers; *Pennsylvania Magazine of History and Biography*, XXX (1906), 361; Greene to [Lincoln], 11 September 1781, Nathanael Greene Papers, William L. Clements Library.

40. William Hooper to Iredell, 1 October 1781, Iredell Papers; *Magazine of History with Notes and Queries*, Extra Number 139, XXV (1928), 73–74; Gibbes, *Documentary History of the American Revolution*, III, 149; Greene to [Lincoln], 11 September 1781, Nathanael Greene Papers, William L. Clements Library.

state troops fell short of the flank of the British right. This inequity exposed it to an enfilade fire of the enemy, especially from Majoribanks's men in the thicket along the creek. Henderson wanted to charge the position, but Greene held him back to protect Pickens's flank and the two remaining artillery pieces. Shortly afterwards a ball broke Henderson's leg and he was no longer able to sit his horse. His troops were in danger of breaking when Colonel Wade Hampton, who succeeded to the command, rallied them and they "resumed their station in perfect tranquility."

The sustained and galling fire was beginning to have its effect upon Sumner's brigade, although Blount's men stood firm until nearly two-thirds of their number were killed or wounded. As the greater enemy firepower began to take effect, the line of the North Carolina Brigade began to sag and then gradually to yield ground. The British, sensing victory, sprang forward and broke their own line in their rush.[41]

This was the opportunity that Greene had been awaiting. A surgeon acting as a temporary aide was sent forward to tell Otho Williams to "sweep the field with his bayonets." The Maryland and Virginia Continentals, who had not been actively engaged until this time, advanced under a shower of grape shot and musket balls. Within forty yards of the enemy the Virginians halted long enough to deliver a volley. Then the men of the entire second line advanced at a trot, their arms at the trail. It was then that the roll of the drums and the shouts of the advancing troops drew every eye upon them and for a moment all action seemed to hang in suspension.[42]

As the second line advanced, the entire British line, including those in front of Sumner, began to fall back. Joined by the infantry of Lee's Legion, the North Carolinians poured in a volley and then fell in with the general charge upon the enemy's ranks. The British left wing was thrown into disorder and began to break away.[43]

The British center held firm until disrupted by the fugitives from the left flank. The enemy front began to yield. Even as the Americans raised their voices in exhuberant shouts, Lieutenant Colonel Richard Campbell fell mortally wounded with a musket ball in his chest.[44]

This was the time to hit the retreating left flank of the enemy with a charge by mounted troops to turn the withdrawal into a rout.

41. Gibbes, *Documentary History of the American Revolution*, III, 150.

42. *Ibid.*, 151–52; *Virginia Magazine of History and Biography*, LI (April, 1943), 148.

43. Hooper to Iredell, 1 October 1781, Iredell Papers.

44. Gibbes, *Documentary History of the American Revolution*, III, 151.

But Lee was with his infantry and his cavalry had remained in place where it had been posted, awaiting orders. Had Lee's men charged at this moment, they may well have dispersed Coffin's dragoons, who were covering the British withdrawal on the left. At the least they would have diverted the attention of the enemy cavalry. With Majoribanks holding fast in the thicket on the British right and their left giving way, their line had executed something of a quarter wheel, and both armies were now in the open ground before the brick mansion.[45]

Greene was now convinced that in the dislodgement of Majoribanks lay the key to victory. William Washington was ordered to charge the enemy right flank, and Hampton was to cooperate with him. By the time Hampton received the order, Washington had galloped forward. Before Hampton could come up, the impetuous Washington attempted to drive Majoribanks from the thicket by a headlong charge. It was impossible for the mounted men to penetrate the tangled underbrush. Washington discovered what he thought to be an opening between the right flank and Eutaw Creek which, if he could gain it, would allow him to hit Majoribanks's flank and rear. As Washington's troops executed the order to wheel by the left by sections, they were brought under the fire of the enemy. A volley swept a number of the Americans from their saddles and many horses fell. Every officer except two were killed or wounded. Washington's horse, struck down, pinned the colonel to the ground. A bayonet thrust in the breast might have proved fatal, had the British soldier wielding the weapon not been stopped by an officer.[46]

The joint account of five officers presented a vivid picture of the field at this moment:

> The field of battle was, at this instant, rich in the dreadful scenery which disfigures such a picture. On the left, Washington's Cavalry, routed and flying, horses plunging as they died, or coursing the field without their riders, while the enemy with pushed bayonets, issued from the thicket, upon the wounded or unhorsed riders. In the fore-ground, Hampton covering and collecting the scattered Cavalry, while Kirkwood, with his bayonets, rushed furiously to avenge their fall, and a road strewed with the bodies of men and horses, and the fragments of dismounted artillery. Beyond these, a scene of indiscribable confusion, viewed over the whole American line advancing rapidly, and in order. And, on the right, Henderson borne off in the arms of

45. Hooper to Iredell, 1 October 1781, Iredell Papers.
46. *South Carolina Historical and Genealogical Magazine*, XVI (July, 1915), 105, XVIII (July, 1917), 140; Hooper to Iredell, 1 October 1781, Iredell Papers; *Graham's Magazine* (December, 1847), p. 257; *Virginia Magazine of History and Biography*, LI (April, 1943), 149.

his soldiers, and Campbell sustained in the saddle by a brave son, who had sought glory at his father's side.[47]

Hampton gathered up the survivors of Washington's command and charged into the thicket. He was driven back. Kirkwood led the Delaware Continentals, bayonets at the ready, into the blackjack oak. Majoribanks, still holding to the thicket, fell back to a new position with one flank resting on the palisaded garden.

Those in the British camp, seeing their lines being driven back upon them, became frightened lest they too be overrun. Commissaries destroyed their stores. Many loyalists and deserters, fearful of falling into American hands, leaped upon draught horses and sped off in the direction of Charleston.

The British army appeared to be in full retreat. Some of the men threw themselves into the palisaded garden. Others sought the protection of a ravine or "hollow way" where they were able to reform. Major Sheridan, of Cruger's command, ordered his New York Volunteers into the brick house. The Legion infantry pursued this last group to the very door of the house, and were so close upon their heels that Sheridan was forced to slam the door in the faces of several of his own officers and men. Fortunately these men were taken prisoner, for the men of the Legion used them as a shield when they retired from the house. The remainder of the British retreated directly through their camp. The tents contained much in the way of booty "to tempt a thirsty, naked and fatigued soldiery to acts of insubordination." The tents likewise offered some concealment from the fire from the mansion house. Many American officers had rushed through the encampment, only to look back and discover that most of their men had abandoned them to plunder the enemy's belongings. Standing in the open beyond the camp, the officers became the primary targets for Sheridan's men. Their troops, rushing about the enemy camp, "fastened upon the liquors and refreshments they afforded, and became utterly unmanageable."[48]

Majoribanks and Coffin took advantage of this confusion to emerge from the thicket on the right and the woods on the left. Greene, not yet aware of the collapse of his infantry, felt that it could handle Majoribanks now that he was out in the open, and sent Cap-

47. Gibbes, *Documentary History of the American Revolution*, II, 152–53.
48. *Ibid.*, II, 143, III, 155; Kirkwood, *Journal and Orderly Book of Captain Robert Kirkwood*, p. 23; Stewart to Cornwallis, 9 September 1781, Cornwallis Papers, PRO 30/11/71; Greene to [Lincoln], 11 September 1781, Nathanael Greene Papers, William L. Clements Library.

tain Nathaniel Pendleton to order Lee to charge the British with his cavalry. Lee could not be found and, according to Pendleton, he had taken "some dragoons with him, as I am informed, and rode about the field, giving orders and directions, in a manner the General did not approve of." Pendleton transmitted the order to Major Joseph Eggleston. When Eggleston led his men in a charge upon Majoribanks, Coffin came forward and drove him back.

Coffin now wheeled to charge those Americans dispersed among the tents of the British camp. He was met by Wade Hampton and after a sharp engagement the British horsemen were driven back. In pursuing Coffin, Hampton's men passed too near Majoribank's position and were subjected to such heavy fire that William Polk thought "every man killed but himself." Hampton rallied his scattered men and sought protection in the skirts of the woods.

The American artillery under Captain Brown had moved forward with the second line. In the excitement of battle, either "by accident or mistake," fieldpieces had been run too far forward and were now within range of the musket fire from the house. Nearly all of those manning Greene's two guns and two six-pounders that had been taken from the enemy were killed or captured. It was then that Majoribanks came forth into the field, captured the guns, and dragged them back under the covering fire furnished by Sheridan's men. Joined by the troops who had taken refuge in the garden, he charged the Americans still in the British camp and drove them before him.[49]

Once they were within the protection of the trees, Greene rallied his men. Majoribank's men were too exhausted and crippled to continue the attack. Greene pulled his army back. The last to leave the field were Kirkwood's Delawares and Edmunds's Virginians, who were still fighting when the rest of the army fell back. They captured an enemy three-pounder, which they brought back behind a horse that they had picked up along the way. After four hours of bitter fighting, American ammunition was exhausted, and the enemy still retained command of the water supply. Greene also reasoned that he would fare better if he could hit Stewart on the march rather than attempt to dislodge the enemy from the battlefield. Collecting his wounded, except those who had fallen within range of the fire from the house, Greene retired to his camp of the night before. A picket un-

---

49. *Pennsylvania Magazine of History and Biography*, XXX (1906), 363; *Southern Literary Messenger*, XXIX (October, 1859), 292; *Graham's Magazine* (December, 1847), p. 257.

der Hampton was left in the vicinity of Eutaw Springs to observe the actions of the enemy.[50]

It had been a bloody battle. Accurate American casualty figures were difficult to obtain. Greene's first total given out shortly after the battle was 525 killed, wounded, and missing. On September 25, 1781, a more accurate count increased the first total to 574, of whom 119 had been killed, 382 wounded, and seventy-eight missing. The North Carolina Brigade suffered greater losses than any other Continental unit: 154 casualties. Four officers, 1 sergeant, and 43 rank and file had been killed; 6 officers, 10 sergeants, and 80 rank and file had suffered wounds; and only 10 rank and file were missing. Over one-third of the casualties of the Continental troops were from Sumner's brigade. Officers killed in action were Captains William Goodman, Christopher Goodwin, and Dennis Porterfield, along with Lieutenant John Dillain. Among the wounded were Captain Joshua Hadley, Lieutenants Charles Dixon, Richard Andrews, Thomas Dudley, and Ensigns James Moore and Abner Lamb.[51]

Stewart's losses are uncertain, but his total casualties must have been between 900 and 1,000. According to his official returns, 85 British soldiers had been killed, 351 wounded, and 257 were missing for a total of 693. On the other hand, Greene reported that he had taken 500 prisoners, 70 of whom were wounded. If Greene's claims were accurate, Stewart's losses could have run as high as 936. But whatever Stewart's casualties, the British were in no condition to fight again in the near future.[52]

Although he had been forced from the field of battle, Greene was jubilant. In general orders the day after the battle he proclaimed, "the Victory is complete." High praise was lavished on all of the

50. Gibbes, *Documentary History of the American Revolution*, III, 152–56; *Pennsylvania Magazine of History and Biography*, XXX (1906), 363; *Magazine of History with Notes and Queries*, Extra Number 139, XXXV (1928), 77; Pendleton Orderly Book; Kirkwood, *Journal and Orderly Book of Captain Robert Kirkwood*, pp. 22–23.

51. Returns of the killed, Missing & Wounded of the Southern Army Commanded by the Honourable Major General Nathanael Greene in the Action of the Eutaw, September 8th 1781, Miscellaneous Papers, 1770–1896, Southern Historical Collection, The University of North Carolina at Chapel Hill, Chapel Hill, N.C.; *State Records*, XV, 638.

52. Stewart to Cornwallis, 9 September 1781, Cornwallis Papers, PRO 30/11/71; Francis V. Greene, *The Revolutionary War and the Military Policy of the United States* (New York, 1911), pp. 256–57; Gibbes, *Documentary History of the American Revolution*, III, 161; *Pennsylvania Magazine of History and Biography*, XXX (1906), 363.

troops, while the North Carolina Brigade "discovered a Confidence which does honour to young Soldiers."[53]

Greene knew that Stewart had been sorely hurt and was of a mind to attack the enemy again when the opportunity presented itself. On the day after the battle, Lee and Marion were sent out to intercept reinforcements or to slow Stewart's march should the British move toward Charleston. But on that same day Stewart's men, working in a steady rain, smashed a thousand stand of arms and threw many of the weapons into the Eutaw Springs. The contents of thirty casks of rum were poured into the creek. Other stores that could not be easily transported were destroyed. Leaving seventy of his wounded on the field, Stewart marched for Charleston along the Nelson Ferry road, felling trees across the road to discourage pursuit. Greene followed until Stewart received a reinforcement of four hundred fresh troops to help cover his withdrawal. Greene halted, resting his weary troops for several days before making his way back to the high hills of the Santee in a series of leisurely marches. His prisoners were sent to Salisbury, escorted by a detachment of the North Carolina Line under Major George Donoho. There they were turned over to a militia group who carried them into Virginia.[54]

Once again Greene had allowed the enemy to claim victory by his withdrawal from the field of battle, and once again he had so weakened his adversary that the latter could not hold the ground he had won. The general was fast proving the assessment of Abner Nash, who in April had told Greene, "I shall have no fears for this [state] as long as you stay with us and possess the peculiar Art of making your Enemies run away from their Victories leaving you master of their Wounded and of all the fertile part of the Country."[55]

53. Pendleton Orderly Book; Greene to [Lincoln], 11 September 1781, Nathanael Greene Papers, William L. Clements Library.

54. *Pennsylvania Magazine of History and Biography*, XXX (1906), 363–65; Gibbes, *Documentary History of the American Revolution*, III, 156–57; Greene to Steuben, 17 September 1781, Steuben Papers; Merritt, *Calendar of the Otho Williams Papers*, p. 51; *Virginia Magazine of History and Biography*, LI (April, 1943), 149; *State Records*, XV, 104; Greene to [Lincoln], 11 September 1781, Nathanael Greene Papers, William L. Clements Library.

55. Nash to Greene, 7 April 1781, Autographs of Americans Collection, Pierpont Morgan Library, New York, N.Y.

Chapter 19

*T*he Beginning of the End

"The goddess of liberty
seems to be the companion of everyone."

Recruiting in North Carolina slacked off after Sumner's departure from the state. It appeared as though the people of North Carolina had lost interest in the war once the fighting had moved away
from them. Yet in all fairness Craig was still in the state and as long
as he held Wilmington the enemy maintained a beachhead from
which a strong drive could be launched. Many prospective recruits
stayed at home trying to scratch a living from ground that had been
raked clean by the maneuverings of two armies. Georgia recruiting
officers slipped through the state, offering generous bounties to North
Carolinians, even those in the field, to join their line. Equally important was a change of heart among the members of the legislature.
They now concluded that the act conscripting the fugitives of Guilford had been unfair and had been applied in an unjust manner.
They had, as early as July 4, petitioned Greene "to discharge those
unhappy men and permit them to return to their Families as soon as
the situation of affairs will admit of such an Act of Benevolence."[1]

1. *State Records,* XVII, 930–31, 975–76; Francis Locke to Greene, 25 August
1781, Revolutionary Collection, Duke University.

Some Continental officers still worked to recruit men. By the end of August Thomas Hogg (who had been exchanged in March, 1781) and James Armstrong had managed to raise seventy men between them but were unable to clothe their recruits. Other officers were in the field attempting to secure the boats at the ferries should Cornwallis decide to march south. Still others were preparing to supply the Pennsylvania Line, which had been ordered south to join Greene, and some were seeking commands in the militia.[2]

Many of those North Carolinians who had been wounded at Eutaw Springs had been returned to the hospital at Charlotte. Even here they were haunted by the specter of Guilford Court House. Many were nearly naked, but because they had been drafted rather than enlisted, those in charge of the hospital were afraid to issue them Continental clothing. Their condition remained unimproved until Greene gave orders that they were to be treated like all other regulars.[3]

And there had been a disarrangement in the executive department of the state government. On June 25 the assembly had elected the one-eyed, pock-marked Thomas Burke as governor of North Carolina. The new governor, according to Greene, had given "energy and a new turn to affairs" in the state. For the first two months Burke had performed the duties of office in Halifax until he received information that the Tories of Orange County were planning to rise and plunder their Whig neighbors. Coupled with this was the news that David Fanning, the notorious partisan leader, was operating in the vicinity, attacking and plundering fortified plantations, sometimes executing the defenders. The latest word was that he planned to sack Hillsborough. In September Burke planned to return to Hillsborough, his home, to organize an extensive campaign against the loyalists.[4]

At this time General John Butler, with a small body of militia, was encamped on the south side of Haw River. Within three days of Burke's arrival in Hillsborough the governor heard that Fanning was now operating in cooperation with the loyalist colonel Hector McNeil and the two were planning to surprise Butler. A messenger was immediately dispatched to Butler with a warning and orders to

2. *State Records*, XV, 628, 629, 633, 639–40, 642; Alexander Martin to Sumner, January 1782, Jethro Sumner Papers, Southern Historical Collection.

3. Merritt, *Calendar of the Otho Williams Papers*, p. 55; Ashe to Sumner, 21 November 1781, Jethro Sumner Papers, Southern Historical Collection.

4. *Pennsylvania Magazine of History and Biography*, XXI (1897), 284; *State Records*, XXII, 566–68, 570–71, 1047–48; Greene to Board of War, 28 July 1781, Nathanael Greene Papers, William L. Clements Library.

move to a place of greater security. Butler retreated toward Hillsborough. Fanning followed.

During the course of these movements Fanning learned that Burke had returned to Hillsborough and was protected by only a small guard. The possibility of capturing the governor excited Fanning's ambition and he set his march toward the town. His tactics were the same as those that had proved successful when he captured Pittsboro on July 18, 1781.[5]

Darkness cloaked Fanning's approach to Hillsborough. A heavy fog obscured the movements of his five hundred men as they slipped into town early Wednesday morning, September 12, 1781. By the time that the townspeople were alerted to their danger, there was no opportunity to organize resistance. The majority of the men chose to remain in their homes to defend their families. The steady fire of the invaders kept them separated and from going to one another's aid.

The Tories gradually converged on the eastern part of the town where Burke's home was located. The governor put up a vigorous defense, aided by his aide de camp, Captain Reid, his secretary, John Huske, and an orderly sergeant of the Continental Line. They were soon overpowered, but Burke refused to surrender his sword because of the hostile posture of the Tories. Only after a British officer accompanying the loyalists assured him that no harm would come to him did the governor give up his weapon. In addition to Governor Burke and several council members, Fanning claimed that he took two hundred prisoners. Thirty loyalists, one of whom was to have been hanged that day, were released from the local jail and their guards locked in their cells. Local houses were plundered and tavern doors were forced so that rum could be brought out. It was nearly two that afternoon before the Tory officers could regain control of their rioting men and march them out of town before the countryside became alarmed.[6]

Robert Mebane, acting as a colonel in the local militia, rode to alert Butler, who immediately set his men in motion to intercept Fanning. Near Lindley's Mill, some eighteen miles from Hillsborough, Butler set an ambush on the high ground commanding the ford at Cane Creek. The easy success of the Tories had made their advance guard under Hector McNeil careless. McNeil fell at the first fire, with three muskets balls in his body, his men thrown into disorder until rallied by Fanning. After sending off the prisoners, Fanning took a part of his force and, moving upstream, crossed Cane

5. Fanning, *Colonel David Fanning*, p. 37.
6. *State Records*, XVI, 12–13; Fanning, *Colonel David Fanning*, p. 33.

Creek and came in on the rear of Butler's force. His first fire threw the militiamen into confusion, but they soon rallied. The ensuing engagement lasted over four hours. When Butler finally withdrew he left behind twenty-four killed, ninety wounded, and ten taken prisoners. Fanning had lost twenty-seven killed and sixty of his men were so badly wounded that they were left on the field. Thirty others were wounded, but they were able to walk when the Tories withdrew. Fanning himself was wounded in the left arm and lost so much blood that he was hidden in the woods, protected by a small guard of three men. The remainder of his command continued on to Wilmington where the prisoners were turned over to Major Craig. Alexander Martin, Speaker of the House, became acting governor in Burke's absence.[7]

The attack on Hillsborough and the capture of Burke further complicated the recruiting of Continentals. Many of those who had been drafted now refused to take the field. A number of the contractors who had been engaged in supplying the Southern Army now refused to leave their homes and families undefended. When Greene heard from Alexander Martin of Burke's capture, he and Sumner discussed the situation over breakfast on September 26. The general ordered Sumner to return to North Carolina "as I fear all things will get into confusion from this untoward event." Lieutenant Colonel John Ashe was left in command of the brigade.[8]

Sumner had his hands full. As the ranking Continental officer on the scene, and with the governor in captivity, the primary responsibility for administering military affairs within North Carolina was his. Now there were the prisoners of war taken in South Carolina to worry about, Continental recruits to be forwarded to Greene's headquarters, and Continental officers to be persuaded to come back into the field. Supplies and provisions collected in the state had to be forwarded to the southern army as quickly as possible. Sumner soon fell ill, his condition complicated by the chronic illness of his wife that was to take her life within the next three years. Yet he stayed on the job when able, and in October met Greene in Charlotte when the general rode up looking for arms.[9]

In Greene's camp there was apprehension that Cornwallis would

7. Fanning, *Colonel David Fanning*, pp. 33–34.

8. *State Records*, XV, 644; Greene to Sumner, 25 September 1781, Jethro Sumner Papers, Southern Historical Collection.

9. *State Records*, XV, 647, 649, 659; Ashe to Sumner, 1 November 1781, Jethro Sumner Papers, N.C. Dept. Arch. & Hist.; Gibbes, *Documentary History of the American Revolution*, III, 185–87, 193; George H. Richmond, *Letters by and to Gen. Nathanael Greene, with Some to His Wife* (New York, 1906), pp. 27–28.

escape the web spun at Yorktown by Washington and Rochambeau and march back to South Carolina. There were grounds for concern. Troops were leaving camp daily and an even greater number were expected to return to their homes in December when the enlistments of the Virginia Line were to expire.[10]

In the North Carolina Line there was unhappiness and discontent, especially among the officers. John Ashe had left the brigade, leaving it under the command of Major John Armstrong. Armstrong's officers sulked; they had long served without pay or proper equipment and now they were almost naked. Supplies destined for the North Carolina troops mysteriously disappeared or were unlawfully confiscated by the militia. Greene was in sympathy with the officers' complaints. He allowed Captain George Doherty to return to North Carolina to present the grievances of the North Carolina officers to the General Assembly. Among other matters, the officers wanted the legislature to make good on its promises of land grants as a reward for their military services and they wished the surveying of these grants to be initiated in the near future. Armstrong explained to Sumner: "Dear General, you are not a stranger to our sufferings, we have our eyes upon you as our support in time of need. I think the officers now in service from our State, must be men of the greatest fortitude & forbearance in the world, they serve without pay, clothing or any regular supplies, of the necessaries allowed them, except Beef and Bread which is allowed the worst Tory in our Provost Guard."[11]

Shortages were complicated when the southern army fell victim to an epidemic of dysentery and fever. In some companies every man was sick. Every doctor in camp had been forced to take to his bed. The sufferings of the wounded were aggravated by disease. "Numbers of my brave fellows," cried Greene, "who have bled in the cause of their country, have been eaten up with maggots, and perish in that miserable situation." Over one-half of the North Carolina Brigade were confined to their tents. Their spirits were lowered even more by the fact that they, along with three-fourths of the southern army, had no blankets to protect them from the crisp November air. The news

10. *Pennsylvania Magazine of History and Biography,* XI (1887), 426; *Year Book: City of Charleston, 1899,* pp. 125–26; *South Carolina Historical and Genealogical Magazine,* XVIII (July, 1917), 159–61.

11. *State Records,* XV, 656–57, XVI, 588–89; Ashe to Sumner, 21 November 1781, Jethro Sumner Papers, N.C. Dept. Arch. & Hist.; Merritt, *Calendar of the Otho Williams Papers,* p. 53; Armstrong to Sumner, 3 February 1782, W. Russell to Sumner, 9 April 1782, Jethro Sumner Papers, Southern Historical Collection.

of the surrender of Cornwallis did raise the spirits of many enough to get out long enough to parade and fire a salute in celebration.[12]

The victory at Yorktown meant more help for Greene. The Pennsylvania, Maryland, and Virginia Lines, along with recruits from Delaware, were sent south under the command of Major General Arthur St. Clair. Two regiments of North Carolina mountaineers under Colonels John Shelby and John Sevier had come into camp.

On November 14, 1781, Major Craig evacuated Wilmington and his garrison was transported to Charleston. Deserters from the British army were coming into Greene's camp at a rate of thirty each week. There would have been an even greater number of deserters, but the British had created a "Negro Horse" whose primary duty was to patrol constantly to apprehend those attempting to steal their way through the lines into the American camp.[13]

Greene, feeling that the British might attempt to break out of Charleston and march overland to Savannah, planned to block such a move by moving his army west of the Edisto River. He broke camp on November 18. He was encamped near Fort Motte when he learned that the back-country men of Shelby and Sevier were leaving the southern army since they, as did all militiamen, counted their time in the field from the time that they had left their homes. The only action experienced by any part of the army had occurred on November 2, when a group of these men under Shelby, along with the command of Colonel Hezikiah Maham, surprised the British hospital at Fair Lawn near Monck's Corner. The patients and medical staff were made prisoners and the hospital was burned. Major General Alexander Leslie had now assumed command of the British forces in the South, and although Leslie's force outnumbered that of Greene, he began to abandon his outposts. Yet there was tension in the air and Armstrong wrote Sumner that "now we are waiting every hour to hear the General beat, we approach in the same manner as we did before the Battle of Eutaw."[14]

Francis Marion sent in the intelligence that Stewart had broken

12. Greene to Alexander Martin, 11 November 1781, Greene to Peter Horry, 11 November 1781, Nathanael Greene Papers, William L. Clements Library; Ashe to Sumner, 21 November 1781, Jethro Sumner Papers, N.C. Dept. Arch. & Hist.

13. *State Records,* XV, 661; Seymour, *A Journal of the Southern Expedition,* pp. 40–41; Smith, *Life . . . of Arthur St. Clair,* I, 564; Merritt, *Calendar of the Otho Williams Papers,* p. 56.

14. *State Records,* XV, 665; Gibbes, *Documentary History of the American Revolution,* III, 213, 215–16; John Armstrong to Sumner, 25 November 1781, Jethro Sumner Papers, Southern Historical Collection; *New England Magazine,* New Series XXVI (May, 1902), 328.

camp at Monck's Corner and had fallen back to Goose Creek, fifteen miles above Charleston. This was not a wise move, for it exposed the British garrison at Dorchester to attack, and Dorchester acted as a check upon the country south of the Edisto River and drew provisions for the army from the surrounding countryside. Although his army was too small to dislodge the enemy garrison by regular siege procedures, Greene decided to make a sudden strike at this post.

Placing the remainder of his army under Otho Williams, Greene made up what he termed a "flying party," composed of the cavalry from Lee's and Washington's corps under Wade Hampton, the Legion infantry, and units from the Maryland and Virginia Continentals, in all about four hundred men. Loyalists reported Greene's circuitous approach to the British. The enemy lay on their arms the night of November 30. There was no sign of Greene.

Late in the morning of December 1 a scouting party of fifty loyalists was sent out. Nearly all these men were put to the sword when they met Hampton's advance guard. After the survivors fled back to their works, British mounted troops rode out to furnish cover for those who might still be coming in. Hampton charged them, killing thirty before driving them back into Dorchester. Greene was recognized by those who had been in the fight and they carried the word that his army was probably following. That night, fearful that the entire American army was moving against him, the British commander destroyed his works and stores and threw his cannon into the river. The British fell back to the Quarter House on Charleston Neck, within five miles of the city. The affair so alarmed those within the city that not only the loyalists but all trustworthy Negro slaves were put under arms.

Greene fell back to Round O where the army under Williams was encamped on the plantation of a Colonel Ferguson.[15]

At Round O the supply situation had fallen into its customary critical state. When William R. Davie pointed out that the people of North Carolina were unable to satisfy their own personal wants and that the specific taxes were inadequate insofar as furnishing provisions for the army was concerned, Greene replied that the state was now free of the enemy and should "give us very great support if the proper exertions are made and a good disposition prevails." One of the prime reasons for the poor response in North Carolina was that a "good disposition" did not prevail in that area and when state cur-

15. *Collections of the New-York Historical Society for 1875*, pp. 495–96; Greene, *Life of Nathanael Greene*, III, 420–21; Lee, *Memoirs of the War in the Southern Department*, pp. 522–23; Johnson, *Sketches of Greene*, II, 264–65.

rency and promissory notes were offered in payment, the people turned them down, claiming them to be "state tricks." Greene's insistence that the army should come first met with little response.

Expedients were adopted in an attempt to relieve some of the sufferings of the officers. Although hunting was generally forbidden in the army, a number of huntsmen were issued permits to kill wild fowl for the officers. When the underbrush was cleared from the campsite, it was burned and the ashes used to make soap. The arrival of a supply of "winter overalls" for issuance to the officers helped but little. John Armstrong complained that "the old disorder or complaint still prevails among the Officers—the want of Clothing for my own part, and I must return home in a short time if I cannot get a supply. We appear ridiculous among those that we are not a Quainted with. We are fed up with promises until we can swallow no more of them."[16]

The troops were kept busy policing the bivouac area, cleaning arms and clothing. Every brigade was on the drill field every afternoon. Rumors from Charleston were that Leslie was expecting reinforcements of five thousand troops from New York, and Greene wanted his army ready for action should this prove true. Christmas was just another day except that general orders carried the message, "The Genl. wishes the Officers & Men of the Army a Merry Christmas. The Troops to draw a proportion of Liquor as usual." That same day Captain Clement Hall arrived in camp with no more than 160 gallons of rum and 2 barrels of coffee for the North Carolina Brigade. He was brought before a court of enquiry to determine how so many stores had disappeared along the route, with an angry Greene declaring that he should be "broken if he has justice done him or the public."[17]

Around eleven o'clock on the foggy morning of January 4, 1782, the Pennsylvania Line under Arthur St. Clair trooped into camp, completing their long march from Yorktown. They were weary, sick, and homesick, complaining of the "poor beef and rice," and heartily wishing themselves back among "the Flesh Pots, the Onions and Garlick of Pennsylvania." Within a week a large detachment under Anthony Wayne had marched for Georgia, its mission to drive the enemy from that state and protect Greene from a surprise attack from

16. Pendleton Orderly Book; Greene to Davie, 26 November 1781, Davie to Greene, 10 December 1781, Greene to Davie, 27 December 1781, Preston Davie Collection, Southern Historical Collection; *State Records*, XVI, 474; Davie to Greene, 6 January 1782, Commissary Correspondence, Military Collection.

17. Pendleton Orderly Book; *State Records*, XVI, 473, 498, 500.

that quarter. Within a month there were reports that Wayne had confined the British in Georgia within Savannah.[18]

Less than a week before the arrival of the Pennsylvania Line a detachment of the North Carolina Brigade was organized under Reading Blount to replace the Virginia Continentals who had been serving with Lee's Legion. Blount's command was made up of three companies and had a total complement of 3 captains, 6 lieutenants, 10 sergeants, 9 corporals, and 150 privates. Within five days, two companies of the Pennsylvania Line, and three from the Maryland Line were added to this force, all under the command of Colonel John Laurens.[19]

This group had been created for a special mission. After the return of Major James Craig from Wilmington, his troops had been posted on John's Island south of Charleston, his original command supplemented by additional infantry and cavalry. Since the South Carolina legislature was soon to meet at Jacksonborough, Craig's presence presented a threat to that body. Laurens had proposed that the British be driven off by a night attack after the Americans had waded across Stono Inlet at low tide. Lee and Laurens were given a joint command of five hundred men for this task. By January 11 Laurens had marched his men for five days. That night there was a dinner for the officers at a nearby plantation, also attended by "some very rich ladies but not handsome."[20]

The approach to Stono Inlet was to be in two columns, one following the other. At sunset, January 12, the men began wading through the swamps. They joined Lee around midnight and continued on toward the Inlet. Somewhere along the way the second column with Blount's men became lost. At the stream crossing Laurens had gone on ahead, leaving the second column under the command of Major James Hamilton of the Pennsylvania Line. Lee and Laurens had led

18. *Pennsylvania Magazine of History and Biography*, XIX (1895), 218–19; Ebeneezer Denny, *Military Journal* (Philadelphia, 1859), p. 146; Greene to General Twiggs, 9 January 1782, Greene Papers, Duke University; *Magazine of American History*, VII (December, 1881), 439; *Collections of the New-York Historical Society for 1875*, pp. 497–99.

19. Pendleton Orderly Book; *State Records*, XVI, 473; *Pennsylvania Magazine of History and Biography*, XIX (1895), 218–19; Armstrong to Sumner, 3 January 1782, Jethro Sumner Papers, Southern Historical Collection; *Pennsylvania Archives*, 2nd Series, XI, 746, XV, 310–11.

20. *Pennsylvania Magazine of History and Biography*, LIV (1940), 310–11; *South Carolina Historical and Genealogical Magazine*, XVI (October, 1915), 139–40; *State Records*, XVI, 499; John Laurens to Greene, 2 January 1782, Revolutionary Collection, Duke University.

the first column through the ford to Stono. After waiting until nearly daybreak for the second column they led the troops back to the mainland to await the arrival of the trailing detachment.[21]

Once the two columns were rejoined they pulled back two miles, there to lie in the woods all day in a cold rain to "eat potatoes." The following day Laurens marched them down to Stono Inlet and had begun a crossing when a dispatch from Greene countermanded former orders, for it had been learned that the enemy had evacuated the island at midnight the night before. A part of the detachment was left on the far side of the inlet to round up Tories and gather horses.[22]

After this Laurens appeared to be leading his troops in aimless wanderings around the countryside in a steady rain and over muddy roads. In reality the movements were something of a patrol in force, with Laurens keeping his men between the enemy and the assembly sitting at Jacksonborough. On February 12 the detached companies were ordered to rejoin their brigades. Two days later they marched into Greene's camp on Pon Pon Creek.[23]

There had been some excitement during their absence. On January 20 Governor Thomas Burke had come into Greene's camp. After his capture by Fanning at Hillsborough Burke had been taken to Wilmington and Craig had sent him on to Charleston. After a period of close confinement on Sullivan's Island Burke was, on November 6, paroled to James's Island. Things ran smoothly until a number of Tory refugees were allowed to camp on the island, some of whom were from North Carolina and to whom Burke was personally obnoxious. Their resentment became evident when Burke's quarters were fired upon one night. Although the governor was not injured, one man was killed and another wounded. When a British officer took into custody one of those suspected of the shooting, his companions rescued him. Burke requested General Leslie to allow him a parole within American lines. Leslie never bothered to reply. The story was that Leslie was agreeable to such action, but that Craig had registered an objection, wishing to keep the governor as a hostage in the event that David Fanning was captured and executed. On the day after Burke broke his parole and took "French leave" a man was shot in the

21. Lee, *Memoirs of the War in the Southern Department*, pp. 528–36; *South Carolina Historical and Genealogical Magazine*, XXV (October, 1925), 211–12.

22. *Pennsylvania Magazine of History and Biography*, XIX (1895), 219; William Henry Egle (ed.), *Journals and Diaries of the War of the Revolution with Lists of Officers and Soldiers, 1775–1783* (Harrisburg, Pa., 1893), pp. 311–12.

23. *Pennsylvania Magazine of History and Biography*, XIX (1895), 219–21.

door of the governor's quarters on the assumption that he was Burke.[24]

Breaking a parole was serious business. On the afternoon that he arrived in Greene's camp, Burke requested a court of enquiry to investigate his conduct and justify the breaking of his parole. All the field officers of the army were called into council, chaired by General St. Clair, to determine whether the governor's conduct could be condoned. After the council had listened to Burke's story, it was reported that Burke had been justified in breaking his parole. But this was mere rumor, and the following month when Colonel Otho Williams was passing through North Carolina on his way to Maryland, he made the statement that the British still had a legal claim on the governor, and the fact that Burke had left headquarters to return home before the enquiry was concluded was felt to be "highly reprehensible and dishonorable to the State."[25]

The Burke case was to linger as a cause for controversy for some time, with Burke insisting that he be exchanged like any paroled officer and Leslie insisting that he be returned unconditionally. The affair occupied more time than it should have when the governor returned to North Carolina and indirectly hampered the recruiting for the Continental Line. Burke was in high spirits when he resumed the chair of chief executive, and soon was "now calling our overgrown fellows in the Public Departments to an account with a very becoming Severity, and is really making some Surprising discoveries," which, if true, may well have been the reason that local politicians made such a great noise about the governor violating the code of honor by breaking his parole.[26]

Burke worried about his public image and was apprehensive of the attitude of the Continental Congress, who he feared might take steps to censure or embarrass him, as "I am but too well acquainted with their modes of proceedings and indeed of thinking." So severe was the criticism by political enemies in North Carolina that the governor wrote Greene that the British "unfortunately place a higher value on me than my own country did, but a little time will make me

24. *State Records*, XVI, 13–19, 238–40, XXII, 606–8; *South Carolina Historical and Genealogical Magazine*, XXVI (October, 1925), 193–94; Burke to Willie Jones, 13 January 1782, Thomas Burke Papers, N.C. Dept. Arch. & Hist.

25. *Pennsylvania Archives*, 2nd Series (1879), XI, 74; *State Records*, XVI, 202, 251–52; Otho Williams to Davie, 24 February 1782, William R. Davie Papers, Southern Historical Collection; Davie to Burke, 23 February 1782, Davie Papers, North Carolina Department of Archives and History, Raleigh, N.C.

26. *State Records*, XVI, 538; Greene to Burke, 31 May 1782, Burke Papers, N.C. Dept. Arch. & Hist.

of no value to either, except as a mere obscure individual, for I am preparing as fast as possible to take a final leave of all public business. . . ." Alexander Martin, on whose shoulders the mantle of government would again fall should Burke carry out his threatened resignation, convinced the governor that his resignation would leave matters in general confusion and that he should remain in office at least until the next meeting of the General Assembly in April.[27]

Little progress had been made in reaching the state's quota of Continentals, despite the return of Burke. Sumner's continuing illness had caused the brigadier to allow military matters to slide. One of the reasons that Greene had sent Sumner back to North Carolina was to gather up all available cloth and have it made into military overalls. Not only had Sumner not executed this mission but he had not taken the trouble to make a report to Greene for the past three months. Since the victory at Yorktown and the gradual withdrawal of the British toward Charleston in South Carolina, the people appeared reluctant to support a war in its last stages. Those cattle collected for the army were "so wretched poor" that it was impossible to move them before spring, for it was diffcult to drive such thin livestock until the grass along the way had grown tall enough to feed them. An outbreak of smallpox in the coastal plains had hampered the collection of swine. Equally serious was the uprising of an estimated five hundred Tories in the area along the Waccamaw River, who prevented cattle drives to the army.

Many expedients were attempted in an effort to sign recruits for the line. A pardon was offered to all those deserters and delinquent draftees who came into the collecting points; few responded. To meet their Continental quota, the assembly had divided the militia into "classes" of twenty men each, with one man of each class to be drafted for eighteen month's service. If it so desired, a class could hire a substitute. In a similar fashion, any two classes, or forty men, could avoid active duty by sending a good wagon and team to serve with the army for eighteen months. The legislators were confident that at least two thousand men could be raised by this system. But the collecting of recruits was but the first of many problems. Many of those who were brought into the collecting points proved so obstreperous that they had to be confined in jails to prevent them from running away, and even then some escaped. When one hundred men were collected in the Wilmington district they were so "very naked" and so poorly

27. *State Records,* XVI, 179–80, 184–86, 214–16, 593; Burke to Greene, 31 January 1782, Burke to Greene, 12 April 1782, Lytle to Burke, 24 October 1782, Thomas Burke Papers, Southern Historical Collection.

armed that their commanding officer refused to march them southward. And when Allen Jones was approached for a loan of weapons from the militia supply he refused. In an attempt to rectify matters an assembly was called to meet at Salem, but not enough members appeared to make a quorum.[28]

The members of the governor's council met with Burke and bestowed upon him all the powers they were authorized to grant. The governor adopted extreme measures in attempting to meet the state's Continental quota. Four men under sentence of death were offered a pardon if they would agree to serve in the state Line for twelve months. Tories were offered an opportunity to regain their citizenship if they enlisted in the regulars, except "those guilty of murder, robbery, house burning, and crimes not justifiable by the Laws of War." Loyalists who had taken up arms against the patriot cause and who now refused to enter Continental service were to be considered prisoners of war eligible for exchange. Those who accepted the governor's offer were to be classified as "restored Citizens," and Burke undertook "immediate measures for bringing them to a decision."[29]

There were further complications in the gathering of supplies and provisions. Recruits were to be supplied by the Continental army, while draftees and substitutes were supplied necessities by their local militia unit. Some arms were procured from Virginia. Many draftees came into collecting points and, finding no responsible Continental officer on hand to receive them, immediately deserted. One-fourth of those brought into the rendezvous at Kinston deserted at the first opportunity.[30]

In Greene's camp there was little to do other than try to combat the boredom that often envelops an army too long in bivouac. Three soldiers of the Pennsylvania Line, one of the Maryland, and one of

28. *State Records,* XVI, 250, 476, 481, 497–98, 503, 510, 515–16, 684–85, 687; Ashe to Sumner, 21 November 1781, Greene to Sumner, 2 February 1782, Greene to Sumner, 30 March 1782, Sumner to Greene, 20 June 1782, Jethro Sumner Papers, Southern Historical Collection; Davie to Greene, 17 February 1782, Davie to Burke, 9 April 1782, William R. Davie Papers, Southern Historical Collection; Malichi Bell to _____, 12 March 1782, Robert Rowan to _____, 6 April 1782, Commissary Correspondence, Military Collection; Alexander Martin to Robert R. Livingston, 24 June 1782, Papers of the Continental Congress; Burke to Greene, 31 January 1782, Thomas Burke Papers, Southern Historical Collection.

29. *State Records,* XVI, 510–12, 522, 589–90; Alexander Martin to Greene, 10 February 1782, William R. Davie Papers, Southern Historical Collection.

30. *State Records,* XVI, 515, 529; John Eaton to William Caswell, 27 April 1782, William Caswell Papers, North Carolina Department of Archives and History, Raleigh, N.C.; Return of Continental Soldiers Rec'd at the Post at Kingston since the 22d of February 1782, Jethro Sumner Papers, Southern Historical Collection.

the North Carolina were hanged as a "dreadful example" before the entire army, their crimes listed only as "villanous conduct." Much time was spent on the drill field. On March 4 a grand review was held. The maneuvers included the firing of blank cartridges on command, "which alarmed the inhabitants," by platoon, battalion, and division. A number of the ladies of the neighborhood came out to witness the spectacle. A month later when a similar exercise was held it was noted that the North Carolina Brigade "made a verry bad fire."[31]

Greene was growing increasingly irritated with the manner in which the state had supported the brigade. Both North and South Carolina, he said, "appear like two great over grown babies who have got out of temper, and who have been accustomed to great indulgence. So little aid does either of those States give us that we cannot get on the public stores for the Army, and such too as we are in the greatest distress for want of." Sumner was chided, "There must be something fundamentally wrong in the mode of managing business in your State that Stores are applied, so contrary to positive orders, and some steps in future must be taken to correct that abuse." In an attempt to solve some of Greene's problems, John Armstrong was sent into the Salisbury district to lend his services in filling up the Continental units. Reading Blount was given leave with the understanding that his services would be available to Sumner in North Carolina should they be desired by the brigadier. Lieutenant Colonel Hardy Murfree assumed command of the brigade.[32]

According to resolves passed by the Continental Congress on October 3 and 30, 1780, it was necessary to rearrange the Continental Line on a proper footing. Because of the general confusion brought about by an enemy invasion and the lack of any considerable number of Continental soldiers in the field, the North Carolina Line had never complied with these directives, although Greene had urged that it do so as quickly as possible. Lieutenant Colonel Henry Dixon was sent south by Sumner, his mission "to Regiment the Officers of the said Line." Murfree was president of a board composed of Dixon, three majors, fifteen captains, and sixteen lieutenants, nearly all of the Continental officers with the southern army. Officers, even those who were still prisoners of war, were assigned, according to seniority, to the four regiments now authorized for North Carolina. For the First

31. *Pennsylvania Archives*, 2nd Series, XI, 753, 754, XV, 319; *Pennsylvania Magazine of History and Biography*, XIX (1895), 222.

32. *State Records*, XVI, 574; Greene to Sumner, 2 February 1782, Greene to Sumner, 30 March 1782, Jethro Sumner Papers, Southern Historical Collection; Greene to Joseph Reed, 27 February 1782, Joseph Reed Papers.

Regiment, Thomas Clark was designated colonel, Hardy Murfree lieutenant colonel, and John Nelson major; for the Second there was John Patten as colonel, Henry Dixon as lieutenant colonel, and Reading Blount as major; the Third Regiment was commanded by Lieutenant Colonel Selby Harney, with Thomas Hogg as second in command and Griffith J. McRee as major; the Fourth Regiment had Lieutenant Colonel Archibald Lytle (only recently exchanged) and Majors John Armstrong and George Donoho. There was an inordinate number of captains; the first three regiments were only allotted a nominal number, while the Fourth Regiment appears to have been designated as something of a catchall, for there were twenty captains assigned to it. Given a choice, Colonel James Armstrong, Lieutenant Colonel James Thackston, and Captain Francis Child chose to retire on half-pay. But the entire arrangement of the line was mostly on paper. A number of supernumerary captains were sent to North Carolina with dispatches and allowed to remain there until there was further need for them in the field. Some field officers pouted in discontent when Hardy Murfree and Henry Dixon were given commissions as lieutenant colonels back-dated to 1778 and given places of preferment in the First and Second Regiments. Seniority posed other problems. When clothing arrived for the officers, those officers still held prisoners in Charleston somehow learned about the issue and demanded their share. Greene refused Murfree's request that he be allowed to complete the First and Second Regiments, for the terms of enlistment for many of the line were running out and he wished to rebuild the regiments with new recruits. Those North Carolina Continentals still in camp Greene wished to use as small detachments for special missions. Around the first of April, a hundred men were discharged and allowed to return to their homes. Others, feeling that the war was over and that they had fulfilled their obligations to the American cause, deserted to return to their families. Still others went over to the enemy.[33]

Both officers and men were growing irritable, so much so that Greene was led to complain, "Our operations this year are as insipid

---

33. *State Records*, XVI, 501, 508, 573, 574, 588–89, 592, 603–4; Proceedings of a Board of Officers, N.C. Line, 6 Feb. 1782 Ponpon, Held to "Regiment the Officers of the Line," Revolutionary War Rolls, Adjutant-General's Office; Dixon to Sumner, 6 February 1782, Murfree to Sumner, 31 March 1782, Approval of Arrangement of North Carolina Line, 24 April 1782, Resolutions of House of Commons, 26 April 1782, Greene to Sumner, 2 July 1782, Jethro Sumner Papers, Southern Historical Collection; Samuel Huntington Circular Letter, 30 November 1780, Lloyd Smith Collection; Greene to Lincoln, 6 February 1782, Nathanael Greene Papers, William L. Clements Library.

as they were important the last." Many blamed the civil authorities for their unhappiness, often venting their annoyance on the governor as the symbol of authority, forgetting that the state constitution and the assembly had stripped that executive of most of his powers. Captain Samuel Jones of the North Carolina Line was brought before a court-martial charged with using strong language against Governor Alexander Martin, which was interpreted as "scandilous and infamous behaviour unbecoming the officer and gentleman." Although the court held that the charges against Jones were "malicious and vexative," Greene observed in his general orders that "although the General does not disapprove the sentence of the Court, he cannot help observing, that the words made use of by Capt. Jones with respect to Governor Martin seem extremely indelicate; that expressions of such a nature, applied to civil officers in high station or authority have a tendency to injure the service, and certainly unworthy the person useing them on any occasion in well bred men."[34]

By May the North Carolina Line was down to but a shadow of its former strength. On March 7, 170 men had come in—without arms. Only 44 recruits had arrived since that time. Others had been enlisted, but had been kept at home because there had been no provisions to feed them on the march to Greene's camp. Those who had been drafted for twelve month's service after Guilford were now clamoring for their discharges. In April the enlistments for 326 troops expired, and 299 left for home in May. Another 141 men were to leave in June. Few would consider re-enlistment. These men, according to North Carolina law, were not liable for further military service for at least a year, but Murfree was convinced that he could persuade a sizable number to re-enlist. He applied to Greene for money to pay bonuses; the general had none. Yet Greene was unhappy to see so many able-bodied soldiers leaving the field and, although against North Carolina law, he ordered Murfree to allow the recruiting officers of Lee's Legion and of the South Carolina Line to try to enlist those whose time had expired or would expire within the following month. Murfree, who had no choice except to comply, saw a number of his men enlisted in the South Carolina forces for a bounty of three Negro slaves for three years' service. Still South Carolinians had the temerity to criticize both North Carolina and Virginia for not having more regiments in the field and because "those states are most shamefully deficient in the quota of troops that they ought to furnish." But by enlisting in other units, the men did have an op-

34. *Pennsylvania Magazine of History and Biography*, XIX (1895), 244; Greene to Reed, 10 July 1782, Joseph Reed Papers.

portunity to secure better clothing, while Murfree's men had "not 1/2 a yard cloathing about them, and are returned not fit for duty, for want of cloathing."[35]

Provisions were equally scarce. Sumner had left his personal baggage wagon in camp when he returned to North Carolina, and Murfree, excusing his actions on the grounds that the provisions were spoiling, took the food from it and issued it to the officers. Not only had Sumner's food been taken, but the waggoner, who had remained with the wagon, stayed drunk off Sumner's brandy most of the time. Part of the shortages were the result of supplies and provisions ordered south by the Continental Congress being "delayed and embezzled along the road." An investigation was ordered.[36]

To many it had now become evident that the war was drawing to an end. Three ships of war convoying sixteen empty transports had dropped anchor in Charleston harbor, and the rumor was that they had come to take the Nineteenth and Thirtieth Regiments either to Georgia or the West Indies. The only enemy activity was in sending out small reconnoitering parties, but once the British were spotted and Greene's army fell out under arms "they loose no time in geting back again." Greene rode down one day to view the enemy works, a part of his escort made up of a detachment from the North Carolina Brigade. British soldiers were captured outside the works, but the main army only fired at the Americans and refused to be provoked into going outside the fortifications. Greene could not bring himself to believe that the war was nearly over; he refused to believe that there could be a cessation of hostilities until France had also made peace with Britain. And there was also the continuing and at times even vicious struggle between Whig and Tory.[37]

The greatest excitement during the spring was a revolt in the Pennsylvania Line. A number of British deserters who had been enlisted in these regiments planned to either seize their officers and carry

35. *South Carolina Historical and Genealogical Magazine*, XXVII (April, 1926), 61; General Orders, 30 April 1782, Return of the expiration of Inlistments of the North Carolina Troops, 1782, Murfree to Sumner, 26 April 1782, Jethro Sumner Papers, Southern Historical Collection; Act of South Carolina General Assembly, 26 February 1782, Papers of the Continental Congress.

36. *State Records*, XVI, 611, 612, 614, 616, 622, 625, 629, 686–88; *Pennsylvania Archives*, 2nd Series, XI, 754, XV, 319; Murfree to Sumner, 1 May 1782, Murfree to Sumner, 1 June 1782, Jethro Sumner Papers, Southern Historical Collection.

37. *State Records*, XVI, 615; *Pennsylvania Archives*, 2nd Series, XV, 320; Murfree to Sumner, 1 May 1782, Murfree to Sumner, 15 May 1782, Jethro Sumner Papers, Southern Historical Collection; Greene to Alexander Martin, 31 May 1782, Greene Papers, Duke University.

them into Charleston or wait until the enemy attacked and then go over to them. A Sergeant Gosnall, a British deserter and leader of the insurgents, was shot. Four British deserters who had enlisted in the Pennsylvania Line and who were suspected of involvement in the plot were sent off under guard into North Carolina, there to work in the laboratory at Frohock's Mill near Salisbury making cartridges, a fate that Greene said soldiers felt to be a disgrace "little less than death."[38]

The Continental officers were concerned about their future. The North Carolina Assembly had now provided for commissioners to lay off bonus lands for its soldiers along the Cumberland River, including 25,000 acres voted to General Greene. To protect their interests, the officers in camp gathered to elect representatives to see that they received their just dues in the survey. They recommended Lieutenant Colonel Selby Harney, Major John Nelson, and Captains Tilghman Dixon and Alexander Brevard. They also suggested that Dr. Thomas Bull be included in the party, not only for his medical skills but because he could speak Spanish fluently and much of the land to be surveyed was along the borders of land where Spanish-speaking people resided.[39]

The monotony of camp routine was broken somewhat by the celebration of Independence Day on July 4. At five that afternoon the army was drawn up in a long single line to salute Greene. Thirteen cannon were fired to celebrate the independence of the thirteen states, followed by a twenty-one gun salute to honor the birth of the new Dauphin of France, then a *feu de joie* of running fire from one end of the line to the other. At the conclusion of the firing the army passed in review, and that night the officers were entertained by General Greene and Governor Rutledge.[40]

It was still a ragged and hungry army that had celebrated independence. Because General Leslie had indicated to the inhabitants that the city would be soon evacuated, too many people assured themselves that the war was over and there was no longer any reason for maintaining an army in the field. Quartermasters now insisted that

38. *State Records,* XVI, 615–16; *Pennsylvania Magazine of History and Biography,* XIX (1895), 225; Greene to Reed, 10 July 1782, Joseph Reed Papers; Balch, *Papers of the Maryland Line,* p. 177; *Pennsylvania Archives,* 2nd Series, XV, 320; Merritt, *Calendar of the Otho Williams Papers,* pp. 54, 66; Murfree to Sumner, 15 May 1782, Jethro Sumner Papers, Southern Historical Collection.

39. *State Records,* XVI, 164–65, 324–25, 621–22, 623–24, 713; Murfree to Sumner, 1 June 1782, Thomas Bull to Sumner, 1 June 1782, Jethro Sumner Papers, Southern Historical Collection.

40. *Pennsylvania Archives,* 2nd Series, XV, 325; *Pennsylvania Magazine of History and Biography,* XIX (1895), 227.

the details of supplying the troops be followed to the letter of the law. When there were wagons available to transport supplies there was a shortage of wagoners, for these men had gone home to plant or harvest their crops. Governor Alexander Martin steadfastly refused to allow militia arms to be issued to Continental recruits. As an example of the inefficiency of the times, a quantity of Continental weapons was discovered, but apparently no one could be found who knew for whom the arms had been intended, or even when they had arrived.[41]

The same lethargy and lack of coordination in the supply situation was evident in the collection of recruits for the line. There seemed to be a reluctance on the part of junior officers to make an appearance at the various rendezvous points to assist in marching recruits southward. Many had no desire to command Tories who, now that the outcome of the war seemed certain, "conscious of their delusion return with the cheerfulness to their allegiance and duty in support of the common cause." An increasing number of officers were offering their resignations because they could no longer bear the financial strain of remaining on duty. A number of the draftees brought in were found to be physically unfit for service; others deserted at the first opportunity. Those who did arrive in Greene's camp were so poorly trained that their drills were described as "amazingly bad."[42]

By August 9 there were reports that not only Charleston but New York was to be evacuated. Hessian and British deserters began slipping out of town to "make their peace with the State." On August 15, 1782, Anthony Wayne led his troops back into camp, Savannah having been evacuated by the enemy on July 11.[43]

Officers continued to harbor a lingering fear concerning their military status. The situation remained confused, brought about by the capture of the North Carolina Brigade at Charleston and resignations and retirements of officers, coupled with the general chaos of the times. Despite the formal arrangements of the line, others feared a retrenchment by an ungrateful government. This gnawing fear was by no means indigenous to the North Carolinians but was present as a persistent apprehension in all state lines. The men also feared

41. *State Records*, XVI, 632, 633, 635–36, 638, 642–43; *Collections of the New-York Historical Society for 1875*, p. 504.

42. *State Records*, XVI, 636–37, 638–42, 644–45; Alexander Martin to Robert R. Livingston, 20 August 1782, Papers of the Continental Congress. *Pennsylvania Archives*, 2nd Series, XV, 321.

43. *Pennsylvania Archives*, 2nd Series, XV, 327; *State Records*, XVI, 640–41.

the capriciousness of state legislatures, who sometimes elevated officers with no regard for seniority.

And now Congress had suggested a new arrangement of Continental units in the field. When this arrangement was completed, it was to be submitted to Major General Benjamin Lincoln, now secretary of war, who was to use this disposition in determining the number of regiments each state was to maintain in the field. To provide guidelines, the Continental Congress, on August 7, 1782, resolved that the various lines should be rearranged into regiments of not less than five hundred men each. If there were additional men after the regiments had been completed, they were to be assigned to company-strength units until there were enough new recruits gathered to build a new regiment. Officers were assigned on a basis of seniority. Surplus officers were to retire, but could be recalled as needed, and during their absence they were to enjoy all the rewards and emoluments of their rank. The new arrangement was to go into effect on January 1, 1783.[44]

On November 10, 1782, Reading Blount assumed the role of president of a board of officers to determine the new arrangement, especially of company-grade ranks. Field-grade officers retained their commands according to the arrangement of February 6, 1782, although Archibald Lytle and John Armstrong were left without active roles since there were only enough men to make up three regiments at this time. The greatest shortage appeared among lieutenants and ensigns. Some of these junior officers who had agreed to march draftees to camp were placed on active duty once they reached the army, occasionally against their wishes. Greene urged Sumner to send forward all available officers named in the new arrangement as "the troops are so raw & undisciplined that every exertion & attention of their Officers will barely fit them for the opening of the ensuing campaign." Greene was so distressed with the new draftees that he dispatched Archibald Lytle to the North Carolina Assembly to protest "some abuses which have been practiced in furnishing the last drafts from your state."[45]

During the hot, sultry days of August and September the southern army was able to do little, for at least one-half of the troops were down with malaria or other endemic fevers of the low country. Since

44. *State Records,* XVI, 391–92, 650–51, 653, 664–65; _____ to Lytle, 2 September 1782, Miscellaneous Papers, 1697–1912; John Armstrong to Sumner, 4 September 1782, Lloyd Smith Collection.

45. Burnett to Sumner, 20 September 1782, Greene to Sumner, 11 November 1782, Jethro Sumner Papers, Southern Historical Collection; *State Records,* XVI, 666–67.

the first of July 106 men of the Pennsylvania Line had died and over 200 of the entire army had found their graves in that swampy land. Deaths were so frequent that Greene ordered that all funeral services be stopped lest they give an even more morbid air to the camp. Both the general and Anthony Wayne suffered severe attacks of disease. Although better acclimated than the Pennsylvanians, of the 305 North Carolinians in camp in mid-September, 107 were ill and between 20 and 30 had died.[46]

On October 23, 1782, there was an agreement for a general prisoner exchange. Included was Thomas Burke, but the cartel had come too late to save his political career. Among others who were exchanged was Lieutenant Colonel Selby Harney, although he was still so handicapped by a hip wound received in Charleston that he was unable to rejoin the army until the musket ball had been removed. Unfortunately Greene had not captured enough field officers to exchange for Colonels Thomas Clark and John Patten or Major John Nelson. Also left in British hands because of the lack of proper ranks to exchange were eight captains, three captain-lieutenants, five lieutenants, and one surgeon.[47]

With South Carolina depending too much on its militia and partisan corps and Virginia falling into a seeming lethargy after Yorktown, Greene was beginning to rely more upon the state of North Carolina for the maintenance of his army. He constantly urged the governor to fill his regiments, explaining that "the Country will be more secure and less ravaged, and the expence is far less, than when the war is carried on with Militia, besides the interruption which calling the militia gives to all kinds of business, the general corruption of morals follows, for want of discipline." By the first of November, however, only about 600 of a promised 1,200 Continental recruits had reached the southern army from North Carolina, the discrepancy a result of the "great supineness of the Militia officers." The general also demanded 3,000 head of cattle from the state, and if they were too thin, he demanded that they be driven to South Carolina where they could be fattened on the rice plantations. He called for

46. *Pennsylvania Archives,* 2nd Series, XV, 330; Denny, *Military Journal,* p. 428; Smith, *Life . . . of Arthur St. Clair,* I, 570; *State Records,* XVI, 659; Greene to Charles Pettit, 27 November 1782, Joseph Reed Papers; Return of the North Carolina Battalion of Foot, Commanded by Lieut. Col. Lytle, Sept. 14, 1782, Revolutionary Papers, Southern Historical Collection.

47. *State Records,* XVI, 444, 661–62, 669, 671–75; American Officers Taken in the Southern Department, 26 November 1782, Bruce Cotten Collection, Southern Historical Collection, The University of North Carolina at Chapel Hill, Chapel Hill, N.C.; Burke to Greene, 1 December 1782, Thomas Burke Papers, N.C. Dept. Arch. & Hist.

measures to be taken against the lawlessness of the citizens who, when quartermasters impressed wagons for the use of the army, rose up and took them away by force. Heavy punishment was recommended for those commissioners who were negligent in collecting the specific tax. But Greene was grasping at straws, for North Carolina had not yet recovered from the demands and ravages of both friendly and enemy military forces.[48]

Governor Alexander Martin did what he could; but not only had he found the specific tax to be a "mere Nullity" but he explained to Greene that "the Executive fettered with restrictions in the Acts of Assembly walk on ticklish ground if they deviate in any uncommon exertions not authorized by Law; which renders it difficult for me to supply the wants of the Army immediately as you request." In a call to the members of the legislature, Martin included the plea, "Let me not forfeit your Confidence by being compelled to wrest from you your provisions by the hand of violence, a measure obnoxious to you, to me, and every free mind. Let me walk with the Legislative aid, lest the road of Discretion be the road of Tyranny." Still the governor was forced to resort to the "odious and disagreeable measure of impressment" when the people refused to give up their cattle by barter, purchase by certificate, by contract, or in voluntary support of the army.[49]

Equally disturbing to Martin was the general atmosphere within the state, for with victory in sight many people were more interested in punishing those who had disagreed with them in political principles than they were in the conduct of the war. In Bladen County an uprising against the Tories was led by Captain Robert Raiford of the Continental Line. The captain, at the head of thirty armed men, burst into the county courthouse and attacked Archibald MacLaine "at the bar with a naked sword, beat and dangerously wounded him, unarmed in the exercise of his profession, before the Court; under the pretence that the said Maclain had given him sometime before abusive language, and was then defending a Tory, the Court endeavouring to quell the disturbance." After beating the clerk, for no apparent reason, the rioters moved back into the street. After electing "field officers," they "marched about the County under the color of apprehending Tories without any order from any commanding offi-

48. *State Records*, XVI, 451, 677–80; Thomas Posey to Greene, 16 March 1782, Miscellaneous Papers, New-York Historical Society; *Pennsylvania Archives*, 2nd Series, XV, 30; Greene to Martin, 11 July 1782, Greene to Martin, 11 July 1782, Greene Papers, Duke University.

49. *State Records*, XVI, 463, 702–05, 707, 712; _____ to Archibald Lytle, 2 September 1782, Miscellaneous Papers, 1697–1912.

cer for this purpose, to the great Terror of the Good Citizens of the State." By the time a warrant was issued against Raiford, he was back with Greene's army where he had been put in command of the light infantry. It was not until a year later that Raiford was brought to trial and then he was acquitted, possibly because of his crying out against the Tories when he attacked MacLaine.[50]

As a result of a resolution by the Continental Congress stating that no troops should remain in the field except those who had enlisted for three years and because of the difficulty of feeding and clothing the troops in the Southern Department, Greene, near the end of 1782, ordered all North Carolina troops home except one regiment. Officers were directed to furlough their men until further orders. Greene's idea was not to dismiss the men altogether, but to allow them to remain at home with no pay, no clothing issue, and no ration allowance.[51]

On Saturday, December 14, 1782, the last great goal in the South was achieved: the British evacuation of Charleston. Greene agreed to a peaceful occupation of the city. Anthony Wayne, with four companies of light infantry, a part of Lee's cavalry, and two artillery pieces, had been allowed to cross the Ashley River and move down near the British works. Leslie notified Wayne that he would pull back his British troops from the works at the firing of the morning gun, at which time Wayne could move his men forward but no nearer than 200 yards from the British rear guard. The agreement was followed to the letter, except that now and then the British would call out that the Americans were too close. By eleven o'clock Wayne was in possession of the statehouse.

By three that afternoon Greene, accompanied by Governor John Mathews of South Carolina, his council, and other prominent citizens, and escorted by a troop of 150 cavalry, rode into Charleston in triumphant procession. The balconies, doors, and windows were crowded as well as the streets, many crying out, "God bless you, Gentlemen! You are welcome home, gentlemen!"[52]

"One universal joy," wrote William Pierce, "seems to reign through the whole country. The fetters of tyranny are taken off, and the goddess of liberty seems to be the companion of everyone." Even in the midst of celebration, however, the general could see nothing but trouble in the future, for he feared the southern states would now

50. *State Records*, XVI, 717, 720, 723–24, 741–42, 991.
51. Pendleton Orderly Book.
52. Moultrie, *Memoirs of the American Revolution*, II, 358; Balch, *Maryland Line*, p. 201; Smith, *Life . . . of Arthur St. Clair*, I, 571.

turn their attentions to their own problems and neglect the army. General Greene just could not seem to convince himself that the British were giving up the fight.[53]

And so the year 1782 came to an end, a year in which there had been less action than at any time since the war began. By the first of January, 1783, there did not appear to be a great deal for the Continentals to do other than mopping up and performing housekeeping chores. Greene rather aptly summed up the situation when he said, "I believe both the people and the Army are tired of war. The one from the expense, the other from getting no pay."[54]

53. *Magazine of American History,* VII (December, 1881), 445; Greene to Charles Pettit, 28 December 1782, Joseph Reed Papers.

54. *Pennsylvania Magazine of History and Biography,* XIV (1890), 83–84.

Chapter 20
*P*eace

*"I hope this may be a happy close
to the southern war."*

Bringing a war to an end is a complex and messy business, especially when that war is a result of a revolution and the traditions and formalities of both war and government have been so long neglected. The fighting was over, although the war had not ended, for in early 1783 there was only a provisional treaty of peace. Yet British trading vessels were already freely entering American ports. The men of the American army were now little more than bystanders awaiting the outcome of diplomatic negotiations.[1]

In North Carolina Governor Alexander Martin was attempting to assemble the legislature, but a majority of the delegates refused to attend, many declaring that they had been so impoverished by the war that they could not afford to make the trip. This delay, in turn, compelled Martin to spread his energies over a wide area of military and civil activities. One problem that complicated the governor's routine was that of Lord Charles Montague, a lieutenant colonel in the British army. Montague, his son, and five other British officers had been captured at sea by a privateer and brought as prisoners into Wil-

---

1. *State Records,* XVI, 729–30.

mington. His lordship requested that he be allowed a parole to New York or some other British post, but Martin refused the petition until he had first investigated rumors regarding Montague's past conduct. It had been said that Montague had gone aboard the prison ships anchored in Charleston harbor and there, by the use of dire threats, had forced prisoners from the North Carolina and Virginia Lines to enlist in his regiment. They had been sent to serve in the West Indies where, it was said, "they have chiefly perished." When the problem was passed on to Greene he investigated and discovered that the enlistments in British service had been voluntary on the part of the men, perhaps to escape their miserable existence aboard the prison hulks.[2]

Greene had by now established himself in Charleston, a town "neither so large or elegant as I expected; and yet it contains a great number of Houses and many of them are spacious and noble buildings. The People are flocking down like Jews to the Temple. I hope this may be a happy close to the southern war."[3]

By the first of January, 1783, most of the army had been posted on James's Island. The troops were immediately put to work clearing away a bivouac area adjacent to a forest of tall, stately pine trees. The encampment became something of a small city, with huts constructed along well laid-out streets, and the whole surrounded by an almost impenetrable wall of stumps and brush. The rank and file were allowed to hunt game in the forest, as well as to fish and gather oysters and stone crabs to provide welcome deviations from an otherwise drab diet. Provisions began to come in at a more generous rate than at any time since the war began. Clothing for the first time in several years was not a critical issue.[4]

The rank and file were frequently exercised on the drill field. At other times they were kept out of mischief by digging out the stumps that had remained when trees were cut to be used in constructing the huts. Off-duty officers were often rowed over to the city for their relaxation. Others, in rotation, dined with Greene at the home of Governor John Rutledge, the general's Charleston headquarters. Even death had taken on a greater dignity and a more profound sense of mourning than had been possible during the war. When Colonel John Stewart of the Maryland Line broke his neck when thrown from his horse into a ditch, every off-duty officer in the army attended the funeral services in Charleston.[5]

2. *Ibid.*, 733, 735, 739-40, 740-41, 742-43, 768.
3. Greene to Charles Pettit, 21 December 1782, Joseph Reed Papers.
4. *State Records*, XXII, 620-21.
5. Denny, *Military Journal*, pp. 50-52; Merrit, *Otho Williams Papers*, pp. 74-75.

The political leaders of South Carolina appeared now to be looking forward to their futures and seemingly regarded the southern army as a necessary nuisance. So apparent was this sentiment that Greene was led to comment that "the spirit of the people here leads to an almost independence of Congress and I fear this disposition will lead to an overturn of the present forms of Government . . . the whole country is so split into parties and factions and they are growing more and more violent every day." The politicians had grown so "jealous" of the military that Greene feared that "we shall starve or feed ourselves by force."[6]

Of the North Carolina Line, there was only the reconstituted First Regiment in Greene's camp, for the Continental Congress had resolved that only those men enlisted for three years or the duration of the war should remain in the field. Although there appeared to be little need for an army, Greene strove to prepare for any eventuality, and requested Governor Alexander Martin to lend him some of North Carolina's heavy artillery to defend Charleston. The knowledge that the enemy still maintained a considerable force at St. Augustine led the general to fear that hostilities could be resumed at almost any time, particularly since he held an abiding distrust of the "turn of politicks in Europe." A number of North Carolina Continental officers, including Lieutenant Colonel Hardy Murfree, retired on the "half-pay establishment" because of the press of personal affairs. They were, in effect, retiring from the service, for a recent resolution of the Congress had stated that those who sought retirement at this time would be "precluded from the right of ever being called into service hereafter" during the remaining days of the war. Greene allowed Sumner to stay in North Carolina to superintend recruiting activities and attend to his personal affairs.[7]

The majority of the North Carolina officers taken at the fall of Charleston were now exchanged, although Colonel Thomas Clark was so ill that he was forced to remain in bed for some time after his release. On September 30, 1783, he was to be brevetted a brigadier general.[8]

Despite assurances of peace, there was a continuing, though half-hearted, attempt to recruit for the North Carolina Line. Those who were persuaded to sign enlistment papers received no supplies. Some

6. Greene to Reed, 23 April 1783, Joseph Reed Papers.

7. *State Records*, XVI, 725, 768, 930–31, XXII, 620–21; Greene to _____, 2 February 1783, Greene Papers, Duke University; Greene to Sumner, 2 February 1783, Greene's Instructions to Lieutenant Colonel Stewart, 26 December 1782, Jethro Sumner Papers, Southern Historical Association.

8. *State Records*, XVI, 934–35, 997.

of those who had signed earlier had remained so long at collecting points that a considerable portion of their terms had gone by. By January 9, however, a few recruits from North Carolina had trickled into Greene's camp, but by then the general had made up his mind to relieve the supply situation by furloughing many of those soldiers who had only a few months to serve.[9]

But by April 23, recruiting and decisions to furlough assumed a relatively unimportant role as news was received in Greene's headquarters of the preliminary peace terms signed in Paris. The Pennsylvania, Maryland, and North Carolina Lines, along with the four artillery companies stationed on James's Island celebrated with a "grand review," followed by feasting, fire works, and dancing for the officers. A number of ladies, accompanied by gentlemen from Charleston, came over to witness and participate in the festivities.[10]

Although there was general satisfaction expressed about the puff and pomp of ceremony, there were many who regarded the army as little more than a vehicle for spectacle. Local politicians not only ignored the needs of the troops but Greene complained that "no sooner was the Enemy gone than those in power began to feel jealous of the Army."[11]

With the tidings of peace, the army grew restless. For many there were crops to be planted and families to be comforted. Others, remembering the summer of 1782 when so many of their comrades had found their graves in the sand clay soil of South Carolina, held no desire to spend another warm season in the area. Despite Greene's directive that "the Army will not relax its discipline," the troops grew irritable and sullen. In May the men of the First Regiment of Virginia Cavalry rode off home and sold their horses, although the animals were the property of the Continental army. They received no punishment. The Legion cavalry almost mutinied until pacified by Greene, and near the first of June the Maryland troops were threatening to pack their gear and march home. The Pennsylvania Continentals murmured, while the Virginia Line verged on outright mutiny. Greene quelled their irascibility by throwing the ringleader into confinement and drawing up the remaining troops in battle formation. The 476 men, present and fit for duty, of the North Carolina Regiment were just as restless, but remained comparatively quiet,

9. Francis Mentges to Steuben, 9 January 1783, Steuben Papers; *State Records,* XVI, 942.
10. Denny, *Military Journal,* pp. 51–52; Greene to Reed, 23 April 1783, Joseph Reed Papers; Frances Mentges to Steuben, 2 April 1783, Steuben Papers.
11. Greene to Reed, 23 April 1783, Joseph Reed Papers.

although 22 men deserted between the April and May inspections. The general spirit of irritability communicated itself to the officers, who resorted to duelling to ease their tensions and frustrations. Others neglected routine duties to engage in private business.[12]

By June 26 Greene had received the resolution of Congress to furlough all troops while awaiting the final signing of the definitive peace treaty. It was suggested that he put this directive into effect as quickly as possible. All military supplies were to be stored in magazines.[13]

Most of the Continentals were to be transported home by ship. As the temperature climbed, so did apprehensions of a return of the fevers. Troops began to drift off in "great numbers" and there were continued whisperings that the entire army might walk away in a body. Not until July did the troop transports begin to drop anchor in Charleston harbor. While those from the more northerly areas began their embarkation, the North Carolina and Virginia troops started on an overland march home. Although the men were supposed to have been given three months' pay when furloughed, there was no money in the Continental treasury and the troops were issued promissory notes rather than cash. Greene paid them tribute "because no Army ever suffered such a variety of distresses." He assured them that they would be "paid with Justice, if not rewarded with Liberality, and this will be done as soon as the Nature of our unsettled Country, and the State of its Finances will admit." And then they marched away. By July 29 Greene was "left like Samson after Delilah cut his locks."[14]

For a victorious army the end came rather quietly, with no great crescendo of victory or hallelujahs to mark its triumph. Not even one last grand review was held to hail success; there was only a gradual melting away of vagabond soldiers, making their way to their homes,

12. Pendleton to Greene, 4 July 1783, Greene to Lincoln, 17 May 1783, Eggleston to Greene, 12 May 1783, Greene to Lincoln, 3 June 1783, Nathanael Greene Papers, William L. Clements Library; Johnson, *Sketches of Greene*, II, 384; Greene's General Orders on the Peace, June 1783, Nathaniel Pendleton Papers, New-York Historical Society, New York, N.Y.; *State Records*, XVI, 930–31; Return of the 1st N.C. Regt., May 1783, Miscellaneous Papers, Military Collection; *Historic Letters from the Collection of the West Chester Normal School* (Philadelphia, 1898), pp. 28–30.

13. Greene to Lyman Hall, 26 June 1783, Greene to Habersham, 26 June 1783, Greene to Hall, 23 July 1783, William Jackson to Greene, 12 April 1783, Greene Papers, Duke University.

14. Greene to Lincoln, 18 June 1873, Greene to Lincoln, 11 July 1783, Nathanael Greene Papers, William L. Clements Library; General Orders, June 1783, Nathaniel Pendleton Papers; Greene to Pettit, 29 June 1783, Joseph Reed Papers; *State Records*, XIX, 945.

satisfying the gnawing in their bellies by begging, stealing, or using force. In a great hurry to get home, they spent little time reflecting upon the injustices they had experienced.[15]

It was Greene who kept memories of the war alive for the people of North Carolina. On August 11, 1783, the general, with two aides, set out in a carriage for the long overland journey to his home in Rhode Island. By August 22 he arrived at Wilmington, a town "not handsomely built or elegantly laid out." The leaders of local society attempted to persuade the general to spend more time with them than he had planned, but he wanted to get on with his journey. While in town, however, he was honored by bonfires in the streets, the firing of guns, and the illumination of houses in the evenings. On August 24 Greene rode north, escorted by Reading Blount. Along the way he visited Alexander Lillington, Thomas Blount, and William Caswell. At every stop as he traveled through Tarboro to Halifax he was lavishly entertained. His impressions of North Carolina are worth repeating:

Our passage through North Carolina had been rendered agreeable as possible by the polite attention of the inhabitants. It will be a long time before this State will begin to feel its importance. Dissipation and idleness are too predominant for either law or reason to control. The people live too remote from each other to be animated by a principle of emulation. When men live more contiguous they warm and rouse the passions of each other, and the desire of excelling inspires one common spirit of industry. What adds to the misfortunes of this State is, morality is at a low ebb and religion almost held in contempt, which are the great pillars of good government and sound policy. Where these evils prevail the laws will be treated with neglect and the magistrate with contempt. Patriotism will have little influence and government continues without dignity.[16]

With the North Carolina Continentals back home and trying to gather together the twisted threads of an interrupted civilian life, and with the last vestiges of the war disappearing as Greene crossed over into Virginia, the people of the state had more time to reflect upon the lessons learned during the past few years of turbulence. Few did, however, for the immediate problems were too pressing. It had been a long and hard war, with North Carolina feeling the heavy hand of the conqueror, which was even more oppressive for a state so poorly endowed with material wealth. Yet North Carolina had carried more than its share of the burden of war, in some ways more so than its wealthier neighboring states.

15. Davie to Greene, 12 December 1783, William R. Davie Papers, Southern Historical Collection.

16. Greene, *Life of Nathanael Greene*, III, 499–504.

Perhaps North Carolina's poverty can best be explained in terms of geography. There were few harbors and consequently few centers of commerce, and this, in turn, had led to a sparseness of stockpiles of supplies at the beginning of the war. And when the small farmers were taken from the land to serve as soldiers, shortages veered onto the acute, a situation sometimes intensified by such natural disasters as floods, droughts, and hurricanes.

In many ways, the state's position among the English colonies must be termed obscure. There had been little to focus attention upon the area. Other than the great plantations in the coastal plain, North Carolina was primarily a community of small farmers lying between two monuments to aristocracy. As late as 1851 a South Carolina writer was to refer to these small farmers as "peasantry." Both neighboring states were grounded in an economic system based on the plantation whose lands were cultivated by slaves. For Virginia and South Carolina this proved to be both a blessing and a handicap. Although slaves could ostensibly produce provisions for an army in the field, it was still necessary that a substantial number of whites remain behind to maintain control over them. Then, too, those of the upper strata of social, economic, and political rank considered themselves to be prime officer material and refused to lower themselves to serve in the ranks. This, however, was only a natural reaction for a society so structured, especially when those of the lower classes had so long looked up to those better educated and socially oriented for guidance and leadership.[17]

It was because of this basic attitude and relatively simple social hierarchy that North Carolina proved to be a fertile recruiting ground for South Carolina, Virginia, and even Georgia. In effect, men in the North Carolina regiments were in some instances stolen, or persuaded to desert, for these wealthier states were able to provide greater enlistment bonuses. A number of desertions credited to the rank and file of the North Carolina Line resulted from the powerful persuasions of recruiting officers of the Continental units of other states. In fact, some of the men of the ranks almost made a military career of deserting, enlisting in another regiment, collecting the bonus, and deserting still another time and enlisting and collecting still another bonus. One member of the North Carolina Line enlisted in five regiments just to collect the inducements.

Still the rate of desertion in the North Carolina Line was lower than in the military units of other states. Of the 6,086 men on the

17. Johnson, *Traditions and Reminiscences . . . of the American Revolution,* p. 551.

North Carolina Continental roster, 641 were listed as deserters, a percentage of 10.5, while the over-all rate of desertion in the Continental army was 18.2 percent. About 30 percent of those who deserted from North Carolina units and who were returned to service deserted another time. The longer a soldier served, the less likely he was to desert. Of those deserting the North Carolina Line, 70 percent had served less than a year, 17 percent one to two years, 8 percent two to three years, and 3 percent three to four years, while only a few took unauthorized leave after serving longer than the above periods. Still it should be pointed out that not many soldiers served longer than three years. There had been three peaks of desertion, the winter of 1777, the last half of 1779, and the first half of 1783.[18]

Not generally recognized, or emphasized as a handicap to the war effort in North Carolina, was the dissension and divided loyalties that ran strong beneath the surface. It has been said that in proportion to its total population North Carolina had more inhabitants of a loyalist bent than any other state. Although the Tories had been defeated at Moore's Creek Bridge they were not long subdued. When Whig spirits ran high, the Tories had lain quiet, but when necessary the latter had come out to disrupt recruiting campaigns and waylay supply trains. When British military support seemed promising these loyalists had come out in force, but their ambitions were frequently blunted by the swift reaction of the Whigs. Yet despite the lack of any notable success the loyalists were able to play a rather significant role, for when they came out in any numbers at all, prospective recruits for the Continental regiments remained at home to protect their homes and families. Some who lived in communities of strong loyalist sentiment were so intimidated that they either remained quietly at home or hid out in the woods. The word "neighbor" often took on a new meaning in North Carolina during the American Revolution.[19]

Equally frustrating for the war effort was the fondness of the state's political leaders for the militia, especially after it had won such stunning victories as Moore's Creek Bridge, Ramsour's Mill, and King's Mountain. Few would admit that these victories had been against their own kind and could not be considered as proof of how they would behave against British regulars. For many politicians the use of the militia proved to be a simple solution to the manpower problem, and they thought it would also cost less to maintain. They clung to this conviction even after it was demonstrated time and time

18. Thad W. Tate, Jr., "Desertions From the American Revolutionary Army" (M.A. thesis, University of North Carolina, 1948), pp. 9–11.
19. DeMond, *Loyalists in North Carolina during the Revolution,* p. vii.

again that these ill-trained, poorly disciplined troops, seldom available in adequate strength when needed and unsteady in battle, were wont to go home after the first spell of bad weather. But this was not a unique situation in North Carolina, for all states sought this solution to recruiting problems and were willing to repeat these same mistakes in the War of 1812 and the Civil War.

At times there were breakdowns in the leadership of the North Carolina Line, fortunately, in most cases, before such men reached the battlefield. A case in point is Abraham Sheppard, a man whose enthusiasm was boundless, but whose efforts bordered on the inept, and who somehow managed to see his command melt away before it reached a war zone. Almost pathetic were the efforts of the Frenchman Monsieur Chariol, who fell victim to petty politics and personal animosities when he attempted to recruit a regiment of southern Frenchmen on the Continental establishment.

On the other hand, there were able leaders whose efforts overshadowed those who failed. Among the regimental commanders, Thomas Clark and John Patten were outstanding, but both had their military careers cut short when they were captured at the fall of Charleston. Other regimental commanders may well have been just as impressive had they been given an opportunity and had not their regiments been consolidated with other units because of the lack of men. Even as supernumeraries many of these officers performed well when placed in critical positions. Clark may have been an outstanding brigadier had not his appointment become entangled in jealousies and trivial politics. Perhaps the leadership among the generals would have reached greater heights had not the careers of James Moore and Francis Nash been terminated by death in the earlier stages of the war. Such an evaluation is not intended to downgrade the ability of James Hogun and Jethro Sumner, for the results of their efforts were almost predestined by the conditions under which they operated. Hogun was competent and reliable, although not a spectacular officer. He performed his duties with thoroughness, but with a seeming lack of imagination. Jethro Sumner, who had been termed a man of "violent principle," but "of a person lusty, rather handsome, with an easy and genteel address," was caught between several fires as the only active brigadier general of the North Carolina Line during the last three years of the war. His labors were complicated by the chronic illness of his wife and his own frequent sicknesses. When given a chance to prove himself, he became a capable battlefield leader at Eutaw Springs. In general, North Carolina military leadership could rank with that of any other state when properly evaluated in light of the conditions under which they were forced to operate.[20]

North Carolina's only major general, Robert Howe, was too much in Continental service to have made significant contributions to the state units. Judging by Howe's performance at the Continental level, however, one is led to suspect that he leaned too much toward the spectacular. To do the man justice, on the other hand, Howe could possibly have been one of the better known officers of the Revolution had his timing been better in that his opportunities came at times when he had not the proper field strength.

One explanation for the weakness of the military establishment was the lack of a strong hand holding the reins of government. This statement is not to disparage the wartime chief executives of the state, but the governors, who should have been prime coordinators of military efforts, found their hands shackled to a great degree by the North Carolina Constitution of 1776, a document that did not allow the executive branch the dictatorial powers sometimes needed in war. And with the creation of a Board of War, and later a Council Extraordinary, to "aid" in the conduct of the war, confusion became a way of life. Equally responsible was the legislature, whose attention to political concerns and whose affinity for the operations and structures of the past did little to aid the total effort. For many, the war seemed an opportunity to achieve future political prominence, while they remained oblivious to the necessary exertions to be made if such opportunities were to be realized.

The financial situation continued in a constant state of crisis. Never a wealthy colony, North Carolina was an even poorer state and, like most other states, won its independence by fighting a war with a treasury that lay empty most of the time. The withdrawal of trade with England and the decline of transportation to other markets had so wrecked trade that little new money found its way into the state. The great quantity of paper money issued by both the Continental Congress and the state resulted in rampant inflation, so much so that by the end of the war it has been estimated that the Continental private was paid, if paid at all, the equivalent of six cents a month. The scarcity of money made taxes difficult to collect, even when payments were demanded in produce.

The continuing jealousies and suspicions between the individual states and a well-grounded distrust of any strong central authority combined to limit concentrated efforts. No state wished to waive authority to a central government, and this lack of trust was accentuated

20. Smyth, *Tour of the United States of America*, pp. 70–71.

by the fear of a highly organized and well-disciplined standing army.

In battle the rank and file of the North Carolina Line behaved as well as could be expected under fire. In the early years of the war when the fighting was concentrated in the northern colonies the North Carolinians did not reach the theater of action until the lines of other states had already been battle-tested. There was great jealousy among regiments concerning who should occupy the place of honor in battle, the most dangerous spot, usually on the flanks. Most of the regiments already in the field had seniority in length of service. As a result the North Carolina Line was customarily assigned a less prestigious position, and under Washington it was usually held in reserve until its men had been bloodied in battle. At Germantown, Stony Point, and Monmouth, when given their chances, the North Carolina Continentals had behaved well, much better, in fact, than they have been given credit for. On the Hudson and in other cantonments to the north they had performed well when called upon.

At Charleston in 1780, when that city fell to the enemy, the North Carolina Line became almost a memory. This disaster forced Jethro Sumner to attempt to rebuild the state's Continental units from almost nothing. There were many complications. The British invasion of North Carolina made recruiting almost impossible. After Greene had returned to South Carolina and Cornwallis had turned north into Virginia it had been necessary to draft those militiamen who had fled at Guilford Courthouse. Yet these men of supposedly capricious valor, had performed well under stress and had stood firm and covered themselves with glory at Eutaw Springs. Their behavior in smaller and lesser known actions had brought praise from General Greene, who held little brief for the militia, even when these men were drafted and playing the role of regulars. When forced into Continental units, they were almost always still referred to as militiamen, thereby denying them the credit they should have received for acting as regulars.

When reviewed in the light of the conditions existing in North Carolina at the time of the American Revolution, it can be concluded that the state and its people did their best under the circumstances and experienced, in the words of one James Campbell when he later applied for a pension, "a series of toils and dangers."[21]

21. *State Records,* XXII, 812.

Works Cited

Unpublished Papers

Adams, Samuel. New York Public Library, New York, N.Y.
Additional Manuscripts 14038, 14039. British Museum, London, Eng.
Admiralty Papers. Public Record Office, London, Eng.
American Loyalist Claims, 1775–1789 (transcripts). North Carolina
    Department of Archives and History, Raleigh, N.C.
Arnold, Benedict. New-York Historical Society, New York, N.Y.
Audit Office Records (transcripts). North Carolina Department of Ar-
    chives and History, Raleigh, N.C.
Autographs of Americans Collection. Pierpont Morgan Library, New
    York, N.Y.
British Headquarters Papers. Colonial Williamsburg, Inc., Williams-
    burg. Va.
Burke, Thomas. North Carolina Department of Archives and History,
    Raleigh, N.C.
————. Southern Historical Collection. The University of North
    Carolina at Chapel Hill, Chapel Hill, N.C.
Bush, John, Orderly Book. Southern Historical Collection. The Uni-
    versity of North Carolina at Chapel Hill, Chapel Hill, N.C.
Caswell, Richard. Duke University, Durham, N.C.
————. North Carolina Department of Archives and History, Ra-
    leigh, N.C.
————. Southern Historical Collection. The University of North
    Carolina at Chapel Hill, Chapel Hill, N.C.

Caswell, William. North Carolina Department of Archives and History, Raleigh, N.C.

Caswell Letterbook. North Carolina Department of Archives and History, Raleigh, N.C.

Clinton, Sir Henry. William L. Clements Library, University of Michigan, Ann Arbor, Mich.

Cogdill, Richard. North Carolina Department of Archives and History, Raleigh, N.C.

Coleman-Tucker Papers. Colonial Williamsburg, Inc., Williamsburg, Va.

Colonial Office Papers. Public Record Office, London, Eng.

Commissions Grants, 25 August 1777. National Archives, Washington, D.C.

Continental Congress, Papers of the. National Archives, Washington, D.C.

Continental Congress Delegates' Papers. North Carolina Department of Archives and History, Raleigh, N.C.

Cornwallis, Charles. Public Record Office (PRO), London, Eng.

Cotten, Bruce, Collection. Southern Historical Collection. The University of North Carolina at Chapel Hill, Chapel Hill, N.C.

Dartmouth Manuscripts (transcripts). North Carolina Department of Archives and History, Raleigh, N.C.

Davie, Preston, Collection. Southern Historical Collection. The University of North Carolina at Chapel Hill, Chapel Hill, N.C.

Davie, William R. North Carolina Department of Archives and History, Raleigh, N.C.

————. Southern Historical Collection. The University of North Carolina at Chapel Hill, Chapel Hill, N.C.

Emmet Collection. New York Public Library (transcripts), North Carolina Department of Archives and History, Raleigh, N.C.

English Records Transcripts, Foreign Office 1783–1794. North Carolina Department of Archives and History, Raleigh, N.C.

Gage, Thomas. William L. Clements Library, University of Michigan, Ann Arbor, Mich.

Gates, Horatio. New-York Historical Society, New York, N.Y.

Germain Papers. William L. Clements Library, University of Michigan, Ann Arbor, Mich.

Governors' Papers. North Carolina Department of Archives and History, Raleigh, N.C.

Graham, Joseph. North Carolina Department of Archives and History, Raleigh, N.C.

Graham, William A. North Carolina Department of Archives and History, Raleigh, N.C.

Greene, Nathanael. Duke University, Durham, N.C.

————. Library of Congress, Washington, D.C.

————. New-York Historical Society, New York, N.Y.

————. North Carolina Department of Archives and History, Raleigh, N.C.

————. William L. Clements Library, University of Michigan, Ann Arbor, Mich.

Greene Letterbook. New York Public Library, New York, N.Y.

Harmar, Josiah, Orderly Book. William L. Clements Library, University of Michigan, Ann Arbor, Mich.

Harnett, Cornelius. Southern Historical Collection. The University of North Carolina at Chapel Hill, Chapel Hill, N.C.

Hart, Oliver, Diary (copy). Duke University, Durham, N.C.

Hayes Collection (transcripts). North Carolina Department of Archives and History, Raleigh, N.C.

Historical Society of Pennsylvania Collection (photostats). North Carolina Department of Archives and History, Raleigh, N.C.

Hooke, George Philip, Journal of. William L. Clements Library, University of Michigan, Ann Arbor, Mich.

Howe, Robert, Orderly Book. William L. Clements Library, University of Michigan, Ann Arbor, Mich.

Howe, Robert. Southern Historical Collection. The University of North Carolina at Chapel Hill, Chapel Hill, N.C.

Hutson, Richard. Duke University, Durham, N.C.

Iredell Papers. Duke University, Durham, N.C.

Johnston, Charles E., Collection. North Carolina Department of Archives and History, Raleigh, N.C.

Johnston, Samuel. North Carolina Department of Archives and History, Raleigh, N.C.

Kirby, Ephraim. Duke University, Durham, N.C.

Kirkwood, Frederic, Collection. Columbia University, New York, N.Y.

Lamb, Gideon. North Carolina Department of Archives and History, Raleigh, N.C.

Lawson, Robert. Duke University, Durham, N.C.

Lillington Papers. Southern Historical Collection. The University of North Carolina at Chapel Hill, Chapel Hill, N.C.

Lincoln, Benjamin. Massachusetts Historical Society, Boston, Mass.

————. Southern Historical Collection. The University of North Carolina at Chapel Hill, Chapel Hill, N.C.

Liverpool Papers. Additional Manuscripts 38374. British Museum, London, Eng.

MacDonald, Donald. North Carolina Department of Archives and History, Raleigh, N.C.

MacDougall, Alexander. New-York Historical Society, New York, N.Y.

McHenry, James, Diary of. William L. Clements Library, University of Michigan, Ann Arbor, Mich.

McLean, Alexander. A Narrative of the Proceedings of a Body of Loyalists in North Carolina, in Genl. Howe's Letter of the 25th April 1776, English Records, Colonial Office, 1776 (transcripts). North Carolina Department of Archives and History, Raleigh, N.C.

Martin Papers, Additional Manuscripts 41361. British Museum, London, Eng.

Military Collection. North Carolina Department of Archives and History, Raleigh, N.C.

Miscellaneous Papers. New-York Historical Society, New York, N.Y.

_____. Public Record Office (PRO), London, Eng.

_____. William L. Clements Library, University of Michigan, Ann Arbor, Mich.

_____, 1697–1912. North Carolina Department of Archives and History, Raleigh, N.C.

_____, 1770–1896. Southern Historical Collection. The University of North Carolina at Chapel Hill, Chapel Hill, N.C.

Nash, Francis. Southern Historical Collection. The University of North Carolina at Chapel Hill, Chapel Hill, N.C.

Office of the Secretary of State, Papers in the. North Carolina Department of Archives and History, Raleigh, N.C.

Peebles, Lieutenant John, Journal of. Cunningham of Thornton Muniments, Scottish Record Office, Edinburgh, Scot.

Pendleton, Nathaniel. New-York Historical Society, New York, N.Y.

_____, Orderly Book. Library of Congress, Washington, D.C.

Reed, Joseph. New-York Historical Society, New York, N.Y.

Return of the Continental Soldiers together with the New Series from Hillsborough and Salisbury Districts . . . Commanded by Col. Jethro Sumner, Jany 29, 1779, in the possession of Curtis Carroll Davis, Baltimore, Md.

Revolutionary Collection. Duke University, Durham, N.C.

Revolutionary Papers. Southern Historical Collection. The University of North Carolina at Chapel Hill, Chapel Hill, N.C.

Revolutionary War Rolls, Adjutant General's Office. National Archives, Washington, D.C.

Schenck, David. North Carolina Department of Archives and History, Raleigh, N.C.

Smith, Lloyd, Collection. Morristown National Historical Park, Morristown, N.J.

Steele, John. North Carolina Department of Archives and History, Raleigh, N.C.

Steuben Papers. New-York Historical Society, New York, N.Y.

Sumner, Jethro. North Carolina Department of Archives and History, Raleigh, N.C.

_____. Southern Historical Collection. The University of North Carolina at Chapel Hill, Chapel Hill, N.C.

_____. William L. Clements Library, University of Michigan, Ann Arbor, Mich.

Turner, Jacob, Orderly Book. North Carolina Department of Archives and History, Raleigh, N.C.

Washington, George. Library of Congress, Washington, D.C.

Wayne, Anthony. Pennsylvania Historical Society, Philadelphia, Pa.

Weedon, George. Chicago Historical Society, Chicago, Ill.

Williams, John. Duke University, Durham, N.C.

Yorktown Papers, Siege of. Pierpont Morgan Library, New York, N.Y.

THESES

Naisawald, Louis van Loan. "The Military Career of Robert Howe." M.A. Thesis, University of North Carolina, 1948.

Tate, Thad W., Jr. "Desertions from the American Revolutionary Army." M.A. thesis, University of North Carolina, 1948.

NEWSPAPERS

Boston Gazette, 1774.
Maryland Gazette (Annapolis), 1775.
Morning Chronicle and London Advertiser, 1777.
New England Chronicle (Boston), 1776.
Newport [Rhode Island] *Gazette*, 1777.
New York Gazette and Weekly Mercury, 1778.
New York Journal, 1778.
North Carolina Gazette, 1777, 1778.
Pennsylvania Evening Post (Philadelphia), 1776.
Pennsylvania Packet (Philadelphia), 1778.
Royal Gazette (Charleston), 1781.
South Carolina and American General Gazette (Charleston), 1776.
Virginia Gazette (Williamsburg), 1775, 1776.

MAGAZINES AND JOURNALS

American Historical Record, 1873.
American Historical Review, 1926.
American Museum: Or Repository of Ancient and Modern Fugitive Pieces, etc., Prose and Poetry, 1789.
Annual Register, 1776–1781.
Bulletin of the New York Public Library, 1905.
Collector, The, 1962.
English Historical Review, 1951.
Gentleman's Magazine, 1776.
Graham's Magazine, 1845, 1847.
Historical Magazine, 1860, 1867.
Journal of American History, 1901.

Journal of Modern History, 1947.
London Magazine: Or Gentleman's Monthly Intelligencer, The, 1781.
Magazine of American History, 1879, 1880, 1881, 1885.
Magazine of History and Biography, 1879.
Magazine of History with Notes and Queries, 1928.
Magnolia: Or Southern Appalachian, 1843.
New England Magazine, 1902.
New Jersey Historical Society Proceedings, 1922–23, 1924.
North American Review, 1826, 1837.
North Carolina Historical and Genealogical Register, 1901.
North Carolina Historical Review, 1927, 1932, 1954.
North Carolina University Magazine, The, 1844, 1857.
Pennsylvania Magazine of History and Biography, 1877, 1878, 1887, 1890, 1892, 1895, 1897, 1898, 1902, 1906, 1908, 1910, 1911, 1939.
Portfolio, 3rd Series, I, 1813.
Proceedings of the American Antiquarian Society, New Series, XL, 1930.
Rhode Island Historical Society Publications, 1927.
Richmond College Historical Papers, 1915.
South Carolina Historical and Genealogical Magazine, 1915, 1917, 1925, 1926, 1937.
Southern Literary Messenger, 1839, 1845, 1859.
Virginia Magazine of History and Biography, 1943.

BOOKS

Abbatt, William (ed.). *Memoirs of Major-General William Heath, by Himself*. New York, 1901.
Adams, Charles Francis (ed.). *Familiar Letters of John Adams and His Wife Abigail Adams*. New York, 1876.
Alden, John Richard. *General Charles Lee: Traitor or Patriot?* Baton Rouge, La., 1951.
_____. *The South in the Revolution, 1763–1789*. Baton Rouge, La., 1957.
Almon, J. *The Remembrancer: Or Impartial Repository of Public Events for the Year 1776*. Part I. London, 1776.
Anderson Galleries. *The Library of Dr. Geo: C. F. Williams*. New York, 1934.
André, John. *Major André's Journal, 1777–1778*, ed. Henry Cabot Lodge. 2 vols. Boston, 1902.
Andrews, John. *History of the War with America, France, Spain, and Holland; Commencing in 1775 and Ending in 1783*. 2 vols. London, 1785.
Anon. *Impartial History of the War in America between Great Britain and Her Colonies, from Its Commencement to the End of the Year 1779*. London, 1780.

Ashe, Samuel A'Court. *History of North Carolina.* 2 vols. Greensboro, N.C., 1908–1925.

Balch, W. Thomas (ed.). *Papers Related Chiefly to the Maryland Line During the Revolution.* Philadelphia, 1857.

Bartlett, John Russell (ed.). *Records of Rhode Island and Providence Plantations in New England.* 10 vols. Providence, R.I., 1864.

Belcher, Henry. *The First American Civil War.* 2 vols. London, 1911.

Bill, Alfred Hoyt. *Valley Forge: The Making of an Army.* New York, 1952.

Billias, George A. (ed.). *George Washington's Generals.* New York, 1964.

Bland, Theodorick. *The Bland Papers,* ed. Charles Campbell. Petersburg, Va., 1840–43.

Brooks, Noah. *Henry Knox, a Soldier of the Revolution.* New York, 1900.

Brown, Lloyd A., and Howard Peckham (eds.). *Revolutionary War Journals of Henry Dearborn.* Chicago, 1939.

Burnett, Edmund C. *The Continental Congress.* New York, 1941.

—————— (ed.). *Letters of Members of the Continental Congress.* 8 vols. Washington, 1921–36.

Caldwell, Charles. *Memoirs of the Life and Campaigns of the Hon. Nathaniel Greene.* Philadelphia, 1819.

Carruthers, E. W. *A Sketch of the Life and Character of the Rev. David Caldwell, D.D.* Greensboro, N.C., 1829.

——————. *Interesting Revolutionary Incidents: And Sketches of Characters, Chiefly in the "Old North State."* Philadelphia, 1854.

Cary, A. D. L., and Stouppe McCace. *Regimental Records of the Royal Welch Fusiliers (Late the 23rd Foot).* London, 1921.

Chastellux, Marquis de. *Travels in North America in the Years 1780, 1781, and 1782,* trans. George Greive. 2 vols. London, 1787.

Clark, Walter (ed.). *The State Records of North Carolina.* 16 vols. Goldsboro, N.C., Winston, N.C., etc., 1895–1914.

Clinton, Sir Henry. *The American Rebellion: Sir Henry Clinton's Narrative of His Campaigns, 1775–1782,* ed. William B. Willcox. New Haven, Conn., 1954.

Collections of the Massachusetts Historical Society. 4th Series. Boston, 1858.

Collections of the New-York Historical Society for the Year 1875. New York, 1875.

Collections of the New-York Historical Society for the Year 1879. New York, 1880.

Collections of the New-York Historical Society for the Year 1882. New York, 1893.

Collections of the Rhode Island Historical Society. Providence, R.I., 1867.

Collins, James P. *Autobiography of a Revolutionary Soldier*, ed. John M. Roberts. Clinton, La., 1859.

Colonial Records. See Saunders, William L.

Connor, George W. (ed.). *Autobiography of Benjamin Rush*. Princeton, N.J., 1948.

Connor, R. D. W. *Cornelius Harnett*. Raleigh, N.C., 1909.

————. *History of North Carolina*. Vol. I. New York, 1919.

Conway, Moncure Daniel (ed.). *The Writings of Thomas Paine*. 2 vols. New York, 1894–96.

Custis, George Washington. *Recollections and Private Memories of Washington*. New York, 1860.

Daves, John C. (ed.). *Minutes of the North Carolina Society of the Cincinnati*. n.p., n.d.

Davidson, Chalmers G. *Piedmont Partisan: The Life and Times of Brigadier-General William Lee Davidson*. Davidson, N.C., 1951.

Dawson, Henry B. *Battles of the United States by Sea and Land*. 2 vols. New York, 1858.

————. *The Assault on Stony Point*. Morrisiana, N.Y., 1863.

DeMond, Robert O. *The Loyalists in North Carolina during the Revolution*. Durham, N.C., 1940.

Denny, Ebenezer. *Military Journal*. Philadelphia, 1859.

Dexter, Franklin Bowditch (ed.). *The Literary Diary of Ezra Stiles, D.D., LL.D., President of Yale College*. 3 vols. New York, 1901.

Dill, Alonzo Thomas. *Governor Tryon and His Palace*. Chapel Hill, N.C., 1955.

Douglas, R. D. (trans, ed.). *Charles Albert, Comte de More, Chevalier de Pontgibaud, a French Volunteer in the War of Independence*. New York, 1898.

Drake, Francis S. *Memorials of the Massachusetts Society of the Cincinnati*. Boston, 1873.

Draper, Lyman C. *King's Mountain and Its Heroes: History of the Battle of King's Mountain October 7th, 1780, and the Events Which Led to It*. Cincinnati, Ohio, 1881.

Drayton, John. *Memoirs of the American Revolution, From Its Commencement to the Year 1776, Inclusive: as Relating to the State of South-Carolina and Occasionally Referring to the States of North-Carolina and Georgia*. 2 vols. Charleston, S.C., 1821.

Duane, William (ed.). *Extracts from the Diary of Christopher Marshall, Kept in Philadelphia and Lancaster, during the American Revolution, 1774–1781*. Albany, N.Y., 1877.

Egle, William Henry (ed.). *Journals and Diaries of the War of the Revolution with Lists of Officers and Soldiers, 1775–1783*. Harrisburg, Pa., 1893.

Ewing, Thomas. *George Ewing, a Gentleman, a Soldier, at Valley Forge*. Yonkers, N.Y., 1928.

Fitzpatrick, John C. (ed.). *The Writings of George Washington.* 39 vols. Washington, 1931–44.

Force, Peter (comp.). *American Archives.* 4th Series. 6 vols. Washington, 1837–46.

Ford, Worthington C., et al. (eds.). *Journals of the Continental Congress, 1774–1789.* 34 vols. Washington, 1904–37.

Fortescue, Sir John. *A History of the British Army.* 13 vols. New York, 1899–1900; London, 1902.

————. (ed.). *The Correspondence of King George the Third from 1760 to December 1783.* 6 vols. New York, 1928.

Fowler, George L. (ed.). *A Narrative of the Life and Travels of John Robert Shaw, the Well Digger, Now Resident in Lexington, Kentucky, Written by Himself.* Lexington, Ky., 1807.

Freeman, Douglas Southall. *George Washington.* 8 vols. New York, 1948–57.

Fries, Adelaide L. (ed.). *Records of the Moravians in North Carolina.* 8 vols. Raleigh, N.C., 1922–47.

Garden, Alexander. *Anecdotes of the American Revolution, Illustrative of the Talents and Virtue of the Heroes of the Revolution, Who Acted the Most Conspicuous Parts Therein.* 3 vols. Brooklyn, N.Y., 1865.

Gibbes, R. W. (ed.). *Documentary History of the American Revolution.* 3 vols. New York, 1853–57.

Godfrey, Carlos E. *The Commander-in-Chief's Guard, Revolutionary War.* Washington, 1904.

Gordon, William. *The History of the Rise, Progress, and Establishment of the Independence of the United States of America: Including an Account of the Late War and of the Thirteen Colonies, from Their Origin to That Period.* 4 vols. London, 1788.

Gottschalk, Louis. *Lafayette Joins the American Army.* Chicago, 1937.

Graham, James. *The Life of General Daniel Morgan, of the Virginia Line of the United States, with Portions of His Correspondence Compiled from Authentic Sources.* New York, 1856.

Graham, William A. *General Joseph Graham and His Papers on North Carolina Revolutionary History.* Raleigh, N.C., 1904.

Graydon, Alexander. *Memoirs of His Own Times with Reminiscences of the Men and Events of the Revolution,* ed. John Stockton Littell. Philadelphia, 1846.

Greene, Francis V. *The Revolutionary War and the Military Policy of the United States.* New York, 1911.

Greene, G. W. *Life of Nathanael Greene.* 3 vols. New York, 1867–71.

Gregg, Alexander. *History of the Old Cheraws.* New York, 1867.

Gunby, *Colonel John Gunby of the Maryland Line.* Cincinnati, Ohio, 1902.

Haiman, Miecislaus. *Kosciuszko in the American Revolution.* New York, 1953.

Hamilton, John C. (ed.). *The Works of Alexander Hamilton.* 7 vols. New York, 1856.

Hammond, Otis G. (ed.). *Letters and Papers of Major-General John Sullivan, Continental Army.* 3 vols. Concord, N.H., 1930–31, 1939.

Hastings, Hugh. *Public Papers of George Clinton, First Governor of New York, 1777–1795—1801–1804.* 9 vols. Albany, N.Y., 1904.

Henkels, Stanley. *Confidential Correspondence of Robert Morris.* Philadelphia, 1917.

Henry, Robert. *Narrative of the Battle of Cowan's Ford.* Greensboro, N.C., 1891.

Higginbotham, Don. *Daniel Morgan: Revolutionary Rifleman.* Chapel Hill, N.C., 1961.

Historical Manuscripts Commission. *Report on the Manuscripts of Mrs. Stopford-Sackville of Drayton House, Northhamptonshire.* 2 vols. London, 1904.

Historic Letters from the Collection of the West Chester Normal School. Philadelphia, 1898.

[Hough, Franklin Benjamin]. *The Siege of Charleston, by British Fleet and Army Under the Command of Admiral Arbuthnot and Sir Henry Clinton.* Albany, N.Y., 1867.

Hough, Franklin B. *The Siege of Savannah, by the Combined American and French Forces, under the Command of Gen. Lincoln, and the Count d'Estaing, in the Autumn of 1779.* Albany, N.Y., 1866.

Hoyt, W. H. (ed.). *The Papers of Archibald D. Murphey.* 2 vols. Raleigh, N.C., 1914.

James, William Dobein. *A Sketch of the Life of Brig. Gen. Francis Marion and a History of His Brigade from Its Rise in June 1780 Until Disbanded in December 1782.* Marietta, Ga., 1948.

Johnson, Joseph. *Traditions and Reminiscences Chiefly of the American Revolution in the South.* Charleston, S.C., 1851.

Johnson, Victor Leroy. *The Administration of the American Commissariat During the Revolutionary War.* Philadelphia, 1941.

Johnson, William. *Sketches of the Life and Correspondence of Nathanael Greene.* 2 vols. Charleston, S.C., 1822.

Johnston, Henry P. (ed.). *Memoirs of Colonel Benjamin Tallmadge.* New York, 1904.

Johnston, Henry P. *The Storming of Stony Point on the Hudson, Midnight, July 15, 1779; Its Importance in the Light of Unpublished Documents.* New York, 1900.

Jooe, Charles C. (ed.). *The Siege of Savannah in 1779, as Described in Two Contemporaneous Journals of French Officers in the Fleet of Count d'Estaing.* Albany, N.Y., 1874.

Kapp, Friedrich. *Life of John Kalb.* New York, 1884.

————. *The Life of Frederick William von Steuben, Major General in the Revolutionary War.* New York, 1859.

Keith, Alice Barnwell (ed.).*The John Gray Blount Papers.* 2 vols. Raleigh, N.C., 1952.

Kirkwood, Robert. *The Journal and Orderly Book of Captain Robert Kirkwood of the Delaware Regiment of the Continental Line,* ed. Joseph Brown Taylor. Wilmington, Del., 1910.

Lafayette, Marquis de. *Memoirs, Correspondence and Manuscripts of General Lafayette.* 3 vols. New York, 1837.

Lamb, R[oger]. *An Original and Authentic Journal of Occurrences During the Late American War, From Its Commencement to the Year 1783.* Dublin, 1809.

Laurens, John. *The Army Correspondence of Colonel John Laurens in the Year 1777–8, Now First Printed from Original Letters Addressed to His Father, Henry Laurens, President of Congress, with a Memoir by William Gilmore Simms.* New York, 1867.

Lawrence, Alexander A. *Storm Over Savannah: The Story of Count d'Estaing and the Siege of the Town in 1779.* Athens, Ga., 1951.

Lazenby, Mary Elinor. *Catawba Frontier, 1775–1781.* Washington, 1950.

Leake, Isaac Q. *Memoirs of the Life and Times of General John Lamb.* Albany, N.Y., 1857.

Lee, Henry. *Memoirs of the War in the Southern Department of the United States,* ed. Robert E. Lee. New York, 1870.

Lee, Henry, [Jr.]. *The Campaign of 1781 in the Carolinas: with Remarks Historical and Critical on Johnson's Life of Greene.* Philadelphia, 1824.

Lee Papers, The, in *Collections of the New-York Historical Society for the Year 1871 . . . 1872 . . . 1873 . . . 1874.* 4 vols. New York, 1872–75.

Lefler, Hugh T., and Albert R. Newsome. *North Carolina: The History of a Southern State.* Chapel Hill, N.C., 1954.

Lefler, Hugh T., and Paul Wager (eds.). *Orange County—1752–1952.* Chapel Hill, N.C., 1953.

Lossing, Benson J. *The Pictorial Field Book of the Revolution; or, Illustrations by Pen and Pencil, of the History, Biography, Scenery, Relics, and Traditions of the War for Independence.* 2 vols. New York, 1851.

Lundin, Leonard. *Cockpit of the Revolution.* Princeton, N.J., 1940.

McCall, Hugh. *The History of Georgia.* 2 vols. Savannah, Ga., 1811–16.

McCrady, Edward. *The History of South Carolina in the Revolution, 1775–1780.* New York, 1901.

Mackenzie, Frederick. *Diary of Frederick Mackenzie.* 2 vols. Cambridge, Mass., 1930.

Mackenzie, Roderick. *Strictures on Lt. Col. Tarleton's History "of the Campaigns of 1780 and 1781, in the Southern Provinces of North America."* London, 1787.

MacLean, J. P. *An Historical Account of the Settlement of Scotch Highlanders in America Prior to the Peace of 1783 together with Notices of Highland Regiments and Biographical Sketches.* Cleveland, Ohio, 1900.

MacMillan, Margaret Burnham. *The War Governors in the American Revolution.* New York, 1943.

McRee, Griffith J. *The Life and Correspondence of James Iredell.* 2 vols. New York, 1857–58.

[Martin, Joseph Plumb]. *A Narrative of Some of the Adventures, Dangers and Sufferings of a Revolutionary Soldier.* Hallowell, Me., 1830.

Merritt, Elizabeth (ed.). *Calendar of the General Otho Williams Papers in the Maryland Historical Society.* Baltimore, Md., 1940.

Montross, Lynn. *Rag, Tag, and Bobtail: The Story of the Continental Army, 1775–1783.* New York, 1952.

Moore, Frank (ed.). *Diary of the American Revolution from Newspapers and Original Documents.* 2 vols. New York, 1863.

Moravian Records. See Fries, Adelaide L.

Moultrie, William. *Memoirs of the American Revolution, So Far as It Related to the States of North and South Carolina, and Georgia.* 2 vols. New York, 1802.

Myers, Theoderas Baily (ed.). *Cowpens Papers: Being the Correspondence of General Morgan and Prominent Actors.* Charleston, S.C., 1881.

Original Papers Relating to the Siege of Charleston, 1780. Charleston, S.C., 1898; reprinted from the *Charleston Year Book for 1897,* Charleston, S.C., 1898.

Palmer, John M. *General von Steuben.* New York, 1937.

Palmer, W. P., et al. (eds.). *Calendar of Virginia State Papers and Other Manuscripts 1652–1781.* 11 vols. Richmond, Va., 1875–93.

Pennsylvania Archives, 2nd Series, XI; 3rd Series, V (Harrisburg, Pa., 1879, 1894).

Pickens, A. L. *Skyagunsta, The Border Wizard Owl: Major-General Andrew Pickens (1739–1807).* Greenville, S.C., 1934.

Pleasants, J. Hall et al. (eds.). *Archives of Maryland.* 63 vols. Baltimore, Md., 1930.

Public Acts of the General Assembly of North Carolina, The. New Bern, N.C., 1804.

Quincy, Josiah. *Memoir of the Life of Josiah Quincy Jun. of Massachusetts.* Boston, 1825.

———— (ed.). *Journal of Major Samuel Shaw, First American Consul at Canton.* Boston, 1847.

Ramsey, David. *The History of the American Revolution.* 2 vols. London, 1793.

———. *The History of the Revolution in South Carolina.* 2 vols. Trenton, N.J., 1785.

Reed, William B. *Life and Correspondence of Joseph Reed.* Philadelphia, 1847.

Report on the Manuscripts of Mrs. Stopford-Sackville. See Historical Manuscripts Commission.

Richmond, George H. *Letters by and to Gen. Nathanael Greene, with Some to His Wife.* New York, 1906.

Robertson, Archibald. *Diaries and Sketches in America.* New York, 1930.

Robinson, Blackwell P. *The Five Royal Governors of North Carolina, 1729–1775.* Raleigh, N.C., 1963.

———. *William R. Davie.* Chapel Hill, N.C., 1957.

Ross, Charles (ed.). *Correspondence of Charles, First Marquis Cornwallis.* 3 vols. London, 1859.

Saunders, William L. (ed.). *The Colonial Records of North Carolina.* 10 vols. Raleigh, N.C., Goldsboro, N.C., etc., 1886–98.

Savory, A. W. (ed.). *Col. David Fanning's Narrative of His Exploits and Adventures as a Loyalist of North Carolina in the American Revolution, Supplying Important Omissions in the Copy Published in the United States.* Toronto, 1908.

Schaw, Janet. *Journal of a Lady of Quality; Being the Narrative of a Journal from Scotland to the West Indies, North Carolina and Portugal, in the Years 1774 to 1776,* ed. Evangeline Walker Andrews and Charles McLean Andrews. New Haven, Conn., 1932.

Scheer, George F., and Hugh F. Rankin. *Rebels and Redcoats.* Cleveland, Ohio, 1957.

Schenck, David. *North Carolina, 1780–81.* Raleigh, N.C., 1889.

Scull, G. D. (ed.). *The Montresor Journals: Collections of the New-York Historical Society for 1881.* New York, 1882.

Serle, Ambrose. *The American Journal of Ambrose Serle, Secretary to Lord Howe, 1776–1778,* ed. Edward H. Tatum, Jr. San Marino, Calif., 1940.

Seymour, William. *A Journal of the Southern Expedition, 1780–1783.* Wilmington, Del., 1896.

Sidelight on History: Being the Letters of James McHenry, Aide-de-Camp of the Marquis de Lafayette to Thomas Sim Lee, Governor of Maryland, Written During the Yorktown Campaign, 1781 Southampton, N.Y., 1931.

Smith, Samuel Stelle. *The Battle of Monmouth.* Monmouth Beach, N.J., 1964.

Smith, W. H. (ed.). *The St. Clair Papers: The Life and Public Service of Arthur St. Clair.* 2 vols. Cincinnati, Ohio, 1882.

Smyth, J. F. D. *A Tour of the United States of America.* 2 vols. London, Dublin, 1784.

Sparks, Jared (ed.). *Correspondence of the American Revolution: Being Letters of Eminent Men to George Washington, From the Time of His Taking Command of the Army to the End of His Presidency.* 12 vols. Boston, 1853.

_____. *The Writings of George Washington.* 4 vols. Boston, 1834–35.

Sprunt, James. *Chronicles of the Cape Fear River.* Raleigh, N.C., 1914.

State Records. See Clark, Walter.

Stedman, Charles. *The History of the Origin, Progress, and Termination of the American War.* 2 vols. London, 1794.

Stevens, Benjamin Franklin (ed.). *Clinton-Cornwallis Controversy Growing Out of the Campaign in Virginia, 1781.* 2 vols. London, 1888.

_____. *Facsimiles of Manuscripts in European Archives Relating to America, 1773–1783.* 25 vols. London, 1889–95.

Stillé, Charles J. *Major-General Anthony Wayne and the Pennsylvania Line in the Continental Army.* Philadelphia, 1893.

Stryker, William S. *The Battle of Monmouth.* Princeton, N.J., 1927.

Talman, James T. (ed.). *Loyalist Narratives from Upper Canada.* Toronto, 1946.

Tarleton, Banastre. *A History of the Campaigns of 1780 and 1781, in the Southern Provinces of North America.* Dublin, 1787.

Thacher, James. *Military Journal During the Revolutionary War.* Boston, 1827.

_____. *Military Journal of the American Revolution.* Hartford, Conn., 1862.

Thayer, Theodore. *Nathanael Greene: Strategist of the Revolution.* New York, 1960.

Tiffany, Osmond. *A Sketch of the Life and Services of Gen. Otho Williams.* Baltimore, Md., 1851.

Tilghman, Oswald. *Memoir of Lieut. Col. Tench Tilghman, Secretary and Aid to Washington, Together with an Appendix, Containing Revolutionary Journals and Letters Hereto Unpublished.* Albany, N.Y., 1876.

Trumbull Papers: Collections of the Massachusetts Historical Society. 7th Series. Boston, 1902.

Uhlendorf, Bernhard A. (trans., ed.). *Revolution in America: Baurmeister Journals—Confidential Letters and Journals 1776–1784 of Adjutant General Major Baurmeister of the Hessian Forces.* New Brunswick, N.J., 1957.

_____. *The Siege of Charleston, with an Account of the Province of South Carolina: Diaries and Letters of Hessian Officers, From the von Jungken Papers in the William L. Clements Library.* Ann Arbor, Mich., 1938.

Waddell, Alfred M. *A History of New Hanover County.* 2 vols. Wilmington, N.C., 1909.

Wallace, David Duncan. *South Carolina: A Short History.* Chapel Hill, N.C., 1951.

Wallace, Willard M. *Appeal to Arms.* New York, 1951.

Walsh, Richard (ed.). *The Writings of Christopher Gadsden, 1746–1805.* Columbia, S.C., 1966.

Ward, Christopher L. *The Delaware Continentals, 1776–1783.* Wilmington, Del., 1941.

————. *The War of the Revolution,* ed. John R. Alden. 2 vols. New York, 1952.

Watson, Winslow C. *Men and Times of the Revolution: or, Memoirs of Elkanah Watson.* New York, 1856.

Wheeler, John H. *Historical Sketches of North Carolina from 1584 to 1851.* Philadelphia, 1851.

White, George (ed.). *Historical Collections of Georgia.* New York, 1855.

Willcox, William B. *Portrait of a General: Sir Henry Clinton in the War of Independence.* New York, 1964.

Year Book: City of Charleston, 1894. Charleston, S.C., 1894.

Year Book of the City of Charleston, 1895. Charleston, S.C., 1895.

Year Book: City of Charleston, S.C., 1899. Charleston, S.C., 1899.

Index

The Ultimate Guide to
Cooking A to Z

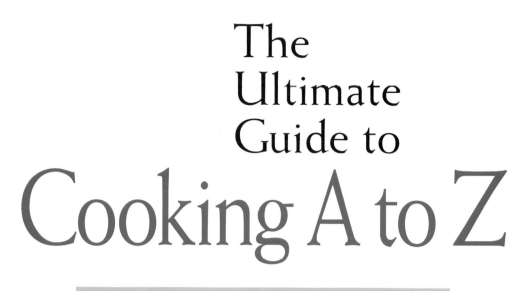

Classic Recipes and More

Publications International, Ltd.

Some of the products listed in this publication may be in limited distribution.

Contributing Writers:
Pat Dailey is a food writer and cookbook author. She writes food feature stories and two regular columns for the food section of the Chicago Tribune. She has authored four cookbooks, including her two most recent, *One-Pot Sunday Suppers* and *The Best Pressure Cooker Cookbook Ever.*

Eleanor H. Hanson, B.S. in Foods and Nutrition, M.B.A., is a food industry consultant and a principal in a company that specializes in identifying, tracking and analyzing consumer food trends. She is also the managing editor of its bi-monthly newsletter for food professionals. She is a former Director of the Kraft Creative Kitchens, Kraft Foods, Inc.

Mary Sue Peterson, B.S. in Foods and Nutrition, is a food industry consultant. Her clients include food companies, advertising agencies and communications firms. She is also a cookbook editor, food writer and recipe developer. She is active in the American Association of Family and Consumer Sciences.

Photo Credits: FPG International: Art Montes De Oca: 488; G&M Kohler: 110; Tom Kelley: 353; Andrea Sperling: 21; **International Stock:** John Michael: 16; Stephen S. Myers: 53, 286; **The Stock Market:** Dick Frank: 138; Dennis M. Gottlieb: 366; Ted Horowitz: 281; McCormick: 478 (top); Molkenthin Studio: 464; Roy Morsch: 44, 216, 518; J. Barry O'Rourke: 422; Palmer/Kane, Inc.: 165; Christel Rosenfeld: 197; **StockFood America:** 480; **Tony Stone Images:** Anthony Blake: 36; Beverly Factor: 394; **Superstock:** 12, 74, 178, 336, 340 (top), 544, 552; Dr. Nigel Smith: 291.

Front cover photography and photography on pages 4–5, 13, 27, 28, 56, 57, 84–85, 86, 96, 154, 182–183, 200, 226–227, 266–267, 276, 292, 298, 322–323, 348–349, 414–415, 438–439, 502–503, 523, 524, 527 by Sacco Productions Limited, Chicago.

Photographer: Marc A. Frisco
Photo Stylists: Melissa J. Frisco, Paula M. Walters
Production: Paula M. Walters
Food Stylists: Kim Hartman, Josephine Orba
Assistant Food Stylists: Liza Brown, Susie Skoog

Pictured on the front cover *(clockwise from top right):* Thai Grilled Beef Salad *(page 442),* Braised Chicken & Snow Peas *(page 464),* Fresh Fruit Tart *(page 512)* and Marinated Roasted Pepper Tapas *(page 508).*
Pictured on the back cover *(top left):* Marinated Tomatoes & Mozzarella *(page 521).*

ISBN: 0-7853-1789-9

Library of Congress Catalog Card Number: 96–69332

Manufactured in U.S.A.

8 7 6 5 4 3 2 1

Microwave Cooking: Microwave ovens vary in wattage. The microwave cooking times given in this publication are approximate. Use the cooking times as guidelines and check for doneness before adding more time. Consult manufacturer's instructions for suitable microwave-safe cooking dishes.

The recipes in this publication have been selected with care by the Editors of Favorite Brand Name Recipes. The Recipe Institute Seal of Quality is your assurance that the recipes are of the highest quality.

The Ultimate Guide to
Cooking A to Z

The Ultimate Guide to Cooking A to Z will appeal to both the novice and experienced cook. Whether you're just getting started in the kitchen or already know your way around it, you'll learn new skills, fascinating food facts and cooking techniques, which will expand your culinary horizons. With over 450 entries, this book is filled with information about all types of foods—how to shop for them, how to store them and how to prepare them. Plus, you'll learn valuable food terminology to improve your understanding of recipes and menus. Clear how-to photos and concise instructions help you master indispensable cooking techniques that you'll use over and over again. You'll also discover tips for equipping your kitchen, choosing the right wine and planning a dinner party. In addition, this book has over 350 delectable recipes, many with beautiful full-color photos.

The Ultimate Guide to Cooking A to Z is simple to use. Entries are listed alphabetically, making it easy to locate information. For example, to make something with apples, turn to the entry titled "Apple." You'll find a listing of six popular varieties, suggested uses for each, the peak seasons for best quality, buying tips, basic preparation information and a few recipes. Also, check the Recipe Index (page 556) for more recipes that contain apples. After choosing a recipe, review it, noting the ingredients, equipment and time needed to prepare it. This complete volume will assist you at every step.

If you're unfamiliar with an ingredient or piece of equipment, just turn to its alphabetical listing to learn more about it. If you cannot find an entry, check the General Index (page 566). Before shopping, refer to the buying tips included. Re-read the recipe thoroughly and familiarize yourself with any new terms or techniques before beginning preparation. Prepare and measure all the ingredients as called for in the ingredient list. Now you're ready to cook.

Are you just starting out and need to equip your kitchen? Read the entries about bakeware, cookware and tools; they will help you to determine the basic equipment you need, even if your budget is small. First-time cooks will benefit from understanding some basic techniques, such as how to chop (page 130), combine (page 147), measure (page 298), peel (page 372) and sauté (page 449). Experienced cooks can fine-tune their preparation techniques, learn more about wild mushrooms, tropical fruits and food safety, and discover the history of some of their favorite dishes.

This comprehensive guide is the only kitchen reference book you'll ever need! Keep it handy to answer your most frequently asked cooking questions. Then, use your newly acquired skills to prepare these delicious recipes, many featuring products from your favorite brand name food companies. Discover the pleasure of cooking and serving sensational meals for family and friends now with more confidence and ease than ever before.

A to B

How does the French phrase *à la* apply to cooking? *Make a delicious wreath out of asparagus.* What does arugula taste like? *Bake a batch of fudgey brownies.* Where are bananas grown? *Learn to knead bread dough.*

❧

Apple Cheesecake (recipe on page 15)

À LA

This French idiom is a contraction of the phrase à la mode de, meaning "in the manner of." In cooking, it indicates the style used to prepare food. For example, à la bourguignonne means "as prepared in Burgundy."

☙

AL DENTE

The literal translation of this Italian phrase is "to the tooth." It indicates a degree of doneness when cooking pasta. Al dente pasta is slightly firm and chewy, rather than soft.

☙

ALMOND PASTE

Almond paste is a prepared product made of ground blanched almonds, sugar and an ingredient, such as glucose, glycerin or corn syrup, to keep it pliable. It is used to make decorations and as an ingredient in confections and baked goods. Almond extract is often added to the paste to intensify the flavor. Almond paste is available in cans and plastic tubes in most large supermarkets or gourmet food markets. After opening, wrap the container tightly and store it in the refrigerator.

☙

Technique for Chocolate Macaroons

Step 4. *Piping dough onto baking sheet.*

Chocolate Macaroons

Chocolate Macaroons

> 12 ounces semisweet chocolate
> 　chips or baking chocolate,
> 　broken into pieces
> 1 can (8 ounces) almond paste
> 2 egg whites
> ½ cup powdered sugar
> 2 tablespoons all-purpose flour
> 　Additional powdered sugar

1. Preheat oven to 300°F. Line 3 baking sheets with parchment paper.

2. Melt chocolate in heavy small saucepan over low heat, stirring constantly. Remove from heat immediately after chocolate is melted; set aside.

3. Beat almond paste, egg whites and ½ cup powdered sugar in large bowl with electric mixer at medium speed 1 minute, scraping down side of bowl once. Beat in melted chocolate until well combined. Beat in flour at low speed, scraping down side of bowl once.

4. Spoon dough into pastry bag fitted with rosette tip. Pipe 1½-inch spirals 1 inch apart onto prepared baking sheets. (Pipe all cookies at once; dough will stiffen upon standing.)

5. Bake 20 minutes or until set. Carefully remove parchment paper to countertop; cool completely.

6. Peel cookies off parchment paper. Place additional powdered sugar in fine-mesh strainer; sprinkle over cookies. Store tightly covered at room temperature or freeze up to 3 months.

Makes about 3 dozen cookies

AMANDINE

The French term amandine in recipe titles refers to dishes prepared or garnished with almonds. It is often misspelled "almondine."

☙

AMBROSIA

Ambrosia was the food that brought immortality to the gods of ancient Greek mythology. Today, the word designates a chilled fruit dessert or salad made with oranges, usually bananas and shredded coconut.

☙

Ambrosia with Honey Lime Cream Dressing

> ¼ cup honey
> 2 tablespoons fresh lime juice
> 3 oranges, peeled, sectioned
> 2 bananas, peeled, sliced
> 1 *each* red and green apple,
> 　cored, cubed
> 1 cup flaked coconut
> 　Honey Lime Cream Dressing
> 　(recipe follows)

1. Combine honey and juice in large bowl; add fruit and toss until coated with honey mixture.

2. Layer fruit alternately with coconut in serving bowl. Top with Honey Lime Cream Dressing.

Makes 4 servings

Honey Lime Cream Dressing

> ½ cup whipping cream
> 2 tablespoons honey
> 1 teaspoon grated lime peel

Beat cream in large bowl with electric mixer at high speed until fluffy. Drizzle in honey; beat until stiff peaks form. Fold in lime peel.

Makes 1 cup dressing

*Favorite recipe from **National Honey Board***

ANTIPASTO

Antipasto is an Italian term literally meaning "before the pasta." It refers to a selection of appetizers that may include sausage, cheese, fish, olives, fruits or marinated vegetables. A sample platter of assorted antipasti might include prosciutto-wrapped melon, ripe figs, provolone cheese, salami, marinated mushrooms and artichokes, garlic olives, anchovies and pickled peppers.

☙

Antipasto with
Marinated Mushrooms

Antipasto with Marinated Mushrooms

Marinated Mushrooms (recipe follows)
4 teaspoons red wine vinegar
½ teaspoon dried basil leaves
½ teaspoon dried oregano leaves
Generous dash ground black pepper
¼ cup olive oil
4 ounces mozzarella cheese, cut into ½-inch cubes
4 ounces prosciutto or cooked ham, thinly sliced
4 ounces provolone cheese, cut into 2-inch sticks
2 jars (6 ounces each) marinated artichoke hearts, drained
1 jar (10 ounces) pepperoncini peppers, drained
8 ounces hard salami, thinly sliced
1 can (6 ounces) pitted ripe olives, drained
Lettuce leaves (optional)
Fresh oregano leaves and chives (optional)

1. Prepare Marinated Mushrooms; set aside.

2. Combine vinegar, basil, dried oregano and black pepper in small bowl. Whisk in oil until well blended. Add mozzarella; stir to coat. Cover; marinate in refrigerator at least 2 hours.

3. Meanwhile, wrap ½ of prosciutto slices around provolone sticks; roll up remaining slices separately.

4. Drain mozzarella, reserving marinade. Arrange mozzarella, prosciutto-wrapped provolone sticks, prosciutto rolls, Marinated Mushrooms, artichokes, pepperoncini, salami and olives on large platter lined with lettuce, if desired. Drizzle reserved marinade over pepperoncini, artichokes and olives. Garnish with fresh oregano and chives, if desired. Serve with small forks or wooden toothpicks.
Makes 6 to 8 servings

Marinated Mushrooms

    3 tablespoons lemon juice
    2 tablespoons chopped fresh
        parsley
    ½ teaspoon salt
    ¼ teaspoon dried tarragon leaves
        Generous dash ground black
        pepper
    ½ cup olive oil
    1 clove garlic
    ½ pound small fresh button
        mushrooms, stems removed

1. To prepare marinade, combine juice, parsley, salt, tarragon and pepper in medium bowl. Whisk in oil until well blended. Lightly crush garlic with flat side of chef's knife or mallet; add to marinade. Add mushrooms; mix well. Cover; marinate in refrigerator 4 hours or overnight, stirring occasionally.

2. To serve, remove and discard garlic.   *Makes about 2 cups*

*Venetian Canapés
(recipe on page 11)*

APPETIZER

An appetizer is a finger food served before a meal to stimulate the appetite and to excite the palate. (The term may be used interchangeably with the French term "hors d'oeuvre.") A variety of foods, hot or cold—including dips, spreads, canapés, crudités and pâtés—may be served as appetizers.

Appetizers are most often served as special occasion fare. In fact, gatherings centering on appetizers, rather than full meals, have been popular since the 1920's and continue to be a very popular form of entertaining. Whether referred to as cocktail parties or appetizer parties, these gatherings are less formal than a sit-down dinner and offer guests the opportunity to mix and mingle while sipping drinks and munching on tidbits.

Canapé: A canapé consists of a small piece of bread (toasted or untoasted) or a cracker that is topped with a savory food, such as cheese or anchovy-flavored spread. For an attractive presentation, the bread is cut into interesting shapes, toppings are piped and garnishes applied.

Crudités: Crudités are fresh raw vegetables that are usually served with a dip or spread. They also may be eaten as a snack or as an accompaniment to a light meal and are suitable lunch box or picnic food. Common crudités are radishes; carrot, celery and zucchini sticks; and cauliflower and broccoli florets. Some cooks like to blanch crudités, especially broccoli, to enhance their color. *See Blanching, page 51.*

Pâté: French for "pie," pâté is a hot or cold seasoned mixture of ground meat, poultry or seafood. The mixture may be enclosed in a pastry crust and baked or molded in a container called a terrine. Some pâtés are spreadable while others are firm enough to slice.

Spicy Orange Chicken Kabob Appetizers

Spicy Orange Chicken Kabob Appetizers

   2 boneless, skinless chicken breast halves
   1 small red or green bell pepper
  24 small fresh button mushrooms
  ½ cup orange juice
   2 tablespoons low sodium soy sauce
   1 tablespoon vegetable oil
 1½ teaspoons onion powder
  ½ teaspoon Chinese five-spice powder

1. Cut chicken and pepper each into 24 (¾-inch) square pieces. Place chicken, pepper and mushrooms in large resealable plastic food storage bag. Combine juice, soy sauce, oil, onion powder and five-spice powder in small bowl. Pour over chicken mixture. Close bag securely; turn to coat. Marinate in refrigerator 4 to 24 hours, turning frequently.

2. Soak 24 small wooden skewers or toothpicks in water 30 minutes. Meanwhile, preheat broiler. Coat broiler pan with nonstick cooking spray.

3. Drain chicken, pepper and mushrooms, reserving marinade. Place marinade in small saucepan; bring to a full boil. Thread 1 piece chicken, 1 piece pepper and 1 mushroom onto each skewer. Place on prepared pan. Brush with marinade; discard remaining marinade. Broil 4 inches from heat source 5 to 6 minutes until chicken is no longer pink in center. Serve immediately.
    Makes 24 appetizers (8 servings)

Fresh Tomato Eggplant Spread

   1 medium eggplant
   2 large ripe tomatoes, seeded, chopped
   1 cup minced zucchini
  ¼ cup chopped green onions
   2 tablespoons red wine vinegar
   1 tablespoon olive oil
   1 tablespoon minced fresh basil
   2 teaspoons minced fresh oregano
   1 teaspoon minced fresh thyme
   1 teaspoon honey
   1 clove garlic, minced
  ⅛ teaspoon ground black pepper
  ¼ cup pine nuts or slivered almonds
  32 melba toast rounds

1. Preheat oven to 375°F.

2. Poke holes in surface of eggplant with fork. Bake 20 to 25 minutes until tender. Cool completely; peel and mince. Place in colander; press to release excess water.

3. Combine eggplant, tomatoes, zucchini, onions, vinegar, oil, basil, oregano, thyme, honey, garlic and pepper in large bowl; mix well. Refrigerate 2 hours to allow flavors to blend.

4. Stir in pine nuts just before serving. Serve with melba toast.
    Makes 8 appetizer servings

Venetian Canapés

    12 slices firm white bread
     5 tablespoons butter or
        margarine, divided
     2 tablespoons all-purpose flour
    ½ cup milk
     3 ounces fresh button mushrooms
        (about 9 medium), finely
        chopped
     6 tablespoons grated Parmesan
        cheese, divided
     2 teaspoons anchovy paste
    ¼ teaspoon salt
    ⅛ teaspoon ground black pepper
        Green and ripe olive slices, red
        and green bell pepper strips
        and rolled anchovy fillets

1. Preheat oven to 350°F.

2. To prepare toast rounds, cut circles out of bread slices with 2-inch round cutter; save bread crusts for another use. Melt 3 tablespoons butter in small saucepan. Brush both sides of bread circles lightly with butter.

3. Bake bread circles on ungreased baking sheet 5 to 6 minutes per side until golden. Remove to wire rack. Cool completely.

4. *Increase oven temperature to 425°F.* Melt remaining 2 tablespoons butter in same small saucepan. Stir in flour; cook and stir over medium heat until bubbly. Whisk in milk; cook and stir 1 minute or until sauce thickens and bubbles. (Sauce will be very thick.) Place mushrooms in large bowl; stir in sauce mixture, 3 tablespoons cheese, anchovy paste, salt and black pepper until well blended.

5. Spread heaping teaspoonful mushroom mixture on top of each toast round; place on ungreased baking sheets. Sprinkle remaining 3 tablespoons cheese over mushroom mixture, dividing evenly. Top with olives, bell pepper and anchovies.

6. Bake 5 to 7 minutes until tops are light brown. Serve warm.

Makes 8 to 10 appetizer servings (about 2 dozen canapés)

Spicy Taco Dip

     1 pound BOB EVANS FARMS®
        Italian Roll Sausage
     1 (13-ounce) can refried beans
     1 (8-ounce) jar medium salsa
     2 cups (8 ounces) shredded
        Cheddar cheese
     2 cups (8 ounces) shredded
        Monterey Jack cheese
     1 (4-ounce) jar sliced black olives,
        drained
     1 cup sliced green onions with
        tops
     2 cups sour cream
     1 (1-pound) bag tortilla chips

Preheat oven to 350°F. Crumble sausage into medium skillet. Cook over medium heat until browned, stirring occasionally. Drain off any drippings. Spread beans in ungreased 2½-quart shallow baking dish, then top with sausage. Pour salsa over sausage; sprinkle with cheeses. Sprinkle olives and onions over top. Bake 20 to 30 minutes or until heated through.

Spread with sour cream while hot and serve with chips. Refrigerate leftovers; reheat in oven or microwave.

Makes 12 to 16 appetizer servings

Spicy Taco Dip

APPLE

Apples can be traced back thousands of years and have played a symbolic role in human history from Adam and Eve to Isaac Newton and Johnny Appleseed to computers. When the Pilgrims first came to America, they brought apples, seeds and cuttings. Today, the United States is the largest producer of apples in the world. Washington, Michigan and New York yield most of the crop.

☙

Varieties: Thousands of apple varieties exist around the world, but less than twenty varieties account for almost all U.S. production and only a handful make up 80 percent of the American apple supply.

• The Red Delicious apple, contributing to almost half the domestic crop, is by far the favorite variety in America. It has a characteristic strawberry shape, a sweet taste and a crisp, juicy texture. It is best eaten raw; when cooked, it disintegrates and loses its flavor.

• A Golden Delicious apple is similar in shape to the Red Delicious apple but has a more delicate flavor. This crisp, juicy and sweet apple is suitable for both eating raw and baking.

• Granny Smith apples, originally developed in Australia, are tart green apples with tough skins and a firm, crunchy texture. They are a good choice for eating raw and for making pies.

• Jonathan apples are bright red, juicy and sweet-tart in flavor. They are fine for eating out of hand and for making pies or applesauce, but they are not recommended for baking whole as they lose their shape. Jonathan apples are more common in Midwest markets than other parts of the country.

• McIntosh apples have an exceptionally smooth, moderately crisp texture and a sweet-tart flavor. Although they appear in markets in September, they do not reach their peak flavor until late September or early October. Later in the fall, they have a sweeter flavor but are less crisp and juicy. McIntosh apples are a good choice for eating raw and for applesauce, but they do not retain their shape in pies or when baked whole.

• Rome Beauty apples are large, round late fall apples. Their dry texture and thick skin make them less suitable for eating out of hand, making applesauce or baking in pies but good for baking whole.

• Other regional and local varieties include Baldwin, Cortland, Crispin or Mutsu, Gala, Gravenstein, Imperial, Northern Spy, Royal Gala, Stayman, Winesap and York.

Availability: Thanks to "controlled atmosphere" (CA) storage, apples are available year-round. CA storage holds the fruit in a high-humidity environment at about 30°F in the presence of a mixture of gases, including oxygen, nitrogen and carbon dioxide, and thus extends their shelf life.

The peak season for domestically grown apples—when flavor and texture are at their best—is September through November. Apples imported from Australia and New Zealand, such as Braeburn, Granny Smith, Gala and Royal Gala, are at their peak from April through July. Since these varieties are also grown in the United States, check labels or ask the produce manager to ensure that spring and summer apples have been imported from the Southern Hemisphere.

Look for local varieties at fall farmers' markets. Apples are also available as canned or jarred applesauce, canned apple pie filling and dried apple slices.

Buying Tips: Choose apples that are firm, fragrant and a bright color. The skin should be tight without bruises, blemishes or punctures. An apple should not yield when squeezed or pinched. Brown streaks, called russeting or scalds, on the skin are present in some varieties but won't affect quality.

Yield: 1 pound apples = 2 large, 3 medium or 4 small apples; 2 to 2½ cups chopped or sliced; about 1¾ cups applesauce.
1 pound dried apples = 4⅓ cups; 8 cups cooked.

Storage: Apples will keep in a cool, dry place for a week or two. For longer storage, place apples in a plastic bag and store in the refrigerator. Apples in good condition can last up to six weeks in the refrigerator. Check them occasionally and discard any that have begun to spoil as one rotten apple can ruin the whole lot.

Basic Preparation: Apples should be washed and may be used peeled or unpeeled. Quarter apples from top to bottom and remove seeds, woody core and stem with a paring knife. To prepare apples for baking whole,

remove a horizontal ½-inch-wide strip of peel from around the middle. Remove the core with an apple corer.

Chunky Applesauce

> 10 McIntosh or Jonathan apples (about 3 pounds), peeled, cored
> ¾ cup packed light brown sugar
> ½ cup apple juice or apple cider
> 1½ teaspoons ground cinnamon
> ⅛ teaspoon salt
> ⅛ teaspoon ground nutmeg

1. Cut apples into quarters; cut quarters into small pieces.

2. Combine apples, sugar, juice, cinnamon, salt and nutmeg in heavy large saucepan; cover. Cook over medium-low heat 40 to 45 minutes until apples are tender, stirring occasionally to break apples into chunks. Remove from heat. Cool completely. Store in airtight container in refrigerator up to 1 month.

Makes about 5½ cups applesauce

Tip

To prevent cut apples from browning when exposed to air, brush with a small amount of lemon or other citrus juice or place in lemon water (six parts water to one part lemon juice).

Grilled Pork Tenderloin with Apple Salsa

1 tablespoon chili powder
½ teaspoon garlic powder
1 pound pork tenderloin
2 Granny Smith apples, peeled, cored, finely chopped
1 can (4 ounces) chopped green chilies
¼ cup fresh lemon juice
3 tablespoons finely chopped fresh cilantro
1 clove garlic, minced
1 teaspoon dried oregano leaves
½ teaspoon salt

1. Generously spray grid with nonstick cooking spray. Prepare grill for direct grilling over medium-hot heat.

2. Combine chili powder and garlic powder in small bowl; mix well. Rub spice mixture over pork to coat well.

3. Grill pork, on uncovered grill, over medium-hot coals 30 minutes or until instant-read thermometer inserted into thickest part of pork registers 155°F, turning occasionally. Remove to platter; cover with foil. Let stand 10 minutes before slicing.

4. Meanwhile, to make apple salsa, combine apples, chilies, juice, cilantro, garlic, oregano and salt in medium bowl; mix well.

5. Slice pork across grain; serve with salsa. Garnish as desired.

Makes 4 servings

Grilled Pork Tenderloin with Apple Salsa

Apple Cheesecake

1 cup graham cracker crumbs
    About 1 cup sugar, divided
1 teaspoon ground cinnamon,
    divided
3 tablespoons margarine, melted
2 packages (8 ounces each) cream
    cheese, softened
2 eggs
½ teaspoon vanilla extract
4 cups peeled, thin Golden
    Delicious apple slices (about
    2½ pounds apples)
¼ to ½ cup chopped pecans

1. Preheat oven to 350°F.

2. Combine crumbs, 3 tablespoons sugar, ½ teaspoon cinnamon and margarine in small bowl; mix well. Press onto bottom and up side of 9-inch pie plate. Bake crust 10 minutes.

3. Meanwhile, beat cream cheese and ½ cup sugar in large bowl with electric mixer at medium speed until well blended. Add eggs, 1 at a time, beating well after each addition. Blend in vanilla; pour into baked crust.

4. Combine ⅓ cup sugar and remaining ½ teaspoon cinnamon in large bowl. Add apples; toss gently to coat. Spoon or arrange apple mixture over cream cheese mixture. Sprinkle with pecans.

5. Bake 1 hour and 10 minutes or until set. Cool completely. Store in refrigerator.

Makes one 9-inch cheesecake

Apple Cheesecake

• Dried apricots may be eaten as a snack or reconstituted and used as an ingredient in vegetable and grain side dishes, stuffings or baked goods.

• Apricot nectar, the juice of fresh apricots, has a velvety texture and makes a delicious beverage or base for fruit drinks.

Varieties: Although there are about a dozen varieties of apricots that differ somewhat in size and color, they vary little in flavor.

Availability: Domestically grown apricots are only available from late May to early August. Imports are found sporadically throughout the rest of the year. Ripe apricots are very fragile; consequently, they must be picked when hard and shipped under refrigeration. Improper handling will prevent ripening. It is best to buy domestically grown apricots rather than imported, since imported fruit may be picked green for shipment. Canned apricots and apricot nectar are also available. Dried apricots have been pitted, but not peeled, before drying. They are treated with sulphur dioxide to preserve their color.

Buying Tips: Ripe apricots are soft to the touch and very juicy. However, since fully ripe apricots travel poorly, you may have to purchase ones that need a day or two to ripen. Unripe apricots are plump and fragrant with a smooth, blemish-free skin. They appear orange-gold in color and may have a slightly pink blush. They may yield to gentle pressure. To prevent bruising, avoid handling the fruit.

APRICOT

Apricots still grow wild in the mountains around Beijing, China, where the fruit was first cultivated over four thousand years ago. They are round, golden fruit about the size of a small plum with an almond-shaped seed and a thin, slightly fuzzy skin. The trees grow best in temperate climates; today California supplies over 90 percent of the domestic crop. Excellent apricots are also grown in Morocco, where the soil and climate are ideal for good flavor development. Chile, Australia and New Zealand export apricots to the United States. Apricots are an excellent source of beta-carotene, which is a vitamin A precursor.

🌾

Uses: Fresh apricots are wonderful eaten raw.

• Fresh apricots may also be poached, grilled, used in fillings or made into preserves.

Tip

Like peaches, the kernel inside an apricot pit contains a small amount of cyanide and should be discarded.

Yield: 1 pound apricots = 8 to 12 whole apricots; 2½ cups halves or slices.
1 pound dried apricots = 2¾ cups dried; 5 cups cooked.

Storage: Apricots may be ripened by placing them in a paper bag at room temperature for up to three or four days. Store ripe apricots in a plastic bag in the refrigerator for a day or two at most; they dry out very quickly under refrigeration.

Basic Preparation: Wash apricots gently under running water just before using them. They almost never need to be peeled. To remove the pit, cut around the seam to the pit, twist gently to separate into halves and pull out the pit. Use immediately or brush the cut surfaces with lemon or other citrus juice to delay browning. To reconstitute (plump) dried apricots, simmer in a small amount of liquid about 15 minutes or until tender.

Fresh Apricot Cobbler

  1 cup all-purpose flour
  ¼ cup granulated sugar
  2 tablespoons nonfat dry milk
     powder
  2 teaspoons baking powder
  ¼ teaspoon baking soda
  ¼ teaspoon salt
  2 tablespoons canola oil
  7 tablespoons buttermilk
  ½ cup firmly packed dark brown
     sugar
 4½ teaspoons cornstarch
  ½ cup water
1½ pounds ripe apricots, pits
     removed, quartered
    Cinnamon Yogurt Topping
    (recipe follows)

1. Preheat oven to 400°F.

2. Combine flour, granulated sugar, milk powder, baking powder, baking soda and salt in medium bowl. Stir in oil until mixture becomes crumbly. Add buttermilk. Stir just until moistened; set aside.

3. Combine brown sugar, cornstarch and water in medium saucepan, stirring until cornstarch is dissolved. Cook over medium heat until thickened, stirring constantly. Add apricots; cook and stir about 3 minutes or until apricots are completely covered in sauce. Pour into ungreased 8-inch square baking pan. Immediately drop reserved flour mixture in small spoonfuls on top of apricot mixture.

4. Bake 25 minutes or until topping is lightly browned. Meanwhile, prepare Cinnamon Yogurt Topping. Serve cobbler warm with Cinnamon Yogurt Topping.   *Makes 6 servings*

Cinnamon Yogurt Topping

  1 envelope unflavored gelatin
  2 tablespoons cold water
  ¼ cup boiling water
  1 cup plain nonfat yogurt
  ¼ cup nonfat dry milk powder
  ¼ cup granulated sugar
  ¼ to ½ teaspoon ground
     cinnamon
1½ teaspoons vanilla extract
  2 cups crushed ice

1. Sprinkle gelatin over cold water in medium bowl; let stand 1 minute to soften. Add boiling water; stir 2 minutes or until gelatin is completely dissolved. Add yogurt; mix well. Refrigerate until jelled.

2. Place yogurt mixture in blender or food processor. Add all remaining ingredients; process until smooth. Serve immediately or cover and store in refrigerator.   *Makes 6 servings*

Fresh Apricot Cobbler

ARTICHOKE

The artichoke, specifically the globe artichoke, is actually the unopened flower bud of a thistlelike plant. A passion of Catherine de Médici in fifteenth-century Florence, Italy, the artichoke was brought to the United States in the nineteenth century, first to Louisiana and later to California. Today California, especially the area around Castroville, produces virtually the entire domestic crop. Artichokes are also grown in abundance in the Mediterranean region where they are a very popular vegetable.

☙

Uses: Artichokes are cooked and served whole, either hot or chilled, as an appetizer or first course. They are sometimes stuffed and often served with a dipping sauce.

• Cooked, canned or frozen artichoke bottoms and hearts may be ingredients in appetizers, soups, salads or vegetable side dishes.

Availability: Artichokes are actually harvested year-round but are most plentiful in the spring and fall. Canned and frozen artichoke hearts and bottoms are also available.

Buying Tips: Artichokes should be compact with tightly closed leaves and feel heavy for their size. Spring artichokes should be soft green and autumn ones olive green. If the leaves are tipped with brown, the artichoke may have experienced some frost damage ("winter's kiss"). However, this will not affect its quality. Avoid artichokes with lots of black spots (a few are fine) or purple color on the leaves, caused by too much sun.

Yield: 1 artichoke = 1 serving.
1 (14-ounce) can of artichoke hearts or bottoms = about 5 pieces.

Storage: Artichokes are best if cooked immediately but may be stored in a plastic bag in the refrigerator for up to four days. Whole cooked artichokes may be kept wrapped in plastic wrap in the refrigerator for four or five days.

Basic Preparation: Wash artichokes under cold running water being sure to remove any dirt caught between the leaves. For stubborn dirt, soak artichokes in warm salted water for 1 hour.

To prepare artichokes for cooking whole, see Pilaf-Stuffed Artichokes (steps 1–3).

To cook whole artichokes, see Pilaf-Stuffed Artichokes (step 4).

To eat a whole artichoke, you need to use your fingers. Break off the leaves, one at a time, and dip the fleshy end into the melted butter, if desired. Then draw the base of the leaf through your teeth to remove the tender portion. Lay the discarded leaves on the side of the plate or place in a small bowl. When all the leaves are consumed scoop out the choke from the center and discard. The remaining bottom may be cut and eaten with a knife and fork. Whole artichokes can be eaten hot with melted butter or lukewarm with herbed vinaigrette or flavored mayonnaise.

Pilaf-Stuffed Artichokes

> 4 medium globe artichokes
> 2 tablespoons fresh lemon juice
> 2 cups water*
> ¼ cup *each* uncooked wild, brown and wehani rices, rinsed*
> ½ teaspoon salt
> 1 large carrot, peeled, cubed
> ¼ cup cubed cooked ham
> 1 tablespoon chopped fresh parsley
> Fresh oregano and purple basil leaves (optional)

Or, substitute ¾ cup uncooked long-grain white rice for the wild, brown and wehani rices. Decrease water to 1½ cups.

Tips

Rub the cut edges of an artichoke with lemon juice to prevent browning.

Don't use a carbon-steel knife to cut artichokes as it will cause the cut surfaces to darken.

1. To prepare artichokes, cut bottom stems from artichokes so that artichokes sit flat and upright. Remove outer, tough leaves; discard.

2. Cut 1 inch off pointed tops of artichokes.

3. Snip tips from remaining leaves with scissors.

4. Use large enough stockpot to allow artichokes to fit in single layer. Add enough water to stockpot to 4-inch depth. Bring to a boil over high heat. Add juice; drop in artichokes so their bases are at the bottom of pot. Reduce heat to low. Cover; simmer 30 to 40 minutes until leaves pull easily from bases and artichoke bottoms are tender when pierced with fork. Drain artichokes upside down in colander; set aside until cool enough to handle.

5. Meanwhile, combine 2 cups water, rices and salt in 2-quart saucepan. Cover; bring to a boil over high heat. Reduce heat to low; simmer 15 minutes. Add carrot; simmer 20 to 25 minutes more until water is absorbed.** Stir in ham and parsley.

6. Preheat oven to 400°F.

7. Carefully spread outer leaves of artichokes. Remove small heart leaves by grasping with fingers, then pulling and twisting. Scoop out fuzzy chokes down to the flat artichoke bottoms with spoon. Fill hollowed artichokes with rice mixture, smoothing leaves upward to close slightly.

8. Place on ungreased baking sheet; bake 10 to 15 minutes until heated through. Garnish with oregano and basil, if desired. Serve immediately.

Makes 4 servings

**If using white rice, simmer only 10 minutes more.*

Techniques for Pilaf-Stuffed Artichokes

Step 2. *Cutting pointed tops off artichokes.*

Step 3. *Snipping remaining leaves with scissors.*

Step 7. *Scooping out the fuzzy choke.*

Pilaf-Stuffed Artichokes

*Garden Greens with
Fennel Dressing*

ARUGULA

Arugula has long been popular in Italy, Greece and southern France but until recently was little known in the United States beyond New York City. Arugula has smooth dark green leaves that resemble dandelion greens or its relative, the radish. Sometimes called rocket, this aromatic but bitter salad green with a spicy mustardlike flavor is considered by many to be an acquired taste.

🐝

Uses: Arugula adds its distinctive flavor to a mixture of tossed salad greens. It is essential to the salad mix known as mesclun, which is a toss of young salad greens and mild herbs.

• For those who are fond of this leafy green, arugula can be served simply dressed with a light vinegar and oil dressing.

• The peppery flavor of arugula adds a special touch to grilled vegetable sandwiches.

• Arugula can also be lightly sautéed for a last minute addition to soups and vegetable dishes.

Availability: Arugula is available all year in large supermarkets and is easily grown in home gardens.

Buying Tips: Arugula is usually sold in small bunches with the roots still attached. The leaves should be bright emerald green and appear fresh and crisp. Avoid limp leaves.

Yield: 1 small bunch arugula = about 1 to 2 cups of torn greens.

Storage: Arugula is very perishable. Wrap the roots in a damp paper towel and store the bunch in a plastic bag in the refrigerator for no more than a day or two. Never wash arugula before refrigerating.

Basic Preparation: Cut off the roots and any thick stems. Arugula leaves can hold a large amount of sand and grit so swish the leaves in a large container of water, let them sit a moment, remove the leaves and pour out the water. Repeat two or three times to remove all traces of dirt. Pat dry with paper towels.

Garden Greens with Fennel Dressing

Dressing

   ½ teaspoon unflavored gelatin
   2 tablespoons cold water
   ¼ cup boiling water
   ½ teaspoon salt
   ½ teaspoon sugar
   ¼ cup raspberry or wine vinegar
   1 tablespoon fresh lemon juice
   ¼ teaspoon dry mustard
   ¼ teaspoon anise extract or
       ground fennel seeds
   ⅛ teaspoon ground black pepper
   1¼ teaspoons walnut or canola oil

Salad

   1 head (10 ounces) Bibb lettuce,
       torn into bite-size pieces
   1 head (10 ounces) radicchio,
       torn into bite-size pieces
   1 cup mâche or spinach leaves,
       torn into bite-size pieces
   1 bulb (8 ounces) fennel, finely
       chopped (reserve fern for
       garnish)
   1 bunch (3 ounces) arugula, torn
       into bite-size pieces
   1 tablespoon pine nuts, toasted

1. To prepare Dressing, sprinkle gelatin over cold water in small bowl; let stand 1 minute to soften. Add boiling water; stir 2 minutes or until gelatin is completely dissolved. Add salt and sugar; stir until sugar is completely dissolved. Add all remaining Dressing ingredients except oil; mix well. Slowly whisk in oil until well blended. Cover; refrigerate 2 hours or overnight. Shake well before using.

2. To prepare Salad, place all Salad ingredients except pine nuts in large bowl. Add Dressing; toss until all leaves glisten. Divide salad among 6 chilled salad plates. Top each salad with ½ teaspoon pine nuts. Garnish with sprig of fennel fern, if desired.

Makes 6 servings

ASPARAGUS

Asparagus, once an anxiously awaited harbinger of spring, is now available almost year-round. However, springtime does bring a plentiful supply at reasonable prices. Whether it's grown wild, cultivated in plots, or carefully tended underground so shoots are completely void of color, asparagus never fails to excite its fans. Asparagus is the tender shoot of a perennial vegetable from the lily family. It grows best in parts of the United States where the ground freezes in winter and the summers are warm. Domestic production is supplemented with imports from Mexico and Chile.

✿

Varieties: Most of the asparagus available in the American markets is green. Purple asparagus, with purple tips and leaves, and the rare and more costly white asparagus, readily available in European markets, are seen infrequently in American produce markets. White asparagus, sometimes called Belgian asparagus, is really green asparagus grown underground so that the spears are never exposed to light. It is considered a delicacy.

Chicken and Asparagus Stir-Fry

Storage: The best storage method is to keep asparagus upright with the stems in several inches of water. Or, wrap the bunch in damp paper towels and place in a plastic bag. Since it loses its natural sugar during storage, asparagus should be refrigerated as quickly as possible and used within a day or two for best flavor.

Basic Preparation: The first consideration is whether to peel. Some purists insist that peeling is necessary, but others are not convinced. Slender stalks do not need to be peeled, unless a more elegant presentation is desired. Stems that are thick or woody are best peeled with a vegetable peeler or paring knife, beginning just under the tip and going all the way to the end in long sweeps. Or, peel only the stem ends.

Peeling improves the texture of the stems and allows them to cook as quickly as the tender tips.

It is often recommended that stems be flexed because they will break where the stem is too tough to eat. This practice, however, wastes too much of the vegetable. It is preferable to trim off ends that appear dried, shriveled or woody and peel as necessary. Leave spears intact or cut into one-inch pieces. A diagonal cut is attractive for asparagus pieces.

Availability: Asparagus is sold in most months, although off-season, at a premium price. Prime season begins in late February or early March. From there, the supply increases dramatically and the price falls to match the abundance. By mid-summer, the domestic supply diminishes and is replaced by imports. Cut and whole spears are also available frozen and canned.

Buying Tips: Select firm, smooth green stems with tightly closed tips; tips that are open are a sign of age. Look for even green shading along the whole length; ends that become lighter in color may be a sign of toughness. Avoid wilted spears and asparagus that has a strong odor. In the produce department, select bunches of asparagus that are kept upright with their bases in water.

Yield: 1 pound asparagus = 12 to 15 spears; 3 cups, cut spears.

Asparagus can be steamed or boiled. In a deep skillet that is large enough to hold the stems (or a large saucepan for pieces), bring water to a boil and then add the asparagus. Boil 4 to 6 minutes or until crisp-tender. Remove whole spears from the water with tongs and transfer them to several layers of paper towels to absorb excess water. (Drain cut pieces in a colander.) If desired, the cooking water can be salted. Stir-frying, roasting and grilling are other methods for preparing this vegetable.

Chicken and Asparagus Stir-Fry

> **1 cup uncooked rice**
> **2 tablespoons vegetable oil**
> **1 pound boneless, skinless chicken breasts, cut into ½-inch-wide strips**
> **2 small red bell peppers, cut into thin strips**
> **½ pound fresh asparagus, cut diagonally into 1-inch pieces**
> **½ cup bottled stir-fry sauce**

1. Cook rice according to package directions.

2. Meanwhile, heat oil in wok or large skillet over medium-high heat until hot. Add chicken; stir-fry 3 to 4 minutes until chicken is no longer pink in center.

3. Stir in peppers and asparagus; reduce heat to medium. Cover; cook 2 minutes or until vegetables are crisp-tender, stirring once or twice. Stir in stir-fry sauce. Serve immediately over rice.

Makes 4 servings

Asparagus Wreath

> **1 pound fresh asparagus**
> **1 tablespoon butter or margarine**
> **1 teaspoon fresh lemon juice**
> **6 thin slices pepperoni, finely chopped**
> **¼ cup seasoned dry bread crumbs**
> **Pimiento strips (optional)**

1. To prepare asparagus, trim off tough ends of spears. To prevent tips from cooking faster than stems, peel stem ends with vegetable peeler.

2. Rinse asparagus and place in steamer basket. Place steamer basket in large saucepan; add 1 inch water.

(Water should not touch bottom of basket.) Cover. Bring to a boil over high heat; steam asparagus 5 to 8 minutes until crisp-tender. Add water, as necessary, to prevent pan from boiling dry.

3. Remove spears from basket and arrange in glass ring mold or make wreath of spears on warm, round serving platter.

4. Melt butter with juice in small saucepan over medium heat; pour over asparagus. Sprinkle pepperoni and bread crumbs over asparagus. Garnish with pimiento, if desired. Serve immediately.

Makes 4 side-dish servings

Tip

Special cookers are available to cook asparagus. These pans are tall and slender so a bundle of asparagus can stand upright. This design allows the tougher stems to boil while the delicate tips are steamed.

Asparagus Wreath

AU JUS

Au jus, the French term meaning "with juice," describes roasted meat, particularly beef, that is served with unthickened natural juices collected from pan drippings and skimmed of fat.

AVOCADO

Avocados, native to Mexico, are widely loved by Americans for their use in guacamole, the lively green Mexican dip. They have a rich, butter-like texture and a mild, almost nutty flavor. The fat content of avocados is high; two thirds is monounsaturated and the remainder is saturated.

Uses: Overwhelmingly, they are used for guacamole, where perfectly ripe, fork-mashed avocadoes are combined with onion, hot chilies, cilantro, fresh lime juice and salt.

• They make great additions to salads and sandwiches, especially cheese and vegetable or turkey and bacon sandwiches.

• Cut into halves, they become "boats," ideal vessels for chicken or shrimp salad.

• Puréed, they form the base for soups and sauces. Also, because of their soft texture, mild taste and store of vitamins and minerals, they make a fine early food for infants.

Varieties: There are two types of avocados in the United States—those from California and those from Florida. California avocados are small and pear-shaped with rough, nubby blackish-green skins that are sometimes marked by a purple tint. Several varieties are grown in California but the Hass is the most common. Florida avocados, which originated in the West Indies, are large with thin, smooth green skins. Their texture is more watery, their flavor is less sweet and they aren't as widely available or as popular as the Hass. California avocados have twice as much fat as their Florida counterparts.

Availability: Avocados are available all year.

Buying Tips: Avocados are picked unripe and are often found unripe in the supermarket too. If you plan on using them right away, look for specimens that yield to gentle pressure. However, they should not feel soft or mushy. If the flesh has shrunken away from the peel, they are overripe and should be avoided. Avocados have no aroma to judge them by. Firm avocados will eventually ripen but avoid those that are rock-hard.

Yield: 1 pound avocados = 2 to 3 California or 1 Florida; 2 cups mashed; 2½ cups diced.

Storage: Ripe avocados should be stored in the refrigerator. Depending on how ripe they are, they will last for five to seven days. Unripe avocados can be left at room temperature until they soften, which can take as little as a day or as long as nine days. Placing them in a sealed brown paper bag will hasten ripening.

Basic Preparation: Avocados usually are served raw. To prepare an avocado, insert a utility knife into the stem end. Slice in half lengthwise to the pit, turning the avocado while

slicing. Remove the knife blade and twist the halves in opposite directions to pull apart.

 Press the knife blade into the pit, twisting the knife gently to pull the pit away from the avocado. Discard pit.

For slicing or dicing, peel away the skin with your fingers. There is no need to peel if you plan to mash the fruit; just scoop the flesh out of the shells. Once peeled, the flesh begins to discolor almost immediately. Lightly brush the avocado with lemon or lime juice; or if mashing, add lemon or lime juice to the mixture.

Classic Guacamole

  4 tablespoons finely chopped
      white onion, divided
1½ tablespoons coarsely chopped
      fresh cilantro, divided
  1 or 2 fresh serrano or jalapeño
      chilies, seeded, finely
      chopped*
¼ teaspoon chopped garlic
      (optional)
  2 ripe large avocados
  1 very ripe medium tomato,
      blanched, peeled
  1 to 2 teaspoons fresh lime juice
¼ teaspoon salt
      Corn tortilla chips
      Additional chilies and fresh
          cilantro sprig (optional)

*Chili peppers can sting and irritate the skin; wear rubber or plastic gloves when handling peppers and do not touch eyes. Wash hands after handling.

1. Combine 2 tablespoons onion, 1 tablespoon chopped cilantro, chopped chilies and garlic, if desired, in large mortar. Grind with pestle until almost smooth. (Mixture can be processed in blender, if necessary, but will become more watery than desired.)

Classic Guacamole

2. Cut avocados lengthwise into halves; remove and discard pits. Scoop avocado flesh out of shells; place in bowl. Add chili mixture. Mash roughly with wooden spoon, bean masher or potato masher, leaving avocado slightly chunky; set aside.

3. Cut tomato crosswise in half. Gently squeeze each half to remove seeds; discard seeds. Chop tomato.

4. Add tomato, remaining 2 tablespoons onion, ½ tablespoon chopped cilantro, juice and salt to reserved avocado mixture; mix well. Serve immediately, or cover and refrigerate up to 4 hours. Serve with chips. Garnish with additional chilies and cilantro, if desired.

Makes about 2 cups guacamole

Technique for Classic Guacamole

Step 2. *Scooping avocado flesh out of shells.*

BAKED ALASKA

Baked Alaska is a showy dessert that consists of a layer of cake, a layer of ice cream and a snowy meringue coating. The dessert is popped into a very hot oven to brown the meringue just before serving. This results in what seems to be magic—the ice cream does not melt. Tiny air bubbles beaten into the egg whites for the meringue provide the perfect insulation from the heat of the oven. Be sure that the ice cream is completely covered with meringue. Store-bought cake can be substituted for easier preparation.

❧

Brownie Baked Alaskas

Brownie Baked Alaskas

2 purchased or prepared
  2½×2½-inch brownies
2 scoops vanilla ice cream (or
  favorite flavor)
⅓ cup semisweet chocolate chips
2 tablespoons light corn syrup or
  milk
2 egg whites
¼ cup sugar
  Strawberry slices (optional)

1. Preheat oven to 500°F. Place brownies on small ungreased baking sheet; top each with scoop of ice cream and place in freezer.

2. Melt chips in small saucepan over low heat, stirring occasionally. Stir in corn syrup; remove from heat. Cover and keep warm.

3. Beat egg whites in small bowl with electric mixer at high speed until soft peaks form. Gradually beat in sugar, beating until stiff peaks form. Spread egg white mixture over ice cream and brownies with small spatula. (Ice cream and brownies should be completely covered with egg white mixture.)

4. Bake 2 to 3 minutes until golden. Spread warm chocolate sauce on serving plates; place baked Alaskas over sauce. Garnish with strawberries, if desired.

Makes 2 servings

Note: Brownies may be cut into round or heart shapes before topping with ice cream.

BAKEWARE

Bakeware is a general term that refers to a wide variety of utensils used for baking foods in the oven. Baking utensils are usually made of metal, glass or ceramic. Should your kitchen include all those utensils described below? Probably not. It is best to know what types of baked goods you will be making and how much storage space your kitchen has before deciding what utensils you need.

Selecting Bakeware: When choosing metal bakeware, buy pans of the heaviest weight and best quality that you can afford—they will produce better results and last longer. Aluminum pans are an excellent conductor of heat, producing uniform baking and browning. However, aluminum can react with acids in food, affecting the flavor and color of the food and damaging the pan. While this is not generally a problem with baked goods, aluminum bakeware can not be used for marinating or for baking dishes that contain tomatoes or citrus juice. On the other hand, stainless steel is a poor conductor of heat. It is nonreactive and easy to clean.

The exterior and interior surface of a pan is another aspect that should be considered. Pans with shiny exteriors are best for cakes, because they produce the light, delicate crusts. Dull or dark-surfaced pans absorb heat more quickly, shorten baking time, and produce crisp, brown crusts that are desirable for breads and pies. Nonstick finishes make cleanup easy, but they should never be scoured because the surface will scratch and the finish will become less effective.

Glass and ceramic bakeware absorb heat more slowly and hold heat better than metal. Both glass and ceramic are good choices for casseroles and acidic foods.

TYPES OF BAKEWARE

Baking Dish: Baking dishes are open utensils in square, rectangular and round shapes. They are made of glass or ceramic. Both materials absorb and hold heat very well and make cleanup easy. The most common sizes of baking dishes are:

8 inch squares (21×21 cm)

11×7 inches, or 2 quarts, or 2 liters (28×18×4 cm)

13×9 inches, or 2½ quarts, or 3 liters (33×23×5 cm)

Baking dishes are best suited for foods that are acidic or for savory foods that require long exposure to even heat, such as casseroles. For the convenience of storing foods in the refrigerator or freezer prior to baking, choose glass baking dishes labeled "freezer-to-oven safe." For microwave cooking, glass baking dishes are a good choice, but ceramic dishes containing metallic powders should not be used. Ceramic dishes suitable for use in a microwave oven are labeled "for microwave use" or "microwave-safe."

Tip

When substituting glass bakeware in recipes that call for baking pans reduce oven temperature by 25°F.

Baking Pan: This metal utensil has a square or rectangular shape and straight sides at least 1½ inches high. The most usual sizes are 8 and 9 inches square; 11×7×2 inches; and 13×9×2 inches. Baking pans (sometimes referred to as cake pans) are designed for cake and cookie batters. Shiny aluminum pans are ideal for producing a tender, lightly browned cake crust. A baking pan may also be used to roast poultry and meat by adding a rack to a rectangular baking pan.

Baking Sheet: A baking sheet (often referred to as a cookie sheet) is a flat, rigid sheet of metal on which stiff dough is baked into cookies, rolls, biscuits, etc. It has a low lip on one or more sides for ease in handling; a lip higher than one half of an inch interferes with surface browning, especially of cookies.

The type of surface also determines the browning characteristics of the baking sheet. Shiny finishes promote even browning. Dark metal baking sheets absorb more heat and cause food to brown quickly. Insulated baking sheets have a layer of air sandwiched between two sheets of aluminum which helps to prevent excess browning but increases baking time. (Some cookie doughs may also spread more on these sheets.) Nonstick finishes minimize sticking and make cleanup easier.

Baking sheets vary in size. Before buying, know the dimensions of your oven. A baking sheet should fit on an oven rack with at least one inch on all sides between the edge of the sheet and the oven wall. Otherwise, heat circulation will be hampered.

Baking Stone: A baking stone is a 12- to 15-inch round or 12×15-inch rectangular piece of unglazed light-colored stone. It is used to duplicate the baking qualities of a commercial brick oven, which produces light, crusty bread and crisp pizza crusts. Baking stones (sometimes known as pizza stones) should be placed on the lowest rack in a cold oven and heated while the oven is preheating. Round bread loaves and pizza are baked directly on the stone. Loaf pans filled with bread dough and baking sheets with roll dough may be placed on the stone to bake. Clean the baking stone by wiping it with a damp cloth, but do not put it in the dishwasher.

Bundt Pan: A bundt pan is a fluted tube pan traditionally used to bake a densely textured bundt cake. The pan has curved indentations that create an attractive sculpted design. Bundt pans usually measure 10 inches in diameter with a 12-cup capacity. They are traditionally made of cast aluminum with a nonstick interior coating but are also available in lightweight aluminum. Generously greasing the fluted sides is extremely important to prevent sticking.

Cake Pan: A cake pan, or layer pan, is round with a straight side at least 1½ inches high. Choose aluminum or heavy-gauge steel to produce a cake with a delicate, tender crust. Besides the most common round 8- or 9-inch cake pans, there Is a wide array of pans available that measure from 3 to 24 inches in diameter. Cake pans also come in a variety of specialty shapes.

Casserole: Casserole refers both to a specific baking utensil and the food it contains. A casserole dish is a deep round or oval ovenproof container with two short handles. It may or may not be covered. This utensil is usually made of glass, earthenware or porcelain. Casserole dishes are measured by their volume in quarts. The most common sizes of casseroles are 1, 1½, 2, 2½ and 3 quarts. This container is designed for slow cooking in the oven. Many casseroles are ideal for microwave cooking and some are suitable for use on the stovetop. Check the manufacturer's label to determine if a casserole can be used in these ways.

Corn Stick Pan: This specialty pan is made of cast iron with five or six molds shaped like ears of corn. It is used to bake corn sticks from corn bread batter. Follow the manufacturer's directions for seasoning to prevent rusting. Grease the pan and preheat it in the oven before filling the molds two-thirds full with corn bread batter. This will ensure that the corn sticks have a crisp browned exterior. Pans with molds of other shapes are also available.

Jelly-Roll Pan: This rectangular baking pan with 1-inch-high sides is used to make a thin sponge cake that can be spread with jelly and rolled into a jelly roll. Jelly-roll pans are also used for making thin sheet cakes or bar cookies. A standard pan measures 15½×10½×1-inch. They are available in aluminum and steel. Jelly-roll pans are not a good choice for baking individual cookies, because the sides interfere with air circulation during baking, which results in uneven browning.

Loaf Pan: Loaf pans are designed for baking yeast-bread loaves, quick-bread loaves, pound cakes, fruit cakes and meat loaf. A standard loaf pan measures 9×5×3 inches with slightly flared sides. Smaller loaf pans measuring 8½×4½×2½ inches and miniature pans measuring 5×4×2 inches are also available. Loaf pans come in a variety of materials including aluminum, steel and glass. Pans with dark exteriors are best for yeast bread. Those with shiny exteriors are best for quick breads and pound cakes.

Madeleine Pan: A madeleine pan has oval-shaped molds with a scalloped shell design. It is used to make madeleines, light sponge cakes that take on the form of the mold. Madeleines are eaten like cookies.

Muffin Pan: Muffin pans (sometimes called muffin tins) are rectangular baking pans with 6 or 12 cup-shaped cavities that hold muffin or cupcake batter. Cavities are greased or lined with paper baking cups and filled three-fourths full. A standard muffin cup measures 2½ inches in diameter and 1½ inches deep. Also available are giant muffin cans with cups measuring 3¼ inches in diameter by 2 inches deep; miniature or gem pans with cups measuring 1½ to 2 inches in diameter and ¾ of an inch deep; and muffin top pans with cups measuring 4 inches in diameter and ½ of an inch deep. Muffin pans are made with aluminum, steel or cast iron.

Tip

Baking utensils with dark finishes will absorb heat more quickly than shiny bakeware; reduce the oven temperature by 25°F when using pans with this finish to prevent overbrowning and crisp crusts.

Pie Pan or Plate: A pie pan or plate is exclusively designed for baking a pie. Pie plate generally refers to a glass or ceramic utensil; pie pan refers to a metal utensil. Both are round, about 1½ inches deep and have a sloping side. They range in diameter from 8 to 12 inches. Nine inches is the most popular. Deep-dish pie pans are 2 inches deep. Glass or dark metal pie pans produce a crisp, golden brown crust. Shiny aluminum pans produce a paler crust.

Pizza Pan: A pizza pan is a round metal sheet with a raised rim used for baking pizza. The bottom of some pans are perforated with hundreds of small holes that allow moisture to escape during baking, creating a crisper and more evenly browned bottom crust. A dark surface also produces a crisper crust. A shiny exterior results in a softer crust. Pizza pans are made of aluminum or black steel, ranging in diameter from 11 to 15 inches. Deep-dish pizza pans measuring 15 inches across by 2 inches deep are also available.

Quiche Dish or Pan: A quiche dish is a fluted, straight-sided ceramic dish. Metal quiche pans also have fluted sides; they often have removable bottoms as well. Both dishes and pans are usually 10 to 12 inches in diameter and 1½ inches deep.

Ring Mold: Ring molds are round pans with a large center hole. They are used to shape gelatin or salad mixtures and to bake breads and cakes. They are available in a variety of sizes and materials.

Shaped Mold: Shaped molds are containers into which foods, such as gelatin, ice cream or rice salad, are placed in order to take on the shape of the container. Molds are available in a wide range of sizes, shapes and materials. Food is poured or packed into the mold and then refrigerated or frozen until firm enough to hold its shape.

Springform Pan: A springform pan is a two-piece round baking pan with an expandable side (secured by a clamp or spring) and a removable bottom. When the clamp is opened, the rim expands and the bottom of the pan can be removed. This makes it easy to remove cheesecakes, cakes and tortes from the pan. The diameter ranges from 6 to 12 inches with 9- and 10-inch pans being the most common.

Tart Pan: A tart pan has a shallow fluted side and a removable bottom. Although round is the most common shape, tart pans are also available in square and rectangular shapes. Typically made of black steel, they range in size from 8 to 12 inches in diameter and 1 to 2 inches deep. Tartlet pans, or miniature tart pans, also have fluted sides and are available in a variety of shapes.

Tube Pan: A tube pan is a round baking pan with a hollow tube in the center, which conducts heat to the center of the cake to promote even baking. The tube also supports delicate batters as they rise in the oven. Most tube pans have a high, slightly flared side. Some, such as the angel food cake pan, have a removable bottom. They are generally 8 to 10 inches in diameter and 3½ to 4 inches high with a 12-cup capacity.

BAKLAVA

Baklava, a sweet dessert pastry, is a classic in Greek, Turkish and Armenian cuisines. It is made of many paper-thin layers of phyllo dough that are brushed with melted butter and interspersed with a mixture of chopped nuts, sugar and spices. While the baked pastry is still warm, it is drenched with a honey-lemon syrup. Baklava is traditionally cut into diamonds before serving.

🐝

BAMBOO SHOOT

Bamboo shoots, the young shoots of an edible species of bamboo, are plucked as soon as they poke through the ground. Prized as a vegetable in Asian cooking, they are crunchy, slightly sweet and mild tasting. Fresh bamboo shoots are rarely, if ever, available in the United States. Sliced bamboo shoots are available in cans; they should be drained and rinsed well before using.

BANANA

Bananas are grown in the warm, humid areas throughout the tropics. A banana plant, which matures in about 15 months, yields only one bunch of bananas weighing 50 to 60 pounds. A bunch consists of 10 to 15 "hands" of 10 to 20 bananas or "fingers." After the bunch is cut, the plant is chopped down and another one is planted. Unlike most fruit, bananas develop a better flavor when picked and shipped green. By the time they reach the supermarket, they are almost ripe.

Uses: Use slightly underripe bananas for baking, sautéing and grilling, because they hold their shape better when cooked.

• Overripe bananas are best used to flavor baked goods, such as cakes, quick breads and muffins.

• Banana leaves are used in many tropical cuisines to wrap foods for steaming.

Varieties: There are hundreds of varieties of bananas. The most common one in American supermarkets is the yellow Cavendish. Some larger supermarkets carry such varieties as the short, chunky red banana and the tiny finger banana; both are known for their sweetness. Plantains are large, firm bananas with rough skins and a squashlike flavor. They are a staple food in the tropics where they are used as a starchy vegetable but they are never eaten raw.

Availability: Fresh bananas are available all year. Dried banana slices, most often used for snacking, are also available.

Buying Tips: Look for bananas with plump, evenly colored yellow skins. Avoid bananas with blemishes or split skins.

Bananas with green tips and ridges will ripen at home within a day or two. Brown speckles are an indication of ripeness. When banana skins develop black patches, they are overripe. A grayish-green color is a sign that the fruit was exposed to cold temperatures and will not ripen properly. Red bananas are dark red with black speckles when ripe.

Lemony Banana-Walnut Bread (recipe on page 32)

Yield: 1 pound Cavendish bananas = 3 medium; 2 cups sliced; 1⅓ cups mashed.
1 pound dried banana slices = 4½ cups slices.

Storage: To ripen bananas, store at room temperature. To speed ripening, place them in an unsealed paper bag at room temperature. To prevent ripe bananas from spoiling, store them, tightly wrapped, in the refrigerator. Although the peel will turn brown, the fruit will retain its creamy color for about three days. Mashed bananas may be frozen for up to six months. Simply stir in 1 teaspoon of lemon juice for each banana to prevent browning and freeze in an airtight container.

Basic Preparation: Once the peel is removed, the fruit should be used immediately or it will begin to brown. To retain its creamy color, the fruit can be dipped in an acidic liquid, such as orange juice or a mixture of lemon juice and water. To mash bananas, use a fork, potato masher or process in a food processor.

Chocolate-Covered Banana Pops

    3 ripe, large bananas
    9 wooden popsicle sticks
    2 cups (12-ounce package)
        HERSHEY᾽S Semi-Sweet
        Chocolate Chips
    2 tablespoons shortening (do not
        use butter, margarine or oil)
 1½ cups coarsely chopped unsalted,
        roasted peanuts

Peel bananas; cut each into thirds. Insert wooden stick into each banana piece; place on waxed paper-covered tray. Cover; freeze until firm. In microwave-safe container, place chocolate chips and shortening. Microwave at HIGH (100% power) 1½ to 2 minutes or until chocolate is melted and mixture is smooth when stirred. Remove bananas from freezer just before dipping. Dip each piece into warm chocolate, covering completely; allow excess to drip off. Immediately roll in peanuts. Cover; return to freezer. Serve frozen.
Makes 9 pops

Variation: HERSHEY᾽S Milk Chocolate Chips or HERSHEY᾽S MINI CHIPS® Semi-Sweet Chocolate may be substituted for Semi-Sweet Chocolate Chips.

Lemony Banana-Walnut Bread

   ⅔ cup vegetable shortening
    1 cup granulated sugar
    2 eggs
 1½ cups mashed ripe bananas
        (about 3 medium)
    7 tablespoons fresh lemon juice
        (about 3 lemons), divided
    2 cups all-purpose flour
    1 teaspoon baking soda
   ½ teaspoon salt
   ½ cup chopped walnuts
    1 tablespoon grated lemon peel
   ½ cup powdered sugar

1. Preheat oven to 325°F. Grease 2 (8½×4½-inch) loaf pans.

2. Beat shortening and granulated sugar in large bowl with electric mixer at medium speed until well blended. Add eggs, 1 at a time, mixing well after each addition. Blend in bananas and 6 tablespoons juice. Combine flour, baking soda and salt in small bowl; add to banana mixture, mixing until blended. Stir in walnuts and lemon peel. Pour evenly into prepared pans.

3. Bake 50 to 60 minutes until wooden toothpick inserted into centers comes out clean. Remove from pans; cool completely on wire racks.

4. Combine powdered sugar and remaining 1 tablespoon juice in small bowl; stir until smooth. Drizzle over cooled loaves.   *Makes 2 loaves*

Ginger Baked Bananas with Cinnamon Cream

4 firm ripe bananas, peeled
¼ cup butter or margarine,
    melted, divided
1 tablespoon fresh lemon juice
¼ cup firmly packed brown sugar
¼ cup uncooked rolled oats
¼ cup chopped pecans or walnuts
1 tablespoon finely chopped
    crystallized ginger
1 teaspoon granulated sugar
½ teaspoon ground cinnamon
½ cup chilled whipping cream

1. Preheat oven to 375°F.

2. Place bananas in baking dish large enough to hold them in single layer. Combine 2 tablespoons butter and juice in small bowl; drizzle evenly over bananas. Combine brown sugar, oats, pecans, ginger and remaining 2 tablespoons butter; sprinkle evenly over bananas.

3. Bake 15 to 18 minutes until bananas are hot and topping is bubbly.

4. To prepare Cinnamon Cream, combine granulated sugar and cinnamon in cup; set aside.

5. Chill large bowl and beaters thoroughly. Pour cream into chilled bowl and beat with electric mixer at high speed until soft peaks form. Gradually beat reserved sugar mixture into whipped cream until stiff peaks form.

6. Serve bananas warm with Cinnamon Cream.

Makes 4 servings

Ginger Baked Bananas with Cinnamon Cream

BARBECUE SAUCE

Barbecue sauce is a thick sauce used to brush on meat, poultry or fish during grilling or baking to add flavor and retain moisture. The sauce is usually prepared with tomatoes or a tomato product, brown sugar or molasses, vinegar, onions, mustard and garlic. It may be prepared at home or purchased bottled. Because its high sugar content can cause charring, barbecue sauce should be used during the last 10 to 30 minutes of cooking. Additional sauce may be served with the cooked meat, but for food safety, sauce used for brushing should not accompany the food after it is cooked.

🐝

Technique for Seasoned Baby Back Ribs

Step 2. *Rubbing spice mixture over ribs.*

Seasoned Baby Back Ribs

    1 tablespoon paprika
 1½ teaspoons garlic salt
    1 teaspoon celery salt
  ½ teaspoon ground black pepper
  ¼ teaspoon ground red pepper
    4 pounds pork baby back ribs, cut
        into 3- to 4-rib portions, well
        trimmed
      Barbecue Sauce (recipe follows)
      Rib rack (optional)
      Orange peel strips (optional)

1. Preheat oven to 350°F.

2. For seasoning rub, combine paprika, garlic salt, celery salt, black pepper and red pepper in small bowl. Rub over all surfaces of ribs with fingers.

3. Place ribs in foil-lined shallow roasting pan. Bake 30 minutes.

4. Meanwhile, prepare grill for direct grilling over medium heat; prepare Barbecue Sauce.

Seasoned Baby Back Ribs

5. Transfer ribs to rib rack, if desired; place on grid. (Or, place ribs directly on grid.) Grill ribs, on covered grill, over medium coals 10 minutes.

6. Remove ribs from rib rack with tongs; brush ½ of Barbecue Sauce evenly over both sides of ribs. Return ribs to rib rack. (Or, brush with ½ of sauce and turn over.) Grill, covered, 10 minutes more or until ribs are tender and browned. Serve with reserved sauce. Garnish with orange peel, if desired. *Makes 6 servings*

Barbecue Sauce

> ½ cup ketchup
> ⅓ cup firmly packed light brown
>   sugar
> 1 tablespoon cider vinegar
> 2 teaspoons Worcestershire sauce
> 2 teaspoons soy sauce

Combine ketchup, sugar, vinegar, Worcestershire and soy sauce in glass measuring cup or small bowl. Reserve ½ of sauce for serving with ribs in separate bowl.
Makes about ⅔ cup sauce

Wyoming Wild Barbecue Sauce

> 1 cup chili sauce
> 1 cup ketchup
> ¼ cup steak sauce
> 3 tablespoons dry mustard
> 2 tablespoons horseradish
> 2 tablespoons TABASCO® pepper
>   sauce
> 1 tablespoon Worcestershire
>   sauce
> 1 tablespoon finely chopped
>   garlic
> 1 tablespoon dark molasses
> 1 tablespoon red wine vinegar

Combine ingredients in medium bowl. Whisk until sauce is well blended. Store in 1-quart covered jar in refrigerator up to 7 days. Use as a baste while grilling beef, chicken, pork or game. (Do not baste meat or poultry during last 5 minutes of grilling.) *Makes 3 cups sauce*

Quick Barbecue Basting Sauce

> ½ cup A.1.® Steak Sauce
> ½ cup ketchup
> ½ teaspoon liquid hot pepper
>   seasoning

In small bowl, combine steak sauce, ketchup and hot pepper seasoning. Use as a baste while grilling beef, ribs or poultry. *Makes 1 cup sauce*

BASTE, TO

Basting is the technique of brushing, spooning or pouring liquids over food, usually meat and poultry, as it cooks. It helps preserve moistness, adds flavor and gives foods an attractive appearance. Melted butter, pan drippings, broth or a combination of these ingredients are frequently used. Sometimes seasonings or flavorings are added. A bulb baster is an inexpensive specialized utensil that will efficiently suction liquid and allow you to squeeze it onto food.

🐝

Basting turkey with pan drippings.

BATTER

Batter is an uncooked liquid mixture that is the base for pancakes, waffles and crêpes and for baked goods such as muffins, cakes and quick breads. Usually made from eggs, milk or water, flour, sugar and a leavener, batter consistency can vary from that of a light cream to a thick cereal, but it is almost always thin enough to pour.

🐝

BEAN

Beans are the seeded pods of the legume family. A food staple in many cultures for thousands of years, beans remain an important part of cuisines all around the world. There are hundreds of varieties of beans. Some are grown for their edible pods while others for their seeds, which are used either fresh or dried. The varieties described here are among the most common in North America.

☙

BLACK BEAN: Also known as turtle beans, black beans are very important to the cuisines of Latin America and the Caribbean. These small jet-black beans have an earthy, meaty flavor and mealy texture. They are eaten as an accompaniment to Latin or Caribbean entrées and are the basis for Cuban black bean soup. Black beans can be added to soups, stews, casseroles and salads. They are available both dried and canned.

BLACK–EYED PEA: This southern favorite is really a bean, not a pea. Black-eyed peas are small tan beans that take their name from the black eye-shaped mark on the inner curve of the bean. Their mealy texture and earthy flavor are enhanced by long, slow cooking with ham or salt pork. These beans are the basis for Hoppin' John, a dish of black-eyed peas and rice. Southerners believe that eating black-eyed peas or Hoppin' John on New Year's Day brings good luck for the year to come. These beans are occasionally available fresh, but for the most part, they are dried or canned.

CANNELLINI BEAN: see Kidney Bean

CHICK–PEA: Also known as garbanzo or ceci beans, chick-peas are larger than green peas. They are round, irregularly shaped tan beans with a firm texture and mild, nutlike flavor. Popular in the Mediterranean region, India and the Middle East, chick-peas are used extensively in these cuisines. Brought to Spain by the Moors, they are often used in Spanish and Mexican cuisines. Chick-peas are the basis for hummus, a mixture of mashed beans, garlic, lemon juice and oil, which is used as a dip or a spread. Chick-peas are also an ingredient in couscous, soups and salads. They are available canned, dried and in some parts of the country, fresh.

CRANBERRY BEAN: Cranberry beans have mottled reddish markings. They are occasionally available fresh and already shelled in the summer months. In some parts of the country fresh cranberry beans in pods can be found at farmers' markets. The pods, which are inedible, are whitish-green in color with red striations. Use cranberry beans in minestrone or other soups and stews.

GREAT NORTHERN BEAN:

Great Northern beans are large white beans with a delicate flavor. They can be used in soups, stews, baked beans and salads. Great Northern beans are available both dried and canned.

KIDNEY BEAN:

This bean gets its name because of its shape. Kidney beans have skins that range from very dark red to pink and flesh that is cream colored. Kidney beans are noted for their robust flavor. Milder flavored white kidney beans, which are more difficult to find, are better known as cannellini beans. Use kidney beans in chilis, soups, stews and salads. Cannellini beans are the traditional beans for the Italian *Pasta e Fagioli* or "pasta and bean soup." Kidney beans and cannellini beans are available both dried and canned.

LIMA BEAN:

Lima beans are relatively large, flat kidney-shaped light green beans. When found fresh in the pod, lima beans are shelled and the tough and stringy beans are discarded. Fresh, already shelled lima beans are sometimes available in the supermarket. Lima beans are cooked and eaten most frequently as a side dish. Combined with corn and sometimes green or red bell pepper, they are used to make succotash.

Varieties: There are two distinct varieties of lima beans. Fordhooks are large, slightly plump pale green beans with a full flavor. Baby limas, which are not immature Fordhooks, but a separate variety, are half the size of Fordhooks and less plump. Dried lima beans are sometimes referred to as butter beans.

Availability: Fresh lima beans are generally available year-round in the pod or shelled. Peak season is August through September. Lima beans are also available dried, frozen and canned.

Buying Tips: Look for green, shiny and pliable pods; beans should fill pods well. Avoid pods with signs of drying. When buying shelled beans, choose plump beans with green to greenish-white skins. Avoid beans with brown blemishes or shriveled skins.

Yield: Half the weight of fresh lima beans is in the pods and is waste. Although yields vary according to the size of the bean, 1 pound lima beans = 1 to 1½ cups shelled beans.

Storage: Refrigerate lima bean pods in a perforated plastic bag for up to three days. Store shelled beans, tightly wrapped in plastic, in the refrigerator for up to three days. Store dried beans in an airtight container in a cool, dry place for up to a year.

Basic Preparation: Snap off the stem and pull the string down the length of the bean. Open the pod at the seam

by pinching the pod between your two thumbs and forefingers

Remove the beans from the pod by pushing them out with your thumb. Discard the pod and string.

Cover beans with water and bring to a boil. Reduce heat to low and simmer, covered, 20 to 25 minutes until tender. Lima beans may also be simmered in milk.

NAVY BEAN:

These small oval-shaped white beans are the bean of choice for commercial baked beans and homemade navy bean soup. Navy beans are so named because they were a food staple for the U.S. Navy in the 1800's. They are available both dried and canned.

> ## Tip
>
> *Quick-cooking beans have been presoaked and redried. They do not need to be presoaked.*

PINTO BEAN: Pinto beans are popular Spanish beans that are pale pink in color with reddish-brown streaks. They are used as the basis for refried beans and are an ingredient in soups and chilis. They are available both dried and canned.

SNAP BEAN: These fresh edible-podded beans are harvested when their seeds are immature. They are eaten pod and all.

Varieties: Edible-podded beans include green or string beans, yellow wax beans and *haricot vert*. Green beans are the most recognized and well liked of the edible-podded beans. Growers have virtually eliminated the tough strings that once characterized these beans. Similar in flavor to green beans but much less popular are yellow wax beans. They are, as their name implies, pale yellow in color. A traditional use of yellow wax beans is as one of the beans in three-bean salad. *Haricot vert* are extremely slender, stringless beans that have long been popular in France. Noted for their tenderness and sweet flavor, they are now grown commercially in the United States. However, they are expensive and difficult to find.

Herbed Green Beans

Availability: Green beans are generally available year-round in the supermarket, but the supply peaks from May through September. *Haricot vert* can be found in some specialty produce markets. Home gardeners find that most edible-podded bean varieties are easy to grow and that seeds for less common varieties are increasingly easy to find. Green beans (cut and French-cut) are also available frozen and canned. Yellow wax beans are available canned.

Buying Tips: Choose brightly colored, unblemished beans. Slenderness is an indication of tenderness. Pods should be crisp. Avoid pods that are limp, moldy or show signs of browning or drying. If the outline of the beans can be seen in the pods, the pods are over-mature.

Yield: 1 pound green beans = $3\frac{1}{2}$ cups whole; $2\frac{3}{4}$ cups pieces.

Storage: Refrigerate edible-podded beans, unwashed, in a perforated plastic bag for three to four days.

Basic Preparation: Wash the beans. If strings are present, snap off the stem ends of the beans, pulling the strings down the length of the beans. Discard the stems and strings. If no strings are present, snap off and discard the stem ends. Break beans into short lengths or cut them French-style. Young, very tender beans may

be left whole. To cut beans French-style, slice beans lengthwise into halves or quarters with a chef's knife on a cutting board.

Beans may be steamed or dropped into a generous amount of rapidly boiling water and boiled, uncovered, until tender. Young tender beans can be sautéed, braised or stir-fried.

TURTLE BEAN: see Black Bean

GUIDE TO COOKING DRIED BEANS

Dried Bean	Amount	Water	Simmering Time	Yield
Black Beans	1 cup	4 cups	2 hours	2 cups
Great Northern Beans	1 cup	3½ cups	2 hours	2 cups
Kidney Beans	1 cup	4 cups	2 hours	2 cups
Navy Beans	1 cup	5 cups	3 hours	2½ cups
Pinto Beans	1 cup	3 cups	2½ hours	2 cups

DRIED BEAN BASICS

Buying Tips: Dried beans are packaged in plastic bags or sold in bulk. Look for beans that are plump and free of blemishes. Avoid discolored or shriveled beans. Tiny holes are an indication of bug infestation.

Yield: 1 pound dried beans = 2½ cups uncooked; 5½ to 6½ cups cooked.

Storage: Store dried beans in an airtight container in a cool, dry place for up to a year. Canned beans can be stored in a cool, dry place for two years.

Basic Preparation: Before using, rinse beans under running water and pick out any debris or blemished beans. Dried beans should soak in water for several hours or overnight to soften before cooking. Soak according to the following directions or see the *Quick-Soak Method.* Place them in a large saucepan or bowl and cover with 3 inches of water. Let stand, covered, for 6 hours or overnight. Do not soak beans longer than 12 hours or they may begin to ferment. Drain beans before cooking.

Quick-Soak Method: Place beans in the pan in which they will be cooked. Cover with 3 inches of water. Bring to a boil and boil for 2 minutes. Remove from the heat; cover and let stand for 1 to 2 hours. Proceed with recipe.

Herbed Green Beans

1 pound fresh green beans, stem ends removed
1 teaspoon extra virgin olive oil
2 tablespoons chopped fresh basil *or* 2 teaspoons dried basil leaves
Fresh basil leaves (optional)

1. Steam green beans 5 minutes or until crisp-tender. Rinse under cold running water; drain and set aside.

2. Just before serving, heat oil over medium-low heat in large nonstick skillet. Add chopped basil; cook and stir 1 minute. Add green beans. Cook until heated through. Garnish with basil leaves, if desired. Serve immediately.

Makes 6 side-dish servings

Tips

Cooking dried beans uncovered will result in a firmer texture. If you want a softer texture, cover them during cooking.

Boiling will cause beans to break apart and the skins to separate from the beans. Maintain a gentle simmer when cooking dried beans.

Navy Bean Bacon Chowder

1. Rinse beans in colander, picking out any debris or blemished beans. Cover beans with 6 cups water; soak overnight.

2. Drain beans; discard water. Combine beans, remaining 4 cups water, carrots, onion, chili powder, cumin, bay leaf and salt in 5-quart Dutch oven. Bring to a boil over high heat. Reduce heat to medium-low; simmer, uncovered, 1½ hours, stirring occasionally.

3. Remove bay leaf; discard. Stir in tomatoes, tomato paste and jalapeño. Bring to a boil over high heat. Reduce heat to medium-low, simmer, uncovered, 15 minutes more, stirring occasionally. Serve over rice.

Makes 6 servings

Navy Bean Bacon Chowder

  8 ounces dried navy beans (about 1¼ cups)
  2 cups cold water
  6 slices bacon
  5 cups canned chicken broth
  1 medium onion, chopped
  1 small turnip, peeled, cut into cubes
  1 rib celery, chopped
  1 teaspoon dry Italian seasoning
  ¼ teaspoon salt
  ⅛ teaspoon ground black pepper
  1 medium carrot, peeled, chopped
  1 cup milk

1. Rinse beans in colander, picking out any debris or blemished beans. Place beans and water in Dutch oven or large saucepan. Bring to a boil over high heat. Reduce heat to medium. Cover and boil 2 minutes. Remove from heat and let stand, covered, about 1 hour. (Or, soak beans in water in bowl overnight in refrigerator.)

2. Cook bacon in small skillet over medium heat until brown and crispy. Remove bacon from skillet; drain on paper towels. Crumble bacon. Reserve 2 tablespoons for garnish.

Three Bean Chili

  ⅔ cup dried kidney beans
  ⅔ cup dried navy beans
  ⅔ cup dried black beans
10 cups cold water, divided
  3 medium carrots, peeled, sliced
  1 medium onion, chopped
  2 teaspoons chili powder
  ½ teaspoon ground cumin
  1 bay leaf
  1 teaspoon salt
  1 can (28 ounces) tomatoes, drained, coarsely chopped
  ⅓ cup tomato paste
  1 fresh jalapeño pepper,* chopped
  2 cups hot cooked rice

*Jalapeño peppers can sting and irritate the skin; wear rubber or plastic gloves when handling peppers and do not touch eyes. Wash hands after handling.

3. Drain beans; discard water. Return beans to Dutch oven. Add broth, onion, turnip, celery, remaining bacon, Italian seasoning, salt and pepper. Bring to a boil over high heat. Reduce heat to medium-low; simmer, uncovered, 1½ hours, stirring occasionally.

4. Stir carrot into soup; simmer, uncovered, 20 minutes more, stirring occasionally.

5. Carefully ladle 2 cups hot soup into food processor or blender container; cover and process until mixture is smooth. Return puréed mixture to Dutch oven. Stir in milk. Simmer, uncovered, over medium heat until hot, stirring occasionally. Serve in bowls; sprinkle with reserved bacon. *Makes 6 servings*

Shotgun Billy's Turkey Chili with Black Beans

> 1 can (28 ounces) tomatoes, undrained, coarsely chopped
> 1 cup coarsely chopped onion
> 1 red bell pepper, chopped
> 2 cloves garlic, minced
> 2 fresh jalapeño peppers,* seeded, minced
> 1 tablespoon chili powder
> 1½ teaspoons ground cumin
> 1½ teaspoons ground coriander
> ½ teaspoon dried oregano leaves
> ½ teaspoon dried marjoram leaves
> ¼ teaspoon crushed red pepper flakes
> ¼ teaspoon ground cinnamon
> 2 cups cooked turkey, cut into ½-inch cubes
> 1 can (16 ounces) black beans, drained, rinsed
> ½ cup coarsely chopped fresh cilantro
> 4 tablespoons shredded reduced fat Cheddar cheese

Jalapeño peppers can sting and irritate the skin; wear rubber or plastic gloves when handling peppers and do not touch eyes. Wash hands after handling.

1. Combine tomatoes with juice, onion, bell pepper, garlic and jalapeños in 3-quart microwave-safe dish. Stir in chili powder, cumin, coriander, oregano, marjoram, pepper flakes and cinnamon; cover.

2. Microwave at HIGH (100% power) 10 minutes, stirring once after 5 minutes. Stir in turkey and beans; cover. Microwave at HIGH 4 minutes more or until heated through; stir in cilantro. To serve, ladle into bowls; sprinkle each serving with 1 tablespoon cheese.
Makes 4 servings

Shotgun Billy's Turkey Chili with Black Beans

BEAN PASTE

Also known as brown bean sauce, yellow bean sauce and miso in Japan, bean paste is an Asian condiment made from fermented yellow soybeans, flour, water and salt. Some varieties of this thick sauce are quite smooth; others contain some whole beans. It adds saltiness, rich flavor and body to bland vegetable and tofu dishes. It is also used to season fish, beef, pork and duck. Hot bean paste, which gets its heat from chilies, is also available. Bean paste may be purchased in cans or jars in Asian markets and larger supermarkets. After opening, transfer canned bean paste to a covered glass jar. Store in the refrigerator for up to one year. If the sauce becomes too thick, stir in a little peanut oil.

☗

Grilled Swordfish with Hot Red Sauce

Grilled Swordfish with Hot Red Sauce

    2 tablespoons Sesame Salt (recipe
        follows)
    4 swordfish or halibut steaks
        (about 1½ pounds total)
¼ cup chopped green onions
    2 tablespoons hot bean paste
    2 tablespoons soy sauce
    1 tablespoon Oriental sesame oil
    4 teaspoons sugar
    4 cloves garlic, minced
⅛ teaspoon ground black pepper

1. Generously spray grid of barbecue grill or broiler rack with nonstick cooking spray. Prepare grill for direct grilling over medium-hot heat or preheat broiler.

2. Prepare Sesame Salt; set aside.

3. Rinse swordfish and pat dry with paper towels. Place in shallow glass dish.

4. Combine onions, bean paste, soy sauce, 2 tablespoons Sesame Salt, oil, sugar, garlic and pepper in small bowl; mix well. Spread ½ of marinade over fish; turn fish over and spread with remaining marinade. Cover with plastic wrap; refrigerate 30 minutes.

5. Remove fish from marinade; discard marinade. Place fish on prepared grid. Grill fish, on uncovered grill, over medium-hot coals or broil 4 to 5 minutes per side until fish is opaque and flakes easily when tested with fork. Garnish as desired.   *Makes 4 servings*

Sesame Salt

½ cup sesame seeds, toasted
¼ teaspoon salt

Crush sesame seeds and salt with mortar and pestle or process in clean coffee or spice grinder. Refrigerate any remaining Sesame Salt in covered glass jar.

BEAT, TO

Beating is the technique of stirring or mixing vigorously. It serves several purposes. Beating introduces air into egg whites, egg yolks and whipping cream; mixes two or more ingredients to form a homogeneous mixture; or makes a mixture smoother, lighter and creamier. Beating can be done with a variety of tools including a spoon, fork, wire whisk, rotary egg beater or electric mixer.

❦

BEER

Beer is a low-alcohol beverage made by malting cereals (principally barley), adding flavor with hops and then fermenting the mixture. Yeast is added to start the fermentation process, which results in alcohol and carbon dioxide. The carbon dioxide, which is not allowed to escape, results in the characteristic fizz. Since beer has a high percentage of water, the quality or the source of the water plays a major role in the flavor and character of beer. There are many types of beer including lager, light, ale, stout and porter. Beer is used in cooking to add flavor to stews, soups and breads.

❦

Brats 'n' Beer

1 can or bottle (12 ounces) beer (not dark) or nonalcoholic beer
4 fresh bratwurst (about 1 pound)
1 large sweet or Spanish onion (about ½ pound), thinly sliced, separated into rings
1 tablespoon olive or vegetable oil
¼ teaspoon salt
¼ teaspoon ground black pepper
4 hot dog rolls, preferably bakery-style or onion, split
Coarse-grain or sweet-hot mustard (optional)
Drained sauerkraut (optional)

1. Prepare grill for direct grilling over medium heat.

2. Pour beer into heavy medium saucepan with ovenproof handle. (If not ovenproof, wrap heavy-duty foil around handle.) Set saucepan on one side of grid. Pierce each bratwurst in several places. Carefully add bratwurst to beer, simmer, on uncovered grill, over medium coals 15 minutes, turning once.*

3. Meanwhile, place onion rings on 18×14-inch sheet of heavy-duty foil. Drizzle with oil; sprinkle with salt and pepper. Wrap in foil. Place on grid next to saucepan. Grill onions, on uncovered grill, 10 to 15 minutes until onions are tender.

4. Transfer bratwurst to grid; remove saucepan using heavy-duty mitt. Discard beer. Grill bratwurst, on covered grill, 9 to 10 minutes until browned and cooked through, turning halfway through grilling time.

5. If desired, place rolls, cut sides down, on grid to toast lightly during last 1 to 2 minutes of grilling. Place bratwurst in rolls. Top each bratwurst with onions. Serve with mustard and sauerkraut, if desired.

Makes 4 servings

If desired, bratwurst may be simmered on rangetop. Pour beer into medium saucepan. Bring to a boil over medium-high heat. Carefully add bratwurst to beer. Reduce heat to low; simmer, uncovered, 15 minutes.

Tip

For maximum flavor, beer should be consumed when fresh. Use it within 3 to 4 months. The flavor diminishes if beer is subjected to repeated temperature fluctuations.

BEET

Beets are a firm, round root vegetable with a fairly high sugar content and edible dark green leaves. Native to the Mediterranean region, beets are known to have been used by the Romans. Only the tops were eaten; the roots were used for medicinal purposes. Today beets are commercially grown in 31 states throughout the United States for both their roots and their tops.

🐝

Uses: Cooked beets are often served with just a little butter.

• Shred or slice small cooked beets to use in salads.

• Harvard Beets, a dish of beets in a sweet-and-sour sauce, and pickled beets are two traditional ways of serving this vegetable.

• Beets are the main ingredient in Red Flannel Hash, a New England specialty made by frying chopped cooked beets, onions, potatoes and bacon.

• Borscht is a traditional Russian and Polish soup made from fresh beets.

Tip

Beet juice can stain wood and plastic cutting boards and your hands. Slice beets on a glass plate and wear disposable plastic gloves.

Varieties: The most common table beet is red with purple-red skin and deep red flesh. Golden-yellow beets, white beets and the Chiogga beet, a new variety with alternating concentric rings of red and white flesh, are sometimes available at farmers' markets. The sugar beet, rarely eaten, is processed for sugar.

Availability: Fresh beets are available all year but are most plentiful from June through October. Canned whole, sliced and diced beets and pickled beets are readily available.

Buying Tips: Buy beets that are firm with smooth skins and tops attached. They should have a deep, rich purple-red color. Choose small to medium beets as they are usually sweeter and more tender. Beet tops should be fresh looking and dark green, not wilted or slimy. The tops are frequently bunched and sold separately as beet greens.

Yield: 1 pound trimmed beets = 2 cups chopped.
1 (16-ounce) can beets = 2 cups chopped.

Storage: To store fresh beets, trim off the leaves, leaving an inch or two of stalk above the bulb. Do not trim the long bottom root. Reserve tops and store them separately if intended for cooking. Store unwashed beets in a plastic bag up to one week in the refrigerator. Place washed and dried beet greens in a plastic bag and store refrigerated up to three days.

Basic Preparation: Gently wash beets to remove dirt and sand, being careful not to pierce the skin. Leave roots, stems and skin intact to minimize bleeding during cooking. Place beets in a saucepan, cover with water and bring to a boil. Simmer, covered, 20 to 40 minutes, depending on the size of the beets or until tender when pierced with a fork. Drain and cool beets. Under cold running water, trim off stems and roots and slip off skins. Slice or cut beets. Cook beet greens as you would spinach (page 472).

Apricot-Glazed Beets

1 large bunch fresh beets *or*
    1 pound loose beets
1 tablespoon cornstarch
1 cup apricot nectar
2 tablespoons cider vinegar or red
    wine vinegar
8 dried apricot halves, cut into
    strips
¼ teaspoon salt
    Additional apricot halves
    (optional)

1. To prevent color from bleeding during boiling, cut tops off beets, leaving at least 1 inch of stem; do not trim root ends. Scrub beets under cold running water with soft vegetable brush, being careful not to break skins.

2. Place beets in medium saucepan; cover with water. Cover saucepan. Bring to a boil over high heat; reduce heat to medium. Simmer about 20 minutes or just until beets are barely firm when pierced with fork and skins rub off easily. Transfer to plate; cool. Rinse pan.

3. Stir cornstarch into apricot nectar in same saucepan until smooth; stir in vinegar. Add apricot strips and salt. Cook over medium heat until mixture thickens, stirring occasionally.

4. Cut roots and stems from beets on plate. Peel, halve and cut beets into ¼-inch-thick slices.

5. Add beet slices to apricot mixture; toss gently to coat. Transfer to warm serving dish. Serve with apricot halves, if desired.

Makes 4 side-dish servings

Technique for Apricot-Glazed Beets

Step 1. *Cutting tops of beets.*

Apricot-Glazed Beets

Techniques for Classic Anise Biscotti

Step 4. *Shaping dough into logs.*

Step 5. *Slicing baked logs.*

Classic Anise Biscotti

BISCOTTO

A traditional Italian cookie, biscotti (plural of biscotto) is baked twice. The dough is first formed into a log and baked. The log is then cut into slices and the slices are baked. This produces the characteristic crunchy texture that is ideal for dipping in coffee or a dessert wine. Biscotti can be flavored with anise seed, hazelnuts or almonds.

☙

Classic Anise Biscotti

> 4 ounces whole blanched almonds (about ¾ cup)
> 2¼ cups all-purpose flour
> 1 teaspoon baking powder
> ¾ teaspoon salt
> ¾ cup sugar
> ½ cup unsalted butter, softened
> 3 eggs
> 2 tablespoons brandy
> 2 teaspoons grated lemon peel
> 1 tablespoon whole anise seeds

1. To toast almonds, preheat oven to 375°F. Spread almonds on ungreased baking sheet. Bake 6 to 8 minutes until toasted and light brown; turn oven off. Remove almonds to cutting board; cool. Coarsely chop almonds; set aside.

2. Combine flour, baking powder and salt in small bowl. Beat sugar and butter in medium bowl with electric mixer at medium speed until light and fluffy. Add eggs, 1 at a time, beating well after each addition and scraping side of bowl often. Stir in brandy and lemon peel. Add flour mixture gradually; stir until smooth. Stir in reserved almonds and anise seeds. Cover; refrigerate 1 hour or until firm.

3. Preheat oven to 375°F. Grease large baking sheet.

4. Divide dough in half. Shape ½ of dough into 12×2-inch log on lightly floured surface. (Dough will be fairly soft.) Pat smooth with lightly floured fingertips. Repeat with remaining ½ of dough to form second log. Bake 20 to 25 minutes until logs are light golden brown. Remove baking sheet from oven to wire rack; turn oven off. Cool logs completely.

5. Preheat oven to 350°F. Cut logs diagonally with serrated knife into ½-inch-thick slices. Place slices flat in single layer on 2 ungreased baking sheets.

6. Bake 8 minutes. Turn slices over; bake 10 to 12 minutes more until cut surfaces are light brown and cookies are dry. Remove cookies to wire racks; cool completely. Store cookies in airtight container up to 2 weeks.

Makes about 4 dozen cookies

BISCUIT

This quick bread is not made from a batter but from a dough leavened with baking powder or baking soda. Solid fat, such as butter, margarine or shortening, is cut into the dry ingredients until the mixture resembles coarse crumbs. Then the combined liquid ingredients are stirred in until the mixture clings together. These doughs require brief kneading to bring the dough together so it can be shaped (see Bread, Yeast, page 63 for technique). Too much kneading will make the biscuits mealy and tough.

Country Buttermilk Biscuits

> 2 cups all-purpose flour
> 1 tablespoon baking powder
> 2 teaspoons sugar
> ½ teaspoon baking soda
> ½ teaspoon salt
> ⅓ cup vegetable shortening
> ⅔ cup buttermilk*

*Or, substitute soured fresh milk. To sour milk, place 2½ teaspoons lemon juice plus enough milk to equal ⅔ cup in 1-cup measure. Stir; let stand 5 minutes before using.

1. Preheat oven to 450°F.

2. Combine flour, baking powder, sugar, baking soda and salt in medium bowl. Cut in shortening with pastry blender or 2 knives until mixture resembles coarse crumbs. Make well in center of dry ingredients. Add buttermilk; stir until mixture forms soft dough that clings together and forms a ball.

3. Turn out dough onto well-floured surface. Knead dough gently 10 to 12 times. Roll or pat dough to ½-inch thickness. Cut out dough with floured 2½-inch biscuit cutter. Place biscuits 2 inches apart on ungreased large baking sheet.

4. Bake 8 to 10 minutes until tops and bottoms are golden brown. Serve warm. *Makes about 9 biscuits*

Drop Biscuits: Prepare Country Buttermilk Biscuits as directed in steps 1 and 2, except grease 2 small baking sheets and increase buttermilk to 1 cup. After adding buttermilk, stir batter with wooden spoon about 15 strokes. *Do not knead.* Drop dough by heaping tablespoonfuls, 1 inch apart, onto prepared baking sheets. Bake as directed in step 4. Makes about 18 biscuits.

Sour Cream Dill Biscuits: Prepare Country Buttermilk Biscuits as directed in steps 1 and 2, except omit buttermilk. Combine ½ cup sour cream, ⅓ cup milk and 1 tablespoon chopped fresh dill *or* 1 teaspoon dried dill weed in small bowl until well blended. Stir into dry ingredients and continue as directed in steps 3 and 4. Makes about 9 biscuits.

Country Buttermilk Biscuits

Technique for Country Buttermilk Biscuits

Step 2. *Cutting in shortening with pastry blender.*

BISQUE

A thick, rich soup that usually consists of puréed shellfish, such as lobster, shrimp or crayfish. Bisques can also be made from vegetables. The origin of this term is not known with certainty. Some believe that it was originally a soup made from game.

☙

Shrimp Bisque

Shrimp Bisque

 1 pound raw medium shrimp, peeled, deveined
¼ cup butter or margarine
 2 green onions, sliced
 1 large clove garlic, minced
¼ cup all-purpose flour
 1 cup Fish Stock (page 486) or canned chicken broth
 3 cups half-and-half
 2 tablespoons white wine (optional)
½ teaspoon salt
½ teaspoon grated lemon peel
   Dash ground red pepper
   Lemon slices, green onion strips and cooked whole shrimp (optional)

1. Coarsely chop raw shrimp into ½-inch pieces.

2. Melt butter in large saucepan over medium heat; add shrimp, onion slices and garlic. Cook and stir until shrimp turn pink and opaque. Remove from heat.

3. Blend in flour. Cook and stir just until bubbly. Stir in stock; cook until bubbly. Cook 2 minutes, stirring constantly. Remove from heat.

4. Process soup in small batches in food processor or blender until smooth. Return puréed soup to saucepan.

5. Stir in half-and-half, wine, if desired, salt, lemon peel and pepper. Heat through. Garnish with lemon slices, onion strips and cooked shrimp, if desired.

Makes 4 servings

Butternut Bisque

Butternut Bisque

1 medium butternut squash
    (about 1½ pounds), peeled
1 teaspoon margarine or butter
1 large onion, coarsely chopped
    (about 1 cup)
2 cans (about 14 ounces each)
    low sodium chicken broth,
    divided
½ teaspoon ground nutmeg or
    freshly grated whole nutmeg
⅛ teaspoon ground white pepper
    Plain nonfat yogurt and chives
    (optional)

1. Cut squash lengthwise in half; discard seeds. Cut flesh into ½-inch pieces; set aside.

2. Melt margarine in large saucepan over medium heat until bubbly; add onion. Cook and stir 3 minutes or until onion is tender. Add 1 can broth and reserved squash. Bring to a boil over high heat; reduce heat to low. Cover; simmer 20 minutes or until squash is very tender.

3. Process squash mixture in 2 batches in food processor until smooth.

4. Return puréed soup to saucepan; add remaining can broth, nutmeg and pepper. Simmer, uncovered, 5 minutes, stirring occasionally.* Ladle into soup bowls. Place yogurt in pastry bag fitted with round decorating tip. Pipe onto soup in decorative design and garnish with chives, if desired.

Makes 6 servings (about 5 cups)

*Soup may be covered and refrigerated up to 2 days before serving. Reheat over medium heat until hot, stirring occasionally.

Cream of Butternut Bisque: Add ½ cup whipping cream or half-and-half with broth in step 4. Proceed as directed.

BLACKBERRY

Blackberries, closely related to raspberries, are the sweet summer fruit of prickly shrubs called brambles. The berries themselves are sometimes called brambles as well. They are a lustrous purplish-black color. Each berry technically is made up of multiple fruits, since each tiny segment contains its own seed. Blackberries grow wild and the careful eye may happen upon them along country roads and trails. Most, however, come from cultivated plots. Although they are often mistaken for black raspberries, the two are quite distinct.

🐝

Uses: When fully ripe, blackberries are excellent for eating plain or with sugar and cream.

• They make delicious pies and cobblers, especially when combined with other berries. The English favor them mixed with apples in pies.

• Blackberries also are used in ice cream, sweet sauces and preserves.

Varieties: Wild and cultivated blackberries are available; the cultivated form have slightly larger berries. There are several varieties of blackberries commercially available, such as Marionberry, Olallie, Cherokee and Evergreen; however, varieties are seldom indicated in the supermarket.

Availability: The season extends from May through August. Oregon, Washington, Michigan, New Jersey, Texas, Oklahoma and Arkansas are large domestic producers. Winter supplies come from Chile and New Zealand. Fresh blackberries are usually sold in half pints. Blackberries canned in syrup are also available.

Buying Tips: Select plump berries that are glossy, almost black in color and feel slightly soft. Hard berries are probably not fully ripe and will be quite tart. If the berries are packed in a clear plastic container, check for moldy and crushed berries. If they are packed in a paperboard container, inspect the bottom and sides of the container for stains, which signal that some berries have been crushed.

Yield: ½ pint blackberries = 1 cup; ½ cup purée.

Storage: Blackberries are highly perishable and should be refrigerated only for a day or two in the original container or spread in a single layer in a pan and covered with a damp paper towel. Before storing them, discard any moldy berries.

Basic Preparation: Do not wash berries until you're ready to use them. Pick through and discard any damaged berries before rinsing lightly with cold water. Spread them on paper towels to dry. A food processor or blender can be used to purée them. Because they have so many seeds, the purée is usually strained through a sieve.

Amaretto Breeze

> 1 (8-ounce) package
>   PHILADELPHIA BRAND®
>   Cream Cheese, softened
> ½ cup sour cream
> ½ cup sugar
> 3 tablespoons almond-flavored
>   liqueur
> 2 tablespoons whipping cream
> 1 pint blackberries or blueberries
> 1 pint strawberries

BEAT cream cheese and sour cream in small mixing bowl at medium speed with electric mixer until well blended. Blend in sugar, liqueur and cream. Chill.

PLACE berries in individual serving dishes; top with cream cheese sauce.

Makes 4 to 6 servings

Prep time: 10 minutes plus chilling

Tip

Blackberry juice can stain, so protect your clothing. To remove berry stains from your hands, rub them with a wedge of lemon.

BLANCH, TO

Blanching means cooking foods, most often vegetables, briefly in boiling water and then quickly cooling them in cold water. Food is blanched for one or more of the following reasons: to loosen and remove skin (tomatoes, peaches, almonds); to enhance color and reduce bitterness (raw vegetables for crudités); and to extend storage life (raw vegetables to be frozen).

Parboiling and blanching are similar processes. Whereas blanched foods cook for a very short time, parboiled foods are cooked halfway. Parboiling is a timesaving technique. Long-cooking vegetables, such as carrots or green beans, can be parboiled before adding to stir-fries and sautés.

BLEND, TO

Blending is the technique of mixing together two or more ingredients until they are thoroughly combined. The ingredients may be blended together with an electric mixer or electric blender, or by hand, using utensils such as a wooden spoon or wire whisk.

Amaretto Breeze

BLINTZE

The blintze (sometimes spelled blintz) is of Eastern European origin. Today blintzes are a classic Jewish-American brunch dish. Similar to a crêpe but somewhat less delicate, the thin and tender pancakes are cooked on one side then filled and folded into a rectangular-shaped package and browned in a skillet or baked. The filling is usually made with cottage cheese or ricotta cheese, but they may also be filled with fruit, such as blueberries or cherries. They are often topped with sour cream.

Cheese Blintzes

    3 eggs
1¼ cups milk
    1 cup all-purpose flour
    1 tablespoon cornstarch
½ teaspoon salt
    About ½ cup (1 stick) butter or margarine, divided
    1 container (15 ounces) ricotta cheese
    2 packages (3 ounces each) cream cheese, softened
    3 tablespoons sugar
¼ teaspoon almond extract
    Fresh fruit or cherry pie filling
    Sour cream (optional)

Techniques for Cheese Blintzes

Step 3. *Swirling pan to cover bottom.*

Step 7. *Folding in edges to enclose filling.*

Cheese Blintzes

1. To prepare batter, combine eggs, milk, flour, cornstarch and salt in food processor or blender; process just until smooth. Pour into 1-quart glass measure; set aside.

2. Peel back wrapper on stick of butter. Rub butter on bottom of 7- or 8-inch nonstick skillet. Heat skillet over medium heat until butter sizzles.

3. Remove skillet from heat. For each blintz, pour about 3 tablespoons batter into bottom of hot pan, swirling pan to cover bottom. Return skillet to heat. Cook 1 to 2 minutes or until bottom of blintz is browned.

4. Invert pan over large plate, flipping blintz onto plate. Rub stick of butter over browned surface of cooked blintz.

5. Repeat steps 2, 3 and 4 with remaining batter, stacking and buttering cooked blintzes on plate.

6. To prepare filling, beat ricotta cheese, cream cheese, sugar and almond extract in large bowl with electric mixer at medium speed just until blended.

7. To fill blintzes, place 2 tablespoons filling in center of unbrowned side of each blintz. Fold in sides about 1 inch, then fold in opposite edges to enclose filling and form rectangular shape.

8. Melt 2 tablespoons butter in large skillet over medium heat. Add blintzes in batches and cook 2 minutes per side or until heated through. Serve warm topped with fruit and sour cream, if desired.

Makes 8 servings
(about 16 blintzes)

BLUEBERRY

Blueberries are round, dark blue berries that grow on bushes. They are native to northern North America, but now they are also grown in other parts of the world, such as Scandinavia. North America, however, produces nearly 95 percent of the world's crop.

❧

Varieties: There are two types of blueberries––wild and cultivated. Wild berries, which grow on low bushes, are small and sometimes tart. Cultivated blueberries, which grow on tall bushes that allow them to be cultivated by machine, are larger and generally sweeter.

Tip

To prevent blueberries from turning green in pancakes and muffins, do not use them in batters that contain baking soda. Baking soda (usually added to batters to counteract an acidic ingredient, such as buttermilk or yogurt) creates an alkaline condition that affects the color of the blueberries. If you're adding blueberries to recipes, it's best to choose recipes that use milk and baking powder.

Availability: A blueberry bush has a short harvest season. However, blueberries are now grown from Florida to Canada, keeping supermarkets supplied with fresh berries from May to September. If you live in an area where blueberries are grown, you will find them in abundance during their short peak season at produce and farmers' markets. Fresh blueberries are available in pints and half pints. Frozen blueberries are packaged in bags. Canned blueberries, both wild and cultivated, are packed in water or a sugar syrup.

Berry Bundt Cake

Buying Tips: Choose firm, plump berries with a silvery bloom. Avoid shriveled blueberries or berries with a green or red tint (an indication of an underripe berry). If the berries are packed in a clear plastic container, turn the container over and check for moldy or crushed berries. If they are packed in a paperboard container, look for juice stains on the bottom of the container, which may indicate that some berries are crushed. Crushed berries mold quickly.

Yield: 1 pint blueberries = 2 cups. 1 (10-ounce) package frozen blueberries = 1½ cups.

Storage: If packaged in plastic, fresh blueberries should be stored in the refrigerator in their original package. If packaged in cardboard, the blueberries should be transferred to an airtight container. Fresh berries may be kept up to ten days. Wash them just before using. Periodically check for moldy and crushed berries and discard them to prevent other berries from decaying. Fresh berries can be frozen immediately after purchasing. Before freezing, wash the berries and discard moldy, underripe and shriveled berries. Place dry blueberries in a single layer on a jelly-roll pan and freeze them until they are hard. Transfer to a freezer bag for storage. Frozen blueberries can be stored in the freezer for up to one year.

Basic Preparation: Wash fresh berries just before using, discarding moldy, underripe or shriveled berries and woody stems. Canned blueberries should be drained and dried on paper towels before using. Frozen blueberries should be added to batters while still frozen. When making pies and cobblers with frozen or canned berries, remember that these berries give off more juice during baking than fresh blueberries do. To compensate, decrease the liquid and increase the thickener when substituting frozen or canned berries for fresh berries.

Berry Bundt Cake

    2 cups all-purpose flour
    1 tablespoon baking powder
    1 teaspoon baking soda
    ¼ teaspoon salt
    1 cup sugar
    ¾ cup buttermilk
    ½ cup cholesterol free egg
        substitute
    ¼ cup vegetable oil
    2 cups frozen unsweetened
        raspberries
    2 cups frozen unsweetened
        blueberries
    Fresh berries (optional)

1. Preheat oven to 350°F. Spray 6-cup Bundt pan with nonstick cooking spray.

2. Combine flour, baking powder, baking soda and salt in large bowl. Combine sugar, buttermilk, egg substitute and oil in medium bowl. Add sugar mixture to flour mixture; stir just until moistened. Fold in raspberries and blueberries; pour into prepared pan.

3. Bake 1 hour or until wooden toothpick inserted into center of cake comes out clean. Cool in pan on wire rack. Serve with fresh berries, if desired. *Makes 12 servings*

Streusel-Topped Blueberry Muffins

    1½ cups *plus* ⅓ cup all-purpose
        flour, divided
    ½ cup *plus* ⅓ cup sugar, divided
    1 teaspoon ground cinnamon
    3 tablespoons butter or
        margarine, cut into small
        pieces
    2 teaspoons baking powder
    ½ teaspoon salt
    1 cup milk
    ¼ cup butter or margarine,
        melted, slightly cooled
    1 egg, beaten
    1 teaspoon vanilla extract
    1 cup fresh blueberries

1. Preheat oven to 375°F. Grease or paper-line 12 (2½-inch) muffin cups.

2. For topping, combine ⅓ cup flour, ⅓ cup sugar and cinnamon in small bowl. Cut in 3 tablespoons butter with pastry blender or 2 knives until mixture resembles coarse crumbs; set aside.

3. Combine remaining 1½ cups flour, ½ cup sugar, baking powder and salt in large bowl. Combine milk, ¼ cup melted butter, egg and vanilla in separate small bowl. Stir into flour mixture just until moistened. Fold in blueberries. Spoon evenly into prepared muffin cups. Sprinkle reserved topping evenly over tops of muffins.

4. Bake 20 to 25 minutes until wooden toothpick inserted into centers comes out clean. Remove from pan to wire racks; cool completely. *Makes 12 muffins*

Tip

For a special treat, top fresh blueberries with a dollop of sour cream and a sprinkling of brown sugar.

BOIL, TO

Bring to a boil means to heat a liquid until bubbles break the surface. Boiling refers to cooking food in boiling water. For a "full rolling boil," bubbles continue vigorously to break the surface and cannot be stirred away. Temperature of boiling water at sea level is 212°F or 100°C. For every 1000 feet above sea level, the boiling point decreases by 2°F.

☙

BOK CHOY

Bok choy, a vegetable popular in Asian cuisines, is a member of the crucifer family, which includes cabbage. Hence, it is sometimes referred to as Chinese cabbage. This creates great confusion since napa cabbage also is often called Chinese cabbage. Bok choy has 8- to 10-inch-long white or greenish-white stalks and large dark green leaves. The stalks are generally wider than those of celery and are not ribbed. Bok choy stalks have a crisp texture and a mild cabbagelike flavor. The leaves take on a mild flavor similar to Swiss chard. Bok choy is also sometimes referred to as Chinese chard, pak choi, white mustard cabbage or Chinese mustard.

Uses: Both stalks and leaves can be used raw in salads.

• Bok choy is popular as an ingredient in stir-fries.

• Baby bok choy can be steamed whole or in halves and served as a side dish.

Varieties: Besides regular bok choy, baby bok choy is now available. Baby bok choy is about six inches long and has a sweeter, nuttier flavor.

Availability: Bok choy is available all year. The regular heads vary in size depending on the season and maturity. It is usually sold by the pound.

Buying Tips: Look for bunches with firm, unblemished white stalks topped with fresh-looking crisp green leaves. Avoid heads with wilted or decaying leaves.

Yield: 2 pounds bok choy = 1 large head; 5 cups sliced stalks and 4 cups torn or sliced leaves.

Storage: Store unwashed bok choy in a perforated plastic bag in the refrigerator. It will keep for three to four days.

Basic Preparation: Trim off and discard the base, any blemished stalks and wilted leaves. Separate stalks from bunch. Rinse bok choy under cold running water and drain well. Slice or chop the stalks and coarsely shred the leaves. Both stalks and leaves can be boiled, steamed or stir-fried, but they have different cooking times. Whereas sliced bok choy stalks require 2 or 3 minutes of boiling or stir-frying, bok choy leaves cook in about 30 seconds. Leave baby bok choy whole when cooking. It is milder in flavor and small enough to boil or steam whole. It can be used halved or quartered in stir-fry dishes.

BORSCHT

Borscht, also borsch or bartch, is a class of soups common in Russian and Polish cuisines. There are several styles, from humble pots of cabbage and beets to abundant meals with sausage, duck and many vegetables. Depending on the style, borscht is served hot or cold, often topped with a dollop of sour cream. A lesser known summer borscht is made with greens, but not beets.

BOUILLABAISSE

A fragrant stew from Marseilles, France, bouillabaisse combines a bounty of fish and seafood in a broth of tomato, garlic, onion and saffron. In France, it may contain as many as a dozen types of seafood, including eel, spiny lobster and whiting. The soup is ladled over toasted slices of French bread that may be spread with a fiery-hot red chili paste called rouille.

BOUILLON

Bouillon is a clear light liquid made by boiling meat, fish, poultry or vegetables in water to extract the flavor. The liquid is strained and served plain as a soup or used as the basis for sauces or more complex soups. Chicken, beef and vegetable bouillon are readily available canned. Bouillon cubes and granules, made from dehydrated concentrated bouillon or stock, are available in chicken, beef and vegetable flavors. They need to be reconstituted in boiling water according to package directions. Bouillon is interchangeable with broth.

BOUQUET GARNI

Bouquet garni, a French term, is a small bundle of herbs tied together in cheesecloth that is used to flavor soups, stews, braised dishes and sauces. Fresh parsley, thyme and bay leaves are the traditional ingredients. However, any herbs or spices (fresh or dried) can be used, depending on the recipe. To make a classic bouquet garni, cut a single thickness of cheesecloth into a 6-inch square and lay it flat. Place 1 or 2 sprigs of parsley, 1 bay leaf and 1 or 2 stems of fresh thyme on the cheesecloth. Gather the edges and secure tightly with kitchen string. Add it to simmering foods for the duration of cooking, making sure to remove it before the dish is served.

Placing herbs on square of cheesecloth.

Tying cheesecloth together to make handle.

BOYSENBERRY

Boysenberry is a hybrid developed by crossing the raspberry, blackberry and loganberry. It was developed in the 1920's by Rudolph Boysen. Similar in appearance to a large raspberry, the boysenberry has a rich purple-red color and pleasantly tart flavor. They can be used like raspberries and blackberries and are especially good in cobblers, ice cream, pies and preserves. Highly perishable, they are seldom seen in supermarkets, so look for them at farmers' markets. Boysenberries should be stored in a single layer in the refrigerator and used within a day or two.

🍂

BRAISE, TO

Braising is a moist-heat cooking method used to tenderize tough cuts of meat or fibrous vegetables. Food is first browned in fat and then gently simmered in a small amount of liquid in a tightly covered skillet until tender. This can be done on the rangetop or in the oven. The liquid, such as water, stock, wine or beer, often has finely chopped vegetables and herbs added for flavor.

🍂

Tip

The most efficient pan for braising is a heavy pan that is not too much larger than the food being cooked.

Savory Pot Roast

1 (2½-pound) bottom round roast
1 tablespoon vegetable oil
½ cup A.1.® Steak Sauce
½ cup ketchup
½ cup REGINA® Red Wine Vinegar
1 teaspoon dry mustard
1 teaspoon garlic powder

In Dutch oven, over medium-high heat, brown roast in hot oil; drain.

In small bowl, blend steak sauce, ketchup, vinegar, mustard and garlic powder; pour over meat. Heat to a boil; reduce heat. Cover and simmer 2½ to 3 hours or until meat is fork-tender, skimming and discarding excess fat as necessary. Slice roast and serve with pan gravy. Garnish as desired.   *Makes 6 servings*

BREAD, QUICK

Quick breads are breads that are leavened without yeast. Baking powder and baking soda are the primary leavening agents, but steam can also act as a leavening agent, as it does in popovers. The list of breads that fall into this category is a long one and includes many American favorites, such as biscuits, corn breads, muffins, tea breads, spoon breads, pancakes, waffles, and some coffee cakes and doughnuts. The term "quick bread" is sometimes used to mean a loaf bread that is leavened with baking powder or baking soda. It is used interchangeably with tea bread.

🍂

Quick breads require very little mixing or kneading and no rising time prior to baking. Bake these breads immediately after they are mixed so that leaveners do not lose their power. Since many quick breads can be made from start to finish in less than one hour, it is understandable why they are a popular choice for home bakers.

For quick-batter breads, such as muffins, coffee cakes and tea breads, add the combined liquid ingredients to the combined dry ingredients and stir with a wooden spoon only until the mixture is evenly moistened. The batter should look lumpy when it goes into the prepared pans. Too much stirring or beating will give the breads a tough texture with lots of holes and tunnels. Muffins and tea breads are completely baked when a wooden toothpick inserted near the center comes out clean. *See Coffee Cake, Corn Bread, Muffin, Pancake and Waffle for additional preparation information and recipes.*

For quick-dough breads, such as biscuits and scones, cut the solid fat into the dry ingredients until the mixture resembles coarse crumbs. Add the combined liquid ingredients and stir the mixture just until the dough clings together. These doughs may be kneaded briefly to bring the dough together so that it can be shaped *(see Bread, Yeast, page 63 for technique)*. Too much kneading will make the breads mealy and tough. Biscuits and scones are done when their top and bottom crusts are an even golden brown color. Follow specific cooling instructions in each recipe. *See Biscuit and Scone for additional preparation information and recipes.*

Store quick breads in plastic bags or wrapped in plastic at room temperature for up to three days. Freeze them in plastic bags or tightly wrapped in heavy-duty foil for up to three months. Reheat frozen breads wrapped in foil in a 300°F oven for 15 to 18 minutes.

Peanut Butter Mini Chip Loaf (recipe on page 60)

Peanut Butter Mini Chip Loaves

3 cups all-purpose flour
1½ teaspoons baking powder
1 teaspoon baking soda
1 teaspoon salt
1 cup creamy peanut butter
½ cup butter or margarine, softened
½ cup granulated sugar
½ cup firmly packed light brown sugar
2 eggs
1½ cups buttermilk*
2 teaspoons vanilla extract
1 cup mini semisweet chocolate chips
Cream cheese (optional)

*Or, substitute soured fresh milk. To sour milk, place 1½ tablespoons lemon juice plus enough milk to equal 1½ cups in 2-cup measure. Stir; let stand 5 minutes before using.

1. Preheat oven to 350°F. Grease 2 (8½×4½-inch) loaf pans.

2. Sift flour, baking powder, baking soda and salt into medium bowl; set aside.

3. Beat peanut butter, butter, granulated sugar and brown sugar in large bowl with electric mixer at medium speed until light and fluffy. Beat in eggs, 1 at a time, scraping down side of bowl after each addition. Beat in buttermilk and vanilla. Gradually add flour mixture. Beat at low speed until well blended. Stir in chips with wooden spoon. Spoon evenly into prepared pans.

4. Bake 45 minutes or until wooden toothpick inserted into centers comes out clean. Cool in pans on wire racks 10 minutes. Remove from pans; cool completely on racks. Serve with cream cheese, if desired.

Makes 2 loaves

Tip

Baking powder can lose its leavening ability if stored improperly or kept too long. Check the "use by" date stamped on the container before purchasing. Store baking powder in a cool, dry place. Use it within six months after opening.

BREAD, TO

Breading means to coat a food with bread, cracker or other crumbs prior to cooking. Foods such as chicken and fish are most often breaded. The purpose of breading is to keep food moist during cooking or to provide a crisp coating. The crumbs may be seasoned with herbs for additional flavor. Breaded foods are usually fried or baked.

🐝

BREAD, YEAST

Bread has been part of the human diet since prehistoric times. Early man pounded native grasses or grains into meal, added water and baked the resulting paste on a hot stone or in the ashes of a fire. The first bread was flat, unleavened and tough, but it became a staple in many early cultures. The discovery that adding yeast to the meal mixture improved flavor, texture and volume changed bread forever. Today the varieties of breads available around the world seems endless. Dense and chewy pumpernickle, mouthwatering Italian focaccia, rich and flaky croissants and the simple tortilla are but a few of the delicious breads that bring much pleasure to everyday meals.

🐝

Breads fall into one of three main categories depending on the leavening agent. Yeast-leavened bread makes up much of the bread available in bakeries and supermarkets. It can also be made at home. Although it requires some time to make, hot bread from the oven is a wonderful reward for your labors. Quick breads are leavened with

Basic White Bread (recipe on page 64)

baking powder, baking soda or steam. As their name suggests, they are quick and easy to make. *See Bread, Quick, page 58, for additional information.* Unleavened breads, such as Middle Eastern lavash, Jewish matzo and Indian chapati, remain a tradition in many cuisines around the world.

Yeast breads contain yeast as a leavening agent. They require stirring or kneading to develop gluten, the protein in wheat flour that gives bread its structure. There are two types of yeast breads: yeast-batter breads and yeast-dough breads. Yeast-batter breads call for stirring and beating rather than kneading because ingredients form a soft dough that is too sticky to knead by hand. Yeast-dough breads are kneaded to produce breads with a chewier texture, finer grain and more volume. These doughs are less sticky and easier to handle than batter breads. They ususally become smooth and elastic with kneading. Sweet-yeast doughs are softer and stickier than regular yeast doughs because they contain more sweeteners and fat. Sweet-yeast breads may also be batter breads.

While baking yeast breads can be very satisfying, it is a lengthy process. Frozen yeast doughs and hot roll mixes are readily available and can simplify your life. They are an especially good choice for pizza crusts and dinner rolls.

*Whole Wheat Loaf
(recipe on page 65)*

YEAST BREAD INGREDIENTS

Flour: Wheat flour is the essential ingredient in all breads because it contains the important protein called gluten. When mixed with liquid and stirred or kneaded, gluten stretches and forms a network of strands that catches the carbon dioxide bubbles produced by yeast. This network helps the dough rise and expand, giving the bread its structure. Most yeast bread is made with either bread flour or all-purpose flour. If you choose to substitute one flour for the other, be aware that the quantities used may differ slightly. Rye flour is low in gluten and must be combined with bread flour or all-purpose flour to produce a loaf that rises well and is

not too dense. Whole wheat flour is usually used in combination with bread or all-purpose flour to avoid overly dense or poorly risen loaves. (The bran in whole wheat flour interferes with gluten development.)

Liquids: Liquids are required in yeast breads to dissolve and activate the yeast and moisten the flour so gluten can develop. Most recipes have at least some water; other liquids contribute differently to a bread's flavor and texture. Water provides a chewy interior and crisp crust. Milk gives bread a mild, sweet flavor and soft, creamy texture; it also keeps breads fresh longer. Buttermilk adds a tangy flavor and light texture.

Yeast: Active dry yeast contributes flavor and aroma in addition to leavening. One package of yeast contains thousands of microscopic living plants that are activated by warm liquid and fed by sugar and starch. Yeast releases carbon dioxide gas bubbles that become trapped in the gluten network, causing doughs and batters to rise and giving shape and texture to breads. Store packages of active dry yeast in a cool, dry place.

Temperature is an important factor when working with yeast. If the dissolving liquid is too cold, yeast action is retarded. Too much heat will kill the yeast altogether. Use an instant-read thermometer to determine accurately if the liquid has reached the proper temperature.

The traditional method for using active dry yeast calls for warm liquids (105° to 115°F) to dissolve the yeast. The bubbly yeast mixture is added to the other ingredients as directed in the recipe. In an alternative method, the yeast is combined with a portion of the flour and the other dry ingredients. Warmer liquid (120° to 130°F) is then added. This method is slightly quicker than the traditional one, as the dissolving step is eliminated and the warmer liquid helps the yeast work faster.

Quick-rising yeast uses the alternative method and significantly reduces rising times. Quick-rising yeast may be substituted for regular yeast. Follow the package directions for recommended rising times. Both types of yeast are commonly available in individual packets containing about one tablespoon.

Sweeteners: Granulated sugar and other sweeteners feed the yeast, as well as add their own flavors to the bread. They also help produce a browner crust and improve texture and tenderness. Brown sugar, honey, maple syrup and molasses are all used in breads; powdered sugar is not used because it contains cornstarch, which may affect flavor and texture.

Salt: Salt adds flavor to breads and also controls the action of the yeast. It slows the rising time, allowing the flavors of the dough to develop. Salt also strengthens the gluten, thus contributing to the texture.

Fats: Fats, such as butter, margarine and oils, impart flavor, richness and tenderness to breads. They help breads stay moist longer.

Eggs: Eggs add flavor, color, strength and nutrients to breads. They give bread a golden color, tender crust and fine crumb.

TECHNIQUES FOR YEAST BREADS

Proofing Yeast: This process ensures that the yeast is still alive before going ahead with the recipe. Yeast that is not living cannot make bread rise. To proof, sprinkle yeast and sugar over warm water using the amounts specified in each recipe and stir until the yeast is dissolved.

Let it stand 5 minutes or until the mixture is bubbly, indicating that the yeast is alive and releasing gas bubbles.

If the yeast does not bubble, it is no longer active. This may be the result of liquid that is too hot or yeast that is too old. (Always check the expiration date on the yeast package.) Discard the yeast mixture and start again with new ingredients.

Kneading the Dough: Kneading is essential to developing and strengthening the gluten. Kneading also incorporates and homogenizes the ingredients in the dough. The dough will be sticky after all the ingredients are mixed in, gradually becoming smoother and elastic as it is kneaded. Bread dough may be kneaded by hand. For an inexperienced bread maker, an electric mixer with a dough hook attachment or a food processor can be used to mix and knead doughs quickly and efficiently.

To knead dough by hand, flour the kneading surface and your hands lightly before beginning in order to make the dough easier to handle. Flatten the dough slightly and fold it in half toward you.

Push the dough away from you with the heels of your hands in a rolling motion.

Rotate the dough one-quarter turn and repeat the folding, pushing and turning steps for the length of time specified by each recipe.

Rising: Letting the dough (or batter) rise means allowing time for the yeast cells to give off carbon dioxide gas. This process gradually expands and develops the dough in flavor and texture as well as structure. To prevent the kneaded dough from drying out and developing a crust, place the dough in a greased bowl and turn it over so the top is greased. (Batters rise in the bowls in which they are mixed.) Cover the dough with a clean kitchen towel and set it in a warm place (80° to 85°F) away from drafts until the dough has doubled or almost doubled in bulk. Use the time guidelines given in each recipe and test the dough as directed in the "Testing for Doubling" section.

Cold temperatures cause batters and doughs to rise slowly, offering the

Proofing the yeast.

Folding the dough in half.

Pushing the dough with the heels of your hands.

Rotating the dough.

Pressing fingertips into dough.

Punching down the dough.

Pushing the edges of the dough into the center.

convenience of beginning a recipe one day and completing it later that day or the next day. For the refrigerator-rising method, batters and doughs are covered with greased plastic wrap and set in the refrigerator to rise for 3 to 24 hours. They are then brought to room temperature and shaped or baked as specified in the recipe.

Testing for Doubling: To test if the dough has risen enough, lightly press two fingertips about one-half inch into the dough. The dough is ready if an indentation remains when fingertips are removed.

Punching Down the Dough: After the dough has risen, it is full of air pockets. To work out the excess carbon dioxide and redistribute the yeast, the dough is punched down. Push down the center of the dough with your fist.

Push the edges of the dough into the center.

With yeast-batter breads, the soft, sticky dough is stirred down with a wooden spoon rather than punched. The dough is now ready to rise again or to be shaped.

Shaping the Dough: Bread recipes call for rolling, cutting or shaping the dough after it has risen. Lightly flour the rolling surface and rolling pin before working with the dough. If only a portion of the dough will be used at a time, keep the remaining dough covered with a towel to prevent it from drying out.

Creating Different Finishes for Breads: Change the look and texture of a bread's crust by varying the ingredients brushed on top of the loaf either before or after baking.

• For a shiny crust, brush with 1 egg white beaten with 1 tablespoon of water before baking.

• For a rich, tender golden brown crust, brush with milk or cream before baking.

• For a soft crust, brush melted butter

or margarine over the crust immediately after baking.

• For a crisp crust, mist unglazed breads quickly with water several times during the first 10 minutes of baking.

Testing for Doneness: To test breads for doneness, tap the tops of the loaves with your fingers or a wooden spoon. A hollow sound means the bread is done. A dull thud means that the bread is still moist inside and requires more baking. Remove yeast breads from pans immediately and cool completely on wire racks to prevent a soggy bottom.

Storing Yeast Breads: Store yeast breads wrapped in plastic at room temperature. If the bread will be kept more than several days, refrigerate it. (Refrigeration dries out the bread somewhat, but it also slows the growth of mold.) Breads containing milk and fat last longer than those containing water and no fat. Yeast breads may be frozen by wrapping them securely in heavy-duty foil or by placing them in resealable freezer bags for up to six months. Seal well.

Reheating: Reheat yeast breads, thawed at room temperature or directly from the freezer, by wrapping in foil and placing in a 350°F oven for 5 to 10 minutes. Microwave ovens may be used to thaw or reheat individual servings, but do not use them for whole loaves of bread, because portions of the bread may become tough before the entire loaf is heated through.

Basic White Bread

2 packages active dry yeast
2 tablespoons sugar
2 cups warm water (105° to 115°F)
6 to 6½ cups all-purpose flour, divided
½ cup nonfat dry milk powder
2 tablespoons vegetable shortening
2 teaspoons salt

1. To proof yeast, sprinkle yeast and sugar over warm water in large bowl; stir until yeast is dissolved. Let stand 5 minutes or until mixture is bubbly.

2. Add 3 cups flour, milk powder, shortening and salt. Beat with electric mixer at low speed until blended. Beat 2 minutes at medium. Stir in enough additional flour, about 3 cups, to make soft dough.

3. On lightly floured surface, knead dough about 10 minutes or until smooth and elastic, adding remaining ½ cup flour to prevent sticking if necessary. Shape into ball; place in large greased bowl. Turn dough over so that top is greased. Cover with towel; let rise in warm place about 1 hour or until doubled in bulk.

4. Punch down dough. Knead dough on lightly floured surface 1 minute. Cover with towel; let rest 10 minutes. Grease 2 (8½×4½-inch) loaf pans.

5. Divide dough in half. Roll out ½ of dough into 12×8-inch rectangle with lightly floured rolling pin. Starting with 1 (8-inch) side, roll up dough jelly-roll style. Pinch seam and ends to seal. Place loaf, seam side down, in prepared pan, tucking ends under. Repeat with remaining dough.

6. Cover with towel; let rise in warm place 1 hour or until doubled in bulk.

7. Preheat oven to 375°F. Bake 30 to 35 minutes until loaves are golden brown and sound hollow when tapped. Immediately remove from pans; cool completely on wire racks.

Makes 2 loaves

Whole Wheat Loaves

    3 cups whole wheat flour, divided
2¼ to 2¾ cups all-purpose flour,
        divided
    ½ cup wheat germ
    2 packages active dry yeast
    2 teaspoons salt
1¼ cups milk
    1 cup water
    ⅓ cup honey
    ¼ cup butter or margarine

1. Combine 2 cups whole wheat flour, 1 cup all-purpose flour, wheat germ, yeast and salt in large bowl.

2. Combine milk, water, honey and butter in 2-quart saucepan. Heat over low heat until mixture is 120° to 130°F. (Butter does not need to completely melt.)

3. Gradually beat milk mixture into flour mixture with electric mixer at low speed. Increase speed to medium, scraping down side of bowl once. Reduce speed to low. Beat in remaining 1 cup whole wheat flour. Increase speed to medium; beat 2 minutes. Stir in enough additional all-purpose flour, about 1¼ cups, with wooden spoon to make soft dough.

4. Turn out dough onto lightly floured surface; flatten slightly. Knead dough 8 to 10 minutes until smooth and elastic, adding remaining ½ cup all-purpose flour to prevent sticking if necessary. Shape dough into a ball; place in large greased bowl. Turn dough over so that top is greased. Cover with towel; let rise in warm place about 1 hour or until doubled in bulk.

5. Punch down dough. Knead dough on lightly floured surface 1 minute. Cover with towel; let rest 10 minutes.

6. Grease 2 (8½×4½-inch) loaf pans.

7. Divide dough in half. Roll out ½ of dough into 12×8-inch rectangle with lightly floured rolling pin. Starting with 1 (8-inch) side, roll up dough jelly-roll style. Pinch seam and ends to seal. Place loaf, seam side down, in prepared pan, tucking ends under. Repeat with remaining dough.

8. Cover with towel; let rise in warm place about 45 minutes or until doubled in bulk.

9. Preheat oven to 350°F. Bake 30 to 35 minutes until loaves are browned and sound hollow when tapped. Immediately remove from pans; cool completely on wire racks.

Makes 2 loaves

Tip

Yeast dough should rise only until it is doubled in size. Longer rising will result in inferior texture. Begin checking yeast dough 10 to 15 minutes early for signs of sufficient rising. Always preheat the oven before rising is completed.

BREAD CRUMBS

There are two kinds of bread crumbs—fresh and dry. Fresh bread crumbs are used for stuffings, coatings and fillers. They are made at home. Dry bread crumbs are fine crumbs, seasoned or unseasoned, that may be purchased or made at home. They are used primarily as coatings or fillers. Unless otherwise indicated, bread crumbs are made with white bread. Whole wheat bread or herb-seasoned bread may be substituted in most recipes for more flavor.

✿

To make fresh bread crumbs, remove crust from fresh or day-old bread slices and tear bread into small pieces. To make bread crumbs in the food processor or blender, remove crust and tear bread slices into three or four pieces and process using an on/off pulsing action until crumbs are of the desired size. Fresh bread crumbs can be stored in an airtight container in the refrigerator for about a week or in the freezer for up to 6 months.

To make dry bread crumbs, bake day-old dry bread crumbs or stale bread slices on a baking sheet in a 325°F oven until very dry and lightly browned. Place them in a food processor or blender and process until fine crumbs are formed. To season dry bread crumbs, add dried herbs to the bread before processing. Or, place toasted bread in a resealable plastic bag and seal. Roll with a rolling pin until fine crumbs are formed.

Special Interest

Broccoli is one of the healthiest foods you can eat! It is loaded with antioxidants and cancer-fighting vitamins, such as vitamins A and C.

BRIOCHE

A brioche is a rich French yeast bread with a fine texture. It has a characteristic round shape with a fluted bottom and round top knot. Brioches can be small rolls or large loaves of bread. Eggs and butter contribute flavor, a golden color and a rich brown exterior. A special mold with a fluted, slightly flared side is needed for its unique shape. The dough can also be shaped in muffin pans or used to enclose a filling.

✿

BROCCOLI

Though grown in Italy centuries ago, broccoli didn't become popular in the United States until the 1920's when it began appearing in the home gardens of Italian immigrants. This vegetable, a member of the cabbage family, has a thick, rigid green stalk topped with deep green or purple-green heads. The heads are made up of hundreds of buds, which if left to grow, would open into yellow flowers. The majority of broccoli in the United States is grown in the Salinas Valley of California.

✿

Availability: Fresh broccoli is available all year with its peak season between October and April. Broccoli florets and spears are also available frozen.

Buying Tips: Choose firm broccoli stems with tightly packed dark green buds and crisp leaves. Avoid heads that are light green in color, have thick, tough stems or a strong odor. The buds should be tightly closed. Open buds or tiny yellow flowers indicate overmaturity. Some supermarkets also offer the broccoli heads without the stalks for a higher price. Since both the heads and stalks are edible, it is not necessary to spend the extra money unless the stalks are woody.

Yield: 1 pound broccoli = 2 cups chopped.
1 (10-ounce) package frozen chopped broccoli = 1½ cups cooked.

Storage: Fresh broccoli should be stored unwashed in a plastic bag. It will keep for four to five days in the refrigerator. Frozen broccoli can be kept up to one year.

Basic Preparation: Rinse broccoli thoroughly under cold running water. Broccoli from home gardens and farmers' markets should be soaked in salted water for 15 minutes to eliminate bugs. Trim off and discard the ends of the stalks and the leaves.

 If desired, the tough outer part of the stalk can be peeled away with a vegetable peeler before cooking.

 To cut the broccoli into spears, cut the stalk and head lengthwise into halves or quarters.

To divide the broccoli head into florets, cut off the large stalk. Separate
 the broccoli head into individual florets to include a little stem with each floret.

The stalks can be peeled and cut into crosswise slices. If the slices are more than ¼ inch thick, they may take longer to cook than the florets, so give them a 2- or 3-minute head start.

Broccoli is most often steamed, boiled or stir-fried until crisp-tender. Overcooking results in mushy broccoli with a strong flavor. Steam florets 5 to 7 minutes and spears 7 to 9 minutes. Drop florets into a small amount of boiling water in a saucepan and boil 5 to 7 minutes; boil spears 7 to 9 minutes. Some cooks believe that broccoli should be boiled in a covered saucepan and others insist that covering results in an unpleasant flavor.

Beef and Broccoli (recipe on page 68)

Broccoli with Sesame Vinaigrette

    1 teaspoon butter or margarine
    1 teaspoon sesame seeds
    1 pound fresh broccoli
    2 tablespoons *plus* 1½ teaspoons
        white wine vinegar
    1 tablespoon water
    2 teaspoons olive or sesame oil
    ½ teaspoon LAWRY'S® Seasoned
        Salt
    ½ teaspoon LAWRY'S® Seasoned
        Pepper

Microwave Directions: On shallow microwave-safe plate, place butter and sesame seeds. Cover with plastic wrap. Microwave on HIGH (100% power) 1 minute or until seeds are toasted; set aside. Trim off large ends of lower broccoli stalks; discard. Place trimmed broccoli in shallow microwave-safe dish; cover. Microwave on HIGH 7 minutes or until broccoli is crisp-tender. Place broccoli on serving platter; keep warm. Combine sesame seeds, vinegar, water, oil, Seasoned Salt and Seasoned Pepper; drizzle over broccoli. Garnish as desired.

Makes 4 servings

Beef and Broccoli

    1 boneless beef top sirloin or
        tenderloin steak, cut 1 inch
        thick (about 1 pound)
    2 teaspoons minced fresh ginger
    2 cloves garlic, minced
    1 tablespoon peanut or
        vegetable oil
    3 cups broccoli florets
    ¼ cup water
    ⅓ cup stir-fry sauce
        Hot cooked rice

Broccoli with Sesame Vinaigrette

1. Cut beef across grain into $\frac{1}{8}$-inch slices; cut each slice into $1\frac{1}{2}$-inch pieces. Toss beef with ginger and garlic in medium bowl.

2. Heat wok or large skillet over medium-high heat. Add oil; heat until hot. Add beef mixture; stir-fry 3 to 4 minutes until beef is barely pink in center. Remove from heat; set aside.

3. Add broccoli and water to wok; cover and steam 3 to 5 minutes until broccoli is crisp-tender.

4. Return beef along with any accumulated juices to wok. Add stir-fry sauce. Cook until heated through. Serve over rice. Garnish as desired.

Makes 4 servings

Stir-Fried Turkey with Broccoli

1 lemon
1 teaspoon dried thyme leaves
$\frac{1}{4}$ teaspoon salt
$\frac{1}{4}$ teaspoon ground white pepper
1 pound turkey cutlets
1 pound fresh broccoli
1 tablespoon cornstarch
1 cup chicken broth
4 cups water
3 tablespoons vegetable oil, divided
1 tablespoon butter
$\frac{1}{4}$ pound fresh mushrooms, sliced
1 medium red onion, sliced, separated into rings
1 can (14 ounces) pre-cut baby corn, rinsed, drained*
Hot cooked rice
Lemon slices (optional)

*Or, substitute 1 can (15 ounces) whole baby corn, cut into 1-inch lengths.

1. Finely grate peel of lemon into large glass bowl. Cut lemon crosswise in half; squeeze lemon and measure 2 tablespoons lemon juice. Add juice, thyme, salt and pepper to lemon peel; stir.

2. Cut turkey cutlets into $2\frac{1}{2}\times1$-inch strips. Add turkey to lemon mixture; coat well. Marinate in refrigerator 30 minutes.

3. To prepare broccoli, trim leaves from stalks. Trim off tough ends; discard. Cut broccoli tops into florets by removing each head to include a piece of stem. Peel stems with vegetable peeler, then diagonally slice stems into 2-inch pieces; set aside.

4. Combine cornstarch and broth in cup until smooth; set aside.

5. Place water in wok. Bring to a boil over medium-high heat; add reserved broccoli stems. Cook 1 minute. Add florets; cook 2 minutes more or until crisp-tender. Drain in colander. Rinse with cold water; set aside.

6. Heat wok over medium-high heat until hot and dry. Add 1 tablespoon oil and butter; heat until hot. Add mushrooms; stir-fry 2 minutes or until mushrooms are wilted. Add onion; stir-fry 2 minutes more. Remove mushroom mixture to large bowl.

7. Heat 1 tablespoon oil in wok. Fry $\frac{1}{2}$ of turkey strips in single layer $1\frac{1}{2}$ minutes or until well browned on all sides and turkey is no longer pink in center, stirring occasionally. Transfer to bowl with mushroom mixture. Repeat with remaining 1 tablespoon oil and turkey.

8. Add baby corn to wok; cook 1 minute. Stir reserved cornstarch mixture; add to wok and cook until bubbly. Add broccoli and turkey mixture; cook and stir until heated through. Serve over rice. Garnish with lemon slices, if desired.

Makes 4 to 6 servings

Tips

When cutting broccoli into florets, do not discard the stalk; it makes a great addition to soups and stir fries.

When using broccoli florets as vegetable dippers, make them bright green by quickly cooking in boiling water 1 minute and then immediately plunging into cold or ice water to stop the cooking.

BROIL, TO

Broiling is the technique of cooking foods a measured distance from a direct source of heat. Both gas and electric ovens provide a means of broiling. Some rangetops have built-in grills that provide another broiling option. Grilling on a barbecue grill also fits this broad definition of broiling. The goal of broiling is to brown the exterior without overcooking the interior. Generally, the thinner the food item the closer it should be to the heat source.

🌾

BROTH

Broth is a thin, clear liquid made from cooking meat, poultry or vegetables in water. It is often used interchangeably with bouillon. Broth rarely is served plain but rather is the basis for sauces, soups and stews. Canned chicken, beef and vegetable broths are an acceptable substitute for homemade. They tend to be salty so do not add salt to recipes using them until the cooking is complete.

🌾

BROWN, TO

Browning is the technique of cooking food quickly until the surface is brown. This gives food an appetizing appearance and adds flavor and aroma. Browning may be done in a skillet on the rangetop, in an oven, under a broiler, on a grill or in a toaster.

🌾

BROWNIE

Brownies are the popular all-American bar cookie. There is no accepted standard. The texture may be either moist and cakelike or dense, rich and fudgy. They may contain nuts and be covered with chocolate frosting. Varieties made with vanilla or butterscotch instead of chocolate are called blondies. Brownies are made in a pan and cut into squares or rectangles. They can be made from scratch or from a mix. Frozen brownies and bakery brownies are also available.

🌾

Quick & Easy Fudgey Brownies

> 4 bars (1 ounce each) HERSHEY'S Unsweetened Baking Chocolate, broken into pieces
> ¾ cup (1½ sticks) butter or margarine
> 2 cups sugar
> 3 eggs
> 1½ teaspoons vanilla extract
> 1 cup all-purpose flour
> 1 cup chopped nuts (optional)
> Quick & Easy Chocolate Frosting (recipe follows)

Heat oven to 350°F. Grease 13×9×2-inch baking pan. In large microwave-safe bowl, place chocolate and butter. Microwave at HIGH (100% power) 1½ to 2 minutes or until chocolate is melted and mixture is smooth when stirred. Add sugar; stir with spoon until well blended. Add eggs and vanilla; mix well. Stir in flour and nuts, if desired; stir until well blended. Spread into prepared pan. Bake 30 to 35 minutes or until wooden pick inserted in center comes out almost clean. Cool completely in pan on wire rack. Prepare Quick & Easy Chocolate Frosting. Spread over brownies. Cut into squares.

Makes about 24 brownies

Quick & Easy Chocolate Frosting

> 3 bars (1 ounce each) HERSHEY'S Unsweetened Baking Chocolate, broken into pieces
> 1 cup miniature marshmallows
> ½ cup (1 stick) butter or margarine, softened
> ⅓ cup milk
> 2½ cups powdered sugar
> ½ teaspoon vanilla extract

In medium, heavy saucepan over low heat, melt chocolate, stirring constantly. Add marshmallows; stir frequently until melted. (Mixture will be very thick and will pull away from sides of pan.) Spoon mixture into small mixer bowl. Add butter; beat well. Gradually add milk, beating until blended. Add powdered sugar and vanilla; beat until smooth and of spreading consistency. Add additional milk, 1 teaspoon at a time, if needed.

Decadent Blonde Brownies

> 1 jar (3½ ounces) macadamia nuts
> 1½ cups all-purpose flour
> 1 teaspoon baking powder
> ½ teaspoon salt
> ½ cup butter or margarine, softened
> ¾ cup granulated sugar
> ¾ cup firmly packed light brown sugar
> 2 eggs
> 2 teaspoons vanilla extract
> 1 package (10 ounces) semisweet chocolate chunks*

If chocolate chunks are not available, cut 10-ounce thick chocolate candy bar into ½-inch pieces to equal 1½ cups.

1. Preheat oven to 350°F. Grease 13×9-inch baking pan.

2. Coarsely chop nuts; measure ¾ cup. Combine flour, baking powder and salt in small bowl. Set aside.

3. Beat butter and sugars in large bowl with electric mixer at medium speed until light and fluffy, scraping down side of bowl once. Beat in eggs and vanilla, scraping down side of bowl once. Add flour mixture. Beat at low speed until well blended, scraping down side of bowl once. Stir in chocolate chunks and reserved nuts with spoon. Spread batter evenly into prepared pan.

4. Bake 25 to 30 minutes until golden brown. Remove pan to wire rack; cool completely. Cut into 3¼×1½-inch bars. Store tightly covered at room temperature or freeze up to 3 months.

Makes 2 dozen brownies

Decadent Blonde Brownies

White Chocolate Chunk Brownies

4 squares (1 ounce each) unsweetened chocolate, coarsely chopped
½ cup butter or margarine
2 eggs
1¼ cups granulated sugar
1 teaspoon vanilla extract
½ cup all-purpose flour
½ teaspoon salt
6 ounces white chocolate, cut into ¼-inch pieces
½ cup coarsely chopped walnuts (optional)
Powdered sugar (optional)

1. Preheat oven to 350°F. Grease 8-inch square baking pan.

2. Melt unsweetened chocolate and butter in heavy small saucepan over low heat, stirring constantly; set aside.

3. Beat eggs in large bowl with electric mixer at medium speed 30 seconds. Gradually add granulated sugar, beating at medium speed about 4 minutes until very thick and lemon-colored. Beat in chocolate mixture and vanilla. Beat in flour and salt at low speed just until blended. Stir in white chocolate and walnuts, if desired, with mixing spoon. Spread batter evenly into prepared pan.

4. Bake 30 minutes or until edges just begin to pull away from sides of pan and center is set.

5. Remove pan to wire rack; cool completely. Cut into 2-inch squares. Place powdered sugar in fine-mesh strainer, if desired; sprinkle over brownies. Store tightly covered at room temperature or freeze up to 3 months.   *Makes 16 brownies*

White Chocolate Chunk Brownies

BRUSCHETTA

Bruschetta is an Italian garlic bread. The traditional preparation involves grilling or toasting bread slices, ideally from a rustic country loaf; rubbing the toasted slices with a cut clove of garlic; sprinkling liberally with coarse salt and pepper; and drizzling with extra-virgin olive oil. Bruschetta is often topped with tomatoes or other simple toppings, such as sautéed mushrooms, sautéed red bell peppers and puréed eggplant. In Italy, bruschetta is served as an appetizer or a light meal.

The American version of bruschetta generally uses less olive oil and often foregoes the salt. Toppings are similar to those used in Italy with vegetable mixture and cheese being common. Serve bruschetta as an appetizer or as an accompaniment to a soup or salad.

🌿

Bruschetta

- 1 can (14½ ounces) DEL MONTE® Fresh Cut™ Diced Tomatoes, drained
- 2 tablespoons chopped fresh basil *or* ½ teaspoon dried basil
- 1 clove garlic, finely minced
- 1 baguette (6 inches) French bread, cut into ½-inch slices
- 1 tablespoon olive oil

In 1-quart bowl, combine tomatoes, basil and garlic; cover and refrigerate at least ½ hour. Brush bread with oil. Broil until golden. Top with tomato mixture; serve immediately. Garnish with basil leaves, if desired.

Makes 6 appetizer servings

BRUSH, TO

Brushing refers to the technique of applying liquid, such as melted butter, barbecue sauce or glaze, to the surface of food prior to or during cooking with a brush. It serves the same purpose as basting—preserving moistness, adding flavor and giving foods an attractive appearance.

🌿

Brushing bread loaf with egg white.

Bruschetta

BRUSSELS SPROUT

The Brussels sprout, a member of the cabbage family, is native to northern Europe. It received its name from the Belgian city of Brussels where it was thought to have first been grown. Today, most of the U.S. crop is grown in California. Brussels sprouts look like miniature heads of cabbage with tight overlapping leaves. Each plant produces as many as one hundred small heads arranged on one long, thick trunklike stalk.

🌾

Varieties: Most common is the green Brussels sprout. A new reddish-purple variety is seen occasionally at farmers' markets.

Availability: Fresh Brussels sprouts are most readily available between October and April. Generally the sprouts are removed from their stalks and sold by the pound or in cardboard containers covered with cellophane. You also may find them at farmers' markets still attached to their stalks. These sprouts are fresher and have better flavor. Do not remove them from the stalk until just before cooking. Frozen Brussels sprouts may also be purchased plain or in sauce.

Buying Tips: Choose firm, compact sprouts with a bright green color. They should feel heavy for their size and free of blemishes. Look for small, young sprouts as they have a sweeter flavor. Older sprouts, ones with wilted or yellowed leaves, have a stronger, almost bitter cabbage flavor and should be avoided.

Yield: 1 pound fresh Brussels sprouts = 4 cups raw; 2½ cups cooked. 1 (10-ounce) package frozen Brussels sprouts = 18 to 24 sprouts.

Storage: Pull off and discard any loose or discolored leaves. Refrigerate fresh Brussels sprouts unwashed in a plastic bag or in their original cardboard container for up to five days. If buying sprouts still on the stalk, refrigerate the entire stalk unwashed until cooking; these will keep up to ten days.

Basic Preparation: Peel off any wilted or discolored leaves and trim stem ends. When cutting off the stem end be sure not to cut too closely to the bottom of the leaves; otherwise, the outer leaves of the sprout will fall off during cooking.

For faster and more even cooking of whole sprouts, cut an "X" deep into the stem ends with a paring knife.

Sprouts may be cut in half before cooking, especially if they are large. Brussels sprouts can be boiled or steamed. To boil, drop them into boiling water and cook, covered, about 10 to 15 minutes or until tender. Do not overcook them or they will develop a strong flavor. Sprouts may also be cooked until almost tender, drained and sautéed in butter for 3 to 5 minutes until tender.

Brussels Sprouts in Mustard Sauce

1½ **pounds fresh Brussels sprouts***
1 **tablespoon butter or margarine**
⅓ **cup chopped shallots or onion**
⅓ **cup half-and-half**
1½ **tablespoons tarragon Dijon**
    mustard or Dusseldorf
    mustard
¼ **teaspoon salt**
⅛ **teaspoon ground black pepper**
    or ground nutmeg
1½ **tablespoons grated Parmesan**
    cheese (optional)
    Carrot curls (optional)

Or, substitute 2 (10-ounce) packages frozen Brussels sprouts for fresh Brussels sprouts. Omit steps 1, 2 and 3. Cook according to package directions; drain.

**Or, substitute 1½ tablespoons Dijon mustard plus ½ teaspoon dried tarragon leaves for tarragon Dijon mustard.*

1. Cut stem from each Brussels sprout and pull off outer bruised leaves.

2. For faster, more even cooking, cross-hatch core by cutting an "X" deep into the stem end of each Brussels sprout. (If some Brussels sprouts are larger than others, cut large sprouts lengthwise into halves.)

Brussels Sprouts in Mustard Sauce

3. Use large enough saucepan to allow Brussels sprouts to fit in a single layer. Bring 2 quarts salted water to a boil in saucepan. Add Brussels sprouts; return to a boil. Boil, uncovered, 7 to 10 minutes until almost tender when pierced with fork. Drain in colander. Rinse under cold running water to stop cooking; drain thoroughly.

4. Melt butter in same saucepan over medium heat until foamy. Add shallots; cook 3 minutes, stirring occasionally. Add half-and-half, mustard, salt and pepper. Simmer 1 minute until thickened. Add drained Brussels sprouts; cook about 1 minute or until heated through, tossing gently with sauce. (At this point, Brussels sprouts may be covered and refrigerated up to 8 hours before serving. Reheat in saucepan over low heat. Or, place in microwave-safe covered dish and reheat in microwave oven at HIGH 3 minutes or until hot.) Just before serving, sprinkle with cheese, if desired. Garnish with carrot curls, if desired. *Makes 6 to 8 side-dish servings (about 4 cups)*

Techniques for Brussels Sprouts in Mustard Sauce

Step 1. *Pulling outer leaves from Brussels sprouts.*

Step 2. *Cutting "X" into core for faster cooking.*

Techniques for Bûche de Noël

Step 6. *Gently rolling up cake in towel.*

White Chocolate Curls: Step 2. *Spreading white chocolate mixture on back of baking pan.*

White Chocolate Curls: Step 3. *Forming curls.*

BÛCHE DE NOËL

Literally translated from French as "yule log," bûche de Noël is a classic French cake shaped to resemble the traditional French Yule log. It is made of thin sponge cake that has been filled and rolled to form a "log." It is covered with chocolate frosting that is made to resemble bark.

❦

Bûche de Noël

¾ **cup cake flour**
½ **teaspoon baking powder**
½ **teaspoon salt**
5 **eggs, separated**
1 **cup granulated sugar, divided**
1 **teaspoon vanilla extract**
½ **cup powdered sugar**
1 **cup semisweet chocolate chips**
¾ **cup whipping cream**
1 **tablespoon rum (optional)**
  Cocoa Frosting (recipe follows)
  White Chocolate Curls (recipe follows, optional)
2 **teaspoons unsweetened cocoa powder (optional)**

1. Preheat oven to 375°F. Grease 15½×10½-inch jelly-roll pan; line pan with waxed paper. Grease again.

2. Combine flour, baking powder and salt in small bowl; set aside.

3. Beat egg yolks and ⅔ cup granulated sugar in small bowl with electric mixer at high speed about 5 minutes or until thick and lemon-colored, scraping down side of bowl once. Beat in vanilla; set aside.

4. Beat egg whites in large bowl with electric mixer at high speed until foamy. Gradually beat in remaining ⅓ cup granulated sugar, 1 tablespoon at a time, until stiff peaks form. Fold flour mixture into egg yolk mixture with rubber spatula until well blended. Fold in egg white mixture.

5. Spread mixture into prepared pan. Bake 12 to 15 minutes until cake springs back when lightly touched.

6. Meanwhile, sift powdered sugar over clean dish towel. Loosen warm cake from edges of pan with spatula; invert onto prepared towel. Remove pan; carefully peel off paper. Gently roll up cake in towel from short end, jelly-roll style. Let cake cool completely on wire rack.

7. For chocolate filling, place chips and cream in heavy 2-quart saucepan. Heat over low heat until chocolate is melted, stirring constantly. Immediately pour into small bowl; stir in rum, if desired. Cover; refrigerate about 1½ hours or until filling is of spreading consistency, stirring occasionally.

8. Prepare Cocoa Frosting. Cover; refrigerate until ready to use. Prepare White Chocolate Curls, if desired. Cover; refrigerate until ready to use.

9. Unroll cake; remove towel. Spread cake with chilled chocolate filling to within ½ inch of edge; reroll cake. Place cake, seam side down, on serving plate. Spread Cocoa Frosting over cake roll. Garnish with White Chocolate Curls. Sprinkle with cocoa, if desired. *Makes 12 servings*

Cocoa Frosting

1 **cup whipping cream**
½ **cup powdered sugar, sifted**
2 **tablespoons unsweetened cocoa powder, sifted**
1 **teaspoon vanilla extract**

Beat cream, sugar, cocoa and vanilla in medium bowl with electric mixer at medium speed until soft peaks form. *Do not overbeat.* Cover; refrigerate until ready to use.
Makes about 2 cups frosting

White Chocolate Curls

1 **package (8 ounces) white chocolate, coarsely chopped**
1 **tablespoon vegetable shortening**

1. Place chocolate and shortening in 2-cup glass measure. Microwave at HIGH (100% power) about 1½ minutes or until chocolate is melted, stirring every 30 seconds.

2. Pour chocolate mixture onto back of baking pan, marble slab or other heat-resistant flat surface. Quickly spread chocolate into thin layer with metal spatula. Refrigerate about 10 minutes or until firm, but still pliable.

3. Holding small straight-edge metal spatula at a 45° angle, push spatula firmly along baking pan, under chocolate, so chocolate curls as it is pushed. (If chocolate is too firm to curl, let stand a few minutes at room temperature. Refrigerate again if it becomes too soft.) Using small skewer or toothpick, transfer curls to waxed paper.

BUFFALO WING

Buffalo wings are deep-fried chicken wings served with a spicy hot sauce and blue cheese dressing. This dish originated at the Anchor Bar in Buffalo, New York, in 1964 when the owner served chicken wings with hot pepper sauce. They became a much requested item and are served throughout the country today.

☙

Buffalo Chicken Wings

  24 chicken wings
   1 teaspoon salt
  ¼ teaspoon ground black pepper
   4 cups vegetable oil for frying
  ¼ cup butter or margarine
  ¼ cup hot pepper sauce
   1 teaspoon white wine vinegar
    Celery sticks
   1 bottle (8 ounces) blue cheese
    dressing

Bûche de Noël

1. Cut tips off wings at first joint; discard tips. Cut remaining wings into two parts at the joint; sprinkle with salt and pepper.

2. Heat oil in deep fryer or heavy saucepan to 375°F. Add half the wings; fry about 10 minutes or until golden brown and crisp, stirring occasionally. Remove with slotted spoon; drain on paper towels. Repeat with remaining wings.

3. Melt butter in small saucepan over medium heat; stir in pepper sauce and vinegar. Cook until thoroughly heated.

4. Place wings on large platter. Pour sauce over wings. Serve warm with celery and dressing for dipping.
Makes 48 appetizers

*Favorite recipe from **National Broiler Council***

BURRITO

Burritos, originating in Mexico, are flour tortillas filled and folded into rectangular-shaped packages. Fillings vary and may include combinations of refried beans, shredded meat, poultry, chorizo, cheese, lettuce, tomatoes and sour cream. Breakfast burritos may be filled with seasoned scrambled eggs or a fruit mixture. Burritos are served without a sauce but may be garnished with sour cream or salsa.

❧

Bean and Cheese Burritos with Tomato-Mango Salsa

Tomato-Mango Salsa (recipe follows)
8 (8-inch) flour tortillas
1 tablespoon vegetable oil
1 cup chopped red onions
1 medium poblano chili, seeded, finely chopped*
1 teaspoon chili powder
½ teaspoon ground cumin
1 can (15 ounces) black beans, drained, rinsed
1 can (15 ounces) red kidney beans, drained, rinsed
1 can (4 ounces) chopped green chilies, drained
2 tablespoons fresh lime juice
Salt and ground black pepper
1 cup (4 ounces) farmer cheese, crumbled

Chili peppers can sting and irritate the skin; wear rubber or plastic gloves when handling chilies and do not touch eyes. Wash hands after handling.

Bean and Cheese
Burritos with Tomato-
Mango Salsa

1. Prepare Tomato-Mango Salsa.

2. To soften and warm tortillas, preheat oven to 350°F. Stack tortillas; wrap in foil. Heat in oven 10 minutes or until tortillas are warm.

3. Heat oil in large skillet over medium heat. Add onions and poblano chili; cook and stir 5 minutes or until onions are tender. Stir in chili powder and cumin; cook 1 minute. Reduce heat to low. Add beans, green chilies and juice to skillet; cook 2 to 3 minutes until heated through. Season with salt and pepper. Remove from heat. Coarsely mash bean mixture with back of wooden spoon.

4. Spoon about ½ cup bean mixture onto center of each tortilla; sprinkle evenly with cheese. To form burrito, fold side edge of tortilla over filling; fold over top and bottom edges, leaving one side open. Serve with Tomato-Mango Salsa. Garnish as desired. *Makes 4 servings*

Tomato-Mango Salsa

   1 small mango
   1 large tomato, seeded, chopped
   ⅓ cup chopped red onion
   ¼ cup minced fresh cilantro
   1 small jalapeño pepper, seeded, finely chopped
   2 tablespoons lime juice

1. To prepare mango, hold mango, stem side up, on cutting board. Make vertical cut on flat side of mango from top to bottom about ½ inch to right of stem and seed. Repeat on opposite flat side of mango. Peel skin from cut sections. Carefully peel skin from mango sections attached to seed. Slice flesh from seed. Chop flesh to measure 1½ cups.

2. Combine all ingredients in small bowl; refrigerate 2 hours.
Makes about 2 cups salsa

Special Beef and Spinach Burritos

   1 pound lean ground beef
   1 small onion, chopped
   1 clove garlic, minced
   ½ teaspoon salt
   ½ teaspoon chili powder
   ¼ teaspoon ground cumin
   ¼ teaspoon ground black pepper
   1 package (10 ounces) frozen chopped spinach, thawed, well drained
   2 jalapeño peppers, seeded, finely chopped*
   1½ cups (6 ounces) shredded Monterey Jack cheese
   4 large (10-inch) *or* 8 medium (8-inch) flour tortillas, warmed
   Lime slices (optional)
   Jalapeño pepper slices (optional)
   1 cup prepared chunky salsa

*Jalapeño peppers can sting and irritate the skin, wear rubber or plastic gloves when handling peppers and do not touch eyes. Wash hands after handling.

1. Brown beef, onion and garlic in large nonstick skillet over medium heat 8 to 10 minutes until beef is no longer pink, stirring occasionally. Pour off drippings. Add salt, chili powder, cumin and black pepper. Stir in spinach and jalapeños; heat through. Remove from heat; stir in cheese.

2. To serve, spoon equal amount of beef mixture into center of each tortilla. Fold bottom edge up over filling. Fold right and left sides to center, overlapping edges. Garnish with lime and jalapeño slices, if desired. Serve with salsa.
Makes 4 servings

*Favorite recipe from **North Dakota Beef Commission***

Tip

Tortillas can be softened and warmed in microwave oven just before using. Stack tortillas; wrap in plastic wrap. Microwave at HIGH (100% power) ½ to 1 minute, turning over and rotating ¼ turn once during heating.

BUTTER

Butter is made from the cream portion of cow's milk. The cream is churned until fat globules come together to form a semisolid mass. It is used as a spread, a medium for browning and sautéing, and as an integral ingredient in pastries, cakes, confections and frostings.

🐝

By law, butter must be at least 80 percent butterfat and have less than 16 percent water. The rest is milk solids. It is the milk solids that will burn if subjected to high heat. It can be dyed with annatto, a natural coloring agent. Butter is scored by the United States Department of Agriculture (USDA) and assigned quality grades based on flavor, body, texture, color and salt. Grade AA (93 score) is the highest grade and the most common grade available in the retail market. Grade A (92 score) is also sold. Lower grades are rarely seen in supermarkets.

Storage: Butter is usually sold in one-pound packages that contain four (4-ounce) sticks. Each stick equals 8 tablespoons or 1/2 cup. Packages should be stamped with a freshness date. At home, butter should be stored in the coldest part of the refrigerator or frozen. Either way, wrap it tightly since it picks up other flavors.

Availability: Unsalted and salted butter are available. Unsalted butter has a more delicate flavor and is preferred by many cooks, especially for sauces and baking. Although it varies by manufacturer, salted butter has about 1 1/2 teaspoons added salt per pound. Whipped butter, sold in tubs, has air beaten into it so it is spreadable at refrigerator temperature. Do not substitute whipped butter for regular butter in baked goods. Butter-margarine blends combine the two in varying

proportions to produce a product with fewer grams of cholesterol while retaining the flavor of butter. As long as the blend has the same percentage of fat as butter (80), it can be used interchangeably with butter.

Butter granules are made from butter extracts by removing the fat and water. They may be sprinkled on food as a flavoring or reconstituted in liquid. They can't be used in baking or for frying.

Citrus Butter

1 orange
1 cup butter, softened
1/4 teaspoon grated lime peel

1. Finely grate colored portion of orange peel; measure 3/4 teaspoon peel. Cut orange in half; remove any visible seeds. Squeeze orange halves; measure 2 tablespoons juice.

2. Place butter, juice, orange peel and lime peel in medium bowl. Beat with electric mixer at medium speed until well blended.

3. Spoon butter mixture into clean, dry decorative crock, packing down with back of spoon; cover. Or, place butter mixture on sheet of waxed paper. Using waxed paper to hold butter mixture, roll it back and forth to form log. Wrap log in plastic wrap. Store in refrigerator up to 2 weeks.

Makes about 1 cup butter

Serving Note: Remove desired amount from crock or roll; refrigerate remaining butter.

Honey Butter: Omit orange peel, juice and lime peel. Beat butter and 1/4 cup honey in medium bowl with electric mixer at medium speed until well blended. Continue as directed in step 3.

Strawberry Butter: Omit orange peel, juice and lime peel. Beat butter and 2/3 cup strawberry preserves in medium bowl with electric mixer at medium speed until well blended. Continue as directed in step 3.

Special Interest

Clarifying is a process of slowly melting unsalted butter so that the water evaporates and the milk solids sink to the bottom. The clear liquid, or clarified butter, consisting of fat and flavor, is carefully spooned or poured off. Clarified butter can be used to fry foods at a higher temperature than regular butter, since it does not burn as easily.

Viennese Hazelnut Butter Thins

1 cup hazelnuts, skins removed
1¼ cups all-purpose flour
¼ teaspoon salt
1¼ cups powdered sugar
1 cup butter, softened
1 egg
1 teaspoon vanilla extract
1 cup semisweet chocolate chips

1. Place hazelnuts in food processor. Process using on/off pulsing action until hazelnuts are ground, but not pasty; set aside. Combine flour and salt in small bowl; set aside.

2. Beat sugar and butter in medium bowl with electric mixer at medium speed until light and fluffy, scraping down side of bowl once. Beat in egg and vanilla. Gradually add flour mixture. Beat in hazelnuts at low speed until well blended.

3. Place dough on sheet of waxed paper. Using waxed paper to hold dough, roll it back and forth to form log 12 inches long and 2½ inches wide. Wrap log in plastic wrap. Refrigerate until firm, at least 2 hours or up to 48 hours.

4. Preheat oven to 350°F. Cut dough crosswise into ¼-inch-thick slices. Place cookies 2 inches apart on ungreased baking sheets.

5. Bake 10 to 12 minutes until edges are very lightly browned. Let cookies stand on baking sheets 1 minute. Remove to wire racks; cool completely.

6. Melt chips in 2-cup glass measuring cup in microwave at HIGH (100% power) 2½ to 3 minutes, stirring once.

7. Dip each cookie into chocolate, coating halfway up sides. Let excess chocolate drip back into cup. Transfer cookies to waxed paper; let stand at room temperature 1 hour or until set.

Makes about 3 dozen cookies

Viennese Hazelnut Butter Thins

BUTTERMILK

Even though its name might suggest otherwise, buttermilk is a low-fat dairy product made from cow's milk. Originally, it was made from the liquid left after milk was churned into butter. Now, it is far more likely to be processed from nonfat or low-fat milk and treated with a special strain of bacteria to thicken it and add its characteristic tang.

In addition to its use as a beverage, buttermilk is used for making salad dressings, chilled soups and as an ingredient in pancake, cake and quick bread recipes. Buttermilk can be found primarily in quart and half gallon containers, although pints are increasingly available. Shake the carton before using. Buttermilk also is sold in powdered form, a welcome convenience for those who use buttermilk only for baking purposes. It is shelf-stable and can be reconstituted with water.

🐝

Premier Pound Cake

    3 cups sifted all-purpose flour
 ½ teaspoon baking powder
 ½ teaspoon baking soda
 ½ teaspoon salt
    1 cup butter or margarine, softened
    2 cups superfine sugar
    2 eggs
    1 teaspoon vanilla extract
    1 teaspoon lemon extract
    1 cup buttermilk
      Starfruit, strawberry slices and orange peel strip (optional)

1. Preheat oven to 350°F. Grease and flour 2 (9×5-inch) loaf pans.

2. Combine flour, baking powder, baking soda and salt in medium bowl; set aside. Beat together butter and sugar in large bowl until light and fluffy. Add eggs, 1 at a time, beating well after each addition. Blend in vanilla and lemon extracts. Add flour mixture alternately with buttermilk, beating well after each addition. Pour into prepared pans.

3. Bake 35 to 40 minutes until wooden toothpick inserted into centers comes out clean. Cool loaves in pans on wire racks 10 minutes. Loosen edges; remove to wire racks. Cool completely. Garnish with fruit, if desired.   *Makes 2 loaves*

Buttermilk Corn Bread Loaf

    1½ cups all-purpose flour
    1 cup yellow cornmeal
 ⅓ cup sugar
    2 teaspoons baking powder
    1 teaspoon salt
 ½ teaspoon baking soda
 ½ cup vegetable shortening
    1⅓ cups buttermilk*
    2 eggs

*Or, substitute soured fresh milk. To sour milk, place 4 teaspoons lemon juice plus enough milk to equal 1⅓ cups in 2-cup measure. Stir; let stand 5 minutes before using.

1. Preheat oven to 375°F. Grease 8½×4½-inch loaf pan.

2. Combine flour, cornmeal, sugar, baking powder, salt and baking soda in medium bowl. Cut in shortening with pastry blender or 2 knives until mixture resembles coarse crumbs.

3. Whisk together buttermilk and eggs in small bowl. Make well in center of dry ingredients. Add buttermilk mixture; stir until mixture forms stiff batter. (Batter will be lumpy.) Turn into prepared pan; spread mixture evenly, removing any air bubbles.

4. Bake 50 to 55 minutes until wooden toothpick inserted into center comes out clean. Cool in pan on wire rack 10 minutes. Remove from pan; cool on rack 10 minutes more. Slice and serve warm.   *Makes 1 loaf*

Buttermilk Pancakes with Blueberry-Orange Sauce

> **Blueberry-Orange Sauce (recipe follows)**
> **2 cups all-purpose flour**
> **1 tablespoon sugar**
> **1½ teaspoons baking powder**
> **½ teaspoon baking soda**
> **½ teaspoon salt**
> **1 egg**
> **1½ cups buttermilk**
> **¼ cup vegetable oil**

1. Prepare Blueberry-Orange Sauce; set aside. Lightly grease and preheat griddle or large skillet over medium heat.

2. Combine flour, sugar, baking powder, baking soda and salt in large bowl; set aside.

3. Place egg in medium bowl; beat with wire whisk. Gradually add buttermilk and oil, whisking continuously until mixture is thoroughly blended. Stir egg mixture into flour mixture just until moistened.

4. For each pancake, pour about ½ cup batter onto hot griddle. Cook until tops of pancakes appear dry; turn with spatula and cook 2 minutes more or until golden brown. Serve with Blueberry-Orange Sauce. Garnish as desired.
Makes 6 to 8 (5-inch) pancakes

Blueberry-Orange Sauce

> **2 tablespoons cornstarch**
> **2 tablespoons cold water**
> **½ cup orange juice**
> **1 tablespoon grated orange peel**
> **1 bag (16 ounces) frozen blueberries, thawed *or* 3½ to 4 cups fresh blueberries**
> **½ cup sugar**
> **2 tablespoons orange-flavored liqueur**

1. Stir cornstarch into water in medium saucepan until smooth. Stir in orange juice and peel.

2. Add blueberries, any accumulated juices and sugar to cornstarch mixture. Cook and stir over high heat until mixture comes to a boil. Reduce heat to medium-low; simmer 2 to 3 minutes (4 to 5 minutes for fresh blueberries) until mixture thickens, stirring occasionally. Remove from heat; stir in liqueur. Serve immediately. *Makes 2¾ cups*

Buttermilk Pancakes with Blueberry-Orange Sauce

C

Is cactus edible? *Decorate a home-baked cake.* What makes a soup a chowder? *Bake a warm berry cobbler.* How is cheese made? *Find out what kind of coffee you're ordering at a coffee house.* How many types of chocolate can you name?

Rich Chocolate Truffle Cake
(recipe on page 94)

Tips

CABBAGE

Cabbage—a member of the crucifer family, including Brussels sprouts, broccoli, cauliflower and kale—has long been a popular vegetable in many of the world's cuisines. It is eaten raw in salads, steamed, sautéed and added to soups. The leaves can be stuffed with a filling before cooking. Pickled cabbage is a staple in China, Germany (sauerkraut) and Korea (kim chee).

Varieties: There are several varieties of this vegetable from the familiar round green cabbage to the exotic napa cabbage.

The most common variety found in the United States, green cabbage is round with tightly packed leaves ranging from light to dark green in color. It has a delicate flavor. The red variety, actually purple-red in color, is similar in shape to green cabbage. Savoy cabbage (often called curly cabbage) is also a round variety. It has beautifully crinkled pale green

leaves. Heads are more loosely packed than the green variety. Used interchangeably with green cabbage, it has a milder flavor and a less crisp, more tender texture. It is principally used for salads.

Also known as Chinese cabbage, napa is a loosely packed elongated head of light green stalks that are slightly crinkled. This variety has a milder flavor and doesn't give off a strong odor when cooked, which endears it to many cooks.

Availability: Heads of green and red cabbage are available all year. Markets sell whole heads as well as preshredded cabbage. Shredded green cabbage, sometimes combined with shredded carrots, may be labeled coleslaw mix. Savoy cabbage is not as easy to find. Look for it in large supermarkets and speciality produce markets. Napa cabbage is also available all year, but winter is its peak season when prices are likely to be lower.

Buying Tips: When buying green and red varieties look for well-trimmed, compact heads that feel heavy for their size. They should have a bright color and be free of withered leaves. Avoid cabbage with badly discolored or dry outer leaves. If you intend to stuff some of the green cabbage leaves, look for heads with outer green leaves still loosely attached. Napa and savoy cabbage should look crisp. Avoid limp or discolored heads.

Yield: 1 pound cabbage = 4 to 4½ cups shredded; 2 cups cooked.

Storage: Fresh heads of cabbage should be stored, unwashed, in plastic bags; they will keep up to two weeks when refrigerated.

Basic Preparation: Remove and discard any wilted or discolored outer leaves. Wash cabbage under cold running water. To prepare cabbage for shredding or chopping, cut head lengthwise through core into quarters with a chef's knife. To core, hold one quarter upright and cut off and discard the white triangular core. (Do not remove the core if cabbage is to be cut into wedges and cooked; the core will help hold the wedges together.)

Place the cabbage wedge, flat side down, on cutting board. Thinly slice the cabbage crosswise into shreds

using a chef's knife or utility knife. Then, if desired, the shreds can be coarsely chopped.

Cabbage can also be shredded using the largest holes of a four-sided grater. The most common cooking methods are braising, steaming and sautéing.

Jalapeño Coleslaw

6 cups preshredded cabbage or coleslaw mix
2 tomatoes, seeded, chopped
6 green onions, coarsely chopped
2 jalapeño peppers, finely chopped*
¼ cup cider vinegar
3 tablespoons honey
1 teaspoon salt

*For a milder coleslaw, discard seeds and veins when chopping the jalapeños. Jalapeño peppers can sting and irritate the skin; wear rubber or plastic gloves when handling peppers and do not touch eyes. Wash hands after handling.

1. Combine cabbage, tomatoes, onions, jalapeños, vinegar, honey and salt in serving bowl; mix well. Cover; refrigerate at least 2 hours.

2. Stir well before serving.
Makes 4 side-dish servings

Red Cabbage with Apples

1 small head red cabbage, shredded
2 large apples, peeled, thinly sliced
½ cup sliced onion
½ cup unsweetened apple juice
¼ cup fresh lemon juice
2 tablespoons raisins
2 tablespoons brown sugar
Salt and ground black pepper (optional)

1. Combine cabbage, apples, onion, apple juice, lemon juice, raisins and sugar in large nonstick saucepan. Bring to a boil over medium-high heat. Reduce heat to medium-low. Cover; simmer 30 minutes or until cabbage is tender.

2. Season with salt and pepper, if desired. Serve immediately.
Makes 8 side-dish servings

Tip

Cook cabbage only until it is crisp-tender as overcooking results in an unpleasant odor and strong flavor.

Jalapeño Coleslaw

CACCIATORE

Cacciatore, Italian for "hunter," refers to dishes prepared "hunter's style." The most popular dish is Chicken Cacciatore. Recipes for this entrée usually include chicken cut into pieces, tomatoes or tomato sauce, mushrooms, onions, garlic and various herbs and spices. Chicken pieces are browned in a skillet, other ingredients are added, and the dish is simmered until the chicken is cooked. Cacciatore sometimes includes wine and may be served with pasta or rice.

🐝

Skillet Chicken Cacciatore

Skillet Chicken Cacciatore

2 tablespoons olive oil
1 cup sliced red onion
1 cup (1 medium) green bell pepper strips
2 cloves garlic, minced
1 pound (about 4) boneless, skinless chicken breast halves
1¾ cups (14-ounce can) CONTADINA® Pasta Ready Chunky Tomatoes with Mushrooms, undrained
¼ cup dry white wine or chicken broth
½ teaspoon salt
¼ teaspoon ground black pepper
Hot cooked rice or pasta
1 tablespoon chopped fresh basil *or* 1 teaspoon dried basil leaves, crushed

In large skillet, heat oil over medium-high heat. Add onion, bell pepper and garlic; sauté for 1 minute. Add chicken; cook until browned on both sides. Add tomatoes and juice, wine, salt and black pepper. Bring to a boil. Reduce heat to low; simmer, uncovered, for 15 to 20 minutes or until chicken is no longer pink in center. Serve over hot cooked rice. Sprinkle with basil.

Makes 6 servings

CACTUS

Cactus refers to two very different and distinct parts of a cactus plant: the cactus pear and cactus pad. The cactus pear, also called prickly pear, is the large, egg-shaped berry of the cactus plant. Its prickly skin ranges in color from green to deep magenta, and its pulp, dotted with black seeds, is yellow-green to gold. It has a melonlike aroma and mild, sweet flavor. Erroneously referred to as leaves, the cactus pads, or nopales, are succulent but crunchy, with a flavor that resembles both asparagus and bell peppers.

🐝

Uses: Prickly pears are most often eaten raw, or they can be cut up for fruit salads.

• Prickly pear pulp may be used for beverages and jams.

• Cactus pads, or nopales, mix well in vegetable side dishes, may be battered and deep fried, and combine especially well with scrambled eggs.

Availability: Prickly pears are available in large supermarkets and produce markets from autumn through spring. Cactus pads are available year-round, but they are more tender and juicy in the spring. Canned nopalitos, which are cactus pads chopped or cut into strips, are available pickled or packed in water.

Buying Tips: Prickly pears should have a deep, even color and yield slightly to pressure. Cactus pads should be small, firm and green with no signs of wrinkling.

Storage: Ripen prickly pears at room temperature until soft and then store in the refrigerator up to one week. Refrigerate cactus pads, tightly wrapped in plastic, for up to a week.

Basic Preparation: The sharp spines of prickly pears are removed before shipping, but the fibrous spines remain in the skin. If these spines become embedded in your skin, they are difficult to remove so it's best to hold the fruit by the ends or wear protective gloves. Cut a slice from each end with a sharp knife. Peel prickly pears using a paring knife or a vegetable peeler. Some cooks suggest scoring the skin from end to end, gripping the skin between the blade of the paring knife and your thumb, and carefully pulling it off. Cut the pulp into slices and remove the seeds. Serve prickly pears chilled.

Use a paring knife or a vegetable peeler to remove the spines and "eyes" from the nopales and to trim the outside edges. Chop or cut them into strips. Although they can be eaten raw, cactus pads are best if steamed or simmered until tender.

CAKE

This large category of baked goods includes a vast array of different cakes. Made from batters that include flour, sugar, eggs, sometimes flavorings, liquid and fat, cakes can be as small as cupcakes or as grand and towering as a multi-tiered wedding cake with countless variations in between.

🌾

Shortened Cakes: Cakes are generally divided into two broad groups based on how they are leavened: chemically leavened (shortened) and air-leavened (foam) cakes.

The first group—which includes pound cakes, butter cakes, chocolate cakes and fruit cakes—uses baking powder or baking soda as the primary leavening agent. These cakes contain fat, such as butter, shortening, margarine or oil. Butter or shortening should be at room temperature. Margarine needs to be softened until it becomes pliable, which generally occurs between 50° to 55°F. Solid fat is beaten (a technique called "creaming") together with sugar until the mixture is smooth, light and fluffy.

There are some basic techniques that should be followed when mixing the batter of shortened cakes. Eggs (or yolks, if the whites are beaten separately) should be at room temperature, added one at a time, and mixed thoroughly after each addition. Combined liquids and flavorings, such as vanilla, should be added alternately with flour that has been mixed with a leavening agent (baking powder or baking soda). The liquid and flour mixtures are generally divided into halves or thirds before adding. As the flour is added, it is important not to overmix or the cake will be tough. If the egg whites are beaten separately, they should be folded in gently with a rubber spatula as the final step. Throughout the mixing process, be sure to scrape the

Tip

To measure flour, spoon flour into the appropriate dry measure until it is overflowing. With a straight-edged metal spatula, sweep across the top of the measure to level the flour. Do not scoop the flour with the measure or tap the measure on the counter, because this will compact the flour.

side and bottom of the bowl with a rubber spatula to ensure that all ingredients are well blended.

Shortened cakes that use vegetable oil or melted fat are mixed differently. Combine all dry ingredients—flour, sugar, baking powder and spices—in a mixing bowl. Add wet ingredients—liquid, fat, eggs and flavorings—one at a time and mix thoroughly after all have been added.

Foam Cakes: The second group—which includes angel food and sponge cakes—relies solely on the air beaten into egg whites or eggs for leavening. They contain no baking powder or baking soda. Angel food cakes are made with egg whites and contain no fat. Sponge cakes contain some fat because they are made with egg yolks as well as egg whites.

When preparing foam cakes, the following general recommendations are useful to remember. (Techniques for sponge and chiffon cakes may vary from these, so be sure to follow each recipe carefully.) The egg yolks should be separated from the egg whites, and the egg whites placed in a very large, perfectly clean bowl. Any trace of fat will interfere with foaming. With an electric mixer on low speed, mix the whites until they are foamy. Add a small amount of cream of tartar to stabilize the egg white foam. Increase the mixer speed to high and beat until soft peaks form. For angel food cake, some sugar should be beaten in, a little at a time, until the whites are thick and glossy. Very gently fold in the flour mixture. (Cake flour is used in angel food cake; it should be sifted at least three times. In angel food and some chiffon cake recipes, part of the sugar is sifted into the flour.) Cake pans for foam cakes are not greased, as grease will prevent satisfactory rising.

Chiffon cakes are a hybrid in that they share characteristics of both shortened cakes (fat in the form of vegetable oil and a chemical leavener, baking powder) and foam

Removing cake layer from pan.

cakes (beaten eggs provide some of the leaven).

Another variation of the foam cake is the flourless chocolate cake, a very rich cake leavened with eggs. Its richness comes from chocolate, egg yolks and some type of fat, usually butter.

Testing for Doneness: To test whether a cake is done, insert a wooden toothpick or cake tester into the center, gently pressing it about halfway down. When the pick is removed, it should be dry and free of crumbs, unless recipe directions indicate otherwise. Begin testing about five minutes before the end of the specified baking time.

Cooling and Removing from Pan: Many cakes are removed from the pan after 10 or 15 minutes of cooling on a wire rack. Two important exceptions are angel food cakes and flourless cakes. Because they have a more delicate structure, they are cooled in the pan. Angel food cakes and some chiffon cakes are cooled in the pan upside down. An angel food cake pan has three metal feet on which the inverted pan stands for cooling. If you use a tube pan instead, invert the pan on a funnel or narrow-necked bottle.

Before attempting to remove a cake from its pan, carefully run a table knife or narrow metal spatula around the outside of the cake to loosen it from the pan. Using oven mitts or hot pads (if the pan is hot), place a wire cooling rack on top of the cake and pan. Turn the cake over so that the wire rack is on the bottom. Gently shake the cake to release it from the pan. Place the rack on a counter and remove the pan.

Tips for Successful Cake Making: Follow recipe directions exactly. If the recipe instructions differ from the general tips listed here, follow the recipe instructions.

• Begin with top quality ingredients, resisting temptations to substitute.

• Measure ingredients carefully, using spoons and measuring cups made especially for this purpose. All measurements are usually level.

• All-purpose flour usually doesn't need to be sifted; simply stir it lightly with a spoon before measuring. When sifted flour is called for, note carefully the wording of the instructions. When the ingredient list calls for "1 cup sifted flour," the flour should be sifted before it is measured. If "1 cup flour, sifted" is required, the flour should be measured before it is sifted. Because it is more finely milled, cake flour has a tendency to form lumps so it should always be sifted or strained before using.

• Use the pan sizes suggested and prepare baking pans carefully as indicated in the recipe. Shortened cakes usually require a greased pan; foam cakes do not. Solid vegetable shortening has superior releasing qualities, and it is the best choice for greasing pans. Sometimes butter is used for flavor. Liquid fats, such as melted butter or vegetable oil, should be avoided. Using a paper towel, waxed paper or pastry brush to apply, coat the entire inside of the pan, paying particular attention to creases and molded shapes. To line a pan with parchment or waxed paper, place it on a piece of paper larger than the pan. Trace around the outside of the pan; cut inside the traced line to form a liner that fits inside the pan. Grease the paper.

• Dusting the inside of the pan with flour helps the cake to develop a thin, crisp crust and prevents the cake from absorbing the fat used to grease the pan. Use all-purpose flour, sprinkling about 1 tablespoon into the pan and then shaking and tilting the pan until the bottom and sides have a fine coating. Hold the pan upside down over the sink and tap it gently on the side so any excess flour falls away.

• When filling two or more cake pans for a layer cake, divide the batter equally among the pans, so that all layers are the same depth.

• Immediately place the pan into a preheated oven. Cake batter should not sit before baking, because chemical leaveners begin working as soon as they are mixed with liquids or because the air in foam batters will begin to dissipate. Place the pan on the center rack of the oven. If two or more pans are used, allow at least an inch of space between the pans and two inches between the pans and the walls of the oven for proper heat circulation.

• Do not open the oven during the first half of the baking time. Cold air will interfere with the rising of the cake.

Chocolate Orange Marble Chiffon Cake (recipe on page 94)

Angel Food Cake

Techniques for Angel Food Cake

Step 3. *Folding flour mixture into egg white mixture.*

Step 5. *Placing inverted pan on bottle.*

Angel Food Cake

1¼ cups cake flour, sifted
1⅓ cups *plus* ½ cup sugar, divided
12 egg whites
1¼ teaspoons cream of tartar
¼ teaspoon salt
1 teaspoon vanilla extract
¼ teaspoon almond extract
   Fresh strawberries (optional)

1. Preheat oven to 350°F.

2. Sift together flour with ½ cup sugar four times in small bowl; set aside.

3. Beat egg whites, cream of tartar, salt and extracts in large bowl with electric mixer at high speed until stiff peaks form. Gradually add remaining 1⅓ cups sugar, beating well after each addition. Fold in flour mixture. Pour into ungreased 10-inch tube pan.

4. Bake 35 to 40 minutes until cake springs back when lightly touched with finger.

5. Invert pan; place on top of clean empty bottle. Allow cake to cool completely in pan before removing from pan. Serve with strawberries, if desired.

Makes one 10-inch tube cake

Bittersweet Chocolate Pound Cake

Cake
2 cups all-purpose flour
1 teaspoon baking soda
1 teaspoon baking powder
1½ cups water
2 tablespoons instant coffee
    granules
4 bars (8 ounces) NESTLÉ®
    Unsweetened Baking
    Chocolate, broken up,
    divided
2 cups granulated sugar
1 cup butter, softened
1 teaspoon vanilla extract
3 eggs

Chocolate Glaze
3 tablespoons butter or margarine
1½ cups sifted powdered sugar
2 to 3 tablespoons water
1 teaspoon vanilla extract
   Powdered sugar (optional)

For Cake: COMBINE flour, baking soda and baking powder in small bowl. Bring water and coffee to a boil in small saucepan; remove from heat. Add *3 bars (6 ounces)* baking chocolate; stir until smooth.

BEAT granulated sugar, butter and vanilla in large mixer bowl until creamy. Add eggs; beat on high speed for 5 minutes. Beat in flour mixture alternately with chocolate mixture. Pour into greased 10-inch Bundt pan.

BAKE in preheated 325°F oven for 50 to 60 minutes until long wooden pick inserted near center of cake comes out clean. Cool in pan on wire rack for 30 minutes. Remove from pan; cool completely. Drizzle with Chocolate Glaze; sprinkle with powdered sugar, if desired.

For Chocolate Glaze: MELT *remaining baking bar (2 ounces)* and 3 tablespoons butter in small, heavy saucepan over low heat, stirring until smooth. Remove from heat. Stir in powdered sugar alternately with water until desired consistency. Stir in vanilla.   *Makes 12 servings*

Yellow Butter Cake

    2 cups all-purpose flour
    4 teaspoons baking powder
    ½ teaspoon salt
  1½ cups sugar
    1 cup milk
    ½ cup butter or margarine,
        softened
    1 teaspoon vanilla extract
    3 eggs

1. Preheat oven to 350°F. Grease and flour cake pan(s)* or grease and line with waxed paper.

2. Sift together flour, baking powder and salt in large bowl. Stir in sugar.

3. Add milk, butter and vanilla; beat with electric mixer at low speed 30 seconds. Beat at medium speed 2 minutes. Add eggs; beat 2 minutes. Pour into prepared pan(s).

4. Bake as directed until wooden toothpick inserted into center(s) comes out clean. Cool in pan(s) 10 minutes. Loosen cake edge(s) from pan(s); invert onto wire rack(s). Remove paper; cool completely. Frost as desired.

Makes 1 cake or 24 cupcakes

*Yellow Butter Cake can be prepared in any of the following pans (follow correct baking times): 1 (13×9-inch) baking pan: 35 to 40 minutes, 1 (10-inch) Bundt pan: 45 to 55 minutes, 2 (9-inch) cake pans: 30 to 35 minutes, 2 (8-inch) cake pans: 35 to 40 minutes, 3 (8-inch) cake pans: 20 to 25 minutes, 24 medium (2¾-inch) muffin cups: 20 to 25 minutes.

Bittersweet Chocolate Pound Cake

Chocolate Orange Marble Chiffon Cake

⅓ **cup HERSHEY'S Cocoa**
¼ **cup hot water**
  3 **tablespoons** *plus* 1½ **cups sugar, divided**
  2 **tablespoons** *plus* ½ **cup vegetable oil, divided**
2¼ **cups all-purpose flour**
  1 **tablespoon baking powder**
  1 **teaspoon salt**
¾ **cup cold water**
  7 **egg yolks**
  1 **cup egg whites (about 8)**
½ **teaspoon cream of tartar**
  1 **tablespoon freshly grated orange peel**
    Orange Glaze (recipe follows)

Remove top oven rack; move other rack to lowest position. Heat oven to 325°F. In medium bowl, stir together cocoa and hot water. Stir in 3 tablespoons sugar and 2 tablespoons oil. In large bowl, stir together flour, remaining 1½ cups sugar, baking powder and salt. Add cold water, remaining ½ cup oil and egg yolks; beat with spoon until smooth. In large mixer bowl on high speed of electric mixer, beat egg whites and cream of tartar until stiff peaks form. Pour egg yolk mixture in a thin stream over egg white mixture, gently folding just until blended. Remove 2 cups batter; add to chocolate mixture, gently folding until well blended. Into remaining batter, fold orange peel. Spoon half the orange batter into ungreased 10-inch tube pan; drop half the chocolate batter on top by spoonfuls. Repeat layers. Gently swirl with knife for marbled effect, leaving definite orange and chocolate areas. Bake 1 hour and 15 to 20 minutes or until top springs back when touched lightly. Immediately invert cake onto heatproof funnel; cool cake completely. Remove cake from pan; invert onto serving plate. Prepare Orange Glaze; spread over top of cake, allowing glaze to run down sides. Garnish as desired.

Makes 12 to 16 servings

Techniques for Rich Chocolate Truffle Cake

Step 1. *Lining bottom of pan with foil.*

Step 6. *Removing side of pan.*

Step 7. *Placing waxed paper strips around edge of plate.*

Orange Glaze

⅓ **cup butter or margarine**
  2 **cups powdered sugar**
  2 **tablespoons orange juice**
½ **teaspoon freshly grated orange peel**

In medium saucepan over low heat, melt butter. Remove from heat; gradually stir in powdered sugar, orange juice and orange peel, beating until smooth and of desired consistency. Add additional orange juice, 1 teaspoon at a time, if needed.

Rich Chocolate Truffle Cake

  2 **packages (8 ounces each) semisweet chocolate (16 squares)**
1½ **cups butter or margarine**
  1 **cup sugar**
½ **cup light cream**
  6 **large eggs**
  2 **teaspoons vanilla extract**
    Chocolate Curls (recipe follows, optional)
    Chocolate Glaze (recipe follows)
    Sweetened whipped cream (optional)
    Fresh mint leaves (optional)

1. Preheat oven to 350°F. Line bottom of springform pan with foil, tucking foil edges under bottom. Attach springform side. Bring foil up around side of pan. Grease foil-lined bottom and side of pan with butter.

2. Heat chocolate, butter, sugar and cream in heavy 2-quart saucepan over low heat until chocolate melts and mixture is smooth, stirring frequently. Remove from heat.

3. Beat eggs and vanilla in large bowl with wire whisk until frothy. Slowly whisk in warm chocolate mixture until well blended. *Do not vigorously beat batter. You do not want to incorporate air into batter.*

4. Pour batter into prepared pan. Bake 45 minutes or until wooden toothpick inserted about 1 inch from edge comes out clean and center is set. Cool completely in pan on wire rack.

5. Prepare Chocolate Curls, if desired; refrigerate curls.

6. When cake is cool, carefully remove side of pan. Leave cake on bottom of pan. Wrap cake in foil. Refrigerate until well chilled, at least 4 hours or overnight.

7. Prepare Chocolate Glaze. Remove foil and pan from cake; place upside down on serving plate. Surround with waxed paper strips. Spread warm glaze over top and side of cake with metal spatula. Remove paper after glaze sets.

8. Spoon sweetened whipped cream into decorating bag fitted with medium star tip, if desired. Pipe cream around edge of cake. Garnish piped cream with Chocolate Curls and mint leaves, if desired. Refrigerate until serving.

Makes 16 to 20 servings

Rich Chocolate Truffle Cake

Chocolate Curls

1 square (1 ounce) semisweet
    chocolate, coarsely chopped
1 teaspoon vegetable shortening

1. Place chocolate and shortening in 2-cup glass measure. Microwave at HIGH (100% power) about 1½ minutes or until chocolate is melted, stirring every 30 seconds.

2. Pour chocolate mixture onto back of baking pan, marble slab or other heat-resistant flat surface. Quickly spread chocolate into thin layer with metal spatula. Refrigerate about 10 minutes or until firm, but still pliable (technique on page 76).

3. Holding small straight-edge metal spatula at a 45° angle, push spatula firmly along baking pan, under chocolate, so chocolate curls as it is pushed (technique on page 76). (If chocolate is too firm to curl, let it stand a few minutes at room temperature. Refrigerate again if it becomes too soft.) Using small skewer, transfer curls to waxed paper.

Chocolate Glaze

1 cup semisweet chocolate chips
2 tablespoons butter or margarine
3 tablespoons half-and-half
2 tablespoons light corn syrup

Heat chips and butter in heavy 1-quart saucepan over low heat, stirring frequently. Remove from heat. Stir in half-and-half and corn syrup until smooth.

Makes about 1¼ cups

CAKE DECORATING

Elaborate cake decorating is an art that turns an ordinary cake into a masterpiece. Requiring much training and practice, it is not for the inexperienced cook. However, there are many simple tricks that anyone can use to create sensational cakes. The easiest tricks are to add garnishes to cakes and special touches to frosting with simple kitchen tools.

❦

Making swirls in frosting.

Making wide ridges in frosting with a metal spatula.

Making narrow ridges in frosting with a cake comb.

CAKES

The perfect cake for decorating is firm and moist, but not crumbly. The Yellow Butter Cake recipe (page 93) and the Quick & Easy Chocolate Cake (page 127) are perfect for decorating. Cake-mix cakes are more difficult to decorate because they are more tender and crumbly. Placing a cooled cake in the freezer for 30 to 45 minutes will make it easier to frost and decorate.

FILLING AND FROSTING

Always cool a cake completely before frosting it. Use a soft pastry brush to remove all loose cake crumbs. If possible, make the cake the day before you plan to frost it; this makes it easier to work with. If you wish to decorate the cake the day it is made, place it in the freezer as directed above while you make the frosting.

The consistency of the frosting is important. Beginners should use uncooked frostings, such as Cream Cheese Frosting (page 224), Easy Fudge Frosting (page 224) and Buttercream Frosting (page 225). Commercially prepared canned frosting can also be used. Frosting that is too soft will not hold its shape. If the frosting is too soft because the kitchen is warm, refrigerate the frosting for about 15 minutes and

keep it chilled while you work. If the frosting is soft because too much liquid was used, beat in some additional sifted powdered sugar. If the frosting is too stiff to spread easily, beat in additional milk, one teaspoon at a time, until the desired consistency is achieved.

Place the bottom cake layer on a flat plate and place waxed paper strips under the cake's edge. Spoon a mound of frosting, about ½ cup, on top of this layer and spread it evenly over the cake with a metal spatula.

Top with a second cake layer. Spread a thin layer of base frosting over the entire cake to seal in crumbs; let the cake stand for at least 15 minutes. Then, spread the side with a thicker final layer of frosting, working from the bottom toward the top and turning the cake as needed. Keep the spatula well coated with frosting so that it doesn't pick up crumbs from the cake. If the spatula does pick up crumbs, wipe it with paper towels before dipping it back into the frosting.

To frost the cake top, spoon a mound of frosting in the center and spread it outward to all edges. Be careful not to mix crumbs into the frosting. Finish off the cake using one of these decorative frosting touches.

Swirls: With a metal spatula or the back of a teaspoon, carefully make swirls in the frosting on the side and top of the cake.

Ridges: With a metal spatula, make wide, evenly spaced ridges in the frosting on the side of the cake by pulling the spatula from the bottom of the cake to the top, cleaning the spatula of excess frosting as necessary. Make ridges on the cake top by sweeping the metal spatula through the frosting from side to side in evenly spaced strokes.

Narrow Ridges: For narrow ridges, drag an icing or cake comb around the top and side of the cake. Turn the cake plate, by hand or on a turntable, for greater ease in decorating.

Piping: Piping can be as elaborate as making bouquets of roses from decorator's frosting or as simple as making straight lines. Secrets to decorating with a pastry bag are many, and much practice is needed to gain proficiency. If this is your interest, join a class where you can learn from an experienced teacher or look for a book devoted to cake decorating. Lines and writing can be done by anyone with decorating gels, which are available in the supermarket.

Garnishes: Coat the side of cake with chopped nuts, flaked coconut or chocolate jimmies while the frosting is still soft. Or cover the top of the cake with chocolate curls (page 76) or a few chocolate leaves (page 231).

CALZONE

This triangular or half-moon–shaped pizza turnover originated in Naples, Italy, where it is sold as street food. The crust, made from a yeast dough, encases traditional pizza toppings, such as cheese, meat and vegetables. It is almost always baked although it can be deep-fried. Tomato sauce is either added to the filling or served separately for dipping.

☙

Calzone Italiano

> Pizza dough for one 14-inch
>   pizza
> 1¾ cups (15-ounce can)
>   CONTADINA® Pizza Sauce,
>   divided
> 3 ounces sliced pepperoni *or*
>   ½ pound crumbled Italian
>   sausage, cooked, drained
> 2 tablespoons chopped green bell
>   pepper
> 1 cup (4 ounces) shredded
>   mozzarella cheese
> 1 cup (8 ounces) ricotta cheese

Divide dough into 4 equal portions. Place on lightly floured, large, rimless cookie sheet. Press or roll out dough to 7-inch circles. Spread *2 tablespoons* pizza sauce onto half of each circle to within ½ inch of edge; divide pepperoni, bell pepper and mozzarella cheese evenly over pizza sauce. Spoon ¼ cup ricotta cheese onto remaining half of each circle; fold dough over. Press edges together tightly to seal. Cut slits into tops of dough to allow steam to escape. Bake in preheated 350°F. oven for 20 to 25 minutes or until crusts are golden brown. Meanwhile, heat *remaining* pizza sauce; serve over calzones.   *Makes 4 servings*

Note: If desired, 1 large calzone may be made instead of 4 individual calzones. To prepare, shape dough into 1 (13-inch) circle. Spread ½ *cup* pizza sauce onto half of dough; proceed as directed. Bake for 25 minutes.

Calzone Italiano

CANDY

Candies are sweet treats composed primarily of sugar and flavoring. They satisfy our cravings for sugar. Textures vary from rock hard to soft and gooey. Most candy is commercially produced, but some can be prepared at home. Holidays, especially Christmas and Valentine's Day, are perfect times to make homemade candies. The whole family can help create these luscious treats. Give them as gifts and wow your friends and family.

🐝

Classic Caramels
(recipe on page 100)

COOKED CANDIES

Most of the classic candies—fudges, fondants, caramels, toffees and brittles—are cooked candies. Cooked candies are formed from a boiling syrup made from sugar, a liquid, and a variety of ingredients for flavor. They are prepared the conventional way on the rangetop in a heavy saucepan and cooked to the proper temperature.

There are three important things to remember when preparing cooked candies. First, it is necessary to prevent large sugar crystals from forming since they cause the candy to become grainy and coarse in texture. To prevent large crystals, the sugar should be completely dissolved. Large crystals can form on the side of the saucepan; they should be washed down before a candy thermometer is placed in the pan.

To wash down the crystals from the side of a pan, use a pastry brush dipped in hot water. Gently brush the crystals down into the syrup or collect them on the brush bristles. Dip the brush frequently in hot water to clean off the bristles. Another easy way to wash down crystals is to place a cover on the pan for 2 or 3 minutes. This allows the trapped steam to wash down the crystals. If you use the cover method, make sure the syrup does not boil over.

Second, it is important to cook candy to the correct temperature. If you make cooked candy often, a candy thermometer is essential. Thermometers are available in cookware stores and some supermarkets. Test the accuracy of your candy thermometer before using. If a candy thermometer is not available, use the cold water test as described in the section titled "Cold Water Test." However, using a thermometer is much easier and more accurate. The proper use and testing for accuracy of candy thermometers are discussed in the section titled "Candy Thermometers."

The shape, size and thickness of the pan will determine the time required for the syrup to reach its final temperature. Times given in recipes are only approximate. It is more important to refer to the temperatures of the syrups. Also, the temperatures are given in ranges. To achieve the proper consistency, the syrup must be heated to at least the minimum temperature without exceeding the higher temperature. Heating the syrup concentrates it. The longer the syrup is heated, the more liquid is evaporated and the more concentrated the syrup becomes. The higher the temperature, the firmer and more brittle the candy will be.

Third, candies, such as fudges, must be cooled to lukewarm before they can be beaten and shaped. This cooling can take almost 2 hours for large fudge recipes, and patience is necessary. *Do not place the hot candy mixture in the refrigerator or freezer to cool unless noted in the recipe.*

Saucepans: Heavy saucepans with flat bottoms will prevent candy from scorching during cooking. Pans should be large enough to prevent syrups from boiling and foaming over the rims. Always use the size pan suggested in the recipe and never double cooked-candy recipes.

Cold Water Test: Place a small amount of the hot syrup into a cup of very cold, but not iced, water. Using your fingers, remove the cooled syrup. If the syrup has not reached the desired stage, continue cooking the candy and test again.

Soft-Ball Stage (234° to 240°F): The cooled syrup can be rolled into a soft ball that flattens when removed from water.

Firm-Ball Stage (244° to 248°F): The syrup can be rolled into a firm ball that does not flatten immediately when removed from water.

Hard-Ball Stage (250° to 266°F): The syrup can be rolled into a firm ball that gives some resistance when pressed.

Soft-Crack Stage (270° to 290°F): The syrup can be stretched into strands that are hard but elastic.

Hard-Crack Stage (300° to 310°F): The syrup forms strands that are hard and brittle and can easily be snapped in half.

Candy Thermometers: Candy thermometers are the most accurate way of determining the temperature of boiling syrup. Always attach the thermometer to the side of the pan after washing down sugar crystals. Make sure that the thermometer does not touch the bottom of the pan. Read the thermometer at eye level.

Verify the accuracy of a candy thermometer by checking its reading in boiling water. Water normally boils at 212°F at sea level. If your thermometer does not read 212°F, either you do not live at sea level or your thermometer is not accurate. (Water always boils at a lower temperature above sea level because there is less air pressure.) To adjust the temperature given on a recipe, add or subtract the difference from 212°F as needed. For example, if your thermometer reads 210°F in boiling water and the recipe temperature is 240°F, cook the candy to 238°F, or 2°F less than the temperature stated in the recipe.

Soft-Ball Stage

Firm-Ball Stage

Hard-Ball Stage

Soft-Crack Stage

Hard-Crack Stage

UNCOOKED CANDIES

Uncooked candies can be as rich and creamy as cooked candies. Truffles and nut clusters are examples of uncooked candies. The ingredients are mixed, then either shaped into balls, coated or pressed into pans or molds. Ingredients typically used for uncooked candies are fruits, nuts, sweetened condensed milk, evaporated milk, powdered sugar, marshmallows and extracts. Some uncooked candies are mixed and topped or coated with melted chocolate. While a heat source is needed to melt the chocolate, these candies are still considered uncooked.

A NOTE ABOUT MELTING CHOCOLATE

To prevent scorching, chocolate should be melted with care. It can be melted in a saucepan over direct heat at a very low setting, in a double boiler or in a microwave oven. See Chocolate, page 127, for detailed melting directions.

A NOTE ABOUT BUTTER

Butter, not margarine, should be used in most candy recipes to ensure the best texture and results. Butter also contributes flavor to candies. Today many margarines have added water to decrease the amount of fat they contain. Margarine-type products marked as "spreads" or those that come in tubs should *not* be used because their water content will cause melted chocolate to become stiff and grainy. Also, the added water will change cooking times for cooked candies. If you must use margarine, use only *stick products labeled as margarine.*

> ## Tip
>
> *Do not store hard candies with other candy. Moisture from soft candies will make hard candies sticky.*

Classic Caramels

2 cups sugar
2 cups light corn syrup
1 cup half-and-half
1 cup unsalted butter
½ teaspoon salt
1 cup whipping cream
1 teaspoon vanilla extract

1. Line 8-inch square pan with heavy-duty foil, pressing foil into corners to cover completely and leaving 1-inch overhang on sides. Lightly butter foil.

2. Combine sugar, syrup, half-and-half, butter and salt in deep heavy 4- or 4½-quart saucepan. Bring to a boil over medium-high heat, stirring occasionally. Wash down sugar crystals with pastry brush, if necessary.

3. Attach candy thermometer to side of pan, making sure bulb is submerged in sugar mixture but not touching bottom of pan. Continue boiling about 25 minutes or until sugar mixture reaches firm-ball stage (244° to 246°F) on candy thermometer, stirring frequently. (If you do not have a thermometer, boil until spoonful of mixture, when dropped into very cold water, forms a firm ball that does not flatten immediately when removed from water.) Remove from heat and gradually stir in cream. Return to medium heat and cook about 15 minutes or until mixture reaches 248°F on candy thermometer, stirring frequently.

4. Remove from heat; stir in vanilla. Immediately pour into prepared pan. (Do not scrape saucepan.) Cool at room temperature 3 to 4 hours until firm, or cover with plastic wrap and let stand overnight. (Candy will be harder to cut if cooled overnight.)

5. Remove from pan by lifting caramels using foil handles. Place on cutting board; peel off foil. Cut into 1-inch strips with long thin-bladed knife. Cut each strip into 1-inch squares with buttered knife or kitchen shears. Wrap caramels individually in small squares of plastic wrap. Store in airtight container at room temperature up to 2 weeks.

Makes 64 caramels
(about 2½ pounds)

Chocolate Caramels: Add 1 bar (4 ounces) chopped sweet dark chocolate to sugar mixture after it comes to a boil. Proceed as directed.

Gingerbread Caramel Corn

10 cups popped, lightly salted popcorn (about ⅔ cup unpopped *or* 1 package [3½ ounces] microwave popcorn)
1 cup lightly salted roasted cashews (optional)
1 cup firmly packed dark brown sugar
½ cup butter (do not use margarine or shortening)
¼ cup light corn syrup
1 teaspoon ground ginger
1 teaspoon ground cinnamon
½ teaspoon baking soda

1. Preheat oven to 250°F. Line 17×11-inch shallow roasting pan with foil or use disposable foil roasting pan.

2. Combine popcorn and cashews in prepared pan; set aside.

3. Combine sugar, butter and syrup in heavy 1½- or 2-quart saucepan. Bring to a boil over medium heat, stirring constantly. Wash down sugar crystals with pastry brush, if necessary.

4. Attach candy thermometer to side of pan, making sure bulb is submerged in sugar mixture but not touching bottom of pan. Continue boiling, without stirring, about 5 minutes or until sugar mixture reaches soft-crack stage (290°F) on candy thermometer. (If you do not

have a thermometer, boil until spoonful of mixture, when dropped into very cold water, can be stretched into threads that are hard but elastic when removed from water.) Remove from heat; stir in ginger, cinnamon and baking soda. Immediately drizzle sugar mixture slowly over popcorn mixture; stir until evenly coated.

5. Bake 1 hour, stirring quickly every 15 minutes. Transfer to large baking sheet lined with foil; spread caramel corn out in single layer. Cool completely, about 10 minutes. Store in airtight container at room temperature.

Makes about 10 cups
caramel corn

Gingerbread
Caramel Corn

Rich Cocoa Fudge

    3 cups sugar
    ²/₃ cup HERSHEY'S Cocoa
    ⅛ teaspoon salt
    1½ cups milk
    ¼ cup (½ stick) butter or
        margarine
    1 teaspoon vanilla extract

Line 8- or 9-inch square pan with foil, extending foil over edges of pan. Butter foil. In heavy 4-quart saucepan, stir together sugar, cocoa and salt; stir in milk. Cook over medium heat, stirring constantly, until mixture comes to a full rolling boil. Boil, without stirring, until mixture reaches 234°F on candy thermometer or until syrup, when dropped into very cold water, forms a soft ball that flattens when removed from water. (Bulb of thermometer should not rest on bottom of saucepan.) Remove from heat. Add butter and vanilla. *Do not stir.* Cool at room temperature to 110°F (lukewarm). Beat with wooden spoon until fudge thickens and just begins to lose some of its gloss. Quickly spread into prepared pan; cool completely. Use foil to lift fudge out of pan; peel off foil. Cut into squares. Store in tightly covered container at room temperature.

Makes about 36 pieces

Rich Cocoa Fudge

Note: For best results, do *not* double this recipe.

Nutty Rich Cocoa Fudge: Beat cooked fudge as directed. Immediately stir in 1 cup chopped almonds, pecans or walnuts; quickly spread into prepared pan.

Marshmallow-Nut Cocoa Fudge: Increase cocoa to ¾ cup. Cook fudge as directed. Add 1 cup marshmallow creme with butter and vanilla. *(Do not stir.)* Cool to 110°F (lukewarm). Beat 8 minutes; stir in 1 cup chopped nuts. Pour into prepared pan. (Fudge will not set until poured into pan.)

CANNING

Canning is a method of preserving food that uses heat to destroy harmful microorganisms, inactivate enzymes that cause spoilage, and create an airtight vacuum-sealed jar. Foods such as fruits, vegetables, stews, sauces and relishes are suitable for canning.

🐝

There are two methods of processing canned foods, depending on the pH (acidity level) of the food. Acidic foods, such as fruits, pickles and some tomatoes, are canned by the boiling water-bath method, which involves cooking the food in canning jars in a 212°F water bath for a period of time specific to the food. Low-acid foods, such as vegetables, meats, poultry and fish, must be processed in a steam-pressure canner, which produces a superheated temperature of 240°F. During the canning process air in the jar is forced out, which creates a vacuum that seals the lid to the jar. This seal is necessary to prevent contamination of the food by harmful organisms.

For additional information and detailed instructions about canning, contact the United States Department of Agriculture, a county agricultural extension agent or consult literature from one of the large canning jar manufacturers. Since canning information has been updated in recent years, make sure that any printed materials are current.

Not all varieties of tomatoes have enough acid to allow them to be safely processed by the boiling water-bath method. Often newer hybrids are lower in acid. Before canning tomatoes, always determine the tomato variety and ask the county agricultural extension agent if it is safe to process by this method. When in doubt, process tomatoes in a steam-pressure canner.

CANNOLI

Cannoli is a rich Italian dessert composed of a tube-shaped pastry shell that has been deep fried to a crispy golden brown. It is filled with a traditional creamy filling of whipped sweetened ricotta cheese, candied fruit, chocolate bits and chopped pistachio nuts.

❦

CAPER

Capers are deep green flower buds of a Mediterranean bush that have been preserved in a vinegary brine. They range slightly in size. They may be as tiny as a peppercorn or as large as a pistachio nut. The smallest variety, called nonpareil, is from France and is considered the best. Capers have a piquant, slightly bitter taste. They are used in salad dressings, as a condiment and in sauces for meat and seafood. Rinse them in cold water to remove excess salt before using.

❦

CARAMELIZE, TO

Caramelizing is the technique of cooking sugar, sometimes with a small amount of water, to a very high temperature (between 310°F and 360°F) so that it melts into a clear brown liquid and develops a characteristic flavor. The color can vary from light golden brown to dark brown. Caramelized sugar, sometimes called "burnt sugar," is used in a variety of desserts and sauces.

❦

Caramelized Nuts

1 cup slivered almonds, pecans or walnuts
⅓ cup sugar
½ teaspoon ground cinnamon (optional)
¼ teaspoon grated nutmeg (optional)

1. To toast nuts, cook and stir in medium skillet over medium heat 9 to 12 minutes until light golden brown. Transfer to small bowl.

2. Sprinkle sugar evenly over bottom of skillet. Cook, without stirring, 2 to 4 minutes until sugar is melted. Remove from heat.

3. Quickly add nuts to skillet; sprinkle with cinnamon and nutmeg, if desired. Return to heat; stir until nuts are coated with melted sugar mixture. Transfer to plate; cool completely.

4. Place nuts on cutting board; coarsely chop. Store in airtight container up to 2 weeks.

Makes 1 cup nuts

Tip

Care should be taken when caramelizing sugar because the melted sugar can cause serious burns if spilled or splattered.

CAROB

Carob, also known as locust bean or St. John's bread, is made from the pulp of the leathery pods of the tropical carob tree. The pulp is dried, roasted and ground into a powder. Its flavor is somewhat like chocolate and thus can be used as a chocolate substitute. Carob powder as well as fresh and dried carob pods may be found in specialty food markets.

CARROT

Carrots can be traced back more than two thousand years to the hills of Afghanistan, where the people were sun-worshipers who believed that eating yellow and orange foods brought virtue and piety. For centuries, carrots were believed to have various curative powers. Today it is known that carrots are an excellent source of beta-carotene, a precursor of vitamin A.

Tip

If carrots become limp, soak them in ice water for 30 minutes to restore their crispness.

Varieties: Other than baby carrots, Americans seldom distinguish among different kinds of carrots. Gardeners can select from numerous varieties of carrot hybrids that are developed to perform in specific kinds of soil.

Availability: Carrots are available year-round in plastic bags. Carrots with the green tops attached are also available in most supermarkets. Growing soil affects the flavor of carrots. Many believe that California soil produces the sweetest carrots. Carrots are also available frozen and canned. Carrot juice may be purchased or prepared at home with a juice extractor.

Buying Tips: Fresh carrots should be slender, firm, smooth and a healthy reddish-orange color. Avoid carrots that are cracked, limp or have begun to send out tiny white roots—these are signs of overly long storage. The top, or "shoulder," of the carrot may be tinged with green but should not be dark or black. The smaller the fibrous middlecore, the sweeter the carrot. Since the core can't be seen until the carrot is cut, note that carrots with thick shoulders are more apt to have large cores. Carrots with green tops attached lose sweetness quickly so purchase them only if you can use them in a day or two. The tops should be bright green and fresh.

Yield: 1 pound carrots = 3 cups chopped or sliced; 2½ cups shredded.

Storage: Store carrots in a plastic bag in the refrigerator's vegetable drawer. Packaged carrots may be kept in the refrigerator up to two weeks. Carrots with green tops (tops should be removed before storing) must be used within a day or two. Avoid storing carrots with apples, pears or other fruits that produce ethylene gas when ripening as this gas can give carrots a bitter taste.

Basic Preparation: Young or baby carrots need only be rinsed before cooking. Older carrots should be rinsed, scrubbed with a vegetable brush if imbedded soil is present, and lightly peeled with a swivel-bladed vegetable peeler or a paring knife. Trim off the stem and root ends. Cut carrots crosswise into slices or one- or two-inch-long chunks. Cutting carrots, whether into slices or chunks, on the diagonal gives an attractive appearance. Small carrots can be left whole.

Carrots may be steamed or boiled in a small amount of liquid until crisp-tender. Cooking until just crisp-tender actually improves the availability of nutrients and enhances the carrots' sweetness. Carrot slices or chunks can also be baked in a covered dish, lightly salted and topped with a little butter, if desired, at 350°F for about 40 minutes or at 400°F for about 30 minutes.

Fresh carrots can be shredded by hand using the large holes of a four-sided grater or with a food processor fitted with the shredding disc. Shredded carrots can be used in salads and carrot cakes.

Orange-Glazed Carrots

1 pound fresh or frozen baby carrots, thawed
⅓ cup orange marmalade
2 tablespoons butter
2 teaspoons Dijon mustard
½ teaspoon grated fresh ginger

1. Bring 1 inch lightly salted water to a boil in 2-quart saucepan over high heat. Immediately add carrots; return to a boil. Reduce heat to low. Cover; simmer 10 to 12 minutes for fresh carrots (8 to 10 minutes for frozen carrots) until crisp-tender. Drain well; return carrots to saucepan.

2. Stir in marmalade, butter, mustard and ginger. Cook, uncovered, over medium heat 3 minutes or until carrots are glazed, stirring occasionally. Garnish as desired. Serve immediately. Or, carrots may be transferred to microwave-safe casserole dish with lid. Cover and refrigerate up to 8 hours before serving. To reheat, microwave at HIGH (100% power) 4 to 5 minutes until hot.

Makes 6 side-dish servings

Note: Recipe may be doubled to serve 10 to 12.

Orange-Glazed Carrots

Toll House® Carrot Cake

      2 cups all-purpose flour
      1 teaspoon baking powder
      1 teaspoon baking soda
      1 teaspoon salt
      1 teaspoon ground cinnamon
      ¼ teaspoon ground nutmeg
      3 eggs
      1¼ cups granulated sugar
      ¾ cup vegetable oil
      1 teaspoon vanilla extract
      1¾ cups shredded carrots
      1 cup (8-ounce can) crushed
            pineapple in juice, undrained
      1 cup chopped nuts
      2 cups (12-ounce package)
            NESTLÉ® TOLL HOUSE® Semi-
            Sweet Chocolate Mini
            Morsels, divided
      Citrus Cream Cheese Frosting
      (recipe follows)

COMBINE flour, baking powder, baking soda, salt, cinnamon and nutmeg in small bowl. Beat eggs, sugar, oil and vanilla in large mixer bowl until well blended. Gradually add flour mixture. Stir in carrots, pineapple and juice, nuts and *1¾ cups* morsels.

POUR into greased and floured 13×9-inch baking pan. Bake in preheated 350°F. oven for 45 to 50 minutes until wooden toothpick inserted into center comes out clean. Cool completely. Spread with Citrus Cream Cheese Frosting and sprinkle with *remaining* morsels.

Makes 16 servings

Citrus Cream Cheese Frosting:
COMBINE 4 ounces softened cream cheese and 2 tablespoons softened butter or margarine in small mixer bowl. Add 3 cups sifted powdered sugar; mix thoroughly. Stir in 1 tablespoon orange juice and 1 tablespoon lemon juice. Add additional orange juice if necessary until frosting is of spreading consistency.

Tip

Carrots add moistness and sweetness to baked goods, such as cake and muffins.

CAULIFLOWER

Although cultivated in Europe and the Mediterranean region since the sixteenth century, major production in the United States only began in the 1920's. Today most of the cauliflower sold here is grown in California. The cauliflower head contains small, tightly compact white florets on thick stems. The entire plant is edible, including the leaves. Cauliflower has a cabbagelike flavor that is milder after cooking. While growing, the outside green leaves envelop the cauliflower head protecting it from bright sunlight. This assures a creamy white head.

🐝

Varieties: Most common is the creamy white variety, but a purple variety is also available.

Availability: Fresh cauliflower is available all year with its peak season from late fall to spring. It is sold in heads and as florets. Frozen cauliflower is also available.

Buying Tips: Choose firm, heavy heads with compact florets. Leaves should be crisp and green without signs of yellowing. Avoid heads that have a speckled appearance or brown spots. A medium head of cauliflower weighs about two pounds.

Yield: 1 pound trimmed cauliflower = 1½ cups florets.
1 (10-ounce) package frozen cauliflower = 2 cups.

Storage: Because cauliflower acquires a strong odor with long storage, plan to use it within one week. Store it unwashed in a perforated plastic bag. Washed raw florets, tightly wrapped in plastic, will keep refrigerated for three to five days. Cooked cauliflower does not store well. It is best to cook only what will be eaten at one meal.

Basic Preparation: Cut the leaves from the cauliflower by slicing through the stem between the head and leaves with a chef's knife. Remove and discard the leaves and stem. Cut around the core with a paring knife; remove and discard the core.

Rinse the head thoroughly under cold running water. Cook whole, or separate the head into florets using a paring knife. Place the whole head, stem side down, in a large pan. Cook it covered in one inch of boiling water until the stem end is tender when pierced with a fork, 10 to 12 minutes. Florets can be steamed, boiled or stir-fried until crisp-tender.

Crumb-Topped Snowball

1 large head cauliflower (about 1¼ pounds)
4 tablespoons butter or margarine
1 cup fresh bread crumbs (about 2 slices)
2 green onions, thinly sliced
2 eggs, hard cooked, finely chopped
2 tablespoons fresh lemon juice
Chopped fresh parsley, lemon peel strips and baby sunburst squash (optional)

1. To prepare cauliflower, cut leaves from cauliflower by slicing through stem between head and leaves; remove and discard leaves and stem.

2. Cut around core, being careful not to separate florets from head; remove and discard core. Rinse.

3. Pour 1 inch water into large saucepan. Place cauliflower, stem side down, in water; cover saucepan. Bring to a boil over high heat; reduce heat to low. Simmer 10 to 12 minutes until crisp-tender; drain. Place cauliflower in ungreased 8×8-inch baking dish.

4. Preheat oven to 375°F. Melt butter in small skillet over medium heat. Stir in crumbs and onions; cook until crumbs are lightly browned. Stir in eggs and juice. Pat crumb mixture evenly over top of cauliflower. Place any extra crumb mixture in baking dish.

5. Bake 10 minutes or until crumb mixture is crispy and lightly browned. Garnish with parsley, lemon peel and squash, if desired. Serve immediately.
Makes 6 side-dish servings

Technique for Crumb-Topped Snowball

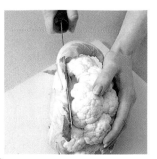

Step 1. *Removing leaves from cauliflower.*

Crumb-Topped Snowball

Microwaved Broccoli & Cauliflower with Mustard Sauce

2 cups broccoli florets
2 cups cauliflorets
⅓ to ½ cup skim milk
1 tablespoon all-purpose flour
1½ teaspoons prepared mustard
¼ teaspoon salt (optional)
Dash garlic powder
Dash ground white pepper

1. Combine broccoli and cauliflower in microwave-safe baking dish; cover. Microwave at HIGH (100% power) 8 to 11 minutes until tender, stirring once. Drain; set aside.

2. Combine milk, flour, mustard, salt, if desired, garlic powder and pepper in medium microwave-safe bowl. Microwave at HIGH 2 to 3 minutes until thickened, stirring every minute. Pour over vegetables; toss to coat. Serve immediately.

Makes 4 side-dish servings

Tip

Limp or wilted celery can be freshened by soaking trimmed ribs in a bowl of ice water for about one hour.

CAVIAR

Caviar, one of the world's most celebrated and expensive appetizers, is simply salted fish eggs (or roe). They may be black, gray, red or gold. The finest and technically the only authentic caviar comes from sturgeon, although other species of fish yield suitable roe. Beluga, osetra and sevruga are the three main types of caviar. Beluga sturgeon from the Caspian Sea, prized for its large eggs, is considered the best. Other less costly caviar comes from lumpfish, whitefish and salmon.

🐝

CELERY

Celery has a rather colorful history compared to its present mundane culinary role. For example, Romans believed that wreaths of celery would protect them from hangovers, and medieval magicians put celery seeds in their shoes in order to fly. A bunch of celery is more precisely referred to as a stalk composed of individual ribs. Celery is often erroneously thought to have "negative calories"; in other words, more calories are used to chew it than it contains. However, at about only 6 calories per rib, it is virtually calorie-free.

🐝

Varieties: Although several varieties of celery ranging from light to dark green are grown in the United States, Pascal celery is the most common. Celery root, or celeriac, comes from a variety of celery that is cultivated specifically for its root. It should not be confused with celery.

Availability: Celery is available all year with California and Florida producing 90 percent of the United States crop. Prepackaged celery hearts are the tender innermost ribs of the celery.

Buying Tips: Choose celery stalks in a tightly formed bunch with shiny bright green ribs; dark green stalks may be stringy. The leaves should look fresh and the leaf stems should be crisp.

Yield: 1 medium celery rib, trimmed of leaves = about ½ cup chopped or sliced.

Storage: Celery is a good keeper. Store it in a plastic bag in the refrigerator for up to two weeks.

Basic Preparation: Separate the ribs from the stalk. Rinse ribs under cold running water to remove sand and dirt, rubbing lightly with a fingertip to loosen soil at the bottom of the rib. Trim off the leaves. They can be saved to flavor soups or stocks. Darker green outer ribs may be stringy, but do not discard them. Remove the strings and use the ribs for cooking. To remove tough strings, snap a short piece from the top of a rib that has been trimmed below the joint, leaving the short piece attached. Pull the piece down the length of the rib. The strings and outer membrane will pull off.

Frenched Beans with Celery

3/4 **pound fresh green beans**
2 **ribs celery**
2 **tablespoons butter, melted**
2 **tablespoons toasted sunflower**
   seeds*
   Carrot slices (optional)

To toast sunflower seeds, heat 1/2 teaspoon oil in small skillet over medium heat. Add shelled sunflower seeds; cook and stir 3 minutes or until lightly browned, shaking pan constantly. Remove with slotted spoon to paper towels.

1. Place beans in colander; rinse well. Snap off stem end from each bean; discard. Slice beans lengthwise; set aside.

2. To prepare celery, trim stem end and leaves from ribs. Reserve leaves for garnish, if desired. Slice ribs into thin diagonal slices.

3. Bring 1 inch water to a boil in 2-quart saucepan over high heat. Add beans and celery. Cover; reduce heat to medium-low. Simmer 8 minutes or until beans are crisp-tender; drain. Toss beans and celery with butter. Transfer to warm serving dish. Sprinkle with sunflower seeds. Garnish with reserved celery leaves and carrot slices, if desired. Serve immediately.

Makes 6 side-dish servings

Frenched Beans with Celery

CHEESE

Cheese, said the ancient Greeks, was a gift of benevolent gods. Then, as now, cheese was a means of preserving milk, making it a useful, versatile food. Cheesemaking has evolved into an art practiced all around the world. There are hundreds of types available today, each with its own distinctive flavor and texture.

☙

Many factors affect the flavor and texture of cheese, but the list can be simplified to include three main elements: the milk source, the cheesemaking process and the aging procedure.

The Cheesemaking Process: Cheesemaking can be reduced to two absolutes: mammal's milk (whether cow, sheep, goat or buffalo's milk) and liquid extraction. Removing liquid matter (or whey) from the milk leaves semisolids (or curd) that contain protein, fat and nutritional value. Cheese is made from the curd. When milk sours, it naturally separates into curds and whey. To make cheese, however, the souring process is hastened in unspoiled milk by adding rennet (an enzyme found in the stomach lining of calves or other small animals) or lactic acid.

The size the curds are cut into determines the moisture in the final cheese. For soft, high-moisture cheeses, the curds are cut into large pieces. For hard cheeses, the curds are cut into small pieces or combed into strands.

Aging: To ripen, the cheese may be soaked in brine, waxed, washed, covered with ashes or left plain. Some cheeses are barely ripened, if at all. Popular unripened (or fresh) cheeses are cottage cheese, cream cheese and ricotta. Other cheeses may be aged for up to four years, during which time the cheesemaker manipulates and controls many conditions. For instance, holey cheeses are turned periodically to disperse holes evenly, and blue-veined cheeses are pierced with needles to add veins.

Categories of Natural Cheeses: Natural cheeses are categorized by the amount of moisture they contain. Categories include hard cheese, such as Parmesan, with 30 percent moisture; firm, such as Cheddar, with 30 to 40 percent moisture; semisoft, such as Monterey Jack, with 40 to 50 percent moisture; soft and ripened, such as Brie, with 50 to 75 percent moisture; and soft and unripened, such as cream cheese, with 80 percent moisture.

Types of Natural Cheeses: Americans have access to an abundant array of cheeses, domestic and imported. Some of the most popular types are listed in the chart (pages 112–113), although there are many others worth exploring.

Cheese Products: Aside from the natural cheeses described above, there are other important cheese products—all made from natural cheeses.

Process cheese (or pasteurized process cheese) is made by grinding together different lots of cheese, some ripe, others "green." Water can be added along with chemical emulsifiers, and the mixture is heated. The advantage of process cheese is that it melts easily and smoothly.

Cheese food (or pasteurized process cheese food) is made much the same way as process cheese, but with added milk solids, moisture, salt and emulsifiers. It has more moisture than process cheese and shares similar melting characteristics.

Cheese spreads (or pasteurized process cheese spreads) are similar to process cheese and cheese food, except they are softer, more spreadable and often have added flavorings or ingredients, such as olives or garlic.

Coldpack cheese is made from several types of natural cheese that are combined into a spreadable product without heat or emulsifiers. This snacking cheese is often flavored or smoked.

Nonfat cheeses are made from skim milk. Special dietary needs may create a niche for them, but they may melt differently than other cheese products.

Storage: Cheese should be refrigerated. Unopened packaged cheese can be left in the original wrapping, but bulk cheese should be wrapped tightly in plastic wrap or foil. With the exception of cream-style cottage cheese, cheese can be frozen for two to three months; however, texture and taste will be affected to some degree. Cheese that has been frozen is best used in cooked dishes rather than for snacking.

Serving: A small amount of surface mold on hard or firm cheese can be cut away and the cheese safely used. With semisoft cheese, it is more difficult to judge the degree of mold penetration. If mold is limited to a small area on the surface, trim that part away as well as the surrounding

area and use the rest immediately. Otherwise, semisoft cheese with several areas of mold should be discarded. Soft and fresh cheeses that show any sign of mold should be discarded.

Serve almost all types of cheese at or near room temperature for the best flavor. This is especially true for appetizer cheese trays and cheese and fruit desserts where cheese is the star. Exceptions are soft, fresh cheeses, such as cottage and cream cheese, although even these are best when not too cold. Cheese grates or shreds better when well chilled.

Baked Apricot Brie
(recipe on page 114)

POPULAR CHEESES IN THE UNITED STATES

Type	Characteristics	Uses
American	mild Cheddar-type processed cheese; often sold sliced	cooking, sandwiches
Blue and Blue-veined	class of sharp, creamy cheeses injected with bacteria, resulting in blue or green veins; made from cow, goat or sheep's milk; aromatic and pungent; flavor increases with age; crumbly in texture; American Maytag blue, French Roquefort, English Stilton, Italian Gorgonzola and Danish Danablue	dessert, snacking, topping for salads
Boursin	soft, spreadable triple-cream (75% milk fat) cow's milk cheese from France; often flavored with garlic and herbs	snacking
Brick	a truly American semisoft cheese from Wisconsin; pungent and lively; modeled after Limburger	cooking, sandwiches, snacking
Brie	flat rounds of ultrarich, creamy French cheese with edible white rind; mildly tangy; very creamy to runny in texture at room temperature	cooking, dessert, snacking
Camembert	French cheese made from cow's milk; mild, soft and creamy with edible gray-white rind	dessert, snacking
Cheddar	named after an English village; white to orange firm cheese with mild to sharp flavor; orange Cheddar is colored with annatto, a natural dye	cooking, sandwiches, snacking, topping for salads
Chèvre	generic name for French and French-style goat's cheese; tangy flavor; mild and creamy; with age, flavor is stronger and texture drier; many variations, such as Montrachet and Bûcheron	cooking, snacking, topping for salads
Chihuahua	soft, mild white cow's milk cheese from Mexico; similar to Monterey Jack	cooking
Colby	Wisconsin-made variation of Cheddar; mild and sweet; lighter, softer and more open textured than Cheddar	cooking, sandwiches, snacking
Cottage cheese	fresh cheese made from whole, low fat or skim milk; moist with small or large curds and a mild flavor; short shelf life; available with flavor additions, such as chives and pineapple	baked in cheesecakes, side dish, snacking
Cream cheese	smooth, spreadable, unripened fresh cheese from cow's milk; Neufchâtel is the lower fat and usually softer version	baked in cheesecakes
Edam	yellow cheese, with small holes and red wax coating, from Holland; semisoft texture with mellow nutty flavor	cooking, dessert, sandwiches, snacking
Emmentaler (Emmental)	buttery-yellow firm cheese made in Switzerland; mild sweet-and-nutty flavor with a distinct network of holes	cooking, dessert, snacking
Farmer	fresh soft cheese similar to dry curd cottage cheese; firmer and higher in fat	cooking
Feta	tangy, sharp, salty, brine-cured goat's milk cheese; made in Greece, Bulgaria, France and the United States; soft, white and crumbly	snacking, topping for salads

POPULAR CHEESES IN THE UNITED STATES, *continued*

Type	Characteristics	Uses
Gouda	Dutch straw-colored cheese; mild flavor when young and sharper flavor as it ages; semisoft texture with small holes; sometimes flavored with herbs; baby Gouda comes in small rounds with red wax coating	cooking, dessert, sandwiches, snacking
Gruyère	dry, firm Swiss-made cheese with a nutty taste and aroma; has small holes; usually aged	cooking
Havarti	rich, creamy Danish cheese with small holes; semisoft texture; mild and tangy when young; sharper flavor when aged; sometimes flavored with dill weed or caraway	cooking, sandwiches, snacking
Limburger	creamy, red-rinded German cheese made from cow's milk; notoriously pungent aroma and strong flavor—an acquired taste; goes well with hearty ales	snacking
Mascarpone	recently popularized soft Italian cheese; very rich, creamy and white; sometimes sweetened and flavored	ingredient in tiramisu, snacking
Monterey Jack (Jack)	from Monterey, California; mild, buttery, semisoft cow's milk cheese; sometimes flavored with jalapeño peppers or garlic; usually not aged; aged Monterey Jack is similar to Cheddar and available only on the West Coast	cooking (especially Tex-Mex), sandwiches, snacking
Mozzarella	popular, mild, stringy melting cheese; made from cow's milk; factory-produced mozzarella is semisoft and chewy with a mild flavor; fresh mozzarella, available in Italian markets, has soft texture and sweet, mild flavor; *mozzarella di bufala*, a highly prized product made from water buffalo's milk	cooking (especially pizza and lasagna), sandwiches, snacking
Muenster (Munster)	originally German and French, now made in the United States; pale yellow with very small holes and orange rind; American Muenster is mild flavored while European Muenster is pungent	cooking, sandwiches, snacking
Parmesan (Parmigiano-Reggiano)	Italian hard cheese; usually aged to a dry, crumbly texture and a pleasantly sharp, salty flavor; excellent for grating	cooking, topping for salads
Provolone	firm Italian cheese with a mild, smoky taste; comes in a variety of shapes, but a pear shape is most common	cooking, snacking
Ricotta	soft, fresh white Italian cheese with a sweet, mellow taste; traditionally made from whey, a by-product of cheesemaking, it is not really a cheese; American ricotta is usually made from a combination of whey and milk	baked in cheesecakes, cooking (especially lasagna and manicotti), filling for cannoli and cassata
Romano (Pecorino Romano)	Italian hard cheese made from sheep's milk; pungent flavor; excellent for grating	cooking
Swiss	generic term for a group of pale yellow cheeses with large holes, mild nutty flavor and firm, slightly dry texture; American Swiss is milder than Emmentaler and Gruyère	cooking, sandwiches, snacking

Baked Apricot Brie

1 round (8 ounces) Brie cheese
⅓ cup apricot preserves
2 tablespoons sliced almonds
  Cracked pepper crackers
  Fresh grapes and grape leaves
  (optional)

1. Preheat oven to 400°F. Place cheese in small baking pan. Spread top of cheese with preserves; sprinkle with almonds.

2. Bake 10 to 12 minutes until cheese begins to melt and lose its shape. Serve hot with crackers. Garnish with grapes and grape leaves, if desired. Refrigerate leftovers; reheat before serving.

Makes 6 appetizer servings

*Fettuccine with
Gorgonzola Sauce*

Fettuccine with Gorgonzola Sauce

½ pound asparagus
8 ounces uncooked fettuccine
2 teaspoons olive oil
1 leek, cleaned well, cut into
  ½-inch pieces
1 medium-size red bell pepper,
  seeded, cut into short strips
2 cloves garlic, minced
1 can (15 ounces) artichoke
  hearts, drained, quartered
1 cup cherry tomato halves
  Gorgonzola Sauce (recipe
  follows)
¼ cup grated Parmesan cheese or
  crumbled Gorgonzola
  Additional cherry tomatoes
  (optional)

1. To prepare asparagus, trim off tough ends of spears; peel stem ends with vegetable peeler. Cut asparagus diagonally into 1-inch pieces.

2. Cook fettuccine according to package directions. Drain in colander. Place in large warm bowl; keep warm.

3. Meanwhile, heat oil in large skillet over medium heat. Add asparagus, leek, pepper and garlic; cook and stir 5 to 7 minutes until asparagus is crisp-tender. Add artichokes and tomato halves; cook 2 to 3 minutes until hot. Add to fettuccine; set aside.

4. Prepare Gorgonzola Sauce.

5. Pour Gorgonzola Sauce over fettuccine mixture; toss to coat. Sprinkle with Parmesan cheese. Garnish with tomatoes, if desired.

Makes 4 servings

Gorgonzola Sauce

3 tablespoons butter or margarine
¼ cup all-purpose flour
2 cups milk
¼ cup canned vegetable broth
½ teaspoon ground black pepper
4 ounces Gorgonzola, crumbled

1. Melt butter in small saucepan over medium heat. Stir in flour. Cook and stir 2 to 3 minutes until bubbly. Gradually stir in milk, broth and pepper. Cook until thickened, stirring constantly.

2. Reduce heat to low. Stir in cheese until melted.

Makes about 2¹/₂ cups sauce

Rigatoni with Four Cheeses

    3 cups milk
    1 tablespoon chopped carrot
    1 tablespoon chopped celery
    1 tablespoon chopped onion
    1 tablespoon fresh parsley sprigs
    ¹/₂ bay leaf
    ¹/₄ teaspoon black peppercorns
    ¹/₄ teaspoon hot pepper sauce
       Dash ground nutmeg
    ¹/₄ cup butter
    ¹/₄ cup all-purpose flour
    ¹/₂ cup grated Wisconsin Parmesan
       cheese
    ¹/₄ cup grated Wisconsin Romano
       cheese
    12 ounces uncooked rigatoni,
       cooked according to package
       directions, drained
    1¹/₂ cups (6 ounces) shredded
       Wisconsin Cheddar cheese
    1¹/₂ cups (6 ounces) shredded
       Wisconsin mozzarella cheese
    ¹/₄ teaspoon chili powder

1. Combine milk, carrot, celery, onion, parsley, bay leaf, peppercorns, pepper sauce and nutmeg in large saucepan. Bring to a boil. Reduce heat to low; simmer 10 minutes. Strain; reserve liquid.

2. Preheat oven to 350°F.

3. Melt butter in medium saucepan over medium heat. Stir in flour. Gradually stir in reserved liquid.

Rigatoni with Four Cheeses

Cook, stirring constantly, until thickened. Remove from heat. Add Parmesan and Romano cheeses; stir until blended. Pour into large bowl. Add cooked rigatoni; toss gently to coat.

4. Combine Cheddar and mozzarella cheeses in medium bowl. Place ¹/₂ of pasta mixture in greased 2-quart casserole; sprinkle with cheese mixture. Top with remaining pasta mixture. Sprinkle with chili powder. Bake 25 minutes or until bubbly. Garnish as desired.

Makes 6 servings

Favorite recipe from **Wisconsin Milk Marketing Board**

Tip

When cooking with cheese, use a low temperature and cook it slowly as high temperatures cause it to become rubbery.

using an electric mixer. The cheesecake is usually baked in a crust of finely crushed, sweetened graham cracker crumbs or cookie crumbs that are mixed with just enough melted butter so they hold together. Some cheesecakes have a light sprinkling of crumbs or a pastry in lieu of a crumb crust. The most familiar size is a 9-inch round, baked in a springform pan that has removable sides. Cheesecakes can be baked at a consistent temperature of about 325°F or combination of a brief time at a high temperature (about 425°F) followed by a longer time at a low temperature (about 250°F). After baking, cheesecakes must be thoroughly chilled before serving. They last for several days in the refrigerator and without toppings, they can be frozen.

Lemon Cheesecake

CHEESECAKE

Cheesecake is a creamy baked dessert made from cheese that is sweetened and flavored. The texture can range from airy and light to dense and heavy. Some are flawlessly smooth and moist while others have a drier and more crumbly consistency. Traditional cheesecakes are simply flavored with vanilla or lemon and topped with sour cream or berries. The popularity of this rich dessert has spawned countless variations, such as pumpkin, white chocolate, crème de menthe and apple cinnamon.

☙

The two cheeses most often used to make cheesecakes are cream cheese and ricotta cheese. Sieved cottage cheese is sometimes used, but the resulting cheesecake lacks the creamy texture of one made with cream cheese. The cheese is thoroughly mixed with eggs, liquid and flavorings

Tip

An unbaked refrigerated dessert made of cream cheese, liquid and gelatin for thickening is sometimes referred to as a cheesecake.

Lemon Cheesecake

Crust
   35 vanilla wafers
   ¾ cup slivered almonds, toasted
   ⅓ cup sugar
   ¼ cup butter or margarine, melted

Filling
   3 packages (8 ounces each) cream
      cheese, softened
   ¾ cup sugar
   4 eggs
   ⅓ cup whipping cream
   ¼ cup fresh lemon juice
   1 tablespoon grated lemon peel
   1 teaspoon vanilla extract

Topping
   1 pint strawberries
   2 tablespoons sugar

1. Preheat oven to 375°F.

2. For crust, combine wafers, almonds and ⅓ cup sugar in food processor; process until fine crumbs form. Combine sugar mixture with melted butter in medium bowl. Press mixture evenly onto bottom and 1 inch up side of 9-inch springform pan; set aside.

3. For filling, beat cream cheese and ¾ cup sugar in large bowl with electric mixer at high speed 2 to 3 minutes until fluffy. Add eggs, 1 at a time, beating after each addition. Add cream, juice, lemon peel and vanilla; beat just until blended. Pour over prepared crust. Place pan on baking sheet.

4. Bake 45 to 55 minutes until set. Cool completely on wire rack. Cover and refrigerate at least 10 hours or overnight.

5. For topping, hull and slice strawberries just before serving. Combine with 2 tablespoons sugar in medium bowl. Let stand at least 15 minutes. Serve over cheesecake.

Makes 16 servings

Chocolate Swirled Cheesecake

      Yogurt Cheese (recipe follows)
   **2 tablespoons graham cracker
         crumbs**
   **1 package (8 ounces) Neufchatel
         cheese (light cream cheese),
         softened**
1½ teaspoons vanilla extract
   ¾ cup sugar
   1 tablespoon cornstarch
   **1 container (8 ounces) frozen egg
         substitute, thawed**
   ¼ cup HERSHEY'S Cocoa
   ¼ teaspoon almond extract

Prepare Yogurt Cheese. Heat oven to 325°F. Spray bottom of 8- or 9-inch springform pan with vegetable cooking spray. Sprinkle graham cracker crumbs on bottom of pan. In large mixer bowl, beat Yogurt Cheese, Neufchatel cheese and vanilla on medium speed of electric mixer until smooth. Add sugar and cornstarch; beat just until well blended. Gradually add egg substitute, beating on low speed until blended. Transfer 1½ cups batter to medium bowl; add cocoa. Beat until well blended. Stir almond extract into vanilla batter. Alternately spoon vanilla and chocolate batters into prepared pan.

With knife or metal spatula, cut through batters for marbled effect.

Bake 35 minutes for 8-inch pan; 40 minutes for 9-inch pan or until edge is set. With knife, loosen cheesecake from side of pan. Cool completely in pan on wire rack. Cover; refrigerate at least 6 hours before serving. Just before serving, remove side of pan. Garnish as desired. Cover; refrigerate leftover cheesecake. *Makes 16 servings*

Yogurt Cheese: Line non-rusting colander or sieve with large piece of double thickness cheesecloth or large coffee filter; place colander over deep bowl. Spoon one 16-ounce container plain low-fat yogurt (no gelatin added) into prepared colander; cover with plastic wrap. Refrigerate until liquid no longer drains from yogurt, about 24 hours. Remove yogurt from cheesecloth and place in separate bowl; discard liquid.

Tip

To prevent cracking, do not overmix a cheesecake batter; beat just until the mixture is blended. Baking a cheesecake in a water bath affords added protection.

Chocolate Swirled Cheesecake

*Turtle Pecan
Cheesecake*

Technique for Turtle Pecan Cheesecake

Step 6. *Drizzling
Chocolate Topping over
cheesecake.*

Turtle Pecan Cheesecake

8 ounces chocolate cookies or
   vanilla wafers
¼ cup butter, melted
2½ packages (8 ounces each) cream
   cheese, softened
1 cup sugar
1½ tablespoons all-purpose flour
1 teaspoon vanilla extract
¼ teaspoon salt
3 eggs
2 tablespoons whipping cream
   Caramel Topping (recipe
   follows)
   Chocolate Topping (recipe
   follows)
1 cup chopped toasted pecans

1. Preheat oven to 450°F.

2. Place cookies in large resealable plastic food storage bag. Squeeze out excess air; seal bag tightly. Finely crush cookies with rolling pin.

3. Combine crumbs and butter in medium bowl; press onto bottom of 9-inch springform pan. Set aside.

4. Beat cream cheese in large bowl until creamy. Add sugar, flour, vanilla and salt; mix well. Add eggs, 1 at a time, beating well after each addition. Blend in cream. Pour over crust.

5. Bake 10 minutes. *Reduce oven temperature to 200°F.* Bake 35 to 40 minutes more until set. Loosen cake from rim of pan; cool before removing rim of pan.

6. Prepare Caramel Topping and Chocolate Topping. Drizzle over cheesecake. Refrigerate cheesecake. Sprinkle with pecans just before serving.

Makes one 9-inch cheesecake

Caramel Topping

½ (14-ounce) bag caramels,
   unwrapped
⅓ cup whipping cream

Place ingredients in small saucepan; stir over low heat until caramels are melted and mixture is smooth.

Chocolate Topping

1 package (4 ounces) dark sweet
   chocolate, coarsely chopped
1 teaspoon butter
2 tablespoons whipping cream

Place ingredients in small saucepan; stir over low heat until chocolate is melted and mixture is smooth.

CHERIMOYA

The cherimoya, also called chirimoya or custard apple, originated in South America and may be the earliest recorded New World fruit. This pinecone-shaped jade green fruit is about the size of a large fist. It has a creamy, sweet-tasting pulp dotted with black seeds. The flavor may have hints of pineapple, papaya, banana, mango or strawberry. It is now grown domestically.

Uses: The cherimoya is most often eaten raw.

• Cherimoya pulp is sometimes used to make sorbet, ice cream or fruit drinks.

Availability: Cherimoyas are available from November through May.

Buying Tips: Cherimoyas are very fragile when ripe. Like avocados, they are picked and shipped hard. Choose cherimoyas that are firm, heavy for their size and free of blemishes or brown spots.

Storage: Allow cherimoyas to ripen at room temperature for a few days until they yield slightly to soft pressure before chilling them. Wrapped carefully to protect from bruising, they may be refrigerated four to five days.

Basic Preparation: Serve cherimoyas chilled. Simply cut the fruit in half lengthwise, discard the seeds and scoop out the pulp with a spoon.

CHERRY

Cherries charmed Billy Boy of nursery rhyme fame, whose sweetheart could "make a cherry pie as fast as you can wink an eye," and apparently kept George Washington from telling a lie, but mostly they are known as the luscious rosy red fruits that develop from the early spring blossoms of a cherry tree. It's likely that they originated in northeastern Asia, but for thousands of years, they have flourished in much of Asia, Europe and North America, areas where they continue to grow today. In the United States, sweet cherries grow primarily in the Pacific Northwest and tart cherries in the Midwest (particularly Door County, Wisconsin and near Traverse City, Michigan).

Uses: Sweet cherries are most often eaten out of hand.

• Sweet cherries can be preserved in brandy or stirred into ice cream to make the flavor New York cherry.

• Tart cherries, also called sour or pie cherries, are excellent for baking pies, cobblers, cakes and crumbles.

• Tart cherries make excellent preserves and jams.

• Cherries are used to make several notable liqueurs, including kirsch (kirschwasser) and Cherry Heering.

• Maraschino cherries are sweet cherries that are pitted, soaked in sugar syrup, flavored and dyed a vivid red or green.

Varieties: Of sweet cherries, Bing is the most popular variety. It is large, sweet and deep purple-red. Other varieties include Lambert, Royal (or Queen) Ann and Windsor. Tart cherries usually are red and slightly smaller than sweet cherries. Principle varieties include Morello and Montmorency.

Tip

A cherry pitter is a tool that holds a single cherry while a plunger pushes out the pit. Automatic pitters that hold several cups of unpitted cherries are also available.

Availability: Cherries remain mainly a summer fruit. Sometimes sweet cherries from Chile are available in January. Tart cherries, available for several weeks in June, are seldom seen in supermarkets. Look for them at farmers' markets in areas where they are grown. Canned sweet and tart cherries are available in syrup. Tart cherries are canned with sugar and thickeners added to make pie filling. Both sweet and tart cherries are available frozen or dried all year.

Buying Tips: Choose plump, firm fruits with glossy skin and no bruises or leakage. Cherries don't ripen after picking, so immature cherries, marked by a small size and poor color, should be avoided. Tart cherries are slightly soft when ripe. Cherries with stems attached keep longer.

Roasted Pork with Tart Cherries

Yield: 1 pound sweet cherries, pitted and stemmed = about 1¾ cups. 1 pound tart cherries, pitted and stemmed = about 2¼ cups. 1 (16-ounce) can tart cherries, drained = 1½ cups. 1 (20-ounce) bag frozen pitted cherries = 2 cups.

Storage: Discard any cherries with broken skin and refrigerate unwashed cherries in a bowl loosely covered with plastic wrap. They will last for several days.

Basic Preparation: For eating out of hand, rinse cherries under cold running water. Remove the stems. When pitted cherries are called for in a recipe, use the tip of a swivel-bladed vegetable peeler, inserted through the stem end, to remove the pit. Work over a bowl to collect the juice. Canned cherries should be drained before using. When baking with frozen cherries, thaw them partially before using.

Roasted Pork with Tart Cherries

> 1 boneless rolled pork roast (3½ to 4 pounds)
> 3 teaspoons bottled grated horseradish, divided
> 1 teaspoon ground coriander
> ½ teaspoon ground black pepper
> 1 can (16 ounces) pitted tart cherries, undrained
> ½ cup chicken broth
> ⅓ cup Madeira wine or dry sherry
> 1 tablespoon brown sugar
> 1 tablespoon Dijon mustard
> ⅛ teaspoon ground cloves
> 4 teaspoons grated orange peel
> Orange peel twist (optional)

1. Preheat oven to 400°F. Place pork on meat rack in shallow roasting pan. Insert meat thermometer into thickest part of roast.

2. Combine 2 teaspoons horseradish, coriander and pepper in small bowl. Rub over pork. Roast pork 10 minutes; remove from oven. *Reduce oven temperature to 350°F.*

3. Add cherries with juice and broth to pan. Cover pan loosely with foil. Roast about 1 hour and 30 minutes, basting every 20 minutes, or until pork registers 155°F on meat thermometer. (Cook, uncovered, during last 20 minutes.)

4. Transfer pork to cutting board; tent with foil. Let stand 10 minutes.

5. Meanwhile, remove meat rack from roasting pan. Pour contents of pan through strainer into small saucepan, reserving cherries. Stir wine, sugar, mustard, remaining 1 teaspoon horseradish, cloves and grated orange peel into saucepan. Bring to a boil over medium-high heat. Boil 10 minutes or until sauce is thickened. Stir in reserved cherries.

6. Carve pork into thin slices; place on serving platter. Pour some of cherry sauce mixture around pork. Serve with remaining cherry sauce mixture. Garnish with orange peel twist, if desired.   *Makes 8 servings*

Cherry Glazed Chocolate Torte

Cherry Glazed Chocolate Torte

  ½ **cup (1 stick) butter or margarine, melted**
  1 cup sugar
  1 teaspoon vanilla extract
  2 eggs
  ½ **cup all-purpose flour**
  ⅓ **cup HERSHEY'S Cocoa**
  ¼ **teaspoon baking powder**
  ¼ **teaspoon salt**
    Cream Layer (recipe follows)
  1 can (21 ounces) cherry pie filling, divided

Heat oven to 350°F. Grease bottom of 9-inch springform pan. In large bowl, stir together butter, sugar and vanilla. Add eggs; using spoon, beat well. In small bowl, stir together flour, cocoa, baking powder and salt; gradually add to egg mixture, beating until well blended. Spread into prepared pan.

Bake 25 to 30 minutes or until cake is set. (Cake will be fudgey; wooden pick inserted in center will not come out clean.) Cool completely in pan on wire rack. Prepare Cream Layer; spread over top of cake. Spread 1 cup cherry pie filling over Cream Layer; refrigerate 3 hours. With knife, loosen cake from side of pan; remove side of pan. Serve with remaining pie filling. Garnish as desired. Cover; refrigerate leftover torte.

Makes 10 to 12 servings

Cream Layer

  1 package (8 ounces) cream cheese, softened
  1 cup powdered sugar
  1 cup frozen non-dairy whipped topping, thawed

In small mixer bowl, beat cream cheese and powdered sugar until well blended. Fold in whipped topping.

CHILI

Chili, often called chile con carne (Spanish for "chili with meat"), can be traced back to San Antonio where these "bowls of red" were sold in the marketplace. A thick, stewlike dish, its main ingredients are cubed or coarsely ground beef and chili peppers or chili powder. The addition of beans can be highly controversial with chili aficionados. Whereas Texans generally do not add beans, others consider beans a necessity.

❦

30-Minute Chili Olé

30-Minute Chili Olé

    1 cup chopped onion
    2 cloves garlic, minced
    1 tablespoon vegetable oil
    2 pounds ground beef
    1 (15-ounce) can tomato sauce
    1 (14½-ounce) can stewed
        tomatoes
  ¾ cup A.1.® Steak Sauce
    1 tablespoon chili powder
    1 teaspoon ground cumin
    1 (16-ounce) can black beans,
        rinsed, drained
    1 (11-ounce) can corn, drained
        Shredded cheese, sour cream
        and chopped tomato, for
        garnish

In 6-quart heavy pot, sauté onion and garlic in oil until tender. Brown beef. Drain; stir in tomato sauce, stewed tomatoes, steak sauce and spices. Heat to a boil; reduce heat to low. Cover; simmer for 10 minutes, stirring occasionally. Stir in beans and corn; simmer, uncovered, for 10 minutes. Serve hot.   *Makes 8 servings*

Classic Texas Chili

  ¼ cup vegetable oil
    3 pounds beef round or chuck,
        cut into 1-inch cubes
 1½ quarts water
    4 to 6 tablespoons chili powder
    3 cloves garlic, minced
    2 teaspoons TABASCO® pepper
        sauce
    2 teaspoons salt
    2 teaspoons dried oregano leaves
    2 teaspoons ground cumin
  ⅓ cup white cornmeal
        Hot cooked rice and beans

Heat oil in large saucepan or Dutch oven. Brown beef on all sides. Add water, chili powder, garlic, TABASCO sauce, salt, oregano and cumin; mix well. Bring to a boil; cover and reduce heat. Simmer 1 hour and 15 minutes, stirring occasionally. Add cornmeal; mix well. Simmer, uncovered, 30 minutes or until beef is tender. Serve with rice and beans.
                    Makes 6 to 8 servings

CHILI OIL

Chili oil is made by infusing sesame, olive or vegetable oil with dried hot chili peppers. Results range from mildly to fiery hot. Traditionally, it was limited to Chinese cuisine, where very small amounts were used in Szechwan-style cooking. As flavored oils were becoming more popular, Italian and Mexican versions appeared. Used judiciously, chili oil has many purposes and can be added to stir-fries, dressings, marinades and sauces.

☙

Spicy Orange Chicken

   2 oranges
   2 teaspoons cornstarch
   ¼ cup mild-flavored molasses
   1 tablespoon soy sauce
   ¾ cup all-purpose flour
   ½ teaspoon salt
   ¼ teaspoon baking powder
   ¾ cup water
   1 pound boneless, skinless
       chicken breasts or thighs
   3 cups vegetable oil
   1 teaspoon chili oil
   4 whole dried chili peppers
   2 cloves garlic, minced
  1½ teaspoons minced fresh ginger
       Orange and chili flowers
       (optional)
       Hot cooked rice

Spicy Orange Chicken

1. Remove ½-inch-wide strips of peel from 1 orange with vegetable peeler. Slice peel into 1-inch pieces; set aside. (Remove colored portion of skin only; white pith has a bitter taste.) Squeeze enough juice from oranges to measure ½ cup. Combine cornstarch, ½ cup juice, molasses and soy sauce in small bowl, stirring until smooth; set aside.

2. Combine flour, salt and baking powder in medium bowl. Whisk in water to form smooth batter. Add chicken; mix well.

3. Heat vegetable oil in wok over medium-high heat until oil reaches 375°F on deep fry thermometer. Shake off excess batter from ⅓ of chicken; carefully add chicken to wok.

4. Cook about 4 minutes or until chicken is golden brown and no longer pink in center, stirring occasionally to break up pieces. Remove chicken with slotted spoon to tray lined with paper towels; drain. Repeat 2 more times with remaining chicken, reheating oil between batches.

5. Pour off all oil from wok. Reheat wok over medium-high heat until hot; add chili oil. Add reserved orange peel, peppers, garlic and ginger; stir-fry about 1 minute or until fragrant.

6. Stir reserved cornstarch mixture; add to wok. Cook and stir until sauce boils and thickens. Return chicken to wok; mix well. Transfer to serving platter. Garnish with orange and chili flowers, if desired. Serve with rice.

Makes 4 servings

CHILI PASTE

Chili paste and garlic chili paste are used extensively in Chinese, Thai, Vietnamese and other Asian cuisines. Made from mashed chili peppers, vinegar, seasonings and often garlic, chili paste is fiery hot. A small dab adds a bolt of heat and a burnished red tint to foods. Depending on the brand and the consistency, the paste is sometimes called Chinese chili sauce, Asian chili sauce or sambal oelek. Chili paste keeps almost indefinitely in the refrigerator.

🌾

Beef with Cashews

Beef with Cashews

- 1 piece fresh ginger (about 1 inch square)
- 1 pound beef rump steak, well trimmed
- 4 tablespoons vegetable oil, divided
- 4 teaspoons cornstarch
- ½ cup water
- 4 teaspoons soy sauce
- 1 teaspoon Oriental sesame oil
- 1 teaspoon oyster sauce
- 1 teaspoon Thai chili paste*
- 8 green onions, cut into 1-inch pieces
- ⅔ cup unsalted roasted cashews (about 3 ounces)
- 2 cloves garlic, minced
  Fresh carrot slices and thyme leaves (optional)

*Thai chili paste is available at some larger supermarkets and at Asian markets.

1. Peel and finely chop ginger; set aside.

2. Cut beef across grain into thin slices about 2 inches long. Heat 1 tablespoon vegetable oil in wok or large skillet over high heat. Add ½ of beef; stir-fry 3 to 5 minutes until browned. Remove from wok; set aside. Repeat with 1 tablespoon vegetable oil and remaining beef.

3. Combine cornstarch, water, soy sauce, sesame oil, oyster sauce and chili paste in small bowl; mix until smooth. Set aside.

4. Heat remaining 2 tablespoons vegetable oil in wok or large skillet over high heat. Add reserved ginger, onions, cashews and garlic; stir-fry 1 minute. Stir cornstarch mixture; add to wok with reserved beef. Cook and stir until liquid boils and thickens. Garnish with carrot slices and thyme, if desired.   *Makes 4 servings*

CHILI SAUCE

Chili sauce is a close kin to ketchup but with a chunkier consistency and a spicy kick. Based on tomatoes, onions and bell peppers, it has a sweet-and-sour flavor achieved by the balance of sugar and distilled vinegar. The slight heat comes from the use of either chili peppers or chili powder. Although chili sauce is generally considered a condiment, it is sometimes used as an ingredient.

☙

Sloppy Joes

> 1 pound lean ground beef
> 1/2 cup chopped onion
> 1/3 cup chopped green bell pepper
> 1 bottle (12 ounces) HEINZ® Chili Sauce
> 1/4 cup water
> 1 to 2 tablespoons firmly packed brown sugar
> 1 tablespoon HEINZ® Worcestershire Sauce
> 1/4 teaspoon salt
> 1/8 teaspoon ground black pepper
> Sandwich buns

In large skillet, cook and stir beef, onion and green pepper until beef is browned and green pepper is tender; drain, if necessary. Stir in chili sauce, water, brown sugar, Worcestershire, salt and black pepper; simmer 10 minutes, stirring occasionally. Serve in sandwich buns.

Makes 6 to 8 servings (about 3 cups)

CHILL, TO

Chilling is the technique of cooling foods, usually in the refrigerator or over ice, to a temperature of 35° to 40°F. A recipe or dish may require several hours or as long as overnight to chill thoroughly.

Stirring foods during chilling hastens cooling. However, do not stir cornstarch-thickened pudding and sauces as they may thin. To chill a large portion of a hot mixture, such as soup or chili, separate the mixture into several small containers for quicker cooling. To chill small amounts of hot food, place the food in a bowl or saucepan over a container of crushed ice or iced water. Or chill the food in the freezer for 20 to 30 minutes. Once chilled, a dish may be transported in a cooler or insulated case, preferably packed with ice packs.

☙

CHIMICHANGA

Chimichangas, or chivichangas, which originated in Mexico, are deep-fried burritos. Flour tortillas are filled and folded into rectangular packages and then deep-fried. Fillings vary, but common ingredients include rice, refried beans, cheese and shredded chicken, beef or pork. Chimichangas are served without a sauce but may be garnished with guacamole, shredded cheese, sour cream or salsa.

☙

Tip

Bloom refers to the white or grey streaks or mottling that appears on the surface of chocolate when it is stored at too high a temperature. The cocoa butter has separated, come to the surface and crystallized. However, the chocolate is not spoiled. The cocoa butter will recombine when the chocolate is melted.

CHOCOLATE

The word chocolate originated from the Aztec word xocolatl, meaning "bitter water"—an unexpected translation since chocolate is loved for its sweetness. The Aztec word, however, described an ancient drink made from unsweetened cocoa beans and spices, which was probably rather bitter. Chocolate comes from the cocoa bean. Cocoa trees are found in tropical climates near the equator, with most cocoa bean production centered in West Africa and South America. The first chocolate factory in this country was opened in Massachusetts a decade prior to the American Revolution by James Baker.

🐝

Production: After harvest, cocoa beans are fermented for a few days, dried in the sun, and then shipped to processing locations, where they are roasted. The roasted beans are cracked open to separate the shells from the kernels, or "nibs." Cocoa shells are sold for animal feed, fertilizer and mulch.

The nibs are over 50 percent cocoa butter (a natural vegetable fat). When the nibs are ground, the cocoa butter melts, and the result is a thick, dark brown liquid called chocolate liquor. At this point the chocolate liquor may be pressed, extracting much of the cocoa butter, in order to form dry, hard cakes, which are ground into cocoa powder. *See Cocoa Powder, page 137.* Or, the chocolate liquor may undergo certain blending and refining processes, during which ingredients such as sugar, cocoa butter and condensed milk may be added, to make different types of chocolate

Cocoa butter is a fat used to give smoothness and flavor to foods (chocolate itself is an example). It is also used in soaps and cosmetics.

TYPES OF CHOCOLATE

Unsweetened Chocolate: Also known as baking or bitter chocolate, this is pure chocolate: no sugar or flavorings have been added. Used for baking rather than eating, it is usually available in packages of individually wrapped one-ounce squares.

Bittersweet Chocolate: This is pure chocolate with some sugar added. Bittersweet chocolate is available in one-ounce squares or in bars. If unavailable, substitute half unsweetened chocolate and half semisweet chocolate.

Semisweet Chocolate: This is pure chocolate combined with sugar and extra cocoa butter. It is sold in a variety of forms, including one-ounce squares, bars, chips and chunks. It is interchangeable with bittersweet chocolate in most recipes.

Sweet Cooking Chocolate: This is pure chocolate combined with extra cocoa butter and sugar. It is available in bars.

Milk Chocolate: This is pure chocolate with sugar, extra cocoa butter and milk solids added. Having a milder flavor than other chocolate, it is widely used for candy bars and is also available in various shapes, such as chips and stars. Milk chocolate can not be used interchangeably with other chocolates because the presence of milk changes its melting and cooking characteristics.

White Chocolate: This is not considered real chocolate since it contains no chocolate liquor. It is a combination of cocoa butter, sugar, milk solids, vanilla and emulsifiers. White chocolate is available in chips and baking bars. Some products labeled "white chocolate" do not contain cocoa butter. They are simply coatings, so check the ingredient list for cocoa butter.

Artificial Chocolate: This is not chocolate; do not substitute it for chocolate as it has different flavor, texture and melting properties.

Unsweetened Cocoa Powder: This is formed by extracting most of the cocoa butter from the nibs of the cocoa bean and grinding the remaining solids into a powder. It is low in fat and contains no additives. *For additional information on cocoa powder, see page 137.*

MELTING
Chocolate should be melted gently to prevent scorching. Follow one of these methods for successful melting.

Direct Heat: Place chopped chocolate or chips in a heavy saucepan over very low heat. Stir constantly. Remove from the heat as soon as it melts. Watch the chocolate carefully since it can easily be scorched.

Double Boiler: This method prevents scorching. Place chocolate in the top pan of a double boiler. The bottom pan should contain hot, not boiling, water. The top pan should not touch the water. Heat, uncovered, until the chocolate melts.

Microwave Oven: Place chocolate in a small microwavable container and heat for 60 seconds per ounce of chocolate. Chocolate may not appear melted, so stir it to determine if it has begun to soften.

If chocolate has been overheated or if liquid is added after melting, the chocolate will "seize up," or form a thick mudlike clump that is virtually impossible to remelt. White chocolate browns easily and should be melted with extreme care.

DRIZZLING
For an easy way to drizzle chocolate, melt it in a resealable plastic bag in the microwave oven. Cut a small corner off the bottom of the bag with scissors. Gently squeeze the bag to drizzle chocolate over food.

Buying: The quality of commercially available chocolate varies a great deal. Generally higher quality chocolate has the best flavor. Make your selection based on your personal taste preference. Fine-quality chocolate breaks evenly, is smooth, not grainy, and has a shiny, unmarked surface.

Storage: Since both heat and moisture adversely affect chocolate, it should be stored at room temperature wrapped in foil or waxed paper, but not plastic wrap. Bittersweet and semisweet chocolate can be stored a very long time, as long as a ten years. Because they contain milk solids, white chocolate and milk chocolate have a much shorter shelf life and should be used within about nine months.

Quick & Easy Chocolate Cake

> 4 bars (1 ounce each) HERSHEY'S Unsweetened Baking Chocolate, broken into pieces
> ¼ cup (½ stick) butter or margarine
> 1⅔ cups boiling water
> 2⅓ cups all-purpose flour
> 2 cups sugar
> ½ cup dairy sour cream
> 2 eggs
> 2 teaspoons baking soda
> 1 teaspoon salt
> 1 teaspoon vanilla extract

Heat oven to 350°F. Grease and flour 13×9×2-inch baking pan. In large mixer bowl, combine chocolate, butter and water; with spoon, stir until chocolate is melted and mixture is smooth. Add flour, sugar, sour cream, eggs, baking soda, salt and vanilla; beat on low speed of electric mixer until smooth. Pour batter into prepared pan. Bake 35 to 40 minutes or until wooden pick inserted in center comes out clean. Cool completely in pan on wire rack. Frost as desired.

Makes 12 to 15 servings

Techniques for drizzling chocolate

Cutting corner off bag.

Squeezing bag to drizzle chocolate.

Fudgy Bittersweet Brownie Pie

12 ounces bittersweet chocolate, broken into pieces
½ cup butter or margarine
2 large eggs
½ cup sugar
1 cup all-purpose flour
½ teaspoon salt
  Vanilla ice cream
  Prepared hot fudge sauce
  Red and white candy sprinkles (optional)

1. Preheat oven to 350°F. Grease 10-inch tart pan with removable bottom or 9-inch square baking pan.

2. Melt chocolate and butter in heavy small saucepan over low heat, stirring constantly; set aside.

Fudgy Bittersweet Brownie Pie

3. Beat eggs in medium bowl with electric mixer at medium speed 30 seconds. Gradually beat in sugar; beat 1 minute. Beat in chocolate mixture, scraping down side of bowl once. Beat in flour and salt at low speed just until combined, scraping down side of bowl once. Spread batter evenly in prepared pan.

4. Bake 25 minutes or until center is just set. Remove pan to wire rack; cool completely. (At this point, brownie may be stored, tightly covered, at room temperature up to 2 days or in freezer up to 3 months.)

5. To serve, cut brownies into 12 wedges (or 12 squares if using square pan). Top each piece with 1 scoop ice cream. Place fudge sauce in small microwave-safe bowl or glass measuring cup. Microwave at HIGH (100% power) until hot, stirring once. Spoon over ice cream; top with candy sprinkles, if desired. Serve immediately.   *Makes 12 brownies*

Swiss Mocha Treats

2 ounces imported Swiss bittersweet chocolate candy bar, broken into pieces
½ cup *plus* 2 tablespoons butter, softened, divided
1 tablespoon instant espresso powder
1 teaspoon vanilla extract
1¾ cups all-purpose flour
½ teaspoon baking soda
½ teaspoon salt
¾ cup sugar
1 large egg
3 ounces imported Swiss white chocolate candy bar, broken into pieces

1. Melt bittersweet chocolate and 2 tablespoons butter in heavy small saucepan over low heat, stirring often. Add espresso powder; stir until dissolved. Remove from heat; stir in vanilla. Let cool to room temperature.

2. Combine flour, baking soda and salt in medium bowl; set aside.

3. Beat remaining ½ cup butter and sugar in large bowl with electric mixer at medium speed until light and fluffy, scraping down side of bowl once. Beat in bittersweet chocolate mixture and egg. Gradually add flour mixture. Beat at low speed until well blended, scraping down side of bowl once. Cover; refrigerate 30 minutes or until firm.

4. Preheat oven to 375°F.

5. Roll tablespoonfuls of dough into 1-inch balls. Place balls 3 inches apart on ungreased baking sheets. Flatten each ball into ½-inch-thick round with fork dipped in sugar.

6. Bake 9 to 10 minutes until set (do not overbake or cookies will become dry). Immediately remove cookies to wire racks; cool completely.

7. Place white chocolate in small resealable plastic freezer bag; seal bag. Microwave at MEDIUM (50% power) 1 minute. Turn bag over; microwave at MEDIUM 1 minute or until melted. Knead bag until chocolate is smooth.

8. Cut off tiny corner of bag; pipe or drizzle white chocolate decoratively onto cooled cookies (technique on page 127). Let stand at room temperature 30 minutes or until set. Store tightly covered at room temperature or freeze up to 3 months.

Makes about 4 dozen cookies

Swiss Mocha Treats

*Double Chocolate
Chunk Cookies*

MELT 1 square chocolate; set aside. Cut 3 squares chocolate into large (½-inch) chunks; set aside.

BEAT margarine, sugars, egg and vanilla until light and fluffy. Stir in 1 square melted chocolate. Mix in flour, baking powder and salt. Stir in chocolate chunks and walnuts. Refrigerate 30 minutes.

HEAT oven to 375°F. Drop dough by heaping tablespoonfuls, about 2 inches apart, onto greased cookie sheets. Bake for 8 minutes or until lightly browned. Cool 5 minutes on cookie sheets. Remove and finish cooling on wire racks.

MELT 4 squares chocolate. Dip ½ of each cookie into melted chocolate. Let stand on waxed paper until chocolate is firm.

Makes about 2 dozen cookies

Prep time: 30 minutes
Chill time: 30 minutes
Bake time: 8 minutes

Double Chocolate Chunk Cookies

4 squares BAKER'S® Semi-Sweet
    Chocolate
½ cup (1 stick) margarine or
    butter, slightly softened
½ cup granulated sugar
¼ cup firmly packed brown sugar
1 egg
1 teaspoon vanilla
1 cup all-purpose flour
½ teaspoon CALUMET® Baking
    Powder
¼ teaspoon salt
¾ cup chopped walnuts (optional)
4 squares BAKER'S® Semi-Sweet
    Chocolate

CHOP, TO

Chopping is the technique of cutting food into small, irregularly shaped pieces. Although the term does not designate a specific size, most cooks would suggest that food be chopped into approximately one-quarter-inch pieces. Chopped food is larger than minced food and more irregularly cut than diced food. Recipe directions may call for a coarsely chopped or a finely chopped ingredient.

A chef's knife is an experienced cook's tool of choice for chopping. (For instructions on using a chef's knife, see page 526.) A food processor, fitted with the metal chopping blade, can also be used to chop. For more even chopping, cut food into one-inch chunks first and process with a series of brief spurts.

🐝

CHOWDER

Chowder is a type of milk- or cream-based soup closely associated with New England. It is most often made with clams, but lobster and cod are other favored seafood ingredients. Regional variations also exist, using chicken, corn or vegetables, but a thick, creamy soup of clams, potatoes and onions is the most common.

❦

Ranch Clam Chowder

¼ cup chopped onion
3 tablespoons butter or margarine
½ pound fresh mushrooms, sliced
2 tablespoons Worcestershire sauce
1½ cups half-and-half
1 can (10¾ ounces) cream of potato soup
¼ cup dry white wine
1 package (1 ounce) HIDDEN VALLEY RANCH® Milk Recipe Original Ranch® Salad Dressing Mix
1 can (10 ounces) whole baby clams, undrained
Chopped fresh parsley

In 3-quart saucepan, cook onion in butter over medium heat until onion is soft but not browned. Add mushrooms and Worcestershire. Cook until mushrooms are soft and pan juices have almost evaporated.

In medium bowl, whisk together half-and-half, potato soup, wine and salad dressing mix until smooth. Drain clam liquid into dressing mixture; stir into mushrooms in pan. Cook, uncovered, until soup is heated through but not boiling. Add clams to soup; cook until heated through. Garnish each serving with parsley.

Makes 6 servings

Ranch Clam Chowder

Chicken and Corn Chowder

1 pound boneless, skinless
     chicken breasts, cut into
     ½-inch pieces
3 cups thawed frozen whole
     kernel corn
¾ cup coarsely chopped onion
     (about 1 medium)
1 to 2 tablespoons water
1 cup diced carrots
2 tablespoons finely chopped
     jalapeño peppers*
½ teaspoon dried oregano leaves
¼ teaspoon dried thyme leaves
3 cups defatted low sodium
     chicken broth
1½ cups 2% milk
½ teaspoon salt

*Jalapeño peppers can sting and irritate the
skin; wear rubber or plastic gloves when
handling peppers and do not touch eyes.
Wash hands after handling.

Chicken and Corn
Chowder

1. Spray large nonstick saucepan with nonstick cooking spray; heat over medium heat until hot. Add chicken; cook and stir about 10 minutes or until browned and no longer pink in center. Remove chicken from saucepan; set aside.

2. Add corn and onion to saucepan; cook and stir about 5 minutes or until onion is tender. Place 1 cup corn mixture in food processor or blender. Process until finely chopped, adding 1 to 2 tablespoons water to liquify mixture; set aside.

3. Add carrots, jalapeños, oregano and thyme to saucepan; cook and stir about 5 minutes or until corn begins to brown. Return reserved chicken to saucepan. Stir in broth, milk, reserved corn mixture and salt; bring to a boil. Reduce heat to low; cover and simmer 15 to 20 minutes. Serve immediately.

Makes 4 main-dish servings

CHUTNEY

Chutney is a spicy fruit-based relish served as a refreshing accompaniment to Indian curries. There are many variations—some raw, others cooked. The most well-known commercial chutney, Major Grey's, is made with mangoes cooked with raisins, tamarind, vinegar, sugar, ginger and spices. Commercial products in glass jars keep indefinitely in the refrigerator. Homemade chutneys are quick-to-fix accompaniments that add flavor and interest to everyday foods. Peaches, apples, tomatoes and bananas are popular ingredients for these preparations.

Cranberry-Apple Chutney

1¼ cups granulated sugar
½ cup water
1 package (12 ounces) fresh or
  frozen cranberries (about
  3½ cups)
2 cups chopped peeled Granny
  Smith apples (about
  2 medium)
1 medium onion, chopped
½ cup golden raisins
½ cup firmly packed light brown
  sugar
¼ cup cider vinegar
1 teaspoon ground cinnamon
1 teaspoon ground ginger
⅛ teaspoon ground cloves
⅛ teaspoon ground allspice
½ cup toasted walnuts or pecans,
  chopped (optional)

1. Combine granulated sugar and water in heavy 2-quart saucepan. Cook over high heat until boiling. Boil gently 3 minutes. Add cranberries, apples, onion, raisins, brown sugar, vinegar, cinnamon, ginger, cloves and allspice. Bring to a boil over high heat. Reduce heat to medium. Simmer, uncovered, 20 to 25 minutes until mixture is very thick, stirring occasionally. Cool; stir in walnuts, if desired.

2. Cover and refrigerate up to 2 weeks before serving. Garnish as desired.

Makes about 3½ to 4 cups chutney

Note: This chutney makes a wonderful appetizer when spooned over cream cheese spread on melba toast rounds.

Cranberry-Apple Chutney

Cioppino

CIOPPINO

Cioppino, a San Francisco wharf-side specialty, is a tomato-based fish stew. It was probably devised by Genoese immigrant fishermen to remind them of home. Onions, garlic, carrots, leeks and celery are cooked in olive oil as the base. Tomatoes, wine, fish stock and an array of fish and shellfish (particularly crab, mussels, shrimp, scallops and snapper) are among the other ingredients.

🐝

Cioppino

2 tablespoons olive or
　vegetable oil
1½ cups (1 medium) chopped onion
1 cup (2 large stalks) chopped
　celery
½ cup chopped green bell pepper
3½ cups (two 14.5-ounce cans)
　CONTADINA® Recipe Ready
　Diced Tomatoes, undrained
2 cups water
¾ cup dry red wine or chicken
　broth
⅔ cup (6-ounce can)
　CONTADINA® Italian Paste
　with Roasted Garlic
1 teaspoon Italian herb seasoning
1 teaspoon salt
½ teaspoon ground black pepper
3 pounds white fish, scallops,
　shrimp, cooked crab, cooked
　lobster, clams and/or oysters
　(in any proportion)

In large saucepan, heat oil. Add onion, celery and bell pepper; sauté until vegetables are tender. Add tomatoes and juice, water, wine, tomato paste, Italian seasoning, salt and black pepper. Bring to a boil. Reduce heat to low; simmer, uncovered, for 15 minutes.

To prepare fish and seafood: Scrub clams and oysters under running water. Place in ½ inch boiling water in separate large saucepan; cover. Bring to a boil. Reduce heat to low; simmer just until shells open, about 3 minutes. Set aside; discard any unopened shells. Cut crab, lobster, fish and scallops into bite-sized pieces. Shell and devein shrimp. Add fish to tomato mixture; simmer for 5 minutes. Add scallops and shrimp; simmer for 5 minutes. Add crab, lobster and reserved clams and oysters; simmer until heated through.

Makes about 14 cups

COAT, TO

To coat means to cover food with an outer layer, usually fine or powdery, using ingredients such as flour, crumbs, cornmeal or sugar. With foods such as chicken, fish fillets and eggplant, this coating is preliminary to frying or baking and provides a crispy exterior. Such foods are often first rolled in eggs or milk so the coating adheres. Some cookies are coated with sugar before or after baking.

☙

COBBLER

Cobblers are popular American fruit-based desserts. Baked in a casserole or baking dish, they are similar to deep-dish pies, but have a rich, thick biscuit topping. Fresh fruit filling is placed in the dish, and a soft biscuit dough is spooned on top of the filling before baking. The dough should not be smoothed but left bumpy and rough, or "cobbled." Cobblers are often served warm with vanilla ice cream or whipped cream.

☙

Berry Cobbler

1 pint (2½ cups) fresh raspberries
1 pint (2½ cups) fresh blueberries
    or strawberries, sliced
2 tablespoons cornstarch
½ to ¾ cup sugar
1 cup all-purpose flour
1½ teaspoons baking powder
¼ teaspoon salt
⅓ cup milk
⅓ cup butter or margarine, melted
2 tablespoons thawed frozen
    apple juice concentrate
¼ teaspoon ground nutmeg

1. Preheat oven to 375°F.

2. Combine berries and cornstarch in medium bowl; toss lightly to coat. Add sugar to taste; mix well. Spoon into 1½-quart or 8-inch square baking dish. Combine flour, baking powder and salt in medium bowl. Add milk, butter and juice concentrate; mix just until dry ingredients are moistened. Drop 6 heaping tablespoonfuls batter evenly over berries; sprinkle with nutmeg.

3. Bake 25 minutes or until topping is golden brown and fruit is bubbly. Cool on wire rack. Serve warm or at room temperature.

Makes 6 servings

Shaking pork cubes with flour to coat.

Berry Cobbler

Spicy Cocktail Sauce

COCKTAIL SAUCE

Cocktail sauce is a ketchup-based condiment flavored with prepared horseradish, lemon juice and hot pepper sauce. It is served with chilled seafood cocktail appetizers, such as shrimp and crab. Cocktail sauce is readily available bottled, but it can easily be made at home with the ingredients listed above in amounts to suit individual taste.

🌸

Spicy Cocktail Sauce

1 cup ketchup
2 cloves garlic, finely chopped
1 tablespoon fresh lemon juice
1 teaspoon prepared horseradish
³/₄ teaspoon chili powder
¹/₂ teaspoon salt
**¹/₄ teaspoon hot pepper sauce *or*
    ¹/₈ teaspoon ground red
    pepper**

1. Combine all ingredients in medium bowl; blend well.

2. Spoon into glass bowl and serve with cooked seafood. Or, pour into clean glass jar and seal tightly. Store up to 1 year in refrigerator.
       *Makes 1¹/₃ cups sauce, enough
              for 1 pound of seafood*

COCOA POWDER

Unsweetened cocoa powder is produced by grinding the dry substance remaining from the processed kernels, or nibs, of cocoa beans. (See Chocolate, page 126.) When the cocoa powder is further treated with alkali, producing a dark mellow-flavored powder, it is called Dutch-processed cocoa. Unsweetened cocoa powder can be stored in a tightly closed container in a cool, dark place for up to two years. Since cocoa powder is naturally lower in fat than other chocolate baking ingredients, it is often used to make lower fat baked goods. Cocoa powder should not be confused with cocoa mixes or instant cocoa that contain cocoa powder combined with sweeteners and often dried milk powder. These products added to milk or water are used to prepare the hot beverage known as cocoa, or hot chocolate.

❦

Hot Cocoa

½ cup sugar
¼ cup HERSHEY'S Cocoa
   Dash salt
⅓ cup hot water
4 cups (1 quart) milk
¾ teaspoon vanilla extract
   Miniature marshmallows or
      sweetened whipped cream
      (optional)

In medium saucepan, stir together sugar, cocoa and salt; stir in water. Cook over medium heat, stirring constantly, until mixture comes to a boil. Boil 2 minutes, stirring constantly. Add milk; heat to serving temperature, stirring constantly. *Do not boil.* Remove from heat; add vanilla. Beat with rotary beater or whisk until foamy. Serve topped with marshmallows or sweetened whipped cream, if desired.

Makes five 8-ounce servings

Spiced Cocoa: Add ⅛ teaspoon ground cinnamon and ⅛ teaspoon ground nutmeg with vanilla. Serve with cinnamon stick, if desired.

Mint Cocoa: Add ½ teaspoon mint extract *or* 3 tablespoons crushed hard peppermint candy *or* 2 to 3 tablespoons white crème de menthe with vanilla. Serve with peppermint candy stick, if desired.

Citrus Cocoa: Add ½ teaspoon orange extract *or* 2 to 3 tablespoons orange liqueur with vanilla.

Swiss Mocha: Add 2 to 2½ teaspoons powdered instant coffee with vanilla.

Canadian Cocoa: Add ½ teaspoon maple extract with vanilla.

Cocoa au Lait: Omit marshmallows or sweetened whipped cream. Spoon 2 tablespoons softened vanilla ice cream on top of each cup of cocoa at serving time.

Slim-Trim Cocoa: Omit sugar. Substitute skim milk for milk. Proceed as directed. Stir in sugar substitute with sweetening equivalence of ½ cup sugar with vanilla.

Quick Microwave Cocoa: To make one serving, in microwave-safe cup or mug, combine 1 heaping teaspoon HERSHEY'S Cocoa, 2 heaping teaspoons sugar and dash salt. Add 2 teaspoons cold milk; stir until smooth. Fill cup with milk. Microwave at HIGH (100% power) 1 to 1½ minutes or until hot. Stir to blend.

Tips

In recipes, cocoa powder may be used in place of unsweetened chocolate. For every ounce of unsweetened chocolate needed, substitute 3 tablespoons unsweetened cocoa powder plus 1 tablespoon butter, margarine or shortening.

To minimize lumps when using cocoa powder to make beverages or syrups, combine it first with the sugar in the recipe before adding the liquid.

Uses: Coconut adds flavor and texture to a wide variety of confections, desserts, salads and entrées.

• Coconut oil, which is made from dried coconut meat, is used commercially as an ingredient in processed foods, such as cookies, candies and snacks. It is not available at retail stores.

• Coconut milk is used in curries. *See Coconut Milk, page 141, for additional information.*

Availability: Fresh coconuts are available all year, peaking in late autumn. Flaked and shredded sweetened coconut is readily available year-round in plastic bags and cans. Unsweetened dried coconut is usually available at produce or Asian markets.

Buying Tips: Choose fresh coconuts that are heavy for their size and sound full of liquid when shaken. Avoid coconuts with damp "eyes."

Yield: 1 medium coconut = 3 to 4 cups grated.

Storage: Fresh unopened coconuts may be stored at room temperature up to six months. Chunks of meat from an opened coconut may be refrigerated in an airtight container for about one week. If possible, pour the juice drained from the coconut over the chunks before refrigerating. Freshly grated coconut may be refrigerated in an airtight plastic bag for about five days or frozen up to six months.

Unopened canned sweetened coconut will last up to 18 months at room temperature. Sweetened coconut packaged in plastic bags may be stored up to six months. Both should be refrigerated after opening.

COCONUT

Coconuts, the fruit of the coconut palm, have been a staple food in the tropics for centuries. Most likely native to Malaysia, coconuts now are grown literally around the world in a band falling within 22 degrees north and south of the equator. Most of those sold in the United States come from Puerto Rico and Central America. Coconut trees flower and bear fruit 10 to 12 times a year and continue producing coconuts for approximately 70 years. Each coconut takes up to a year to mature. The smooth brown outer covering of the coconut is removed before shipping. The hairy shell of the coconuts sold in supermarkets is actually the second layer. This shell is marked by three indentations, or "eyes." Coconuts are high in saturated fat but a good source of potassium.

Special Interest

The spread of coconut palms around the world is due to coconuts floating on ocean currents and taking root wherever they happen to land.

COCONUT MILK

Coconut milk and a richer coconut cream may be purchased in Asian markets or specialty food stores. They may also be prepared at home. Used in many tropical and Asian dishes, coconut milk and cream add flavor to curries, puddings and sauces. Coconut milk should not be confused with the thin liquid that may be drained from a fresh coconut before the meat is removed.

🐝

To make coconut milk, simmer together equal amounts of water and shredded fresh coconut until foamy. Remove from the heat and allow to stand covered for 15 minutes. Strain through cheesecloth or a very fine strainer, squeezing out as much liquid as possible. The coconut may be simmered once more with fresh water for a second batch and then discarded. The resulting coconut milk may be stored in the refrigerator in a covered container up to five days.

Coconut cream may be prepared in a similar fashion except the amount of coconut should be increased to 4 parts coconut to 1 part water. For richer cream, milk may be used in place of water. This mixture should not be confused with "cream of coconut," a sweetened canned product used for desserts and mixed drinks.

Thai Shrimp Curry

½ cup vegetable oil
2 large shallots, peeled, thinly sliced
1 lime
1 can (14 ounces) unsweetened coconut milk, divided
1 teaspoon red Thai curry paste*
⅓ cup water
1 tablespoon brown sugar
1 tablespoon fish sauce*
1 pound raw large shrimp, peeled, deveined
½ cup fresh basil leaves, sliced into ¼-inch strips
Hot cooked jasmine rice
2 cups fresh pineapple wedges (optional)
½ cup peanuts (optional)
Fresh basil leaves (optional)

Thai curry paste and fish sauce are available at specialty stores and at Asian markets.

1. Heat oil in wok over high heat until oil reaches 375°F on deep-fry thermometer. Add shallots; fry until crisp and golden brown. Remove from wok with slotted spoon; drain on paper towels. Reserve for garnish.

2. Remove colored portion of lime peel with vegetable peeler. Finely chop peel; set aside. Reserve lime for another use.

3. Pour ½ of coconut milk into large skillet. Bring to a boil over medium heat, stirring occasionally. Cook 5 to 6 minutes. Stir in curry paste. Cook and stir 2 minutes.

4. Stir together remaining coconut milk and water. Add to curry paste mixture in skillet. Stir in sugar, fish sauce and reserved lime peel. Cook over medium-low heat 10 to 15 minutes until sauce reduces and thickens.

5. Add shrimp and basil strips; reduce heat to low. Cook 3 to 5 minutes until shrimp turn pink and opaque. Serve over rice; sprinkle with reserved shallots. Garnish with pineapple, peanuts and basil leaves, if desired.

Makes 4 servings

Tip

To cut basil leaves into thin strips, layer several leaves with the largest leaves on the bottom. Roll up leaves, starting at one side. Slice the roll crosswise into slices with a sharp knife. Separate slices into strips.

COFFEE

Coffee is native to Ethiopia and has been prepared as a hot drink in Arabic countries for centuries. Today, the two largest producers of coffee are Brazil and Colombia. All of the coffee produced comes from only two commercially viable plant species grown throughout the equatorial ribbon. Coffea arabica grows well at high altitudes and produces beans with delicate but complex flavors. These beans are lower in caffeine. Caffea robusta (or Canephora) grows well at lower elevations and produces beans with more neutral flavors. Caffea robusta beans are high in caffeine.

☙

Coffee Manufacture: After harvest, coffee beans are removed from the berries that encase them, dried, and shipped for roasting at their destination. The temperature and length of time coffee beans are roasted affect color and flavor. (See section titled "Roasts.") A variety of beans are often mixed together to create different flavor blends.

For decaffeinated coffee, coffee beans are treated prior to roasting. There are two methods available. Caffeine may be removed by chemically extracting it with a solvent (which is rinsed away before the beans are dried) or by steaming the coffee beans and then scraping away the caffeine-rich outer layers.

Instant powdered coffees are the result of removing water from brewed coffee through drying.

Freeze-dried granules or crystals come from brewed coffee that is frozen to a slush. The water is then evaporated.

Roasts: Regular (American) is a medium roast resulting in a moderate brew.

French is a heavy roast for strong coffee.

Italian is a heavy roast for espresso.

European is two-thirds heavy-roast and one-third regular-roast beans.

Viennese is two-thirds regular-roast and one-third heavy-roast beans.

Buying Tips and Storage: For the freshest flavor, buy coffee beans and grind only as much as you intend to use. Store unused beans in a tightly sealed container in a cool, dry place for up to two weeks, or freeze for up to three months.

Ground coffee that is purchased already ground becomes stale at room temperature in only a day or two after opening. Refrigerated, it will last about two weeks in an airtight container.

Instant and freeze-dried coffees should be stored in a cool place.

Styles: Espresso is a very strong coffee usually served in small cups often with a twist of lemon peel. It is usually brewed in a special appliance under steam pressure, using finely ground Italian-roast beans.

Café macchiato is espresso served in a small cup and topped with the foam of steamed milk.

Cappuccino is espresso with steamed milk added to the mix. It is served in a standard-size cup and topped with the foam of steamed milk. It may be dusted with sweetened cocoa powder and cinnamon.

Café latte is espresso with steamed milk served in a tall mug and topped with the foam of steamed milk.

Café au lait consists of coffee and hot milk in equal amounts.

Café brûlot (diable, royal) is coffee with orange, cloves and brandy that is flamed before serving.

Café mocha is coffee with milk and chocolate added.

Technique for Viennese Coffee

Step 2. *Making chocolate shavings.*

Irish coffee is sweetened coffee with Irish whisky served in a tall glass mug topped with whipped cream.

Thai coffee is coffee mixed with sweetened condensed milk.

Turkish coffee is a strong coffee made by boiling grounds, water and sugar. It is prepared in a special pot.

Coffee Tips: Always use cold water to make coffee. If tap water has a mineral taste it may adversely affect the coffee flavor. Use bottled water instead.

• 1 coffee measure = 2 tablespoons coffee. Use one measure of ground coffee for every 6 ounces of water.

• The flavor of coffee can deteriorate very easily. Never boil coffee. Never reheat coffee. Never leave coffee on a heating element for more than fifteen minutes.

• Never reuse coffee grounds.

• Always clean the coffee grinder and pot after using to remove residual oils, which may become rancid.

Viennese Coffee

> 1 cup whipping cream, divided
> 1 teaspoon powdered sugar
> 1 bar (3 ounces) bittersweet or
>   semisweet chocolate
> 3 cups strong freshly brewed hot
>   coffee
> ¼ cup crème de cacao or Irish
>   cream (optional)

1. Chill bowl, beaters and cream before whipping. Place ⅔ cup cream and sugar into chilled bowl. Beat with electric mixer at high speed until soft peaks form. *Do not overbeat.* Cover; refrigerate up to 8 hours.

2. To make chocolate shavings for garnish, place waxed paper under chocolate. Holding chocolate in one hand, make short, quick strokes across chocolate with vegetable peeler; make enough shavings for garnish and set aside. Break remaining chocolate into pieces.

3. Place remaining ⅓ cup cream in heavy medium saucepan. Bring to a simmer over medium-low heat. Add chocolate pieces; cover and remove from heat. Let stand 5 minutes or until chocolate is melted; stir until smooth. Add hot coffee to chocolate mixture. Heat over low heat just until bubbles form around edge of pan and coffee is heated through, stirring frequently. Remove from heat; stir in crème de cacao, if desired. Pour into 4 warmed mugs. Top with reserved whipped cream; garnish with reserved chocolate shavings.

Makes 4 servings

Viennese Coffee

Tiramisu

> 2 packages (8 ounces each) cream
>   cheese, softened
> ²⁄₃ cup sugar
> ¼ cup marsala wine
> 2 teaspoons vanilla extract
> 2 cups whipping cream, whipped
> 1 cup strong coffee or espresso,
>   chilled
> 2 tablespoons almond liqueur *or*
>   1 teaspoon almond extract
> 2 packages (3 ounces each)
>   ladyfingers (24 ladyfingers)
> 1 cup HEATH® Bits

In mixing bowl, beat cream cheese
and sugar until light and fluffy. Blend
in wine and vanilla. Fold in whipped
cream. In small bowl or measuring
cup, combine coffee and liqueur.

Tiramisu

To assemble dessert, split each
ladyfinger in half horizontally and
vertically. Place four pieces in each of
eight dessert or wine glasses. Drizzle
ladyfingers with coffee mixture. Top
with about ¼ cup cream mixture and
several teaspoons Heath® Bits. Repeat
layers twice with remaining
ladyfingers, coffee mixture, cream
mixture and Heath® Bits. Cover;
refrigerate at least 2 hours before
serving.   *Makes 8 servings*

COFFEE CAKE

*Coffee cakes form a large and diverse
category of sweetened breads traditionally served in the morning but
also appropriate for afternoon tea.
They may be purchased at supermarkets and bakeries or made at home.
Homemade coffee cakes can be made
with yeast (a lengthy process) or leavened with baking powder or baking
soda (an easier and less time-consuming process). Either type can be
frosted with a light glaze, dusted with
powdered sugar or served plain.*

Cherry Coconut Cheese Coffee Cake

> 2½ cups all-purpose flour
> ¾ cup sugar
> ½ teaspoon baking powder
> ½ teaspoon baking soda
> 2 packages (3 ounces each) cream
>   cheese, softened, divided
> ¾ cup milk
> 2 tablespoons vegetable oil
> 2 eggs
> 1 teaspoon vanilla extract
> ½ cup flaked coconut
> ¾ cup cherry preserves
> 2 tablespoons butter or margarine

1. Preheat oven to 350°F. Grease and flour 9-inch springform pan.

2. Combine flour and sugar in large bowl. Reserve ½ cup flour mixture. Stir baking powder and baking soda into flour mixture in large bowl. Cut in 1 package cream cheese with pastry blender or 2 knives until mixture resembles coarse crumbs; set aside.

3. Combine milk, oil and 1 egg in medium bowl. Add to cream cheese mixture; stir just until moistened. Spread dough on bottom and 1 inch up side of prepared pan. (Dough should be about ¼ inch thick on sides.)

4. Combine remaining package cream cheese, remaining egg and vanilla in small bowl; stir until smooth. Pour over dough, spreading to within 1 inch of edge. Sprinkle coconut over cheese mixture. Spoon preserves evenly over coconut.

5. Cut butter into reserved flour mixture with pastry blender or 2 knives until mixture resembles coarse crumbs. Sprinkle over preserves.

6. Bake 55 to 60 minutes until browned and wooden toothpick inserted into coffee cake crust comes out clean. Cool in pan on wire rack 15 minutes. Remove side of pan. Serve warm or cool completely.

Makes 10 servings

Cherry Coconut Cheese Coffee Cake

Maple Nut Twist

Sweet Yeast Dough (recipe follows)
2 tablespoons butter or margarine, melted
2 tablespoons honey
½ cup chopped pecans
¼ cup granulated sugar
2½ teaspoons maple extract, divided
½ teaspoon ground cinnamon
1 cup sifted powdered sugar
5 teaspoons milk

1. Prepare Sweet Yeast Dough; let rise as directed.

2. Combine butter and honey in custard cup; set aside. Combine pecans, granulated sugar, 2 teaspoons maple extract and cinnamon in small bowl. Toss to coat pecans; set aside.

3. Grease 2 baking sheets. Cut dough into quarters. Roll out 1 piece of dough into 9-inch circle on lightly floured surface with lightly floured rolling pin. (Keep remaining dough covered with towel.) Place on prepared baking sheet.

4. Brush ½ of butter mixture over dough. Sprinkle ½ of pecan mixture over butter mixture.

5. Roll another piece of dough into 9-inch circle. Place dough over pecan filling, stretching dough as necessary to cover. Pinch edges to seal.

6. Place 1-inch biscuit cutter* in center of circle as cutting guide. *(Do not cut into dough.)* Cut dough into 12 wedges, with scissors or sharp

Technique for Maple Nut Twist

Step 6. *Twisting wedges.*

Maple Nut Twist

knife, from edge of circle to edge of biscuit cutter, cutting through all layers. Pick up wide edge of 1 wedge, twist several times and lay back down on baking sheet. Repeat twisting procedure with remaining 11 wedges. Remove biscuit cutter.

7. Repeat with remaining 2 pieces of dough, butter mixture and pecan mixture. Cover coffee cakes with towels; let rise in warm place about 1 hour or until almost doubled in bulk.

8. Preheat oven to 350°F. Bake on 2 racks in oven 20 to 25 minutes until coffee cakes are golden brown and sound hollow when tapped. (Rotate baking sheets top to bottom halfway through baking.) Immediately remove from baking sheets; cool on wire racks about 30 minutes. (Place pieces of waxed paper under wire racks to keep counter clean.)

9. Combine powdered sugar, milk and remaining ½ teaspoon maple extract in small bowl until smooth. Drizzle over warm coffee cakes.

Makes 24 servings
(2 coffee cakes)

*Or, use the lid of an herb or spice jar if biscuit cutter is not available.

Sweet Yeast Dough

---

    4 to 4¼ cups all-purpose flour,
        divided
    ½ cup granulated sugar
    2 packages active dry yeast
    1 teaspoon salt
    ¾ cup milk
    4 tablespoons butter or margarine
    2 eggs
    1 teaspoon vanilla extract

---

1. Combine 1 cup flour, sugar, yeast and salt in large bowl; set aside.

2. Combine milk and butter in 1-quart saucepan. Heat over low heat until mixture is 120° to 130°F. (Butter does not need to completely melt.)

3. Gradually beat milk mixture into flour mixture with electric mixer at low speed. Increase speed to medium; beat 2 minutes, scraping down side of bowl once. Reduce speed to low. Beat in eggs, vanilla and 1 cup flour. Increase speed to medium; beat 2 minutes, scraping down side of bowl once. Stir in enough additional flour, about 2 cups, with wooden spoon to make soft dough.

4. Turn out dough onto lightly floured surface; flatten slightly. Knead dough about 5 minutes or until smooth and elastic, adding remaining ¼ cup flour to prevent sticking if necessary (technique on page 63). Shape dough into a ball; place in large greased bowl. Turn dough over so that top is greased. Cover with towel; let rise in warm place 1½ to 2 hours until doubled in bulk.

5. Punch down dough (technique on page 64). Knead dough on lightly floured surface 1 minute. Cover with towel; let rest 10 minutes.

Refrigerator Sweet Yeast Dough:
Prepare Sweet Yeast Dough as directed in steps 1 through 4, except cover with greased plastic wrap and refrigerate 3 to 24 hours. Punch down dough. Knead dough on lightly floured surface 1 to 2 minutes. Cover with towel; let dough rest 20 minutes before shaping and second rising. (Second rising may take up to 1½ hours.)

COMBINE, TO

Combining is the process of mixing two or more liquid or dry ingredients together to make them a uniform substance. This can be done with any number of tools, such as a spoon, fork, rubber spatula, mixer, blender or food processor.

🐝

COMPOTE

A compote is a combination of fruits, usually cooked in a light syrup, served for dessert or breakfast. The fruits may be fresh or dried. Although traditionally they are chilled, warm compotes are a welcome treat on cold winter days. The syrup, made with sugar and water or wine, is infused with spices, such as cinnamon, cloves, and possibly citrus rind. Liqueurs or brandy may be added.

☙

CONDIMENT

Condiments are accompaniments to food, chosen to enhance flavors or textures of foods. Ketchup, mustard and mayonnaise are among the most common. Other examples are chutney, chili sauce, pickle relish and salsa.

☙

CONSOMMÉ

Consommé is a clear soup made from meat or poultry stock. The stock may be cooked further to reduce and concentrate it. The stock is clarified by adding egg whites (and sometimes egg shells) and simmering 10 to 15 minutes. The sediment becomes entangled with the coagulated egg whites and rises to the surface where it is skimmed off with a slotted spoon. Then the liquid is strained through a cheesecloth-lined sieve. Consommé can be enriched with other ingredients, such as small meat dumplings, diced vegetables or filled pasta.

☙

COOKIE

The word cookie comes from the Dutch word koejke, which means "little cake." However, cookies are truly universal. Whether they are called biscuits in England, galletas in Spain, keks in Germany or biscotti in Italy, almost every country has its own classic cookie. The term covers such a myriad of morsels that it is difficult to define. A very broad definition of cookie is a flour-based, hand-held sweet treat that can range from a thin, crisp butter round to a one-inch-thick cakey bar cookie. Cookies can be eaten as a snack, dessert or with afternoon tea. Special cookies are often tied closely to holiday traditions and family celebrations.

☙

TYPES OF COOKIES

The seemingly endless variety of cookies can be divided into five basic types: bar, drop, refrigerator, rolled and shaped.

Bar Cookies: These cookies are made by spreading or pressing a batter or soft dough into a baking pan. After baking, cookies are cooled, sometimes frosted and cut into squares or rectangles. One reason for the popularity of bar cookies is their ease of preparation. Always use the size pan specified in the recipe to ensure proper doneness. If using a glass baking dish instead of a metal baking pan, reduce oven temperature by 25°F. For easier cutting and cleanup, line the baking pan with foil, allowing the foil to cover the sides of the pan. Grease the foil if the recipe directions recommend greasing the pan. After baking and cooling, remove the cookies from the pan using the foil. Peel off the foil. Place the cookies on a cutting board and cut as directed.

Drop Cookies: Made by dropping spoonfuls of thick dough onto a baking sheet, drop cookies are the most common type of cookie in the United States, with chocolate chip and oatmeal raisin dominating. Use regular tableware rather than measuring spoons for dropping dough. To easily shape dough, use an ice cream scoop with a release bar. The handiest sizes for cookies are 40, 50 and 80. The size usually is stamped on the release bar. Cookies that are uniform in size and shape will finish baking at the same time. Space dough 2 inches apart on baking sheets to allow for spreading, unless the recipe directs otherwise.

Refrigerator Cookies: The dough is shaped into logs, refrigerated until firm and then sliced for baking. Shaping is easier if you first place the dough on a piece of waxed paper or plastic wrap. Then roll it back and forth to form a log. Before chilling, wrap the rolls securely in plastic wrap to prevent the dough from drying out. To keep a log of cookie dough round during slicing, roll it a quarter turn every four or five slices. For easier slicing, finely chop the ingredient pieces, such as nuts and fruit.

Rolled Cookies: The dough is rolled with a rolling pin until it is a certain thickness, usually $1/8$- to $1/4$-inch thick. Then the dough is cut into shapes with cookie cutters. Chill the cookie dough for easier handling. Remove only enough dough from the refrigerator to work with at one time. Save any trimmings and reroll them together to prevent the dough from becoming tough. To minimize sticking of dough when using cookie cutters, dip cutters in flour or spray with vegetable spray. After baking, these cookies are often frosted and decorated.

Shaped (or Molded) Cookies: These cookies are made by one of several methods. Dough can be shaped by hand into various shapes, such as balls, crescents or logs. Or, it can be forced through a cookie press to form more complex shapes, such as the shape of spritz cookies. Dough for shortbread, madeleines and sometimes springerle is pressed into decorative molds, which imprint their designs on the cookies. If the recipe calls for butter, do not substitute margarine. Since margarine produces a softer dough, the cookie dough may not hold its shape.

Technique for refrigerator cookies

Forming dough into log.

No-Bake Cherry Crisps (recipe on page 152)

BAKING COOKIES

Baking Sheets: Shiny, heavy-gauge aluminum baking sheets promote even browning of cookies; dark pans absorb more heat causing cookies to brown too quickly. To use dark sheets, reduce oven temperature by 25°F. Nonstick finishes minimize sticking and make cleanup easier.

Grease baking sheets only if directed to do so in the recipe. Most cookie recipes are high enough in fat that they will not stick while baking. Use vegetable shortening or nonstick vegetable spray. Grease sheets for cookies that are rolled in sugar since sugar scorches easily.

Baking: Preheat oven to desired temperature about 15 minutes before beginning to bake. For even baking and browning, place only one baking sheet at a time in the center of the oven. Allow at least two inches of space between the baking sheet and the wall of the oven for proper air circulation. If the cookies brown unevenly, rotate the cookie sheet from front to back halfway through the baking time.

When baking more than one sheet of cookies at a time, rotate them from the top rack to the bottom rack halfway through the baking time.

When reusing the same baking sheets for several batches, cool the sheets completely before placing dough on them. Dough will soften and begin to spread on a hot sheet.

To avoid overbaking cookies, check them at the minimum baking time. If more time is needed, watch them carefully to make sure they do not overbake. It is better to slightly underbake than overbake cookies.

Cool individual cookies on a wire rack. If the cookies seem too tender or begin to fall apart when removed from the pan, allow them to cool a minute or two before transferring to the cooling rack. Cool bar cookies in their pan, unless the recipe directs otherwise.

Storage: Completely cool all cookies before storing in airtight containers. Store each kind of cookie separately to prevent transfer of flavor and changes in texture.

To keep moist cookies soft, store them in a tightly covered container for a day or two with 2 or 3 thick apple slices. Remember to remove the apple slices at the end of the two- or three-day period. Apple slices may also be added to a storage container to soften stale or overbaked cookies.

Most cookies freeze well for several months. Store unfrosted cookies in sealed plastic bags or airtight containers with plastic wrap or waxed paper between layers of cookies. Most cookies thaw at room temperature in 10 to 15 minutes.

Black and White Cutouts

2¾ **cups** *plus* **2 tablespoons all-purpose flour, divided**
1 **teaspoon baking soda**
¾ **teaspoon salt**
1 **cup butter or margarine, softened**
¾ **cup granulated sugar**
¾ **cup packed light brown sugar**
2 **eggs**
1 **teaspoon vanilla extract**
¼ **cup unsweetened cocoa powder**
1 **white chocolate baking bar (4 ounces), broken into ½-inch pieces**
4 **ounces semisweet chocolate chips**

1. Combine 2¾ cups flour, baking soda and salt in small bowl; set aside.

2. Beat butter and sugars in large bowl with electric mixer at medium speed until light and fluffy, scraping down side of bowl once. Beat in eggs, 1 at a time, scraping down side of bowl after each addition. Beat in vanilla. Gradually add flour mixture. Beat at low speed, scraping down side of bowl once.

Technique for Black and White Cutouts

Step 7. *Kneading bag of white chocolate drizzle.*

3. Remove ½ of dough from bowl; set aside. To make chocolate dough, beat cocoa into remaining dough with mixing spoon until well blended. To make butter cookie dough, beat remaining 2 tablespoons flour into reserved dough. Flatten each piece of dough into a disc; wrap in plastic wrap and refrigerate about 1½ hours or until firm. (Dough may be refrigerated up to 3 days before baking).

4. Preheat oven to 375°F.

5. Working with 1 type of dough at a time, place dough on lightly floured surface. Roll out dough with lightly floured rolling pin to ¼-inch thickness. Cut dough into desired shapes with cookie cutters. Place cutouts 1 inch apart on ungreased baking sheets.

6. Bake 9 to 11 minutes until set. Let cookies stand on baking sheets 2 minutes. Remove cookies to wire racks; cool completely.

7. For white chocolate drizzle, place white chocolate pieces in small resealable plastic freezer bag; seal bag. Microwave at MEDIUM (50% power) 2 minutes. Turn bag over; microwave at MEDIUM 2 to 3 minutes until melted. Knead bag until white chocolate is smooth. Cut off tiny corner of bag; drizzle white chocolate onto chocolate cookies. Let stand about 30 minutes or until white chocolate is set.

8. For chocolate drizzle, place chips in small resealable plastic freezer bag; seal bag. Microwave at HIGH (100% power) 1 minute. Turn bag over; microwave at HIGH 1 to 2 minutes until melted. Knead bag until chocolate is smooth. Cut off tiny corner of bag; drizzle chocolate onto butter cookies. Let stand about 40 minutes or until chocolate is set.

Makes 3 to 4 dozen cookies

Black and White Cutouts

Almond Milk Chocolate Chippers

1. To toast almonds, preheat oven to 350°F. Spread almonds on baking sheet. Bake 8 to 10 minutes until golden brown, stirring frequently. Remove almonds from pan; set aside.

2. *Increase oven temperature to 375°F.*

3. Combine flour, baking soda and salt in small bowl; set aside.

4. Beat butter and sugars in large bowl with electric mixer at medium speed until light and fluffy, scraping down side of bowl once. Beat in egg until well blended. Beat in liqueur. Gradually add flour mixture. Beat at low speed until well blended, scraping down side of bowl once. Stir in chips and toasted almonds.

5. Drop rounded teaspoonfuls of dough 2 inches apart onto ungreased baking sheets.

6. Bake 9 to 10 minutes until edges are golden brown. Let cookies stand on baking sheets 2 minutes. Remove to wire racks; cool completely. Store tightly covered at room temperature or freeze up to 3 months.
Makes about 3 dozen cookies

Almond Milk Chocolate Chippers

½ **cup slivered almonds**
1¼ **cups all-purpose flour**
½ **teaspoon baking soda**
½ **teaspoon salt**
½ **cup butter or margarine, softened**
½ **cup firmly packed light brown sugar**
⅓ **cup granulated sugar**
1 **egg**
2 **tablespoons almond-flavored liqueur**
1 **cup milk chocolate chips**

No-Bake Cherry Crisps

¼ **cup butter or margarine, softened**
1 **cup powdered sugar**
1 **cup peanut butter**
1⅓ **cups crisp rice cereal**
½ **cup maraschino cherries, drained, dried, chopped**
¼ **cup *plus* 2 tablespoons mini semisweet chocolate chips**
¼ **cup chopped pecans**
1 **to 2 cups flaked coconut**

1. Beat butter, sugar and peanut butter in large bowl with electric mixer at medium speed until light and fluffy. Stir in cereal, cherries, chips and pecans; mix well.

2. Shape teaspoonfuls of dough into 1-inch balls. Roll in coconut. Place on baking sheet; refrigerate 1 hour or until firm. Store in refrigerator.
Makes about 3 dozen treats

Choco-Coco Pecan Crisps

> ½ cup butter or margarine,
>   softened
> 1 cup packed light brown sugar
> 1 egg
> 1 teaspoon vanilla extract
> 1½ cups all-purpose flour
> 1 cup chopped pecans
> ⅓ cup unsweetened cocoa powder
> ½ teaspoon baking soda
> 1 cup flaked coconut

1. Beat butter and sugar in large bowl with electric mixer at medium speed until light and fluffy. Beat in egg and vanilla. Combine flour, pecans, cocoa and baking soda in small bowl. Add to butter mixture, blending until stiff dough forms.

2. Sprinkle coconut on work surface. Divide dough into 4 parts. Shape each part into 1½-inch-wide log; roll in coconut until thickly coated. Wrap in plastic wrap; refrigerate until firm, at least 1 hour or up to 2 weeks. (For longer storage, freeze up to 6 weeks.)

3. Preheat oven to 350°F. Line baking sheets with parchment paper or leave ungreased. Cut rolls into ⅛-inch-thick slices. Place 2 inches apart on baking sheets.

4. Bake 10 to 13 minutes until firm, but not overly browned. Remove to wire racks; cool completely. Store tightly covered at room temperature.

Makes about 6 dozen cookies

Peanut Butter Chips and Jelly Bars

> 1½ cups all-purpose flour
> ½ cup sugar
> ¾ teaspoon baking powder
> ½ cup (1 stick) cold butter or
>   margarine
> 1 egg, beaten
> ¾ cup grape jelly
> 1⅔ cups (10-ounce package)
>   REESE'S® Peanut Butter Chips,
>   divided

Heat oven to 375°F. Grease 9-inch square baking pan. Stir together flour, sugar and baking powder; with pastry blender, cut in butter until mixture resembles coarse crumbs. Add egg; blend well. Reserve half of mixture; press remaining mixture onto bottom of prepared pan. Spread jelly over crust. Sprinkle 1 cup peanut butter chips over jelly. Stir together reserved crumb mixture with remaining ⅔ cup chips; sprinkle over top. Bake 25 to 30 minutes or until lightly browned. Cool completely in pan on wire rack. Cut into bars.

Makes about 16 bars

Chocolate-Dipped Almond Horns

> 1½ cups powdered sugar
> 1 cup butter or margarine,
>   softened
> 2 egg yolks
> 1½ teaspoons vanilla extract
> 2 cups all-purpose flour
> ½ cup ground almonds
> 1 teaspoon cream of tartar
> 1 teaspoon baking soda
> 1 cup semisweet chocolate chips,
>   melted
> Additional powdered sugar

1. Preheat oven to 325°F.

2. Beat 1½ cups powdered sugar and butter in large bowl with electric mixer at medium speed until creamy, scraping bowl often. Add egg yolks and vanilla; beat until well mixed. Beat in flour, almonds, cream of tartar and baking soda at low speed until well mixed, scraping bowl often.

3. Shape dough into 1-inch balls. Roll balls into 2-inch ropes; shape into crescents. Place 2 inches apart on ungreased baking sheets. Flatten slightly with bottom of glass.

4. Bake 8 to 10 minutes until set. (Cookies will not brown.) Cool completely. Dip ½ of each cookie into chocolate; sprinkle remaining half with powdered sugar. Refrigerate until set.

Makes about 3 dozen cookies

COOKWARE

Cookware is one of the most important purchases you will make for the kitchen. Select pots and pans that suit your particular style of cooking and your specific needs. Matched sets are an economical choice. Select additional pieces, one at a time, as you find a need for them. Choose the best quality cookware you can afford. Although the initial expense of a good quality pan may be higher, it can last a lifetime.

🐝

Selecting Cookware: When buying cookware, look for medium or heavyweight pans. Thin, inexpensive cookware dents easily and can develop hot spots that cause food to burn. Good quality cookware can be heavy. Make sure you can handle a heavy pan with the added weight of food. Also, look for materials that conduct heat quickly and evenly. Resist the temptation to choose something that looks good but isn't a good heat-conducting material. The characteristics of available cookware materials (various metals, glass and ceramic) and the appropriate uses for each are discussed in the section "Cookware Materials."

The overall construction of the skillet or saucepan should also be examined. Handles should be sturdy and snugly attached. For every day rangetop use, choose handles that stay cool, such as those made from heat-resistant plastic. A medium or large skillet with an ovenproof metal handle may be a consideration. Make sure all pans have tight-fitting covers. Interiors should be easy to clean and free of ridges or crevices that can trap food. When making decisions about size, make sure that your rangetop can accommodate two pans, such as a large skillet and a large saucepan, at the same time.

Basic cookware for a starter kitchen include the following:

> 7- or 8-inch sloping-sided skillet or omelet pan with lid

> 10- or 12-inch skillet with straight or sloped sides and lid

> 1-, 2- and 3- *or* 4-quart covered saucepans (one of each)

> 5- to 8-quart Dutch oven or stockpot

Cookware Materials:

Aluminum is relatively inexpensive, lightweight and responds quickly to temperature change. It works well for browning and sautéing. However, unclad aluminum reacts with acidic ingredients, such as tomatoes and wine, and can give these foods an off flavor. Manufacturers now produce aluminum cookware coated with enamel that solves the problem with acidic ingredients but may reduce the aluminum's heat response. Anodized aluminum cookware browns food well and doesn't react to acid but can darken some delicate foods.

Cast iron is inexpensive, heavy and durable. It heats slowly and evenly. A good choice for frying, cast iron produces crisp and brown foods. If not kept well seasoned, it can rust.

Clad metals, a combination of two or more layers of metals, take advantage of the best qualities of different metals. Often aluminum is sandwiched between two thin layers of stainless steel. Aluminum has good heat conductivity while stainless steel is nonreactive to acid and cleans easily.

Copper is an excellent conductor of heat but is expensive and requires special attention to keep it looking its best. It is best used for cooking sauces and for candymaking. All copper pans must be lined with tin or stainless steel because copper reacts chemically with many foods. Worn copper pans must be relined.

Enameled metals are cast iron or drawn steel that are coated with porcelain enamel. When combined with a nonstick coating, enameled metals can be an economical choice.

Glass and glass-ceramic combinations conduct heat poorly but retain heat well. They are best used for oven cooking. For greater versatility choose glass-ceramic combinations that can resist sudden temperature changes without breaking.

Stainless steel is a poor heat conductor but is nonreactive, durable and easy to clean. It is best when clad on the bottom with a better conductor such as copper or aluminum.

TYPES OF COOKWARE

Double Boiler: A double boiler consists of two stacked pans and a cover. The top pan, which holds food, nestles in the bottom pan, which holds simmering water. The purpose of a double boiler is to protect heat-sensitive foods from direct heat. Use it for melting chocolate or for cooking delicate sauces.

Dutch Oven: This large, heavy covered pot with two short handles is used for the slow, moist cooking of a large quantity of food. It is ideal for soups and stews and for braising large pieces of meat. Choose one with ovenproof handles if you would like the convenience of using it in the oven as well as on the rangetop. Dutch ovens range in size from 5 to 8 quarts. Larger pots are generally referred to as stockpots.

Griddle: This heavy, flat pan is used for cooking foods, such as pancakes, with a minimum of fat. Griddles generally are square with very shallow rims on all sides. Round and rectangular griddles are also available. The typical square griddle measures 12 or 14 inches across. Choose a material that heats evenly and well, such as cast iron or aluminum. Nonstick finishes often eliminate the need for fat.

Tip

If a recipe suggests a heavy saucepan and you don't have one, place a lightweight saucepan in a skillet. The extra layer of metal will provide just the right amount of insulation.

Omelet Pan: This shallow pan with a sloping side and flat bottom was originally designed for making omelets. The sloping side allows an omelet to slide around the pan while cooking and facilitates easy turning and removal. Because this pan has proved so versatile, skillets are now sold with a sloping side for sautéing and may not be labeled as omelet pans. Choose a heavy pan that is 6 to 8 inches in diameter. A tight-fitting cover will increase its versatility. Some have nonstick finishes.

Pressure Cooker: This large pan has a locking airtight cover that allows steam under pressure to reach temperatures much higher than the boiling point of water. A valve system regulates the internal pressure. As steam builds up inside the pan, foods cook at a very high temperature. Cooking time is cut by up to two thirds without losing the nutrient value of the food. New ones have improved safety controls. Be sure to read the manufacturer's directions before using. Pressure cookers are primarily used for cooking tough cuts of meat and soups or for canning.

Saucepan: This round cooking utensil, with a deep straight or slightly flared side, a long handle and tight-fitting cover, is very versatile. It is used for cooking sauces, vegetables, grains and pasta as well as reheating, warming and melting. It should be made of a material that heats quickly and evenly, is easy to clean, nonreactive to acidic foods and not too heavy. Saucepans range in size from 2 cups to 4 quarts.

Sauté Pan: The traditional sauté pan is a wide pan with a straight or slightly curved side that is slightly higher than a skillet and has a long handle. This pan is designed for quick cooking over high heat. Use it for browning and stir-frying as well. A large skillet can be substituted for a sauté pan.

Skillet: Also known as a frying pan, this round, shallow pan has a straight or slightly sloping side. It is used for frying and sautéing. Choose a heavy pan that conducts heat evenly and has a tight-fitting cover. Skillets range in size from 6 to 12 inches. A large skillet with a second short handle opposite the long handle is much easier to lift.

Steamer: This two-piece covered pan is used for steaming. The bottom surface of the top pan is perforated to allow steam to rise from the simmering water in the bottom pan. A tight-fitting cover prevents steam from escaping. An inexpensive perforated steamer insert can turn most large covered saucepans into steamers. The principle is the same—food is held above simmering water and the steam from the water cooks the food. When steaming, water should not touch the top pan or the insert. Allow at least one inch of head room.

Stockpot: This large, deep pot is ideal for the slow, gentle cooking of liquids. Less moisture is lost in this tall, narrow pot with a tight-fitting cover. A stockpot should have two handles and a thick bottom to prevent scorching. Stockpots are usually larger than 8 quarts but the name may be used interchangeably with the smaller Dutch oven.

CORE, TO

Coring means to remove the center seed-bearing structure of a fruit or vegetable. The most commonly cored foods are apples, pears, pineapple, zucchini and cucumbers. Coring can be accomplished with a small knife by first cutting the food into quarters and then cutting out the center core. A utensil specially designed to remove the core of specific whole fruits and vegetables is known as a corer. The most common corers are for apples, pears and pineapple.

🐝

CORN

Corn is one of a handful of indigenous American crops. It has played an important and sustaining role in American culinary history. Pilgrims, arriving at Plymouth with barley and wheat plants, followed Native American ways and planted corn. It was fortuitous, as their barley and wheat plants failed while the corn thrived. Since then, it has become a major United States crop. Although most corn is grown as animal feed, it is also an important food source. Many uniquely American foods, such as corn bread, corn chowder, corn fritters, corn pudding and succotash, are based on it. It can be used fresh, dried or ground into meal for use in cereals and snack foods. Dried, hulled and treated, it becomes hominy, which can be cooked in stews or ground into a coarse meal known as grits. A variety known as popcorn is dried and then heated until it puffs. Corn also provides fuel (ethanol) and important secondary products, such as corn oil, cornstarch and corn syrup.

☙

Varieties: Sweet corn has been significantly improved through hybridization. There are now more than 200 varieties with sweetness being one of the most desired attributes. In the 1950's, super-sweet strains were developed and those were further improved with "sugar-enhanced" hybrids. Names such as Butter and Sugar, Silver Queen, Sugar Loaf and Golden Nectar indicate their sweet nature. White, or shoepeg corn, is a type of sweet corn with small, sweet kernels. Other major types include field corn, which is used as animal feed; flint, or Indian corn, of which blue corn is a variety; and popcorn.

Availability: Corn from the midwestern Corn Belt comes in season in mid July, peaks in August and ends by early September. Crops from Florida lengthen the season at both ends. A small demand for corn exists all year, filled by the Mexican supply. Canned and frozen corn kernels, as well as frozen ears, are widely used. Canned ears of baby corn, used in Thai and Chinese cooking, also are available.

Grilled Coriander Corn (recipe page 158)

Buying Tips: Ears of corn are sold both shucked and unshucked. The convenience of shucked corn is not usually enough to offset the loss of quality. Select ears with soft, pliable outer husks free of worm holes. The silks should be golden and soft, like grass. Limit the habit of pulling back husks to inspect the corn as exposed kernels lose quality more quickly.

Yield: 1 ear of corn = 1/2 cup kernels. 1 (10-ounce) package frozen corn = 1 3/4 cups. 1 (12-ounce) can drained, whole kernel corn = 1 1/2 cups.

Storage: The recommendation has long been to take corn from field to pot as quickly as possible since the sugar in corn begins a conversion to starch as soon as it is picked. Sugar-enhanced corn stores longer and does not need to be cooked immediately. However, corn should be bought at a supermarket with high turnover or local farmers' markets and used quickly. Store ears in the refrigerator, husks and silk intact. Ideally, it should be used within 24 hours, especially when served on the cob.

Basic Preparation: Removing husks and silk from an ear of corn is called shucking. To shuck corn, pull outer husks down the ear to the base. Snap off the husks and stem at the base.

Strip away the silk from the corn by hand. Remove any remaining silk with a dry vegetable brush or a corn-silk brush.

Trim any blemishes from the corn and rinse under cold running water.

Traditionally, corn on the cob is boiled in water and served plain or with butter and salt. Cooking time varies from 3 to 7 minutes. Corn toughens if it is overcooked. Drop ears of corn in boiling unsalted water in a Dutch oven and cook until tender. Always cover the Dutch oven so the steam can cook the portions of the ears that are not submerged. Corn microwaves well; follow manufacturer's directions.

Technique for Grilled Coriander Corn

Step 3. *Spreading butter mixture over kernels.*

To cut kernels from the ear, holding the tip of one ear, stand the corn upright on its stem end on a cutting board or in a shallow dish. Cut down the side of the cob with a utility knife, releasing kernels without cutting the cob. Repeat while rotating the ear until all kernels are removed. Kernels can be used for salads, soups and relishes.

For cream-style corn, chowders and corn puddings, press down along each cob with the dull edge of a knife to release the milky liquid, which is a great addition to these dishes.

Grilled Coriander Corn

4 ears fresh corn
3 tablespoons butter or
margarine, softened
1 teaspoon ground coriander
1/4 teaspoon salt (optional)
1/8 teaspoon ground red pepper

1. Pull husks to base of each ear of corn; leave husks attached to ear. (If desired, remove 1 strip of husk from inner portion of each ear; reserve for later use.) Strip away silk by hand. Remove remaining silk with dry vegetable brush. Cover corn with cold water; soak 20 to 30 minutes.

2. Meanwhile, prepare grill for direct grilling over medium-hot heat.

3. Remove corn from water; pat dry with paper towels. Combine butter, coriander, salt, if desired, and pepper in small bowl. Spread evenly with spatula over kernels.

4. Bring husks back up each ear of corn; secure at top with paper-covered metal twist-ties. (Or, use reserved strips of corn husk to tie knots at the top of each ear.)

5. Place corn on grid. Grill corn, on covered grill, over medium-hot coals 20 to 25 minutes until corn is hot and tender, turning halfway through grilling time. Garnish as desired. Serve immediately.

Makes 4 side-dish servings

Note: For ember cooking, prepare corn as directed, but omit soaking in cold water. Wrap each ear securely in heavy-duty foil. Place directly on coals. Grill corn, in covered grill, on medium-hot coals 25 to 30 minutes until corn is hot and tender, turning every 10 minutes.

Southwestern Bean and Corn Salad

> 1 can (about 15 ounces) pinto beans, rinsed, drained
> 1 cup fresh (about 2 ears) or thawed frozen whole kernel corn, cooked
> 1 red bell pepper, finely chopped
> 4 green onions, finely chopped
> 2 tablespoons cider vinegar
> 2 tablespoons honey
> ½ teaspoon salt
> ½ teaspoon dry mustard
> ½ teaspoon ground cumin
> ⅛ teaspoon ground red pepper
> Lettuce leaves (optional)

1. Combine beans, corn, bell pepper and onions in large bowl.

2. Whisk vinegar and honey in small bowl until smooth. Stir in salt, mustard, cumin and ground red pepper. Drizzle over bean mixture; toss to coat. Cover; refrigerate 2 hours. Serve on lettuce leaves, if desired.

Makes 4 side-dish servings

Southwestern Bean and Corn Salad

Clockwise from bottom right: Corn Muffin, Corn Bread, Corn Stick

CORN BREAD

Corn bread is a simple, slightly sweet quick bread that uses cornmeal to replace some or all of the flour. There are regional variations, most of them southern or southwestern in origin. The most common is cakelike in appearance and texture. The same batter also can be baked in a cast iron skillet, cast iron molds or muffin pans. Southwestern variations often have other ingredients, such as chopped chilies, shredded cheese and chopped onions, added to the batter. Regional variations include Johnnycake, corn pone, spider cake and hush puppies. Corn bread mixes are also available.

🌾

Corn Bread

1 cup all-purpose flour
1 cup yellow cornmeal
⅓ cup sugar
2 teaspoons baking powder
½ teaspoon salt
1 cup milk
⅓ cup vegetable oil
1 egg

1. Preheat oven to 400°F. Grease 8-inch square baking pan.

2. Combine flour, cornmeal, sugar, baking powder and salt in large bowl. Combine milk, oil and egg in small bowl until blended. Stir milk mixture into flour mixture just until moistened.

3. Spoon batter quickly into prepared pan, spreading evenly.

4. Bake 20 to 25 minutes until golden brown and wooden toothpick inserted into center comes out clean. Cut into squares. Serve warm.

Makes 9 servings

Corn Muffins: Preheat oven to 400°F. Prepare batter as directed in steps 1 and 2. Spoon batter into 12 (2½-inch) greased or paper-lined muffin cups. Bake 20 minutes or until golden brown and wooden toothpick inserted into centers comes out clean. Immediately remove from pan; cool on wire rack 10 minutes. Serve warm. Makes 12 muffins.

Corn Sticks: Preheat oven to 425°F. Heat cast-iron corn stick pan in oven while preparing batter as directed in steps 1 and 2. Carefully brush hot pan with additional vegetable oil before spooning ½ of batter into prepared pan. Bake 10 to 15 minutes until lightly browned. Immediately remove from pan; cool on wire racks 10 minutes. Repeat with remaining ½ of batter. Serve warm. Makes 14 corn sticks.

CORNMEAL

Cornmeal, not to be confused with cornstarch, is a meal ground from dried corn kernels. There are two grades: coarse, used for polenta (an Italian cereal) and for cornmeal mush; and fine, ground from white, yellow or blue corn and used in quick breads, as a coating and occasionally as a thickener. Fine grade is more common. Either grade can be stone-ground, in which the germ and hull of the corn is ground too, so the meal has more vitamins but is also more perishable. More typical is steel-ground cornmeal, produced by a modern process that removes the husk and germ so the meal is more highly refined.

🐝

CORNSTARCH

Cornstarch, a smooth powder that is made from the endosperm (center) of dried corn kernels, is used as a thickener. It has about twice the thickening ability of flour. Unlike flour, cornstarch becomes clear when cooked. For this reason, it is often preferred for Asian stir-fry sauces, dessert sauces and puddings. In order to avoid lumps, it should be mixed with a cold liquid until smooth before cooking or adding it to a hot liquid. In sweet sauces and puddings, mixing cornstarch with the granulated sugar in the recipe before adding cold liquid helps to prevent lumps. If sauces made with cornstarch are overcooked or stirred too long, they will become thin.

🐝

CORN SYRUP

Corn syrup is a thick, sweet and highly refined liquid made by treating cornstarch with acids and enzymes that cause it to liquefy. It is an important ingredient in pecan pie and can be flavored with maple extract for pancake syrup. Corn syrup also is invaluable in making candy and frostings since it prevents sugar from crystallizing. (Sugar crystals make candy grainy and coarse.) Light and dark corn syrups are available. Light syrups are clear; whereas, dark syrups have an amber color and a subtle taste.

🐝

Chocolate Peanut Butter Cups

¾ **cup sifted confectioners sugar**
¼ **cup KARO® Light or Dark Corn Syrup**
¼ **teaspoon salt**
¼ **cup SKIPPY® Super Chunk® or Creamy Peanut Butter**
1 **package (11½ ounces) milk chocolate chips, melted**

Place 36 (1 × ¾-inch) foil or paper petit-four cups on a tray. In small bowl with mixer at low speed, beat confectioners sugar, corn syrup and salt until smooth. Stir in peanut butter; knead until blended.

Shape scant teaspoonfuls of peanut butter mixture into 36 balls; place on waxed paper. Spoon 1 rounded teaspoonful melted chocolate into each cup. Place a peanut butter ball in each cup; gently push down. Refrigerate until firm.

Makes 36 candies

Prep time: 25 minutes plus cooling

Tip

For easy cleanup, before measuring corn syrup, lightly coat the measuring cup with nonstick cooking spray. The corn syrup will slip right out without sticking.

Classic Pecan Pie

3 eggs
1 cup sugar
1 cup KARO® Light or Dark Corn
    Syrup
2 tablespoons MAZOLA®
    Margarine, melted
1 teaspoon vanilla
1½ cups pecan halves
1 (9-inch) unbaked or frozen
    deep-dish pie crust*

To use prepared frozen pie crust, do not thaw. Preheat oven and a cookie sheet. Pour filling into frozen crust. Bake on cookie sheet.

Preheat oven to 350°F. In medium bowl beat eggs slightly. Add sugar, corn syrup, margarine and vanilla; stir until well blended. Stir in pecans. Pour into pie crust.

Bake 50 to 55 minutes or until knife inserted halfway between center and edge comes out clean. Cool on wire rack.   *Makes 8 servings*

Prep time: 10 minutes
Bake time: 55 minutes plus cooling

Almond Amaretto Pie: Substitute 1 cup sliced almonds for pecans. Add 2 tablespoons almond-flavored liqueur and ½ teaspoon almond extract to filling.

California Pecan Pie: Stir ¼ cup sour cream into eggs until blended.

Kentucky Bourbon Pecan Pie: Add up to 2 tablespoons bourbon to filling.

Chocolate Pecan Pie: Reduce sugar to ⅓ cup. Melt 4 squares (1 ounce each) semisweet chocolate with margarine.

Top to bottom: Almond Amaretto Pie, Classic Pecan Pie

Couscous

Couscous, or semolina, is coarsely ground durum wheat. It is a staple in North African cuisines. Similar in texture and flavor to rice, it has the shape of very tiny beads. Most of the couscous found in the United States is very fast cooking as it is precooked or instant. Couscous is usually served as a side dish. The term couscous also refers to a North African meat stew in which semolina or cracked wheat is steamed in the top part of a special pot called a couscoussière.

☙

Mediterranean Stew

8 ounces fresh okra *or* 1 package
   (10 ounces) frozen cut okra,
   thawed
1 medium butternut or acorn
   squash
2 tablespoons olive oil
1½ cups chopped onions
1 clove garlic, minced
½ teaspoon ground cumin
½ teaspoon ground turmeric
¼ teaspoon ground cinnamon
¼ teaspoon ground red pepper
¼ teaspoon paprika
2 cups cubed unpeeled eggplant
2 cups sliced zucchini
1 medium carrot, peeled, sliced
1 can (8 ounces) tomato sauce
½ cup canned vegetable broth
1 can (15½ ounces) chick-peas,
   drained
1 medium tomato, chopped
⅓ cup raisins
   Salt
6 to 8 cups hot cooked couscous
   Minced fresh parsley (optional)

1. Cut okra into ¾-inch slices. Peel squash; trim off stem end. Cut squash lengthwise into halves; discard seeds. Cut flesh into 1-inch pieces. Set aside.

2. Heat oil in Dutch oven over high heat until hot. Add onions and garlic; cook and stir 5 minutes or until tender. Stir in cumin, turmeric, cinnamon, pepper and paprika; cook and stir 2 to 3 minutes.

3. Add okra, squash, eggplant, zucchini, carrot, tomato sauce and broth. Bring to a boil over high heat; reduce heat to low. Simmer, uncovered, 5 minutes, stirring occasionally.

4. Stir in chick-peas, tomato and raisins; cover and simmer 30 minutes. Season with salt. Serve over couscous. Garnish with parsley, if desired.   *Makes 6 servings*

Mediterranean Stew

Chicken and Vegetable Couscous

    1 tablespoon vegetable oil
    3 boneless, skinless chicken
         breast halves (3 ounces each),
         cut into 3-inch cubes
  ½ cup chopped green onions
    3 cloves garlic, minced
 1¼ cups tomato sauce
 1¾ cups water, divided
 1¼ cups chopped carrots
    1 cup rinsed and drained canned
         Great Northern beans
    1 large potato, peeled, cubed
    1 yellow squash, chopped
    1 medium tomato, chopped
  ¼ cup chopped red bell pepper
  ¼ cup raisins
    2 tablespoons packed brown
         sugar
    2 teaspoons ground cumin
  ¾ teaspoon ground cinnamon
    3 to 4 drops hot pepper sauce
    1 cup dry couscous

1. Heat oil in medium skillet until hot; add chicken. Cook over medium heat until chicken is browned on all sides. Add onions and garlic; cook and stir 1 minute. Stir in tomato sauce and ¼ cup water. Add remaining ingredients except 1½ cups water and couscous. Bring to a boil; reduce heat to low. Cook 15 minutes, stirring occasionally.

2. Meanwhile, bring remaining 1½ cups water to a boil; add couscous. Cover and remove from heat; let stand 5 minutes. Serve chicken and vegetables over couscous.

Makes 6 servings

*Chicken and
Vegetable Couscous*

CRANBERRY

The cranberry is a fruit native to North America. The Pilgrims thought the shape of the pink cranberry blossom resembled the shape of a crane's head and neck. They called the berry "crane berry," which has been shortened to cranberry. Cranberries are small, round red berries grown in large marshy areas on low-lying vines. Raw cranberries have a very tart flavor and firm, crunchy texture. There are two methods for harvesting cranberries, dry and wet. In dry harvesting a mechanical picker combs the berries off the vines. Most of these berries are used for cooking and baking. In wet harvesting, the bogs are flooded with water. The next day a water reel stirs up the water to loosen the cranberries from the vines. The berries float to the surface where they are collected. These berries are mostly processed for juice and sauces. Massachusetts and Wisconsin are the leading producers of cranberries in the United States.

🌾

Uses: Cranberries are best known as the basis for cranberry sauce (jellied and whole berry) and cranberry relish.

• Cranberries can be mixed with apples or pears for pies, tarts and crisps.

• They are a great addition to muffins, breads, chutneys and desserts.

• Cranberry juice is the basis for many commercial beverages.

• Dried cranberries can be eaten as a snack or used like raisins for baking.

Availability: Fresh cranberries are readily available September through December. Since they are not available fresh other months of the year, buy an extra bag or two for the

freezer. Cranberries are most commonly sold in 12-ounce plastic bags. They are also sold canned as whole-berry or jellied sauce. Sweetened dried cranberries are now available in many large supermarkets.

Buying Tips: Look for plump, firm and unblemished red berries. The color may vary from light to dark.

Yield: 1 (12-ounce) bag = 3 cups whole berries; 2½ cups chopped.

Storage: Fresh unwashed cranberries can be kept in an unopened plastic bag for up to one month in the refrigerator and for up to one year in the freezer. Double wrap the bag with freezer wrap before freezing. Dried cranberries should be kept in an airtight container and will keep indefinitely.

Basic Preparation: Fresh cranberries should be rinsed under cold running water and sorted. Discard any soft or blemished berries before cooking. Add whole or chopped fresh cranberries or unthawed frozen cranberries to quick breads. They are most easily chopped in a food processor with the chopping blade using an on/off pulsing action.

Special Interest

Wild cranberries were an important source of vitamin C to Native Americans who used them to make a survival cake known as pemican.

Cranberry Oat Bread

¾ **cup honey**
⅓ **cup vegetable oil**
2 **eggs**
½ **cup milk**
2½ **cups all-purpose flour**
1 **cup uncooked rolled oats**
1 **teaspoon baking soda**
1 **teaspoon baking powder**
½ **teaspoon salt**
½ **teaspoon ground cinnamon**
2 **cups fresh or frozen cranberries**
1 **cup chopped nuts**

1. Combine honey, oil, eggs and milk in large bowl; mix well. Combine flour, oats, baking soda, baking powder, salt and cinnamon in medium bowl; mix well. Stir into honey mixture. Fold in cranberries and nuts. Spoon evenly into two greased and floured 8½×4½×2½-inch loaf pans.

Cranberry Oat Bread

2. Bake in preheated 350°F oven 40 to 45 minutes or until wooden toothpick inserted near center comes out clean. Cool in pans on wire racks 15 minutes. Remove from pans; cool completely on wire racks.

Makes 2 loaves

Favorite recipe from **National Honey Board**

Cranberry Sauce

2 **cups fresh or thawed frozen cranberries, drained**
1 **cup orange juice**
¾ **cup sugar**
2 **teaspoons cornstarch**
2 **teaspoons cold water**
1 **tablespoon grated lemon peel**
2 **to 3 tablespoons cranberry- or orange-flavored liqueur (optional)**

1. Combine cranberries, juice and sugar in medium saucepan. Bring to a boil over high heat, stirring frequently; reduce heat to medium-low. Cover; simmer 10 minutes or until cranberries are tender and pop. Remove saucepan from heat.

2. Remove ½ of cranberries from saucepan; set aside in medium bowl. Mash remaining cranberries with back of spoon.

3. Blend cornstarch and water in small bowl until smooth. Add cornstarch mixture and lemon peel to saucepan; blend well. Simmer over medium heat 2 minutes or until thickened, stirring frequently. Stir in reserved whole cranberries. Remove saucepan from heat. Cool completely. Stir in liqueur to taste, if desired. Store in airtight container in refrigerator up to 3 weeks.

Makes about 2 cups

CREAM

Cream is the thick part of milk that contains a rich concentration of butterfat. Before the advent of homogenization, milk naturally separated into two layers—cream at the top and milk on the bottom that was almost fat-free. Now, cream is separated out of milk by centrifugal force.

❧

Cream has many uses, both savory and sweet, as well as some properties that give it distinct advantages over milk. Because the protein in cream is diluted by a large proportion of butterfat, cream is less likely than milk to form a skin on the surface when boiled. Also, cream is less likely than milk to curdle when mixed with acidic ingredients, such as lemon juice or tomatoes.

TYPES OF CREAM
Different types of cream are based on their percentage of butterfat. Each has specific uses.

Half-and-Half: This cream is made from equal parts cream and milk. With 10½ to 15 percent butterfat, it is used as coffee whitener but also can be used in sauces and cream soups. In fact, it is often substituted for whipping cream in these foods because it has less fat.

Light Cream: Also called coffee cream, light cream contains about 20 percent fat, although the fat content can go as high as 30 percent. Even though it will not whip, light cream can replace whipping cream in many recipes, such as sauces, ice cream, soups and puddings. Light cream is not available everywhere. If it is not available in your area, substitute half-and-half for it.

Whipping Cream: Also called heavy cream, whipping cream has 35 to 40 percent butterfat or occasionally more. It is used in many preparations, including sauces, soups, ice creams and custards. It is the only cream suitable for whipping. Almost all whipping cream is now ultrapasteurized, a process of heating that considerably extends its shelf life by killing bacteria and enzymes. Cream that is not ultrapasteurized is preferred by some cooks who cite its superior taste and whipping qualities. It is available in some specialty markets and natural food stores.

To Whip Cream: Use a bowl that is deep enough to allow cream to double in volume. Cream whips better if it is well chilled. It also is helpful to chill the bowl and beaters. Begin with an electric mixer on low speed. After several seconds, increase to high speed and beat to the desired consistency. Softly whipped cream should hold soft peaks when the beater is lifted. To test for soft peaks, turn off mixer and lift beaters from whipped cream; it should have droopy but definite peaks.

In stiffly whipped cream, the beater will leave furrows through the cream and it will hold firm peaks when the beaters are lifted. Watch carefully because at this stage the cream is close to becoming butter. If the cream develops small curds and a yellow tint, it has been beaten too long.

If sugar and flavorings are to be added, add them to the cream just before it is fully whipped. Adding them earlier will prevent the cream from reaching full volume. Although it is best to use whipped cream immediately, it can be refrigerated for several hours. It can rewhipped briefly to stiffen it, but it will not have the volume it had initially.

Aerosol whipped cream is sold in pressurized cans in the dairy section of the supermarket. It is real cream, but it is not truly whipped. Instead, it is expanded by a gas, such as nitrous oxide. This product is sweetened and contains stabilizers and emulsifiers. Aerosol dessert toppings are also available, but these do not include cream and should not be confused with whipped cream.

Testing for soft peaks.

Testing for stiff peaks.

Tip

If you overbeat cream and it becomes buttery, carefully whisk in additional whipping cream, 1 tablespoon at a time, until the yellow curds disappear.

Crème fraîche is a cultured, thickened French cream with a smooth texture and subtle nutty taste. It is used as a dessert topping and in cooked sauces and soups, where it has the advantage of not curdling when boiled. In France, *crème fraîche* is made from unpasteurized cream that thickens from the lactic acid contained in it. A version can be made at home by combining 2 tablespoons buttermilk and 1 cup whipping cream in a covered glass jar and letting it stand at room temperature for about 24 hours, until it thickens. It then can be refrigerated for about one week.

CREAM, TO

Creaming is the technique of mixing ingredients (usually solid fat, such as butter, margarine or shortening, and sugar) until light and fluffy. The purpose is both to blend the ingredients and incorporate some air into the mixture. Shortened cakes rely on the air incorporated during the creaming process for a part of their leavening. Butter and shortening should be at room temperature for creaming. Margarine must be softened but not liquefied. Although creaming may be done with a mixing spoon, it is less time consuming to use an electric mixer.

Tip

Leftover whipped cream can be frozen; spoon it into mounds on a baking sheet lined with waxed paper or parchment. Freeze it, uncovered, until firm. Then place the mounds in a plastic bag and seal it. It will keep up to one week. Remove mounds from freezer and place them on the dessert to thaw. Thawing takes about five minutes. If the dessert is warm, serve immediately.

Classic Crème Brûlée

CRÈME BRÛLÉE

Crème brûlée, meaning "burnt cream," is a rich, chilled custard that is topped with brown or granulated sugar just before serving and quickly broiled until the sugar is caramelized. This creates a delicious brittle coating for the cold creamy custard. Some chefs prefer to caramelize the sugars with a blow torch.

Classic Crème Brûlée

> 2 cups whipping cream
> 4 egg yolks, beaten
> ¼ cup granulated sugar
> 1 teaspoon vanilla extract
> Brown sugar

1. Preheat oven to 325°F.

2. Place cream in heavy medium saucepan. Heat over medium-low heat until small bubbles appear around the edge of the pan (130° to 140°F).

3. Whisk egg yolks briefly in medium bowl. Whisk in sugar until blended. Stir in hot cream. Add vanilla until well blended. Pour into 6 small ovenproof custard cups. Place cups in 13×9 baking pan. Fill with hot water halfway up side of cups.

4. Bake on middle rack of oven 50 to 55 minutes until knife inserted in center comes out clean. (The custard may still look thin but will set upon cooling.) Refrigerate until well chilled at least 4 hours or up to a day before you plan to serve it.

5. Preheat broiler.

6. Press brown sugar through sieve with back of spoon. Sprinkle ¼-inch-thick layer of sifted brown sugar over tops of custards. Broil 6 inches from heat, rotating occasionally, to brown sugar evenly. Broil until a fine, golden crust forms. Serve immediately.

Makes 6 servings

CRÈME CARAMEL

Crème caramel is a light custard mixture that is poured into a caramel-coated mold and baked in a water bath. After baking and chilling, this dessert is turned out onto a serving plate. The melted caramel then forms a topping and sauce for the custard. This dish is known as crema caramella in Italy, flan in Spain and Mexico and crème renversée in France.

CRÊPE

Crêpe is the French word for "pancake," but crêpes are not at all like American pancakes. The crêpe, made from a thin batter of eggs, milk and flour, is a paper-thin wrapper for a filling. Thin unleavened batter is poured into a crêpe pan or small skillet with sloping sides and then tilted so the batter flows quickly over the bottom of the pan forming a thin layer. Crêpes are cooked only until lightly browned on one side and dry on the other side. Fillings can be either savory or sweet. Crêpe Suzette, the most well-known crêpe dish, is composed of folded crêpes without filling that are heated in an orange-butter sauce and finished with flaming liqueur. This dish is usually prepared at the table, making for a spectacular presentation.

Tip

Crêpes can be made ahead. Wrap them in stacks of six with foil. Store them in the refrigerator for up to two days or in the freezer for up to two months. Thaw frozen crêpes at room temperature for one hour.

Seafood Crêpes

Technique for Basic Crêpes

Step 3. *Swirling crêpe batter to cover bottom of pan.*

Seafood Crêpes

Basic Crêpes (recipe follows)
3 tablespoons butter or margarine
⅓ cup finely chopped shallots or
    sweet onion
2 tablespoons dry vermouth
3 tablespoons all-purpose flour
1½ cups *plus* 2 tablespoons milk,
    divided
¼ to ½ teaspoon hot pepper sauce
    (optional)
8 ounces cooked peeled and
    deveined shrimp, coarsely
    chopped (about 1½ cups)
8 ounces lump crabmeat or
    imitation crabmeat, shredded
    (about 1½ cups)
2 tablespoons snipped fresh
    chives or green onion tops
3 tablespoons freshly grated
    Parmesan cheese
Fresh chives and red onion rings
    (optional)

1. Prepare Basic Crêpes.

2. Preheat oven to 350°F.

3. Melt butter over medium heat in medium saucepan. Add shallots; cook and stir 5 minutes or until shallots are tender. Add vermouth; cook 1 minute. Add flour; cook and stir 1 minute. Gradually stir in 1½ cups milk and pepper sauce, if desired. Bring to a boil, stirring frequently. Reduce heat to low; cook and stir 1 minute or until mixture thickens.

4. Remove from heat; stir in shrimp and crabmeat. Measure ½ cup seafood mixture; set aside.

5. To assemble crêpes, spoon about ¼ cup seafood mixture down center of each crêpe. Roll up crêpe jelly-roll style. Place, seam side down, in well-greased 13×9-inch baking dish.

6. Stir chives and remaining 2 tablespoons milk into reserved seafood mixture. Spoon seafood mixture over center of crêpes; sprinkle cheese evenly over top.

7. Bake, uncovered, 15 to 20 minutes until heated through. Garnish with chives and red onion, if desired. Serve immediately.

Makes 6 servings

Basic Crêpes

1½ cups milk
1 cup all-purpose flour
2 eggs
¼ cup butter or margarine,
    melted, cooled, divided
¼ teaspoon salt

1. Combine milk, flour, eggs, 2 tablespoons butter and salt in food processor; process until smooth. Let stand at room temperature 30 minutes.

2. Heat ½ teaspoon butter in 7- or 8-inch crêpe pan or skillet over medium heat. Process crêpe batter again until blended.

3. Pour ¼ cup batter into hot pan. Immediately rotate pan back and forth to swirl batter over entire surface of pan. Cook 1 to 2 minutes until crêpe is brown around edges and top is dry. Carefully turn crêpe with spatula and cook 30 seconds more. Transfer crêpe to waxed paper to cool. Repeat with remaining batter, adding remaining butter only as needed to prevent sticking.

4. Separate each crêpe with sheet of waxed paper. Cover and refrigerate up to 1 day or freeze up to 1 month before serving.

Makes about 1 dozen crêpes

CRISP

A crisp is a baked fruit dessert topped with a crisp, crunchy topping. Fruit is first placed in the dish and then a crumbled topping, usually flour, sugar and butter, is sprinkled over the top. The dessert is then baked and the crumb topping becomes crisp and crumbly. Crisps are often topped with whipped cream and are best served warm.

🌾

Cranberry Apple Crisp

⅓ to ½ cup sugar
3 tablespoons ARGO® or KINGSFORD'S® Corn Starch
1 teaspoon ground cinnamon
½ teaspoon ground nutmeg
5 to 6 cups cubed peeled tart apples
1 cup fresh or frozen cranberries
½ cup KARO® Light Corn Syrup
1 teaspoon grated orange peel

Topping
½ cup chopped walnuts or uncooked oats
⅓ cup packed brown sugar
¼ cup all-purpose flour
¼ cup (½ stick) MAZOLA® Margarine

Preheat oven to 350°F. In large bowl combine sugar, corn starch, cinnamon and nutmeg. Add apples, cranberries, corn syrup and orange peel; toss to mix well. Spoon into 8-inch square baking dish.

For Topping, combine nuts, brown sugar and flour. With pastry blender or 2 knives, cut in margarine until mixture resembles very coarse crumbs. Sprinkle over cranberry mixture.

Bake 50 minutes or until apples are tender and juices that bubble up in center are shiny and clear. Cool slightly; serve warm.

Makes 6 to 8 servings

Prep time: 15 minutes
Bake time: 50 minutes plus cooling

Cranberry Apple Crisp

CRISP, TO

Crisping is a term meaning to refresh or to make firm and brittle. To crisp vegetables that have lost their snap, such as carrots or celery, soak them in ice water until they have become crisp again. Other foods that have lost their freshness, such as pretzels or crackers, may be crisped by being heated in a 300°F oven until they are brittle again and have regained their flavor.

CROISSANT

Croissant is the French word for crescent, which is the shape of this flaky, buttery yeast pastry adapted by the French from an Austrian pastry. Many layers of yeast dough or puff pastry are layered with butter, cut into triangles and then rolled, and formed into the crescent shape. Although usually served for breakfast in France, they are often used as a meal accompaniment or for sandwiches in America.

CROUTON

Probably derived from the French word croûte meaning crust, crouton refers to a small piece or cube of bread that has been crisped by baking or browning in a pan. Croutons are widely used as garnishes on soups, salads and casseroles. They may be purchased prepackaged or prepared at home. Croutons come plain or flavored with cheese, herbs or other seasonings.

Special Interest

Croissants originated in the seventeenth century when Austria was at war with Turkey. Austrian bakers alerted their army that Turkish soldiers were tunneling under their kitchens in order to attack. The bakers were rewarded by being asked to create a commemorative pastry. The result symbolized the crescent of the Turkish flag.

CRUMBLE

A crumble is a dessert of fresh fruit topped with a crumbly pastry mixture that becomes brown and crispy when baked. It is believed to have its origin in Great Britain.

CRUMBLE, TO

To crumble means to break food into small pieces of irregular size. It is usually done with the fingers. Ingredients often crumbled are blue cheese and bacon. Both foods can be purchased in the supermarket already crumbled.

CRUSH, TO

Crushing means reducing a food, such as crackers, to small fine particles by rolling with a rolling pin or pounding with a mortar and pestle. A food processor or blender also works well. Fruit can be crushed to extract its juices. Garlic is sometimes crushed with the flat side of a knife blade or garlic press to release its flavor.

CRUST

Crust is the crisp outer layer of a food, such as bread, or the thin layer of pastry that serves as the shell and topping of a pie. Crusts can be made from a wide range of ingredients. The traditional pastry crust combines flour, fat and liquid. Cookie crumbs, graham cracker crumbs, ground nuts and biscuit dough are also used for crusts. Today pastry, cookie and graham cracker crusts can be purchased already made. In fact, ready-made crumb crusts and frozen unbaked pastry crusts are already formed in a foil pie pan eliminating all work for the consumer except baking. Sticks of pie crust dough and refrigerated pre-rolled pie crusts are also available in supermarkets. The term crust may also refer to the crisp, browned exterior of a baked, fried or roasted food.

☙

Classic Crisco® Crusts

Ingredients for 9-inch Classic Crisco Single Crust
- 1⅓ cups all-purpose flour
- ½ teaspoon salt
- ½ CRISCO Stick *or* ½ cup CRISCO All-Vegetable Shortening
- 3 tablespoons cold water

Ingredients for 9-inch Classic Crisco Double Crust
- 2 cups all-purpose flour
- 1 teaspoon salt
- ¾ CRISCO Stick *or* ¾ cup CRISCO All-Vegetable Shortening
- 5 tablespoons cold water

Ingredients for 10-inch Classic Crisco Double Crust
- 2⅔ cups all-purpose flour
- 1 teaspoon salt
- 1 CRISCO Stick *or* 1 cup CRISCO All-Vegetable Shortening
- 7 to 8 tablespoons cold water

1. Spoon flour into measuring cup and level. Combine flour and salt in medium bowl.

2. Cut in shortening using pastry blender or 2 knives until flour is blended to form pea-size chunks.

3. Sprinkle with water, 1 tablespoon at a time. Toss lightly with fork until dough forms a ball.

4. Press dough between hands to form 5- to 6-inch "pancake." Flour rolling surface and rolling pin lightly. Roll dough into circle. Trim circle 1 inch larger than upside-down pie plate. Carefully remove trimmed dough. Set aside to reroll and use for pastry cutout garnish, if desired.

5. Fold dough into quarters. Unfold and press into pie plate. Fold edge under. Flute.

6. For recipes using a baked pie crust, heat oven to 425°F. Prick bottom and side thoroughly with fork (50 times) to prevent shrinkage. Bake at 425°F for 10 to 15 minutes or until lightly browned.

7. For recipes using an unbaked pie crust, follow baking directions given for that recipe.

8. For double crust pies, follow steps 1 through 3 for Classic Crisco Crusts. Divide dough in half. Roll out each half separately as described in step 4. Transfer bottom crust to pie plate as described in step 5. Trim edge even with plate. Add desired filling to unbaked crust. Moisten pastry edge with water. Lift top crust onto filled pie. Trim ½ inch beyond edge of pie plate. Fold top edge under bottom crust. Flute. Cut slits in top crust to allow steam to escape. Follow baking directions given for that recipe.

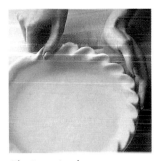

Folding dough into quarters.

Fluting single crust

Fluting double crust.

Chocolate Nut Crust

**6 squares BAKER'S® Semi-Sweet
   Chocolate
1 tablespoon margarine or butter
1½ cups toasted finely chopped
   nuts**

LINE 9-inch pie plate with foil.

MICROWAVE chocolate and
margarine in large microwavable
bowl on HIGH 2 minutes or until
margarine is melted. Stir until
chocolate is completely melted.

STIR in nuts. Press mixture onto
bottom and up side of prepared pie
plate. Refrigerate until firm, about
1 hour.

REMOVE crust from pie plate; peel off
foil. Return crust to pie plate or place
on serving plate. Refrigerate.

Makes one 9-inch crust

Prep time: 15 minutes
Chill time: 1 hour

Fiesta Beef Pot Pie

Fiesta Beef Pot Pie

Crust
**1⅔ cups all-purpose flour
⅓ cup yellow cornmeal
2 tablespoons toasted wheat germ
1 teaspoon salt
¾ CRISCO® Stick or ¾ cup
   CRISCO All-Vegetable
   Shortening
⅓ cup shredded Cheddar cheese
5 to 7 tablespoons cold water**

Filling
**1 pound boneless beef chuck, cut
   into ½-inch chunks
1 tablespoon CRISCO All-
   Vegetable Shortening
½ cup chopped green bell pepper*
½ cup chopped onion*
1 can (14½ ounces) Mexican-style
   stewed tomatoes,* undrained
1 can (8½ ounces) whole kernel
   corn, drained
1 can (4 ounces) sliced
   mushrooms, drained
½ cup water
⅓ cup tomato paste
2 teaspoons sugar
1 teaspoon chili powder
½ teaspoon ground cumin
¼ teaspoon salt
⅛ teaspoon crushed red pepper
   flakes (optional)
⅓ cup sliced black olives**

Glaze and Topping
**1 egg, beaten
¼ teaspoon salt
⅓ cup shredded Cheddar cheese**

**If Mexican-style tomatoes are unavailable,
use plain stewed tomatoes. Increase green
pepper and onion to ⅔ cup each. Add
1 tablespoon minced jalapeño pepper and
¼ teaspoon garlic powder.*

1. For crust, combine first four
ingredients in large bowl. Cut in ¾
cup shortening and ⅓ cup cheese.
Sprinkle with water, 1 tablespoon at a
time. Toss lightly with fork until
dough forms a ball. Divide dough in
half. Roll out bottom crust. Press
bottom crust into 9-inch pie plate;
flute. *Do not bake.*

2. For filling, brown beef in 1 tablespoon shortening in large skillet. Remove beef with slotted spoon. Add green pepper and onion to skillet; cook until tender. Add beef, tomatoes with liquid, corn, mushrooms, water, tomato paste, sugar, chili powder, cumin, ¼ teaspoon salt and red pepper, if desired. Cover. Bring to a boil. Reduce heat and simmer 30 minutes, stirring occasionally. Remove from heat. Stir in olives. Spoon hot filling into unbaked pie crust. Moisten pastry edge with water.

3. Heat oven to 425°F. Roll top crust. Lift onto filled pie. Trim ½ inch beyond edge of pie plate. Fold top edge under bottom crust. Flute. Cut slits or design in top crust to allow steam to escape.

4. For glaze and topping, combine egg and ¼ teaspoon salt. Brush lightly over top crust. Bake at 425°F for 30 to 40 minutes or until crust is golden brown. Sprinkle with cheese. Let stand 10 minutes before cutting and serving. Serve hot or warm. Refrigerate leftover pie.

Makes one 9-inch pie

Graham Cracker Crumb Crust

22 to 24 square graham crackers*
⅓ cup sugar
¼ to ⅓ cup butter or margarine, melted

Substitute 1½ cups purchased graham cracker crumbs for graham crackers and proceed with step 3.

1. Preheat oven to 350°F.

2. Place crackers in food processor, breaking into smaller pieces if necessary. Process using on/off pulses until finely crushed.

3. Combine cracker crumbs, sugar and butter in medium bowl; mix well. Press firmly onto bottom and up side of 8 or 9 inch pie plate.

4. Bake about 8 minutes or until browned. Cool completely before filling.

Makes one 8- or 9-inch crust

Note: For vanilla wafer or chocolate cookie crust, substitute 1⅔ cups cookie crumbs for the graham crackers. Prepare as directed.

CUBE, TO

To cube means to cut food, especially meat and cheese, into cubes of uniform size. The size depends on the food and how it will be prepared or presented, but cubed food is always larger in size than diced food. The smallest cube is about one-half inch.

☙

CUCUMBER

Cucumber seeds found near the Burma-Thailand border have been carbon-dated to reveal that cucumbers were grown as far back as 7750 B.C. Christopher Columbus brought cucumber seeds to America. A refreshing appetite stimulator and more than 95 percent water, the cucumber fits the saying "cool as a cucumber."

☙

Uses: The majority of cucumbers are eaten raw as relishes and crudités.

• Cucumbers are used as ingredients in salads, sandwiches or chilled soups.

• Although less common, cucumbers may be baked, braised, boiled, sautéed or steamed as a vegetable side dish.

• Small varieties of cucumbers are pickled.

> **Tip**
>
> *Cucumber skin can be bitter. To be sure, cut off a piece of the skin and taste it—if it's bitter, peel the cucumber.*

Tip

To add a decorative touch to cucumber slices, score the skin of a cucumber by pulling the tines of a dinner fork along the length of the cucumber. Rotate the cucumber and repeat until completely scored. Then cut the cucumber crosswise into slices.

Varieties: There are two basic types of cucumbers—those eaten fresh and those used for pickling. The most common slicing cucumbers are the field variety, about six to nine inches long with dark green skin and tapered ends. Greenhouse-grown slicing cucumbers are gaining popularity. Referred to as European or English cucumbers, they are long (one to two feet) and thin with a smooth skin and almost no seeds. Because most of the flavor is in the seeds, European cucumbers have less flavor than field-grown varieties. Most pickling varieties go directly to the processor, except for the kirby, which is used to make commercial dill pickles. These can sometimes be found at farmers' markets for home pickling but they can also be eaten raw.

Availability: Slicing cucumbers are available all year but are at their best from May through July. Mostly grown domestically, cucumber supplies are supplemented in fall and winter months by Mexican imports. Cucumbers are easily grown in home gardens and readily available at farmers' markets.

Buying Tips: Select cucumbers that are firm with an even shape and with smooth, deep green skin. Avoid those with bruises, dark spots or shriveled tips. Slender cucumbers usually have fewer seeds than thick cucumbers. Greenhouse cucumbers are usually sold in plastic wrapping.

Yield: 1 (7-inch) cucumber, peeled = 2 cups sliced or chopped.

Storage: Whole cucumbers may be stored in the vegetable drawer of the refrigerator for at least a week. Cut cucumbers, securely wrapped in plastic wrap, may be refrigerated for two or three days.

Basic Preparation: Most field-grown cucumbers found in supermarkets are waxed to improve shelf life and should be peeled with a paring knife or swivel-bladed vegetable peeler. If not waxed, the skin is edible and a good source of dietary fiber. Wash unpeeled cucumbers before using. The seeds are edible but may be removed, if desired. To seed, cut the

cucumber in half lengthwise and scoop out the seeds with the tip of a small spoon.

Cucumbers may be sliced, chopped, cut into sticks or shredded. When shredding cucumbers, first remove the seeds.

Cucumber-Jicama Salad

> 1 cucumber, unpeeled
> 1 jicama (1¼ to 1½ pounds)
> ½ cup thinly slivered mild red onion
> 2 tablespoons fresh lime juice
> ½ teaspoon grated lime peel
> 1 clove garlic, minced
> ¼ teaspoon salt
> ⅛ teaspoon crumbled dried de árbol chili or crushed red pepper flakes
> 3 tablespoons vegetable oil
> Leaf lettuce
> Additional red onion slivers and lime wedges (optional)

1. Cut cucumber lengthwise in half; scoop out and discard seeds. Cut halves crosswise into ⅛-inch-thick slices. Peel jicama. Cut lengthwise into 8 wedges; cut wedges crosswise into ⅛-inch-thick slices.

2. Combine cucumber, jicama and ½ cup onion in large bowl; toss lightly to mix; set aside.

3. Combine juice, lime peel, garlic, salt and chili in small bowl.

Gradually add oil, whisking continuously, until dressing is thoroughly blended.

4. Pour dressing over salad; toss lightly to coat. Cover; refrigerate 1 to 2 hours to blend flavors.

5. Serve salad in lettuce-lined salad bowl. Garnish with onion slivers and lime wedges, if desired.

Makes 6 servings

CURDLE

To curdle is to cause a change, usually undesirable, in which liquid separates into clots (curds) and watery matter (whey). It occurs with dairy products, especially milk, that are cooked to a high temperature or that have acidic ingredients, such as lemon juice, vinegar or tomatoes, added. Custards and certain egg or cheese preparations also can curdle during heating. In cake making, creamed sugar and butter will curdle if cold eggs are added.

🐝

CURE, TO

Curing is a technique used to preserve foods, usually meat, poultry or fish, while imparting a distinctive flavor. The two most common methods are salt curing, when food is either soaked in brine or dried and packed in salt, and smoke curing, when food is smoked for long periods at low temperatures. Common cured foods include ham, corned beef, bacon, pickled herring and salt cod.

🐝

Cucumber-Jicama Salad

CURRANT

Two very different fruits share the name "currant." One is a tiny, smooth fresh berry and the other a small dried fruit resembling a raisin. Fresh currants have a shiny skin and tart, tangy flavor. They can be red, black or white. Although they grow wild in the United States, cultivation is currently restricted since this prickly shrub carries a fungus that kills the white pine.

The dried currant is a small, seedless raisinlike fruit made from a Corinth grape. Many currants are still imported from the Mediterranean region. Black Corinth grapes are now grown in California for dried currants.

🐝

Uses: Fresh currants are eaten out of hand or used for jellies and syrups.

• Fresh currants are the basis for some liqueurs, notably cassis.

• Dried currants can be used whenever raisins are called for, mainly for baking.

Varieties: There are three varieties of fresh currants: red (the most common type), black and white. Black ones are generally used for liqueurs, syrups and preserves.

Availability: Fresh currants are available June through August. Dried currants are available all year.

Buying Tips: Choose plump, brightly colored fresh currants.

Yield: 1 pound fresh currants = 2 to 2½ cups.

Storage: Refrigerate unwashed berries in a plastic bag up to four days. Fresh currants can also be frozen for up to one year. Dried currants should be stored in an airtight container and will keep for a year, if unopened, and two to three months, if opened.

Basic Preparation: Fresh berries should be washed just before using. Gently wash in a bowl full of water. Then carefully drain, dry, and remove stems.

Honey Currant Scones

2½ cups all-purpose flour
2 teaspoons grated orange peel
1 teaspoon baking powder
½ teaspoon baking soda
½ teaspoon salt
½ cup butter or margarine
½ cup dried currants
½ cup sour cream
⅓ cup honey
1 egg, slightly beaten

1. Combine flour, orange peel, baking powder, baking soda and salt in large bowl; mix well. Cut in butter until mixture resembles size of small peas. Stir in currants.

2. Combine sour cream, honey and egg in medium bowl; mix well. Stir honey mixture into dry mixture to form soft dough. Knead dough on lightly floured surface 10 times. Shape dough into 8-inch square. Cut into 4 squares; cut each square diagonally into 2 triangles. Place triangles on greased baking sheet.

3. Bake in preheated 375°F oven 15 to 20 minutes or until golden brown. Serve warm.

Makes 8 scones

Favorite recipe from **National Honey Board**

Currant Spice Muffins

1½ **cups all-purpose flour**
⅓ **cup sugar**
2 **teaspoons baking powder**
1½ **teaspoons pumpkin pie spice**
½ **teaspoon baking soda**
½ **teaspoon salt**
½ **cup milk**
½ **cup sour cream**
3 **tablespoons butter or**
   margarine, melted
1 **egg, beaten**
½ **teaspoon maple extract**
½ **cup dried currants**

1. Preheat oven to 400°F. Grease or paper-line 24 (1¾-inch) mini-muffin cups.

2. Combine flour, sugar, baking powder, pumpkin pie spice, baking soda and salt in large bowl. Combine milk, sour cream, butter, egg and maple extract in small bowl until blended; stir into flour mixture just until moistened. Fold in currants. Spoon into prepared muffin cups, filling almost full.

3. Bake 14 to 16 minutes until wooden toothpick inserted into centers comes out clean. Remove from pans; cool on wire racks. Store tightly covered at room temperature.

Makes 24 mini muffins

CURRY

Curry can refer to both a wide range of hot, spicy sauce-based dishes of the East Indian cuisine and the integral spice blend used to make them. The characteristically bright yellow spice blend known as curry powder is based on garam masala, the Indian spice mixture prepared by pounding or grinding dried spices together. The mixture varies greatly as Indian cooks each make their own unique blends. Common ingredients for curry powder are cinnamon, cardamom, cloves, cumin, coriander, tumeric and ground red or black pepper. Curry powder is seldom prepared from scratch in the American kitchen and is readily available in grocery stores.

❦

Honey Currant Scones

Chicken Curry

4 to 6 boneless, skinless chicken
   thighs, cut into 1-inch cubes
1 cup plain yogurt, divided
2 cloves garlic, minced, divided
1 teaspoon salt
3 tablespoons butter
1 cinnamon stick, broken
1 teaspoon coriander seeds
½ teaspoon cumin seeds
¼ teaspoon cardamom seeds
¼ teaspoon whole black
   peppercorns
¼ teaspoon ground turmeric
1 large onion, chopped
2 teaspoons finely chopped fresh
   ginger
½ cup chicken broth
1 Granny Smith or Jonathan
   apple, unpeeled, cut into
   ½-inch pieces
   Hot cooked rice (optional)
   Flaked coconut, raisins,
   chopped nuts and fresh
   cilantro for condiments
   (optional)

1. Place chicken into medium bowl. Combine ½ cup yogurt, ½ of garlic and salt in small bowl. Pour over chicken; toss to coat well. Cover; refrigerate at least 30 minutes or up to 2 hours, stirring occasionally.

2. To clarify butter, melt in small saucepan over low heat. Skim off white foam with spoon; discard. Continue skimming until only clear butter remains. Strain butter through cheesecloth into container. Discard milky white residue at bottom of saucepan; set aside.

3. To prepare curry powder, process cinnamon stick, coriander, cumin, cardamom and peppercorns in clean coffee or spice grinder. (Or, use mortar and pestle to pulverize.) Stir in turmeric.

4. Heat 2 tablespoons clarified butter in large skillet over medium heat. Add curry powder; cook and stir 2 minutes. Add onion, remaining

Chicken Curry

garlic and ginger; cook and stir 5 minutes or until onion is softened. Push mixture to side of skillet. Heat remaining 1 tablespoon clarified butter. Add chicken with yogurt marinade; cook and stir about 4 to 5 minutes or until chicken begins to turn white.

5. Whisk remaining ½ cup yogurt into broth. Add mixture to skillet; bring to a boil, stirring constantly. Reduce heat to medium-low; cover and cook 20 to 25 minutes until chicken is no longer pink in center. Cook, uncovered, 5 minutes. Stir in apple; cook 2 minutes more. Serve with rice and condiments, if desired.

Makes 4 servings

CUSTARD

Custard is a sweetened puddinglike egg-and-milk mixture in which the egg acts as the thickening agent during cooking. There are two general types of custard: stirred, or soft, custard and baked custard. Both types require slow cooking to avoid curdling. Stirred custards are best made in a double boiler to prevent separation or curdling. They have a pourable consistency and are often used as sauces. Baked custard is generally baked in custard cups in a water bath. It is firm enough to hold its shape when unmolded. Sometimes custards are flavored.

☙

Stirred Custard

2 cups milk
3 eggs
⅓ cup sugar
⅛ teaspoon salt
1 teaspoon vanilla

1. Heat milk in small saucepan until hot (instant-read thermometer should register 170°F). *Do not boil.*

2. Whisk eggs in top of double boiler until well blended. Add sugar and salt; whisk until blended. Stir in hot milk.

3. Fill bottom of double boiler with water to 1 inch *below* level of top pan. Bring water just to a boil; reduce heat to low. Place top of double boiler over hot, not boiling, water.

4. Cook and stir over low heat 10 to 12 minutes until egg mixture thickens and instant-read thermometer registers about 170°F. (Mixture should coat back of spoon. Run fingertip across back of spoon; if mark remains, mixture is ready.) *Do not boil.* The custard will thicken as it cools.

5. Immediately remove top of double boiler from heat. Stir in vanilla. For a smoother texture, strain through wire mesh sieve into medium bowl; cover and refrigerate until ready to use.

Makes 2½ cups custard

CUT IN, TO

Cutting in is the technique used to combine a chilled solid fat such as shortening or butter with dry ingredients, such as flour, so that the resulting mixture is in coarse, small pieces. A fork, two table knives, fingers or a pastry blender may be used. If using a food processor, be careful not to overmix the ingredients. This process is used to make biscuits, scones, pie pastry and some cookies.

☙

Tip

Slow cooking over gentle heat is essential to prevent curdling of a stirred custard. If the water in the bottom of the double boiler begins to simmer, reduce the heat until the water no longer simmers.

D ^{to} F

How is dicing different from chopping? *Learn to beat egg whites.* What type of flour needs to be stored in the refrigerator? *Discover how much fresh fish to buy per serving.* What do nasturtiums taste like? *Whip up a bowl of creamy frosting.*

Top to bottom: French Raisin Toast (recipe on page 221) and Encore Eggs Benedict (recipe on page 192)

DASH

A dash refers to a very small amount of a dry or liquid ingredient, most often a seasoning. Although it is not an exact measure, a dash is generally more than $1/16$ and less than $1/8$ of a teaspoon. When the seasoning is spicy hot, such as ground red pepper, use $1/16$ of a teaspoon and taste the dish before adding more.

🐝

DEGLAZE, TO

Deglazing is the technique used to retrieve the flavorful bits that adhere to a pan after a food, usually meat, has been browned and the excess fat has been drained. While the pan is still hot, a small amount of liquid (water, wine or broth) is added and stirred to loosen the browned bits in the pan. The resulting liquid is used as a base for sauces and gravies.

🐝

DEGREASE, TO

Degreasing is a technique used to remove fat from the surface of a liquid, such as soup or stock. It can be accomplished in several ways. First remove the soup or stock from the heat and allow it to stand briefly until the fat rises. The quickest degreasing method is to skim off the fat using a large spoon. If the fat to be removed is animal fat, the liquid may be chilled; the animal fat will harden, making it easy to lift off. To remove fat from stock or broth, quickly pull a paper towel across the surface, allowing the towel to absorb the fat.

Pulling a paper towel across the surface of stock.

A utensil called a fat separator is a good choice for small amounts of stock or broth. It has a spout at the bottom of the container that allows the broth to be poured out without disturbing the fat at the surface. It is available at cookware shops.

🐝

DEVIL, TO

To devil is to mix with hot seasonings, especially mustard, hot pepper sauce or ground red pepper, to create a deviled dish. The seasonings can be incorporated into a chopped or ground mixture, as in deviled eggs, deviled crab and deviled ham; or they can be applied to the surface of cooked meat, as in deviled short ribs.

🐝

DICE, TO

To dice is to cut food into small cubes that are uniform in size. The smallest dice, which is about $1/8$ of an inch, is best suited for delicate garnishing. More typical are sizes between $1/4$ and $1/2$ of an inch. Dicing is distinguished from chopping and mincing by the care taken to achieve a uniform size for an attractive presentation.

🐝

DILUTE, TO

Diluting is to make a mixture thinner or less concentrated by adding liquid, usually water. Condensed soups and flavored bases are examples of foods that are diluted before using.

🐝

DIM SUM

Dim sum refers to small servings of food traditionally served in Chinese tea houses. Today, dim sum has achieved limited popularity in the United States. Dumplings and other small wrapped bundles of food, such as shrimp balls and spring rolls, are generally served accompanied by tea in a dim sum restaurant. The patron chooses the items, usually from carts or trays, which are circulated throughout the establishment.

❧

Spring Rolls

1 cup preshredded cabbage or coleslaw mix
½ cup finely chopped cooked ham
¼ cup finely chopped water chestnuts
¼ cup sliced green onions
3 tablespoons plum sauce, divided
1 teaspoon Oriental sesame oil
3 (6- to 7-inch) flour tortillas

1. Combine cabbage, ham, water chestnuts, onions, 2 tablespoons plum sauce and oil in medium bowl; mix well.

2. Spread remaining 1 tablespoon plum sauce evenly over tortillas. Spread about ½ cup cabbage mixture on each tortilla to within ¼ inch of edge; roll up.

3. Wrap each tortilla tightly in plastic wrap. Refrigerate at least 1 hour or up to 24 hours.

4. To serve, cut each tortilla into 4 pieces. Garnish as desired.
Makes 12 appetizer servings

Spring Rolls

A dollop of whipped cream.

DOLLOP

A dollop is a portion of a soft, creamy food, such as whipped cream or sour cream, used to give a finishing touch to a serving of food. For example, a slice of pumpkin pie is often topped with a dollop of whipped cream. Occasionally, the term dollop is used to mean a splash of a liquid.

❦

DOT, TO

This term, generally used in cooking as "to dot with butter," refers to cutting butter (or margarine) into small bits and scattering them over a food. This technique allows the butter to melt evenly. It also keeps the food moist, adds richness and can promote browning.

❦

DOUGHNUT

Doughnuts (also spelled "donuts") are individual cakelike pastries often in the shape of a ring. They are usually deep-fried but may be baked. Raised doughnuts are leavened with yeast; cake doughnuts are leavened with baking powder. Jelly doughnuts, also known as bismarcks, are round or rectangular without holes and filled with jelly. Crullers are two strips of doughnut dough twisted together before frying.

DRIPPINGS

Drippings refer to the mixture of melted fat and sometimes juices that accumulate in a pan or skillet after a food, usually meat or poultry, is cooked. They may be used as a base for sauces and gravies and are occasionally used as a medium to cook foods, such as Yorkshire pudding.

❦

DU JOUR

Du jour, a French phrase meaning "of the day," refers to a restaurant dish, such as soup du jour, that is prepared for a particular day. It is often a special that is not on the standard menu.

❦

DUMPLING

Dumplings are usually made from a savory biscuitlike dough that is dropped by spoonfuls into a simmering soup or stew. They are cooked until firm to the touch and wooden toothpicks inserted into the centers come out clean. Dumpling dough may have herbs or seasonings added or may ocassionally be stuffed with meat, cheese or vegetable fillings before cooking. Chinese dumplings are made by wrapping dough around a savory filling and then steaming. Dessert dumplings are fruit-filled packages of pastry dough that are baked and often served warm with a sauce.

❦

Bean Ragoût with Cilantro-Cornmeal Dumplings

- **1 tablespoon vegetable oil**
- **2 large onions, chopped**
- **1 poblano chili, seeded, chopped***
- **3 cloves garlic, minced**
- **3 tablespoons chili powder**
- **2 teaspoons ground cumin**
- **1 teaspoon dried oregano leaves**
- **1 can (28 ounces) tomatoes, undrained, chopped**
- **2 small zucchini, cut into ½-inch pieces**
- **2 cups chopped red bell peppers**
- **1 can (15 ounces) pinto beans, drained**
- **1 can (15 ounces) black beans, drained**
- **¾ teaspoon salt, divided**
  Ground black pepper
- **½ cup all-purpose flour**
- **½ cup cornmeal**
- **1 teaspoon baking powder**
- **2 tablespoons vegetable shortening**
- **¼ cup (1 ounce) shredded Cheddar cheese**
- **1 tablespoon minced fresh cilantro**
- **½ cup milk**

Chili peppers can sting and irritate the skin; wear rubber or plastic gloves when handling peppers and do not touch eyes. Wash hands after handling.

1. Heat oil in Dutch oven over medium heat. Add onions; cook and stir 5 minutes or until tender. Add chili, garlic, chili powder, cumin and oregano; cook and stir 1 to 2 minutes. Add tomatoes with juice, zucchini, bell peppers, beans and ¼ teaspoon salt; bring to a boil. Reduce heat to medium-low. Simmer, uncovered, 5 to 10 minutes until zucchini is tender. Season with salt and black pepper.

2. To prepare dumplings, combine flour, cornmeal, baking powder and remaining ½ teaspoon salt in medium bowl; cut in shortening with pastry blender or 2 knives until mixture resembles coarse crumbs. Stir in cheese and cilantro. Pour milk into flour mixture; blend just until dry ingredients are moistened.

3. Drop dumpling dough into 6 mounds on top of simmering ragoût. Cook, uncovered, 5 minutes. Cover; cook 5 to 10 minutes more until wooden toothpick inserted into dumplings comes out clean. Garnish as desired. Serve immediately.

Makes 6 servings

Bean Ragoût with Cilantro-Cornmeal Dumpling

*Navajo Lamb Stew
with Cornmeal
Dumpling*

Navajo Lamb Stew with Cornmeal Dumplings

2 pounds lean lamb stew meat
   with bones, cut into 2-inch
   pieces *or* 1½ pounds lean
   boneless lamb, cut into
   1½-inch pieces
1 teaspoon salt
½ teaspoon ground black pepper
2½ tablespoons vegetable oil,
   divided
1 large onion, chopped
1 clove garlic, minced
4 cups water
2 tablespoons tomato paste
2 teaspoons chili powder
1 teaspoon ground coriander
3 small potatoes, cut into 1½-inch
   pieces
2 large carrots, cut into 1-inch
   pieces
1 package (10 ounces) frozen
   whole kernel corn
⅓ cup coarsely chopped celery
   leaves
   Cornmeal Dumplings (recipe
   follows)
   Whole celery leaves (optional)

1. Sprinkle lamb with salt and pepper. Heat 2 tablespoons oil in 5-quart Dutch oven over medium-high heat. Add lamb in batches; cook until browned. Transfer meat to medium bowl.

2. Heat remaining ½ tablespoon oil in same pan over medium heat. Add onion and garlic; cook until onion is tender. Stir in water, tomato paste, chili powder and coriander. Return meat to Dutch oven. Add potatoes, carrots, corn and chopped celery leaves. Bring to a boil. Cover; reduce heat to low. Simmer 1 hour and 15 minutes or until meat is tender.

3. During last 15 minutes of cooking, prepare Cornmeal Dumplings. Drop dough onto stew to make 6 dumplings. Cover; simmer 18 minutes or until dumplings are firm to the touch and wooden toothpick inserted into center comes out clean. To serve, spoon stew onto individual plates; top each with 1 dumpling. Garnish with whole celery leaves, if desired.

Makes 6 servings

Cornmeal Dumplings

½ cup yellow cornmeal
½ cup all-purpose flour
1 teaspoon baking powder
¼ teaspoon salt
2½ tablespoons cold butter or
   margarine
½ cup milk

Combine cornmeal, flour, baking powder and salt in medium bowl. Cut in butter with fingers, pastry blender or 2 knives until mixture resembles coarse crumbs. Make well in center; pour in milk. Stir with fork until mixture forms dough.

DUST, TO

Dusting is a technique used to lightly coat a food, before or after cooking, with a powdery ingredient, such as flour or powdered sugar. The ingredient may be sprinkled on using your fingers or shaken from a small sieve or a container with holes on the top. A greased baking pan can be dusted with flour before it is filled, a technique also known as flouring.

❦

EGG

Eggs are one of the world's most versatile foods. They can be prepared in many ways—from simple scrambled eggs to an elegant omelet. They provide an inexpensive and easy-to-prepare source of protein. In addition, eggs perform several important functions in cooking and baking.

❦

Functions: Beating or whipping eggs, especially egg whites, creates a foam that leavens angel food, sponge and chiffon cakes. Foams also provide volume to meringues and soufflés.

• Eggs function as a thickener for cooked foods, such as custards, puddings and sauces.

• Eggs function as an emulsifier, holding in suspension ingredients that do not naturally mix. For example, eggs hold oil and lemon juice (or vinegar) together in mayonnaise.

• Eggs bind ingredients together in foods, such as meatloaf, and help crumbs to adhere to food for frying.

• A combination of beaten egg and water or milk brushed on pastries or breads before baking produces a shiny glaze on the surface of the baked food.

Types, Grades and Sizes: There are many different types of eggs, but the chicken egg is most commonly used in cooking. The color of the egg shell (white or brown) is determined by the breed of the chicken. The color of the shell does not affect flavor, quality, nutrients or cooking characteristics of the egg.

Eggs are sold by grade and size. The grade of an egg is not the measure of its freshness. The grade is based on attributes, such as thickness of the white, firmness of the yolk and size of the interior air pocket. There are three grade classifications for eggs: AA, A and B. High grade eggs (AA) have firm, compact, round yolks with thick whites.

There are six size classifications for eggs: jumbo, extra large, large, medium, small and peewee. The classification is determined by the minimum weight allowed per dozen. For example, a dozen large eggs weighs a minimum of 24 ounces. Any size egg can be used for scrambling, frying, poaching, etc. However, most recipes that call for eggs were developed using large eggs. Unless otherwise specified in the recipe, always use large eggs.

Buying Tips: Select clean, unbroken grade AA or A eggs from refrigerated cases. Purchase eggs as fresh as possible. The USDA requires that egg cartons display the packing date. The date is indicated by a number representing the day of the year. For example, January 1 is day 1 and December 31 is day 365. An expiration date (month and day) may also be displayed. This is the last sale date and must not exceed 30 days after the packing date.

Storage: Refrigerate eggs immediately after purchasing. To prevent them from absorbing odors from other foods, store them in the original carton. For best flavor, use eggs within a week after purchasing. However, they will keep for five weeks after the packing date without loss of nutrients or functional

Tip

To add a shiny glaze to the surface of pastries and breads, brush with an egg wash before baking. To prepare an egg wash, beat 1 egg with 1 tablespoon water until just combined. (For a golden color, substitute an egg yolk for the whole egg.) Lightly brush pastry or bread dough with the egg wash just before baking.

properties. Longer storage may affect the appearance of fried and poached eggs. For hard cooking, choose eggs that are at least a week old. They will peel more easily.

Separating Eggs: Eggs separate more easily when cold. To separate an egg yolk from a white, gently tap the egg in the center with a table knife or against a hard surface, such as the side of a bowl. Gently break the egg in half over a small bowl. Holding a shell half in each hand, gently transfer the yolk back and forth between the two shell halves, allowing the white to drip into the bowl. Place the yolk into another bowl. An egg separator is a useful tool that will facilitate this job. *See Tools, page 525, for additional information.*

Separating the egg yolk from the egg white.

Breakfast Hash (recipe on page 192)

Beating Egg Whites: Egg whites reach the fullest volume if they are allowed to stand at room temperature for 30 minutes before beating. Egg whites must be completely free of egg yolk. To remove any traces of yolk, use a cotton swab or the corner of a paper towel. Always check that the bowl and beaters are clean and dry. The smallest trace of yolk, fat or water can prevent the whites from obtaining maximum volume. Do not use plastic bowls, because they may have an oily film even after repeated washings.

Beat the egg whites slowly with an electric mixer at low speed until the whites are foamy. Then increase the speed to high. Add a pinch of salt or cream of tartar to stabilize the foam. Beat until the whites are stiff but not dry. Immediately fold beaten egg whites into another mixture so volume is not lost.

COOKING METHODS

The basic principle of egg cookery is to cook eggs until the whites are completely coagulated (thickened) and the yolks begin to thicken. Yolks should not be runny, but they should not be hard either. Cook slowly over gentle heat, and once cooked, serve immediately. Keep in mind that too much heat will result in tough, rubbery eggs. The following are guidelines for basic egg-cooking methods.

Eggs Cooked in the Shell: For hard-cooked eggs, place the eggs in a single layer in a saucepan. Add cold water to cover the eggs by one inch. Cover and bring to a boil over high heat. Remove from the heat. Let stand 15 minutes. Immediately pour off the water, cover with cold water or ice water and let stand until cooled.

To peel hard-cooked eggs, crack the shell all over by tapping the egg on the counter. Gently roll the egg across the counter with the palm of your hand to loosen the shell. Peel away the shell under cold running water.

For soft-cooked eggs, place the eggs in a single layer in a saucepan. Add enough cold water to cover the eggs by one inch. Bring to a boil over high heat. Reduce the heat so the water is just below simmering. Cover and cook 4 to 5 minutes, depending on desired doneness. Remove from the heat and drain. Immediately run cold water over the eggs or place in ice water until cool enough to handle.

To serve out of the shell, crack the shell through the middle with a knife. With a teaspoon, scoop the egg out of each shell half into a serving dish. To serve in an egg cup, place the egg in the egg cup, small end down. Slice off the large end of the egg with a small knife or egg scissors and eat from the shell with a spoon.

Eggs Cooked out of the Shell: For fried eggs, melt 1 to 2 tablespoons butter or margarine over medium heat in an 8-inch skillet, swirling to coat the bottom of the skillet. Break two eggs into the pan. Cook 2 to 4 minutes spooning butter over eggs several times. Or, cover and cook 2 to 4 minutes or until the eggs are set. Makes 1 serving.

For scrambled eggs, combine 2 eggs, 2 tablespoons milk, salt and black pepper to taste in a small bowl. Beat with a fork or until completely blended. Melt 1 teaspoon butter or margarine in a 7- to 8-inch skillet over medium-low heat. Pour in the egg mixture. As the mixture begins to set, gently stir it with a wooden spoon, lifting the cooked portions and letting the uncooked egg flow underneath. Cook until the eggs are just set, but still moist looking. *Do not stir the eggs constantly.* Makes 1 serving.

For poached eggs, bring 2 to 3 inches of water, milk, broth or other liquid to a boil over medium-high heat in a medium saucepan. Reduce the heat to keep the water at a simmer. Break 1 egg into a small dish or custard cup. Holding the dish close to the surface of the water, carefully slip the egg into the water. Repeat with another egg. Cook 3 to 5 minutes or until the yolks are just set. Remove the eggs from the saucepan with a slotted spoon and drain on paper towels. Makes 1 serving.

A NOTE ABOUT SALMONELLA

A very small percentage of eggs are contaminated with salmonella, a bacteria that causes a type of food poisoning. To avoid illness caused by this bacteria, follow these simple guidelines:

• Keep eggs refrigerated. If a recipe calls for room temperature eggs, remove only the number of eggs needed and let them stand on the counter for 30 minutes before using.

• Do not eat raw eggs or foods containing raw eggs, such as homemade eggnog and mayonnaise. Avoid lightly cooked eggs. Whites should be set and yolks should be thickened. A temperature of 160°F kills salmonella.

• After handling raw eggs, wash your hands before touching other food or equipment. Keep equipment and counter surfaces clean.

• At buffets and picnics, keep cold foods cold and hot foods hot.

See Food Safety, page 219, for additional information.

Egg Products: Developed for use in commercial and food service applications, processed liquid egg products are now available in cholesterol-free versions for the retail consumer. They are available refrigerated and frozen. Cholesterol-free products generally contain egg whites, nonfat milk, emulsifiers, stabilizers, gums and color. These products can be substituted for whole eggs in cooking and baking. Pasteurized liquid eggs that contain both whites and yolks are also available. Although these are not cholesterol-free, they are a good choice for use in lightly cooked egg dishes or homemade eggnog.

Tip

When poaching eggs, add white vinegar to the poaching water (1 tablespoon vinegar for each 2 cups of water). This helps the egg whites to coagulate, resulting in a more compact shape.

Encore Eggs Benedict

Breakfast Hash

- 1 pound BOB EVANS FARMS®
  Special Seasonings or Sage
  Roll Sausage
- 2 cups chopped potatoes
- ¼ cup chopped red and/or green
  bell peppers
- 2 tablespoons chopped onion
- 6 eggs
- 2 tablespoons milk

Crumble sausage into large skillet.
Add potatoes, peppers and onion.
Cook over low heat until sausage is
browned and potatoes are fork-
tender, stirring occasionally. Drain off
any drippings. Whisk eggs and milk
in small bowl until blended. Add to
sausage mixture; scramble until eggs
are set but not dry. Serve hot.
Refrigerate leftovers.

Makes 6 to 8 servings

Serving Suggestion: Serve with fresh
fruit.

Encore Eggs Benedict

- Hollandaise Sauce (recipe
  follows)
- 16 slices Canadian bacon
- 8 eggs
- 4 English muffins, split, toasted,
  buttered

1. Prepare Hollandaise Sauce; set
aside.

2. Cook bacon in large skillet over
medium-low heat until heated
through, turning occasionally.
Remove from heat.

3. To poach eggs, bring 2 inches of
water in separate large skillet to a boil
over medium-high heat. Reduce heat
to medium-low. Break 1 egg into
small dish or custard cup. Holding
dish close to surface of water,
carefully slip egg into water. Repeat
with remaining eggs. Simmer 3 to
5 minutes until yolks are just set.
Remove eggs with slotted spoon;
drain on paper towels. Transfer to
warm plate; keep warm.

4. Top each English muffin half with
2 slices bacon, 1 poached egg and
1 tablespoon Hollandaise Sauce.
Serve immediately.

Makes 4 servings

Hollandaise Sauce

- 3 egg yolks
- 1 tablespoon fresh lemon juice
- 1 teaspoon dry mustard
- ¼ teaspoon salt
  Dash ground red pepper
  (optional)
- ½ cup butter, cut into 8 pieces

1. Beat egg yolks, juice, mustard, salt
and pepper, if desired, in small
saucepan with wire whisk until
blended; add ½ of butter.

2. Cook over low heat, stirring with
wire whisk until butter is melted. Add
remaining ¼ cup butter; whisk
constantly until butter is melted and
sauce is thickened.

Makes ¾ cup sauce

EGGNOG

Eggnog is a rich, creamy beverage made of milk, eggs, sugar and flavorings. It is most often served during the Christmas season. Brandy, rum, whiskey or some other alcohol is a common addition. Eggnog was traditionally made with raw eggs, but now raw eggs introduce a risk of bacterial contamination. Consequently, when preparing homemade eggnog, be certain to choose a recipe that uses a cooked egg custard base or use a pasteurized liquid whole egg product in place of raw eggs. Commercially prepared eggnog is made with pasteurized eggs, thus eliminating any danger of contamination. It is available in the supermarket dairy section from October through December.

🌰

EGGPLANT

Eggplants originated in Asia, probably India, but most Americans associate them with the cuisine of southern Italy where they have been popular for hundreds of years. Many varieties of eggplants have been cultivated since ancient times. The most common variety in America is the large, elongated dark purple eggplant. The pale yellowish-white flesh, which becomes soft when cooked, has a mild almost bland taste that combines well with many flavors.

🌰

Uses: Eggplant can be breaded or battered and fried. When baked with tomato sauce and cheese it becomes the popular Eggplant Parmigiana.

 It is an important ingredient in pasta sauces and stews.

• Caponata, a Sicilian dish served as a salad, side dish or relish, is made with eggplant, onion, tomato and seasonings.

• Eggplant is the main ingredient in the Greek lamb-and-eggplant casserole, moussaka.

• Grilled eggplant, which is served as a side dish or layered with other grilled vegetables in vegetarian sandwiches, is gaining in popularity in the United States.

Varieties: Western eggplant is the most common in the United States. It is large and cylindrical with smooth, glossy dark purple skin. It can become bitter as it ages.

Japanese eggplant is slender and 5 to 7 inches long. It can be purple or purple and white striped. Its flavor is sweeter and milder than the Western variety.

Sicilian Caponata (recipe on page 194)

Italian eggplant looks like a miniature version of the western eggplant with a more delicate skin and flesh.

White eggplant is small, white and egg shaped with a tough skin that requires peeling. It has a firm, sweet flesh.

Chinese eggplant is long, slender and lavender in color or round, tiny and white.

Availability: The common western eggplant is available all year with the peak months of August and September. Other varieties are less readily available. Look for them in large supermarkets, specialty produce markets or farmers' markets.

Buying Tips: Choose firm, smooth-skinned eggplants that feel heavy for their size. Avoid those with blemishes or soft spots. The stem should be bright green and look fresh. Usually, the smaller the eggplant the sweeter and more tender it is.

Yield: 1 pound eggplant = 1 medium; 3 to 4 cups chopped.

Storage: Eggplant becomes bitter with age. Purchase them within a few days of using. Store unwashed in a cool,

Cutting eggplant into slices.

Eggplant & Pepper Cheese Sandwich

dry place for a day or two or in a plastic bag in the refrigerator for up to five days.

Basic Preparation: Rinse eggplant under cold running water; pat dry with a paper towel. Trim off and discard the stem end. Young eggplants have delicious, edible skin; older eggplants and white eggplants should be peeled. Peeling can be done with a vegetable peeler or a paring knife. Since the flesh of eggplant discolors rapidly, peel it just before using. Cut eggplant into crosswise or lengthwise slices with a chef's knife.

To remove any bitterness, draw off moisture and reduce the amount of oil absorbed during cooking, the western variety of eggplant is often salted before cooking. Begin by slicing the eggplant according to recipe directions and placing the slices in a colander. Sprinkle cut sides with salt. Allow to drain for 30 minutes; then rinse and pat dry with paper towels. An alternative method is to allow salted eggplant slices to stand between several sheets of paper towels weighted with a heavy plate for 30 minutes. Then rinse, drain and pat the eggplant slices dry with paper towels.

Sicilian Caponata

    5 **tablespoons olive or vegetable oil, divided**
    8 **cups (1½ pounds) cubed unpeeled eggplant**
 2½ **cups onion slices**
    1 **cup chopped celery**
 1¾ **cups (14.5-ounce can) CONTADINA® Pasta Ready Chunky Tomatoes with Olive Oil, Garlic and Spices, undrained**
  ⅓ **cup chopped pitted ripe olives, drained**
  ¼ **cup balsamic or red wine vinegar**
    2 **tablespoons capers**
    2 **teaspoons granulated sugar**
  ½ **teaspoon salt**
     Dash of ground black pepper

In medium skillet, heat *3 tablespoons* oil. Add eggplant; sauté for 6 minutes. Remove eggplant from skillet. In same skillet, heat *remaining* oil. Add onion and celery; sauté for 5 minutes or until vegetables are tender. Stir in tomatoes and juice and eggplant; cover. Bring to a boil. Reduce heat to low; simmer for 15 minutes or until eggplant is tender. Stir in olives, vinegar, capers, sugar, salt and pepper; simmer, uncovered, for 5 minutes, stirring occasionally.

Makes 4½ cups caponata

Eggplant & Pepper Cheese Sandwiches

    1 (8-ounce) eggplant, cut into
        18 slices
    Salt and pepper, to taste
    ⅓ cup GREY POUPON®
        COUNTRY DIJON® Mustard
    ¼ cup olive oil
    2 tablespoons REGINA® Red Wine
        Vinegar
    ¾ teaspoon dried oregano leaves
    1 clove garlic, crushed
    6 (4-inch) pieces French bread,
        cut in half
    1 (7-ounce) jar roasted red
        peppers, cut into strips
    1½ cups shredded mozzarella
        cheese (6 ounces)

Place eggplant slices on greased baking sheet, overlapping slightly. Sprinkle lightly with salt and pepper. Bake at 400°F for 10 to 12 minutes or until tender.

Blend mustard, oil, vinegar, oregano and garlic. Brush eggplant slices with ¼ cup mustard mixture; broil eggplant for 1 minute.

Brush cut sides of French bread with remaining mustard mixture. Layer 3 slices eggplant, a few red pepper strips and ¼ cup cheese on each bread bottom. Place on broiler pan with roll tops, cut sides up; broil until cheese melts. Close sandwiches with bread tops and serve immediately; garnish as desired.

Makes 6 sandwiches

EGG ROLL

An egg roll is a Chinese appetizer, consisting of a cylindrical package of thin dough that is filled with finely chopped cooked shrimp, meat and shredded vegetables, such as cabbage, carrots and mushrooms. Traditionally, they are deep-fried and served with sweet-and-sour sauce for dipping. Frozen egg rolls are available. Egg roll wrappers, or skins, are available in the refrigerated section of large supermarkets for those cooks who wish to make these appetizers at home.

☙

EMPANADA

Empanadas are Mexican or Spanish filled pastries similar to turnovers. Usually in the shape of a half circle or triangle, they may be deep-fried or baked. Fillings may be savory or sweet. Empanadas range in size from those that serve several people to small, bite-size versions called empanaditas.

☙

ENCHILADA

Enchiladas are Mexican entrées prepared by rolling softened corn tortillas around a filling of shredded meat, chicken or cheese. They are baked with a topping of sauce and usually cheese. Enchilada sauces can be made of tomatoes and chilies, green tomatillos or cream.

☙

Chicken Enchiladas

3 fresh poblano chilies
1 whole frying chicken (about
    3 pounds), cut into 8 pieces
1 large tomato, peeled, seeded,
    chopped
½ cup finely chopped white onion
1 clove garlic, minced
½ teaspoon ground cumin
¼ teaspoon salt
½ cup chicken broth
1½ cups whipping cream
12 (6-inch) corn tortillas
2 cups (8 ounces) shredded queso
    Chihuahua or Monterey Jack
    cheese
   Green onions and slivered red
    bell pepper (optional)
   Mexican rice (optional)

Chicken Enchiladas

1. Preheat broiler. Place chilies on foil-lined broiler pan; roast chilies 2 to 3 inches from heat source until evenly blistered and charred, turning as needed. Place roasted chilies in plastic bag; close bag. Let stand 20 minutes.

2. Peel chilies under cold running water, pulling off charred skin. Cut open; carefully pull out and discard seeds and veins. Rinse well; pat dry with paper towels. Chop chilies.

3. Place chicken in single layer in 12-inch skillet. Sprinkle with chilies, tomato, white onion, garlic, cumin and salt; add broth. Bring to a boil over medium-high heat. Reduce heat. Cover; simmer 1 hour or until fork can be inserted into chicken with ease and juices run clear, not pink.

4. Remove chicken from skillet, shaking off vegetable pieces. Let stand until cool enough to handle.

5. Skim and discard fat from broth mixture. Bring broth mixture to a boil over medium-high heat. Boil 4 to 8 minutes until mixture is reduced to 2 cups. Pour reduced broth mixture into 13×9-inch baking dish.

6. Remove and discard skin and bones from chicken. Shred chicken into coarse pieces.

7. Preheat oven to 375°F. Heat cream in medium skillet over medium heat to just below boiling; remove from heat.

8. Dip 1 tortilla in cream a few seconds or until limp. Remove, shaking off excess cream. Spread about 3 tablespoons chicken down center of tortilla. Roll up; place, seam side down, on sauce in baking dish. Repeat with remaining tortillas, cream and chicken. Pour any remaining cream over enchiladas. Sprinkle cheese over enchiladas. Bake 25 to 30 minutes until sauce is bubbly and cheese is melted. Garnish with green onions and bell pepper, if desired. Serve with Mexican rice, if desired.   *Makes 4 to 6 servings*

ENDIVE

Endive and chicory are often used as interchangeable terms, but they actually refer to two different families of greens. To further confuse matters, European and American or common and scientific definitions may switch. The three rather different varieties of endive are: Belgian endive, curly endive and escarole.

Clockwise from upper left: watercress, Belgian endive, radicchio and curly endive.

Uses: Belgian endive and curly endive may be eaten fresh in salads. The sweet inner leaves of escarole are also good in salads.

• The slim scoop-shaped leaves of Belgian endive are well designed for use as dippers or to hold fillings.

• Belgian endive may also be served braised or baked as a side dish.

• Curly endive and escarole may be steamed or cooked briefly for side dishes or as ingredients in soups.

Varieties: Belgian endive, also called French endive, is grown as a small (4 to 6 inches long), tightly packed oblong head. The white to very pale green color is the result of a tedious cultivation process that involves growing the heads in complete darkness. Belgian endive has a slightly sharp, piquant flavor.

Curly endive is the variety often mistakenly called chicory. The large heads shaped like an open flower have dark green outer leaves and light green to cream-colored leaves at the center. The curly notched leaves have a slightly bitter taste and are curled tightly at the tips, giving them a prickly feel.

Escarole is similar in shape and color to curly endive with smoother, broader leaves and a milder flavor.

Availability: Belgian endive is available September through May with its peak season being November through April. Curly endive and escarole are available year-round and are most plentiful from June to October.

Buying Tips: For Belgian endive, choose crisp, firm creamy-white heads with well-formed light yellow tips. For curly endive and escarole, select crisp heads that are free of insect damage or discoloration.

Yield: 1 (4-inch-long) head of Belgian endive = 1 serving.

1 pound head of curly endive or escarole = 3 cups torn greens.

Storage: Belgian endive begins to turn pale green and taste bitter when exposed to light. Wrap it in paper towels and store it in a plastic bag in the refrigerator for only a day or two. Curly endive and escarole, well wrapped, will keep in the refrigerator about one week. All greens should be stored unwashed.

Basic Preparation: Belgian endive should be rinsed under cold water. When used as dippers or to hold fillings, separate heads into individual leaves. For cooking, cut heads in half lengthwise.

To clean either curly endive or escarole, separate leaves from the head and swish the leaves in a large bowl or sinkful of water. Repeat this process several times, if necessary, to remove embedded sand or soil. Drain and pat dry. Tear into bite-size pieces for salads or cut crosswise into slices or shreds for cooking.

Special Interest

Growing Belgian endive is a time-consuming process. A special variety of chicory known as witloof chicory is grown for its roots. The roots are dug, stored and then replanted indoors away from light. The crisp pale green heads that sprout from the roots are Belgian endive.

ENGLISH PEA

The English pea, also known as the green, shell or common garden pea, is a round seed of the legume family that grows in pods on a bush or vine. English peas are sweet and crisp when fresh but, like corn, begin converting their sugar to starch soon after picking. For the best flavor, buy peas from local farmers' markets rather than the supermarket or try growing them in your garden.

🌾

Peas with Cukes 'n' Dill

Availability: Fresh peas are available in supermarkets year-round. Since peas are a cool weather crop, the peak season for locally grown English peas is April through July and sometimes again in the fall. They are also available frozen and canned. *Petits pois*, or tiny young peas, popularized by French cooks, are available frozen and canned.

Buying Tips: Choose small, plump pods that are firm, shiny and bright green. The pods should appear well filled. Avoid pods that are yellow, shriveled, limp or dry.

Yield: 1 pound unshelled English peas = 1 cup shelled peas.
1 (10-ounce) package frozen peas = 2 cups.
1 (16-ounce) can peas = 2 cups.

Storage: Store peas unwashed in a plastic bag in the refrigerator for up to three days.

Basic Preparation: Shell English peas just before cooking. To prepare peas, snap off the stem and pull the string down the length of the pod. Press each pod between your thumbs and forefingers to open.

Push the peas out of the pod with

your thumb into a colander. Discard the pods, stems and strings. Rinse under cold running water and drain.

To cook peas, steam them in a vegetable steamer for 4 to 5 minutes, or in ¼ inch of simmering water in a covered saucepan for 3 minutes, or until crisp-tender. Drained peas are often served with butter or cream and seasoned with salt or chopped fresh parsley.

Sugar Snap Peas: A hybrid of the English pea and the snow pea, the sugar snap pea has a pod that remains sweet, tender and edible after the peas have fully developed. Look for crisp, tender and shiny pods with prominent peas. They should not be confused with snow peas, which have flatter pods with tiny peas. *See Snow Pea, page 464.* Sugar snap peas are available all year but are at their peak in the spring. Store them unwashed in a plastic bag in the refrigerator for a day or two.

Wash sugar snap peas under cold running water. They can be eaten raw in salads. Steam them as you would English peas for 2 to 3 minutes or until crisp-tender. They are also ideal for stir-frying. Do not overcook peas or the pods will lose their bright green color and fresh flavor. Cook only until they are crisp-tender.

Peas with Cukes 'n' Dill

 2 pounds fresh peas*
 ½ medium cucumber, peeled
 2 tablespoons butter or margarine
 1 teaspoon dried dill weed
 Salt and ground black pepper
 Fresh dill, pineapple sage leaves and edible flowers, such as pansies (optional)

Or, substitute 1 (10-ounce) package frozen peas, thawed, for fresh peas.

1. To prepare peas, press each pea pod between thumbs and forefingers to open. Push peas out with thumb into colander; discard pods. Rinse peas under running water. Drain well; set aside.

2. Cut cucumber lengthwise in half. Scrape out seeds with spoon; discard. Cut into ¼-inch slices.

3. Heat butter in medium skillet over medium-high heat until melted and bubbly. Add peas and cucumber; cook and stir 5 minutes or until vegetables are crisp-tender. Stir in dill weed; season with salt and pepper. Transfer to warm serving dish. Garnish with fresh dill, sage and edible flowers, if desired. Serve immediately.

Makes 4 side-dish servings

ENTERTAINING

There are many styles of entertaining—casual, formal and informal—but the goal is always the same: to extend a warm welcome to invited guests and to put them at ease in a pleasant social setting. Food is usually a key component.

☙

Although rigid rules are not necessary, some guidelines can help create a smooth-flowing affair. Whether you're planning a bridal shower, a casual brunch, or an elegant party, organization is very important. Once you decide on the style and size of the party, you can make appropriate decisions about food, beverages, flowers, table settings, etc. Make lists, consider options, anticipate all sorts of what-ifs. If you are a beginner at entertaining, do not let lack of experience deter you. Start with small, simple get-togethers and work your way up to more elaborate parties.

Casual Entertaining: Casual parties include barbecues, Sunday-football parties, potluck dinners, etc. This type of entertaining is the most free-form. Casual parties are often planned at the last minute, with invitations issued by phone.

Food can be simple, either homemade or take-out. It is acceptable for close friends and family to bring food, especially if they offer. Serving alcohol is a personal choice that depends on the particular party. If you do serve alcohol, it may be limited to beer and wine. If you offer mixed drinks, it is acceptable for guests to mix their own.

Paper plates and plastic flatware are fine if they suit the mood of the party. Choose from a variety of festive patterns for paper plates and napkins. Buy good-quality plastic utensils so that guests do not struggle when cutting meats.

Tip

When entertaining, keep notes with the menu listing any preparation problems encountered, costs and suggestions for improvements to the menu. This will make it easy to reuse the menu with another group of guests. Just be sure to include a guest list to avoid repetition.

An informal table setting

should be available immediately. Appetizers may be as simple as glazed nuts or spiced olives in bowls set around the room in convenient spots or as fancy as an assortment of light appetizers passed on trays. Since the guests will presumably be standing and holding drinks, make sure that appetizers can be handled easily with one hand and eaten without the benefit of utensils.

Concerning food selection, there are broad parameters of acceptability. It does not have to be elaborate. Most cooks have a few recipes in their repertoire that they are comfortable with and that they make especially well. These are probably more likely to succeed than new and untried recipes. Eliminate as much last-minute work as possible by choosing recipes that can be made ahead of time. You do not want to be caught in the frenzy of trying to greet guests while having to run back into the kitchen to check on dishes. Roasts, whether beef, lamb or chicken, are good choices. Vegetables can be easily overcooked, so blanch them ahead of time and then quickly reheat them with butter and herbs in a skillet or microwave oven.

It is also perfectly acceptable to make some recipes and buy others. Bakeries, take-out shops and delis have wonderful selections and these places can be ideal for bread or rolls, dessert, relish or a side dish. Place the food in a nice serving dish and add a little flourish of fresh herbs or other garnish.

Whether you have place cards or not, it is a good idea for the host to assign seats. It is not mandatory for couples to be seated next to each other. Make arrangements so that the conversation will be lively, interesting and friendly. The host should be in a central spot, easily accessible to the kitchen but also in the midst of the group in order to mediate any uneasy moments in the conversation.

Informal Entertaining: Informal entertaining includes a broad spectrum of events, such as family holiday dinners, birthday and surprise parties, brunches, buffets and open houses. It involves advance planning and notice. Invitations should be issued at least two weeks in advance or even earlier, depending on the season and the guest list. Holiday party invitations should be issued three to four weeks ahead of time. Although the phone is an acceptable means of inviting guests, invitations sent by mail are a nice touch.

Advance planning should be reflected in the details. The table should be neatly set with table decorations. The food selected should be given careful thought. For dinner parties, plan to serve the meal approximately one hour after the guests' arrival time. Beverages and appetizers, however,

Whether you serve the meal in courses or family style depends on the event. A simple starter course is a nice prelude although not a necessity. If a salad or chilled appetizer is served first, it should already be at the table when guests are seated. The main course may be put on plates in the kitchen and brought to the table or served on platters from the dining room. The table should always be cleared before dessert and coffee are served.

Formal: Formal entertaining is appropriate for a fancy occasion, such as New Year's Eve, a wedding reception or an anniversary bash. Formal parties may be held at special locations, such as a banquet hall, yacht or hotel. Invitations are always sent by mail. The food is mostly catered and may be served as a sit-down dinner or buffet style. Because this type of entertaining requires extensive planning and much attention to detail, it cannot be covered fully here.

A WORD ABOUT MENU PLANNING

The purpose of menu planning is to create a meal that is satisfying to the eye as well as to the palate. The goal is to achieve balance between foods with contrasting colors, textures and tastes.

Appearance: When planning a menu, select the entrée first and then pair it with dishes that will complement it in appearance. Colors and shapes should work together to create a pleasing presentation. A meal of three foods of a similar color is not visually interesting. If the entrée is eye-catching, such as a chicken breast with a colorful salsa, team it with a simple rice dish and steamed green beans. On the other hand, dress up a main dish of grilled flounder with colorful side dishes.

Texture: Foods served together should offer some contrast in texture. Soft cheese spreads with crisp crackers,

creamy dips with crunchy chips and tender meats with crisp salads are good examples of foods that complement each other.

Flavors: Complementary flavors make meals interesting. Half the pleasure of eating a spicy burrito is knowing that cooling sour cream and a cold beer are close at hand. Balance hot foods with ones that will quench the fire. Combine bland foods with flavorful ones. Do not repeat strong flavors, such as tomato, garlic and ginger, in the same meal.

Richness: Balance and moderation are important. Do not serve too many rich, creamy dishes and do not get carried away with too much ethnic fusion at the same meal. A rich or filling main course followed by a rich dessert will send your guests home moaning. Finish a rich meal with a light and refreshing fresh fruit dessert. If you want to serve a spectacularly rich dessert, choose a main course that is light.

Special Dietary Needs: Keep in mind any special dietary needs of your guests. If a vegetarian, diabetic or cardiac patient is on the guest list, have an appropriate meal in mind that does not single out this person as an oddball. Guests with allergies should of course be accommodated.

GENERAL GUIDELINES

Always make sure that there is enough food for all the guests, especially if you plan to serve the food buffet style. Many people may take big portions of everything! Also make sure that there is adequate seating for guests to comfortably enjoy the meal.

Something that should not be lost even in the grandness of a fancy party is the role of the host. Regardless of the size or style of the party, the host, by making introductions, guiding conversations and seeing that everyone is getting enough to eat, must make the guests feel welcome and comfortable.

Tip

When guests are seated at a table, always serve food from the left and remove plates from the right. Beverages may be served from the right, since glasses and cups are on the right of the place setting.

EXTRACT AND FLAVORING

Extracts are very concentrated flavorings derived from a variety of foods. Well-known extracts include vanilla, lemon and almond. A pure extract is made by distilling and concentrating the natural oils in a food and mixing them with alcohol. Small amounts, usually a teaspoon or less, provide a lot of flavor impact without adding volume or moisture.

Imitation flavorings are chemical replications of their natural counterparts or creations of flavors that are not available in a natural extract form, such as coconut or maple. A wide variety of extracts and flavorings are available in the spice section of the supermarket. A basic kitchen pantry should have vanilla, almond and lemon extracts and maple flavoring. Extracts are sensitive to heat and light. To prevent evaporation and loss of flavor, keep bottles tightly closed and stored in a cool, dark place.

❦

Vanilla: Probably the most popular and often-used extract is vanilla. It is derived from the long, thin pod of a tropical orchid. Through a lengthy and labor-intensive curing process, the pods are transformed into intensely flavored dark brown vanilla beans. Thus, pure vanilla products remain relatively expensive. Vanilla beans are grown in Madagascar, Mexico and Tahiti. Madagascar provides the majority of the world's supply.

Tip

The flavor of extracts diminishes quickly when cooked. To prevent flavor loss, add extracts to cooked foods that have cooled slightly.

Vanilla Beans: Vanilla beans are available in some large supermarkets, specialty stores and through mail order. They may be stored tightly wrapped in an airtight jar and refrigerated for about six months.

Vanilla beans may be slit lengthwise to scrape out the seeds, which can be used to flavor puddings, custards, cake batters and homemade ice cream. The seeds are visible as tiny black specks in the finished dish.

Vanilla beans can be utilized to make vanilla sugar. This fragrant sugar may be used in place of sugar and vanilla extract in desserts, powdered sugar for sprinkling on cakes, and regular sugar for sweetening coffee. To make vanilla sugar, place two vanilla beans in a pound of granulated or powdered sugar and store in an airtight container for about a week. Remove the beans and store them for up to six months. The beans can be used again to make vanilla sugar.

FAJITA

Fajitas originated in Texas. The traditional dish is prepared by marinating beef skirt steak in oil, lime juice, garlic and ground red pepper before grilling it. The steak is cut into thin strips and rolled in flour tortillas. Fajitas now often include grilled bell peppers and onions. They are served with sour cream, guacamole and salsa. Sometimes the dish is prepared with beef flank steak, chicken strips or shrimp.

❦

Chicken Fajitas

1 pound chicken tenders
¼ cup lime juice
4 cloves garlic, minced, divided
1 cup sliced red bell pepper
1 cup sliced green bell pepper
1 cup sliced yellow bell pepper
¾ cup onion slices (about
    1 medium)
½ teaspoon ground cumin
¼ teaspoon salt
¼ teaspoon ground red pepper
8 teaspoons low-fat sour cream
8 (6-inch) flour tortillas, warmed
Green onion tops (optional)
Salsa (optional)

1. Arrange chicken in 10×7-inch glass baking dish; add lime juice and ½ of garlic. Toss to coat. Cover; marinate in refrigerator 30 minutes, stirring occasionally.

2. Spray large nonstick skillet with nonstick cooking spray; heat over medium heat until hot. Add chicken mixture; cook and stir 5 to 7 minutes until browned and no longer pink in center. Remove chicken from skillet; set aside. Drain excess liquid from skillet, if necessary.

3. Add bell peppers, onion and remaining garlic to skillet; cook and stir about 5 minutes or until peppers are tender. Sprinkle with cumin, salt and ground red pepper. Return chicken to skillet. Cook and stir 1 to 2 minutes.

4. Spread 1 teaspoon sour cream on 1 side of each tortilla. Spoon chicken and pepper mixture evenly over sour cream; roll up tortillas. Tie each tortilla with green onion top, if desired. Serve with salsa, if desired.

Makes 4 servings

Tip: To heat tortillas in conventional oven, wrap in foil and place in 350°F oven about 10 minutes. To heat tortillas in microwave oven, wrap loosely in damp paper towel. Microwave at HIGH (100% power) 1 minute.

Chicken Fajitas

Skillet Steak Fajitas

½ **cup A.1.® Steak Sauce**
½ **cup prepared mild, medium or
    hot salsa**
1 **(1-pound) beef flank or bottom
    round steak, thinly sliced**
1 **medium onion, thinly sliced**
1 **medium green bell pepper, cut
    into strips**
1 **tablespoon FLEISCHMANN'S®
    Margarine**
8 **(6½-inch) flour tortillas,
    warmed**
   Favorite fajita toppings, optional

In small bowl, blend steak sauce and salsa. Place steak in glass dish; coat with ¼ cup salsa mixture. Cover; chill 1 hour, stirring occasionally.

In large skillet, over medium-high heat, cook onion and pepper in margarine for 3 minutes or until tender. Remove with slotted spoon; set aside. In same skillet, cook and stir steak for 5 minutes or to desired doneness. Add remaining salsa mixture, onion and pepper; cook until heated through. Serve with tortillas and your favorite fajita toppings, if desired. Garnish as desired.   *Makes 4 servings*

FENNEL

Fennel (also called Florence fennel, bulb fennel, sweet anise and finocchio) originated in southern Europe. It is most widely used as a vegetable in Mediterranean cuisines. The bulbous base, which slightly resembles celery in appearance and texture, is white to pale green with several slender stalks topped with a fringe of feathery green leaves. Fennel has a crisp texture and a slightly sweet licoricelike flavor, which mellows when cooked.

🌿

Special Interest

Although they are related, bulb fennel should not be confused with fennel seeds that are commonly used in Italian sausage. The seeds are harvested from common fennel, a bulbless variety from the same family.

Uses: Paper-thin slices of the fennel bulb are used raw in salads.

• When cooked, fennel is most commonly braised, sautéed or added to soups.

• Fennel can be topped with Parmesan cheese and baked, mixed with mashed potatoes, or grilled.

Availability: Fennel is in season in the fall, winter and early spring. It is increasingly available all year. It can be found at many large supermarkets as well as Italian markets.

Buying Tips: Select bulbs that are firm, clean and unblemished, with fresh feathery tops. Small bruises on the outermost layer can be trimmed away. If the feathery tops have been trimmed away, it may indicate that the bulb is not fresh. Between the large and small bulbs, there is not a noticeable difference in taste or texture. However, small bulbs usually have a higher percentage of waste.

Yield: 1 pound fennel = 1 large bulb; approximately 2½ cups of trimmed slices.

Storage: Store fennel in the refrigerator in a plastic bag. The bulb will keep for one week; the green tops for two or three days.

Basic Preparation: The bulb typically is the only part that is eaten. The stalks can be tough and the feathery leaves have little flavor. The leaves, which resemble dill in appearance,

can be reserved for use as a garnish. To prepare fennel, wash the bulb under cold water. Trim off the stalks.

Trim the bottom of the bulb, leaving ⅛ inch of the base. Remove any dry or discolored outer layers. For braising, the whole bulb is usually cut  lengthwise into quarters. For salads and soups, the bulb can be sliced crosswise or chopped after quartering.

4. Whisk together flour, half-and-half and sherry in small bowl until smooth. Stir flour mixture into fennel mixture. Cook over medium heat until mixture thickens, stirring constantly. *Do not boil.*

5. To serve, ladle soup into soup bowls; sprinkle each serving with 1 ounce blue cheese and 1½ tablespoons walnuts. Garnish with reserved feathery leaves, if desired.

Makes 4 servings

Fennel and Potato Bisque

Fennel and Potato Bisque

    1 leek, trimmed, cleaned well
  ⅔ pound fennel bulb
    3 tablespoons butter or margarine
    3 cups milk
    1 tablespoon vegetable bouillon
        granules
  ½ teaspoon ground white pepper
    2 cups cubed peeled red boiling
        potatoes
    2 tablespoons all-purpose flour
    1 cup half-and-half
    3 tablespoons dry sherry
    4 ounces blue cheese, crumbled
  ¼ cup *plus* 2 tablespoons finely
        chopped toasted walnuts

1. Cut leek lengthwise in half; cut each half into thin slices. Set aside.

2. To prepare fennel, wash fennel bulb. Trim stalks from top of bulb, reserving feathery leaves for garnish. Trim bottom of bulb, leaving ⅛ inch of base. Remove any dry or discolored outer layers. Cut bulb into quarters; trim core from wedges. Cut into thin slices; cut slices crosswise in half. Set aside.

3. Melt butter in large saucepan over medium heat. Add reserved leek; cook and stir 10 minutes or until tender. Add milk, bouillon granules and pepper. Bring to a boil over medium-high heat. Add fennel slices and potatoes. Reduce heat to low. Cover; simmer 15 to 20 minutes until fennel is very tender.

FIG

Figs have been grown in warm climates for centuries. They were enjoyed by the ancient Egyptians, Romans and Greeks. Spanish monks brought figs to California in the early eighteenth century when they were building missions. The fig is a small fruit with an edible skin, soft flesh and many tiny edible seeds. When ripe, the fig is among the sweetest of fruits. In the United States the majority of figs are grown in California.

❦

Uses: Fresh figs may be eaten whole as a snack or sliced and served with a squeeze of lemon or lime juice. They may be served with milk or cream for breakfast or dessert.

• Figs are often poached or baked.

• Dried figs can be used like any other dried fruit. Chop and add them to cookies, cakes and chutney.

Varieties: There are hundreds of varieties of figs. The most common varieties in the United States are the Black Mission with purplish-black skin and pink flesh, available fresh and dried; the Calimyrna, the variety most commonly dried, seldom available fresh; and the Kadota, with yellow-green skin and pinkish-purple flesh, available most often canned.

Fresh figs are picked when just turning ripe and sold immediately. Figs that are to be dried are allowed to fully ripen on the tree until all the sugar has developed. Partially dried when they are harvested, they are then further dried in the sun or by commercial means.

Availability: Fresh figs are available June until October. Dried and canned figs are available all year.

Buying Tips: Fresh figs should be plump, bright in color and slightly firm to the touch. Avoid ones that are bruised or splitting. Handle with care as their delicate skin bruises easily.

Yield: 1 pound fresh figs = 8 large or 14 small; 2½ cups chopped.
8 ounces dried figs = 20 to 24; 1 to 1¼ cups chopped.

Storage: Fresh figs are extremely perishable and should be used soon after purchase. Store them unwashed in the refrigerator for two or three days. Dried figs stored in an airtight container will keep up to one year.

Basic Preparation: Trim off the hard portion of the stem end of a fresh fig with a sharp knife. Wash them under cold running water. The skin may be peeled, if desired. The most common way to cook fresh figs is to poach them in water, fruit juice or a light sugar syrup.

FILLET

A fillet (filet is the French spelling) is a boneless piece of lean meat or fish. When referring to beef, the fillet is the tenderloin portion, which may be cut into steaks, tournedos or filet mignons. To fillet is to cut a fish or a piece of meat into boneless pieces.

❦

FISH

It is no surprise that cooks are serving more fish than ever before. Fish is versatile, delicious and nutritious. It also cooks quickly. Although there are literally hundreds of species of fish, only a small number are readily available across the country.

❦

Fresh fish are generally separated into two categories—lean and fatty. Lean fish contain from 1 to 5 percent fat. Fatty fish contain from 5 to 35 percent fat, which makes their flesh darker, richer and stronger tasting than lean fish. The type of fish is an important factor when preparing and cooking fish. For an easy reference to types of fish, their availability and preferred cooking methods, refer to the chart on page 208.

Cuts of Fish: Fish come in various forms. The most readily available forms of fish are whole, dressed, pandressed, fillets and steaks. Fillets and steaks are a good choice for inexperienced cooks.

• Whole fish are sold with the head, tail, fins and scales intact and must be gutted before cooking. These are the most economical, but they are best left to experienced cooks.

• Dressed fish are gutted and scaled with the head, tail and fins intact.

• Pan-dressed fish are dressed and have the head and tail cut off so that the fish fits into a skillet.

• Fillets are sold boneless and may or may not be skinless.

• Steaks are the cross sections from large, round fish (fish with rounder bodies and eyes on both sides of the head). Steaks vary from ¾ to 1 inch in thickness. They contain part of the backbone, and the outside edge is covered with skin.

Buying Tips: It is important to know what to look for when purchasing fresh fish. One can find fresh fish at most large supermarkets or at a retail fish market. An independent retail fish market usually buys its fish on a daily basis, whereas chain stores order in large quantities and often do not receive daily shipments.

When buying whole fish, look for bright, clear and protruding eyes rather than dull, hazy sunken ones.

Southern Breaded Catfish (recipe on page 210)

The skin should be moist and shiny, the gills red or pink and the flesh firm and elastic. A fresh fish should have a mild, slightly oceanlike odor rather than a fishy or sour smell.

Fish fillets and steaks should have moist flesh that is free from discoloration and skin that is shiny and resilient. Again, if the fillet or steak has a strong odor, it is not fresh.

Frozen fish should have its original shape with the wrapper intact. There should be no ice crystals, visible blood or discoloration on the skin and flesh. Do not allow frozen fish to thaw on the way home from the store.

Storing: When storing fresh fish, wrap it tightly in plastic wrap. If possible, place the package on ice and store in

FISH INFORMATION CHART

Fish	Availability	Type of Fish	Cooking Methods
Bluefish	year-round	fatty	baking, broiling, grilling
Cod	year-round	lean	baking, broiling, frying, grilling, poaching, stewing
Flounder	year-round	lean	baking, broiling, frying, grilling, poaching
Grouper	year-round	lean	baking, broiling, frying, grilling, poaching, stewing
Haddock	year-round	lean	baking, broiling, frying, grilling, poaching, stewing
Hake	year-round	lean	baking, broiling, frying, grilling, poaching, stewing
Halibut	early spring to early fall	lean	baking, broiling, frying, grilling, poaching
Mahi Mahi	year-round	medium-fatty	broiling, grilling
Monkfish	year-round	lean	baking, broiling, frying, grilling, poaching, stewing
Orange Roughy	year-round	lean	baking, broiling, frying, grilling, poaching, stewing
Perch	year-round	lean	baking, broiling, frying, grilling, poaching
Red Snapper	summer	lean	baking, broiling, frying, grilling, poaching, stewing
Salmon	summer to fall	fatty	baking, broiling, grilling, poaching
Sea Bass	year-round	lean	baking, frying, poaching, stewing
Shark	year-round	lean	baking, broiling, frying, grilling, poaching, stewing
Skate	year-round	lean	broiling, frying, grilling, poaching, stewing
Sole	year-round	lean	broiling, frying, grilling, poaching, stewing
Swordfish	late spring to early fall	medium-fatty	baking, broiling, grilling, poaching
Trout	year-round	fatty	baking, broiling, frying, grilling, stewing
Tuna	late spring to early fall	fatty	baking, broiling, grilling, stewing

Tip

How Much to Buy:
The amount of fish to purchase per serving varies according to the cut. Here are general guidelines to follow:

Whole fish:
³⁄₄ to 1 pound

Dressed fish:
¹⁄₂ to ³⁄₄ pound

Pan-dressed fish:
¹⁄₃ pound

Fillets:
¹⁄₄ to ¹⁄₃ pound

Steaks:
¹⁄₄ to ¹⁄₃ pound

the coldest part of the refrigerator. Be sure that melting ice drains away from the fish. If the flesh comes in contact with moisture, it may become discolored. Fresh fish should be used within a day.

Cooking Methods: The most common methods of cooking fish are pan frying, deep-frying, sautéing, poaching, broiling, grilling, baking and microwaving.

Before cooking, rinse fish under cold running water and pat it dry with paper towels. Fish cooks quickly. Be careful not to overcook it as this makes the fish tough and destroys flavor. Fish is done when the flesh turns opaque and begins to flake easily when tested with a fork. Cooking times vary with each fish and cut. The following is a guideline for cooking times:

- 10 minutes per inch of fish

- 15 minutes per inch of fish cooked in a sauce

- 20 minutes per inch of frozen fish

Red Snapper Vera Cruz

    4 red snapper fillets (1 pound)
    ¼ cup fresh lime juice
    1 tablespoon fresh lemon juice
    1 teaspoon chili powder
    4 green onions with 4 inches of
        tops, sliced into ½-inch
        pieces
    1 tomato, coarsely chopped
    ½ cup chopped Anaheim or green
        bell pepper
    ½ cup chopped red bell pepper

1. Microwave Directions: Place snapper in shallow microwave-safe baking dish. Combine lime juice, lemon juice and chili powder. Pour over snapper. Marinate 10 minutes, turning once or twice.

2. Sprinkle onions, tomato and peppers over snapper. Cover dish loosely with plastic wrap. Microwave at HIGH (100% power) 6 minutes or just until snapper flakes easily when tested with fork, rotating dish every 2 minutes. Let stand, covered, 4 minutes before serving. Garnish as desired. *Makes 4 servings*

Red Snapper Vera Cruz

Herbed Haddock Fillet

Herbed Haddock Fillets

    3 slices whole wheat bread
    1 clove garlic, peeled
    6 chive stems
    ½ cup loosely packed fresh parsley
    ¼ cup loosely packed fresh basil
    2 tablespoons fresh oregano
    3 to 4 tablespoons plain nonfat
        yogurt
    1 tablespoon olive oil
    1 teaspoon Dijon mustard
    4 haddock fillets (5 to 6 ounces
        each)

1. Preheat oven to 400°F. Tear bread into pieces. Place in food processor or blender. Process until fine crumbs are formed. Measure 1 cup crumbs; place in medium bowl. Place garlic in food processor or blender; process until minced. Add chives, parsley, basil and oregano; process until chopped, scraping sides of bowl if necessary. Stir herb mixture into bread crumbs; set aside.

2. Combine 3 tablespoons yogurt, oil and mustard in small bowl. Stir into bread crumb mixture. Stir until blended and soft ball forms. (If mixture is dry, stir in additional 1 tablespoon yogurt.)

3. Line baking sheet with aluminum foil. Place haddock on foil. Spread bread crumb mixture over fillets. Bake 15 minutes or until fish flakes easily when tested with fork. Serve immediately.   *Makes 4 servings*

Southern Breaded Catfish

    ⅓ cup pecan halves
    ¼ cup cornmeal
    2 tablespoons all-purpose flour
    1 teaspoon paprika
    ¼ teaspoon ground red pepper
    2 egg whites
    4 catfish fillets (about 1 pound)
    4 cups hot cooked rice

1. Place pecans in food processor or blender; process until finely chopped. Combine pecans, cornmeal, flour, paprika and pepper in shallow bowl.

2. Beat egg whites in separate shallow bowl with wire whisk until foamy. Roll catfish fillets in pecan mixture, then in egg whites. Roll again in pecan mixture, coating fillets well with pecan mixture. Place fillets on plate; cover and refrigerate at least 15 minutes.

3. Spray large nonstick skillet with nonstick cooking spray; heat over medium-high heat. Place catfish fillets in single layer in skillet.

4. Cook fillets 2 minutes per side or until golden brown. Serve over rice. Garnish as desired.

          Makes 4 servings

Grilled Salmon with Cilantro Butter

1 clove garlic, peeled
⅓ cup packed fresh cilantro leaves
¼ cup butter or margarine, softened
½ teaspoon grated lime or lemon peel
¼ teaspoon ground black pepper
4 salmon fillets (about 6 ounces each)
Salt (optional)
Lime or lemon wedges

1. Drop garlic through feed tube of food processor with motor running. Add cilantro; process until cilantro is coarsely chopped. Add butter, lime peel and pepper to cilantro mixture; process until well combined and cilantro is finely chopped.

2. Place butter mixture on sheet of waxed paper; roll mixture back and forth into 1-inch-diameter log. Wrap paper around butter mixture to seal; refrigerate about 30 minutes or until firm.

3. Meanwhile, prepare grill for direct grilling over medium heat.

4. Lightly sprinkle salmon with salt, if desired. Place salmon, skin side down, on grid. Grill salmon, on covered grill, over medium coals 8 to 10 minutes until salmon flakes easily when tested with fork. Transfer salmon to serving plates. Cut butter log crosswise into 8 slices; top each fillet with 2 slices. Serve with lime wedges.   *Makes 4 servings*

Grilled Salmon with Cilantro Butter

Pad Thai

FISH SAUCE

As common in Southeast Asia as soy sauce is in China, this pungent, thin liquid is made from salted, fermented fish. It is both an ingredient and a condiment in several cuisines. Fish sauce is called nuoc mam in Vietnam, nam pla in Thailand and shottsuru in Japan. The strong aroma dissipates in cooking. Fish sauce from the first pressing (sometimes called "virgin") is preferred for its light taste and amber color.

🌿

Pad Thai

8 ounces flat rice noodles (⅛ to ¼ inch wide)

¼ cup water

3 tablespoons ketchup

3 tablespoons fish sauce*

2 tablespoons packed brown sugar

1 tablespoon fresh lime juice

1 jalapeño pepper, seeded, finely chopped**

1 teaspoon curry powder

2 tablespoons peanut oil, divided

1 pound raw medium shrimp, peeled, deveined

3 cloves garlic, minced

3 eggs, lightly beaten

2 cups fresh bean sprouts, divided

⅔ cup roasted skinless peanuts, chopped

3 green onions, thinly sliced

1 small carrot, shredded

¾ cup shredded red or green cabbage

½ cup fresh cilantro, coarsely chopped

1 lime, cut into wedges

Fish sauce is available at some larger supermarkets and at Oriental markets.

**Jalapeño peppers can sting and irritate the skin; wear rubber or plastic gloves when handling peppers and do not touch eyes. Wash hands after handling.*

1. Place noodles in large bowl; cover with hot water. Let stand 10 to 30 minutes or until soft and pliable; drain.

2. To prepare sauce, combine ¼ cup water, ketchup, fish sauce, sugar, juice, jalapeño and curry in medium bowl; set aside.

3. Heat wok or large skillet over high heat. Add 1 tablespoon oil and swirl to coat surface. Add shrimp; stir-fry 2 minutes or until shrimp turn pink and opaque. Transfer to bowl with slotted spoon.

4. Reduce heat to medium. Add remaining 1 tablespoon oil and heat 15 seconds. Add garlic; stir-fry 20 seconds or until golden. Add eggs; cook 2 minutes or just until set, turning and stirring every 30 seconds to scramble. Stir in reserved sauce.

5. Increase heat to high. Add softened noodles; stir to coat with sauce. Cook 2 to 4 minutes, stirring often, until noodles are tender. (Add water, 1 tablespoon at a time, if sauce is absorbed and noodles are still dry.)

6. Add cooked shrimp, 1½ cups bean sprouts, peanuts and onions; cook and stir 1 to 2 minutes until heated through. To serve, transfer mixture to large serving platter. Pile remaining ½ cup sprouts, carrot, cabbage, cilantro and lime wedges around noodles. Squeeze lime over noodles before eating.   *Makes 4 servings*

FLAKE, TO

To flake refers to the technique of separating or breaking off small pieces or layers of a food using a utensil, such as a fork. For example, cooked fish fillets may be flaked for use in a salad or main dish. When cooking fish, flaking is an indication of doneness.

🌿

FLAKY

Flaky is a word used to describe foods that are dry and tender in texture and easily separated into thin layers. Examples include pie and puff pastry. The secret to flaky, tender pastry is to minimize handling and to distribute the fat evenly.

🌿

FLAMBÉ

Flambé is a French term that refers to the flaming of a dish, usually a dessert, with alcohol for a dramatic tableside presentation. This adds flavor to a dish. It can be done at home if care is exercised. Brandy and rum complement most desserts. Fruit-based liquors that are compatible with the dish are also a good choice. For instance, kirsch, a cherry-based brandy, complements desserts with cherries or plums. The best known flamed dishes are crêpes suzette and cherries jubilee.

To flame a dish, choose a liquor with a proof of about 70. Do not use 150-proof alcohol because its high percentage of alcohol can cause a small explosion. Carefully heat a small amount of alcohol in a small saucepan over low heat until bubbles appear at edge of pan. Pour the warmed alcohol over the hot dish. Carefully ignite the fumes with a long match. The flames will die when all the alcohol has been burned off.

🌿

FLAN

A flan is a Spanish dessert in which custard is topped with caramel. The custard is baked in a dish that has first been coated with caramel. After baking, the flan is chilled. The custard is then inverted onto a serving plate. The caramel will be on top. The term flan also refers to a shallow French pastry tart with a sweet or savory filling.

🌿

Tip

If a dish will not flame, it may be for one of several reasons. The food may not be hot enough or the alcohol may have been heated too long, causing the alcohol to evaporate.

Techniques for Caramel Flan

Step 2. *Melting sugar in skillet.*

Step 3. *Coating ring mold with hot caramelized sugar.*

Caramel Flan

    1 cup sugar, divided
    2 cups half-and-half
    1 cup milk
    1½ teaspoons vanilla extract
    6 eggs
    2 egg yolks
    Hot water
    Fresh whole and sliced
       strawberries (optional)

1. Preheat oven to 325°F. Heat 5½- to 6-cup ring mold in oven 10 minutes or until hot.

2. Heat ½ cup sugar in heavy medium skillet over medium-high heat 5 to 8 minutes until sugar is completely melted and a deep amber color, stirring frequently. *Do not allow sugar to burn.*

3. Immediately pour caramelized sugar into ring mold. Holding mold with potholder, quickly rotate to coat bottom and sides evenly with sugar. Place mold on wire rack. (**Caution:** Caramelized sugar is very hot; do not touch.)

Caramel Flan

4. Combine half-and-half and milk in heavy 2-quart saucepan. Heat over medium heat until almost simmering; remove from heat. Add remaining ½ cup sugar and vanilla, stirring until sugar is dissolved; set aside.

5. Lightly beat eggs and egg yolks in large bowl until blended but not foamy; gradually stir in reserved milk mixture. Pour egg mixture into mold.

6. Place mold in large baking pan; pour hot water into baking pan to depth of ½ inch. Bake 35 to 40 minutes until knife inserted into center of custard comes out clean. Remove mold from water bath; place on wire rack. Let stand 30 minutes. Cover and refrigerate 1½ to 2 hours until thoroughly chilled.

7. To serve, loosen inner and outer edges of flan with tip of small knife. Cover mold with rimmed serving plate; invert and lift off mold. Garnish with strawberries, if desired. Spoon some of melted caramel over each serving.   *Makes 6 to 8 servings*

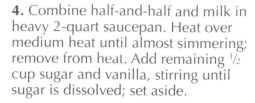

FLOUR

Flour is the very finely ground meal of edible grains, such as wheat, rye and rice. Most grain is ground with huge high-speed steel rollers. This process strips away the nutritious bran and germ and destroys vitamins. Therefore, federal standards in the United States require that steel-ground flour be enriched with some of these lost vitamins. Historically, in America, grain was ground between two rotating stones to produce stone-ground flour. This process, which does not waste the wheat germ and vita-mins, results in a more nutritious product. Stone-ground flours are available in some large supermarkets, health food stores and by mail order.

🐝

TYPES OF FLOUR

Flour contains protein. The most important is glutenin (commonly known as gluten), the substance that provides the structure in baked goods. Flours are categorized by the grain from which they come and, in the case of wheat flour, by the variety of the grain and the processing method used. Listed below are the most common flours available.

All-Purpose Wheat: To produce a flour with a moderate amount of gluten, high-gluten hard wheat and low-gluten soft wheat are combined. This creates a product that can be used for most baking. It contains neither the germ nor the bran. Bleached flour is whitened with chemical agents. Wheat flour naturally whitens through oxidation if allowed to age for a month or two. Bleached and unbleached flour can be used interchangeably. Most all-purpose flour comes presifted, eliminating the need to sift unless specified in a recipe.

Bread: This flour is ground entirely from high-gluten hard wheat. Bakers prefer bread flour for yeast breads, because it produces breads with the best taste, volume and texture.

Cake or Pastry: This flour is made from low-gluten soft wheat. It has a fine texture and is a good choice for cakes, pastries and quick breads.

Rye: Milled from rye grain, this flour contains less gluten than wheat flour. It needs to be mixed with wheat flour (all-purpose or bread) to produce a loaf that rises well and is not too dense. Rye flour is available in light, medium and dark varieties. The medium variety is the most commonly available. Rye flour is used to make rye and pumpernickel bread.

Self-Rising: Made from all-purpose wheat flour to which baking powder (a leavener) and salt have been added, self-rising flour is popular in southern states. Use it only when a recipe calls for it.

Whole Wheat (or Graham): Milled from the entire wheat kernel, whole wheat flour retains all of the grain's natural flavor, color and nutrients. It is generally used in combination with all-purpose or bread flour to avoid overly dense or poorly risen loaves.

Storage: Store all-purpose, bread, cake, rye and self-rising flour in an airtight container in a cool, dry place for up to six months. Temperatures above 70°F encourage bug infestations and mold. For longer storage, refrigerate or freeze flour in moistureproof wrapping. Whole wheat flour is more perishable than other types of flour, so purchase it in small amounts and store it in the refrigerator for up to three months. Allow chilled flour to return to room temperature before using.

FLOUR, TO

To flour means to apply a light coating of flour to a food or piece of equipment. Applied to food, the flour dries the surface. This helps food brown better when frying or sautéing or keeps food, such as raisins, from sticking together. Baking pans are floured for better release characteristics and to produce thin, crisp crusts. Rolling pins, biscuit cutters, cookie cutters and work surfaces are floured to prevent doughs from sticking to them.

❧

Special Interest

Instant flour is specially processed to allow it to dissolve easily in either hot or cold liquid. It is used primarily for thickening sauces and gravies.

FLOWER, EDIBLE

Edible flowers have been used in cooking for centuries to flavor dishes. Today, they are most often used as a garnish or a salad ingredient. Popular edible flowers include peppery nasturtiums and their leaves; delicate, fruity violas and pansies; and perfumy roses. Herb flowers, such as chive, rosemary, thyme and oregano, taste much like the herbs themselves. Other edible flowers are lavender, marigolds, chrysanthemums, daisies, violets and scented geraniums. Many taste similar to their fragrance. Blossoms from both summer and winter squashes are edible. The large yellow or orange blossoms are often large enough to stuff. Stuffed squash blossoms are baked or batter-dipped and fried.

Not all flowers are edible, some due to natural characteristics and others because of where or how they were grown and handled. Choose flowers from supermarkets, specialty produce markets, farmers' markets or mail-order sources. Use flowers from your own garden only if you are positive that they are not a poisonous variety and that they have not been sprayed with pesticides.

Avoid picking wild flowers because they may be mistakenly identified as an edible variety; they may be growing in areas exposed to exhaust fumes or other toxic substances; or they may be endangered varieties and thus illegal to pick. Never use flowers from florists since they almost certainly have been treated with pesticides.

Flowers may be stored in the refrigerator in an airtight container or plastic bag for about one week.

🐝

FOCACCIA

This thin, chewy bread is originally from Genoa, Italy. Focaccia is almost always rustically shaped in an oblong pan or in a round loaf. It is traditionally brushed with olive oil and sprinkled with salt before baking. Focaccia is often found today topped with herbs, garlic, sun-dried tomatoes, onions or vegetables. Serve it as a snack, as an accompaniment to soups and salads or as an appetizer. Increasingly popular in the United States, it is sometimes split and used for sandwiches.

🐝

Tomato-Artichoke Focaccia

1 package (16 ounces) hot roll
 mix
2 tablespoons wheat bran
1¼ cups hot water
4 teaspoons olive oil, divided
1 cup thinly sliced onions
2 cloves garlic, minced
4 ounces dry sun-dried tomatoes,
 rehydrated,* cut into strips
1 cup canned artichoke hearts,
 sliced
1 tablespoon minced fresh
 rosemary
2 tablespoons freshly grated
 Parmesan cheese

*To rehydrate sun-dried tomatoes, simply pour
1 cup boiling water over tomatoes in small
heatproof bowl. Let tomatoes soak 5 to
10 minutes until softened; drain well.

1. Preheat oven to 400°F.

2. Combine dry ingredients and yeast
packet from hot roll mix in large
bowl. Add bran; mix well. Stir in hot
water and 2 teaspoons oil. Knead
dough about 5 minutes or until
ingredients are blended.

3. Spray 15½×11½-inch baking pan
or 14-inch pizza pan with nonstick
cooking spray. Press dough onto
bottom of prepared pan. Cover; let
rise 15 minutes.

4. Heat 1 teaspoon oil in medium
skillet over low heat. Add onions and
garlic; cook and stir 2 to 3 minutes
until onions are tender. Brush surface
of dough with remaining 1 teaspoon
oil. Top dough with onion mixture,
tomatoes, artichokes and rosemary.
Sprinkle with Parmesan.

5. Bake 25 to 30 minutes until lightly
browned on top. To serve, cut into
squares. *Makes 16 servings*

FOLD, TO

Folding is a specialized technique for combining two ingredients or mixtures, one of which usually has been aerated, such as whipped cream or egg whites. It is best done by placing the airy mixture on top of the other and with a rubber spatula, gently but quickly cutting through to the bottom and turning the ingredients over with a rolling motion. The bowl is rotated a quarter turn each time and the process repeated until the mixtures are combined, with as little loss in volume as possible. Care must be taken not to stir, beat or overmix. Fruit pieces, chips or nuts may be folded into an airy mixture using the same technique.

🐝

Folding cherry pie filling into whipped cream.

Tomato-Artichoke Focaccia

Cheesy Fondue

FONDUE

Fondue comes from the French word fondre meaning "to melt." It originally referred only to fondue au fromage ("cheese fondue"), a combination of hot melted cheese, such as Emmentaler or Gruyère, and wine. Using long, slender forks, diners dipped chunks of French bread into the melted mixture. The word has now come to include food cooked or served at the table in a communal pot.

Fondue bourguignonne is prepared by cooking bite-size pieces of beef in a pan of hot oil. The cooked meat is dipped into savory sauces before eating. To lighten the dish, contemporary recipes may use a broth to cook the meat instead of oil. Chocolate fondue is melted chocolate often combined with cream and a liqueur. Small pieces of pound cake, angel food cake or fruit are used as dippers. Fondue forks are used for dipping and transferring food to plates. Then the diners eat the food with their individual dinner forks. This prevents transfer of germs and eliminates the risk of being burned with a hot fork.

🌿

Cheesy Fondue

2 cups (8 ounces) shredded Swiss cheese
2 cups (8 ounces) shredded Monterey Jack cheese
2 tablespoons all-purpose flour
1½ cups dry white wine or apple juice
Dash ground nutmeg
Dash ground red pepper
1 French bread loaf, cut into cubes
1 large Granny Smith apple, cut into wedges, or other fruit pieces

1. Combine cheeses and flour in large bowl; toss lightly to coat. Set aside.

2. Bring wine to a simmer over medium heat in fondue pot. Gradually add reserved cheese mixture until melted, stirring constantly. Stir in nutmeg and pepper. Serve with bread cubes and apple for dipping. Keep warm, stirring occasionally.   *Makes 4 servings*

FOOD COLORING

Food colorings are edible dyes, usually red, green, blue and yellow, used to tint frostings and candies. The most popular are liquid colors available at supermarkets. Paste colors, which are sold at specialty stores, come in a wider variety of colors and are well suited to foods that don't mix well with liquid. Both types impart intense color and should initially be used sparingly, a drop or two at a time. When stored tightly closed in a cool, dry place, liquid colors will last four years and paste colors will store indefinitely.

🌿

FOOD SAFETY

A report by the Institute of Food Technologists states that most cases of food-borne illness occur because of mistakes made at home rather than in restaurants or food service settings. As a consequence, it is essential for all cooks to become familiar with the basic tenets of food safety, especially those that change as microbes in the food supply become more adaptable and resistant.

✾

Remember to follow these important guidelines:

• Always wash your hands with hot soapy water before handling and preparing food. Rewash hands after touching your nose or mouth or caring for children. Do not cough or sneeze on food during preparation.

• Avoid contaminating other foods with raw eggs or juices from raw poultry, meat or seafood by washing your hands after handling these items.

• Keep raw meat and poultry packages away from other food items, especially produce and unwrapped items. The juices can drip and contaminate other foods.

• Utensils and work surfaces should be kept clean. All work surfaces, including knives and cutting boards, should be thoroughly cleaned with hot soapy water after touching raw poultry, meat, seafood or eggs.

• Rinse poultry and fish under cold running water to remove surface dirt and bone fragments.

• Rinse fruits and vegetables, scrubbing with a brush to remove embedded soil, if necessary.

• Marinate foods in the refrigerator instead of at room temperature. A marinade drained from poultry can be used as a baste during cooking—just be sure to allow the meat to cook on the grill at least 5 minutes after the last application. You can also serve drained marinade as a dipping sauce if you cook it first. Place the marinade in a small saucepan, bring to a boil and boil for at least 1 minute.

• Cook foods thoroughly. Use a meat thermometer to test poultry and meat, ensuring that they reach the minimum temperature for safety. *See Eggs, Fish, Meat, Poultry and Shellfish for additional information.*

• Reheat leftover protein dishes to 165°F before serving.

• Organisms that cause food-borne illness thrive at temperatures between 40° and 140°F. Thaw foods in the refrigerator rather than on the counter at room temperature. At picnics and on buffet tables keep hot foods hot (above 140°F) and cold foods cold (below 40°F). Do not let cooked foods stand longer than 2 hours. Any cooked food that has remained unrefrigerated for more than two hours must be discarded.

• The refrigerator should be set between 34° and 40°F. Set the freezer at 0°F. Wipe shelves and walls of the refrigerator regularly. Do not overfill the refrigerator or freezer; this prevents efficient, even chilling.

• Chill leftovers quickly. Do not transfer a large pot of food directly from the range to the refrigerator. Divide it into several smaller containers so it chills quickly.

• Check all packages of perishables at the supermarket, noting the freshness date and the packaging. Do not buy any package that looks as though it has been opened, damaged or otherwise mishandled.

• Infants, the elderly and people with weak immune systems are more likely to experience serious complications or death from food poisoning. Extra caution should be exercised when preparing food for them.

• A good rule of thumb is that if there is any doubt at all about the safety or quality of food, throw it out.

MAXIMUM RECOMMENDED STORAGE FOR FOODS KEPT AT 0°F*

Fresh Uncooked Meats

Beef, Veal, Lamb (cuts)	6 to 8 months
Beef, Veal, Lamb (ground)	3 to 4 months
Beef, Veal, Lamb organ meats	3 to 4 months
Pork roasts, chops	3 to 4 months
Pork, ground (including fresh sausage)	1 to 3 months

Smoked Meats

Ham, Slab bacon, Frankfurters	1 to 2 months
Sausages	1 to 2 months

Cooked Meats

Beef, Veal, Lamb, Pork roasts	2 to 3 months
Stews, Meats in sauce, Hash, Meat loaves, Patties, Casseroles	2 to 3 months

Fresh Uncooked Poultry

Chicken	8 to 10 months
Turkey, Duck, Goose, Game birds	6 months

Cooked Poultry

All types	2 to 4 months

Fresh Uncooked Seafood

All types	2 to 3 months

Cooked Seafood

All types	1 to 2 months
Vegetables	9 to 12 months

Dairy Products

Butter	6 months
Cheeses, hard	4 to 6 months
Cheeses, soft	2 months
Milk	not recommended
Ice cream, Sherbet, Frozen yogurt	1 to 3 months

Eggs

Beaten yolks, loose whites	8 months

Breads

Quick	2 to 4 months
Yeast	6 to 8 months

Cakes and Cookies

Baked cakes and cookies without frosting	4 to 8 months
Cheesecakes	4 to 6 months
Cookie dough	2 to 4 months

Pastries

Unbaked pie shells	2 to 3 months
Unbaked fruit pies	6 to 8 months
Baked fruit pies	2 to 4 months

The type of freezer, amount of food stored and how often the freezer is opened affect the quality of frozen foods. These are only guidelines. Assuming that foods have stayed solidly frozen for the duration of storage, quality will deteriorate, but safety will not.

FREEZE, TO

Freezing is a simple and effective means of preserving, a fact that easily gets lost amid the cartons of ice cream and frozen dinners. Of all methods of preserving, it causes the least amount of change in taste, color, texture and nutritive value. Many foods can be frozen, allowing cooks to stock the freezer with uncooked foods, leftovers and specially prepared dishes.

☙

Frozen Food Storage and Handling: Set the freezer at 0°F or lower, keep it free of frost and do not overload it. Proper wrapping is important. The extra effort results in tremendous benefits. Air and moisture are culprits in freezer burn so wrap foods as tightly as possible, ideally in a double layer of moisture-proof wrapping or in rigid freezer containers. Make sure all seals are airtight and that as much air as possible is squeezed out before sealing. In containers of foods that are liquid at room temperature, leave 1/4 to 1/2 inch of headspace to allow the food to expand as it freezes. Label packages with the contents and date.

Ideally, food should be thawed in the refrigerator. Alternatively, it can be thawed in a microwave oven, if it is carefully watched to prevent edges from cooking before other areas are thawed. Poultry, meat and seafood thawed in a microwave oven should be cooked immediately.

Power Failures: If there is a lapse in power, do not open the freezer and allow cold air to escape. Many variables influence how quickly foods thaw. A fully loaded upright freezer will keep foods frozen 24 hours or more if the door is not opened. Food in the freezer compartment of a refrigerator (as well as food in a partially full freezer) will stay frozen for less time. Adding dry ice can increase the holding time.

When power is restored, food that contains ice crystals can be refrozen. Refrozen foods may experience some loss in quality. Foods that are thawed but still thoroughly chilled can be stored in the refrigerator and used within one to two days. All foods above 40°F, with the exception of breads, rolls, plain muffins and cakes, should be discarded.

FRENCH TOAST

French toast, usually served as a breakfast entrée, is prepared by pan-frying bread slices that have been dipped in a mixture of beaten eggs and milk. Thick-cut French or Italian bread is a good choice for this dish. French toast is often served topped with syrup, preserves or powdered sugar.

French Raisin Toast

2 tablespoons granulated sugar
1 teaspoon ground cinnamon
4 eggs, lightly beaten
½ cup milk
8 slices raisin bread
4 tablespoons butter or
        margarine, divided
Powdered sugar

1. Combine granulated sugar and cinnamon in wide shallow bowl. Beat in eggs and milk. Add bread; let stand to coat, then turn to coat other side.

2. Heat 2 tablespoons butter in large skillet over medium-low heat. Add 4 bread slices; cook until brown. Turn and cook other side. Remove; keep warm. Repeat with remaining butter and bread. Sprinkle with powdered sugar. Garnish as desired. Serve immediately.   *Makes 4 servings*

Tip

Freezer burn, which is indicated by dry white or gray patches on the surface of frozen foods, is caused by improper wrapping. Food that is freezer burned is safe to eat. Just trim off the affected areas because they have an unpleasant flavor.

French Raisin Toast

FRICASSEE

Fricassee is a stewlike mixture of poultry that is floured and sautéed (but not browned) in butter and then gently simmered in broth and sometimes white wine. Vegetables, especially carrots and onions, are added. The sauce is traditionally finished with cream or egg yolks, so the resulting dish is light in color. For health conscious cooks, milk can be substituted. Rabbit and veal may also be prepared in this manner.

🌿

Chicken Fricassee

Chicken Fricassee

   3 **pounds chicken pieces (breasts, legs and/or thighs)**
      All-purpose flour
   3 **cups low sodium chicken broth**
   1 **bay leaf**
   1 **pound whole baby carrots**
   ¾ **cup onion wedges**
   1 **tablespoon margarine**
   3 **tablespoons all-purpose flour**
   ¾ **cup skim milk**
   1 **tablespoon fresh lemon juice**
   3 **tablespoons minced fresh dill** *or*
      2 **teaspoons dried dill weed**
   1 **teaspoon sugar**
   ½ **teaspoon salt**
   6 **cups hot cooked noodles**
      Fresh dill sprigs (optional)

1. Coat chicken pieces very lightly with flour. Spray large nonstick skillet with nonstick cooking spray; heat over medium heat until hot. Add chicken; cook 10 to 15 minutes until browned on all sides. Drain fat from skillet.

2. Add broth and bay leaf to skillet; bring to a boil over high heat. Reduce heat to low; simmer, covered, about 1 hour or until fork can be inserted into chicken with ease and juices run clear, not pink. Add carrots and onion during last 20 minutes of cooking.

3. Transfer chicken and vegetables with slotted spoon to platter; keep warm. Bring broth to a boil over high heat; boil until broth is reduced to 1 cup. Discard bay leaf.

4. Melt margarine in small saucepan over low heat; stir in 3 tablespoons flour. Cook and stir 1 to 2 minutes. Stir in reduced broth, milk and juice; bring to a boil over high heat. Boil until thickened, stirring constantly. Stir in minced dill, sugar and salt. Arrange chicken over noodles on 6 individual serving plates; top with sauce. Garnish with dill sprigs, if desired. Serve immediately.

Makes 6 servings

FRITTATA

A frittata is an Italian omelet in which the eggs are combined, before cooking, with other ingredients, such as meat, vegetables and herbs. The egg mixture is poured into a heavy skillet and cooked slowly over low heat. The top of the frittata may be finished either by turning over the omelet or by placing it under the broiler. The frittata is then cut into wedges and served.

☙

Chicken Broccoli Frittata

  1 cup chopped fresh broccoli
      flowerettes
  ½ cup chopped cooked chicken
  ¼ cup chopped tomato
  ¼ cup chopped onion
  ¼ teaspoon dried tarragon leaves
  1 tablespoon FLEISCHMANN'S®
      Margarine
  1 cup EGG BEATERS® Healthy
      Real Egg Product

In 10-inch nonstick skillet, over medium heat, sauté broccoli, chicken, tomato, onion and tarragon in margarine until tender-crisp. Reduce heat to low. Pour Egg Beaters evenly into skillet over chicken mixture. Cover; cook for 5 to 7 minutes or until cooked on bottom and almost set on top. Slide onto serving platter; cut into wedges to serve.   *Makes 2 servings*

Prep time: 15 minutes
Cook time: 11 minutes

Vegetable Frittata

  2 tablespoons butter or margarine
  1 bag (16 ounces) BIRDS EYE®
      frozen Farm Fresh Mixtures
      Broccoli, Corn and Red
      Peppers
  8 eggs
  ½ cup water
  1 tablespoon Tabasco® pepper
      sauce
  ¾ teaspoon salt

• Melt butter in 12-inch nonstick skillet over medium heat. Add vegetables; cook and stir 3 minutes.

• Lightly beat eggs, water, Tabasco® sauce and salt.

• Pour egg mixture over vegetables in skillet. Cover and cook 10 to 15 minutes or until eggs are set.

• To serve, cut into wedges.
          Makes about 4 servings

Prep time: 5 minutes
Cook time: 20 minutes

Serving Suggestion: Serve with warm crusty bread and a green salad.

FRITTER

A fritter is made by deep-frying a small portion of batter or dough that often contains small pieces of fruit or vegetable. It may be sweet or savory depending on the ingredients used. Some of the more common types of fritters are corn, apple or banana.

☙

FROSTING

Frostings are sweet, smooth mixtures spread on cakes, cookies and pastries as a finishing touch. Also called icings, these mixtures may be cooked (seven-minute frosting) or uncooked (butter-cream frosting). The consistency can vary widely, from a very thin glaze to a thick, billowy pouf of frosting. Chocolate, fudge and vanilla are the most common flavors, but there are many possibilities, including caramel, citrus, mocha and fruit flavors. Frosting can be spread in a smooth layer using a metal spatula or applied in a thick layer and swirled. The back of a spoon, a serrated cake comb or a pastry bag with an array of tips can be used for decorative frostings. See Cake Decorating, page 96, for additional information.

🐝

Technique for Cream Cheese Frosting

Step 1. *Sifting powdered sugar.*

Cream Cheese Frosting

> 4 cups (16-ounce box) powdered sugar
> 1 package (8 ounces) cream cheese, softened
> ½ cup butter or margarine, softened
> 1 teaspoon vanilla extract

1. Sift powdered sugar into large bowl with fine-meshed sieve or sifter; set aside.

2. Beat cream cheese, butter and vanilla in another large bowl with electric mixer at medium speed until smooth, scraping down side of bowl occasionally. Gradually add sifted powdered sugar. Beat with electric mixer at low speed until well blended, scraping down side of bowl occasionally.
> *Makes about 1½ cups frosting*

Easy Fudge Frosting

> 4 squares BAKER'S® Unsweetened Chocolate
> 2 tablespoons margarine or butter
> 4 cups powdered sugar
> ½ cup milk
> 1 teaspoon vanilla

MICROWAVE chocolate and margarine in large microwavable bowl on HIGH 1 minute or until margarine is melted. **Stir until chocolate is completely melted.**

STIR in sugar, milk and vanilla until smooth. Let stand, if necessary, until of spreading consistency, stirring occasionally. Spread quickly. (Add 2 to 3 tablespoons additional milk if frosting becomes too thick.)
> *Makes about 2½ cups or enough to frost tops and sides of 2 (8- to 9-inch) layer cakes*

Prep time: 10 minutes

Seven-Minute Frosting

> 1½ cups sugar
> ½ cup water
> 2 egg whites
> 1 tablespoon light corn syrup
> Dash salt
> 1 teaspoon vanilla extract

1. Mix sugar, water, egg whites, corn syrup and salt in top of double boiler. Beat with electric mixer at medium speed about 1 minute to blend thoroughly. Place top of double boiler over boiling water in bottom of double boiler. Beat constantly with electric mixer at high speed about 7 minutes or until stiff peaks form, scraping side occasionally with rubber scraper.

2. Remove from boiling water. Immediately pour into large bowl. Add vanilla; beat 1 minute more or until thick enough to spread.
> *Makes about 5⅓ cups frosting*

Buttercream Frosting

6 cups powdered sugar, sifted, divided
¾ cup butter or margarine, softened
¼ cup vegetable shortening
6 to 8 tablespoons milk, divided
1 teaspoon vanilla extract

1. Place 3 cups sugar, butter, shortening, 4 tablespoons milk and vanilla in large bowl. Beat with electric mixer until smooth.

2. Add remaining powdered sugar; beat at medium speed until light and fluffy, adding more milk, 1 tablespoon at a time, as needed for good spreading consistency.

Makes about 3½ cups frosting

FRUITCAKE

A fruitcake is a traditional holiday cake made from dried and candied fruits, fruit peels, and nuts that are held together by a dense batter. It is often baked in a loaf or tube pan at a low temperature. Liquor, such as brandy, is often an ingredient or can be added after baking. Wrapped in cheesecloth and moistened with liquor as needed, fruitcakes can last for months stored in a cool, dry place.

FRUIT LEATHER

Fruit leather is prepared by spreading puréed fruit, sometimes with sugar or honey added, in a very thin layer and allowing it to dry at a low heat. The dried sheets may be cut in strips or rolled up for snacking. Fruit leather is available in most supermarkets or can be made at home.

FRY, TO

Frying refers to the technique of cooking foods in hot fat, usually vegetable oil. Proper fat temperature is critical to a successful result. The ideal temperature produces a crisp exterior and a moist, perfectly cooked interior. Too high a temperature will burn the food. Too low a temperature will result in food absorbing excessive fat. A deep-fat thermometer is essential to determining the temperature of the fat. Deep-fried foods are submerged or floated in hot fat in a large heavy saucepan or Dutch oven. Electric deep fryers fitted with wire baskets are available. Panfrying refers to cooking food in a skillet in a small amount of fat that does not cover the food.

Frying Tips: To avoid spattering, foods should be free of surface moisture before frying.

• For safety, when deep-frying, fill the cooking pan no more than half full of fat to allow space for food.

• If possible, use a deep-fat thermometer. If one is not available, drop a cube of white bread in the hot oil. The bread will brown evenly in 1 minute at approximately 350° to 365°F, 40 seconds at 365° to 380°F, and 20 seconds at 380° to 390°F.

• Fry foods in small batches to make them crisp and less greasy.

• The best fats for frying have a high smoke point (the temperature at which fat smokes and begins to breakdown). Good choices are vegetable oils, such as corn, peanut and safflower oils.

• Fat should not be allowed to smoke. Smoking is a sign that the fat is beginning to break down and this will affect the flavor.

Tip

Do not leave hot fat unattended. Oil that is allowed to get too hot can ignite. If this happens, immediately cover the pan to cut off oxygen to the flames. Baking soda or salt thrown on the flames will also extinguish them. Do not attempt to douse a grease fire with water. Water will only spread the flames.

G to H

What is elephant garlic?

Decorate a cake with a delectable

garnish of chocolate leaves

How far does the average

honeybee travel in a day?

Make a hearty shrimp gumbo.

What is the difference

between a spice and

an herb?

America's Favorite Cheddar Beef Burgers
(recipe on page 254)

GANACHE

Ganache is a dense, smooth mixture of melted chocolate and whipping cream that can be used as a glaze for cakes, a filling for tarts and pastries or as a center for chocolate truffles. Sometimes liquor or flavoring may be added to the ganache.

GARLIC

A member of the lily family, garlic is a cousin to onions, leeks, chives and shallots. The edible bulb or head grows beneath the ground and, like the onion, is encased in a papery covering. But unlike its relatives, each garlic bulb is comprised of 12 to 15 cloves each in a closely fitting papery skin.

Tip

A whole peeled garlic clove can impart a delicate flavor when rubbed inside a salad bowl or placed on the tines of a fork when beating eggs for an omelet.

Garlic Skewered Shrimp

Throughout history, folklore has credited garlic with many powers—increasing physical strength, protecting against disease and curing various ills. It is said that garlic was fed to the Egyptian slaves building the ancient pyramids in order to enhance and prolong their physical strength. During the Middle Ages it was believed to protect one from evil spirits, the plague and the common cold. Cures for consumption and even snake bites have been attributed to garlic in the past. Today, many studies are being conducted to determine the effectiveness of garlic as a weapon against heart disease.

Uses: Cloves of garlic may be used whole, sliced, crushed, chopped or minced to flavor a wide variety of savory foods. Although usually cooked, finely chopped or minced garlic may be added raw to salad dressings, appetizers or dips.

• Whole heads of garlic or individual garlic cloves may be baked (or roasted) until the garlic has a buttery consistency. This can be used to flavor foods or as a spread.

Varieties: The best known and most readily available variety, American garlic, has white skin and a strong flavor. Use American garlic unless the recipe indicates otherwise.

Mexican, or Italian, garlic has a milder flavor and can be identified by its mauve- or purple-colored skin.

Elephant garlic has heads as large as a small grapefruit and individual cloves two or more inches in length. It has a very mild flavor.

Processed garlic is available in flakes (minced), powder, salt, juice and packed in oil (chopped or whole). While these may be convenient, they all lack the true flavor of fresh garlic.

Availability: Garlic is abundant and available all year.

Buying Tips: Look for garlic that is sold loose so you can judge whether it feels heavy and solid in your hand. Avoid bulbs that are lightweight for their size, because they may be partially dried and shriveled. Bulbs should be plump, firm and compact.

Yield: 1 medium clove garlic (American, Italian or Mexican) = ½ teaspoon minced.
⅛ teaspoon garlic powder or dried minced garlic may be substituted for 1 clove garlic.

Storage: Store garlic bulbs, loosely covered, in a cool, dark location with good air circulation. A specialized covered terra-cotta container with holes for air circulation is available for storing garlic bulbs. Bulbs may be stored up to two months. Once broken from the bulb, individual unpeeled cloves will keep up to ten days. After peeling, they may be tightly wrapped in plastic and refrigerated for a day or two.

Basic Preparation: To quickly peel a garlic clove, place the clove on a cutting board. Slightly crush the clove under the flat side of a chef's knife blade; peel away the skin with your fingers.

Garlic may be chopped, minced, pressed in a garlic press or crushed under the flat side of a knife blade to release its oils. These methods result in a stronger garlic flavor than coarsely chopping, slicing or leaving cloves whole. Some cooks insist that pressing and crushing garlic damages cell walls so severely that the resulting garlic is unpleasantly strong.

To mince garlic, chop a peeled clove with a chef's knife until the garlic is in uniform fine pieces.

To peel a head of garlic or many cloves at once, blanch them in boiling water for 5 to 10 seconds or microwave them for a few seconds. Plunge the head into cold water to separate it into cloves and peel away the skins.

To roast or bake a head of garlic, cut off the top third of the garlic head (not the root end) to expose the cloves. Discard the top.

Place the head of garlic in a small baking dish. Roast in a preheated 400°F oven for 30 to 40 minutes until the papery skin darkens and the head is softened. When cool enough to handle, gently squeeze the softened garlic head from the root end so that the roasted cloves slip out of their skins into a small bowl.

Garlic Skewered Shrimp

> 1 pound raw large shrimp, peeled, deveined
> 2 tablespoons low sodium soy sauce
> 1 tablespoon vegetable oil
> 3 cloves garlic, minced
> ¼ teaspoon crushed red pepper flakes (optional)
> 3 green onions, cut into 1-inch pieces
> Lettuce leaves

1. Preheat broiler. Soak 4 (12-inch) skewers in water 20 minutes.

2. Meanwhile, place shrimp in large resealable plastic food storage bag. Combine soy sauce, oil, garlic and pepper flakes, if desired, in cup; mix well. Pour over shrimp. Close bag securely; turn to coat. Marinate at room temperature 10 to 15 minutes.

3. Drain shrimp; reserve marinade. Alternately thread shrimp and onions onto skewers. Place on rack of broiler pan. Brush with reserved marinade; discard remaining marinade.

4. Broil 5 to 6 inches from heat 5 minutes. Turn shrimp over; broil 5 minutes more or until shrimp turn pink and opaque. Serve on lettuce-lined plate. Garnish as desired.

Makes 4 servings

Crushing garlic clove.

Chopped garlic.

Cutting off top third of garlic head.

Squeezing roasted garlic head.

Rosemary-Garlic Mashed Potatoes

Rosemary-Garlic Mashed Potatoes

    1 large head garlic*
2½ pounds Yukon Gold potatoes
      (about 5 medium)
1½ teaspoons salt, divided
   ½ cup whipping cream
   ½ cup milk
    2 tablespoons butter
    1 tablespoon minced fresh
      rosemary *or* 1 teaspoon dried
      rosemary, crushed
   ⅛ teaspoon ground white pepper

The whole garlic bulb is called a head.

1. Preheat oven to 400°F. Cut off top third of garlic head (not root end) to expose cloves; discard top. Place head of garlic, cut side up, in small baking dish. Roast in oven 30 to 40 minutes until papery skin darkens and head is softened. Set aside until cool enough to handle.

2. Gently squeeze softened garlic head from root end toward cut end so that roasted cloves slip out of their skins into small bowl; discard skins. Mash garlic with fork; set aside.

3. Peel potatoes; cut lengthwise into quarters. Cut quarters into 1-inch pieces. Place potato pieces in 3-quart saucepan; add water to cover and 1 teaspoon salt. Bring to a boil over high heat. Reduce heat to medium-low; simmer, uncovered, about 12 to 15 minutes until potato pieces are tender when pierced with fork. (Do not overcook.) Drain water from pan. Transfer potatoes to large bowl. Cover; set aside.

4. Place cream, milk, butter and rosemary in small saucepan; heat over medium-high heat about 3 minutes or until butter melts and mixture simmers, stirring often.

5. Uncover potatoes; mash with potato masher until smooth. Add reserved garlic and milk mixture to potatoes. Stir with large whisk until smooth. Whisk in remaining ½ teaspoon salt and pepper. Serve immediately.
    Makes 4 to 6 side-dish servings

Dijon Garlic Bread

   ½ cup FLEISCHMANN'S®
      Margarine, softened
   ¼ cup GREY POUPON® Dijon
      Mustard
    1 teaspoon dried oregano leaves
    1 clove garlic, crushed
    1 (16-inch-long) loaf Italian bread

Preheat oven to 400°F. In small bowl, blend margarine, mustard, oregano and garlic. Slice bread crosswise into 16 slices, cutting ¾ of the way through. Spread margarine mixture on each cut side of bread. Wrap in foil. Bake 15 to 20 minutes or until heated through.
    Makes 16 servings

GARNISH, TO

Garnishing is the term used to describe the technique of adding an edible ornament to a finished dish for the purpose of enhancing its visual appearance. Garnishes can be as simple as a sprig of parsley or as elegant as green onion brushes. Colors and textures should be chosen with both the food and the serving piece in mind. The following recipes demonstrate both savory and sweet garnishes. (See Bûche de Noël, page 76, for instructions on preparing chocolate curls.)

Chocolate Leaves

> **Semisweet chocolate (squares or bars)**
> **Vegetable shortening**
> **Nontoxic leaves, such as rose, lemon or camellia**

1. Place chocolate on cutting board; shave into small pieces with paring knife. Place shavings in glass measuring cup. Add shortening. (Use 1 teaspoon of shortening for every 2 ounces of chocolate.) Fill saucepan about 1 inch deep with warm (not hot) water.

2. Place measuring cup in water to melt chocolate, stirring frequently with rubber spatula until smooth. *(Be careful not to get any water into chocolate.)*

3. Wash leaves; dry well with paper towels. Brush melted chocolate onto *underside* of each leaf with paintbrush or pastry brush, coating leaf thickly and evenly. Repeat brushing with a second coating of chocolate, if desired, for a sturdier leaf.

4. Carefully wipe off any chocolate that may have run onto front of leaf.

5. Place leaves, chocolate sides up, on waxed paper. Let stand in cool dry place until chocolate is firm. *(Do not chill in refrigerator.)*

6. When chocolate is firm, carefully peel leaves away from chocolate; refrigerate until ready to use.

Orange Peel Rose

> **1 orange**
> **2 or 3 fresh mint leaves**

1. Peel orange, starting at top, with vegetable peeler, cutting continuous narrow strip of peel in spiral fashion around entire orange and pressing firmly with peeler.

2. Wrap strip around itself to form coil. Continue wrapping peel tightly, tapering bottom as much as possible.

3. Insert one or two wooden toothpicks horizontally into base to secure. Tuck mint leaves under base of orange peel rose.

Makes 1 orange peel rose

Green Onion Brushes

> **6 medium green onions with tops**
> **Cold water**
> **10 ice cubes**

1. To prepare green onions, trim off roots. For each onion, cut crosswise into one 4-inch piece, leaving about 2 inches of both white onion and green top.

2. Using sharp scissors or kitchen shears, cut each section of green stems lengthwise into very thin strips almost down to beginning of stems, cutting 6 to 8 strips in each stem section. (Do not cut all the way through.) Leave other end uncut.

3. Fill large bowl about ½ full with cold water. Add green onions and ice cubes. Refrigerate about 1 hour or until onions curl; drain.

Makes 6 onion brushes

Techniques for Chocolate Leaves

Step 3. *Brushing leaves with melted chocolate.*

Step 6. *Peeling leaves from chocolate.*

Technique for Orange Peel Rose

Step 2. *Wrapping peel into coil.*

GAZPACHO

Gazpacho is a spicy Spanish soup that is served cold. It is made of a puréed mixture of fresh tomatoes, green bell peppers, onions and cucumbers. It is most often flavored with garlic, olive oil and vinegar. This refreshing summer soup is often served garnished with croutons, chopped tomato, chopped green bell pepper and green onion slices.

☙

Gazpacho

Gazpacho

3 cups tomato juice
4 tomatoes, chopped
1 green bell pepper, chopped
1 cucumber, chopped
1 cup chopped celery
1 cup chopped green onions
3 tablespoons red wine vinegar
2 tablespoons FILIPPO BERIO®
   Olive Oil
1 tablespoon chopped fresh
   parsley
1 to 2 teaspoons salt
1 clove garlic, finely minced
   Freshly ground black pepper or
   hot pepper sauce

In large bowl, combine tomato juice, tomatoes, bell pepper, cucumber, celery, green onions, vinegar, olive oil, parsley, salt and garlic. Cover; refrigerate several hours or overnight before serving. Season to taste with black pepper or hot pepper sauce. Serve cold.

Makes 10 to 12 servings

GELATIN

A colorless and tasteless thickening agent, unflavored gelatin is used to give body to chilled aspics, gelatin salads and molded desserts. Originally obtained from natural sources, such as calves' feet, now it is commercially made. Most gelatin is granulated, although it is available in sheets (known as sheet or leaf gelatin) in some gourmet shops. A ¼-ounce envelope of unflavored gelatin contains 1 tablespoon, which is enough to gel 2 cups of most clear liquids. Certain raw foods contain an enzyme that prevents gelatin from thickening. These include figs, ginger root, guava, kiwifruit, papaya and pineapple. Cooking and canning destroys the enzyme. Sweetened, flavored gelatin mixes are also readily available.

Before using, unflavored gelatin must be softened. To soften, place ¼ cup of the cold liquid used in the recipe in a small bowl or saucepan and evenly sprinkle the liquid with 1 tablespoon gelatin. Let it stand for 5 minutes. To dissolve gelatin, place the bowl in a larger container of hot water. Let it stand until all the crystals have dissolved. Softened gelatin can also be added to a hot mixture or heated in a saucepan over very low heat until dissolved. Do not let the softened gelatin boil, because this will destroy its thickening powers.

☗

Chocolate Mousse

1 teaspoon unflavored gelatin
1 tablespoon cold water
2 tablespoons boiling water
½ cup sugar
¼ cup HERSHEY'S Cocoa or HERSHEY'S European Style Cocoa
1 cup (½ pint) cold whipping cream
1 teaspoon vanilla extract

In small cup, sprinkle gelatin over cold water; let stand 2 minutes to soften gelatin. Add boiling water; stir until gelatin is completely dissolved and mixture is clear. Cool slightly. In cold small mixer bowl, stir together sugar and cocoa. Add whipping cream and vanilla. Beat on medium speed of electric mixer, scraping bottom of bowl occasionally, until mixture is stiff. Add gelatin mixture; beat until well blended. Spoon into serving dishes. Refrigerate about 30 minutes before serving. Garnish as desired. Cover; refrigerate leftover desserts.   *Makes 4 servings*

Note: For double recipe, use 1 envelope gelatin; double remaining ingredients. Follow directions above, using cold large mixer bowl.

GINGER

Fresh ginger (also known as ginger root) has been a basic flavoring in Asian dishes for centuries and was also used in ancient Rome as well as medieval England. It has a pungent and spicy flavor. Native to tropical Asia, ginger is more likely to be used in its fresh or pickled form in Asian cuisines and in its dried or crystallized form in European and American cooking.

Ginger can also be dried and ground into a powder. This is not an appropriate substitute in recipes calling for fresh ginger. Crystallized (or candied) ginger has been cooked in a sugar syrup and coated with coarse sugar. Pickled ginger has been preserved in vinegar.

☗

Uses: Fresh ginger may be sliced, slivered or grated for use in savory dishes, such as stir-fries, vegetable side dishes, soups and fish dishes.

• Ground dried ginger is used in desserts and baked goods, such as gingerbread and pumpkin pie.

• Crystallized (or candied) ginger can be used as an ingredient in desserts or as a confection.

• Pickled ginger is used as a garnish for savory Asian dishes.

Varieties: Fresh ginger is available in two forms—young and mature. The skin of young ginger is tender enough that it does not require peeling, but the tough skin of mature ginger should be peeled away before using. Most ginger available in supermarkets is mature ginger. Ground dried ginger is readily available in the spice section of the supermarket. Crystallized ginger is available in some large supermarkets and Asian markets. Pickled ginger can be found in Asian markets.

Availability: Ginger in all its forms is available throughout the year.

Buying Tips: Buy fresh mature ginger that is firm with a smooth tan skin and a pungent fragrance. Avoid ginger with wrinkled skin. This is an indication that it is past its prime.

Storage: Fresh unpeeled ginger, tightly wrapped, may be refrigerated for three weeks. It may be frozen up to six months wrapped in plastic wrap and sealed in a plastic freezer bag. To use, slice off what is needed and return the remaining ginger to the freezer.

Ground dried ginger should be stored no more than four to six months or it will begin to lose its flavor. Crystallized ginger can be stored indefinitely in a tightly sealed container. Pickled ginger should be stored in its brine in the refrigerator. It will keep for up to six months.

Basic Preparation: To peel fresh ginger, use a paring knife with a sharp blade, taking care to remove only the tough outer skin since the most flavorful flesh is just below the surface. A vegetable peeler can also be used. The ginger root skin can be scraped off with the edge of a metal tableware spoon. Peel only as much as you need. Chop, mince or grate the ginger. Sliced ginger can be stir-fried in oil for flavor, then removed before serving.

Gingered Chicken Thighs

   1 tablespoon peanut or vegetable oil
  ½ teaspoon hot chili oil
   8 chicken thighs (1½ to 2 pounds)
   2 cloves garlic, minced
  ¼ cup sweet and sour sauce
   1 tablespoon soy sauce
   2 teaspoons minced fresh ginger
     Fresh cilantro sprigs and orange peel strips (optional)

Chopped, peeled ginger

Tip

To lengthen the storage time of fresh ginger, cover it with dry sherry in a small glass jar and store it in the refrigerator for as long as three months. Remove the ginger root from the sherry to use. It will have a slight sherry flavor. The ginger-flavored sherry may later be used for cooking, especially in stir-fries.

1. Heat large nonstick skillet over medium-high heat. Add peanut oil and chili oil; heat until hot. Add chicken, skin side down; cook 4 minutes or until golden brown. Reduce heat to low; turn chicken. Cover; cook 15 to 18 minutes until fork can be inserted into chicken with ease and juices run clear, not pink.

2. Spoon off fat. Increase heat to medium. Stir in garlic; cook 2 minutes. Combine sweet and sour sauce, soy sauce and ginger in cup. Brush ½ of mixture over chicken; turn chicken over. Brush remaining mixture over chicken. Cook 5 minutes, turning once more, until sauce has thickened and chicken is browned. Transfer chicken to serving platter; pour sauce evenly over chicken. Garnish with cilantro and orange peel, if desired. Serve immediately.   *Makes 4 servings*

GINGERBREAD

Gingerbread may refer to either one of two traditional desserts—gingerbread cake or gingerbread cookies. Gingerbread cake is a dark, moist cake flavored with molasses, ginger and other spices. It is usually baked in a square baking pan and cut into squares to be served unfrosted with a simple topping of whipped cream or lemon sauce. Gingerbread cookies date back to medieval times. They range from thin and crisp to thick and chewy. They are often cut out in the shape of people.

🌿

Gingered Chicken Thighs

Spicy Gingerbread with Cinnamon Pear Sauce

2 cups all-purpose flour
½ cup packed light brown sugar
1 teaspoon baking soda
1 teaspoon ground ginger
1 teaspoon ground cinnamon
¼ teaspoon ground cloves
¼ teaspoon salt
1 cup light molasses
¾ cup buttermilk
½ cup butter or margarine, softened
Cinnamon Pear Sauce (recipe follows)

1. Preheat oven to 325°F. Grease and lightly flour 9×9-inch baking pan.

2. Combine all ingredients except Cinnamon Pear Sauce in large bowl. Beat with electric mixer at low speed until well blended, scraping side of bowl with rubber spatula frequently. Beat at high speed 2 minutes more. Pour into prepared pan.

3. Bake 50 to 55 minutes until wooden toothpick inserted into center comes out clean. Cool in pan on wire rack about 30 minutes. Cut into squares; serve warm with Cinnamon Pear Sauce.   *Makes 9 servings*

Cinnamon Pear Sauce

2 cans (16 ounces each) pear halves in syrup, undrained
2 tablespoons granulated sugar
1 teaspoon fresh lemon juice
½ teaspoon ground cinnamon

Drain pear halves, reserving ¼ cup syrup. Place pears, reserved syrup, granulated sugar, juice and cinnamon in food processor or blender; cover. Process until smooth. Just before serving, place pear sauce in medium saucepan; heat until warm.

Makes 2 cups sauce

Special Interest

Gingerbread houses that are made of thick, sturdy gingerbread add a whimsical touch to the Christmas season.

GLAZE

A glaze is a thin, shiny coating applied to the surface of certain foods, both sweet and savory. Baked ham may be glazed with a corn syrup or brown sugar mixture; a cake may be glazed with a thin coating of chocolate or melted preserves. Yeast breads may be glazed with an egg wash before baking.

🌿

Basic Ham Glaze

> 1 cup KARO® Light or Dark Corn Syrup
> ½ cup packed brown sugar
> 3 tablespoons prepared mustard
> ½ teaspoon ground ginger
> Dash ground cloves

In medium saucepan combine corn syrup, brown sugar, mustard, ginger and cloves. Stirring constantly, bring to boil over medium heat and boil 5 minutes. Brush on ham frequently during last 30 minutes of baking.

Makes about 1 cup glaze

Prep time: 8 minutes

Microwave Directions: In 1½-quart microwavable bowl combine all ingredients. Microwave on High (100%) 6 minutes. Glaze as directed.

Royal Glaze

> 8 bars (1 ounce each) HERSHEY'S Semi-Sweet Baking Chocolate, broken into pieces
> ½ cup whipping cream

In small saucepan, combine chocolate pieces and whipping cream. Cook over very low heat, stirring constantly, until chocolate is melted and mixture is smooth; *do not boil.* Remove from heat. Cool, stirring occasionally, until mixture begins to thicken, 10 to 15 minutes.

Makes about 1 cup glaze

GNOCCHI

Italian for "dumpling," gnocchi are made from potatoes, flour and sometimes eggs or cheese. Gnocchi are shaped into little balls, squares or strips and simmered in water. They are served with butter and Parmesan cheese or a pasta sauce. The dough can also be chilled, sliced into squares or strips and then baked or fried. Gnocchi are often served as a first course in Italy, but they are usually a meal accompaniment in America.

🌿

GOOSEBERRY

These small, tart round fruits, either green, white, red or yellow, look like small striated grapes. They are popular in Europe. The availability of fresh gooseberries is very limited in the United States, but they may sometimes be found at farmers' markets in the summer. Canned gooseberries also are available. They are best known for their use in gooseberry fool, an English dessert that combines cooked berries with whipped cream. They also make excellent pies and preserves.

🌿

GOULASH

Goulash, or gulyás, is a Hungarian stew prepared with meat, usually beef, and vegetables. It is also seasoned with Hungarian paprika. It may be served with buttered egg noodles and topped with sour cream.

Hungarian Beef Goulash

    ¼ cup all-purpose flour
    1 tablespoon Hungarian sweet
        paprika
    1½ teaspoons salt
    ½ teaspoon Hungarian hot paprika
    ½ teaspoon ground black pepper
    2 pounds beef stew meat
        (1¼-inch pieces)
    4 tablespoons vegetable oil,
        divided
    1 large onion, chopped
    3 cloves garlic, minced
    2 cans (about 14 ounces each)
        single-strength beef broth
    1 can (14½ ounces) stewed
        tomatoes, undrained
    1 cup water
    1 tablespoon dried marjoram
        leaves, crushed
    3 cups (6 ounces) uncooked thin
        egg noodle twists
    1 large green bell pepper,
        chopped
    Sour cream

1. Combine flour, sweet paprika, salt, hot paprika and black pepper in resealable plastic food storage bag. Add ½ of beef. Seal bag; shake to coat well. Repeat with remaining beef.

2. Heat 1½ tablespoons oil in Dutch oven over medium heat. Add ½ of beef; brown on all sides. Transfer to large bowl. Repeat with 1½ tablespoons oil and remaining beef; transfer to same bowl.

3. Heat remaining 1 tablespoon oil in same Dutch oven; add onion and garlic. Cook 8 minutes or until tender, stirring often.

4. Return beef and any juices to Dutch oven. Add broth, tomatoes with liquid, water and marjoram. Bring to a boil over medium-high heat. Reduce heat to medium-low; cover and simmer 1½ hours or until meat is tender, stirring once.

5. When meat is tender, stir in noodles and bell pepper; cover. Simmer about 8 minutes or until noodles are tender, stirring once. To serve, ladle into 8 soup bowls. Dollop with sour cream.

Makes 8 servings

Hungarian Beef Goulash

Tabbouleh Salad (recipe on page 240)

GRAIN

Grain is the edible seed kernel of cereal plants or grasses. The most common cereal grains in America are barley, corn, oats, quinoa, rice, rye, wheat and wild rice. These inexpensive sources of protein and complex carbohydrates provide food for people throughout the world. In vegetarian cultures and areas where meat is in short supply, grains are an important part of every meal.

☙

Grain undergoes processing of various kinds before it reaches the marketplace. Some grains have tough inedible husks that must be removed. Grains are often processed to prolong their shelf life or make them easier to cook. Polishing grains removes the bran and germ from the kernel. Steaming softens kernels. Cracking or grinding shortens cooking time. Since the bran and germ contain much of the B vitamins and fiber and some of the protein, polished grains are not as nutritious as whole grains.

TYPES OF GRAINS

Barley: Barley, native to Ethiopia, is available in several forms. Hulled barley has only the husk removed so that its bran and germ are intact. Scotch barley and barley grits have been further processed by grinding or cracking. All of these forms can be found in health food stores. The most common form of barley is pearled, meaning that it has been polished many times to remove the bran and most of the germ. Pearled barley is also available in a quick-cooking form. Pearl and quick-cooking barley are readily available in supermarkets. All forms of barley have a nutty flavor and slightly chewy texture.

Buckwheat: Although buckwheat is technically not a grain, but the fruit of a leafy plant, it is used like other grains in cooking. Unpolished buckwheat kernels, called groats, and ground kernels, called buckwheat grits, are available in health food stores. Toasted groats, known as kasha, are also available. This grain has a strong, nutty flavor that is more pronounced if the groats are toasted.

Bulgur: Bulgur is a processed form of

wheat produced by steaming, drying and crushing wheat kernels. It has a tender, chewy texture.

Corn: *See Corn, page 157, for additional information.*

Oats: Oats are one of the most nutritious of grains. Whole oats must be processed before they can be eaten. They are cleaned, toasted and hulled to make oat groats. Scotch oats, steel-cut oats and Irish oatmeal are groats that have been cut into pieces but not rolled. They are available in health food stores. They are used to make cereal. Most of the oats sold in America have been further processed. Groats are steamed and flattened into flakes to make regular rolled oats, often called old-fashioned oats. Further processing yields quick-cooking rolled oats. Regular rolled oats need about 7 minutes of cooking; whereas quick-cooking rolled oats take only 1 minute to cook. These two products are interchangeable in baking recipes. Instant oats have been precooked and dried, requiring only the addition of boiling water. The more processed the oats, the less chewy the texture they have when cooked. In addition to their use as a cooked cereal, rolled oats are used as an ingredient in cookies, muffins and granola.

Rice: *See Rice, page 429, for additional information.*

Rye: Rye is the unpolished whole kernels or berries of rye grass. It is best known as the source of rye flour, but the kernels can be cooked and used as other grains. It has a strong, distinct flavor. Rye berries are available at health food stores.

Wheat: This grain plays an important part in the cuisines of much of the world. There are thousands of varieties of wheat. The three most common types are hard, soft and durum. Hard wheats are high in the proteins, glutenin and gliadin. When moistened these proteins form gluten, the elastic substance that creates the structure of baked goods and traps

the gases that cause them to rise. Hard wheat flour is used primarily for yeast breadmaking; soft wheat for cakes, cookies and quick breads; and durum wheat for pasta. Unprocessed wheat kernels (berries) can be cooked like any other grain. Wheat kernels are cut with steel blades to form cracked wheat, which can be cooked and served as a breakfast cereal or used in stuffings and breads.

Wild Rice: *See Wild Rice, page 542, for additional information.*

Buying Tips: Grains containing the bran and the germ (whole-grain products) are more nutritious but also more perishable than polished (processed) grains. When purchasing grains in bulk, choose a store with rapid turnover where grains are stored in covered containers in a cool, dry place.

Storage: Because of their tendency to become rancid, unpolished whole grains should be bought in small quantities and stored in the refrigerator in an airtight container. They will keep up to six months. Polished kernels stored in a cool, dry place in an airtight container will keep up to one year.

Basic Preparation: Each grain has its optimum cooking time and each requires a different amount of cooking liquid. As a general rule, most uncooked grains will expand two to three times their original size during cooking so choose a saucepan that will hold the expanded grain. A general reference for cooking grains is provided on page 240. Many grains are added to boiling salted water. Some must be added to cold water. For specific directions about an individual grain, read label directions carefully. Most grains should be cooked until tender but firm and until all cooking liquid has been absorbed.

COOKING GRAINS

Grain (1 cup)	Amount of Water	Cooking Time	Yield
Barley (pearl)	4 cups	45 minutes	3½ cups
Barley (quick-cooking)	1½ cups	10 to 12 minutes	2½ cups
Buckwheat groats or kasha	2 cups	15 minutes	2½ cups
Bulgur	2 cups	Simmer, covered, 12 to 15 minutes	3 cups
Oats (quick-cooking)	2 cups	1 minute	2 cups
Oats (regular)	2 cups	5 to 7 minutes	2 cups
Rye berries	3 cups	1 hour	3 cups
Wheat berries	2 cups	30 to 40 minutes	2¾ cups
Wheat (cracked)	2 cups	30 to 40 minutes	2⅔ cups

Tabbouleh Salad

¾ cup bulgur, cooked
¾ cup chopped green bell pepper
½ cup chopped fresh parsley
2 tablespoons thinly sliced green onion
¼ cup fresh lemon juice
2 tablespoons water
4 teaspoons vegetable oil
2 teaspoons chopped fresh dill *or* ½ teaspoon dried dill weed
1 teaspoon sugar
¼ teaspoon salt
Lettuce leaves
½ cup chopped seeded tomato

1. Place bulgur in colander. Rinse under cold water; drain. Combine bulgur, bell pepper, parsley and onion in medium bowl; set aside.

2. Place juice, water, oil, dill, sugar and salt in jar with tight-fitting lid. Cover; shake well. Add to reserved bulgur mixture; toss to combine. Cover; refrigerate at least 4 hours or up to 24 hours.

3. Line salad bowl with lettuce. Top with bulgur mixture and tomato.

Makes 4 servings

Greens, White Bean and Barley Soup

1½ pounds collard greens, cleaned well
2 tablespoons olive oil
½ pound carrots, chopped
1½ cups chopped onions
2 cloves garlic, minced
1½ cups sliced fresh button mushrooms
6 cups Vegetable Stock (page 487) or canned vegetable broth
2 cups cooked pearl barley
1 can (16 ounces) Great Northern beans, drained, rinsed
2 bay leaves
1 teaspoon sugar
1 teaspoon dried thyme leaves
1 tablespoon white wine vinegar
Hot pepper sauce
Red bell pepper strips (optional)

1. To remove stems from greens, fold each leaf in half. With fingers, pull stem toward top of leaf. Discard stem. Coarsely chop greens to measure 7 cups; set aside.

2. Heat oil in Dutch oven over medium heat. Add carrots, onions and garlic; cook and stir 3 minutes. Add mushrooms; cook and stir 5 minutes or until tender. Add stock, barley, beans, bay leaves, sugar and thyme. Bring to a boil over high heat. Reduce heat to low. Cover; simmer 5 minutes. Add reserved greens; simmer 10 minutes or until greens are tender. Remove bay leaves; discard. Stir in vinegar. Season to taste with pepper sauce. Garnish with bell pepper, if desired. Serve immediately.

Makes 8 servings

GRANOLA

Granola is a cereal made of various combinations of grains, mainly oats, nuts and dried fruits that are sweetened with brown sugar or honey and flavored with spices or vanilla. Some granolas contain coconut. Granola may be purchased at supermarkets or health food stores or made at home. Use it as a snack, breakfast food or as an ingredient in baked goods. Granola should be stored in an airtight container in a cool, dry place for up to one month or refrigerated for no longer than three months.

☙

Date-Nut Granola

2 cups uncooked rolled oats
2 cups barley flakes
1 cup sliced almonds
⅓ cup vegetable oil
⅓ cup honey
1 teaspoon vanilla extract
1 cup chopped dates

1. Preheat oven to 350°F. Grease 13×9-inch baking pan.

2. Combine oats, barley flakes and almonds in large bowl; set aside.

3. Combine oil, honey and vanilla in small bowl. Pour honey mixture over oat mixture; stir well. Pour into prepared pan.

4. Bake about 25 minutes or until toasted, stirring frequently after first 10 minutes. Stir in dates while mixture is still hot. Cool completely. Store tightly covered at room temperature.

Makes 6 cups granola

GRAPE

Grapes are small fruit that grow in clusters on bushes or climbing vines. This fruit is one of the oldest known to man. There are thousands of varieties, shaped either oval or round, with smooth green, red, purple or purple-black skin. Some are seedless; others have several seeds. Grapes are classified by use (table, wine-making or processing). Table grapes have a low acid content and are sweeter; grapes for wine have high acidity and are often too tart for eating. Most of the domestic wine and table grapes are grown in California.

☙

California Pearlettes are round, light green seedless table grapes with a sweet flavor and crisp texture.

Concord grapes are medium to large in size with purplish-blue color and a mild flavor. They are too fragile for shipping. They are used primarily for juice and jelly.

Emperor grapes are large, elongated table grapes with a light reddish-purple color and a mild cherry flavor.

Exotic grapes are shiny and black with juicy, meaty flesh and a subtle sweetness. They are table grapes.

Flame Seedless are purplish-red oval table grapes with a firm, crunchy texture. They are mildly sweet yet slightly tart table grapes.

Italia Muscat are large, yellow-green table grapes with a rich winelike flavor. They complement the flavor of cheese, making them an excellent choice for dessert. They are also used to make raisins.

Red Flame are round, red seedless table grapes.

Ribier are plump, purple-black meaty table grapes. They are mildly sweet.

Tip

Frozen grapes make a great snack. Wash thoroughly and dry. Remove grapes from stems. Place them on a tray in the freezer. When frozen solid, store them in a resealable plastic freezer bag. They will keep frozen for up to three months.

Thompson Seedless grapes are green in color with a crisp, firm texture and a light, sweet flavor. This variety is a widely available table grape. It is also used to make raisins.

Tokay grapes are bright red in color. These large, round table grapes have a mild, sweet flavor.

Availability: Fresh grapes can be found all year. Imports supplement the domestic crop during the winter months. White, purple and red grapes are used for juice, which is available frozen, canned or bottled.

Buying Tips: Buy firm, well-formed grapes that are firmly attached to their stems. A dusty bloom on the skin is an indication of freshness. Avoid bunches with bruised, moldy or soft grapes.

Yield: 1 pound seedless grapes = 2½ cups.

Tuna Veronique

Storage: Remove any crushed grapes before storing the bunch unwashed in a plastic bag in the refrigerator for up to one week.

Basic Preparation: Thoroughly wash grapes with a gentle spray of cold water. Blot dry with paper towels. To serve, cut the larger bunch into smaller bunches using kitchen shears or gently pull the grapes off the stems. Grapes may be cut in half using a paring knife. Remove seeds with the tip of the knife.

Tuna Veronique

    2 leeks or green onions
    ½ cup thin carrot strips
    1 stalk celery, cut diagonally into
        slices
    1 tablespoon vegetable oil
 1¾ cups or 1 can (14½ ounces)
        chicken broth
    2 tablespoons cornstarch
    ⅓ cup dry white wine
 1¼ cups seedless red and green
        grapes, cut into halves
    1 can (12 ounces) STARKIST®
        Tuna, drained and broken into
        chunks
    1 tablespoon chopped chives
    ¼ teaspoon ground white or black
        pepper
 4 to 5 slices bread, toasted and
        cut into quarters *or* 8 to
        10 slices toasted French bread

If using leeks, wash thoroughly between leaves. Cut off white portion; trim and slice ¼ inch thick. Discard green portion. For green onions, trim and slice ¼ inch thick. In large nonstick skillet, sauté leeks, carrot and celery in oil for 3 minutes. In small bowl, stir together chicken broth and cornstarch until smooth; stir into vegetables. Cook and stir until mixture thickens and bubbles. Stir in wine; simmer 2 minutes. Stir in grapes, tuna, chives and pepper. Cook 2 minutes more to heat through. To serve, ladle sauce over toast.   *Makes 4 to 5 servings*

Prep time: 20 minutes

GRAPEFRUIT

Compared to many other fruits, grapefruit is relatively new on the scene. Present-day grapefruit are descendents of an Asian fruit, the pomelo. Pomelos were large fruits with rough, thick skins, lots of seeds and a slightly sour flavor. Grapefruit have been grown in Florida since the 1830's, but not until the turn of the century were they shipped outside the state. The United States produces the majority of the world's supply of grapefruit, with Florida leading all other states in production. Grapefruit are also commercially grown in California, Texas and Arizona.

✿

Uses: Grapefruit can be cut into halves and served for breakfast. The halves can be lightly sprinkled with sugar or salt.

• Grapefruit can be peeled and separated into segments for use in salads and entrées.

• For a light dessert, grapefruit halves can be sprinkled with sugar (granulated or brown), dotted with butter and broiled until the sugar melts.

• Grapefruit are commercially processed to extract the juices. This can also be done at home.

Varieties: Grapefruit are grouped by color of the flesh—white (yellow-white) and pink (yellow-pink to deep pink). The skins of all varieties are yellow, some with a pink blush. They can also be classified as seeded or seedless. Common varieties of white grapefruit are Marsh (seedless) and Duncan. Pink grapefruit varieties include pink Marsh, Ruby Red (seedless) and Star Ruby.

Availability: Grapefruit is available all year. The Florida and Texas season begins in November and continues through June. Fruit from California and Arizona is available from January through August.

Buying Tips: Grapefruit should be firm with shiny, smooth thin skins. Fruit that feels heavy for its size is probably juicy. Avoid lightweight grapefruit with rough skins.

Yield: 1 medium grapefruit = 1 cup juice; 1½ cups segments.

Storage: While grapefruit can be stored at room temperature for two or three days, they keep better if stored in a plastic bag in the refrigerator. They will keep up to two weeks.

Basic Preparation: For serving grapefruit halves, a serrated grapefruit knife is ideal for separating the segments from the peel and membranes before serving. A paring knife can also be used. The segments can be eaten with a spoon.

To section, place the grapefruit on a cutting board. Cut a slice from the top and bottom of the grapefruit. Then starting at the top and working towards the bottom, slice the peel and white pith off the grapefruit in wide strips, following the curve of the grapefruit. Repeat until all the peel and pith are removed. Make "V-shaped" slices into the center of the grapefruit just inside of the membrane to remove grapefruit segments (technique on page 344).

GRATE, TO

Grating refers to the technique of making very small particles from a firm food like carrots, lemon peel or Parmesan cheese by rubbing it along a coarse surface with small, sharp protrusions, usually a metal kitchen grater. Food may also be grated in a food processor using the metal blade.

✿

Tip

Grating and shredding cheese are often confused. Only hard cheeses, like Parmesan and romano, can be grated. All other cheeses, like Cheddar, Swiss and mozzarella, are shredded.

GREENS

Greens often refer to a number of pungently flavored dark green leaves including, but not limited to, collard greens, dandelion greens, mustard greens and turnip greens. Throughout history most greens have had curative powers attributed to them. Generally, all are good sources of various nutrients including beta carotene, vitamin C, iron and calcium.

☙

Uses: Most greens can be eaten raw when they are very young and tender.

• Greens are more commonly cooked when mature to enhance their flavor. They are served as a side dish often flavored with bits of smoked ham or vinegar.

• Chopped greens may be added to soups, stews and stir-fries. They mix well with other highly flavored ingredients.

Varieties: Collard greens, a staple of soul food, is a member of the cabbage family. Collard greens are often confused with kale. Its flavor is a cross between cabbage and kale.

• Mustard greens, also a soul food ingredient, are cousins to collard greens. The leaves are very dark green and have a pungent, mustardlike flavor.

• Dandelion greens have a slightly bitter, tangy flavor and grow both wild and cultivated.

• Turnip greens, another popular soul food, are one of the sharpest tasting greens when mature. Turnips grown for their tops don't develop full-grown roots.

• Other greens include kale *(see page 276)*, beet greens, spinach *(see page 472)* and Swiss chard.

Availability: Collard greens are available all year with January through April as their peak season.

• Mustard greens are most abundant from December through March but may be found year-round in some areas. They may also be purchased canned or frozen.

• Dandelion greens are at their peak in the early spring when the plants have not yet flowered.

• Turnip greens are available year-round with their peak season from October through February.

Buying Tips: All greens should be chosen for their crisp, bright and even-colored leaves. Avoid greens that are wilted, yellowed, spotted or have thick, fibrous stems. When choosing dandelion greens, the smaller, the better. Leaves less than 6 inches long are best.

Yield: 1 pound fresh greens = approximately 3 cups cooked.

Storage: All greens should be stored in plastic bags in the refrigerator. Collard and dandelion greens will keep for up to five days; mustard greens one week; turnip greens up to three days.

Basic Preparation: Greens can be sandy. Soak them in a sinkful of cool water for a few minutes. Then swish them to remove sand and dirt. Repeat this process several times, if necessary, with fresh water.

Collard greens may have tough stems that should be removed before cooking. To remove the stems, fold each leaf in half. With your fingers, pull the stem toward the top of the leaf. Discard the stems. Greens may be blanched, braised, sautéed, simmered, steamed or stir-fried.

Swishing collard greens in cold water.

Removing stem from leaf.

GRILL, TO

Grilling refers to the technique of cooking foods, usually meat, poultry and seafood but also vegetables, fruits and breads, directly over a heat source, such as hot coals or an open gas flame. The goal of cooking foods by grilling is to sear and brown the outside, giving the food its characteristically grilled flavor, while concentrating the moisture and juices inside.

The terms barbecue and grill are usually used interchangeably. When a distinction is made, barbecue refers to long, slow cooking, sometimes on a spit or in a pit, of large pieces of meat kept moist with a highly seasoned sauce. Barbecuing in this form is likely done for large groups or gatherings. By contrast, grilling implies quicker, lighter cooking of a wider variety of foods including poultry, seafood, vegetables and fruits, using seasonings, spice rubs, marinades and light sauces.

☙

Types of Grills: The most common open grills or braziers for charcoal cooking have large metal firebowls secured to long legs. The cooking racks can be raised and lowered in order to adjust the cooking distance of foods from the heat source. Since these open grills can be very inexpensive, their quality varies widely. Look for equipment with stable legs and a sturdy firebowl.

The popular kettle charcoal grill is similar to the brazier but has a cover, vents and a stationary rack. Cooking is more controlled, because the grill is covered and the vents can be used to adjust air flow and thus heat intensity. Food cooks more evenly, cooking time is reduced and smoked flavor is increased.

Gas grills for outdoor use provide lava stones or briquette-shaped rocks in place of charcoal. They heat up quickly and avoid the mess of charcoal. Gas grills are fueled either by a refillable gas canister or through a permanent hookup to a natural gas line.

Electric grills for use outdoors are manufactured with exterior-grade materials, wiring and plug.

Hibachis are small brazier-type grills with a cast iron bottom kettle that holds the coals and an open grill rack held in place on notched upright supports. Common to Asian cooking, they usually hold small amounts of food, for example four hamburgers.

Hickory Beef Kabob (recipe on page 248)

*Blackened Sea Bass
(recipe on page 248)*

Indoor grills may be free-standing electric countertop appliances or cooktops that are installed as part of a gas or electric range or counter cooking surface. Electric countertop grills have an electric element as their heat source and are considered smokeless. Built-in gas and electric grill tops use lava stones as a heat source and need generous venting, which is often part of the appliance.

Grill Supplies: Charcoal briquettes are manufactured by burning wood in the absence of oxygen until it is reduced to carbon, which is pressed into the briquette shapes in combination with starch binders, ground coal and sometimes added chemicals. The process was invented by Henry Ford as a way to use the wood left from making his car frames. Briquettes that are presoaked with lighter fluid are also available.

Charcoal lighter fluid can assist in starting a fire and imparts no flavor to the cooking food since it burns away within a few minutes after the fire is lit. Alcohol, gasoline and kerosene should never be used to light charcoal. Also, never add lighter fluid to a fire that is already lit.

Hardwood and fruitwood chips or chunks can impart additional flavor to charcoal-grilled foods. Choices include mesquite, hickory, apple, cherry, maple, peach, pecan and walnut. If you chip your own wood, never use soft woods, such as cedar, pine or spruce; these emit resins that can give food an unpleasant taste. Soak wood chips in water for at least 20 minutes before sprinkling over hot coals.

A spray bottle filled with water is useful to control wild sparks and very small flare-ups on a charcoal grill. Care should be taken not to overuse the water spray and inadvertently extinguish the coals. Do not use water to quench flare-ups on a gas grill. Simply close the hood and turn down the heat until the flames subside.

Grill cleaning utensils such as wire brushes and steel wool pads make cleanup after grilling much easier.

Cooking Equipment, Utensils and Supplies: Rotisseries are often available as attachments for larger grills. The unit consists of a spit that is inserted through the food to be cooked and then placed in a motor-driven assembly that rotates the food during cooking, allowing it to baste in its own juices and cook more evenly.

Basting brushes, tongs, turners and forks are all useful utensils. If possible, choose ones with long handles. Some brushes are designed with angled handles for ease of use. Avoid using forks to pierce meat during cooking as this will result in lost juices. Never set these utensils directly on a hot grill as they can get very hot and even melt or burn.

Hinged wire baskets, available in a variety of shapes, are especially useful when cooking fish, which has a tendency to fall apart if cooked directly on the grill grid. Baskets may also be used to cook vegetables and other small foods that are not skewered.

Skewers are threaded with small chunks or strips of meat, poultry, vegetables and sometimes fruit to make kabobs for grilling. Metal skewers are best for heavier foods like chunks of meat. Long, thin wooden skewers work well for individual servings consisting of small pieces of meat, vegetables and fruits. Soak wooden skewers in water for about 30 minutes before using to prevent burning.

Heavy-duty foil is useful to shield foods on the grill from intense heat, to make drip pans, and to wrap and cover foods being cooked on the grill.

A meat thermometer can be useful for determining the doneness of foods.

Preparing Grill for Cooking: Grease grill grid with oil or cooking spray before use to minimize food sticking to the grid and to assist cleanup. However, do not spray the grill over the fire as this could cause a flare-up.

To start a charcoal fire, pile the briquettes in a loose pyramid, soak with charcoal lighting fluid and allow the fluid to soak in for a minute or two before lighting. Or, use an electric charcoal starter by following the manufacturer's instructions.

Charcoal briquettes are ready for cooking when they are glowing red and their surface is covered with gray ash. Coals will take anywhere from 20 to 40 minutes to reach this stage. Using tongs, coals may then be spread out for even heat.

For direct grilling, arrange hot coals in a single layer to extend 1 to 2 inches beyond the area of the food on the grid. This method is for quick-cooking foods, such as hamburgers, steaks, chicken breasts and fish.

For indirect grilling, the food is placed on the grid over a metal or disposable foil drip pan with coals banked either to one side or both sides of the pan. This method is used for slow-cooking foods, such as large roasts and whole chickens.

To determine the degree of heat intensity, place your hand just above the grid. Count "one-thousand one, one-thousand two, etc." until your hand feels hot. Your time corresponds to heat intensity: 2 seconds for hot; 3 seconds for medium-hot; 4 seconds for medium; 5 seconds for medium-low. If you can keep your hand at that level for more than 5 seconds, the coals are low.

Electric or gas grills should be preheated according to the manufacturer's instructions.

If you want to start cooking and the coals are too hot, use tongs to spread them apart. Or, remove a few of the coals and partially close the vents to slow the fire. Or, adjust the grilling rack so the food will be farther from the heat.

To speed cooking, meats and vegetables may be partially cooked in the microwave before completing the cooking on the grill. Foods should not be allowed to stand after microwaving. For safety sake, immediately place them on the grill.

Do not crowd pieces of food on the grill. Food will cook more evenly with a ¾-inch space between pieces.

Sauces and marinades add flavor and moisture to grilled foods. Brush foods with sauces during the last 30 minutes of cooking to avoid excess charring. For food safety, allow the meat or poultry to cook on the grill at least 5 minutes after the last application of sauce. If using leftover marinade for basting or as a sauce over cooked food, boil it for at least 1 minute.

For food safety, do not use the same pan or platter for both raw and cooked foods.

Arranging coals in a pyramid shape.

Charcoal arranged for direct grilling.

Arranging charcoal for indirect grilling.

Special Interest

Cooking over an open fire has been practiced since the time man recognized and harnessed fire as a source of light and heat. Archeological remains indicate the existence of fire pits to cook food tens of thousands of years ago. Writings from early civilizations refer to spit-roasted animals. Throughout history great banquets, feasts and celebrations have included spit-roasted meats. Early explorers to America wrote of seeing native Indians cooking and smoking fish and game over open flames.

Hickory Beef Kabobs

> 2 ears fresh corn,* shucked
> 1 pound boneless beef top sirloin or tenderloin steak, cut into 1¼-inch pieces
> 1 red or green bell pepper, cut into 1-inch squares
> 1 small red onion, cut into ½-inch wedges
> ½ cup beer or nonalcoholic beer
> ½ cup chili sauce
> 1 teaspoon dry mustard
> 2 cloves garlic, minced
> 1½ cups hickory chips
> 3 cups hot cooked white rice
> ¼ cup chopped fresh parsley
> Fresh parsley sprigs and plum tomatoes (optional)

*Four small ears frozen corn, thawed, can be substituted for fresh corn.

1. Cut corn crosswise into 1-inch pieces. Place beef, bell pepper, onion and corn in large resealable plastic food storage bag. Combine beer, chili sauce, mustard and garlic in small bowl; pour over beef and vegetables. Seal bag tightly, turning to coat. Marinate in refrigerator at least 1 hour or up to 8 hours, turning occasionally.

2. Prepare grill for direct grilling over medium-hot heat.

3. Meanwhile, cover hickory chips with cold water; soak 20 minutes.

4. Drain beef and vegetables; reserve marinade. Alternately thread beef and vegetables onto 4 (12-inch-long) metal skewers. Brush with reserved marinade.

5. Drain hickory chips; sprinkle over coals. Place kabobs on grid. Grill kabobs, on covered grill, over medium-hot coals 5 minutes. Brush with reserved marinade; turn and brush again. Discard remaining marinade. Continue to grill, covered, 5 to 7 minutes for medium or until beef is desired doneness.

6. Combine rice and chopped parsley; serve kabobs over rice mixture. Garnish with parsley sprigs and tomatoes, if desired.

Makes 4 servings

Blackened Sea Bass

> Hardwood charcoal*
> 2 teaspoons paprika
> 1 teaspoon garlic salt
> 1 teaspoon dried thyme leaves
> ¼ teaspoon ground white pepper
> ¼ teaspoon ground red pepper
> ¼ teaspoon ground black pepper
> 3 tablespoons butter or margarine
> 4 skinless sea bass or catfish fillets (4 to 6 ounces each)
> Lemon halves
> Fresh dill sprigs (optional)

*Hardwood charcoal takes longer than regular charcoal to become hot but results in a hotter fire than regular charcoal. A hot fire is necessary to seal in the juices and cook fish quickly. If hardwood charcoal is not available, scatter dry hardwood, mesquite or hickory chunks over hot coals to create a hot fire.

1. Prepare grill for direct grilling over high heat using hardwood charcoal.

2. Meanwhile, combine paprika, garlic salt, thyme and peppers in small bowl; mix well. Set aside.

3. Melt butter in small saucepan over medium heat. Pour melted butter into pie plate or shallow bowl. Cool slightly.

4. Dip sea bass into melted butter, evenly coating both sides. Sprinkle both sides of sea bass evenly with reserved paprika mixture. Place sea bass on grid. (Fire will flare up when sea bass is placed on grid, but will subside when grill is covered.) Grill sea bass, on covered grill, over hot coals 4 to 6 minutes until sea bass is blackened and flakes easily when tested with fork, turning halfway through grilling time. Serve with lemon halves. Garnish with dill, if desired.   *Makes 4 servings*

Micro-Grilled Pork Ribs

1 tablespoon firmly packed brown
   sugar
2 teaspoons ground cumin
1 teaspoon salt
½ teaspoon black pepper
   Dash ground red pepper
   (optional)
3 pounds pork back ribs
⅓ cup water
½ cup K.C. MASTERPIECE®
   Barbecue Sauce
   Grilled Sweet Potatoes (recipe
   follows)

Combine brown sugar, cumin, salt
and peppers in small bowl. Rub onto
ribs. Arrange ribs in single layer in
13×9-inch microwave-safe baking
dish. Pour water over ribs, cover
loosely with plastic wrap. Microwave
on MEDIUM-HIGH (70% power)
15 minutes, rearranging ribs and
rotating dish halfway through cooking
time.

Arrange medium-hot KINGSFORD®
Briquets on one side of grill. Place
ribs on grid area opposite briquets.
Barbecue ribs, on a covered grill,
15 to 20 minutes, turning every
5 minutes and basting with barbecue
sauce the last 10 minutes. Ribs
should be browned and cooked
through. Serve with Grilled Sweet
Potatoes.   *Makes 4 servings*

**Grilled Sweet Potatoes or Baking
Potatoes:** Slice potatoes into ¼-inch-
thick rounds, allowing about ⅓
pound potatoes per serving. Brush
both sides of slices lightly with oil.
Place on grid around edges of
medium-hot KINGSFORD® Briquets.
Cook potatoes, on a covered grill,
10 to 12 minutes until golden brown
and tender, turning once.

Micro-Grilled Pork Ribs

Shrimp on the Barbie

**1 pound raw large shrimp,
    shelled, deveined**
**1 *each* red and yellow bell
    pepper, seeded, cut into
    1-inch chunks**
4 slices lime (optional)
**½ cup prepared smoky-flavor
    barbecue sauce**
**2 tablespoons FRENCH'S®
    Worcestershire Sauce**
**2 tablespoons FRANK'S® Original
    RedHot® Cayenne Pepper
    Sauce**
1 clove garlic, minced

Thread shrimp, peppers and lime, if
desired, alternately onto metal
skewers. Combine barbecue sauce,
Worcestershire, RedHot sauce and
garlic in small bowl; mix well. Brush
on skewers.

Shrimp on the Barbie

Place skewers on grid, reserving
sauce mixture. Grill over hot coals
15 minutes or until shrimp turn pink,
turning and basting often with sauce
mixture. (Do not baste during last
5 minutes of cooking.) Serve warm.

Makes 4 servings

Prep time: 10 minutes
Cook time: 15 minutes

Beijing Chicken

3 pounds frying chicken pieces
**½ cup KIKKOMAN® Teriyaki
    Marinade & Sauce**
1 tablespoon dry sherry
**2 teaspoons minced fresh ginger
    root**
½ teaspoon fennel seed, crushed
½ teaspoon grated orange peel
½ teaspoon honey

Rinse chicken under cold water; pat
dry with paper towels. Combine
teriyaki sauce, sherry, ginger, fennel,
orange peel and honey; pour over
chicken in large plastic food storage
bag. Press air out of bag; close top
securely. Refrigerate 8 hours or
overnight, turning bag over
occasionally. Reserving marinade,
remove chicken; place on grill 5 to
7 inches from hot coals. Cook 30 to
40 minutes, or until chicken is no
longer pink in center, turning over
and basting occasionally with
reserved marinade. (Or, place
chicken on rack of broiler pan. Broil
5 to 7 inches from heat 40 minutes,
or until chicken is no longer pink in
center, turning over and brushing
occasionally with reserved marinade.)

Makes 4 servings

Grilled Sweet Potato Packets with Pecan Butter

        4 sweet potatoes (about 8 ounces
            each), peeled
        1 large sweet or Spanish onion,
            thinly sliced and separated
            into rings
        3 tablespoons vegetable oil
        ⅓ cup butter or margarine,
            softened
        2 tablespoons packed light brown
            sugar
        ¼ teaspoon salt
        ¼ teaspoon ground cinnamon
        ¼ cup chopped pecans, toasted

1. Prepare grill for direct grilling over medium heat.

2. Slice potatoes crosswise into ¼-inch-thick slices. Alternately place potato slices and onion rings on four 14×12-inch sheets of heavy-duty foil. Brush tops and sides with oil.

3. For each packet, bring long sides of foil together above food; fold down in series of locked folds, allowing space for heat circulation. Crimp short ends closed to seal foil packet.

4. Place foil packets on grid. Grill packets, on covered grill, over medium coals 25 to 30 minutes until potatoes are fork-tender.

5. Meanwhile, to prepare Pecan Butter, combine butter, sugar, salt and cinnamon in small bowl; mix well. Stir in pecans. Open packets carefully; top each with dollop of Pecan Butter.

Makes 4 side-dish servings

GRIND, TO

Grinding refers to the technique of reducing a food to very small pieces. Different equipment may be used depending on the firmness of the food. Coffee, spice, pepper or meat are examples of foods that use different grinders.

☙

GRITS

Grits, also known as hominy grits, are a cereal made of dried, milled white or yellow corn kernels. Grits are sold all over the country, but they are most common in the South, where they are standard breakfast fare. They are cooked in liquid, usually water though sometimes milk or cream, in an open saucepan and stirred frequently. They can be served as cereal, either plain, with a pat of butter or a drizzling of maple syrup. Grits pair up well with cheese, and many popular grit dishes include it.

Quick-cooking grits are finely ground so they cook in less than 5 minutes instead of the 20 or 30 minutes required for regular grits. Instant grits have been precooked and dehydrated. Stone-ground grits usually are coarser than most commercial types and contain some of the germ. Except for stone-ground grits, which should be refrigerated, grits should be stored in a tightly sealed container and placed in a cool, dry place.

☙

Technique for Grilled Sweet Potato Packets with Pecan Butter

Step 3. *Sealing the foil packet.*

Bacon and Maple Grits Puff

Bacon and Maple Grits Puff

8 slices bacon
2 cups milk
1¼ cups water
1 cup quick-cooking grits
½ teaspoon salt
½ cup pure maple syrup
4 eggs
Fresh chives (optional)

1. Preheat oven to 350°F. Grease 1½-quart round casserole or soufflé dish; set aside.

2. Cook bacon in large skillet over medium-high heat about 7 minutes or until crisp. Remove bacon to paper towel; set aside. Reserve 2 tablespoons bacon drippings.

3. Combine milk, water, grits and salt in medium saucepan. Bring to a boil over medium heat, stirring frequently. Simmer 2 to 3 minutes until mixture thickens, stirring constantly. Remove from heat; stir in syrup and reserved 2 tablespoons bacon drippings. Crumble bacon; reserve ¼ cup for garnish. Stir remaining crumbled bacon into grits mixture.

4. Beat eggs in medium bowl. Gradually stir small amount of grits mixture into eggs, then stir back into remaining grits mixture. Pour into prepared casserole dish.

5. Bake 1 hour and 20 minutes or until knife inserted into center comes out clean. Top with reserved ¼ cup bacon. Garnish with chives, if desired. Serve immediately.

Makes 6 to 8 servings

Note: Puff will fall slightly after removing from oven.

GUACAMOLE

This popular Mexican dish is made from mashed ripe avocados, minced onion, chilies, lime juice and cilantro. A small amount of finely diced tomato may be added. Prone to discoloring, it must be served quickly once it is made. Its most popular use is as a dip with tortilla chips, but it is also used as a component in such dishes as tostados and tacos.

GUAVA

Guava is an aromatic, sweet tropical fruit that grows in its native South America as well as in California, Florida and Hawaii. The fruit is allowed to ripen on the trees until it falls. Guavas are round or slightly oval in shape, two to three inches in diameter with several small, hard edible seeds.

Varieties: Guavas are available in many sizes and colors. Skin color can range from pale yellow to red to purple-black. The sweet, juicy flesh is off-white to bright red in color.

Availability: Guavas are available fresh only in areas where they are locally grown. They are in season from August through October. Most of the domestic crop is canned or processed into juice, jellies and sauces.

Buying Tips: Choose guavas with a fragrant aroma that yield to gentle pressure. Avoid fruit with blemishes or any soft spots.

Yield: 6 large guavas = 1 cup pulp.

Storage: To ripen, allow green guavas to stand uncovered and out of direct sunlight at room temperature. Store ripe guavas in the refrigerator for up to four days.

Basic Preparation: Wash the guava and cut off the blossom end. Cut in half lengthwise with a utility knife and scoop out the pulp with a spoon or melon baller. To slice, peel off the skin with a paring knife and cut the flesh as desired.

GUMBO

A Creole specialty that can most likely be traced to Africa, this New Orleans classic is a hearty, spicy stew that usually includes combinations of meat, sausage, poultry, seafood, tomatoes and vegetables. It begins with a roux of flour and fat that has been allowed to brown over low heat to develop a rich flavor. The gumbo may also include okra or filé powder (obtained from sassafras root) for thickening.

☙

Spicy Shrimp Gumbo

- ½ cup vegetable oil
- ½ cup all-purpose flour
- 1 large onion, chopped
- ½ cup chopped fresh parsley
- ½ cup chopped celery
- ½ cup sliced green onions
- 6 cloves garlic, minced
- 4 cups chicken broth or water*
- 1 package (10 ounces) frozen sliced okra, thawed (optional)
- 1 teaspoon salt
- ½ teaspoon ground red pepper
- 2 pounds raw medium shrimp, peeled, deveined
- 3 cups hot cooked rice
  Fresh Italian parsley leaves (optional)

*Traditional gumbo's thickness is like stew. If you prefer it thinner, add 1 to 2 cups additional broth.

1. For roux, blend oil and flour in large heavy stockpot. Cook over medium-high heat 10 to 15 minutes until roux is dark brown, stirring often.

2. Add chopped onion, chopped parsley, celery, green onions and garlic to roux. Cook over medium-high heat 5 to 10 minutes until vegetables are tender. Add broth, okra, salt and pepper. Cover; simmer 15 minutes. Add shrimp; simmer 3 to 5 minutes until shrimp turn pink and opaque.

3. Place about ⅓ cup rice into each of 8 soup bowls; top with gumbo. Garnish with Italian parsley, if desired.   *Makes 8 servings*

Technique for Spicy Shrimp Gumbo

Step 1. *Cooking roux until dark brown.*

HAMBURGER

A hamburger is traditionally a hot sandwich consisting of a cooked patty of ground beef served in a round bun. The ground beef may be mixed with chopped onion and seasonings. Toppings for hamburgers include cheese, ketchup, mustard, relish, pickle slices, onion slices, tomato slices and lettuce. Hamburger patties should be cooked until they are gray rather than pink in the center. See Meat (Testing for Doneness), page 302, for additional information. The term hamburger can also refer to the ground beef itself.

🌾

America's Favorite Cheddar Beef Burgers

> 1 pound ground beef
> ⅓ cup A.1.® Steak Sauce, divided
> 1 medium onion, cut into strips
> 1 medium green or red bell pepper, cut into strips
> 1 tablespoon FLEISCHMANN'S® Margarine
> 4 ounces Cheddar cheese, sliced
> 4 hamburger rolls
> 4 tomato slices

In medium bowl, combine ground beef and 3 tablespoons steak sauce; shape mixture into 4 patties. Set aside.

In medium skillet, over medium heat, cook onion and pepper in margarine until tender, stirring occasionally. Stir in remaining steak sauce; keep warm.

Grill burgers over medium heat for 4 minutes on each side or until no longer pink in center. When almost done, top with cheese; grill until cheese melts. Spoon 2 tablespoons onion mixture onto each roll bottom; top each with burger, tomato slice, some of remaining onion mixture and roll top. Serve immediately.

Makes 4 servings

Mexicali Burgers

> Guacamole (recipe follows)
> 1 pound ground chuck
> ⅓ cup purchased salsa or picante sauce
> ⅓ cup crushed tortilla chips
> 3 tablespoons finely chopped fresh cilantro
> 2 tablespoons grated onion
> 1 teaspoon ground cumin
> 4 slices Monterey Jack or Cheddar cheese
> 4 Kaiser rolls or hamburger buns, split
> Lettuce leaves (optional)
> Sliced tomatoes (optional)

1. Prepare grill with rectangular metal or foil drip pan. Bank briquets on either side of drip pan for indirect cooking.

2. Meanwhile, prepare Guacamole.

3. Combine ground chuck, salsa, chips, cilantro, onion and cumin in medium bowl. Mix lightly but thoroughly. Shape mixture into four ½-inch-thick burgers, 4 inches in diameter.

4. Place burgers on grid. Grill burgers, on covered grill, over medium coals 8 to 10 minutes for medium or to desired doneness, turning halfway through grilling time.

5. Place 1 slice cheese on each burger to melt during last 1 to 2 minutes of grilling. If desired, place rolls, cut sides down, on grid to toast lightly during last 1 to 2 minutes of grilling. Place burgers between rolls; top burgers with Guacamole. Serve with lettuce and tomatoes, if desired.

Makes 4 servings

Guacamole

> 1 ripe avocado, seeded
> 1 tablespoon purchased salsa or picante sauce
> 1 teaspoon fresh lime or lemon juice
> ¼ teaspoon garlic salt

1. Scoop avocado flesh out of shells; place in medium bowl. Mash roughly with fork, leaving avocado slightly chunky.

2. Stir in salsa, juice and garlic salt. Let stand at room temperature while grilling burgers. Cover; refrigerate if preparing in advance. Bring to room temperature before serving.

Makes about ½ cup guacamole

HERB AND SPICE

Herbs are the aromatic leaves of herbaceous plants (plants with stems that are soft rather than woody). They are valued in the kitchen for their natural aromatic oils, which are used to accent and enhance the flavor of foods or, on occasion, to provide the essential ingredient in a recipe, such as basil in pesto and dill in dill sauce. Herbs are also used as fragrances, medicines, cosmetics, teas, dyes and ornaments.

Spices come from the seeds, bark, roots, fruit or flowers of plants. They add flavor and color to both sweet and savory dishes. Like herbs, they are a component of fragrances and medicines. For thousands of years spices were an important world commodity, actively traded and in part responsible for expeditions that led to the discovery of the New World. During the Middle Ages the demand for spices in Europe was so great that they were considered as valuable as gold.

✿

Availability: Fresh herbs for cooking have enjoyed a surge in popularity in recent years. Some of the more common fresh herbs, such as basil, chives, dill, mint, oregano, rosemary, sage, tarragon and thyme, are available year-round in large supermarkets. They can be found either cut or potted. Most herbs are easily grown in the home garden. Dried herbs and spices, both leaf and ground form, are readily available all year in any supermarket.

Buying Tips: When purchasing fresh herbs, look for brightly colored, fresh-looking leaves without any brown spots or signs of wilting.

Storage: Fresh herbs are very perishable, so purchase them in small amounts. For short-term storage, place the herb stems in water. Cover leaves loosely with a plastic bag or plastic wrap and store in the refrigerator. They will last from two days (basil, chives, dill, mint, oregano) to five days (rosemary, sage, tarragon, thyme).

Tip

When herbs are dried their oils become more pungent. As a general rule of thumb, when substituting dried herbs for fresh, use 1 teaspoon dried herbs for 1 tablespoon chopped fresh herbs.

Clockwise from top left: chives, rosemary, curly parsley, lemon thyme, basil, tarragon, dill, Italian parsley

HERBS AND SPICES

HERB OR SPICE	COMMON FORM	CULINARY USE
Allspice (spice)	whole, ground	fruit dishes, stews, pumpkin pie, spicy baked goods
Basil (herb)	fresh, dried, ground	Italian dishes, pesto, salads, soups, stews, tomatoes
Bay leaf (herb)	whole dried	sauces, casseroles, meat dishes
Caraway (spice)	whole seeds	cheese, bread, pickling, pork, vegetables
Cardamom (spice)	pod, whole seeds	Scandinavian baking, spiced wine, pudding
Celery seed (spice)	whole seeds	potato salad, pickles
Chervil (herb)	fresh, dried, ground	salads, sauces
Chives (herb)	fresh, dried, frozen	eggs, sour cream, salads, cottage cheese, dips
Cilantro (herb)	fresh	Latin and Thai dishes, salsas
Cinnamon (spice)	whole sticks, ground	baking, meat, sauces, pickles, custards, cocoa
Cloves (spice)	whole, ground	hot beverages, ham, baked goods, vegetables
Coriander (spice)	whole seeds, ground	Scandinavian baking, pickling, curry blends
Cumin (spice)	whole seeds, ground	chili, curry, chili powder
Dill seed (spice)	whole seeds	dill pickles
Dill weed (herb)	fresh, dried	salads, vegetables, meat, fish, sauces
Fennel seed (spice)	whole seeds, ground	pickles, fish, meat, soup
Ginger (spice)	fresh, dried	soups, curry, meat, baked goods
Mace (spice)	ground	fruit pies, puddings, baked goods, vegetables
Marjoram (herb)	fresh, dried, ground	salads, sauces, cooked green vegetables, meat
Mint (herb)	fresh, dried, ground	beverages, lamb, fruit, cooked vegetables, salads
Mustard (spice)	whole seeds, ground	sauces, pickling, dressings, meat, cheese dishes
Nutmeg (spice)	whole, ground	egg dishes, baked goods, custard, eggnog, fruit
Oregano (herb)	fresh, dried, ground	Italian dishes, pizza, cheese, vegetables, salads
Paprika (spice)	ground	used as garnish and in savory dishes, such as goulash
Parsley (herb)	fresh, dried	sauces, eggs, butters, fish, meat
Pepper, black and white (spice)	whole, ground	used in almost all types of savory dishes
Red cayenne pepper (spice)	ground	adds heat to vegetables, meat, eggs, sauces
Rosemary (herb)	fresh, dried, ground	soups, vegetables, meat, fish, eggs, dressings
Saffron (herb)	whole threads, ground	Spanish breads, bouillabaisse, paella
Sage (herb)	fresh, dried, ground	cheese dishes, salad dressings, pork, beans
Savory (herb)	fresh, dried	pâtés, soups, meat, fish, beans
Tarragon (herb)	fresh, dried, ground	French dishes, sauces, chicken, fish
Thyme (herb)	fresh, dried, ground	vegetables, meat, soups, sauces
Turmeric (spice)	ground	curry, mustard, noodles, rice

When purchasing dried herbs or spices, mark each container with the purchase date and discard any remaining after six months. Buy small quantities of infrequently used herbs and spices. Store in a cool, dry place in tightly covered lightproof containers. Do not place above the range as heat and moisture will cause the flavor to deteriorate more quickly.

Spice Blends: There are many herb-and-spice blends available at the supermarket. Most are composed of spices and herbs found in the spice section of grocery stores. Spice blends have the advantage of convenience. Some of the more common blends are: *bouquet garni, fines herbes, herbes de Provence,* Italian seasoning, poultry seasoning, apple pie spice, celery salt, chili powder, curry powder, five-spice powder, garlic salt, pizza spice, pumpkin pie spice and seasoned salt.

Herbal Oils: Simple-to-make herb-flavored oils make perfect gifts for cooks. For an attractive presentation, choose glass jars and bottles that have appealing shapes and colors. Since oil is used sparingly in cooking, select small containers. Choose a high-quality olive oil or any flavorless vegetable oil, such as canola or soybean. To ensure freshness, use recently purchased oil.

To make herbal oil, start with clean, odor-free covered glass jars. (Do not use the jars that will hold the finished oil.) Sterilize them by submerging them in a Dutch oven of boiling water for 15 minutes. Remove with tongs and let stand until cool.

Chop fresh, clean herbs that have been thoroughly dried. Pack them loosely in sterilized jars, about one-third to one-half full. Fill the jars with room temperature oil. Cap the jars and place them in a warm location. Stir or gently shake them daily for three to five days.

Remove herbs by pouring the mixture through a cheesecloth-lined sieve. Taste the oil. If the herb flavor isn't strong enough, add fresh herbs to the oil and store again for three to five days.

Sterilize the jars and bottles you have selected for gift giving. When cool, fill with herbal oil. Label and date the oil.

For preparation information about herbal vinegars, see page 538.

Salmon with Dill-Mustard Sauce

> **2 tablespoons fresh lemon juice**
> **2 tablespoons fresh lime juice**
> **4 salmon fillets (8 ounces each)**
> **¼ cup fat free mayonnaise**
> **1 tablespoon Dijon mustard**
> **1 tablespoon chopped fresh dill**
> **Fresh dill sprigs and lemon wedges (optional)**

1. Combine juices in glass baking dish. Rinse salmon; pat dry. Place salmon in juices; marinate 10 minutes, turning once.

2. For sauce, combine mayonnaise, mustard and chopped dill in small bowl; set aside.

3. Preheat broiler. Spray rack of broiler pan with nonstick cooking spray. Remove salmon from juices; pat dry. Place on rack. Broil, 4 inches from heat, 3 to 4 minutes on each side until salmon flakes easily when tested with fork. Serve salmon with sauce. Garnish with dill sprigs and lemon, if desired.

Makes 4 servings

Techniques for Herbal Oils

Covering the herbs with oil.

Removing the herbs from the oil.

Labeling the jar.

Balsamic Chicken

3. Bake about 10 minutes or until chicken is golden brown and no longer pink in center. If pan is dry, stir in another 1 to 2 tablespoons water to loosen drippings. Drizzle vinegar over chicken in pan. Transfer chicken to plates. Stir liquid in pan; drizzle over chicken. Garnish as desired. Serve immediately.

Makes 6 servings

Beef with Dry Spice Rub

> 3 tablespoons firmly packed brown sugar
> 1 tablespoon black peppercorns
> 1 tablespoon yellow mustard seeds
> 1 tablespoon whole coriander seeds
> 4 cloves garlic
> 1½ to 2 pounds beef top round steak or London broil (about 1½ inches thick)
> Vegetable or olive oil
> Salt
> Grilled Mushrooms (recipe follows)
> Grilled New Potatoes (recipe follows)

Place brown sugar, peppercorns, mustard seeds, coriander seeds and garlic in blender or food processor; process until seeds and garlic are crushed. Rub beef with oil, then pat on spice mixture. Season generously with salt.

Oil hot grid to help prevent sticking. Grill beef, on covered grill, over medium-low KINGSFORD® Briquets, 16 to 20 minutes for medium doneness, turning once. Let stand 5 minutes before slicing. Cut across the grain into thin, diagonal slices. Serve with Grilled Mushrooms and Grilled New Potatoes.

Makes 6 servings

Balsamic Chicken

> 6 boneless, skinless chicken breast halves
> 1½ teaspoons fresh rosemary, minced *or* ½ teaspoon dried rosemary, crushed
> 2 cloves garlic, minced
> ¾ teaspoon ground black pepper
> ½ teaspoon salt
> 1 tablespoon olive oil
> ¼ cup balsamic vinegar

1. Rinse chicken; pat dry. Combine rosemary, garlic, pepper and salt in small bowl; mix well. Place chicken in large bowl; drizzle chicken with oil and rub with spice mixture. Cover; refrigerate overnight.

2. Preheat oven to 450°F. Spray heavy roasting pan or iron skillet with nonstick cooking spray. Place chicken in pan; bake 10 minutes. Turn chicken over, stirring in 3 to 4 tablespoons water if drippings are beginning to stick to pan.

Grilled Mushrooms: Thread fresh mushrooms, 1½ to 2 inches in diameter, on metal or bamboo skewers. Brush lightly with oil; season with salt and pepper. Grill 7 to 12 minutes, turning occasionally.

Grilled New Potatoes: Cook or microwave small new potatoes until barely tender. Thread on metal or bamboo skewers. Brush lightly with oil; season with salt and pepper. Grill 10 to 15 minutes, turning occasionally.

Note: Bamboo skewers should be soaked in water for at least 20 minutes to keep them from burning.

Cinnamon-Date Scones

¼ **cup sugar, divided**
¼ **teaspoon ground cinnamon**
2 **cups all-purpose flour**
2½ **teaspoons baking powder**
½ **teaspoon salt**
5 **tablespoons cold butter or margarine**
½ **cup chopped pitted dates**
2 **eggs**
⅓ **cup half-and-half or milk**

1. Preheat oven to 425°F.

2. Combine 2 tablespoons sugar and cinnamon in small bowl; set aside. Combine flour, baking powder, salt and remaining 2 tablespoons sugar in medium bowl. Cut in butter with pastry blender or 2 knives until mixture resembles coarse crumbs. Stir in dates; set aside.

3. Beat eggs in separate small bowl with fork. Add half-and-half; beat until well blended. Reserve 1 tablespoon egg mixture in small cup; set aside. Stir remaining egg mixture into flour mixture until soft dough forms. Turn out dough onto well floured surface. Knead dough gently 10 to 12 times. Roll out dough with lightly floured rolling pin into 9×6-inch rectangle. Cut dough into 6 (3-inch) squares. Cut each square diagonally in half, making 12 triangles.

4. Place triangles 2 inches apart on ungreased baking sheets. Brush triangles with reserved egg mixture; sprinkle with reserved sugar mixture. Bake 10 to 12 minutes until golden brown. Immediately remove from baking sheets. Cool on wire racks 10 minutes. Serve warm or cool completely.   *Makes 12 scones*

Cinnamon Date Scones

Moravian Spice Crisps

⅓ **cup vegetable shortening**
⅓ **cup packed brown sugar**
¼ **cup unsulfured molasses**
¼ **cup dark corn syrup**
1¾ **to 2 cups all-purpose flour,**
　　divided
2 **teaspoons ground ginger**
1¼ **teaspoons baking soda**
1 **teaspoon ground cinnamon**
½ **teaspoon ground cloves**
　Powdered sugar

1. Melt shortening in small saucepan over low heat. Remove from heat; stir in brown sugar, molasses and corn syrup. Set aside; cool.

2. Combine 1½ cups flour, ginger, baking soda, cinnamon and cloves in large bowl. Beat in shortening mixture with electric mixer at medium speed, scraping down side of bowl once. Gradually beat in additional flour until stiff dough forms, scraping down side of bowl once.

3. Knead dough on lightly floured surface, adding more flour if too sticky. Form dough into 2 discs; wrap in plastic wrap and refrigerate 30 minutes or until firm.

4. Preheat oven to 350°F. Grease baking sheets.

5. Working with 1 disc at a time, unwrap dough and place on lightly floured surface. Roll out dough with lightly floured rolling pin to ¹⁄₁₆-inch thickness. Cut dough with floured 2⅜-inch scalloped cookie cutter. (If dough becomes too soft, refrigerate several minutes before continuing.) Gently press dough trimmings together; reroll and cut out more cookies. Place cookies ½ inch apart on prepared baking sheets.

6. Bake 8 minutes or until firm and lightly browned. Remove cookies to wire racks; cool completely.

7. Place small strips of cardboard or parchment paper over cookies; dust with sifted powdered sugar. Carefully remove cardboard. Store tightly covered at room temperature or freeze up to 3 months.

Makes about 6 dozen cookies

Moravian Spice Crisps

HIGH ALTITUDE

Foods cook and bake differently at altitudes above 3,000 feet because the air pressure is lower than at sea level. This requires some recipe modifications for successful cooking and baking. Keep notes with each recipe indicating what modifications you tried and the results of those changes. For additional information, contact the United States Department of Agriculture, a county extension agent or read labels of food products.

🐝

Here are some examples of the differences that may occur at high altitudes:

• Water boils at a lower temperature (see chart) so foods cooked in boiling water take longer. Solution: Increase cooking times and taste foods to check for doneness.

• Foods take longer to cook. Solution: Increase cooking times when roasting meat and poultry and use a meat thermometer to judge doneness. Increase baking times for casseroles and frozen foods, such as pizza. Increase baking temperatures for cakes, cookies and quick breads by 25°F and decrease baking times slightly.

• Baked goods leavened with baking powder and baking soda rise more at higher altitudes. Solution: Reduce amount of leavener used (see chart).

• Baked goods whose primary or secondary leavener is beaten egg whites (angel food cakes, sponge cakes and some shortened cakes) also rise more. Solution: Beat egg whites less to form soft peaks rather than stiff peaks.

• Cakes leavened with beaten whole eggs, such as some flourless chocolate cakes, also rise more. Solution: Beat eggs for a shorter time.

• Liquids evaporate more quickly. Solution: Increase the liquid in foods especially longer-cooking foods, such as dried beans, casseroles and soups. Increase liquid in baked goods (see chart).

• Sugars become more concentrated at higher altitudes. Solution: Decrease sugar in baked goods (see chart).

• Yeast doughs may rise faster. Solution: Check doughs early. For better flavor development of yeast doughs at high altitudes, always let the doughs rise twice. If the baked bread is dry, increase liquid or decrease flour the next time.

BOILING TEMPERATURES OF WATER AT VARIOUS ALTITUDES

Altitude	Boiling Point
Sea Level	212°F (100°C)
2,000 feet	208°F (98°C)
5,000 feet	203°F (95°C)
7,500 feet	198°F (92°C)
10,000 feet	194°F (90°C)

MODIFICATIONS FOR HIGH-ALTITUDE BAKING

Altitude in Feet	Reduce each Teaspoon of Baking Powder by	Reduce each Cup of Sugar by	Increase each Cup of Liquid by
3,000 to 5,000	⅛ teaspoon	1 tablespoon	3 tablespoons
5,000 to 7,000	⅛ to ¼ teaspoon	2 tablespoons	2 to 3 tablespoons
7,000 to 10,000	¼ teaspoon	2 to 3 tablespoons	3 to 4 tablespoons

HOISIN SAUCE

A brownish-red Chinese sauce made from soybean paste, garlic, vinegar, sugar, spices and flavorings. It is both sweet and mildly spicy with a texture that typically is thick and creamy. It is used in many Asian dishes, including stir-fries and braised meat, but most commonly, it is brushed on barbecued meats. Hoisin sauce lasts indefinitely when stored in a glass jar in the refrigerator.

☙

Hoisin-Roasted Chicken with Vegetables

> 1 whole frying chicken (about 2 pounds), cut into serving pieces
> 3 tablespoons hoisin sauce
> 1 tablespoon dry sherry
> 1 tablespoon Oriental sesame oil
> 6 ounces medium or large fresh button mushrooms
> 2 small red or yellow onions, cut into thin wedges
> 1 package (9 or 10 ounces) frozen baby carrots, thawed

1. Preheat oven to 375°F. Place chicken, skin side up, in lightly oiled foil-lined shallow roasting pan.

2. Combine hoisin sauce, sherry and oil in small bowl. Brush ½ of hoisin mixture evenly over chicken; bake 20 minutes.

3. Scatter mushrooms, onions and carrots around chicken. Brush remaining hoisin sauce mixture over chicken and vegetables; bake 20 minutes more or until fork can be inserted into chicken with ease and juices run clear, not pink. Serve immediately.

Makes 4 to 6 servings

Special Interest

It takes the gatherings of 500 bees from 2 million flowers to produce a pound of honey. The average bee travels 1 mile from the hive and may make as many as 25 round trips a day.

HONEY

This sweet and thick amber liquid is made by honey bees from the nectar of flowers. Honey is one of the oldest sweeteners. Its earliest known representation appears on a cave painting in Spain dating to the Stone Age. Today, it is most popularly used as a sweetener for tea, a spread for toast and biscuits or as an ingredient in breads, pastries and confections, such as Greek baklava. The color and flavor of the honey is determined by the type of flower from which the nectar originated. The color of honey ranges from a delicate pale gold to a deep amber. The taste usually reflects the color—the lighter the color, the milder the flavor. In this country, some of the most popular honeys are orange blossom, clover, acacia, tupelo, thyme, buckwheat and heather honey, each bearing its own distinct character. Much of the honey sold in supermarkets is mild enough for all-purpose use. Some honey flavors, such as heather, pine flower and buckwheat honey, have pronounced flavors and should be used only in dishes that are compatible with their strong flavors.

☙

Availability: Honey is sold in one of three forms. Comb honey, taken directly from the hive, has the liquid honey still stored in the waxy comb, which is edible. Chunk honey includes small bits of the comb. By far the most common is extracted liquid honey, which has been removed from the comb by centrifugal force, heated, strained, filtered and often pasteurized to prevent crystallization. It is sold in jars or squeeze bottles.

Creamed honey is honey that has been agitated to become a creamy, opaque spread. Honey butter is a mixture of honey and butter. Both products are usually used as spreads for toast or biscuits.

Storage: Do not refrigerate honey as it will become grainy and too thick to use. It can be stored up to a year in a cool, dry and dark place in a tightly sealed jar. (Comb or chunk honey can be stored for six months.) When spooning honey from the jar, be sure not to contaminate it with other ingredients, which may cause the honey to become moldy.

Baking with Honey: In baked goods, honey adds sweetness while imparting its distinct taste. Its use results in a moist, dense product. In most cases, substituting honey for sugar in baked goods is not recommended although using honey in place of other liquid sweeteners, such as maple syrup, corn syrup and molasses, usually is successful.

German Honey Bars

2¾ cups all-purpose flour
2 teaspoons ground cinnamon
1 teaspoon baking powder
½ teaspoon baking soda
½ teaspoon salt
½ teaspoon ground cardamom
½ teaspoon ground ginger
½ cup honey
½ cup dark molasses
¾ cup packed brown sugar
3 tablespoons butter, melted
1 egg
½ cup chopped toasted almonds (optional)
Lemon Glaze (recipe follows)

1. Preheat oven to 350°F. Grease 15×10-inch jelly-roll pan.

2. Combine flour, cinnamon, baking powder, baking soda, salt, cardamom and ginger in medium bowl; set aside.

3. Combine honey and molasses in medium saucepan; bring to a boil over medium heat. Remove from heat; cool 10 minutes. Stir in brown sugar, butter and egg.

4. Place brown sugar mixture in large bowl. Gradually add reserved flour mixture. Beat at low speed with electric mixer until dough forms, scraping down side of bowl once. Stir in almonds, if desired. (Dough will be slightly sticky.) Spread dough evenly into prepared pan.

5. Bake 20 to 22 minutes until golden brown and set. Remove pan to wire rack; cool completely.

6. Prepare Lemon Glaze. Spread over cooled bar cookies. Let stand about 30 minutes or until set. Cut into 2×1-inch bars. Store tightly covered at room temperature or freeze up to 3 months.

Makes about 6 dozen bars

Lemon Glaze: Combine 1¼ cups powdered sugar, 3 tablespoons fresh lemon juice and 1 teaspoon grated lemon peel in medium bowl until smooth.

Tip

If honey crystallizes, place the container in a pan of hot water and gently stir the honey until it liquifies. It can also be liquified by removing the lid and microwaving at HIGH for 20 to 60 seconds.

German Honey Bars

Honey Glazed Carrots

3 cups sliced carrots
¼ cup honey
2 tablespoons butter or margarine
2 tablespoons chopped fresh parsley *or* 2 teaspoons dried parsley flakes
1½ to 2 teaspoons prepared mustard (optional)

Heat 2 inches salted water in medium saucepan to a boil over high heat. Add carrots; return to a boil. Reduce heat to medium-high. Cover and cook 8 to 12 minutes or until carrots are crisp-tender. Drain carrots; return to saucepan. Stir in honey, butter, parsley and mustard, if desired. Cook and stir over low heat until carrots are glazed.

Makes 6 side-dish servings

Favorite recipe from **National Honey Board**

HORSERADISH

Horseradish is a large, white root with a pungent flavor. It is usually grated and used raw as a condiment with beef and fish. It can also be used as an ingredient in sauces (cocktail and horseradish sauces) and in creamy dressings for beets and coleslaw. Horseradish is seldom cooked because its flavor easily vaporizes when exposed to heat. It can be found fresh occasionally in produce markets, but it is most commonly found grated, preserved in vinegar and packed in jars in the refrigerated section of the supermarket. It is referred to as prepared horseradish in recipes. Once opened it loses its pungency quickly so plan to use it within a few weeks.

Creamy Horseradish Sauce

1 (8-ounce) package cream cheese, softened
⅓ cup A.1.® Steak Sauce
3 tablespoons prepared horseradish, drained
2 tablespoons chopped green onion

In medium bowl, blend cream cheese, steak sauce and horseradish; stir in onion. Cover; chill at least 1 hour or up to 2 days. Serve cold or at room temperature with cooked beef, sausage, fish or baked potatoes.

Makes 1½ cups sauce

Barbecued Pork Sandwiches

2 pork tenderloins (about 1½ pounds total)
⅓ cup prepared barbecue sauce
½ cup prepared horseradish
4 pita bread rounds, cut into halves
1 onion, thinly sliced
4 romaine lettuce leaves
1 red bell pepper, cut lengthwise into ¼-inch-thick slices
1 green bell pepper, cut lengthwise into ¼-inch-thick slices

1. Preheat oven to 400°F. Place pork tenderloins in roasting pan; brush with barbecue sauce.

2. Bake tenderloins 15 minutes; turn and bake 15 minutes more or until instant-read thermometer inserted into thickest part of pork registers 155°F. Cover with foil; let stand 15 minutes.

3. Slice pork across grain. Spread horseradish in pita bread halves; stuff evenly with pork, onion, lettuce and bell peppers. Garnish as desired. Serve immediately.

Makes 4 servings

HUMMUS

Hummus is a Middle Eastern dish prepared with mashed chick-peas combined with lemon juice, garlic and oil. When tahini, a paste made from sesame seeds, is added, the mixture is known technically as hummus bi tahini. Hummus is most often served as a dip with wedges of pita bread. It can be purchased canned or fresh in Middle Eastern markets and many large supermarkets. Hummus can also easily be made at home.

🌼

Vegetable-Topped Hummus

> 1 can (about 15 ounces) chick-peas, rinsed, drained
> 2 tablespoons tahini
> 2 tablespoons fresh lemon juice
> 1 clove garlic
> ¾ teaspoon salt
> 1 tomato, finely chopped
> 2 green onions, finely chopped
> 2 tablespoons chopped fresh parsley
> Pita bread wedges or assorted crackers

1. Place chick-peas, tahini, juice, garlic and salt in food processor or blender; process until smooth. Set aside.

2. Combine tomato, onions and parsley in small bowl. Place reserved bean mixture in medium serving bowl; spoon tomato mixture evenly over top. Serve with pita bread.
Makes 8 appetizer servings

Vegetable-Topped Hummus

I to M

Where was ice cream created? *Learn how to make julienne strips of carrots.* How did the kiwifruit get its name? *Make a pitcher of refreshing lemonade.* What is a madeleine? *Indulge yourself with a decadent chocolate mousse.*

Left to right: Double Almond Ice Cream (recipe on page 270) and Crunchy Nutty Ice Cream Sundae (recipe on page 270)

Italian Ice

ICE

The dessert ice (known as granita in Italy and granité in France) is a frozen mixture of sugar and liquid, such as fruit juice, wine or coffee. It has a slightly granular texture that is created by stirring the mixture during the freezing process (the manufacturing term for this process is churn-freezing). Sweet ices are usually served as dessert, but savory or slightly acidic ices, like lemon or grapefruit, may be served between courses as a palate refresher.

☙

Italian Ice

1 cup fruity white wine
1 cup water
1 cup sugar
1 cup fresh lemon juice
2 egg whites*
Fresh berries (optional)
Fresh mint leaves (optional)

*Use only clean uncracked grade A eggs.

1. Place wine and water in small saucepan; stir in sugar. Cook over medium-high heat until sugar has dissolved and syrup boils, stirring frequently. Cover; boil 1 minute. Uncover; adjust heat to maintain simmer. Simmer 10 minutes without stirring. Remove from heat. Refrigerate 1 hour or until syrup is completely cool.

2. Stir juice into cooled syrup. Pour into round cake pan. Freeze 1 hour.

3. Stir mixture with fork to break up ice crystals. Freeze 1 hour or until firm but not solid. Place medium bowl in freezer to chill.

4. Beat egg whites in small bowl with electric mixer at high speed until stiff peaks form. Remove lemon ice mixture from cake pan to chilled bowl. Immediately beat ice with whisk or fork until smooth. Fold in egg whites; mix well. Spread egg mixture evenly into same cake pan.

5. Freeze 30 minutes. Immediately stir with fork; cover cake pan with foil. Freeze at least 3 hours or until firm. Serve with berries and garnish with mint leaves, if desired.

Makes 4 servings

ICE CREAM

Ice cream, which can be traced back to sixteenth century France, enjoys greater popularity in America than in other countries of the world. At its simplest, ice cream includes cream, milk, sweeteners and flavorings. Sometimes pasteurized eggs and small pieces of food, such as nuts, fruit or chocolate bits, are added. The majority of ice cream eaten in America is commercially produced, although homemade ice cream is easy to make with just a few ingredients and an ice cream maker.

Commercial Ice Cream: Commercial ice creams usually include emulsifiers and stabilizers to prevent the formation of large ice crystals, ensure smooth texture, extend shelf life and control melting. Flavorings (both natural and artificial) are also added. Air is pumped into the ice cream during the freezing process to soften it. The industry term for the amount of air incorporated in a ice cream is "overrun," which is given as a percentage. The less overrun the harder the ice cream and the more a given amount will weigh.

Ice cream is categorized as premium, regular, low-fat and nonfat. Premium products are more expensive than regular ice cream. They have higher levels of butterfat (sometimes as much as 20 percent) and generally less overrun. Regular ice cream has less butterfat and more overrun than premium ice cream. Low-fat ice cream must contain 3 grams of fat or less per serving. Nonfat ice cream has less than one-half gram of fat per serving.

Store commercial ice cream in airtight containers at 0°F for up to two months. Ice cream in opened containers will develop large ice crystals. Covering the surface of the ice cream will delay this process and help prevent the ice cream from absorbing odors from the freezer.

Homemade Ice Cream: Homemade ice cream when properly made is smooth and creamy with fine ice crystals. For best results, carefully read the manufacturer's directions for the ice cream maker. Homemade ice cream develops large ice crystals after two or three days, resulting in a coarse texture, so try to eat it within a day or two of making it. The following tips will help produce smooth, creamy homemade ice cream:

• Thoroughly chill the ice cream mixture before freezing it to ensure a smooth texture. Chilling also cuts freezing time.

• Fill the canister no more than two-thirds full to allow the mixture to expand.

• Layer the crushed ice and rock salt around the canister, replenishing as needed. Use 6 cups ice to 1 cup salt.

• The ice cream mixture must be constantly stirred during the freezing process.

• After freezing, the ice cream needs to stand for at least four hours to develop flavor. This can be done in the ice cream maker by packing it with additional ice and salt (4 cups ice to 1 cup salt—the higher proportion of salt lowers the temperature of the ice cream). The alternative method is to transfer the ice cream to a covered freezer container and place it in a 0°F freezer.

Tip

Do not use egg yolks in ice cream unless they are heated to 160°F. The heating destroys harmful bacteria.

Double Almond Ice Cream (recipe on page 270)

Double Almond Ice Cream

> 3 cups whipping cream
> 1 cup milk
> ¾ cup *plus* 2 tablespoons sugar,
>   divided
> 4 egg yolks, beaten
> 1 tablespoon vanilla extract
> 2 teaspoons almond extract
> 2 tablespoons butter
> 1½ cups BLUE DIAMOND®
>   Chopped Natural Almonds

Combine cream, milk and ¾ cup sugar in medium saucepan. Cook and stir over medium heat until sugar is dissolved and mixture is hot. Gradually add 1 cup cream mixture to beaten egg yolks, whisking constantly. When mixture is smooth, strain into double boiler. Gradually pour in remaining cream mixture, whisking constantly. Cook over simmering water until mixture thickens slightly and coats back of spoon, about 8 minutes, stirring constantly. *Do not boil.* Stir in extracts. Cool.

Meanwhile, melt butter and stir in remaining 2 tablespoons sugar in small saucepan. Cook and stir over medium heat until sugar begins to bubble, about 30 seconds. Add almonds; cook and stir over medium heat until golden and well coated. Cool. Stir almonds into ice cream mixture. Pour into ice cream maker container. Freeze according to manufacturer's instructions.

Makes 1 quart ice cream

Crunchy Nutty Ice Cream Sundaes

> Peanut Butter Sauce (recipe
>   follows)
> Coconut Crunch (recipe
>   follows)
> 1 pint vanilla ice cream

Prepare Peanut Butter Sauce and Coconut Crunch. Scoop ice cream into sundae dishes. Spoon prepared sauce over ice cream; sprinkle prepared crunch over top. Serve immediately.

Makes 4 to 6 servings

Peanut Butter Sauce

> 1 cup REESE'S® Peanut Butter
>   Chips
> ⅓ cup milk
> ¼ cup whipping cream
> ¼ teaspoon vanilla extract

In medium saucepan over low heat, heat peanut butter chips, milk and whipping cream until chips are melted, stirring constantly. Remove from heat; stir in vanilla. Cool to room temperature.

Coconut Crunch

> ½ cup MOUNDS® Sweetened
>   Coconut Flakes
> ½ cup chopped nuts
> 1 tablespoon butter or margarine

Heat oven to 325°F. In shallow baking pan, combine all ingredients. Toast in oven 6 to 8 minutes or until mixture is very lightly browned, stirring occasionally. (Watch carefully.) Cool to room temperature.

JAM

Jam is a sweet, thick spread made from crushed fruit cooked with sugar. It is similar to fruit preserves in how it is made, but unlike preserves, it seldom contains identifiable fruit pieces. Jam is used as a spread for toast and bread, a filling for cookies, tortes and pastries or as an ingredient.

🌾

JAMBALAYA

Jambalaya is a Creole dish that combines rice with ham, sausage, shrimp or chicken in a tomato-based sauce containing onion, green pepper and seasonings. The name is thought to have come from the French word for ham, "jambon." Because jambalaya makes good use of leftovers, the ingredients vary widely from cook to cook.

☙

Louisiana Jambalaya

1½ **pounds chicken tenders**
½ **teaspoon salt**
½ **teaspoon ground black pepper**
1 **tablespoon vegetable oil**
¾ **pound smoked turkey sausage,**
   cut into ¼-inch slices
2 **medium onions, chopped**
1 **large green bell pepper,**
   chopped
1 **cup chopped celery**
1 **clove garlic, minced**
2 **cups uncooked rice***
¼ **to ½ teaspoon ground red**
   pepper
2½ **cups chicken broth**
1 **cup sliced green onions**
1 **medium tomato, chopped**
   Celery leaves (optional)

*Recipe based on regular-milled long-grain white rice.

Season chicken with salt and black pepper. Heat oil in large saucepan or Dutch oven over high heat until hot. Add chicken, stirring until brown on all sides. Add sausage; cook 2 to 3 minutes. Remove chicken and sausage from saucepan; set aside. Add chopped onions, green pepper, celery and garlic to same pan; cook and stir over medium-high heat until crisp-tender. Stir in rice, red pepper, broth and reserved chicken and sausage; bring to a boil. Reduce heat to low; cover and simmer 30 minutes.

Stir in green onions and tomato. Garnish with celery leaves, if desired. Serve immediately.

Makes 8 servings

Microwave Directions: Season chicken with salt and black pepper. Place oil in deep 3-quart microproof baking dish. Add chicken; cover with wax paper and cook on HIGH 3 minutes, stirring after 2 minutes. Add sausage; cover with wax paper and cook on HIGH 1 minute. Remove chicken and sausage with slotted spoon; set aside. Add chopped onions, green pepper, celery and garlic to same dish. Cover and cook on HIGH 4 minutes, stirring after 2 minutes. Stir in rice, red pepper, broth and reserved chicken and sausage; cover and cook on HIGH 8 minutes or until boiling. Reduce setting to MEDIUM (50% power); cover and cook 30 minutes, stirring after 15 minutes. Stir in green onions and tomato. Let stand 5 minutes before serving. Garnish with celery leaves, if desired. Serve immediately.

*Favorite recipe from **USA Rice Council***

Louisiana Jambalaya

JELLY

A clear, sweet mixture of fruit juice cooked with sugar, jelly is used primarily as a spread for bread and toast or as a filling for cakes and doughnuts. It can be melted over low heat and used as a glaze for fruit, especially on tarts. Natural thickeners in the fruit, called pectin, thicken the mixture. When made at home commercial pectin is often used in the jelly-making process.

❦

JELLY ROLL

A jelly roll is made from a thin, oblong cake, usually a sponge cake that is spread with a thin layer of jelly or jam and then rolled. The log-shaped cake can be finished with a thin glaze, whipped cream or dusted with powdered sugar. Other fillings, such as whipped cream and frosting, can be used in place of the jelly. The dessert is then referred to as a cake roll. The pan used to make the cake portion is called a jelly-roll pan (see page 29).

❦

Chocolate Cream-Filled Cake Roll

Chocolate Cream-Filled Cake Roll

¾ **cup sifted cake flour**
¼ **cup unsweetened cocoa powder**
½ **teaspoon baking powder**
¼ **teaspoon salt**
4 **eggs**
¾ **cup granulated sugar**
1 **tablespoon water**
1 **teaspoon vanilla extract**
Powdered sugar
Cream Filling (recipe follows)
Chocolate Stars (recipe follows, optional)
Sweetened whipped cream (optional)
Fresh raspberries and mint leaves (optional)

1. Preheat oven to 375°F. Grease bottom of 15½×10½×1-inch jelly-roll pan. Line with waxed paper. Grease paper and sides of pan; dust with flour.

2. Combine ¾ cup flour, cocoa, baking powder and salt in small bowl; set aside.

3. Beat eggs in medium bowl with electric mixer at high speed about 5 minutes or until thick and lemon colored. Add granulated sugar, a little at a time, beating well at medium speed; beat until thick and fluffy. Stir in water and vanilla. Beat in flour mixture at low speed until smooth. Spread evenly in prepared pan.

4. Bake 12 to 15 minutes until wooden toothpick inserted into center comes out clean.

5. Sprinkle clean kitchen towel with powdered sugar. Loosen cake edges and turn out onto prepared towel. Carefully peel off waxed paper. Roll up cake with towel inside, starting with narrow end. Cool, seam side down, 20 minutes on wire rack.

6. Meanwhile, prepare Cream Filling and Chocolate Stars, if desired. Unroll cake and spread with Cream Filling. Roll up again, without towel. Cover and refrigerate at least 1 hour.

7. Just before serving, dust with additional powdered sugar. If desired, place star tip in pastry bag; add sweetened whipped cream. Pipe rosettes onto cake. Place Chocolate Stars into rosettes. Garnish with raspberries and mint, if desired. Store tightly covered in refrigerator.

Makes 8 to 10 servings

Cream Filling

> 1 teaspoon unflavored gelatin
> ¼ cup cold water
> 1 cup whipping cream
> 2 tablespoons powdered sugar
> 1 tablespoon orange-flavored
>   liqueur

1. Sprinkle gelatin over cold water in small saucepan; let stand 1 minute to soften. Heat over low heat until dissolved, stirring constantly. Cool to room temperature.

2. Beat cream, powdered sugar and liqueur in small chilled bowl with electric mixer at high speed until stiff peaks form. Fold in gelatin mixture. Cover; refrigerate 5 to 10 minutes.

Chocolate Stars: Melt 2 squares (1 ounce each) semisweet chocolate in heavy small saucepan over low heat, stirring frequently. Immediately remove from heat; pour onto baking sheet lined with waxed paper. Spread

to ⅛-inch thickness with small metal spatula. Refrigerate about 15 minutes or until firm. Cut out stars with small cookie cutter. Carefully lift stars from waxed paper using metal spatula or knife. Refrigerate until ready to use.

JICAMA

Jicama is a large, round root vegetable with a rough brown skin. Many think it resembles a large turnip. The flesh is white with a sweet, crunchy texture. It is most often eaten raw but can be cooked. Both flavor and texture resemble that of water chestnuts. Jicama is important in Mexican and Central American cuisines.

🌿

Uses: Raw jicama can be served with dips or added to salads

• In Mexico, slices of jicama are served as an appetizer with ground chilies and lime juice.

• Cooked jicama retains its crispness but is more mellow in flavor. Use it in stir-fries and add it to soups during the last few minutes of cooking.

Availability: Jicama is available all year, but its peak season is from November through May.

Buying Tips: Choose a firm jicama without blemishes. It should be heavy for its size with a smooth root. Small jicamas are less fibrous.

Yield: 1 pound jicama = about 3 cups sliced or chopped.

Storage: Store jicama in a cool, dry place or in the refrigerator for two or three weeks.

Basic Preparation: Trim off the root. Scrub the jicama with a vegetable brush under cold running water. Peel off the skin with a paring knife. If the flesh underneath the skin is very fibrous, peel off an additional layer.

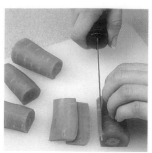

Cutting carrot into thin slices.

Cutting carrot slices into julienne strips.

Jicama Slaw

Jicama Slaw

  2 to 3 large oranges
  ½ cup minced red onion
  ½ cup lightly packed fresh
     cilantro, coarsely chopped
  ⅓ cup reduced calorie mayonnaise
  2 tablespoons frozen orange juice
     concentrate, thawed
  1 tablespoon sugar
  1 jalapeño or serrano pepper,
     seeded, minced*
  4 cups shredded jicama**
  3 cups shredded green cabbage
     Orange peel strips (optional)

*Jalapeño peppers can sting and irritate the skin; wear rubber or plastic gloves when handling peppers and do not touch eyes. Wash hands after handling.

**Peel jicama with sharp knife, removing brown outer skin and thin coarse layer of flesh underneath. Shred jicama in food processor.

1. Grate peel from 1 orange with grater or zester; measure 1 tablespoon. Place in large bowl; set aside. Cut away remaining white pith from oranges. Separate oranges into segments; set aside.

2. Add onion, cilantro, mayonnaise, juice concentrate, sugar and jalapeño to grated orange peel; stir until blended. Add jicama and cabbage; stir to combine. Reserve several orange segments for garnish; cut remaining segments in half and stir into slaw. Transfer slaw to serving bowl. Garnish with orange strips. Serve immediately.

Makes 6 side-dish servings

JUICE, TO

Juicing refers to the extraction of juice from fruits, most often citrus fruits. Reamers and juicers are inexpensive tools designed for this purpose (page 525). Electric juicers are best for juicing vegetables and large quantities of fruit. Often, it is desirable to strain the juice to remove the pulp; this is done with a filtering device on the juicer or a sieve.

🌾

JULIENNE, TO

To julienne is to cut food, most often vegetables, into thin, four-sided strips, sometimes called matchsticks. It is done by first slicing the vegetable into thin slices (about ⅛ to ¼ inch thick). The slices are then stacked and cut again into strips of the same thickness. A julienne salad consists of julienne strips of cheese, meat or vegetables arranged over a bed of lettuce.

🌾

KABOB

A kabob (also spelled "kebab") refers to small pieces of meat, poultry, fish and sometimes vegetables that are threaded onto a skewer before grilling or broiling. The kabob components are often marinated before cooking. Examples of skewered dishes include the French brochette, the Italian spiedini, the Russian shashlik, the Middle Eastern shish kebab and the Indonesian saté. Fresh fruit kabobs are used as appetizers; they may or may not be heated.

🐝

Oriental Shrimp & Steak Kabobs

   1 envelope LIPTON® RECIPE
        SECRETS® Savory Herb with
        Garlic or Onion Soup Mix
   ¼ cup soy sauce
   ¼ cup lemon juice
   ¼ cup olive or vegetable oil
   ¼ cup honey
   ½ pound uncooked medium
        shrimp, peeled and deveined
   ½ pound boneless sirloin steak,
        cut into 1-inch cubes
  16 cherry tomatoes
   2 cups mushroom caps
   1 medium green bell pepper, cut
        into chunks

In 13×9-inch glass baking dish, blend savory herb with garlic soup mix, soy sauce, lemon juice, oil and honey; set aside. On skewers, alternately thread shrimp, steak, tomatoes, mushrooms and green pepper. Add prepared skewers to baking dish; turn to coat. Cover and marinate in refrigerator, turning skewers occasionally, at least 2 hours.

Oriental Shrimp & Steak Kabobs

Remove prepared skewers, reserving marinade. Grill or broil, turning and basting frequently with reserved marinade, until shrimp turn pink and steak is done. Do not brush with marinade during last 5 minutes of cooking.   *Makes about 8 servings*

Menu Suggestion: Serve with corn-on-the-cob, a mixed green salad and grilled garlic bread.

KALE

Kale was perhaps the first form of cabbage to be cultivated as long as two thousand years ago. It may even date back to prehistoric times as evidenced by fossil impressions from the dinosaur era. A cousin to cabbage and collards, kale is quickly identified by its very curly leaves arranged like a bouquet. The color of the leaves ranges from deep blue-green to delicate green to a rich reddish-purple. Because this nutritious vegetable grows best in cool climates and can be harvested after frost, kale is popular in northern European countries, such as Scotland, Germany, Norway and Sweden. Flowering kale, which is popular as an ornamental accent in home gardens, is edible and may be seen in colors from white to pink to lavender.

🐝

Uses: Kale may be eaten raw when very young and tender. It is seldom available at this stage except at some farmers' markets.

• Cooking enhances the flavor of mature kale. It is served blanched or steamed as a side dish.

• Kale can be added to soups, stews, stir-fries and other one-dish entrées. It pairs especially well with other highly flavored ingredients like onion, garlic, ham and bacon.

Availability: Kale is available year-round but its flavor is best during the winter months.

Buying Tips: Choose kale in small bunches with firm leaves in a rich, deep color. Avoid bunches with limp, wilted or discolored leaves.

Yield: 1 pound kale = about 3 cups cooked.

Storage: Store kale in a plastic bag in the refrigerator. Use it within two or three days; its flavor becomes stronger if stored longer.

Basic Preparation: Kale can be sandy. Soak the leaves in a sinkful of cool water for a few minutes. Then swish them to remove any sand and dirt. Repeat this process several times, if necessary, with fresh water. Drain kale to remove excess water.

Kale has tough stems that should be removed before cooking. To trim away tough stems, make a "V-shaped" cut at the stem end, discarding stems. Stack the leaves and cut them into pieces. Kale can be blanched, braised, sautéed, simmered, steamed or stir-fried.

KETCHUP

In the past, ketchup has referred to a group of thick sauces made from ingredients, such as walnuts, mushrooms and mangoes. In America, ketchup (or catsup) almost universally refers to a thick, deep-red condiment, made from tomatoes, sweeteners, vinegar and spices.

🐝

KIM CHEE

Kim chee, also kimchi, is a hot-and-spicy vegetable mixture served at almost every Korean meal. The name means pickled vegetables. This condiment is made of pickled vegetables, usually cabbage, which are traditionally packed into tightly sealed jars and then buried in the ground to ferment. Today it is available in the produce section of large supermarkets and in Asian markets. It will keep for a long time when stored refrigerated.

🐝

KIWIFRUIT

First known as the Chinese gooseberry, kiwifruit (also kiwi) received its current name from New Zealand exporters who wanted to avoid confusion with the American gooseberry and also have it identified with their country. It is named after the New Zealand kiwi bird. This vine-grown fruit is shaped like a large oval egg with a fuzzy brown exterior. Its flesh is a sparkling emerald green with tiny edible black seeds. The flavor is delicately sweet-tart and thought to have a taste reminiscent of strawberry or pineapple. Kiwifruit is grown in California and imported from New Zealand.

🐝

Uses: Kiwifruit can be peeled and sliced or cubed for eating out of hand. Or, simply cut it in half and scoop the flesh from the skin with a spoon.

• Add kiwifruit to fruit salads for a bright touch of color. Do not add it to gelatin salads, because it contains an enzyme that prevents gelatin from thickening.

• One of most popular uses for kiwi in New Zealand is Pavlova, a baked meringue shell filled with sweetened whipped cream and topped with thin slices of kiwifruit.

Availability: Kiwifruit is available all year. California kiwifruit is in markets from October through May, and New Zealand kiwis from June to October.

Buying Tips: Ripe kiwifruit yields to gentle pressure. Most need additional ripening after purchase. Choose fruit without mold or soft spots.

Yield: 1 large kiwifruit = $\frac{1}{3}$ to $\frac{1}{2}$ cup slices.

Storage: To ripen, store kiwifruit at room temperature out of direct sunlight or place in a paper bag. Turn them occasionally until they yield to gentle pressure. Ripe kiwis can then be stored unpeeled in the refrigerator for one week.

Basic Preparation. To peel, remove the skin with a paring knife. An alternative method is to cut off the two ends and peel the remaining skin with a vegetable peeler. For an attractive slice, cut kiwifruit crosswise to show the decorative pattern of seeds. Cooking kiwifruit is not recommended as it turns an unattractive olive-green color.

KNEAD, TO

Kneading refers to the technique of manipulating bread dough in order to develop the protein in flour, called gluten, to ensure the structure of the finished product. Kneading also aids in combining the dough ingredients. Biscuit dough is lightly kneaded only about ten times whereas yeast doughs may be vigorously kneaded for several minutes. For additional information about kneading, see page 63.

🐝

Tips

Slices or wedges of kiwifruit make colorful garnishes that will not discolor.

Contrary to popular belief, the skin of kiwifruit is edible. Gently rub the excess fuzz off with a clean kitchen towel.

KOLACKY

Kolacky, also spelled kolachke, are small filled yeast rolls or rich cookies that originated in Eastern Europe. Typical fillings are poppy seed, prune, cheese and apricot. Yeast dough is cut into small circles or squares and a small depression is made in the middle of the dough to hold the filling. When cookie dough is used, the edges of the dough are folded over to partially cover the filling.

❧

Kolacky

Kolacky

½ cup butter or margarine, softened
3 ounces cream cheese, softened
1 teaspoon vanilla extract
1 cup all-purpose flour
⅛ teaspoon salt
¼ cup fruit preserves, assorted flavors
1 egg
1 teaspoon cold water
Powdered sugar (optional)

1. Combine butter and cream cheese in large bowl; beat with electric mixer until smooth and creamy. Blend in vanilla.

2. Combine flour and salt in small bowl; gradually add to butter mixture, mixing until mixture forms soft dough. Divide dough in half; wrap each half in plastic wrap. Refrigerate until firm.

3. Preheat oven to 375°F.

4. Roll out ½ of dough on lightly floured pastry cloth or board to ⅛-inch thickness. Cut with top of glass or biscuit cutter into 3-inch rounds. Spoon ½ teaspoon preserves onto center of each dough circle. Beat egg with water in separate small bowl; lightly brush onto edges of dough circles. Bring three edges of dough up over fruit spread; pinch edges together to seal. Place on ungreased baking sheets; brush with egg mixture. Repeat with remaining dough, fruit spread and egg mixture.

5. Bake 12 minutes or until golden brown. Let stand on baking sheets 1 minute; transfer to wire racks. Cool completely. Sprinkle with powdered sugar, if desired. Store tightly covered at room temperature.

Makes about 2 dozen cookies

KOSHER

Kosher is the word used to describe food that is prepared following strict Jewish biblical dietary laws. The word kosher means "proper" or "pure." To be kosher, food must come from an acceptable food group, be prepared correctly and not be combined with certain other foods. Only animals such as cattle, sheep, goats and deer can be eaten. Dietary laws require that these animals be raised in a certain way. Pork, game birds and rabbits are forbidden. Fish with fins and scales can be eaten, but not shellfish, such as shrimp. Meat and dairy foods can not be cooked or eaten together. All dishes and utensils used to prepare meat and dairy dishes must also be kept separate. To meet kosher standards and receive the kosher seal, commercial foods must be prepared under a rabbi's supervision. Kosher products are often marked by a K alone or a U or K in a circle. Kosher foods are available in most supermarkets.

KUCHEN

Kuchen, the German term for cake, generally refers to a coffee cake made from a sweet yeast dough that is served at breakfast and sometimes as a dessert. It is often filled with fruit or cheese and topped with a combination of sugar, spices and nuts before baking.

LARD

A firm, snowy white fat obtained from rendered pork fat. Although it is high in saturated fat and cholesterol, and therefore has fallen out of favor in the United States, lard is integral to many ethnic cuisines, including Mexican and Chinese. It is excellent for pastry crusts, biscuits and deep-frying.

LEEK

Leeks have traditionally been more popular in Europe than in the United States. Looking rather like a monster version of the scallion, the leek has a milder flavor than its relatives, the onion and garlic. The leek has a thick, cylindrical white base usually an inch or more in diameter that may widen at the root end. The top portion of the stalk is composed of broad, flat dark green leaves that are tightly wrapped.

Uses: Tender young leeks may be very thinly sliced and added to a salad.

• Leeks may be sliced or split lengthwise, steamed, braised or sautéed.

• Chopped leeks may be added to soups and egg or cheese dishes, such as omelets and quiches.

• Leeks are a classic ingredient in the chilled potato soup *vichyssoise* and the Scottish soup *cock-a-leekie.*

Availability: Leeks can be found year-round, but they are most plentiful from fall to early spring.

Buying Tips: Although sometimes sold individually, leeks are usually displayed in bunches of three or four. The smaller the leek, the more tender it will be. Leeks over 1½ inches in diameter can be tough and woody. Choose ones with firm bright green stalks and white blemish-free bases. Avoid leeks with split or oversize bases. Leeks from a farmers' market or produce stand may contain more hard-to-clean garden soil between the leaves than their supermarket counterparts.

Yield: 1 pound leeks = 2 cups chopped.

Storage: Leeks may be stored, loosely wrapped in plastic, in the refrigerator for up to a week.

Basic Preparation: To prepare leeks, trim off the roots. Remove any withered outer leaves. Use a chef's knife to cut off the leaf tops down to where the dark green begins to pale. The green tops are too tough to eat but may be used to flavor stocks.

Leeks are notorious for collecting soil and grit between the leaf layers. Make a deep cut into each leek lengthwise to within an inch of the root end. (If the leek is cut into halves it will fall  apart.) Rinse leeks thoroughly under cold running water to remove embedded soil.

To remove stubborn dirt, soak them in a bowl of water for 15 minutes, changing the water until it is clear and the leeks are free of dirt.

The leeks can be cut into halves or quarters, then sliced or chopped, if desired. Leeks may be braised, steamed or sautéed. Avoid overcooking them. Overcooked leeks will be soft and slimy. Cook them until they are crisp-tender.

Potatoes and Leeks au Gratin

>   5 tablespoons butter or margarine, divided
>   2 large leeks
>   2 tablespoons minced garlic
>   2 pounds baking potatoes (about 4 medium), peeled, cut into $1/16$-inch-thick slices
>   1 cup whipping cream
>   1 cup milk
>   3 eggs
>   2 teaspoons salt
> $1/4$ teaspoon ground white pepper
>   2 to 3 slices dense, day-old white bread, such as French or Italian
>   2 ounces Parmesan cheese, grated

1. Preheat oven to 375°F. Generously butter shallow oval 10-cup baking dish with 1 tablespoon butter.

Potatoes and Leeks au Gratin

2. To prepare leeks, remove any withered outer leaves. Cut off leaf tops down to where dark green begins to pale. Cut off roots. Discard tops and roots. Make deep cut into leek to within an inch of root end. Rinse under cold running water several times, washing thoroughly to remove all grit and embedded soil. Cut leeks completely in half. Cut leeks crosswise into ¼-inch slices.

3. Melt 2 tablespoons butter in large skillet over medium heat. Add leeks and garlic. Cook and stir 8 to 10 minutes until leeks are softened. Remove from heat; set aside.

4. Layer ½ of potato slices in prepared baking dish. Top with ½ of leek mixture. Repeat layers once with remaining potato slices and leek mixture.

5. Whisk together cream, milk, eggs, salt and pepper in medium bowl until well blended; pour evenly over leek mixture. Set aside.

6. Tear bread slices into 1-inch pieces and place in food processor or blender; process until fine crumbs form. Measure ¾ cup crumbs and place in small bowl; stir in cheese. Melt remaining 2 tablespoons butter in small saucepan; pour over crumb mixture, tossing to blend thoroughly. Sprinkle crumb mixture evenly over cream mixture.

7. Bake 50 to 60 minutes until top is golden and potatoes in center are tender when pierced with tip of sharp knife. Remove from oven; let stand 5 to 10 minutes before serving. Garnish as desired.

Makes 6 to 8 side-dish servings

LEMON

These vibrant yellow fruits, which probably originated in the Indus Valley of Asia about 2500 years ago, have a remarkable range of culinary possibilities. Lemons are essential to lemonade, lemon meringue pie, lemon bars and lemon cake. A squirt of lemon enhances tomato juice, ice tea, fish, shellfish, many vegetables and melon. It can be used in salad dressings as a refreshing change from vinegar and lends homemade mayonnaise a wonderful flavor. Most domestic lemons come from groves in California, although a few are grown in Arizona and Florida.

🌾

Availability: There is an abundant supply of lemons all year. They are, however, easily damaged by frost and an unseasonable cold spell may cause prices to rise. Bottled and frozen lemon juice are readily available, with frozen having a truer flavor than bottled.

Buying Tips: Lemons should be firm and heavy for their size, with a sheen to the skin. Avoid those that have any sign of green, which indicates that they are unripe. Thin-skinned lemons usually yield more juice, but it is easier to remove the zest and the peel of thick-skinned ones.

Tip

To release more juice from refrigerated lemons, warm them in a microwave oven at HIGH for about 30 seconds before juicing.

*Lemon Poached
Halibut with Carrots*

*Grating lemon peel on a
box-shaped grater.*

*Juicing a lemon with a
reamer.*

A vegetable peeler also works if used carefully not to remove any of the white pith underneath, as this has a bitter taste. The large pieces then can be sliced into paper-thin strips for use as a garnish or minced for use as an ingredient.

More juice will be available if the lemons are at room temperature. Roll them around on the counter under the flat of your hand before cutting them in half. This releases juice from the small sacs of the lemon. A reamer or juicer, either hand (technique on page 287) or electric, can be used to extract juice.

Lemon Poached Halibut with Carrots

    3 medium carrots, cut into
        julienne strips
  ¾ cup water
  ¼ cup dry white wine
    2 tablespoons fresh lemon juice
    1 teaspoon dried rosemary,
        crushed
    1 teaspoon dried marjoram leaves
    1 teaspoon chicken or fish
        bouillon granules
  ¼ teaspoon ground black pepper
    4 fresh or frozen halibut steaks,
        cut 1 inch thick (about
        1½ pounds)
  ½ cup sliced green onions
    Lemon slices (optional)

1. Combine carrots, water, wine, juice, rosemary, marjoram, bouillon granules and pepper in large skillet. Bring to a boil over high heat. Carefully place fish and onions in skillet. Return just to boiling. Reduce heat to medium-low. Cover; simmer 8 to 10 minutes until fish flakes easily when tested with fork.

2. Carefully transfer fish to serving platter with slotted spatula. Spoon vegetables over fish. Garnish with lemon slices, if desired.

Makes 4 servings

Yield: 1 pound lemons = 3 large or 5 medium.
1 lemon = 3 tablespoons juice and about 2 teaspoons grated peel.

Storage: Store lemons in a plastic bag in the refrigerator for up to three weeks. Check them periodically for signs of mold. A cut lemon tightly wrapped in plastic will keep for two or three days before its flavor begins to deteriorate.

Basic Preparation: If the peel is to be used, the lemons must be thoroughly scrubbed with warm, soapy water to remove wax and any traces of insecticide. To remove the peel or zest (colored portion only), use a box-shaped grater or a special tool called a zester (zester technique on page 344).

Zesty Fresh Lemon Bars

Crust
½ cup butter or margarine, softened
½ cup granulated sugar
Grated peel of ½ SUNKIST® Lemon
1¼ cups all-purpose flour

Filling
1 cup packed brown sugar
1 cup chopped walnuts
2 eggs, slightly beaten
¼ cup all-purpose flour
Grated peel of ½ SUNKIST® Lemon
¼ teaspoon baking powder

Glaze
1 cup powdered sugar
1 tablespoon butter or margarine, softened
2 tablespoons fresh-squeezed SUNKIST® Lemon Juice

To prepare crust, preheat oven to 350°F. In medium bowl, beat ½ cup butter, granulated sugar and lemon peel. Gradually stir in 1¼ cups flour to form soft dough. Press evenly on bottom of ungreased 13×9×2-inch pan. Bake 15 minutes.

To prepare filling, in medium bowl, combine all filling ingredients. Spread over baked crust. Bake 20 minutes. Meanwhile, prepare glaze.

To prepare glaze, in small bowl, gradually blend small amount of powdered sugar into 1 tablespoon butter. Add lemon juice and remaining powdered sugar; stir to blend well. Drizzle glaze over hot lemon filling. Cool in pan on wire rack; cut into bars. Store tightly covered at room temperature.

Makes about 3 dozen bars

Lemonade

1 cup Time-Saver Sugar Syrup (recipe follows)
1⅓ cups squeezed lemon juice
4 cups water

Prepare Time-Saver Sugar Syrup. Combine Time-Saver Sugar Syrup, lemon juice and water. Mix thoroughly; serve over ice. Garnish as desired.

Makes 1½ quarts lemonade

Time-Saver Sugar Syrup

1 cup water
2 cups sugar

Combine water and sugar in medium saucepan. Cook and stir over medium heat until sugar dissolves. Cool to room temperature; strain through sieve. Refrigerate until chilled.

Makes about 2 cups syrup

*Favorite recipe from **The Sugar Association, Inc.***

LENTIL

Lentils are small disk-shaped seeds of a legume (bean) plant. They are the oldest cultivated legume with historical references dating back to 2400 B.C. Today, they are grown in Asia, Africa and Europe. Known as the "fast food" member of the legume family, lentils cook in less than 30 minutes.

🌾

Uses: Lentils can be used as a side dish or combined with other ingredients, such as chicken, smoked sausage and ham, for main dishes.

• Lentils are the basis for lentil soup.

• Lentils can be combined with other ingredients, such as vegetables, cooked poultry and ham, and dressed with a simple vinaigrette for a change-of-pace salad.

*Spiced Orange
Chicken with Lentils*

water or broth (2 cups of liquid to each 1 cup of lentils) in a saucepan. Bring to boil. Reduce heat to low. Simmer, covered, for 15 to 20 minutes or until tender.

Spiced Orange Chicken with Lentils

> 3 tablespoons all-purpose flour
> 1 teaspoon ground coriander
> 1 teaspoon ground cumin
> ½ teaspoon salt
> ½ teaspoon dried mixed herbs (thyme, marjoram and rosemary)
> ¼ teaspoon freshly ground black pepper
> 8 chicken drumsticks
> 2 tablespoons FILIPPO BERIO® Olive Oil, divided
> Finely grated peel and juice of 1 orange
> 1 large onion, finely chopped
> 2 cloves garlic, minced
> 2½ cups chicken broth
> 8 ounces dried lentils (about 1¼ cups), rinsed and drained
> Additional salt and freshly ground black pepper
> 1 to 2 tablespoons honey
> Orange wedges and chopped fresh parsley (optional)

• *Dal* is a spicy Indian dish made with lentils, tomatoes, onions and seasonings. This mixture is often puréed and served with curries.

Varieties: Lentils come in brown (the most common), red and yellow. All varieties can be used interchangeably in cooking.

Availability: Lentils are available all year and are sold in 1-pound packages and in bulk.

Buying Tips: Choose plump-looking lentils. Avoid shriveled or blemished ones.

Yield: 1 cup dried lentils = 2½ cups cooked.

Storage: Store lentils in an airtight container in a cool, dry place for up to one year.

Basic Preparation: Sort through lentils, discarding any debris or blemished lentils. Place the lentils in a colander. Rinse with cold running water. Unlike dried beans, lentils do not need to be soaked before cooking. Combine lentils with cold

In small brown paper bag or plastic food storage bag, combine flour, coriander, cumin, ½ teaspoon salt, dried herbs and ¼ teaspoon pepper; shake until well mixed. Place 1 chicken drumstick at a time into flour mixture; shake well to coat evenly. In large skillet, heat 1 tablespoon olive oil over medium-high heat until hot. Add drumsticks; cook 5 minutes or until brown, turning occasionally. Stir orange peel and juice into skillet. Cover; reduce heat to low and simmer 20 minutes or until chicken is no longer pink in center and juices run clear.

Meanwhile, in another large skillet, heat remaining 1 tablespoon olive oil over medium heat until hot. Add onion and garlic; cook and stir

Tip

When cooking lentils with acidic ingredients, such as tomatoes or wine, the cooking time will increase, sometimes by as much as 10 or 15 minutes.

5 minutes or until onion is softened. Add chicken broth and lentils; bring to a boil. Cover; reduce heat to low and simmer 20 minutes or until lentils are tender and broth is absorbed. Season to taste with additional salt and pepper. Arrange lentils on serving plate; place drumsticks on top. Stir honey into chicken juices remaining in skillet. Heat through, stirring occasionally. Spoon over chicken and lentils. Garnish with orange wedges and parsley, if desired.

Makes 4 servings

Middle Eastern Lentil Soup

1 cup dried lentils
2 tablespoons olive oil
1 onion, chopped
1 red bell pepper, chopped
½ teaspoon ground cumin
1 teaspoon fennel seeds
¼ teaspoon ground red pepper
4 cups water
½ teaspoon salt
1 tablespoon fresh lemon juice
2 tablespoons chopped fresh parsley
½ cup plain yogurt

1. Rinse lentils, discarding any debris or blemished lentils; drain. Set aside.

2. Heat oil in large saucepan over medium-high heat. Add onion and bell pepper; cook and stir 5 minutes or until tender. Add cumin, fennel and ground red pepper; cook and stir 1 minute. Add water and reserved lentils. Bring to a boil. Reduce heat to low. Cover and simmer 20 minutes. Stir in salt. Simmer 5 to 10 minutes more until lentils are tender. Refrigerate, covered, overnight or up to 2 days.

3. Reheat soup over medium heat until hot. Stir in juice. Meanwhile, stir parsley into yogurt in small bowl. Serve soup topped with yogurt mixture.

Makes 4 servings

Middle Eastern Lentil Soup

LETTUCE

The family of lettuce includes hundreds of varieties from tender, buttery soft leaves to crisp, crunchy heads. By far the most common is iceberg lettuce, a head lettuce that is used in salads and sandwiches. Although it is often criticized by some for having little flavor and practically no nutritive value, iceberg continues to be the top seller in the lettuce category. Most supermarkets offer other more flavorful varieties.

❦

Varieties: The following varieties are the most common in American supermarkets.

• Bibb lettuce is related to Boston lettuce but is smaller, crisper and more expensive.

• Boston is a round, loosely packed head lettuce with soft green leaves. It is sweeter and more tender than any other lettuce.

• Iceberg was developed in the 1920's by producers who wanted a less perishable lettuce that would withstand cross-country shipping. It has a mild taste, crisp texture and pale green color. It keeps well.

• Leaf lettuce (red and green) is less sweet than Boston and Bibb. Its soft leaves with curly edges are ideal for sandwiches and make a good addition to salads. The red variety is more fragile than the green, but both can deteriorate quickly.

• Romaine lettuce has elongated heads with dark green outer leaves and lighter, more tender hearts. The leaves are very crisp and sturdy. The dark green color makes romaine more nutritious than any other lettuce.

• Oak leaf lettuce, frisee and chicory are less common salad greens. They are often included as components in baby-lettuce mixes.

Availability: Almost all of the major types of lettuce are available all year. Ready-to-eat blends of lettuces and other salad greens are also available in plastic bags.

Buying Tips: Select crisp-looking specimens with no signs of rusty color, rot or wilted leaves. All outer leaves of heads should look vibrant and fresh. Iceberg heads should feel slightly springy rather than hard. Leaf lettuce with pale pink on the stems have experienced wet growing conditions and will rot quickly.

Yield: 1 pound lettuce = about 6 cups of torn leaves.

Storage: Store lettuce in the vegetable drawer of the refrigerator. Whether it is washed before storing or just before serving is a matter of choice. The leaves should be dry before storing to discourage mold and rot. Leaf lettuce will keep from two to five days. Iceberg and romaine lettuce lasts five to seven days. Bags of salad mixes are stamped with a freshness date.

Basic Preparation: Before washing, discard bruised or wilted leaves and remove the central core from iceberg lettuce. Wash lettuce thoroughly under cold water, taking care to separate the leaves so that any buried mud or grits will be rinsed away. (Soak especially dirty lettuce in water

Tips

If you purchase lettuce from a supermarket that periodically mists vegetables, dry the leaves before storing or add paper towels to bags of damp lettuce to absorb the moisture.

Lettuce can be torn or cut into bite-size pieces for salads. To prevent browning, cut lettuce with a knife that has a stainless steel blade rather than a carbon-steel blade.

for 5 minutes, then swish to remove dirt.) Drying the lettuce is very important, both for its keeping qualities and so that salads are not diluted by excess water. Salad spinners are invaluable for the job.

LIME

Puckery and tart, to be sure, limes possess an elusive perfumed aroma and slightly exotic taste. These vibrant, green citrus fruits are overshadowed by lemons in popularity. Nonetheless, they are indispensible, quite unique and valuable in their own right. They grow in most tropical and subtropical regions, including the Caribbean, Mexico, Florida and California.

☙

Uses: An indispensible ingredient in a well-stocked bar, limes are used as garnish in such drinks as gin and tonic and rum and Coca-Cola. Their juice forms the tart, refreshing base for margaritas, gimlets, daiquiris and many other tropical drinks.

• Lime juice is used to "cook" fish and scallops in the Latin American dish known as *seviche.*

• It is added to guacamole and many Mexican soups and marinades.

• A wedge of lime is served along with the Italian appetizer of melon and prosciutto.

• It is a favorite flavor for sherbet and, of course, is used in Key lime pie.

Varieties: The Persian lime, grassy green in color and somewhat oval, is by far the most common in the United States. Key limes, from Florida and the Caribbean, are smaller, rounder and tarter. They have an obvious yellow tint to the skin and a marked floral aroma.

Availability: Persian limes are in ready supply all year, with Mexican imports supplementing domestic supplies at certain times of the year. Lime juice is available bottled and frozen. Key limes are only occasionally available outside Florida. Specialty markets may carry bottled Key lime juice.

Buying Tips: Select firm, heavy specimens that have a natural sheen to their skin. Avoid those that appear to be dried out or that are light for their size. Small brown patches on the skin, called scald, are not indicative of poor quality.

Yield: 1 pound Persian limes = 6 to 8 medium.
1 medium lime = 1½ tablespoons juice and 1½ teaspoons grated peel.

Storage: Store limes in a plastic bag in the refrigerator for up to two weeks.

Basic Preparation: If the peel is to be used, the limes must be thoroughly scrubbed with warm, soapy water to remove wax and any traces of insecticide. To remove the peel or zest (colored part only), use a box-shaped grater (technique on page 282) or a special tool called a zester (technique on page 344).

A vegetable peeler also works if used carefully not to remove any of the white pith underneath, as this has bitter taste. The large pieces of peel can then be sliced into paper-thin strips for use as a garnish or minced for use as an ingredient.

More juice will be available if the limes are at room temperature. Roll them around on the counter under the flat of your hand before cutting them in half. This releases juice from the small juice-filled sacs. Use a reamer (technique on page 282) or juicer, either hand or electric, to extract juice.

Juicing a lime with a juicer.

Chicken Picante

- ½ cup medium-hot chunky taco sauce
- ¼ cup Dijon mustard
- 2 tablespoons fresh lime juice
- 3 boneless, skinless chicken breasts, halved (about 2 pounds)
- 2 tablespoons butter or margarine
  Chopped fresh cilantro (optional)
  Plain yogurt

1. Combine taco sauce, mustard and juice in large bowl. Add chicken, turning to coat. Cover; marinate in refrigerator at least 30 minutes.

2. Melt butter in large skillet over medium heat until foamy. Remove chicken from marinade; reserve marinade. Add chicken to skillet; cook about 10 minutes or until browned on both sides. Add marinade. Increase heat to medium-high; cook chicken about 5 minutes or until chicken is glazed and no longer pink in center. Remove chicken to serving platter. Pour any remaining sauce over chicken. Garnish with cilantro, if desired. Serve with yogurt.

Makes 6 servings

Favorite recipe from **National Broiler Council**

Chicken Picante

LINGONBERRY

A lingonberry is a small, tart red wild berry, related to the cranberry, that grows in mountainous areas, especially in Sweden. It is rarely, if ever, sold fresh in this country. The berries are prepared and sold as preserves and sauces. They are used on crêpes, Swedish-style pancakes, puddings and as a sauce for certain duck dishes.

🐝

LIQUEUR

Liqueur is the result of infusing an alcoholic beverage, such as brandy or whiskey, with a natural flavoring ingredient, such as fruit, herbs, nuts and cocoa. They are generally served as after-dinner drinks or used as ingredients in cocktails and in cooking and baking. Liqueurs commonly used in cooking and baking include amaretto (almond), crème de cacao (chocolate), crème de menthe (mint), Grand Marnier (orange), Kahlúa (coffee) and Triple Sec (orange).

🐝

Chocolate Amaretto Squares

½ cup (1 stick) butter (do not use margarine), melted
1 cup sugar
2 eggs
½ cup all-purpose flour
⅓ cup HERSHEY'S Cocoa or HERSHEY'S European Style Cocoa
2 tablespoons almond flavored liqueur *or* ½ teaspoon almond extract
1¼ cups ground almonds
Sliced almonds (optional)

Heat oven to 325°F. Grease 8-inch square baking pan. In large bowl, beat butter and sugar until creamy. Add eggs, flour and cocoa; beat well. Stir in almond liqueur and ground almonds. Pour batter into prepared pan. Bake 35 to 40 minutes or just until set. Cool completely in pan on wire rack. Cut into squares. Garnish with sliced almonds, if desired.

Makes about 16 squares

Kahlúa® Ice Cream Pie

1 (9-ounce) package chocolate wafer cookies
½ cup unsalted butter, melted
10 tablespoons KAHLÚA®, divided
1 teaspoon espresso powder
3 ounces semisweet chocolate, chopped
1 tablespoon unsalted butter
1 pint vanilla, coffee or chocolate chip ice cream
1 pint chocolate ice cream
¾ cup whipping cream, whipped
Chocolate-covered coffee beans (optional)

Preheat oven to 325°F. Place ½ of cookies in food processor, breaking cookies into pieces. Process to make fine crumbs. Repeat with remaining cookies. Add ½ cup melted butter and process with on-off pulses, just to blend. Press crumb mixture evenly onto bottom and up side to rim of 9-inch pie plate. Bake 10 minutes. Cool completely.

In small saucepan, heat 6 tablespoons Kahlúa® and espresso powder over low heat until warm and espresso powder dissolves. Stir in chocolate and 1 tablespoon butter until melted and smooth. Cool completely.

Transfer vanilla ice cream to electric mixer bowl and allow to soften slightly. Add 2 tablespoons Kahlúa® and beat at low speed until blended. Spread over bottom of cooled crust and freeze until firm.

Spread cooled chocolate mixture over ice cream mixture. Freeze until firm.

Transfer chocolate ice cream to mixer bowl and allow to soften slightly. Add remaining 2 tablespoons Kahlúa® and beat at low speed until blended. Spread over frozen chocolate mixture. Freeze until firm.

To serve, pipe decorative border of whipped cream on pie around inside edge. Garnish with chocolate-covered coffee beans, if desired.

Makes one 9-inch pie

LITCHI

A litchi is a subtropical fruit grown in China, Mexico and the United States (California, Florida and Hawaii). It is a small oval fruit with a rough, bright red hull. Beneath the hull is milky white flesh surrounding a single seed. The flesh is sweet and juicy. The fresh litchi is a delicacy in China. They are available fresh at Asian markets in the United States in early summer. Canned litchis are readily available. They are most often served as dessert.

☙

Chocolate Chip Macaroons

2. Drop dough by rounded teaspoonfuls 2 inches apart onto greased baking sheets. Press dough gently with back of spoon to flatten slightly.

3. Bake 10 to 12 minutes until light golden brown. Let cookies stand on baking sheets 1 minute. Remove cookies to wire racks; cool completely. Store tightly covered at room temperature.

Makes about 3½ dozen cookies

MADELEINE

Madeleine refers to a small, light cakelike cookie that is baked in a special pan with scalloped indentations, known as a madeleine pan. The cookies often accompany coffee or tea. Although usually simply flavored with lemon or orange, recipe variations may include cocoa, nuts or almond paste.

❦

Chocolate Madeleines

> 3 teaspoons butter, softened, divided
> 1¼ cups cake flour or all-purpose flour
> ¼ cup unsweetened cocoa powder
> ¼ teaspoon salt
> ¼ teaspoon baking powder
> 1 cup granulated sugar
> 2 eggs
> ¾ cup butter, melted, cooled
> 2 tablespoons almond-flavored liqueur or kirsch
> Powdered sugar

1. Preheat oven to 375°F. Grease 3 madeleine pans with softened butter, 1 teaspoon per pan; dust with flour. (If only 1 madeleine pan is available, thoroughly wash, dry, grease and flour after baking each batch. Cover remaining dough with plastic wrap; let stand at room temperature.)

MACAROON

A cookie with a crisp, yet chewy texture, a macaroon is traditionally made from egg whites and sugar that are flavored with ground almonds or almond paste. A variation with coconut substituted for almonds is almost more popular than the original. Chocolate and cherries are sometimes added to macaroons.

❦

Chocolate Chip Macaroons

> 2½ cups flaked coconut
> ⅔ cup mini semisweet chocolate chips
> ⅔ cup sweetened condensed milk (not evaporated milk)
> 1 teaspoon vanilla extract

1. Preheat oven to 350°F. Combine coconut, chips, milk and vanilla in medium bowl; mix until well blended.

Technique for Chocolate Madeleines

Step 1. *Greasing madeleine pan.*

2. Combine flour, cocoa, salt and baking powder in medium bowl. Beat sugar and eggs in large bowl with electric mixer at medium speed 5 minutes or until mixture is light in color and falls in wide ribbons from beaters, scraping down side of bowl once. Beat in flour mixture at low speed until well blended, scraping down side of bowl once. Beat in melted butter and liqueur until just blended. Spoon level tablespoonfuls of batter into each prepared madeleine mold.

3. Bake 12 minutes or until puffed and golden brown. Let madeleines stand in pan 1 minute. Carefully loosen cookies from pan with point of small knife. Invert pan over wire racks; tap lightly to release cookies. Let stand 2 minutes; cool completely.

4. Dust with sifted powdered sugar. Store tightly covered at room temperature up to 24 hours or freeze up to 3 months.

Makes about 2 dozen madeleines

MANGO

Although largely overlooked by most Americans until recently, this lushly aromatic and flavorful fruit is one of the most popular fruits in the world. It is used abundantly in Indian, Mexican and Caribbean cuisines. Native to Southeast Asia, mangoes have been cultivated for more than 6,000 years. Now, there are hundreds of varieties, ranging in weight from less than half a pound to four pounds or more. When properly ripe, mangoes have a floral aroma, succulent orange flesh and tropical fruity taste.

🌿

Uses: Mangoes are generally eaten plain or with a squirt of fresh lime juice.

• They can be diced and added to fresh salsas, fruit salads and desserts. They are especially good with poultry and smoked meats.

• Green, unripe mangoes are the basis for a cooked mango chutney, which often accompanies curry dishes.

• Mango purée can be used as the foundation for sorbets, ice cream, beverages or as a sweet dessert sauce.

Varieties: Many varieties of mangoes show up in the American marketplace but they rarely are labeled. In almost all cases, markets offer one variety. Almost without exception, mangoes in American markets are somewhat flat ovals, weighing from slightly less than a pound to almost two pounds. Their skin color is usually green with a blush that ranges from yellow to orange to rose.

Availability: A small percentage of mangoes in our markets are grown in Florida and California. Others are imported from Haiti and Mexico. Florida and California mangoes are in season in the summer months. The imports enjoy a longer season that begins in January and slows to a trickle by autumn. Some large

Special Interest

Mangoes belong to the same family as poison ivy and poison oak. They contain an oil that may cause a mild allergic reaction in some people. Generally, it is the mango skin and not the flesh that is an irritant.

supermarkets stock jars of mango spears in light syrup in the refrigerator case. Canned mango nectar and canned sliced mangoes in heavy syrup are available in some markets.

Buying Tips: Mangoes should be firm but not hard. The flesh should yield slightly to pressure. Somewhat hard ones will ripen at home although rock-hard mangoes most likely will rot before they ripen. The skin should be taut, smooth and free of black spots and shriveled ends. Black speckling on the skin is perfectly acceptable. A sweet, fruity aroma around the stem end is indicative of a good specimen.

Yield: 1 pound mango = about 2½ cups peeled, diced fruit.

Storage: Ripe mangoes should be stored in the refrigerator and used within two to four days. Unripe fruit can be placed in a perforated brown paper bag and allowed to stand at room temperature for a day or two to ripen.

Basic Preparation: Mangoes have a large central seed that clings tenaciously to the flesh. Do not try to cut the mango in half and twist the two halves apart, as is often directed. To prepare a mango, hold it, stem end up, on a cutting board. Using a utility knife, make a vertical cut on the flat side of the mango from the top to the

bottom about ½ inch to the right of the stem and seed. Repeat on the opposite flat side of the mango.

To make spears, peel the skin from the cut sections and the sections still attached to the seed. Slice the flesh from the seed. Cut the flesh into spears.

To cube a mango, do not peel the skin from the cut sections. Score the flesh, but not the skin, with the tip of a paring knife. Holding the scored

section in two hands, gently push from the skin side toward you so that the flesh separates.

To separate the cubes from the skin, gently run a table knife or the edge of a spoon between the skin and the flesh. Peel the sections still attached to the mango and slice the flesh from the seed. Cut the flesh into cubes.

Tropical Frozen Mousse

2½ cups mango chunks (1 or 2 mangoes, peeled, cut into bite-size pieces)
⅓ cup sugar
1 tablespoon kirsch
1 teaspoon grated lime peel
¼ teaspoon fresh lime juice
2 cups whipped cream
Mango slices and fresh mint leaves (optional)

1. Place mango chunks in food processor or blender; process until smooth. Transfer to large bowl. Blend in sugar, kirsch, lime peel and juice. Fold whipped cream into mango mixture. Pour into sherbet glasses or 8-inch square pan. Cover; freeze 4 hours or until firm.

2. Let stand at room temperature 30 minutes before serving. Garnish with mango slices and mint, if desired.   *Makes 6 servings*

Hawaiian Shrimp Kabobs

- 1 can (6 ounces) pineapple juice
- ⅓ cup packed brown sugar
- 4 teaspoons cornstarch
- 1 tablespoon rice vinegar
- 1 tablespoon reduced sodium soy sauce
- 1 clove garlic, minced
- ¼ teaspoon ground ginger
- 1 medium-size green bell pepper
- 1 medium-size red bell pepper
- 1 medium onion
- 1 cup fresh pineapple chunks
- 1 cup fresh mango or papaya chunks (1 mango, peeled, cut into bite-size pieces)
- 1 pound raw large shrimp, peeled, deveined
- 2½ cups hot cooked white rice
  Red onion rings and fresh herb sprigs (optional)

1. For sauce, combine juice, sugar, cornstarch, vinegar, soy sauce, garlic and ginger in saucepan. Cook over medium-high heat until mixture comes to a boil and thickens, stirring frequently; set aside.

2. Preheat broiler. Cut peppers and onion into 1-inch squares. Thread peppers, onion, pineapple, mango and shrimp onto 10 metal skewers. Place kabobs in large glass baking dish. Brush reserved sauce over kabobs.

3. Spray rack of broiler pan with nonstick cooking spray. Place kabobs on rack. Broil, 3 to 4 inches from heat, 3 minutes. Turn and brush with sauce; discard any remaining sauce. Broil 3 minutes more or until shrimp turn pink and opaque. Serve with rice. Garnish with onion rings and herbs, if desired.

Makes 5 servings

Hawaiian Shrimp Kabobs

MAPLE SYRUP

Maple syrup comes from the sap of certain species of maple trees. A tap inserted into the tree trunk during sugaring season drains the sap, which is then boiled and concentrated to form the thick, sweet liquid known as maple syrup. Further boiling to evaporate the liquid results in maple sugar. Maple-flavored syrup is a mixture of a less expensive syrup, usually corn syrup, and maple syrup. Pancake syrup is artificially flavored. Once opened, maple syrup should be refrigerated.

🐝

Special Interest

Maple syrup is graded according to flavor and color. Fancy, or Grade AA, is the lightest in color and the most delicate in flavor. Other grades are A, B and C.

MARGARINE

Developed 100 years ago as a less costly substitute for butter, this hydrogenated vegetable oil (usually soy or corn oil) now is widely used because it has less cholesterol than butter. It does, however, have the same amount of fat as butter, but most of the fat is polyunsaturated rather than saturated. By law, stick margarine must be 80 percent fat. It is sold salted and occasionally unsalted. Margarine can be used in place of butter for all cooking and baking uses, although flavor will vary and in some cases the texture of baked goods may be different.

🐝

A margarine-type product with less than 80 percent fat must be labeled as a spread. Spreads contain more water than margarine, which limits the way they can be used. Spreads with at least 70 percent fat can be substituted for margarine in cooking and baking with two exceptions. Dough for shaped cookies, such as spritz, will not hold the shape, and buttercream-type frostings may be too soft. Frosting can be adjusted by adding additional powdered sugar. Spreads with less than 70 percent fat will produce less tender cakes and less crisp cookies, which will stale quickly. Some spreads may not be satisfactory for sautéing because of the added water.

Some products may be blends of margarine and butter (usually 60 percent margarine, 40 percent butter). They have the flavor of butter but less cholesterol.

Soft margarine and spreads, which come in a tubs, are spreadable at refrigerated temperature. Liquid margarine and spreads, which come in squeeze bottles, are a convenient way to add flavor to vegetables, popcorn and quick breads.

MARINADE

A marinade is a well-seasoned liquid mixture used as a preliminary step in the preparation of many foods, primarily meat, poultry and fish. The marinade flavors foods and sometimes tenderizes meats by breaking down the collagen in animal protein. It is usually a mixture of oil for moistness; an acidic ingredient, such as vinegar, wine, citrus juice or yogurt, for flavor and tenderizing; and seasonings, such as herbs and garlic. For additional information about marinades and food safety, see page 219.

Dry marinades (also called dry rubs) are mixtures of herbs and spices that are rubbed onto the surface of meat and poultry and allowed to stand before cooking. The flavor of the herbs and spices permeates the meat and generally produces a more intense flavor than a liquid marinade.

🐝

Marinating Tips: When a marinade contains an acid, place it in a glass, not a metal container, for marinating food.

• For best flavor, a liquid marinade should completely cover the food. Marinating in a resealable plastic food storage bag allows for better coverage and makes cleanup easy.

• Marinate foods in the refrigerator, not at room temperature.

• If using leftover marinade as a sauce over cooked food, for food safety, the marinade should first be boiled for at least one minute.

• Fish should marinate briefly to prevent changes in texture. Chicken should be marinated for 30 minutes to 2 hours. Meats can be marinated up to 24 hours.

New Mexico Marinade

> 1½ cups beer
> ½ cup chopped fresh cilantro
> 3 cloves garlic
> ½ cup lime juice
> 2 teaspoons chili powder
> 1 teaspoon TABASCO® pepper
>   sauce
> 1½ teaspoons ground cumin

Place ingredients in food processor or blender; process until well combined. Store in 1-pint covered jar in the refrigerator up to 3 days. Use to marinate beef, pork or chicken in refrigerator.

Makes 2 cups marinade

Grilled Marinated Chicken

> 8 chicken thighs with drumsticks
>   attached (about 3½ pounds)
> 6 ounces frozen lemonade
>   concentrate, thawed
> 2 tablespoons white wine vinegar
> 1 tablespoon grated lemon peel
> 2 cloves garlic, minced
>   Curly endive and lemon peel
>   strips (optional)

1. Remove skin and all visible fat from chicken. Place chicken in 13×9-inch glass baking dish. Combine lemonade, vinegar, grated lemon peel and garlic in small bowl; blend well. Pour over chicken; turn to coat. Cover; refrigerate 2 hours or overnight, turning occasionally.

2. To prevent sticking, spray grid of grill with nonstick cooking spray. Prepare grill for direct grilling over medium-hot heat.

3. Place chicken on grid 4 inches from medium-hot coals. Grill, on uncovered grill, 20 to 30 minutes until fork can be inserted into chicken with ease and juices run clear, not pink, turning occasionally. (Do not overcook or chicken will be dry.) Garnish with curly endive and lemon peel strips, if desired. Serve immediately.   *Makes 8 servings*

Grilled Marinated Chicken

Dijon Teriyaki Marinade

⅓ cup GREY POUPON® Dijon
    Mustard
2 tablespoons teriyaki sauce
2 tablespoons packed brown
    sugar

In small bowl, blend all ingredients.
Use as a marinade for pork or poultry.
Makes ½ cup marinade

Thai Marinade

½ cup A.1.® Steak Sauce
⅓ cup peanut butter
2 tablespoons soy sauce

In small nonmetal bowl, combine
steak sauce, peanut butter and soy
sauce. Use to marinate beef, poultry
or pork for about 1 hour in
refrigerator.

Makes 1 cup marinade

Balsamic Marinade

2 pounds beef, pork, lamb or veal
½ cup FILIPPO BERIO® Olive Oil
½ cup balsamic vinegar
2 cloves garlic, slivered
1 teaspoon dried oregano leaves
½ teaspoon salt
½ teaspoon dried marjoram leaves
¼ teaspoon freshly ground black
    pepper

Place meat in shallow glass dish. In
small bowl, whisk together olive oil,
vinegar, garlic, oregano, salt,
marjoram and pepper. Pour marinade
over meat, using about ½ cup for
each pound. Turn to coat both sides.
Cover; marinate in refrigerator several
hours or overnight, turning
occasionally. Remove meat; boil
marinade 1 minute. Grill meat as
desired, brushing frequently with
marinade. (Do not brush meat during
last 5 minutes of cooking.)
Makes 1 cup marinade

Thai Marinade

MARMALADE

*Marmalade is a thick, spreadable fruit
mixture that contains bits of the fruit's
rind. Usually citrus fruits, most often
Seville oranges, which grow in the
Mediterranean region, are used to
make marmalade. Although the tart-
ness and bitterness of the Seville orange make it unsuitable for eating out
of hand, it is ideal for making marmalade. Marmalade is used as a
spread for toast and English muffins
and as an ingredient in baked goods
and some meat sauces.*

MARZIPAN

Marzipan is a mixture made from ground almonds, sugar and liquid egg whites. It is pliable and often colored. Marzipan is used to make fanciful shapes, such as small animals and fruits. It also can be rolled into sheets to cover tortes and cakes or used for garnishing. It is sold in tubes and cans in most large supermarkets. Marzipan should not be confused with almond paste or almond filling.

MASA HARINA

Masa harina is a specially prepared corn flour used in Mexican cooking to make corn tortillas, tamales and other corn-based doughs. It is available in most large supermarkets in 5-pound bags.

MASH, TO

To mash is to crush a food into a soft, smooth mixture, as in mashed potatoes or bananas. It can be done with a tool called a potato masher or with an electric mixer. Small amounts of food, such as one or two bananas or a few hard-cooked egg yolks, can be mashed with a fork. For best results, make sure that potatoes are fully cooked so they are soft enough to become completely smooth.

MATZO

Matzo is unleavened bread in thin sheets usually made from flour and water. It is perforated to make breaking it apart easy. Traditionally served during the Jewish Passover holiday, the bread commemorates the flight of Israelites who had to flee Egypt before their bread had time to rise. This bread is also ground and used as flour in other recipes.

MATZO BALL

Matzo ball is a small, round dumpling usually cooked in chicken soup. It can also be served as a substitute for potatoes. The stiff batter is made with matzo meal, eggs, chicken fat and seasonings.

MATZO MEAL

Matzo meal is made by grinding matzo, Jewish unleavened bread. It is available in two textures, fine and medium, in Jewish markets and most large supermarkets. This meal is traditionally used to make matzo balls, pancakes and gefilte fish. It is also used as a thickener for soups and stews and as a breading for fried foods.

MAYONNAISE

Mayonnaise is a thick, creamy dressing made from egg yolks, oil, a small amount of lemon juice or vinegar, and seasonings. It is used as a spread for sandwiches, a sauce for cold meats and fish, and as the basis for dips and salads dressings. Classic mayonnaise is not a cooked dressing but rather an emulsion. Egg yolks act as the emulsifying agent, keeping the oil and acidic ingredients from separating. Almost all mayonnaise is commercially produced. Homemade mayonnaise should not be made from raw eggs as it once was, but rather from cooked or pasteurized eggs.

🌾

Blender Olive Oil Mayonnaise

        1 cup FILIPPO BERIO® Olive Oil,
            divided
    ¼ cup liquid egg substitute
        1 tablespoon chopped onion
        1 teaspoon salt
        1 teaspoon dry mustard
    ¼ teaspoon minced garlic
    ¼ teaspoon sugar
        2 tablespoons lemon juice
        1 tablespoon cider vinegar

In blender container, combine ¼ cup olive oil, egg substitute, onion, salt, mustard, garlic and sugar; blend until thoroughly mixed. While blender is running, very slowly add ½ cup olive oil, lemon juice and vinegar, stopping to scrape down sides several times. While blender is running, add remaining ¼ cup olive oil, 1 tablespoon at a time. Store mayonnaise, in tightly covered container, in refrigerator up to 3 weeks.

Makes about 1 cup mayonnaise

Leveling flour in a 1-cup dry measure.

MEASURE, TO

Careful measuring of ingredients in cooking and baking contributes to a successful result and ensures that this result can be repeated. Do not be fooled by experienced cooks who appear not to measure ingredients—they may add a pinch of this and a splash of that. Long practice has made those pinches and splashes accurate measures. Measuring with the correct tools is a must for novice cooks.

🌾

Measuring Dry Ingredients: The tools needed for measuring dry ingredients include a set of four metal or plastic dry measures (1 cup, ½ cup, ⅓ cup and ¼ cup) and a set of measuring spoons (1 tablespoon, 1 teaspoon, ½ teaspoon, ¼ teaspoon and sometimes ⅛ teaspoon).

To measure accurately, fill the measure to overflowing and with a straight edge of a metal spatula, sweep across the top of the measure to level the ingredient. Flour should be spooned into the cup. Do not dip the measuring cup into the flour, because this will compact the flour and result in an inaccurate measure.

BASIC MEASURES

1 tablespoon	=	3 teaspoons
1 cup	=	16 tablespoons
1 cup	=	8 ounces
1 pint	=	2 cups
1 pint	=	16 ounces
1 quart	=	4 cups (2 pints)
1 quart	=	32 ounces
1 gallon	=	16 cups (8 pints, 4 quarts)

Measuring Liquid Ingredients: Use clear glass measuring cups with calibrations marked on the side when measuring liquid ingredients.

To measure liquid accurately, place the measuring cup on the counter so it is level. Fill to the desired mark. Compare the ingredient amount with the cup calibration at eye level. Do not pick up the cup because you may not hold it level, resulting in a error in measuring. An ideal set of liquid measures include 1-cup, 2-cup and 4-cup measures. Small amounts of liquid (under ¼ cup) can be measured with measuring spoons by filling the spoon to the rim.

MEAT

Meat is the edible portion of cattle, swine or sheep. The common use of the terms beef, veal and pork dates back to the Norman invasion of England in 1066. While William the Conqueror maintained the former names for the animals, once they were slaughtered and cooked, the latter terminology originated from the French words boeuf, veau and porc.

Until recently meat was often the food around which the rest of the menu revolved. As Americans have become more health conscious, they are eating more grain-based foods, fruits and vegetables and less meat. In response to this decrease in demand the meat industry is now producing products that are leaner than ever. Beef is 27 percent leaner than it was 20 years ago due to leaner animals and closer trimming of fat. Pork is 50 percent leaner than it was in the late 1960's because of better feeding practices and improved genetics.

☙

Fat: Varying amounts of fat may be found in several locations. Fat may be found beneath the skin, around the muscles and within the muscles. The fat found within the muscles is referred to as marbling. Fat can usually be trimmed from under the skin and around the muscles, but the amount of marbling is directly related to the way the animal is fed and raised prior to slaughter.

Meat Inspection and Grading: Since 1906 the federal government through the United States Department of Agriculture has conducted a program of meat inspection to ensure that meat comes only from healthy animals processed in facilities and with equipment that meet sanitation standards. The USDA also regulates the packaging and labeling of both fresh and cooked meat, monitors the use of additives and oversees imported meat.

*Italian-Style Meat Loaf
(recipe on page 305)*

The USDA administers a voluntary program that grades meat carcasses for quality and yield. The grade is indicated by a shield-shaped purple stamp on the carcass. The most familiar grades are those used for beef—Prime, Choice, Select and Standard. Choice is the most common in supermarkets. Veal and lamb have similar grades.

Availability: Meats may be sold fresh, frozen and cured (for example, ham, bacon, sausages or corned beef). Cooked meat products are available canned, frozen or freeze-dried.

Buying Tips: Choose fresh meat that has good color (pink for pork, veal and lamb; red for beef). Avoid meat that is pale or gray-colored. Any fat should be firm and creamy white, not yellow. The meat should have no odd odors. The surface should be moist but not slimy. Always check the "sell-by" date and purchase on or before that date. Meat should only be purchased from a refrigerated case and should be securely wrapped and transported home quickly for immediate refrigeration.

When determining the amount of meat to purchase per person, allow four to five ounces for boneless cuts; eight ounces for bone-in cuts, such as steaks and chops; and ten ounces for mostly-bone cuts, such as ribs and shanks.

Storage and Handling: Meat is very susceptible to contamination and spoilage so care should be taken in handling and storage to maintain quality and food safety. After working with fresh meat, either to prepare for storage or for cooking, always wash your hands and all utensils and surfaces that have been in contact with the meat before continuing another task.

Meat may be stored in its original supermarket wrap unless the package is leaking. Store fresh meat in the

Barbecued Pork Loin (recipe on page 304)

coldest part of the refrigerator, about 36° to 40°F, and use within two to three days. If not used within this time, wrap in moistureproof material, label, date and freeze at 0°F or lower. *For additional information on freezing meat, see page 220.* After cooking, meat may be refrigerated three days or frozen for three months.

Thaw meat, still wrapped, in the refrigerator about four to seven hours per pound, usually overnight. Once meat is thawed completely, it should be used within a day or two and not refrozen. Meat can also be thawed in a microwave oven. Follow the microwave oven manufacturer's directions for thawing, being careful not to begin cooking the edges of the meat. Use meat that has been thawed in the microwave immediately.

Tenderizing Meat: Less tender and tough cuts of meat may be tenderized by one of several methods.

• Aging meat after slaughter tenderizes it and develops flavor. Aging occurs within the first ten days after slaughter and requires closely controlled conditions of temperature and humidity best achieved by the processor. Thus aging is not recommended as a home method of tenderizing meat.

• Meat may be tenderized manually by pounding it with a meat mallet and grinding or chopping it into small pieces. Avoid tenderizing a piece of meat by piercing it with a fork as this will cause the loss of meat juices during cooking.

• Slicing meat across the grain in very thin slices or strips, either before cooking, such as for stir-fries, or after cooking results in a more tender product. Raw meat is easier to slice thinly if it is partially frozen before slicing.

• Marinades and commercial meat tenderizers can be applied to meat to tenderize the meat to about ½ inch below the surface. Always place meat in the refrigerator when marinating or tenderizing it for more than 30 minutes.

• Moist-heat cooking methods like stewing and braising are designed to tenderize tough pieces of meat.

Common Cuts and Cooking Methods: *See also chart on page 303.* A good rule of thumb for determining whether a cut of fresh meat is tough or tender is the original location of the cut on the carcass. Less tender cuts come from the shoulder, leg and rump muscles of the animal because these muscles are used more. The muscles of the midsection of the animal provide more tender cuts.

Generally, dry-heat cooking methods may be used for tender cuts or tough cuts that have been tenderized. Moist-heat cooking methods are appropriate for tough cuts. The moisture tenderizes the connective tissue between the muscle fibers. A word of caution: Any cut will dry out if overcooked.

Dry-Heat Cooking Methods: Oven broiling and grilling are suitable for thin cuts of meat, such as steaks, chops and burgers. Preheat the broiler or prepare the grill for direct grilling. Place the meat on the rack of the broiler pan so that fat can drip off during cooking. Place thin cuts (¾ to 1 inch thick) two to three inches and thicker cuts three to six inches from the heat source. If broiling or grilling less tender cuts, such as flank steak, marinate the meat first. Small tender roasts, such as pork and beef tenderloin, also work well with this method. For large roasts, prepare the grill for indirect cooking. *For more information about grilling, see page 245.*

Panbroiling, well suited to thin steaks and chops, sears the outside of the meat. Preheat a heavy nonstick skillet or griddle and cook meat over medium-high heat, turning to ensure even cooking and draining any fat the accumulates.

Panfrying is similar to panbroiling except a small amount of fat is added to the skillet. Use this method for thin cuts of lean meat, thin strips of meat,

Tip

It is easier to cut beef or pork into thin strips for stir-frying if the meat is partially frozen. Place the meat in the freezer for 30 minutes (thin cuts) or 60 minutes (thick cuts) before slicing.

meat that has been pounded to tenderize it, and cuts that have been floured or breaded. Cook, uncovered, over medium heat until done, turning occasionally.

Roasting, usually used for large tender cuts of meat, is done in an oven. To roast meat, place the meat, fat side up, on a rack in a shallow open baking pan. Do not add water. Insert a meat thermometer in the thickest part of the meat. Roast in an oven preheated at 300°F to 350°F following recipe directions until the thermometer registers 5° to 10°F *below* the desired temperature. Allow the meat to stand for 15 to 20 minutes before carving. (Internal temperature will rise 5° to 10°F.) Slicing will be easier after standing. This method is best for large cuts of meat, at least 2 inches thick, such as beef and pork roasts and hams.

Stir-frying is a fast way to cook meat that is cut in uniform small pieces, such as thin strips or small cubes, and other foods, such as vegetables. Stir-frying is best done in a wok or a large skillet over medium-high heat, adding just enough oil to coat the wok. Cook the meat in batches to avoid overcrowding. Meat and other ingredients must be kept in constant motion by stirring. *See Stir-Fry, To, page 484, and Wok, page 546, for additional information.*

Moist-Heat Cooking Methods:
Braising is a moist-heat method for preparing beef roasts, tough cuts of steak, shanks and briskets. To braise, first brown the meat in a small amount of fat in a heavy skillet or Dutch oven. (The meat may be coated with flour before browning.) Drain off the fat and add a small amount of liquid. Bring the liquid to a simmer and cook, tightly covered, until the meat is tender. It is important not to let the liquid boil and to cook the meat at a low, even temperature to prevent it from becoming tough. After cooking the liquid can be thickened with flour to make gravy. Sometimes a flavorful liquid is

reduced by boiling to thicken and concentrate it. This can be done after the meat is removed from the skillet. The thickened mixture, known as a reduction, is served as a sauce.

Simmering or stewing consists of first browning the meat before covering it with liquid and simmering, covered, until fork-tender. Other ingredients, such as vegetables, pasta and seasonings, are often added. This method is used for making soups and stews and poaching various cuts of meat. Cuts that work best include shanks, stew meat, ribs and tough roasts.

Testing for Doneness: A meat thermometer is the best way to determine doneness for large pieces of meat that are roasted or grilled. Insert the thermometer at a slight angle or through the end of the roast so the tip of the thermometer is in the thickest part of the meat but not near a bone. For food safety, beef and lamb should reach a minimum internal temperature of 140°F for rare. Beef, lamb, veal and pork should be 160°F for medium and 170°F for well done. Fully cooked ham may be heated to 140°F. These temperatures are final temperatures and take into account the standing time necessary for roasts; that is, roasts should be removed from the oven or grill 5° to 10°F below the desired internal temperature and allowed to stand 15 to 20 minutes while the temperature rises to the desired level.

For thin pieces of meat that are broiled, grilled or pan-fried, check for doneness by cutting a small slit in the center or near the bone. The meat should be light pink to beige when done. To kill bacteria in ground beef, the USDA recommends cooking to at least medium doneness (160°F) or until centers are no longer pink and the juices run clear.

Use a fork to test for doneness of meat cooked by moist-heat methods, such as pot roast or stew. A fork will slide in easily and meat should be "fork tender" when done.

Tip

To carve roasts and large pieces of meat, cut across the grain to prevent stringiness and to ensure tenderness. To cut across the grain, look for long thin parallel fibers along the meat and cut or slice across them.

COMMON RETAIL MEAT CUTS

LOCATION	BEEF	VEAL	LAMB	PORK
BREAST	Brisket/M	Breast/M	Breast/M	Spareribs/D
FORE SHANK	Shank/M	Shank/M	Shank/M	Shank/M
SHOULDER/ CHUCK	Pot roast/M	Blade steak of roast/M	Shoulder	Picnic roast/M Blade roast/M
	Blade steak/M			
	Chuck eye steak/M			
	Short ribs/M			
RIB	Rib roast/D	Rib chops or roast/D	Rib chops or roast/D	Rib chops/D
	Rib eye steak/D	Crown roast/D	Crown roast/D	Center rib roast/D
LOIN	Porterhouse steak/D	Loin chops or roast/D	Double loin chops/D	Loin blade chops/D
	T-Bone steak/D		Loin chops or roast/D	Loin chops/D
	Tenderloin or Filet mignon/D			Center loin roast/D
	Top loin/D			Tenderloin/D
				Top loin chops/D
				Country-style ribs/D
				Backribs/D
SIRLOIN	Sirloin steak or roast/D	Sirloin steak or roast/D	Sirloin chops or roast/D	Sirloin chops or roast/D
	Sirloin roast/D			
	Top sirloin steak/D			
LEG/ROUND	Bottom round/M	Round roast/M	Leg/D	Ham/D
	Eye of round/M	Rump roast/M		
	Top round/M	Round steak/M		
	Rump/M			
	Round tip/M			
FLANK	Flank steak/D/M			

Recommended Cooking Methods
D = Dry-Heat Cooking Methods (see page 301)
M = Moist-Heat Cooking Methods (see page 302)

Indonesian Pork Chop 'n' Zesty Relish

Indonesian Pork Chops 'n' Zesty Relish

¼ **cup A.1.® Steak Sauce**
¼ **cup coconut milk**
2 **tablespoons firmly packed light brown sugar**
2 **cloves garlic, minced**
1 **teaspoon grated fresh ginger**
½ **cup finely diced, seeded, peeled cucumber**
¼ **cup finely chopped radishes**
¼ **cup finely chopped onion**
¼ **cup shredded coconut, toasted**
6 **(4-ounce) boneless loin pork chops**

In small bowl, combine steak sauce, coconut milk, brown sugar, garlic and ginger; reserve ¼ cup for basting. Stir cucumber, radishes, onion and coconut into remaining sauce; chill.

Grill pork chops over medium heat for 10 minutes or until no longer pink in center, turning occasionally and brushing often with reserved sauce. Serve hot with cucumber relish.

Makes 6 servings

Barbecued Pork Loin

2 **teaspoons LAWRY'S® Seasoned Salt**
1 **(3- to 3½-pound) boneless pork loin**
1 **cup orange juice**
¼ **cup soy sauce**
1 **teaspoon LAWRY'S® Garlic Powder with Parsley**
½ **teaspoon LAWRY'S® Seasoned Pepper**
Vegetable oil

Sprinkle Seasoned Salt onto all sides of meat. In large resealable plastic bag or shallow glass baking dish, place meat; let stand 10 to 15 minutes. Combine orange juice, soy sauce, Garlic Powder with Parsley and Seasoned Pepper; pour over meat. Seal bag or cover dish. Refrigerate at least 2 hours or overnight, turning occasionally. Heat grill; brush with vegetable oil. Remove meat from marinade, reserving marinade. Add meat to grill; cook 30 minutes or until internal meat temperature reaches 170°F, turning and brushing frequently with reserved marinade. Remove meat from grill; let stand about 10 minutes before thinly slicing. Meanwhile, in small saucepan, bring reserved marinade to a boil; boil 1 minute.

Makes 6 servings

Presentation: Serve sliced meat with extra heated marinade poured over top. Garnish with fresh herb sprigs. Serve with steamed vegetables.

Conventional Directions: Marinate meat as directed. Remove meat from marinade, reserving marinade. Place meat in shallow roasting pan; brush with reserved marinade. Bake, uncovered, in 350°F oven 1 hour or until internal temperature reaches 170°F, brushing frequently with reserved marinade. Discard any remaining marinade.

Italian-Style Meat Loaf

   1 egg
1½ pounds lean ground beef or
      turkey
   8 ounces hot or mild Italian
      sausage, casings removed
   1 cup CONTADINA® Seasoned
      Bread Crumbs
   1 cup (8-ounce can)
      CONTADINA® Tomato Sauce,
      divided
   1 cup finely chopped onion
   ½ cup finely chopped green bell
      pepper

In large bowl, beat egg lightly. Add
ground beef, sausage, bread crumbs,
¾ cup tomato sauce, onion and bell
pepper; mix well. Press into
ungreased 9×5-inch loaf pan. Bake,
uncovered, in preheated 350°F. oven
for 60 minutes. Spoon *remaining*
tomato sauce over meat loaf. Bake for
an additional 15 minutes or until no
longer pink in center; drain. Let stand
for 10 minutes before serving.

Makes 8 servings

Herb-Roasted Racks of Lamb

   2 whole racks (6 ribs each) loin
      lamb chops (2½ to 3 pounds)
   ½ cup mango chutney, chopped
   2 to 3 cloves garlic, minced
   1 cup fresh French or Italian
      bread crumbs
   1 tablespoon chopped fresh
      thyme *or* 1 teaspoon dried
      thyme leaves
   1 tablespoon chopped fresh
      rosemary *or* 1 teaspoon dried
      rosemary, crushed
   1 tablespoon chopped fresh
      oregano *or* 1 teaspoon dried
      oregano

1. Preheat oven to 400°F.

2. Trim fat from racks of lamb.
Combine chutney and garlic in small
bowl; spread evenly over meaty side
of lamb. Combine remaining
ingredients in separate small bowl;
pat crumb mixture evenly over
chutney mixture. Place lamb racks,
crumb sides up, on rack in shallow
roasting pan.

3. Roast in oven about 30 minutes or
until instant-read thermometer
inserted into lamb, but not touching
bone, registers 135°F for medium-rare
or to desired doneness. Slice between
ribs into individual chops. Garnish as
desired. Serve immediately.

Makes 4 servings

Technique for Herb-Roasted Racks of Lamb

Step 2. *Trimming fat from rack of lamb.*

Herb-Roasted Racks of Lamb

Peppered Beef Tenderloin Roast

  1 (3- to 4-pound) beef tenderloin, fat trimmed
  5 cloves garlic, finely chopped
  2 tablespoons finely chopped fresh rosemary
  1 tablespoon green peppercorns in brine, drained, finely chopped
  1 teaspoon ground black pepper
  1 teaspoon salt
  2 tablespoons olive oil or vegetable oil
 1¼ cups beef stock or broth

1. Place beef on sheet of plastic wrap. Combine remaining ingredients except oil and beef stock; rub over roast. Wrap tightly and refrigerate at least 4 hours but no longer than 48 hours. Return to room temperature before cooking.

2. Preheat oven to 425°F. In large ovenproof skillet or roasting pan, heat oil over medium-high heat. Place roast in skillet; brown on all sides, about 4 minutes per side.

3. Carefully lift roast with large carving fork; place roasting rack in skillet. Place roast on rack. *Do not cover.* Insert meat thermometer into thickest part of roast.

4. Roast in oven until meat thermometer registers 155°F or to desired doneness. (Roast will increase about 5°F after removal from oven.)

5. Remove to cutting board; let stand in warm place 15 minutes before carving.

6. Meanwhile, heat skillet with pan drippings over high heat until hot. Stir in beef stock. Cook until reduced to about ¾ cup, stirring occasionally. Strain mixture into sauce pitcher; serve with sliced roast.

Makes 10 to 12 servings

Favorite recipe from **California Beef Council**

Tip

Always let a roast stand at room temperature for 15 minutes after removing it from the oven. During this time, the temperature of the inside portion of the roast will increase by 5° to 10°F as heat is transferred from the hotter outside layers. The juices will "set" as the roast stands, resulting in less moisture loss when it is carved.

MEDALLION

Medallions are small, rather thin round or oval pieces of meat, usually beef, pork or veal taken from the tenderloin. When referring to beef, the term is used interchangeably with "tournedos."

MELBA SAUCE

This sweet dessert sauce was devised in the late nineteenth century by the French chef Auguste Escoffier for the opera singer Dame Nellie Melba. It is made from puréed raspberries, red currant jelly and sugar. When served with peaches and vanilla ice cream, the dessert is called peach Melba. Without ice cream, the dish of peaches and sauce is called peaches cardinale.

MELBA TOAST

A type of crisp toast, Melba toast is made by slicing day-old bread into very thin slices, trimming the crust and baking the slices in an oven at a low temperature until they are pale golden brown and crisp. It is used as a base for canapés and spreads and as an accompaniment for soups and salads. Melba toast is available packaged in supermarkets.

MELON

Melons are members of the gourd family. They grow on trailing vines. Melons are large, round or oval fruits with thick rinds and soft, juicy flesh. All melons require a long frost-free growing season and are handpicked when mature. Most melons have many seeds that are all contained in the central cavity of the melon. Watermelons have seeds that are distributed throughout the fleshy part of the melon.

❧

Varieties: There are many types of melons, varying in shape, size, color, flavor and texture. Descriptions of the most common melons follow:

Cantaloupe has a coarse, cream-colored raised netting over a yellowish-green rind. The flesh is salmon colored with a pungent aroma and sweet, juicy taste.

Casaba is a large, globe-shaped melon that is slightly pointed at the blossom end. It has a rough, furrowed, mostly yellow rind. The flesh is creamy white, sweet and juicy. Casabas have little aroma.

Crenshaw melons have a large, round base and pointed stem end. The rind is smooth and a goldish-green color. The salmon-colored flesh is juicy with a slightly spicy taste.

Honeydew, a large oval-shaped melon, has a smooth whitish-green to creamy yellow rind. The light green flesh is faintly fragrant, very sweet and juicy.

Muskmelons are larger than cantaloupes with deep grooves and loose netting. The soft salmon-colored flesh is sweeter than cantaloupe. Muskmelons are most likely to be found at local farmers' markets. Since they are very juicy and fragile, they do not ship well.

Persian melons are similar in shape to cantaloupes, but they are larger with a deep green rind and fine netting. The orange-pink flesh has a pleasant aroma and mildly sweet taste.

Santa Claus melons (or Christmas melons) are shaped a little like footballs. Their green rind has yellow-gold stripes. The flesh is creamy white to yellow with a mildly sweet and juicy flavor.

Watermelons are large oblong or round melons with a smooth green rind that is yellowish on the underside. The pink or red flesh is very juicy and sweet. Other varieties of watermelon with flesh color ranging from white to yellow to pink are sometimes available at farmers' markets.

Crab and Pasta Salad in Cantaloupe (recipe on page 308)

Tip

When using only half of a melon, such as cantaloupe or honeydew, do not remove the seeds from the remaining half. It will stay fresher longer if stored with its seeds.

Availability: Most melons are available fresh almost all year. However, peak seasons for certain varieties are as follows:

Cantaloupe – May to October
Casaba – August to November
Crenshaw – July to October
Honeydew – June to October
Muskmelon – August to September
Persian – July to October
Santa Claus – December
Watermelon – May to September

In addition, melon balls in syrup or juice are sold frozen.

Buying Tips: A ripe watermelon will have a shrunken and discolored stem and will produce a hollow sound when thumped with your knuckles. When choosing cut watermelon, look for bright-colored flesh with black seeds. The end nearest the stem is usually the sweetest. Avoid cut melon with coarse pale flesh, dark wet-looking flesh (overripe) or an abundance of small white seeds (underripe).

All other melons should feel heavy for their size and appear well shaped. A ripe melon should give to slight pressure at the blossom end and have a pleasant fragrance. Avoid bruised, dented or wet fruit.

Yield: 1 pound melon = about 1 cup cubes.

Storage: Most melons, except watermelons, continue to ripen after picking. If underripe, store at room temperature for a few days. When ripe, refrigerate and use within three to four days. Wrap cut melons with plastic food wrap, refrigerate and eat within two to three days.

Basic Preparation: To prepare, cut the melon into halves. Scoop out and discard the seeds. Cut the melon into quarters or wedges to serve. The flesh can be eaten with a spoon or a knife and fork. Watermelons can be cut into halves and then into slices or wedges for serving. The flesh of melons may be formed into balls with a tool called a melon baller.

Crab and Pasta Salad in Cantaloupe

1½ cups uncooked rotini pasta
  1 cup seedless green grapes
  ½ cup chopped celery
  ½ cup fresh pineapple chunks
  1 small red onion, chopped
  6 ounces canned, fresh or frozen crabmeat, drained, shredded
  ½ cup plain nonfat yogurt
  ¼ cup whipped salad dressing
  2 tablespoons fresh lemon juice
  2 tablespoons honey
  2 teaspoons grated lemon peel
  1 teaspoon Dijon mustard
  2 small cantaloupes

1. Cook rotini according to package directions, omitting salt; drain. Rinse in cold water; drain. Set aside.

2. Combine grapes, celery, pineapple, onion and crabmeat in large bowl. Combine yogurt, salad dressing, juice, honey, lemon peel and mustard in small bowl. Add yogurt mixture and reserved pasta to crabmeat mixture. Toss to coat evenly. Cover and refrigerate.

3. Just before serving, cut cantaloupes in half. Remove and discard seeds. Remove some of cantaloupe with spoon, leaving about ¾-inch-thick shell. Fill cantaloupes with salad.

Makes 4 servings

MELT, TO

Melting is the technique of using heat to turn a solid, such as chocolate, butter or preserves, into a liquid. Use either a small pan on the rangetop or in a microwave oven. Gentle heat (or reduced power) and frequent stirring result in even melting without burning. Take special care when melting chocolate and butter as they will easily scorch. See Butter, Cheese and Chocolate for additional information.

❦

MERINGUE

Meringue is a mixture of egg whites and sugar that is beaten to a stiff foam. For a smooth texture the sugar must dissolve completely. To accomplish this, while beating the egg whites, add the sugar in small increments, a tablespoon at a time. There are two types of meringues, soft and hard. A soft meringue has less sugar than a hard meringue. Soft meringues are used as toppings for pies or baked Alaska. They are popped into the oven for browning. A hard-meringue mixture is generally spooned or piped with a pastry bag onto a parchment-lined baking sheet to form shells or small mounds. Meringues require long baking (one hour or more) at a low temperature (200° to 250°F) until they are firm and crisp. Allowing meringues to stand in the oven with the heat off for an additional hour or more ensures thorough drying.

☙

Lemon Meringue Pie

Lemon Meringue Pie

 1⅓ cups sugar, divided
 ¼ cup ARGO® or KINGSFORD'S® Corn Starch
 1½ cups cold water
 3 egg yolks, slightly beaten
  Grated peel of 1 lemon
 ¼ cup lemon juice
 1 tablespoon MAZOLA® Margarine
 1 baked (9-inch) pie crust
 3 egg whites

Preheat oven to 350°F. In medium saucepan combine 1 cup sugar and corn starch. Gradually stir in water until smooth. Stir in egg yolks. Stirring constantly, bring to a boil over medium heat; boil 1 minute. Remove from heat. Stir in lemon peel, lemon juice and margarine. Spoon hot filling into pie crust. In small bowl with mixer at high speed beat egg whites until foamy. Gradually beat in remaining ⅓ cup sugar; continue beating until stiff peaks form. Spread meringue evenly over hot filling, sealing to edge of crust. Bake 15 to 20 minutes or until golden. Cool on wire rack; refrigerate.

Makes one 9-inch pie

Microwave Directions: In large microwavable bowl combine 1 cup sugar and corn starch. Gradually stir in water until smooth. Stir in egg yolks. Microwave on HIGH (100%), stirring twice with fork or wire whisk, 6 to 8 minutes or until mixture boils; boil 1 minute. Stir in lemon peel, lemon juice and margarine. Spoon hot filling into pie crust. Continue as directed.

Fruited Meringue Heart Melba

3. Preheat oven to 250°F. Spoon meringue into large pastry bag fitted with medium star tip; pipe heart outlines on parchment paper. Fill in heart shapes with meringue. Then pipe second row on top of first row of meringue around outside edges of hearts to form rims.

4. Bake 1 hour or until meringues are firm and crisp to touch. Turn off oven; leave meringues in oven with door closed at least 2 hours.

5. Meanwhile, prepare Melba Sauce; set aside.

6. Fill meringue hearts with fruit. Spoon about ¼ cup sauce onto each dessert plate and place filled hearts on sauce. Garnish with mint, if desired.　　*Makes 6 servings*

Melba Sauce

> **1 package (16 ounces) frozen unsweetened raspberries, thawed, drained**
> **¼ cup sugar**

Place raspberries and sugar in food processor or blender; process until smooth. Strain and discard seeds.　　*Makes 1½ cups sauce*

Fruited Meringue Hearts Melba

> **6 egg whites**
> **¼ teaspoon cream of tartar**
> **¼ teaspoon ground allspice**
> **1½ cups sugar**
> **Melba Sauce (recipe follows)**
> **3 cups sliced assorted fruit (berries, melon, grapes)**
> **Fresh mint leaves (optional)**

1. Line large baking sheet with parchment paper; draw 6 (3×3-inch) hearts on paper.

2. Beat egg whites in large bowl with electric mixer until foamy. Add cream of tartar; beat until soft peaks form. Add allspice. Beat in sugar, 1 tablespoon at a time, beating at high speed until stiff peaks form, about 5 minutes.

METRIC SYSTEM

The metric system is a decimal system of weights and measures that is based on the gram for weight and meter for length. It is used throughout most of the world with the major exception of the United States. To use a recipe published in another country, the following chart serves as a guide to metric conversions.

METRIC CHART

VOLUME MEASUREMENTS (dry)

1/8 teaspoon = 0.5 mL

1/4 teaspoon = 1 mL

1/2 teaspoon = 2 mL

3/4 teaspoon = 4 mL

1 teaspoon = 5 mL

1 tablespoon = 15 mL

2 tablespoons = 30 mL

1/4 cup = 60 mL

1/3 cup = 75 mL

1/2 cup = 125 mL

2/3 cup = 150 mL

3/4 cup = 175 mL

1 cup = 250 mL

2 cups = 1 pint = 500 mL

3 cups = 750 mL

4 cups = 1 quart = 1 l

VOLUME MEASUREMENTS (fluid)

1 fluid ounce (2 tablespoons) = 30 mL

4 fluid ounces (1/2 cup) = 125 mL

8 fluid ounces (1 cup) = 250 mL

12 fluid ounces (1 1/2 cups) = 375 mL

16 fluid ounces (2 cups) = 500 mL

WEIGHTS (mass)

1/2 ounce = 15 g

1 ounce = 30 g

3 ounces = 90 g

4 ounces = 120 g

8 ounces = 225 g

10 ounces = 285 g

12 ounces = 360 g

16 ounces = 1 pound = 450 g

OVEN TEMPERATURES

250°F = 120°C

275°F = 140°C

300°F = 150°C

325°F = 160°C

350°F = 180°C

375°F = 190°C

400°F = 200°C

425°F = 220°C

450°F = 230°C

DIMENSIONS

1/16 inch = 2 mm

1/8 inch = 3 mm

1/4 inch = 6 mm

1/2 inch = 1.5 cm

3/4 inch = 2 cm

1 inch = 2.5 cm

BAKING PAN SIZES

Utensil	Size in Inches/ Quarts	Metric Volume	Size in Centimeters
Baking or Cake Pan (square or rectangular)	8 × 8 × 2	2 L	20 × 20 × 5
	9 × 9 × 2	2.5 L	22 × 22 × 5
	12 × 8 × 2	3 L	30 × 20 × 5
	13 × 9 × 2	3.5 L	33 × 23 × 5
Loaf Pan	8 × 4 × 3	1.5 L	20 × 10 × 7
	9 × 5 × 3	2 L	23 × 13 × 7
Round Layer Cake Pan	8 × 1 1/2	1.2 L	20 × 4
	9 × 1 1/2	1.5 L	23 × 4
Pie Plate	8 × 1 1/4	750 mL	20 × 3
	9 × 1 1/4	1 L	23 × 3
Baking Dish or Casserole	1 quart	1 L	—
	1 1/2 quart	1.5 L	—
	2 quart	2 L	—

MILK

Milk is a popular and nutritious beverage obtained from mammals, usually cows in the United States. It is pasteurized and vitamin-enriched. Whole milk contains about 3½ percent butterfat; lowfat milk may have either 2 percent or 1 percent butterfat; and nonfat or skim milk has less than ½ percent butterfat. Lactose-reduced milk is available for those who can not digest the lactose, a naturally occuring sugar in milk. Acidophilus milk has lactobacillus culture, good bacteria, added. Some believe that this helps the digestive tract. Most milk cartons are freshness dated. Fresh milk should be refrigerated in its original container. It is generally recommended that milk not be frozen.

Dry milk is a powder made from milk that has the moisture removed. It is readily available in nonfat form and can be reconstituted with water. It does not require refrigeration, making it convenient when refrigerator space is limited. It is also economical. When reconstituted, its flavor is different from fresh milk. It is best used for baking. Canned evaporated milk, both whole and skim, has about 60 percent of the water removed. It is then sealed in cans and heat treated. It also does not need refrigeration so, like dry milk powder, it is convenient. When substituting evaporated milk for fresh milk, reconstitute it with an equal amount of water. Evaporated milk should not be confused with sweetened condensed milk (page 499).

Tips

Milk will keep up to a week beyond the freshness date if properly handled and stored.

To keep milk fresh, do not let it stand at room temperature. To serve milk at the table, transfer it to a pitcher. Do not return the unused milk to the original container.

MINCE, TO

Mincing refers to the technique of chopping food into very tiny, irregular pieces. Minced food is smaller than chopped food. Flavorful seasonings, such as garlic and fresh herbs, are often minced to distribute their flavor more evenly throughout a dish.

MIX, TO

To mix means to combine two or more foods together by stirring or beating until they are thoroughly blended or until ingredient bits, such as chips and nuts, are evenly distributed throughout a mixture. Mixing may be done by hand using a spoon or a rubber spatula or with an electric mixture.

MOCHA

The term mocha is used to indicate that coffee, or coffee and chocolate, have been added to a food for flavor. Originally, mocha was the name of a strong coffee that was exported from Arabia. It can also refer to a hot chocolate-flavored coffee beverage.

Smooth Mocha Coffee

¾ cup hot brewed coffee
2 tablespoons HERSHEY'S Syrup
Whipped cream (optional)
Ground cinnamon (optional)

In mug or cup, stir together coffee and syrup. Garnish with whipped cream and cinnamon, if desired. Serve immediately.

Makes 1 serving

Mocha Parfait

1½ tablespoons margarine
⅓ cup unsweetened cocoa powder
1 cup boiling water
½ cup sugar
1 tablespoon instant coffee granules
1 teaspoon vanilla extract
1 pint coffee-flavored nonfat frozen yogurt
12 whole coffee beans (optional)

1. Melt margarine in heavy saucepan over low heat. Add cocoa; cook and stir 3 minutes. Add boiling water, sugar and coffee; cook and stir until thickened. Remove from heat; stir in vanilla. Cool completely.

2. Place 2 tablespoons frozen yogurt in bottom of each of 4 parfait glasses. Top each with 1 tablespoon cocoa mixture. Top with another 2 tablespoons frozen yogurt; top frozen yogurt with 2 tablespoons cocoa mixture. Repeat layers twice. Garnish top of each parfait with 3 coffee beans, if desired. Serve immediately.

Makes 4 servings

Mocha Parfait

MOLASSES

Molasses is a dark, strong-flavored liquid used as a sweetener in cakes, cookies, puddings, muffins and baked beans. It is a secondary product in the production of sugar from cane or beets, obtained after the cane juice has been boiled until it crystallizes to become table sugar. The remaining liquid is molasses. Molasses taken after the first boiling is called first strike, or light. It is the highest quality and sweetest. It is best for table use. The liquid may be boiled again to extract more sugar. The resulting molasses is called second strike, or dark, a good choice for baking. Blackstrap molasses, the darkest and thickest, is taken after the third boiling. It has a bitter flavor and is generally not recommended for cooking purposes. Sulfur is sometimes used in the processing of the sugar cane juice, resulting in a darker molasses with a hint of sulfur in the taste. Molasses should be refrigerated after opening.

☙

Soft Spicy Molasses Cookies

    2 cups all-purpose flour
    1 cup sugar
    ¾ cup butter, softened
    ⅓ cup light molasses
    3 tablespoons milk
    1 egg
    ½ teaspoon baking soda
    ½ teaspoon ground ginger
    ½ teaspoon ground cinnamon
    ½ teaspoon ground cloves
    ⅛ teaspoon salt
      Additional sugar

1. Combine flour, 1 cup sugar, butter, molasses, milk, egg, baking soda, ginger, cinnamon, cloves and salt in large bowl. Beat with electric mixer at low speed 2 to 3 minutes until well mixed, scraping bowl often. Cover; refrigerate at least 4 hours.

2. Preheat oven to 350°F.

3. Shape rounded teaspoonfuls of dough into 1-inch balls. Roll in additional sugar. Place, 2 inches apart, on ungreased baking sheets. Bake 10 to 12 minutes until slightly firm to touch. Remove immediately to wire racks; cool completely.

Makes about 4 dozen cookies

MOLE

Mole is a reddish-brown or green sauce popular in Mexican cooking. There are many variations of this complex sauce, but most recipes include ground dried chilies, ground seeds (sesame or pumpkin), tomatoes (for red mole), tomatillos (for green mole), onions, garlic and spices. Other ingredients may include ground nuts, raisins or chocolate. Chocolate adds a hint of sweetness to mole poblano.

☙

MOUSSAKA

One of the best known of all Greek dishes, moussaka is a layered casserole that almost always includes sliced eggplant, ground lamb or beef, and a topping of a creamy white sauce to which eggs and cheese have been added. Other ingredients may include zucchini, potatoes, tomatoes and onions.

☙

MOUSSE

Mousse, a French word meaning "frothy" or "foamy," is a name given to a light and airy dish that may be either sweet or savory. Sweet dessert mousses are made by folding something foamy, such as beaten egg whites or whipped cream, into a cooked egg yolk or gelatin mixture that is flavored with puréed fruit or chocolate. They are served cold. Savory mousses are made with ground fish, meat, poultry, cheese or vegetables that are usually blended with cream or egg yolks. Beaten egg whites are added to produce the light texture. Savory mousses are baked and served hot.

❧

Decadent Chocolate Mousse

> 1¼ **cups semisweet chocolate chips, divided**
> 2 **cups chilled whipping cream, divided**
> 5 **egg yolks**
> 1 **teaspoon vanilla extract**
> ¼ **cup sugar**
> 1½ **teaspoons butter or margarine**

1. Heat 1 cup chips in medium saucepan over low heat until melted, stirring frequently. Remove from heat; stir in ¼ cup cream.

2. Place egg yolks in medium bowl. Whisk ½ of chocolate mixture into egg yolks; whisk egg yolk mixture back into chocolate mixture in saucepan. Cook over low heat 2 minutes, whisking constantly. Remove from heat; cool 3 to 5 minutes.

3. Beat remaining 1¾ cups cream and vanilla in medium bowl with electric mixer at medium speed until soft peaks form. Gradually beat in sugar; beat at high speed until stiff peaks form. Stir about ¼ of whipped cream mixture into chocolate mixture; fold chocolate mixture into remaining whipped cream until completely combined.

4. Pour chocolate mixture into serving bowl or individual dessert dishes; cover and refrigerate 8 hours or until set. (Mousse may be refrigerated up to 2 days.)

5. Heat remaining ¼ cup chocolate chips in small saucepan over low heat until melted, stirring frequently; stir in butter until smooth. Spoon mixture into small resealable plastic food storage bag. Cut tiny corner off bottom of bag with scissors. Pipe designs on plate lined with waxed paper; refrigerate 15 minutes or until firm. (Designs may be refrigerated up to 3 days.)

6. To serve, carefully peel waxed paper from chocolate designs; place on mousse. *Makes 6 servings*

Decadent Chocolate Mousse

MUESLI

Muesli, the German word for "mixture," is a breakfast cereal that combines a variety of toasted grains (such as oats, wheat and barley) with bran, nuts and dried fruit. It was developed in the late 1800's by a Swiss nutritionist as a health food. It originally was intended to be soaked in milk for several hours before serving, resulting in a slurry. Now, it is sold as a packaged cereal and is usually served with milk.

🐝

Raspberry-Sesame Muffins

MUFFIN

Muffins are small, round quick breads with a cakelike texture. They can be sweet or savory. Muffins can be flavored with fruit, vegetables, cheese or chocolate. Muffins are made from batters rather than doughs. Usually the combined liquid ingredients (such as eggs and milk) are stirred into the dry ingredients (such as flour, sugar and leavening). To avoid overbeating, mixing is done by hand only until the dry ingredients are moistened. Too much stirring or beating will give the muffins a tough texture with lots of holes and tunnels and a peaked top. The batter should look lumpy when it goes into the prepared muffin pans.

English muffins are yeast-raised breads that are baked on a griddle. Although they can be made at home, they are usually purchased.

🐝

Raspberry-Sesame Muffins

  1 cup nonfat milk
  ¼ cup Prune Purée (recipe
      follows) or prepared prune
      butter
  1 egg
  2 cups all-purpose flour
  ⅓ cup sugar
  3 tablespoons toasted sesame
      seeds, divided
  1 tablespoon baking powder
  ½ teaspoon salt
  2 tablespoons butter or
      margarine, melted
  1 cup fresh or frozen raspberries

1. Preheat oven to 400°F. Coat 12 (2¾-inch) muffin cups with vegetable cooking spray.

2. In medium bowl, beat milk, Prune Purée and egg until well blended. In large bowl, combine flour, sugar, 2 tablespoons sesame seeds, baking powder and salt. Add milk mixture to flour mixture; stir just until blended. Mix in butter. Fold in raspberries. Spoon batter into prepared muffin cups, dividing equally. Sprinkle with remaining 1 tablespoon sesame seeds.

3. Bake, in center of oven, 15 to 20 minutes until lightly browned and springy to the touch. Remove muffins to wire rack to cool slightly. Serve warm. *Makes 12 muffins*

Prune Purée: Combine 1⅓ cups (8 ounces) pitted prunes and 6 tablespoons hot water in food processor or blender. Pulse on and off until prunes are finely chopped and smooth. Store leftovers in covered container in refrigerator up to 2 months. *Makes 1 cup*

*Favorite recipe from **California Prune Board***

MUSHROOM

Mushrooms are members of the fungus family. They grow on decaying material and are reproduced from spores. Mushrooms have grown wild since ancient times, surviving wherever there is decaying material to support their growth. There are thousands of mushrooom species varying by color, shape, size and flavor. The cultivated button mushroom is the most common variety found in supermarkets. Several varieties of wild mushrooms have become popular in recent years. Some of these varieties are now cultivated. Pennsylvania produces half of the United States mushroom crop. Mushrooms are cultivated in special windowless buildings where temperature, humidity and ventilation are controlled.

🌾

Rice Cakes with Mushroom Walnut Ragoût (recipe on page 320)

Varieties: There are many varieties of fresh mushrooms available in supermarkets and specialty markets in the United States.

Button (or Field) Mushrooms are the most common mushrooms grown and sold. They are plump and dome-shaped with a smooth texture and mild flavor. The color of button mushrooms varies from white to pale tan.

Chanterelle mushrooms, which are yellowish-orange in color, grow wild in Pacific Northwest forests and in Europe. They have a flared trumpetlike shape, delicate flavor and fruity fragrance. Chanterelles are available fresh, but in limited supply, in the late spring. They are more commonly available dried.

Enoki are Japanese mushrooms that are now cultivated in California. They have long, thin stems with tiny caps. They are creamy white in color with a delicate, slightly fruity flavor. Enoki mushrooms are very perishable and should be used within two or three days. Unlike other mushrooms they do not require cleaning, but any mass at the base of the stems should be removed. They are best eaten fresh.

Morels are wild mushrooms that are difficult to cultivate. They have an elongated spongelike dome and a rich, intense earthy flavor. Look for them in the spring.

Oyster mushrooms are wild mushrooms from Asia that are now cultivated in the United States. They have a broad shell shape. Oyster mushrooms are creamy white to pale brown in color with a strong peppery flavor when raw but a milder cooked flavor. They are very perishable and should be used within two or three days.

Portobello mushrooms have large pancake-shaped dark brown caps on thick tough stems. They have a firm texture when cooked and a beeflike flavor. Because of their large size and sturdiness, they are a good choice for grilling. They are sometimes substituted for beef in vegetarian sandwiches, stir-fries and fajitas.

Shiitake are wild mushrooms from Japan that are easily cultivated. They have brown caps, a firm texture and thin tough stems, which are usually trimmed away. Their woodsy odor and rich, smoky mushroom flavor contribute to their popularity.

Straw mushrooms, an Asian variety with a deep umbrella-shaped cap, are more commonly seen canned than fresh. Look for fresh straw mushrooms at Asian markets. They have a mild flavor.

The following dried mushrooms are usually available in large supermarkets and specialty markets:

Chanterelle mushrooms are yellow-orange in color and have a flared, hornlike shape.

Porcini mushrooms (also known as cèpes) are tan to pale brown in color. They have a pungent, woodsy flavor.

Wood ears (also known as cloud ears and tree ears) are popular in Asian cuisines. They are available in Asian markets and large supermarkets.

Availability: Button mushrooms are available all year but the peak season is fall and winter. They are sold in 8- and 16-ounce packages and in bulk. Cultivated wild mushrooms are generally available all year. Morels and chanterelles, which are not cultivated, can be found in large supermarkets in the late spring. Button mushrooms are also available canned.

Buying Tips: Mushrooms should be firm and evenly colored with tightly closed caps. Avoid ones that are slimy or have any soft dark spots.

Yield: 1 pound fresh mushrooms = 6 cups slices; 2 cups cooked slices. 1 (4-ounce) can sliced mushrooms = $2/3$ cup.

Storage: Fresh mushrooms with the exception of enoki and oyster mushrooms will keep for five to seven days in the refrigerator. Enoki and oyster mushrooms should be used within two or three days. Wrap in paper towels and refrigerate unwashed in a plastic bag. Dried mushrooms should be stored in a cool, dry place for up to six months.

Basic Preparation: Wipe mushrooms with a damp paper towel, brush with a mushroom brush or soft toothbrush, or rinse briefly under cold running water to remove the dirt. (Do not wash enoki mushrooms.) Pat dry before using. Never soak in water because they absorb water and will become mushy. Trim and discard stem ends. (Shiitake and portobello mushrooms have tough stems that should be discarded.) Slice mushrooms through stem or chop.

Tip

Because many wild mushrooms are poisonous, it is extremely important that the picking of wild mushrooms be left to experienced gatherers.

To reconstitute dried mushrooms, soak in warm water until softened, about 20 to 30 minutes or in boiling water for 15 to 20 minutes. Drain off the soaking liquid and save it for use in soups and stews. Swish reconstituted dried mushrooms in a bowl of fresh warm water to remove any embedded dirt. Drain mushrooms on paper towels.

Mushrooms Rockefeller

    18 large fresh button mushrooms
        (about 1 pound)
     2 slices bacon
    ¼ cup chopped onion
     1 package (10 ounces) frozen
        chopped spinach, thawed,
        squeezed dry
     1 tablespoon fresh lemon juice
     1 teaspoon grated lemon peel
    ½ jar (2 ounces) chopped
        pimiento, drained
        Lemon slices and lemon balm
        (optional)

1. Lightly oil 13×9-inch baking dish. Preheat oven to 375°F.

2. To prepare mushrooms, brush dirt from mushrooms; clean by wiping mushrooms with damp paper towel. Pull entire stem out of each mushroom cap; set aside stems. Place caps in single layer in prepared baking dish.

3. Cut thin slice from base of each reserved stem; discard. Chop stems; set aside.

4. Cook bacon in medium skillet over medium heat until crisp. Remove bacon to paper towel; set aside.

5. Add reserved stems and onion to hot drippings in skillet. Cook and stir until onion is soft. Add spinach, juice, lemon peel and pimiento; blend well. Stuff mushroom caps with spinach mixture. Crumble reserved bacon and sprinkle on top of mushrooms.

6. Bake 15 minutes or until heated through. Garnish with lemon slices and lemon balm, if desired. Serve immediately. *Makes 18 appetizers*

Technique for Mushrooms Rockefeller

Step 2. *Removing stem from mushroom cap.*

Mushrooms Rockefeller

Rice Cakes with Mushroom Walnut Ragoût

2/3 **cup uncooked Arborio rice**
1 **whole egg**
1 **egg white**
1/2 **cup grated Parmesan cheese**
3 **tablespoons minced green onions**
1 **ounce dried porcini mushrooms**
1 **cup boiling water**
1 **tablespoon olive oil**
1 **medium onion, sliced**
2 **cloves garlic, minced**
8 **ounces fresh button mushrooms, sliced**
1 **teaspoon dried oregano leaves**
1 **can (14 1/2 ounces) tomato wedges, undrained**
2 **teaspoons lemon juice**
1/4 **teaspoon salt**
1/2 **teaspoon ground black pepper**
1/3 **cup chopped toasted walnuts**
   Asiago or Parmesan cheese wedge
   Fresh herb sprigs (optional)

1. Cook rice according to package directions. Uncover and cool.

2. Preheat oven to 350°F. Spray 8-inch square baking pan with nonstick cooking spray.

3. For rice cakes, beat egg and egg white in medium bowl until blended. Add rice, grated cheese and green onions; mix well. Press into prepared pan. Cover; refrigerate.

4. Soak dried mushrooms in boiling water in small bowl 15 to 20 minutes until soft. Drain, reserving liquid. Chop mushrooms.

5. Bake rice cakes 20 to 25 minutes until set.

6. Meanwhile for ragoût, heat oil in large nonstick skillet over medium heat. Add onion and garlic; cook and stir 5 minutes. Add fresh mushrooms, dried mushrooms and oregano; cook and stir 5 minutes or until fresh mushrooms are tender. Drain tomatoes, reserving 1/4 cup juice. Add tomatoes, reserved juice, reserved mushroom liquid, lemon juice, salt and pepper to skillet. Bring to a boil over high heat. Reduce heat to low. Simmer, uncovered, 15 minutes or until sauce thickens. Stir in walnuts.

7. Cut rice cakes into 8 rectangles; top with ragoût. Shave Asiago cheese with vegetable peeler; sprinkle shavings over ragoût. Garnish with herbs, if desired. Serve immediately.

Makes 4 servings

Technique for Rice Cakes with Mushroom Walnut Ragoût

Step 7. *Shaving Asiago cheese.*

MUSTARD

Prepared mustard is a pungent, hot condiment made from ground seeds of the same plant that produces mustard greens. The seeds are mixed with vinegar, water or wine and a variety of spices to make prepared mustard.

🦋

There are two kinds of mustard seeds: white (or yellow) and brown (Asian). Yellow, or American-style mustard, is tinted a vibrant gold by the addition of the spice turmeric. It is made from white mustard seeds. The famous French Dijon mustard is made with brown mustard seeds and white wine. Bright yellow English mustard, resulting from a mixture of white and brown seeds and turmeric, is very hot. German mustards, chiefly Dusseldorf, are made from brown seeds and have a mild sweet-and-sour flavor. Thin and pale of color, Chinese mustard is generally the hottest of all. Coarse-grained mustards have crushed seeds blended into the finished product. Sugar or honey are sometimes added for a sweet finish. Raspberries, horseradish, wine, bourbon and herbs are among the ingredients found in specialty mustards.

Mustards can be used in salad dressings and marinades, as a condiment with grilled meats, on sandwiches and spread on poultry before cooking. Prepared mustards should be refrigerated after opening. If they are not contaminated by other foods, they will keep indefinitely.

A combination of mustard seeds is ground to a powder to make the spice that is typically called dry mustard. *See Herb and Spice, page 256, for additional information.*

Spicy German Mustard

½ cup mustard seeds
2 tablespoons dry mustard
½ cup cold water
1 cup cider vinegar
1 small onion, chopped
2 cloves garlic, minced
3 tablespoons packed brown sugar
¾ teaspoon salt
¼ teaspoon dried tarragon leaves
¼ teaspoon ground cinnamon

1. Combine mustard seeds, dry mustard and water in small bowl. Cover; let stand at least 4 hours or overnight.

2. Combine vinegar, onion, garlic, sugar, salt, tarragon and cinnamon in nonmetal heavy 1-quart saucepan. Bring to a boil over high heat; reduce heat to medium. Boil, uncovered, about 7 to 10 minutes until mixture is reduced by half.

3. Pour vinegar mixture through fine sieve into food processor bowl. Rinse saucepan. Add mustard mixture to vinegar mixture; process about 1 minute or until mustard seeds are chopped but not puréed. Pour into same saucepan. Cook over low heat until mustard is thick, stirring constantly. Store tightly covered or in decorative gift jars up to 1 year in refrigerator.

Makes about 1 cup mustard

Smoked Turkey and Provolone Croissants

⅓ cup GREY POUPON®
    COUNTRY DIJON® Mustard
2 tablespoons mayonnaise*
1 tablespoon chopped fresh basil leaves
4 croissants, split horizontally
1 cup fresh spinach leaves
6 ounces deli sliced smoked turkey breast
1 small red onion, thinly sliced
4 ounces deli sliced provolone cheese
1 medium tomato, thinly sliced

*Low-fat mayonnaise may be substituted for regular mayonnaise.

In small bowl, blend mustard, mayonnaise and basil. Spread mustard mixture on cut sides of each croissant. Layer spinach leaves, turkey, onion, cheese and tomato on croissant bottoms; replace croissant tops. Serve immediately.

Makes 4 sandwiches

Smoked Turkey and Provolone Croissants

N to O

What does *à la niçoise* mean? *Bake a pan of sticky pecan buns.* What is the connection between okra and gumbo? *Learn how to stop crying over onions.* Why is an orange orange? *Cook up a scrumptious omelet.*

Classic French Onion Soup
(recipe on page 341)

Nachos Olé

NACHO

Nachos, which originated in the American Southwest, may be as simple as corn chips covered with cheese sauce and chilies or as elaborate as a layered combination of tortilla chips, refried beans, shredded beef or chicken, melted cheese, guacamole, sour cream, tomatoes and chilies. Nachos are usually served as a hearty snack or an appetizer.

❦

Nachos Olé

1½ **cups canned refried beans**
1½ **cups (6 ounces) shredded
    Monterey Jack cheese**
1½ **cups (6 ounces) shredded
    Cheddar cheese**
6 **dozen corn tortilla chips**
1 **large tomato, seeded, chopped**
½ **cup thinly sliced canned
    jalapeño peppers**

1. Warm refried beans in small skillet over low heat.

2. Preheat oven to 400°F. Combine cheeses in small bowl; set aside.

3. Spread 1 teaspoon beans on each tortilla chip. Arrange chips in single layer with edges overlapping slightly on 2 to 3 baking sheets or large ovenproof plates. Sprinkle chips evenly with tomato and jalapeños; sprinkle with reserved cheeses.

4. Bake 5 to 8 minutes until cheeses are bubbly and melted. Garnish as desired. Serve immediately.
Makes 4 to 6 appetizer servings

NAPOLEON

A Napoleon is a rich elegant dessert pastry consisting of thin crisp sheets of puff pastry layered with a creamy filling or whipped cream. The top may be glazed with a thin frosting. It is unclear whether Napoleons originated in France, Italy or Denmark. They are oblong in shape and just large enough for one serving.

❦

NECTARINE

The word nectarine derived most likely from the Greek nektar, or "drink of the gods." Nectarines are smooth-skinned cousins to the peach. They are generally sweeter, firmer and juicier than peaches with skins that are deep yellow under a red blush. Almost all the domestic crop is grown in California.

Uses: Nectarines are most often eaten as a snack but may also be pitted and sliced for fruit salads.

• Sliced nectarines can top waffles, pancakes or French toast. Chopped nectarines may be used as an ingredient in salsas, relishes and chutneys. Purée nectarines with milk or fruit juices as a beverage.

• Slightly underripe nectarines may be poached in sugar syrup.

• Nectarines may be substituted in most recipes using peaches.

Varieties: Although there are over 150 varieties of nectarines, they differ very little in color, shape, texture, taste and size. Like peaches, they may be clingstone or freestone.

Availability: Nectarines are available throughout the summer, but they are most flavorful at the end of the summer in August and early September. Those found in markets in the winter and early spring most likely come from South America and the Middle East and may be less sweet.

Buying Tips: Choose firm nectarines with a pleasant fruity fragrance and bright-colored skins that yield slightly to pressure. Hard, green-looking fruit will not ripen properly. Avoid fruit that is bruised, shriveled or mushy.

Yield: 1 pound nectarines = 4 small or 3 medium; 2½ cups chopped.

Storage: Ripen fruit for two or three days at room temperature in a paper bag. When ripe, nectarines may be stored for three to five days in the refrigerator. Longer chilling may diminish flavor and juiciness.

Basic Preparation: Wash nectarines under cold running water before eating. Nectarines do not need to be peeled.

Fruit-Filled Chocolate Dreams

> 1 envelope (1.3 ounces) dry whipped topping mix
> 1 tablespoon HERSHEY'S Cocoa
> ½ cup cold skim milk
> ½ teaspoon vanilla extract
> Assorted fresh fruit, cut up
> Chocolate Sauce (recipe follows)

Place foil on cookie sheet. In small mixer bowl, stir together topping mix and cocoa. Add milk and vanilla. Beat on high speed of electric mixer until stiff peaks form. Spoon topping into 5 mounds onto prepared cookie sheet. With spoon, shape into 4-inch shells. Freeze until firm, about 1 hour. To serve, fill center of each frozen shell with about ⅓ cup assorted fresh fruit; drizzle with 1 tablespoon Chocolate Sauce. Garnish as desired. Serve immediately.

Makes 5 servings

Chocolate Sauce

> ¾ cup sugar
> ⅓ cup HERSHEY'S Cocoa
> 1 tablespoon cornstarch
> ¾ cup water
> 1 tablespoon margarine
> 1 teaspoon vanilla extract

In small saucepan, combine sugar, cocoa and cornstarch; gradually stir in water. Cook over medium heat, stirring constantly, until mixture comes to a boil; boil 1 minute. Remove from heat; add margarine and vanilla, stirring until smooth. Cover; refrigerate until cold.

Tip

The flesh of nectarines browns quickly when cut. When using nectarines raw in salads and desserts, dip cut pieces in a mixture of water and lemon juice (6 parts water to 1 part lemon juice).

NIÇOISE

Niçoise, which is shortened from à la niçoise, means "as prepared in Nice," the city on the French Riviera. These dishes have a Mediterranean influence and include ingredient such as tomatoes, garlic, black olives, anchovies and sometimes olive oil and capers. The classic salad niçoise contains these ingredients plus tuna, green beans, onions, hard-cooked eggs and herbs. Niçoise olives are small dark olives that are cured in brine and packed in oil.

❧

Salad Niçoise

Salad Niçoise

1 clove garlic, halved
1 small head iceberg lettuce, leaves separated
8 ounces fresh green beans, trimmed and steamed until tender-crisp
1 (6½-ounce) can tuna packed in water, drained and flaked
3 tomatoes, cut into wedges
2 hard-boiled eggs, shelled and cut into wedges
1 green bell pepper, seeded and cut into rings
1 small red onion, thinly sliced
¼ cucumber, sliced
1 (2-ounce) can anchovy fillets, drained
12 oil-cured black olives
¼ cup FILIPPO BERIO® Olive Oil
3 tablespoons white wine vinegar
1 to 2 tablespoons chopped fresh herbs (chives, parsley or marjoram)
1 teaspoon Dijon-style mustard
½ teaspoon sugar
Salt and freshly ground black pepper

Rub inside of large bowl with cut garlic. Line bowl with lettuce leaves. Arrange green beans, tuna, tomatoes, eggs, bell pepper, onion, cucumber, anchovies and olives over lettuce, keeping each ingredient in a separate group.

In small screw-top jar, combine olive oil, vinegar, herbs, mustard and sugar. Cover; shake vigorously until well blended. Drizzle over salad. Season to taste with salt and black pepper.

Makes 4 servings

NUT

Nuts today are almost all commercially grown, unlike the early days in the United States when families gathered nuts in forests. Nuts are the dry fruit of trees. The outside covering of most nuts is the shell, the inside edible part is called the "meat." Some foods we call nuts are actually seeds, but they are included here. For example, peanuts are seeds of a legume and Brazil nuts are seeds of a South American tree.

🌱

Varieties: There are many kinds of nuts available in a variety of forms. Following is a description of the most common types of nuts sold in the United States:

Almonds are oval, flat white nuts with thin brown skin and light tan pitted shells. There are two types of almonds, bitter and sweet. The bitter variety contains toxic prussic acid when raw. The acid is destroyed by heating, so commercial processors use this stronger flavored almond to make extract and liqueurs. Sweet almonds have a delicate, slightly sweet flavor and are used for baking and cooking.

Cashews are the seeds of a tropical fruit called a cashew apple. The nut grows on the outside of the fruit at its base. This nut has a kidney-shaped shell which is highly toxic. The shell is removed commercially, and the nut is cleaned before marketing. The nut itself is kidney-shaped with a sweet, buttery flavor and crunchy texture. Cashews are 48 percent fat. They are generally used for snacking and cooking, especially in Chinese stir-fries.

Macadamia nuts are native to Australia, but most of the commercial crop is now grown in Hawaii. This small, round nut has a hard brown shell with cream colored meat and a

Almond Butter Chicken (recipe on page 328)

buttery rich, slightly sweet flavor. Most are sold shelled, either roasted or raw. They are used for snacking and baking.

Peanuts are grown throughout the southern part of the United States and have a soft, thin netted tan-colored shell. The nuts have a reddish-brown papery skin, ivory-colored flesh and a buttery, nutty flavor that is intensified by roasting. They are used for snacking, baking and for peanut butter.

Pecans are native to the United States and a member of the hickory family. They are widely grown in Georgia, Oklahoma and Texas. The nut has a smooth tan shell which is thin, but hard. The flesh is beige with a thin brown exterior. These nuts are widely eaten out of hand and used in a variety of sweet and savory dishes.

Pine nuts are found inside pine cones. The cones are generally heated to extract the nuts. This labor-intensive process makes these nuts expensive. They have a long, narrow ivory-colored "meat" and a faint pine flavor. They are used in Mediterranean cooking and are an important ingredient in pesto.

Tip

Because nuts become rancid in a relatively short time, buy them at a store with rapid turnover. Always taste nuts before using them. Rancid nuts will ruin the flavor of a dish.

Pistachio nuts have a hard tan shell which is sometimes dyed pink or blanched until white. They are grown in California, Iran, Italy and Turkey. The inside meat has a pale green color and a delicate, subtly sweet flavor. Generally eaten as an out-of-hand snack, pistachios may also be used in baking and cooking.

Walnuts are encased in a hard, light brown shell. The two most popular varieties are the English and the black walnut. The English variety is most common and has a milder flavor. Black walnuts have a strong, rich flavor. The black walnut shell is extremely difficult to crack and can stain your skin.

Availability: Shelled nuts are available all year and are sold in bulk, vacuum-packed in cans and jars, or in cellophane bags. Depending on the specific type of nut, they may be sold oil- or dry-roasted and salted or unsalted. They are sometimes sweetened with sugar or honey, seasoned with spices or covered with chocolate. Unshelled nuts are available in bulk especially during November and December.

Buying Tips: When purchasing nuts in their shell look for clean, unbroken shells without cracks or splits. Nuts should feel heavy for their size and appear well shaped. Shelled nuts should be plump, crisp and uniform in size and color.

Yield: 1 pound unshelled nuts = 3 to 4 cups chopped.

Storage: Store unshelled nuts in a cool, dry and dark place. Heat, light and moisture encourage rancidity. They can be kept for several months. Shelled nuts will keep in an airtight container up to 4 months refrigerated and 6 months if frozen.

Basic Preparation: Toasting gives nuts a rich, fuller flavor. To toast nuts spread them in single layer on a baking sheet and toast them in a preheated 350°F oven for 8 to 10 minutes. Watch carefully and stir

them once or twice for even browning. An alternative method is to stir the nuts in a heavy skillet over low heat for 3 to 4 minutes until brown. Always cool nuts before adding them to other ingredients.

Almond Butter Chicken

2 boneless, skinless chicken breasts, halved (about 1¼ pounds)
2 tablespoons all-purpose flour
½ teaspoon salt
½ teaspoon ground black pepper
1 egg, beaten
1 package (2¼ ounces) sliced almonds
¼ cup butter
Orange Sauce (recipe follows)

1. Place each chicken breast half between 2 pieces of plastic wrap. Pound to ¼-inch thickness. Coat chicken with flour. Sprinkle with salt and pepper.

2. Dip 1 side of each chicken breast into egg; press with almonds.

3. Melt butter in large skillet over medium-high heat. Add chicken, almond side down; cook 3 to 5 minutes until almonds are toasted. Turn chicken. Reduce heat to medium-low; cook 10 to 12 minutes until chicken is no longer pink in center. Serve, almond side up, with Orange Sauce. Garnish as desired.

Makes 4 servings

Orange Sauce

1 tablespoon brown sugar
2 teaspoons cornstarch
Juice of 1 orange (about ½ cup)
2 tablespoons butter
1 teaspoon grated orange peel

Combine sugar and cornstarch in saucepan. Stir in juice, butter and orange peel. Cook over medium heat until thickened, stirring constantly.

Makes ⅔ cup sauce

*Favorite recipe from **Wisconsin Milk Marketing Board***

Tip

To reduce the risk of overprocessing when grinding nuts in a food processor, add a small amount of the flour or sugar from the recipe. If they are overprocessed, nuts will become nut butter.

White Chocolate Chunk & Macadamia Nut Brownie Cookies

1½ cups firmly packed light brown
    sugar
⅔ **CRISCO®** Stick *or* ⅔ cup
    CRISCO All-Vegetable
    Shortening
1 tablespoon water
1 teaspoon vanilla
2 eggs
1½ cups all-purpose flour
⅓ cup unsweetened cocoa powder
½ teaspoon salt
¼ teaspoon baking soda
1 cup white chocolate chunks or
    chips
1 cup coarsely chopped
    macadamia nuts

1. Heat oven to 375°F. Place sheets of foil on countertop for cooling cookies.

2. Place brown sugar, shortening, water and vanilla in large bowl. Beat at medium speed of electric mixer until well blended. Add eggs; beat well.

3. Combine flour, cocoa, salt and baking soda. Add to shortening mixture; beat at low speed just until blended. Stir in white chocolate chunks and macadamia nuts.

4. Drop dough by rounded measuring tablespoonfuls 2 inches apart onto ungreased baking sheet.

5. Bake one baking sheet at a time at 375°F for 7 to 9 minutes or until cookies are set. *Do not overbake.* Cool 2 minutes on baking sheet. Remove cookies to foil to cool completely.

Makes about 3 dozen cookies

White Chocolate Chunk & Macadamia Nut Brownie Cookies

Killer Brownies

Killer Brownies

> ½ **cup hazelnuts or unblanched almonds**
> ¾ **cup butter or margarine**
> 2 **cups sugar**
> ¾ **cup unsweetened cocoa powder**
> 3 **eggs, slightly beaten**
> 2 **teaspoons vanilla extract**
> 1 **cup all-purpose flour**
> 1½ **cups fresh or thawed frozen raspberries**
>   **White Chocolate Ganache (recipe follows)**
>   **Chocolate Ganache (recipe follows)**
> 3 **to 4 tablespoons raspberry jam**

1. Preheat oven to 350°F. To remove skins from hazelnuts, spread in single layer on baking sheet. Bake 10 to 12 minutes until skins begin to flake off; let cool slightly. Wrap hazelnuts in heavy kitchen towel; rub against towel to remove as much of the skins as possible.

2. Place hazelnuts in food processor; process using on/off pulsing action until hazelnuts are finely chopped, but not pasty. Set aside.

3. Lightly grease 2 (8-inch) square baking pans. Line bottoms of pans with foil; lightly grease foil.

4. Melt butter in medium saucepan over medium heat, stirring occasionally. Remove saucepan from heat. Stir in sugar and cocoa until well blended. Stir in eggs and vanilla until smooth. Stir in flour just until blended. Pour batter evenly into prepared pans. Place raspberries on top of batter, pressing gently into batter.

5. Bake 15 to 20 minutes until center is just set. *Do not overbake.* Cool brownies completely in pans on wire racks.

6. Run knife around edges of pans to loosen brownies from sides. Gently work flexible metal spatula down edges and slightly under brownies to loosen from bottoms of pans. Hold wire rack over top of 1 pan; invert to release brownie. Remove foil; discard. Invert brownie onto plate.

7. Prepare White Chocolate Ganache and Chocolate Ganache. Reserve 2 tablespoons White Chocolate Ganache; spread remaining White Chocolate Ganache evenly on brownie with spatula. Spread raspberry jam on top of ganache.

8. Unmold remaining brownie as directed in Step 6. Place, flat side down, on bottom layer, pressing gently to seal. Spread Chocolate Ganache evenly on top layer. Drizzle reserved 2 tablespoons White Chocolate Ganache over Chocolate Ganache. Sprinkle with hazelnuts. Cut into 16 squares. Store tightly covered in refrigerator up to 1 week.

Makes 16 brownies

White Chocolate Ganache

1 cup (6 ounces) white chocolate chips or chopped white chocolate, divided
3 tablespoons whipping cream
½ teaspoon almond extract

1. Combine ½ cup chocolate and whipping cream in medium saucepan. Heat over medium heat until chocolate is half melted, stirring occasionally.

2. Remove saucepan from heat. Stir in remaining ½ cup chocolate and almond extract until mixture is smooth. Keep warm. (Ganache is semi-firm at room temperature.)

Makes ¾ cup ganache

Chocolate Ganache

2 tablespoons whipping cream
1 tablespoon butter
½ cup (2 ounces) semisweet chocolate chips or chopped semisweet chocolate
½ teaspoon vanilla extract

1. Combine whipping cream and butter in small saucepan. Heat over medium heat until mixture boils, stirring frequently.

2. Remove saucepan from heat. Stir in chocolate and vanilla until mixture is smooth, returning to heat for 20- to 30-second intervals as needed to melt chocolate. Keep warm.

Makes ¾ cup ganache

Maple-Cinnamon Almonds

¼ cup maple-flavored syrup
3 tablespoons butter
2 tablespoons sugar
1½ teaspoons ground cinnamon
¼ teaspoon salt
1 pound blanched whole almonds
¼ cup crystallized vanilla sugar* (optional)

*Look for crystallized sugar where either gourmet coffees or cake decorating supplies are sold.

1. Preheat oven to 325°F. Line 15×10×1-inch jelly-roll pan with foil.

2. Combine syrup, butter, sugar, cinnamon and salt in heavy medium saucepan. Bring to a boil over high heat, stirring frequently. Boil 30 seconds. Remove from heat; stir in almonds, tossing to coat evenly.

3. Spread almonds in single layer in prepared pan. Bake about 40 minutes or until almonds are crisp and dry, stirring every 15 minutes. Immediately transfer almonds to baking sheet lined with foil; sprinkle with crystallized sugar. Cool completely. Store in airtight container at room temperature up to 1 week.

Makes about 3½ cups nuts

Note: If almonds become tacky upon storing, place on baking sheet lined with foil. Bake at 325°F 15 to 20 minutes; cool.

Maple-Cinnamon Almonds

Spicy Tuna and Linguine with Garlic and Pine Nuts

2 tablespoons olive oil
4 cloves garlic, minced
2 cups sliced mushrooms
½ cup chopped onion
½ teaspoon crushed red pepper
2½ cups chopped plum tomatoes
1 can (14½ ounces) chicken broth *plus* water to equal 2 cups
½ teaspoon salt
¼ teaspoon coarsely ground black pepper
1 package (9 ounces) uncooked fresh linguine
1 can (12 ounces) STARKIST® Solid White Tuna, drained and chunked
⅓ cup chopped fresh cilantro
⅓ cup toasted pine nuts or almonds

In 12-inch skillet, heat olive oil over medium-high heat; sauté garlic, mushrooms, onion and red pepper in oil until golden brown. Add tomatoes, chicken broth mixture, salt and black pepper; bring to a boil.

Spicy Tuna and Linguine with Garlic and Pine Nuts

Separate linguine into strands; place in skillet and spoon sauce over. Reduce heat to simmer; cook, covered, 4 minutes more or until cooked through. Toss gently; add tuna and cilantro. Toss again. Sprinkle with pine nuts. Garnish as desired. Serve immediately.

Makes 4 to 6 servings

Prep time: 12 minutes

Quicky Sticky Buns

3 tablespoons packed brown sugar, divided
¼ cup KARO® Light or Dark Corn Syrup
¼ cup coarsely chopped pecans
2 tablespoons softened MAZOLA® Margarine, divided
1 can (8 ounces) refrigerated crescent dinner rolls
1 teaspoon ground cinnamon

Preheat oven to 350°F. In small bowl combine 2 tablespoons brown sugar, corn syrup, pecans and 1 tablespoon margarine. Spoon about 2 teaspoons mixture into each of 9 (2½-inch) muffin pan cups. Unroll entire crescent roll dough; pinch seams together to form 1 rectangle. Combine remaining 1 tablespoon brown sugar and cinnamon. Spread dough with remaining 1 tablespoon margarine; sprinkle with cinnamon mixture. Roll up from short end. Cut into 9 slices. Place one slice in each prepared muffin pan cup. Bake 25 minutes or until golden brown. Immediately invert pan onto cookie sheet or tray; cool 10 minutes.

Makes 9 buns

Prep time: 15 minutes
Bake time: 25 minutes, plus cooling

Barbecued Peanuts

¼ cup barbecue sauce
2 tablespoons butter or
   margarine, melted
¾ teaspoon garlic salt
⅛ teaspoon ground red pepper*
1 jar (16 ounces) dry roasted
   lightly salted peanuts

*For Spicy Barbecued Peanuts, increase
ground red pepper to ¼ teaspoon.*

1. Preheat oven to 325°F. Grease
13×9-inch baking pan.

2. Whisk together barbecue sauce,
butter, garlic salt and pepper in
medium bowl until well blended.
Add peanuts; toss until evenly coated.
Spread coated peanuts in single layer
in prepared baking pan.

3. Bake 20 to 22 minutes until
peanuts are glazed, stirring
occasionally. Cool completely in pan
on wire rack, stirring occasionally to
prevent sticking.

4. Spoon into clean dry decorative
tin. Store tightly covered at room
temperature up to 2 weeks.
Makes about 4 cups nuts

Orange-Walnut Chippers

½ cup all-purpose flour
¼ teaspoon baking soda
¼ teaspoon salt
½ cup butter or margarine,
   softened
1 cup packed light brown sugar
1 large egg
1 tablespoon grated orange peel
1½ cups uncooked rolled oats
1 cup semisweet chocolate chips
½ cup coarsely chopped walnuts

1. Preheat oven to 375°F. Lightly
grease baking sheets.

2. Combine flour, baking soda and
salt in small bowl; set aside.

3. Beat butter and sugar in large bowl
with electric mixer at medium speed
until light and fluffy, scraping down
side of bowl once. Beat in egg and
orange peel, scraping down side of
bowl once. Add reserved flour
mixture. Beat at low speed, scraping
down side of bowl once. Stir in oats
with spoon. Stir in chips and walnuts.
Drop teaspoonfuls of dough 2 inches
apart onto prepared baking sheets.

4. Bake 10 to 12 minutes until golden
brown. Let cookies stand on baking
sheets 2 minutes. Remove cookies to
wire racks; cool completely. Store
tightly covered at room temperature
or freeze up to 3 months.
Makes about 3 dozen cookies

OIL

*Cooking oils are obtained from plant
sources, such as seeds, nuts and
beans. Their culinary uses are many.
Since they are fats, oils provide flavor,
richness, lubrication and are a means
of browning foods.*

☙

When selecting oils, two
considerations must be kept in mind:
flavor and smoke point (the
temperature at which heated oil
begins to burn and decompose). An
inexperienced cook may wish to have
only two oils on hand. An all-purpose
oil for sautéing and frying is a must.
Choose a flavorless oil, such as
soybean or safflower. Olive oil adds
flavor to salad dressing and
Mediterranean dishes. Purchase other
oils only as you need them.

Common Cooking Oils: Corn oil has
little flavor and a high smoke point. It
is good for frying.

Olive oil is produced when tree-
ripened olives are pressed. The best
olive oils are extracted using a
chemical-free process. They can be
classified as extra-virgin or virgin.
Both are cold-pressed oils from the

first pressing of the olives. Extra-virgin has a lower acidity and a full-bodied fruity flavor. It is the most expensive of olive oils. Use it when the fruity flavor will lend a pleasing note to foods, such as in salad dressings, for dipping bread and in vegetable dishes. Products labeled olive oil are an all-purpose blend of olive oils. They are less expensive and blander in flavor, making them an economical choice for most uses. Light olive oil is olive oil that has been filtered to make it lighter in flavor. Filtering also increases its smoke point making it a good choice for sautéing and pan-frying.

Peanut oil has a faint peanut flavor and a high smoke point. It is a good oil for frying and stir-frying.

Safflower oil is flavorless and has a high smoke point, making it an ideal choice for frying.

Sesame oil is amber-colored oil pressed from toasted sesame seeds. It has a strong, nutty flavor that when used sparingly adds a unique flavor to foods, such as stir-fries, Asian noodles and fish dishes. It is not used for frying. There is also a pale-colored cold-pressed sesame oil that is available in health food stores. It is used for cooking and as a salad oil. The two types are not interchangeable.

Soybean oil has little flavor and a high smoke point. It is excellent for frying and is the most common cooking oil in the United States.

Walnut oil is made from walnuts. This expensive oil is usually imported from France. It has a pleasant nutty flavor and is often added to salad dressings. Look for it in large supermarkets and gourmet food stores. Buy walnut oil in small quantities because a little goes a long way.

Flavored oils are oils to which herbs, spices and seasonings, such as garlic and chili peppers, have been added. Use them when you need a quick burst of flavor.

> ## Tip
>
> *To remove the fuzz from fuzzy varieties of okra, rinse pods under cold running water and scrub lightly with a vegetable brush.*

Storage: Oils should be stored in a cool, dark place. Cold-pressed sesame oil is more perishable and should always be refrigerated. Oils will keep from three to six months. If a cool spot is not available they should be refrigerated. Buy small quantities of oils that you use infrequently. Heat, light and time will turn oils rancid. A rancid oil will ruin any dish it is used in.

OKRA

Okra is native to Northern Africa and Asia. It is most commonly grown and used in the South, particularly in Creole cooking. It is a member of the edible hibiscus family. Okra are slender, bright green pods filled with many small white seeds. Some pods are fuzzy. When cooked, okra develops a gumminess that makes it a good thickener for soups and stews. Known as ngumbo in Africa, okra lent its name to gumbo, the Creole stew that it thickens. Okra has a mild flavor similar to that of green beans.

☙

Uses: Okra is used in stews and soups, especially gumbo. It teams especially well with tomatoes.

• Okra can be pickled.

Availability: Fresh okra is available all year in the southern United States. In other markets the peak season is May through October. It is also available canned and frozen.

Buying Tips: Look for firm, brightly colored pods measuring under four inches in length. Longer pods are often tough and fibrous. Avoid pods which are dull, limp or blemished.

Yield: 1 pound okra = 2¼ cups sliced.
1 (10-ounce) package frozen okra = 1¼ cups.

Storage: Store fresh okra unwashed in a plastic bag in the refrigerator for up to three days.

Basic Preparation: Rinse okra under cold running water. Tiny okra pods may be used whole; avoid piercing

the pods. To prepare larger pods, trim the stem ends. Discard the stem ends. Cut the okra into slices or leave whole.

To prevent okra from becoming gummy, avoid long cooking and take care to leave the pods whole. Okra that has been sautéed or breaded and fried will not be gummy. If you wish to take advantage of the gumminess, use sliced okra in long-cooking dishes, such as stews and soups.

Shrimp Okra Gumbo

¼ cup *plus* 1 tablespoon vegetable oil, divided
¼ cup all-purpose flour
1 medium onion, chopped
1 small green bell pepper, chopped
2 cloves garlic, minced
2½ cups water
1 can (14½ ounces) tomatoes, cut-up, undrained
½ teaspoon dried thyme leaves
½ teaspoon salt
¼ teaspoon ground red pepper
2 bay leaves
8 ounces fresh or thawed frozen okra
1 pound raw medium shrimp, peeled, deveined
5 cups hot cooked rice
Fresh herb sprig (optional)

1. To make roux, cook and stir ¼ cup oil and flour together in medium saucepan over medium-low heat 20 minutes or until mixture is a light brown color; set aside.

2. Heat remaining 1 tablespoon oil in 5-quart Dutch oven or large saucepan over medium-high heat. Add onion, bell pepper and garlic; cook and stir until bell pepper is crisp-tender. Stir in water, tomatoes with liquid, thyme, salt, red pepper and bay leaves. Bring to a boil over high heat. Reduce heat to medium-low; simmer, uncovered, 15 minutes.

3. Meanwhile wash okra; cut into ¾-inch slices. Stir roux and okra into tomato mixture. Bring to a boil over high heat. Reduce heat to medium-low; simmer, uncovered, 20 minutes, stirring occasionally.

4. Add shrimp and cook 5 minutes or until shrimp turn pink and opaque. Discard bay leaves. Serve gumbo over rice. Garnish with herb sprig, if desired.   *Makes 5 servings*

Technique for Shrimp Okra Gumbo

Step 1. *Stirring roux until light brown in color.*

Shrimp Okra Gumbo

OLIVE

The olive is a fruit native to the sunny Mediterranean region. Hardy olive trees now flourish in other subtropical areas, such as California, Arizona, New Mexico and Latin America. Olives are grown both for their fruit and oil. There are dozens of varieties, each bearing a small, oily fruit containing a pit. Olives vary in size and color by their specific type. All fresh olives have a bitter flavor. They are either pressed for oil or cured for eating. The curing process removes the bitterness and produces the characteristic flavor and shiny appearance.

☙

Uses: Olives are eaten as an appetizer or meal accompaniment.

• Ripe (black) olives are used in Latin and Mediterranean cuisines.

• Spanish-style olives are added to sandwich fillings, potato and pasta salads, and martinis.

• Tapenade is an olive spread flavored with anchovy, garlic and capers from southern France. It is traditionally made with ripe olives and spread on bread.

Varieties: Black, or Mission, olives are ripe green olives that obtain their characteristic black color and flavor from lye-curing and oxygenation. Black olives are often referred to as ripe olives. They have a mellow, smooth taste and are sold pitted, unpitted, sliced and chopped.

Dry-cured olives have been packed in salt to remove their moisture. They are available pitted, unpitted and stuffed with herbs.

Kalamata olives are from Greece. They are almond-shaped with a dark purplish-black color. They are soaked in a wine vinegar marinade and have a rich, fruity flavor. These olives are generally sold unpitted.

Niçoise olives from the Provence region of France are small, dark olives that are cured in brine and then packed in olive oil. They are sold whole.

Spanish-style, or green olives, are picked underripe, soaked in lye and then fermented for six months or more. They have a tart, salty taste and are sold pitted, unpitted and stuffed with pimiento.

Availability: Both pitted ripe black olives and stuffed Spanish olives are readily available all year in jars in supermarkets. Some markets also offer a variety of other imported and domestic olives. Dry-cured olives are available in jars at some large supermarkets or at gourmet food markets.

Storage: Leftover opened jars of olives should be kept refrigerated in their brine or oil in a tightly covered container. Leftover canned olives should be transferred to a glass jar for storage. Olives will keep for several weeks. When the olives begin to turn soft, discard them. Unopened cans and jars of olives can be stored for up to two years.

Quick Mediterranean Fish

1 medium onion, sliced
2 tablespoons olive oil
1 clove garlic, crushed
1 can (14½ ounces) DEL MONTE® Italian Recipe Stewed Tomatoes
4 tablespoons DEL MONTE Thick & Chunky Salsa, Medium
¼ teaspoon ground cinnamon
1½ pounds firm fish (such as halibut, red snapper or sea bass)
12 stuffed green olives, halved crosswise

Microwave Directions: In 1½-quart microwavable dish, combine onion, oil and garlic. Cover and microwave on HIGH 3 minutes; drain. Stir in tomatoes, salsa and cinnamon. Top with fish and olives. Cover and microwave on HIGH 3 to 4 minutes or until fish flakes easily with fork. Garnish with chopped parsley, if desired. *Makes 4 to 6 servings*

Prep time: 7 minutes
Microwave cook time: 7 minutes

Provençal Pasta Shells

12 uncooked jumbo pasta shells
1 can (6 ounces) pitted ripe olives, drained
2 tablespoons olive oil
1 teaspoon fresh lemon juice
½ teaspoon dried thyme leaves
1½ cups (6 ounces) shredded Gruyère or mozzarella cheese, divided
⅓ cup herb-seasoned bread crumbs
1 teaspoon bottled minced garlic
1 jar (14 ounces) purchased chunky spaghetti sauce

1. Microwave Directions: Cook pasta according to package directions; drain. Rinse with cool water; drain again.

2. Meanwhile, combine olives, oil, juice and thyme in food processor; process until puréed. Transfer to small bowl; stir in 1¼ cups cheese, bread crumbs and garlic. Set aside.

3. Spread spaghetti sauce into 10×7-inch shallow baking dish. Stuff each pasta shell with 2 tablespoons olive mixture. Arrange stuffed shells on sauce. Sprinkle with remaining ¼ cup cheese. Cover with plastic wrap, turning back corner to vent. Microwave at HIGH 3 to 4 minutes or until cheese is melted and sauce is hot. *Makes 4 servings*

Provençal Pasta Shells

OMELET

An omelet is made of beaten eggs and seasonings and cooked in an omelet pan (see page 156) or a skillet with sloping sides until set and the top is still moist. An omelet can be topped with a filling, then folded into halves or thirds to enclose the filling. Common fillings include cheese, ham, sausage, vegetables and herbs. The omelet may be served with a sauce.

There is another type of omelet known as the puffy omelet. The egg whites and yolks are beaten separately and then folded together to create a light, airy omelet. A puffy omelet is cooked on top of the range until the bottom is set and then finished in a preheated oven. An oven-proof omelet pan or skillet is needed. Puffy omelets are often filled or topped with a sauce.

☙

Roasted Vegetable Omelet with Fresh Salsa

    Fresh Salsa (recipe follows)
  4 small red boiling potatoes, cut into quarters
⅓ cup coarsely chopped red bell pepper
  2 slices bacon, chopped
  1 green onion, cut into thin slices
  3 eggs
  1 tablespoon water
    Salt and ground black pepper
  1 tablespoon butter or margarine
⅓ cup shredded Colby cheese
    Fresh cilantro sprigs (optional)

Roasted Vegetable Omelet with Fresh Salsa

1. Prepare Fresh Salsa.

2. Preheat oven to 425°F. Combine potatoes, bell pepper, bacon and onion in greased 15×10-inch jelly-roll pan.

3. Bake 30 minutes or until potatoes are fork-tender, stirring occasionally.

4. Meanwhile, whisk together eggs, water, salt and black pepper to taste in small bowl. Melt butter in 10-inch skillet over medium-high heat. Pour egg mixture into skillet; cook until eggs begin to set. Gently lift cooked edges with spatula to allow uncooked eggs to flow under cooked portion.

5. When omelet is set, but not dry, and bottom is light golden brown, remove from heat. Place roasted vegetable mixture over ½ of omelet; sprinkle with cheese. Gently fold omelet in half with spatula. Transfer to serving plate. Serve with Fresh Salsa. Garnish with cilantro, if desired. *Makes 2 servings*

Fresh Salsa

> 3 medium plum tomatoes, seeded, chopped
> 2 tablespoons chopped onion
> 1 small jalapeño pepper, stemmed, seeded, minced*
> 1 tablespoon chopped fresh cilantro
> 1 tablespoon fresh lime juice
> ¼ teaspoon salt
> ⅛ teaspoon ground black pepper

Jalapeño peppers can sting and irritate the skin; wear rubber or plastic gloves when handling peppers and do not touch eyes. Wash hands after handling.

Stir together tomatoes, onion, jalapeño, cilantro, juice, salt and black pepper. Refrigerate until ready to serve. *Makes 1 cup salsa*

Three-Egg Omelet

> 1 tablespoon butter or margarine
> 3 eggs, lightly beaten
> Salt and ground black pepper
> Fillings: Shredded cheese, shredded crabmeat, cooked sliced mushrooms, cooked chopped onion, avocado slices, chopped ham, cooked small shrimp, cooked chopped bell pepper, chopped tomatoes, cooked chopped asparagus and/or cooked chopped broccoli

1. Melt butter in 10-inch skillet over medium heat. Add eggs; lift cooked edges with spatula to allow uncooked eggs to flow under cooked portion. Season with salt and black pepper. Shake pan to loosen omelet. Cook until set.

2. Place desired fillings on ½ of omelet. Fold in half. Transfer to serving plate. Serve immediately. *Makes 1 serving*

ONION

Onions have been used since prehistoric times. They continue to play an essential role in cuisines around the world. Like asparagus and garlic, onions are a member of the lily family. They are used as both a seasoning and as a vegetable.

☙

Varieties: There are two types of onions: green and dry.

Green onions, or scallions, are onions that are harvested when immature. They are long and finger-thin with white bases and green tops, both of which are edible. They are sold in bunches. Green onions are easy to grow in a home garden. If you plant them every few weeks, you will have a constant supply during the entire growing season.

Tip

When onions are cut, they release sulfur compounds that bring tears to the eyes. Try one of these suggestions for minimizing tears:

- *Wear glasses or goggles.*

- *Place the onion in the freezer for 20 minutes before chopping.*

- *Chew a piece of bread while peeling and chopping.*

- *Chop onions with your mouth closed.*

- *Work under an exhaust fan.*

- *Work as quickly as possible, never touching your eyes.*

- *Wash your hands, knife and cutting surfaces when finished.*

Red onions (also called Italian onions) may be round, oval or slightly flat. They are covered with a dark red to purple skin. When cut, their rings of whitish flesh are outlined in purple. Red onions are generally sweet unless they have been stored for a long time.

Spanish onions are large and round with a caramel-colored skin. These are fairly sweet and can be eaten raw.

Vidalia, Maui and Walla Walla are all very sweet onions. They have taken their names from the areas where they grow: Vidalia, Georgia; Maui, Hawaii; and Walla Walla, Washington. Vidalia are generally the sweetest.

Availability: Green onions are available all year. They are most abundant in the spring and summer. Bermuda, Spanish and red onions are available all year but they are sweeter in the late summer and early fall. Sweet onion varieties have short seasons: Maui from April to July, Vidalia from May to June, Walla Walla from June to September.

Buying Tips: Green onions should have firm white bottoms and crisp green tops. Dry onions should feel heavy for their size, dry and firm to the touch with no soft spots or sprouts. Onions should smell mild when purchased. Avoid excess dirt or dark spots as this may indicate that mold is present.

Yield: 1 pound onions = 3 large or 4 medium onions; 2 to 3 cups chopped.
1 green onion = 1 or 2 tablespoons sliced or chopped.

Storage: Store green onions in the refrigerator in a plastic bag for up to five days. All other onions should be stored in a cool, dry area with good air circulation for up to two months. Sweet onions may not store for quite as long. Check them periodically and discard any soft onions.

All other onions are classified as dry onions, meaning that they are harvested when mature and then allowed to dry until their skins are papery. This group includes: Bermuda, globe, pearl, red, Spanish, Vidalia, Maui and Walla Walla.

Bermuda onions are mild-flavored onions with an oval shape and white skin that has subtle vertical green stripes. They are sweet during the peak of the season (early fall), when they are good raw, but become stronger when stored.

Globe onions (also called yellow onions) are the most common of the dry onions. They are round and small or medium in size with yellowish-gold skins and a strong flavor. Use them for cooking. Globe onions are generally more economical and they keep for some time.

Pearl onions are tiny white onions with a mild flavor. They are usually cooked whole; they make good additions to stews. Pearl onions are also pickled.

Chopping onion with a utility knife.

Cutting onion into thin slices.

Basic Preparation: To prepare green onions, wash them thoroughly and trim off the roots. Remove any wilted or discolored layers. Green onions may be sliced, chopped, cut into lengths or used whole. The green tops can be cooked, but they cook more quickly than the white bases.

To peel dry onions, slice off the stem and root ends, make a shallow lengthwise slit through the papery skin and remove the outer layer of the onion. To peel pearl onions, drop them into boiling water for about two minutes. Drain the onions and plunge them into cold water to stop the cooking. Cut off the stem end. Squeeze the onions between your thumb and forefinger to separate them from the skins.

To slice dry onions, peel the skin. Cut in half through the root end with a utility knife. Place the onion half, cut side down, on a cutting board. Cut into thin vertical slices. Onions may also be cut crosswise into slices. The slices may be separated into rings. To chop onions, place the cut side down on a cutting board. Cut the onion into slices perpendicular to the root end, holding the onion with your fingers to keep it together. Turn the onion half and cut it crosswise. Repeat with the remaining half.

Classic French Onion Soup

    3 tablespoons peanut oil
    3 large yellow onions (about
        2 pounds), halved, sliced
    1 cup dry white wine
    3 cans (about 14 ounces each)
        beef or chicken broth
    ½ teaspoon salt
    ¼ teaspoon ground white pepper
    1 bouquet garni*
    4 slices (1 inch thick) French bread
    4 ounces grated Gruyère cheese
        Fresh thyme sprigs (optional)

*To prepare bouquet garni, tie together 3 sprigs parsley, 2 sprigs thyme and ½ bay leaf with cotton string or enclose herbs in square piece of cheesecloth secured with string.

1. Heat oil in Dutch oven over medium-high heat until hot. Add onions; cook 15 minutes or until lightly browned, stirring frequently. Reduce heat to medium; cook 30 to 45 minutes until onions are deep golden brown, stirring occasionally.

2. Preheat broiler. Add wine to Dutch oven; cook over high heat 3 to 5 minutes until liquid is reduced by half. Add broth, salt, pepper and bouquet garni; bring to a boil. Reduce heat to low. Simmer 15 to 20 minutes. Remove bouquet garni; discard.

3. Toast bread under broiler about 3 minutes per side.

4. Ladle soup into 4 heatproof bowls; top with bread and cheese. Broil, 4 inches from heat, 2 to 3 minutes until cheese is bubbly and browned. Serve immediately. Garnish with thyme, if desired.

Makes 4 servings

Classic French Onion Soup

Onions Baked in Their Papers

**4 medium-size yellow onions
    (about 2½ inches in
    diameter)***
**1½ teaspoons mixed dried herbs,
    such as thyme, sage and
    tarragon**
1 teaspoon sugar
½ teaspoon salt
**   Dash crushed red pepper flakes**
¼ cup butter or margarine, melted
½ cup fresh bread crumbs

Choose onions with skins intact.

1. Preheat oven to 400°F. Line square baking pan with foil.

2. Slice off stem and root ends of onions; discard. Cut 1½×1½-inch cone-shaped indentation in top of each onion. Set onions in prepared pan on root ends.

3. Stir herbs, sugar, salt and pepper flakes into melted butter. Add bread crumbs; mix until blended. Spoon equal amounts of crumb mixture into indentations in onions.

4. Bake about 1 hour or until fork-tender. Garnish as desired.

Makes 4 side-dish servings

Onions Baked in Their Papers

Two-Onion Pork Shreds

½ teaspoon Szechuan
    peppercorns*
1 teaspoon cornstarch
4 teaspoons soy sauce, divided
4 teaspoons dry sherry, divided
7½ teaspoons vegetable oil, divided
8 ounces boneless lean pork
2 teaspoons red wine vinegar
½ teaspoon sugar
2 cloves garlic, minced
½ small yellow onion, cut into
    ¼-inch slices
8 green onions, cut into 2-inch
    pieces
½ teaspoon Oriental sesame oil

*Szechuan peppercorns are deceptively potent. Wear rubber or plastic gloves when crushing them and do not touch your eyes or lips when handling.

1. For marinade, place peppercorns in small skillet. Cook over medium-low heat about 2 minutes or until fragrant, shaking skillet frequently. Let cool. Crush peppercorns with mortar and pestle, or place peppercorns between paper towels and crush with hammer. Transfer peppercorns to medium bowl. Add cornstarch, 2 teaspoons soy sauce, 2 teaspoons sherry and 1½ teaspoons vegetable oil; stir until smooth.

2. Slice pork into ⅛-inch-thick strips; cut strips into 2×½-inch pieces. Add to marinade; stir to coat well. Let stand 30 minutes.

3. Combine remaining 2 teaspoons soy sauce, 2 teaspoons sherry, vinegar and sugar in small bowl; mix well. Set aside.

4. Heat remaining 6 teaspoons vegetable oil in wok or large skillet over high heat. Stir in garlic. Add pork with marinade; stir-fry about 2 minutes or until pork is no longer pink in center. Add yellow onion; stir-fry 1 minute. Add green onions; stir-fry 30 seconds. Add reserved soy sauce mixture; cook and stir 30 seconds. Stir in sesame oil. Serve immediately.

Makes 2 to 3 servings

ORANGE

Sweet, juicy and universally loved, oranges are multifaceted fruits. They are valued for eating whole as well as for their juice and peel. Like many other fruits, they originated in Southeast Asia, but today, the largest supply of oranges comes from the United States, with Florida and California both contributing significant numbers to the total.

☙

Varieties: There are three broad categories of oranges: sweet, loose skinned and bitter.

Navel oranges, so named because of a protuberance at the blossom end that resembles a navel, are the most well-known in retail markets. Large, sweet, juicy and seedless, they are ideal for peeling and eating.

Valencias, sometimes labeled as juice oranges, are very juicy (and seedy) and most often are squeezed for juice.

Loose-skinned oranges are generally smaller and have peels that easily separate from the flesh. This category includes tangerines, tangelos, temple oranges, honey oranges, mandarin oranges and clementines. All are sweet and juicy and excellent for snacking. Their peels can be used in recipes.

Bitter oranges are rarely, if ever, seen fresh. Types include Seville oranges and bergamot, both of which are used commercially for preserves, flavorings and liqueurs.

Availability: Navel oranges are available all year with the peak season from January through April. Valencias are available almost all year with the winter and spring supply from Florida and the summer supply from California. Loose-skinned varieties come to market in late fall and stay through much of the winter.

Tip

The oil, which is the flavorful part of the peel, dissipates quickly, so the peel, or zest, should be grated just before using.

Orange juice is available in cartons, bottles and as frozen juice concentrate. Canned mandarin oranges are readily available.

Buying Tips: Americans like their oranges to be vibrant orange, without any sign of their natural greenish tinge showing through. This means that most oranges are dyed, making color an unreliable guide to quality. Instead, select heavy, firm fruits with no signs of mold on the skin or softening at the blossom end. The skin should have a natural luster; avoid those that look dull.

Yield: 1 pound oranges = 3 medium oranges or 2 large; 1 cup juice.

Storage: Oranges should be kept in the refrigerator, where they will last up to two weeks. When using them for juice, they should not be juiced until just before serving or there will be a significant loss in vitamin C.

Basic Preparation: When the peel will be used, scrub the orange thoroughly, using soap and water. This removes pesticide residues as well as the wax coating. The peel can be grated with the fine side of a box grater (technique page 282).

Techniques for Grilled Swordfish à l'Orange

Step 3. *Slicing peel and pith from orange.*

Step 4. *Making "V-shaped" slices.*

To zest an orange, draw a zester (see page 529) across the surface of the orange in short strokes.

The peel can be removed in large strips with a vegetable peeler. Be careful to remove only the colored part, not the bitter white pith. The peel may be cut into thin strips for garnishing or it may be minced. Once the peel is removed from the fruit, the fruit will dry out so it should be used within a day or two. Juice can be extracted with reamers (technique on page 282), hand juicers (technique on page 287) or electric juicers.

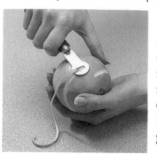

To make orange strips, remove the colored portion of the peel, not the white pith, in long, thin strips using a citrus stripper. The strips can be curled or tied in knots for garnishing.

To section an orange, place it on a cutting board. Cut a slice from the top and bottom of the orange with a utility knife. Then starting at the top and working towards the bottom, slice the peel and white pith off the orange in wide strips, following the curve of the orange. Repeat until all the peel and pith are removed. Make "V-shaped" slices into the center of the orange just inside of the membrane to remove the segments.

Grilled Swordfish à l'Orange

> **4 swordfish, halibut or shark steaks (about 1½ pounds)**
> **1 orange**
> **¾ cup orange juice**
> **1 tablespoon fresh lemon juice**
> **1 tablespoon sesame oil**
> **1 tablespoon soy sauce**
> **1 teaspoon cornstarch**
> **Salt and ground black pepper**

1. Rinse swordfish; pat dry with paper towels.

2. Grate orange peel using finest side of box-shaped grater, being careful to remove only the outermost layer of skin and not any of the bitter white pith. Grate enough peel to measure 1 teaspoon; set aside.

3. To section orange, cut off slice from top and bottom; set orange flat on cutting board. Starting at top and working toward bottom, slice remaining peel and pith off orange in wide strips, following curve of orange.

4. Make "V-shaped" slices into center of orange just inside of membranes to remove orange segments; set aside. Discard orange membranes.

5. Combine orange juice, lemon juice, oil and soy sauce in small bowl. Pour ½ of orange juice mixture into shallow glass dish. Add ½ teaspoon grated orange peel to orange juice mixture. Coat fish in mixture; cover and allow to marinate in refrigerator at least 1 hour.

6. Prepare grill for direct grilling over medium heat.

7. Place remaining ½ of orange juice mixture in small saucepan. Stir in cornstarch and remaining ½ teaspoon orange peel. Heat over medium-high heat 3 to 5 minutes until sauce thickens, stirring constantly; set aside.

8. Remove fish from marinade; discard remaining marinade. Lightly sprinkle fish with salt and pepper to taste. Grill swordfish, on uncovered grill, over medium coals 3 to 4 minutes per side until fish is opaque and flakes easily when tested with fork. Top with orange sections and orange sauce. Serve immediately.

Makes 4 servings

Fresh Citrus Salad

   3 oranges, peeled and sliced
   1 grapefruit, peeled and sliced
   ⅓ cup thinly sliced ripe olives
   1 clove garlic, minced
   ¼ cup FILIPPO BERIO® Extra
      Virgin Olive Oil
   Freshly ground black pepper

On medium platter, arrange slices of oranges and grapefruit. Sprinkle with olives and garlic. Drizzle with olive oil. Season to taste with pepper.

Makes 4 servings

Grilled Swordfish à l'Orange

ORGANIC FOOD

Organic food is defined by the California Organic Food Act of 1979 as "food grown without applied coloring or synthetically compounded materials by the grower, processor or other handler." It has to be "harvested, distributed, stored, processed and packaged without application of synthetically compounded fertilizers, pesticides or growth regulators." Organically grown foods use only biological and botanical pesticides and other chemicals that are not harmful to man.

🌿

An organic food or product can be certified by an independent organization or a state government agency. There are currently about 50 independent organizations that provide third-party organic certification. These organizations verify that the producer or grower has followed the standard set of production practices for growing or producing organic food. The soil must be inspected and the growing methods checked for the specific product or produce to be labeled "certified organically grown." Fish, poultry, meat and wild game can be certified organic if they have been fed only organic feed and have not been given any regular antibiotics or hormones. There are currently 31 states that have their own laws governing organic foods. The U.S. Department of Agriculture is currently developing certification standards for the entire organic foods industry.

PRO: Today many foods in our supermarkets are imported from countries where the growers use agricultural chemicals currently banned in the United States. It is often difficult to determine where the foods you purchase at the grocery store, particularly fresh fruits and vegetables, were grown. Choosing organic food assures the absence of unwanted chemicals.

CON: Although most consumers assume products labeled organic are indeed "pure," in reality there are presently no consistent regulations guiding or governing the standards of organic food producers. This means that chemical cross-contamination through shipping, chemical spraying, water leeching and wind can occur, making it difficult to guarantee that food is really free of chemical contamination. Organic products are often more costly. Today, major manufacturers add vitamins and minerals back to processed food to make them healthier and closer to whole (unprocessed) food.

OYSTER SAUCE

Oyster sauce is a thick, brown Chinese sauce made from oysters that are boiled with soy sauce and seasonings before being strained. It adds a surprisingly delicate taste to meat and vegetable dishes. Its salty and fishy taste dissipates when cooked with other ingredients. Oyster sauce is sold in many large supermarkets. It will last indefinitely in the refrigerator if stored in a glass jar.

🌿

Lo Mein Noodles with Shrimp

12 ounces uncooked Chinese-style thin egg noodles
2 teaspoons Oriental sesame oil
   Chinese chives*
4½ teaspoons oyster sauce
4½ teaspoons soy sauce
½ teaspoon sugar
¼ teaspoon salt
¼ teaspoon ground white pepper
2 tablespoons vegetable oil
1 teaspoon minced fresh ginger
1 clove garlic, minced
8 ounces raw medium shrimp, peeled, deveined
1 tablespoon dry sherry
8 ounces bean sprouts

*You can substitute ¼ cup domestic chives, cut into 1-inch pieces, and 2 green onions, cut into 1-inch pieces, for Chinese chives.

1. Cook noodles according to package directions 2 to 3 minutes until tender but still firm; drain. Rinse under cold running water; drain again.

2. Combine noodles and sesame oil; toss lightly to coat.

3. Cut enough chives into 1-inch pieces to measure ½ cup; set aside.

4. Combine oyster sauce, soy sauce, sugar, salt and pepper in small bowl; set aside.

5. Heat vegetable oil in wok or large skillet over high heat. Add ginger and garlic; stir-fry 10 seconds. Add shrimp; stir-fry about 1 minute or until shrimp begin to turn pink. Add sherry and reserved chives; stir-fry about 15 seconds or until chives begin to wilt. Add ½ of bean sprouts; stir-fry 15 seconds. Add remaining bean sprouts; stir-fry 15 seconds. Add reserved oyster sauce mixture and noodles. Cook and stir about 2 minutes or until heated through. Serve immediately.

Makes 4 servings

Lo Mein Noodles with Shrimp

P

Are papaya seeds edible?
Create a sensational pear tart.
How much water is needed
to cook one pound of pasta?
*Learn how to beat the heat of
chili peppers.* What is a new
potato? *Roast a holiday turkey.*
What does primavera mean?

Penne with Fresh Herb Tomato Sauce
(recipe on page 365) and Homemade Pizza
(recipe on page 388)

PAELLA

Paella is a classic Spanish dish of saffron-flavored rice that originated in Valencia, Spain. It may include a variety of shellfish and meat (such as clams, mussels, shrimp, chicken, chorizo and pork), onions, garlic, tomatoes and often peas. There is no standard recipe. Paella varies from region to region and from cook to cook. It is made and served in a wide, shallow round pan known as a paella pan.

❦

Paella

Paella

¼ cup **FILIPPO BERIO®** Olive Oil
1 **pound boneless skinless chicken breasts, cut into 1-inch strips**
½ **pound Italian sausage, cut into 1-inch slices**
1 **onion, chopped**
3 **cloves garlic, minced**
2 **(14½-ounce) cans chicken broth**
2 **cups uncooked long grain white rice**
1 **(8-ounce) bottle clam juice**
1 **(2-ounce) jar chopped pimento, drained**
2 **bay leaves**
1 **teaspoon salt**
¼ **teaspoon saffron threads, crumbled (optional)**
1 **pound raw shrimp, shelled and deveined**
1 **(16-ounce) can whole tomatoes, drained**
1 **(10-ounce) package frozen peas, thawed**
12 **littleneck clams, scrubbed**
¼ **cup water**
   Fresh herb sprig (optional)

Preheat oven to 350°F. In large skillet, heat olive oil over medium heat until hot. Add chicken; cook and stir 8 to 10 minutes or until brown on all sides. Remove with slotted spoon; set aside. Add sausage to skillet; cook and stir 8 to 10 minutes or until brown. Remove with slotted spoon; set aside. Add onion and garlic to skillet; cook and stir 5 to 7 minutes or until onion is tender. Transfer chicken, sausage, onion and garlic to large casserole.

Add chicken broth, rice, clam juice, pimento, bay leaves, salt and saffron, if desired, to chicken mixture. Cover; bake 30 minutes. Add shrimp, tomatoes and peas; stir well. Cover; bake an additional 15 minutes or until rice is tender, liquid is absorbed and shrimp are opaque. Remove bay leaves; discard.

Meanwhile, combine clams and water in stockpot or large saucepan. Cover; cook over medium heat 5 to

10 minutes or until clams open; remove clams immediately as they open. Discard any clams with unopened shells. Place clams on top of paella. Garnish with herb sprig, if desired.   *Makes 4 to 6 servings*

PANBROIL, TO

Panbroiling is a technique used to cook meats and fish on the rangetop with little or no added fat. The method is well suited to thinner steaks, chops and fish fillets. It sears the outside of the meat in a similar manner to oven broiling. To panbroil, preheat a heavy nonstick skillet and cook meat or fish over medium-high heat, draining any fat that accumulates. A rangetop grill with bottom ridges will continuously drain away fat.

PANCAKE

Pancakes, also known as flapjacks, griddlecakes or hotcakes, are one of the world's simplest and most versatile forms of bread. They are prepared from a pourable quick-bread batter of flour, eggs, liquid and usually leavening. Pancakes come in many forms, ranging from the traditional 4-inch rounds to the skillet-size puffy baked pancakes to the thin unleavened French crêpes wrapped around a filling. Although pancakes are primarily a breakfast food, they can be served at other meals. Crêpes are most often served as a main dish or a sweet dessert. See Blintze, page 52, and Crêpe, page 169, for additional information and recipes.

Sunrise Pancakes

Vanilla Cream Syrup (recipe follows)
1 cup all-purpose flour
2 tablespoons sugar
1 teaspoon baking powder
½ teaspoon baking soda
½ teaspoon salt
2 eggs, slightly beaten
½ cup plain yogurt
½ cup water
2½ to 3 tablespoons butter or margarine, melted, divided

1. Prepare Vanilla Cream Syrup; set aside.

2. Combine flour, sugar, baking powder, baking soda and salt in large bowl. Combine eggs, yogurt and water in medium bowl. Whisk in 2 tablespoons butter. Pour liquid ingredients, all at once, into dry ingredients; stir until moistened.

3. Heat griddle or large skillet over medium heat; brush with ½ tablespoon butter. For each pancake, pour about ¼ cup batter onto hot griddle; spread batter out to make 5-inch circle. Cook until tops of pancakes are bubbly and appear dry; turn and cook about 2 minutes or until browned. (Brush griddle with additional butter, if needed, to prevent sticking.) Serve pancakes with Vanilla Cream Syrup.
        Makes about 8 pancakes

Vanilla Cream Syrup

½ cup sugar
½ cup light corn syrup
½ cup whipping cream
1 fresh nectarine, chopped
1 teaspoon vanilla extract

Combine sugar, corn syrup and cream in 1-quart saucepan. Cook over medium heat until sugar is dissolved, stirring constantly. Simmer 2 minutes or until syrup thickens slightly. Remove from heat. Stir in nectarine and vanilla.
        Makes 1 cup sauce

Tips

Overmixing pancake batter produces tough pancakes. Mix the batter only until the dry ingredients are moistened. The batter may still be lumpy.

Do not be tempted to press the pancake with the turner during cooking. This will give the pancake a dense and heavy texture.

Puff Pancake with Summer Berries

Puff Pancake with Summer Berries

      Summer Berries (recipe follows)
  4 tablespoons butter or
      margarine, divided
  2 eggs
  ½ cup all-purpose flour
  ½ cup milk
  1 tablespoon sugar
  ¼ teaspoon salt

1. Preheat oven to 425°F. Meanwhile, prepare Summer Berries; set aside.

2. Place 2 tablespoons butter in ovenproof skillet. Place skillet in oven 3 minutes or until butter is bubbly. Swirl pan to coat bottom and sides.

3. Beat eggs in medium bowl with electric mixer at high speed. Add flour, milk, remaining 2 tablespoons butter, sugar and salt; beat until smooth. Pour batter into prepared skillet. Bake 15 minutes.

4. *Reduce oven temperature to 350°F.* Bake 10 to 15 minutes more until pancake is puffed and golden brown. Serve pancake in skillet with Summer Berries.   *Makes 6 servings*

Summer Berries

  2 cups blueberries
  1 cup sliced strawberries
  1 cup raspberries
    Sugar to taste
    Whipped cream (optional)

Combine blueberries, strawberries and raspberries in medium bowl. Gently toss with sugar. Let stand 5 minutes. Top with cream, if desired.

Swedish Pancakes

  1 cup milk
  1 egg
  ½ cup all-purpose flour
  2 teaspoons sugar
  ¼ teaspoon salt
    Melted butter
    Lingonberry preserves* (or
      other berry preserves) or
      fresh berries
    Sour cream

*Lingonberries are tart red berries that grow wild in the mountains of Scandinavia. The preserves are available at specialty food shops.

1. Place milk, egg, flour, sugar and salt in food processor or blender; process until smooth.

2. Heat griddle or large nonstick skillet over medium heat; brush with melted butter. Stir batter. For each pancake, pour 1 tablespoon batter onto hot griddle; spread batter with spatula to form thin 3-inch round pancake. Cook 2 minutes per side or until browned. (Brush griddle with additional butter as needed to prevent sticking.) Serve pancakes with preserves and sour cream.
   Makes 20 (3-inch) pancakes

PAPAYA

After visiting the West Indies, Christopher Columbus wrote in his journal about a large melon that sustained the natives and made them "very strong." He called it "fruit of the angels." He was referring to a subtropical fruit commonly known as the papaya. The papaya is native to the Western Hemisphere, most likely the Caribbean, but early in its history, it spread to other subtropical areas. Today, the fruit is grown in Brazil, Costa Rica, India, China, Japan, Malaysia, the Philippines and Hawaii. Most of the papayas sold in the United States are domestically grown in Hawaii or imported from Central or South America.

The fruits, which are shaped like elongated melons or pears, vary in size from about ½ pound to 15 pounds or more (a huge specimen that can provide a feast for a dozen or so diners). Smooth and green when unripe, the exterior develops a yellow-gold color as it ripens. Inside, the deep yellow flesh is succulent and sweet, with more natural sugar than most fruits. It has a musky melonlike taste. The inner cavity contains a wealth of small black seeds, which are often discarded. However, the seeds are edible. They have a pungent, peppery bite.

❦

Uses: Papayas are eaten raw, often seasoned with salt, ground pepper and a squirt of lime juice.

• Papayas also can be used in salads and salsas or puréed and used in puddings and mousses.

• Their flesh has a natural tenderizing effect so it can be puréed and used to marinate meats.

• The enzyme papain, which is responsible for its tenderizing abilities, also inhibits gelatin from thickening. Therefore, raw papaya is not suitable for any preparation containing gelatin. However, cooked papaya presents no problem.

• Unripe, green papayas are cooked and eaten as a vegetable rather than as a fruit. They are also pickled or cooked in chutneys.

• Use papaya seeds as a garnish on sliced papaya or fruit salads.

Availability: Many large supermarkets stock papayas all year. Summer is the peak season.

Tip

Papaya seeds can be dried, ground and used as a spice or a tenderizer for meat.

Buying Tips: Unripe papayas are green. They turn yellow as they ripen. Papayas are fragile when ripe, so completely ripe ones are not usually found in the supermarket. Select fruit that has begun to yellow and yields to gentle pressure. Avoid papayas that are green, shriveled or marked with dark spots. Check for signs of rot at the small end.

Yield: 1 pound papaya = about 3 cups chopped and ½ cup seeds.

Storage: Unripe papayas should be kept at room temperature until they are fully ripened. Ripe fruits can be stored in the refrigerator for two or three days.

Basic Preparation: For the simplest presentation, the fruit can be cut lengthwise into halves, the seeds scooped out and the flesh eaten with a spoon. For sliced or cubed papaya, peel the papaya with a vegetable peeler or a paring knife. Cut the fruit into halves, remove the seeds and slice or cube the flesh.

Scooping seeds out of papaya.

Calypso Pork Chops

1 ripe medium papaya
1 teaspoon paprika
½ teaspoon dried thyme leaves
¼ teaspoon salt
¼ teaspoon ground allspice
4 center-cut pork loin chops
    (about 1½ pounds), cut
    ¾ inch thick
5 tablespoons fresh lime juice,
    divided
2 tablespoons *plus* 1½ teaspoons
    seeded, chopped jalapeño
    peppers,* divided
1 tablespoon vegetable oil
1½ teaspoons grated fresh ginger,
    divided
1 teaspoon sugar
¼ cup finely chopped red bell
    pepper
    Lime wedges (optional)

*Jalapeño peppers can sting and irritate the skin; wear rubber or plastic gloves when handling peppers and do not touch eyes. Wash hands after handling.

1. Peel papaya with paring knife or vegetable peeler; slice in half lengthwise. Scrape out seeds with spoon; discard. Chop papaya flesh into ¼-inch pieces. Chop enough papaya to measure 1½ cups; set aside.

2. Combine paprika, thyme, salt and allspice in small bowl; rub over both sides of pork chops with fingers. Place chops in large resealable plastic food storage bag. Combine 3 tablespoons juice, 2 tablespoons jalapeños, oil, 1 teaspoon ginger and sugar in small bowl; pour over chops. Seal bag tightly, turning to coat. Marinate in refrigerator 1 to 2 hours.

3. Combine papaya, bell pepper, remaining 2 tablespoons juice, 1½ teaspoons jalapeños and ½ teaspoon ginger in separate small bowl. Cover; refrigerate until ready to serve.

4. Prepare grill for direct grilling over medium heat.

5. Meanwhile, drain chops; discard marinade. Place chops on grid. Grill chops, on covered grill, over medium coals 10 to 12 minutes until pork is juicy and barely pink in center, turning once. Serve chops topped with papaya mixture. Garnish with lime wedges, if desired.

Makes 4 servings

PAPILLOTE

The term "en papillote" refers to a cooking technique in which savory foods, such as meat, chicken, seafood and vegetables, are enclosed in heavy parchment paper before baking to retain their flavor and aroma. To serve the food, cut the paper across the top in a crisscross pattern and peel it back. Papillote is a French term for the frilled paper decorations used on the tips of the rib bones of pork or lamb crown roasts.

🐝

Orange Roughy in Parchment Hearts

8 ounces fresh asparagus,
    cleaned, peeled, diagonally
    cut into 2-inch pieces
Parchment paper or foil
4 orange roughy fillets (about
    1½ pounds)
Butter
1 yellow bell pepper, cut into
    16 thin strips
1 red bell pepper, cut into 16 thin
    strips
1 medium carrot, cut into
    julienne strips
¼ cup dry white wine
3 tablespoons Dijon mustard
2 tablespoons fresh lemon juice
1 teaspoon dried marjoram leaves
¼ teaspoon ground black pepper

1. Steam asparagus in large saucepan 2 to 3 minutes until asparagus turns bright green.

2. Preheat oven to 375°F. Cut parchment paper into 4 (12-inch) squares. Fold each square in half diagonally and cut into half heart shape.

3. Rinse orange roughy; pat dry with paper towels. Lightly butter inside of each heart. Place 1 piece fish on 1 side of each heart. Divide steamed asparagus, yellow and red peppers, and carrot evenly over fish.

4. Combine wine, mustard, juice, marjoram and black pepper in small bowl. Drizzle wine mixture over fish, dividing evenly.

5. Fold parchment hearts in half. Beginning at top of heart, fold edges together, 2 inches at a time. At tip of heart, fold paper up and over to seal. Place hearts on large baking sheet. Bake 20 to 25 minutes until fish flakes easily when tested with fork. To serve, place hearts on plates and cut an "X" through top layer of parchment, folding paper back.
Makes 4 servings

Orange Roughy in Parchment Heart

PAPRIKASH

Paprikash (paprikás in Hungarian) is a traditional Hungarian stew made with chicken. Paprika is the primary seasoning. It is prepared by first browning chicken pieces and chopped onions in fat (often bacon fat) and then braising the mixture until tender in chicken broth. Sour cream is then added to the broth to make a rich sauce. Paprikash is usually served over egg noodles.

❧

PARE, TO

Paring is the technique used to remove the thin outer covering or skin of a food, usually a fruit or vegetable. A paring knife or vegetable peeler may be used.

❧

Techniques for Orange Roughy in Parchment Hearts

Step 3. Placing fish on side of parchment heart.

Step 5. Folding edges of heart together.

PARFAIT

A parfait refers to a dessert layered in tall footed clear glasses known as parfait glasses. One layer is usually creamy, for example ice cream or pudding. The second layer may consist of fruit, whipped cream or a second creamy layer of an ingredient with a different flavor and color.

❧

Two Great Tastes Pudding Parfaits

> 1 package (4-serving size) vanilla cook & serve pudding and pie filling mix*
> 3½ cups milk
> 1 cup REESE'S® Peanut Butter Chips
> 1 cup HERSHEY'S Semi-Sweet Chocolate Chips or Semi-Sweet Chocolate Chunks
> Whipped topping (optional)

Do not use instant pudding mix.

In large heavy saucepan, combine pudding mix and 3½ cups milk (rather than amount listed in package directions). Cook over medium heat, stirring constantly, until mixture comes to a full boil. Remove from heat; divide hot mixture between 2 heatproof medium bowls. Immediately stir peanut butter chips into mixture in one bowl and chocolate chips into mixture in second bowl. Stir both mixtures until chips are melted and mixtures are smooth. Cool slightly, stirring occasionally.

In parfait glasses, wine glasses or dessert dishes, alternately layer peanut butter and chocolate mixtures. Place plastic wrap directly onto surface of each dessert; refrigerate several hours or overnight. Remove plastic wrap; top each dessert with dollop of whipped topping, if desired.

Makes 4 to 6 servings

PARMIGIANA

Parmigiana, which is shortened from the Italian "alla parmigiana," is a term used to refer to dishes prepared with Parmesan cheese. The most well-known preparations are veal parmigiana and eggplant parmigiana. Each preparation begins by breading and frying the main ingredient and then cooking or baking it in tomato sauce. Parmesan cheese is usually included in the bread-crumb breading but may be used as a topping. Sometimes mozzarella cheese is used as a topping.

❧

Veal Parmigiana

> 4 veal cutlets, cut ⅜ inch thick (about 4 ounces each)
> 4 tablespoons olive oil, divided
> 1 small red bell pepper, finely chopped
> 1 medium onion, finely chopped
> 1 rib celery, finely chopped
> 1 clove garlic, minced
> 1 can (14½ ounces) whole peeled tomatoes, undrained, finely chopped
> 1 cup chicken broth
> 1 tablespoon tomato paste
> 1 tablespoon chopped fresh parsley
> 1 teaspoon sugar
> ¾ teaspoon dried basil leaves
> ½ teaspoon salt
> ⅛ teaspoon ground black pepper
> 1 egg
> ¼ cup all-purpose flour
> ⅔ cup fine dry bread crumbs
> 2 tablespoons butter
> 1½ cups (6 ounces) shredded mozzarella cheese
> ⅔ cup freshly grated Parmesan cheese
> Fresh basil leaves (optional)
> Hot cooked pasta

1. Pound veal with meat mallet to ¼-inch thickness. Pat dry with paper towels; set aside.

Veal Parmigiana

Techniques for Veal Parmigiana

Step 1. *Pounding veal to ¼-inch thickness.*

Step 3. *Coating veal with bread crumbs.*

2. To make tomato sauce, heat 1 tablespoon oil in medium saucepan over medium heat. Add bell pepper, onion, celery and garlic; cook and stir 5 minutes. Stir in tomatoes with juice, broth, tomato paste, parsley, sugar, dried basil, salt and black pepper. Cover; simmer over low heat 20 minutes. Uncover; cook over medium heat 20 minutes more or until sauce thickens, stirring frequently; set aside.

3. Beat egg in shallow bowl; spread flour and bread crumbs on separate plates. Dip reserved veal cutlets first in flour, then in egg, then in bread crumbs to coat both sides evenly. Press crumb coating firmly onto veal.

4. Heat butter and 2 tablespoons oil in large skillet over medium-high heat. Add veal. Cook 3 minutes per side or until browned.

5. Preheat oven to 350°F.

6. Remove veal with slotted spatula to ungreased 13×9-inch baking dish. Sprinkle mozzarella cheese evenly over veal. Spoon reserved tomato sauce evenly over cheese. Sprinkle Parmesan cheese over tomato sauce. Drizzle remaining 1 tablespoon oil over top. Bake, uncovered, 25 minutes or until veal is tender and cheese is golden. Garnish with fresh basil, if desired. Serve with pasta.

Makes 4 servings

PARSNIP

Parsnips, more popular than potatoes in medieval times, have never been an American favorite. This ivory-colored cousin to the carrot has a similar shape but is broader at the top. Parsnips have a distinctly nutty and sweet flavor. Harvested in the late fall, parsnips become sweeter the longer they are left in the ground. The green leafy tops are not eaten.

Cutting parsnip into 1-inch pieces.

Uses: Parsnips may be used in many of the same ways as cooked carrots. They are good for soups, stews and vegetable side dishes. Their flavor pairs well with herbs, such as rosemary, chives, thyme or tarragon.

Their sweetness is enhanced by brown sugar, apples, orange zest and spices like cinnamon, ginger or nutmeg.

• Chopped parsnips may be cooked and used in salads in place of potatoes.

• Parsnips can be eaten raw in salads. They contribute a pungent, peppery flavor similar to radishes.

Availability: Fresh parsnips are available almost year-round, with supplies peaking in the fall and winter. They may be in short supply during hot summer months.

Guinness Chicken

Buying Tips: Choose parsnips that are firm, unblemished and small or medium in size (about 8 inches long). Large parsnips may have woody centers but, unlike carrots, broad tops are not an indication of woody cores. Parsnips range in color from pale yellow to creamy white. Avoid limp, shriveled or blemished parsnips with moist spots or a lot of tiny hairlike roots.

Yield: 1 pound parsnips = 4 medium; 2 cups peeled and chopped.

Storage: Store parsnips in a plastic bag in the refrigerator for up to two weeks.

Basic Preparation: Rinse and scrub parsnips with a vegetable brush to remove embedded soil. Peel parsnips with a swivel-bladed vegetable peeler or paring knife. Trim off ends and discard. For even cooking, parsnips are best chopped, cubed, sliced or cut into strips before cooking. Parsnips may be steamed, sautéed, baked or boiled. After steaming or boiling they may be mashed or puréed.

Guinness Chicken

  5 carrots, peeled
  2 parsnips, peeled
  2 tablespoons vegetable oil
  1 medium onion, chopped
  2 cloves garlic, minced
  1 whole frying chicken (3 to 4 pounds), cut into serving pieces
  1 teaspoon dried thyme leaves
  ¾ teaspoon salt
  ½ teaspoon black pepper
  ¾ cup Guinness Stout
  ½ pound fresh button mushrooms
  ¾ cup frozen peas
  Fresh parsley (optional)

1. Cut carrots and parsnips into 1-inch pieces; set aside.

2. Heat oil in large skillet over medium heat until hot. Add onion and garlic; cook and stir 3 minutes or until tender. Remove with slotted spoon to small bowl; set aside.

3. Arrange chicken in single layer in same skillet. Cook over medium-high heat 5 minutes per side or until lightly browned. Add reserved onion and garlic, carrots, thyme, salt and pepper. Pour stout over chicken and vegetables. Bring to a boil over high heat; reduce heat to low. Cover; simmer 35 minutes. Add parsnips, mushrooms and peas to skillet. Cover; cook 10 minutes more.

4. Increase heat to medium. Cook, uncovered, 10 minutes or until sauce is slightly reduced and fork can be inserted into chicken with ease and juices run clear, not pink. Garnish with parsley, if desired. Serve immediately.   *Makes 4 servings*

Honey-Mustard Parsnips

  1½ pounds parsnips
  ¾ cup defatted low sodium chicken broth
  ⅓ cup julienned red bell pepper
  1 tablespoon honey
  2 teaspoons Dijon mustard
  ⅓ cup 1% low-fat milk

1. Peel parsnips; trim ends. Cut parsnips into 2-inch lengths; cut each length into ½-inch wide matchsticks.* Combine parsnips and broth in medium saucepan. Bring to a boil over high heat. Cook, covered, 7 minutes, stirring occasionally. Add pepper; cook 1 minute more.

2. Meanwhile, blend honey and mustard in small bowl; gradually stir in milk. Add honey mixture to parsnips; cook and stir about 2 minutes or until sauce is slightly thickened. Serve immediately.
   Makes 4 side-dish servings

*Remove central core of parsnips if woody.

> ## Tip
> *Parsnips become mushy when overcooked. When adding them to soups and stews, do so during the last 10 to 15 minutes of cooking.*

PASTA

Pasta is believed to have originated in central Asia around 1000 B.C., but it was Italian cooks who popularized pasta in America. Italian pasta is made from durum wheat, water and sometimes eggs. Durum wheat is high in gluten and is used only for pasta, never baking. Coarsely ground durum wheat is called semolina. The Asian form of pasta, called noodles or threads, may be made of rice, soybean, wheat, potato or other flours. Polish pierogi, Italian gnocchi and German spaetzle are considered forms of pasta. (They may also be referred to as dumplings.)

🐝

Types of Pasta: Pasta is categorized as dry or fresh. Both forms are commercially made; fresh pasta also can be made at home. Commercially made dry pasta begins with hard durum wheat and water. The ground durum wheat, or semolina, works well because it makes a firm, elastic dough that is sturdy enough to be shaped by machine. The dough is shaped by pushing it through a die or mold. It is then dried in large commercial ovens. This type of pasta should be stored in a cool, dry place in a tightly covered container or tightly closed package. It will keep almost indefinitely. The exceptions are whole wheat pasta and Japanese soba noodles made from buckwheat. These must be used within a month, so buy only as much as you will use in that period of time.

Fresh pasta is generally limited to long goods, such as spaghetti, linguine and fettuccine, or filled pastas, such as ravioli and tortellini. The dough is made by combining all-purpose wheat flour, whole eggs,

Penne with Fresh Herb Tomato Sauce (recipe on page 365)

sometimes oil for easier handling and salt for flavoring. It is blended, and kneaded and rolled out by hand or machine. It is then cut into the desired widths. Commercially made fresh pasta is sold in bulk in Italian markets and a few supermarkets or prepackaged in many supermarkets. Fresh bulk pasta is very perishable; it must be refrigerated tightly wrapped and used within four or five days. Prepackaged fresh pastas contain preservatives. These are stamped with a "use by" date. Frozen filled pasta is available in most supermarkets. It can be stored frozen for up to four months. It should not be thawed before using but cooked from the frozen state.

Specialty pastas, both dry and fresh, are also available. They have ingredients, such as vegetables, herbs and seasonings, added to them. Spinach results in a green color, carrots in an orange color, beets or tomatoes in a red color and squid ink in a black color. Common herb and seasoning additions include basil, black pepper, garlic and lemon peel.

Pasta Yields: 1 pound dry macaroni-type pasta = 9 cups cooked.
1 pound dry spaghetti or linguine = 7 cups cooked.

Cooking Dry Pasta: To cook pasta, use plenty of rapidly boiling water. For 1 pound of pasta use 4 to 6 quarts water. Add 2 teaspoons of salt, if desired. Gradually add pasta, stirring gently until the water returns to a boil. Stirring prevents the pasta from sticking to the pan and allows it to cook more evenly. Keep water boiling continuously and cook the pasta, uncovered, until desired doneness, stirring occasionally. Cooking times vary by the type and sometimes the brand of pasta. Always check the package for the manufacturer's recommended cooking time. Begin testing for doneness at the minimum recommended time by removing a piece or strand of pasta and biting into it. If it's tender but still firm (*al dente*), it is done. Immediately drain

pasta by pouring it into a colander. Serve it immediately. Pasta should only be rinsed if it is to be used in a salad. Rinsing cools the pasta and washes away excess starch, which causes sticking. Pasta that is to be baked, such as lasagna noodles, should be slightly undercooked or it will be too soft after baking.

As a general rule, 2 ounces of dry pasta is equal to a first-course or side-dish serving. Use 3 to 4 ounces dry pasta per person for each main-dish serving. Spaghetti and macaroni products usually double in amount when cooked, but egg noodles do not expand significantly. Fresh pasta is much moister and does not expand, so use 3 ounces of fresh pasta for each side-dish serving and 4 to 5 ounces for each main-dish serving.

Tip

A pasta cooker is a large pan with a perforated inner basket. After cooking, the inner basket containing the pasta is lifted out and the cooking water drains away.

Rolling dough with pasta machine.

Cutting dough with pasta machine.

Preparing Fresh Pasta: Making pasta is really very simple. Begin by mounding the combined flour and salt on a clean work surface, such as a cutting board, or in a large bowl. Make a well in the flour. Whisk together the eggs and oil. Pour the egg mixture into the well. Mix the egg mixture into the flour mixture with a fork or your fingertips to form a ball of dough. A food processor may be used to mix the dough ingredients; follow the recipe directions or the manufacturer's directions for processing times. The dough must be kneaded (technique on page 63) to thoroughly blend the ingredients and develop the gluten, which gives the pasta its sturdiness. Roll out the dough on a lightly floured surface with a lightly floured rolling pin to the desired thickness. Cut the pasta into the desired widths or shapes for filling. To prevent pasta from sticking together when cooked, dry it for 5 or 10 minutes before cooking by arranging it on a clean kitchen towel or hanging it on a wooden pasta rack.

Rolling out the dough is a tedious task. If you plan to prepare pasta often, it is wise to invest in a pasta machine. A hand-cranked machine kneads and rolls out the dough. An attachment is needed to cut the dough into the desired widths. (Pasta may be cut by hand.) An electric pasta machine mixes, kneads and extrudes the dough into the desired shape. Follow the manufacturer's directions for using pasta machines.

Hearty Manicotti

    8 to 10 dry manicotti shells, cooked, drained
    2 cups (15-ounce container) ricotta cheese
    1 package (10 ounces) frozen chopped spinach, thawed, squeezed dry
    1 egg, lightly beaten
    ½ cup (2 ounces) grated Parmesan cheese
    ⅛ teaspoon ground black pepper
    1⅓ cups (two 6-ounce cans) CONTADINA® Italian Paste with Roasted Garlic
    1⅓ cups water
    ½ cup (2 ounces) shredded mozzarella cheese

Hearty Manicotti

In medium bowl, combine ricotta cheese, spinach, egg, Parmesan cheese and pepper; mix well. Spoon into manicotti shells. Place in ungreased 12×7½-inch baking dish. In small bowl, combine tomato paste and water; pour over manicotti. Sprinkle with mozzarella cheese. Bake in preheated 350°F. oven for 30 to 40 minutes or until heated through.   *Makes 4 to 5 servings*

Classic Fettuccine Alfredo

Homemade Fettuccine (recipe
   follows) *or* ¾ pound
   uncooked dry fettuccine
6 tablespoons unsalted butter
⅔ cup whipping cream
½ teaspoon salt
   Generous dash ground white
     pepper
   Generous dash ground nutmeg
**1 cup (about 3 ounces) freshly
   grated Parmesan cheese**
**2 tablespoons chopped fresh
   parsley**
   Fresh Italian parsley sprig
     (optional)

1. Prepare and cook Homemade Fettuccine or cook dry fettuccine in large pot of boiling salted water 6 to 8 minutes until al dente (tender but still firm); remove from heat. Drain well; return to dry pot.

2. Place butter and cream in heavy large skillet over medium-low heat. Cook and stir until butter melts and mixture bubbles. Cook and stir 2 minutes more. Stir in salt, pepper and nutmeg. Remove from heat. Gradually stir in cheese until thoroughly blended and smooth. Return briefly to heat to completely blend cheese if necessary. (Do not let sauce boil or cheese will become lumpy and tough.)

3. Pour sauce over fettuccine in pot. Stir and toss over low heat 2 to 3 minutes until sauce is thickened and fettuccine is evenly coated. Sprinkle with chopped parsley. Garnish with parsley sprig, if desired. Serve immediately.

     Makes 4 servings

Homemade Fettuccine

2 cups all-purpose flour
¼ teaspoon salt
3 eggs
1 tablespoon milk
1 teaspoon olive oil

1. Combine flour and salt on pastry board, cutting board or countertop; make well in center. Whisk eggs, milk and oil in small bowl until well blended; gradually pour into well in flour mixture while mixing with fork or fingertips to form ball of dough.

2. Place dough on lightly floured surface; knead 5 minutes or until smooth and elastic, adding more flour to prevent sticking if necessary. Wrap dough in plastic wrap; let stand 15 minutes.

3. Unwrap dough; knead briefly. Using lightly floured rolling pin, roll out dough to ⅛-inch-thick circle on lightly floured surface. Let stand until dough is slightly dry but can be handled without breaking.

4. Lightly flour dough circle; roll loosely on rolling pin. Slide rolling pin out; press dough roll gently with hand and cut into ¼-inch-wide strips with sharp knife. Carefully unfold strips.* Cook fettuccine in large pot of boiling salted water 1 to 2 minutes until al dente (tender but still firm); drain well.

     Makes about ¾ pound pasta

Fettuccine can be dried and stored at this point. Hang fettuccine strips over pasta rack. Dry at least 3 hours; store in airtight container in refrigerator up to 4 days. To serve, cook fettuccine in large pot of boiling salted water 3 to 4 minutes until al dente (tender but still firm); drain well.

Techniques for Classic Fettuccine Alfredo

Homemade Fettuccine: Step 1. *Mixing egg mixture into flour to form dough.*

Homemade Fettuccine: Step 4. *Cutting dough into strips.*

Italian Garden Fusilli

Italian Garden Fusilli

8 ounces dry fusilli, cooked, drained, kept warm

1¾ cups (14.5-ounce can) CONTADINA® Recipe Ready Diced Tomatoes, undrained

1 cup (4 ounces) cut fresh green beans

¼ teaspoon dried rosemary leaves, crushed

½ teaspoon garlic salt

1 cup (1 small) thinly sliced zucchini

1 cup (1 small) thinly sliced yellow squash

1 cup (12-ounce jar) marinated artichoke hearts, undrained

1 cup frozen peas

½ teaspoon salt, or to taste

¼ teaspoon ground black pepper, or to taste

¼ cup (1 ounce) shredded Parmesan cheese

In large skillet, combine tomatoes and juice, green beans, rosemary and garlic salt. Bring to a boil. Reduce heat to low; cover. Simmer for 3 minutes. Add zucchini and yellow squash; cover. Simmer for 3 minutes or until vegetables are tender. Stir in artichoke hearts and juice, peas, salt and pepper; heat through. Add pasta; toss to coat well. Sprinkle with Parmesan cheese just before serving.

Makes 6 to 8 servings

Penne with Fresh Herb Tomato Sauce

> 1 pound uncooked penne pasta
> 4 ripe large tomatoes, peeled and seeded*
> ½ cup tomato sauce
> ¼ cup FILIPPO BERIO® Olive Oil
> 1 to 2 tablespoons lemon juice
> 2 teaspoons minced fresh parsley or 1 teaspoon dried parsley
> 1 teaspoon minced fresh rosemary, oregano or thyme or 1 teaspoon dried Italian seasoning
> Salt and freshly ground black pepper
> Shavings of Parmesan cheese

For chunkier sauce, reserve 1 peeled, seeded tomato. Finely chop; stir into sauce.

Cook pasta according to package directions until al dente (tender but still firm). Drain; transfer to large bowl. Process tomatoes in blender container or food processor until smooth. Add tomato sauce. While machine is running, very slowly add olive oil. Add lemon juice, parsley and herbs. Process briefly at high speed. Spoon sauce over hot or room temperature pasta. Season to taste with salt and pepper. Top with cheese.   *Makes 4 servings*

Easy Lasagna

> 1 pound lean ground beef
> 1 jar (28 ounces) meatless spaghetti sauce
> 1 pound cottage cheese
> 8 ounces sour cream
> 8 uncooked lasagna noodles
> 3 packages (6 ounces each) sliced mozzarella cheese (12 slices)
> ½ cup grated Parmesan cheese
> 1 cup water

1. For meat sauce, cook beef in large skillet over medium-high heat until meat is brown, stirring to separate meat; drain. Add spaghetti sauce. Reduce heat to low. Heat through, stirring occasionally; set aside.

2. Preheat oven to 350°F.

3. Combine cottage cheese and sour cream in medium bowl; blend well.

4. Spoon 1½ cups of meat sauce in bottom of 13×9-inch baking dish. Layer with 4 uncooked noodles, ½ of cheese mixture, 4 slices mozzarella cheese, ½ of remaining meat sauce and ¼ cup Parmesan cheese. Repeat layers starting with uncooked noodles. Top with remaining 4 slices mozzarella cheese. Pour water around sides of dish. Cover tightly with foil.

5. Bake lasagna 1 hour. Uncover; bake 20 minutes more or until bubbly. Let stand 15 to 20 minutes before cutting. Garnish as desired. Serve immediately.

Makes 8 to 10 servings

Tip

If hot cooked pasta is not served immediately it will become sticky. If this happens, just pour boiling water over the pasta to separate.

Easy Lasagna

PASTEURIZATION

Pasteurization is the process of using heat to sterilize a liquid. Milk, liquid egg mixtures, beer, wine and apple cider are the most common foods that are pasteurized. The temperature should be high enough to destroy microorganisms that cause disease but not so high as to cause a change in the flavor of the liquid. Pasteurization is used to destroy bacteria that cause undesirable fermentation in beer, but it does not kill the bacteria that cause milk to sour. Ultrapasteurization holds the liquid at the high temperature for a longer period of time, destroying enzymes that cause foods to deteriorate. This process prolongs the freshness. Ultrapasteurization is used with such products as whipping cream and half-and-half.

🌾

PASTRY

Pastry is a general term used for a rich, unleavened dough made with flour, fat (butter, margarine or lard) and a little water. Pie pastry is mostly used to make pie crusts but can also be used for sweet or savory turnovers. Puff pastry is an especially rich pastry prepared by layering pastry dough with bits of butter. When baked the moisture in the butter creates steam, causing the dough to separate into hundreds of paper-thin, flaky layers. The term pastry is also used to refer to sweet baked items, such as Danish pastries, cream puffs and sweet rolls.

🌾

PEACH

Peaches, which probably originated in China, were planted along the Eastern Seaboard of the United States as early as the mid-1700's. Georgia is known for its peaches, but at least 30 states now grow peaches commercially. Peaches that are found in supermarkets are not as fuzzy as they were in the past; now they are often mechanically defuzzed after harvesting.

🌾

Varieties: Peaches are classified as freestone, meaning that the pit is easily removed from the flesh, and clingstone, meaning that the flesh adheres to the pit and must be cut away. Nearly all varieties sold fresh in markets are freestone. Clingstone peaches are used for commercial purposes, although they can sometimes be found at farmers' markets.

Availability: Domestic peaches are available from April to October with supplies peaking during the summer months. Imported varieties may be found in supermarkets from November to April. Sliced peaches and peach halves are available canned. Frozen peach slices are also available.

Buying Tips: Locally harvested peaches purchased at farmers' markets or produce stands will probably be sweeter than those found in the supermarket. Choose peaches that yield slightly to pressure along the seam, have a yellow, not green, background color and a fruity fragrance. The amount of pink or red blush relates to the variety and not to ripeness. Avoid green, hard, dark-colored, bruised (soft spots) or mushy fruit.

Yield: 1 pound peaches – 4 medium peaches; 2³/₄ cups sliced; 2¹/₄ cups chopped.

Storage: Firm peaches may be ripened by placing them in a closed paper bag at room temperature for one or two days. The peaches will soften and become juicier but will not necessarily get sweeter. Store ripe peaches in the refrigerator for three to five days. Longer chilling results in loss of juiciness.

Marinated Poached Peaches
(recipe on page 368)

Basic Preparation: Fresh peaches may be served chilled or at room temperature, although their flavor intensifies at room temperature. Wash peaches before using. Peel with a paring knife. Remove pits from freestone peaches by cutting the fruit in half around the pit and twisting the halves in opposite directions. To slice or quarter clingstone varieties, use a paring knife to make cuts toward the center of the fruit and then around the pit, lifting out each slice. Cut peaches turn brown quickly when exposed to air. To retard browning, dip cut surfaces in lemon or orange juice. Peaches used for cooking should be peeled.

Marinated Poached Peaches

    10 medium peaches
     2 tablespoons whole allspice
    10 cinnamon sticks
    ½ cup sugar
        Fresh mint leaves and
        raspberries (optional)

1. Place peaches in large saucepan or stockpot. Cover with water; add allspice and cinnamon. Bring to a boil over high heat. Boil 2 minutes; remove peaches.

2. Peel peaches when cool enough to handle. Add sugar to poaching water; boil 5 minutes. Add peaches and simmer 2 minutes more.

3. Remove from heat; cool to room temperature in poaching liquid. Place peaches and liquid in airtight container. Refrigerate 3 hours or overnight. Serve peaches cold with syrup. Garnish with mint and raspberries, if desired.

Makes 10 servings

Peach Cobbler

     4 cups sliced peeled peaches *or*
       2 (29-ounce) cans sliced
       peaches, drained
     1 cup fresh or frozen blueberries
       (optional)
    ⅔ cup all-purpose flour, divided
    ⅓ cup sugar, divided
     2 tablespoons lemon juice
    ⅓ cup FLEISCHMANN'S®
       Margarine, softened, divided
    20 NILLA® Wafers, finely crushed
       (about ¾ cup crumbs)
     2 tablespoons water

In large bowl, toss peaches and blueberries with 2 tablespoons flour, 3 tablespoons sugar and lemon juice. Place in greased 8×8×2-inch baking dish; dot with 1 tablespoon margarine.

In medium bowl, combine wafer crumbs with remaining flour and sugar; cut in remaining margarine until mixture resembles coarse crumbs. Stir in water until mixture holds together; shape into ball. Roll dough out between 2 sheets of lightly floured waxed paper to 7½-inch circle. Remove 1 sheet of waxed paper. Cut 1-inch circle out of center of dough. Invert dough over fruit mixture; peel off paper. Sprinkle with additional sugar if desired.

Bake at 400°F for 35 to 40 minutes or until pastry is browned. Cool slightly before serving.   *Makes 8 servings*

Tip

To peel a large quantity of peaches, blanch them in boiling water for about 30 seconds. Remove the peaches from the boiling water with a slotted spoon and plunge them into cold water. Pull off the skins with a paring knife.

PEANUT BUTTER

Peanut butter is a blend of ground roasted peanuts, vegetable oil and salt. Some brands contain sugar or a stabilizer that prevents the oil from separating. By law it must contain at least 90 percent peanuts. There are two types of peanut butter: creamy and chunky. Chunky has chopped peanuts added. Commercial brands of peanut butter can be stored after opening for three months at room temperature or longer if refrigerated. Natural peanut butters that are 100 percent peanuts contain no additives to keep them from separating. They need to be stirred before using. Natural peanut butters should always be refrigerated after opening. They will keep up to 6 months. Peanut butter is used primarily as a bread spread and as an ingredient in cookies, candies, and sweet and savory sauces.

Peanut Butter Thumbprints

1¼ cups firmly packed light brown
     sugar
¾ cup creamy peanut butter
½ CRISCO® Stick *or* ½ cup
     CRISCO All-Vegetable
     Shortening
3 tablespoons milk
1 tablespoon vanilla
1 egg
1¾ cups all-purpose flour
¾ teaspoon baking soda
¾ teaspoon salt
     Granulated sugar
¼ cup strawberry jam,* stirred

Substitute your favorite jam or jelly for strawberry jam, if desired.

1. Heat oven to 375°F. Place sheets of foil on countertop for cooling cookies.

2. Place brown sugar, peanut butter, shortening, milk and vanilla in large bowl. Beat at medium speed of electric mixer until well blended. Add egg; beat just until blended.

3. Combine flour, baking soda and salt. Add to shortening mixture; beat at low speed just until blended.

4. Shape dough into 1-inch balls. Roll in granulated sugar. Place 2 inches apart on ungreased baking sheets.

5. Bake one baking sheet at a time at 375°F for 6 minutes. Press centers of cookies immediately with back of measuring teaspoon. Bake 3 minutes longer or until cookies are set and just beginning to brown. *Do not overbake.* Cool 2 minutes on baking sheet. Spoon jam into center of each cookie. Remove cookies to foil to cool completely.

Makes about 4 dozen cookies

Peanut Butter Thumbprints

PEAR

Pears are juicy fruits grown in temperate climates around the world. Most of the domestic crop is grown in California, Oregon and Washington. Pears are second only to apples in worldwide fruit production. There are two types of pears: the more common European pear and the Asian pear. European pears are one of the few fruits that are better if picked before they are completely ripe. Ripening off the tree results in a better flavor and a finer texture.

☙

MOST COMMON EUROPEAN PEARS

Variety	Characteristics	Peak Season
Anjou	autumn pear; oval shape with short neck; greenish-yellow skin; yellowish-white flesh; buttery, sweet flavor	October to March
Bartlett	summer pear; yellow skin; white flesh; highly aromatic; sweet and juicy	late July to mid-September
Bosc	autumn pear; elongated shape; golden russet skin; white flesh; firm when ripe; buttery, sweet and juicy; good for poaching	October to March
Comice	autumn pear; large and round; thick yellowish-gold skin with red blush; white flesh; very soft when ripe; highly aromatic; buttery texture and great flavor	August to March
Seckel	autumn pear; tiny pear; range from dark green with dark red blush to mostly red; grainy texture and sweet flavor; often used for preserving	August to January
Red Anjou	autumn pear; smaller and firmer than the Anjou; red skin; white flesh; spicy and juicy	October to March
Red Bartlett	summer pear; bell-shaped; bright crimson skin; white flesh; similar flavor to yellow Bartlett	late July to mid-September

Varieties: European varieties have the typical pear shape and soft flesh. They are further grouped as summer or autumn pears. Summer pears are best eaten raw rather than cooked. Autumn pears are more versatile; they can be eaten raw, cooked or baked. They keep longer than summer pears.

Asian pears, also known as apple pears, are juicy like European pears but have the crisp texture of an apple. Unlike European pears, they are sold fully ripened. They are round and have a greenish-yellow or russet-colored skin. Their crisp texture works well in salads and for snacking. Until recently they were imported from Asia but now are cultivated in California and Washington.

Availability: See the chart (left) for availability of fresh European pears. They are also available canned and as pear nectar. Asian pears are available year-round. Domestically grown pears can be found from August to December.

Buying Tips: Ripe European pears are seldom seen in markets. Unripe pears should be free of blemishes. Ripe pears are fragile so they may have a few blemishes. Choose ones that are fragrant without any soft spots.

Asian pears should have a bright color and smooth skin. Most blemishes are only skin deep.

Yield: 1 pound European pears = 3 to 4 medium; 2 cups slices.
1 pound Asian pears = 2 large; 2 cups slices.
1 (16-ounce) can pear halves = 6 to 10 halves.

Storage: Store European pears in a paper bag at room temperature until they give to slight pressure. It is best to turn pears occasionally while ripening. Refrigerate ripened pears and use within three or four days. Asian pears may be stored at room temperature for up to one week. They will keep up to two months in the refrigerator.

Basic Preparation: Most pears are eaten fresh with the skin on. If the skin is removed or the pear is cut, dip it in lemon water (six parts water to one part lemon juice) to prevent the flesh from browning.

When pears are to be used for cooking, use fruit that is still firm. It is best to remove the skin; it toughens and darkens as it cooks. To peel the skin use a vegetable peeler. Bosc and Anjou are the best varieties for cooking. To poach pears, peel, halve and core before simmering pear halves in liquid (light sugar syrup, fruit juice or wine) until tender when pierced with fork.

Chocolate and Pear Tart

> **Chocolate Tart Crust (recipe follows)**
> **1 cup milk**
> **2 egg yolks, beaten**
> **2 tablespoons sugar**
> **⅛ teaspoon salt**
> **1 cup HERSHEY'S Semi-Sweet Chocolate Chips**
> **3 large fresh pears**
> **Apricot Glaze (recipe follows)**

Prepare Chocolate Tart Crust; set aside. In top of double boiler over hot, not boiling, water, scald milk; gradually stir in egg yolks, sugar and salt. Cook over hot water, stirring constantly, until slightly thickened; do not boil. Remove from heat; immediately add chocolate chips, stirring until chips are melted and mixture is smooth. Pour into baked Chocolate Tart Crust; refrigerate several hours or until firm. Core and peel pears; cut into thin slices. Place in circular pattern on top of filling. Immediately prepare Apricot Glaze. Spoon over top of fruit, covering completely. Refrigerate several hours or until firm. Remove rim of pan. Serve cold. Cover; refrigerate leftovers. *Makes 12 servings*

Chocolate Tart Crust: Preheat oven to 325°F. Grease and flour 9-inch round tart pan with removable bottom. In small mixer bowl, stir together ¾ cup

Chocolate and Pear Tart

all-purpose flour, ¼ cup powdered sugar and 1 tablespoon HERSHEY'S Cocoa. At low speed of electric mixer, beat in 6 tablespoons cold butter or margarine until blended and smooth. Press evenly onto bottom and up side of prepared pan. Bake 10 to 15 minutes; cool.

Apricot Glaze

> **¾ teaspoon unflavored gelatin**
> **2 teaspoons cold water**
> **½ cup apricot nectar**
> **¼ cup sugar**
> **1 tablespoon arrowroot**
> **1 teaspoon lemon juice**

In small bowl or cup, sprinkle gelatin over cold water; let stand several minutes to soften. In small saucepan, combine apricot nectar, sugar, arrowroot and lemon juice; cook over medium heat, stirring constantly, until mixture is thickened. Remove from heat; immediately add gelatin mixture. Stir until smooth.

Pear Brown Betty

8 medium pears, cored, peeled,
   sliced
¾ cup frozen unsweetened apple
   juice concentrate, thawed
½ cup golden raisins
¼ cup *plus* 3 tablespoons all-
   purpose flour, divided
1 teaspoon ground cinnamon
⅓ cup uncooked rolled oats
3 tablespoons firmly packed dark
   brown sugar
3 tablespoons margarine, melted

1. Preheat oven to 375°F. Spray 10×7-inch baking dish with nonstick cooking spray.

2. Combine pears, juice concentrate, raisins, 3 tablespoons flour and cinnamon in large bowl; mix well. Spoon mixture into prepared baking dish.

3. Combine oats, remaining ¼ cup flour, brown sugar and margarine in medium bowl; mix until coarse crumbs form. Sprinkle evenly over pear mixture. Bake 1 hour or until golden brown. Cool in pan on wire rack. *Makes 12 servings*

PEEL, TO

To peel is to remove the outer coating, such as the skin or peel, from foods, usually fruits and vegetables. Tools used for peeling include a paring knife and a swivel-bladed vegetable peeler. Of course, you can use your hands to peel loose-skinned oranges.

🐝

PEPPER

Hundreds of pepper varieties exist in a multitude of shapes, sizes and colors. They range in flavor from mild and sweet to fiery hot. All are members of the Capsicum family and are native to tropical areas of the Western Hemisphere. Peppers were introduced to Europe and Asia after Christopher Columbus brought back to Spain, along with other New World treasures, the plant that produces peppers.

🐝

SWEET BELL PEPPERS

Varieties: The most familiar sweet pepper is the green pepper, also known as the bell pepper for its bell-like shape. Green peppers are picked before they ripen. When ripe, a bell pepper is red, yellow, orange, white or purple, depending on the variety. They are sweeter and crisper than green peppers. Pimientos are large, heart-shaped red sweet peppers. Banana peppers are long, tapered pale yellow peppers. They have thin walls and a sweet flavor.

Availability: Green peppers are grown in almost every state in the United States and are abundantly available year-round in supermarkets. Their season peaks between July and November. Red peppers are generally more expensive because the yield is lower from each plant. However, they are more abundant and, consequently, less expensive toward the end of the green pepper season. Most speciality colored peppers are imported from Holland and are becoming more available in supermarkets. They tend to be very expensive.

Buying Tips: All peppers should be firm, crisp and feel heavy for their size. They should be shiny and brightly colored and their stems should be green and hard. Avoid peppers that have wrinkles, soft spots or bruises. If you plan to stuff or peel peppers, purchase round, blocky peppers rather than oddly-shaped peppers.

Yield: 1 large bell pepper = 1 cup chopped; 1¼ cups strips.

Storage: Store unwashed sweet peppers in the refrigerator. Green peppers begin to lose their crispness after three to four days, and red peppers are even more perishable. Once cut, refrigerate peppers, wrapped in plastic wrap, and use them quickly.

Basic Preparation: Peppers should be washed under cold running water before using. To slice or chop, stand a bell pepper on its end on a cutting board. Cut off 3 to 4 lengthwise slices from the sides with a utility knife, cutting close to, but not through, the stem.

Discard the stem and seeds. Scrape out any remaining seeds and rinse the inside of the pepper under cold running water. Slice each piece lengthwise into long strips or cut into pieces.

To prepare a pepper for stuffing or slicing into rings, the stem must be removed. Make a circular cut around the top of the pepper with a paring knife. Pull the stem from the pepper to remove it. Carefully cut out the membrane and seeds; discard. Rinse the inside of the pepper under cold running water. To form rings, slice crosswise through the pepper with a utility knife.

To roast bell peppers, preheat the broiler. Place whole peppers on a foil-covered broiler pan 4 inches from the heat source. Broil 15 to 20 minutes until blackened on all sides, turning the peppers every 5 minutes with tongs.

To loosen their skins, steam blackened peppers by placing them in a paper bag immediately after roasting. Close the bag and set it aside to cool for 15 to 20 minutes. To peel peppers, cut around the cores, twist and remove them. Cut peppers in half; place on a cutting board. Peel off their skins with a paring knife and rinse them under cold water to remove the seeds. Lay the halves flat and slice them lengthwise into ¼-inch strips with a utility knife.

Cutting sides from pepper.

Removing stem from pepper before stuffing.

Roasting peppers.

Peeling skin from roasted peppers.

Ratatouille-Stuffed Pepper Halves (recipe on page 376)

From left to right: Anaheim, jalapeño, poblano and serrano chili peppers

CHILI PEPPERS

Varieties: Chili peppers make up 90 percent of the Capsicum family. There are over 100 varieties of chili peppers in Mexico alone, each with its own distinct flavor. Chilies are sold both fresh and dried. A general rule to follow is that the smaller the chili, the hotter the taste (although this is not guaranteed). The heat of chilies can even vary within a variety. Cayenne, paprika, hot pepper sauce, red pepper flakes, chili oil, chili powder and harissa are all products from chilies. The most common varieties of chilies available in the United States follow:

• Anaheim chilies, also known as California green chilies, are light green with a mild flavor and a slight bite. They are 4 to 6 inches long, about 1½ inches wide and have a rounded tip.

• Ancho peppers are fairly large, triangular-shaped dried poblano chilies. They are medium to dark reddish-brown in color. Anchos are full-flavored, ranging from mild to medium-hot. They are often ground for use in cooked sauces, such as mole.

• Chipotles are smoked, dried red jalapeño peppers. They have a rich, smoky, very hot flavor. They are commonly canned in adobo sauce.

• De árbol chili peppers are very small, slender dried chilies with a smooth, bright red skin and a very hot flavor.

• Jalapeño peppers are small, dark green chilies, normally 2 to 3 inches long and about ¾ of an inch wide with a blunt or slightly tapered end. Their flavor varies from hot to very hot. Ripe jalapeño peppers are red and sweeter than the green jalapeño. They are also sold canned or pickled.

• Mulatos are large, triangular-shaped dried chilies that have wrinkled, blackish-brown skin. Its flavor is rich, pungent and medium-hot. Mulatos are often used in red mole sauce.

• Pasillas are long, slender medium-sized dried chilies with wrinkled, blackish-brown skin. Their flavor is pungent, ranging from mild to hot.

• Poblano peppers are very dark green, large triangular-shaped chilies with pointed ends. Poblanos are usually 3½ to 5 inches long. This is the pepper most frequently used for *chiles rellenos,* a dish of stuffed chilies. Their flavor ranges from mild to quite hot. For a milder flavor, Anaheims can be substituted.

• Serrano peppers are very small, medium-green or red chilies with a very hot flavor. Serranos are also available pickled.

Availability: Chili peppers, especially jalapeños, are becoming more popular and are finding their way into more supermarkets. The availability of fresh chili peppers varies according to the variety and the season, but they are most likely to be found in supermarkets between July and November when sweet peppers are in season. Not all varieties are available in all areas at all times but substitutions can be made. Latin markets stock a large variety of chilies. Dried chilies are available year-round either loose or in packages and canned.

Buying Tips: All varieties of chili peppers should be firm, crisp and have unblemished skins. They should have shiny, bright coloring and green stems. Avoid limp chilies that have soft spots or wrinkled skin.

Storage: Fresh chilies will keep for several weeks refrigerated in a plastic bag lined with paper towels. Dried chilies should be kept in an airtight container in a cool, dry place. They will keep for six months.

Basic Preparation: All fresh chilies should be rinsed and patted dry with paper towels. To limit the amount of heat in a dish, remove the veins and seeds from the chili. Cut them lengthwise into halves with a utility  knife. Scrape out and discard the stems, seeds and veins, if desired. Cut the peppers into coarse pieces.

To use dried chilies, place them in a saucepan, cover them with water and bring them to a boil over medium-high heat. Remove the saucepan from the heat and let the chilies stand until they are softened. Remove the stems and seeds. Chop or purée the peppers in a blender with a small amount of water to form a paste.

A Note of Caution: The heat of the chilies comes from a substance known as capsaicin located in the seeds, in the veins (the thin inner membranes to which the seeds are attached) and in the parts nearest the veins. The oils from the seeds and veins can be very irritating to the skin and can cause painful burning of the hands, eyes and lips. Use rubber or plastic gloves when handling chilies and do not touch your face or eyes. Wash your hands well in warm soapy water after handling. If you eat too much chili pepper at once, resist the urge to drink water, which spreads the capsaicin. Bread, rice or yogurt work well to put the fire out.

Baked Chilies Rellenos

4 small to medium poblano chili peppers
1 cup cooked brown rice
½ cup cooked corn (fresh, canned or frozen)
¼ cup GUILTLESS GOURMET® Spicy Nacho Dip
1 tablespoon chopped fresh cilantro
¼ cup low-fat sour cream
¼ cup GUILTLESS GOURMET® Salsa (mild, medium or hot)

1. Preheat broiler. Place peppers on baking sheet; broil about 10 minutes, turning as skin blisters. (Avoid charring peppers; blister peppers evenly.) Remove peppers from oven; turn off broiler. Immerse peppers in bowl of ice water; allow to cool. Remove peppers from ice water and gently scrape away blistered skin, being careful not to tear the flesh.* Make lengthwise slit in each pepper and carefully scrape out seeds and membranes.

2. Preheat oven to 350°F.

3. Combine rice, corn, nacho dip and cilantro in small bowl. Stuff peppers evenly with rice mixture; press peppers to close, squeezing with fingertips. Arrange peppers in small baking dish.

4. Bake 20 to 30 minutes until heated through. To serve, dollop each pepper with 1 tablespoon sour cream and 1 tablespoon salsa.

Makes 4 servings

*Chili peppers can sting and irritate the skin; wear rubber or plastic gloves when handling peppers and do not touch eyes. Wash hands after handling.

Technique for Ratatouille-Stuffed Pepper Halves

Step 1. *Scraping out seeds and membranes.*

Jerked Pork

Jerked Pork

2 jalapeño peppers
4 green onions, coarsely chopped
2 tablespoons brown sugar
1 tablespoon dried thyme leaves
½ teaspoon ground cinnamon
½ teaspoon ground nutmeg
½ teaspoon ground allspice
½ teaspoon ground cloves
½ teaspoon ground black pepper
6 pork chops (5 to 6 ounces each), well trimmed
Fresh thyme sprigs (optional)

1. Rinse jalapeños; pat dry with paper towels. Cut jalapeños lengthwise into halves. Scrape out and discard stems, seeds and veins. Cut halves crosswise into thirds.* Combine onions, jalapeños, sugar, dried thyme, cinnamon, nutmeg, allspice, cloves and black pepper in food processor; process until onions and jalapeños are finely chopped.

2. Rub both sides of pork with spice mixture.

3. Preheat broiler. Broil pork on broiler pan, 2 to 3 inches from heat, 5 to 6 minutes per side until pork is juicy and barely pink in center. Garnish with fresh thyme, if desired. Serve immediately.

Makes 6 servings

*Jalapeño peppers can sting and irritate the skin; wear rubber or plastic gloves when handling peppers and do not touch eyes. Wash hands after handling.

Ratatouille-Stuffed Pepper Halves

3 large bell peppers (1 red, 1 yellow and 1 green or any combination)
¼ cup olive oil
1 small eggplant (about ¾ pound), unpeeled, cut into ½-inch cubes
1 small onion, thinly sliced
1 large tomato, seeded, coarsely chopped
1 cup sliced fresh button mushrooms
1 clove garlic, minced
½ teaspoon dried basil leaves
½ teaspoon dried oregano leaves
½ teaspoon salt
Dash ground black pepper
Dash ground red pepper
1 zucchini, quartered, cut into ½-inch chunks

1. Cut bell peppers in half lengthwise through stems. Scrape out seeds and membranes, being careful not to cut through shells. Rinse out pepper halves; drain.

2. Place steamer basket in large saucepan or stockpot; add 1 inch of water. Place pepper halves, cut sides up, in steamer basket; cover. Bring to a boil; steam 5 minutes or until pepper halves are crisp-tender. Plunge pepper halves into ice water to stop cooking. Place pepper halves in 13×9-inch baking dish; set aside.

3. Heat oil in large skillet over medium heat. Add eggplant and onion; cook 10 minutes or until vegetables are soft, stirring occasionally. Add tomato, mushrooms, garlic, basil, oregano, salt, black pepper and ground red pepper. Bring to a boil over medium-high heat; reduce heat to medium-low. Simmer about 5 minutes, stirring occasionally. Add zucchini; simmer 5 minutes more or until mixture thickens slightly.

4. Preheat oven to 350°F.

5. Spoon mixture evenly into pepper halves.* Bake 15 minutes or until heated through. Garnish as desired. Serve immediately.

Makes 6 side-dish servings

*Pepper halves may be refrigerated up to 4 days at this point.

PEPPER SAUCE

Pepper sauce, or hot pepper sauce, is a thin, spicy liquid, usually red in color, made from chili peppers (such as cayenne, jalapeño and serrano), vinegar and seasonings. Widely used in Cajun, Creole and Caribbean cooking, it is used both as an ingredient and table condiment. There are many brands, each with a unique taste and widely varying levels of heat.

🌿

PERSIMMON

Persimmons are orange fruits with a glossy skin and green cap. They are found in produce markets in autumn. There are two distinct varieties of persimmons, one is native to America and the other to Asia. They differ in size and flavor. The American persimmon tree grows wild in southern states and in southern Indiana. The fruits are small, only slightly larger than a golf ball. Picked off the tree, they tend to be tart. But harvested from the ground, where they fall as soon as they ripen, their custardlike flesh is succulent and sweet, ideal for making puddings, cakes and candy. Native persimmons rarely are sold commercially and do not ship well so they are regional. Occasionally, canned or frozen persimmon pulp can be found.

Asian persimmons are larger than native persimmons. Two varieties are available in many supermarkets: the Hachiya and Fuyu. Their taste is less complex than the native persimmons, although they can be used in many of the same preparations. Select plump fruits with smooth, waxy skin and vibrant orange color. Rock-hard Asian persimmons will not fully ripen but firm ones can be ripened at room temperature in a paper bag for several days. The Hachiya is the more common variety. It is oval in shape and soft when ripe. The Fuyu is round in shape and is slightly firm when ripe. Once ripened, persimmons can be refrigerated for several days.

🌿

Tip

To eat a persimmon, rinse it under cold water and eat as you would an apple or pear. The skin is edible. A soft, ripe persimmon may be wrapped in plastic and partially frozen for a special treat.

Technique for Classic Pesto with Linguine

Step 3. *Adding oil through feed tube while processing.*

PESTO SAUCE

From the Italian word meaning paste, this green uncooked sauce from the Ligurian region of Italy is made from fresh basil, garlic, pine nuts, Parmesan cheese and olive oil. The ingredients are mashed together, traditionally in a mortar and pestle, but today, more likely in a food processor. Pesto sauce is primarily served with pasta, but it is also added to minestrone soup, marinades and salad dressings. Variations of the classic pesto are now seen in restaurants with various herbs substituted for the traditional basil.

❦

Classic Pesto with Linguine

Classic Pesto with Linguine

Homemade Linguine *or*
　　³/₄ **pound dry uncooked linguine, cooked, drained**
　2 **tablespoons butter or margarine**
　¹/₄ **cup *plus* 1 tablespoon olive oil, divided**
　2 **tablespoons pine nuts**
　1 **cup tightly packed fresh basil leaves, stems removed**
　2 **cloves garlic**
　¹/₄ **teaspoon salt**
　¹/₄ **cup (about 1 ounce) freshly grated Parmesan cheese**
1¹/₂ **tablespoons freshly grated Romano cheese**
　　Additional fresh basil leaves (optional)

1. To prepare Homemade Linguine, make dough following steps 1 and 2 of Homemade Fettuccine (page 363). In step 3, roll out dough to ¹/₁₆-inch-thick circle. In step 4, cut dough into ¹/₈-inch-wide strips. Cook as directed. Toss hot linguine with butter; keep warm.

2. Heat 1 tablespoon oil in small skillet over medium-low heat. Add pine nuts; cook 30 to 45 seconds until light brown, shaking pan constantly. Remove with slotted spoon; drain on paper towels.

3. Place toasted pine nuts, 1 cup basil, garlic and salt in food processor or blender. With processor running, add remaining ¹/₄ cup oil in slow steady stream until evenly blended and pine nuts are finely chopped. Transfer basil mixture to small bowl. Stir in Parmesan and Romano cheeses.*

4. Combine hot linguine and pesto sauce in large serving bowl; toss until well coated. Garnish with additional basil, if desired. Serve immediately.

Makes 4 servings (about ³/₄ cup pesto sauce)

*Pesto sauce can be stored at this point in airtight container; pour thin layer of olive oil over pesto and cover. Refrigerate up to 1 week. Bring to room temperature. Proceed as directed in step 4.

Sun-Dried Tomato Pesto

1 tablespoon vegetable oil
½ cup pine nuts
2 cloves garlic
1 jar (8 ounces) sun-dried
    tomatoes packed in oil,
    undrained
1 cup tightly packed fresh Italian
    parsley leaves, stems removed
½ cup (about 2 ounces) freshly
    grated Parmesan cheese
¼ cup coarsely chopped pitted
    kalamata olives
2 teaspoons dried basil leaves
¼ teaspoon crushed red pepper
    flakes

1. Heat oil in small skillet over medium-low heat. Add pine nuts; cook 30 to 45 seconds until lightly browned, shaking pan constantly. Remove with slotted spoon; drain on paper towels.

2. Place toasted pine nuts and garlic in food processor; process using on/off pulsing action until mixture is finely chopped. Add undrained tomatoes; process until finely chopped. Add parsley, cheese, olives, basil and pepper flakes; process until mixture resembles thick paste, scraping down side of bowl occasionally.

3. Spoon pesto into clean decorative crock or jar with tight-fitting lid; cover. Store tightly covered in refrigerator up to 1 month.

Makes about 1½ cups pesto

PETIT FOUR

Petit four generally refers to a tiny fancy individual cake covered on the top and sides with a cooked fondant icing and topped with tiny decorations. The French also apply the term to small fancy cookies.

🐝

Sun-Dried Tomato Pesto

*Raspberry Cheesecake
Blossom*

PHYLLO

*Phyllo, which literally translated
means "leaf" in Greek, refers to the
tissue-thin, almost transparent sheets
of pastry dough made of flour and
water that are used in a variety of
Greek and Middle Eastern dishes.
Phyllo, also spelled filo, is an integral
ingredient in both baklava, the Greek
dessert, and spanakopitta, the savory
spinach cheese pie. Although similar
to strudel dough, phyllo sheets are
much thinner.*

*Phyllo dough is seldom prepared at
home but may be purchased refrigerated in Greek markets and frozen at*

*supermarkets. Unopened packages of
phyllo leaves will keep in the refrigerator up to one month and frozen up
to one year. Thaw frozen dough in the
refrigerator overnight. Thawed and
opened packages, if wrapped securely,
will keep in the refrigerator two or
three days. Phyllo becomes brittle if
refrozen.*

*Once opened, the dough dries out
very quickly, crumbles easily and becomes unmanageable. So, keep phyllo
leaves wrapped until all ingredients
are assembled and the dough is ready
to be used. Once you begin working
with the phyllo, keep unused sheets
covered with plastic wrap and a damp
towel. Avoid laying the towel directly
on the dough sheets as they will become moist and tear easily.*

❦

Raspberry Cheesecake Blossoms

  3 packages (10 ounces each)
    frozen raspberries, in syrup,
    thawed
¼ cup butter, melted
  8 sheets phyllo dough*
  1 package (8 ounces) cream
    cheese, softened
½ cup cottage cheese
  1 egg
½ cup *plus* 3 tablespoons sugar,
    divided
  4 teaspoons fresh lemon juice,
    divided
½ teaspoon vanilla extract
    Fresh raspberries and sliced
    kiwifruit (optional)

*Cover with plastic wrap, then a damp
kitchen towel to prevent dough from
drying out.

Technique for Raspberry Cheesecake Blossoms

Step 3. *Fitting phyllo
dough into muffin cups.*

1. Drain thawed raspberries in fine-meshed sieve over 1-cup glass measure. Reserve syrup.

2. Preheat oven to 350°F. Grease 12 (2½-inch) muffin cups.

3. Brush melted butter onto 1 phyllo sheet. Cover with second phyllo sheet; brush with butter. Repeat with remaining sheets of phyllo and butter. Cut stack of phyllo dough in thirds lengthwise and then in fourths crosswise, to make a total of 12 squares. Gently fit each stacked square into prepared muffin cup.

4. Place cream cheese, cottage cheese, egg, 3 tablespoons sugar, 1 teaspoon juice and vanilla in food processor or blender; process until smooth. Divide cheese mixture evenly over phyllo squares.

5. Bake 10 to 15 minutes until lightly browned. Carefully remove cheesecake blossoms from muffin cups to wire racks; cool completely.

6. Meanwhile, to prepare raspberry sauce, bring reserved raspberry syrup to a boil in small saucepan over medium-high heat. Cook until reduced to ¾ cup, stirring occasionally.

7. Place thawed raspberries in food processor or blender; process until smooth. Press through fine-meshed sieve with back of spoon to remove seeds; discard seeds. Combine raspberry purée, reduced syrup, remaining ½ cup sugar and 3 teaspoons juice in small bowl; mix well. To serve, spoon raspberry sauce onto 12 dessert plates. Place 1 cheesecake blossom on each plate. Garnish with fresh raspberries and kiwifruit, if desired.

Makes 12 servings

PIE

A pie is a sweet or savory baked dish with a crust and a filling. Dessert pies may be baked or chilled. They are usually made in a pie pan. They feature a variety of crusts made from pastry dough, graham cracker crumbs or cookie crumbs. Savory pies are baked and generally served hot. These have crusts made from pastry dough, biscuit dough or corn bread. They are often made in a casserole or baking dish. Pies are thought to have originated in England during the fourteenth or fifteenth century.

🌾

The most common types of sweet dessert pies:
Chiffon pies are single-crust chilled pies with a light, airy filling made by folding whipped cream or stiffly beaten egg whites into a gelatin-, cream- or cream cheese-based mixture.

Best Ever Apple Pie (recipe on page 382)

Techniques for Best Ever Apple Pie

Step 2. *Rolling out dough.*

Step 6. *Cutting slits in dough around edge of pie.*

Step 6. *Cutting slits in top crust to allow steam to escape.*

Cream pies are single-crust chilled pies with a rich, sweet puddinglike filling. They are usually topped with meringue, whipped cream or fruit.

Custard pies are single-crust baked pies with a sweet, rich custard filling made from eggs and milk.

Frozen pies have a single crust. They are filled with an ice cream, cream cheese or chiffon filling.

Fruit pies may have single or double crusts. They are filled with fresh, canned or frozen fruit and baked.

The most common types of savory pies:

Pot pies are baked with a single bottom or top crust or both. They are filled with a mixture of meat or poultry, vegetables and gravy.

Quiches are single-crust baked pies with a savory custard filling that includes cheese and often seafood or meat and vegetables. They are baked in either a pie pan or a specialty quiche pan.

Tips for Fruit Pies: Do not fill the pie crust with fruit filling until just before baking as the bottom crust can become soggy. To make ahead, cover filling and crust separately and refrigerate until ready to bake.

• To prevent major oven cleanups, place juicy fruit pies on a baking sheet when baking.

• For double-crust pies, cut slits in the top crust to allow the steam to escape during baking.

• If the pie crust is browning too quickly, cover the edges with strips of aluminum foil. An alternative is to cut the bottom out of a foil pie pan and invert it over the pie.

• Common thickeners for fruit pies are flour, cornstarch and tapioca. Flour gives the filling a more opaque appearance, while cornstarch and tapioca create a translucent filling.

Tips for Custard-Type Pies: To avoid messy spills, place the pie crust in the oven, then pour in the filling.

• To test for doneness, insert the blade of a tableware knife about one inch from the center. If the knife comes out clean, the pie is done.

Tips for Cream and Chiffon Pies: To bake an unfilled pastry crust, pierce the crust with the tines of a fork at ¼-inch intervals. Cut a square of foil about 4 inches larger than the pie plate. Line the crust with the foil. Fill with dried beans, uncooked rice or ceramic pie weights. Partially bake the crust, then gently remove the foil lining and beans. Continue to bake until the crust is lightly brown. Cool the beans; store them in an airtight container in a cool, dry place and reuse them as pie weights.

• To prevent a baked crust from becoming soggy, cool it before filling it with a cool filling.

• When cutting cream pies, the slices will cut better if the knife is wiped with a damp cloth or paper towel between cuts.

Storage: When storing pies, remember that any type made with eggs or dairy products, such as chiffon, cream and custard pies, should always be kept refrigerated. Fruit pies may be stored at room temperature for a day or two. After that they should also be refrigerated.

Best Ever Apple Pie

    2⅓ cups all-purpose flour, divided
     ¾ cup *plus* 1 tablespoon sugar, divided
     ½ teaspoon baking powder
     ½ teaspoon salt
     ¾ cup cold unsalted butter
     4 to 5 tablespoons ice water
     1 egg, separated
     7 medium apples, such as Jonathan, McIntosh or Granny Smith, peeled, cored, sliced
     1 tablespoon fresh lemon juice
    1¼ teaspoons ground cinnamon
     3 tablespoons unsalted butter, cut into small pieces
     1 tablespoon sour cream

1. Combine 2 cups flour, 1 tablespoon sugar, baking powder and salt in large bowl until well blended. Cut in ¾ cup butter using pastry blender or 2 knives until mixture resembles coarse crumbs. Add water, 1 tablespoon at a time. Toss with fork until mixture holds together. Form dough into 2 (6-inch) discs. Wrap discs in plastic wrap; refrigerate 30 minutes or until firm.

2. Working with 1 disc at a time, roll out dough on lightly floured surface into 12-inch circle. Place dough over 9-inch glass pie plate. Trim dough leaving ½-inch overhang; brush with egg white. Set aside.

3. Preheat oven to 450°F.

4. Place apple slices in large bowl; sprinkle with juice. Stir together remaining ⅓ cup flour, ¾ cup sugar and cinnamon in small bowl. Add to apple mixture; toss to coat apples evenly. Spoon filling into prepared pie crust; place 3 tablespoons butter on top of filling.

5. Moisten edge of dough with water. Roll out remaining disc. Place over filled pie. Trim dough leaving ½-inch overhang.

6. To flute, press dough between thumb and forefinger to make stand-up edge. Cut slits in dough at ½-inch intervals around edge to form flaps. Press 1 flap in toward center of pie and the next out toward rim of pie plate. Continue alternating in and out around edge. Cut 4 small slits in top of dough to allow steam to escape.

7. Combine egg yolk and sour cream in small bowl until well blended. Cover; refrigerate until ready to use.

8. Bake pie 10 minutes; *reduce oven temperature to 375°F.* Bake 35 minutes. Brush egg yolk mixture evenly on pie crust with pastry brush. Bake 20 to 25 minutes until crust is deep golden brown. Cool completely in pie plate on wire rack. Store loosely covered at room temperature 1 day or refrigerate up to 4 days.

Makes one 9-inch pie

Hershey's Cocoa Cream Pie

  ½ **cup HERSHEY'S Cocoa**
1¼ **cups sugar**
  ⅓ **cup cornstarch**
  ¼ **teaspoon salt**
  3 **cups milk**
  3 **tablespoons butter or margarine**
1½ **teaspoons vanilla extract**
  1 **baked 9-inch pie crust or graham cracker crumb crust, cooled**

In medium saucepan, stir together cocoa, sugar, cornstarch and salt. Gradually add milk, stirring until smooth. Cook over medium heat, stirring constantly, until mixture comes to a boil; boil 1 minute. Remove from heat; stir in butter and vanilla. Pour into prepared crust. Press plastic wrap directly onto surface. Cool to room temperature. Refrigerate 6 to 8 hours. Garnish as desired. Cover and refrigerate leftover pie. *Makes 6 to 8 servings*

Hershey's Cocoa Cream Pie

Beef Tamale Pie

4. Bake 30 minutes or until corn muffin mixture is slightly browned and begins to pull away from edge of pan. Sprinkle with cheese; let stand 5 minutes before serving.

Makes 4 servings

*Favorite recipe from **National Cattlemen's Beef Association***

Beef Tamale Pie

2½ cups (12 ounces) cooked beef, cut into ½-inch pieces
1 can (15¾ ounces) mild chili beans in chili sauce
1 can (4 ounces) chopped green chilies
¼ cup sliced green onions
¼ teaspoon ground cumin
¼ teaspoon ground black pepper
1 package (8½ ounces) corn muffin mix
1 cup cold water
½ cup (2 ounces) shredded sharp Cheddar cheese

1. Preheat oven to 425°F.

2. Combine beef, beans, chilies, onions, cumin and pepper in large bowl; mix well. Set aside.

3. Combine corn muffin mix and water (mixture will be very thin). Grease sides and bottom of 9-inch square baking pan or 10-inch metal skillet. Pour corn muffin batter into pan. Spoon reserved beef mixture into center of corn muffin mixture, leaving 1-inch border.

PIEROGI

Pierogis are traditional Polish filled dumplings. Fillings include pork and onions, cottage cheese, potatoes, cabbage and mushrooms. The dumplings are cooked in boiling water, drained and sometimes sautéed in butter. They are most often served as a side dish. Pierogi dough may also be filled with fruit, then boiled or deep-fried and served as a dessert.

PILAF

Pilaf is a Middle Eastern rice or bulgur side dish. The rice is first browned in butter or oil to give it a nutty flavor and then cooked in broth with seasonings until tender. Vegetables and sometimes meat, seafood and poultry are added to the pilaf.

PINCH

A pinch is a measurement of dry ingredients, such as sugar or salt, that is equivalent to the amount that can be held between thumb and forefinger. It is generally considered to equal about ¹⁄₁₆ of a teaspoon.

PINCH, TO

In cooking and baking, to pinch is to squeeze together dough between the thumb and forefinger for the purpose of creating a tight seal, a decorative edge or both. Filled pasta, turnovers and double-crust pies are pinched to seal their edges. A single crust pastry shell is pinched to form a decorative edge.

☸

PINEAPPLE

Pineapples were first grown in Central and South America. Today most of the domestic supply is grown in Hawaii and Central America. Since they do not ripen after picking, pineapples are picked when ripe and shipped by air to their destination. The distinct pineapple shape has been used as a symbol of hospitality for centuries. This fragrant, juicy, sweet fruit is shaped like a large cylindrical pinecone with long, sharp pointed leaves.

☸

Varieties: There are three major varieties of pineapples: Cayenne from Hawaii and Central America; Red Spanish from Florida and Puerto Rico; and Sugar Loaf from Mexico. The majority sold at supermarkets is Cayenne.

Availability: Fresh whole pineapple is available all year with the peak season from March to July. Peeled and cored fresh pineapples are now seen in some supermarkets. Crushed, chunked, sliced and tidbit pineapple is sold canned in its own juice and in syrup. Pineapple is also available candied and dried. Pineapple juice, both canned and frozen, is readily available.

Buying Tips: Although a pineapple does not ripen or become sweeter after picking, it can become juicier and less acidic. Choose fruit that is plump with a bright green crown and a strong sweet aroma at the stem end. The color should be changing from green to golden yellow. (Red Spanish will be tinged with red.) Avoid pineapples that are green, have soft spots, dry looking leaves or a fermented aroma.

Yield: 2 pounds pineapple = 1 medium; 2 cups cubed.
1 (29-ounce) can = 3¾ cups chunks or tidbits; 3¾ cups crushed.

Singapore Rice Salad (recipe on page 386)

Storage: If the aroma of the pineapple is not strong, allow it to stand at room temperature for two or three days until it softens slightly and its aroma increases. Refrigerate ripe pineapple for three to five days. Leftover canned or fresh pineapple can be stored in an airtight, nonmetallic container in the refrigerator and used within three to four days. Leftover pineapple may be frozen and used for blender drinks.

Preparation: To prepare a pineapple, twist off the crown. Use a chef's knife to cut the pineapple lengthwise into halves and then into quarters. Trim off the ends and remove the core. To remove the fruit from the shell, carefully run the blade of a utility knife between the shell and the fruit. Cut the fruit into wedges or chunks.

For pineapple boats, cut the pineapple in half lengthwise through the crown. Remove the fruit from the shell with a curved grapefruit knife or utility knife, leaving the shell intact. Cut the fruit into quarters and remove the core. Cut the fruit as desired.

Removing pineapple from shell.

Tip

Fresh or frozen pineapple cannot be combined with gelatin mixtures as it contains a natural enzyme that will prevent gelatin from thickening. Heating destroys the enzyme so canned pineapple can be used.

Calypso Grilled Pineapple

  ½ **cup FRENCH'S® Worcestershire Sauce**
  ½ **cup honey**
  ½ **cup (1 stick) butter or margarine**
  ½ **cup packed light brown sugar**
  ½ **cup dark rum**
  1 **pineapple, cut into 8 wedges, cored***
     Vanilla ice cream

*You may substitute other fruits, such as halved peaches, nectarines or thick slices of mangos, for the pineapple.

To prepare sauce, combine Worcestershire, honey, butter, sugar and rum in 3-quart saucepan. Bring to a full boil over medium-high heat, stirring often. Reduce heat to medium-low. Simmer 12 minutes or until sauce is slightly thickened, stirring often. Remove from heat; cool completely.

Brush pineapple wedges with some of the sauce. Place pineapple on oiled grid. Grill over hot coals 5 minutes or until glazed, turning and basting often with sauce. Serve pineapple with ice cream and remaining sauce. Garnish as desired. Refrigerate any leftover sauce.**

    Makes 8 servings (1½ cups sauce)

Prep time: 15 minutes
Cook time: 20 minutes

**Leftover sauce may be reheated in microwave. Microwave, stirring every 30 seconds, until heated through.

Singapore Rice Salad

  1 **can (8 ounces) pineapple tidbits or chunks in pineapple juice, undrained**
  3 **cups chilled cooked white rice, prepared in salted water**
  1 **cup finely chopped cucumber**
  1 **red bell pepper, finely chopped**
  1 **cup shredded carrots**
  ½ **cup sliced green onions**
  2 **tablespoons fresh lime juice**
  2 **tablespoons dry sherry**
  1 **tablespoon rice vinegar**
  1 **teaspoon minced fresh ginger**
  2 **tablespoons chopped fresh cilantro**
  1 **tablespoon chopped unsalted peanuts**
     Cucumber slices (optional)

1. Drain pineapple, reserving 3 tablespoons juice. Set juice aside.

2. Combine pineapple, rice, chopped cucumber, pepper, carrots and onions in large bowl. Combine lime juice, sherry, vinegar, ginger and reserved pineapple juice in small bowl; mix well. Pour over rice mixture; toss to coat. Cover; refrigerate at least 2 hours.

3. Sprinkle with cilantro and peanuts just before serving. Garnish with cucumber slices, if desired.

    Makes 6 side-dish servings

No-Bake Pineapple Marmalade Squares

1 cup graham cracker crumbs
2 tablespoons sugar
¼ cup light margarine, melted
1 cup fat free or light sour cream
4 ounces light cream cheese, softened
½ cup sugar
¼ cup orange marmalade or apricot fruit spread, divided
1 can (20 ounces) DOLE® Crushed Pineapple
1 envelope unflavored gelatin

• **Combine** crumbs, 2 tablespoons sugar and margarine in 8-inch square glass baking dish; pat mixture firmly and evenly onto bottom of dish. Freeze 10 minutes.

• **Beat** sour cream, cream cheese, ½ cup sugar and 1 tablespoon marmalade in medium bowl until smooth and blended; set aside.

• **Drain** pineapple; reserve ¼ cup juice.

• **Sprinkle** gelatin over reserved juice in small saucepan; let stand one minute. Cook and stir over low heat until gelatin dissolves.

• **Beat** gelatin mixture into sour cream mixture until well blended. Spoon mixture evenly over crust.

• **Stir** together pineapple and remaining 3 tablespoons orange marmalade in small bowl until blended. Evenly spoon over sour cream filling. Cover and refrigerate 2 hours or until firm.

Makes 16 servings

Prep time: 20 minutes
Chill time: 2 hours

No-Bake Pineapple Marmalade Squares

PITA

Pita, also known as pocket bread, is a round, flat Middle Eastern bread made from white or whole wheat flour. It is usually about six to seven inches in diameter. The bread splits horizontally to form a pocket, which can be filled with a variety of ingredients to make a sandwich. Pita bread may also be cut into wedges, toasted and used as dippers for Middle Eastern dishes like hummus.

PIZZA

Pizza literally translated means "pie," but today it can refer to any of a wide variety of flat crusts with toppings. The "classic" American pizza usually is made with a thin, crisp crust or thick breadlike crust topped with seasoned tomato sauce, mozzarella cheese and ingredients, such as Italian sausage, pepperoni, onions, mushrooms, green pepper and olives. Other convenient choices for pizza crusts are bagels, pita bread, English muffins and tortillas. Today's trendy toppings include goat cheese, duck sausage, artichokes and sun-dried tomatoes. Dessert pizzas are made with cookie dough crusts and topped with cream cheese or ice cream and fruit or candy toppings.

Tip

To produce the authentic crisp crust of a pizzeria pizza, bake homemade and frozen pizzas on a preheated baking stone.

Homemade Pizza

4½ teaspoons active dry yeast
1 teaspoon sugar, divided
½ cup warm water (105°F to 115°F)
1¾ cups all-purpose flour, divided
¾ teaspoon salt, divided
2 tablespoons olive oil, divided
1 medium onion, chopped
1 clove garlic, minced
1 can (14½ ounces) whole peeled tomatoes, undrained, finely chopped
2 tablespoons tomato paste
1 teaspoon dried oregano leaves
½ teaspoon dried basil leaves
⅛ teaspoon ground black pepper
1¾ cups (7 ounces) shredded mozzarella cheese
½ cup (about 2 ounces) freshly grated Parmesan cheese
½ small red bell pepper, cut into ¾-inch pieces
½ small green bell pepper, cut into ¾-inch pieces
4 fresh button mushrooms, thinly sliced
1 can (2 ounces) flat anchovy fillets, drained
⅓ cup pitted ripe olives, halved

1. To proof yeast, sprinkle yeast and ½ teaspoon sugar over warm water in small bowl; stir until yeast is dissolved. Let stand 5 minutes or until mixture is bubbly.

2. Place 1½ cups flour and ¼ teaspoon salt in medium bowl; stir in yeast mixture and 1 tablespoon oil, stirring until a smooth, soft dough forms. Place dough on lightly floured surface; knead using as much of remaining flour as needed to form a stiff, elastic dough. Shape into a ball; place in large greased bowl. Turn to grease entire surface. Cover with clean kitchen towel; let dough rise in warm place 30 to 45 minutes until doubled in bulk.

3. Meanwhile, to prepare sauce, heat remaining 1 tablespoon oil in medium saucepan over medium heat. Add onion; cook 5 minutes or until soft. Add garlic; cook 30 seconds

Homemade Pizza

more. Add tomatoes with juice, tomato paste, oregano, basil, remaining ½ teaspoon sugar, ½ teaspoon salt and black pepper. Bring to a boil over high heat; reduce heat to medium-low. Simmer, uncovered, 10 to 15 minutes until sauce thickens, stirring occasionally. Pour into small bowl; cool.

4. Punch dough down. Knead briefly on lightly floured surface; let dough stand 5 minutes more. Flatten dough into circle on lightly floured surface. Roll out dough, starting at center and rolling to edges, into 10-inch circle. Place circle in greased 12-inch pizza pan; stretch and pat dough out to edges of pan. Cover; let stand 15 minutes.

5. Preheat oven to 450°F.

6. Spread cooled sauce evenly over pizza dough. Mix mozzarella and Parmesan cheeses in small bowl. Sprinkle pizza with ⅔ cheese mixture. Arrange bell peppers,

mushrooms, anchovies and olives over top. Sprinkle with remaining cheese mixture.

7. Bake 20 minutes or until crust is golden brown. To serve, cut into wedges.   *Makes 4 to 6 servings*

PLUM

Plums, related to apricots, cherries, peaches and nectarines, are drupes, or fleshy fruits with a single pit in the center and a thin flexible skin. Plums grow on every continent except Antarctica and come in more varieties than any other drupe. Wild American plums were among the foods eaten at the first Thanksgiving dinner, although they were soon replaced by European varieties.

Uses: Fresh plums are popular eaten raw for snacking.

• Plums may be added to salads, baked goods and desserts.

• Sauces or preserves made from plums may be used with poultry and in Chinese sweet-and-sour dishes.

• Certain varieties of plums are dried to make prunes.

Varieties: Plums come in almost every color of the rainbow including red, yellow, lime green and bluish-black. More than 100 varieties are cultivated in the United States. California and the Pacific Northwest produce the majority of the domestic crop, but the Midwest and New England grow a variety of plums as well. Plum varieties are categorized as Japanese and European.

Japanese-type plums are clingstone varieties, meaning that the flesh adheres to the pit and must be cut away. They range in color from red to green to yellow. Their flesh is juicy and yellow to reddish in color. The most common varieties follow:

• Santa Rosa is a popular Japanese variety with crimson-red skin and a sweet, tart flavor. It accounts for about one third of the domestic crop.

• Kelsey, Wickson and greengage are green and yellow-skinned Japanese varieties.

• Other Japanese varieties include Red Beaut, El Dorado, French, Friar, Nubiana, Queen Rosa, Casselman, Laroda and Simka.

European-type plums are freestone varieties, meaning that the pit is easily removed from the flesh. They are smaller, less juicy and less flavorful than Japanese varieties and their skins are always blue or purple. European varieties are used for making prunes and are well suited for baking and stewing.

• Damson plums are a small, tart European variety usually used for making prunes and preserves.

• Other European-type plums are the Empress, Italian, President, Stanley and Tragedy.

Availability: Various varieties of plums are available from May through October. The sweeter, juicier Japanese-type varieties are the first to arrive at markets, peaking in supply in August. The European-type varieties, used more for baking, cooking and preserves, come to the market in the fall.

Buying Tips: Choose plump plums with a good color for their variety. Ripe plums yield to gentle pressure. Firm plums can be ripened at home. Avoid those that are bruised, discolored or have soft spots or shriveled skin. A dull white film, or "bloom," over the skin is harmless and is nature's way of waterproofing the surface.

Hazelnut Plum Tart

Yield: 1 pound plums = 6 to 8 medium; 3 cups sliced or chopped.

Storage: To ripen plums at home, place in a closed paper bag and let them stand at room temperature until ripe. Ripe plums may be stored in the refrigerator up to three or four days.

Basic Preparation: Wash plums under cold running water. To remove the pits from freestone plums, cut the plums in half around the pit, then twist the halves in opposite directions to separate. Pull out the pit. Clingstone varieties are more difficult to pit. Slice or quarter these plums, using a paring knife to separate the fruit from the pit. Both fresh and cooked plums are usually eaten with the skins left on. If you wish, a plum may be peeled after blanching it for about 30 seconds in boiling water and plunging it in cold water.

Hazelnut Plum Tart

1 cup hazelnuts, skins removed
¼ cup firmly packed light brown
    sugar
1 cup all-purpose flour
⅓ cup FILIPPO BERIO® Olive Oil
1 egg, separated
    Pinch salt
3 tablespoons granulated sugar
2 teaspoons cornstarch
½ teaspoon grated lime peel
    Pinch ground nutmeg
    Pinch ground cloves
1¼ pounds plums (about 5 large),
    halved and pitted
3 tablespoons currant jelly
    Sweetened whipped cream
    (optional)

Preheat oven to 375°F. Grease 9-inch tart pan with removable bottom with olive oil.

Place hazelnuts in food processor; process until coarsely chopped. Remove ¼ cup for garnish; set aside. Add brown sugar; process until nuts are finely ground. Add flour, olive oil, egg yolk and salt; process until combined. (Mixture will be crumbly.)

Spoon mixture into prepared pan. Press firmly in even layer on bottom and up side. Brush inside of crust with egg white. Place in freezer 10 minutes.

In large bowl, combine granulated sugar, cornstarch, lime peel, nutmeg and cloves. Cut each plum half into 4 wedges. Add to sugar mixture; toss until combined. Arrange plums in overlapping circles in crust; spoon any remaining sugar mixture over plums. Place tart on baking sheet.

Bake 45 to 50 minutes or until fruit is tender and juices are thickened. Cool 30 minutes on wire rack. Place currant jelly in small saucepan; heat over low heat, stirring frequently, until melted. Brush over plums; sprinkle with reserved hazelnuts. Serve tart warm or at room temperature with whipped cream, if desired.   *Makes 6 servings*

PLUM SAUCE

This thick, amber-brown Asian sauce is made from fruit, usually plums but also apricots, cooked with vinegar, sugar, hot chili peppers and spices. Originally made in China to preserve the plums that grow there, it can range from excessively sweet to sweet-and-hot, depending on the brand. It is often served with duck or pork but may be most familiar to Americans as the sauce spread on the pancakes used to make moo shu pork.

Tip

Once opened, plum sauce will keep up to a year in a tightly closed glass jar in the refrigerator.

Chicken with Walnuts

1 cup uncooked instant rice
½ cup chicken broth
¼ cup Chinese plum sauce
2 tablespoons soy sauce
2 teaspoons cornstarch
2 tablespoons vegetable oil, divided
3 cups frozen bell peppers and onions
1 pound boneless, skinless chicken breasts, cut into ¼-inch slices
1 clove garlic, minced
1 cup walnut halves

1. Cook rice according to package directions; set aside.

2. Combine broth, plum sauce, soy sauce and cornstarch until smooth; set aside.

3. Heat 1 tablespoon oil in wok or large skillet over medium-high heat. Add frozen peppers and onions; stir-fry 3 minutes or until crisp-tender. Remove vegetables from wok. Drain; discard liquid.

4. Heat remaining 1 tablespoon oil in wok. Add chicken and garlic; stir-fry 3 minutes or until chicken is no longer pink in center. Stir broth mixture; add to wok. Cook and stir 1 minute or until sauce thickens. Stir in reserved vegetables and walnuts; cook 1 minute more. Serve with rice.

Makes 4 servings

POACH, TO

Poaching refers to the technique of cooking food slowly and gently in a simmering, but not boiling, liquid that just covers the food. The poaching liquid may be flavored or seasoned. This flavor will transfer to the food during cooking.

☙

Technique for Poached Salmon with Tarragon Cream Sauce

Step 2. Simmering fish in poaching liquid.

Poaching Tips: When poaching eggs, add a small amount of vinegar to the water to help the eggs maintain their shape.

• Poaching fruit in a sugar or wine syrup helps the fruit retain its shape. Wine also adds flavor.

• Begin poaching fish and poultry in a cold liquid, such as broth or stock, to ensure even cooking. This will also prevent fish from falling apart.

Poached Salmon with Tarragon Cream Sauce

2 tablespoons butter or margarine
3 tablespoons finely chopped shallot
1 clove garlic, minced
1 cup dry white wine, divided
½ cup clam juice
½ cup whipping cream
1 tablespoon chopped fresh parsley
½ teaspoon dried tarragon leaves
2 salmon steaks, 1 inch thick (about 8 ounces each)
Fish Stock (page 486), clam juice or water
Fresh tarragon leaves (optional)

1. To make Tarragon Cream Sauce, melt butter in medium saucepan over medium heat. Add shallot and garlic; reduce heat to low and cook 5 minutes or until shallot is tender. Add ½ cup wine and juice to shallot mixture. Bring to a boil; reduce heat to low. Simmer 10 minutes or until sauce is reduced to ½ cup. Add cream; simmer 5 minutes or until sauce is reduced by half. (Sauce should heavily coat back of metal spoon.) Stir in parsley and dried tarragon; keep warm over very low heat.

2. Rinse salmon; pat dry with paper towels. To poach fish, place fish in saucepan just large enough to hold fillets. Add remaining ½ cup wine and enough Fish Stock to barely cover fish. Bring liquid to a simmer over medium heat. (*Do not boil. This* *will cause fish to break apart.)* Adjust heat, if necessary, to keep liquid at a simmer. Simmer 10 minutes or until center is no longer red and fish flakes easily when tested with fork.

3. Remove fish with slotted spatula; transfer to serving plates. To serve, top fish with Tarragon Cream Sauce. Garnish with fresh tarragon, if desired. *Makes 2 servings*

POLENTA

Polenta, an integral part of Northern Italian cuisine, is made from cornmeal. It is prepared by cooking cornmeal and water together to a thick spoonable consistency. Americans would call this dish "mush." It may be served as a hot cereal or side dish with butter and sometimes Parmesan cheese. When allowed to cool and become firm, it can be sliced or cut into squares and fried, broiled or baked. Fried polenta is usually eaten as a first course or a side dish often topped with tomato sauce or a mushroom or other vegetable mixture.

☙

Classic Polenta

6 cups water
2 teaspoons salt
2 cups yellow cornmeal
¼ cup vegetable oil

1. Bring water and salt to a boil in heavy large saucepan over medium-high heat. Stirring water vigorously, add cornmeal in very thin but steady stream (do not let lumps form). Reduce heat to low. Cook, uncovered, 40 to 60 minutes until very thick, stirring frequently. Polenta is ready when spoon will stand upright by itself in center of mixture. Polenta can be served at this point.*

Classic Polenta

2. Spray 10×7-inch baking pan with nonstick cooking spray. Spread polenta mixture evenly into baking pan. Cover; let stand at room temperature at least 6 hours or until completely cooled and firm.

3. Unmold polenta onto cutting board. Cut polenta crosswise into 1¼-inch-wide strips. Cut strips into 2- to 3-inch-long pieces. Heat oil in heavy large skillet over medium-high heat; reduce heat to medium. Fry polenta pieces, in 2 batches, 4 to 5 minutes until golden on all sides, turning as needed. Garnish as desired.

Makes 6 to 8 side-dish servings

*Hot freshly made polenta, as prepared in step 1, can be mixed with ⅓ cup butter and ⅓ cup grated Parmesan cheese and served as a first course. Or, pour onto a large platter and top with prepared bolognese sauce or other hearty meat sauce for a main dish.

POMEGRANATE

These bright coral-red, leathery-skinned fruits are a sure sign of fall. Cultivated for centuries, probably first in Persia or Afghanistan, pomegranates were a symbol of fertility to early Greeks. Pomegranate juice was used historically for medicinal purposes and as a dye. Once the skin is broken, the fruit yields an abundance of garnet-colored seeds that are juicy and flavorful. They have a tantalizing, sweet-and-sour taste. They are notorious for their ability to stain the skin and clothing. Wear rubber gloves while handling them and proceed with caution as the juice can squirt and splatter as the seeds pop open.

🌾

Uses: Primarily used for eating out of hand in this country, the edible seeds are also used as a garnish for salads and baba ghanouj, a Middle Eastern eggplant relish.

• Pomegranate juice can be used in marinades, sherbets, ices and sauces.

• Grenadine syrup was originally flavored and colored with pomegranate juice, but today the syrup is more likely to include artificial flavor and color instead.

Availability: The California supply of pomegranates begins to enter markets in September, peaks in October and November and continues through the winter holidays.

Buying Tips: A firm, heavy fruit with a rich, even color is the best choice. A shiny skin is an indication of a waxy coating; in their natural state, the skin has a dull patina. Avoid fruits that are broken or have soft spots.

Yield: 1 (4-inch) pomegranate = about 1 cup of seeds or ¾ cup juice.

Storage: The leathery skin protects pomegranates, allowing them to be stored for up to a week at room temperature or two months in the refrigerator. The juice and seeds can be frozen for several months.

Basic Preparation: Preparation is almost always limited to extracting seeds or juice from the fruit. Both tasks are somewhat labor intensive although worth the effort. To remove seeds, lightly score the skin from top to bottom. Peel back the skin, taking care not to pop the seeds. As the seeds are exposed, remove them from the bitter membrane with your fingers.

To juice, roll the fruit around on the counter, pressing lightly with the palm of your hand. This releases some of the juice. Then, carefully cut the fruit in half crosswise and gently press the halves onto a citrus juicer to extract the juice. Do not exert too much force or the membrane will add a bitter taste to the juice.

POPPY SEED

Poppy seeds are the very tiny bluish-grey to black ripe seeds of the opium poppy plant, which is native to the Mediterranean region. It takes about 900,000 seeds to make one pound. They are available whole, ground and as a sweetened poppy seed filling. Roasting or crushing poppy seeds enhances their nutty flavor. Ground sweetened poppy seeds are used as a filling for a variety of pastries, cakes, coffee cakes and other baked goods. Whole poppy seeds are used in salad dressings and sprinkled on breads and baked goods. They are popular in Middle Eastern, Indian and Central European cuisines, especially German and Bohemian.

❦

Lemon Poppy Seed Muffins

    3 cups all-purpose flour
    1 cup sugar
    3 tablespoons poppy seeds
    1 tablespoon grated lemon peel
    2 teaspoons baking powder
    1 teaspoon baking soda
    ½ teaspoon salt
    1 container (16 ounces) low-fat
        plain yogurt
    ½ cup fresh lemon juice
    ¼ cup vegetable oil
    2 eggs, beaten
    1½ teaspoons vanilla extract

1. Preheat oven to 400°F. Grease 12 (3½-inch) large muffin cups.

2. Combine flour, sugar, poppy seeds, lemon peel, baking powder, baking soda and salt in large bowl. Combine yogurt, juice, oil, eggs and vanilla in small bowl until blended; stir into flour mixture just until moistened. Spoon into prepared muffin cups, filling ⅔ full.

3. Bake 25 to 30 minutes until wooden toothpick inserted into centers comes out clean. Cool in pans on wire racks 5 minutes. Remove from pans. Cool on wire racks.   *Makes 12 jumbo muffins*

POTATO

Potatoes are grown all around the world, making them one of the world's most important vegetables. The potato may have its roots in ancient Peru but today it is grown in more than 80 countries. Originally thought to be poisonous, this underground tuber became a staple food in Ireland until failure of the crop led to widespread famine and massive emigration in the 1840's. Potatoes, when prepared with little additional fat, are low in calories and a good source of vitamins, minerals and fiber.

❦

Varieties: Potatoes in America can be categorized as russets, long whites, round whites and round reds.

• Russets are popular for baking and for French fries. They are large (often up to 18 ounces each) and oval in shape with rough brown skin and starchy flesh. Russet Burbank, also referred to as Idaho or russet, is the leading variety.

• Long whites are an all-purpose potato with thin pale brown skin. They average about eight ounces each. They can be baked, boiled or fried.

• Round whites are good for boiling and mashing. Smaller than long whites with a light tan skin, they are similar to round red potatoes.

• Round reds have a smooth red skin, and because of their lower starch and higher moisture content, they are good for boiling and mashing.

Tip

Because of their high oil content, poppy seeds have a tendency to become rancid if stored at room temperature. If kept refrigerated, they will keep for up to six months.

• A number of specialty varieties are becoming available in some supermarkets and farmers' markets. Yukon gold potatoes, with a skin and flesh that ranges from yellow to buttery gold, have a rich moist texture that is ideal for mashing. Blue potatoes have a delicate flavor with blue to purple skin and flesh.

• New potatoes are freshly dug young potatoes. They may be any variety, but most often are round reds. New potatoes can be as small as marbles or almost as large as full-size potatoes, but they should have a very thin wispy skin. The sugar in these young potatoes has not completely converted to starch so they have a crisp, waxy texture.

Swiss-Style Twice Baked Potatoes

Availability: Fresh potatoes are commercially grown in 48 states in overlapping growing seasons, so at least one or two varieties are always available. Potatoes in many forms are also available frozen, refrigerated, dehydrated and canned.

Buying Tips: Select potatoes based on their intended use. Choose potatoes that are clean, firm, smooth, well-shaped and free from sprouts. Any "eyes" should be minimal and shallow. Skins should be dry and without wrinkles or cracks. Avoid potatoes with green-tinged skins or black spots.

Yield: 1 pound potatoes = 2 to 3 medium; 3½ cups cooked, sliced or chopped; 2 to 3 cups mashed.

Storage: Store potatoes in a cool, dry dark location (light and warmth encourage sprouting) for up to two weeks. They may be stored in a paper or burlap bag. Check them occasionally and remove any potatoes that have sprouted or begun to shrivel. One rotten potato can spoil the whole lot. Avoid storing potatoes and onions together as the gases given off by the onions can cause the potatoes to spoil more quickly. Avoid storing potatoes in the refrigerator as the starch turns to sugar making them overly sweet. New potatoes, if not used within in a few days, should be refrigerated.

Basic Preparation: Scrub potatoes before cooking with a vegetable brush to remove embedded dirt. For many uses, potatoes do not need to be peeled. When peeling, use a swivel-bladed vegetable peeler rather than a knife. The skin and the flesh below the skin are rich in vitamins, so peel away as little of the flesh as possible. Cut out the "eyes" and any blemishes. A green-tinged flesh is an indication that the potato has been exposed to sunlight. Trim away any green skin or flesh, because it can be toxic in large amounts. Peeled potatoes should be immediately covered with water as the surface discolors quickly. Sliced or cut-up potatoes speed up cooking. Pieces of similar thickness ensure even cooking. Before baking or microwaving potatoes, pierce the skin with a fork to allow steam to escape and prevent them from exploding.

Swiss-Style Twice Baked Potatoes

4 large, evenly shaped baking potatoes (about 2½ pounds)
4 teaspoons butter or margarine, softened
⅔ cup grated Gruyère cheese*
⅔ cup grated Emmentaler cheese*
½ teaspoon caraway seeds (optional)
½ teaspoon minced garlic
½ teaspoon salt
4 teaspoons dry white wine
2 teaspoons kirsch (cherry brandy)

*Gruyère and Emmentaler are imported Swiss cheeses that tend to be aged longer than domestic Swiss. If unavailable, any Swiss cheese may be used.

1. Preheat oven to 425°F.

2. Scrub potatoes; dry well. Rub each potato with 1 teaspoon butter. Place in shallow baking dish at least 1 inch apart. Bake 30 minutes; remove from oven and pierce top of each potato several times with fork to allow steam to escape. Return to oven; bake 20 to 30 minutes more until potatoes are tender when pierced in center with sharp knife.

3. Meanwhile, place cheeses and caraway seeds, if desired, in small bowl. Toss well; set aside.

4. Allow potatoes to cool for several minutes. Cut off top ⅓ of potatoes, holding potatoes with oven mitt. Scoop out potato pulp from bottom sections to within ¼ inch of skins. Place pulp in large bowl, reserving shells. Add pulp from potato tops to bowl; discard top skins. Mash potatoes with potato masher until smooth. Add garlic, salt, wine and

kirsch. Mash to blend; stir in cheese mixture. Mash lightly just until all ingredients are blended.

5. Spoon potato mixture into potato shells, mounding evenly. Place potatoes in same baking dish.

6. Bake 20 to 25 minutes more until tops are lightly browned and potatoes are heated through. Garnish as desired. Serve immediately.

Makes 4 side-dish servings

Beef Stroganoff and Zucchini Topped Potatoes

4 baking potatoes (8 ounces each)
¾ pound lean ground beef
¾ cup chopped onion
1 cup sliced fresh button mushrooms
1 beef bouillon cube
2 tablespoons ketchup
1 teaspoon Worcestershire sauce
¼ teaspoon ground black pepper
¼ teaspoon hot pepper sauce
1 medium zucchini, cut into julienne strips
½ cup low-fat sour cream, divided

1. Pierce potatoes in several places with fork. Place in microwave oven on paper towel. Microwave potatoes at HIGH (100% power) 15 minutes or until softened. Wrap in paper towels. Let stand 5 minutes.

2. Heat large nonstick skillet over medium-high heat until hot. Add beef and onion. Cook and stir 5 minutes or until beef is browned. Add all remaining ingredients except zucchini and sour cream. Cover; simmer 5 minutes. Add zucchini. Cover; cook 3 minutes more. Remove from heat. Stir in ¼ cup sour cream. Cover; let stand 5 minutes.

3. Cut potatoes open. Divide beef mixture evenly among potatoes. Dollop with remaining ¼ cup sour cream. Serve immediately.

Makes 4 servings

Technique for Swiss-Style Twice Baked Potatoes

Step 4. *Scooping potato pulp from skins.*

Favorite Potato Salad

8 medium white potatoes, peeled,
   cubed and cooked
1 cup sliced green onions,
   including tops
⅔ cup chopped celery
½ cup mayonnaise
¼ cup chopped pimiento
2 teaspoons prepared mustard
1½ teaspoons LAWRY'S® Seasoned
   Salt
½ teaspoon LAWRY'S® Seasoned
   Pepper
⅛ teaspoon cayenne pepper
2 hard-cooked eggs, finely
   chopped
Paprika (garnish)

In large glass or ceramic bowl,
combine all ingredients except eggs
and paprika; toss gently, being careful
not to mash potatoes. Add chopped
eggs; toss gently. Garnish with
paprika.

Makes 6 to 8 side-dish servings

*Cheesy Potato
Chowder*

Cheesy Potato Chowder

1½ cups water
3 medium red boiling potatoes,
   peeled, cut into ½-inch cubes
1 rib celery, sliced
1 medium carrot, chopped
¼ cup butter or margarine
3 green onions, sliced
¼ cup all-purpose flour
1 teaspoon salt
⅛ teaspoon ground black pepper
4 cups milk
2 cups (8 ounces) shredded
   American cheese
1 cup (4 ounces) shredded Swiss
   cheese
½ teaspoon caraway seeds
Oyster crackers (optional)
Fresh chervil (optional)

1. Combine water, potatoes, celery
and carrot in medium saucepan.
Bring to a boil over high heat. Reduce
heat to medium; simmer, uncovered,
10 minutes or until vegetables are
tender.

2. Meanwhile, melt butter in large
saucepan over medium heat. Add
onions; cook and stir 2 minutes or
until tender but not brown. Stir in
flour, salt and pepper. Cook and stir
about 1 minute.

3. Stir milk and potato mixture into
flour mixture; cook and stir over
medium heat until bubbly. Cook and
stir 1 minute more. Stir in cheeses
and caraway seeds. Reduce heat to
low; simmer, uncovered, until
cheeses are melted and mixture is
hot, stirring constantly. Serve with
oyster crackers and garnish with
chervil, if desired.

Makes 6 servings

POULTRY

Poultry was once a luxury enjoyed only by the rich. After World War II, modern production methods and better transportation made poultry accessible to almost every American. For a long time it was considered the bargain-priced alternative to more costly meats, but it is increasingly becoming a dinner mainstay. Price continues to be an attraction, but nutritional qualities, versatility and convenience are factors that are driving its popularity. Poultry is typically lower in fat and calories than most meats. Certain cuts can be cooked very quickly and in a variety of ways. Brillat-Savarin, the famous French gastronome, wrote in the 19th century that "poultry is for the cook what canvas is to the painter." It is as true now as it was then.

☙

CHICKEN

Chicken consumption continues to increase with busy cooks stocking up on convenient, quick-cooking cuts, such as skinless and boneless breast halves and economical whole chickens. Whatever their form, chickens are among the most versatile of foods. They can be cooked by any number of methods and their mild taste is complemented by a great variety of flavors.

Types of Chicken: Whole chickens range in size from about 2½ to 10 pounds. The smallest, called frying chickens (also, broiler-fryers or broilers) are the most common and the most economical. As the name indicates, they are intended for frying and broiling but can also be used for braising, baking, grilling and poaching. They are young, usually about 2½ months old, and weigh from 2½ to 3½ pounds. They are sold whole or cut into parts.

Stuffed Chicken with Apple Glaze (recipe on page 405)

Larger chickens are called roasters. They weigh from 2½ to 5 pounds or more. Somewhat older than fryers, they have more fat, making them well-suited to oven roasting. They usually are sold whole. Capons are roosters that have been castrated at an early age. This allows them to become quite meaty and plump, weighing from 4 to 10 pounds. Their tender, juicy flesh is also ideal for roasting.

Increasingly hard to find are stewing hens (also known as fowl). These older birds weigh from 3 to 6 pounds and are characterized by tough but flavorful meat. They are excellent for stewing and making soups and stocks.

Cornish game hens, also called game hens, are hybrids of small chickens. They weigh from 1 to 1½ pounds and are sold whole. Their tender, juicy meat makes game hens excellent for roasting and grilling, either whole or cut into halves. One hen is often considered a serving.

Cuts of Chicken: Supermarkets and butcher shops offer chicken parts, with cuts and packages tailored to changing consumption patterns. Cut-up chickens are whole chickens that

*Chicken Cordon Bleu
(recipe on page 404)*

have generally been cut into eight pieces: two breast halves, thighs, legs and wings. The backbone may or may not be cut apart from the breasts. However, some markets may divide the bird differently, sometimes as quarters or with labels such as "choice-cuts," which can mean different things; the label usually explains exactly what is in the package. Read carefully to make sure that you are getting what you want. Whole chickens, whether whole or cut-up, contain the giblets (neck, gizzard, liver and heart). Be sure to remove them before cooking.

Chicken breasts, the white meat of the chicken, are a popular cut and one of the more costly. Breasts are available whole, with both skin and bone intact. They can also be purchased with the bone removed but the skin intact or with the skin and bone both removed. The breast is often split. Recipe references to chicken breasts usually mean a chicken breast half. The convenience of split skinless and boneless breasts

is obvious, but those that are cooked on the bone often result in a juicier and more flavorful dish. Studies have shown that the breast is juicier if cooked with the skin attached. After removing and discarding the skin, the chicken does not have any more fat than chicken cooked without the skin.

Chicken "tenders" or "supremes" are the lean, tender strips that are found on the underside of the breast. They are skinless and boneless and have virtually no waste.

Other cuts include legs, also called drumsticks. These may be sold as legs only, but many are still attached to the thigh. Thighs also are available separately. Increasingly, they can be found with the skin and bone removed, making them an excellent choice for quick sautés. They can be used in place of boneless chicken breasts in many recipes, allowing cooks to take advantage of their lower price. Thighs and legs are considered dark meat, which is higher in fat but more flavorful than chicken breasts. Wings, also called drumettes, are available. These are used for appetizers or main dishes, often marinated and baked. In addition, ground chicken and chicken sausages are sold in many markets.

Free-range chickens are available in some large supermarkets, gourmet food shops and butcher shops. These chickens are raised differently than mass-produced chickens. They are allowed more freedom to roam, usually outdoors as well as indoors. In most cases they are fed a vegetarian diet that is free of antibiotics, hormones and growth enhancers. This is said to result in a better tasting product. Free-range chickens are more expensive than mass-produced chickens.

Buying Tips: Choose chicken that is plump looking and has no unpleasant odors. The skin should be creamy white to yellow in color (diet dictates the color of the skin). Check the "freshness date" on the package, which indicates the last sale date. Chicken should keep at least two days beyond this date. Chicken is very perishable and must be handled with care. Buy it just before returning home and refrigerate it as soon as possible. Special care must be taken in warm weather to keep chicken cold when traveling back home from the supermarket.

Storage: If chicken is wrapped only in butcher paper or if the package has tears or is leaking, rewrap it in plastic wrap before refrigerating. Chicken should be stored in the coldest part of the refrigerator and used within two days after its "last sale date." However, if the chicken has an unpleasant odor or if it is slimy, discard it, regardless of the freshness date.

If you plan on freezing chicken, freeze it immediately after purchasing. Chicken should be tightly wrapped for the freezer, preferably with freezer paper or a double thickness of other wrapping. This prevents freezer burn and ensures good quality when cooked. When freezing parts, consider wrapping them individually in plastic wrap. Wrap several pieces together with freezer paper or place them in a resealable freezer bag. This will allow you to remove only the amount you need. The chicken will also thaw more quickly when separated into small packages. Ideally, the giblets should be removed from whole chickens and frozen separately; they will freeze more quickly than if left inside the bird. Also, the giblets deteriorate more quickly than chicken so they should be used within two to three months.

Thawing Chicken: To thaw chicken, transfer it from the freezer to the refrigerator and allow three to four hours per pound to defrost. Or, for quicker thawing, chicken can be immersed in cold water, changing the water frequently so the chicken remains cold. Make sure the bird is wrapped in watertight packaging before immersing it in water. Cook it as soon as it is thawed. Chicken may be thawed in the microwave, following manufacturer's directions. Watch the chicken carefully so that the edges do not begin to cook before the chicken is completely thawed. The chicken must be cooked immediately, because all or part of it will reach room temperature when thawed in the microwave. Bacteria multiply rapidly at room temperature and care must be taken to minimize their growth. Never thaw chicken at room temperature.

Preparing and Cooking Chicken: Rinse chicken under cold running water to remove surface dirt and bone fragments. Most cooks remove all excess visible fat. Clumps of fat tend to gather around the neck and tail and can be removed by tugging with the fingers or trimming with kitchen shears or a utility knife. Each breast half has a white tendon that runs down the length of the underside. This toughens as it cooks so you may wish to remove it, when possible. To do so, grasp it at one end and use a paring knife to scrape it away from the flesh.

Some recipes call for flattening chicken breasts, so they can be filled and rolled or cooked more quickly. To flatten uncooked boneless chicken breasts, place one chicken breast half between two sheets of waxed paper or plastic wrap. Using the flat side of a meat mallet or a rolling pin, gently pound the chicken from the center to the outside until it is of the desired thickness.

Flattening chicken breasts with meat mallet.

There are many cooking methods that can be applied to chicken. One of the most successful is roasting a whole chicken. After removing the giblets, rinsing and removing excess fat, place the chicken in a shallow roasting pan, breast side up. It is preferable to place it on a rack, so it is about one inch off the bottom of the pan. However, this is not absolutely essential. The surface of the chicken can be lightly rubbed with butter or oil and seasoned with salt and pepper or other seasonings, if desired. Whole chickens are usually roasted at 350°F, although they may go into an oven that is preheated to a higher temperature for a brief time.

Bone-in chicken parts can be broiled, poached, grilled, braised or baked. Boneless cuts can be prepared in the same way. In addition, they can be sautéed, panfried or stir-fried. In other words, almost any cooking method works. Because chicken has a mild flavor, marinades or dry rubs are welcome additions. The purpose of this step is not to tenderize, since the meat already is tender, but to add flavor. Therefore, keep in mind that marinating can be completed in 20 to 30 minutes. Chicken should not be left in acidic marinades for more than several hours or the acid will break down the tissue and the flesh will become mushy. Many flavors are complementary to chicken, including garlic, onion, mustard, most fresh and dried herbs, curry, chilies, citrus juice and wine. These can be added to marinades or simple sauces.

Testing for Doneness: There are a number of ways to determine if chicken is thoroughly cooked and ready to eat. For whole chickens, a meat thermometer inserted into the thickest part of the thigh, but not near any bone or fat, should register 180°F before removing the chicken from the oven. If a whole chicken is stuffed, insert an instant-read thermometer into the center of the body cavity; when the stuffing registers 165°F, it is done. (Chicken should be stuffed immediately before roasting; never stuff a chicken ahead of time.) Roasted whole chicken breasts are done when they register 170°F on a meat thermometer.

To test bone-in chicken pieces, you should be able to insert a fork into the chicken with ease and the juices should run clear; however, the meat and juices nearest the bones might still be a little pink even though the

chicken is cooked thoroughly. Boneless chicken pieces are done when the centers are no longer pink; you can determine this by simply cutting into the chicken with a paring knife.

Cornish game hens can be roasted whole at 375°F for 1 to 1½ hours. If they are stuffed, add an additional 15 to 20 minutes to the cooking time. For grilling, the hens can be split by cutting through the breastbone and backbone with a utility knife or kitchen shears. This allows them to rest flat on the grill for even cooking and easier eating. The backbone may be trimmed away before grilling.

TURKEY

If Ben Franklin's wish had prevailed, the native American turkey, not the bald-headed eagle, would have been chosen as the national emblem. Of course, on Thanksgiving, it is the turkey that symbolizes all-things American. Recently, the popularity of turkey has increased. Like chicken, turkey is economical, nutritious and versatile.

Types of Turkey: Almost all turkeys sold in the United States are of the White Holland variety, a type that is bred to have mild, juicy meat with a high proportion of white meat, which Americans favor. Toms (male) and hens (female) are available. Hens are somewhat smaller on the average. The overall trend is toward smaller turkeys. Although it is increasingly difficult to find birds larger than 25 pounds, smaller families welcome the 10-pound turkeys now available on the market.

Fresh and frozen turkeys are available. Both can be of excellent quality. Many are self-basting, which helps to keep the breast meat moist. If fat content is a consideration, read the ingredient list carefully, because some turkeys are basted with butter or vegetable oil. Those with broth are lower in fat.

Special Interest

The term "poultry" refers to any domesticated bird raised for its eggs or meat. Chicken, turkey, Cornish game hen, capon, duck and goose are examples.

Cuts of Turkey: An array of turkey parts is available. Many of them are breast parts. Turkey breasts, sold whole or as halves, are available with the bone in, boned and rolled, as boneless halves, and as breast cutlets. Except for the cutlets, the breast parts can be roasted, stewed, grilled, braised or cut into pieces and used in stews and sautés. Cutlets can be sautéed or braised. Drumsticks and thighs also are available. They can be prepared by the same methods as the breast parts. Fresh ground turkey is sold in most supermarkets and can be used in place of ground beef in many recipes. It has soared in popularity due to a lower fat content. Read the label carefully; if skin or fat is ground along with the meat, the amount of fat and cholesterol will increase.

Buying Tips: Choose fresh whole turkey that is plump looking and has no unpleasant odors. Packaging should be free of tears. Check "freshness date" on the package, which indicates the last sale date. Always keep turkey cold.

Storage: Store fresh turkey in the coldest part of the refrigerator and use within two days of the "last sale date."

Remove stuffing from a whole turkey immediately after roasting. Leftover roast turkey stuffing should be refrigerated within two hours after cooking. Large amounts of stuffing and a large turkey should be divided into several smaller packages to allow quick chilling. Stuffing will keep up to two days and turkey up to four days. If you intend to freeze some of the leftover turkey, do so the day it is cooked, not after several days of refrigerator storage.

Thawing Turkey: Whole turkey must be thawed in the refrigerator. When thawing a whole turkey, remember that this is a lengthy process, taking as long as four days for a large 25-pound bird. It is preferable to thaw turkey parts in the refrigerator. *For speedier thawing of turkey parts, see Thawing*

Chicken on page 401. However, turkey thawed by these alternative methods must be cooked immediately. Never thaw turkey at room temperature.

After thawing, remove the giblets from the neck and body cavities. Wash the inside and outside of the turkey under cold water and drain well. Do not stuff a turkey until you are ready to cook it. Never put hot stuffing in a cold turkey.

Preparing and Cooking Turkey: Whole turkeys are usually roasted in an open pan at 325°F. Timing for an unstuffed turkey is about 20 minutes per pound; allow a little more time if the turkey is stuffed. Let the turkey stand, covered loosely with foil, for 15 to 20 minutes before slicing. During this standing time, the internal temperature will rise at least 5°F and the juices set up, making it easier to carve. Be sure to allow for standing time when planning a meal.

Turkey Gyro (recipe on page 405)

Testing for Doneness: A meat thermometer inserted into the thickest part of the thigh, but not near any bone or fat, should register 180° to 185°F before removing the turkey from the oven. If a turkey is stuffed, a thermometer may be inserted into the center of the body cavity; when the stuffing registers 165°F, the turkey should be done. However, it is essential to also check the temperature of the thigh.

Poultry and Salmonella: Poultry, especially chicken, may be contaminated with salmonella bacteria, a harmful microorganism that causes food poisoning, so careful handling is essential. Do not let the juices from uncooked poultry mingle with other foods, either in the grocery cart at the store, in the refrigerator or on the counter at home. Wash any surfaces and utensils, including your hands, that have come in contact with raw poultry, using hot, soapy water. Always cook poultry thoroughly. *See Testing for Doneness for more information.* Care also needs to be taken when transporting, storing and thawing poultry. *See Buying Tips, Storage and Thawing on page 403 for additional information.*

Glazed Cornish Hens

> 2 fresh or thawed frozen Cornish game hens (1½ pounds each)
> 3 tablespoons fresh lemon juice
> 1 clove garlic, minced
> ¼ cup orange marmalade
> 1 tablespoon coarse-grain or country-style mustard
> 2 teaspoons grated fresh ginger

1. Remove giblets from cavities of hens; reserve for another use. Split hens in half on cutting board with sharp knife or poultry shears, cutting through breastbones and backbones. Rinse hens with cold water; pat dry with paper towels. Place hen halves in large resealable plastic food storage bag.

2. Combine juice and garlic in small bowl; pour over hens in bag. Seal bag tightly, turning to coat. Marinate in refrigerator 30 minutes.

3. Meanwhile, prepare grill for direct grilling over medium-hot heat.

4. Drain hens; discard marinade. Place hens, skin sides up, on grid. Grill hens, on covered grill, over medium-hot coals 20 minutes.

5. Meanwhile, combine marmalade, mustard and ginger in small bowl. Brush ½ of marmalade mixture evenly over hens. Grill, covered, 10 minutes. Brush with remaining mixture. Grill, covered, 5 to 10 minutes more until fork can be inserted into hens with ease and juices run clear, not pink. Serve immediately.　　*Makes 4 servings*

Chicken Cordon Bleu

> 6 boneless, skinless chicken breast halves (about 1¼ pounds)
> 1 tablespoon Dijon mustard
> 3 slices (1 ounce each) lean ham, cut into halves
> 3 slices (1 ounce each) reduced fat Swiss cheese, cut into halves
> Nonstick cooking spray
> ¼ cup unseasoned dry bread crumbs
> 2 tablespoons minced fresh parsley
> 3 cups hot cooked rice
> Fresh dill sprig (optional)

1. Preheat oven to 350°F.

2. Pound chicken breasts between 2 pieces of plastic wrap to ¼-inch thickness using flat side of meat mallet or rolling pin. Brush mustard on 1 side of each chicken breast; layer ½ slice *each* ham and cheese over mustard. Roll up each chicken breast from short end; secure with wooden toothpicks. Spray tops of chicken rolls with cooking spray; sprinkle with bread crumbs.

---

3. Arrange chicken rolls in 10×7-inch baking pan. Cover; bake 10 minutes. Uncover; bake about 20 minutes more or until chicken is no longer pink in center.

4. Stir parsley into rice; serve with chicken. Garnish with dill, if desired.

Makes 6 servings

Stuffed Chicken with Apple Glaze

1 whole frying chicken (3½ to
  4 pounds)
½ teaspoon salt
¼ teaspoon ground black pepper
2 tablespoons vegetable oil
1 package (6 ounces) chicken-
  flavored stuffing mix *plus*
  ingredients to prepare mix
1 large apple, chopped
½ teaspoon grated lemon peel
¼ cup chopped walnuts
¼ cup raisins
¼ cup thinly sliced celery
½ cup apple jelly
1 tablespoon fresh lemon juice
½ teaspoon ground cinnamon
  Celery leaves and lemon peel
  twists (optional)

1. Preheat oven to 350°F.

2. Sprinkle inside of chicken with salt and pepper; rub outside with oil. Set aside.

3. Prepare stuffing mix in large bowl according to package directions. Add apple, grated lemon peel, walnuts, raisins and celery to prepared stuffing; mix thoroughly. Stuff body cavity of chicken loosely with stuffing mixture.

4. Place chicken in shallow baking pan; insert meat thermometer into thickest part of thigh not touching bone. Cover loosely with foil; roast in oven 1 hour.

5. Meanwhile, combine jelly, juice and cinnamon in small saucepan. Simmer over low heat 3 minutes, stirring often, until jelly dissolves and mixture is well blended; keep warm.

6. Remove foil from chicken; brush with jelly glaze. Roast chicken, uncovered, brushing frequently with jelly glaze, 30 minutes more or until meat thermometer registers 180°F. Let chicken stand 15 minutes before carving. Garnish with celery leaves and lemon peel twists, if desired.

Makes 4 servings

Turkey Gyros

1 turkey tenderloin (8 ounces)
1½ teaspoons Greek seasoning
1 cucumber
⅔ cup plain nonfat yogurt
¼ cup finely chopped onion
2 teaspoons dried dill weed
2 teaspoons fresh lemon juice
1 teaspoon olive oil
4 pita breads
1½ cups washed, shredded romaine
  lettuce
1 tomato, thinly sliced
2 tablespoons crumbled feta
  cheese

1. Cut turkey across the grain into ¼-inch slices. Place turkey slices on plate; lightly sprinkle both sides with Greek seasoning. Let stand 5 minutes.

2. Cut ⅔ of cucumber into thin slices. Finely chop remaining cucumber. For yogurt-cucumber sauce, combine chopped cucumber, yogurt, onion, dill weed and juice in small bowl; set aside.

3. Heat oil in large skillet over medium heat. Add reserved turkey. Cook 2 minutes on each side or until no longer pink in center.

4. Wrap 2 pita breads in paper towels. Microwave at HIGH (100% power) 30 seconds or just until warmed. Repeat with remaining pita breads. Divide lettuce, tomato, cucumber slices, turkey, cheese and yogurt-cucumber sauce evenly among pita breads. Fold edges over and secure with wooden toothpicks. Serve immediately.

Makes 4 servings

Roast Turkey with Pan Gravy

> **Sausage Corn Bread Stuffing (page 492) or your favorite stuffing (optional)**
> **1 fresh or thawed frozen turkey (12 to 14 pounds),* giblets and neck reserved**
> **2 cloves garlic, minced (optional)**
> **½ cup butter or margarine, melted**
> **Turkey Broth with Giblets (recipe follows)**
> **1 cup dry white wine or vermouth**
> **3 tablespoons all-purpose flour**
> **Salt and ground black pepper**

*A 12- to 14-pound turkey should take 2 to 3 days to thaw in the refrigerator. Do not thaw at room temperature.

1. Preheat oven to 450°F.

2. Prepare stuffing, if desired.

3. Rinse turkey; pat dry with paper towels. Stuff body and neck cavities loosely with stuffing, if desired. Fold skin over openings and close with skewers. Tie legs together with cotton string or tuck through skin flap, if provided. Tuck wings under turkey. Place turkey on meat rack in shallow roasting pan. Insert meat thermometer into thickest part of thigh not touching bone. Stir garlic into butter, if desired. Brush ⅓ of butter mixture evenly over turkey.

4. Place turkey in oven; *reduce oven temperature to 325°F.* Roast 18 to 20 minutes per pound for unstuffed turkey or 22 to 24 minutes per pound for stuffed turkey, brushing with butter mixture after 1 hour and then after 1½ hours. Baste with pan juices every hour of roasting. (Total roasting time should be 4 to 5 hours.) If turkey is overbrowning, tent with foil. Turkey is done when meat thermometer registers 180°F and legs move easily in sockets.

5. Meanwhile, prepare Turkey Broth with Giblets.

6. Transfer turkey to cutting board; tent with foil. Let stand 15 minutes.

7. Meanwhile, pour off and reserve all juices from roasting pan. To deglaze pan, pour wine into pan. Place over burners and cook over medium-high heat, scraping up browned bits and stirring constantly 2 to 3 minutes until mixture has reduced by half.

8. Spoon off ⅓ cup fat from pan drippings;** discard any remaining fat. Place ⅓ cup fat in large saucepan. Add flour; cook over medium heat 1 minute, stirring constantly. Slowly stir in Turkey Broth, defatted turkey drippings from pan and deglazed wine mixture from pan. Cook over medium heat 10 minutes, stirring occasionally. Stir in reserved chopped giblets; heat through. Season with salt and pepper.

9. Carve turkey. Serve immediately with gravy. Garnish as desired.

Makes 12 servings (3½ cups gravy)

**Or, substitute ⅓ cup butter or margarine for turkey fat.

Creamy Turkey Gravy: Stir in 1 cup whipping cream with giblets; proceed as directed. Makes 4½ cups gravy.

Turkey Broth with Giblets

> **Reserved giblets and neck from turkey (discard liver or reserve for another use)**
> **4 cups water**
> **1 can (about 14 ounces) chicken broth**
> **2 medium carrots, coarsely chopped or sliced**
> **1 medium onion, cut into quarters**
> **4 large parsley sprigs**
> **1 bay leaf**
> **1 teaspoon dried thyme leaves**
> **10 whole black peppercorns**

Techniques for Roast Turkey with Pan Gravy

Step 3. *Tucking wings under turkey.*

Step 3. *Inserting meat thermometer into thigh.*

1. For Turkey Broth, combine giblets, neck, water and broth in 3-quart saucepan. Bring to a boil over high heat; skim off any foam. Stir in carrots, onion, parsley, bay leaf, thyme and peppercorns. Reduce heat to low. Simmer, uncovered, 1½ to 2 hours, stirring occasionally. (If liquid evaporates too quickly, add additional ½ cup water.) Cool to room temperature.

2. Strain broth; set aside giblets and neck. Discard vegetables and seasonings. If broth measures less than 3 cups, add water to equal 3 cups liquid. If broth measures more than 3 cups, bring to a boil and heat until liquid is reduced to 3 cups.

3. Remove meat from neck and chop giblets finely; set aside.

4. Broth may be prepared up to 1 day before serving. Cover giblets and broth separately; refrigerate

Makes 3 cups broth

Maple-Glazed Turkey Breast

Maple-Glazed Turkey Breast

> 1 bone-in turkey breast (5 to 6 pounds)
> Roast rack (optional)
> ¼ cup pure maple syrup
> 2 tablespoons butter or margarine, melted
> 1 tablespoon bourbon (optional)
> 2 teaspoons grated orange peel
> Fresh bay leaves (optional)

1. Prepare grill for indirect grilling over medium heat.

2. Insert meat thermometer into center of thickest part of turkey breast not touching bone. Place turkey, bone side down, on roast rack or directly on grid over drip pan. Grill turkey, on covered grill, over medium coals 55 minutes, adding 4 to 9 briquets to both sides of the fire after 45 minutes to maintain medium coals.

3. Meanwhile, combine maple syrup, butter, bourbon, if desired, and orange peel in small bowl; brush ½ of syrup mixture over turkey. Grill, covered, 10 minutes. Brush with remaining mixture; grill, covered, about 10 minutes more or until meat thermometer registers 170°F.

4. Transfer turkey to carving board; tent with foil. Let stand 10 minutes before carving. Cut turkey into thin slices. Garnish with bay leaves, if desired. Serve immediately.

Makes 6 to 8 servings

For hickory-smoked flavor, cover 2 cups hickory chips with cold water; soak 20 minutes. Drain; sprinkle over coals just before placing turkey on grid.

PRESERVE, TO

To preserve is to apply one of many methods of preparing or handling foods so they can be stored for long periods of time without spoiling or decaying. Among the commonly used methods are pickling, drying, canning, freezing, smoking and salting.

PRIMAVERA

Primavera is an Italian word meaning "springtime." It is used as a term in the title of recipes that contain fresh spring vegetables, either raw or blanched. Pasta primavera is the dish most familiar to Americans. Pasta is tossed with cooked vegetables and a light Parmesan cheese sauce.

PRESERVES

Preserves are a sweet mixture of fruit and sugar cooked together to make a spread for bread, biscuits, scones and muffins. Similar to jam, preserves are distinguished by having chunky bits of fruit left intact in the mixture.

Seafood Primavera

- ⅓ cup olive oil
- 1 medium onion, chopped
- 4 green onions, chopped
- 3 carrots, julienned
- 1 zucchini, julienned
- 1 *each* small red and yellow bell pepper, julienned
- 3 ounces fresh snow peas (Chinese pea pods), stems removed
- ⅓ cup sliced fresh button mushrooms
- 3 cloves garlic, minced
- ½ pound scallops
- ½ pound shrimp, peeled, deveined
- ⅔ cup clam juice
- ⅓ cup dry white wine
- 1 cup whipping cream
- ½ cup (about 2 ounces) freshly grated Parmesan cheese
- ⅔ cup shredded crabmeat
- 2 tablespoons fresh lemon juice
- 2 tablespoons chopped fresh parsley
- ¼ teaspoon dried basil leaves
- ¼ teaspoon dried oregano leaves
  Ground black pepper to taste
- 1 package (8 ounces) uncooked linguine, cooked, drained
  Additional freshly grated Parmesan cheese (optional)

Seafood Primavera

1. Heat oil in large skillet over medium-high heat. Add onions; cook and stir until soft. Add remaining vegetables and garlic; reduce heat to low. Cover; simmer until vegetables are tender. Remove to large bowl; set aside.

2. Add scallops and shrimp to same skillet; cover and cook over medium-low heat until seafood turns opaque. Remove with slotted spoon to same large bowl; reserve liquid in skillet.

3. Add juice to skillet; bring to a boil over medium-high heat. Add wine; cook 3 minutes, stirring constantly. Reduce heat to low; add cream, stirring constantly. Add ½ cup cheese; stir until smooth. Cook until thickened.

4. Add reserved vegetables, shrimp, scallops and crabmeat to cream sauce mixture; heat through. Add remaining ingredients except linguine and additional cheese. Pour over linguine in large bowl; toss gently to coat. Serve with additional cheese, if desired.   *Makes 6 servings*

PRUNE

Prunes, which are dried plums, can be traced back to the Roman Empire. The entire domestic prune supply and 70 percent of the world's supply come from California. About three to four pounds of fresh plums are needed to produce each pound of prunes. Prunes are made by allowing plums to mature on the tree for maximum sweetness. After harvesting, they are dried for 15 to 24 hours under carefully controlled conditions.

🌱

Uses: Prunes are perfect for snacking.

• Prunes may also be chopped and used like dates or raisins in muffins and other quick breads.

• Whole pitted prunes may be added to stews or cooked with pork, beef or poultry.

• Prunes stewed in fruit juice, wine or liqueurs and spices may be served alone or mixed with other fruits in compotes.

• Prune purée may be used as a filling for coffee cakes.

Varieties: The best prunes are made from European-type plum varieties which have firmer flesh and more sugar then other varieties. Although often labeled small, medium and large, quality is not related to size.

Availability: Prunes are available all year.

Buying Tips: Choose prunes that are blemish-free with a bluish-black skin. They should be moist and somewhat flexible. Packages should be tightly sealed to ensure freshness and minimize moisture loss. Whole prunes with pits are usually less expensive than pitted prunes.

Yield: 1 pound prunes = 2½ cups; 4 to 4½ cups reconstituted or cooked.

Storage: Store prunes in a tightly sealed container to retain moisture in a cool, dry place.

Basic Preparation: Pit prunes by slitting them with a paring knife and pushing out the pit.

PUDDING

Pudding is a term that most often describes a creamy cooked dessert made with milk, sugar, flavoring and a thickener, such as eggs, cornstarch or tapioca. Puddings can be homemade or prepared from mixes, which require only the addition of milk. Other types of puddings include baked puddings, such as bread pudding and rice pudding, and steamed puddings, such as plum pudding. Less common are savory puddings, such as corn pudding and Yorkshire pudding.

🌱

Tip

To plump or reconstitute prunes, simmer equal amounts of prunes and liquid, such as water, fruit juice or wine, in a saucepan for about 7 to 10 minutes or pour boiling liquid over prunes, cover and refrigerate overnight. Soften prunes that have lost moisture by sprinkling with water and microwaving them for 2 minutes.

1. Trim crusts from bread; reserve crusts for another use. Tear bread into pieces; place in large bowl. Pour milk over bread; let soak 30 minutes.

2. Preheat oven to 350°F. Lightly grease 9×5×3-inch loaf pan.

3. Add butter, sugar, cinnamon, ¼ teaspoon nutmeg and cloves to bread mixture; beat with electric mixer at low speed about 1 minute until smooth. Beat in egg. Stir in dried fruit, apple and nuts. Pour mixture into prepared pan.

4. Bake 1 hour 15 minutes to 1 hour 30 minutes until wooden toothpick inserted near center comes out clean. Cool pudding in pan 10 minutes. Remove from pan; cool on wire rack until slightly warm. Cut into slices. Serve warm with whipped cream sprinkled with nutmeg, if desired. Garnish with berries and mint, if desired.   *Makes 6 to 8 servings*

Rice Pudding with Raspberry Sauce and Crème Anglaise

1⅓ **cups cooked rice**
1⅓ **cups warm low-fat milk**
 ¼ **cup sugar**
 ⅛ **teaspoon salt**
 2 **eggs, beaten**
 1 **teaspoon vanilla extract**
   Raspberry Sauce (recipe follows)
   Crème Anglaise (recipe follows)
   Fresh raspberries and mint leaves (optional)

Combine rice, milk, sugar and salt in medium bowl; whisk in eggs and vanilla. Pour rice mixture into 8 greased ovenproof molds or custard cups. Place molds in baking pan. Pour hot water in pan to 1-inch depth. Bake at 350°F 30 to 35 minutes until knife inserted into centers comes out clean. Cool

English Bread Pudding

English Bread Pudding

14 **slices day-old firm-textured white bread (about 12 ounces)**
1½ **cups milk**
 ⅓ **cup butter or margarine, softened**
 ⅓ **cup packed light brown sugar**
 1 **teaspoon ground cinnamon**
 ¼ **teaspoon ground nutmeg**
 ¼ **teaspoon ground cloves**
 1 **egg**
 1 **package (6 ounces) mixed dried fruit, chopped**
 1 **medium apple, peeled, chopped**
 ⅓ **cup chopped nuts**
   Sweetened whipped cream and additional ground nutmeg (optional)
   Assorted fresh berries and mint leaves (optional)

completely. To serve, pour equal amounts of Raspberry Sauce and Crème Anglaise on individual serving plates. Unmold pudding over sauces. Garnish with raspberries and mint, if desired.   *Makes 8 servings*

Raspberry Sauce

> 1 package (10 ounces) frozen sweetened raspberries, thawed
> 2 teaspoons cornstarch

Combine raspberries and cornstarch in small saucepan over medium heat. Cook 5 to 7 minutes until thickened, stirring constantly. Strain mixture; cool completely.

Crème Anglaise

> 1 cup low-fat milk
> 2 tablespoons sugar
> 2 teaspoons cornstarch
> 1 egg yolk, beaten

Combine milk, sugar and cornstarch in small saucepan over medium heat. Cook 5 to 7 minutes until almost thickened, stirring constantly. Whisk 2 tablespoons of hot mixture into egg yolk; stir back into hot mixture. Heat 1 to 3 minutes, stirring constantly. Cool completely.

Favorite recipe from **USA Rice Council**

Classic Chocolate Pudding

> 2 bars (1 ounce each) HERSHEY'S Unsweetened Baking Chocolate, broken into pieces
> 2½ cups milk, divided
> 1 cup sugar
> ¼ cup cornstarch
> ½ teaspoon salt
> 3 egg yolks, slightly beaten
> 1 tablespoon butter (do not use margarine)
> 1 teaspoon vanilla extract
> Sweetened whipped cream (optional)

In medium saucepan, combine chocolate with 1½ cups milk; cook over low heat, stirring constantly with whisk, until chocolate is melted and mixture is smooth. In medium bowl, stir together sugar, cornstarch and salt; blend in remaining 1 cup milk and egg yolks. Gradually stir into chocolate mixture. Cook over medium heat, stirring constantly, until mixture comes to a boil; boil 1 minute, stirring constantly. Remove from heat; stir in butter and vanilla. Pour into bowl; press plastic wrap directly onto surface. Refrigerate 2 to 3 hours or until cold. Just before serving, garnish with sweetened whipped cream, if desired.

Makes 4 to 6 servings

PUFF PASTRY

Puff pastry, called pâte feuilletée in French, is a rich but delicate and flaky multilayered pastry. It is prepared by repeatedly layering thin sheets of pastry dough with bits of butter and rolling and folding. When baked, the moisture in the melting butter creates steam, causing the pastry to puff and separate into crispy layers. Puff pastry is used to make pastry shells and Napoleons. It is also the method used to make croissants. Ready-to-bake pastry shells and puff pastry dough may be purchased frozen in most large supermarkets.

☙

PUMPKIN

Related to squash, the pumpkin is a member of the gourd family. The word is derived from the French word pompion and the Greek word pepon meaning "cooked by the sun." The stringy yellowish-orange flesh has a sweet flavor and can be used in recipes calling for winter squash. Pumpkins vary in weight from several pounds to as much as 100 pounds. Indigenous to the United States, pumpkins were used by Native Americans who boiled them, baked them, added them to soups, and made breads and puddings with ground dried pumpkin meal. Since pumpkins were introduced to the early settlers, pumpkin pie has been a traditional Thanksgiving dessert. Because of the lengthy preparation time for cooking and puréeing pumpkin, many cooks purchase processed pumpkin for baking and cooking.

Varieties: Most of the pumpkins sold in October for jack-o'-lanterns are field pumpkins. Pumpkins for baking and cooking are called sugar or cheese pumpkins. They are much smaller in size and have a deep, rich sweet flavor and a meaty, less stringy texture than jack-o'-lantern pumpkins.

Availability: Fresh pumpkins can be purchased September through November. Canned pumpkin is available all year. Pumpkin seeds are dried and sold roasted and salted; they may or may not be hulled. Pumpkin seeds are used for snacking and in Mexican cooking. They are called *pepitas* in Spanish.

Buying Tips: Choose pumpkins that are heavy for their size and free of blemishes.

Yield: 3 pounds fresh pumpkin = 3 cups cooked, mashed.
1 (16- to 17-ounce) can = 2 cups pumpkin purée.

Storage: Fresh whole pumpkins can be stored at room temperature for up to one month or in the refrigerator for several months. Canned pumpkin can be kept in a cool, dry place for up to one year. Refrigerate any opened canned pumpkin in a tightly covered nonmetal container for five days.

Basic Preparation: Wash pumpkin under cold running water to remove dirt. To purée a sugar pumpkin, cut off the top and bottom with a chef's knife. Place the pumpkin on a cutting board on one end. Starting at the top and working towards the bottom, slice off the skin in wide strips, following the curve of the pumpkin. Cut the pumpkin in half and scoop out the seeds. Cut the flesh into 2-inch chunks. Steam over boiling water for 15 to 20 minutes or until tender. Purée the pumpkin in batches in a food processor or mash with a potato masher until smooth.

Harvest Pumpkin Cookies

2 cups all-purpose flour
1 teaspoon baking powder
1 teaspoon ground cinnamon
½ teaspoon baking soda
½ teaspoon salt
½ teaspoon ground allspice
1 cup butter or margarine, softened
1 cup sugar
1 cup canned pumpkin
1 egg
1 teaspoon vanilla extract
1 cup chopped pecans
1 cup dried cranberries (optional)
Pecan halves (about 36)

1. Preheat oven to 375°F.

2. Combine flour, baking powder, cinnamon, baking soda, salt and allspice in medium bowl. Beat butter and sugar in large bowl with electric mixer at medium speed until light and fluffy, scraping down side of

Tip

To toast pumpkin seeds, carefully separate the seeds from fibers. Wash, drain and dry seeds on paper towels. Coat the seeds lightly with vegetable oil. If desired, season seeds with a mixture of 2 tablespoons Worcestershire sauce and ½ teaspoon ground red pepper. Spread seeds on a baking sheet. Bake in a 275°F oven, stirring occasionally, until golden brown.

bowl once. Beat in pumpkin, egg and vanilla. Gradually add flour mixture. Beat at low speed until well blended, scraping down side of bowl once. Stir in chopped pecans and cranberries, if desired.

3. Drop heaping tablespoonfuls dough 2 inches apart onto ungreased baking sheets. Flatten mounds slightly with back of spoon. Press 1 pecan half into center of each mound.

4. Bake 10 to 12 minutes until golden brown. Let cookies stand on baking sheets 1 minute. Remove cookies to wire racks; cool completely. Store tightly covered at room temperature or freeze up to 3 months.

Makes about 3 dozen cookies

Pumpkin Cheese-Swirled Pie

1 package (3 ounces) cream cheese, softened
½ cup KARO® Light Corn Syrup, divided
½ teaspoon vanilla
1 cup canned solid pack pumpkin
2 eggs
½ cup evaporated milk
¼ cup sugar
2 teaspoons pumpkin pie spice
¼ teaspoon salt
1 (9-inch) unbaked or frozen deep dish pie crust*

To use prepared frozen pie crust, do not thaw. Preheat oven and a cookie sheet. Pour filling into frozen crust. Bake on cookie sheet.

Preheat oven to 325°F. In small bowl with mixer at medium speed, beat cream cheese until light and fluffy. Gradually beat in ¼ cup corn syrup and vanilla until smooth; set aside. In medium bowl combine pumpkin, eggs, evaporated milk, remaining ¼ cup corn syrup, sugar, pumpkin pie spice and salt. Beat until smooth. Pour into pie crust. Drop tablespoonfuls of cream cheese mixture onto pumpkin filling. With knife or small spatula, swirl mixture to give marbled effect.

Pumpkin Cheese-Swirled Pie

Bake 50 to 60 minutes or until knife inserted halfway between edge and center comes out clean. Cool completely on wire rack.

Makes 8 servings

Prep time: 20 minutes
Bake time: 50 minutes plus cooling

PURÉE, TO

To purée means to mash or strain a soft or cooked food until it has a smooth consistency. This can be done with a food processor, sieve, blender or food mill. For best results, the food must be naturally soft, such as raspberries or ripe pears, or cooked until it is completely tender. Puréed foods are used as sauces and as ingredients in other sweet or savory dishes. The term also refers to the foods that result from the process.

🌿

Q to R

Where did the quiche originate? *Make a satisfying ragoût.* What part of the rhubarb plant is toxic? *Make an eye-catching raspberry shortcake.* What is a reduction? *Learn the many ways to cook rice.* What does the term rocky road mean?

Chocolate Raspberry Tart
(recipe on page 424)

QUESADILLA

Quesadillas are one of Mexico's most popular snacks. They are made from flour tortillas topped with shredded cheese, such as Monterey Jack or Chihuahua. Then they are folded into half moons and toasted on a griddle or in a skillet until the cheese melts. An alternate method is to place the filling ingredients on a large tortilla. The filling is then topped with a second tortilla, and the quesadilla is toasted on a griddle. This large quesadilla is cut into wedges to serve. Usually served as an appetizer or entrée, quesadillas may be garnished with guacamole and salsa. Other popular fillings include refried beans, chorizo, chicken and vegetables.

❧

Cheese and Bean Quesadillas

Cheese and Bean Quesadillas

    1 can (15 ounces) pinto beans, rinsed, drained
    ½ cup salsa
    1 teaspoon chili powder
    4 (10-inch) flour tortillas
    1 cup (4 ounces) shredded low sodium, reduced fat Monterey Jack cheese
    ¼ cup chopped fresh cilantro
    ¼ cup low-fat sour cream
      Fresh cilantro sprigs (optional)

1. Place beans in medium saucepan. Mash beans with potato masher or fork. Stir in salsa and chili powder. Cook and stir over medium heat until bubbly. Reduce heat to low. Simmer 5 minutes, adding more salsa if mixture becomes dry.

2. To prepare first quesadilla, spray griddle with nonstick cooking spray. Heat over medium heat until hot. Brush 1 tortilla lightly on both sides with water. Heat on griddle until lightly browned. Turn tortilla. Spread with ½ of bean mixture; sprinkle with ½ cup cheese and 2 tablespoons chopped cilantro. Top with second tortilla; press lightly. Brush top of tortilla with water. Carefully turn to brown second side. Remove from heat. Repeat to make second quesadilla with remaining tortillas, bean mixture, cheese and chopped cilantro.

3. Cut each quesadilla into 6 wedges. Serve with sour cream. Garnish with cilantro sprigs, if desired.

Makes 6 appetizer servings

QUICHE

A quiche is a savory tart or pie with an egg custard filling flavored with cheese and sometimes meat, seafood or vegetables. It is generally baked in a pie plate or quiche dish (page 30). Quiches originated in the Alsace-Lorraine region of France. Quiche Lorraine, which is flavored with bacon, is a well-known quiche. It contains no cheese. Other popular versions include Cheddar cheese and ham, Cheddar cheese and broccoli, and Swiss cheese and onion. Quiches are served as an appetizer or entrée.

❧

Two-in-One Quiche

Pie Crust (recipe follows)
1 pound fresh spinach, washed, stemmed
1 tablespoon butter or margarine
1 medium shallot, chopped
¼ cup chopped red bell pepper
1½ cups (6 ounces) shredded Swiss cheese
2 tablespoons all-purpose flour
6 eggs
1 cup half-and-half
½ teaspoon salt
¼ teaspoon ground black pepper
⅛ teaspoon ground nutmeg

1. Preheat oven to 425°F. Meanwhile, prepare Pie Crust. Pierce bottom and side of Pie Crust about 40 times with fork.

2. Bake pie crust 10 minutes; cool on wire rack. *Reduce oven temperature to 350°F.*

3. To blanch spinach, bring 1 quart salted water to a boil in 2-quart saucepan over high heat. Add spinach; boil 2 to 3 minutes until crisp-tender. Drain spinach; immediately plunge into cold water. Drain again; let stand until cool enough to handle. Squeeze spinach

to remove excess moisture; finely chop.

4. Melt butter in small skillet over medium-high heat; add shallot and bell pepper. Cook and stir 3 to 5 minutes until bell pepper is tender; remove from heat. Stir in spinach; set aside.

5. Combine cheese and flour in medium bowl; spread on bottom of cooled Pie Crust.

6. Beat eggs, half-and-half, salt, black pepper and nutmeg in large bowl until blended.

7. Stir spinach mixture into egg mixture until well blended. Pour over cheese mixture. Bake 40 to 50 minutes until knife inserted near center comes out clean. Let stand 10 minutes. To serve, cut into wedges. Garnish as desired.

Makes 6 servings

Variation: Substitute 1 pound fresh broccoli, cut into florets, for spinach, Cheddar cheese for Swiss cheese and ground red pepper for nutmeg. Proceed as directed.

Pie Crust

1½ cups all-purpose flour
¾ teaspoon salt
½ cup vegetable shortening
4 tablespoons cold water

1. Combine flour and salt in large bowl. Cut in shortening with pastry blender or 2 knives until mixture forms pea-sized pieces.

2. Sprinkle with water, 1 tablespoon at a time. Toss with fork until mixture holds together. Form into a ball.

3. Press dough between hands to form 5- to 6-inch disc. Roll out dough on lightly floured surface with lightly floured rolling pin into circle at least 1 inch larger than inverted pie plate. Carefully lift dough over pie plate. Ease dough into pie plate with fingertips. Do not stretch dough. Trim crust, leaving ½-inch overhang. Fold overhang under. Flute as desired.

Tip

Leftover quiche does not have to be heated. It is delicious when served slightly chilled. Remove it from the refrigerator and let it stand for 20 or 30 minutes before serving.

RADICCHIO

Radicchio, the Italian name for a red-leafed variety of chicory, has become a popular salad ingredient in America in recent years. Young radicchio is green. It turns red when the weather becomes cool, resembling a very small head of red cabbage. Radicchio has a sharp, slightly bitter flavor similar to Belgian endive. Most of the United States supply is imported from Italy.

❦

Uses: Radicchio is a colorful addition to tossed salads.

• Radiccho may be baked, grilled or braised and served as a side dish.

• It is often used as a garnish.

Varieties: Several varieties of radicchio are grown in Italy, but the two most available in the United States are radicchio di Verona, a loose head of deep burgundy leaves, and radicchio di Treviso, a tight tapered head of leaves that range from pink to dark red.

Availability: Radicchio is available all year in most large supermarkets with supplies peaking from November to March. Because much of it is imported, radicchio tends to be more expensive than other salad greens.

Buying Tips: Choose heads with crisp, well-colored leaves and no signs of browning or wilting.

Storage: Radicchio should be stored, unwashed, in a plastic bag in the refrigerator for about one week.

Basic Preparation: Wash the head under cold running water and shake off the excess moisture. Separate the head into individual leaves for salads.

To cook radicchio, cut it into halves or quarters. Brush it with olive oil or melted butter. Grill radicchio for 5 minutes or sauté for 3 minutes in olive oil or butter over medium heat.

Tip

When purchasing radishes, avoid those that yield to slight pressure. This may be an indication that the centers are hollow or woody.

RADISH

Radishes are root vegetables that were first cultivated thousands of years ago in China. They belong to the crucifer family, which includes cabbage and broccoli. Radishes range from the common small red spheres to one- to two-pound Japanese daikon roots. All radishes have distinctive flavors ranging from peppery to pungent.

❦

Uses: Common red radishes and the more rare white icicle radishes are eaten raw in salads and as appetizers.

• Red and icicle radishes may be steamed or sautéed.

• Daikon radishes are eaten raw and added to stir-fries.

Varieties: Red globe is the most common American variety. Averaging about one inch in diameter, it has a bright red skin, snowy white interior, crispy texture and sharp flavor.

• Slender, white icicle radishes have a milder flavor than the red globe.

• Daikon radishes, native to Japan, are large (up to 18 inches in length) and carrot shaped with light tan skin and white flesh. They are hotter than the red globe radish.

Availability: Red globe radishes are available year-round in supermarkets. Less common varieties can be found at specialty produce markets.

Buying Tips: Choose radishes that are free of blemishes and firm to the touch. Radishes with tops attached generally have a better color, are less likely to be woody and keep longer.

Yield: 1 pound red globe radishes = 1⅔ cups slices.

Storage: If radishes are purchased with tops attached, remove and discard the tops. Store red, icicle and daikon radishes in a plastic bag in the refrigerator for up to two weeks.

Basic Preparation: Wash radishes under cold running water. Trim roots and stem ends. Daikon radishes may be peeled with a vegetable peeler or paring knife to reduce their pungency. Cut them into small pieces or grate them. Red radishes may be served raw, whole or sliced. Icicle radishes should be sliced. Cooking diminishes the pungent taste of radishes. All varieties can be steamed, stir-fried or sautéed.

Ragoût

A ragoût is a thick stew made from pieces of meat, poultry or fish that are browned in fat and then cooked slowly with stock and seasonings. Vegetables are often added as well. Typically French, ragoûts are similar to simple stews and braises. The terms are often used interchangeably.

❧

Chicken and Vegetable Ragoût

2 tablespoons olive or
    vegetable oil
½ cup chopped onion
3 cloves garlic, minced
1 pound (about 4) boneless,
    skinless chicken breast halves,
    cut into ½-inch pieces
1¾ cups (14.5-ounce can)
    CONTADINA® Recipe Ready
    Diced Tomatoes, undrained
1 cup water or chicken broth
1 cup sliced peeled carrots
⅔ cup (6-ounce can)
    CONTADINA® Italian Paste
    with Tomato Pesto
1 cup halved zucchini slices
1 cup red or green bell pepper
    strips
1 teaspoon Italian herb seasoning
½ teaspoon salt
⅛ teaspoon ground black pepper
    Hot cooked rice or pasta
    (optional)

In large skillet, heat oil. Add onion and garlic; sauté for 2 to 3 minutes or until onion is tender. Add chicken; cook until browned, stirring frequently. Add tomatoes and juice, water, carrots and tomato paste; cover. Bring to a boil. Reduce heat to low; simmer for 10 minutes, stirring occasionally. Add zucchini, bell pepper, Italian seasoning, salt and black pepper; cover. Simmer for 15 to 20 minutes or until chicken is no longer pink in center and vegetables are tender. Serve over hot cooked rice or pasta.   *Makes 6 servings*

Chicken and Vegetable Ragoût

Tasty Pork Ragoût

½ **pound pork loin, cubed**
1 **small onion, chopped**
1 **large clove garlic, pressed**
½ **teaspoon dried rosemary,**
    crumbled
2 **tablespoons margarine**
    Salt and pepper
1 **bouillon cube, any flavor**
½ **cup boiling water**
2 **cups DOLE® Cauliflower**
    flowerets
1 **cup sliced DOLE® Carrots**
1 **cup hot cooked rice**

• **Brown** pork with onion, garlic and rosemary in margarine. Season with salt and pepper to taste.

• **Dissolve** bouillon in water; stir into pork mixture. Cover; simmer 20 minutes.

• **Add** cauliflower and carrots. Cover; simmer 5 minutes longer or until vegetables are tender-crisp. Serve with rice.   *Makes 2 servings*

Prep time: 10 minutes
Cook time: 25 minutes

RAISIN

Raisins are simply dried grapes. They are one of the oldest processed foods. Bunches of grapes are hand-picked, dried, graded, cleaned and packed. They are dried either naturally by the sun or by artificial heat. Like other dried fruit, raisins have a chewy texture and very sweet flavor due to their high natural concentration of sugar. California is the largest producer of raisins, accounting for about half the world's supply. The most common type of grape used to make raisins is the Thompson seedless. Zante, Muscat and Sultana grapes are also used.

Varieties: Dark seedless raisins are generally made from Thompson seedless grapes. They are sun-dried in the vineyard for several weeks until they are shriveled and dark in color. Their sweet flavor makes them ideal for snacking and for cooking and baking.

• Golden seedless raisins are also made from Thompson seedless grapes, but they are processed differently. The grapes are treated with sulfur dioxide, which prevents the raisins from darkening, and dried with artificial heat resulting in a moist, plump amber-colored raisin. They have a tangy flavor that some prefer for snacking. They are also used for cooking and baking.

• Muscat raisins are made from Muscat grapes. They are large sun-dried raisins that are dark in color. They are very sweet with a fruity flavor. Muscat raisins are good for cooking and baking.

• Sultanas are small dark raisins made from Sultana grapes. They are sun-dried and used primarily for commercial purposes.

• Currants are made from Zante grapes. They are tiny dried fruit that resemble raisins. *See Currant, page 178, for additional information.*

Availability: Dark seedless and golden raisins are readily available in supermarkets. Bulk food stores are more likely to carry several varieties of raisins.

Buying Tips: When buying in bulk, look for moist-looking raisins.

Yield: 1 pound seedless raisins = 2¾ cups.

Storage: After opening, wrap raisins securely in plastic wrap or store in an airtight container at room temperature. They will keep for several months. If refrigerated in a tightly covered container, raisins will keep for up to one year.

Basic Preparation: Raisins are sometimes soaked in a liquid to plump them (make them soft and moist) before cooking and baking. This may be necessary if raisins are dry and hard. Water is generally used, but fruit juice, brandy or other liquids can be used to add flavor. To plump raisins in water for recipe use, cover them with very warm water and soak for 3 to 5 minutes. Or, place raisins in a small saucepan, cover with water and bring to a boil. Remove the saucepan from the heat and let the raisins stand for 5 minutes. Drain off the liquid and use the raisins as directed in the recipe. To plump and flavor raisins in other liquids, soak them at room temperature for several hours or overnight. Drain them before using.

Pineapple-Raisin Muffins

 ¼ cup finely chopped pecans
 ¼ cup packed light brown sugar
 2 cups all-purpose flour
 ¼ cup granulated sugar
 2½ teaspoons baking powder
 ¾ teaspoon salt
 ½ teaspoon ground cinnamon
 6 tablespoons cold butter or margarine
 ½ cup raisins
 1 can (8 ounces) crushed pineapple in juice, undrained
 ⅓ cup unsweetened pineapple juice
 1 egg

1. Preheat oven to 400°F. Grease or paper-line 12 (2½-inch) muffin cups.

2. Combine pecans and brown sugar in small bowl; set aside.

3. Combine flour, granulated sugar, baking powder, salt and cinnamon in large bowl. Cut in butter with pastry blender or 2 knives until mixture resembles fine crumbs. Stir in raisins. Combine undrained pineapple, pineapple juice and egg in small bowl until blended; stir into flour

mixture just until moistened. Spoon evenly into prepared muffin cups, filling ⅔ full. Sprinkle with reserved pecan mixture.

4. Bake 20 to 25 minutes until golden brown and wooden toothpick inserted into centers comes out clean. Remove from pan. Cool on wire rack 10 minutes. Serve warm or cool completely. Store tightly covered at room temperature.

Makes 12 muffins

Raisin Scones

 2 cups all-purpose flour
 2 tablespoons sugar
 2 teaspoons baking powder
 ½ teaspoon baking soda
 ½ teaspoon salt
 ½ teaspoon ground nutmeg
 ½ cup butter or margarine, cut into chunks
 1 cup SUN-MAID® Raisins
 ¾ cup buttermilk
 1 egg white, lightly beaten, for glaze
 Sugar, for glaze

Preheat oven to 425°F. Coat 2 baking sheets with vegetable cooking spray.

Combine flour, 2 tablespoons sugar, baking powder, baking soda, salt and nutmeg in large bowl. Cut in butter until mixture resembles coarse crumbs. Stir in raisins; mix in buttermilk with fork. Gather dough into ball and knead on lightly floured surface about 2 minutes. Roll or pat dough into circle, ¾ inch thick. With sharp knife, cut into 3-inch wedges. Place 2 to 3 inches apart on prepared baking sheets. Brush tops with egg white; sprinkle with sugar.

Bake about 15 minutes or until nicely browned. Serve warm with butter or jam. *Makes about 1 dozen scones*

Tip

To prevent raisins from sinking to the bottom of a cake or muffin batter, toss them with a little of the flour used in the recipe. If the raisins are clumped together, separate with your fingers, making sure all raisins are coated with flour.

RASPBERRY

If ancient mythology is to be believed, raspberries once were pure white, that is until a nymph went looking for something to calm the crying baby Zeus and pricked herself on the thorns of a raspberry bush. Her blood stained the berries red and so they have remained red ever since. Their vibrant color, intense flavor and high price have made raspberries an elegant and extravagant fruit. Fortunately, summer abundance results in lower prices, bringing them within the means of most fans.

🐝

Uses: Raspberries are delicious when served plain, with a sprinkling of sugar or with a little cream.

• Raspberries can be puréed and mixed with sugar for a simple sauce or used as the base for ice creams, sorbets, mousses and soufflés.

• Combine raspberries with other berries or peaches for pies and cobblers.

• Raspberries are a popular topping for fruit tarts, puddings and ice creams.

• They also make excellent jam or preserves.

Varieties: Red raspberries are the most common, but black and golden raspberries are also cultivated.

Availability: Summer is the prime season for domestic raspberries. Winter supplies come from Chile and New Zealand. They are available in half-pint containers. Frozen berries are sold in 10-ounce containers.

Buying Tips: Plump berries that have a rich color and a sweet, berrylike aroma are apt to be sweet and luscious. Avoid berries that have a hull attached in the center. This is a sign that they were picked before fully ripening and they are likely to be tart. Raspberries are extremely fragile so avoid containers with crushed or moldy berries.

Yield: ½ pint raspberries = 1 cup berries; ½ cup purée.

Storage: Raspberries are extremely perishable. Buy small quantities and plan on using them within a day or two. Never wash berries before storing. Remove any crushed berries, because they will mold quickly. Store in the refrigerator. Red raspberries are very fragile. If you want the berries to look perfect, remove them from the original container and store them in a single layer in a shallow glass dish, covered with a damp paper towel. This will prevent crushing.

To freeze, spread berries in a single layer on a jelly-roll pan and freeze them until the berries are firm. Then, transfer them to a freezer bag or airtight container. They will keep for nine months. Raspberry purée can also be frozen.

Tip

Use frozen raspberries without thawing. Thawed berries will not hold their shape, so they are best used for cooking or puréeing.

Basic Preparation: Raspberries should be lightly rinsed under cold running water and well drained just before serving. To purée raspberries, process them in a food processor or blender until the mixture is smooth. Strain the purée through a sieve to remove the seeds.

Raspberry Shortcake

1½ **cups whole raspberries, frozen, divided**
6 **tablespoons sugar, divided**
1 **cup all-purpose flour**
1 **teaspoon baking powder**
¼ **teaspoon baking soda**
1 **tablespoon margarine**
1 **egg white**
⅓ **cup evaporated skim milk**
¼ **teaspoon almond extract**
¾ **cup 1% low-fat cottage cheese**
1 **teaspoon fresh lemon juice**

1. Preheat oven to 450°F. Spray baking sheet with nonstick cooking spray.

2. Toss 1¼ cups raspberries with 2½ tablespoons sugar; refrigerate.

3. Combine flour, additional 2 tablespoons sugar, baking powder and baking soda in medium bowl. Cut in margarine with pastry blender or 2 knives until coarse crumbs form. Beat egg white, milk and almond extract in separate bowl; add to flour mixture. Mix lightly. Knead slightly on lightly floured board. Roll out dough to ½-inch thickness. Cut out 8 biscuits with 2½-inch biscuit cutter. Place biscuits on baking sheet.

4. Bake 10 minutes or until slightly brown on top.

5. Meanwhile, place cheese, remaining 1½ tablespoons sugar and juice in food processor or blender; process until smooth. Transfer cheese mixture to medium bowl. Fold in remaining ¼ cup raspberries.

6. Split baked biscuits in half; place bottom half on each serving dish. Top each with 2 tablespoons chilled raspberries and 1 tablespoon cheese mixture; cover with biscuit top. Top biscuits evenly with remaining raspberries and cheese mixture. Serve immediately. *Makes 8 servings*

*Favorite recipe from **The Sugar Association, Inc.***

Raspberry Shortcake

Chocolate Raspberry Tart

1 package (4-serving size) JELL-O® Pudding and Pie Filling, Vanilla Flavor
1¾ cups half and half or milk
1 Chocolate Crumb Crust (recipe follows), baked in 9-inch tart pan and cooled
1 pint raspberries
2 squares BAKER'S® Semi-Sweet Chocolate, melted

MICROWAVE pie filling mix and half and half in large microwavable bowl on HIGH 3 minutes; stir well. Microwave 3 minutes longer; stir again. Microwave 1 minute or until mixture comes to a boil. Cover surface with plastic wrap. Refrigerate at least 4 hours.

SPOON filling into Chocolate Crumb Crust just before serving. Arrange raspberries on top of filling. Drizzle with melted chocolate.

Makes one 9-inch tart

Prep time: 30 minutes
Chill time: 4 hours

Chocolate Crumb Crust

3 squares BAKER'S® Semi-Sweet Chocolate
3 tablespoons margarine or butter
1 cup graham cracker crumbs

HEAT oven to 375°F.

MICROWAVE chocolate and margarine in microwavable bowl on HIGH 2 minutes or until margarine is melted. Stir until chocolate is completely melted.

STIR in crumbs. Press mixture onto bottom and up sides of 9-inch tart pan or pie plate. Freeze 10 minutes. Bake for 8 minutes. Cool on wire rack.   *Makes one 9-inch crust*

Prep time: 5 minutes
Freezing time: 10 minutes
Baking time: 8 minutes

Chocolate Raspberry Tart

RATATOUILLE

Ratatouille is a vegetable stew from the Provence region of France. It is made of eggplant, zucchini, tomato, onion, garlic and seasonings, usually basil and thyme. The ingredients are cooked together until tender. The vegetables may also be cooked separately and then combined. Ratatouille can be served hot or cold as an appetizer or side dish.

🐝

Ratatouille

1 small eggplant, cut into ½-inch
  cubes
2 medium green peppers, diced
1 medium onion, sliced
1 clove garlic, minced
¼ cup olive oil
1 can (14½ ounces) DEL MONTE®
  Zucchini With Italian-Style
  Tomato Sauce
1 can (14½ ounces) DEL MONTE
  Original Recipe Stewed
  Tomatoes
½ teaspoon salt
⅛ teaspoon pepper

Cook eggplant, green peppers, onion
and garlic in oil over medium-high
heat, stirring constantly. Add
zucchini, tomatoes, salt and pepper.
Cover and simmer 30 minutes. Serve
with grated Parmesan cheese, if
desired.   *Makes 6 to 8 servings*

Microwave Directions: Reduce oil to
2 tablespoons and add 2 tablespoons
water. In 3-quart microwavable
casserole, combine eggplant, onion,
garlic, oil and water. Cover and
microwave on HIGH 10 minutes,
stirring halfway through. Add green
pepper, zucchini, tomatoes, salt and
pepper. Microwave 10 to 12 minutes,
stirring halfway through.

Prep time: 15 minutes
Cook time: 40 minutes
Microwave cook time: 22 minutes

RECONSTITUTE, TO

To reconstitute is to add liquid, usu-
ally water, to a dry or concentrated
food in order to return it to its origi-
nal consistency. Juice concentrates,
beverage mixes, bouillon granules and
dry milk powder are some examples
of foods that are dried or concen-
trated and need to be reconstituted.

❧

REDUCE, TO

To reduce is to boil a liquid, usually a
sauce, until its volume has been de-
creased through evaporation. This re-
sults in a more intense flavor and
thicker consistency. Typically sauces
are reduced by one third or one half
of their original volume. Use a pan
with a wide bottom to shorten prepa-
ration time. The reduced product is
referred to as a reduction. Since the
flavor of the seasonings will also be-
come concentrated when a sauce is
reduced, add the seasonings to the
sauce after it has been reduced.

❧

RELISH

A relish is a simple accompaniment to
a meal. It may be a raw vegetable,
such as celery or carrot sticks, or a
pickled item, such as pickles or olives.
The relish serves as an accent or con-
trast to the main course.

The term relish often refers to a
sweet-and-sour mixture of finely
chopped pickled vegetables. Relishes
are served chilled as a condiment.
Examples include pickle relish for hot
dogs and hamburgers, chowchow,
piccalilli and corn relish.

❧

Tip

Low-fat sauces can
be made by reducing
liquids used to
simmer meats and
poultry. Just be sure
to use liquids without
fat. For example,
orange juice flavored
with soy sauce,
garlic, thyme and
black pepper can be
used to simmer pork
chops and then
reduced to a sauce
consistency. Or add
puréed vegetables,
wine and herbs to
chicken or beef stock
and reduce it to
make a sauce.

Top to bottom: Sweet & Sour Relish and Gazpacho Relish

Gazpacho Relish

4 teaspoons tomato paste
2 teaspoons red wine vinegar
2 teaspoons lime juice
1½ teaspoons olive oil
½ pound tomatoes, peeled, seeded* and chopped
¼ cup minced green bell pepper
¼ cup peeled and chopped cucumber
4 canned artichoke hearts, chopped
2 teaspoons minced shallots
2 teaspoons chopped fresh dill
¼ teaspoon black pepper
3 to 6 drops hot pepper sauce to taste

*To easily peel tomatoes, first blanch in boiling water 30 to 45 seconds. Immediately plunge in cold water; peel. Cut tomatoes in half; scoop out seeds with spoon.

Place tomato paste, vinegar, juice and oil in blender or food processor; process until smooth. Transfer mixture to medium bowl and stir in remaining ingredients. Cover and refrigerate several hours before serving. Serve cold. Refrigerate leftovers.

Makes 1 cup relish

Serving Suggestion: Serve as an accompaniment to grilled BOB EVANS FARMS® Sandwich Patties or chicken.

Sweet & Sour Relish

1 medium onion, chopped
1 stalk celery, chopped
½ cup prepared chili sauce
2 tablespoons dark brown sugar
2 tablespoons cider vinegar
Dash dried tarragon leaves

Combine ingredients in medium saucepan. Bring to a boil over medium-high heat. Reduce heat to low; simmer 5 minutes, stirring occasionally. Serve hot or cold. Refrigerate leftovers and reheat if necessary. *Makes 1 cup relish*

Serving Suggestion: Serve with BOB EVANS FARMS® Bratwurst, Smoked Sausage or Kielbasa.

Cranberry-Orange Relish

4 large oranges, divided
7 (½-pint) jelly jars with lids and screw bands
2 cups sugar
½ cup water
2 packages (12 ounces each) fresh cranberries, washed, drained

1. Remove peel from white part of 2 oranges in long strips with sharp paring knife, making sure there is no white pith on the peel. Stack strips; cut into thin slivers. Measure ¼ cup; set aside.

2. Add orange peel to 1 inch boiling water in 1-quart saucepan. Boil over medium heat 5 minutes. Drain; set aside. Peel remaining 2 oranges. Remove white pith from all 4 oranges; discard peel and pith. Separate oranges into sections. With fingers, remove pulp from membrane of each section over 2-cup measure to save juice, discarding membrane. Dice orange sections into same cup. Add additional water to orange mixture to make 2 cups, if necessary; set aside.

3. Wash jars, lids and bands. Leave jars in hot water. Place lids and bands in large pan of water.

4. Combine sugar and water in heavy 6-quart saucepan or Dutch oven. Bring to a boil over medium heat. Add reserved orange peel, orange mixture and cranberries. Bring to a boil, stirring occasionally. Boil about 10 minutes or until mixture thickens and cranberries pop.

5. Bring water with lids and bands to a boil. Ladle hot mixture into hot jars leaving ¹/₂-inch space at top. Run metal spatula around inside of jar to remove air bubbles. Wipe tops and sides of jar rims clean. Place hot lids and bands on jars. Screw bands tightly, but do not force. To process, place jars in boiling water; boil 10 minutes. Remove jars with tongs; cool on wire racks. (Check seals by pressing on lid with fingertip; lid should remain concave.) Label and date jars. Store unopened jars in a cool dry place up to 12 months. Refrigerate after opening up to 6 months.

Makes about seven ¹/₂-pint jars

RHUBARB

Rhubarb is technically a vegetable, but it is used as a fruit. The long, thick pink or red celerylike stalks are the only edible portion of the plant. The leaves and roots should never be eaten. They contain oxalic acid and are toxic. Rhubarb stalks are not eaten raw. Cooked rhubarb is very tart and must be prepared with sugar.

🌺

Uses: The simplest way to prepare rhubarb is to stew it with sugar and a little water. Stewed rhubarb may be served warm or cold as a dessert.

• Combine stewed rhubarb with an equal amount of whipped cream to make rhubarb fool, a popular English dessert.

• Rhubarb and strawberries combine well. They make a popular filling for pies and cobblers.

• The tart flavor of rhubarb is complimented by apples, ginger, cinnamon, honey, maple syrup and pineapple.

Varieties: Field-grown and hothouse-grown rhubarb are the two main varieties. Field-grown rhubarb has bright red stalks and green leaves. It is easily grown in home gardens. Hothouse-grown rhubarb has pink or light red stalks and yellow leaves. It is less stringy and slightly less tart than the field-grown variety.

Availability: Field-grown rhubarb is available from April through July and the hothouse variety from January through June. Rhubarb is also available frozen.

Buying Tips: Choose rhubarb with crisp, straight firm stalks. Avoid limp stalks or ones that are obviously dried out.

Yield: 1 pound rhubarb stalks = 3 cups pieces; 2 cups cooked.

Tip

To make stewed rhubarb, combine 3 cups rhubarb pieces (1 inch long), ¹/₂ cup sugar and ¹/₄ cup water in a medium saucepan. Cover and cook over medium heat for 5 to 7 minutes or until the rhubarb is tender.

Storage: Store rhubarb in the refrigerator in a plastic bag. It will keep for about three to five days. Cleaned and dried rhubarb stalks can be cut into 1-inch pieces and frozen in a plastic freezer bag for up to nine months.

Basic Preparation: Always discard leaves as they are poisonous. Wash stalks under cold running water, rubbing lightly with your fingertip if they are particularly dirty. Trim off the ends of the stalks. If the rhubarb is field grown, remove the fibrous strings. Cut the stalks into 1- or 2-inch pieces. Combine the pieces with a mixture of granulated sugar, a thickener and seasonings for use as fillings in pies and cobblers.

Sumptuous Strawberry Rhubarb Pie

Sumptuous Strawberry Rhubarb Pie

Crust
> **9-inch Classic Crisco® Double Crust (page 173)**

Filling
> **4 cups fresh cut rhubarb (½-inch pieces)**
> **3 cups sliced strawberries**
> **1⅓ cups sugar**
> **⅓ cup *plus* ¼ cup all-purpose flour**
> **2 tablespoons *plus* 1½ teaspoons quick-cooking tapioca**
> **½ teaspoon grated orange peel**
> **½ teaspoon ground cinnamon**
> **¼ teaspoon ground nutmeg**
> **2 tablespoons butter or margarine**

Glaze
> **1 egg, beaten**
> **1 tablespoon sugar**

1. Prepare 9-inch Classic Crisco® Double Crust; roll out and press bottom crust into 9-inch pie plate. *Do not bake.* Heat oven to 425°F.

2. For filling, combine rhubarb and strawberries in large bowl. Combine 1⅓ cups sugar, flour, tapioca, orange peel, cinnamon and nutmeg in medium bowl; stir well. Add to fruit. Toss to coat. Spoon filling into unbaked pie crust. Dot with butter. Moisten pastry edge with water.

3. Roll out top crust. Lift onto filled pie. Trim ½ inch beyond edge of pie plate. Fold top edge under bottom crust; flute. Cut desired shapes into top crust to allow steam to escape.

4. For glaze, brush crust with egg. Sprinkle with 1 tablespoon sugar.

5. Bake at 425°F for 40 to 50 minutes or until filling in center is bubbly and crust is golden brown. Cover edge with foil, if necessary, to prevent overbrowning. Cool until barely warm or to room temperature before serving.   *Makes one 9-inch pie*

RICE

Rice is the seed kernel of an annual grass. The plant sprouts a number of fine 3- to 6-feet-tall stalks. Each grain is covered with an inedible husk. Rice is the staple food of half of the world's population. There are two types of cultivated rice: aquatic and hill grown. Aquatic, or paddy-grown rice, is grown in flooded fields. Since this is generally of higher quality and yields more per acre than hill-grown rice, it is the most common source of commercial rice. Hill-grown rice can be grown on most terrains in tropical or subtropical climates. In the United States, rice is grown in Arkansas, California, Louisiana, Mississippi, Missouri and Texas.

🌾

Varieties: There are three commercial grades of rice: long, medium and short grain. The length of the rice kernel affects the texture of the cooked rice. Long-grain rice kernels are four to five times longer than they are wide with tapered ends. They are lower in starch than shorter-grained kernels, resulting in a less sticky finished product. It is a good choice for pilafs and rice salads. Medium-grain rice has a high starch content. When cooked, the kernels tend to be moist and sticky. Medium-grain rice is perfect for croquettes and molded dishes. Short-grain rice, which is almost round, is the preferred type in Asia, because it is easy to eat with chopsticks. It is also used for risotto, rice pudding and other sweet rice dishes. The most common rice varieties available in the United States are as follows:

• Arborio is a translucent short-grain Italian rice that is very high in starch. It is traditionally used to make risotto, because it produces the characteristic creamy texture.

• Basmati is a long-grain aromatic rice grown in the foothills of the Himalaya Mountains, where the soil and climate contribute to its special taste. It has a perfumy aroma and nutlike flavor. Look for it in large supermarkets and Indian markets. A less expensive aromatic rice, known as jasmine rice, is grown in Thailand.

• Brown rice grains are unpolished with only the inedible husk removed. Since it contains the bran and the germ, it is more nutritious than white rice. It also takes longer to cook. Light tan in color, it has a chewy texture and nutty flavor. Quick brown rice (cooks in 15 minutes) and instant brown rice (cooks in 10 minutes) are also available.

• Converted, or parboiled rice, is the unhulled grain that is soaked, processed by steam pressure and dried before milling. The result is a rice kernel that is more nutritious and less starchy than polished white rice. It takes longer to cook than white rice and absorbs more liquid during cooking.

• Flavored rices have seasonings added to them. They are available in a variety of flavors. Quick-cooking varieties are also available.

• Texmati rice is a Texas-grown variety of the basmati-type rice.

• White rice has been polished to remove the husk, bran and germ. Vitamins and minerals are then added to most white rice to replace the nutrients lost in the milling process. It is available in short-, medium- and long-grain grades. Instant or quick-cooking rice has been fully or partially cooked before being dehydrated and packaged. It only takes a few minutes to prepare but does not have the same texture or flavor as polished white rice.

Special Interest

Rice was considered the symbol of life and fertility in ancient China. This explains the custom of showering bridal couples with grains of rice.

Storage: Store rice in an airtight container in a cool, dry place. It will keep indefinitely. Brown rice is subject to rancidity because the bran is intact. It can be stored for only six months.

Basic Preparation: It is not necessary to rinse rice before cooking. Basmati rice may contain some chaf and small stones. Remove any debris before cooking and rinse, if necessary.

Rice has a reputation for being difficult to cook. Since rice can be cooked by several methods, the choice is dependent upon the result you desire. To prepare brown, converted, flavored or quick-cooking rices, follow the package directions. The two most common cooking methods for polished white rice are the boiling method and the pilaf method.

Boiling Method: Boiling rice in a measured amount of water is the most common cooking method. To boil rice, bring 2 cups of water with 1 teaspoon of salt to a boil in a medium saucepan over medium-high heat. Slowly add 1 cup of rice so that the water continues to boil. Stir briefly. Reduce heat to low. Cook, covered, for 14 minutes or until the rice is tender. If all of the water has evaporated, but the rice is not tender, add ¼ cup of hot water. Cover and continue to cook until the rice is tender. If the rice is tender but all the water has not evaporated, remove the cover and cook over low heat until the water has evaporated. Boiling rice in a measured amount of water preserves the vitamins and results in moist rice. Long-grain rice will be slightly sticky and short-grain rice will be very sticky. For added flavor, substitute canned broth for the water and reduce the salt to ½ teaspoon.

Rice may also be boiled in a large quantity of water as pasta is cooked. To boil rice, bring 2 quarts of water to a boil in a large saucepan or Dutch oven over high heat. Slowly add 1 to 2 cups of rice so that water continues

to boil. Boil, uncovered, for 15 minutes or until the rice is tender. Drain well in a sieve or colander. This method allows the starch to drain away leaving cooked rice kernels that are fluffy and separate. However, much of the vitamins are drained away with the starch.

Pilaf Method: Use this method to make rice that is not sticky. Heat 1 or 2 tablespoons of oil (or melt 1 or 2 tablespoons butter or margarine) in a medium saucepan. Add 1 cup rice. Cook and stir the rice over medium heat for 4 to 5 minutes until it turns opaque. Carefully add 2 cups boiling water. Add 1 teaspoon salt. Cover and cook over low heat for 14 minutes or until the rice is tender and the water has evaporated. For the nutty flavor, characteristic of a traditional pilaf, allow the rice kernels to brown slightly before adding the water. For added flavor, substitute canned broth for the water and reduce the salt to ½ teaspoon.

Chicken Thighs with Lentils and Rice

    8 boneless, skinless chicken thighs
    ½ teaspoon salt
    ½ teaspoon ground black pepper
    1 tablespoon vegetable oil
    1 medium onion, chopped
    2 medium carrots, thinly sliced
    1 rib celery, thinly sliced
    2 cans (14½ ounces each) chicken broth
    1 cup dried lentils
    ½ teaspoon dried thyme
    1 bay leaf
    3 cups hot cooked brown rice
    2 tablespoons chopped fresh parsley *or* 2 teaspoons dried parsley

1. Sprinkle chicken with salt and pepper. Heat oil in large skillet over medium-high heat until hot. Add chicken; cook 3 to 4 minutes on each side or until light brown. Remove chicken; keep warm.

Tips

Do not stir rice while it is cooking. This will make it more sticky.

Adding 1 or 2 teaspoons of butter or oil to rice while it cooks will prevent it from boiling over.

Rice cooked with acidic ingredients, such as tomatoes, will require longer cooking and a little extra liquid.

2. Spoon off excess fat from skillet; add onion, carrots and celery. Cook 3 to 4 minutes or until crisp-tender. Stir in broth, lentils, thyme and bay leaf. Return chicken to skillet. Bring to a boil; reduce heat to medium. Cover; simmer 25 to 30 minutes or until lentils are tender and chicken is no longer pink in center. Remove bay leaf; discard. Serve over hot rice. Sprinkle with parsley.

Makes 4 servings

Favorite recipe from **USA Rice Council**

Green Bean Rice Amandine

2 tablespoons reduced calorie margarine
½ cup finely chopped onion
1¼ cups low sodium chicken broth
½ teaspoon lemon pepper seasoning
1 cup diagonally sliced green beans
1¼ cups uncooked instant white rice
3 tablespoons sliced almonds, toasted

1. Melt margarine in medium saucepan over medium heat; add onion. Cook and stir 5 minutes or until onion is tender. Add broth and lemon pepper seasoning; bring to a boil over high heat. Add beans; cover. Reduce heat to low. Simmer 7 minutes or until beans are tender, stirring occasionally.

2. Stir rice into saucepan; cover. Remove from heat. Let stand 5 minutes or until liquid is absorbed and rice is tender. Fluff rice mixture with fork; stir in almonds until well blended. Serve immediately. Garnish as desired.

Makes 6 side-dish servings

Green Bean Rice Amandine

Vegetable Risotto

Risotto

Risotto is a classic rice dish of northern Italy. It is made by first sautéing short-grain rice, preferably Arborio rice, in butter or olive oil. A small amount of hot broth or stock is added and the mixture is cooked over low heat with constant stirring until the broth has been absorbed. This process is repeated until all the broth has been added and absorbed. Risotto has a characteristically creamy texture. It is typically served as a first course or side dish. It can be made with a wide variety of ingredients. Parmesan cheese, shellfish, white wine, vegetables and herbs are popular additions.

☙

Vegetable Risotto

2 tablespoons olive oil, divided
1 medium zucchini, cut into
   ½-inch cubes
1 medium yellow summer squash,
   cut into ½-inch cubes
1 cup fresh shiitake mushroom
   slices
1 cup chopped onions
1 clove garlic, minced
6 plum tomatoes, quartered,
   seeded
1 teaspoon dried oregano leaves
3 cups Vegetable Stock (page 487)
   or canned vegetable broth
¾ cup uncooked arborio or short-
   grain rice
¼ cup (about 1 ounce) freshly
   grated Parmesan cheese
   Salt and ground black pepper
½ cup frozen peas, thawed
   Fresh oregano leaves and cherry
   tomato (optional)

1. Heat 1 tablespoon oil in large saucepan over medium heat. Add zucchini and summer squash; cook and stir 5 minutes or until crisp-tender. Place in medium bowl; set aside.

2. Add mushrooms, onions and garlic to saucepan; cook and stir 5 minutes or until tender. Add plum tomatoes and dried oregano; cook and stir 2 to 3 minutes until tomatoes are soft. Add to bowl with zucchini mixture. Wipe saucepan clean with paper towels.

3. Place stock in medium saucepan; bring to a boil over medium heat. Reduce heat to medium-low to keep stock hot, but not boiling.

4. Meanwhile, heat remaining 1 tablespoon oil in same large saucepan over medium heat. Add rice; cook and stir 2 minutes.

5. Using ladle or measuring cup, add ¾ cup hot stock to rice. Reduce heat to medium-low, maintaining a simmer until step is completed. Cook and stir until rice has absorbed stock. Repeat, adding stock 3 more times and cooking and stirring until rice has absorbed stock. (Total cooking time of rice will be about 20 to 25 minutes.)

6. Remove from heat. Stir cheese into rice mixture. Season with salt and pepper. Stir in reserved vegetables and peas; cook until heated through. Serve immediately. Garnish with fresh oregano and cherry tomato, if desired.   *Makes 4 to 6 servings*

ROAST, TO

Roasting involves cooking poultry and large tender cuts of meat in the oven in an uncovered pan. Roasting produces a nicely browned exterior and a moist interior. Roasting vegetables intensifies their natural sweetness. Vegetables, such as onions and carrots, can be roasted alongside meat. Many vegetables can be roasted and served as a side dish or used as ingredients in other dishes.

☙

Prime Rib

    3 cloves garlic, minced
    1 teaspoon ground black pepper
    1 (3-rib) standing beef roast,
        trimmed* (about 6 to
        7 pounds)

*Ask meat retailer to remove chine bone for easier carving. Fat should be trimmed to ¼-inch thickness.

1. Preheat oven to 450°F.

2. Combine garlic and pepper; rub over all surfaces of roast. Place roast, bone side down, in shallow roasting pan. Insert meat thermometer into thickest part of roast not touching bone or fat.

3. Roast in oven 15 minutes. *Reduce oven temperature to 325°F.* Roast 20 minutes per pound or until meat thermometer registers 120° to 130°F for rare or 135° to 145°F for medium. Transfer roast to cutting board; tent with foil.

4. Let stand 20 to 30 minutes to allow for easier carving. (Temperature of roast will continue to rise about 10°F during stand time.) Carve; serve immediately. Garnish as desired.
        Makes 6 to 8 servings

Prime Rib

Techniques for Prime Rib

Step 2. *Inserting the meat thermometer.*

Step 3. *Tenting the roast with foil.*

Fettuccine with Roasted Vegetables

Dijon Vinaigrette (recipe
   follows)
Nonstick cooking spray
2 large sweet potatoes, unpeeled
1 medium eggplant, unpeeled
3 large bell peppers (1 red,
   1 green and 1 yellow), cut
   into 1-inch strips
1 large red onion, cut into wedges
2 large tomatoes, cut into wedges
12 ounces uncooked fettuccine
   Salt and ground black pepper
½ cup pine nuts, toasted
   Red bell pepper curls and fresh
   basil sprigs (optional)

1. Prepare Dijon Vinaigrette; set aside.

2. Preheat oven to 475°F. Line two 15×10-inch jelly-roll pans with foil; spray with cooking spray.

3. Cut potatoes and eggplant into ½-inch-thick slices. Cut potato slices into halves; cut eggplant slices into quarters. Arrange eggplant, potatoes, bell pepper strips and onion on prepared pans; spray generously with cooking spray.

4. Bake 15 minutes. Add tomatoes; bake about 30 minutes or until vegetables are fork-tender and browned.

5. Cook fettuccine according to package directions; drain. Place in large warm bowl. Add roasted vegetables and reserved Dijon Vinaigrette; toss. Season with salt and black pepper. Sprinkle with nuts. Garnish with bell pepper curls and basil, if desired.

Makes 4 to 6 servings

Dijon Vinaigrette

⅓ cup olive oil
2 tablespoons red wine vinegar
1 tablespoon chopped fresh basil
   or 1 teaspoon dried basil
   leaves
1½ teaspoons Dijon mustard
¼ teaspoon salt

Whisk together all ingredients in small bowl.

Makes about ½ cup dressing

*Fettuccine with
Roasted Vegetables*

ROCKY ROAD

Rocky road is a type of candy that contains a mixture of whole marshmallows, most often the miniature size, nuts and chocolate, usually in chunks. The name refers to the bumpy texture that resembles the appearance of a rough road. The term may also describe a food, such as ice cream, that contains these ingredients.

❦

Rocky Road Brownies

½ cup butter or margarine
½ cup unsweetened cocoa powder
1 cup sugar
1 egg
½ cup all-purpose flour
¼ cup buttermilk
1 teaspoon vanilla extract
1 cup miniature marshmallows
1 cup coarsely chopped walnuts
1 cup (6 ounces) semisweet
   chocolate chips

1. Preheat oven to 350°F. Lightly grease 8 inch square baking pan.

2. Combine butter and cocoa in heavy medium saucepan over low heat, stirring constantly until smooth. Remove from heat; stir in sugar, egg, flour, buttermilk and vanilla. Mix until smooth. Spread batter evenly in prepared pan.

3. Bake 25 minutes or until center feels dry. (Do not overbake or brownies will be dry.)

4. Remove from oven; sprinkle marshmallows, walnuts and chips over top. Return to oven; bake 3 to 5 minutes more just until topping is warmed enough to melt together. Cool in pan on wire rack. Cut into 2-inch squares. Store tightly covered at room temperature.

Makes 16 brownies

Rocky Road Brownies

ROLL OUT, TO

To roll out means to flatten dough into an even layer using a rolling pin. To roll out pastry or cookie dough, place the dough, which should be in the shape of a disk, on a floured surface, such as a counter, pastry cloth or a large cutting board. Lightly flour your hands and the rolling pin. Place the rolling pin across the center of the dough. With several light strokes, roll the rolling pin away from you toward the edge of the dough. Turn the dough a quarter turn and roll again from the center to the edge. Repeat this process until the dough is the desired thickness. If the dough becomes sticky, dust it and the rolling pin with flour. If the dough sticks to the surface, gently fold back the edge of the dough and dust the surface underneath the dough with flour.

Rolling out dough.

❦

ROUX

A roux is a mixture of flour and fat, usually butter or margarine, that is cooked for use as a thickener for gravies and sauces. There are three types of roux: white, blond and brown. Their color is determined by the length of time they are cooked. The white roux, which is cooked for 1 or 2 minutes until the raw flour taste has dissipated, is used to thicken delicately flavored sauces. Blond roux is cooked a few minutes longer than white roux until it is golden brown in color and has a pleasantly mild flavor. Blond roux is used in lightly colored sauces and gravies. A brown roux is generally a combination of beef or pork drippings, or oil, and flour, which is slowly cooked to a rich brown color. It has a nutty aroma and flavor. It is used to flavor and thicken rich dark soups and sauces. Cajun and Creole dishes are often flavored with brown roux.

❦

Honey Nut Rugelach

RUGELACH

Rugelach refers to small crescent-shaped eastern European pastries or cookies. They are usually made with a cream-cheese dough that is cut into triangles and shaped around a filling of raisins (or other dried fruit) and nuts, jam, chocolate or sweetened ground poppy seed paste. Rugelach are often part of the Jewish celebration of Hanukkah.

❦

Honey Nut Rugelach

  1 cup butter or margarine, softened
  3 ounces cream cheese, softened
½ cup honey, divided
  2 cups all-purpose flour
  1 teaspoon fresh lemon juice
  1 teaspoon ground cinnamon, divided
  1 cup finely chopped walnuts
½ cup dried cherries or cranberries

1. Beat butter and cream cheese in medium bowl with electric mixer until fluffy. Add 3 tablespoons honey; mix well. Mix in flour until dough holds together. Form into a ball; wrap dough with plastic wrap and refrigerate at least 2 hours.

2. Divide dough into 4 equal portions. On floured surface, roll one portion of dough into 9-inch circle. Combine 2 tablespoons honey and lemon juice in small bowl; mix well. Brush dough with ¼ of lemon juice mixture; sprinkle with ¼ teaspoon cinnamon. Combine walnuts and cherries in separate small bowl; drizzle with remaining 3 tablespoons honey and mix well. Spread ¼ of walnut mixture onto circle of dough, stopping ½ inch from outer edge. Cut circle into 8 wedges. Roll up dough starting at wide outer edge and rolling toward tip. Gently bend both ends to form a crescent. Place on oiled parchment paper on baking sheet; refrigerate 20 minutes or longer. Repeat with remaining dough, lemon juice mixture, cinnamon and walnut filling.

3. Bake at 350°F 20 to 25 minutes or until golden brown. Cool on wire racks. Store tightly covered at room temperature. *Makes 32 cookies*

Freezing Tip: Unbaked cookies can be placed in freezer-safe containers or bags and frozen until ready to bake.

Favorite recipe from **National Honey Board**

RUMAKI

Rumaki is a Hawaiian-inspired appetizer made from water chestnuts, chicken livers and bacon. The liver, which is marinated in a mixture of ginger, garlic and soy sauce, and a slice of water chestnut are wrapped in a strip of bacon. They are placed on a skewer before grilling or broiling. Rumaki is served hot.

🐝

RUTABAGA

Rutabagas are round root vegetables that resemble turnips, but they are, in fact, a separate species that is a cross between a cabbage and a turnip. Rutabagas are yellow to tan in color with a dark purple color around the leaves. The pale yellow flesh has a sweeter and stronger flavor than the turnip. Sometimes called the yellow turnip, the rutabaga is larger than the turnip, averaging 4 or more inches in diameter.

🐝

Uses: Rutabagas may be used interchangeably with turnips.

• Although they can be eaten raw, their strong flavor mellows with cooking.

• Rutabagas can be boiled and mashed or puréed.

• They can be roasted, baked or added to soups, stews, chowders and casseroles.

• Their flavor is compatible with sweet spices, such as ginger and cloves, and citrus flavors, such as orange and lemon.

Varieties: Most rutabagas have pale yellow flesh. There is a white-fleshed variety that is not readily available.

Availability: Rutabagas are available year-round. Peak season is in the fall and winter months.

Buying Tips: Choose rutabagas that are firm, smooth and heavy for their size. If they are coated with a layer of clear wax to resist moisture loss, the skin that is visible through the wax should be free of blemishes. For best flavor and texture, choose rutabagas about 4 inches in diameter. Avoid those that are soft or spongy.

Yield: 1 pound rutabagas = about 2½ cups chopped.

Storage: Rutabagas should be stored in a plastic bag in the refrigerator. They will keep for up to two weeks.

Basic Preparation: Wash rutabagas under cold running water. Peel them with a paring knife. Slice or cube them before cooking. Avoid overcooking rutabagas in order to retain their mild flavor.

S

Why should salad greens be dry before adding salad dressing? *Serve hot buttered scones for afternoon tea.* What type of shellfish has a beard? *Toss together a sizzling stir-fry.* What makes brown sugar brown? *Enjoy an oven-baked sweet potato topped with sour cream.*

Strawberry Shortcake (recipe on page 462)

SALAD

The earliest salads were probably limited to freshly picked leaves and herbs until the Romans introduced the concept of an oil-and-vinegar salad dressing. By the 18th century Europeans were adding other ingredients, such as vegetables and cooked poultry, to salads for a more formal presentation. Historically, in America, salads were summer fare made from locally grown lettuce and vegetables. With the development in the 1920's of a variety of lettuce that could be shipped long distances (iceberg lettuce), salads began to appear at other times.

Apple Slaw with Poppy Seed Dressing

Today the term salad refers to a diverse assortment of dishes. Salads may contain lettuce, vegetables, fruits, cheeses, meats, seafood or poultry. They may be tossed together, artistically arranged, or added to gelatin mixtures and molded. They are served chilled, at room temperature or warm. Salads are often served as a first course to stimulate the appetite, as an accompaniment to an entrée or following the entrée to perk up the taste buds. A main-dish salad, containing meat, poultry or seafood, can be the star of the meal.

❦

Tips for Making Salads: To make salads of leafy greens, choose ingredients that provide a good contrast in flavors, colors and textures. Strong-flavored ingredients should be used in small quantities. Otherwise they will overpower milder greens.

• Dry greens thoroughly before dressing them to prevent diluting the salad dressing. In addition, dressing will not cling to wet greens.

• To keep salad greens crisp, toss them with dressing just before serving. Too much dressing will make delicate lettuces soggy and will overpower mild-flavored ingredients.

• Salad greens and raw vegetables are best served very cold to ensure crispness. Serving green salads on chilled plates will help keep them crisp.

• Potato salad should be made with new potatoes or long whites, round whites or round reds (see page 395). Russet potatoes will not hold their shape after cooking. Cook the potatoes with their skins on to retain more of the nutrients. Whether you peel them or not after cooking is a personal preference.

• For pasta salads, boil pasta in lots of water. Noodles and long strands of pasta, such as linguine and fettuccine, should be rinsed of excess starch before they are combined with other ingredients. Use cold water to hasten cooling, if desired.

• Potatoes and pasta can be dressed with either a vinaigrette-type dressing or a creamy mayonnaise-type dressing. Add a vinaigrette dressing to hot potatoes and pasta if you want them to absorb more dressing for added flavor. Cool the mixture before adding other vegetables or herbs. Mayonnaise should be combined with room temperature ingredients to prevent the mayonnaise from separating. Chilling salads for several hours will also allow them to develop flavor, but serve them cool, not cold, for more flavor.

• Meat and poultry salads can be made from leftovers. If the meat or poultry is dry, marinate it in the vinaigrette for an hour or two.

Apple Slaw with Poppy Seed Dressing

   1 cup coarsely chopped unpeeled
         Jonathan apple
   1 teaspoon fresh lemon juice
   2 tablespoons nonfat sour cream
4½ teaspoons skim milk
   1 tablespoon frozen apple juice
         concentrate, thawed
   1 teaspoon sugar
   ¾ teaspoon poppy seeds
   ½ cup sliced carrot
   ⅓ cup shredded green cabbage
   ⅓ cup shredded red cabbage
   2 tablespoons finely chopped
         green bell pepper
      Cabbage leaves (optional)

1. Combine apple and juice in resealable plastic food storage bag. Seal bag; toss to coat.

2. Combine sour cream, milk, juice concentrate, sugar and poppy seeds in medium bowl until well blended. Add apple mixture, carrot, cabbages and pepper; toss to coat. Serve over cabbage leaves, if desired.

Makes 2 servings

Chicken-Asparagus Salad

   1 can (14½ ounces) chicken broth
   1 bay leaf
   1 green onion, cut into 1-inch
         pieces
   1 slice (¼ inch thick) fresh ginger
   4 boneless, skinless chicken breast
         halves (about 1 pound)
      Mustard Vinaigrette (recipe
         follows)
   ½ pound asparagus spears, cut in
         half, cooked until crisp-
         tender
   1 (8¾-ounce) can whole baby
         sweet corn, drained, rinsed
      Spinach or lettuce leaves
   3 small tomatoes, chopped

1. Combine broth, bay leaf, onion and ginger in medium saucepan. Bring to a boil. Add chicken; reduce heat to low. Cover; simmer 8 minutes or until chicken is no longer pink in center. Remove chicken from broth; cool slightly. (Reserve broth for another use, if desired.)

2. Meanwhile, prepare Mustard Vinaigrette.

3. Cut chicken diagonally into narrow strips; place in medium bowl with asparagus and corn. Add Mustard Vinaigrette; toss lightly. Marinate at room temperature 15 minutes. Drain, reserving vinaigrette.

4. Arrange chicken, asparagus and corn on individual spinach-lined salad plates. Top with tomatoes. Serve with reserved vinaigrette.

Makes 4 servings

Mustard Vinaigrette

   2 tablespoons country-style Dijon
         mustard
   ½ cup seasoned rice vinegar
   ¼ cup vegetable oil
   ½ teaspoon Oriental sesame oil
      Dash ground black pepper

Whisk together all ingredients in small bowl.

Tip

To make a tossed salad ahead, place the firm vegetables and meat or poultry in the bottom of the salad bowl and add the salad dressing. Top with the salad greens but do not toss. Refrigerate the mixture for up to 2 hours. Toss the salad just before serving.

Layered Southwest Salad

Technique for Layered Southwest Salad

Step 2. Cutting jicama into thin triangles.

Layered Southwest Salad

Creamy Ranch-Style Buttermilk Dressing (page 443)
4 large eggs, hard-cooked, cooled
1 jicama (³/₄ pound)
1 can (15 ounces) black beans, drained, rinsed
²/₃ cup salsa
¹/₂ cup finely chopped red onion
10 ounces fresh spinach, washed, stemmed, cut into ¹/₄-inch-wide strips
1 package (10 ounces) frozen whole kernel corn, cooked, drained, cooled
1¹/₂ cups (6 ounces) shredded Cheddar cheese
Fresh oregano (optional)

1. Prepare Creamy Ranch-Style Buttermilk Dressing; set aside.

2. Peel eggs; cut into slices. Peel jicama; cut lengthwise into 8 wedges. Cut wedges crosswise into ¹/₈-inch-thick slices. Combine beans, salsa and onion in medium bowl.

3. Layer ¹/₂ each of spinach, jicama, bean mixture, corn, eggs and Creamy

Ranch-Style Buttermilk Dressing in large salad bowl. Repeat first 5 layers once; sprinkle with cheese. Drizzle with remaining dressing. Cover; refrigerate 1 to 2 hours before serving. Garnish with oregano, if desired.   *Makes 6 servings*

Thai Grilled Beef Salad

1 pound beef flank steak
3 tablespoons Thai seasoning, divided
2 red Thai chilies* *or* 1 red jalapeño pepper
1 tablespoon finely chopped lemon grass*
1 clove garlic, minced
2 tablespoons chopped fresh cilantro
2 tablespoons chopped fresh basil
1 tablespoon minced red onion
1 tablespoon fish sauce*
Juice of 1 lime
1 large carrot, peeled, grated
1 cucumber, chopped
4 cups assorted salad greens

*Thai chilies, lemon grass and fish sauce are available at some larger supermarkets and at Asian markets.

1. Prepare grill for direct grilling over medium heat.

2. Place beef on plate. Sprinkle 1 tablespoon Thai seasoning over beef; turn to coat. Cover; marinate 15 minutes.

3. Meanwhile, rinse chilies; pat dry with paper towel. Cut chilies** lengthwise into halves; scrape out and discard stems, seeds and veins. Cut halves lengthwise into thin slivers.

4. Grill beef, on uncovered grill, over medium coals or broil 5 to 6 minutes per side or to desired doneness. Cool 10 minutes on cutting board.

5. Meanwhile, to prepare dressing, combine remaining 2 tablespoons Thai seasoning, chilies, lemon grass, garlic, cilantro, basil, onion, fish sauce and juice in medium bowl; mix well. Set aside.

6. Thinly slice beef across grain; if strips are too long, cut into halves. Add beef strips, carrot and cucumber to reserved dressing; toss to coat. Arrange beef mixture on bed of salad greens. *Makes 4 servings*

**Chili peppers can sting and irritate the skin; wear rubber or plastic gloves when handling chilies and do not touch eyes. Wash hands after handling.

SALAD DRESSING

Salad dressing refers to several different types of mixtures. Vinaigrette is a mixture of oil, an acidic ingredient (such as vinegar or lemon juice) and seasonings (such as prepared mustard, garlic or herbs). It is a two-phase dressing that will easily separate into its oil and vinegar portions when allowed to stand. This type of dressing can be made at home or purchased. See Vinaigrette, page 537, for preparation information and recipes.

Single-phase salad dressings are creamy dressings that do not separate upon standing. They include mayonnaise, cooked dressings and sour cream- or buttermilk-type dressings. Single-phase dressings can be purchased as well as homemade.

☙

Creamy Ranch-Style Buttermilk Dressing

⅔ cup cottage cheese
½ cup buttermilk
1 tablespoon white wine vinegar
1 clove garlic
½ teaspoon salt
½ teaspoon ground black pepper
½ teaspoon ground cumin
½ teaspoon dried oregano leaves

Combine all ingredients in blender; cover and process until smooth. Cover; refrigerate 1 hour before serving. *Makes 1¼ cups dressing*

Thousand Island Dressing

12 ounces (2 cartons) ALPINE LACE® Fat Free Cream Cheese with Garden Vegetables
½ cup 2% low fat milk
⅓ cup fat free sour cream
¼ cup chili sauce
¼ cup minced dill pickles
2 to 3 tablespoons minced red onion
2 tablespoons fresh lemon juice
¼ teaspoon hot red pepper sauce

1. In a medium-size bowl, whisk all of the ingredients together until well blended. Refrigerate until ready to serve.

2. Serve this dressing over fish, meat or green salads.
Makes 2¼ cups dressing

French Salad Dressing

1 clove garlic, crushed
½ teaspoon salt
¼ teaspoon dry mustard
¼ teaspoon freshly ground black pepper
¼ teaspoon dried salad seasoning
¼ cup FILIPPO BERIO® Olive Oil
¼ cup white wine vinegar* or lemon juice, divided

*Dressing may be varied by using tarragon vinegar.

In small bowl, combine garlic, salt, mustard, pepper and salad seasoning. Whisk in olive oil and vinegar until thoroughly mixed. Store dressing, in tightly covered container, in refrigerator up to 1 week. Shake well before using.
Makes about ½ cup dressing

SALSA

Salsa is the Spanish word for sauce. In America, it is a generic term that refers to a large, diverse group of chunky, usually highly seasoned mixtures. Salsa has become a staple in America due to the popularity of Mexican and Tex-Mex cooking. This cooking popularized salsa cruda, an uncooked salsa made from tomatoes and chili peppers. Salsa verde is a green salsa made from tomatillos, green chilies and cilantro. Salsas can be made at home from fresh ingredients or purchased. They are used as a dip for chips, an ingredient for recipes and as a topping for tacos and burgers. Trendy salsas based on fruits (such as papaya, mango and peaches), corn, black beans and vegetables are gaining in popularity.

🌿

Black Bean Salsa

Fresh Tomato Salsa

1 medium tomato, finely chopped
¼ cup coarsely chopped fresh cilantro
2 tablespoons finely chopped white onion
1 jalapeño pepper, seeded, finely chopped*
1 tablespoon fresh lime juice

*Jalapeño peppers can sting and irritate the skin; wear rubber or plastic gloves when handling peppers and do not touch eyes. Wash hands after handling.

Combine all ingredients in small bowl; mix well. Let stand, covered, at room temperature 1 to 2 hours to blend flavors.

Makes about ¾ cup salsa

Black Bean Salsa

1 can (14½ ounces) black beans, rinsed, drained
1 cup frozen whole kernel corn, cooked, drained
1 large tomato, chopped
¼ cup chopped green onions
2 tablespoons chopped fresh cilantro
2 tablespoons fresh lemon juice
1 tablespoon vegetable oil
1 teaspoon chili powder
¼ teaspoon salt
6 corn tortillas
Lemon wedges and fresh cilantro sprig (optional)

1. For salsa, combine beans, corn, tomato, onions, chopped cilantro, juice, oil, chili powder and salt in medium bowl; mix well.

2. Preheat oven to 400°F.

3. Cut each tortilla into 8 wedges; place on ungreased baking sheet. Bake 6 to 8 minutes until edges begin to brown. Serve tortilla wedges warm or at room temperature with salsa. Garnish with lemon wedges and cilantro sprig, if desired.

Makes 6 appetizer servings

SATÉ

Saté (also satay) is a dish popular in Indonesia and Malaysia. It consists of pieces or strips of meat, poultry or seafood that have been marinated and then threaded onto skewers for grilling. Saté is generally served with a spicy peanut sauce. In Indonesia and Malaysia, saté is cooked to order by street vendors over portable charcoal braziers.

☫

Chicken Saté with Peanut Sauce

½ cup fresh lime Juice
⅓ cup reduced sodium soy sauce
¼ cup packed brown sugar
4 cloves garlic, minced
¼ teaspoon ground red pepper
3 boneless, skinless chicken breast halves (about 1¼ pounds)
18 (10- to 12-inch) bamboo skewers
¼ cup peanut butter
¼ cup thick unsweetened coconut milk* or Thick Coconut Milk Substitute (recipe follows)
¼ cup finely chopped onion
1 teaspoon paprika
1 tablespoon minced fresh cilantro

*Coconut milk separates in can. Spoon thick cream (consistency may be soft like yogurt or firm like shortening) from top. If less than ¼ cup, add enough remaining thin coconut milk to measure ¼ cup.

1. Stir juice, soy sauce, sugar, garlic and red pepper in medium bowl until sugar dissolves. Set ⅓ cup aside in cup.

2. Slice chicken lengthwise into ⅓-inch-thick strips. Add to juice mixture in bowl; stir to coat evenly. Cover; set aside at room temperature 30 minutes or refrigerate up to 12 hours.

3. Meanwhile, prepare grill for direct grilling over high heat. Cover skewers with cold water. Soak 20 minutes to prevent them from burning; drain.

4. Place peanut butter in medium bowl. Stir in ⅓ cup reserved juice mixture, 1 tablespoon at a time, until smooth. Stir in coconut milk, onion and paprika. Transfer sauce to small serving bowl; set aside.

5. Drain chicken; discard marinade. Weave 1 or 2 strips chicken onto each skewer.

6. Grill chicken, on uncovered grill, over hot coals or broil 2 to 3 minutes per side until chicken is no longer pink in center. Transfer to serving platter. Sprinkle sauce with cilantro; serve with chicken. Garnish as desired.

Makes 6 appetizer servings

Thick Coconut Milk Substitute

⅓ cup milk
1 teaspoon cornstarch
½ teaspoon coconut extract

Combine milk and cornstarch in small saucepan. Stir constantly over high heat until mixture boils and thickens. Immediately pour into small bowl; stir in extract.

Techniques for Chicken Saté with Peanut Sauce

Step 2. *Slicing chicken into strips.*

Step 5. *Weaving chicken strips onto skewers.*

SAUCE

A sauce is generally defined as a thickened, seasoned liquid that is served with a food to add flavor and moisture and to enhance its appearance. It can be thick or thin, hot or cold, savory or sweet. Many sauces, especially the classic French sauces, can be classified by the way in which they are thickened.

❦

Flour-thickened sauces include two classics—white sauce and brown sauce—that are the basis for many variations. White sauce (known as béchamel sauce in France) is made by thickening milk or cream with a roux made of butter or margarine and flour. The roux is cooked for a minute or two until the raw taste of the flour has dissipated. Then the milk is gradually added and the mixture is brought to a boil while being constantly stirred. Boiling for 2 or 3 minutes will eliminate any residual raw flour taste. The white sauce can then be seasoned with salt and pepper. This rich, creamy sauce is the basis for cheese sauces, cream sauces, savory soufflés and cream soups. Variations of the white sauce are made by substituting chicken or fish stock for milk. Egg yolks and cream are sometimes added for extra richness and white wine for flavor.

White sauces can be made in different thicknesses. The thickness of the sauce is determined by the proportion of flour and butter to liquid. Consult the chart below for appropriate ingredient proportions. Thin white sauce can be served as an accompaniment to vegetables or used as a thickening agent for delicately flavored soups. Medium white sauce is generally served over food or used as an ingredient in casseroles. Thick white sauce is combined with vegetables for creamed vegetables or used as the base for soufflés.

Brown sauce is made by thickening a rich meat stock with a roux made of flour and fat, such as butter, margarine, oil or meat drippings. The roux is cooked for 15 to 20 minutes until it is a rich brown color. Brown sauce is the basis for gravies, mushroom sauce, bordelaise sauce and Madeira sauce. It also acts as a thickener for stews, gumbos and meat soups. Like white sauce, brown sauce can be made in different thicknesses by altering ingredient proportions.

Egg-thickened sauces include hollandaise and béarnaise (savory sauces) and custard (dessert sauce). Hollandaise and béarnaise sauces are cooked emulsions of egg yolks, an acidic ingredient and butter. The egg yolks also act as a thickener. The acidic ingredient in hollandaise sauce is lemon juice. Béarnaise contains vinegar, white wine, shallots and tarragon. To prevent separation, these sauces should be whisked constantly over low heat. Egg-thickened sauces should never be allowed to boil, because this will coagulate the egg, resulting in a lumpy sauce. Egg sauces should not be prepared ahead. Hollandaise sauce (page 192) is served with eggs, vegetables,

Tip

When making a flour-thickened sauce, melting the fat before stirring in the flour allows the fat to coat the flour particles. This helps prevent lumps from forming when the liquid is added.

WHITE & BROWN SAUCE PROPORTIONS

	Thin Sauce	Medium Sauce	Thick Sauce
Butter	1 tablespoon	1½ tablespoons	2 tablespoons
Flour	1 tablespoon	1½ tablespoons	2 tablespoons
Liquid	1 cup	1 cup	1 cup

especially asparagus, and poached fish. The rich flavor of béarnaise sauce is a good accompaniment to beef and lamb. Custard sauce is a cooked dessert sauce of milk, sugar and flavoring that is thickened with egg. Unlike emulsified sauces, it can be made ahead.

Butter sauces are rich emulsions of butter and liquid. They can be difficult to make if the butter separates from the liquid, causing the sauce to become watery and unattractive. *Beurre blanc* is the classic French butter sauce made of a reduction (page 425) of wine, vinegar and shallots into which chunks of cold butter are whisked to form a thick, smooth sauce. It is traditionally served with fish, poultry, eggs and vegetables. This sauce cannot be reheated because it will separate. Stir any leftover sauce into hot cooked vegetables, pasta or rice.

Cornstarch thickened sauces can be savory or sweet. Cornstarch gives sauces a clear, glossy appearance. Most common are Asian stir-fry sauces and dessert sauces, such as lemon and orange sauces. Cornstarch must be dissolved in cold liquid before cooking.

Dessert sauces include butterscotch, caramel and chocolate. These are generally lightly cooked sauces that can be made at home or purchased.

Fruit purées are simple sauces that contain no thickeners. Fruit may be raw (raspberries) or cooked (persimmons). Some cooked vegetables, such as red bell peppers, can also be puréed and used as sauces.

Reductions are liquids that are simmered in order to evaporate liquid and concentrate flavor. The result is a sauce that contains no thickener. Flourless cream sauces and reduced meat stocks are examples of reductions.

Tomato sauces can be made from either fresh or canned tomatoes. When using fresh tomatoes, the quality of the sauce is dependent on the ripeness of the tomatoes. If the tomatoes are commercially grown, they may be pale and lacking in flavor. For more flavor, add a tablespoon or two of tomato paste or a tablespoon of chopped sun-dried tomatoes. Cooking time affects the thickness and the flavor of tomato sauces. Longer cooking results in a more full-bodied flavor.

SAUERBRATEN

Sauerbraten, meaning "sour roast" in German, is a traditional German main dish. It is prepared by marinating a boneless beef roast, usually round or rump, in a seasoned vinegar marinade for as long as several days. Other variations use buttermilk or wine for the marinade. The roast is browned and then simmered in the marinating liquid until tender. It is often served with dumplings, potatoes or noodles. The cooking liquid is used to make a sauce that is served with the roast. Gingersnaps are often added to the sauce for flavor.

❧

Special Interest

An emulsion is a mixture of two liquids, such as oil and vinegar, that do not naturally combine and an emulsifying agent. One ingredient (the oil) is separated into tiny globules and suspended in the other liquid (vinegar). This is accomplished by rapidly mixing the two liquids with an emulsifier that binds the two liquids together. The result is a stable mixture that is no longer liquid or translucent, but rather thick and opaque. Mayonnaise, for example, is an emulsion of oil, vinegar and egg yolk. The lecithin in the egg yolk is the emulsifier that holds the liquids in suspension.

Techniques for Sauerbraten with Gingersnap Gravy

Step 2. *Pouring marinade over roast.*

Step 3. *Browning roast on all sides.*

Sauerbraten with Gingersnap Gravy

> 3 cups water
> 1 cup cider vinegar
> 1 onion, thinly sliced
> 3 tablespoons brown sugar
> 1½ teaspoons salt
> 1 teaspoon ground ginger
> 1 teaspoon whole allspice
> 1 teaspoon whole cloves
> ½ teaspoon juniper berries
> 2 cloves garlic, crushed
> 1 beef rump roast (about 4 pounds)
> 2 tablespoons vegetable oil
> 2 tablespoons all-purpose flour
> ¼ cup crushed gingersnaps

1. To prepare marinade, bring water and vinegar to a boil in large saucepan over high heat. Remove from heat; add onion, sugar, salt, ginger, allspice, cloves, juniper berries and garlic. Cool slightly.

2. Place roast in large glass bowl or large resealable plastic food storage bag; pour marinade over roast. Cover or seal bag; refrigerate at least 8 hours, turning occasionally.

Sauerbraten with Gingersnap Gravy

3. Remove roast from marinade, reserving marinade. Pat dry with paper towels. Heat oil in Dutch oven over medium-high heat. Brown roast on all sides. To braise roast, add marinade to Dutch oven. Reduce heat to low. Cook, covered, 2½ to 3 hours until fork-tender. Remove roast from Dutch oven; set aside.

4. Strain braising liquid through fine-meshed sieve into large bowl; discard spices and onion. Skim fat from braising liquid with spoon; discard. Measure 2 cups braising liquid; discard remaining braising liquid. Place 1½ cups liquid in Dutch oven. Place flour in small bowl; gradually whisk remaining ½ cup braising liquid into flour. Stir mixture into liquid in Dutch oven. Add gingersnaps; mix well. Bring to a boil.

5. Return roast to Dutch oven. Reduce heat to low; cook, covered, 15 to 20 minutes until flavors blend and sauce thickens. Slice roast and serve with thickened sauce.

Makes 6 to 8 servings

SAUERKRAUT

Sauerkraut, a popular German food, is chopped or shredded cabbage that is salted and fermented in its own juice. The brine preserves the cabbage and gives the sauerkraut its distinct sour flavor. The German process is probably the adaptation of an ancient Chinese process of fermenting cabbage with rice wine. Sauerkraut is served as a side dish with pork dishes and is an essential ingredient in a Reuben sandwich. It is available fresh in bags in the refrigerated section of the supermarket or canned.

🌿

SAUTÉ

The word sauté is derived from the French word sauter, meaning "to jump." Sautéing is the technique of rapidly cooking or browning food in a small amount of fat in a skillet or sauté pan. The food is constantly stirred, turned or tossed to keep it from sticking or burning. Thin, tender cuts of meat, such as steaks, lamb chops, sliced pork tenderloin, flattened chicken breasts and fish fillets are candidates for sautéing. The objective is to brown the food on the outside in the time needed to cook the interior. This requires medium-high heat. Oil can withstand the higher heat needed for sautéing. For flavor, a little butter can be added to the oil, but do not use only butter or margarine, because it will burn before the food browns. However, clarified butter (page 80) may be used in place of the oil.

❦

Tender vegetables are often sautéed to improve their flavor and color before being used in soups, side dishes and entrées. It is generally not necessary to brown vegetables but only to soften them. Medium or medium-low heat is sufficient.

The following tips will ensure successful sautéing:

• Food must be dry or it will steam instead of sauté.

• Do not crowd the food in the pan. Crowding will reduce the temperature of the fat, resulting in less browning and crisping. Sauté foods in batches, if necessary.

• The fat must be hot to produce good browning and crisping and to minimize sticking.

SCALD, TO

Scalding refers to the technique of heating milk to just below the boiling point. The best indicator of this stage is when tiny bubbles begin to form around the edge. Before routine pasteurization, this technique was necessary to destroy bacteria. Although scalding is no longer necessary for sanitary reasons, it is a useful technique to shorten cooking time (for example, when making custard) and to improve flavor. When adding hot milk to egg mixtures it is best to let the milk cool a little to prevent it from curdling the eggs.

❦

SCALE, TO

Scaling is the technique of removing scales from the skin of fish. Scales are the small, flat rigid plates that cover the outside surface of a fish. This is done to prepare the fish for cooking. A special utensil called a fish scaler does this job quickly, but the edge of a table knife will also work. Scaling is necessary for freshly caught fish, but fish purchased at a supermarket is usually already scaled. To scale a whole fish, place it in the sink and hold it by the tail. Scrape the skin in long strokes from tail to head. Rinse the fish under cold running water before proceeding with preparation.

❦

Tip

To make sauerkraut less salty and milder in flavor, place it in a strainer and rinse it with cold running water. Drain it well before using it in casseroles, side dishes or sandwiches. Dress up sauerkraut with chopped apple, apple juice, brown sugar and caraway seeds.

Scalloped Red Skin
Potatoes

SCALLOP, TO

To scallop refers to the technique of preparing a food by slicing or cutting it into small pieces and layering it in a casserole with a creamy sauce. The finished dish may be topped with cracker or bread crumbs before baking. Scalloped potatoes and scalloped oysters are probably the best known dishes prepared this way. A simpler method for preparing scalloped potatoes is to coat potato slices with flour, layering them in a casserole and adding hot milk. To scallop may also refer to the technique of crimping or fluting the edge of pastry dough when making a pie.

Scalloped Red Skin Potatoes

    2 pounds red boiling potatoes,
        scrubbed, cut into ¼-inch
        slices
    2 tablespoons all-purpose flour
    4 tablespoons butter or
        margarine, divided
      Salt, ground black pepper and
        paprika
  1¼ cups milk
      Fresh thyme sprig (optional)

1. Preheat oven to 350°F.

2. Place potato slices on waxed paper; sprinkle with flour, tossing to coat. Grease 9-inch round baking dish with 1 tablespoon butter. Place ⅓ of potatoes in dish; sprinkle with salt, pepper and paprika to taste. Dot with 1 tablespoon butter. Repeat layers twice.

3. Heat milk in small saucepan over medium heat until hot. *(Do not boil.)* Pour over potatoes; sprinkle with salt, pepper and paprika. Cover with lid or foil.

4. Bake 35 minutes. Uncover; bake 20 minutes more or until potatoes are fork-tender. Garnish with thyme, if desired. Serve immediately.

Makes 6 side-dish servings

SCONE

Scones are a classic Scottish quick bread. Originally made of oats and cooked on a griddle, scones are now made of flour and baked. They are flavored with ingredients such as currants, almonds and bits of chocolate. Scones are similar to the American biscuit, but they are sweeter and richer. Traditional ingredients include cream or eggs in addition to butter. Scones are served for breakfast or afternoon tea.

To make scones, cut butter into the dry ingredients before the liquid ingredients are added. Brief kneading (page 63) is necessary to assure a thorough blending of ingredients. Overkneading produces tough scones. See Breads, Quick, page 58, for additional information.

⚜

Orange-Currant Scones

1½ **cups all-purpose flour**
¼ **cup *plus* 1 teaspoon sugar, divided**
 1 **teaspoon baking powder**
¼ **teaspoon salt**
¼ **teaspoon baking soda**
⅓ **cup dried currants**
 1 **tablespoon grated fresh orange peel**
 6 **tablespoons chilled butter or margarine, cut into small pieces**
½ **cup buttermilk, plain yogurt, or regular or nonfat sour cream**

1. Preheat oven to 425°F. Lightly grease baking sheet.

2. Combine flour, ¼ cup sugar, baking powder, salt and baking soda in large bowl. Stir in currants and orange peel. Cut in butter with pastry blender or 2 knives until mixture resembles coarse crumbs. Add buttermilk; stir until mixture forms soft dough that clings together. (Dough will be sticky.)

3. Lightly flour hands and shape dough into a ball. Pat dough into 8-inch round on prepared baking sheet. Cut dough into 8 wedges. Sprinkle wedges with remaining 1 teaspoon sugar.

4. Bake 18 to 20 minutes until lightly browned. Serve warm.

Makes 8 scones

SEAR, TO

Searing is the technique of exposing meat to a very high heat to quickly brown the outside while sealing the juices inside. It can be done in a skillet, under a broiler, on a grill or in a very hot oven. Searing is often the first step in the braising or roasting process.

⚜

SEASON, TO

To season refers to two very different culinary techniques. In cooking, to season means to add salt, herbs or spices to foods to enhance their flavor. Some recipes call for "seasoning to taste with salt and pepper." This means adding enough salt and pepper to make the flavor of the food acceptable to the cook. It is a good idea for inexperienced cooks to add only a small amount of seasoning and then taste the food before adding additional seasoning.

Seasoning is also the term for the process of pretreating new cookware or bakeware, usually cast iron, to minimize foods from sticking during cooking and to prevent rusting. Seasoning is usually accomplished by brushing the inside of the pan with vegetable oil (soybean oil) and heating it in a 350°F oven for about 1 hour. Or, follow the manufacturer's directions.

⚜

Tip

When doubling a recipe, do not double the seasoning. It is better to increase the seasoning by only 1½ times and then taste the finished dish, making any necessary adjustments.

SESAME SEED

Sesame seeds are the seeds of a leafy green plant that is native to East Africa and Indonesia. These tiny round seeds are usually ivory colored, but brown, red and black sesame seeds are available. Sesame seeds, regardless of color, have a slightly sweet, nutty flavor. They are widely available packaged in supermarkets and are sold in bulk in specialty stores and ethnic markets. Because of their high oil content, they easily turn rancid and are best stored in the refrigerator where they will keep up to six months or they may be frozen up to a year.

Sesame seeds are used in many ethnic cuisines including those of Africa, India and China. The Middle Eastern spread tahini is a thick paste made from sesame seeds. The confection halvah is made from ground sesame seeds and honey. Sesame seeds are used in India in rice pilafs and in candy. In the United States they are used in and as a topping for baked goods and sweets. Sesame seeds are the source of two types of vegetable cooking oil. Dark sesame oil is a common ingredient in Asian dishes. Light sesame oil is used for cooking. For additional information about sesame oil, see page 334.

🌾

Sesame Crunch Banana Muffins

Sesame Crunch Banana Muffins

Sesame Crunch Topping (recipe follows)
2 ripe medium bananas, mashed
1 cup low-fat milk
2 egg whites
2 tablespoons vegetable oil
1 teaspoon vanilla extract
1½ cups uncooked rolled oats
½ cup all-purpose flour
½ cup whole wheat flour
2 tablespoons granulated sugar
1 tablespoon baking powder
½ teaspoon salt

1. Prepare Sesame Crunch Topping; set aside. Spray muffin cups with nonstick cooking spray or use paper liners.

2. Preheat oven to 400°F.

3. Combine bananas, milk, egg whites, oil and vanilla in large bowl. Combine oats, flours, sugar, baking powder and salt in medium bowl; stir into banana mixture until just moistened. (Batter will be lumpy.) Fill prepared muffin cups about ¾ full. Sprinkle 2 teaspoons Sesame Crunch Topping over batter in each cup.

4. Bake 20 to 25 minutes until golden on top and wooden toothpick inserted into centers comes out clean. Cool slightly in pan before transferring to wire rack. Serve warm.
Makes about 16 muffins

Sesame Crunch Topping

4 tablespoons packed brown sugar
2 tablespoons chopped walnuts
2 tablespoons whole wheat flour
1 tablespoon sesame seeds
1 tablespoon margarine
¾ teaspoon ground nutmeg
¼ teaspoon ground cinnamon

Combine all ingredients; mix well.
Makes about ¾ cup topping

*Favorite recipe from **The Sugar Association, Inc.***

SEVICHE

Seviche, also spelled ceviche, refers to a dish of raw fish or shellfish, popular in Mexico and Latin America. The dish is prepared by marinating raw fish or shellfish in lime juice. The acid in the lime juice firms the fish and turns it opaque, thus mimicking cooking. Usually served as an appetizer, the dish is most often made with pompano, red snapper, sole, shrimp or squid. It may also include chopped tomatoes, green peppers and onions.

☙

Seviche

½ pound sea scallops, halved
½ pound fresh firm white fish, cubed
¼ cup lime juice
¼ cup lemon juice
1 large tomato, seeded and chopped
2 tablespoons chopped red onion
2 tablespoons olive or vegetable oil
1 tablespoon diced green chiles
1 tablespoon chopped fresh cilantro
1 teaspoon LAWRY'S® Seasoned Salt
¼ teaspoon LAWRY'S® Garlic Powder with Parsley
¼ teaspoon dried oregano, crushed

In large glass bowl, combine scallops and fish with lime juice and lemon juice. Cover and refrigerate 4 hours or overnight, stirring occasionally. Drain; stir in remaining ingredients.
Makes 8 appetizer or 4 main-dish servings

Presentation: Serve on lettuce leaves with lemon or lime wedges.

Hint: Be sure to use the freshest possible scallops and fish.

SHALLOT

*Shallots are believed to have origi-
nated in Palestine. Although they resemble garlic in appearance, they are
a member of the onion family. Each
head is made up of two or three
cloves, and each clove is covered with
a papery skin that ranges in color
from light reddish tan to gold. The
flesh is off-white with a hint of purple.*

🌾

Availability: Shallots are available
year-round.

Buying Tips: Choose firm shallots with
dry skins. Avoid those that are
wrinkled or beginning to sprout,
which are signs that the shallots are
past their prime.

Storage: Shallots will keep for up to a
month if stored in a cool, dry and
well-ventilated location.

Basic Preparation: Shallot cloves are
easier to separate than garlic because
they are not enclosed in a second
papery sheath. To peel the papery
covering, cut off and discard the stem
and root ends. The skin should slip off
easily. If shallots are difficult to peel,
blanch them in boiling water for 1
minute before peeling.

Lime and Lemon Cream Dressing

    **Finely grated peel and juice of
      1 lime
    Finely grated peel and juice of
      1 lemon
  2 teaspoons sugar
  3 tablespoons FILIPPO BERIO®
     Olive Oil
  ½ cup half-and-half
    Few drops hot pepper sauce
  2 shallots, finely chopped
    Salt and freshly ground black
     pepper**

In small bowl, combine lime peel and
juice, lemon peel and juice and
sugar. Whisk in olive oil. Gradually
whisk in half-and-half and hot pepper
sauce. Stir in shallots. Season to taste
with salt and pepper. Store dressing,
in tightly covered container, in
refrigerator 1 to 2 days.

Makes about ¾ cup dressing

SHELL, TO

*Shelling is the technique of removing
the tough outer covering from foods,
such as hard-cooked eggs, shrimp,
English peas, pod beans and nuts. The
method used depends on the food.
The shells of hard-cooked eggs are
cracked and then peeled away with
your fingers (page 190). Shrimp are
peeled, or "shelled," by first pulling
off the legs and then peeling the shells
by hand (page 458). Peeling eggs and
shrimp is easier if done under cool
running water. To shell beans, such as
limas, break off the stems from the
pods and pull the strings down the
seams. Then the pods should be gently squeezed between your thumbs
and forefingers to open them (page
198) and to remove the contents.
Shelling most nuts requires more effort and a tool called a nutcracker.
For easier shelling, place the nuts
lengthwise rather than crosswise in
the nutcracker.*

🌾

Tips

*Although shallots
have a more delicate
flavor than onions,
they may be used in
many of the same
ways. Use shallots for
a more subtle flavor.*

*When a recipe calls
for one shallot, one
clove should be
used, not the whole
bulb.*

SHELLFISH

Shellfish are separated into two categories: crustaceans and mollusks. Crustaceans have elongated bodies and external shells with jointed parts. Crab, lobster and shrimp are examples of crustaceans. Mollusks have soft, tender bodies that are in most cases covered by a shell. Mollusks are classified as univalves, bivalves and cephalopods. Univalves, or single-shelled mollusks, include abalone, sea urchins and conch. Bivalves, or double-shelled mollusks, include clams, oysters and mussels. Cephalopods have ink sacs and tentacles. Octopus and squid are two examples of cephalopods.

🐝

Clams are found along both the Atlantic and Pacific coasts of the United States. Clams may have a hard or a soft shell. Atlantic soft-shell clams include steamers and longneck clams. Atlantic hard-shell clams include the small littleneck, the medium cherrystone and the large chowder clams. All but the chowder clams may be eaten raw. Pacific hard-shell clams include littleneck and butter varieties. Pacific soft-shell clams are the razor and geoduck clams. Pacific clams are cooked, since they are generally too tough to eat raw.

Several forms of crabs are available in the United States. Dungeness crabs from the Pacific Northwest and blue crabs from the Atlantic and Gulf of Mexico coasts have edible bodies and claws. Alaska king crabs from the northern Pacific have edible meat in the claws and legs. Stone crabs, which come from the waters around Florida, have edible meat only in the claws. Canned crabmeat is usually taken from snow crabs, although sometimes it is taken from Alaska king or Dungeness crabs.

Two forms of lobsters are found in the waters surrounding the United States. The most common is the American or Maine lobster from New England. The meat, which is contained in the tail and the claws, is sweet and tender. Spiny lobsters, which are also known as rock lobsters, come from California and the Gulf of Mexico. They have rough reddish-brown shells and no claws. The meat comes from the tail.

Mussels can be found in the waters of both the Pacific and Atlantic coasts. However, most mussels found in markets are farm raised. They have bluish-black shells and are usually sold in the shell.

Oysters are found on the Atlantic, Pacific and Gulf of Mexico coasts and in Puget Sound in the Pacific Northwest. The oysters from the Pacific coast are quite large (up to a foot long) and those from Puget Sound are small (1½ inches). Pacific oysters are cut up and cooked, whereas those from Puget Sound are eaten raw. Atlantic oysters, or Eastern

Tip

Lump crabmeat is the large pieces of white crabmeat usually used for salads. Backfin crabmeat is the smaller pieces that are used when appearance is less important (for example, crab cakes).

Chesapeake Crab Cake (recipe on page 459)

oysters, better known by their place of origin (such as Blue Point, Chesapeake and Indian River), are the most common oysters. They range in size from 3 to 5 inches in length. They are eaten raw on the half shell or cooked. Many of these varieties are now farm raisied.

Shrimp are found in most of the waters surrounding the United States. Shrimp are grouped for retail purposes by their size. The most common sizes are jumbo (11–15 per pound), large (21–30), medium (31–35) and small (36–45).

Buying Tips: All fresh shellfish should have a mild aroma and smell of the sea. Avoid shellfish that have a strong fishy odor. Fresh shellfish are very perishable. To find the freshest shellfish available, buy from a reputable fish market or supermarket that has a rapid turnover. If you are in doubt about the freshness of any shellfish, do not buy it. If you are purchasing live shellfish, it is best to buy them as close to the time you plan to cook them as possible. Fresh shellfish should be cooked on the day they are purchased. Frozen shellfish

should be packaged in a close-fitting moisture-proof package that is intact at the time of purchase.

Live lobsters and crabs should feel heavy for their size and actively move their claws. Lobsters should flap their tail tightly against their chests or curl their tail under their shell when picked up. However, if the lobsters and crabs have been refrigerated, they will not be as active. Do not purchase any lobsters or crabs that do not show these signs of life. Frozen lobster tails should be intact in packaging and free of ice crystals and juices. Whole crabs and crabmeat should smell sweet, not fishy.

Shrimp are available raw or cooked, fresh or frozen, and unshelled or peeled. All should feel firm to the touch. Cooked shelled shrimp should be plump. Raw shrimp should not smell of ammonia.

Clams, mussels and oysters should have moist shells free of cracks and chips. All hard-shell clams, mussels and oysters should have tightly closed shells or slightly open shells that snap tightly closed when tapped. If they do

---

Tip

The veins of large and jumbo shrimp are gritty; they must always be removed. The veins of medium and small shrimp are not gritty and need not be removed unless you wish a more elegant presentation.

SHELLFISH INFORMATION CHART

Shellfish	Availability	Type of Shellfish	Cooking Methods
Clams	summer	mollusk	baking, steaming
Crabs	summer to winter	crustacean	poaching, steaming, stewing
Lobster	spring to summer	crustacean	grilling, poaching, steaming
Mussels	early fall to spring	mollusk	baking, grilling, steaming
Oysters	early fall to spring	mollusk	baking, broiling, frying, grilling, stewing
Scallops, Bay	fall	mollusk	baking, broiling, frying, poaching, sautéing, stewing
Scallops, Sea	mid fall to spring	mollusk	baking, broiling, frying, poaching, sautéing, stewing
Shrimp	year-round	crustacean	baking, broiling, frying, grilling, poaching, sautéing, steaming, stewing

not close when tapped, they are dead and should be discarded. The soft-shell clam is unable to close its shell completely. To determine if it is alive, gently touch the protruding neck of the clam to see if it will retract. If the neck does not retract slightly, discard the clam. Freshly shucked clams are packaged in their liquor and should be plump and moist. Their color varies from grayish-green to beige to dark orange depending on the variety. Shucked mussels should be plump and their liquor clear. Freshly shucked oysters should be surrounded by a clear, slightly milky white or light gray liquid. Oysters are usually creamy white but the color varies depending on the variety. Freshly shucked scallops vary in color from creamy white to pink.

How Much to Buy (per person):

Lobster (in shell)—10 to 14 ounces

Large shrimp (unshelled)—10 ounces

Large shrimp (shelled)—3 ounces

Crab (in shell)—14 ounces to 1 pound

Oysters—6 to 12

Scallops—2 to 3

Mussels, Clams—14 ounces

Storage: Shellfish are highly perishable and it is best to use them within 24 hours of purchase. They need to be handled carefully before cooking to keep them fresh or alive. The most important factor is to keep them in a cold, moist environment. Keep fresh or thawed shellfish as close to 32°F as possible.

Store shrimp and shucked shellfish in a leakproof bag or covered container in the refrigerator. Store live shellfish in a shallow dish covered with a damp towel. If available, you may also want to keep the shellfish covered with seaweed. Never put live shellfish in an airtight container or fresh water, since they can suffocate and die. Some shells may open during storage. If so, tap them. They will close if still alive.

Frozen shellfish can be stored in the freezer for three to six months. The longer it is stored, the greater the loss of flavor, texture and moisture.

Cleaning and Preparation Techniques: To clean clams, begin by scrubbing the shellfish thoroughly with a stiff brush under cold running water to eliminate seaweed, sand and filaments. Soak them in salted water (1/3 cup salt to 1 gallon water) for 20 minutes to remove any sand. Drain water; repeat two more times. Place clams on a tray and refrigerate them for 1 hour so that they relax, making them easier to open. To shuck clams, take a clam knife in one hand and a thick towel or glove in the other. With the towel, grip the shell in the palm of the hand. Keeping the shell level, insert the tip of the knife between the shells next to the hinge; twist to pry the shell until it snaps. (Use the knife as leverage, but do not force it.)

Twist to open the shell, keeping it level at all times to save the liquor. Cut the muscle from shell and discard the top shell.

To crack a steamed crab, place the crab on its back. With your thumb or the point of a paring knife, pry off the "apron" flap (the "pull-tab" looking shell in the center) and discard it.

Turn the crab over. Lift off the top shell and discard it.

Break off the toothed claws and set them aside. With the edge of a paring knife, scrape off the 3 areas of lungs and debris over the hard semi-transparent membrane covering the edible crabmeat.

Hold the crab at each side; break it apart at the center. Discard the legs. Remove the membrane cover with the knife, exposing the large chunks of meat; remove the meat with your fingers or a knife.

Crack claws with a mallet or knife handle to expose the meat.

Sliding clam knife between clam shells.

Prying off "apron" flap of crab.

Scraping off lungs from crab.

Breaking crab apart.

Boiled Whole Lobster with Burned Butter Sauce

Removing beard from mussel.

Deveining shrimp.

To clean mussels, scrub with a stiff brush under cold running water. To debeard mussels, pull the threads from the shells with your fingers. Soak, relax and open following instructions for clams. Mussels die soon after debearding. Use them immediately.

To peel shrimp, remove the legs by gently pulling them off the shell. Loosen the shell with your fingers, then slide it off.

To devein shrimp, cut a shallow slit along the back of the shrimp with a paring knife. Lift out the vein. (You may find this easier to do under cold running water.)

Testing for Doneness: Most shellfish take very few minutes to cook and it is very important not to overcook them. If shellfish are cooked too long, they become tough and dry and lose much of their flavor. Heat precooked shellfish just to the desired temperature and not longer.

Lobsters are cooked according to weight. When boiling, the cooking time begins once the water returns to a boil. Cook lobsters from 10 to 18 minutes depending on their size.

1-pound lobster—10 minutes

1¼-pound lobster—12 minutes

1½-pound lobster—15 minutes

2-pound lobster—18 minutes

Lobster is opaque when cooked. A bright red shell is not an indication of doneness, because the shell turns color when it comes in contact with boiling water. Crabs are cooked until their shells turn red and the meat is white. Shrimp turn pink and opaque when cooked.

Clams and mussels are done when their shells open. Remove them as they open and continue cooking until all are opened. Discard any that do not open. Shucked shellfish, such as clams, mussels and oysters, become opaque when done. Oyster edges start to curl. If they are overcooked, oysters shrink. Scallops become opaque and firm when cooked.

Boiled Whole Lobster with Burned Butter Sauce

 ½ **cup butter**
 2 **tablespoons chopped fresh**
  parsley
 1 **tablespoon cider vinegar**
 1 **tablespoon capers**
 2 **live lobsters***

*Purchase live lobsters as close to time of cooking as possible. Store in refrigerator.

1. Fill 8-quart stockpot with enough water to cover lobsters. Cover stockpot; bring water to a boil over high heat.

2. Meanwhile, to make Burned Butter Sauce, melt butter in medium saucepan over medium heat. Cook and stir butter until it turns dark chocolate brown. Remove from heat. Add parsley, vinegar and capers. Pour into 2 ramekins; keep warm.

3. For each lobster, hold lobster by its back and submerge headfirst in boiling water. Cover and continue to heat. When water returns to a boil, cook lobsters 10 to 18 minutes. (Cook 1-pound lobsters 10 minutes, 1¼-pound lobsters 12 minutes, 1½-pound lobsters 15 minutes and 2-pound lobsters 18 minutes.)

4. Transfer lobsters to 2 large serving platters. Remove bands restraining claws. Serve lobster meat with Burned Butter Sauce. Garnish as desired.

5. To remove meat from claws, first break claws from body. Pull off "thumb" part of claw. Using metal nutcracker, crack claw gently to avoid damaging meat. Using seafood fork, gently remove claw meat (it should come out in 1 piece).

6. To remove meat from legs, crack legs gently with nutcracker. Pick out meat.

7. To remove tail meat, place lobster tail on plate with underside facing up. With kitchen scissors, cut through underside of shell. Pull shell apart and slide your index finger between meat and shell to loosen meat; gently pull out meat from shell.

Makes 2 servings

Chesapeake Crab Cakes

Tartar Sauce (page 512)
1 pound backfin crabmeat
½ cup soft bread crumbs
1 tablespoon minced onion
1 tablespoon finely chopped bell
    pepper
1 tablespoon chopped fresh
    parsley
¼ cup mayonnaise
1 egg
2 teaspoons white wine
    Worcestershire sauce
2 teaspoons fresh lemon juice
1 teaspoon prepared mustard
½ teaspoon salt
¼ teaspoon ground white pepper
    Vegetable oil for frying
    (optional)

1. Prepare Tartar Sauce; refrigerate until ready to serve.

2. To remove cartilage and shell from crabmeat, gently squeeze a teaspoonful at a time between fingers. Feel carefully for small bits. The shells may be white or orange and cartilage milky white and thin. To shred, flake with fork.

3. Place crabmeat in medium bowl. Add bread crumbs, onion, bell pepper and parsley; set aside.

4. Mix remaining ingredients except oil and Tartar Sauce in small bowl. Stir well to combine. Pour mayonnaise mixture over crabmeat mixture. Gently mix so large lumps will not be broken. Shape mixture into 6 large (¾-inch-thick) cakes (or 36 bite-size cakes).

5. To pan fry crab cakes, pour enough oil into 12-inch skillet to cover bottom. Heat oil over medium-high heat until hot. Add crab cakes; fry 10 minutes for large cakes (6 minutes for bite-size cakes) or until cakes are lightly browned on bottom, turning halfway through cooking.

6. To broil crab cakes, preheat broiler. Place crab cakes on broiler pan. Broil 4 to 6 inches below heat 10 minutes for large cakes (6 minutes for bite-size cakes) or until cakes are lightly browned on surface, turning halfway through cooking.

7. Serve immediately with Tartar Sauce. Garnish as desired.

Makes 6 servings

Serving Suggestions: Serve large crab cakes on plate or as sandwiches with round buns. Serve bite-size cakes on plate with toothpicks as appetizers.

Techniques for Boiled Whole Lobster with Burned Butter Sauce

Step 5. *Pulling off "thumb" part of claw.*

Step 5. *Removing claw meat.*

Step 7. *Pulling out tail meat.*

Oysters Romano

1 dozen oysters
1 cup salt
2 slices bacon, cut into 1-inch pieces
½ cup Italian-seasoned dry bread crumbs
2 tablespoons butter or margarine, melted
½ teaspoon garlic salt
6 tablespoons grated Romano, Parmesan or provolone cheese
Fresh chives (optional)

1. Scrub oysters thoroughly with stiff brush under cold running water. Soak oysters in mixture of ⅓ cup salt to 1 gallon water 20 minutes. Drain water; repeat 2 more times.

2. Place oysters on tray; refrigerate 1 hour to help them relax.

3. To shuck oysters, take pointed oyster knife in 1 hand and thick towel or glove in the other. With towel, grip shell in palm of hand. Keeping oyster level with knife, insert tip of knife between shell next to hinge; twist to pry shell until you hear a snap. (Use knife as leverage; do not force.) Twist to open shell, keeping oyster level at all times to save liquor.* Cut muscle from shell; discard top shell. Cut muscle from lower shell, being careful not to spill liquor. (Do not remove oyster from shell.)

4. Preheat oven to 375°F.

5. Place shells with oysters on baking sheet. Top each oyster with 1 piece bacon. Bake 10 minutes or until bacon is crisp.

6. Meanwhile, combine bread crumbs, butter and garlic salt in small bowl. Spoon mixture over oysters; sprinkle with cheese. Bake 5 to 10 minutes until cheese melts. Serve immediately. Garnish with chives, if desired.

Makes 4 appetizer servings

*Liquor is the term used to describe the natural juices of an oyster.

Techniques for Oysters Romano

Step 3. *Inserting tip of knife between shells next to hinge.*

Step 3. *Twisting to open shell.*

Step 3. *Cutting oyster from shell.*

Stir-Fry Shrimp and Snow Peas

¾ cup defatted low sodium chicken broth
1 tablespoon oyster sauce
1 teaspoon rice vinegar
1 tablespoon cornstarch
½ teaspoon sugar
2 teaspoons peanut oil
1 small red onion, cut into thin wedges
1 teaspoon minced fresh ginger
1 clove garlic, minced
½ pound raw medium shrimp, peeled, deveined
2 cups fresh snow peas (Chinese pea pods), stems removed, cut diagonally into 1-inch pieces
3 cups hot cooked white rice, prepared in unsalted water

1. Blend broth, oyster sauce and vinegar into cornstarch and sugar in small bowl until smooth; set aside.

2. Heat oil in wok or large nonstick skillet over medium heat. Add onion, ginger and garlic; stir-fry 2 minutes. Add shrimp and snow peas. Stir-fry 3 minutes or until shrimp turn pink and opaque.

3. Stir reserved broth mixture; add to wok. Cook 1 minute or until sauce comes to a boil and thickens. Serve over rice.   *Makes 4 servings*

SHERBET

Sherbet refers to a frozen low-fat dessert made from fruit, fruit juices, sugar, stabilizers and flavorings. In the United States, sherbet often contains milk solids. Sorbet is the French term and sorbetto the Italian term for sherbet. Neither contains milk products, and they are usually fat free.

🐝

SHORTBREAD

Shortbread, which originated in Scotland, is a thick, rich cookie made with a high proportion of butter to flour and sugar. Traditionally served for Christmas and New Year's celebrations, shortbread was often pressed into round decorative molds. After baking, the shortbread was cut into wedges called petticoat tails. Today, shortbread may be shaped into rectangles or rounds called highlanders or it may be half-dipped in chocolate for royal shortbread. Chopped nuts, spices and candied fruit are sometimes added.

☫

Molded Scotch Shortbread

1½ cups all-purpose flour
¼ teaspoon salt
¾ cup butter, softened
⅓ cup sugar
1 egg
10-inch diameter ceramic shortbread mold

1. Preheat oven to temperature recommended by shortbread mold* manufacturer.

2. Combine flour and salt in medium bowl. Beat butter and sugar in large bowl with electric mixer at medium speed until light and fluffy, scraping down side of bowl once. Beat in egg. Gradually add flour mixture. Beat at low speed until well blended, scraping down side of bowl once.

3. Spray shortbread mold with nonstick cooking spray. Press dough firmly into mold. Bake, cool and remove from mold according to manufacturer's directions. Store tightly covered at room temperature or freeze up to 3 months.

Makes 1 shortbread mold

Molded Scotch Shortbread

*If mold is not available, shortbread cookies may be made. Preheat oven to 350°F. Roll tablespoonfuls of dough into 1-inch balls. Place balls 2 inches apart on ungreased baking sheets; press with fork to flatten. Bake 18 to 20 minutes until edges are lightly browned. Let cookies stand on baking sheets 2 minutes. Remove cookies to wire racks; cool completely. Store as directed. Makes 2 dozen cookies.

SHORTCAKE

Shortcake in its classic American form consists of a sweet, rich biscuit that is cut in half, filled with fruit (most often strawberries) and topped with whipped cream. Sponge cake, angel food cake and pound cake may also be used for this dessert. Unsweetened biscuits filled and topped with savory mixtures like chicken à la king may also be called shortcakes.

☫

Strawberry Shortcake

Strawberry Shortcake

Cake
　　1 package DUNCAN HINES®
　　　　Moist Deluxe French Vanilla
　　　　Cake Mix
　　3 eggs
　1¼ cups water
　　½ cup butter or margarine,
　　　　softened

Filling and Topping
　　2 cups whipping cream, chilled
　　⅓ cup sugar
　　½ teaspoon vanilla extract
　　1 quart fresh strawberries, rinsed,
　　　　drained and sliced
　　Mint leaves, for garnish

1. Preheat oven to 350°F. Grease two 9-inch round cake pans with butter or margarine. Sprinkle bottom and sides with granulated sugar.

2. For cake, combine cake mix, eggs, water and butter in large bowl. Beat at medium speed with electric mixer for 2 minutes. Pour evenly into pans. Bake at 350°F for 30 to 35 minutes or until toothpick inserted in center comes out clean. Cool in pan 10 minutes. Invert onto cooling rack. Cool completely.

3. For filling and topping, beat whipping cream, sugar and vanilla extract until stiff in large bowl. Reserve ⅓ cup for garnish. Place one cake layer on serving plate. Spread with half the whipped cream and sliced strawberries. Repeat with second layer. Garnish with reserved whipped cream and mint leaves. Refrigerate until ready to serve.

Makes 12 servings

SHUCK, TO

Shucking refers to the technique of removing oysters or clams from their shells (pages 457 and 460). Oysters can be opened with a special tool known as an oyster knife. The tool used to open clams is a clam knife. The pointed end of a can or bottle opener will also work to open both shellfish. Shucking may also refer to pulling the husk from an ear of fresh corn.

🐝

SIEVE, TO

To sieve refers to the technique of straining liquid or semiliquid through the wire mesh of a sieve or small holes of a strainer. The purpose is to separate particles from the liquid. Examples include separating stock into its liquid and solid components, sieving a stirrred custard to make it smoother and straining fresh lemon juice to separate the seeds.

The technique is also used to separate small particles from large ones (fine bits of nuts and skin from chopped nuts) and to purée soft foods (fruits, such as raspberries and strawberries, and hard-cooked egg yolks). The terms sieve and strain are sometimes used interchangeably.

SIFT, TO

Sifting is the technique of passing a dry ingredient, such as flour or powdered sugar, through the fine mesh of a sieve or sifter for the purpose of breaking up lumps and making it lighter in texture. Sifting results in finer baked goods and smoother frostings. Most all-purpose flour is presifted, eliminating the need for sifting. Cake flour is generally sifted before using. Spoon the ingredient into the sieve and push it through the mesh screen using a metal spoon or rubber spatula. See page 528 for information on sieves and page 525 for information on flour sifters.

SIMMER, TO

To simmer is to cook a liquid or a food in a liquid with gentle heat just below the boiling point. Simmering is indicated by small bubbles slowly rising to the surface of the liquid.

SKIM, TO

The technique of skimming refers to removing a substance, such as a fat, from the top of a liquid using a spoon or ladle. A bulb baster also works well for removing fat. The term to skim also refers to removing the foam from stock or jelly after boiling.

SLIVER, TO

To sliver is the technique of cutting food into thin strips or pieces. Basil and garlic are two ingredients that may be identified as slivered in a recipe. The word sliver may also refer to a long, thin strip of food or a small wedge of a pie.

SMOKE, TO

Smoking is the technique of curing foods, usually meats or fish but also cheese, by using smoke for long periods of time at low temperatures. Smoking may take several days at temperatures around 150° to 200°F. Aromatic woods, vines or herbs may be used to impart various smoked flavors. The chemicals present in the smoke assist in the preservation of the food. Smoking of foods is usually done commercially, but with specialized equipment it can be done at home.

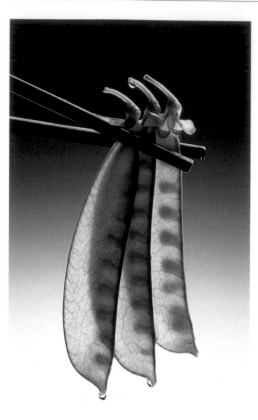

SNOW PEA

A snow pea is a slender, almost translucent green pod containing undeveloped seeds. It is also called the Chinese pea pod and the Mennonite pea in Pennsylvania. This type of edible pea pod contains tiny peas inside a flat, crisp tender pod which measures about 3 to 4 inches long. They are often used in Asian dishes where they are prized for their crispness, color and delicate flavor.

🌾

Uses: Snow peas are most commonly used as an ingredient in stir-fry recipes.

• They can also be steamed for use as vegetable side dish.

• Blanched snow peas make great additions to salads.

• Snow peas are served raw or blanched with dips or stuffed for appetizers.

Availability: Snow peas are available all year with peak season from May to September. They are also available frozen.

Yield: ½ pound fresh snow peas, trimmed = 2 cups.

Storage: Store snow peas in a plastic bag in the refrigerator for up to three days.

Buying Tips: Choose firm, crisp bright green pods with small seeds. Avoid limp or wrinkled pods.

Basic Preparation: Wash snow peas under cold running water. Break off the stem ends and remove the strings that run the length of the pod. Pods can be cut in half crosswise, diagonally or lengthwise.

Braised Chicken & Snow Peas

   ¼ **cup soy sauce**
   2 **tablespoons dry sherry**
   1 **teaspoon sugar**
   1 **whole frying chicken (3 to 3½ pounds), cut into serving pieces**
 12 **ounces fresh snow peas (Chinese pea pods)**
  ⅔ **cup** *plus* **1 tablespoon cornstarch, divided**
   ¼ **cup vegetable oil**
   1 **piece fresh ginger (about 1 inch square), peeled, cut into 4 slices**
   2 **cloves garlic, crushed**
   1 **cup chicken broth**
   1 **large yellow onion, coarsely chopped**
     Yellow squash, zucchini, carrot and red bell pepper crescents (optional)

1. To prepare marinade, combine soy sauce, sherry and sugar in large bowl; mix well. Add chicken; stir to coat well. Cover; refrigerate 1 hour to marinate, stirring occasionally.

2. Meanwhile, to de-stem snow peas, pinch off stem end from each pod, pulling string down pod to remove if present; set aside.

3. Drain chicken, reserving marinade. Place ⅔ cup cornstarch in shallow dish or pie plate. Coat chicken pieces with cornstarch. Combine remaining 1 tablespoon cornstarch with marinade; mix well.

4. Heat wok over medium-high heat about 1 minute or until hot. Drizzle oil into wok; heat 30 seconds. Add ginger and garlic; cook and stir about 1 minute or until oil is fragrant. Remove and discard ginger and garlic with slotted spoon. Add chicken to oil; fry about 10 to 15 minutes until well browned on all sides.

5. Add broth and onion to wok; bring to a boil. Cover; reduce heat to low. Simmer chicken about 20 minutes or until fork can be inserted into chicken with ease and juices run clear, not pink, turning occasionally. Move chicken up side of wok and add reserved snow peas to bottom of wok. Cover; cook 3 to 5 minutes until peas are crisp-tender. Stir cornstarch mixture and add to wok. Cook and stir until sauce thickens and boils. Transfer to serving platter. Garnish with vegetable crescents, if desired. Serve immediately.

Makes 2 to 4 servings

Hawaiian-Style Stir-Fry

  1 can (8 ounces) pineapple chunks in juice
  2 teaspoons cornstarch
  1 tablespoon oil
  1 red bell pepper, cut into strips
  1 teaspoon curry powder
  8 ounces (about 3 cups) fresh snow peas (Chinese pea pods), stems removed
  ⅓ cup diagonally sliced green onions
  2 teaspoons light soy sauce

1. Drain pineapple, reserving juice. Combine juice and cornstarch in small bowl until smooth; set aside.

2. Heat large skillet or wok 1 minute over medium-high heat. Add oil, red pepper and curry; stir-fry 1 minute. Add pineapple chunks; stir-fry 1 minute. Add pea pods; stir-fry 1 minute. Add cornstarch mixture; cook and stir 1 minute or until clear and thickened. Stir in onions and soy sauce. Serve immediately.

Makes 6 side-dish servings

SORBET

Sorbet is the French term for sherbet but, unlike sherbet, it contains no milk products. This frozen mixture of fruit juice, fruit purée, water and sugar is more similar to an ice than to sherbet. Sorbet is known as sorbetto in Italy. Sorbet may be served as a palate refresher between courses or as a dessert.

☙

Lime Sorbet

  ½ cup fresh lime juice (about 4 limes)
  1 tablespoon grated lime peel
1½ cups hot water
  6 tablespoons sugar
  1 egg white, slightly beaten
  1 drop *each* green and yellow food color
  Mint leaves or citrus leaves (optional)

1. Combine juice and lime peel in medium bowl. Combine hot water and sugar in small bowl; stir to dissolve. Add sugar mixture, egg white and food color to juice mixture; pour into shallow pan. Cover; freeze until firm, stirring once an hour to break up ice crystals.

2. Remove sorbet from freezer about 20 minutes before serving. Garnish with mint, if desired.

Makes 6 servings

*Favorite recipe from **The Sugar Association, Inc.***

Tip

For an elegant appetizer, wrap chilled cooked shrimp with chilled blanched snow peas; secure with a toothpick. Serve with a dipping sauce of ¼ cup soy sauce and 1 tablespoon rice vinegar.

California Plum Sorbet

12 fresh California plums, halved,
   pitted and sliced
3 tablespoons sugar
1 cup orange juice
1 tablespoon grated orange peel

1. Add plums, sugar, orange juice and orange peel to food processor or blender; process until smooth. Pour into loaf pan; freeze about 4 hours.

2. Process again 30 minutes before serving. Freeze until ready to serve.

Makes 6 servings

Favorite recipe from **California Tree Fruit Agreement**

SOUFFLÉ

The term soufflé is applied to two different dishes. The most common is a light, airy baked egg-based dish that may be savory or sweet. A soufflé begins with a white sauce to which egg yolks and flavorings are added. Egg whites, which are beaten until stiff peaks form, are folded into the sauce mixture. The air in the beaten egg whites causes the soufflé to rise, often above the top of the dish. Soufflés are generally baked in a straight-sided round casserole known as a soufflé dish. Savory soufflés usually contain cheese and vegetables, such as asparagus, broccoli and spinach. Sweet soufflés are often flavored with chocolate or fruit. Both are served hot and puffy from the oven.

Classic Spinach Soufflé

A chilled soufflé is a light, creamy dessert that is stablized with gelatin. It is generally made with whipped cream or cream cheese and sometimes cooked egg yolks. Flavorings include chocolate and fruit purées.

☙

Tips for a Perfect Baked Soufflé: Egg whites should be beaten only until stiff peaks form. Overbeating egg whites will result in a soufflé that fails to rise properly (page 190).

• Gently fold in the beaten egg whites. A heavy hand will deflate the whites. To make this process easier, lighten the sauce mixture by stirring in a spoonful of the egg whites. This will make it easier to fold in the remaining egg whites.

• Serve a soufflé immediately after removing it from the oven. A delay in serving will cause the soufflé to deflate.

Classic Spinach Soufflé

> 1 pound fresh spinach, washed, stemmed
> 1/4 cup butter or margarine
> 2 tablespoons finely chopped onion
> 1/4 cup all-purpose flour
> 1/4 teaspoon salt
> 1/4 teaspoon ground nutmeg
> 1/8 teaspoon ground black pepper
> 1 cup milk
> 4 eggs, separated
> 1 cup (4 ounces) shredded sharp Cheddar cheese
> Carrot strips and green onion curl (optional)

1. Preheat oven to 375°F. Grease 1½- or 2-quart soufflé dish.

2. Heat 1 quart slightly salted water in 2-quart saucepan over high heat. Bring to a boil; add spinach. Return to a boil; cook 2 to 3 minutes until spinach is crisp-tender. Drain spinach; immediately plunge into cold water. Drain spinach again; let stand until cool enough to handle. Squeeze spinach to remove excess moisture. Finely chop spinach; set aside.

3. Melt butter in large saucepan over medium heat. Add onion; cook and stir 2 to 3 minutes. Stir in flour, salt, nutmeg and pepper. Gradually stir in milk. Cook and stir until mixture comes to a boil and thickens. Remove from heat. Stir egg yolks into flour mixture until well blended. Add reserved spinach and cheese; mix well. Set aside.

4. Beat egg whites in clean large bowl with electric mixer at high speed until stiff peaks form. Carefully, fold egg whites into spinach mixture with rubber spatula. Pour into prepared dish.

5. Bake 35 to 40 minutes until puffed and wooden skewer inserted into center comes out clean. Garnish with carrot strips and onion curl, if desired. Serve immediately.

Makes 4 servings

Tip

To prevent a soufflé from falling during baking, do not open the oven door until the last quarter of the baking time.

SOUP

A soup is a liquid, usually hot, but sometimes cold, that has been cooked with added ingredients, such as meat and vegetables. Soups are far more interesting and diverse than such a definition suggests. The simplest are clear liquids, such as consommés and bouillons, which may be served plain or garnished with bits of vegetables, meat or dumplings. Most soups are heartier, filled with a number of ingredients, such as meat, fish, poultry, vegetables, pasta, dumplings or rice. Soups may be served as smooth purées or left chunky. Depending on the ingredients, they can be served as a main course or a first course.

☙

Cream of Broccoli Soup

(page 486)

1 bunch broccoli (about
    1½ pounds)
1 medium onion, chopped
1 carrot, chopped
1 rib celery, chopped
1 potato, peeled, chopped
1 clove garlic, minced
½ teaspoon dried basil leaves
3 cups Chicken Stock (page 486)
    or canned chicken broth
2 tablespoons butter
2 tablespoons all-purpose flour
1½ cups milk
1 cup half-and-half
½ cup (2 ounces) shredded
    Cheddar cheese
½ teaspoon salt
¼ teaspoon ground black pepper
6 to 8 teaspoons sour cream
    (optional)
Fresh basil leaves and red bell
    pepper curl (optional)

1. Trim leaves and ends from broccoli stalks; discard. Peel stalks. Cut broccoli into ½-inch pieces; set aside.

2. Combine onion, carrot, celery, potato, garlic, dried basil and Chicken Stock in large saucepan. Bring to a boil over high heat. Reduce heat to low; simmer 10 minutes. Add reserved broccoli to saucepan. Simmer 10 minutes or until vegetables are fork-tender. Cool at room temperature 20 to 30 minutes. *Do not drain.*

3. Remove vegetables in small batches with slotted spoon to food processor or blender; process until smooth. Set aside.

4. Melt butter in Dutch oven over medium heat; add flour, stirring until mixture is smooth. Cook 1 minute more. Gradually whisk in milk and half-and-half. Stir in cheese, salt and black pepper. Add puréed vegetables. Cook 3 to 5 minutes until mixture thickens, stirring occasionally. To serve, ladle soup into bowls. Top each serving with small dollops of sour cream. Allow sour cream to melt, then swirl in attractive pattern with tip of knife. Garnish with fresh basil and red pepper, if desired.

Makes 8 servings

Tip

To prevent cheese from becoming tough and stringy in soup, heat the soup over low or medium heat. High heat should be avoided.

SOUR CREAM

This thick, tangy dairy product is made by commercially treating cream with lactic acid, a process that thickens the cream and adds an acidic taste. Sometimes renin, gelatin or stabilizers are added. The fat content of sour cream is typically between 18 and 20 percent. Light sour cream is made from half-and-half or other lower fat dairy products. It can usually be used in place of regular sour cream. Nonfat sour cream also is available. Made with nonfat milk, it is thickened with added ingredients, such as starches and stabilizers. Nonfat sour cream may be substituted for regular sour cream in most uses, but it may not produce an acceptable result in baked goods.

Sour cream has a wide range of culinary uses. It is used as a topping for baked potatoes, soups and Mexican entrées. It is an ingredient in cakes, especially those of Eastern European origin, cheesecakes, dips and sauces. Special care must be taken when adding sour cream to sauces during cooking. Sour cream will separate, or break, if it is boiled. Add it to most dishes after cooking has completed and the pan has been removed from the heat. To minimize risk, blend a spoonful or two of the hot liquid into the sour cream and then stir the sour cream mixture into the liquid.

Linguine with Paprikash Sauce

- 12 ounces uncooked linguine
- 2 red bell peppers, cut into thin strips
- 2 tablespoons olive oil
- 1 medium onion, sliced
- 1 clove garlic, minced
- 2 tablespoons all-purpose flour
- 4 teaspoons sweet Hungarian paprika
- ½ teaspoon salt
- ¼ teaspoon ground black pepper
- 1 can (8 ounces) tomato sauce
- 1 cup canned vegetable broth
- ½ cup sour cream
  Fresh herb sprigs (optional)

1. Cook linguine according to package directions. Drain in colander. Place in large warm bowl; keep warm.

2. Cut pepper strips crosswise into halves. Heat oil in large skillet over medium heat. Add pepper strips, onion and garlic; cook and stir 8 to 10 minutes until peppers are very soft.

3. Combine flour, paprika, salt and black pepper in small bowl. Stir into bell pepper mixture. Cook over medium heat 3 minutes, stirring occasionally.

4. Combine tomato sauce and broth; stir into pepper mixture. Bring to a boil, stirring constantly. Reduce heat to low; simmer, uncovered, until sauce thickens. Remove from heat; place sour cream in small bowl. Stir several spoonfuls hot mixture into sour cream. Stir sour cream mixture back into hot mixture in skillet. Cook over low heat 1 minute or until heated through. *Do not boil.* Pour over warm linguine; toss. Garnish with herbs, if desired. Serve immediately.

Makes 5 to 6 servings

Tip

Small spots of mold on sour cream indicate mold throughout the container, so always discard the entire container when mold is present.

Linguine with Paprikash Sauce

Cocoa Sour Cream Bundt Cake

¾ cup (1½ sticks) butter or
        margarine, softened
1⅔ cups sugar
2 eggs
1 teaspoon vanilla extract
¾ cup dairy sour cream
2 cups all-purpose flour
⅔ cup HERSHEY'S Cocoa
½ teaspoon salt
2 teaspoons baking soda
1 cup buttermilk or sour milk*

To sour milk: Use 1 tablespoon white vinegar plus milk to equal 1 cup.

Heat oven to 350°F. Grease and flour 9- or 12-cup fluted tube pan. In large mixer bowl on medium speed of electric mixer, beat butter, sugar, eggs and vanilla until light and fluffy; blend in sour cream. Stir together flour, cocoa and salt. Stir baking soda into buttermilk; add alternately with dry ingredients to butter mixture, beating well after each addition. Beat an additional 2 minutes. Pour into prepared pan. Bake 45 to 50 minutes or until wooden pick inserted in cake comes out clean. Cool 10 minutes; remove from pan to wire rack. Cool completely. Glaze as desired.

Makes 10 to 12 servings

SOY SAUCE

A crucial ingredient in Chinese and Japanese cooking, soy sauce is a dark, salty liquid made by fermenting boiled soy beans and wheat or barley. Although there are different varieties available, such as dark and light, the major commercial brands sold in the United States are all-purpose. Reduced-sodium (or lite) soy sauce is also available.

🐝

Castillian Grilled Chicken

3 tablespoons KIKKOMAN® Lite
        Soy Sauce
2 tablespoons water
1 tablespoon olive oil
1 clove garlic, pressed
½ teaspoon dried oregano leaves,
        crumbled
¼ teaspoon ground cumin
¼ to ½ teaspoon ground red
        pepper (cayenne)
6 boneless, skinless chicken breast
        halves

Blend lite soy sauce, water, oil, garlic, oregano, cumin and pepper; pour over chicken in large plastic food storage bag. Press air out of bag; close top securely. Refrigerate 1 hour, turning bag over occasionally. Remove chicken from marinade; place on grill 4 to 5 inches from hot coals. Cook chicken 5 minutes on each side, or until no longer pink in center. (Or, place chicken on rack of broiler pan. Broil 4 to 5 inches from heat 5 to 6 minutes on each side, or until no longer pink in center.)

Makes 6 servings

Spicy Pork Stir-Fry

1 can (about 14 ounces) defatted
        low sodium chicken broth,
        divided
2 tablespoons reduced sodium soy
        sauce
2 tablespoons cornstarch
1 tablespoon grated orange peel
1 pork tenderloin (about
        10 ounces)
2 tablespoons peanut oil, divided
1 tablespoon sesame seeds
2 cloves garlic, minced
2 cups broccoli flowerets
2 cups sliced carrots
1 teaspoon Szechuan seasoning*
6 cups hot cooked rice

Szechuan seasoning is available at some larger supermarkets and at Asian markets.

Spicy Pork Stir-Fry

1. Combine 1 ½ cups broth, soy sauce, cornstarch and orange peel in medium bowl until smooth; set aside.

2. Cut pork lengthwise, then cut crosswise into ¼-inch slices. Heat 1 tablespoon oil in wok or large skillet over high heat. Add pork, sesame seeds and garlic. Stir-fry 3 minutes or until pork is barely pink in center. Remove from wok to large bowl.

3. Heat remaining 1 tablespoon oil in wok. Add broccoli, carrots, Szechuan seasoning and remaining 2 tablespoons broth. Cook and stir 5 minutes or until vegetables are crisp-tender. Add pork mixture. Stir broth mixture; add to wok. Cook and stir over medium heat until sauce is thickened. Serve over rice.

Makes 6 servings

SPAETZLE

Spaetzle, also spelled spätzle, is a tiny German dumpling or noodle made from a dough of flour, egg and water or milk. The soft dough is pressed through the large holes of a colander or spaetzle maker into boiling liquid. A firmer dough can be rolled and cut into small pieces. Spaetzle are cooked when they float to the top of the water. Spaetzle is served as a side dish tossed with butter or topped with a sauce or gravy.

☙

SPINACH

Spinach is said to have been culti-vated in Persian gardens thousands of years ago to please their much-prized cats. Today, spinach is a popular part of American cuisine and, although eating a lot of it will not make you strong as the comic strip character Popeye suggests, it is a healthy addi-tion to the diet. Spinach is an excel-lent source of fiber and beta-carotene. If eaten raw it supplies a good amount of vitamin C.

☕

Uses: Fresh spinach is an ingredient in mixed green salads and the basis for spinach salad. Traditional spinach salad is made with bacon, hard-cooked eggs and a sweet-and-sour dressing. It is served both fresh or "wilted" with warmed dressing.

• Spinach is a cooked ingredient in a wide variety of appetizers, side dishes and entrées. Popular spinach dishes include spinach dip, creamed spinach and spinach soufflé.

• Cooked spinach can be served as a side dish, alone or in a cream sauce.

Varieties: There are many varieties of spinach, but they are generally grouped by leaf type—flat and curly. Savoy and semisavoy spinach has curly, crinkly dark green leaves. It has a crisp crunchy texture but the leaves are more difficult to clean. Flat or smooth-leaf spinach has tender spade-shaped leaves. This type is often used in canned or frozen products.

Availability: Fresh spinach is available year-round either loose, in bunches or packaged in plastic bags. Flat-leaf spinach is most often found in bunches and curly-leaf spinach is usually bagged. Spinach is also available canned and frozen.

Buying Tips: If choosing loose spinach, look for leaves with good color and a crisp texture. Avoid limp, wilted, bruised, spotted or discolored leaves. The leaves should have a fresh aroma, not a sour or musty odor. Avoid leaves with thick coarse stems as they are a sign of overgrown spinach, which can be tough and bitter. Thick stems also mean more waste, since they are removed and discarded. If purchasing spinach prepackaged, squeeze the bag to check if the contents are resilient and thus fresh and crisp.

Yield: 1 pound spinach = about 10 to 12 cups torn pieces; about 1 cup cooked.
1 (10-ounce package) thawed and drained frozen spinach = about 1½ cups.

Storage: Do not wash spinach before storing. Store loose spinach lightly packed in a plastic bag in the refrigerator. Leave prepackaged spinach in its original plastic bag. It will keep for three or four days.

Basic Preparation: All spinach should be well washed and rinsed to remove the sand and grit that adheres to the leaves. Remove any roots or slimy leaves and soak the spinach leaves in a sinkful of cold water for a few minutes. Then swish the leaves gently to remove dirt and sand. Repeat this process several times, if necessary, with fresh water. Prepackaged spinach may only need one cleaning, whereas loose spinach may need to be rinsed several times.

To remove the stems from the spinach  leaves, fold each leaf in half, then with your hand pull the stem toward the the top of the leaf. Discard the stem.

For salads and other fresh uses, dry spinach leaves with paper towels or in a salad spinner. Wrap loosely in paper towels in a plastic bag and refrigerate for no more than two or three hours to crisp the leaves. If spinach is to be cooked, there is usually just enough water adhering to the leaves so that they can be steamed in a saucepan without additional liquid.

Spinach can be steamed, sautéed or stir-fried. Cook it only until it is wilted. It should still be bright green.

Wilted Spinach Mandarin

½ **pound fresh spinach**
1 **tablespoon oil**
1 **cup bean sprouts**
1 **can (11 ounces) mandarin oranges, drained**
2 **tablespoons reduced sodium soy sauce**
2 **tablespoons orange juice**
   Quartered orange slices (optional)

1. Separate spinach into leaves. Swish in cold water. Repeat several times with fresh water to remove sand and grit. Pat dry with paper towels. To remove stems from spinach leaves, fold each leaf in half, then with hand pull stem toward top of leaf. Discard stem.

2. Heat oil in wok or large skillet over medium-high heat; add spinach, bean sprouts and mandarin oranges. Stir fry 1 to 2 minutes just until spinach wilts. Transfer to serving dish. Heat soy sauce and juice in wok; pour over spinach and toss gently to coat. Garnish with orange slices, if desired. Serve immediately.

Makes 4 side-dish servings

Wilted Spinach Mandarin

Florentine-Stuffed Shells

24 uncooked jumbo pasta shells for filling
1 package (10 ounces) frozen chopped spinach, thawed
1 egg, slightly beaten
2 cups (15 ounces) SARGENTO® Ricotta Cheese*
1½ cups (6 ounces) SARGENTO® Classic Supreme® Shredded or Fancy Supreme® Shredded Mozzarella Cheese
⅓ cup finely chopped onion
2 cloves garlic, minced
¼ teaspoon salt
⅛ teaspoon ground nutmeg
2 cups meatless spaghetti sauce
½ cup (2 ounces) SARGENTO® Grated Cheese**

*SARGENTO® Old Fashioned Ricotta, Part Skim Ricotta or Light Ricotta can be used.

**SARGENTO® Parmesan, Parmesan and Romano or Italian-Style Grated Cheese can be used.

Cook pasta shells according to package directions; drain. Meanwhile, squeeze spinach to remove as much moisture as possible. Combine egg, spinach, Ricotta cheese, Mozzarella cheese, onion, garlic, salt and nutmeg; stir to blend well. Stuff shells with Ricotta mixture, using about 2 tablespoons mixture for each shell. Place in lightly greased 13×9-inch baking dish. Pour spaghetti sauce over shells. Sprinkle with grated cheese; cover. Bake at 350°F, 30 to 40 minutes or until thoroughly heated.

Makes 8 servings

Florentine-Stuffed Shells

SPOON BREAD

Spoon bread is a soft, moist egg-based dish made with cornmeal and sometimes corn kernels. It is baked in a casserole dish. This "bread" is more like a pudding than bread and, as its name indicates, it can be served with a spoon. This Southern favorite is served as a side dish in place of bread, potatoes or rice.

🌾

Denver Spoon Bread

> 3 tablespoons butter or margarine, divided
> 2 tablespoons freshly grated Parmesan cheese
> ½ cup chopped onion
> ¼ cup chopped green bell pepper
> ¼ cup chopped red bell pepper
> 2½ cups milk
> 1 cup yellow cornmeal
> 1 teaspoon salt
> 1½ cups (6 ounces) shredded Cheddar cheese
> 4 eggs, separated
> Red and green bell pepper strips (optional)

1. Preheat oven to 350°F. Grease 1½-quart soufflé dish with 1 tablespoon butter. Sprinkle bottom and side of dish evenly with Parmesan cheese.

2. Melt remaining 2 tablespoons butter in heavy medium saucepan over medium heat. Add onion and chopped peppers; cook 5 to 7 minutes or until tender, stirring occasionally. Transfer mixture to small bowl; set aside.

3. Combine milk, cornmeal and salt in same saucepan. Bring to a boil over high heat. Reduce heat to medium; cook and stir 5 minutes or until mixture thickens. Remove from heat. Stir in Cheddar cheese until cheese is melted. Stir in reserved onion mixture; set aside.

4. Beat egg whites in large bowl with electric mixer at high speed until stiff but not dry; set aside.

5. Beat egg yolks in separate large bowl with fork. Stir into reserved cornmeal mixture. Stir ⅓ of egg whites into cornmeal mixture to lighten. Fold remaining egg whites into cornmeal mixture until all egg whites are evenly incorporated. Pour into prepared soufflé dish.

6. Bake about 50 minutes or until puffed and golden brown. Serve immediately. Garnish with pepper strips, if desired.   *Makes 6 servings*

SPRING ROLL

A spring roll is a delicate version of the egg roll. This Chinese appetizer is made with a paper-thin translucent wrapper. It is filled with vegetables, pork, shrimp and seasonings. Spring rolls are served on the first day of the Chinese New Year.

🌾

SPROUT

Sprouts are the very first young tender growth of various beans, grains and seeds. Asian cultures have long appreciated the crunchy appeal of mung and soy bean sprouts. In America, the addition of alfalfa sprouts to salads and sandwiches has been popularized by vegetarians. All sprouts are eaten raw, but only mung bean and soybean sprouts are sturdy enough to be stir-fried.

🌾

*Hummus Pita
Sandwich*

Varieties: Alfalfa, clover and radish sprouts are thin hairlike sprouts with tiny tan to light green tips.

• Mung bean and soybean sprouts are thick white sprouts that are more likely to be used in cooked dishes, such as stir-fries.

• Wheat berry, lentil, pea and red bean sprouts all have short tiny sprouts protruding from small crunchy seeds.

Availability: Sprouts are available year-round since they are grown indoors. They may be purchased in bulk, but they are usually packaged in plastic bags or in clear plastic boxes in which they have been sprouted. Canned mung bean sprouts are available in most markets.

Buying Tips: Choose sprouts that are fresh and crisp. Avoid sprouts that look slimy or have a musty odor.

Storage: Store sturdy sprouts (mung and soybean) refrigerated in a plastic bag, no more than three days. Other sprouts may be refrigerated in the packages in which they are purchased for two days.

Basic Preparation: Wash sprouts just before using and pat dry with paper towels. Use sprouts raw to preserve their crispness. If cooked, choose the sturdy varieties and cook no more than thirty seconds.

Hummus Pita Sandwiches

    1 can (15 ounces) chick-peas,
       undrained
    1 to 2 cloves garlic, peeled
    ¼ cup loosely packed parsley
    3 tablespoons fresh lemon juice
    1 tablespoon olive oil
    ¼ teaspoon ground black pepper
    2 tablespoons sesame seeds,
       toasted
    4 pita breads
    2 tomatoes, thinly sliced
    1 cucumber, sliced
    1 cup alfalfa sprouts, rinsed,
       drained
    2 tablespoons crumbled feta
       cheese

1. Drain chick-peas; reserve liquid.

2. For hummus, place garlic in food processor. Process until minced. Add chick-peas, parsley, juice, oil and pepper. Process until almost smooth, scraping sides of bowl once. If mixture is very thick, stir in 1 to 2 tablespoons reserved chick-pea liquid. Pour hummus into medium bowl. Stir in sesame seeds.

3. Cut pita breads in half. Spread about 3 tablespoons hummus in each pita bread half. Divide tomatoes, cucumber and sprouts evenly among pita breads. Sprinkle with cheese. Garnish as desired. Serve immediately.　　　*Makes 4 servings*

SPUMONI

Spumoni is a molded Italian dessert with two layers of ice cream, usually vanilla and chocolate, separated by a layer of whipped cream that is usually flavored with rum, candied fruits and nuts. Spumoni is served in slices and often topped with a sauce.

SQUASH

Squash, a member of the gourd family, is available in a wide variety of shapes, sizes and colors. In the garden, these plants can be recognized by their long trailing vines, large leaves and handsome blossoms. Squashes are native to the Western Hemisphere and have been an important source of food and medicine to Native Americans for thousands of years. Today it is commercially grown in most states, Florida being the leader. This vegetable can be divided into two categories, summer squash and winter squash.

SUMMER SQUASH

Summer squashes are harvested when immature. They have edible skins, small soft seeds and a mild, delicate flavor. Their flesh has a high water content and cooks quickly. The different types can easily be interchanged in recipes.

Varieties: Some of the most common varieties are listed here.

Pattypan is a bowl-shaped squash with a scalloped rim. It is 3 to 4 inches in diameter and pale green or white in color.

Yellow crookneck squash has a slender curved neck and a slight bulbous base.

Yellow straight-neck squash, a related variety, has a straight, slender shape, yellow skin and creamy flesh.

Zucchini is a straight, slender dark green squash with creamy flesh. *See Zucchini, page 552, for additional information.*

Availability: Summer squashes are available all year in supermarkets, but summer is their peak season. Look for the crookneck variety at farmers' markets.

Buying Tips: Choose small to medium-size squashes that are firm with smooth, glossy unblemished skins. They should feel heavy for their size. Large squashes are less tender.

Yield: 1 pound summer squash = 3 medium; 2½ cups chopped; 1⅔ cups cooked.

Storage: Refrigerate summer squashes, unwashed, in a plastic bag for up to five days.

Basic Preparation: Wash squash under cold running water. Do not peel. Trim off and discard both ends. Cut into chunks or slices. Summer squashes are generally steamed, sauteed, grilled, stir-fried, and breaded or battered and panfried.

Cheese-Stuffed Pattypans (recipe on page 478)

WINTER SQUASH

Winter squashes are harvested in the fall when they are mature. They will keep for a month or two because of their thick, hard shells. They need to be peeled and the seeds removed before eating. Their flavor and texture vary widely so they can not be easily interchanged in recipes.

Varieties: Some of the most common varieties are listed here.

Acorn squash has an acorn shape and weighs from one to three pounds. The skin is dark green with patches of orange and the flesh is a deep orange. It has a sweet flavor.

Butternut squash, which weighs from two to five pounds, is cylindrical with a slight bulbous base. The skin is creamy tan and the flesh is a yellowish-orange. The flavor is sweet and slightly nutty.

Hubbard squash is large (about 10 pounds) with a grayish-green to bright orange bumpy skin and a yellowish-orange grainy flesh.

Spaghetti squash, which weighs from three to five pounds, is oblong with creamy yellow skin and pale yellow flesh. It gets its name because the flesh separates into spaghettilike strands when cooked.

Techniques for Cheese-Stuffed Pattypans

Step 2. *Slicing tops off squash.*

Step 2. *Scooping seeds from squash.*

Turban squash has, as its name suggests, a turban-shaped top. The hard, bumpy shell varies greatly in color from orange to green to yellow. Although they can be cooked, they are often used for decoration.

Availability: Winter squashes are usually available all year with peak season from September to March. Some varieties are difficult to find in summer.

Buying Tips: Choose squashes that are heavy for their size with hard, thick shells. Avoid those with any signs of decay, soft spots or cuts in the shells.

Yield: 1 pound winter squash = 1 cup cooked and mashed.

Storage: Store whole unwashed squashes in a cool (50°F), dry, dark place with good ventilation for up to two months. Smaller varieties do not keep as long as larger ones. Do not wrap them or place them in a plastic bag. Wrap cut pieces securely in plastic food wrap and refrigerate for up to five days.

Basic Preparation: Rinse with cold running water. To cube or slice the squash, peel with a swivel-bladed vegetable peeler. Cut squash into halves or quarters. Remove and discard the seeds. Cut into cubes or slices for baking, boiling or steaming. Winter squashes may also be baked or microwaved whole or cut into halves.

Cheese-Stuffed Pattypans

> 4 pattypan squash (about 3 inches in diameter)
> 4 tablespoons butter or margarine
> 2 ribs celery, chopped
> ½ cup chopped onion
> ½ cup water
> 1 cup dry herb-seasoned stuffing mix
> 1 cup (4 ounces) shredded sharp Cheddar cheese

1. Preheat oven to 350°F.

2. Wash squash and slice off tops, above scalloped edges; discard. Scoop out seeds from center; discard.

3. Place squash shells in large skillet. Pour ¼ inch of water into skillet; cover. Bring to a boil over high heat; reduce heat to medium-low. Simmer 5 minutes. Transfer squash, cut side up, to greased 8×8-inch baking dish with slotted spoon; set aside.

4. Heat butter in large skillet over medium-high heat until melted and bubbly. Add celery and onion; cook and stir until tender. Add water and stuffing mix. Stir to absorb water. Stir in cheese. Spoon mixture into squash shells.

5. Bake 20 to 30 minutes until squash is fork-tender and stuffing is lightly browned. Garnish as desired. Serve immediately.

Makes 4 side-dish servings

Sesame Peanut Spaghetti Squash

1 spaghetti squash (3 pounds)
⅓ cup sesame seeds, toasted
⅓ cup vegetable broth
2 tablespoons reduced sodium soy sauce
1 tablespoon sugar
2 teaspoons Oriental sesame oil
1 teaspoon cornstarch
1 teaspoon crushed red pepper flakes
1 teaspoon Worcestershire sauce
1 tablespoon vegetable oil
2 medium carrots, cut into julienne strips
1 large red bell pepper, thinly sliced
¼ pound fresh snow peas (Chinese pea pods), stems removed, cut diagonally into halves
½ cup coarsely chopped unsalted peanuts
⅓ cup minced fresh cilantro

1. Preheat oven to 350°F. Spray 13×9-inch baking dish with nonstick cooking spray.

2. Wash squash; cut in half lengthwise. Remove and discard seeds. Place squash, cut side down, in prepared dish. Bake 45 minutes to 1 hour or until just tender.

3. Using fork, remove spaghettilike strands from hot squash; place strands in large bowl. Cover; keep warm.

4. Place sesame seeds, broth, soy sauce, sugar, sesame oil, cornstarch, pepper flakes and Worcestershire in blender or food processor; process until mixture is coarsely puréed. Set aside.

5. Heat wok or large skillet over medium-high heat 1 minute or until hot. Drizzle vegetable oil into wok and heat 30 seconds. Add carrots; stir-fry 1 minute. Add bell pepper; stir-fry 2 minutes or until vegetables are crisp-tender. Add snow peas; stir fry 1 minute. Stir sesame seed mixture; add to wok. Cook and stir 1 minute or until sauce thickens. Pour vegetable mixture over spaghetti squash. Add peanuts and cilantro; toss well. Garnish as desired. Serve immediately. *Makes 4 servings*

Technique for Sesame Peanut Spaghetti Squash

Step 3. *Removing spaghettilike strands from squash.*

Sesame Peanut Spaghetti Squash

Jamaican Seafood Salad

- 6 ounces uncooked vermicelli noodles
- 6 ounces lump crabmeat or imitation crabmeat, shredded
- 4 ounces cooked medium shrimp
- 1 cup diagonally sliced yellow squash
- 1 cup diagonally sliced zucchini
- 1 tablespoon rice vinegar
- 1 tablespoon reduced sodium soy sauce
- 1 tablespoon minced fresh cilantro
- 1 tablespoon fresh lime juice
- 2 teaspoons Oriental sesame oil
- 2 teaspoons grated fresh ginger
- 1 teaspoon grated lime peel
- 1/8 teaspoon ground cinnamon

1. Cook noodles according to package directions, omitting salt. Drain and rinse well under cold water until pasta is cool; drain well.

2. Combine crabmeat, shrimp, yellow squash and zucchini in medium bowl. Combine remaining ingredients in small bowl; pour over seafood mixture. Toss to coat evenly. Serve over reserved noodles at room temperature or refrigerate until ready to serve. Garnish as desired.

Makes 6 servings

Glazed Acorn Squash

- 2 medium acorn squash, halved and seeded
- 1 1/2 cups cold tap water
- 1/3 cup KARO® Light or Dark Corn Syrup
- 1 tablespoon MAZOLA® Margarine or butter, melted
- 1/2 teaspoon ground cinnamon
- 1/4 teaspoon salt

Place squash, cut side down, in 13×9×2-inch baking dish; add water. Bake in 400°F oven 30 minutes or until squash is fork-tender. Turn squash cut-side up. In small bowl combine corn syrup, margarine, cinnamon and salt. Spoon corn syrup mixture into squash cavities.

Bake in 350°F oven 15 minutes or until fork-tender, basting occasionally.

Makes 4 side-dish servings

Prep time: 5 minutes
Bake time: 45 minutes

STAR FRUIT

Star fruit is the common name for the carambola. This fragrant fruit is small and oval-shaped ranging from 3 to 5 inches long with four to six deep lengthwise grooves. It has an edible thin, waxy bright yellow skin and sweet, juicy almost translucent yellow flesh. Its taste is similar to a combination of lemon, pineapple and apple. It can vary from sweet to slightly tart. When it is sliced crosswise, the slices are is shaped like stars, thus its common name, star fruit. It is native to Malaysia and now an important crop in the tropical and subtropical regions of Asia, the Caribbean, Hawaii and southern Florida. Its interesting shape makes it attractive for fruit baskets, salads and as a garnish for beverages and meat.

Varieties: There are two types of star fruit, tart and sweet. Tart varieties generally have narrowly spaced ribs; sweet varieties have thick, fleshy ribs.

Availability: Star fruit is generally available from August through March.

Buying Tips: Choose firm, bright, evenly colored fruit. Ribs often have a slightly brown tinge when ripe. Avoid fruit with brown, shriveled ribs. Slightly green fruit will ripen at home, but avoid fruit that is all green. Star fruit is also available dried.

Yield: 2 large or medium star fruit = 2 cups slices.

Storage: If purchased slightly green, ripen at room temperature uncovered and out of direct sunlight. Turn frequently, until they are bright yellow in color and fragrant. Ripe fruit should be stored at room temperature for two to three days or refrigerated, unwashed, in a tightly covered container or plastic bag for up to one week.

Basic Preparation: Star fruit is easy to prepare, because it does not require peeling or seeding. It can be eaten out of hand after it has been washed. Wash under cold running water. Cut it crosswise into thin slices. If the skin is unappealing, simply peel it off with a paring knife.

STEAM, TO

Steaming is a method of cooking food, usually vegetables, in the steam given off by boiling water. The food is held above, but not in, the boiling or simmering water in a covered pan. The steam swirls around the food and cooks it with an intense, moist heat. Steaming helps to retain flavor, color, shape, texture and many of the vitamins and minerals. Steaming requires a two-pan steamer, a steamer basket or a bamboo steamer.

There are several points to remember when steaming food: never allow the steamer to boil dry (this will ruin the steamer and burn the food); the water should never touch the food; and the water should be kept boiling (otherwise, it may result in improperly cooked food).

☙

STEAMING TIMES FOR COMMON VEGETABLES

Asparagus	8 to 10 minutes
Beans, green	5 to 15 minutes
Broccoli florets	5 to 6 minutes
Broccoli spears	8 to 15 minutes
Cabbage, shredded	5 to 8 minutes
Cabbage wedges	6 to 9 minutes
Carrots, whole	10 to 15 minutes
Carrot slices	4 to 5 minutes
Cauliflower, whole	15 to 20 minutes
Cauliflower florets	6 to 10 minutes
Eggplant cubes or slices	5 to 6 minutes
Peas	3 to 5 minutes
Peppers, bell, slices	2 to 4 minutes
Spinach	5 to 6 minutes
Squash, summer, slices	3 to 6 minutes
Squash, winter, cubes or slices	9 to 12 minutes
Zucchini slices	3 to 6 minutes

STEEP, TO

Steeping refers to the technique of soaking a dry ingredient in a liquid that is usually hot in order to transfer its flavor and color to the liquid. The food is often discarded after steeping, and the liquid is consumed or used as an ingredient to flavor other foods. Tea leaves, ground coffee beans, herbs and spices are examples of ingredients that are steeped.

❦

STEW

A stew is a dish of meat, chicken or fish and vegetables that is prepared by long simmering in a covered pan. This method is called stewing. Stewing blends flavors and tenderizes less tender but economical cuts of meat.

❦

Technique for Favorite Beef Stew

Step 2. *Browning beef cubes.*

Favorite Beef Stew

Favorite Beef Stew

1½ pounds beef stew meat, trimmed, cut into ¾-inch cubes
3 tablespoons all-purpose flour
1 teaspoon salt
½ teaspoon ground black pepper
2 tablespoons vegetable oil
1 cup Beef Stock (page 487) or canned beef broth
1 can (16 ounces) whole tomatoes, chopped, undrained
1 clove garlic, minced
1 bay leaf
1 tablespoon Worcestershire sauce
½ teaspoon dried thyme leaves
¼ teaspoon dried basil leaves
2 potatoes
1 cup frozen pearl onions
2 carrots, cut into ½-inch pieces
2 ribs celery, cut into ½-inch pieces
Onion rings and fresh herb leaves (optional)

1. Place beef in large bowl; sprinkle with flour, salt and pepper. Toss lightly to coat.

2. Heat oil in 5-quart Dutch oven over medium-high heat. Add floured beef; brown on all sides, stirring frequently. Add Beef Stock, tomatoes with juice, garlic, bay leaf, Worcestershire, thyme and basil; bring to a boil over high heat. Reduce heat to low; simmer, uncovered, 1½ hours, stirring occasionally.

3. Peel potatoes and cut into ½-inch cubes. Increase heat to medium. Add potatoes, onions, carrots and celery; bring to a boil. Reduce heat to low; simmer, uncovered, 30 minutes more or until beef and vegetables are tender. Garnish with onion rings and herbs, if desired. Serve immediately.

Makes 6 servings

Pork Stew

2 tablespoons vegetable oil
3 pounds lean fresh boneless pork
    butt, cut into 1½-inch cubes
2 medium white onions, cut
    lengthwise into thin slices
3 cloves garlic, minced
1 teaspoon salt
1 teaspoon ground cumin
¾ teaspoon dried oregano leaves
1 cup fresh tomatillos, husked *or*
    1 can (8 ounces) tomatillos,
    drained, chopped
3 or 4 fresh Anaheim chilies,
    seeded, deveined, finely
    chopped *or* 1 can (4 ounces)
    diced green chilies
1 large tomato, peeled, coarsely
    chopped
¼ cup chopped fresh cilantro
¾ cup chicken broth
2 teaspoons fresh lime juice
4 cups hot cooked white rice
½ cup toasted slivered almonds
    Fresh cilantro sprig and radish
    slices (optional)

1. Heat oil in 5-quart Dutch oven over medium heat. Add pork, about ⅓ at a time; brown about 10 minutes, turning occasionally. Remove to plate. Repeat with remaining pork.

2. Remove and discard all but 2 tablespoons drippings from pan. Add onions and garlic to drippings. Cook and stir 4 minutes or until onions are soft. Stir in salt, cumin and oregano. Add tomatillos, chilies, tomato and chopped cilantro. Stir in broth. Bring to a boil over high heat. Return pork to pan. Reduce heat to low. Cover; simmer 1½ to 2 hours until pork is tender.

3. Increase heat to medium. Simmer, uncovered, 20 to 30 minutes until sauce is thickened, stirring occasionally. Stir in juice. Serve pork stew over rice; sprinkle with almonds. Garnish with cilantro sprig and radish slices, if desired.

Makes 10 to 12 servings

Pork Stew

STIR, TO

To stir is to mix one or more foods with a spoon or whisk. It can be done with a circular or a figure-eight motion or a combination of the two. Stirring performs several functions: blending ingredients; making mixtures smooth; ensuring even heating; preventing food from sticking and burning during cooking; and preventing lumps from forming when making a thickened sauce. Recipe directions may call for constant stirring, frequent stirring (every minute or two) or occasional stirring (every few minutes).

☙

Beef with Peppers

STIR-FRY, TO

Stir-frying is the method of quickly cooking bite-size pieces of meat and vegetables over high heat in a small amount of oil. Ingredients are stirred constantly to ensure even cooking and to prevent burning. Traditionally, a wok or a sloping-sided skillet is used. This technique, which is associated with Chinese cooking, preserves the flavors, colors and textures of foods. The stir-frying technique is simple, but it does necessitate some preparation. The speed of the method requires that all ingredients be prepared in advance. Vegetables should be chopped or sliced into pieces, meat, poultry or fish sliced into strips, and spices and flavorings measured before beginning to stir-fry. This preparation can be done ahead of time and the ingredients should be stored in the refrigerator. The finished dish is referred to as a stir-fry.

Beef with Peppers

- 1 ounce dried Oriental mushrooms
- 1 teaspoon cornstarch
- 1 teaspoon instant beef bouillon granules
- 1/4 cup water
- 1 tablespoon soy sauce
- 1 teaspoon Oriental sesame oil
- 1 pound beef tenderloin, trimmed
- 2 1/2 tablespoons vegetable oil
- 1 clove garlic, minced
- 1/4 teaspoon Chinese five-spice powder
- 2 small yellow onions, cut into wedges
- 1 green bell pepper, thinly sliced
- 1 red bell pepper, thinly sliced
- 8 ounces Chinese-style thin egg noodles, cooked, drained (optional)

1. Place mushrooms in bowl; cover with hot water. Let stand 30 minutes; drain.

2. Squeeze excess water from mushrooms. Remove and discard stems. Slice caps into thin strips; set aside.

3. Combine cornstarch, bouillon granules, water, soy sauce and sesame oil in small bowl until smooth; set aside.

4. Cut beef into thin slices 1 inch long; set aside.

5. Heat vegetable oil in wok or large skillet over high heat. Add garlic and five-spice powder; stir-fry 15 seconds. Add reserved beef to wok; stir-fry about 5 minutes or until browned. Add onions; stir-fry 2 minutes. Add reserved mushrooms and peppers; stir-fry about 2 minutes or until peppers are crisp-tender. Stir cornstarch mixture; add to wok. Cook and stir until liquid boils and thickens. Serve over hot noodles, if desired.   *Makes 4 servings*

Chinese-Style Fried Brown Rice

2 cups uncooked long-grain
    brown rice
3½ cups water
3 tablespoons vegetable oil,
    divided
2 eggs, lightly beaten
1 medium yellow onion, coarsely
    chopped
1 slice (8 ounces) smoked or
    baked ham, cut into julienne
    strips
1 cup frozen green peas, thawed
1 to 2 tablespoons soy sauce
1 tablespoon Oriental sesame oil
Fresh cilantro leaves (optional)

1. Combine rice and water in wok. Cover; bring to a boil over high heat. Reduce heat to low; simmer rice about 40 to 45 minutes until rice is tender and all water is absorbed, stirring occasionally with fork. Remove from heat; let stand, covered, 10 minutes.

2. Fluff rice with fork; spread onto greased baking sheet. Cool to room temperature, about 30 to 40 minutes. Rinse out wok.

3. Heat wok over medium heat about 30 seconds or until hot. Drizzle 1 tablespoon vegetable oil into wok; heat 15 seconds. Add eggs; cook 1 minute or just until set on bottom. Turn eggs over; stir to scramble until cooked but not dry. Remove eggs to bowl; set aside.

4. Add remaining 2 tablespoons vegetable oil to wok; heat 30 seconds or until hot. Add onion; stir-fry about 3 minutes or until tender. Stir in ham and increase heat to medium-high; stir-fry 1 minute. Add cooked rice, peas, soy sauce to taste and sesame oil; cook 5 minutes, stirring frequently. Stir in reserved eggs; cook until heated through. Transfer to warm serving dish. Garnish with cilantro, if desired. Serve immediately.   *Makes 6 servings*

Chinese-Style Fried Brown Rice

STOCK

Stock is the flavorful liquid that results from the long cooking of meat (beef or veal), poultry or fish and bones in water. Vegetables (such as onion, celery, leeks and carrots), herbs and spices contribute to the flavor. The ingredients are simmered gently, and the amount of time depends on the ingredients: beef and chicken stock may take several hours whereas fish stock cooks in 30 to 40 minutes. The stock is then strained and the excess fat is removed. The stock may be concentrated by further simmering. A lighter, meatless variation of stock is made with vegetables only.

Stocks are an integral part of classic French cooking. They are the basis for sauces, soups and stews. Because of the time needed to make stocks, they are used less frequently in everyday cooking. Instead canned broth and bouillon are used, but they are not as rich and flavorful as a good homemade stock. Stocks are not difficult to make. Since most recipes make large quantities, they can be frozen in small batches for later use.

🐝

Tips

Stock is economical to make, because bones and tough cuts of meat can be used.

Roasting beef, veal or poultry in a 450°F oven before simmering produces a stock that is richer in flavor and color.

Technique for Chicken Stock

Step 2. *Straining stock through cheesecloth.*

Chicken Stock

　　1 capon (about 5 pounds),* cut
　　　　into pieces
　　2 medium onions, cut into wedges
　　2 medium carrots, halved
　　2 ribs celery including leaves, cut
　　　　into halves
　　1 clove garlic, crushed
　　1 bay leaf
　　6 sprigs fresh parsley
　　8 black peppercorns
　½ teaspoon dried thyme leaves
　　3 quarts cold water

*Capon provides a wonderfully rich flavor, but can be expensive. You may substitute chicken.

1. Place capon, onions, carrots, celery, garlic, bay leaf, parsley, peppercorns, thyme and water into stockpot or 6-quart Dutch oven. Bring to a boil over high heat. Reduce heat to medium-low; simmer, uncovered, 3 to 4 hours, skimming foam that rises to surface.

2. Remove stock from heat; cool slightly. Remove large bones. Strain stock through large sieve or colander lined with several layers of damp cheesecloth; discard bones and vegetables. Use immediately or refrigerate stock in tightly covered container up to 2 days. (Stock can be frozen in freezer containers for several months.)

　　　　Makes about 10 cups stock

Fish Stock

　1¾ pounds fish skeletons and heads
　　　　from lean fish, such as red
　　　　snapper, cod, halibut or
　　　　flounder
　　2 medium onions, cut into wedges
　　3 ribs celery, cut into 2-inch
　　　　pieces
　2½ quarts cold water
　　2 slices lemon
　　¾ teaspoon dried thyme leaves
　　8 black peppercorns
　　1 bouquet garni*

*To prepare bouquet garni, tie together 3 sprigs parsley, 2 sprigs thyme and ½ bay leaf with cotton string or enclose herbs in square piece of cheesecloth secured with string.

1. Rinse fish; cut out gills and discard.

2. Place fish skeletons and heads, onions and celery in stockpot or 6-quart Dutch oven. Add water, lemon, thyme, peppercorns and bouquet garni. Bring to a boil over high heat. Reduce heat to medium-low; simmer, uncovered, 30 minutes, skimming foam that rises to surface.

3. Remove stock from heat; cool slightly. Strain stock through large sieve or colander lined with several layers of damp cheesecloth; discard all bones, vegetables and seasonings. Use immediately or refrigerate stock in tightly covered container up to 2 days. (Stock can be frozen in freezer containers for several months.)

Makes about 10 cups stock

Beef Stock

4 pounds meaty beef bones
2 large onions, cut into wedges
2 large carrots, halved
4 ribs celery, halved
3½ quarts cold water, divided
8 sprigs fresh parsley
2 bay leaves
1 teaspoon dried thyme leaves
6 black peppercorns
3 whole cloves

1. Preheat oven to 450°F.

2. Rinse bones in cold water; arrange in large roasting pan. To brown bones, roast in oven 30 minutes, turning once.

3. Arrange onions, carrots and celery over bones. Roast 30 minutes more.*

4. Remove bones and vegetables from roasting pan; place in stockpot or 5-quart Dutch oven. Skim fat from roasting pan.

5. To deglaze pan, pour 2 cups water into pan. Place over burners; cook over medium-high heat 2 to 3 minutes until mixture has reduced by about half, scraping up brown bits and stirring constantly. Transfer mixture to stockpot. Add remaining 3 quarts water, parsley, bay leaves, thyme, peppercorns and cloves. Bring to a boil over high heat. Reduce heat to medium-low; simmer, uncovered, 3 to 4 hours, skimming foam that rises to surface.

6. Remove stock from heat; cool slightly. Remove large bones. Strain stock through large sieve or colander lined with several layers of damp cheesecloth; discard bones and vegetables. Use immediately or refrigerate stock in tightly covered container up to 2 days. (Stock can be frozen in freezer containers for several months.)

Makes about 6 cups stock

*For added zip, you may spread 3 ounces tomato paste over bones at this point. Roast 15 minutes more. Proceed as directed.

Vegetable Stock

2 tablespoons vegetable oil
2 medium onions, cut into wedges
2 leeks, well cleaned, cut into 2-inch pieces
3 ribs celery, cut into 2-inch pieces
2 quarts cold water
6 medium carrots, cut into 1-inch pieces
1 potato, peeled, cut into chunks
1 turnip, peeled, cut into chunks (optional)
2 cloves garlic, crushed
4 fresh parsley sprigs
1 teaspoon dried thyme leaves
¼ teaspoon ground black pepper
2 bay leaves

1. Heat oil in stockpot or 5-quart Dutch oven over medium-high heat. Add onions, leeks and celery; cook and stir 5 minutes or until vegetables are limp but not brown. Add water, carrots, potato, turnip, if desired, garlic, parsley, thyme, pepper and bay leaves. Bring to a boil over high heat. Reduce heat to medium-low; simmer, uncovered, 1½ hours.

2. Remove stock from heat; cool slightly. Strain stock through large sieve or colander. Press vegetables lightly with slotted spoon to remove extra liquid; discard vegetables. Use immediately or refrigerate stock in tightly covered container up to 2 days. (Stock can be frozen in freezer containers for several months.)

Makes about 7 cups stock

Technique for Beef Stock

Step 2. *Arranging beef bones in pan.*

STOLLEN

Stollen is the traditional Christmas bread of Germany. It is made from a rich, sweet yeast dough studded with dried or candied fruits. Traditionally, the dough is shaped into an oval and folded in half before baking so that the finished loaf is tapered at each end with a crescent-shaped ridge down the center. Stollens are often topped with a simple powdered sugar glaze and decorated with nuts or candied cherries.

❦

STRAIN, TO

Straining refers to the technique of pouring a liquid through the small holes of a strainer or the wire mesh of a sieve to remove lumps or unwanted particles. Straining may also refer to puréeing soft foods, such as raspberries or cooked vegetables, by pressing them through a sieve or strainer to produce a smooth texture. For example, baby foods are often strained. The terms sieve and strain are sometimes used interchangeably.

❦

Tip

Many supermarkets periodically offer huge strawberries with long stems. These berries are ideal for dipping in melted semisweet baking chocolate or chocolate fondue.

STRAWBERRY

Strawberries, America's most beloved berries, were once a sure sign of summer. Now thanks to air transport these bright red, seed-speckled berries are available virtually all year long. Present-day American strawberries resulted from the crossbreeding of a wild Virginian strawberry and a Chilean berry over 200 years ago.

Varieties: Because strawberries are naturally fragile, most supermarket strawberries are varieties that have been developed to withstand shipping and short storage. This has taken some toll on their natural sweetness and flavor, although work has been done to improve the flavor. When locally grown berries are in the market, it is worth the effort to seek them out.

Availability: California strawberries are in season about 10 months of the year, taking a brief hiatus in December and January. Florida berries are available from January to May. With Chilean and Mexican crops filling in the gap during winter months, there is an uninterrupted supply. In most of the United States, locally grown berries reach the market in May and June. These berries are generally sweeter than supermarket berries. Look for them at farmers' markets. Frozen berries, either loose-packed or in syrup, are also available.

❦

Buying Tips: Look for berries that are shiny, bright red and fragrant. The green caps should be vibrant and the berries should be reasonably clean. Green or pale red berries are underripe. There is nothing you can do to ripen them further. Avoid strawberries with soft spots, mildew or leakage. These are signs of deterioration.

Yield: 1 pound strawberries = about 1 pint; 2 cups slices.

Storage: Strawberries can be refrigerated, unwashed, for up to three days. Or, they may be frozen. To freeze strawberries, hull them and arrange them in a single layer on a jelly-roll pan. Place them in the freezer until they are frozen solid and then transfer and tightly seal them in storage containers. They will keep for up to nine months.

Basic Preparation: Wash berries quickly under cold running water just before using, with the stem and cap still attached. Do not the soak the berries in water, because they may become waterlogged. Remove the cap using a paring knife or a specialized tool called a strawberry huller. Dry the berries on paper towels. Use them whole or sliced.

Strawberries with Honeyed Yogurt Sauce

1 quart fresh strawberries
1 cup plain low-fat yogurt
1 tablespoon orange juice
1 to 2 teaspoons honey
   Ground cinnamon

Rinse and hull strawberries. Combine yogurt, juice, honey and cinnamon to taste in small bowl; mix well. Serve sauce over berries.

Makes 4 servings

Strawberry Devonshire Tart

1 package (9-inch) sponge cake
   layer or dessert shell
⅓ cup tropical juice blend or
   orange juice
½ cup sour cream
1 tub (8 ounces) COOL WHIP®
   Whipped Topping, thawed
1 pint strawberries, hulled
⅓ cup strawberry jelly, melted
   Fresh mint leaves

BRUSH cake layer with juice.

STIR sour cream and 2½ cups of the whipped topping with wire whisk in medium bowl until blended. Spread over cake layer. Arrange strawberries, hulled side down, in center; brush with jelly. Garnish with remaining whipped topping and mint leaves.

REFRIGERATE until ready to serve.

Makes 8 servings

Strawberry Devonshire Tart

STREUSEL

Streusel, a word meaning "sprinkle" in German, is a crumbly mixture of flour, sugar, spices and sometimes nuts. This mixture is used to top coffeecakes, muffins, pies and tea breads before they are baked. The resulting crunchy, crumbly topping adds both flavor and texture to baked goods.

Sour Cream Graham Streusel Cake

¾ cup crushed graham cracker crumbs
¼ cup chopped pecans
2 tablespoons packed brown sugar
½ teaspoon ground cinnamon
3 tablespoons butter or margarine, melted
1 cup all-purpose flour
½ teaspoon baking powder
½ teaspoon baking soda
½ cup butter or margarine, softened
¼ cup granulated sugar
½ teaspoon vanilla extract
½ teaspoon grated lemon peel
½ cup sour cream

Sour Cream Graham Streusel Cake

1. Preheat oven to 350°F. Grease 8-inch round cake pan.

2. Combine cracker crumbs, pecans, brown sugar and cinnamon in small bowl. Add melted butter; stir until well blended. Set aside.

3. Sift together flour, baking powder and baking soda into medium bowl. Beat softened butter and granulated sugar in large bowl with electric mixer at medium speed until light and fluffy, scraping down side of bowl once. Beat in vanilla and lemon peel. Reduce speed to low. Add flour mixture alternately with sour cream; beat well after each addition.

4. Spoon ½ of batter into prepared pan, spreading evenly. Sprinkle ⅔ crumb mixture evenly over batter. Spoon remaining batter over crumbs, spreading carefully. Sprinkle remaining crumb mixture over batter; press crumbs lightly into batter.

5. Bake 30 to 35 minutes until wooden toothpick inserted into center comes out clean. Cool cake in pan on wire rack 10 minutes. Remove from pan; cool completely on wire rack, crumb side up.   *Makes 8 servings*

Apple Strudel (recipe on page 492)

STROGANOFF

Stroganoff, a classic Russian dish created for the 19th century Count Paul Stroganov, consists of thin slices or strips of very tender beef (usually tenderloin or top loin), onions and mushrooms. These ingredients are sautéed quickly and then simmered in broth or stock. Sour cream is stirred into the mixture just before serving. Beef stroganoff is usually served over egg noodles or rice.

❦

STRUDEL

Strudel, from the German word for whirlwind, is a pastry made with many layers of very thin pastry dough. The dough is rolled and stretched until it is paper thin, sometimes sprinkled with bread crumbs, spread with filling, and then rolled and baked. The traditional filling consists of apples and raisins, but other common fillings include cherries, ground poppy seeds and nuts as well as savory fillings, such as meat, cheese and vegetables.

❦

Apple Strudel

1 sheet (½ of a 17¼-ounce
    package) frozen puff pastry
1 cup (4 ounces) shredded
    ALPINE LACE® Reduced Fat
    Cheddar Cheese
2 large Granny Smith apples,
    peeled, cored and sliced
    ⅛ inch thick (12 ounces)
⅓ cup golden raisins
2 tablespoons apple brandy
    (optional)
¼ cup granulated sugar
¼ cup packed light brown sugar
½ teaspoon ground cinnamon
2 tablespoons unsalted butter
    substitute, melted

1. To shape the pastry: Thaw the pastry for 20 minutes. Preheat the oven to 350°F. On a floured board, roll the pastry into a 15×12-inch rectangle.

2. To make the filling: Sprinkle the cheese on the dough, leaving a 1-inch border. Arrange the apples on top. Sprinkle with the raisins, then the brandy, if you wish. In a small cup, mix both of the sugars with the cinnamon, then sprinkle over the apple filling.

3. Starting from one of the wide ends, roll up jelly-roll style. Place on a baking sheet, seam side down, tucking the ends under. Using a sharp knife, make 7 diagonal slits on the top, then brush with the butter. Bake for 35 minutes or until golden brown.

Makes 18 servings

Tip

Do not stuff poultry until just before cooking it. Harmful bacteria may multiply during storage. If you wish to make stuffing ahead of time, refrigerate it in a covered container.

STUFFING

Sometimes called dressing, stuffing is a savory mixture used to fill, or "stuff," the cavity of poultry before roasting. After roasting, the stuffing is served as an accompaniment to the chicken or turkey. (Stuffing may also be baked in a casserole.) It usually is made with bread cubes or crumbs, although rice may also be used. Typical flavorings include onions, sausage, oysters, chestnuts and sage. In addition to whole chicken or turkey, the cavity of whole fish and various cuts of meat and poultry are stuffed. For example, thin cuts of tender beef or pork are rolled around a stuffing mixture. Pockets are cut into pork chops, pork roasts and veal or chicken breasts to hold stuffing. Stuffing for meat may or may not include bread. Other common ingredients include herbs, spices, vegetables, cheese and fruit.

🐝

Sausage Corn Bread Stuffing

1 recipe day-old Corn Bread*
    (recipe follows)
8 ounces bulk pork sausage
    (regular or spicy)
½ cup butter or margarine
2 medium onions, chopped
2 cloves garlic, minced
2 teaspoons rubbed sage
1 teaspoon poultry seasoning
¾ to 1¼ cups chicken broth
    Fresh sage leaves (optional)

*Or, substitute 1 package (16 ounces) prepared dry corn bread crumbs for homemade corn bread. Omit step 1.

1. Preheat oven to 350°F. Crumble Corn Bread coarsely. Crumble enough to make 6 cups. Spread evenly in 15×10-inch jelly-roll pan. Bake 20 to 25 minutes until dry.

2. Meanwhile, brown sausage in large skillet over medium-high heat until no longer pink, stirring to separate meat. Drain sausage on paper towels; set aside. Wipe skillet with paper towels to remove grease.

3. Melt butter in same skillet over medium heat until foamy. Add onions and garlic; cook 10 minutes or until onions are softened. Stir in rubbed sage and poultry seasoning; cook 1 minute more.

4. Combine Corn Bread crumbs, sausage and onion mixture in large bowl.

5. If stuffing is to be cooked in a turkey, drizzle ¾ cup broth over stuffing; toss lightly until evenly moistened. Stuff body and neck cavities loosely with stuffing. Stuffing may be prepared up to 1 day before using. *Do not stuff the turkey until just before you are ready to roast it.* Roast according to directions given on page 403 or according to instructions given with turkey.

6. If stuffing is to be cooked separately, drizzle 1¼ cups broth over stuffing; toss stuffing lightly until evenly moistened. Transfer to 3-quart casserole. (Sausage Corn Bread Stuffing may be covered and refrigerated up to 1 day before baking.) Preheat oven to 350°F. Bake 45 minutes (55 to 60 minutes if refrigerated) or until heated through. For a drier stuffing, uncover during last 15 minutes of baking. Garnish with fresh sage, if desired.

Makes 12 cups stuffing

Corn Bread

> 1¼ **cups yellow cornmeal**
> ¾ **cup all-purpose flour**
> 2 **tablespoons sugar**
> 1 **tablespoon baking powder**
> ¾ **teaspoon salt**
> 1 **egg**
> 1 **cup milk**
> 3 **tablespoons butter or margarine, melted, cooled**

1. Preheat oven to 425°F. Grease 9-inch square baking pan.

2. Combine cornmeal, flour, sugar, baking powder and salt in medium bowl. Combine egg, milk and butter in small bowl; add to flour mixture. Stir just until dry ingredients are moistened. Pour into prepared pan.

3. Bake 20 to 25 minutes until golden brown and wooden toothpick inserted into center comes out clean. Cool completely on wire rack. Corn Bread may be prepared up to 2 days before using as stuffing. Cover; let stand at room temperature.

Makes 6 cups corn bread crumbs

Sausage Corn Bread Stuffing

SUGAR

Once a precious and expensive commodity, sugar is the favored fuel for America's sweet tooth. Granulated sugar, made from highly refined cane or beet sugar, is the most common form for table use and cooking purposes. It is white and free-flowing. Granulated sugar is also formed into sugar cubes. Crystallized, or pearl, sugar is a coarse granulation that is usually used for decorating purposes. Superfine, or bar, sugar is finely granulated so that it dissolves readily in liquids, making it a good choice for cold beverages and meringues.

Powdered sugar, also called confectioners' or icing sugar, is granulated sugar that has been pulverized into a powder. A small amount of cornstarch is added to prevent caking. Powdered sugar, which dissolves readily, is used in creamy uncooked frostings and in some cake and cookie recipes. It can also be sprinkled on top of cakes and cookies for decoration.

Brown sugar is granulated sugar with molasses added to it. The molasses imparts both the tawny color and moisture associated with brown sugar. Light and dark varieties are available. The dark variety has a slightly stronger taste.

Raw sugar looks somewhat like brown sugar although the two are different. Raw sugar is a product made from the residue left after molasses is extracted from cane sugar. It contains many impurities. Only raw sugar that has been processed to remove impurities is available in the United States.

Sugar Cookies

1 cup sugar
1 cup butter or margarine
2 eggs
½ teaspoon lemon extract
½ teaspoon vanilla extract
3 cups all-purpose flour
1 teaspoon baking powder
¼ teaspoon salt
  Egg Yolk Paint (recipe follows)
  Royal Icing (recipe follows)
  Decorator Frosting (recipe follows)

Equipment and Decorations
  Liquid or paste food coloring
  Small paintbrushes
  Sponges

1. Beat sugar and butter in large bowl with electric mixer at medium speed until light and fluffy. Beat in eggs and extracts at medium speed until well blended, scraping down side of bowl occasionally. (Mixture will look grainy.) Beat in 1 cup flour, baking powder and salt at medium speed until well blended. Gradually add remaining 2 cups flour. Beat at low speed until soft dough forms, scraping down side of bowl once. Form dough into 3 discs. Wrap discs in plastic wrap; refrigerate 2 hours or until dough is firm.

2. Preheat oven to 375°F.

3. Working with 1 disc at a time, unwrap dough; place on lightly floured surface. Roll out dough with lightly floured rolling pin to ⅛-inch thickness. Cut dough with lightly floured 3- to 4-inch cookie cutters. Place cutouts 1 inch apart on ungreased baking sheets. Gently press dough trimmings together; reroll and cut out more cookies. (If dough is sticky, pat into disc; wrap in plastic wrap and refrigerate until firm before rerolling.)

4. To paint cookies before baking, prepare Egg Yolk Paint. Divide paint among several bowls; tint with liquid food coloring, if desired. Paint onto unbaked cookies with paintbrush.

5. Bake 7 to 9 minutes until cookies are set. Remove to wire rack; cool completely.

6. To sponge paint cooled cookies, prepare Royal Icing. Divide icing among several bowls; tint with liquid or paste food coloring. Spread thin layer of icing on cookies to within ⅛ inch of edges. Let stand 30 minutes at room temperature or until icing is set. Cut clean kitchen sponge into 1-inch squares with scissors. Dip sponge into tinted icing, scraping against side of bowl to remove excess icing. Gently press sponge on base icing several times until desired effect is achieved. Let stand 15 minutes or until set.

7. To pipe additional decorations on cookies, prepare Decorator Frosting. Divide frosting among several bowls; tint with different food coloring, if desired. Place each color frosting in pastry bag fitted with small writing tip or resealable plastic freezer bags with tiny corner cut off. Decorate as desired. Let cookies stand at room temperature until set. Store loosely covered at room temperature up to 1 week.

Makes about 3 dozen cookies

Egg Yolk Paint

2 egg yolks
2 teaspoons water

Combine egg yolks and water in small bowl until blended.
Makes about ⅓ cup yolk paint

Note: Use this paint only on unbaked cookies.

Royal Icing

4 egg whites*
4 cups powdered sugar, sifted
1 teaspoon lemon extract or clear vanilla extract**

Use only clean, uncracked grade A eggs.

**Use clear extracts to keep frosting white.*

Beat egg whites in large bowl with electric mixer at high speed until foamy. Gradually add sugar and lemon extract. Beat at high speed until thickened.
Makes 2 cups icing

Decorator Frosting

¾ cup butter, softened
4½ cups powdered sugar, sifted, divided
3 tablespoons water
1 teaspoon vanilla extract
¼ teaspoon lemon extract

Beat butter in medium bowl with electric mixer at medium speed until smooth. Add 2 cups sugar. Beat at medium speed until light and fluffy. Add water and extracts. Beat at low speed until well blended, scraping down side of bowl once. Beat in remaining 2½ cups sugar until mixture is creamy.
Makes 2 cups frosting

Note: This frosting is perfect for piping, but is less durable than Royal Icing. Bumping, stacking and handling may damage decorations.

Technique for Sugar Cookies

Step 6. *Pressing sponge on base icing.*

Sugar Cookies

SUKIYAKI

Sukiyaki is a dish that became popular in Japan in the late 1800's after foreign visitors introduced beef. It consists of thin strips of beef, vegetables and sometimes tofu that are simmered in a mixture of soy sauce and rice wine. It is usually prepared at the table. Japanese diners may dip each bite into raw beaten egg before eating. The heat of the food cooks the egg, which provides the food pieces with a coating.

🌸

SUNFLOWER SEED

Sunflower seeds come from the huge centers of the sunflower plant, a daisy-shaped flower that is very tall, often six feet or more. The seeds are oval shaped with a hard black-and-white or grey-and-white striped shell. The shell is removed and only the kernel of the seed is eaten. The kernels, which are referred to as seeds, may be dried or roasted and salted. Sunflower seeds may be eaten as a snack, sprinkled on salads and sandwiches, or used as nuts in baked goods or cooked dishes.

🌸

Tip

Since sunflower seeds are high in fat, they should be stored in the refrigerator to prevent them from becoming rancid. Dried or roasted seeds will keep up to four months. For longer storage (eight months), freeze sunflower seeds.

SUSHI

Sushi is a Japanese specialty of flavored boiled rice that is rolled in thin strips of raw fish or seaweed. There are many varieties made with ingredients enclosed in the rice mixture, such as chopped vegetables, seafood, tofu and egg. Sushi rolls are a finger food eaten as an appetizer, snack or as a meal accompaniment. Soy sauce is often served as a dipping sauce.

🌸

SWEET AND SOUR

"Sweet and sour" is a descriptive term for dishes that have a flavor balanced between tart and sweet. The tart taste comes from an acidic ingredient, such as vinegar or lemon juice, and the sweet taste usually comes from sugar. The two contrasting ingredients are added in amounts that allow both sensations to be apparent in the finished dish. Chinese, Jewish and German cuisines are noted for sweet-and-sour dishes.

🌸

Sweet and Sour Sauce

4 teaspoons cornstarch
1 cup water
½ cup distilled white vinegar
½ cup sugar
¼ cup tomato paste

Combine all ingredients in small saucepan. Bring to a boil over medium heat, stirring constantly. Boil 1 minute, stirring constantly.

Makes about 1 cup sauce

Sweet and Sour Chicken

2 tablespoons rice vinegar

3 cloves garlic, minced

2 tablespoons low sodium soy sauce

½ teaspoon minced fresh ginger

¼ teaspoon crushed red pepper flakes (optional)

6 ounces boneless, skinless chicken breasts, cut into ½-inch strips

1 teaspoon vegetable oil

3 green onions, cut into 1-inch pieces

1 large green bell pepper, cut into 1-inch squares

1 tablespoon cornstarch

½ cup defatted low sodium chicken broth

2 tablespoons apricot fruit spread

1 can (11 ounces) mandarin orange segments

2 cups hot cooked white rice or Chinese egg noodles

Orange slices and fresh herb leaves (optional)

1. Combine vinegar, garlic, soy sauce, ginger and pepper flakes in medium bowl. Add chicken; toss to coat. Marinate 20 minutes at room temperature.

2. Heat oil in wok or large nonstick skillet over medium heat. Drain chicken, reserving marinade. Add chicken to wok; stir-fry 3 minutes or until no longer pink in center. Stir in onions and bell pepper.

3. Stir cornstarch into reserved marinade. Stir broth, fruit spread and marinade mixture into wok. Cook and stir 1 minute or until sauce boils and thickens. Add orange segments; heat through. Serve over rice. Garnish with orange slices and herbs, if desired. *Makes 4 servings*

Sweet and Sour Chicken

Sweet and Sour Pork

Sweet and Sour Pork

   1 **egg yolk, lightly beaten**
  ¼ **cup soy sauce**
 4½ **teaspoons dry sherry**
   2 **teaspoons sugar**
   2 **pounds boneless lean pork, cut
      into 1-inch pieces**
 10 **tablespoons cornstarch, divided**
   1 **can (20 ounces) pineapple
      chunks in syrup, undrained**
  ¼ **cup rice vinegar**
   3 **tablespoons tomato sauce**
   1 **cup water**
   1 **medium cucumber**
   3 **cups *plus* 3 tablespoons
      vegetable oil, divided**
   1 **large yellow onion, thinly sliced**
   8 **green onions, diagonally cut
      into 1-inch pieces**
   1 **red or green bell pepper,
      chopped**
   4 **ounces fresh button
      mushrooms, cut into quarters**
   2 **ribs celery, diagonally cut into
      ½-inch slices**
    **Celery leaves and red bell
      pepper curls (optional)**

1. For marinade, combine egg yolk, soy sauce, sherry and sugar in large bowl. Add pork; stir to coat well. Cover; refrigerate 1 hour, stirring occasionally.

2. Drain pork, reserving marinade. Measure 8 tablespoons cornstarch into large bowl. Add pork; toss to coat well. Set aside.

3. Drain pineapple, reserving syrup. Add syrup to reserved marinade. Stir in vinegar and tomato sauce; set aside.

4. Combine remaining 2 tablespoons cornstarch and water in another small bowl until smooth; set aside.

5. Cut cucumber in half lengthwise; remove seeds. Cut cucumber into ¼-inch pieces; set aside.

6. Heat 3 cups oil in wok or large skillet over high heat until oil reaches 375°F on deep-fry thermometer. Add ½ of pork. Cook about 5 minutes or until pork is no longer pink in center; drain on paper towels. Repeat with remaining pork. Discard oil.

7. Heat remaining 3 tablespoons oil in wok over high heat. Add cucumber, onions, chopped pepper, mushrooms and celery; stir-fry 3 minutes. Stir reserved cornstarch mixture. Add to wok with pineapple syrup mixture; cook and stir until sauce boils and thickens. Add pork and pineapple; stir-fry until thoroughly heated. Garnish with celery leaves and pepper curls, if desired.   *Makes 4 servings*

SWEETENED CONDENSED MILK

Sweetened condensed milk is a canned product that is the result of evaporating about half of the water from whole milk and adding cane sugar or corn syrup to sweeten and preserve the milk. The thick milk is used for desserts and candy. It should not be confused with evaporated milk.

☙

No-Fuss Bar Cookies

> 2 cups graham cracker crumbs (about 24 graham cracker squares)
> 1 cup semisweet chocolate chips
> 1 cup flaked coconut
> ³/₄ cup coarsely chopped walnuts
> 1 can (14 ounces) sweetened condensed milk

1. Preheat oven to 350°F.

2. Combine crumbs, chips, coconut and walnuts in medium bowl; toss to blend. Add milk; mix until blended. Spread into greased 13×9-inch baking pan.

3. Bake 15 to 18 minutes until edges are golden brown. Cool completely in pan on wire rack. Cut into 2¼-inch squares.   *Makes about 20 cookies*

Easy Turtle Fudge

> 1 package (12 ounces) semisweet chocolate chips (2 cups)
> 2 ounces bittersweet or semisweet chocolate, chopped
> 1 cup sweetened condensed milk
> ¼ teaspoon salt
> 30 individually wrapped caramel candies, unwrapped
> 1 tablespoon water
> 40 pecan halves

1. Grease 10×7-inch pan.

2. Melt chips in heavy medium saucepan over very low heat, stirring *constantly* to prevent scorching. Remove from heat as soon as chocolate is melted; stir in chopped chocolate until melted. Stir in milk and salt until smooth. Spread evenly in prepared pan; cover with foil. Refrigerate until firm.

3. Cut fudge into 40 squares by cutting 5 sections lengthwise and 8 sections crosswise. Transfer to baking sheet lined with waxed paper, placing squares ½ inch apart.

4. Place caramels and water in heavy small saucepan. Heat over low heat until melted, stirring frequently. Drizzle or top fudge pieces with caramel mixture. Top each piece with 1 pecan half. Store candies in airtight container in freezer. Bring to room temperature before serving.
Makes 40 candies

Technique for Easy Turtle Fudge

Step 4. *Drizzling fudge with caramel mixture.*

Easy Turtle Fudge

SWEET POTATO

Sweet potatoes, native to America, were a chief means of sustenance to soldiers during the Revolutionary War. Not truly a potato, this tuberous root is a member of the morning glory family. Naturally sweet, they are an excellent source of beta-carotene. Although the words yam and sweet potato are sometimes used interchangeably, they are two distinct vegetables.

🌾

Uses: Like white potatoes, sweet potatoes can be baked and served with butter or sour cream.

• Boiled sweet potatoes can be sliced or cubed and served buttered or glazed with honey, brown sugar or a flavored sugar syrup. Boiled sweet potatoes can be mashed or cubed and added to stews.

Sweet Potato Gratin

• Sweet potato pie, which has a sweet custardlike filling, is a popular dessert in the southern United States.

• Sliced sweet potatoes may be batter-dipped for tempura.

• Thin, crisp sweet potato chips are served in some restaurants and available in specialty stores.

Varieties: The most common variety of sweet potato in the United States is the dark orange sweet potato with moist orange flesh. This is the variety that is most often mistakenly referred to as a yam. Less common varieties include the dark red-skinned variety that has yellow flesh or the pale orange-skinned variety that has white flesh. These varieties have a dry crumbly texture much like a white russet potato. Both varieties may be used interchangeably in recipes but avoid combining the two in the same recipe since their different textures may be noticeable.

Availability: Sweet potatoes are available year-round with the supplies peaking in the fall and winter. Most sweet potatoes undergo a curing process in a heated high-humidity environment, which causes the starch to be converted to sugar. The first sweet potatoes that are harvested may not be cured but sent directly to the market in late summer. Uncured sweet potatoes are less sweet. Canned and frozen sweet potatoes are available, but are often mislabeled as yams.

Buying Tips: Sweet potatoes should be heavy for their size, firm, smooth and free of bruises or blemishes. Check for decay, which often begins at the tips. Choose potatoes of similar size and shape if they are to be cooked whole.

Yield: 1 pound sweet potatoes = 3 medium; 3 cups chopped or sliced. 1 (16-ounce) can sweet potatoes = about 2 cups.

Storage: After purchasing sweet potatoes, brush off any dirt but do not wash them. Sweet potatoes should be handled gently since their skins are very thin. Store them in a cool, dry and dark location. They will keep for up to two weeks at room temperature or a month at about 55°F. Do not refrigerate sweet potatoes because they can develop an off flavor.

Basic Preparation: Sweet potatoes need not be peeled but should be scrubbed under cold running water before cooking. Cooking with skins intact retains more nutrients. They may be baked or boiled whole and then peeled and sliced or cubed. Sweet potatoes may be peeled first if they are going to be added raw to stews or soups.

To bake, pierce sweet potatoes with a fork or paring knife to allow steam to escape during cooking. Bake sweet potatoes on a baking sheet or foil rather than directly on the oven rack because sticky sweet juices seep out of the potatoes during baking. Bake them in a preheated 400°F oven for 40 to 45 minutes or until soft.

Sweet Potato Gratin

> 3 pounds sweet potatoes (about 5 large)
> ½ cup butter or margarine, divided
> ¼ cup *plus* 2 tablespoons packed light brown sugar, divided
> 2 eggs
> ⅔ cup orange juice
> 2 teaspoons ground cinnamon, divided
> ½ teaspoon salt
> ¼ teaspoon ground nutmeg
> ⅓ cup all-purpose flour
> ¼ cup uncooked rolled oats
> ⅓ cup chopped pecans or walnuts
> Quartered orange slices (optional)

1. Preheat oven to 350°F. Bake potatoes 1 hour or until fork-tender.

2. While potatoes are hot, cut lengthwise into halves. Scrape hot pulp from skins into large bowl. Add ¼ cup butter and 2 tablespoons sugar. Beat with electric mixer at medium speed until butter is melted. Beat in eggs, juice, 1½ teaspoons cinnamon, salt and nutmeg, scraping down side of bowl once. Beat until smooth. Pour mixture into ungreased 1½-quart baking dish or gratin dish; smooth top.

3. For topping, combine flour, oats, remaining ¼ cup sugar and remaining ½ teaspoon cinnamon in medium bowl. Cut in remaining ¼ cup butter with pastry blender or 2 knives until mixture resembles coarse crumbs. Stir in pecans. Sprinkle evenly over potatoes. (At this point, Sweet Potato Gratin may be covered and refrigerated up to 1 day. Let stand at room temperature 1 hour before baking.)

4. Preheat oven to 350°F.

5. Bake 25 to 30 minutes until potatoes are heated through. For a crisper topping, broil 5 inches from heat 2 to 3 minutes until golden brown. Garnish with orange slices, if desired. Serve immediately.
Makes 6 to 8 side-dish servings

Sweet Potato Apple Bake

> 3 cups mashed sweet potatoes
> 2 to 3 medium apples, peeled, sliced
> Ground cinnamon
> ½ cup apple jelly

Preheat oven to 350°F. Spray 9-inch glass pie plate with nonstick cooking spray. Fill dish evenly with mashed sweet potatoes. Arrange apple slices on top. Sprinkle apples with cinnamon. Melt apple jelly over low heat in small saucepan. Brush over apples. Bake 30 minutes or until apples are tender.
Makes 6 side-dish servings

Favorite recipe from **New York Apple Association, Inc.**

T to Z

What is tapenade? Discover *the type of fruit used in a tasty tarte tatin*. At what time is high tea served in Scotland? *Bake a savory sausage turnover.* Where does watercress grow? *Make a batch of fruity frozen yogurt.* What do the English call zucchini?

Marinated Summer Salad
(recipe on page 553)

Far East Tabbouleh

Far East Tabbouleh

¾ **cup uncooked bulgur**
1¾ **cups boiling water**
2 **tablespoons reduced sodium teriyaki sauce**
2 **tablespoons fresh lemon juice**
1 **tablespoon olive oil**
¾ **cup finely chopped seeded cucumber**
¾ **cup finely chopped seeded tomato**
½ **cup thinly sliced green onions**
½ **cup minced fresh cilantro or parsley**
1 **tablespoon minced fresh ginger**
1 **clove garlic, minced**

1. Combine bulgur and water in small bowl. Cover with plastic wrap; let stand 45 minutes or until bulgur is puffed, stirring occasionally. Drain in wire mesh sieve; discard liquid.

2. Combine cooked bulgur, teriyaki sauce, juice and oil in large bowl. Stir in cucumber, tomato, onions, cilantro, ginger and garlic until well blended. Cover; refrigerate 4 hours before serving, stirring occasionally. Garnish as desired.

Makes 4 side-dish servings

TABBOULEH

Tabbouleh is a Middle Eastern salad made of bulgur wheat mixed with tomato, parsley, lemon juice and fresh mint leaves. It is traditionally served cold with lavash, a crisp crackerlike bread. In America tabbouleh is often served as an appetizer with wedges of pita bread or romaine lettuce leaves.

❦

TACO

A taco is a popular Mexican-style dish consisting of a corn tortilla folded around a filling of ground or shredded cooked beef, chicken, chorizo or re-fried beans. Other ingredients include cheese, tomato, onion and shredded lettuce. Tacos are often topped with sour cream and salsa. In the United States, tortillas are usually deep-fried to form a U-shaped vessel to hold the ingredients, although soft tacos are growing in popularity. In Mexico, soft tortillas rolled around a filling are more common.

❦

Quick 'n' Easy Tacos

  1 **pound ground beef**
  1 **can (14½ ounces) whole peeled tomatoes, undrained and coarsely chopped**
  1 **medium green bell pepper, finely chopped**
  1 **envelope LIPTON® Recipe Secrets® Onion Soup Mix**
  1 **tablespoon chili powder**
  3 **drops hot pepper sauce (optional)**
  8 **taco shells**
     Taco Toppings*

*Taco Toppings: Use shredded Cheddar or Monterey Jack cheese, shredded lettuce, chopped tomatoes, sliced pitted ripe olives, sour cream or taco sauce.

In 10-inch skillet, brown ground beef over medium-high heat; drain. Stir in tomatoes, green pepper, onion soup mix, chili powder and hot pepper sauce. Bring to a boil, then simmer 15 minutes or until slightly thickened. Serve in taco shells with assorted Taco Toppings.   *Makes 4 servings*

• Also terrific with Lipton® Recipe Secrets® Onion-Mushroom or Beefy Mushroom Soup Mix.

Soft Turkey Tacos

  8 **(6-inch) corn tortillas***
1½ **teaspoons vegetable oil**
  1 **pound ground turkey**
  1 **small onion, chopped**
  1 **teaspoon dried oregano leaves**
     Salt and ground black pepper
     Chopped tomatoes
     Shredded lettuce
     Salsa

*Substitute 8 (10-inch) flour tortillas for corn tortillas, if desired.

1. Wrap tortillas in foil. Place in cold oven; set temperature to 350°F.**

2. Meanwhile, heat oil in large skillet over medium heat. Add turkey and onion; cook until turkey is no longer pink, stirring occasionally. Stir in oregano. Season with salt and pepper; keep warm.

3. For each taco, fill warm tortilla with turkey mixture; top with tomatoes, lettuce and salsa.
     Makes 4 servings

**To warm tortillas in microwave oven, wrap loosely in damp paper towels. Microwave at HIGH (100% power) 2 minutes or until hot.

Soft Turkey Tacos

Tip

Because of its high oil content, tahini should be stored in the refrigerator after opening. It will keep for two months. Tahini has a tendency to separate, so stir it before using.

TAHINI

Tahini is a thick, mild Middle Eastern paste made from ground sesame seeds. It has a rich, nutty flavor. It is a key ingredient in such preparations as hummus and baba ghanouj. It should not be confused with Asian sesame seed paste, which is made from roasted sesame seeds, resulting in a more pronounced flavor.

🐚

TAMALE

Tamales are a Mexican dish in which corn flour (masa harina) is made into a dough and filled with savory, and sometimes sweet, ingredients. The tamale is wrapped in dried corn husks and steamed until it is cooked through. The husks are peeled away at serving time. Traditional savory fillings include shredded beef, pork, turkey and chicken mixed with a spicy sauce. Sweet tamales are filled with fruits.

🐚

TAMARILLO

A tamarillo is a South American fruit. It is shaped like an egg, with flawlessly smooth skin. Depending on the variety, it may be a striking purple-red or golden hue. The skin is very bitter. The pinkish-gold flesh is peppered with seeds. It is somewhat tart even when fully ripened, but a little sugar makes it palatable.

Although tamarillos are still a novelty in the United States, they are popular in Latin American countries, Australia and New Zealand. They are available in Latin markets and some large supermarkets. When ripe, they should be fragrant and firm but not hard. They will continue to ripen at room temperature and can be stored in the refrigerator for at least one week. Tamarillos are peeled and eaten fresh or cooked in both sweet and savory dishes.

🐚

TAMARIND

Also known as Indian date, the tamarind comes from the pod of a tropical tree native to Asia and northern Africa. The pods of this tree produce a refreshingly astringent pulp that is used in Indian and Middle Eastern cuisines much the same way Americans use lemon juice. It is added to curries, chutneys and is a key component of Worcestershire sauce. It also is used as a flavoring for soft drinks.

🐚

TANDOORI

Tandoori is a term used to describe Indian food that is cooked over a very hot, smoky fire in a tandoor oven. Chicken or meat are often threaded onto skewers before baking. The oven is also used to cook the traditional bread of India, naan.

🐚

Tandoori Chicken

4 chicken legs, thighs and
drumsticks attached (about
2¼ pounds)*
1 tablespoon fresh lemon juice
1 teaspoon yellow food coloring
½ teaspoon red food coloring
1½ tablespoons ground coriander
1 tablespoon paprika
1 tablespoon ground cumin
2 teaspoons salt
1¼ cups plain yogurt
1 tablespoon grated fresh ginger
1 teaspoon minced garlic
¼ cup melted butter or vegetable
oil, divided
Lemon wedges

*Tandoori Chicken can be made with chicken
breasts in place of legs; reduce cooking time
to about 10 minutes per side.

1. Remove skin and excess fat from
chicken; discard. Mix juice and food
coloring in cup. Brush chicken with
juice mixture. Mix coriander, paprika,
cumin and salt in cup. Sprinkle
mixture over chicken in shallow glass
bowl or casserole, turning chicken
and spreading spices to evenly coat.

2. Mix yogurt, ginger and garlic in
small bowl. Pour yogurt mixture over
chicken, turning pieces to coat.
Cover; marinate in refrigerator 4 to
6 hours, turning pieces occasionally.
Let chicken stand in marinade,
covered, at room temperature 1 hour
before cooking.

3. Preheat oven to 500°F.

4. Remove chicken from bowl,
shaking off as much marinade as
possible; discard marinade. Place
chicken in single layer in greased
shallow baking pan; brush chicken
with 2 tablespoons butter. Bake
chicken 12 minutes. Turn pieces over;
brush with remaining 2 tablespoons
butter. Bake about 13 minutes more
or until fork can be inserted into
chicken with ease and juices run
clear, not pink. Serve immediately
with lemon wedges.

Makes 4 servings

*Shrimp Tapas in Sherry
Sauce (recipe on
page 509)*

TAPA

**Tapas are Spanish appetizers that are
served in bars and restaurants to stave
off hunger until the late evening
Spanish dinner. These dishes range
from something as simple as a cube of
cheese to more elaborate prepara
tions, such as cold potato omelets and
shrimp cooked in sherry sauce. Tapas
can also serve as an entire meal. They
are generally accompanied by sherry
or other cocktails. Tapas bars and
restaurants are becoming popular in
many large American cities.**

🌑

Marinated Roasted Pepper Tapas

1 large red bell pepper
1 large yellow bell pepper
3 tablespoons olive oil
1 tablespoon sherry wine vinegar
   or white wine vinegar
1 tablespoon capers, rinsed,
   drained
1 clove garlic, thinly sliced
1 teaspoon sugar
½ teaspoon cumin seeds
1 loaf French bread
   Fresh basil leaves (optional)

1. Cover broiler pan with foil. Preheat broiler.

2. Place peppers on foil. Broil peppers 4 inches from heat source 15 to 20 minutes until blackened on all sides, turning peppers every 5 minutes. To steam peppers and loosen skin, place peppers in paper bag for 30 minutes.

3. Meanwhile, whisk together oil, vinegar, capers, garlic, sugar and cumin seeds in small bowl until well blended; set aside.

4. To peel peppers, cut around core; twist and remove. Cut peppers into halves. Peel off skin with paring knife; rinse under cold water to remove seeds. Cut each half into triangular or square-shaped pieces. Place in resealable plastic food storage bag. Pour reserved oil mixture over peppers. Cover; refrigerate at least 2 hours or overnight, turning occasionally. Bring to room temperature before serving.

5. To serve, slice bread into rounds; toast, if desired. Arrange peppers on top of rounds. Garnish with basil, if desired.

Makes 4 to 6 appetizer servings

Marinated Roasted Pepper Tapas

Shrimp Tapas in Sherry Sauce

1 slice thick-cut bacon, cut into ¼-inch strips
2 tablespoons olive oil
2 ounces fresh cremini or button mushrooms, cut into quarters
½ pound raw large shrimp (about 16), peeled, deveined
2 cloves garlic, thinly sliced
2 tablespoons medium dry sherry
1 tablespoon fresh lemon juice
¼ teaspoon crushed red pepper flakes
Fresh herb sprig and lemon wedge (optional)

1. Cook bacon in large skillet over medium heat until brown and crispy. Remove from skillet with slotted spoon; drain on paper towels. Set aside.

2. Add oil to bacon drippings in skillet. Add mushrooms; cook and stir 2 minutes. Add shrimp and garlic; cook and stir 3 minutes or until shrimp turn pink and opaque. Stir in sherry, juice and pepper flakes. Remove shrimp to serving bowl with slotted spoon. Cook sauce 1 minute or until reduced and thickened. Pour over shrimp. Sprinkle with reserved bacon. Garnish with herb sprig and lemon wedge, if desired.

Makes 4 appetizer servings

TAPENADE

Tapenade is a condiment from the Provence region of France. It is made from ground black niçoise olives, anchovies, garlic, capers and olive oil. This inky black paste is pungent and flavorful. It is used as a spread or as a dip for raw vegetables.

❧

TAPIOCA

Tapioca is a starch obtained from the roasted root of the cassava, or manioc, plant that is grown in South America and Africa. Tapioca is used both as a thickener, particularly for fruit pies, and as a creamy dessert pudding. Tapioca is available in several forms: pearl tapioca, granulated tapioca and tapioca flour. Pearl tapioca must be soaked before using. Granulated or quick-cooking tapioca, which is precooked and dehydrated, is also available. Cooked pearl and granulated tapioca do not completely dissolve but become soft and almost transparent. Tapioca flour, or starch, dissolves completely and is used as a thickener. Tapioca is a good thickener for foods that will be frozen, because freezing and thawing do not affect its thickening properties.

❧

Chocolate Tapioca

¾ cup sugar
¼ cup HERSHEY'S Cocoa
3 tablespoons quick-cooking tapioca
⅛ teaspoon salt
2¾ cups milk
1 egg, slightly beaten
1 teaspoon vanilla extract

Combine sugar, cocoa, tapioca and salt in medium saucepan; blend in milk and egg. Let stand 5 minutes. Cook over medium heat, stirring constantly, until mixture boils. Remove from heat; stir in vanilla. Pour into bowl; press plastic wrap directly onto surface. Cool; refrigerate. Spoon into individual dessert dishes.

Makes 4 to 6 servings

Tip

To thicken fruit pie fillings, substitute quick-cooking tapioca for flour. Use an equal amount of tapioca.

TART

The word tart comes from the French word "tarte," meaning an open-faced pastry. Tarts are generally baked in a shallow, straight-sided tart pan with a fluted side and a removable bottom. They are usually round in shape but can be square or rectangular. The pastry shell may be baked and then filled with a cooked or uncooked filling. Or the shell may be baked with a filling. Fillings may be sweet or savory. Tarts come in many sizes: 8 to 10 inches in diameter to serve six to ten, 4 inches in diameter to serve one, and 1 inch in diameter for bite-size appetizers.

🌿

Amaretto Cheesecake Tart

Crust
> ¾ **cup amaretti cookie crumbs**
> ¾ **cup zwieback crumbs**
> 1 **tablespoon sugar**
> ¼ **cup Prune Purée (page 317) or prepared prune butter**

Filling
> 1 **carton (16 ounces) nonfat cottage cheese**
> 4 **ounces fat free cream cheese, softened**
> 2 **eggs**
> 2 **tablespoons almond-flavored liqueur**

Topping & Glaze
> 2 **oranges, peeled and sliced into rounds**
> 1 **kiwifruit, peeled and sliced into rounds**
> 2 **tablespoons apple jelly, melted**
> **Fresh raspberries, orange peel and mint leaves, for garnish**

Amaretto Cheesecake Tart

1. Preheat oven to 325°F.

2. To prepare crust, in medium bowl, combine crumbs and sugar. Cut in Prune Purée with pastry blender until mixture resembles coarse crumbs. Press onto bottom and side of 9-inch tart pan with removable bottom.

3. To prepare filling, process cottage cheese and cream cheese in food processor 3 to 5 minutes or until smooth. Add eggs and liqueur; process until blended. Pour into prepared crust. Bake in center of oven 30 minutes until filling is set. Cool on wire rack; refrigerate until completely chilled.

4. Arrange fruit on top of filling. Brush fruit with jelly. Garnish with raspberries, orange peel and mint. Cut into wedges.

Makes 10 servings

Favorite recipe from **California Prune Board**

Tarte latin

> **Pie Crust (recipe follows)**
> **8 Granny Smith apples (about 3 pounds)**
> **½ cup granulated sugar**
> **½ cup butter**
> **½ cup dark brown sugar, loosely packed**
> **1 tablespoon Calvados or other apple brandy**
> **Sweetened whipped cream and fresh mint leaves (optional)**

1. Prepare Pie Crust.

2. Preheat oven to 375°F.

3. Peel and core apples; cut into halves. Place apple halves, core sides up, in 13×9-inch baking dish. Sprinkle with granulated sugar. Bake 45 minutes; remove from oven. *Increase oven temperature to 425°F.* (Bake apples immediately after cutting to prevent browning.)

4. Remove dough from refrigerator. Flatten dough into 5- to 6-inch disc. Roll dough on lightly floured surface with lightly floured rolling pin into circle at least 1 inch larger than inverted 9 inch pie plate.

5. Melt butter in small saucepan over medium heat. Pour into 9-inch pie pan. Quickly spread brown sugar over butter. Sprinkle with Calvados. Arrange cooked apples, core sides up, in concentric circles. Carefully lift dough and place over apples. Gently press dough around fruit. Trim crust even with edge of pie plate. Turn under edge of crust to seal. Prick several holes in crust with fork to release steam.

6. Bake 20 to 25 minutes until crust is golden brown and apples are tender. Let tart stand 10 minutes before inverting onto serving platter. Garnish with whipped cream and mint, if desired. Serve immediately.

Makes 8 servings

Pie Crust

> **1 cup all-purpose flour**
> **Grated peel of 1 lemon**
> **¼ teaspoon salt**
> **4 tablespoons cold unsalted butter**
> **2 to 3 tablespoons water**

Combine flour, lemon peel and salt in large bowl. Cut in butter with pastry blender or 2 knives until mixture resembles coarse crumbs. Sprinkle mixture with water, 1 tablespoon at a time. Toss with fork until mixture holds together. Press together to form ball. Wrap dough in plastic wrap; refrigerate at least 30 minutes.

Makes one 9-inch pie crust

Tip

To prebake a pastry tart shell before filling it, prick the shell all over with a fork, line it with foil or parchment, and fill it with dried beans or rice. Bake the shell in a preheated oven; remove the liner and beans during the last few minutes of baking to allow the shell to brown. The beans (or rice) can be cooled, stored in an airtight container, and reused in the same way. Ceramic or metal pie weights are also available.

Techniques for Fresh Fruit Tart

Step 1. *Processing until dough leaves side of bowl.*

Step 3. *Pressing dough onto bottom and up side of tart pan.*

Fresh Fruit Tart

Fresh Fruit Tart

  1⅔ **cups all-purpose flour**
   ⅓ **cup sugar**
   ¼ **teaspoon salt**
   ½ **cup butter or margarine, softened**
   1 **egg yolk**
   2 **to 3 tablespoons milk**
   1 **package (8 ounces) cream cheese, softened**
   ⅓ **cup strawberry jam**
   2 **to 3 cups assorted fresh fruit, such as sliced bananas, blueberries, halved grapes, sliced nectarines, sliced peaches, sliced plums, raspberries or halved strawberries**
   ¼ **cup apple jelly, melted**
   ¼ **cup toasted sliced unblanched almonds (optional)**

1. Place flour, sugar and salt in food processor or blender; process until just combined. Cut butter into 6 pieces; add to flour mixture. Process using on/off pulsing action until mixture resembles coarse crumbs. Add egg yolk and 2 tablespoons milk; process until dough leaves side of bowl. Add additional milk by teaspoons, if necessary. Shape dough into a disc. Wrap in plastic wrap; refrigerate 30 minutes or until firm.

2. Preheat oven to 350°F.

3. Roll dough out on lightly floured surface to ¼-inch thickness with floured rolling pin. Cut 12-inch circle; transfer to ungreased 10-inch tart pan with removable bottom. Press lightly onto bottom and up side of pan; trim edges even with edge of pan.

4. Bake 16 to 18 minutes until light golden brown. Cool on wire rack.

5. Combine cream cheese and jam in small bowl; mix well. Spread evenly over cooled crust. Arrange fruit decoratively over cheese layer. Brush fruit with jelly. Sprinkle with almonds, if desired. Refrigerate up to 2 hours before serving.   *Makes 8 servings*

TARTAR SAUCE

Tartar sauce is a mayonnaise-based condiment that is traditionally flavored with finely chopped capers, dill pickles, onions and lemon juice. Although it is typically served with fried fish and shellfish, tartar sauce can also be served with broiled or grilled fish. Tartar sauce may be purchased or made at home from purchased mayonnaise.

🌿

Tartar Sauce

   1 **cup mayonnaise**
   2 **tablespoons chopped cornichons or dill relish**
   1 **clove garlic, minced**
   1 **teaspoon fresh lemon juice**
   1 **teaspoon prepared horseradish**
   2 **to 3 dashes ground red pepper**
   3 **tablespoons sun-dried tomatoes packed in oil (optional)**

1. Combine mayonnaise, cornichons, garlic, juice, horseradish and red pepper in small bowl.

2. Drain sun-dried tomatoes; pat dry with paper towels. Slice tomatoes lengthwise into thin strips and cut in half. Fold tomatoes into mayonnaise mixture. Serve immediately or store, covered, in refrigerator up to 1 day.

Makes about 1 cup sauce

TEA

Tea refers to the beverage prepared by steeping dried leaves in boiling water. Tea also refers to the leaves themselves of the shrub from which they come. The drink was first served in China 4,000 years ago. By the eighth century A.D. the Japanese had discovered it. Tea arrived in England in the 1700's. By the end of that century its import had increased ten-thousand fold with a specific daily meal, called tea or high tea, devoted to it. Tea is grown in tropical and subtropical regions of Asia, especially China, India, Indonesia and Japan. The choicest tea is grown at high altitudes.

🌽

Varieties: All tea plants are of the same species but differences in cultivation, climate and processing result in a wide variety of tea types.

• Green tea, popular in Asia, is produced by withering, rolling, and then firing or drying the tea leaves.

• Black tea is the result of fermenting the leaves before they are fired. Black tea is favored by Westerners. Well-known black teas are Darjeeling, English and Irish breakfast, Earl Grey and Ceylon.

• Oolong tea leaves are only partially fermented prior to firing.

• Specialty teas may have various

spices, blossoms or dried fruits mixed with the leaves.

• Herbal teas contain no leaves from the tea shrub but a blend of dried herbs, flowers and spices. Chamomile and mint are popular herbal teas.

Availability: Tea may be purchased loose or in individual premeasured bags. Many of the black teas sold in America and Great Britain are blends of several teas. Black teas are categorized by the size of leaf: orange pekoe (small), pekoe (medium) and souchong (large). Instant tea, often with lemon and sweeteners added, dissolves quickly in water and is most often used for making iced tea. Tea will keep up to a year. Bottled tea and tea-flavored beverages are also available.

Tips for Making Tea: For the perfect pot of tea, allow 6 ounces of cold water for each cup of tea and bring it to a boil. Using a ceramic or glass, not metal, pot to steep the tea, allow one tea bag or one heaping teaspoon of loose tea for each cup. Pour the boiling water over the tea in the pot, stir once, cover and allow to steep for 3 to 6 minutes for black tea and 6 to 8 minutes for green tea. If using loose tea, pour the tea into cups through a strainer (or place the loose tea in a tea ball or tea infuser before steeping). Tea may be served with milk, lemon or sugar.

Iced Tea

2½ tablespoons Time-Saver Sugar
Syrup (page 283)
1 cup double-strength hot tea
Crushed ice

Add Time-Saver Sugar Syrup to tea; stir well. Fill 2 glasses with crushed ice; pour tea mixture over ice. Serve cold. *Makes 2 servings*

Note: To prepare double-strength tea, bring 1 cup water to a boil; add 2 tea bags. Steep 3 to 5 minutes. Discard tea bags.

*Favorite recipe from **The Sugar Association, Inc.***

TEMPURA

Tempura had its beginnings in the deep-fried foods, especially shrimp, that were introduced to Japan by Portuguese traders in the 1500's. This Japanese specialty is prepared by deep-frying shrimp, pieces of fish or pieces of vegetables that have been dipped in a light batter. The deep-fried foods should be eaten immediately for their crispy coating to be enjoyed. They may be dipped in a soy sauce for added flavor.

🌿

Cut chicken into 1½-inch-square pieces. Thread skewers alternately with chicken and green onion pieces. (Spear green onion pieces crosswise.) Place skewers in shallow pan. Combine soy sauce, sugar, oil, ginger and garlic in small bowl; pour over skewers. Brush chicken thoroughly with sauce. Cover; marinate in refrigerator 30 minutes. Drain marinade; reserve. Place skewers on rack of broiler pan. Broil 3 minutes; turn over and brush with reserved marinade. Broil for an additional 5 minutes or until chicken is no longer pink in center.

Makes 4 servings

TERIYAKI

Teriyaki is a Japanese preparation of grilled meat or poultry that has first been marinated in a mixture of soy sauce, sake (Japanese rice wine), sugar and seasonings. The soy sauce and sugar combine to give the cooked food an appealing brown glaze. Teriyaki also can refer to a sauce made with these ingredients. It is sold bottled in most supermarkets and can be used for marinating or for adding flavor to simple stir-fry preparations.

🌿

Chicken Teriyaki Kabobs

　1½ pounds chicken breasts, skinned and boned
　8 (6-inch) bamboo skewers
　1 bunch green onions, cut into 1-inch lengths
　½ cup KIKKOMAN® Soy Sauce
　2 tablespoons sugar
　1 teaspoon vegetable oil
　1 teaspoon minced fresh ginger root
　1 clove garlic, minced

Technique for Tiramisu

Step 3. *Brushing ladyfingers with espresso mixture.*

TIRAMISU

Tiramisu is a rich Italian dessert made from ladyfingers or sponge cake that is soaked in a mixture of espresso and brandy. These are layered with mascarpone cheese (a very rich and creamy Italian cheese), shaved chocolate and whipped cream.

🌿

Tiramisu

　Zabaglione (recipe follows)
　⅔ cup whipping cream, chilled
　4 tablespoons sugar, divided
　1 pound mascarpone cheese* (about 2¼ cups)
　⅓ cup freshly brewed espresso or strong coffee, cooled
　¼ cup Cognac or brandy
　1 tablespoon vanilla extract
　3 packages (3 ounces each) ladyfingers, split
　3 ounces bittersweet or semisweet chocolate, grated
　1 tablespoon unsweetened cocoa powder
　Edible flowers (optional)

*If mascarpone cheese is unavailable, blend 2 packages (8 ounces each) softened cream cheese with ½ cup whipping cream and 5 tablespoons sour cream.

1. Prepare Zabaglione. Cover; refrigerate until well chilled.

2. Beat cream and 2 tablespoons sugar in large bowl until soft peaks form. Gently fold in mascarpone cheese, then Zabaglione. (If Zabaglione has separated, beat until well mixed before folding into mascarpone.) Refrigerate 3 hours or until well chilled.

3. Combine espresso, Cognac, remaining 2 tablespoons sugar and vanilla in small bowl. Layer ¼ of ladyfingers in flower-petal design in 2-quart glass bowl with straight side or trifle dish. Generously brush ladyfingers with espresso mixture. Spoon ¼ of chilled cheese mixture over ladyfingers to within 1 inch of side of bowl. Sprinkle with ¼ of grated chocolate. Repeat layers 3 more times using remaining ladyfingers, espresso mixture, cheese mixture and grated chocolate. (For garnish, sprinkle remaining ¼ of grated chocolate around edge of dessert, if desired.)

4. Sift cocoa powder over top with small sieve. Cover; refrigerate at least 30 minutes before serving. Garnish with flowers, if desired.

Makes 8 to 10 servings

Zabaglione

> 5 egg yolks
> ¼ cup sugar
> ½ cup marsala wine, divided
> ¼ cup dry white wine

1. Place egg yolks in top of double boiler; add sugar. Beat with portable electric mixer at medium speed or rotary beater until mixture is pale yellow and creamy. Place water in bottom of double boiler. Bring to a boil over high heat; reduce heat to low. Place top of double boiler over hot water. Gradually beat ¼ cup marsala into egg yolk mixture. Beat 1 minute. Gradually beat in remaining ¼ cup marsala and white wine.

2. Cook 6 to 10 minutes until mixture is fluffy and thick enough to form soft mounds when dropped from beaters, beating constantly and scraping bottom and side of pan frequently. (*Do not overcook* or custard will curdle.) Remove top of double boiler from water. Whisk custard briefly. If not using for Tiramisu recipe, pour into 4 individual serving dishes. Serve immediately with fresh berries and/or cookies.   *Makes 4 servings*

Tiramisu

TOAST, TO

Toasting is the technique of browning foods by means of dry heat. Bread products, nuts, seeds and coconut are commonly toasted. Toasting is done in a toaster, toaster oven, oven, skillet or under the broiler. The purpose of toasting bread is to brown, crisp and dry it. Nuts, seeds and coconut are toasted to intensify their flavor.

🌿

TOFU

Tofu, also known as soybean curd, is made by coagulating soy milk, draining it and pressing the curds in a method similar to cheesemaking. It is used extensively in Asian cooking. Tofu is white or cream-colored with a creamy smooth texture. It has a bland, slightly nutty taste, but readily takes on the flavor of foods it is cooked with. It is available in three forms: soft, firm and extra firm. Soft tofu can be whipped or blended for use in dips, fillings and scrambled eggs. Firm and extra-firm tofu can be cubed and used in stir-fries. Fresh tofu is packed in water and available in the refrigerated section of many large supermarkets. It should be stored refrigerated and covered with water. The water should be changed daily. Fresh tofu will keep up to a week. Tofu is also available in aseptic packages (a form of vacuum packaging). This form is shelf stable and needs only to be stored in a cool place. Refrigerate leftover tofu, covered with water, in the refrigerator.

🌿

Szechuan Vegetable Stir-Fry

Szechuan Vegetable Stir-Fry

8 ounces firm tofu, drained, cut
    into cubes
1 cup vegetable broth, divided
½ cup orange juice
⅓ cup soy sauce
1 to 2 teaspoons hot chili oil
½ teaspoon fennel seeds
½ teaspoon ground black pepper
2 tablespoons cornstarch
3 tablespoons vegetable oil
1 cup sliced green onions and
    tops
3 medium carrots, diagonally
    sliced
3 cloves garlic, minced
2 teaspoons minced fresh ginger
¼ pound fresh button mushrooms,
    sliced
1 medium red bell pepper, cut
    into 1-inch squares
¼ pound fresh snow peas (Chinese
    pea pods), stems removed,
    cut diagonally into halves
8 ounces broccoli florets, steamed
½ cup peanuts
4 to 6 cups hot cooked rice

1. Place tofu in 8-inch glass baking dish. Combine ½ cup broth, juice, soy sauce, chili oil, fennel seeds and black pepper in 2-cup measure; pour over tofu. Let stand 15 to 60 minutes. Drain, reserving marinade.

2. Combine cornstarch and remaining ½ cup broth in medium bowl; stir until smooth. Stir in reserved marinade; set aside.

3. Heat vegetable oil in wok or large skillet over high heat. Add onions, carrots, garlic and ginger; stir-fry 3 minutes. Add tofu, mushrooms, bell pepper and snow peas; stir-fry 2 to 3 minutes until vegetables are crisp-tender. Add broccoli; stir-fry 1 minute or until heated through. Stir cornstarch mixture. Add to wok; cook 1 to 2 minutes until bubbly. Stir in peanuts. Serve over rice. Garnish as desired.   *Makes 4 to 6 servings*

TOMATILLO

A tomatillo looks like a small green tomato with a papery tan husk. Tomatillos are related to tomatoes, since both are members of the nightshade family. Tomatillos are sometimes called Chinese lantern plants, an obvious reference to the outer husk. They have been a cherished ingredient in Mexican kitchens since the days of the Aztecs but are seldom used in other cuisines. Tomatillos have a refreshingly herbal taste with a hint of lemon. Cooking mellows the flavor. Although botanically a fruit, tomatillos are treated as a vegetable. Tomatillos are used primarily in sauces and salsa, pairing well with pork, poultry and seafood.

🌾

Availability: Fresh tomatillos are available all year in many large supermarkets and Latin markets. They are also available canned.

Buying Tips: Select solid, firm tomatillos with smooth, unbroken skins and clean husks that are not blackened by mildew or softened by juice. Unlike tomatoes, tomatillos are ready to use while still quite firm.

Yield: 1 pound tomatillos – 6 to 8 medium; 2 cups finely chopped.

Storage: Tomatillos keep in the refrigerator up to 3 weeks. Check them periodically and discard any that have begun to rot.

Basic Preparation: Remove the husk by peeling it away. The skin will feel sticky. Rinse the tomatillo thoroughly to clean the skin. Core and chop as directed.

Tip

Tofu must be drained before being stir-fried or deep-fried. Remove any remaining water by placing the block of tofu on several layers of paper towels and covering it with additional paper towels weighted down with a heavy plate. Let it stand for 15 to 20 minutes before slicing or cubing the tofu, as the recipe directs.

TOMATO

Tomatoes are the third most widely consumed vegetable in the United States, lagging behind potatoes and lettuce. It is estimated that more than 85 percent of home gardeners plant tomatoes. Tomatoes are one of a few foods that are native to the Western Hemisphere. It is generally believed that they originated in the coastal highlands of western South America. They appeared later in Central America where Mayan Indians used them as food. With the conquest of Mexico in 1519, tomatoes were carried eastward to Europe. Although Europeans at first believed tomatoes to be poisonous, the Spaniards and Italians eventually found many culinary uses for them. By the early 1900's, tomatoes were considered a staple of American cookery, invaluable both canned and fresh.

🌱

Varieties: There are literally hundreds of varieties of tomatoes, but consumers are limited to what the market offers. Most supermarkets offer three types: globe, plum and cherry tomatoes. Globe tomatoes are the common all-purpose tomatoes. Some varieties are yellow. They are served raw or cooked. Plum tomatoes, sometimes called Italian tomatoes, are small and oval in shape. Since they are fleshier than most globe tomatoes, they are a good choice for sauce making. Cherry tomatoes are small tomatoes, 1-inch in diameter, that are ideal for snacking, salads and garnishes. Yellow cherry tomatoes and small yellow pear tomatoes are occasionally available. These tomatoes are less acidic than red tomatoes. Green tomatoes are unripened. Firm and tart, green tomatoes are excellent for pickling and frying.

Availability: Fresh tomatoes are available all year although locally grown summer tomatoes are superior to all others. The best hybrids are found at farmers' markets. Depending on the area, tomato season usually begins in mid-summer and lasts through September. Winter tomatoes often are labeled as "vine-ripened," when, in fact, they have been picked green and ripened with ethylene gas so they can be shipped and stored. This process prevents them from reaching their full flavor potential and burdens them with a mealy texture. Tomatoes from Israel also help fill the winter gap. Occasionally, these are of better quality, especially if they are sold still attached to the vine. Plum tomatoes are often a better off-season choice for salads than globes. Canned tomatoes are a good alternative to off-season tomatoes, especially for cooking purposes. There are many forms of canned tomatoes, including whole, diced, wedges, stewed, crushed and puréed. Some are flavored. Sun-dried tomatoes, either dry-packed or in oil, have an intense tomato flavor and chewy texture.

Buying Tips: In season, tomatoes should be plump and heavy with a vibrant color and a pleasant aroma. They should be firm but not hard. A soft tomato will either be watery or overripe. Avoid those that are cracked or have soft spots.

Yield: 1 pound tomatoes = 3 medium globe; 8 plum; 2 cups chopped.

Storage: Tomatoes should never be refrigerated before cutting, because cold temperatures cause their flesh to become mealy and lose flavor. Store them at room temperature. Ripening can be hastened by placing them in a paper bag.

Basic Preparation: To prepare tomatoes for salads or sandwiches, wash tomatoes under cold running water. Cut out the stems and core the tomatoes with a paring knife. Tomatoes do not need to be peeled for these uses. Slice tomatoes with a serrated knife, if possible. Otherwise, puncture the skin with the point of a knife and then slice with a sharp utility knife.

To prepare tomatoes for cooking, they should generally be peeled and seeded. Tomato skins will shrivel and toughen when cooked, and tomato seeds in sauces are not attractive. To peel tomatoes, cut an "X" in the skin of the bottom of each tomato. Drop the tomatoes into a pan of boiling water. Cook ripe tomatoes 10 to 15 seconds or firm tomatoes 20 seconds. Remove the tomatoes with a slotted spoon and plunge them

into a bowl of cold water. When the tomatoes are cool, slip off the skins with a paring knife.

Marinated Tomatoes & Mozzarella
(recipe on page 521)

To seed a tomato, cut it in half crosswise. Holding each tomato half over a bowl, cut side down, gently squeeze the  tomato to remove the seeds. An alternative method is to remove the seeds with a small spoon.

To soften dry sun-dried tomatoes, cover them with hot water for 30 minutes or boiling water for 5 minutes. Drain them before using. Drain oil-packed sun-dried tomatoes before using. They may be rinsed in hot water to remove the oil.

Marinated Tomato Salad

Marinated Tomato Salad

Marinade
- 1½ **cups tarragon or white wine vinegar**
- ½ **teaspoon salt**
- ¼ **cup finely chopped shallots**
- 2 **tablespoons finely chopped chives**
- 2 **tablespoons fresh lemon juice**
- ¼ **teaspoon ground white pepper**
- 2 **tablespoons extra virgin olive oil**

Salad
- 6 **ripe plum tomatoes, quartered lengthwise**
- 2 **large yellow tomatoes, sliced crosswise into ½-inch slices**
- 16 **red cherry tomatoes, halved lengthwise**
- 16 **small yellow pear tomatoes, halved lengthwise**
- **Sunflower sprouts (optional)**

1. To prepare marinade, combine vinegar and salt in large bowl; stir until salt is completely dissolved. Add shallots, chives, juice and pepper; mix well. Slowly whisk in oil until well blended.

2. Add tomatoes to marinade; toss well. Cover and let stand at room temperature 2 to 3 hours. To serve, divide tomatoes among 8 salad plates. Garnish with sunflower sprouts, if desired.

Makes 8 servings

Tomato Sauce

- 2 **pounds ripe Italian plum tomatoes***
- 2 **tablespoons olive oil or butter**
- 1 **clove garlic, minced**
- 1 **teaspoon sugar**
- ¼ **cup finely chopped prosciutto or cooked ham (optional)**
- 1 **tablespoon finely chopped fresh basil**
- **Salt and ground black pepper**

*If good-quality tomatoes are unavailable, substitute 2 cups drained canned plum tomatoes for the fresh.

1. To easily remove tomato peels, cut skin-deep "X" on bottom of each tomato. Place no more than 2 tomatoes at a time in saucepan of simmering water for 10 seconds. Remove with slotted spoon; plunge immediately into bowl of cold water for another 10 seconds. Remove tomato peels with paring knife.

2. To seed tomatoes, cut each tomato in half crosswise. Hold each tomato half over bowl, cut side down, and squeeze to remove seeds; discard seeds. Chop tomatoes.

3. Heat oil in medium saucepan over medium heat. Add garlic. Cook 30 seconds or until fragrant. Stir in tomatoes and sugar. Cook 10 minutes or until most of liquid is evaporated. Stir in prosciutto, if desired, and basil. Cook 2 minutes. Season with salt and pepper.

Makes about 2 cups sauce

Marinated Tomatoes & Mozzarella

> 1 medium bunch fresh basil leaves, divided
> 1 pound Italian (plum) tomatoes, sliced
> ½ pound fresh packed buffalo mozzarella cheese, sliced
> ¼ cup olive oil
> 3 tablespoons chopped fresh chives
> 2 tablespoons red wine vinegar
> 2 teaspoons sugar
> ½ teaspoon dried oregano
> ½ teaspoon LAWRY'S® Seasoned Pepper
> ½ teaspoon LAWRY'S® Garlic Powder with Parsley

Divide basil in half; reserve one half for garnish. Chop remaining basil leaves; set aside. In shallow dish, place tomato slices and cheese. Combine all remaining ingredients except reserved whole and chopped basil leaves; pour over tomatoes and cheese. Cover. Refrigerate at least 30 minutes. To serve, arrange tomato and cheese slices on serving plate. Sprinkle with chopped basil leaves. Garnish with reserved whole basil leaves.   *Makes 4 to 6 servings*

Presentation: Serve with grilled chicken sandwiches or as a zesty Italian appetizer.

Plum Tomato Sauce

> ⅓ cup butter or margarine
> 1 clove garlic, minced
> 1 can (28 ounces) Italian plum tomatoes, undrained
> 1 can (8 ounces) tomato sauce
> ¾ teaspoon salt
> ½ teaspoon ground allspice
> ½ teaspoon dried basil leaves
> ½ teaspoon dried rosemary leaves, crushed
> ⅛ teaspoon ground black pepper

Heat butter in large saucepan over medium heat until melted and bubbly; add garlic. Cook and stir 30 seconds. Press tomatoes with juice through sieve into garlic mixture; discard seeds. Stir in tomato sauce, salt, allspice, basil, rosemary and pepper. Cover; simmer 30 minutes. Uncover; simmer 15 minutes more or until sauce thickens, stirring occasionally.

Makes about 2 cups sauce

Tip

When making tomato sauce, add a pinch or two of sugar. For long-cooking sauces, add a little grated carrot for a touch of sweetness.

Pesto-Pasta Stuffed Tomatoes

3 ounces uncooked star or other small pasta
4 large ripe tomatoes
1 cup loosely packed fresh basil
1 clove garlic, minced
3 tablespoons reduced calorie mayonnaise
1 tablespoon skim milk
¼ teaspoon ground black pepper
1 cup shredded zucchini
4 teaspoons grated Parmesan cheese

1. Cook pasta according to package directions, omitting salt. Drain and rinse; set aside in medium bowl.

2. Cut tops from tomatoes. Scoop out and discard all but ½ cup tomato pulp. Chop tomato pulp; add to pasta. Place tomatoes, cut sides down, on paper towels; let drain 5 minutes.

3. Preheat oven to 350°F.

4. Place basil and garlic in blender or food processor; process until finely chopped. Add mayonnaise, milk and pepper; process until smooth. Add zucchini and basil mixture to pasta mixture; toss to coat evenly. Place tomatoes, cut sides up, in 8-inch baking dish. Divide pasta mixture evenly among tomatoes, mounding filling slightly. Sprinkle with cheese.

5. Bake 10 to 15 minutes until heated through. Serve immediately.

Makes 4 servings

Pesto-Pasta Stuffed Tomatoes

TOOLS

A basically equipped kitchen requires not only cookware and bakeware but also a variety of kitchen tools. The following list includes basic tools needed to prepare the recipes in this book. Not everyone will need all of these tools. If you are equipping your first kitchen, read through the list and determine which tools you need based on the type of cooking you intend to do. Buy other tools as you find a need for them.

🌾

Apple Corer: An apple corer is an inexpensive utensil that removes the core of an apple while leaving the apple whole. An apple corer/slicer is a wheel-shaped utensil that not only removes the core of an apple or pear but also cuts it into wedges.

Blender, Electric: Blenders are excellent for mixing drinks, grinding spices, puréeing foods and making smooth sauces. An immersion blender serves some of the functions of a regular blender but has the added convenience of being immersible in saucepans, bowls and glasses.

Bowl, Mixing: Bowls suitable for food preparation can be made of ceramic, metal, glass or plastic. A basic kitchen should have a variety of bowls, such as 1-, 2- and 3-quart bowls as well as a bowl large enough for bread dough.

Brush: Brushes made of natural bristles, such as boar bristles, or nylon are used to brush crumbs off cakes, brush excess flour from doughs and apply syrups, glazes and melted butter. Brushes should be washed by hand with hot, soapy water and then air dried. Boar bristle brushes are more expensive but last longer.

Cake Comb: This triangular metal or plastic tool with saw-tooth edges is used to make patterns in frosting.

Cake Tester: A cake tester is a long wire used to test cakes for doneness. Wooden toothpicks can also be used in place of a cake tester.

Carving Board: A carving board, usually made of hardwood, is similar to a cutting board, but it has a "gutter" around the edges or down the center to catch meat juices.

Cheesecloth: Cheesecloth is an inexpensive, white cotton that is sold in various weaves, from fine to coarse. It is used for making *bouquet garni (page 57)*, straining liquids and juicing fruits for jelly making.

Cheese Grater, Rotary: This hand-held utensil, which consists of a food container with a grating cylinder and a hand-turned crank, is designed to grate hard cheeses, such as Parmesan. Most rotary graters will also grate chocolate. Hard cheeses may also be grated on a box grater or flat metal grater with small holes.

Tip

Electric blenders are not interchangeable with food processors. A blender will not chop, slice or shred foods; a food processor is needed for these operations.

Citrus Stripper: A citrus stripper is a small tool with a head that has a single notched groove. It is used to remove thin strips of citrus peel to use as garnishes *(page 344)*. Or, it may be used to remove strips of peel at equally spaced intervals to add a decorative touch to the fruit.

Colander: A colander is a bowl-like utensil made of metal or plastic with equally spaced holes that allow liquids to drain away from solids. Many colanders are raised to facilitate draining. Others have handles that allow them to be suspended over a sink or saucepan. Two or three colanders of different sizes are handy, but if you decide to buy only one colander it should be large enough to drain a pound of cooked pasta.

Cookie Cutter: Cookie cutters of metal or plastic cut round, square or decorative shapes from cookie dough. The cutters come in a wide variety of shapes and sizes. Round cutters are also used to cut biscuit dough.

Cookie Press: A cookie press consists of a tube that is filled with cookie dough and a mechanism that pushes the dough through decorative disks. Use cookie presses only with recipes that were developed for them, because dough consistency is very important to its successful operation.

Cooling Rack: A cooling rack is a raised wire rack used to cool baked goods. It is raised to allow air circulation around the baking pan, which hastens cooling and prevents steam accumulation. When cakes or breads are removed from pans, they are also cooled on cooling racks. Individual cookies are removed from baking sheets and cooled on cooling racks. Cooling racks come in various sizes.

Custard Cup: Custard cups are individual dishes made of ovenproof glass or ceramic suitable for desserts such as baked custard and crème brûlée. Sizes vary from 4 ounces to 12 ounces. They are also useful for holding small amounts of ingredients.

Cutting Board: A cutting board is a flat piece of wood or plastic that is used as a cutting surface, protecting both knife blades and countertops. It can also be used to roll out cookie and pastry doughs. Sizes vary. If you wish to buy only one, select a large cutting board. The cutting board should be stable during cutting. Wooden boards need special care; they must be washed by hand, thoroughly air dried before storage, oiled periodically and sanded occasionally.

Dough Scraper: A dough scraper is a rectangular implement, usually with a wooden handle and a metal blade. It is used for loosening and turning dough and for scraping excess dough from the work surface. It can also be used for cutting dough and for transferring chopped ingredients from a cutting board to a pan.

Egg Separator: An egg separator is a metal or plastic utensil that allows the egg white to fall through openings, leaving the egg yolk separate and intact.

Egg Slicer: An egg slicer is a tool designed to cut perfect slices of hard-cooked eggs with thin wires.

Electric Mixer: Electric mixers come in many styles and sizes. Portable hand-held and stand mixers are available. Portable mixers can do most of the operations of stand mixers, but they sometimes have difficulty with heavy doughs. (They also leave you with only one free hand.) The frequent baker may find the stand mixer more practical. Select one with a dough hook and whip for more versatility. If you choose to have only a portable mixer, buy a high quality one that is comfortable to hold.

Flour Sifter: A flour sifter consists of a fine mesh screen and a mechanism to push flour through the mesh. A sifter with a 2- or 3-cup capacity and a crank-type handle is a good choice. A strainer can be used instead.

Food Processor: This multipurpose electric appliance can be used to chop, slice, shred, mix, purée, knead and sometimes whip with efficiency. Although a kitchen can function without one, a frequent cook with limited time may find a food processor useful.

Funnel: Specially designed funnels are available for canning, sausage-stuffing and confectionary purposes, but most cooks will find a general-purpose funnel useful for filling jars and bottles.

Garlic Press: A garlic press is a hand tool that presses one or two cloves of garlic through small openings to mash them. Garlic presses can be difficult to clean. Some cooks believe that crushing garlic results in a harsh flavor, but many prefer the convenience of a garlic press.

Grater/Shredder: A four sided box-shaped grater/shredder is a versatile and inexpensive tool that has several different size openings for grating vegetables and cheese. Graters that are flat sheets of metal with similar openings and a wire handle are also available. These often come in sets.

Juicer/Reamer: Juicers and reamers are used to extract juice from citrus fruit. Juicers, which often strain out seeds and large pieces of pulp, may be used over a small bowl or cup, although some juicers come with a container to hold the juice. A reamer is a hand-held tool, often wooden, that is inserted into a citrus half and twisted to extract the juice.

Kitchen Shears: Kitchen shears are a very useful tool for cutting. They are an excellent choice for trimming fat from poultry and cutting fresh herbs, pastry, canned tomatoes, dried fruit, paper, cheesecloth and string. Select heavy-duty shears made for the kitchen. Some shears separate into two parts for easier cleaning. Poultry shears are designed to cut raw poultry; they are strong enough to cut through bone and cartilage.

Tip

With regards to food safety and cutting boards, there is no definitive answer as to what material is safest for use with foods that may contain bacteria, such as poultry and meat. No matter what the material, it must always be thoroughly washed in hot, soapy water after it comes in contact with poultry or meat and before it is used with any other foods.

Kitchen String: Kitchen string is a medium-weight, all-cotton string that is used for trussing poultry, tying certain meat roasts and securing a *bouquet garni.*

Knife: Good quality, sharp knives are absolutely essential in the kitchen. Most good knives are made from a combination of carbon steel and stainless steel. Carbon steel is superior for holding a sharp edge; however, it pits and stains easily. Mixing carbon steel with stainless steel makes a sturdier and easier to maintain blade. Knives are available with wood or hardened plastic handles. A high quality knife has a full tang, meaning that the blade runs the entire length of the handle. It should be securely riveted to the handle in several places. When selecting knives, pick them up to see if they feel comfortable in your hand. Which knives you select depends on your cooking style, but every kitchen needs at least three knives: a paring knife, utility knife and chef's knife. Other knives can be purchased as the need arises. A sharpening steel is a good investment for keeping knives sharpened. Good cutlery should be washed by hand as dishwashers are often too hot.

A paring knife has a short 3- or 4-inch-long blade. It is used for peeling, slicing fruit and vegetables, chopping herbs and other fine work. A utility knife has a 6-inch-long blade. It is a general purpose knife for slicing fruit, vegetables, meat, poultry, fish and cheese. A chef's knife has a wide, slightly curved blade from 7 to 12 inches long. This knife is used primarily for chopping food using a rocking motion. To use a chef's knife, grasp the handle of the knife with one hand, rest the fingertips lightly on the top of the blade near the tip end and rock the blade back and forth over the food.

Other specialized knives include serrated, boning, slicing, carving, Asian knives and cleavers. Serrated knives are good choices for slicing bread and tomatoes. Boning knives have a slender blade that make them ideal for removing bones from meat and poultry. Slicing and carving knives are designed to cut cooked meat and poultry. Meat requires a wide rigid blade and poultry a thinner blade. Asian knives perform many tasks from slicing to chopping, but it takes practice to perfect the techniques. Cleavers are generally heavier than Asian knives and are strong enough to chop through bone.

Ladle: A ladle has a deep bowl attached to a long handle for reaching into deep pans and removing liquids.

Measuring Cup: *See Measure, To, page 298, for information about measuring cups.*

Measuring Spoon: *See Measure, To, page 298, for information about measuring spoons.*

Meat Mallet: Also called a meat tenderizer, a meat mallet is a hammerlike tool that has a head marked with a waffled surface. It flattens the meat while breaking surface fibers. The flat side of the mallet can be used to flatten tender cuts.

Melon Baller: A melon baller is a small tool that shapes melon into perfect balls. It is also useful for coring apple halves and scooping out cherry tomatoes prior to stuffing.

Metal Spatula: Metal spatulas are tools with narrow thin metal blades attached to plastic or wooden handles. They are ideal for spreading. Some are 8 inches long and rigid whereas others are shorter and flexible. A flat spatula forms a straight line from handle to blade. An offset spatula is angled near the handle, causing the handle to be raised slightly.

Tip

Wooden knife handles require a little extra care, since they must be oiled periodically and protected from long exposure to water and heat. They should never be washed in the dishwasher.

Mortar and Pestle: Unsurpassed for grinding small amounts of herbs, spices, nuts and seeds, a mortar and pestle is a useful tool for an experienced cook. Marble is the best choice since it does not absorb the odors of food as wood does.

Parchment: Parchment is heavy paper that is impervious to grease and moisture. It is sold in sheets and in rolls. There are many uses for it in the kitchen, including making sealed envelopes for cooking *en papillote* (page 354) and lining baking sheets for cookies, meringues and cream puffs. It allows for easy removal.

Pastry Bag: A pastry bag is a cone-shaped bag made of canvas, plastic or plastic-lined cloth. It is used to pipe foods, such as frosting, whipped cream, cream puff dough and mashed potatoes, in a decorative pattern. It is open at both ends. The food to be piped is placed in the larger opening. The smaller opening can be fitted with decorative tips.

Pastry Blender: This hand-held tool consists of several u-shaped wires or metal blades attached to a handle. It is used to cut butter or shortening into flour, which is an essential step in pastry making. Although two knives can be used to accomplish the same task, the pastry blender is more practical.

Pastry Cloth: Made of canvas, a pastry cloth is used to roll out pastry. When well floured, it minimizes sticking. Some pastry cloths are marked with concentric circles that serve as guidelines. It does require thorough cleaning to remove oils before they become rancid. A large cutting board can also be used for rolling out pastry.

Pizza Wheel: A pizza wheel is a round metal wheel attached to a handle. It can be rolled across pizza to cut it. Choose one with a sharp heavy-duty blade.

Rolling Pin: Rolling pins are used to roll pastry and cookie dough. They can be made from hardwood or marble. The typical American rolling pin is made of wood with a handle on each end. It rolls on bearings. The French version has no handles. A heavy rolling pin allows for the most efficient rolling, because the weight of the pin does most of the work, requiring less effort from the user. A marble rolling pin is used to make pastry. It stays cool and does not warm the butter; however, it is very expensive and unnecessary for someone who seldom makes pastry.

Rubber Spatula: A flexible utensil with a paddlelike rubber, plastic or nylon head attached to a handle, a rubber spatula is ideal for mixing, folding and scraping mixtures from bowls and cookware. A wide variety of sizes is available, and most cooks will find it useful to have several. Some are stain resistant and heat resistant.

Scoop: Ice cream scoops, sometimes called dishers, are used not only for portioning ice cream but also for portioning cookie dough, muffin batter or mashed potatoes. Many are designed with a scraping blade that aids in releasing the food from the scoop. Scoops come in a variety of sizes and are labeled with a number from 8 to 100. The smaller the number, the larger the bowl of the scoop. Good sizes for cookie batter are 40, 50 and 80. Muffin batter can be scooped with a number 16 or 30. Choose a sturdy metal scoop if it will be used for frozen foods.

Skewer: Metal or bamboo skewers are used for kabobs, saté and appetizers. They are available in a variety of lengths. Select skewers that are flat rather than round, if possible, so that the food will not slip around when the skewers are turned on the grill. Bamboo skewers, which are disposable, must be soaked in water for 30 minutes before using on a grill to prevent them from burning.

Spoon, Mixing: Every kitchen needs several spoons for mixing and stirring. Spoons are available in plastic, wood and metal. Choose plastic or wood for nonstick surfaces, because metal will scratch these surfaces. A long-handled spoon is a good choice for tall pans. Whatever the material, select spoons that are stamped from a single piece; joints break and are more difficult to clean. If wooden spoons crack, they can harbor bacteria so it is best to discard them. Wooden spoons will last longer if they are not subjected to the dry heat of the dishwasher.

Spoon, Slotted: The bowl of a slotted spoon has slots that make it useful for removing foods from liquids.

Strainer/Sieve: Strainers consist of wire mesh that is stabilized by a rigid handle or ring. They are used to separate liquid from solid ingredients, to sift flour, to separate fine particles from foods and purée soft foods. Most kitchens should have at least one strainer. A medium-size strainer with handles that will allow it to be suspended over a bowl is a good choice. The wire mesh should be sturdy and made of stainless steel to prevent rusting.

Thermometer: There are many specialized kitchen thermometers. A mercury thermometer for the oven is recommended for every kitchen. It allows the cook to read the actual oven temperature, which often varies from the dial setting. Remember that the oven temperature of a normal electric oven fluctuates continuously in a range as wide as 75°F. When checking the dial setting for accuracy, check the oven temperature on the thermometer frequently through the glass of the oven door if possible. Meat thermometers are inserted into meat or poultry before roasting to measure the internal temperature of the meat. An instant-read thermometer is used to quickly check the temperature of a food. It cannot be left in the oven. A candy thermometer records higher temperatures than meat or instant-read thermometers allowing it to be used for candy syrups. Deep-fat thermometers measure even higher temperatures. *See Candy, page 99, and Frying, page 225, for additional information.*

Timer: Many ranges, ovens and microwave ovens have built-in timers. Free-standing timers are also available. These come in a range of prices; some are portable and some need a source of electricity. A few high-tech timers can be programmed to time several items simultaneously.

Tongs: Tongs are indispensable for turning foods, especially meat that is best not pierced with a fork. Two basic types are available—heavy wire tongs that are joined like scissors and lightweight metal tongs that have a spring at the end.

Turner: Turners are ideal for turning and lifting foods. They may be made of metal or plastic. Choose sturdy metal ones for most uses. A wide surface is often useful. Choose plastic turners for nonstick surfaces. A wedge-shaped turner is a good choice for serving pie and cake.

Vegetable Peeler: A swivel-bladed vegetable peeler is designed to remove a paper-thin layer, such as the peel, from fruits and vegetables. Used with long, sweeping motions down the length of the food, it is an efficient alternative to the paring knife for such foods as carrots, potatoes and apples.

Wire Whisk: Made of wires that loop to form a bulbous shape, wire whisks are designed to aerate and mix. Select whisks with sturdy wires and handles that are easy to grip.

Zester: A zester has several tiny sharp holes on a curved head attached to a short handle. The purpose of this tool is to remove fine shreds of citrus peel, called zest.

TORTE

Torte, the German word for cake, refers to a rich cakelike dessert made with butter, sugar, eggs and little or no flour. Bread crumbs or ground nuts are often substituted for most or all of the flour. Tortes are often made in bakeware with removable bottoms, such as spingform pans, for easier removal. Tortes come in single-layered or multilayered forms. Tortes made of multiple layers are filled with jam or whipped cream.

🦅

Linzer Torte

  ½ **cup toasted whole almonds***
1½ **cups all-purpose flour**
  1 **teaspoon ground cinnamon**
  ¼ **teaspoon salt**
  ¾ **cup granulated sugar**
  ½ **cup butter or margarine**
  ½ **teaspoon grated lemon peel**
  1 **egg**
  ¾ **cup raspberry or apricot jam**
    Powdered sugar

*To toast almonds, spread in single layer on baking sheet. Bake in a preheated 350°F oven 8 to 10 minutes or until golden brown, stirring frequently. Remove from sheet to cool.

1. Place almonds in food processor. Process using on/off pulsing action until almonds are finely ground. Measure enough to make ½ cup.

2. Preheat oven to 375°F.

3. Combine flour, almonds, cinnamon and salt in medium bowl.

4. Beat granulated sugar, butter and lemon peel in large bowl using electric mixer at medium speed about 15 minutes or until light and fluffy, scraping down side of bowl once. Beat in egg until well blended.

5. Beat in flour mixture at low speed until well blended. Spoon ⅔ of dough onto bottom of 10-inch tart pan with removable bottom. Pat dough evenly over bottom and up side of pan. Spread jam over dough.

6. Roll remaining ⅓ of dough on lightly floured surface with lightly floured rolling pin into 10×6-inch square. Cut dough into 10×½-inch strips using a knife or pizza wheel.

7. Arrange 4 to 5 strips of dough lengthwise across jam. Arrange another 4 to 5 strips of dough crosswise across top. Press ends of dough strips into edge of crust.

8. Bake 25 to 35 minutes or until crust is golden brown. Cool completely in pan on wire rack. Remove torte from pan. Cut into wedges. Sprinkle with powdered sugar.   *Makes 12 servings*

Special Interest

One of the most well-known tortes is the classic Sacher torte, a rich dessert of chocolate cake layers spread with apricot jam and topped with chocolate glaze. It was created in Vienna by Franz Sacher in the 1830's.

Lemon Cream Almond Torte

½ **cup sifted cake flour**
½ **teaspoon baking powder**
⅛ **teaspoon salt**
½ **cup butter or margarine, softened**
¾ **cup granulated sugar**
1 **cup BLUE DIAMOND®
   Blanched Almond Paste**
3 **eggs**
1 **tablespoon brandy**
1 **teaspoon vanilla**
⅛ **teaspoon almond extract
   Lemon Cream (recipe follows)
   Powdered sugar (optional)
   Lemon slices (optional)**

Preheat oven to 325°F. In small bowl, combine flour, baking powder and salt. In large bowl, beat butter and granulated sugar until creamy. Add almond paste; beat until smooth. Add eggs, 1 at a time, beating after each addition. Mix in brandy, vanilla and almond extract. Stir in flour mixture until well blended. Pour into greased and floured 8-inch round pan.

Bake 45 minutes or until wooden toothpick inserted into center comes out clean. Let cool in pan on wire rack 15 minutes. Loosen edge; remove from pan. Cool completely on wire rack.

Meanwhile, prepare Lemon Cream. Slice cake horizontally in half. Spread Lemon Cream over cut side of bottom layer; top with second layer, cut side down. Refrigerate until serving time. To serve, if desired, place lace doily over top of torte. Sift powdered sugar evenly over top; carefully remove doily. Garnish with lemon slices, if desired.   *Makes 8 to 10 servings*

Lemon Cream

3 **egg yolks**
⅓ **cup granulated sugar**
2 **tablespoons all-purpose flour**
1 **cup milk, scalded**
2 **teaspoons grated lemon peel**
2 **tablespoons lemon juice**
½ **teaspoon vanilla**

In medium saucepan, beat egg yolks and sugar until thick and pale yellow. Stir in flour. Gradually pour in hot milk, stirring constantly. Stir in lemon peel. Bring mixture to a boil over medium heat, stirring constantly. Boil and stir 1 minute. Remove from heat; add lemon juice and vanilla. Cool completely, stirring occasionally.

TORTILLA

A tortilla is a round, thin unleavened Mexican bread that is baked on a griddle. It can be made of either corn or wheat flour, water and a little salt. Traditionally the dough is shaped and flattened by hand and cooked on both sides on a hot griddle until dry and flecked with brown. Tortillas are a staple of Mexican and Tex-Mex cooking. They can be eaten plain or used as a base for tacos, burritos, enchiladas and many other dishes. Both corn and flour tortillas are available in supermarkets and Mexican markets either shelf stable or refrigerated.

☙

Sweet Tortilla Chips

1 **tablespoon margarine**
1½ **teaspoons water**
¼ **cup firmly packed brown sugar**
6 **(6- to 7-inch) flour tortillas**

1. Place margarine and water in small microwave-safe bowl. Microwave at HIGH (100% power) 15 seconds or until margarine melts. Stir in brown sugar until smooth. Spread equal amount of sugar mixture over top of each tortilla, leaving ½-inch border. Cut each tortilla into 8 wedges. Arrange ½ of wedges in single layer on large baking sheet (edges may overlap slightly).

2. Bake 7 to 9 minutes until sugar melts and chips feel firm. (Do not let tortillas brown.) Remove chips to plate; cool completely. Repeat with remaining wedges. Store tightly covered at room temperature.

Makes 6 appetizer servings

Cinnamon-Sugar Chips: Add 1½ teaspoons cinnamon to sugar mixture before spreading over tortillas. Cut and bake as directed.

Fiery Sweet Chips: Prepare chips as directed. Lightly sprinkle wedges with ground red pepper before baking.

Baked Tortilla Chips

> **6 (7- to 8-inch) flour tortillas *or*
> 6 (6-inch) corn tortillas
> Paprika, chili powder or
> cayenne pepper**

1. Preheat oven to 375°F.

2. Sprinkle 1 tortilla with water to dampen; shake off excess water. Lightly sprinkle top with paprika. Repeat with remaining tortillas. Cut each flour tortilla into 8 wedges or each corn tortilla into 6 wedges. Arrange ½ of wedges in single layer on large baking sheet (edges may overlap slightly).

3. Bake 4 minutes. Rotate sheet. Bake 2 to 4 minutes more until chips are firm and flour tortillas are spotted with light golden color. (Do not let corn tortillas brown.) Remove chips to plate; cool completely. Repeat with remaining wedges. Store tightly covered at room temperature.

Makes 6 appetizer servings

Parmesan Chips: Prepare Baked Tortilla Chips as directed, omitting paprika. Sprinkle each tortilla with 1 tablespoon grated Parmesan cheese and ¼ teaspoon dried oregano leaves. Cut and bake as directed.

Baked Tortilla Chips

TORTONI

Tortoni is a rich frozen Italian dessert made of sweetened whipped cream that is flavored with rum or sherry and mixed or topped with chopped almonds, chopped maraschino cherries or crumbled amaretti cookies (crisp Italian macaroons). When the dessert is served in individual paper cups, it is often called biscuit tortoni. In America, ice cream is sometimes substituted for the whipped cream.

☙

Tortoni

¾ **cup amaretti cookie crumbs**
¾ **cup graham cracker crumbs**
1 **tablespoon sugar**
¼ **cup Prune Purée (page 317) or
   prepared prune butter**
1 **quart fat free vanilla ice cream
   or nonfat frozen yogurt**
½ **cup drained maraschino
   cherries, halved**
¼ **cup grated or coarsely chopped
   semisweet chocolate**

1. Preheat oven to 350°F.

2. In medium bowl, combine crumbs and sugar. With pastry blender, cut in Prune Purée until well blended. Arrange in even layer on baking sheet. Bake in center of oven 10 minutes, stirring once after 5 minutes; cool.

3. Line twelve 2¾-inch (⅓-cup capacity) muffin cups with paper or foil cupcake liners. Spoon 1 tablespoon crumb mixture into each cup. In large bowl, soften ice cream slightly. Stir in cherries and chocolate. Spoon into muffin cups, dividing equally. Top with remaining crumb mixture, dividing equally and patting down lightly. Cover; freeze at least 2 hours. Remove from freezer 5 minutes before serving.

Makes 12 servings

Favorite recipe from **California Prune Board**

TOSTADA

A tostada is a Mexican dish composed of a crisp, flat fried tortilla covered with various toppings. Corn tortillas are commonly used and toppings include refried beans, seasoned meat or poultry mixtures, shredded lettuce, chopped tomatoes and shredded cheese. Tostadas are usually served as entrées.

🌿

Chicken Tostadas

Fresh Tomato Salsa (page 444)
**Lime-Cumin Dressing (recipe
   follows)**
Vegetable oil
4 **(10-inch) flour tortillas *or*
   8 (6-inch) corn tortillas**
2 **cups canned refried beans**
4 **cups shredded iceberg lettuce**
3 **cups shredded cooked chicken**
1 **small carrot, shredded**
1 **cup (4 ounces) shredded mild
   Cheddar cheese, divided**
1 **large ripe avocado, pared,
   pitted, sliced**
½ **cup sour cream (optional)**

1. Prepare Fresh Tomato Salsa and Lime-Cumin Dressing. Set aside.

2. Preheat oven to 250°F. Heat 1 inch oil in deep heavy large skillet over medium-high heat until oil reaches 375°F on deep-fry thermometer; adjust heat to maintain temperature. Line baking sheet with paper towels.

Chicken Tostada

3. Fry tortillas, 1 at a time, in oil 1 minute or until crisp and light brown, turning once. Drain on paper towels. Keep warm in oven on prepared baking sheet.

4. Heat refried beans in medium saucepan. Combine lettuce, chicken and carrot in large bowl. Add reserved dressing; toss to mix. Place 1 flour or 2 corn tortillas on each serving plate. Spread warm beans to within ½ inch of edge of each tortilla. Sprinkle ¾ cup cheese evenly over tostadas. Top with chicken mixture and avocado. Garnish with remaining ¼ cup cheese. Serve with Fresh Tomato Salsa and sour cream, if desired. *Makes 4 servings*

Lime-Cumin Dressing

> 2 tablespoons fresh lime juice
> ¼ teaspoon grated lime peel
> ¼ teaspoon salt
> ¼ teaspoon ground cumin
> ¼ cup vegetable oil

Combine juice, lime peel, salt and cumin in small bowl. Whisk in oil until thoroughly blended. Cover; store in refrigerator.
Makes about ⅓ cup dressing

TRIFLE

Trifle is a layered dessert of English origin that has been on American menus since colonial times. A trifle begins with a layer of ladyfingers or sponge cake pieces that are sprinkled with sherry or another liquor, spread with jam and topped with custard. The layers are usually repeated. It is refrigerated for several hours before serving to allow the flavors to blend. Trifle is generally served in a glass bowl to display the layers. Just before serving, it is topped with whipped cream and garnished with fruit or nuts.

Chocolate Raspberry Trifle

Chocolate Custard
> 3 tablespoons cornstarch
> 1 tablespoon granulated sugar
> ⅛ teaspoon salt
> 2 cups milk
> 3 egg yolks
> 2 cups (11½-ounce package) NESTLÉ® TOLL HOUSE® Milk Chocolate Morsels, divided

Trifle
> 1 cup heavy whipping cream
> 1 tablespoon granulated sugar
> 1 (10¾-ounce) frozen pound cake, thawed
> 2 tablespoons crème de cacao, divided
> ¼ cup seedless raspberry jam

For Chocolate Custard: COMBINE cornstarch, sugar and salt in medium, heavy saucepan. Gradually add milk. Whisk in egg yolks until smooth. Cook over medium heat, stirring constantly, until mixture comes to a boil; boil for 1 minute. Remove from heat. Add *1½ cups* morsels; stir until melted and smooth. Press plastic wrap on surface; chill.

For Trifle: BEAT cream and sugar until stiff peaks form. Cut cake into ½-inch-thick slices. Cut 1 slice into thin strips; reserve for top. In 2-quart straight-sided bowl, layer ½ cake slices, ½ crème de cacao, ½ jam, ½ chocolate custard and ½ whipped cream. Repeat cake, crème de cacao, jam and chocolate custard layers. Top with reserved cake strips, ¼ cup morsels, remaining whipped cream and *remaining* morsels. Chill.
Makes 8 to 10 servings

TRUFFLE

A truffle is an edible fungus that grows underground near the roots of oak trees, especially in France and Italy. Although unattractive, it is much loved for its fragrance and delicate earthy flavor. There are several varieties, but the black truffle is the most prized. Truffles must be hunted by dogs or pigs that are trained to sniff them out. Because truffles cannot be cultivated and the harvesting process is time consuming, it is one of the world's most expensive foods.

Chocolate truffles, so named because of their similarity in appearance to truffles, are a rich, elegant uncooked French candy. They are made of chocolate, butter, cream and sugar. They are flavored with liqueur, coffee, nuts or fruit. The mixture is formed into balls and rolled in unsweetened cocoa, powdered sugar or chopped nuts.

Tip

Avoid cooking turnips or turnip greens in aluminum or iron pans; the metal may darken the flesh of the turnips or impart a metallic flavor to the greens.

TURNIP

Turnips were probably one of the vegetables eaten by primitive humans. Since they are easy to cultivate, they have been a mainstay in human diets throughout history, especially during lean times. During affluent periods, turnips were relegated to livestock feed. Today turnips are more popular in the South than in other parts of the United States. They are root vegetables, which grow partially above the ground. In fact, the purple tops result from exposure to sunlight.

Uses: Turnips may be eaten raw. They are usually shredded for use in coleslaw or sliced for crudités.

• The strong flavor of turnips is mellowed by cooking. They may be roasted, baked, and added to soups, stews and casseroles.

• A popular way to serve turnips is to mash or purée them and serve them alone or with potatoes.

• Cooked turnip greens are a popular southern food. Raw turnip greens, when young and tender, may be used in salads.

Varieties: The most common variety of turnip found in supermarkets has a creamy white skin that changes to purple, lavender or green at the top.

Availability: Turnips are available year-round, but the supply peaks from October to February.

Buying Tips: Choose turnips that are about 2 inches in diameter. Larger turnips have a coarse texture and less sweet flavor. Select ones that are firm and heavy for their size with a smooth unblemished skin. Avoid turnips that are soft, shriveled and have many root hairs. If greens are attached, they should be fresh, crisp and a bright color.

Yield: 1 pound turnips without tops = about 2½ cups chopped.

Storage: If turnips are purchased with tops attached, remove and store them separately. Store turnips in a plastic bag in the refrigerator for up to two weeks. Store turnip greens, unwashed, in the refrigerator in a plastic bag for several days.

Basic Preparation: Wash turnips under cold running water, scrubbing them with a brush, if necessary, to remove soil. Trim off the top and roots. Peel turnips with a paring knife. (Very young, fresh turnips may not need peeling.) Slice, cube or cut them into strips. In order to retain their mild flavor, avoid overcooking turnips.

TURNOVER

A turnover is a triangular-shaped filled pastry made with pastry dough. Sometimes turnovers are in the shape of a half moon. Fillings may be sweet or savory. Turnovers are usually baked. They are served as appetizers, entrées or desserts.

Savory Sausage Mushroom Turnovers

Savory Sausage Mushroom Turnovers

  1 (12-ounce) package frozen bulk
      pork sausage, thawed
  1 cup chopped mushrooms
  $\frac{1}{3}$ cup chopped onion
  $\frac{1}{2}$ cup shredded Swiss cheese
      (2 ounces)
  $\frac{1}{3}$ cup GREY POUPON®
      COUNTRY DIJON® Mustard
  2 tablespoons diced red bell
      pepper
  $\frac{1}{2}$ teaspoon dried thyme leaves
  2 (8-ounce) packages refrigerated
      crescent dinner roll dough
  1 egg, beaten
    Sesame or poppy seed

In large skillet, over medium heat, cook sausage, mushrooms and onion until sausage is cooked, stirring occasionally to break up sausage. Remove from heat. Stir in cheese, mustard, bell pepper and thyme.

Separate each package of dough into 4 rectangles; press perforations together to seal. On floured surface, roll each rectangle into 6-inch square. Cut each square into quarters, making 32 squares total. Place 1 scant tablespoon sausage mixture on each square; fold dough over filling to form triangle. Press edges with fork to seal. Place on greased baking sheets.

Brush triangles with beaten egg and sprinkle with sesame or poppy seed. Bake at 375°F for 10 to 12 minutes or until golden brown. Serve warm.

Makes 32 appetizers

Golden Apple Turnovers

  2 cups diced WASHINGTON
      Golden Delicious apples
      (about 2 apples)
  $\frac{1}{4}$ cup raisins
  2 tablespoons chopped walnuts
  2 teaspoons grated orange peel
  $\frac{1}{3}$ cup granulated sugar
    Pastry for 2-crust 9-inch pie
    Orange Glaze (recipe follows)

Preheat oven to 400°F. Combine apples, raisins, nuts, 2 teaspoons orange peel and sugar. Roll pastry to $\frac{1}{8}$-inch thickness; cut into 10 to 12 ($4\frac{1}{2}$-inch) circles. Divide apple mixture evenly among pastry circles. Fold circles in half; seal edges with fork. Cut steam vents into tops of pastry. Bake 25 to 30 minutes or until golden. Drizzle with Orange Glaze while still warm.

Makes 10 to 12 turnovers

Orange Glaze: Combine $\frac{3}{4}$ cup powdered sugar, 1 tablespoon orange juice, $\frac{1}{4}$ teaspoon grated orange peel and dash salt.

*Favorite recipe from **Washington Apple Commission***

UPSIDE-DOWN CAKE

An upside-down cake is a single-layered cake that is served upside down. It is prepared by coating the bottom of a cake pan with a mixture of butter and brown sugar and then arranging pieces of fruit in a decorative pattern. Cake batter is poured over the fruit. After baking, the cake is inverted onto a serving plate so that the fruit and caramelized sugar mixture provide a topping for the cake. Pineapple and peach upside-down cakes are the most common types.

🐝

Ginger Pear Upside-Down Cake

Ginger Pear Upside-Down Cake

8 tablespoons (½ cup) softened MAZOLA® Margarine, divided
¾ cup KARO® Dark Corn Syrup, divided
½ cup *plus* 2 tablespoons packed brown sugar, divided
1 can (16 ounces) pear halves, well drained*
½ cup walnut halves
1⅓ cups all-purpose flour
1 teaspoon ground ginger
½ teaspoon baking soda
½ teaspoon ground cinnamon
¼ teaspoon salt
1 egg
½ cup buttermilk

*Well-drained canned peaches, pineapple or apricots are excellent substitutes for pears.

Preheat oven to 350°F. In small saucepan melt 2 tablespoons margarine. Stir in ¼ cup corn syrup and 2 tablespoons brown sugar. Spread evenly in ungreased 9-inch round cake pan. Arrange pears and walnuts, rounded sides down, over corn syrup mixture. In medium bowl combine flour, ginger, baking soda, cinnamon and salt. In large bowl with mixer at medium speed, beat remaining 6 tablespoons margarine, ½ cup corn syrup and ½ cup brown sugar. Add egg and buttermilk; beat until well blended. Add flour mixture; beat 1 minute or until thoroughly combined. Carefully spoon batter over pears and walnuts, smoothing top. Bake 55 to 60 minutes or until toothpick inserted into center comes out clean. Immediately run spatula around edge of pan and invert cake onto serving plate.

Makes 8 servings

Prep time: 25 minutes
Bake time: 60 minutes

VICHYSSOISE

A cold creamy potato and leek soup, vichyssoise is often erroneously thought to be of French origin. The soup was actually developed by Louis Diat, chef at the Ritz-Carlton Hotel in New York, sometime between 1910 and 1920. Potatoes and leeks are cooked in chicken broth or stock, and the mixture is puréed until smooth. Cream is added and then the soup is chilled.

VINAIGRETTE

A vinaigrette is a mixture of oil, vinegar and sometimes seasonings or fresh herbs. It is used primarily as a dressing for salads. It may also be served over chilled meat, fish or vegetables or used as a marinade. Considered one of the classic sauces of French cuisine, a traditional vinaigrette is made with three parts oil to one part vinegar.

Herbed Vinaigrette

  ⅓ cup olive oil
  2 tablespoons minced fresh basil
  2 tablespoons minced fresh
     oregano
  2 tablespoons fresh lemon juice
  1 tablespoon balsamic vinegar
  1 teaspoon Dijon mustard
  ½ teaspoon ground black pepper

Whisk all ingredients in small bowl until blended. Serve with favorite mixed greens.

Makes about ⅔ cup dressing

Lime Vinaigrette

  3 tablespoons finely chopped
     fresh cilantro or parsley
  3 tablespoons plain low-fat yogurt
  3 tablespoons orange juice
  2 tablespoons fresh lime juice
  2 tablespoons white wine vinegar
  2 tablespoons water
  1 tablespoon sugar
  1 teaspoon chili powder
  ½ teaspoon onion powder
  ½ teaspoon ground cumin

In small jar with tight-fitting lid, place all ingredients. Cover; shake well. Refrigerate until ready to use. Shake before serving. Serve with seafood or chicken salads.

Makes about ¾ cup dressing

VINEGAR

The word vinegar is a derivation of the French term vin aigre, which means "sour wine." It is produced by adding bacteria to alcohol, changing it to acetic acid in a controlled fermentation process. The alcohol can be made from grapes (red or white wine vinegar), grain (distilled white vinegar), apples (cider vinegar) or rice (rice wine vinegar). Balsamic vinegar is made from sweet white grapes and aged in barrels for years to develop the typical brown color and mellow sweet-and-sour flavor. Wine vinegars and balsamic vinegars contain sulfites to control unwanted bacterial activity. There has been an explosion of interest in vinegars and many types are available in supermarkets and specialty markets. Vinegar is an ingredient in salad dressings, marinades and sweet-and-sour sauces. Vinegar may also be used as a condiment and for preserving and pickling.

Tip

Vinegar should be stored in a cool, dark place. Opened vinegar will keep for six months. Unopened vinegar will keep indefinitely.

Making Herbal Vinegar: Herb-flavored vinegars are very easy to make. Always start with a pleasant-tasting wine vinegar, since the original flavor can only be altered, not improved, by the addition of herbs. For attractive containers to hold the finished herbal vinegar, select bottles that have appealing shapes and colors.

To make herbal vinegar, wash and sterilize a clean, odor-free glass jar. (Do not use the bottles that will hold the finished vinegar.) Sterilize the jar by submerging it in a Dutch oven of boiling water for 15 minutes. Remove it with tongs; let it stand until cool.

Chop fresh, clean herbs that have been thoroughly dried. Pack them loosely in the glass jar, about one-third to one-half full. Fill the jar with simmering vinegar. Cap the jar with an acid-resistant cover and store it at room temperature. Stir or shake it once each day for two weeks.

Remove the herbs by pouring the mixture through a cheesecloth-lined sieve. Taste the vinegar. If it is too strong, dilute it with plain vinegar.

Sterilize the bottles you have selected for the finished vinegar. When they are cool, fill them with the herbal vinegar. Add fresh sprigs of each of the herbs used, if you wish, for decoration. Label and date the vinegar. Herbal vinegar may be stored in the refrigerator for up to six months.

Pouring vinegar over herbs.

Straining vinegar to remove herbs.

Adding fresh herb sprigs to vinegar.

Basil Garlic Vinegar

½ cup coarsely chopped fresh
    basil leaves
2 cloves garlic, peeled and split
1 bottle (16 ounces) HEINZ® Wine
    or Distilled White Vinegar
Fresh basil leaves, for garnish

Place chopped basil and garlic in sterilized pint jar. Heat vinegar to *just* below boiling point. Fill jar with vinegar and seal tightly. Allow to stand 3 to 4 weeks. Strain vinegar, discarding basil and garlic. Pour vinegar into clean sterilized jar, adding basil leaves for garnish, if desired. Seal tightly. Use in dressings for rice, pasta, salads or in mayonnaise.

Makes 2 cups vinegar

WAFFLE

Waffles are crisp quick breads with a unique honeycomb design of pockets and ridges. They require an appliance known as a waffle iron to make them. Waffles are prepared by pouring a batter similar to that used for pancakes onto one side of a very hot waffle iron and closing the second side over the batter. The waffle batter should be allowed to cook several minutes until crisp and brown. The cooking surfaces of a waffle iron impress the design into the waffle batter. Most often eaten for breakfast topped with syrup, waffles may also be served as dessert or topped with savory mixtures for an entrée. Dessert waffles are usually topped with ice cream, a sweet sauce or fruit. Entrée waffles are topped with creamy mixtures of meat and vegetables, such as creamed chicken and mushrooms. Belgian waffles have deeper, larger pockets and ridges; they require a Belgian waffle iron to make them. They are often topped with strawberries and whipped cream.

❦

Waffles

2¼ cups all-purpose flour
2 tablespoons sugar
1 tablespoon baking powder
½ teaspoon salt
2 eggs
2 cups milk
¼ cup vegetable oil
Crab apples and fresh mint
    sprigs (optional)

1. Lightly grease and preheat waffle iron.

2. Combine flour, sugar, baking powder and salt in large bowl. Beat eggs in medium bowl with wire whisk. Whisk in milk and oil until mixture is thoroughly blended. Stir egg mixture into flour mixture just until moistened.

3. For each waffle, pour about ¾ cup batter into waffle iron. Close lid and bake until steaming stops.* Transfer waffles to serving plate. Garnish with apples and mint, if desired.

Makes about 6 round waffles

Check manufacturer's directions for recommended amount of batter and baking time.

WATER BATH

The term water bath refers to the technique of placing a bowl or pan containing food in another pan filled with hot water. Water baths are used for several purposes: keeping food hot, melting food, such as chocolate and butter, and gently cooking or baking food. In recipes, the term water bath is used most often to refer to the method of baking delicate foods (such as custards, cheesecakes and bread puddings) with gentle, even heat in a pan of shallow hot water.

This method does not necessarily require a special piece of equipment. A water bath may be done with two baking pans of different sizes, one pan to hold the food and a second larger pan for the hot water. A double boiler is a type of water bath and is used on the rangetop to melt foods or to cook delicate foods, such as stirred custards and hollandaise sauce.

☙

Waffle

Chicken with Mandarin Orange and Water Chestnut Sauce

WATER CHESTNUT

Water chestnuts are the edible fruit of an aquatic plant native to Southeast Asia. They are encased in a black skin that must be peeled away. The flesh is crisp, white and slightly sweet. Since they are quite starchy, water chestnuts are used as a vegetable in Asian cooking and also ground to make water chestnut powder (or flour), which is a thickener similar to cornstarch. Fresh water chestnuts can usually be found in Asian markets, but the bulk of the American supply comes canned either whole or sliced. Typically used as an ingredient in stir-fries, water chestnuts are also added to salads, pilafs and entrées for their crunchiness.

❦

Chicken with Mandarin Orange and Water Chestnut Sauce

2 teaspoons cornstarch
¼ cup water
1 can (11 ounces) mandarin oranges, drained
1 can (8 ounces) sliced water chestnuts, drained
4 teaspoons packed brown sugar
2 tablespoons white vinegar
1 tablespoon soy sauce
1½ cups chicken broth or stock
4 split chicken breast halves, skinned and boned

1. Dissolve cornstarch in water in small saucepan. Stir in mandarin oranges, water chestnuts, brown sugar, vinegar and soy sauce. Cook 4 to 5 minutes until liquid is clear and mixture thickens, stirring occasionally. Remove from heat.

2. Bring broth to a boil over high heat in large skillet. Pound chicken breasts with meat mallet to ½-inch thickness. Place chicken in broth; reduce heat to medium-low. Cover; simmer 8 to 10 minutes until chicken is no longer pink in center. Remove chicken to serving platter; discard poaching liquid. Heat sauce if needed; spoon over chicken. Serve immediately.
Makes 4 servings

*Favorite recipe from **The Sugar Association, Inc.***

WATERCRESS

Watercress, sometimes referred to simply as "cress," has small, crisp dark green leaves and a sharp peppery flavor. Grown in the shaded areas of streams, watercress can be found in the wild. The supermarket supply comes from cultivated sources. Watercress can be added to salads, dips and sandwich fillings. It is also the basis for watercress soup.

❦

Availability: Watercress is available year-round with supplies peaking in the spring. It can be found in small bunches in most large supermarkets.

Buying Tips: Choose watercress with crisp-looking dark green leaves. Look for stems with lots of leaves. Smaller leaves will have a milder flavor. Avoid yellow, limp or wilted leaves.

Storage: Watercress should be refrigerated with its stems in a glass of water and covered with a plastic bag. It will last for up to five days.

Basic Preparation: The stems as well as the leaves of watercress are edible. Remove and discard any yellow leaves or thick stems. Wash watercress under cold running water and shake it dry before using.

Citrus Salad with Bibb Lettuce, Watercress and Balsamic Dressing

> 1 medium pink grapefruit, peeled, white pith removed and sectioned
> 2 large oranges, peeled, white pith removed and sectioned
> 2 tangerines, peeled and sectioned
> 1 bunch watercress, rinsed and patted dry
> 3 tablespoons orange juice
> 1 tablespoon balsamic vinegar
> ¼ teaspoon salt
> 1 tablespoon canola or vegetable oil
> 1 large head Bibb lettuce, separated, rinsed and patted dry
> Peel of 1 orange, cut into julienne strips

1. Combine grapefruit, oranges, tangerines and watercress in medium bowl. Combine orange juice, vinegar and salt in small bowl. Add oil; whisk dressing until combined. Pour over fruit and watercress; gently toss to combine.

2. Line 4 serving plates with lettuce. Divide fruit mixture among plates. Garnish each with orange peel.
Makes 4 servings

Favorite recipe from **Florida Department of Citrus**

Citrus Salad with Bibb Lettuce, Watercress and Balsamic Dressing

WHIP, TO

To whip refers to the technique of beating ingredients, such as egg whites and whipping cream, with a wire whisk or electric mixer in order to incorporate air and increase their volume. This results in a light, fluffy texture.

❧

WHISK, TO

Whisking is the technique of stirring, beating or whipping foods with a wire whisk. If you do not have a whisk, you can use a wooden spoon if the purpose is to blend ingredients. For whipping foods, an electric mixer can be used instead.

❧

WILD RICE

Wild rice was called rice by early explorers because they found it growing in water, but it is not really rice. It is actually the seed of a marsh grass. This long, slender grain, dark to light brown in color, is the only cereal grain native to North America. It has a chewy texture and nutty, earthy flavor. Wild rice grows wild in the lakes of Minnesota, where it is harvested by local Indians, and is also commercially cultivated in California. It can be ground into flour and used in combination with white flour to make bread, pancakes, muffins and baked goods.

❧

Artichoke Wild Rice Salad

Basic Preparation: Wild rice should be thoroughly rinsed before cooking to remove any debris remaining after processing. To rinse, place raw rice in a bowl with cold water, stir and allow it to sit until the debris floats to the surface. Remove the debris and drain. Wild rice requires longer cooking than other rices. Avoid overcooking, because it will lose its characteristic chewy texture.

To make 3 cups of wild rice, bring 2½ cups water to a boil in a medium saucepan over medium-high heat. Add 1 cup rinsed and drained wild rice and ½ teaspoon salt. Return water to a boil. Reduce heat to low. Cover and cook for 40 to 45 minutes until all the water is absorbed and the rice is tender.

Artichoke Wild Rice Salad

1 jar (6 ounces) marinated
    artichoke hearts, undrained
2 cups cooked wild rice
1 cup frozen peas, thawed
1 can (8 ounces) sliced water
    chestnuts, drained
1 cup (4 ounces) shredded
    mozzarella cheese (optional)
1 jar (2 ounces) diced pimiento,
    drained
2 tablespoons canola oil
1 tablespoon balsamic vinegar
½ teaspoon dried tarragon leaves
½ teaspoon Dijon mustard
2 to 3 drops hot pepper sauce

1. Drain artichokes, reserving 2 tablespoons liquid.

2. Combine artichokes, rice, peas, water chestnuts, cheese and pimiento in large bowl. Combine oil, reserved liquid from artichokes, vinegar, tarragon, mustard and hot pepper sauce in small bowl; pour over rice mixture and toss. Refrigerate 4 hours or overnight to allow flavors to blend. Serve cold.   *Makes 6 to 8 servings*

Favorite recipe from **Minnesota Cultivated Wild Rice Council**

Orange Wild Rice

¾ cup wild rice, rinsed well
1 small onion, chopped
2 tablespoons margarine
    Juice of 1 medium orange *plus*
      chicken broth to equal
      1¼ cups
    Finely grated peel of 1 small
      orange
½ teaspoon LAWRY'S® Seasoned
    Pepper
¼ teaspoon LAWRY'S® Garlic
    Powder with Parsley
1 package (10 ounces) frozen
    peas, thawed
⅓ cup chopped pecans
    Mandarin orange sections
    (garnish)

In large saucepan, sauté rice and onion in margarine, stirring frequently. Add combined orange juice and broth, orange peel, Seasoned Pepper and Garlic Powder with Parsley. Bring to a boil; reduce heat. Cover; simmer 35 minutes or until liquid is almost absorbed. Stir in peas and pecans; simmer 3 to 5 minutes longer. Garnish with mandarin orange sections.
    Makes 4 to 6 side-dish servings

Presentation: Serve with roast pork.

Tip

Because wild rice is expensive, combine it with white or brown rice. Cook the rices separately, since they have different cooking times, and combine them after cooking.

WINE

Wine, which is grape juice that has been fermented and aged in a painstaking process, is at its best when enjoyed with food. Sometimes this simple fact is forgotten among the endless array of wines and the complex set of rules for serving them. With a little knowledge and some experimentation, you can gain the confidence needed to serve wine with meals.

Wine Terms:
Fortified wines are wines that have brandy or other alcohol added to them for the purpose of increasing their alcoholic content. Examples include sherry, Madeira, marsala and port. Fortified wines are served before or after dinner.

Nonvintage wines are made from the juice of grapes harvested during different years. The label, therefore, does not include a year.

Sparkling wines contain carbon dioxide, which gives them their characteristic bubbly quality. France's Champagne, the most well-known sparkling wine, and Italy's spumante are examples. They are most often served before dinner.

Still wines are nonsparkling wines. They can be further classified by color (white, red and rosé) and by flavor (dry, semisweet and sweet). Dry and semisweet still wines are primarily dinner wines. They are also served before dinner. Sweet wines are served with dessert.

Table wines are usually inexpensive and meant for everyday use. They are generally blends of different varieties of grapes. Table wines may be white, red or rosé.

Varietal wines are made from one kind of grape. Thus they have the characteristic of that grape. Varietals may be vintage or nonvintage wines. Examples include Cabernet Sauvignon, Chardonay, Chenin Blanc, Pinot Noir and Zinfandel.

Vintage wines are made mostly from grapes harvested in the same year. That year appears on the label.

Serving Wine:
The often-heard rule of serving white wine with fish and chicken and red wine with meat certainly has some merit, but there are exceptions and the rule fails to mention meatless dishes. Some fish, such as salmon, pair well with lighter red wines while an assertive white wine can hold its own with some meat. Sweeter wines require careful partnering with food. The sweetest wines are best served after dinner rather than with meals. When pairing a sweet wine with a dessert, the wine should be sweeter than the dessert or the flavor of the wine will be lost.

Listed below are some common pairings of food and wine. Use them as your guidelines when selecting wine to serve with food. Learn about wines by tasting them alone and with different foods. When you dine out, order wine by the glass. Ask waiters for their recommendations. Attend wine tastings at wine shops. When entertaining, select your menu and then the wine. Ask a knowledgeable wine store clerk or friend for guidance. The more you experiment, the more you will learn. Soon you will have a list of good wine and food combinations that you can serve with confidence.

White wine is best served at 50° to 55°F. Place it in the refrigerator for two hours before serving. Store red wine in a cool (65°F) place or chill it for about 15 minutes prior to serving. Red wines often benefit from being opened 10 to 15 minutes before serving; this allows them to "breath." Tradition suggests special glasses for different types of wine. Red wine glasses generally are larger than white wine glasses to allow enough room in the glass for the more aromatic red wines to be swirled. However, many perfectly suitable "all-purpose" wine glasses are sold.

Cooking with Wine:
Wines of all sorts are used in cooking. Special cooking wines available in supermarkets are not recommended because they are often inferior in quality and contain salt. However, there is no need to use fine vintages for cooking. It is not economical. Leftover wine that is no longer good for drinking can be used in cooking. Wine can be omitted in most recipes that call for it, although adjustments in the amount of liquid may be required.

Storing Wine:
Wine should be stored in a cool place with a consistent temperature between 45° and 65°F (55°F is ideal). Store it away from light and vibration. Do not turn or move stored wine. If this preferred way of storing wine is not possible in your home, buy wine only as you need it. To prevent corks from drying out and air from entering bottles, store wine on its side.

Wine loses flavor quickly when exposed to oxygen. Leftover wine should be sealed tightly and stored in the refrigerator for a day or two. Wine stores sell canned gases that can be injected into a partially full bottle of wine that will protect the flavor of wine for slightly longer storage.

> **Tip**
>
> *Fill wine glasses only half full. This allows room for the wine to be swirled thus releasing its aroma, or bouquet.*

PAIRING WINE WITH FOOD

Food	Wine
Asian and spicy foods	Gewürztraminer
Beef, Lamb	Cabernet Sauvignon, Chianti, Merlot, red Bordeaux, Zinfandel
Chicken, Pork, Veal	Beaujolais, Chardonnay, Riesling, white Rhone
Fish, lean	Chardonnay, white Burgundy
Fish, moderate and high fat	Chardonnay, Pinot Noir, Sauvignon Blanc, white Burgundy, white Zinfandel
Pasta with tomato sauce	Zinfandel, Chianti
Pasta with vegetables	Riesling, Sauvignon Blanc, Valpolicella
Shellfish	Chablis, Chardonnay, Mâcon Blanc, Sauvignon Blanc

Tip

Iron and carbon steel woks need to be protected from rusting by a process called seasoning, which is done when woks are new. Follow the manufacturer's directions for seasoning and caring for seasoned woks.

Coq au Vin

1 pint pearl onions
4 slices thick-cut bacon
1 cup sliced fresh button
    mushrooms
1 tablespoon peanut oil
1 whole frying chicken (3 to
    4 pounds), cut into serving
    pieces
3 tablespoons all-purpose flour
¼ cup tomato paste
1 can (about 14 ounces) chicken
    broth
1 cup dry red wine
1 clove garlic, minced
1 tablespoon fresh thyme leaves
    or 1 teaspoon dried thyme
    leaves
½ teaspoon salt
⅛ teaspoon ground black pepper
    Fresh herb sprigs (optional)

1. To blanch onions, bring 1 quart water to a boil in 2-quart saucepan over high heat. Add onions; boil 2 minutes. Drain onions and plunge into cold water to stop cooking. Cut off stem end of onions; squeeze onions between thumb and forefinger to separate from skins.

Coq au Vin

2. Preheat oven to 350°F.

3. Cut bacon into ½-inch pieces. Cook in ovenproof Dutch oven over medium heat until brown and crispy. Remove bacon with slotted spoon; drain on paper towels.

4. Add onions to bacon drippings; cook 7 minutes or until golden, stirring occasionally. Reduce heat to low. Cover; cook 5 minutes. Remove onions to bowl; set aside.

5. Heat bacon drippings over medium-high heat. Add mushrooms. Cook and stir 3 to 4 minutes until tender. Add mushrooms to onions. Add oil to bacon drippings. Add chicken; cook 5 minutes per side or until browned. Remove chicken from Dutch oven; set aside.

6. Remove all but 2 tablespoons drippings from Dutch oven. Add flour; cook and stir 1 minute. Stir in tomato paste; cook 1 minute. Add broth, wine, garlic, thyme, salt and pepper; bring to a boil. Return chicken, onions, mushrooms and bacon to Dutch oven. Cover; bake in oven 45 minutes to 1 hour until fork can be inserted into chicken with ease and juices run clear, not pink. Garnish with herbs, if desired. Serve immediately.   *Makes 4 servings*

WOK

The wok, the primary cooking vessel of Asia, was developed centuries ago as a result of fuel shortages. Its rounded shape and long sloping side provide an extended cooking surface, which may be heated to very high temperatures with little fuel. The wok is commonly associated with the technique of stir-frying, but it can also be used to braise, deep-fry, roast, simmer, smoke and steam.

Traditionally a wok was made from thin tempered iron and had a rounded bottom for fast, even conduction of heat. In addition to iron, woks are now made of aluminum, stainless steel and carbon steel. Woks with flat bottoms are made for use on smooth-top cooking surfaces. There are electric woks with nonstick finishes and automatic thermostatic controls. The customary side handles made of metal are sometimes replaced with a single long handle made of material that stays cool. Woks range in size from 12 to 24 inches in diameter. The 14-inch wok is a good choice because it can handle most cooking techniques without interfering with other burners on the range.

❧

Herb-Smoked Chicken

   ¼ **cup hoisin sauce**
   2 **tablespoons finely chopped**
       green onion
   1 **tablespoon soy sauce**
   1 **teaspoon sugar**
   1 **teaspoon Chinese five-spice**
       powder
 1½ **teaspoons Oriental sesame oil,**
       divided
   2 **cloves garlic, minced**
   1 **whole frying chicken**
       (3½ pounds)
   ½ **cup uncooked white rice**
   ½ **cup packed brown sugar**
   ¼ **cup dried tarragon leaves**
   3 **bay leaves, crushed**

1. Combine first 5 ingredients, 1 teaspoon oil and garlic in small bowl; set aside.

2. Remove neck and giblets from chicken; save for another use. Rinse chicken and cavity under cold water; pat dry with paper towels. Skewer neck skin to back and bend chicken wings underneath. Fill body cavity with hoisin mixture and close opening with skewers. Tie legs together with string. Place chicken, breast side up, in shallow 9-inch baking dish. Insert meat thermometer into thickest part of thigh not touching bone.

3. Place wire rack in wok. Add water to 1 inch *below* rack. Cover wok; bring water to a boil over high heat. Place dish with chicken on rack. Cover; reduce heat to medium-high. Steam chicken 45 minutes or until meat thermometer registers 180° to 185°F. Add boiling water to wok to keep water at same level, if necessary. Carefully remove dish from wok.

4. Let chicken cool about 20 minutes. Remove rack from wok; discard water. Rinse and dry wok. Line wok with 34-inch-long piece of heavy-duty foil, allowing excess to extend *evenly* above wok edge. Place rice, sugar, tarragon and bay leaves on foil; mix well. Place wire rack over rice mixture. Pour juices from dish into small saucepan. Remove skewers and string from chicken. Drain hoisin mixture from body cavity into same saucepan; set aside juice mixture. Place chicken (without dish) on wire rack in wok. Bring 2 cut edges of foil up over chicken and seal at top, leaving space on top of chicken for smoke to circulate. Fold and crimp foil on each side of chicken to seal and enclose chicken. (Turn on exhaust fan or open window.)

5. Cover wok; heat over medium-high heat about 2 minutes or until wok begins to smoke. Reduce heat to medium-low and smoke chicken 20 minutes or until golden brown.

6. Meanwhile, skim off fat from chicken juice mixture with spoon; discard. Bring to a boil over medium heat; keep warm.

7. Unwrap chicken. Transfer chicken to serving platter. Brush chicken lightly with remaining ½ teaspoon oil. Carve chicken into 2½×1-inch pieces. Serve with warmed juice mixture. Garnish as desired.

Makes 4 to 6 servings

Techniques for Herb-Smoked Chicken

Step 4. *Placing smoking seasonings in wok on foil.*

Step 4. *Sealing foil over chicken.*

WONTON

A wonton is a Chinese filled dumpling made from wonton wrappers filled with a meat, seafood or vegetable mixture. Wonton wrappers, or skins, are thin, soft squares of dough made from flour, eggs and water. The wrappers are sold as squares or circles both refrigerated or frozen. Filled wontons are either fried, boiled or steamed. They are served as appetizers or snacks with various dipping sauces.

Wonton soup is a Chinese specialty in which the wontons are cooked and served in a clear broth. The broth is usually flavored with slivers of green onions and julienned strips of pork or chicken.

🐝

Ginger Wonton Soup

4 ounces lean ground pork
½ cup reduced fat ricotta cheese
1½ teaspoons minced fresh cilantro
½ teaspoon ground black pepper
⅛ teaspoon Chinese five-spice powder
20 fresh or thawed frozen wonton skins
1 teaspoon vegetable oil
⅓ cup chopped red bell pepper
1 teaspoon grated fresh ginger
2 cans (14½ ounces each) low sodium chicken broth
2 teaspoons reduced sodium soy sauce
4 ounces fresh snow peas (Chinese pea pods), stems removed
1 can (8¾ ounces) baby corn, drained, rinsed
2 green onions, thinly sliced

1. For filling, cook pork in small nonstick skillet over medium-high heat 4 minutes or until no longer pink. Cool slightly; stir in cheese, cilantro, black pepper and five-spice powder.

2. Place 1 teaspoon filling in center of each wonton skin. Fold top corner of wonton over filling. Lightly brush remaining corners with water. Fold left and right corners over filling. Tightly roll filled end toward remaining corner in jelly-roll fashion. Moisten edges with water to seal. Cover; set aside.

3. Heat oil in large saucepan. Add bell pepper and ginger; cook 1 minute. Add broth and soy sauce; bring to a boil. Add snow peas, corn and wontons. Reduce heat to medium-low; simmer 4 to 5 minutes until wontons are tender. Sprinkle with green onions. Serve immediately.   *Makes 4 servings*

Ginger Wonton Soup

Easy Wonton Chips

  1 tablespoon low sodium soy sauce
  2 teaspoons peanut or vegetable oil
  ½ teaspoon sugar
  ¼ teaspoon garlic salt
  12 fresh or thawed frozen wonton skins

1. Preheat oven to 375°F.

2. Combine soy sauce, oil, sugar and garlic salt in small bowl; mix well. Cut each wonton skin diagonally in half. Place wonton skins on 15×10-inch jelly-roll pan coated with nonstick cooking spray. Brush soy sauce mixture lightly but evenly over both sides of each wonton skin.

3. Bake 4 to 6 minutes until crisp and lightly browned, turning after 3 minutes. Transfer to cooling rack; cool completely. Store lightly covered at room temperature.

Makes 4 appetizer servings

WORCESTER-SHIRE SAUCE

Worcestershire sauce is a dark, savory sauce developed in India and named after the English town, Worcester, where it was first bottled. Made from a complex and seemingly incompatible mix of ingredients, including anchovies, tamarind paste, molasses, onions, garlic and soy sauce, it is used as a seasoning in sauces, gravies and soups. It also is commonly added to the Bloody Mary cocktail.

☙

Deviled Burgers

Deviled Burgers

  2 slices bread, finely chopped
  ¼ cup finely chopped onion
  ¼ cup ketchup
  1 tablespoon Worcestershire sauce
  2 teaspoons prepared mustard
  2 teaspoons creamy horseradish
  ½ teaspoon garlic powder
  ½ teaspoon chili powder
  1 pound extra-lean ground beef
  6 hamburger buns

1. Preheat broiler.

2. Combine bread, onion, ketchup, Worcestershire, mustard, horseradish, garlic powder and chili powder in large bowl until well blended. Gently blend beef into mixture. *(Do not overwork.)* Shape mixture into 6 (3-inch) patties. Place patties on ungreased broiler pan.

3. Broil burgers 4 inches from heat source 4 minutes per side or to desired doneness. Serve on buns. Garnish as desired.

Makes 6 servings

YAM

YOGURT

A yam is a tropical tuber popular in Central and South America, Africa and Asia. In the United States, the term is used interchangeably, but incorrectly, with sweet potatoes. In fact, they are different and distinct vegetables. To further the confusion, canned and frozen sweet potatoes are often labeled as yams. True yams are seldom grown in the United States and not widely marketed here.

🌿

Uses: Yams may be used in place of sweet potatoes in most recipes.

Varieties: There are more than 150 varieties of yams grown around the world. They can range widely in size from small yams, weighing 6 ounces to yams that are more than 7 feet long, weighing over 100 pounds. The skin color may vary from dark brown to off-white. The texture of the flesh may be moist and tender or coarse, dry and grainy. The color of the flesh ranges from white or yellow to pink or purple.

Availability: Yams are most apt to be found in Latin markets. They may be sold whole or cut into chunks.

Buying Tips: Select firm yams with smooth unblemished skins.

Storage: Yams may be stored in a cool, dark, dry location for up to two weeks. Do not store them in the refrigerator.

Basic Preparation: Yams should be washed under cold running water and scrubbed with a vegetable brush, if necessary, to remove soil. Peel yams and prepare them as you would sweet potatoes.

Yogurt is a creamy, somewhat tart cultured dairy product made by fermenting whole, low-fat or skim milk with a bacterial culture. It has been a staple in the Middle East and Eastern Europe for centuries, but it was not commercially available in the United States until 1940 and did not become popular until the 1970's. Yogurt is available plain, flavored and frozen. Flavored yogurt is available with fruit on the bottom (sundae-style), with fruit blended throughout (Swiss- or French-style) and also without fruit pieces but with added flavors. Frozen yogurt resembles soft-serve ice cream.

Yogurt, popular for its health benefits, is a good source of calcium and protein. The active bacteria used to culture yogurt can be beneficial to the digestive system. Check the package label to know if the cultures are "active," or "living," or if they have been destroyed during heat treatment.

🌿

Fruitful Frozen Yogurt

1 envelope gelatin
¼ cup cold water
1½ cups puréed fresh fruit
1 carton (16 ounces) vanilla low-fat yogurt
¼ to ½ cup sugar

1. Sprinkle gelatin over cold water in small saucepan; let stand 5 minutes to soften. Stir over low heat until gelatin dissolves. Remove from heat. Stir in fruit purée, yogurt and sugar to taste. Pour into 9-inch square pan; freeze until almost firm.

Tip

Plain yogurt can be substituted for its higher-fat cousin, sour cream, in dips, salad dressings and sauces. However, the heat of cooking and baking will destroy the beneficial active bacteria found in some brands.

2. Coarsely chop mixture; spoon into chilled bowl. Beat with electric mixer until smooth. Cover; store in freezer.

Makes 5 servings

*Favorite recipe from **Wisconsin Milk Marketing Board***

Tandoori Chicken Breast Sandwiches with Yogurt Sauce

12 ounces boneless, skinless
    chicken breast halves
    (4 pieces)
1 tablespoon fresh lemon juice
¼ cup plain nonfat yogurt
2 large garlic cloves, minced
1½ teaspoons minced fresh ginger
¼ teaspoon ground cardamom
¼ teaspoon ground red pepper
    Yogurt Sauce (recipe follows)
2 whole wheat pitas, cut into
    halves
½ cup grated carrot
½ cup finely shredded red
    cabbage
½ cup finely chopped red bell
    pepper

1. Lightly slash chicken breast halves 3 or 4 times with sharp knife. Place in medium bowl; sprinkle with juice and toss to coat. Combine yogurt, garlic, ginger, cardamom and ground red pepper in small bowl; add to chicken. Coat all pieces well with marinade. Cover; refrigerate at least 1 hour or overnight.

2. Remove chicken from refrigerator 15 minutes before cooking. Preheat broiler. Prepare Yogurt Sauce; set aside.

3. Line broiler pan with foil. Arrange chicken on foil (do not let pieces touch) and brush with any remaining marinade. Broil 3 inches from heat about 5 to 6 minutes per side or until chicken is no longer pink in center.

4. Place 1 chicken breast half in each pita half with 2 tablespoons each of carrot, cabbage and bell pepper. Drizzle sandwiches with Yogurt Sauce. Garnish as desired.

Makes 4 servings

Yogurt Sauce

½ cup plain nonfat yogurt
2 teaspoons minced red onion
1 teaspoon minced fresh cilantro
¼ teaspoon ground cumin
¼ teaspoon salt
    Dash ground red pepper

Blend all ingredients in small bowl. Cover; refrigerate until ready to use.

Makes about ½ cup sauce

Tandoori Chicken Breast Sandwich with Yogurt Sauce

ZEST

Zest is the colorful, outermost part of the peel of citrus fruit. It is distinguished from the white pith which is bitter. The zest contains rich aromatic oils that are used to add flavor to food. Zest is removed from fruit by one of several methods. It can be grated on a box-shaped grater (page 525) or removed with a tool known as a zester (page 529). The verb zest refers to the technique of removing zest from citrus fruit.

☙

ZUCCHINI

Zucchini is a popular summer squash with a thin edible skin and soft edible seeds. It has a cylindrical shape and a slightly curved, smaller stem end. The skin is light or dark green in color and it sometimes has faint yellow stripes. The off-white flesh is tinged with green. It has a mild, delicate flavor.

Zucchini are grown on vines from flowers that are sometimes eaten. The most common market length for zucchini is 4 to 8 inches long, but they can vary greatly from finger size to almost 2 feet long. The large specimens are usually home grown. Zucchini is also known as Italian squash in the United States or courgettes in both Great Britain and France.

☙

Uses: Zucchini can be eaten raw in salads and as appetizers.

• It is often cooked alone or used as an ingredient in soups, stews, casseroles, vegetable dishes and quick breads. It is also stuffed.

• Zucchini is a major ingredient in Mediterranean dishes, such as ratatouille and moussaka.

Varieties: There are several varieties of zucchini. There are light green and dark green slender vegetables as well as round green globes.

Availability: Zucchini are available all year with their peak season from July to September.

Buying Tips: Choose zucchini that are heavy for their size, firm and well shaped. They should have a bright color and be free of cuts and any soft spots. Small zucchini are more tender because they have been harvested when they were young.

Yield: 1 pound zucchini = 3 medium; $2\frac{1}{2}$ cups cubed.

Storage: Refrigerate zucchini, unwashed, in a perforated plastic bag for up to 5 days.

Basic Preparation: Rinse zucchini under cold running water, scrubbing lightly with a vegetable brush. Trim off both ends with a utility knife. Peeling is not necessary. Cut the zucchini into slices or chunks before cooking.

Since zucchini has such a high water content, it does not require long cooking. Cook zucchini only until it is crisp-tender. It may be boiled, steamed, sautéed or fried. Its mild flavor combines well with many other vegetables, especially tomatoes and green bell peppers.

Double Chocolate Zucchini Muffins

2⅓ cups all-purpose flour
1¼ cups sugar
⅓ cup unsweetened cocoa powder
2 teaspoons baking powder
1½ teaspoons ground cinnamon
1 teaspoon baking soda
½ teaspoon salt
1 cup sour cream
½ cup vegetable oil
2 eggs, beaten
¼ cup milk
1 cup milk chocolate chips
1 cup shredded zucchini

1. Preheat oven to 400°F. Grease 12 (3½-inch) large muffin cups.

2. Combine flour, sugar, cocoa, baking powder, cinnamon, baking soda and salt in large bowl. Combine sour cream, oil, eggs and milk in small bowl until blended; stir into flour mixture just until moistened. Fold in chips and zucchini. Spoon into prepared muffin cups, filling ½ full.

3. Bake 25 to 30 minutes until wooden toothpick inserted into centers comes out clean. Cool in pans on wire racks 5 minutes. Remove from pans. Cool on wire racks. Store tightly covered at room temperature.

Makes 12 jumbo muffins

Zucchini with Pimiento

2 cups thinly sliced zucchini
1 small onion, chopped
1 jar (2 ounces) pimiento, drained, finely chopped
½ teaspoon salt (optional)
½ teaspoon dried oregano leaves
⅛ teaspoon garlic powder
⅛ teaspoon ground red pepper

Microwave Directions: Combine all ingredients in 2-quart microwave-safe casserole; cover. Microwave at HIGH (100% power) 6 to 7 minutes until fork-tender, stirring after 3 minutes. Serve immediately.

Makes 4 side-dish servings

Marinated Summer Salad

4 medium zucchini, diced
1 can (8 ounces) garbanzo beans, drained
½ cup chopped red onion
1 medium tomato, diced
1 can (2¼ ounces) sliced pitted ripe olives, drained
¾ cup LAWRY'S® Herb and Garlic Marinade with Lemon Juice

In large bowl, combine all ingredients; toss lightly. Cover. Refrigerate at least 30 minutes. Serve and garnish as desired.

Makes 4 servings

Presentation: Serve on lettuce-covered platter as a side dish with sandwiches or your favorite chicken recipe.

Tip

To cook vegetables until they are crisp-tender, cook until they have a slight crunch to them. They are tender but not soft.

Zesty Zucchini Chick-Pea Salad

    3 medium zucchini
    ½ teaspoon salt
    5 tablespoons white vinegar
    1 clove garlic, minced
    ¼ teaspoon dried thyme leaves
    ½ cup olive oil
    1 cup canned chick-peas, drained
    ½ cup sliced pitted ripe olives
    3 green onions, minced
    1 canned chipotle chili pepper in
        adobo sauce, drained, seeded,
        minced
    1 ripe avocado
    ⅓ cup crumbled feta *or*
        3 tablespoons grated Romano
        cheese
    Boston lettuce leaves
    Sliced tomato and fresh cilantro
        sprigs (optional)

1. Cut zucchini lengthwise into halves; cut halves crosswise into ¼-inch-thick slices. Place slices in medium bowl; sprinkle with salt. Toss to mix. Spread zucchini on several layers of paper towels. Let stand at room temperature 30 minutes to drain.

2. Combine vinegar, garlic and thyme in large bowl. Gradually whisk in oil until dressing is thoroughly blended. Pat zucchini dry; add to dressing. Add chick-peas, olives and onions; toss lightly to coat. Cover; refrigerate at least 30 minutes or up to 4 hours, stirring occasionally.

3. Stir in chili pepper just before serving. Peel, pit and cut avocado into ½-inch cubes. Add avocado and cheese to salad; toss lightly to mix. Serve salad in lettuce-lined bowl. Garnish with tomato and cilantro, if desired.   *Makes 4 to 6 servings*

Zesty Zucchini Chick-Pea Salad

ZWIEBACK

Zwieback, meaning "twice baked" in German, refers to bread that is baked, sliced and baked again until it is crisp and dry. It may also be called rusk or, in French, biscotte. Zwieback, which is slightly sweet, is easy to digest. For this reason it is often served to very young children and anyone with digestive difficulties.

🍃

ACKNOWLEDGMENTS

**The publisher would like to thank the companies and organizations
listed below for the use of their recipes and photographs
in this publication.**

Alpine Lace Brands, Inc.
Best Foods, a Division of CPC International Inc.
Birds Eye
Blue Diamond Growers
Bob Evans Farms®
California Beef Council
California Prune Board
California Tree Fruit Agreement
Del Monte Corporation
Dole Food Company, Inc.
Filippo Berio Olive Oil
Florida Department of Citrus
Guiltless Gourmet, Incorporated
Heinz U.S.A.
Hershey Foods Corporation
The HVR Company
Kahlúa Liqueur
Kikkoman International Inc.
The Kingsford Products Company
Kraft Foods, Inc.
Lawry's® Foods, Inc.
Leaf®, Inc.
Thomas J. Lipton Co.
McIlhenny Company
Minnesota Cultivated Wild Rice Council
Nabisco, Inc.
National Broiler Council
National Cattlemen's Beef Association
National Honey Board
Nestlé Food Company
New York Apple Association, Inc.
North Dakota Beef Commission
The Procter & Gamble Company
Reckitt & Colman Inc.
Sargento Foods Inc.®
StarKist Seafood Company
The Sugar Association, Inc.
Sunkist Growers, Inc.
Sun•Maid Growers of California
USA Rice Council
Washington Apple Commission
Wisconsin Milk Marketing Board

☯

Note: The page numbers that appear in boldface refer to entry headings.

Note: The page numbers that appear in boldface refer to entry headings.

Note: The page numbers that appear in boldface refer to entry headings.

Note: The page numbers that appear in boldface refer to entry headings.

Note: The page numbers that appear in boldface refer to entry headings.

Note: The page numbers that appear in boldface refer to entry headings.

Note: The page numbers that appear in boldface refer to entry headings.

Note: The page numbers that appear in boldface refer to entry headings.

Note: The page numbers that appear in boldface refer to entry headings.

Note: The page numbers that appear in boldface refer to entry headings.

VOLUME MEASUREMENTS (dry)

$1/8$ teaspoon = 0.5 mL

$1/4$ teaspoon = 1 mL

$1/2$ teaspoon = 2 mL

$3/4$ teaspoon = 4 mL

1 teaspoon = 5 mL

1 tablespoon = 15 mL

2 tablespoons = 30 mL

$1/4$ cup = 60 mL

$1/3$ cup = 75 mL

$1/2$ cup = 125 mL

$2/3$ cup = 150 mL

$3/4$ cup = 175 mL

1 cup = 250 mL

2 cups = 1 pint = 500 mL

3 cups = 750 mL

4 cups = 1 quart = 1 L

VOLUME MEASUREMENTS (fluid)

1 fluid ounce (2 tablespoons) = 30 mL

4 fluid ounces ($1/2$ cup) = 125 mL

8 fluid ounces (1 cup) = 250 mL

12 fluid ounces ($1 1/2$ cups) = 375 mL

16 fluid ounces (2 cups) = 500 mL

WEIGHTS (mass)

$1/2$ ounce = 15 g

1 ounce = 30 g

3 ounces = 90 g

4 ounces = 120 g

8 ounces = 225 g

10 ounces = 285 g

12 ounces = 360 g

16 ounces = 1 pound = 450 g

OVEN TEMPERATURES

250°F = 120°C

275°F = 140°C

300°F = 150°C

325°F = 160°C

350°F = 180°C

375°F = 190°C

400°F = 200°C

425°F = 220°C

450°F = 230°C

DIMENSIONS

$1/16$ inch = 2 mm

$1/8$ inch = 3 mm

$1/4$ inch = 6 mm

$1/2$ inch = 1.5 cm

$3/4$ inch = 2 cm

1 inch = 2.5 cm

BAKING PAN SIZES

Utensil	Size in Inches/ Quarts	Metric Volume	Size in Centimeters
Baking or Cake Pan (square or rectangular)	$8 \times 8 \times 2$	2 L	$20 \times 20 \times 5$
	$9 \times 9 \times 2$	2.5 L	$22 \times 22 \times 5$
	$12 \times 8 \times 2$	3 L	$30 \times 20 \times 5$
	$13 \times 9 \times 2$	3.5 L	$33 \times 23 \times 5$
Loaf Pan	$8 \times 4 \times 3$	1.5 L	$20 \times 10 \times 7$
	$9 \times 5 \times 3$	2 L	$23 \times 13 \times 7$
Round Layer Cake Pan	$8 \times 1 1/2$	1.2 L	20×4
	$9 \times 1 1/2$	1.5 L	23×4
Pie Plate	$8 \times 1 1/4$	750 mL	20×3
	$9 \times 1 1/4$	1 L	23×3
Baking Dish or Casserole	1 quart	1 L	—
	$1 1/2$ quart	1.5 L	—
	2 quart	2 L	—